Sports Collectors Digest

COMPLETE GUIDE TO

FOOTBALL, BASKETBALL & HOCKEY

MEMORABILIA

THE DEFINITIVE REFERENCE FOR NFL, NBA AND NHL COLLECTIBLES

Mark K. Larson

Published by

 **krause
publications**

700 E. State Street • Iola, WI 54990-0001
Telephone: 715/445-2214

Please call or write for our free catalog of sports publications. Our toll-free number to place an order or obtain a
free catalog is 800-258-0929 or please use our regular business telephone 715-445-2214 for editorial comment
and further information.

Library of Congress Catalog Number: 95-77312
ISBN: 0-87341-383-0
Printed in the United States of America

Contents

Preface

I'd forgotten about that elusive Wayne Gretzky Panini sticker, until I found the dog-eared Feb. 23, 1990, Sports Collectors Digest column in my desk drawer...

When I saw it, I couldn't help but chuckle. My then 8-year-old nephew, Drew (who's now three days shy of 13 as I write this), had called me on a Sunday afternoon. He wanted to know where he could get more of the 1990 Panini hockey stickers that I'd given to him for Christmas.

("That's not what you called him for," yelled his father in the background. Actually, his dad wanted me to know Drew had scored his first goal ever in a youth hockey game. Drew, however, didn't realize he'd scored until the coach told him. So, he's a goalie now...)

We'd sat together on the living room floor on Christmas Day, ripping open packs, looking for Drew's favorite player, "The Great One," Wayne Gretzky. But we didn't find one. So Drew called, seeking my wisdom. Eventually, he tracked one down. And I'm sure he had a great big smile on his face when he saw it.

Drew probably owns more hockey memorabilia than I do. He's even got a Wayne Gretzky autographed Edmonton Oilers 5x7 photo, which he'd sent to Gretzky in care of the team to have signed. Quite some time later it did come back signed; I'm not sure if it's authentic, but that really doesn't matter to Drew or me. It's the excitement he had when he got it back in the mail that counts...

And me, I've got the memories of watching him and his brother, Nick, as they've progressed through the ranks, from pee wees to squirts to midgets, or whatever the order is. Watching them is something more valuable to me than any Gretzky photo would ever be worth. And it's kept me young, too, as I've daydreamed back to the early 1970s when I, 8, was just becoming interested in professional sports.

I'd be bouncing a Nerf ball off the basement walls, "pounding" it into the middle, taking it to the hoop as my beloved Milwaukee Bucks, led by Oscar Robertson and Lew Alcindor, dominated the Walt Frazier-Willis Reed-Dave DeBusschere-Bill Bradley New York Knicks, or the Bob Love-Jerry Sloan-Norm Van Lier Chicago Bulls. Or, I'd be Green Bay Packer kicker Chester Marcol, lining up the Nerf football for that game-winning 45-yard field goal against the Minnesota Vikings, which in reality was a 15-yard shot over the left-to-right ascending fence, against a one-apple, two-apple, three-apple rush by two or three kids younger than I.

I've always followed professional basketball and football, and know who's who and what they did. But as far as hockey goes, I'm a wide-eyed big kid who's only recently jumped on the NHL bandwagon. There's all sorts of history to relive, names to learn, games to watch, things to collect, books to read. It's exciting, and I'm sure there will be several terrific memories along the way, ones which I won't be able to put a value on. And that's what this book is really all about...

Introduction

This book follows the same format as Sports Collectors Digest's *Complete Guide to Baseball Memorabilia*. It's meant to serve collectors who want checklists and fair, accurate prices for football, basketball and hockey memorabilia, with the exception of sports cards. The information and prices reflected are a compilation of material taken from advertisements appearing in SCD from January 1995 through September 1995. In most cases, at least two comparable sources have been used to determine the prices and ranges of the items, some of which are being catalogued for the first time ever. The condition of the items being priced is, unless noted, Excellent to Mint. Remember, the buyer and seller ultimately determine an item's value.

Chapter 2, Uniforms, has terms which have appeared in SCD in Dave Miedema's column titled "Shirt Off My Back." Chapter 3, Equipment, has terms which appear in David Bushing's book *Sports Equipment Price Guide*, published by Krause Publications. Chapter 5, Yearbooks/Media Guides, most likely has room to grow; collectors who have information to add to the yearbook/media guide checklists are encouraged to send them to the author for inclusion in future editions. Chapter 8, Books, has an overview, which, written by Mike Shannon, originally appeared in both editions of the *Complete Guide to Baseball Memorabilia*. Chapter 15, Auctions, gives prices realized from some of the bigger recent auctions, along with presale estimates for earlier auctions. The chapter has several fascinating photos, too. Chapter 16, Miscellaneous, has items which don't warrant a chapter in and of themselves, but still deserve coverage. That's the fun stuff in this book.

It is hoped that this first edition will lead to a bigger and better second edition. Therefore, the author and publisher would be interested in your thoughts regarding this book - what's good, what you disliked, what needs to be added or deleted, or explained in more detail. Also, there are items which will invariably turn up at someone's garage sale which haven't been mentioned in this book. So, send descriptions, pictures and checklists along, too. Thanks.

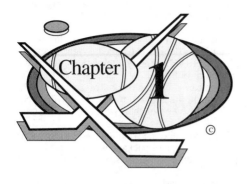

## Chapter 1

Autographs

Troy Aikman and Brett Favre signed for fans attending a quarterback challenge.

The most common memorabilia which is autographed includes basketballs, footballs, sticks, pucks, index cards, photographs and postcards, Hall of Fame plaques and postcards, equipment (shoes, skates, helmets, jerseys, trunks), programs and books, letters and documents, bank checks, and cut signatures, which have been taken from another piece of writing, such as a manuscript, letter or check.

Autographs can be obtained by several ways. The most personable, and perhaps memorable, experience would be acquiring the autograph from the player at the stadium or arena. This is the best place to catch a player, and the best time to get his signature. But get there early, before practice; once a player is into his game routine he doesn't want to be distracted. Give yourself an edge over fans who are rude and obnoxious with their requests by being polite and courteous. Having a pen ready and keeping your request simple and fast also helps.

Another alternative is at a baseball card show. Show promoters often impose time/or quota limitations, so if you know a player is going to be signing at a show it's wise to get tickets in advance and get there early.

Dealers and card show promoters also often hold private signings with the players, during which the player fills the mail-order requests sent to the dealer. Non-flat items which are signed sometimes require an extra fee. These private signings are usually advertised in hobby publications. Authenticity is generally guaranteed, and most dealers also have a return policy.

Direct requests can be sent to the player via the mail in care of his team's address, which is the best way, or his home, but the results can be unpredictable, due to the amount of mail the players receive. Some players also believe mail sent to their homes is an invasion of their privacy, so your request might go unheeded.

When dealing through the mail, send less valuable items; you don't want the post office to lose or damage them. Always include a self-addressed, stamped envelope or package with the required postage for its return. A courteous, creative, brief request, which distinguishes and sets off your letter from the others, will yield better results.

Specify if the item is to be personalized or dated, and don't ask the player to sign more than two items. Perhaps you can include an extra for the player to keep, but players are becoming wary of those who request several autographs, perhaps to be sold at a later date. Thus, sometimes the player, in return for his autograph, might ask for a donation to his favorite charity.

Auctions are another source for autographed material. These events, whether by telephone or live, often offer quality material. Items may also turn up at antique shops and flea markets, but questions regarding authenticity, value, condition and scarcity may occur if the seller has limited knowledge of the item.

Trading is always another easy means in acquiring material. A trading network can be established if you take out a classified advertisement in a hobby publication such as Sports Collectors Digest.

Prices for autographed materials are set by the principles of supply and demand, based on regional interest, scarcity, condition (not faded, dirty, shellacked, smudged, scuffed, ripped), player popularity, and significance of the event commemorated. Factors for autographed basketballs and footballs also include the signature form (style, placement, nickname), type of ball and writing medium used.

Individually-signed balls usually have the autograph on the sweet spot, the shortest distance between two seams. Team balls, those which should include the signatures of all the key players, starters and bench players, generally reserve the sweet spot for the coach's signature.

The more complete the ball is with key players, the more valuable it is. It's also easier to pinpoint the year being represented. But having other signatures, such as those of umpires and broadcasters, detracts from the value.

Some items have just select players who have signed it. These group-signed balls commemorate a particular accomplishment or event, such as a world championship, or the living members of hockey's 500 goal club.

When examining an item for authenticity, consider the writing medium used. Was the player alive when the ink, such as in a felt-tip pen or ballpoint pens, was available? Ballpoints became prominent in the 1940s, felt tips in the 1960s and Sharpies in the 1970s. However, whatever medium is used, don't retrace the signature.

Realize, too, that signatures can vary, based on the writing tool, item being signed, person's age, popularity, health and mood, time spent during a signing session, and circumstances when it was signed. Learn the player's signature evolution. Slant, size, characters, flamboyancy, legibility and capitalization may all change during a player's career and after.

Forgeries can sometimes be detected by uncommon breaks, peculiarities in pressure and movement in strokes, and changes in thickness in the letters. Facsimile signatures also exist; they are exact reproductions which are printed or screened on the item, often through computer-based technology. Rubber stamps and ghost writers have also been used by players to sign their mail.

When collecting autographed material, become familiar with collector terminology in your area of interest. Utilize the knowledge of skilled, reputable, experienced dealers and maintain good rapport with them. They can be future sources in helping you build a collection.

Also, the All Sport Autograph Guide, by Mark Allen Baker, or hobby publications, such as Sports Collectors Digest, are good sources, too. But in the end, before buying, use your own best judgment. Don't buy an item if it's questionable.

Collections can be stored in a file cabinet or display case, with background information on the event and purchase also included. The best conditions for display cases are when effective, indirect lighting is used, so as to not damage or fade the item. The ideal temperature and humidity conditions are 65 to 70 degrees and 50 percent humidity. More valuable items can be kept in safe-deposit boxes.

It's wise to periodically check your collection for signs of deterioration, but avoid excessive handling. Restoration is best left to a professional conservator who's done that type of work before.

*At left is Dwight Clark,
above is Roger Craig.*

*Above is Len Dawson,
at right is Ronnie Lott.*

*At left is O.J. Simpson,
above is Kenny Stabler.*

Football Hall of Famers

I means the item is impossible
U means the item is unlikely

Herb Adderley (1939-) 1980

Football	$75-$85
Cut signature	$3-$7
Goal Line art	$15
3x5 index card	$5-$9
8x10 photograph	$15-$20

Lance Alworth (1940-) 1978

Football	$75-$100
Cut signature	$8-$10
Goal Line art	$25
3x5 index card	$7-$10
8x10 photograph	$20

Doug Atkins (1930-) 1982

Football	$75-$85
Cut signature	$2-$6
Goal Line art	$15
3x5 index card	$5-$9
8x10 photograph	$15-$20

Morris "Red" Badgro (1902-) 1981

Football	$75-$100
Cut signature	$3-$5
Goal Line art	$30
3x5 index card	$5-$8
8x10 photograph	$18-$20

Lem Barney (1945-) 1992

Football	$85-$100
Cut signature	$4-$5
Goal Line art	$15
3x5 index card	$7
8x10 photograph	$12-$18

Cliff Battles (1910-1981) 1968

Football	U
Cut signature	$40-$65
Goal Line art	I
3x5 index card	$40-$50
8x10 photograph	$100-$200

Sammy Baugh (1914-) 1963

Football	$250-$300
Cut signature	$10-$15
Goal Line art	$60
3x5 index card	$20-$25
8x10 photograph	$35-50

Chuck Bednarik (1925-) 1967

Football	$75-$100
Cut signature	$3-$5
Goal Line art	$20
3x5 index card	$5-$8
8x10 photograph	$12-$20

Bert Bell (1895-1959) 1963

Football	U
Cut signature	$100
Goal Line art	I
3x5 index card	$150
8x10 photograph	$400

Bobby Bell (1940-) 1983

Football	$75-$100
Cut signature	$4-$6
Goal Line art	$20
3x5 index card	$7-$12
8x10 photograph	$15-$20

Raymond Berry (1933-) 1973

Football	$75-$100
Cut signature	$10
Goal Line art	$20
3x5 index card	$5-$7
8x10 photograph	$15-$18

Charles Bidwill (1895-1947) 1967

Football	U
Cut signature	$150
Goal Line art	I
3x5 index card	$450
8x10 photograph	$750

Fred Biletnikoff (1943-) 1988

Football	$80-$100
Cut signature	$6-$10
Goal Line art	$20
3x5 index card	$6-$9
8x10 photograph	$20-$25

George Blanda (1927-) 1981

Football	$100-$125
Cut signature	$5-$10
Goal Line art	$50
3x5 index card	$8-$11
8x10 photograph	$25

Pittsburgh Steeler Mel Blount had a Hall of Fame career as a defensive back.

Mel Blount (1948-) 1989

Football	$75
Cut signature	$3-$6
Goal Line art	$15
3x5 index card	$5-$9
8x10 photograph	$20

Terry Bradshaw (1948-) 1989

Football	$150
Cut signature	$7-$10
Goal Line art	$25
3x5 index card	$10
8x10 photograph	$30

Jim Brown (1936-) 1971

Football	$150
Cut signature	$7-$10
Goal Line art	$25
3x5 index card	$12
8x10 photograph	$25-$35

Paul Brown (1908-1991) 1967

Football	$150-$250
Cut signature	$10-$15
Goal Line art	$50
3x5 index card	$18-$25
8x10 photograph	$75

Roosevelt Brown (1932-) 1975

Football	$75
Cut signature	$5-$10
Goal Line art	$15
3x5 index card	$7
8x10 photograph	$20

Willie Brown (1940-) 1984

Football	$75
Cut signature	$3-$6
Goal Line art	$20
3x5 index card	$5-$6
8x10 photograph	$15-$20

Buck Buchanan (1940-1992) 1990

Football	$150-$200
Cut signature	$7-$8
Goal Line art	$50
3x5 index card	$15
8x10 photograph	$40-$60

Dick Butkus (1942-) 1979

Football	$125-$150
Cut signature	$10
Goal Line art	$25
3x5 index card	$8-$12
8x10 photograph	$25

Earl Campbell (1955-) 1991

Football	$100-$125
Cut signature	$10-$12
Goal Line art	$15
3x5 index card	$5-$10
8x10 photograph	$20

Tony Canadeo (1919-) 1974

Football	$75
Cut signature	$3-$4
Goal Line art	$20
3x5 index card	$5
8x10 photograph	$20

Joe Carr (1880-1939) 1963

Football	U
Cut signature	$500
Goal Line art	I
3x5 index card	$700
8x10 photograph	$1,000

Guy Chamberlain (1894-1967) 1965

Football	U
Cut signature	$60
Goal Line art	I
3x5 index card	$75
8x10 photograph	$150

Jack Christiansen (1928-1986) 1970

Football	U
Cut signature	$15
Goal Line art	I
3x5 index card	$40
8x10 photograph	$100-$150

Dutch Clark (1906-1978) 1963

Football	U
Cut signature	$15
Goal Line art	I
3x5 index card	$40
8x10 photograph	$100

George Connor (1925-) 1975

Football	$75
Cut signature	$3-$6
Goal Line art	$25
3x5 index card	$5
8x10 photograph	$15

Jimmy Conzelman (1898-1970) 1964

Football	U
Cut signature	$75
Goal Line art	I
3x5 index card	$100
8x10 photograph	$350

Larry Csonka (1946-) 1987

Football	$75-$125
Cut signature	$6
Goal Line art	$35
3x5 index card	$7-$10
8x10 photograph	$20

Al Davis (1929-) 1992

Football	$125
Cut signature	$10
Goal Line art	$75-$100
3x5 index card	$20
8x10 photograph	$35-$50

Willie Davis (1934-) 1981

Football	$75
Cut signature	$3-$7
Goal Line art	$15
3x5 index card	$6-$7
8x10 photograph	$15-$20

Len Dawson (1935-) 1987

Football	$125
Cut signature	$5-$8
Goal Line art	$25
3x5 index card	$7-$8
8x10 photograph	$25

Mike Ditka (1939-) 1988

Football	$100-$150
Cut signature	$10-$12
Goal Line art	$20
3x5 index card	$7-$10
8x10 photograph	$20-$30

Art Donovan (1925-) 1968

Football	$75
Cut signature	$3-$7
Goal Line art	$20
3x5 index card	$5
8x10 photograph	$20

Tony Dorsett (1954-) 1994

Football	$125-$150
Cut signature	$3
Goal Line art	$40
3x5 index card	$5
8x10 photograph	$25

Paddy Driscoll (1896-1968) 1965

Football	U
Cut signature	$100
Goal Line art	I
3x5 index card	$200
8x10 photograph	$250-$350

Bill Dudley (1921-) 1966

Football	$75
Cut signature	$5-$6
Goal Line art	$15
3x5 index card	$5-$7
8x10 photograph	$15

Turk Edwards (1907-1973) 1969

Football	U
Cut signature	$80
Goal Line art	I
3x5 index card	$125
8x10 photograph	$300

Weeb Ewbank (1907-) 1978

Football	$75
Cut signature	$3-$6
Goal Line art	$15
3x5 index card	$7-$10
8x10 photograph	$20

Tom Fears (1923-) 1970

Football	$85
Cut signature	$3-$7
Goal Line art	$15
3x5 index card	$5-$9
8x10 photograph	$15

Jim Finks (1904-1994) 1995

Football	$150
Cut signature	$5
Goal Line art	I
3x5 index card	$10
8x10 photograph	$30

Ray Flaherty (1904-1994) 1976

Football	$150
Cut signature	$5
Goal Line art	$40
3x5 index card	$10
8x10 photograph	$25

Len Ford (1926-1972) 1976

Football	U
Cut signature	$25-$30
Goal Line art	I
3x5 index card	$50
8x10 photograph	$200

Dan Fortmann (1916-) 1985

Football	U
Cut signature	$20
Goal Line art	I
3x5 index card	$25
8x10 photograph	$50-$75

Dan Fouts (1951-) 1993

Football	$100
Cut signature	$4
Goal Line art	$25
3x5 index card	$7
8x10 photograph	$35

Frank Gatski (1922-) 1985

Football	$75
Cut signature	$3
Goal Line art	$15
3x5 index card	$3
8x10 photograph	$15-$20

Bill George (1930-1982) 1974

Football	U
Cut signature	$40-$50
Goal Line art	I
3x5 index card	$75
8x10 photograph	$250

Frank Gifford (1930-) 1977

Football	$100-$150
Cut signature	$6-$7
Goal Line art	$35
3x5 index card	$10-$15
8x10 photograph	$35

Red Grange and Otto Graham were two of the game's greatest at their positions.

Sid Gillman (1911-) 1983

Football	$75
Cut signature	$3-$6
Goal Line art	$15
3x5 index card	$6
8x10 photograph	$20

Otto Graham (1921-) 1965

Football	$125-$150
Cut signature	$7-$9
Goal Line art	$20
3x5 index card	$5-$8
8x10 photograph	$20

Red Grange (1903-1991) 1963

Football	$475-$600
Cut signature	$35
Goal Line art	$200
3x5 index card	$25
8x10 photograph	$125

Bud Grant (1927-) 1994

Football	$85
Cut signature	$3
Goal Line art	$30
3x5 index	$5
8x10 photograph	$25

Joe Greene (1946-) 1987

Football	$75-$125
Cut signature	$3
Goal Line art	$25
3x5 index card	$7
8x10 photograph	$35

Forrest Gregg (1933-) 1977

Football	$75
Cut signature	$7-$9
Goal Line art	$20
3x5 index card	$6
8x10 photograph	$15

Bob Griese (1945-) 1990

Football	$125
Cut signature	$4-$6
Goal Line art	$30
3x5 index card	$7
8x10 photograph	$20

Lou Groza (1924-) 1974

Football	$100
Cut signature	$3-$6
Goal Line art	$15
3x5 index card	$6
8x10 photograph	$15-$20

Pittsburgh Steeler Hall of Famer Franco Harris was once a spokesman for Score.

Joe Guyon (1892-1971) 1966

Football	U
Cut signature	$35
Goal Line art	I
3x5 index card	$75
8x10 photograph	$300

George Halas (1895-1983) 1963

Football	$250-$300
Cut signature	$20-$25
Goal Line art	I
3x5 index card	$50
8x10 photograph	$175-$250

Jack Ham (1948-) 1988

Football	$75-$100
Cut signature	$3
Goal Line art	$15
3x5 index card	$7-$10
8x10 photograph	$15-$20

John Hannah (1951-) 1991

Football	$75
Cut signature	$3-$6
Goal Line art	$20
3x5 index card	$5-$8
8x10 photograph	$20

Franco Harris (1950-) 1990

Football	$125
Cut signature	$10-$12
Goal Line art	$40
3x5 index card	$8
8x10 photograph	$25

Ed Healey (1894-1978) 1964

Football	$150
Cut signature	$60
Goal Line art	I
3x5 index card	$50-$75
8x10 photograph	$250

Mel Hein (1909-1992) 1963

Football	$175
Cut signature	$10-$15
Goal Line art	I
3x5 index card	$12-$15
8x10 photograph	$40-$60

Ted Hendricks 1990

Football	$75
Cut signature	$3-$6
Goal Line art	$20
3x5 index card	$6
8x10 photograph	$15-$20

Pete Henry (1897-1952) 1963

Football	U
Cut signature	$50
Goal Line art	I
3x5 index card	$75
8x10 photograph	$275

Cal Hubbard (1900-1977) 1963

Football	U
Cut signature	$25
Goal Line art	I
3x5 index card	$50
8x10 photograph	$200-$250

Arnie Herber (1910-1969) 1966

Football	U
Cut signature	$75
Goal Line art	I
3x5 index card	$125
8x10 photograph	$400-$500

Sam Huff (1934-) 1982

Football	$100
Cut signature	$3
Goal Line art	$20
3x5 index card	$6
8x10 photograph	$25

Bill Hewitt (1909-1947) 1971

Football	U
Cut signature	$100
Goal Line art	I
3x5 index card	$200
8x10 photograph	$600

Lamar Hunt (1932-) 1972

Football	$75
Cut signature	$6-$8
Goal Line art	$15
3x5 index card	$8
8x10 photograph	$20

Clarke Hinkle (1909-1988) 1964

Football	$200
Cut signature	$10
Goal Line art	I
3x5 index card	$30
8x10 photograph	$50

Don Hutson (1913-) 1963

Football	$75
Cut signature	$8-$10
Goal Line art	$40
3x5 index card	$10
8x10 photograph	$25-$35

Elroy Hirsch (1923-) 1968

Football	$125
Cut signature	$5
Goal Line art	$15
3x5 index card	$8
8x10 photograph	$20

Jimmy Johnson (1938-) 1994

Football	$75
Cut signature	$3
Goal Line art	$20
3x5 index card	$5
8x10 photograph	$20

Paul Hornung (1935-) 1986

Football	$125
Cut signature	$5-$10
Goal Line art	$30
3x5 index card	$8
8x10 photograph	$20-$25

John Henry Johnson (1929-) 1987

Football	$75
Cut signature	$6-$7
Goal Line art	$20
3x5 index card	$6-$8
8x10 photograph	$15

Ken Houston (1944-) 1986

Football	$75
Cut signature	$7-$10
Goal Line art	$15
3x5 index card	$6
8x10 photograph	$15-$20

Deacon Jones (1938-) 1980

Football	$100
Cut signature	$3
Goal Line art	$15
3x5 index card	$7
8x10 photograph	$15

Stan Jones (1931-) 1991

Football	$75
Cut signature	$5-$6
Goal Line art	$15
3x5 index card	$6
8x10 photograph	$12-$15

Henry Jordan (1935-1976) 1995

Football	U
Cut signature	$50
Goal Line art	I
3x5 index card	$100
8x10 photograph	$175

Sonny Jurgensen (1934-) 1983

Football	$125
Cut signature	$5
Goal Line art	$25-$30
3x5 index card	$5
8x10 photograph	$20

Leroy Kelly (1942-) 1994

Football	$100
Cut signature	$3
Goal Line art	$15
3x5 index card	$5
8x10 photograph	$15

Walt Kiesling (1903-1962) 1966

Football	U
Cut signature	$75
Goal Line art	I
3x5 index card	$150
8x10 photograph	$100-$200

Frank "Bruiser" Kinard (1914-1965) 1971

Football	U
Cut signature	$50
Goal Line art	I
3x5 index card	$75
8x10 photograph	$300

Curly Lambeau (1898-1965) 1963

Football	U
Cut signature	$125
Goal Line art	I
3x5 index card	$200
8x10 photograph	$300-$400

Jack Lambert (1952-) 1990

Football	$150
Cut signature	$3
Goal Line art	$30
3x5 index card	$6
8x10 photograph	$22-$25

Tom Landry (1924-) 1990

Football	$125
Cut signature	$5
Goal Line art	$25
3x5 index card	$7
8x10 photograph	$25-$35

Dick Lane (1928-) 1974

Football	$75
Cut signature	$3
Goal Line art	$15
3x5 index card	$6
8x10 photograph	$15

Jim Langer (1948-) 1987

Football	$75-$100
Cut signature	$5-$8
Goal Line art	$15
3x5 index card	$6-$8
8x10 photograph	$15

Willie Lanier (1945-) 1986

Football	$75
Cut signature	$3
Goal Line art	$15
3x5 index card	$6
8x10 photograph	$15

Steve Largent (1954-) 1995

Football	$125
Cut signature	$4
Goal Line art	I
3x5 index card	$8
8x10 photograph	$20

Yale Lary (1930-) 1979

Football	$75
Cut signature	$3
Goal Line art	$15
3x5 index card	$5
8x10 photograph	$15

Dante Lavelli (1923-) 1975

Football	$75
Cut signature	$3
Goal Line art	$15
3x5 index card	$6
8x10 photograph	$15

Bobby Layne (1926-1986) 1967

Football	$400-$500
Cut signature	$15
Goal Line art	I
3x5 index card	$35
8x10 photograph	$65-$85

Tuffy Leemans (1912-1979) 1978

Football	U
Cut signature	$75
Goal Line art	I
3x5 index card	$125
8x10 photograph	$200

Bob Lilly (1939-) 1980

Football	$100
Cut signature	$3
Goal Line art	$20
3x5 index card	$6
8x10 photograph	$15

Larry Little (1945-) 1993

Football	$75
Cut signature	$5
Goal Line art	$15
3x5 index card	$5
8x10 photograph	$15

Vince Lombardi (1913-1970) 1971

Football	$1,500-$1,750
Cut signature	$75-$100
Goal Line art	I
3x5 index card	$150
8x10 photograph	$400-$500

Sid Luckman (1916-) 1965

Football	$125
Cut signature	$3
Goal Line art	$30
3x5 index card	$6
8x10 photograph	$17-$20

Link Lyman (1898-1972) 1964

Football	U
Cut signature	$75
Goal Line art	I
3x5 index card	$100
8x10 photograph	$200

John Mackey (1941-) 1992

Football	$75
Cut signature	$3
Goal Line art	$15
3x5 index card	$6
8x10 photograph	$15

Tim Mara (1887-1959) 1963

Football	U
Cut signature	$200
Goal Line art	I
3x5 index card	$300
8x10 photograph	$700

Gino Marchetti (1927-) 1972

Football	$75
Cut signature	$3
Goal Line art	$15
3x5 index card	$5
8x10 photograph	$15

George Marshall (1887-1969) 1963

Football	U
Cut signature	$125
Goal Line art	I
3x5 index card	$200
8x10 photograph	$400

Ollie Matson (1930-) 1972

Football	$75
Cut signature	$3
Goal Line art	$20
3x5 index card	$6
8x10 photograph	$15

Don Maynard (1935-) 1987

Football	$100
Cut signature	$3-$7
Goal Line art	$20
3x5 index card	$6
8x10 photograph	$15

George McAfee (1918-) 1966

Football	$75
Cut signature	$7
Goal Line art	$15
3x5 index card	$5
8x10 photograph	$15

Mike McCormack (1930-) 1984

Football	$75
Cut signature	$3-$5
Goal Line art	$15
3x5 index card	$5
8x10 photograph	$15

Hugh McElhenny (1928-) 1970

Football	$100
Cut signature	$10
Goal Line art	$20
3x5 index card	$10-$13
8x10 photograph	$25

John McNally (1903-1985) 1963

Football	$500
Cut signature	$25
Goal Line art	I
3x5 index card	$50
8x10 photograph	$100-$150

Mike Michalske (1903-1983) 1964

Football	$400
Cut signature	$20
Goal Line art	I
3x5 index card	$40
8x10 photograph	$150-$200

Wayne Millner (1913-1976) 1968

Football	U
Cut signature	$75
Goal Line art	I
3x5 index card	$100
8x10 photograph	$300

Bobby Mitchell (1935-) 1983

Football	$75
Cut signature	$3
Goal Line art	$20
3x5 index card	$5
8x10 photograph	$15-$20

Ron Mix (1938-) 1979

Football	$75
Cut signature	$5-$6
Goal Line art	$20
3x5 index card	$6
8x10 photograph	$15

Lenny Moore (1933-) 1975

Football	$75
Cut signature	$6-$7
Goal Line art	$20
3x5 index card	$6-$9
8x10 photograph	$15

Marion Motley (1920-) 1968

Football	$75
Cut signature	$3-$8
Goal Line art	$15
3x5 index card	$6-$10
8x10 photograph	$15

George Musso (1910-) 1982

Football	$75
Cut signature	$3-$5
Goal Line art	$15
3x5 index card	$5
8x10 photograph	$15

Bronko Nagurski (1908-1990) 1963

Football	$350
Cut signature	$25
Goal Line art	I
3x5 index card	$35-$50
8x10 photograph	$100-$150

Joe Namath (1943-) 1985

Football	$150
Cut signature	$10-$12
Goal Line art	$60
3x5 index card	$20-$30
8x10 photograph	$40

Earle "Greasy" Neale (1891-1973) 1969

Football	U
Cut signature	$50-$75
Goal Line art	I
3x5 index card	$100
8x10 photograph	$300

Ernie Nevers (1903-1976) 1963

Football	U
Cut signature	$50
Goal Line art	I
3x5 index card	$80
8x10 photograph	$150-$250

Alan Page (1945-) 1988

Football	$75-$100
Cut signature	$3
Goal Line art	$15
3x5 index card	$6
8x10 photograph	$15

Ray Nitschke (1936-) 1978

Football	$100
Cut signature	$3-$6
Goal Line art	$25
3x5 index card	$6
8x10 photograph	$20

Ace Parker (1912-) 1972

Football	$75
Cut signature	$3
Goal Line art	$15
3x5 index card	$6
8x10 photograph	$15

Chuck Noll (1932-) 1993

Football	$75
Cut signature	$3
Goal Line art	$15
3x5 index card	$6
8x10 photograph	$15

Jim Parker (1934-) 1973

Football	$75
Cut signature	$3
Goal Line art	$15
3x5 index card	$5
8x10 photograph	$15

Leo Nomellini (1924-) 1969

Football	$75
Cut signature	$3-$10
Goal Line art	$20
3x5 index card	$6
8x10 photograph	$15-$20

Walter Payton (1954-) 1993

Football	$150
Cut signature	$6-$8
Goal Line art	$30-$35
3x5 index card	$8-$10
8x10 photograph	$25-$30

Merlin Olsen (1940-) 1982

Football	$75-$100
Cut signature	$5-$7
Goal Line art	$20
3x5 index card	$10
8x10 photograph	$25-$30

Joe Perry (1927-) 1969

Football	$100
Cut signature	$3-$8
Goal Line art	$25
3x5 index card	$7-$8
8x10 photograph	$20

Jim Otto (1938-) 1980

Football	$75
Cut signature	$3-$6
Goal Line art	$20
3x5 index card	$6
8x10 photograph	$15

Pete Pihos (1923-) 1970

Football	$75
Cut signature	$3
Goal Line art	$15
3x5 index card	$6
8x10 photograph	$15

Steve Owen (1898-1964) 1966

Football	U
Cut signature	$200
Goal Line art	I
3x5 index card	$400
8x10 photograph	$750

Hugh Ray (1884-1956)1966

Football	U
Cut signature	$200
Goal Line art	I
3x5 index card	$350-$400
8x10 photograph	$750

Bears running back Gale Sayers is from the Hall of Fame's Class of 1977.

Dan Reeves (1912-1971) 1967

Football	U
Cut signature	$50-$75
Goal Line art	I
3x5 index card	$100
8x10 photograph	$300-$400

John Riggins (1949-) 1992

Football	$125
Cut signature	$5-$6
Goal Line art	$25
3x5 index card	$8
8x10 photograph	$50

Jim Ringo (1931-) 1981

Football	$75
Cut signature	$3-$5
Goal Line art	$20
3x5 index card	$15
8x10 photograph	$15

Andy Robustelli (1925-) 1971

Football	$100
Cut signature	$3
Goal Line art	$15
3x5 index card	$6
8x10 photograph	$15

Art Rooney (1901-1988) 1964

Football	$300
Cut signature	$7-$10
Goal Line art	I
3x5 index card	$25
8x10 photograph	$75-$125

Pete Rozelle (1926-) 1985

Football	$125
Cut signature	$7-$10
Goal Line art	$40
3x5 index card	$15
8x10 photograph	$30

Bob St. Clair (1931-) 1990

Football	$75
Cut signature	$3-$6
Goal Line art	$30
3x5 index card	$6
8x10 photograph	$15

Gale Sayers (1943-) 1977

Football	$125
Cut signature	$4-$7
Goal Line art	$30
3x5 index card	$7-$10
8x10 photograph	$20

Quarterback Bart Starr led the Green Bay Packers to two Super Bowl wins.

Joe Schmidt (1932-) 1973

Football	$75
Cut signature	$3
Goal Line art	$15
3x5 index card	$6-$9
8x10 photograph	$15

Tex Schramm (1920-) 1991

Football	$75
Cut signature	$3-$6
Goal Line art	$15
3x5 index card	$6-$9
8x10 photograph	$15

Lee Roy Selmon (1954-) 1995

Football	$70-$85
Cut signature	$3
Goal Line art	I
3x5 index card	$5
8x10 photograph	$15

Art Shell (1946-) 1989

Football	$75-$100
Cut signature	$4
Goal Line art	$15
3x5 index card	$6
8x10 photograph	$15

O.J. Simpson (1947-) 1985

Football	$250
Cut signature	$25
Goal Line art	I
3x5 index card	$35
8x10 photograph	$60-$75

Jackie Smith (1940-) 1994

Football	$75
Cut signature	$3
Goal Line art	$15
3x5 index card	$5
8x10 photograph	$15

Bart Starr (1934-) 1977

Football	$100-$125
Cut signature	$4
Goal Line art	$30
3x5 index card	$8
8x10 photograph	$25

Roger Staubach (1942-) 1985

Football	$150
Cut signature	$5-$7
Goal Line art	$40
3x5 index card	$8
8x10 photograph	$25-$40

Some collectors try to get footballs signed by Super Bowl MVPs.

Ernie Stautner (1925-) 1969

Football	$75
Cut signature	$4
Goal Line art	$15
3x5 index card	$7
8x10 photograph	$20

Jan Stenerud (1942-) 1991

Football	$75
Cut signature	$3-$5
Goal Line art	$15
3x5 index card	$6
8x10 photograph	$15

Ken Strong (1906-1979) 1967

Football	U
Cut signature	$40
Goal Line art	I
3x5 index card	$60
8x10 photograph	$200

Joe Stydahar (1912-1977) 1967

Football	U
Cut signature	$40
Goal Line art	I
3x5 index card	$60
8x10 photograph	$25

Fran Tarkenton (1940-) 1986

Football	$150
Cut signature	$5-$10
Goal Line art	$40
3x5 index card	$10
8x10 photograph	$25-$30

Charley Taylor (1941-) 1984

Football	$75
Cut signature	$3
Goal Line art	$20
3x5 index card	$6
8x10 photograph	$15

Jim Taylor (1935-) 1976

Football	$75
Cut signature	$3
Goal Line art	$20
3x5 index card	$5
8x10 photograph	$15

Jim Thorpe (1888-1953) 1963

Football	$6,000
Cut signature	$500
Goal Line art	I
3x5 index card	$700
8x10 photograph	$1,500

Colts' quarterback Johnny Unitas was famous for his arm, and hightops.

Y.A. Tittle (1926-) 1971

Football	$100
Cut signature	$4
Goal Line art	$25
3x5 index card	$6
8x10 photograph	$25

George Trafton (1896-1971) 1964

Football	U
Cut signature	$75
Goal Line art	I
3x5 index card	$125
8x10 photograph	$250

Charley Trippi (1922-) 1968

Football	$75
Cut signature	$3
Goal Line art	$15
3x5 index card	$6
8x10 photograph	$18-$20

Emlen Tunnell (1925-1975) 1967

Football	U
Cut signature	$40
Goal Line art	I
3x5 index card	$75
8x10 photograph	$200

Bulldog Turner (1919-) 1966

Football	$100
Cut signature	$4
Goal Line art	$25
3x5 index card	$7
8x10 photograph	$20

Johnny Unitas (1933-) 1979

Football	$150
Cut signature	$5-$10
Goal Line art	I
3x5 index card	$8
8x10 photograph	$20

Gene Upshaw (1945-) 1987

Football	$75
Cut signature	$3-$7
Goal Line art	$15
3x5 index card	$6
8x10 photograph	$15

Norm Van Brocklin (1926-1983) 1971

Football	$350
Cut signature	$40
Goal Line art	I
3x5 index card	$75
8x10 photograph	$200-$225

Steve Van Buren (1920-) 1965

Football	$75
Cut signature	$3
Goal Line art	$20
3x5 index card	$5
8x10 photograph	$15

Doak Walker (1927-) 1986

Football	$100
Cut signature	$3
Goal Line art	$25
3x5 index card	$5
8x10 photograph	$20

Bill Walsh (1931-) 1993

Football	$125
Cut signature	$5
Goal Line art	$50
3x5 index card	$10
8x10 photograph	$25

Paul Warfield (1942-) 1983

Football	$75
Cut signature	$3
Goal Line art	$15
3x5 index card	$6
8x10 photograph	$15-$20

Bob Waterfield (1920-1983) 1965

Football	$350
Cut signature	$30-$40
Goal Line art	I
3x5 index card	$75
8x10 photograph	$175-$250

Arnie Weinmeister (1923-) 1984

Football	$75
Cut signature	$3
Goal Line art	$15
3x5 index card	$5
8x10 photograph	$15

Bill Willis (1921-) 1977

Football	$75
Cut signature	$3
Goal Line art	$20
3x5 index card	$6
8x10 photograph	$15

Larry Wilson (1938-) 1978

Football	$75
Cut signature	$3
Goal Line art	$15
3x5 index card	$6
8x10 photograph	$15

Kellen Winslow (1957-) 1995

Football	$100
Cut signature	$3
Goal Line art	I
3x5 index card	$5
8x10 photograph	$15

Alex Wojciechowicz (1915-1992) 1968

Football	$200
Cut signature	$8
Goal Line art	$150
3x5 index card	$10
8x10 photograph	$35-$50

Willie Wood (1936-) 1989

Football	$75
Cut signature	$3
Goal Line art	$15
3x5 index card	$5
8x10 photograph	$15

Retired players

Player	8x10 photo/football	
Julius Adams	$10	$65
Lyle Alzado	$50	$115
Alan Ameche	$30	$85
Donny Anderson	$12	$70
Ken Anderson	$20	$75
Neal Anderson	$15	$65
Ottis Anderson	$14	$65
Coy Bacon	$15	$70
Jim Bakken	$15	$70
Tom Banks	$12	$65
Steve Bartkowski	$13	$70
Rolf Bernirschke	$15	$70
Bill Bergey	$15	$70
Elvin Bethea	$15	$70
Glenn Blackwood	$10	$65
Lyle Blackwood	$10	$70
Rocky Bleier	$15	$70
Emerson Boozer	$15	$75
Brian Bosworth	$8	$60
Ken Bowman	$15	$70
Cliff Branch	$20	$75
John Brockington	$15	$70
John Brodie	$25	$80

Autographs

Bobby Bryant	$17	$72
Kelvin Bryant	$15	$70
Willie Buchanon	$11	$66
Norm Bulaich	$13	$68
Nick Buoniconti	$18	$73
Ken Burrough	$10	$65
Dave Butz	$13	$68
Dennis Byrd	$10	$65
John Cappelletti	$15	$70
Harold Carmichael	$20	$75
Harry Carson	$20	$75
Dave Casper	$17	$72
Bob Chandler	$7	$60
Don Chandler	$17	$72
Wes Chandler	$8	$50
Raymond Chester	$14	$69
Todd Christensen	$15	$65
Dwight Clark	$20	$75
Mark Clayton	$10	$65
Paul Coffman	$10	$65
Cris Collinsworth	$15	$70
Al Cowlings	$15	$70
Fred Cox	$12	$67
Roger Craig	$15	$70
Randy Cross	$10	$65
Isaac Curtis	$15	$70
Dave Dalby	$12	$67
Gary Danielson	$10	$65
Ben Davidson	$15	$70
Joe DeLamielleure	$15	$70
Tom Dempsey	$20	$75
Eric Dickerson	$25	$80
Lynn Dickey	$10	$65
Dan Dierdorf	$35	$90
Conrad Dobler	$20	$75
Bobby Douglass	$12	$67
Boyd Dowler	$16	$71
Fred Dryer	$17	$72
Mark Duper	$10	$65
Billy Joe DuPree	$10	$65
John Dutton	$13	$68
Carl Eller	$15	$70
Joe Ferguson	$12	$67
Pat Fischer	$17	$67
Tom Flores	$15	$70
Doug Flutie	$15	$70
Chuck Foreman	$13	$68
Russ Francis	$15	$70
Roman Gabriel	$20	$75
Walt Garrison	$15	$70
Roy Gerela	$15	$70
Pete Gogolak	$13	$68
Mel Gray	$12	$67
L.C. Greenwood	$18	$73
Archie Griffin	$15	$70
Steve Grogan	$13	$68
Ray Guy	$15	$70
John Hadl	$20	$75
Dan Hampton	$12	$67
Cliff Harris	$13	$65
Tim Harris	$10	$65
Jim Hart	$15	$70
Bob Hayes	$15	$70
Lester Hayes	$10	$65
Efren Herrera	$16	$70
Calvin Hill	$17	$72
Bo Jackson	$25	$75
Tom Jackson	$17	$72
Ron Jaworski	$13	$68
John Jefferson	$15	$70
Roy Jefferson	$15	$70
Jim Jensen	$10	$65
Billy Johnson	$16	$76
Charley Johnson	$14	$69
Jimmy Johnson	$20	$75
Norm Johnson	$10	$65
Pete Johnson	$10	$65
Charlie Joiner	$20	$75
Bert Jones	$18	$73
Ed "Too Tall" Jones	$18	$73
Lee Roy Jordan	$13	$68
Jack Kemp	$25	$80
Jim Kiick	$14	$69
Billy Kilmer	$20	$75
Joe Klecko	$12	$67
Chuck Knox	$10	$65
Jerry Kramer	$15	$70
Tim Krumrie	$10	$65
Bob Kuechenberg	$13	$68
Daryle Lamonica	$20	$75
Greg Landry	$12	$67
MacArthur Lane	$15	$70
Pat Leahy	$13	$68
D.D. Lewis	$15	$70
Floyd Little	$17	$72
James Lofton	$20	$75
Neil Lomax	$8	$63
Howie Long	$18	$73
Tom Mack	$12	$67
John Madden	$35	$90
Mark Malone	$10	$65
Archie Manning	$15	$70
Chester Marcol	$8	$63
Ed Marinaro	$35	$90
Jim Marshall	$17	$72
Harvey Martin	$20	$75
John Matuszak	$40	$90
Larry McCarren	$10	$65
"Wahoo" McDaniel	$10	$65
Reggie McKenzie	$18	$73
Steve McMichael	$10	$65
Karl Mecklenberg	$15	$70
Terry Metcalf	$17	$72
Matt Millen	$15	$70
Lydell Mitchell	$15	$70
Joe Montana	$40	$95
Mercury Morris	$18	$73
Craig Morton	$15	$70
Mark Moseley	$13	$68
Haven Moses	$12	$67

Anthony Munoz	$15	$70
Brad Muster	$10	$65
Robert Newhouse	$15	$70
Ozzie Newsome	$17	$75
Tommy Nobis	$17	$72
Ken O'Brien	$8	$63
John Offerdahl	$12	$67
Christian Okoye	$8	$63
Jim Otis	$13	$68
Lemar Parrish	$15	$70
Bob Parsons	$10	$65
Dan Pastorini	$17	$72
Drew Pearson	$15	$70
Preston Pearson	$12	$67
Brian Piccolo	$275	$330
Jim Plunkett	$25	$80
Greg Pruitt	$13	$68
Mike Pruitt	$13	$68
Ahmad Rashad	$25	$80
Mel Renfro	$15	$70
Ken Riley	$15	$70
Tobin Rote	$20	$75
Reggie Rucker	$18	$73
Charlie Sanders	$13	$68
Jake Scott	$17	$72
Sterling Sharpe	$30	$90
Donnie Shell	$15	$70
Phil Simms	$15	$70
Billy Sims	$13	$68
Mike Singletary	$15	$70
Brian Sipe	$15	$70
Otis Sistrunk	$18	$73
Jackie Slater	$13	$68
Bubba Smith	$17	$72
Norm Snead	$17	$72
Matt Snell	$18	$73
Jack Snow	$17	$72
Steve Spurrier	$15	$70
Ken Stabler	$25	$80
John Stallworth	$10	$65
Dwight Stephenson	$12	$67
Don Strock	$17	$72
Jack Tatum	$15	$70
Lawrence Taylor	$30	$85
Joe Theismann	$20	$75
Fuzzy Thurston	$8	$68
Mick Tinglehoff	$13	$68
Richard Todd	$13	$68
Al Toon	$15	$70
Bob Trumpy	$17	$72
Jim Turner	$15	$70
Wendall Tyler	$15	$70
Rick Upchurch	$15	$70
Steve Van Buren	$20	$75
Mark van Eeghen	$13	$68
Jeff Van Note	$15	$70
Brad Van Pelt	$15	$70
Randy Vataha	$15	$70
Curt Warner	$13	$68
Mike Webster	$15	$70
Roger Wehrli	$15	$70
Ray Wersching	$13	$68
Danny White	$15	$70
Dwight White	$12	$67
Charlie Waters	$15	$70
Delvin Williams	$12	$67
Doug Williams	$15	$70
Ickey Woods	$12	$67
Ron Yary	$15	$70
Garo Yepremian	$15	$70
Jack Youngblood	$17	$72
Jim Youngblood	$13	$68
Jim Zorn	$15	$70

Active players

Player	8x10 photo/football	
Troy Aikman	$30	$85
Eric Allen	$8	$63
Marcus Allen	$25	$80
Terry Allen	$10	$65
Morton Andersen	$15	$70
"Flipper" Anderson	$8	$63
Gary Anderson (k)	$13	$68
Steve Atwater	$11	$66
Mark Bavarro	$10	$65
Don Beebe	$15	$70
Cornelius Bennett	$15	$70
Edgar Bennett	$8	$63
Rod Bernstine	$10	$65
Steve Beuerlein	$13	$68
Jerome Bettis	$15	$70
Dean Biasucci	$10	$65
Bennie Blades	$10	$65
Brian Blades	$12	$67
Drew Bledsoe	$25	$80
Steve Bono	$10	$65
Bubby Brister	$8	$63
Reggie Brooks	$8	$63
Tim Brown	$20	$75
Kevin Butler	$8	$63
LeRoy Butler	$10	$65
Marion Butts	$10	$65
Earnest Byner	$10	$65
Mark Carrier (Bears)	$13	$68
Anthony Carter	$10	$65
Cris Carter	$15	$70
Gary Clark	$10	$65
Ben Coates	$15	$70
Curtis Conway	$8	$63
Randall Cunningham	$20	$75
Kenneth Davis	$12	$67
Richard Dent	$20	$75
Henry Ellard	$13	$68
John Elway	$30	$85

Emmitt Smith poses with the promoters of a Tri-Star Sports show in Phoenix.

Steve Emtman	$10	$65
Craig Erickson	$10	$65
Boomer Esiason	$15	$70
Jim Everett	$15	$70
Marshall Faulk	$30	$85
Brett Favre	$20	$75
William Floyd	$12	$67
Barry Foster	$20	$75
Irving Fryar	$15	$70
Jeff George	$15	$70
Eric Green	$10	$65
Charles Haley	$15	$70
Rodney Hampton	$15	$70
Jim Harbaugh	$8	$63
Ronnie Harmon	$10	$65
Alvin Harper	$15	$70
Tim Harris	$10	$65
Mike Haynes	$10	$65
Garrison Hearst	$15	$70
Bobby Hebert	$8	$63
Randal Hill	$12	$67
Jeff Hostetler	$13	$75
Desmond Howard	$8	$63
Stan Humphries	$15	$70
Michael Irvin	$25	$80
Rocket Ismail	$15	$70
Keith Jackson	$10	$65
Rickey Jackson	$12	$67
Haywood Jeffires	$10	$65
Johnny Johnson	$10	$65
Daryl Johnston	$15	$70
Jim Kelly	$25	$80
Cortez Kennedy	$10	$65
Terry Kirby	$8	$63
David Klingler	$8	$63
Bernie Kosar	$18	$75
Dave Krieg	$10	$65
Louis Lipps	$10	$65
Ronnie Lott	$25	$80
Nick Lowery	$13	$68
Dan Marino	$35	$90
Eric Martin	$10	$65
Bruce Matthews	$10	$65
Dan McGwire	$8	$63
Jim McMahon	$20	$75
Natrone Means	$15	$70
Dave Meggett	$10	$65
Eric Metcalf	$10	$65
Chris Miller	$10	$65
Sam Mills	$10	$65
Rick Mirer	$15	$70
Scott Mitchell	$13	$68
Art Monk	$25	$80
Warren Moon	$25	$80
Herman Moore	$10	$65
Rob Moore	$10	$65
Eddie Murray	$10	$65
Browning Nagle	$8	$63
Tom Newberry	$10	$65
Nate Newton	$13	$68

Ken Norton Jr.	$15	$70	Shannon Sharpe	$15	$70
Neil O'Donnell	$10	$65	Clyde Simmons	$15	$70
Stephone Paige	$12	$67	Bruce Smith	$15	$70
Bryce Paup	$15	$70	Emmitt Smith	$35	$90
Rodney Peete	$8	$63	Irv Smith	$8	$63
Erric Pegram	$8	$63	Chris Spielman	$13	$68
William Perry	$8	$63	Pete Stoyanovich	$15	$70
Mike Pritchard	$8	$63	Pat Swilling	$10	$65
Tom Rathman	$13	$68	John Taylor	$8	$63
Andre Reed	$15	$70	Vinny Testaverde	$10	$65
Frank Reich	$13	$68	Derrick Thomas	$15	$70
Errict Rhett	$15	$75	Thurman Thomas	$25	$80
Jerry Rice	$45	$100	Tommy Vardell	$10	$65
Andre Rison	$15	$70	Herschel Walker	$15	$70
Willie Roaf	$13	$68	Andre Ware	$8	$63
Reggie Roby	$10	$65	Chris Warren	$15	$70
Ken Ruettgers	$10	$65	Ricky Watters	$15	$70
Leonard Russell	$10	$65	Reggie White	$25	$80
Mark Rypien	$10	$65	Wade Wilson	$10	$65
Barry Sanders	$25	$80	Rod Woodson	$15	$70
Deion Sanders	$35	$90	Steve Young	$40	$95
Junior Seau	$20	$75			

Retired players

Player	8x10 photos
Dan Abramowicz	$7
Mike Adamle	$10
George Allen	$35
Pete Banaszak	$8

Greg Bell	$12
Ricky Bell	$45
Verlon Biggs	$6
Mark Bortz	$6
Mike Bragg	$10

Pat Summerall has remained in the football spotlight as an announcer.

Zeke Bratkowski	$9	Stanley Morgan	$10
Jim Breech	$7	Earl Morrall	$12
Tom Brookshier	$12	Joe Morris	$10
Dave Brown	$10	Mercury Morris	$15
Larry Brown	$15	Chuck Muncie	$10
Dexter Bussey	$10	Steve Nelson	$8
Don Cockroft	$7	Dave Osborn	$10
Jack Concannon	$8	Ed Podolak	$10
Joe Cribbs	$7	Dave Robinson	$8
Sam Cunningham	$8	Rafael Septien	$10
Mouse Davis	$8	Darryl Stingley	$75
Vince Ferragamo	$6	Pat Sullivan	$12
Wayne Fontes	$8	Pat Summerall	$15
Tony Franklin	$7	Duane Thomas	$25
John Fuqua	$9	Pat Tilley	$7
Tony Galbreath	$7	Bob Tucker	$7
Bruce Gossett	$14	Uwe von Schamann	$7
Roy Green	$12	Wesley Walker	$10
Rosey Grier	$12	Gene Washington (49ers)	$12
Chris Hanburger	$10	Gene Washington (Vikings)	$10
Marv Hubbard	$10	Ed White	$10
Spider Lockhart	$35	Ken Willard	$9
Max McGee	$12	Marc Wilson	$8
Wilbert Montgomery	$8		

Individual footballs

Troy Aikman Super Bowl XXVII football	$225	Bernie Kosar Quarterback Club football	$125
Troy Aikman Wilson NFL white panel	$140	Howie Long Wilson NFL white panel	$90
Troy Aikman Quarterback Club football	$140	John Madden Wilson NFL 75th anniversary	$100
Marcus Allen official NFL Wilson	$150	Rick Mirer Quarterback Club football	$125
Jerome Bettis Wilson NFL white panel	$90	Joe Montana official Wilson NFL football	$160
Drew Bledsoe Wilson NFL white panel	$140	Warren Moon Wilson NFL white panel	$90
Drew Bledsoe Quarterback Club football	$125	Warren Moon Quarterback Club football	$125
Randall Cunningham Quarterback Club football	$125	Joe Namath official Wilson NFL football	$160
Mike Ditka Wilson NFL 75th anniversary	$80	Ray Nitschke Wilson NFL 75th anniversary	$80
John Elway Wilson NFL white panel	$125	Jerry Rice game-used NFL ball, signed	$350
Boomer Esiason Quarterback Club football	$125	Andre Rison Wilson NFL white panel	$70
Brett Favre Quarterback Club football	$125	Barry Sanders official Wilson NFL football	$150
Dan Fouts Wilson NFL white panel	$120	Deion Sanders Wilson NFL white panel	$90
Bob Griese Wilson NFL 75th anniversary	$90	Gale Sayers Wilson NFL white panel	$90
Rodney Hampton Wilson NFL white panel	$85	Sterling Sharpe Wilson NFL white panel	$85
Franco Harris Wilson NFL white panel	$90	Emmitt Smith Wilson NFL 75th anniversary	$100
Garrison Hearst Wilson NFL white panel	$75	Roger Staubach official Wilson NFL football	$140
Jeff Hostetler Quarterback Club football	$125	Lawrence Taylor official Wilson NFL football	$150
Michael Irvin Wilson NFL white panel	$90	Thurman Thomas Wilson NFL white panel	$85
Jim Kelly Wilson NFL white panel	$125	Herschel Walker Wilson NFL white panel	$80
Jim Kelly Quarterback Club football	$125	Steve Young Wilson NFL 75th anniversary	$100
Bernie Kosar official Wilson NFL football	$135	Steve Young game-used NFL ball, signed	$300

Multiple and team-signed footballs

- Franco Harris/Tony Dorsett official Wilson white-paneled ball, 75th anniversary $140
- Steve Young/Jerry Rice game-used NFL ball, signed by both $400
- Fearsome Foursome football, white-paneled, signed by Merlin Olsen, Deacon Jones, Lamar Lundy and Rosie Grier $150

- 23 years of Super Bowl MVPs, signed by 17 of them, including Fred Biletnikoff, Terry Bradshaw, Larry Csonka, Len Dawson, Joe Montana, Joe Namath, Jim Plunkett, Jerry Rice, Bart Starr, Roger Staubach and others ... $2,500
- 1948 Green Bay Packers, with 41 signatures, including Walt Kiesling, Don Hutson, Tony Canadeo and Curly Lambeau $4,000

This football, signed by Bears players of the 1940s, is worth $1,200-$1,500.

- Cleveland Browns 1967 team-autographed football with 43 signatures, including Paul Warfield and Lou Groza $300
- 1967 Los Angeles Rams, with 33 signatures, including Roman Gabriel, Jack Pardee, Deacon Jones and Merlin Olsen $175
- 1972 Pittsburgh Steelers, with 52 signatures, including Art Rooney, Mel Blount, Joe Gilliam, Terry Hanratty, Jack Ham, Joe Greene, Rocky Bleier, Franco Harris and Terry Bradshaw $500
- 1974 Los Angeles Rams, with 39 signatures, including James Harris, Jim Youngblood, Tom Mack and Isiah Robertson $195
- Green Bay Packers Super Bowl reunion ball, with 18 signatures, including Jim Taylor, Willie Wood, Lionel Aldridge, Herb Adderly, Ken Bowman and Fuzzy Thurston $225
- 1981-82 Cincinnati Bengals, signed by 40 players, including Ken Anderson, Cris Collinsworth and Anthony Munoz $150
- Cleveland Browns 1986 team-autographed football with 34 signatures, including Ozzie Newsome, Bernie Kosar and Bob Golic ... $250
- 1990-91 New York Giants football autographed by 17 players from the Super Bowl Champs, including Bart Oates and Lawrence Taylor $225
- Monday Night Football NFL Wilson white-paneled ball, signed by Frank Gifford, Al Michaels and Dan Dierdorf $135
- 1994 Arizona Cardinals star-signed official white-paneled ball, signed by Steve Beuerlein, Garrison Hearst, Gary Clark, Seth Joyner, Eric Swann and Buddy Ryan $125
- 1994 Dallas Cowboys star-signed white-paneled ball, signed by Emmitt Smith, Troy Aikman and Michael Irvin $250
- 1994 Houston Oilers star-signed white-paneled ball, signed by Cody Carlson, Gary Brown, Haywood Jeffires, Ernest Givens, Ray Childress and Jack Pardee $125
- 1994 Los Angeles Raiders star-signed white-paneled ball, signed by Jeff Hostetler, Tim Brown, Rocket Ismail, James Jett and Alexander Wright $140
- 1994 San Diego Chargers star-signed white-paneled ball, signed by Stan Humphries, Junior Seau and Natrone Means $105
- 1994 San Francisco 49ers star-signed white-paneled ball, signed by Steve Young, Jerry Rice and John Taylor $180

1994 team-signed footballs

1994 Houston Oilers	$160
1994 Los Angeles Rams	$165
1994 San Diego Chargers	$200
1994 Pittsburgh Steelers	$200
1994 Detroit Lions	$175
1994 Denver Broncos	$200
1994 Los Angeles Raiders	$175

Basketball Hall of Famers

Kareem Abdul-Jabbar began his NBA career as Lew Alcindor.

* deceased

Kareem Abdul-Jabbar (1947-) 1995

Basketball	$150
Cut signature	$15
3x5 index card	$25
8x10 photograph	$30-$40

Nate Archibald (1948-) 1991

Basketball	$90-$110
Cut signature	$6
3x5 index card	$10
8x10 photograph	$15-$20

Paul Arizin (1928-) 1977

Basketball	$100
Cut signature	$5
3x5 index card	$10
8x10 photograph	$30

Red Auerbach 1968

Basketball	$150-$175
Cut signature	$8-$10
3x5 index card	$12
8x10 photograph	$25-$30

Thomas Barlow * 1980

Basketball	$100
Cut signature	$5
3x5 index card	$8
8x10 photograph	$35

Rick Barry (1944-) 1987

Basketball	$125
Cut signature	$7-$10
3x5 index card	$12
8x10 photograph	$20

Elgin Baylor (1934-) 1976

Basketball	$150
Cut signature	$7-$10
3x5 index card	$12-$15
8x10 photograph	$20

John Beckman * 1972

Basketball	$100
Cut signature	$4
3x5 index card	$10
8x10 photograph	$40

Clair Bee * 1967

Basketball	$100
Cut signature	$5
3x5 index card	$10
8x10 photograph	$40

Walt Bellamy (1939-) 1992

Basketball	$75-$100
Cut signature	$5
3x5 index card	$10
8x10 photograph	$15-$20

Dave Bing (1943-) 1990

Basketball	$100-$110
Cut signature	$4-$5
3x5 index card	$10
8x10 photograph	$15-$18

Bennie Borgmann * 1961

Basketball	$100
Cut signature	$4
3x5 index card	$8
8x10 photograph	$40

Bill Bradley (1943-) 1982

Basketball	$125-$150
Cut signature	$8-$12
3x5 index card	$15
8x10 photograph	$30-$35

Joseph Brennan * 1974

Basketball	$100
Cut signature	$5
3x5 index card	$10
8x10 photograph	$35

Lou Carnesseca 1991

Basketball	$100
Cut signature	$7
3x5 index card	$10
8x10 photograph	$12-$16

Alfred Cervi (1917-) 1984

Basketball	$100
Cut signature	$4-$6
3x5 index card	$10
8x10 photograph	$12-$14

Wilt Chamberlain (1936-) 1978

Basketball	$250-$300
Cut signature	$20
3x5 index card	$40
8x10 photograph	$75-$100

Charles Cooper (1926-1984) 1976

Basketball	$100
Cut signature	$15
3x5 index card	$17
8x10 photograph	$35

Bob Cousy (1928-) 1970

Basketball	$150
Cut signature	$9-$10
3x5 index card	$25
8x10 photograph	$25-$30

Dave Cowens (1948-) 1991

Basketball	$100-$125
Cut signature	$6-$7
3x5 index card	$7
8x10 photograph	$130

Billy Cunningham (1943-) 1986

Basketball	$110
Cut signature	$6-$7
3x5 index card	$9
8x10 photograph	$15-$17

Robert Davies (1920-1990) 1969

Basketball	$100
Cut signature	$20
3x5 index card	$25
8x10 photograph	$45

Forrest DeBernardi * 1961

Basketball	$100
Cut signature	$15
3x5 index card	$18
8x10 photograph	$35

Dave DeBusschere (1940-) 1982

Basketball	$125-$150
Cut signature	$5-$6
3x5 index card	$8
8x10 photograph	$15-$20

Henry Dehnert * 1968

Basketball	$100
Cut signature	$7
3x5 index card	$9
8x10 photograph	$12-$17

Paul Endacott 1971

Basketball	$100
Cut signature	$6
3x5 index card	$10
8x10 photograph	$12-$17

Julius Erving (1950-) 1992

Basketball	$175-$225
Cut signature	$15
3x5 index card	$25
8x10 photograph	$30

Bud Foster 1964

Basketball	$125
Cut signature	$30
3x5 index card	$35
8x10 photograph	$50

Walt Frazier (1945-) 1987

Basketball	$100-$125
Cut signature	$15
3x5 index card	$20
8x10 photograph	$20

Marty Friedman * 1971

Basketball	$100
Cut signature	$15
3x5 index card	$20
8x10 photograph	$40

Joe Fulks (1921-1976) 1977

Basketball	$100
Cut signature	$20
3x5 index card	$25
8x10 photograph	$50

Clarence Gaines 1981

Basketball	$100
Cut signature	$7-$9
3x5 index card	$15
8x10 photograph	$20

Laddie Gale 1976

Basketball	$100
Cut signature	$7
3x5 index card	$12
8x10 photograph	$15

Harry Gallatin (1927-) 1990

Basketball	$110
Cut signature	$6-$8
3x5 index card	$15
8x10 photograph	$15-$18

William Gates 1988

Basketball	$125
Cut signature	$8-$10
3x5 index card	$12
8x10 photograph	$20-$25

Tom Gola (1933-) 1975

Basketball	$80-$100
Cut signature	$4
3x5 index card	$7
8x10 photograph	$14

Hal Greer (1936-) 1981

Basketball	$120
Cut signature	$4
3x5 index card	$3-$6
8x10 photograph	$17-$22

Robert Gruenig * 1963

Basketball	$125
Cut signature	$10-$15
3x5 index card	$12
8x10 photograph	$25-$35

Cliff Hagan (1931-) 1977

Basketball	$125
Cut signature	$4-$7
3x5 index card	$6
8x10 photograph	$20

Victor Hanson * 1960

Basketball	$125
Cut signature	$10-$14
3x5 index card	$15
8x10 photograph	$40

John Havlicek (1940-) 1983

Basketball	$150-$160
Cut signature	$10
3x5 index card	$15
8x10 photograph	$25

Connie Hawkins (1942-) 1991

Basketball	$125
Cut signature	$8
3x5 index card	$10
8x10 photograph	$22

Elvin Hayes (1945-) 1990

Basketball	$125
Cut signature	$8
3x5 index card	$12
8x10 photograph	$17

Tommy Heinsohn (1934-) 1985

Basketball	$125
Cut signature	$6
3x5 index card	$8
8x10 photograph	$17

Nat Holman (1945-) 1964

Basketball	$150
Cut signature	$15
3x5 index card	$20
8x10 photograph	$100

Red Holzman (1920-) 1985

Basketball	$125
Cut signature	$8-$10
3x5 index card	$15
8x10 photograph	$22-$27

Robert Houbregs (1932-) 1986

Basketball	$110
Cut signature	$5-$7
3x5 index card	$10
8x10 photograph	$15

Chuck Hyatt * 1959

Basketball	$100
Cut signature	$5
3x5 index card	$10
8x10 photograph	$25

Henry Iba * 1968

Basketball	$150
Cut signature	$10
3x5 index card	$15
8x10 photograph	$30

Dan Issel (1948-) 1992

Basketball	$115
Cut signature	$7
3x5 index card	$12
8x10 photograph	$15

William Johnson * 1976

Basketball	$125
Cut signature	$5
3x5 index card	$10
8x10 photograph	$30

Neil Johnston (1929-1978) 1989

Basketball	$110
Cut signature	$10
3x5 index card	$15
8x10 photograph	$35

K.C. Jones (1932-) 1988

Basketball	$100
Cut signature	$6
3x5 index card	$8
8x10 photograph	$15

Sam Jones (1933-) 1983

Basketball	$120
Cut signature	$6-$7
3x5 index card	$8
8x10 photograph	$20

Bobby Knight (1931-) 1990

Basketball	$100
Cut signature	$10
3x5 index card	$12
8x10 photograph	$15

Edward Krause 1975

Basketball	$110
Cut signature	$5
3x5 index card	$10
8x10 photograph	$20

Bob Kurland 1961

Basketball	$110
Cut signature	$5
3x5 index card	$10
8x10 photograph	$15-$20

Bob Lanier (1948-) 1992

Basketball	$100
Cut signature	$7
3x5 index card	$10
8x10 photograph	$15

Joe Lapchick * 1966

Basketball	$150
Cut signature	$10
3x5 index card	$15
8x10 photograph	$35

Clyde Lovellette (1929-) 1987

Basketball	$110
Cut signature	$4-$7
3x5 index card	$9
8x10 photograph	$15-$17

Jerry Lucas (1940-) 1979

Basketball	$125
Cut signature	$5
3x5 index card	$10
8x10 photograph	$15-$20

Hank Luisetti 1959

Basketball	$125
Cut signature	$7
3x5 index card	$12
8x10 photograph	$15-$25

Ed Macauley (1928-) 1960

Basketball	$150
Cut signature	$15
3x5 index card	$20
8x10 photograph	$30

Pete Maravich (1947-1988) 1987

Basketball	$500-$600
Cut signature	$10
3x5 index card	$15
8x10 photograph	$225-$250

Slater Martin (1925-) 1981

Basketball	$130
Cut signature	$4-$6
3x5 index card	$9
8x10 photograph	$17

Branch McCracken * 1960

Basketball	$100
Cut signature	$7
3x5 index card	$10
8x10 photograph	$20

Jack McCracken * 1962

Basketball	$100
Cut signature	$7
3x5 index card	$10
8x10 photograph	$20

Bobby McDermott 1987

Basketball	$110
Cut signature	$6-$7
3x5 index card	$14
8x10 photograph	$15-$20

Al McGuire (1928-) 1991

Basketball	$75-$100
Cut signature	$5
3x5 index card	$10
8x10 photograph	$15

Dick McGuire (1926-) 1992

Basketball	$75-$100
Cut signature	$5
3x5 index card	$10
8x10 photograph	$20

Frank McGuire 1976

Basketball	$110
Cut signature	$7
3x5 index card	$9
8x10 photograph	$16-$18

Ray Meyer 1978

Basketball	$125
Cut signature	$15
3x5 index card	$20
8x10 photograph	$30

George Mikan (1924-) 1959

Basketball	$125
Cut signature	$7
3x5 index card	$10
8x10 photograph	$20-$25

William Mokray *   1965

Basketball	$100
Cut signature	$10
3x5 index card	$15
8x10 photograph	$35

Earl Monroe (1944-) 1989

Basketball	$125
Cut signature	$8-$10
3x5 index card	$12
8x10 photograph	$15-$20

Calvin Murphy (1948-) 1992

Basketball	$100
Cut signature	$6
3x5 index card	$8
8x10 photograph	$15

Charles Murphy * 1960

Basketball	$100
Cut signature	$7-$10
3x5 index card	$12
8x10 photograph	$15-$20

James Naismith * 1959

Basketball	$1,000
Cut signature	$200
3x5 index card	$300
8x10 photograph	$500

Larry O'Brien * 1990

Basketball	$125
Cut signature	$25
3x5 index card	$15
8x10 photograph	$65

Harlan Page * 1962

Basketball	$100
Cut signature	$5
3x5 index card	$10
8x10 photograph	$20

Bob Pettit (1932-) 1970

Basketball	$150
Cut signature	$10
3x5 index card	$15
8x10 photograph	$20-$25

Andy Phillip (1922-) 1961

Basketball	$100
Cut signature	$5-$7
3x5 index card	$7
8x10 photograph	$15-$16

Maurice Podoloff * 1973

Basketball	$100
Cut signature	$5
3x5 index card	$7
8x10 photograph	$20

Jim Pollard * 1977

Basketball	$100
Cut signature	$5
3x5 index card	$10
8x10 photograph	$15

Frank Ramsey (1931-) 1981

Basketball	$100
Cut signature	$6-$7
3x5 index card	$10
8x10 photograph	$15

Jack Ramsey 1991

Basketball	$125
Cut signature	$7
3x5 index card	$10
8x10 photograph	$20

Willis Reed (1942-) 1981

Basketball	$100
Cut signature	$9
3x5 index card	$12
8x10 photograph	$20

Oscar Robertson (1938-) 1979

Basketball	$125
Cut signature	$8
3x5 index card	$10
8x10 photograph	$25-$35

John Roosma * 1961

Basketball	$100
Cut signature	$5
3x5 index card	$10
8x10 photograph	$15

Adolph Rupp * 1968

Basketball	$100
Cut signature	$5
3x5 index card	$10
8x10 photograph	$50

Bill Russell (1934-) 1974

Basketball	$500-$550
Cut signature	$30
3x5 index card	$40
8x10 photograph	$200

John Russell * 1974

Basketball	$150
Cut signature	$20
3x5 index card	$25
8x10 photograph	$45

Abe Saperstein * 1970

Basketball	$150
Cut signature	$10
3x5 index card	$20
8x10 photograph	$75

Dolph Schayes (1928-) 1972

Basketball	$125
Cut signature	$10
3x5 index card	$15
8x10 photograph	$15-$20

Ernest Schmidt * 1973

Basketball	$110
Cut signature	$7
3x5 index card	$12
8x10 photograph	$20-$30

John Schommer * 1959

Basketball	$100
Cut signature	$5
3x5 index card	$10
8x10 photograph	$15

Barney Sedran * 1962

Basketball	$100
Cut signature	$5
3x5 index card	$7
8x10 photograph	$15

Bill Sharman (1926-) 1975

Basketball	$100
Cut signature	$5
3x5 index card	$7
8x10 photograph	$20

Bill Walton followed Kareem Abdul-Jabbar's path from UCLA to the Hall of Fame.

Dean Smith 1982

Basketball	$100
Cut signature	$15-$18
3x5 index card	$20
8x10 photograph	$25-$35

Amos Alonzo Stagg * 1959

Basketball	$150
Cut signature	$7
3x5 index card	$15
8x10 photograph	$30

Christian Steinmetz * 1961

Basketball	$110
Cut signature	$8
3x5 index card	$12
8x10 photograph	$20-$30

John Thompson * 1962

Basketball	$100
Cut signature	$8
3x5 index card	$10
8x10 photograph	$30

Nate Thurmond (1941-) 1984

Basketball	$115
Cut signature	$6-$8
3x5 index card	$12
8x10 photograph	$15-$20

Jack Twyman (1934-) 1982

Basketball	$125
Cut signature	$6-$9
3x5 index card	$9
8x10 photograph	$15-$18

Wes Unseld (1946-) 1987

Basketball	$110
Cut signature	$6-$10
3x5 index card	$9
8x10 photograph	$15-$20

Robert Vandivier * 1974

Basketball	$100
Cut signature	$5
3x5 index card	$7
8x10 photograph	$25

Edward Wachter * 1961

Basketball	$100
Cut signature	$6
3x5 index card	$8
8x10 photograph	$35

Bill Walton (1952-) 1992

Basketball	$125
Cut signature	$6
3x5 index card	$10
8x10 photograph	$20-$25

Robert Wanzer (1921-) 1986

Basketball	$125
Cut signature	$5-$6
3x5 index card	$10
8x10 photograph	$16-$17

Jerry West (1938-) 1979

Basketball	$150
Cut signature	$7
3x5 index card	$10
8x10 photograph	$25-$30

Lenny Wilkens (1937-) 1988

Basketball	$100
Cut signature	$6-$10
3x5 index card	$20
8x10 photograph	$12-$15

John Wooden 1972

Basketball	$115
Cut signature	$8-$10
3x5 index card	$15
8x10 photograph	$15-$20

Retired players

Player	8x10 photo/ball	
Zaid Abdul-Aziz	$6	$30
Alvan Adams	$10-$12	$70
Rick Adelman	$8-$10	$60
Mark Aguirre	$10-$11	$65
Danny Ainge	$15	$100
Lucius Allen	$10	$50
Curly Armstrong	$25	$75
Al Attles	$12-$14	$90
Dennis Awtrey	$7	$30
Greg Ballard	$9-$10	$50
Mike Bantom	$8	$30
Marvin Barnes	$12	$50
Jim Barnett	$7	$30
Dick Barnett	$20	$75
Butch Beard	$7	$30
Zelmo Beatty	$15-$16	$90
Byron Beck	$7	$30
Ron Behagen	$7	$30
Kent Benson	$7	$30
Walter Berry	$6	$30
Henry Bibby	$10	$70
Larry Bird	$35	$200
Otis Birdsong	$10-$12	$70
John Block	$7	$30
Tom Boerwinkle	$10-$11	$65
Ron Boone	$20	$100
Bob Boozer	$20	$100
Dudley Bradley	$6	$30
Carl Braun	$20-$22	$90
Jim Brewer	$7	$30
Ron Brewer	$7	$30
Junior Bridgeman	$12	$85
Bill Bridges	$7	$30
Allan Bristow	$8	$35
Michael Brooks	$7	$30
Fred Brown	$12-$14	$75
Quinn Buckner	$7	$30
Tom Burleson	$8-$9	$65
Joe Caldwell	$15	$50
Corky Calhoun	$8	$40
Mack Calvin	$9	$65
Austin Carr	$12-$13	$100
Kenny Carr	$8	$30
M.L. Carr	$15	$100
Joe Barry Carroll	$6-$10	$55
Harvey Catchings	$7-$10	$50
Maurice Cheeks	$8-$13	$95
Phil Chenier	$8-$10	$80
Jim Chones	$10-$12	$85
Archie Clark	$15-$18	$90
Jim Cleamons	$6	$30
John Clemens	$6	$30
Sweetwater Clifton	$35	$100
Doug Collins	$18	$100
Darwin Cook	$7	$30
Michael Cooper	$8-$12	$85
Larry Costello	$18	$100
Charlie Criss	$6	$30
Dick Cunningham	$6-$8	$30-$50
Adrian Dantley	$14-$17	$100
Louie Dampier	$15	$95
Bob Dandridge	$15-$16	$95
Mel Daniels	$14	$75
Adrian Dantley	$14-$16	$100
Brad Davis	$7-$8	$50
Mickey Davis	$6-$7	$40
Walter Davis	$12-$14	$95
Darryl Dawkins	$12-$13	$90
Connie Dierking	$15-$18	$70
Coby Dietrick	$7	$30
Ernie DiGregorio	$12	$85
James Donaldson	$8-$10	$60
John Drew	$6	$35

Autographs

Charles Dudley	$6	$30
Walter Dukes	$35	$100
Mike Dunleavy	$12	$75
T.R. Dunn	$8	$50
James Eakins	$6	$30
Dike Eddleman	$15	$70
LeRoy Ellis	$14	$70
Len Elmore	$6	$30
Wayne Embry	$14	$70
Alex English	$15-$20	$85
Gene Englund	$22	$100
Keith Erickson	$9	$60
Julius Erving	$35-$40	$175
Mike Evans	$6	$30
Joseph Fabel	$25	$100
Mike Farmer	$8	$45
Bob Ferry	$9	$60
Ken Fields	$6	$30
Hank Finkel	$7	$30
Jerry Fleishman	$10	$80
Chris Ford	$7	$30
Phil Ford	$14	$85
Fred Foster	$6	$30
James Fox	$7	$30
Nat Frankel	$25	$75
World B. Free	$16	$100
Donnie Freeman	$14	$60
Bill Gabor	$20	$75
Elmer Gainer	$20	$75
Mike Gale	$6	$30
Dave Gambee	$9	$50
Jack George	$15	$75
Gus Gerard	$7	$35
George Gervin	$15	$100
John Gianelli	$9	$40
Herm Gilliam	$9	$40
Artis Gilmore	$15-$25	$90
George Glamack	$20	$75
Mike Glenn	$6	$30
Mike Gminski	$8	$55
Gail Goodrich	$15	$90
Gerald Govan	$6	$30
Joseph Graboski	$20	$100
Michael Green	$6	$30
Sihugo Green	$18	$75
David Greenwood	$8	$40
Kevin Grevey	$9	$45
Paul Griffin	$7	$30
Bob Gross	$9	$35
Ernie Grunfeld	$12	$70
Richie Guerin	$22	$100
Matt Guokas	$9	$50
Happy Hairston	$12-$14	$100
Dale Hamilton	$22	$75
Alex Hannum	$18	$75
Bill Hanzlik	$6	$30
Clem Haskins	$10	$50
Steve Hawes	$6	$30
Tom Hawkins	$14	$60
Spencer Haywood	$22	$100
Garfield Heard	$8	$40
Clarence Hermsen	$14	$70
Fred Hetzel	$6	$30
William Hewitt	$6	$30
Arthur Heyman	$10	$45
Wayne Hightower	$10	$45
Armond Hill	$7	$40
Darnell Hillman	$9	$50
Craig Hodges	$8-$12	$70
Lionel Hollins	$9-$14	$75
Bailey Howell	$20	$100
Phil Hubbard	$7	$50
Lou Hudson	$18	$80
Rod Hundley	$12	$60
Warren Jabali	$6	$35
Phil Jackson	$15	$75
Charles Johnson	$6	$30
Clem Johnson	$6	$30
Dennis Johnson	$12-$15	$100
Eddie Johnson	$9	$75
George L. Johnson	$6	$30
George T. Johnson	$6	$30
Gus Johnson	$35	$150
Magic Johnson	$45	$225
Marques Johnson	$12	$50
Mickey Johnson	$8	$35
Ollie Johnson	$8	$45
Bobby Jones	$15	$90
Caldwell Jones	$12	$70
Steve Jones	$12-$16	$90
Wali Jones	$6-$8	$45
George Karl	$8-$10	$55
Richard Kelley	$7	$35
Clark Kellogg	$7	$40
Greg Kelser	$6	$30
Larry Kenon	$12	$80
Toby Kimball	$7	$35
Bernard King	$15-$16	$85
James King	$6	$30
Robert Kinney	$25	$100
Walter Kirk	$10	$65
Billy Knight	$10-$13	$70
Don Kojis	$12	$50
Jim Krebs	$35	$125
Steve Kuberski	$7	$35
Kevin Kunnert	$7	$35
Mitch Kupchak	$8-$13	$80
Sam Lacey	$10-$13	$75
Tom Lagarde	$6	$30
Bill Laimbeer	$12-$14	$90
Jeff Lamp	$6	$30
Mark Landsberger	$6	$30
Bob Lanier	$15-$18	$110
Allen Leavell	$8	$40
Clyde Lee	$8	$40
George Lee	$8	$40
Keith Lee	$7	$35
Ronnie Lee	$7	$35
Bob Leonard	$18	$100
Fred Lewis	$8	$40

Michael Lewis	$8	$40
Reggie Lewis	$50	$200
Scott Lloyd	$6	$30
Don Lofgran	$28	$125
John Logan	$25	$125
John Loscutoff	$15	$100
Kevin Loughery	$12	$70
Bob Love	$15-$16	$65
John Lucas	$16	$75
Maurice Lucas	$12-$14	$75
Raymond Lumpp	$10	$60
Kyle Macy	$7	$45
John Mahnken	$12	$65
Rick Mahorn	$9-$13	$70
Moses Malone	$20	$115
Ed Manning	$6	$30
Press Maravich	$35	$125
Jack Marin	$14	$90
Wes Mathews	$6	$30
Cedric Maxwell	$14	$90
Don May	$6	$30
Scott May	$6	$30
Bob McAdoo	$13	$90
John McCarthy	$8	$40
Theodore McClain	$7	$30
Bill McGill	$7	$30
George McGinnis	$15	$80
Jon McGlocklin	$10-$12	$60
Kevin McHale	$15-$20	$125
Kevin McKenna	$6	$30
Stan McKenzie	$8	$40
Horace McKinnney	$14	$75
William McKinney	$6	$30
McCoy McLemore	$7	$35
Jack McMahon	$25	$125
Tom McMillen	$15	$85
James McMillian	$7	$35
Mark McNamara	$6	$30
Larry McNeill	$6	$30
Bill Melchionni	$9	$50
Dean Meminger	$7	$40
John Mengelt	$8	$40
Joe Meriweather	$7	$35
David Meyers	$10	$60
Vern Mikkelsen	$16-$18	$100
Eddie Miles	$8	$40
Walter Miller	$25	$100
Steve Mix	$9	$40
Paul Mokeski	$6	$30
Sidney Moncrief	$12-$15	$80
Eric Money	$6	$30
Eugene Moore	$6	$30
John Moore	$6	$30
Jack Moreland	$35	$125
Rick Mount	$12	$85
Edwin Mueller	$6	$30
Jeff Mullins	$15	$85
Swen Nater	$9-$11	$65
Lloyd Neal	$8	$40
Don Nelson	$12-$14	$75
Bob Netolicky	$8	$40
Mike Newlin	$9	$45
Kurt Nimphius	$6	$30
Norm Nixon	$9-$12	$70
Willie Norwood	$7	$35
Mike O'Koren	$6	$30
Mark Olberding	$8	$40
Jawann Oldham	$6	$30
Enoch Olsen	$7	$35
Louis Orr	$7	$35
Tom Owens	$9	$45
Togo Palazzi	$9	$45
Robert Parish	$15	$120
Billy Paultz	$10-$13	$65
John Paxson	$14	$75
John Pelkington	$12	$70
Curtis Perry	$9	$45
Geoff Petrie	$12	$80
Drazen Petrovic	$45	$130
Ben Poquette	$6	$30
Howard Porter	$6	$30
Kevin Porter	$7	$35
Clifford Ray	$7	$40
Kevin Restani	$6	$30
Michael Ray Richardson	$7	$35
Pat Riley	$12	$100
Mike Riordan	$7	$35
Bill Robinzine	$7	$35
Dave Robisch	$7	$35
Red Rocha	$18	$100
Tree Rollins	$7	$40
Dan Roundfield	$10	$70
Curtis Rowe	$7	$40
Jeff Ruland	$9	$65
Cazzie Russell	$16-$18	$100
Herman Schaefer	$25	$100
Fred Schaus	$25	$100
Dale Schlueter	$6	$30
Alvin Scott	$6	$30
Charlie Scott	$14	$70
Lonnie Shelton	$8	$50
Charles Shipp	$35	$125
Purvis Short	$9	$60
Gene Shue	$12-$18	$55
John Shumate	$8	$40
Jack Sikma	$10-$14	$75
James Silas	$15	$75
Paul Silas	$15	$75
Ralph Simpson	$8	$40
Jerry Sloan	$10	$80
Bobby Smith	$8	$45
Elmore Smith	$12	$60
Greg Smith	$7	$35
Phil Smith	$7	$35
Randy Smith	$12	$
Dick Snyder	$8	$45
Rory Sparrow	$7-$11	$60
Kevin Stacom	$6	$30
Dave Stallworth	$8	$40
Larry Steele	$7	$35

Autographs

Steve Stipanovich	$7	$35
Brian Taylor	$7	$40
Thomas Thacker	$7	$35
Reggie Theus	$10-$13	$70
Isiah Thomas	$15-$20	$125
David Thompson	$18	$95
George Thompson	$14	$70
Mychal Thompson	$8	$40
Rudy Tomjanovich	$12-$16	$75
Dick Van Arsdale	$12-$15	$80
Tom Van Arsdale	$12-$15	$80
Jan Van Breda Kolff	$10	$65
Butch Van Breda Kolff	$15	$80
Norm Van Lier	$12	$90
Kiki Vandeweghe	$12	$70
Neal Walk	$12	$60
Chet Walker	$20	$80
Foots Walker	$7-$10	$65
Kermit Washington	$9	$60
Richard Washington	$6	$30
Slick Watts	$15	$75
Marvin Webster	$8	$45
Scott Wedman	$9	$60
Robert Weiss	$7	$35
Walter Wesley	$7	$35
Paul Westphal	$9-$11	$70
JoJo White	$9-$12	$75
Sidney Wicks	$12-$14	$80
Jamaal Wilkes	$15-$18	$80
Chuck Williams	$6	$30
Freeman Williams	$8	$40
Ron Williams	$6	$30
Sly Williams	$6	$30
Brian Winters	$16	$75
Willie Wise	$9	$50
David Wohl	$6	$30
Orlando Woolridge	$9	$60
James Worthy	$14	$100

Active players

Player	8x10	Photo/ball
Michael Adams	$10	$60
Ken Anderson	$13	$95
Greg Anthony	$10	$70
B.J. Armstrong	$10	$95
Stacey Augmon	$14	$100
Thurl Bailey	$11	$70
Vin Baker	$13	$95
Charles Barkley	$30	$150
Dana Barros	$12	$80
Benoit Benjamin	$6	$60
Rolando Blackman	$10	$60
Muggsy Bogues	$13	$80
Manute Bol	$9-$11	$65
Sam Bowie	$7-$10	$75
Frank Brickowski	$6	$30
Michael Cage	$7	$35
Anoine Carr	$8-$10	$95
Bill Cartwright	$12-$13	$95
Sam Cassell	$15	$100
Cedric Ceballos	$13	$70
Tom Chambers	$11	$75
Rex Chapman	$8-$12	$85
Calbert Cheaney	$14	$95
Derrick Coleman	$13	$75
Lester Conner	$6	$35
Terry Cummings	$14	$90
Del Curry	$12	$70
Brad Daugherty	$13	$90
Johnny Dawkins	$6-$10	$70
Vlade Divac	$12	$75
Clyde Drexler	$17-$20	$100
Kevin Duckworth	$6-$10	$70
Joe Dumars	$14	$85
Mark Eaton	$10	$65
Blue Edwards	$12	$70
Sean Elliott	$13	$85
Dale Ellis	$10	$65
Patrick Ewing	$25	$150
Danny Ferry	$8	$60
Rick Fox	$8	$60
Eric Floyd	$9-$10	$70
Armon Gilliam	$8-$9	$75
Harvey Grant	$10	$70
Horace Grant	$15	$100
A.C. Green	$12	$85
Darrell Griffith	$10	$70
Anfernee Hardaway	$18	$125
Tim Hardaway	$15-$20	$95
Derek Harper	$9-$12	$90
Ron Harper	$10	$70
Hersey Hawkins	$12	$90
Grant Hill	$25	$125
Jeff Hornacek	$12	$70
Robert Horry	$16	$115
Bobby Hurley	$13	$90
Marc Iavaroni	$8	$60
Jimmy Jackson	$13	$95
Mark Jackson	$14	$100
Kevin Johnson	$15	$100
Larry Johnson	$20	$115
Michael Jordan	$50	$275
Shawn Kemp	$18-$25	$125
Steve Kerr	$16	$80
Jerome Kersey	$10-$12	$70
Jon Koncak	$10	$65
Toni Kukoc	$14	$100
Chrisitan Laettner	$20	$100
Alton Lister	$8	$30
Brad Lohaus	$6	$30
Grant Long	$6	$30
Dan Majerle	$20	$100
Jeff Malone	$12	$75
Karl Malone	$18	$125

Danny Manning	$12	$110	Alvin Robertson	$8	$45
Donyell Marshall	$14	$70	Cliff Robinson	$12	$80
Jamal Mashburn	$13	$95	David Robinson	$18	$125
Don MacLean	$10	$65	Glenn Robinson	$16	$115
Xavier McDaniel	$10-$15	$60	Dennis Rodman	$18	$115
Harold Miner	$11	$70	Rodney Rodgers	$10	$70
Eric Montross	$12	$70	Jalen Rose	$12	$80
Alonzo Mourning	$20	$125	John Salley	$8-$10	$65
Chris Mullin	$13	$115	Ralph Sampson	$12	$75
Larry Nance	$13	$80	Detlef Schrempf	$14	$75
Johnny Newman	$10	$60	Byron Scott	$13	$70
Ken Norman	$10	$60	Rony Seikaly	$13	$80
Charles Oakley	$12	$65	Lionel Simmons	$10	$65
Hakeem Olajuwon	$25-$30	$135	Scott Skiles	$10	$65
Shaquille O'Neal (Magic)	$35	$200	Kenny Smith	$15	$80
Billy Owens	$12	$65	Steve Smith	$10	$50
Gary Payton	$12	$85	Rik Smits	$12	$65
Anthony Peeler	$10	$65	Latrell Sprewell	$10	$90
Will Perdue	$8	$50	John Starks	$12	$70
Sam Perkins	$11	$55	John Stockton	$15	$95
Ricky Pierce	$9-$12	$75	Rod Strickland	$12	$75
Ed Pinckney	$10	$60	Roy Tarpley	$10	$65
Scottie Pippen	$25	$125	Otis Thorpe	$13	$75
Olden Polynice	$7	$35	Sedale Threatt	$13	$75
Terry Porter	$13	$95	Wayman Tisdale	$10-$12	$80
Paul Pressey	$7-$8	$55	Nick Van Exel	$12-$15	$95
Mark Price	$14	$85	C. Weatherspoon	$13	$75
Kurt Rambis	$8-$14	$75	Spud Webb	$13	$75
Glen Rice	$13	$80	Chris Webber	$20	$100
Isaiah Rider	$14	$95	Mark West	$10	$50
Mitch Ritchmond	$12	$75	Dominique Wilkins	$18-$20	$115
Doc Rivers	$9-$13	$90	Walt Williams	$10-$14	$60
Fred Roberts	$6-$8	$50	Kevin Willis	$10	$70

Basketballs

- NBA synthetic leather Spalding autographed basketballs by Jason Kidd $100, Hakeem Olajuwon $125, David Robinson $135, Magic Johnson $250, Wilt Chamberlain $175, Julius Erving Rawlings $135, Chris Webber $100/$295, Charles Barkley $250, Elgin Baylor $125, Larry Bird $250, Magic Johnson $295, Alonzo Mourning $200, Shaquille O'Neal $295, Scottie Pippen $150, David Robinson $225
- Charles Barkley synthetic leather $135
- Synthetic leather signed by Shaquille O'Neal $175
- Charles Barkley official NBA ball $145
- Elgin Baylor single-signed NBA model ball.. .... $150
- Larry Bird single-signed NBA model ball $250
- Wilt Chamberlain single-signed NBA model ball $350
- Bob Cousy single-signed NBA model ball . $125

- Dave DeBusschere single-signed NBA model ball.. $150
- Clyde Drexler single-signed NBA model ball $150
- Julius Erving single-signed NBA model ball $150
- John Havlicek single-signed NBA model ball $150
- Connie Hawkins official NBA ball $105
- Magic Johnson single-signed NBA model ball.. $300
- Magic Johnson official NBA ball $400
- Michael Jordan single-signed NBA model ball.. $295
- Shawn Kemp official NBA ball $135
- Calvin Murphy official NBA ball $105
- David Robinson single-signed NBA model ball.. $150
- Barkley/Mullin/Pippen/Robinson models are each $150

Multiple and team-signed balls

- 1990 NBA All-Star ball, with 25 signatures on a regulation NBA ball, includes Magic Johnson, Larry Bird, Scottie Pippen, Charles Barkley, John Stockton, David Robinson, Clyde Drexler, James Worthy, Byron Scott, Kevin McHale, Robert Parish, Kevin Johnson, Reggie Lewis, Kareem Abdul-Jabbar, Isiah Thomas and Hakeem Olajuwon $795
- NBA synthetic leather basketball autographed by 12 1992 NBA All-Stars, including Patrick Ewing, Magic Johnson and Michael Jordan $395
- MVP ball, signed by Charles Barkley, Larry Bird, Julius Erving, Magic Johnson, Michael Jordan and Hakeem Olajuwon $325
- Dream Team II basketball, signed by 12 players, including Derrick Coleman, Joe Dumars, Kevin Johnson, Larry Johnson, Shawn Kemp, Dan Majerle, Reggie Miller, Alonzo Mourning, Shaquille O'Neal, Mark Price, Steve Smith and Dominique Wilkins $750
- 1983-84 Boston Celtics official Spalding NBA ball, signers include by Larry Bird, Kevin McHale, Dennis Johnson, Danny Ainge, Robert Parish, Scott Wedman and K.C. Jones.................... $1,195
- 1985-86 Boston Celtics world championship team-signed regulation NBA basketball, with 11 signatures, including Larry Bird, Kevin McHale, Danny Ainge, Dennis Johnson, Bill Walton, Robert Parish and K.C. Jones $1,095
- Boston Celtics 1992-93 green-and-white Celtics ball signed by 16 players, including Dee Brown, Reggie Lewis, Xavier McDaniel, Kevin McHale and Robert Parish........... $300
- 1993-94 Boston Celtics autographed team basketball................................ $350
- 1994-95 Boston Celtics NBA model ball. $95
- 1994-95Boston Celtics official NBA ball $145
- 1992-93 Charlotte Hornets NBA model ball.. .... $200
- 1990-91 Chicago Bulls Wilson basketball signed by 12 players from the World Championship team, including Bill Cartwright, Michael Jordan and Scottie Pippen...........................$475-$500
- 1990-91 Chicago Bulls team-signed NBA basketball................................ $900
- 1991-92 Chicago Bulls team-signed NBA basketball................................ $800
- 1992-93 Chicago Bulls World Champions $750
- 1992-93 Chicago Bulls team-signed NBA basketball................................ $700
- 1994-95 Chicago Bulls team-signed ball, official NBA Spalding indoor/outdoor ...$200
- 1992-93 Cleveland Cavaliers NBA ball..$175
- 1991-92 Denver Nuggets team-signed ball, with Dan Issel, Mark Macon, Dikembe Mutombo....................................$175
- Denver Nuggets NBA model ball, includes Dan Issel, Mark Macon and Dikembe Mutumbo....................................$175
- 1990-91 Detroit Pistons NBA ball.........$200
- 1987-88 Golden State Warriors ball, with Manute Bol, Chris Mullin, Mitch Richmond $175
- 1991-92 Golden State Warriors Spalding synthetic leather ball with 11 signatures, including Tim Hardaway, Chris Mullins, Billy Owens, Tyrone Hill and Sarunas Marciulionis $175
- 1993-94 Golden State Warriors team autographed ball....................................$350
- 1990-91 Houston Rockets ball, with Sleepy Floyd, Hakeem Olajuwon, Robert Smith.....$275
- 1991-92 Houston Rockets NBA ball $175
- 1993-94 Houston Rockets NBA model ball, signed by 11 players, including Robert Horry, Vernon Maxwell, Hakeem Olajuwon, Kenny Smith and Rudy Tomjanovich $450
- 1994-95 Houston Rockets team-signed ball, official NBA Spalding indoor/outdoor $250
- 1992 Los Angeles Clippers basketball signed by nine players, including Ron Harper, Danny Manning, Ken Norman, Loy Vaught $135
- 1987-88 Los Angeles Lakers ball autographed by 11 players, including Kareem Abdul-Jabbar, Michael Cooper, A.C. Green, Magic Johnson, Byron Scott, James Worthy $600
- 1989-90 Los Angeles Lakers ball autographed by 12 players, including Byron Scott, Magic Johnson and James Worthy $495
- 1991-92 Los Angeles Lakers Spalding synthetic leather ball with 12 signatures, including Magic Johnson, James Worthy, Byron Scott, A.C. Green, Vlade Divac and Mike Dunleavy....................................$295
- 1992-93 Los Angeles Lakers Spalding synthetic leather ball with 15 signatures, including Nick Van Exel, Vlade Divac, James Worthy, Kurt Rambis, Anthony Peeler and Sedale Threatt $195

Getting all members of a team poses a difficult challenge for collectors.

- 1994-95 Los Angeles Lakers team-signed ball, official NBA Spalding indoor/outdoor $200
- 1990-91 Miami Heat ball, includes Sherman Douglas, Rony Seikaly, Glen Rice $230
- .. 1993-94 New York Knicks team ball, NBA Spalding.. $300
- 1993-94 Minnesota Timberwolves autographed team basketball $350
- 1992-93 Orlando Magic NBA ball......... $600
- 1993-94 Orlando Magic NBA ball......... $700
- 1990-91 Philadelphia 76ers NBA ball.... $200
- 1992-93 Philadelphia 76ers NBA model ball, includes Armon Gilliam, Hersey Hawkins.. $175
- 1993-94 Philadelphia 76ers basketball signed by 11 players on a red, white and blue ball $125
- 1989-90 Phoenix Suns basketball signed by 10 players, including Tom Chambers, Jeff Hornacek, Kevin Johnson and Dan Majerle $210
- 1990-91 Phoenix Suns basketball, with Tom Chambers, Jeff Hornacek, Dan Majerle $275
- 1992-93 Phoenix Suns NBA model, includes Danny Ainge, Charles Barkley, Tom Chambers and Kevin Johnson $275
- 1993-94 Phoenix Suns basketball signed by 13 players, including Charles Barkley, A.C. Green and Kevin Johnson..................... $225

- 1991-92 Portland Trailblazers, including Danny Ainge, Clyde Drexler and Buck Williams... $250
- 1992-93 Portland Trailblazers NBA ball.... $225
- 1990-91 San Antonio Spurs basketball signed by 14 players, including Kenny Anderson, Larry Brown, Terry Cummings, Sean Elliott and David Robinson............................... $210
- 1993-94 San Antonio Spurs team ball, NBA Spalding $295
- 1994-95 San Antonio Spurs team-signed ball, official NBA Spalding indoor/outdoor $200
- 1992-93 Seattle Supersonics NBA model ball $145
- 1993 Seattle Supersonics 1993 team ball, NBA Spalding $295
- 1993-94 Seattle Supersonics autographed team ball $350
- 1994-95 Seattle Supersonics Wilson model ball... $145
- 1989-90 Utah Jazz basketball signed by 10 players, including Thurl Bailey, Mark Eaton, Darrell Griffith, Karl Malone and John Stockton $210
- 1989-90 Washington Bullets NBA rubber ball signed by Harvey Grant, Bernard King, Jeff Malone $100

Doc Rivers, above
Bill Cartwright, left

Shaquille O'Neal, above
Sergei Fedorov, right

Manon Rheaume, above
Gordie Howe, left

Hockey Hall of Famers

*deceased
U/I means unlikely or impossible

Sid Abel 1969

Puck	$15
1965-66 Topps card	$10
Cut signature	$2-$5
8x10 photograph	$12-$15

Jack Adams * 1959

Puck	$35
Hockey card	U/I
Cut signature	$12-$15
8x10 photograph	$35-$50

Syl Apps 1961

Puck	$70
1955-56 Parkhurst card	$20
Cut signature	$5-$7
8x10 photograph	$70

George Armstrong 1975

Puck	$25
1970-71 Topps card	$10
Cut signature	$5
8x10 photograph	$15

Ace Bailey * 1975

Puck	$40
1955-56 Parkhurst card	$30
Cut signature	$5
8x10 photograph	$40

Don Bain * 1945

Puck	$35
Hockey card	U/I
Cut signature	$15-$20
8x10 photograph	$35-$50

Hobey Baker 1945

Puck	$25
Hockey card	U/I
Cut signature	$10
8x10 photograph	$25

Bill Barber 1990

Puck	$15
1974-75 Topps card	$10
Cut signature	$5-$7
8x10 photograph	$10-$15

Marty Barry * 1965

Puck	$20
Hockey card	U/I
Cut signature	$9-$12
8x10 photograph	$17-$25

Andy Bathgate 1978

Puck	$20
1968-69 Topps card	$15
Cut signature	$6-$11
8x10 photograph	$15-$20

Jean Beliveau 1972

Puck	$25
1970-71 Topps card	$15
Cut signature	$6-$12
8x10 photograph	$20-$25

Clint Benedict * 1965

Puck	$40
Hockey card	U/I
Cut signature	$15-$18
8x10 photograph	$30-$40

Doug Bentley * 1964

Puck	$35
Hockey card	U/I
Cut signature	$15
8x10 photograph	$25-$35

Max Bentley * 1966

Puck	$40
1953-54 Parkhurst card	$20
Cut signature	$15-$16
8x10 photograph	$35-$45

Toe Blake 1966

Puck	$25
1966-67 Topps card	$10
Cut signature	$8-$12
8x10 photograph	$20

Leo Boivin 1986

Puck	$20
1964-65 Topps card	$15
Cut signature	$5-$10
8x10 photograph	$20-$25

Dickie Boon * 1952

Puck	$40
Hockey card	U/I
Cut signature	$18
8x10 photograph	$40

Mike Bossy 1991

Puck	$25-$40
1980-81 Topps card	$20
Cut signature	$5
8x10 photograph	$25

Butch Bouchard 1966

Puck	$15
1955-56 Parkhurst card	$7
Cut signature	$5
8x10 photograph	$12

Frank Boucher * 1958

Puck	$40
Hockey card	U/I
Cut signature	$15
8x10 photograph	$35

George Boucher * 1960

Puck	$45
Hockey card	U/I
Cut signature	$18
8x10 photograph	$40

John Bower 1976

Puck	$15-$25
1968-69 Topps card	$10
Cut signature	$7
8x10 photograph	$15-$20

Dubbie Bowie * 1945

Puck	$45
Hockey card	U/I
Cut signature	$18
8x10 photograph	$40

Frank Brimsek 1966

Puck	$20
Hockey card	U/I
Cut signature	$7
8x10 photograph	$15-$18

Punch Broadbent * 1962

Puck	$35
Hockey card	U/I
Cut signature	$15
8x10 photograph	$35

Turk Broda * 1967

Puck	$35
Hockey card	U/I
Cut signature	$22-$30
8x10 photograph	$35-$50

John Bucyk 1981

Puck	$20-$30
1970-71 Topps card	$10
Cut signature	$5
8x10 photograph	$15

Billy Burch 1974

Puck	$15
Hockey card	U/I
Cut signature	$5
8x10 photograph	$10

Harry Cameron * 1962

Puck	$50
Hockey card	U/I
Cut signature	$20
8x10 photograph	$45

Gerry Cheevers 1985

Puck	$35
1971-72 Topps card	$10
Cut signature	$6
8x10 photograph	$15-$25

King Clancy * 1958

Puck	$30
Hockey card	U/I
Cut signature	$12
8x10 photograph	$25-$30

Dit Clapper * 1947

Puck	$35
Hockey card	U/I
Cut signature	$5
8x10 photograph	$35

Bobby Clarke 1987

Puck	$30-$40
1974-75 Topps card	$10
Cut signature	$5
8x10 photograph	$15-$25

Sprague Cleghorn * 1958

Puck	$45
Hockey card	U/I
Cut signature	$18
8x10 photograph	$40-$50

Neil Colville 1967

Puck	$15
Hockey card	U/I
Cut signature	$3
8x10 photograph	$10

Charlie Conacher 1961

Puck	$15
Hockey card	U/I
Cut signature	$3
8x10 photograph	$12

Alex Connell * 1958

Puck	$40
Hockey card	U/I
Cut signature	$18
8x10 photograph	$40

William Cook * 1952

Puck	$50
Hockey card	U/I
Cut signature	$20
8x10 photograph	$45

Art Coulter 1974

Puck	$20
Hockey card	U/I
Cut signature	$5
8x10 photograph	$15

Yvan Cournoyer 1982

Puck	$25
1970-71 Topps card	$10
Cut signature	$5
8x10 photograph	$12-$15

Bill Cowley 1968

Puck	$40
Hockey card	U/I
Cut signature	$7
8x10 photograph	$30-$40

Rusty Crawford * 1962

Puck	$35
Hockey card	U/I
Cut signature	$15
8x10 photograph	$35

Jack Darragh * 1962

Puck	$40
Hockey card	U/I
Cut signature	$18
8x10 photograph	$40

Scotty Davidson * 1950

Puck	$50
Hockey card	U/I
Cut signature	$20
8x10 photograph	$45

Hap Day   1961

Puck	$15
Hockey card	U/I
Cut signature	$5
8x10 photograph	$12

Alex Delvecchio 1977

Puck	$25
1973-74 Topps card	$8
Cut signature	$5
8x10 photograph	$10-$15

Cy Denneny * 1959

Puck	$40
Hockey card	U/I
Cut signature	$18
8x10 photograph	$40

Gordie Drillon * 1975

Puck	$40
Hockey card	U/I
Cut signature	$18-$25
8x10 photograph	$40

Graham Drinkwater * 1950

Puck	$60
Hockey card	U/I
Cut signature	$25
8x10 photograph	$55-$60

Ken Dryden 1983

Puck	$75-$100
1972-73 Topps card	$40
Cut signature	$8
8x10 photograph	$75-$100

Woody Dumart 1992

Puck	$50
Hockey card	U/I
Cut signature	$15
8x10 photograph	$50

Thomas Dunderdale *   1974

Puck	$55
Hockey card	U/I
Cut signature	$25
8x10 photograph	$55

Bill Durnan * 1964

Puck	$45
Hockey card	U/I
Cut signature	$18
8x10 photograph	$45

Red Dutton * 1958

Puck	$30
Hockey card	U/I
Cut signature	$10
8x10 photograph	$25-$30

Babe Dye * 1970

Puck	$50
Hockey card	U/I
Cut signature	$18
8x10 photograph	$45

Phil Esposito 1984

Puck	$25-$40
1973-74 Topps card	$15
Cut signature	$6
8x10 photograph	$20-$30

Tony Esposito 1988

Puck	$25
1973-74 Topps card	$15
Cut signature	$6
8x10 photograph	$20

Arthur Farrell * 1965

Puck	$40
Hockey card	U/I
Cut signature	$15
8x10 photograph	$35

Fern Flaman 1990

Puck	$15
1990-91 Score card	$10
Cut signature	$5
8x10 photograph	$15

Frank Foyston * 1958

Puck	$45
Hockey card	U/I
Cut signature	$20
8x10 photograph	$45

Bernie "Boom Boom" Geoffrion was elected to the Hall of Fame in 1972.

Frank Frederickson * 1958

Puck	$45
Hockey card	U/I
Cut signature	$20
8x10 photograph	$45

Bill Gadsby 1970

Puck	$15
1965-66 Topps card	$10
Cut signature	$6
8x10 photograph	$12-$15

Bob Gainey 1992

Puck	$15
1979-80 Topps card	$8
Cut signature	$4
8x10 photograph	$12-$15

Chuck Gardiner * 1945

Puck	$55
Hockey card	U/I
Cut signature	$25
8x10 photograph	$55

Herb Gardiner * 1958

Puck	$40
Hockey card	U/I
Cut signature	$15
8x10 photograph	$35

Jimmy Gardner * 1962

Puck	$45
Hockey card	U/I
Cut signature	$15
8x10 photograph	$40

Bernie Boom Boom Geoffrion 1972

Puck	$15-$20
1967-68 Topps card	$10
Cut signature	$6
8x10 photograph	$15-$20

Eddie Gerard * 1945

Puck	$70
Hockey card	U/I
Cut signature	$30
8x10 photograph	$65

Eddie Giacomin 1987

Puck	$15-$25
1971-72 Topps card	$10
Cut signature	$6
8x10 photograph	$15-$20

Rod Gilbert 1982

Puck	$20
1971-72 Topps card	$10
Cut signature	$6
8x10 photograph	$20

Billy Gilmour * 1962

Puck	$50
Hockey card	U/I
Cut signature	$18
8x10 photograph	$45

Moose Goheen * 1952

Puck	$45
Hockey card	U/I
Cut signature	$20
8x10 photograph	$45

Ebbie Goodfellow * 1963

Puck	$30
Hockey card	U/I
Cut signature	$12
8x10 photograph	$30

Mike Grant * 1950

Puck	$40
Hockey card	U/I
Cut signature	$15
8x10 photograph	$35

Wilf Green * 1962

Puck	$20
Hockey card	U/I
Cut signature	$7
8x10 photograph	$15

Si Griffis * 1950

Puck	$70
Hockey card	U/I
Cut signature	$30
8x10 photograph	$65

George Hainsworth * 1961

Puck	$45
Hockey card	U/I
Cut signature	$18
8x10 photograph	$40

Glenn Hall 1975

Puck	$20
1969-70 Topps card	$12
Cut signature	$7
8x10 photograph	$15-$25

Joe Hall * 1961

Puck	$20
Hockey card	U/I
Cut signature	$5
8x10 photograph	$15

Doug Harvey 1973

Puck	$300
1952-53 Parkhurst card	$150
Cut signature	$15
8x10 photograph	$300

George Hay * 1958

Puck	$50
Hockey card	U/I
Cut signature	$20
8x10 photograph	$45

Riley Hern * 1962

Puck	$40
Hockey card	U/I
Cut signature	$18
8x10 photograph	$40

Bryan Hextall * 1969

Puck	$45
Hockey card	U/I
Cut signature	$18
8x10 photograph	$45

Hap Holmes * 1972

Puck	$35
Hockey card	U/I
Cut signature	$15
8x10 photograph	$35

Tom Hooper * 1962

Puck	$45
Hockey card	U/I
Cut signature	$18
8x10 photograph	$45

Red Horner 1965

Puck	$12-$15
Hockey card	U/I
Cut signature	$5
8x10 photograph	$12

Tim Horton * 1977

Puck	$300
1954-55 Parkhurst card	$150
Cut signature	$15
8x10 photograph	$300

Gordie Howe 1972

Puck	$30
1979-80 Topps card	$15
Cut signature	$7
8x10 photograph	$20-$25

Sydney Howe * 1965

Puck	$45
Hockey card	U/I
Cut signature	$20
8x10 photograph	$45

Harry Howell 1979

Puck	$15
1970-71 Topps card	$10
Cut signature	$6
8x10 photograph	$15

Bobby Hull is a popular guest on the card show circuit.

Bobby Hull 1983

Puck	$25-$30
1979-80 Topps card	$15
Cut signature	$7
8x10 photograph	$20-$25

J.B. Hutton 1962

Puck	$40
Hockey card	U/I
Cut signature	$18
8x10 photograph	$40

Harry Hyland * 1962

Puck	$45
Hockey card	U/I
Cut signature	$20
8x10 photograph	$45

Dick Irvin * 1958

Puck	$50
Hockey card	U/I
Cut signature	$22
8x10 photograph	$50

Busher Jackson 1971

Puck	$40
Hockey card	U/I
Cut signature	$20
8x10 photograph	$40

Ching Johnson * 1958

Puck	$30
Hockey card	U/I
Cut signature	$12
8x10 photograph	$30

Ernie Johnson * 1952

Puck	$30
Hockey card	U/I
Cut signature	$12
8x10 photograph	$30

Tom Johnson 1970

Puck	$40
1962-63 Parkhurst card	$20
Cut signature	$15
8x10 photograph	$40

Aurel Joliat * 1947

Puck	$75
Hockey card	U/I
Cut signature	$35
8x10 photograph	$75

Duke Keats * 1958

Puck	$50
Hockey card	U/I
Cut signature	$22
8x10 photograph	$50

Red Kelly 1969

Puck	$15
1967-68 Topps card	$10
Cut signature	$5
8x10 photograph	$15

Teeder Kennedy 1966

Puck	$15
1955-56 Parkhurst card	$10
Cut signature	$6
8x10 photograph	$15

Dave Keon 1986

Puck	$15-$20
1969-70 Topps card	$10
Cut signature	$6
8x10 photograph	$15-$20

Elmer Lach 1966

Puck	$15-$20
Hockey card	U/I
Cut signature	$6
8x10 photograph	$15-$20

Guy Lafleur 1988

Puck	$25-$40
1976-77 Topps card	$15
Cut signature	$6
8x10 photograph	$25

Newsy Lalonde * 1950

Puck	$65
Hockey card	U/I
Cut signature	$30
8x10 photograph	$65

Jacques Laperriere 1987

Puck	$15
1967-68 Topps card	$10
Cut signature	$5
8x10 photograph	$12-$15

Jack Laviolette * 1962

Puck	$30
Hockey card	U/I
Cut signature	$12
8x10 photograph	$30

Hugh Lehman * 1958

Puck	$50
Hockey card	U/I
Cut signature	$22
8x10 photograph	$50

Jacques Lemaire 1984

Puck	$20
1969-70 Topps card	$15
Cut signature	$5
8x10 photograph	$20

Percy LeSueur * 1961

Puck	$45
Hockey card	U/I
Cut signature	$20
8x10 photograph	$45

Herb Lewis * 1989

Puck	$45
Hockey card	U/I
Cut signature	$20
8x10 photograph	$45

Ted Lindsay 1966

Puck	$20
1959-60 Topps card	$25
Cut signature	$6
8x10 photograph	$20

Harry Lumley 1980

Puck	$20
Hockey card	U/I
Cut signature	$10
8x10 photograph	$20

Mickey MacKay * 1952

Puck	$50
Hockey card	U/I
Cut signature	$20
8x10 photograph	$45

Frank Mahovlich 1981

Puck	$25-$40
1972-73 Topps card	$10
Cut signature	$7
8x10 photograph	$20-$25

Joe Malone * 1950

Puck	$65
Hockey card	U/I
Cut signature	$30
8x10 photograph	$65

Sylvio Mantha * 1960

Puck	$25
Hockey card	U/I
Cut signature	$12
8x10 photograph	$25

Jack Marshall * 1965

Puck	$40
Hockey card	U/I
Cut signature	$18
8x10 photograph	$40

Fred Maxwell * 1962

Puck	$45
Hockey card	U/I
Cut signature	$20
8x10 photograph	$45

Lanny McDonald 1992

Puck	$30
1975-76 Topps card	$10
Cut signature	$5
8x10 photograph	$30

Frank McGee * 1945

Puck	$75
Hockey card	U/I
Cut signature	$35
8x10 photograph	$75

Billy McGimsie * 1962

Puck	$50
Hockey card	U/I
Cut signature	$20
8x10 photograph	$45

George McNamara * 1958

Puck	$40
Hockey card	U/I
Cut signature	$15
8x10 photograph	$35

Stan Mikita 1983

Puck	$20-$25
1972-73 Topps card	$10
Cut signature	$7
8x10 photograph	$20

Dickie Moore 1974

Puck	$20
1962-63 Parkhurst card	$10
Cut signature	$5
8x10 photograph	$20

Paddy Moran * 1958

Puck	$45
Hockey card	U/I
Cut signature	$18
8x10 photograph	$45

Howie Morenz * 1945

Puck	$450
Hockey card	U/I
Cut signature	$200
8x10 photograph	$450

Bill Mosienko * 1965

Puck	$25
Hockey card	U/I
Cut signature	$10
8x10 photograph	$25-$40

Frank Nighbor * 1947

Puck	$65
Hockey card	U/I
Cut signature	$30
8x10 photograph	$65

Reg Noble * 1962

Puck	$45
Hockey card	U/I
Cut signature	$18
8x10 photograph	$45

Buddy O'Connor * 1988

Puck	$40
Hockey card	U/I
Cut signature	$18
8x10 photograph	$35

Harry Oliver * 1967

Puck	$45
Hockey card	U/I
Cut signature	$20
8x10 photograph	$45

Bert Olmstead 1985

Puck	$12-$15
1961-62 Parkhurst card	$10
Cut signature	$5
8x10 photograph	$12-$15

Bobby Orr 1979

Puck	$60-$75
1973-74 Topps card	$35
Cut signature	$25
8x10 photograph	$50

Bernie Parent 1984

Puck	$15-$25
1973-74 Topps card	$10
Cut signature	$6
8x10 photograph	$15-$25

Brad Park 1988

Puck	$20-$30
1972-73 Topps card	$12
Cut signature	$6
8x10 photograph	$15-$25

Lester Patrick * 1947

Puck	$75
Hockey card	U/I
Cut signature	$35
8x10 photograph	$75

Lynn Patrick * 1980

Puck	$75
Hockey card	U/I
Cut signature	$35
8x10 photograph	$75

Gil Perreault 1990

Puck	$20-$30
1973-74 Topps card	$10
Cut signature	$6
8x10 photograph	$15-$20

Tommy Phillips * 1945

Puck	$65
Hockey card	U/I
Cut signature	$30
8x10 photograph	$65

Pierre Pilote 1975

Puck	$15-$25
1968-69 Topps card	$10
Cut signature	$6
8x10 photograph	$15

Didier Pitre * 1962

Puck	$50
Hockey card	U/I
Cut signature	$20
8x10 photograph	$45

Jacques Plante * 1978

Puck	$175
1958-59 Topps card	$250
Cut signature	$25
8x10 photograph	$300

Denis Potvin 1991

Puck	$20-$25
1975-76 Topps card	$15
Cut signature	$5
8x10 photograph	$20

Babe Pratt * 1966

Puck	$35
Hockey card	U/I
Cut signature	$15
8x10 photograph	$35

Joe Primeau * 1963

Puck	$50
Hockey card	U/I
Cut signature	$25
8x10 photograph	$50

Marcel Pronovost 1978

Puck	$15
1967-68 Topps card	$10
Cut signature	$6
8x10 photograph	$15

Bob Pulford 1991

Puck	$45
1960-61 Parkhurst card	$30
Cut signature	$20
8x10 photograph	$45

Harvey Pulford * 1945

Puck	$45
Hockey card	U/I
Cut signature	$20
8x10 photograph	$45

Bill Quackenbush 1976

Puck	$15
Hockey card	U/I
Cut signature	$5
8x10 photograph	$12

Frank Rankin * 1961

Puck	$50
Hockey card	U/I
Cut signature	$18
8x10 photograph	$45

Jean Ratelle 1985

Puck	$20-$30
1969-70 Topps card	$10
Cut signature	$5
8x10 photograph	$15-$20

Chuck Rayner 1973

Puck	$20
Hockey card	U/I
Cut signature	$5
8x10 photograph	$15-$20

Ken Reardon 1966

Puck	$25
Hockey card	U/I
Cut signature	$5
8x10 photograph	$20-$25

Henri Richard 1979

Puck	$15-$20
1969-70 Topps card	$10
Cut signature	$6
8x10 photograph	$15-$25

Maurice Richard 1961

Puck	$20
1955-56 Parkhurst	$75
Cut signature	$7
8x10 photograph	$20

George Richardson * 1950

Puck	$75
Hockey card	U/I
Cut signature	$35
8x10 photograph	$75

Gordie Roberts * 1971

Puck	$50
Hockey card	U/I
Cut signature	$18
8x10 photograph	$45

Art Ross * 1945

Puck	$50
Hockey card	U/I
Cut signature	$20
8x10 photograph	$45

Blair Russel * 1965

Puck	$35
Hockey card	U/I
Cut signature	$15
8x10 photograph	$35

Ernie Russell * 1965

Puck	$45
Hockey card	U/I
Cut signature	$18
8x10 photograph	$40

Jack Ruttan * 1962

Puck	$60
Hockey card	U/I
Cut signature	$25
8x10 photograph	$55

Maurice Richard was nicknamed "The Rocket."

Serge Savard 1986

Puck	$20
1970-71 Topps card	$10
Cut signature	$5
8x10 photograph	$20

Terry Sawchuck * 1971

Puck	$300
1953-54 Parkhurst card	$250
Cut signature	$30
8x10 photograph	$300

Fred Scanlan * 1965

Puck	$45
Hockey card	U/I
Cut signature	$18
8x10 photograph	$40

Milt Schmidt 1961

Puck	$15-$20
1965-66 Topps card	$10
Cut signature	$6
8x10 photograph	$15

Sweeney Schriner * 1962

Puck	$45
Hockey card	U/I
Cut signature	$20
8x10 photograph	$45

Earl Seibert 1963

Puck	$15
Hockey card	U/I
Cut signature	$6
8x10 photograph	$15

Eddie Shore * 1947

Puck	$200
Hockey card	U/I
Cut signature	$25
8x10 photograph	$60

Steve Shutt 1993

Puck	$15
1975-76 Topps card	$10
Cut signature	$5
8x10 photograph	$15

Babe Siebert * 1964

Puck	$45
Hockey card	U/I
Cut signature	$20
8x10 photograph	$45

Joe Simpson * 1962

Puck	$45
Hockey card	U/I
Cut signature	$20
8x10 photograph	$45

Darryl Sittler 1989

Puck	$15
1974-75 Topps card	$10
Cut signature	$5
8x10 photograph	$15

Alfred Smith * 1962

Puck	$45
Hockey card	U/I
Cut signature	$20
8x10 photograph	$45

Billy Smith 1993

Puck	$25
1974-75 Topps card	$10
Cut signature	$5
8x10 photograph	$25

Clint Smith 1991

Puck	$15
Hockey card	U/I
Cut signature	$5
8x10 photograph	$12

Hooley Smith * 1972

Puck	$40
Hockey card	U/I
Cut signature	$18
8x10 photograph	$40

Tommy Smith * 1973

Puck	$40
Hockey card	U/I
Cut signature	$15
8x10 photograph	$35

Allan Stanley 1981

Puck	$15
1967-68 Topps card	$10
Cut signature	$5
8x10 photograph	$15

Barney Stanley * 1962

Puck	$30
Hockey card	U/I
Cut signature	$15
8x10 photograph	$30

Jack Stewart * 1964

Puck	$30
Hockey card	U/I
Cut signature	$15
8x10 photograph	$30

Nels Stewart * 1962

Puck	$50
Hockey card	U/I
Cut signature	$22
8x10 photograph	$50

Bruce Stuart * 1961

Puck	$45
Hockey card	U/I
Cut signature	$20
8x10 photograph	$45

Fred Taylor * 1947

Puck	$45
Hockey card	U/I
Cut signature	$18
8x10 photograph	$40

Tiny Thompson * 1959

Puck	$50
Hockey card	U/I
Cut signature	$20
8x10 photograph	$50

Vladislav Tretiak 1989

Puck	$50-$75
Hockey card	U/I
Cut signature	$22
8x10 photograph	$50-$75

Harry Trihey * 1950

Puck	$65
Hockey card	U/I
Cut signature	$30
8x10 photograph	$65

Norm Ullman 1982

Puck	$15
1968-69 Topps card	$10
Cut signature	$6
8x10 photograph	$15

Georges Vezina * 1945

Puck	$250
Hockey card	U/I
Cut signature	$100
8x10 photograph	$250

Jack Walker * 1960

Puck	$45
Hockey card	U/I
Cut signature	$20
8x10 photograph	$45

Marty Walsh * 1962

Puck	$45
Hockey card	U/I
Cut signature	$22
8x10 photograph	$45

Harry Watson * 1962

Puck	$55
Hockey card	U/I
Cut signature	$25
8x10 photograph	$55

Cooney Weiland * 1971

Puck	$50
Hockey card	U/I
Cut signature	$22
8x10 photograph	$50

Harry Westwick * 1962

Puck	$55
Hockey card	U/I
Cut signature	$25
8x10 photograph	$55

Fred Whitcroft * 1962

Puck	$55
Hockey card	U/I
Cut signature	$25
8x10 photograph	$55

Gordon Wilson * 1962

Puck	$40
Hockey card	U/I
Cut signature	$15
8x10 photograph	$35

Gump Worsley 1980

Puck	$25
1968-69 Topps card	$15
Cut signature	$10
8x10 photograph	$25

Roy Worters 1969

Puck	$40
Hockey card	U/I
Cut signature	$18
8x10 photograph	$40

Active players

Active players	Autographed 8x10s
Tony Amonte	$12-$13
Glenn Anderson	$8
Dave Andreychuk	$6
Tom Barrasso	$8
Don Beaupre	$7
Brian Bellows	$12
Ray Bourque	$18
Jeff Beukeboom	$10
Ray Bourque	$20
Neal Broten	$8
Pavel Bure	$20
Sean Burke	$10
Guy Carbonneau	$9
Bob Carpenter	$12
Jon Casey	$9
Chris Chelios	$8
Dino Ciccarelli	$12
Paul Coffey	$15-$20
Shayne Corson	$6
Geoff Courtnall	$8
Russ Courtnall	$7
Murray Craven	$7
Adam Creighton	$8
Ulf Dahlen	$7
Alexandre Daigle	$22
Alex Delvecchio	$10
Kevin Dineen	$4
Pat Falloon	$12-$17
Sergei Fedorov	$12
Ron Francis	$10
Grant Fuhr	$12
Mike Gartner	$14
Tony Granato	$6-13
Dirk Graham	$7
Wayne Gretzky	$35-$45
Dale Hawerchuk	$12
Glenn Healy	$7
Ron Hextall	$12-$15
Kelly Hrudey	$12
Brett Hull	$20
Dale Hunter	$8
Al Iafrate	$12
Jaromir Jagr	$20-$25
Curtis Joseph	$18-$20
Petr Klima	$9
Jari Kurri	$12-$15
Pat LaFontaine	$14
Reggie Lemelin	$10
Claude Lemieux	$10
Mario Lemieux	$30-$40
Eric Lindros	$25-$30
Ken Linseman	$8
Al MacInnis	$7
John MacLean	$9
Craig MacTavish	$7
Basil McRae	$6
Marty McSorley	$7
Rick Meagher	$8
Mark Messier	$20-$30
Rick Middleton	$7-$15
Alexander Mogilny	$28
Mike Modano	$10
Andy Moog	$12-$15
Joe Mullen	$14
Kirk Muller	$9

Mats Naslund $11	Denis Savard.. $14
Cam Neely... $25	Teemu Selanne $15
Bernie Nicholls............................. $10-$14	Brendan Shanahan ....$15-$20
Joe Nieuwendyk .... $15-$17	Peter Stastny $12
Adam Oates................................... $12-$15	Gary Suter.. $10
Dave Poulin $8	Brent Sutter.. $10
Bob Probert $8	Dave Taylor $10
Rob Ramage $6	Esa Tikkanen $8
Mark Recchi $12	Mark Tinordi... $6
Manon Rheaume .... $15-$20	Rick Tocchet... $15
Mike Richter... $7	Darren Turcotte..................................... $12
Luc Robitaille .... $12-$15	Pierre Turgeon $10
Jeremy Roenick.................................... $20	John Vaniesbrouck $12
Patrick Roy... $20	Mike Vernon... $10
Christian Ruuttu $8	Steve Yzerman.............................$20-$30
Joe Sakic...................................... $12-$17	Zarley Zalapski $6
Thomas Sandstrom...................... $10-$14	

Retired players

Lou Angotti $12	Reggie Fleming..................................... $10
Wayne Babych $8	Bill Flett.. $8
Ralph Backstrom $12	Val Fonteyne.. $8
Dave Balon $9	Louie Fontinato.................................... $12
Murray Bannerman $10	Jean-Guy Gendron $9
Bobby Bauer... $12	Gilles Gilbert $8
Bob Baun.. $12	Clark Gillies... $10
Red Rerenson $12	Bill Goldsworthy $9
Dan Bouchard.. $8	Butch Goring $12
Andre Boudrias $8	Phil Goyette.. $12
Rob Brown $12	Danny Grant $10
Charlie Burns $7	Vic Hadfield $15
Wayne Cashman.................................. $12	Alan Haworth $9
Guy Charron... $11	Andy Hebenton..................................... $12
Bill Clement $8	Anders Hedberg...................................... $9
Real Cloutier $7	Camille Henry....................................... $12
Roy Conacher...................................... $18	Dennis Hextall.. $8
Roger Crozier.. $9	Larry Hillman $10
Marcel Dionne...................................... $20	Ken Hodge $12
Clark Donatelli $9	Marty Howe $6
Ted Donato.. $9	Mark Howe $10
Gary Dornhoefer $9	Dennis Hull... $15
Jude Drouin $7	Dave Hunter... $7
Dick Duff $14	Rick Kehoe $12
Don Edwards.. $10	Ted Kennedy... $12
Ron Ellis.. $14	Orest Kindrachuk.................................... $8
Mike Eruzionne.................................... $12	Jerry Korab $6
Bill Fairbairn $8	Orland Kurtenbach $9
Doug Favell... $7	Leo Labine $8
Bernie Federko $12	Guy Lapointe $9
John Ferguson $10	Claude Larose $12

Autographs

Pierre Larouche $14	Dean Prentice $12
Reggie Leach $14	Jean Pronovost $12
Gaetz Link $8	Claude Provost $8
Ross Lonsberry $9	Glenn Resch $9
Jim Lorentz $9	Bobby Rousseau $8
Rick MacLeish $10	Gary Sabourin $8
Pete Mahovlich $12	Frank St. Marseille $8
Chico Maki $12	Derek Sanderson $8
Cesare Maniago $9	Bobby Schmautz $10
Gilles Marotte $8	Milt Schmidt $10
Pit Martin $14	Charlie Simmer $11
Rick Martin $14	Glen Skov $8
Dennis Maruk $14	Dallas Smith $8
Tommy McCarthy $18	Fred Stanfield $9
Ab McDonald $10	Vic Stasiuk $10
Walt McKechnie $10	Pete Stemkowski $9
John McKenzie $11	Brian Sutter $14
Peter McNab $15	Dave Taylor $13
Gilles Meloche $11	Walt Tkaczuk $11
Doug Mohns $11	Gilles Tremblay $10
Gord Murphy $8	Mario Tremblay $12
Lou Nanne $9	Bryan Trottier $22
Eric Nesterenko $12	Perry Turnbull $8
Bob Nevin $12	Garry Unger $15
Willie O'Ree $20	Rogie Vachon $12
Terry O'Reilly $10	Carol Vadnais $11
Wilf Paiement $11	John Van Boxmeer $11
Jim Pappin $9	Mike Walton $9
J.P. Parise $9	Ed Westfall $9
Noel Picard $8	Kenny Wharram $11
Pierre Plante $8	Juha Widing $9
Willi Plett $8	

Autographed pucks

Ray Bourque $15-30	Pat LaFontaine $25
Dino Ciccarelli $25	John LeClair $20
Pat Falloon $35	Mario Lemieux Pittsburgh Penguins puck .. $40
Sergei Fedorov Red Wings puck $40	Mario Lemieux Stanley Cup puck $50
Sergei Fedorov 1994 All-Star game puck ... $40	Eric Lindros $25
Wayne Gretzky autographed photo puck, signed and numbered, commemorates his breaking Gordie Howe's 1,850 career total points $75	Barry Melrose $18
	Stan Mikita Silver Puck "Hall of Famer" edition, 1,467 produced $65
Wayne Gretzky 1993 or 1994 All-Star puck $60	Alexander Mogilny $25
	Cam Neely $45
Ron Hextall $22	Bob Probert $20
Bobby Hull Silver Puck "Golden Jet" edition, 3,670 produced $65	Jeremy Roenick $25
	Patrick Roy $40
Joe Juneau $20	Denis Sevard $15
Vladimir Konstantinov $18	Mike Vernon $25
	Steve Yzerman $28

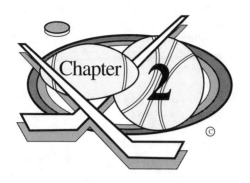

Chapter 2

Uniforms

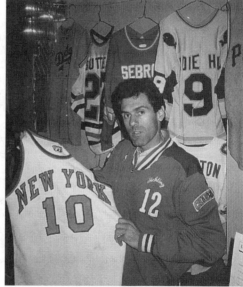

Reputable dealers often have a variety of jerseys, which can make up nice displays, such as this one devoted to St. Louis Blues star Brett Hull.

Until the early 1980s, most professional sports teams didn't make uniforms available to fans; the average fan was unworthy of owning a hallowed piece of history. Some jerseys, however, made it into circulation through charity auctions or the occasional lucky fan who, having written to a team, actually got one back in the mail. But, unfortunately, much of what did circulate in those days was either stolen or obtained through bribes and payoffs to clubhouse people and security personnel. Thus, many authentic shirts were "hot."

Changes in the pro teams' elitist mindset occurred in 1978, when the Philadelphia Phillies sold an entire lot of 1977 game-used jerseys to a New Jersey dealer, who then advertised them in hobby papers. Many teams have since continued this practice of bulk sales to dealers, selling all of the items at once, at a set price per shirt. This eliminates requiring team employees to individually price the items. Some teams, however, do filter individually-priced items into the market through their own outlets and shops, publicity caravans, or through charity auctions. These auctions are not as popular with mainstream collectors because the bidding often escalates to ridiculously high levels.

Shirts bought in bulk from the teams generally make their way to buyers at baseball card shows, through mail order catalogs, and in advertisements in hobby publications. Because the initial seller was the team itself, the authenticity of these jerseys is virtually uncontested.

Game-used equipment collectors consider a truly authentic item as one having been issued by the team, whose logo or name appears on the jersey. It must have discernibly been worn by the player in question. It doesn't have to be falling apart, but it shouldn't be fresh off the rack, either; it should show evidence of laundering.

Two points to consider in establishing authenticity include wear and tagging. A jersey used for an entire season should show some signs of wear. The collar and perhaps the armpits should indicate sweat, or laundering out of that perspiration. Letters and numbers on the jersey should feature an even degree of wear; the edges of the characters may be a bit frayed, the letters and numbers may be loose in one or several locations, and the numbers or scripting may be wrinkled or shrunken a wee bit.

Several types of tags exist, in various colors, designs and locations. Year tags depict the year of issuance for a jersey. Most often, these embroideries are done on a piece of fabric that is then affixed to the jersey. Strip tags are either embroidered or printed (screened). They are shaped in strip fashion, having an accentuated rectangular shape with a line of information running horizontally on an even plane. Flag tags are any tags attached to the jersey on only one edge, normally underneath an adjoining, larger tag (such as a manufacturer's label). Sometimes it may be attached underneath a jersey seam or to the jersey.

Name tags identify the name of a player who was originally issued the jersey. With only rare exceptions, name tags have only a player's last name. They are generally embroidered, and affixed to a strip-style tag that is sewn into the jersey. Name tags come in two varieties, based on their location on the jersey. Tags affixed to the inside back of the shirt collar are classified as "name in collar" tags, usually referred to on sale lists and in inventories as "NIC." Or, the tag may be included in the shirt's tail, with the corresponding notation being "NIT," for "name in tail." Variations of "NIT" include "NOT" (name on tail) and "NIF" or "NOF" (name in/on flap). Extra length tags indicate extra inches added into a jersey's sizing, usually done for taller players.

Your best bet for obtaining authentic items secondhand (i.e., not from the team directly nor from team outlets) is to visit experienced dealers in the field. Their identities can be learned through reading hobby publications and magazines, through recommendations from card and hobby shops, or by visiting card shows. Many dealers issue mail order catalogs, often available for as little as a self-addressed, stamped envelope.

Dealers who have purchased bulk quantities from one or several teams are a good bet, as are dealers with proven experience and longevity in the field. A dealer with an inventory featuring a varied mix of commons, minor stars and superstars is a better possibility than someone who only carries top-of-the-line players in ample quantities.

Most dealers utilize straight sales, although some will auction off rare or unusual pieces. Major consignment dealers with multi-page advertisements for all types of memorabilia often include uniforms and equipment in their ads. These, as well as auction house events, are generally geared towards higher-end material, but some mainstream, affordable equipment may also be included.

If questions arise concerning a jersey's authenticity, seek a second opinion. Most dealers will not object to this practice, but the time needed for an outside appraisal should be agreed upon beforehand, and stressed to the third party whose opinions are being sought.

Many dealers sell their wares at card shows.

Many forged jerseys, normally baseball knits, are subject to "simulated" wear, such as a uniform forger using sandpaper, a sharp instrument, or other foreign object to abrade and damage portions of the jersey. This gives it the appearance of moderate to extreme game usage.

Jersey tags may be clandestinely doctored by removing legitimate tags from a lesser-valued authentic jersey and placing them into a phony item capable of being passed off as a high-ticket item. Doctoring is defined as taking an authentic jersey of a common player and changing tagging, numbering, or other factors pertinent to the jersey, to upgrade the identity of the player.

Restoration, however, involves attempting to bring jerseys (especially flannels) back to their original appearance as close as possible. Where restorations differ from doctoring and gain acceptability in the majority of hobby quarters is that, first, no attempt is made to change or upgrade the identity of the professional athlete.

Legitimate restorations never attempt to restructure or refurbish tags, because too much potential for having a restoration slip into the dark side of the realm (doctoring) exists. Tagging is generally what is used to establish just who wore an item in the first place, and how to go about arranging the restoration process - what year and player were involved - so that the proper script or insignia or numbers can be used. A legitimate restoration tries to put things back the way they originally were, not embellish identities or years of usage to make an item more attractive or saleable.

Restorations are generally accepted by hobbyists if four conditions are met: 1) The restoration is true and accurate to the original identity of the jersey's wearer, with no illicit attempts to upgrade that wearer's identity. 2) The restoration should try to match as closely as possible the original appearance of the item being restored. 3) Potential buyers or traders should know in advance about any restorations. 4) Restorations should have a slight mark-down in price, depending on how many were done and the degree of quality of them.

In most instances, teams issue two of each jersey style to players under their employment. Three sets of attire is not uncommon, but this practice of three homes/three roads is not as common. In rare instances, set 4 and even set 5 shirts have surfaced. Apart from that, extra shirts tend to appear only when replacements are needed for damaged or stolen uniforms. In the 1980s, especially, some stars have had several jerseys issued to them to be donated to fund-raisers and charity auctions, to be given to friends, or for team employees to perhaps bar-ter with collectors. Thus, some star jerseys from the last several years may exist in more com-mon than twos or threes for a given style, and some may only evidence minor wear.

The jersey market has a wide variety of dollar amounts assigned to its items. Certain commons of less popular teams and styles can be had for well under $200, while some to-tally original, authentic flannels have commanded five-figure sums in highly publicized auctions. Factors which may cause a notable markup in a jersey from the lower end of the scale include:

Scarcity: Supply/demand considerations affect the price guide scale in the equipment market. The highest dollars come with teams whose jerseys are not only scarce, but also sought by a wide range of collectors.

New releases: Higher prices are generally seen for styles that have recently been intro-duced and whose numbers within the hobby are restricted due to limited time for release, until greater quantities appear.

Sleeve adornments: Although a regularly-issued logo patch will only minimally in-crease a shirt's price, a commemorative, memorial, or other specially-issued patch often creates a notable price increase.

High popularity: Some teams' prices, even though their attire is readily available, are driven up due to long-standing fan following or current popularity due to recent on-field success.

Striking styles: Other times, a style, be it rare, common or in-between, hits a chord with collectors and finds a niche as a high-priced item, due to demand for the style itself.

Dave Miedema, a longtime Sports Collectors Digest columnist whose efforts include "Up Autograph Alley" and "The Shirt Off My Back," has defined some of the terminology and acronyms used by uniform collectors.

Airknit: Similar to mesh, but with a shinier finish and extremely small holes. Also called micromesh, this has been used in varying degrees since the mid-1980s by the NHL, NBA and NFL.

Arched lettering: Lettering that forms an arc shape on the front or back of a jersey. Ex-amples include the NOBs on Utah Jazz (and many other) NBA jerseys. Charity jersey: This is a non game-worn jersey, either team/game-issued or specially ordered, made specifically for fund-raising activities such as a charity auction. Since they are specially ordered, slight differences may exist between these jerseys and those actually used by team members.

Commemorative patch: Sleeve or jersey body insignia worn for a limited time to note a historical moment in the team or city's history. It can be done for sports-related history (1994 NFL 75th Anniversary patch), general history or specific events.

Crest: The large patch that is found on the front of an NFL jersey. Examples include the Blackhawks Indian head crest, the Blues song note crest and the "B" crest on Bruins attire.

Doctored: Illegitimate, unethical restoration, i.e., taking a B.J. Armstrong Chicago Bulls jersey and trying to pass it off as a Michael Jordan jersey.

Dual autographed: Refers to an equipment item that, used in pairs, is autographed on both items. Most commonly refers to NBA game sneakers and other sports footwear, but can also apply to hockey gloves.

Game-used jerseys are those which have experienced actual game action.

Dual tagging: Denotes jerseys with a manufacturer/size tag and also a second tag, often with "exclusive" specifics. Most often associated with the NBA, and to a lesser degree, the NFL, and usually refers to jerseys manufactured by Champion.

Exclusive tag: A tag placed by a manufacturer of a game-issued item that declares the item to be made "exclusively" for the team or league. Used almost exclusively by Sand-Knit, Starter and Champion.

Extra length not tagged but evident: Authentication tags describe a jersey with obvious extra length sized into the jersey body, but with no specific tagging included to indicate the existence or amount of extra length. This is common with pre-1986 NBA attire, and often found on pro football jerseys, too.

Fishnet mesh: A mesh jersey with very large holes in the jersey body, but not in the shoulders or sleeves. These are limited to use in the NFL and college football.

Flag tag: A small square tag that is fastened underneath a larger tag on the left-hand side so that it resembles a little flag. Used most frequently by Rawlings, but other manufacturers have used them, too.

Game-issue: Refers to a jersey that was made for a player, but for some reason was not actually used. This could occur when a jersey was made for a player, who was later traded, or when an excessive amount of jerseys were made for a player. Also referred to as "team issue."

Game-used: Describes a uniform that is used by a player for actual game action. The term "game-worn" is identical in meaning.

Inspirational patch: Logo worn in tribute to a living person affiliated with the team, for either honor or support in difficulty. An example would be the Chicago Bears patches worn once in the final home game of retired linebacker Mike Singletary.

Jerry West logo: NBA league logo, added to game jerseys in 1986-87, also worn in large patch form on many warm-up tops and shooting shirts a few years beforehand. The logo features a player, dribbling a basketball, modeled after a photo of the Lakers legend.

Memorial band: Similar in purpose to a memorial patch, but reflected by a black mourning band on the sleeve or, in the NBA, on the shoulder strap (1993-94 Bulls band for James Jordan, father of Michael Jordan).

Memorial patch: This sleeve or body insignia is issued in honor of a deceased person, such as a player, manager or team-related employee.

Mesh: A jersey with a consistent pattern of small holes in the body and sleeves, used extensively in the NFL and NBA and frequently in the NHL. Baseball jerseys issued prior to the early 1970s were flannels (flannel, wool and cotton mixes); since then, major league baseball teams have worn knit jerseys.

Nameplate: A piece of fabric, usually arched, sometimes bar-shaped, depending on the team, upon which NOBs letters are attached. This allows for an easier means of removing NOBs by the team; the equipment manager merely needs to remove the entire nameplate, rather than individual letters attached directly to the jersey.

NIC: Name in collar. A tag that features a player's name is found in the back of the collar inside the jersey neck.

NIF/NOF: Name in/on flap.

NIT/NOT: Name in (on) tail. Name tag is affixed to shirt tail.

NIW: Name in waist. Describes a name tag affixed in the waistband of pants.

NNOB: Abbreviation for "no name on back," it applies to a jersey issued without ever having a name on the back, as opposed to one which has had the NOB removed (NOBR).

NOB: Name on back. Every NFL, NHL and NBA team uses this jersey feature.

NOBR: Name on back removed. Teams, especially in baseball, often send jerseys down to a minor league affiliate, having removed the former player's name from the back first. In most cases, however, the names have been stripped off the back. NOBR jerseys generally sell for half or less of what an original NOB does.

Number change: A time and cost saving procedure used by teams for a player who has just joined the team via a trade. He's given a jersey issued to or worn by a departed player, but the numbers have been changed to reflect the new player's identity. It can often apply to a NOB, too. Legitimate number and/or name changed jerseys generally sell for between 1/2 to 3/4 the value of an unaltered jersey, depending on the obviousness of the changes.

Official supplier: Since the mid-1980s, each major league has had an official supplier, a designated manufacturer to outfit the league's member teams with uniform attire (jerseys and pants/trunks). In the NBA and NHL, the agreement has been exclusive - NBA used Sand-Knit from 1986-87 through 1989-90 and Champion from 1990-91 through the past season, while the NHL has used CCM. In the NFL, several companies are currently official suppliers, including Champion, Russell, Wilson, Starter and Apex. Official suppliers can use the company's logo or insignia on attire, other suppliers can not.

Practice jerseys (non-baseball): Refers to jerseys worn by NFL, NHL and NBA players for practices and workouts away and apart from those prior to scheduled league games. They are usually done in team colors and logos, but are generally inferior in quality of appearance to the team's game attire. For example, they are usually without NOBs, have screened on numbers and logos instead of sewn on ones, or are mesh instead of knit.

Pre-game jersey: Applies to knit NBA warmup togs and knit shooting shirts. They are often worn by players on the bench, too.

Provenance: A term often seen in auction catalogs, this refers to the source, usually outside the hobby, from which a choice piece was obtained. This could include an equipment manager, locker room attendant, or relatives of the player.

Restored: Some collectors will research the identity of the jersey's original wearer and/or the team it was issued for and restore the logos, letters and numbers back to their original appearance, or as close as possible. This is an accepted practice provided the changes are accurate (keeping the player and team identity the same as originally made) and advance notice is given that the jersey has been restored.

Salesman's sample: A special jersey made by a manufacturer to show to team representatives to preview style or aesthetics changes or to provide a prototype for what a finished product would look like if the team and manufacturer agree to do business. They often bear the uniform of a star or retired great player from the team it was made for, but are only occasionally tagged. Many of these originally legitimate jerseys are doctored by unscrupulous types to attempt to reflect game-used status.

Set number: A tagging element that indicates what specific jersey one is in the group a player is issued for a given year. Traditionally, teams used to receive two home and two road jerseys. But today, teams may issue more, most notably the NBA. In recent years, the NHL has occasionally used set number tags; the NFL and NBA have rarely used them.

Simulated wear: Wear added artificially to a brand new, non game-used jersey in an attempt to give it a game-used look. This could include smudging dirt or grass on it, ripping it, sandpapering the logos or hacking up trim.

Spandex side inserts: Strips of fabric added to the sides of football jerseys to assist in tightening the jersey on the player's body, to reduce holding by opposing players grabbing the jersey. Unique to football.

Strip tag: Multi-item tag that depicts at least two pieces of tagged information, such as "Jackson 78 1" (name, year, set) or "23 84 2 42" (uniform number, year, set, size).

Sweater: A term used largely by Canadian fans and collectors to describe hockey jerseys, i.e. "hockey sweaters."

Tags: Labels, either embroidered or screened, which are added to a jersey or pants, but are not found on non game-issued items. Tags could indicate a manufacturer, but also indicate numeric or name information, such as years, set numbers, inventory numbers, sizes, uniform numbers or player names.

Tags washed out: Legitimate depreciation that results from repeated washing. It can take the form of either a sewn-in tag made out of a weak fabric (such as felt) disintegrating from excess washings or a printed tag having the print fade to the point of being unreadable. A jersey with tags washed out should display consistency of wear - a shirt with a felt NIC tag reduced to almost nothing should not display crisp, bright numbers or logos.

Tearaway: A flimsy knit jersey used in the NFL in the 1960s and 1970s, designed to tear off the body of a player when an opposing player attempted to tackle or grab him. The NFL eventually outlawed these types of jersey.

Trim: Stripes which encircle the edge or tip of a jersey sleeve or collar.

Untagged: Describes a jersey with no tags other than a manufacturer's label. This is a common occurrence for NBA jerseys before 1987, NFL jerseys before 1990 and up to the current time for NHL jerseys.

Vertical arch: A lettering style, usually related to NOBs, where the tops and bottoms of letters are arched, rather than the arrangement of the letters themselves. Most commonly used on NOBs of jerseys issued by Wilson, although other companies have used them, too. Examples include 1979-86 Chicago Cubs baseball road jersey NOBs.

A Walter Payton Bears jersey can bring $3,000 if it's from his rookie season.

Below, a Joe Namath New York Jets jersey.

Below, Lynn Swann's Pittsburgh Steelers jersey.

At left, John Elway's Broncos jersey.

Game-used football jerseys

Julius Adams: mid-1980s New England Patriots Russell, game worn $250
Troy Aikman: 1993 Dallas Cowboys issued, unused $695
Troy Aikman: 1994 Dallas Cowboys throwback, NOB, game worn....................$2,000
Marcus Allen: mid-1980s Los Angeles Raiders white, NOB,
game worn..$1,150
Marcus Allen: Kansas City Chiefs red, game worn $1,495
Lance Allworth: San Diego Chargers blue, game worn $2,750
Ken Anderson: Cincinnati Bengals home, game worn.................................$795
Neal Anderson: 1989 Chicago Bears home, game worn $650
Willie "Flipper" Anderson: 1990 Los Angeles Rams white, NOB,
game worn..$350
Stacey Bailey: 1980s Atlanta Falcons, NOB, game worn $195
Bill Bain: Los Angeles Rams white, NOB, with 40th anniversary patch,
game worn..$225
Chip Banks: Cleveland Browns white mesh, game worn............................$175
Greg Bell: 1988 Los Angeles Rams Russell, game worn............................$300
Cornelius Bennett: 1993 Buffalo Bills, game worn.....................................$395
Jerome Bettis: 1993 Los Angeles Rams white, with pants, game worn $1,300
Jerome Bettis: 1994 Pro Bowl jersey, game worn, autographed $1,295
Fred Biletnikoff: early-1970s Oakland Raiders black home, NOB,
game worn..$1,850
George Blanda: 1974 Oakland Raiders home, NOB, game worn $2,000
Drew Bledsoe: 1994 New England Patriots home blue, game worn $1,500
Steve Bono: 1992 San Francisco 49ers red, autographed, game worn....................$450
Brian Bosworth: 1989 Seattle Seahawks white, NOB, team issued
but not game used $295
Terry Bradshaw: mid-1970s AFC Pro Bowl jersey, game worn.....................$3,950
Terry Bradshaw: 1970s Pittsburgh Steelers home, game worn $3,750
Cliff Branch: late-1970s Oakland Raiders, white, game worn,
autographed...$895
John Brodie: 1970s San Francisco 49ers road, NOB, game worn $1,750
Jim Brown: Cleveland Browns home, game worn $9,750
Jerome Brown: Philadelphia Eagles, white, NOB, game worn $1,195
Tim Brown: 1994 Los Angeles Raiders home, game worn..........................$1,100
Willie Brown: 1970s Oakland Raiders home, game worn, autographed...............$1,500
Bob Brudzinski: 1984 Miami Dolphins road, game worn $325
Jeff Bryant: 1983 Seattle Seahawks white, NOB, game worn $225
Ed Budde: 1970s Kansas City Chiefs home, game worn.............................$500
Dick Butkus: Chicago Bears home, game worn $3,250
Leroy Butler: 1993 Green Bay Packers white, game worn,
autographed...$495
Marion Butts: San Diego Chargers white mesh, #35....................$345-$395
Earl Campbell: late-1970s Houston Oilers home, game worn $2,200
Cris Carter: 1988 Philadelphia Eagles white mesh, game worn,
autographed...$1,100
Tony Casillas: 1994 New York Jets white, game worn.................................$350

Mark Clayton: 1993 Green Bay Packers home, game worn $575
Dwight Clark: 1990s San Francisco 49ers red, game worn $500
Jim Collins: 1980s Los Angeles Rams white mesh, game worn $275
Cris Collinsworth: 1980s Cincinnati Bengals black mesh, game worn...................$575
Shane Conlan: late-1980s Buffalo Bills blue fishnet, game worn $450
Roger Craig: 1980s San Francisco 49ers home, game worn..................................$650
Joe Cribbs: 1980s San Francisco 49ers red, NOB, game worn $325
Randy Cross: mid-1980s San Francisco 49ers white, NOB, game worn........................$550
Larry Csonka: mid-1970s Miami Dolphins white, game worn,
  autographed..$2,500
Curley Culp: 1979-80 Houston Oilers home, game worn.....................................$400
Randall Cunningham: 1992 Philadelphia Eagles home, game worn,
  autographed..$895
Gary Danielson: 1970s Detroit Lions white mesh, game worn.............................$450
Willie Davis: 1992-93 Kansas City Chiefs white, game worn...............................$400
Jeff Dellenbach: 1992 Miami Dolphins white mesh, game worn...........................$250
Eric Dickerson: Los Angeles Rams white, NOB, team issued
  but not game used $575
Eric Dickerson: 1985 Los Angeles Rams blue, game worn $900
Eric Dickerson: early-1990s Atlanta Falcons black, game worn............................$995
Curtis Dickey: mid-1980s Baltimore Colts white, game worn...............................$475
Lynn Dickey: 1980s Green Bay Packers white, game worn....................................$500
Mike Ditka: early-1970s Dallas Cowboys road, game worn $3,500
Tony Dorsett: late-1970s Dallas Cowboys home, game worn $1,700
Tony Dorsett: 1988 Denver Broncos home, game worn.......................................$400
Kenny Easley: 1986 Seattle Seahawks home, game worn $400
Henry Ellard: 1988 Los Angeles Rams home, game worn autographed $250
John Elway: 1990s Denver Broncos home, game worn $900
Boomer Esiason: late-1980s Cincinnati Bengals black, game worn $650
Jim Everett: Los Angeles Rams white, NOB, team issued
  but not game used $395
Jim Everett: early-1990s Los Angeles Rams home, game worn..............................$795
Marshall Faulk: 1994 Indianapolis Colts home, game worn $2,000
Brett Favre: 1993 Green Bay Packer home green, game worn............................$1,250
Brett Favre: 1994 Green Bay Packer throwback, 75th anniversary patch,
  game worn..$900
Tom Fears: mid-1950s Los Angeles Rams gold, NNOB, game worn,
  autographed..$2,495
William Floyd: 1994 San Francisco 49ers throwback, game worn...........................$850
Barry Foster: Pittsburgh Steelers black, 60-year patch, game worn.....................$1,200
Dan Fouts: late-1970s San Diego Chargers home, game worn...........................$2,500
Bill Fralic: Atlanta Falcons red, NOB, game worn $450
Irving Fryar: 1993 Miami Dolphins complete home uniform,
  game worn..$750
Roman Gabriel: late-1960s Los Angeles Rams home, game worn..........................$700
Mark Gastineau: mid-1980s New York Jets green, game worn $850
Frank Gatski: 1957 Detriot Lions home, game worn $1,200
Jeff George: 1990 Indianapolis Colts home, game worn....................................$300

Jimmy Giles: late-1980s Philadelphia Eagles white, NOB, game worn $225
Ernest Givins: 1990 Houston Oilers home, game worn $300
Mel Gray: 1970s St. Louis Cardinals road, NOB, game worn $350
Kevin Greene: late-1980s Los Angeles Rams white, NOB, game worn $350
Burt Grossman: early-1990s San Diego Chargers white mesh,
   game worn $395
Lou Groza: 1950s Cleveland Browns home, game worn $4,750
Ray Guy: 1980s Oakland Raiders home, game worn $650
Carl Hairston: mid-1980s Cleveland Browns white knit, game worn $175
Ali Haji-Sheikh: 1980s New York Giants white mesh, game worn $275
Jack Ham: early-1970s Pro Bowl jersey, game worn $1,395
Dan Hampton: 1990 NFC Pro Bowl jersey, blue, game worn $795
Ronnie Harmon: 1991 San Diego Chargers white, game worn $400
Jim Harbaugh: early-1990s Chicago Bears white, game worn $425
Ronnie Harmon: early-1990s San Diego Chargers blue mesh,
   game worn $275
Alvin Harper: 1994 Dallas Cowboys throwback, NOB, game worn $1,000
Tim Harris: 1991 Green Bay Packers white, NOB, game worn $375
Jim Hart: 1970s St. Louis Cardinals home, game worn $650
Jim Hart: 1970s St. Louis Cardinals road, NOB, game worn $1,250
Ken Harvey: 1980s St. Louis Cardinals maroon mesh, game worn,
   autographed $295
Bob Hayes: mid-1970s Dallas Cowboys blue, game worn $1,200
Ted Hendricks: late-1970s Oakland Raiders white, game worn,
   autographed $1,200
Kent Hill: late-1970s Los Angeles Rams blue, NOB, game worn $200
Rodney Holman: late-1980s Cincinnati Bengals, white, NOB,
   game worn $225
Estus Hood: early-1980s Green Bay Packers white mesh, game worn $125
Jeff Hostetler: 1994 Los Angeles Raiders black, game worn,
   autographed $895
Desmond Howard: 1992 Washington Redskins home white,
   game worn $600
Leroy Irvin: mid-1980s Los Angeles Rams blue, NOB, game
   worn, autographed $350
Michael Irvin: 1994 Pro Bowl jersey, game worn, autographed $1,150
Michael Irvin: 1994 Dallas Cowboys throwback, NOB, game worn $1,500
Qadry Ismail: 1993 Minnesota Vikings purple, game worn,
   autographed $550
Raghib "Rocket" Ismail: 1994 Los Angeles Raiders black, game worn,
   autographed $995
Bo Jackson: 1990 Los Angeles Raiders black, game worn $2,500
Harold Jackson: 1970s Los Angeles Rams road, NOB, game worn $450
Rickey Jackson: 1990s New Orleans Saints black mesh, game worn $575
Ron Jaworski: 1987-88 Miami Dolphins white, NOB, game worn $375
Jim Jensen: 1980s Miami Dolphins aqua mesh, game worn $225
Billy "White Shoes" Johnson: early-1980s Houston Oilers blue mesh,
   game worn $250
Johnny Johnson: 1990s Phoenix Cardinals white mesh, game worn $275

Norm Johnson: 1989 Seattle Seahwaks white, team issued
but not game used, autographed $225
Swede Johnson: 1934 St. Louis Gunners, game worn $5,500
Daryl Johnston: 1994 Dallas Cowboys throwback jersey, game worn $595
Brent Jones: 1992 San Francisco 49ers red jersey, worn in NFC
Championship game $700
Deacon Jones: late-1960s Los Angeles Rams home, game worn $900
Henry Jones: 1993 Buffalo Bills home, game worn $400
Sonny Jurgensen: 1970s Washington Redskins home, game worn $3,700
Keith Kartz: 1991 Denver Broncos white, NOB removed, game worn $100
Jim Kelly: 1994 Buffalo Bills blue, game worn, autographed $995
Jim Kelly: 1990 Buffalo Bills road, NOB, game worn, autographed $950
Mike Kenn: mid-1980s Atlanta Falcons red, NOB, game worn $295
Terry Kirby: 1993 Miami Dolphins white, game worn, autographed $500
Bernie Kosar: 1993 Cleveland Browns road, game worn $695
Paul Krause: 1970s Minnesota Vikings white, game worn $950
David Krieg: 1991 Seattle Seahawks blue, game worn, autographed $450
Tim Krumrie: 1994 Cincinnati Bengals black mesh throwback,
game worn $495
Willie Lanier: 1970s Kansas City Chiefs home, NOB, game worn $1,500
Steve Largent: 1987 Seattle Seahawks home, game worn $1,500
Steve Largent: 1989 Seattle Seahawks white, game worn $995
D.D. Lewis: 1970s Dallas Cowboys home, game worn $750
Bob Lilly: early-1970s Dallas Cowboys blue, game worn $1,800
James Lofton: early-1980s Green Bay Packers home, game worn $700
Howie Long: 1991 Los Angeles Raiders black, game worn $900
Ronnie Lott: 1992 Los Angeles Raiders home, NOB, game worn $950
Ronnie Lott: 1993 New York Jets road, NOB, game worn, autographed $900
Tony Mandarich: early-1990s Green Bay Packers green, NOB,
game worn $475
Dan Marino: mid-1980s Miami Dolphins road, game worn $4,000
Dan Marino: 1985 Pro Bowl white, game worn $1,900
Dan Marino: 1993 Miami Dolphins aqua, NOB, game worn,
autographed $2,200
Todd Marinovich: 1992 Los Angeles Raiders home, game worn,
autographed $450
Harvey Martin: 1980s Pro Bowl jersey, NOB, game worn $750
Dan McGwire: 1991 Seattle Seahawks home, game worn, autographed $650
Travis McNeal: 1989 Seattle Seahwaks blue, NOB, game worn $225
Dave Meggett: 1980s New York Giants blue, game worn, autographed $650
Eric Metcalf: 1994 Cleveland Browns white, game worn, autographed $550
Anthony Miller: 1993 San Diego Chargers white, game worn $495
Anthony Miller: 1993 Pro Bowl jersey, with pants, game worn $600
Chris Miller: 1994 Los Angeles Rams blue, game worn $250
Art Monk: 1993 Washington Redskins road, NOB, game worn $1,200
Joe Montana: 1989 San Francisco 49ers home, game worn,
autographed $3,500

Emmitt Smith's Dallas Cowboys jersey has a ways to go before it reaches the value of Jim Brown's jersey.

Brian Piccolo's game-used Chicago Bears jersey could cost you $4,000.

Joe Montana: early-1990s San Francisco 49ers scarlet, NOB,
game worn, autographed..$2,500
Joe Montana: 1993 Kansas City Chiefs road, game worn $2,295
Rob Moore: 1992 New York Jets road, NOB, game worn $700
Joe Morris: late-1980s New York Giants white, game worn $695
Keith Mularkey: 1990s Minnesota Vikings purple mesh, game worn.......... $250
Mike Munchak: mid-1980s Houston Oilers home, game worn $550
Chuck Muncie: late-1970s New Orleans Saints white, game worn..........$350
Joe Namath: 1972 New York Jets home, game worn, autographed......................$6,000
Joe Namath: New York Jets practice jersey, autographed $1,400
Ozzie Newsome: mid-1980s Cleveland Browns home, game worn..........$900
Ray Nitschke: 1960s Green Bay Packers home, game worn....................$2,450
Jay Novacek: 1986 St. Louis Cardinals maroon, game worn.................$350
Jay Novacek: 1994 Dallas Cowboys throwback, NOB, game worn $1,000
Christian Okoye: 1992 Kansas City Chiefs home, game worn,
autographed..$500
Merlin Olsen: 1975 Los Angeles Rams home, game worn, autographed....................$1,750
Leslie O'Neal: early-1990s San Diego Chargers blue, game worn $495
Jim Otto: 1970s Oakland Raiders home, game worn, autographed....................$1,450
Walter Payton: 1977 Chicago Bears home, game worn....................$3,000
Walter Payton: 1985 Chicago Bears home, game worn, autographed $2,200
Rodney Peete: 1990s Detroit Lions blue mesh, game worn, autographed....................'$475
Steve Pelluer: 1991 Kansas City Chiefs home, game worn $225
Gerald Perry: early-1990s Denver Broncos white, NOB, game worn $200
Brian Piccolo: late-1960s Chicago Bears home, game worn $4,000
Jim Plunkett: mid-1980s Oakland Raiders black, game worn....................$900
John Rade: 1983 Atlanta Falcons red, NOB, game worn....................$250
Ahmad Rashad: late-1970s Minnesota Vikings white, game worn $1,100
Tom Rathman: late-1980s San Francisco 49ers red, game worn,
autographed..$395
Andre Reed: 1990s Buffalo Bills road, NOB, game worn $750
Andre Reed: 1993 Buffalo Bills home, game worn $575
Jerry Rice: 1994 San Francisco 49ers red, game worn....................$1,495
Jerry Rice: 1994 San Francisco 49ers white, game worn....................$1,595
Jerry Rice: 1994 Pro Bowl jersey, blue, NOB, game worn....................$1,495
John Riggins: late-1970s Washington Redskins home, game worn....................$1,950
Reggie Roby: 1992 Miami Dolphins aqua mesh, game worn....................$350
Dan Ross: Cincinnati Bengals white, NOB, game worn, autographed $200
Mark Rypien: 1991 Washington Redskins home, game worn,
autographed..$700
Barry Sanders: 1990s Detroit Lions blue, game worn $1,495
Deion Sanders: 1992 Atlanta Falcons home, game worn, autographed....................$1,500
Deion Sanders: 1994 San Francisco 49ers throwback home,
game worn..$1,900
Ken Sanders: 1978 Detroit Lions blue, game worn $200
Gale Sayers: Chicago Bears home, game worn....................$4,950
Junior Seau: 1994 San Diego Chargers home, game worn....................$1,500
Luis Sharpe: late-1980s St. Louis Cardinals, game worn $400

Sterling Sharpe: 1993 Green Bay Packers white, game worn,
autographed..$1,250
Phil Simms: 1989 New York Giants home blue, game worn $3,000
O.J. Simpson: 1979 San Francisco 49ers red, game worn $7,000
Jackie Slater: early-1990s Los Angeles Rams home, game worn $450
Bruce Smith: 1993 Buffalo Bills home, NOB, game worn......................................$950
Emmitt Smith: 1994 Dallas Cowboys throwback, NOB, game worn $1,795
Emmitt Smith: 1994 Dallas Cowboys home white, game worn..........................$1,695
John Stallworth: 1987 Pittsburgh Steelers home, NOB, game worn........................$1,000
Bart Starr: Green Bay Packers home, game worn, autographed.............................$3,750
Roger Staubach: 1969 Dallas Cowboys road, game worn $6,000
Lynn Swann: mid-1970s Pittsburgh Steelers home, game worn............................$2,350
Lynn Swann: mid-1970s AFC Pro Bowl, game worn...$1,800
Pat Swilling: 1994 Detroit Lions blue mesh, throwback, game worn $650
Fran Tarkenton: 1969-70 New York Giants road, game worn................................$5,000
Fran Tarkenton: Minnesota Vikings home, game worn...$3,795
Charley Taylor: 1977 Washington Redskins red, game worn...............................$1,700
John Taylor: 1994 San Francisco 49ers throwback, game worn............................$850
John Taylor: 1994 San Francisco 49ers red or white, game worn $595
Lawrence Taylor: 1992 New York Giants white, game worn,
autographed..$2,000
Vinny Testaverde: 1990s Tampa Bay Buccaneers home, game worn.......................$450
Blair Thomas: 1992 New York Jets white, NOB, game worn................................$500
Derrick Thomas: 1989 Kansas City Chiefs white, game worn $950
Thurman Thomas: 1994 Buffalo Bills blue, game worn...$750
Al Toon: 1991 New York Jets road, NOB, game worn $700
Al Toon: 1992 New York Jets home, game worn..$625
Wendell Tyler: 1970s Los Angeles Rams home, NOB, game worn.......................$350
Gene Upshaw: 1970s Pro Bowl, NOB, game worn $700
Norm Van Brocklin: mid-1950s Los Angeles Rams gold, NNOB,
game used..$2,495
Herschel Walker: mid-1980s New Jersey Generals, game worn............................$750
Herschel Walker: 1989 Minnesota Vikings white, game worn $775
Herschel Walker: late-1980s Dallas Cowboys home, game worn.......................$1,000
Curt Warner: 1980s Seattle Seahawks road, NOB, game worn.............................$400
Curt Warner: 1989 Seattle Seahawks white, NOB, team issued
but not game used $275
Bob Waterfield: 1950s Los Angeles Rams home, game worn...............................$5,000
Ricky Watters: 1994 San Francisco 49ers red or white, game worn,
autographed..$750
Mike Webster: 1992 Kansas City Chiefs road, game worn....................................$225
Danny White: mid-1980s Dallas Cowboys white, game worn $850
Reggie White: 1990s Green Bay Packers white, game worn $1,400
Steve Wilson: early-1980s Tampa Bay Buccaneers white, fishnet,
game worn...$150
Wade Wilson: 1980s Minnesota Vikings white mesh, game worn.........................$375
Rod Woodson: early-1990s Pittsburgh Steelers black, game worn $750
Vince Workman: 1991 Green Bay Packers, NOB, game worn $375

Louis Wright: 1970s Denver Broncos home, NOB, game worn $600
Steve Young: 1994 San Francisco 49ers red, game worn....................................$1,295
Steve Young: 1994 San Francisco 49ers white, game worn................................$1,395
Jack Youngblood: early-1980s Los Angeles Rams, game worn,
    autographed...$2,350
Tony Zendejas: 1994 Los Angeles Rams road white, game worn $150

Replica football jerseys

Troy Aikman: Dallas Cowboys replica, white, autographed.................................$250
Ken Anderson: Cincinnati Bengals replica, black, autographed $190
Fred Biletnikoff: Oakland Raiders replica, black, autographed $250
Drew Bledsoe: New England Patriots replica, blue, autographed $250
Brian Bosworth: Seattle Seahawks replica, white..$75
Jim Brown: Cleveland Browns throwback replica, autographed $250
Dick Butkus: Chicago Bears throwback replica, autographed $195
Earl Campbell: Houston Oilers replica, blue, autographed....................................$250
Roger Craig: San Francisco 49ers replica, red, autographed $175
Roger Craig: Los Angeles Raiders replica, black, autographed.............................$175
Eric Dickerson: Baltimore Colts replica, blue, autographed $250
John Elway: Denver Broncos replica, orange, autographed....................................$275
Marshall Faulk: Indianapolis Colts replica, blue, autographed.............................$275
Brett Favre: Green Bay Packers replica, green, autographed $250
Jack Ham: Pittsburgh Steelers replica, black, autographed....................................$250
Jim Harbaugh: Chicago Bears replica, navy blue, autographed $150
Alvin Harper: Dallas Cowboys throwback replica, autographed $250
Franco Harris: Pittsburgh Steelers replica, black, autographed $250
Michael Irvin: Dallas Cowboys replica, white, autographed..................................$250
Bo Jackson: Los Angeles Raiders replica, black, autographed $200
Sonny Jurgensen: Washington Redskins replica, red, autographed.........................$225
Jim Kelly: Buffalo Bills replica, blue, autographed $225
Jack Lambert: Pittsburgh Steelers replica, black $275
Steve Largent: Seattle Seahawks replica, blue or white, autographed $250
Howie Long: Los Angeles Raiders replica, black, autographed..............................$250
Joe Montana: San Francisco 49ers replica, red, autographed.................................$275
Warren Moon: Houston Oilers replica, blue, autographed......................................$150
Anthony Munoz: Cincinnati Bengals replica, black, autographed..........................$200
Christian Okoye: Kansas City Chiefs replica, red $150
Walter Payton: Chicago Bears replica, navy blue, autographed $295
Jerry Rice: San Francisco 49ers replica, scarlet, autographed................................$250
Mark Rypien: Washington Redskins replica, maroon, autographed $225
Barry Sanders: Detroit Lions replica, blue, autographed.......................................$225
Deion Sanders: Atlanta Falcons replica, black, autographed.................................$250
Gale Sayers: Chicago Bears replica, white, autographed $250
Sterling Sharpe: Green Bay Packers replica, white, autographed $225
O.J. Simpson: Buffalo Bills replica, blue, autographed ....$425-$1,500
Mike Singletary: Chicago Bears replica, white, autographed $225
Emmitt Smith: Dallas Cowboys replica, white, autographed..................................$250
Ken Stabler: Oakland Raiders replica, black, autographed.....................................$225

Bart Starr: Green Bay Packers replica, white, autographed....................................$225
Roger Staubach: Dallas Cowboys replica, white, autographed $250
John Taylor: San Francisco 49ers replica, red, autographed $200
Lawrence Taylor: New York Giants replica, blue, autographed $275
Vinny Testaverde: Tampa Bay Buccaneers replica, orange,
    autographed..$175
Y.A. Tittle: San Francisco 49ers replica, red, autographed...................................$250
Johnny Unitas: Baltimore Colts replica, blue, autographed $275
Reggie White: Green Bay Packers replica, green, autographed............................$275
Steve Young: San Francisco 49ers replica, red, autographed...............................$225

Game-used basketball jerseys

Mark Price, Derrick Coleman and Dominique Wilkins jerseys might set you back $2,000-$3,000.

Kareem Abdul-Jabbar: early-1980s Los Angeles Lakers home,
    game worn..$3,450
Kareem Abdul-Jabbar: 1988 Los Angeles Lakers road, NOB,
    game worn..$2,500
Danny Ainge: 1989-90 Sacramento Kings home, game worn,
    autographed..$650
Mark Aguirre: 1992-93 Los Angeles Clippers home, NOB, game worn $395
B.J. Armstrong: 1993-94 Chicago Bulls home jersey and pants,
    game worn..$1,000
Thurl Bailey: 1980s Utah Jazz road, game worn $295
Greg Ballard: 1983 Washington Bullets home, NOB, game worn...............................$425

Charles Barkley: 1992-93 Phoenix Suns playoffs home, game worn.........................$2,495
Charles Barkley: 1993-94 Phoenix Suns purple, NOB, game worn..............$2,295-$2,750
Dana Barros: 1994-95 Philadelphia 76ers road, game worn $375
Elgin Baylor: 1970 Los Angeles Lakers home knit, NOB, game worn $11,500
Benoit Benjamin: 1990-91 Los Angeles Clippers road, NOB,
game worn...$495
Larry Bird: 1987-88 Boston Celtics road green, game worn ....$3,250-$3,500
Larry Bird: 1991-92 Boston Celtics road, NOB, game worn ....$1,995-$2,495
Muggsy Bogues: 1993-94 Charlotte Hornets road, game worn $875
Manute Bol: 1992-93 Philadelphia 76ers road, game worn $250
Ron Boone: 1975 ABA West All-Star, NOB, game worn $1,250
Sam Bowie: 1994-95 Los Angeles Lakers road, game worn $350
Shawn Bradley: 1993-94 Philadelphia 76ers home, game worn $1,000
Randy Breuer: 1991-92 Minnesota Timberwolves road, game worn $350
Dee Brown: 1991-92 Boston Celtics home, game worn $425
Tony Campbell: 1991-92 Minnesota Timberwolves road, game worn...................$400
Cedric Ceballos: 1993-94 Phoenix Suns white, game worn............................$500
Wilt Chamberlain: 1963-64 Philadelphia 76ers home, game worn $10,000
Tom Chambers: 1980s Seattle Supersonics road, game worn $650
Rex Chapman: 1991-92 Charlotte Hornets home, game worn.........................$995
Maurice Cheeks: 1988-89 Philadelphia 76ers road, with pants,
game worn...$500
Tyrone Corbin: 1990-91 Minnesota Timberwolves home, game worn.......................$400
Dave Corzine: 1990-91 Orlando Magic road knit, game worn $250
Dave Cowens: 1978 NBA All-Star game, NOB, game worn...............................$4,000
Patrick Cummings: mid-1980s New York Knicks road, with trunks,
game worn...$195
Louis Dampier: 1970s Kentucky Colonels ABA, NOB, game worn $1,000
Brad Daugherty: 1988-89 Cleveland Cavaliers white, autographed,
game worn...$695
Vlade Divac: 1992-93 Los Angeles Lakers home, NOB, game worn $700
John Drew: 1970s Atlanta Hawks road, game worn $350
Clyde Drexler: 1993-94 Portland Trailblazers black, game worn $1,250
Joe Dumars: 1990-91 Detroit Pistons home, game worn.............................$525
Mark Eaton: 1988-89 Utah Jazz road, with trunks, game worn $395
James Edwards: 1992-93 Los Angeles Lakers home, NOB, game worn....................$295
Sean Elliott: 1991-92 San Antonio Spurs home, game worn $700
Dale Ellis: 1991-92 San Antonio Spurs home, game worn $495
Alex English: 1989-90 Denver Nuggets home, game worn $750
Julius Erving: 1978-79 Philadelphia 76ers blue road, NOB,
game worn...$1,495
Patrick Ewing: 1985-86 New York Knicks road, game worn $2,495
Patrick Ewing: 1985-86 New York Knicks home, game worn..........................$1,850
Patrick Ewing: 1987-88 New York Knicks home, game worn $1,500
Patrick Ewing: 1992-93 New York Knicks home, NOB, autographed,
game worn...$1,200

Walt Frazier: 1970s New York Knicks road, with shorts, NOB,
game worn $3,500
Walt Frazier: 1969 New York Knicks orange shooting shirt, NOB,
game worn $5,000
Kevin Gamble: 1992-93 Boston Celtics road, game worn $375
Kendall Gill: 1990-91 Charlotte Hornets road, game worn.................................... $950
Armon Gilliam: 1992-93 Philadelphia 76ers home, NOB, game worn $200
Artis Gilmore: mid-1980s Chicago Bulls home, game worn $750
Mike Gminski: 1989-90 Philadelphia 76ers road, with pants,
game worn $300
Gary Grant: 1990-91 Los Angeles Clippers road red, NOB, game worn $195
Horace Grant: 1994-95 Orlando Magic black road, game worn $1,200
A.C. Green: 1990-91 Los Angeles Lakers road, game worn $475
A.C. Green: 1993-94 Phoenix Suns road, game worn $500
Hal Greer: 1964 All-Star East, game worn $1,750
Tom Gugliotta: 1994-95 Washington Bullets road, game worn $750
Cliff Hagan: 1961 All-Star West, game worn $2,950
Anfernee Hardaway: 1993-94 Orlando Magic road, game worn $4,400
Anfernee Hardaway: 1993-94 Orlando Magic home, game worn $2,495
Anfernee Hardaway: 1994-95 Orlando Magic road, game worn....................... $1,495
Tim Hardaway: 1994-95 Golden State Warriors white mesh,
game worn $600
Ron Harper: 1993-94 Los Angeles Clippers road, NOB, game worn $395
Ron Harper: 1990-91 Los Angeles Clippers road, NOB, game worn $495
Hersey Hawkins: 1991-92 Philadelphia 76ers red, game worn,
autographed $600
Tom Heinsohn: 1957 All-Star East with shorts, game worn .... $3,000-$3,750
Grant Hill: 1994-95 Detroit Pistons white home mesh, game worn $2,700
Grant Hill: 1994-95 Detroit Pistons road blue, game worn................................. $2,700
Jeff Hornacek: 1992-93 Philadelphia 76ers road, game worn $375
Jeff Hornacek: 1992-93 Philadelphia 76ers home, NOB, game worn..................... $550
Juwan Howard: 1994-95 Washington Bullets road, game worn......................... $1,950
Jay Humphries: 1993-94 Utah Jazz black pre-game.. $50
Bobby Hurley: 1993-94 Sacramento Kings road, game worn,
autographed $550
Marc Iavaroni: 1987-88 Utah Jazz road, game worn $190
Jimmy Jackson: 1994-95 Dallas Mavericks white mesh, game worn.................. $1,400
Mark Jackson: 1992-93 Los Angeles Clippers road, game worn.......................... $300
Kevin Johnson: 1989-90 Phoenix Suns road, game worn, autographed $1,195
Kevin Johnson: 1993-94 Phoenix Suns purple, game worn $700
Larry Johnson: 1991-92 Charlotte Hornets road teal jersey and shorts,
game worn $1,495
Larry Johnson: 1992-93 Charlotte Hornets road, NOB, game worn $1,250
Magic Johnson: 1990-91 Los Angeles Lakers road, NOB, game worn $3,950
Magic Johnson: 1990 Los Angeles Lakers gold, game worn $3,000
Sam Jones: 1964 All-Star East, NOB, game worn... $4,500

*Magic Johnson and Larry Bird captured
the attention of NBA fans.*

Michael Jordan: 1987-88 Chicago Bulls home white, game worn $6,750
Michael Jordan: 1992-93 Chicago Bulls white, game worn $4,250
Michael Jordan: 1992 NBA All-Star game jersey, game worn $9,950
Shawn Kemp: 1991-92 Seattle Supersonics road, NOB, game worn $1,600
Shawn Kemp: 1993 All-Star game jersey, game worn $1,100
Steve Kerr: 1992-93 Orlando Magic road, game worn $185
Jason Kidd: 1994-95 Dallas Mavericks white home mesh, game worn $1,500
Toni Kukoc: 1993-94 Chicago Bulls home white, game worn $1,295
Bill Laimbeer: 1991-92 Detroit Pistons home, game worn............................... $450
Andrew Lang: 1992-93 Philadelphia 76ers home, NOB, game worn $200
Bob Lanier: 1970s Detroit Pistons home, game worn, autographed $4,750
Bob Lanier: 1970s Detroit Pistons road, game worn, autographed $2,000
Meadowlark Lemon: 1970s Harlem Globetrotters, with shorts, NOB, game worn.. $3,750
Reggie Lewis: 1992-93 Boston Celtics road, NOB, game worn............................ $1,200
Luc Longley: 1992-93 Minnesota Timberwolves blue, NOB, game worn $400
Dan Majerle: 1993-94 Phoenix Suns road, game worn $950
Jeff Malone: 1993-94 Philadelphia 76ers road, game worn $225
Karl Malone: 1990-91 Utah Jazz home, game worn, autographed $2,250
Karl Malone: 1994-95 Utah Jazz purple, NOB, game worn $1,495
Moses Malone: 1993-94 Philadelphia 76ers road, game worn............................. $750
Moses Malone: 1993 Philadelphia 76ers home, game worn $1,250
Danny Manning 1993-94 Los Angeles Clippers home, NOB $750
Pace Mannion: 1983-84 Golden State Warriors gold, NOB, game worn.................... $195
Jamal Mashburn: 1994 Dallas Mavericks home white, game worn $1,000
George McGinnis: 1977 All-Star game, NOB, game worn $775
Kevin McHale: 1991-92 Boston Celtics road, game worn.................................. $1,000
Reggie Miller: 1994-95 Indiana Pacers road, NOB, game worn............................ $1,295
Terry Mills: 1991-92 Detroit Pistons home, NOB, game worn $350
Harold Miner: 1993-94 Miami Heat road, game worn....................................... $500
Earl Monroe: 1976 New York Knicks home, NOB, game worn.......................... $2,700
Alonzo Mourning: 1992-93 Charlotte Hornets home, NOB, game worn $2,750
Alonzo Mourning: 1993-94 Charlotte Hornets road, with trunks, game worn, autographed... $3,200
Chris Mullin: 1992 Olympic uniform with shorts, NOB, game worn, autographed.. $3,500
Chris Mullin: 1992-93 Golden State Warriors road, game worn............................ $800
Dikembe Mutombo: 1992-93 Denver Nuggets blue, game worn.......................... $1,450
Pete Myers: 1993-94 Chicago Bulls red, game worn $500
Norm Nixon: early-1980s Los Angeles Lakers home, game worn........................... $650
Charles Oakley: 1994-95 New York Knicks away, game worn, autographed.. $800
Hakeem Olajuwon: 1988-89 Houston Rockets home, game worn...................... $2,295
Hakeem Olajuwon: 1993-94 Houston Rockets home, game worn....................... $1,695
Shaquille O'Neal: 1992-93 Orlando Magic road, NOB, game worn $5,500
Shaquille O'Neal: 1993-94 Orlando Magic home, game worn $3,995

Shaquille O'Neal: 1994-95 Orlando Magic black road mesh,
game worn..$3,300
Billy Owens: 1994-95 Miami Heat home, game worn..............................$495
Robert Parish: 1990-91 Boston Celtics home, game worn $1,000
Anthony Peeler: 1992-93 Los Angeles Lakers home, game worn $750
Drazen Petrovic: 1990-91 New Jersey Nets home, game worn $650
Scottie Pippen: 1992-93 Chicago Bulls white, game worn....................$2,250
Scottie Pippen: 1994 All-Star game jersey, blue, game worn..............$4,500
Kevin Porter: 1980-81 Washington Bullets home, game worn $325
Mark Price: 1992 Cleveland Cavaliers home, NOB, game worn $650
Mark Price: 1994-95 Cleveland Cavaliers black road, game worn...........$895
Kurt Rambis: 1993-94 Los Angeles Lakers home, game worn................$385
Glen Rice: 1993-94 Miami Heat home, game worn.................................$950
Glen Rice: 1990-91 Miami Heat road, game worn.................................$675
Pooh Richardson: 1993 Los Angeles Clippers white, game worn.........$450
Mitch Richmond: 1992-93 Sacramento Kings home, autographed,
game worn...$425
J.R. Rider: 1993-94 Minnesota Timberwolves road, game worn,
autographed..$1,700
Fred Roberts: 1986-87 Boston Celtics home, knit, game worn...............$350
David Robinson: 1993 NBA All-Star game, game worn $2,450
David Robinson: 1990-91 San Antonio Spurs road, game worn,
autographed..$2,295
David Robinson: 1993-94 San Antonio Spurs black, game worn $1,395
Dennis Rodman: 1992-93 Detroit Pistons home, game worn $595
Byron Scott: 1990-91 Los Angeles Lakers road, game worn,
autographed..$500
Rony Seikaly: 1990-91 Miami Heat road, game worn $495
Brian Shaw: 1989 Boston Celtics home, NOB, game worn....................$325
Steve Smith: 1993 Miami Heat road, game worn....................................$600
Tony Smith: 1992-93 Los Angeles Lakers purple road, game worn........$285
Rik Smits: 1990-91 Indiana Pacers home, autographed, game worn......$600
Rory Sparrow: 1986-87 New York Knicks blue, NOB, game worn.......$200
Latrell Sprewell: 1994-95 Golden State Warriors home mesh,
game worn..$1,100
John Stockton: 1987-88 Utah Jazz home, game worn...........................$1,795
John Stockton: 1992-93 Utah Jazz road, game worn............................$1,100
John Stockton: 1993-94 NBA All-Star jersey, game worn $2,295
Isiah Thomas: 1984 All-Star East, NOB, game worn, autographed $1,750
Isiah Thomas: 1991-92 Detroit Pistons home, game worn $750
Sedale Threatt: 1990-91 Los Angeles Lakers home, game worn............$295
Trent Tucker: early-1980s New York Knicks road, game worn $225
Loy Vaught: 1990-91 Los Angeles Clippers road, game worn, NOB.....$250
Bill Walton: 1986-87 Boston Celtics home, NOB, game worn,
autographed..$2,250
Clarence Weatherspoon: 1993-94 Philadelphia 76ers road,
game worn...$575

Clarence Weatherspoon: 1992-93 Philadelphia 76ers home, NOB, game worn...$650
Spud Webb: 1993-94 Sacramento Kings blue, NOB, game worn $450
Chris Webber: 1993 Golden State Warriors home, game worn...........................$2,500
Chris Webber: 1994-95 Washington Bullets home, game worn..........................$1,450
Doug West: Minnesota Timberwolves road, with trunks, game worn......................$750
Jerry West: 1973 Los Angeles Lakers road, NOB, game worn $4,000
Jerome Whitehead: late 1970s San Diego Clippers home, NOB, game worn..$300
Jamaal Wilkes: late 1970s Los Angeles Lakers road, NOB, game worn......................$750
Dominique Wilkins: 1993-94 Los Angeles Clippers home, NOB, game worn...$1,000
Buck Williams: 1984-85 New Jersey Nets road, game worn................................$450
Orlando Woolridge: 1993-94 Philadelphia 76ers road, game worn......................$195
James Worthy: 1993-94 Los Angeles Lakers gold home, game worn.........................$895

Replica basketball jerseys

Kareem Abdul-Jabbar: Los Angeles Lakers replica, gold, autographed...$275
Charles Barkley: Phoenix Suns home replica, autographed $195
Larry Bird: Boston Celtics green replica, autographed...$250
Larry Bird: Olympic jersey replica, white, autographed.......................................$275
Shawn Bradley: Philadelphia 76ers home replica, autographed....................$110
Calbert Chaney: Washington Bullets replica, autographed $225
Clyde Drexler: Portland Trailblazers replica, autographed.................................$225
Julius Erving: Philadelphia 76ers scarlet replica, autographed $295
Patrick Ewing: Olympic jersey replica, white, autographed $250
Patrick Ewing: New York Knicks road replica, autographed.................................$225
Anfernee Hardaway: Orlando Magic home, autographed $150
Tim Hardaway: Golden State Warriors road, autographed..................................$140
Grant Hill: Detroit Pistons replica, blue, autographed $150
Jimmy Jackson: Dallas Mavericks home replica, autographed.............................$110
Magic Johnson: Los Angeles Lakers replica, autographed $395
Magic Johnson: Olympic jersey replica, autographed...$395
Michael Jordan: Chicago Bulls replica, red, autographed $375
Michael Jordan: University of North Carolina, replica, autographed.....................$395
Shawn Kemp: Olympic jersey replica, autographed..$150
Jason Kidd: Dallas Mavericks replica, autographed $175
Tony Kukoc: Chicago Bulls replica, road $100
Christian Laettner: Olympic jersey replica, white, autographed $225
Christian Laettner: Minnesota Timberwolves replica, autographed.........................$125
Reggie Lewis: Boston Celtics replica, green, autographed.....................................$575
Dan Majerle: 1994 USA Dream Team II replica, autographed $150
Karl Malone: Utah Jazz home replica, autographed $250
Moses Malone: Philadelphia 76ers replica, white $125

From left to right are jerseys for Bob Cousy, Michael Jordan and Lew Alcindor.

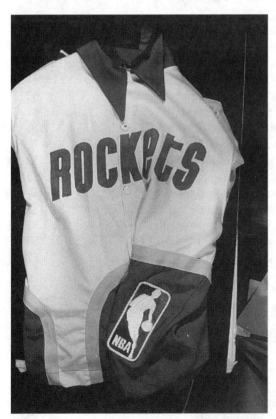 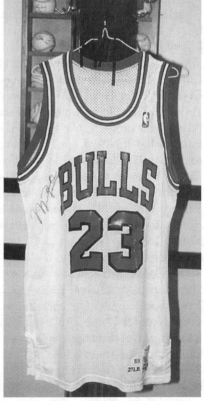

Hakeem Olajuwon and Michael Jordan jerseys would be centerpieces in any collection.

Danny Manning: Los Angeles Clippers road $125
Jamal Mashburn: Dallas Mavericks road replica, autographed $125
Reggie Miller: 1994 USA Dream Team II replica, autographed....................$150
Harold Miner: Miami Heat road, autographed $110
Alonzo Mourning: Charlotte Hornets home replica, autographed....................$175
Alonzo Mourning: 1994 USA Dream Team II replica....................................$175
Chris Mullin: Golden State Warriors road replica $140
Hakeem Olajuwon: Houston Rockets road replica, autographed $175
Shaquille O'Neal: Orlando Magic replica, autographed................................$250
Shaquille O'Neal: 1994 USA Dream Team II replica, autographed $250
Robert Parish: Boston Celtics green, autographed....................................$275
Gary Payton: Seattle Supersonics home replica, autographed................................$100
Scottie Pippen: Olympic jersey replica, white, autographed $250
Scottie Pippen: Chicago Bulls road replica, autographed....................................$175
Mark Price: Cleveland Cavaliers home replica, autographed $125
Mark Price: 1994 USA Dream Team II replica, autographed....................$175
David Robinson: San Antonio Spurs replica, black, autographed....................$150-$175
Glenn Robinson: Milwaukee Bucks replica, green, autographed....................$150
Dennis Rodman: San Antonio Spurs replica, road $140
Bill Russell: Boston Celtics replica, green, autographed $475
Latrell Sprewell: Golden State Warriors replica, autographed $125
John Stockton: Olympic replica, white, autographed............................$375
Isiah Thomas: Indiana Hoosiers replica, white............................$95
Chris Webber: Golden State Warriors replica, autographed $175
Dominique Wilkins: Atlanta Hawks scarlet replica, autographed....................$225
James Worthy: Los Angeles Lakers home, autographed $150

Game-used hockey jerseys

Syl Apps: early-1980s Los Angeles Kings gold mesh, NOB, game worn....................$295
Brent Ashton: Winnipeg Jets blue mesh, NOB, game worn....................................$250
Tom Barrasso: 1990-91 Pittsburgh Penguins home, game worn....................$950
Brian Bellows: 1990-91 Minnesota North Stars green knit, game worn....................$600
Ric Bennett: 1991-92 New York Rangers blue mesh, game worn $350
Rob Blake: 1990-91 Los Angeles Kings road, game worn, NOB $895
Doug Bodger: 1990-91 Buffalo Sabres road, with 20th anniversary patch,
    NOB, game worn..$550
Dan Bourchard: Quebec Nordiques home white, NOB, game worn $295
Ray Bourque: 1991-92 All-Star white knit, throwback, game worn,
    autographed..$995
Aaron Broten: New Jersey Devils red mesh, game worn $295
Mike Bullard: Pittsburgh Penguins black mesh, NOB, game worn....................$225
Ted Bulley: late-1970s Chicago Blackhawks home, game worn, NOB $450
Pavel Bure: 1994-95 Vancouver Canucks playoffs road jersey,
    game worn, autographed..$3,000
Pavel Bure: CCCP Red Russian Army lightweight jersey, game worn....................$1,750

Having all the team members sign a game-used jersey poses a difficult challenge.

Billy Carroll: 1984-85 New York Islanders white mesh, game worn $400
Gerry Cheevers: late-1970s Boston Bruins white mesh, game worn....................$2,500
Alain Chevrier: New Jersey Devils road knit NOB, game worn.............................$350
Paul Coffey: 1993 All-Star game, game worn, autographed $1,995
Ed Courtenay: San Jose Sharks 1992-93 white knit, game worn $500
Russ Courtnall: Minnesota North Stars 1991-92, game worn................................$595
Russ Courtnall: 1993-94 Dallas Stars black knit, game worn.................................$650
Murray Craven: Philadelphia Flyers, orange knit, game worn.............................$275
Glen Currie: Washington Capitals white knit, NOB, game worn...........................$275
Ken Daneyko: 1980s New Jersey Devils red knit, game worn $425
Kevin Dineen: 1992-93 Philadelphia Flyers road, NOB, game worn $550
Marcel Dionne: 1983-84 Los Angeles Kings home, NOB, game worn $2,000
Stephane Fiset: 1993-94 Quebec Nordiques white knit, game used........................$675
Pat Flatley: 1984 New York Islanders blue mesh, game worn.................................$650
Theo Fleury: 1990-91 Calgary Flames playoff jersey, game worn $850
Grant Fuhr: 1993-94 Buffalo Sabres blue, game worn $2,000
Grant Fuhr: 1991-92 Toronto Maple Leafs home, game worn $2,695
Greg Gilbert: 1980s New York Islanders blue knit, game worn $400
Curt Giles: Minnesota North Stars white mesh, NOB, game worn..........................$225
Doug Gilmour: 1990-91 Calgary Flames playoff jersey, game worn......................$750
Dirk Graham: 1991-92 Chicago Blackhawks road, Captain "C" patch,
  NOB, game worn $800
Tony Granato: 1988-89 New York Rangers home, NOB, game worn $1,450

Tony Granato: 1990 Los Angeles Kings playoff jersey, game worn $450
Adam Graves: 1991-92 New York Rangers blue, game worn...........................$1,750
Rick Green: 1989 Montreal Canadiens playoff red, game worn $550
Wayne Gretzky: Los Angeles Kings mid-1980s home, game worn $7,900
Wayne Gretzky: Los Angeles Kings 1988-89 white, game worn,
 autographed..$6,500
Dominik Hasek: 1992-93 Buffalo Sabres blue and white, game worn.................$2,500
Derian Hatcher: 1993-94 Dallas Stars black knit, game worn...............................$650
Tim Higgins: New Jersey Devils red, white and green jersey, NOB,
 game worn...$175
Gordie Howe: 1947-48 Detroit Red Wings, game worn $30,000
Gordie Howe: 1970 Detroit Red Wings, game worn, autographed.......................$9,750
Gordie Howe: 1978-79 New England Whalers home, game worn $7,000
Kelly Hrudey: 1980s New York Islanders blue knit, game worn $475
Brett Hull: 1989-90 St. Louis Blues white knit, game worn $2,700
Brett Hull: 1994 All-Star game jersey, game worn $3,500
Al Iafrate: 1993-94 Washington Capitals red, knit, game worn $850
Jaromir Jagr: 1992-93 Pittsburgh Penguins white knit, game worn.....................$2,750
Al Jensen: early-1980s Washington Capitals home jersey, NOB,
 game worn...$175
Alexei Kasatonov: CCCP Russian red mesh, NOB, game worn...........................$450
Steve Kasper: early-1980s Los Angeles Kings white, NOB, game worn.....................$350
Derek King: 1990-91 New York Islanders home, NOB, game worn $650
Petr Klima: Detroit Red Wings white knit, 60-year patch, game worn...................$975
Vladimir Konstantinov: CCCP Russian lightweight orange,
 game worn...$695
Uwe Krupp: Buffalo Sabres 1986-87 blue knit, game worn $295
Jari Kurri: 1992-93 Los Angeles Kings road, game worn...................................$2,200
Jari Kurri: 1992 All-Star game jersey, game worn, autographed $1,200
Guy Lafleur: 1975-76 Montreal Canadiens red, NOB, game worn $4,800
Pat LaFontaine: 1980s New York Islanders white or blue, game worn $1,750
Pat LaFontaine: 1992-93 Buffalo Sabres away, with Captain "C" patch,
 game worn...$1,400
Rod Langway: late-1980s Washington Capitals home, Captain "C" patch,
 NOB, game worn $625
Steve Larmer: 1980s Chicago Blackhawks white knit, game worn $950
Kevin LaVallee: St. Louis Blues white knit, NOB, game worn $250
Brian Leetch: 1993-94 New York Rangers home, game worn.............................$2,250
Claude Lemieux: 1991-92 New Jersey Devils red, NOB, game worn....................$650
Mario Lemieux: 1990 Pittsburgh Penguins home knit, game worn $3,000
Mario Lemieux: 1990 All-Star game jersey, Wales white, game worn $6,500
Mario Lemieux: 1992 All-Star game jersey, game worn $3,500
Dave Lewis: early-1980s Los Angeles Kings purple mesh, NOB,
 game worn...$325
Dave Lewis: early-1980s Los Angeles Kings gold mesh, with Captain "C" patch,
 NOB, game worn $325

Teams often retire the uniform numbers of Hall of Fame players.

Marty McSorley
Frank Mahovlich

Gordie Howe
Larry Robinson

Trevor Linden: 1990s Vancouver Canucks home jersey, Captain "C" patch,
game worn $900
Brett Lindros: 1994-95 New York Islanders blue, game worn $1,500
Morris Lukowich: Winnipeg Jets 1984-85 blue mesh, game worn $350
Al MacInnis: 1990-91 Calgary Flames playoff jersey, game worn........................$895
Al MacInnis: 1992-93 Calgary Flames white knit, game worn................................$775
Frank Mahovlich: 1957 Toronto rookie jersey, game worn $5,000
Dave Manson: 1994-95 Winnipeg Jets blue knit, game worn................................$850
Brad Maxwell: Winnipeg Jets blue knit, NOB, game worn....................................$225
Mike McEwen: 1983-84 New York Islanders white mesh, game worn $325
Kirk McLean: 1992-93 Vancouver Canucks white, 100-year Stanley Cup patch,
game worn..$1,500
Basil McRae: 1992-93 Tampa Bay Lightning white knit, game worn....................$750
Marty McSorley: 1990 Los Angeles Kings playoff jersey, game worn..................$450
Wayne Merrick: 1983-84 New York Islanders blue mesh, game worn..................$575
Mark Messier: 1991-92 New York Rangers home white, game worn $2,500
Mark Messier: 1993-94 New York Rangers playoff jersey, game worn....................$3,000
Mike Milbury: 1970s Boston Bruins white mesh, game worn $425
Mike Modano: 1991-92 Minnesota North Stars white knit, game worn $1,200
Mike Modano: 1992-93 All-Star game, black knit, game worn $1,650
Andy Moog: 1993-94 Dallas Stars black, game worn $1,250
Andy Moog: mid-1980s Edmonton Oilers white mesh, game worn....................$1,750
Ken Morrow: 1980s New York Islanders blue knit, game worn $575
Kirk Muller: late-1980s New Jersey Devils home, game worn $900
Larry Murphy: 1991-92 Pittsburgh Penguins home, NOB, game worn....................$1,195
Cam Neely: 1992-93 Boston Bruins black knit, Stanley Cup patch,
game worn..$1,095
Joe Nieuwendyk: 1991-92 Calgary Flames home, Captain "C" patch,
NOB, game worn $625
Adam Oates: 1990s St. Louis Blues white, NOB, game worn............................$1,500
Adam Oates: 1991-92 Boston Bruins black, 75-year NHL patch,
game worn..$1,100
Joel Otto: 1990 Calgary Flames playoff, autographed, game used.........................$495
Peter Peeters: 1978-79 Philadelphia Flyers white mesh, game used $550
Michel Petit: 1985-86 Vancouver Canucks gold knit, game worn.........................$350
Denis Potvin: 1980s New York Islanders blue, Captain "C" patch,
game worn..$3,000
Pat Price: late-1970s New York Islanders white mesh, game worn $450
Rob Ramage: Calgary Flames away, red, game worn, autographed,
with 1988 Olympic patch...$375
Mark Recchi: 1992-93 Philadelphia Flyers white knit, game worn........................$850
Joe Reekie: 1992-93 Tampa Bay Lightning home, with Stanley Cup patch,
NOB, game worn $750
Chico Resch: New Jersey Devils white mesh, game worn $525
Maurice "Rocket" Richard: mid-1950s Montreal Canadiens,
game worn..$8,000

Mike Richter: 1993-94 New York Rangers away, with All-Star patch,
game worn..$2,500
Larry Robinson: 1989 Montreal Canadiens playoff jersey, red,
game worn..$2,500
Larry Robinson: 1990-91 Los Angeles Kings home, game worn,
autographed..$1,250
Luc Robitaille: 1990-91 Los Angeles Kings home, NOB, game worn,
autographed..$1,500
Jeremy Roenick: 1992-93 Chicago Blackhawks playoff jersey,
game worn..$2,750
Jeremy Roenick: Team USA Canada Cup jersey, game worn.............................$1,600
Patrick Roy: 1991 All-Star game jersey, game worn.....................................$2,000
Joe Sakic: late-1980s Quebec Nordiques home, with Captain "C" patch,
game worn..$1,750
Joe Sakic: 1991-92 All-Star game jersey, game worn, autographed....$1,650
Borje Salming: 1984 Toronto Maple Leafs blue, game worn.................$900
Thomas Sandstrom: 1990 Los Angeles Kings playoff, game worn.......................$450
Gary Sargent: early-1980s Los Angeles Kings purple mesh, NOB,
game worn..$325
Teemu Selanne: 1992-93 Winnipeg Jets blue knit, game worn.......................$2,395
Brendan Shanahan: 1991-92 St. Louis Blues, white, 25th anniversary
team patch, game worn $1,950
Steve Shutt: 1972-73 Montreal Canadiens red knit, NNOB, game worn...................$2,500
Charlie Simmer: mid-1980s Los Angeles Kings road purple, NOB,
game worn..$750
Darryl Sittler: mid-1970s Toronto Maple Leafs home, game worn.....................$1,200
Darryl Sittler: 1981-82 Philadelphia Flyers orange mesh, game worn...................$950
Brian Skrudland: 1991-92 Montreal Canadiens red knit, game worn.................$475
Doug Smith: early-1980s Los Angeles gold mesh, NOB, game worn.....................$295
Tommy Soderstrom: 1994-95 New York Islanders blue knit,
game worn..$750
Peter Stastny: 1987-88 Quebec Nordiques road, Captain "C" patch,
NOB, game worn $2,000
Scott Stevens: 1992-93 New Jersey Devils home, with Stanley Cup
and Captain "C" patches, game worn $1,200
Mats Sundin: 1992-93 Quebec Nordiques blue knit, game worn $950
Gary Suter: 1980s Calgary Flames red knit, game worn $395
Gary Suter: 1990-91 Calgary Flames playoff jersey, game worn...........................$550
Brent Sutter: 1984-85 New York Islanders white mesh, game worn.....................$575
Bob Sweeney: Boston Bruins home white, NOB, game worn..............................$250
Dave Taylor: 1989-90 Los Angeles Kings home, with Captain "C" patch,
NOB, game worn $1,000
Steve Thomas: 1980s Chicago Blackhawks red, game worn,
autographed..$650
Kevin Todd: 1993-94 Chicagio Blackhawks throwbacks, NOB,
game worn..$600
Darren Turcotte: 1989-90 New York Rangers road, game worn $850
Mike Vernon: 1990-91 Calgary Flames playoff jersey, game worn.......................$695

Since San Jose is a newer team, there isn't an abundance of jerseys on the market yet.

Mike Vernon: late-1980s Calgary Flames red knit, game worn $550
Darcy Wakaluk: 1993-94 Dallas Stars black knit, game worn $750
Doug Weight: 1991-92 New York Rangers blue mesh, game worn $750
Doug Wilson: 1985-86 Chicago Blackhawks home, NOB, game worn.....................$1,000
Steve Yzerman: 1991-92 All-Star game red knit, throwback style,
    game worn...$1,895
Steve Yzerman: 1991-92 Detroit Red Wings home, game worn.................$1,850
Zarley Zalapski: 1991-92 Hartford Whalers road, with 75th anniversary
    patch, game worn..$500
Rob Zamuner: 1991-92 New York Rangers blue mesh, game worn......................$495

Replica hockey jerseys

Alexandre Daigle: Ottawa Senators home or away replica.....................................$289
Sergei Fedorov: Detroit Red Wings home replica..$229
Brett Hull: St. Louis Blues replica, white, autographed $225
Wayne Gretzky: Los Angeles Kings replica, autographed.....................................$350
Jaromir Jagr: Pittsburgh Penguins home replica, autographed...........................$249
Mario Lemieux: Pittsburgh Penguins replica, autographed.........................$350
Bobby Orr: Boston Bruins home replica $300
Manon Rheaume: Tampa Bay home or away replica..$289
Kevin Stevens: Pittsburgh Penguins home replica...$239
Steve Yzerman: Detroit Red Wings home replica $229

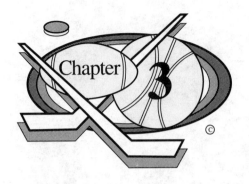

Chapter 3

Equipment

David Bushing, in his Krause Publications' book titled "Sports Equipment Price Guide," lists several styles of helmet, from the simple leather head coverings, with little or no padding, used at the turn of the century, to today's sophisticated models. General values in Near Mint/Excellent condition for what a collector might expect to get if he's selling the item include:

Stocking cap: the earliest form of head apparel, similar to a cotton or wool knitted cap ($800).

Aviator style: all-leather from the turn of the century to the late teens, similar to an airplane pilot's hat ($500).

Flat top: from 1900 until the late 1920s, has a flat top, leather with felt padding ($650).

Strap helmet: a leather style made up of straps which all connect at a central point on top of the head, with felt padding, popular from the late 19th century to the 1920s ($600).

Soft shell: like the aviator style, but stiffer and lacks flexibility, popular during the late teens and 1920s ($350).

Executioner style: used during the 1920s, the leather covers most of the face, with holes for the eyes and nose ($1,200).

Grange style: popular during the 1920s and 1930s, all leather, with a high crown with contrasting straps of leather running both vertically and horizontally across the crown, and padding which has a combination of canvas or leather crown straps and heavy felt or leather side construction ($350).

Hard shells: the crown of the helmet is hard molded composition material covered with straps of leather, with leather sides, used during the 1930s and 1940s ($250).

Composition helmets: with leather inside only, and outer hard molded composition material, introduced into the NFL in the 1940s ($75-$150).

Late all-leather helmets, similar in style to the composition helmets, except they are all leather, used until the 1950s ($250).

This display features equipment used by players from the Miami Dolphins.

Nose guards, used to cover the nose and mouth from 1890-mid-1920s, can be worth up to $300. They were made with hard rubber with an elastic strap that went around the head; some also included a removable mouthpiece. Shoulder pads from the early 1900s are generally worth around $75-$100. These flat pads were basically felt and leather which were laid on the shoulders and fastened under the arm. Harder pads were made later; they were made of composition with heavy padding and are worth between $25-$50. High top shoes with wooden cleats are also desirable among collectors, who should expect to pay between $50-$75 for a pair.

Football weights and shapes have varied little throughout the ages. Rugby style footballs from the turn of the century, official American Football League balls and white Duke balls (used in 1956 for a few years, up to $600) are the most desirable among collectors. Official NFL Dukes (1941-69, up to $200), Spalding J5-V models (NFL ball for 1920-40, up to $200, and also used in the AFL from 1960-69, $300) and facsimile autographed models are also collected. Prewar team models can bring up to $300, while individual Hall of Famer models can be worth up to $150.

Concerning basketballs, American Basketball Association balls are the most highly coveted balls to collect, with those in Near Mint to Mint condition bringing upwards of $300. Laced basketballs, having a lacing system similar to footballs, were used up until the 1950s and can bring up to $150, as can early NBA balls and prewar Hall of

Equipment, such as this early football ware, can be found for sale in auctions.

Famer stamped models, which have player endorsements on them. The value is enhanced if a football or basketball has actually been autographed by a player or members of a team.

Basketball shoes which are endorsed by a player, whose picture is on the shoe box, can be worth up to $200 if the player is a Hall of Famer who played before 1960, or $150 if he's a star. Hall of Famer models from after 1960 can be worth up to $150, or $100 if he's a star.

Hockey skates and pucks are all collected, but there isn't a lot of material out there yet. In general, player-endorsed skates with pictures of the player on the box can bring up to $500 if the player is a prewar Hall of Famer, or $200 if he's a postwar Hall of Famer. Other star models can bring between $100-$300. Resin goalie masks from the 1940s can be worth $400-$500. Pucks with logos from obsolete NHL teams on them can fetch up to $100, while those with old NHL logos still intact can bring $50.

When selling an item, condition is one of the most important factors in determining a value. Other contributing factors which enhance the value include whether the original box is in tact and in good shape; what player is pictured on the box or who may have endorsed the product with a facsimile autograph; regional interest; supply and demand; if the product is a child's model, which detracts from the value compared to adult versions; if the material is game-used and by what player; and if it is autographed.

Football items

Single-signed authentic helmets

Note: game-used are unsigned unless noted

These are helmets signed by O.J. Simpson and Warren Moon.

Troy Aikman: Dallas Cowboys authentic Riddell, signed.......................................$265
Raul Allegre: 1990s New York Giants Riddell, game used $425
Marcus Allen: Los Angeles Raiders authentic Riddell, signed...............................$260
Marcus Allen: Kansas City Chiefs authentic Riddell, signed $250
Jerome Bettis: Los Angeles Rams authentic Riddell, signed...................................$275
Fred Biletnikoff: Oakland Raiders replica helmet, signed $150
Drew Bledsoe: New England Patriots authentic Riddell, signed............................$270
Mel Blount: 1970s Pittsburgh Steelers helmet, game used....................................$695
Terry Bradshaw: Pittsburgh Steelers authentic Riddell, signed $230
Jim Brown: Cleveland Browns authentic Riddell, signed $240
Dick Butkus: Chicago Bears authentic Riddell, signed...$275
Marv Cook: 1991 New England Patriots helmet, game used...................................$195
Randall Cunningham: 1987 Philadelphia Eagles helmet, game-used,
    signed $1,000
Randall Cunningham: Philadelphia Eagles authentic Riddell, signed $225
Len Dawson: Kansas City Chiefs authentic Riddell, signed $250
Eric Dickerson: 1989 Indianapolis Colts helmet, game-used................................$1,250
Eric Dickerson: Indianapolis Colts replica, signed..$175
Mike Ditka: Chicago Bears authentic Riddell, signed..$250
Tony Dorsett: Dallas Cowboys authentic Riddell..$235
Henry Ellard: 1990s Los Angeles Rams helmet, game used..................................$450

Jumbo Elliott: 1980s New York Giants Riddell, game used $525
John Elway: Denver Broncos authentic Riddell, signed $265
Boomer Esiason: New York Jets authentic Riddell, signed $175
Jim Everett: Los Angeles Rams authentic Riddell, signed $175
Brett Favre: Green Bay Packers authentic Riddell, signed.....................................$275
Marshall Faulk: Indianapolis Colts authentic Riddell, signed $280
Vince Ferragamo: 1985 Green Bay Packers helmet, game used $300
Barry Foster: Pittsburgh Steelers authentic Riddell, signed $250
Bill Fralic: late-1980s Atlanta Falcons Riddell, game used.................................$450
Eugene Goodlow: 1983 New Orleans Saints Riddell, game used $395
Mean Joe Greene: Pittsburgh Steelers authentic Riddell, signed...........................$280
Bob Griese: Miami Doplphins replica helmet, signed $150
Myron Guyton: New York Giants Super Bowl helmet, with flag decal, game used $445
Jim Harbaugh: Chicago Bears authentic Riddell, signed...................................$175
Franco Harris: Pittsburgh Steelers authentic Riddell, signed..............................$250
Ron Holmes: 1990s Denver Broncos Riddell helmet, with face shield, game used $400
Desmond Howard: Washington Redskins authentic Riddell, signed.....................$200
Mark Higgs: 1993 Miami Dolphins Riddell, game used................................$375
Michael Irvin: Dallas Cowboys replica helmet, signed $155
Steve Jordan: 1990 Minnesota Vikings Riddell, game used................................$495
Sonny Jurgensen: Washington Redskins authentic Riddell, signed $235
Jim Kelly: Buffalo Bills authentic Riddell, signed.................................$250
Jim Kelly: Buffalo Bills replica helmet, signed $180
Bernie Kosar: Cleveland Browns authentic Riddell, signed.................................$250
Bernie Kosar: Dallas Cowboys authentic Riddell, signed $250
Jack Lambert: Pittsburgh Steelers authentic Riddell, signed $250
Ronnie Lott: Los Angeles Raiders authentic Riddell, signed..............................$230
Duval Love: 1992 Pittsburgh Steelers Riddell, game used $395
Dan Marino: 1990 Miami Dolphins Riddell, game used $2,330
Dan Marino: Miami Dolphins authentic Riddell, signed $300
Dan Marino: Miami Dolphins replica helmet, signed.....................................$170
Leonard Marshall: 1980s New York Giants Riddell, game used..........................$400
Jim McMahon: Chicago Bears authentic Riddell, signed $275
Natrone Means: San Diego Chargers authentic Riddell, signed $275
Rick Mirer: Seattle Seahawks authentic Riddell, signed.................................$275
Joe Montana: San Francisco 49ers authentic Riddell, signed..............................$300
Warren Moon: Houston Oilers authentic Riddell, signed $250
Rob Moore: 1992 New York Jets Riddell, game used................................$495
Joe Namath: old-style New York Jets authentic Riddell, signed $255
Jay Novacek: Dallas Cowboys authentic Riddell, signed $240
Walter Payton: Chicago Bears authentic Riddell, signed.................................$250
Jerry Rice: 1993 San Francisco 49ers helmet, game used.................................$2,750
Jerry Rice: San Francisco 49ers authentic Riddell, signed...................................$260

Jerry Rice: San Francisco 49ers replica helmet, signed $130
Andre Rison: Atlanta Falcons authentic Riddell, signed..$175
Mark Rypien: Washington Redskins authentic Riddell, signed $190
Barry Sanders: Detroit Lions authentic Riddell, signed...$250
Deion Sanders: Atlanta Falcons authentic Riddell, signed $269
Deion Sanders: 1990 Atlanta Falcons helmet, with Desert Storm flag,
     game used...$1,800
Junior Seau: San Diego Chargers authentic Riddell, signed....................................$260
Sterling Sharpe: Green Bay Packers authentic Riddell, signed............................$250
Art Shell: Oakland Raiders authentic Riddell, signed..$230
Kenneth Sims: 1980s New England Patriots helmet, game used...........................$250
Phil Simms: New York Giants authentic Riddell, signed $270
O.J. Simpson: old-style Buffalo Bills authentic Riddell, signed................................$295
O.J. Simpson: Buffalo Bills new-style replica helmet, signed $175
Mike Singletary: Chicago Bears authentic Riddell, signed $240
Emmitt Smith: Dallas Cowboys authentic Riddell, signed..$275
Emmitt Smith: Dallas Cowboys replica helmet, signed $175
Emmitt Smith: Florida Gaters helmet, game used..$2,500
Ken Stabler: Oakland Raiders authentic Riddell, signed $260
Bart Starr: Green Bay Packers authentic Riddell, signed $225
Roger Staubach: Dallas Cowboys authentic Riddell, signed $275
Roger Staubach: Dallas Cowboys replica helmet, signed...$195
Pat Swilling: New Orleans Saints replica helmet, signed $75
Fran Tarkenton: Minnesota Vikings authentic Riddell, signed............................$275
Lawrence Taylor: New York Giants authentic Riddell, signed $275
Joe Theismann: Washington Redskins authentic Riddell, signed $260
Thurman Thomas: 1991 Buffalo Bills helmet, game used.......................................$750
Thurman Thomas: Buffalo Bills authentic Riddell, signed....................................$250
Reyna Thompson: New York Giants Super Bowl helmet, flag decal, game used.............$445
Johnny Unitas: Baltimore Colts authentic Riddell, signed $250
Mike Webster: mid-1980s Pittsburgh Steelers helmet, game used......................$500
Wade Wilson: 1985 Minnesota Vikings Riddell, game used $300
Barry Word: 1990s Kansas City Chiefs helmet, game used $395
Steve Young: San Francisco 49ers helmet, game used...$1,850
Steve Young: San Francisco 49ers authentic Riddell, signed.................................$260
Steve Young: San Fransico 49ers replica helmet, signed......................................$160

Multiple-signed football helmets

Troy Aikman, Jim Kelly, Dan Marino authentic Riddell, autographed $225
Troy Aikman, Michael Irvin, Emmitt Smith authentic Dallas Cowboys Riddell,
     autographed...$375
Marcus Allen, Howie Long, Warren Moon authentic Riddell, autographed $215
Jerome Bettis, Eric Dickerson, Ronnie Lott authentic Riddell, autographed..............$195

Drew Bledsoe, Garrison Hearst, Ricky Watters authentic Riddell, autographed..........$195
Mike Ditka, Gale Sayers authentic Chicago Bears Riddell, autographed...................$325
Mike Ditka, Gale Sayers Chicago Bears replica, autographed $175
Tony Dorsett, Emmitt Smith authentic Dallas Cowboys Riddell, autographed...........$260
John Elway, Joe Montana, Lawrence Taylor authentic Riddell, autographed $225
Boomer Esiason, Derrick Thomas authentic Riddell, autographed $215
Brett Favre, Barry Foster, Reggie White authentic Riddell, autographed..................$195
Michael Irvin, Steve Young authentic Riddell, autographed $225
Michael Irvin, Emmitt Smith authentic Dallas Cowboys Riddell, autographed $295
Joe Montana, Jerry Rice authentic San Francisco 49ers Riddell, autographed...........$350
Joe Namath, Jerry Rice, Emmitt Smith authentic Riddell, autographed $225
Jerry Rice, Steve Young San Francisco 49ers authentic Riddell, autographed.............$325
Mark Rypien, Barry Sanders authentic Riddell, autographed....................................$195

Multiple Hall of Famers

Baltimore Colts helmet: signed by Raymond Berry, Art Donovan, Gino Marchetti,
 Lenny Moore and Johnny Unitas...$400
Cleveland Browns helmet: signed by Jim Brown, Frank Gatski, Otto Graham,
 Lou Groza, Dante Lavelli, Marion Motley and Paul Warfield $380
Dallas Cowboys helmet: signed by Tony Dorsett, Tom Landry, Bob Lilly, Roger
 Staubach and Randy White...$425
Green Bay Packers Riddell: signed by Paul Hornung, Ray Nitschke, Bart Starr,
 Jim Taylor and Willie Wood..$400
Kansas City Chiefs Riddell: signed by Bobby Bell, Len Dawson, Willie Lanier
 and Jan Stenerud $350
Miami Dolphins Riddell: signed by Larry Csonka, Bob Griese, Jim Kiick
 and Paul Warfield $310
Oakland Raiders ProLine helmet: signed by Fred Biletnikoff, Cliff Branch,
 Willie Brown, Lester Hayes, Daryle Lamonica, Howie Long, Jim Otto, Ken
 Stabler and Jack Tatum $250
San Francisco 49ers helmet: signed by Hugh McElhenney, Leo Nomellini,
Joe Perry, Bob St. Clair and Y.A. Tittle..$290
Washington Redskins helmet: signed by Ken Houston, Sam Huff, Sonny Jurgensen
 and Charley Taylor $290
1994 AFC Pro Bowl helmet, authentic Riddell, signed by the team...........................$750
1994 NFC Pro Bowl helmet, authentic Riddell, signed by the team...........................$750

Team-signed helmets

1994 Atlanta Falcons team-autographed Riddell $325
1993 Buffalo Bills team-autographed Riddell...$475
1992 Chicago Bears team-autographed Riddell, 40 signatures...................................$495
1993 Chicago Bears team-autographed Riddell $375
1993 Cincinnati Bengals team-autographed Riddell, 35 signatures............................$350
1994 Cleveland Browns team-autogoraphed Riddell..$325
1992 Dallas Cowboys team-autographed Riddell, 33 signatures.................................$500

1993 Dallas Cowboys team-autographed Riddell $495
1992 Detroit Lions team-autographed Riddell, 42 signatures....................................$375
1992 Denver Broncos team-autographed Riddell, 29 signatures $350
1994 Denver Broncos team-autographed Riddell throwback $325
1992 Green Bay Packers team-autographed Riddell, 50 signatures.............................$450
1993 Green Bay Packers team-autographed Riddell $360
1994 Green Bay Packers team-autographed Riddell...$325
1992 Kansas City team-autographed Riddell..$295
1993 Kansas City Chiefs team-autographed Riddell...$475
1994 Kansas City Chiefs team-autographed Riddell...$350
1991 Los Angeles Raiders team-autographed Riddell, 47 signatures.........................$495
1992 Los Angeles Raiders team-autographed Riddell, 46 signatures.........................$495
1993 Los Angeles Raiders team-autographed Riddell, 30 signatures.........................$500
1992 Los Angeles Rams team-autographed Riddell, 38 signatures $350
1994 Los Angeles Rams team-autographed Riddell $325
1993 Miami Dolphins team-autographed Riddell $375
1992 Minnesota Vikings team-autographed Riddell, 41 signatures............................$495
1993 Minnesota Vikings team-autographed Riddell..$350
1994 New England Patrtiots team-autographed Riddell $325
1992 New Orleans Saints team-autographed Riddell, 34 signatures $350
1993 New Orleans Saints team-autographed Riddell..$340
1990-91 New York Giants Super Bowl Championship team-autographed Riddell,
    39 signatures $900
1993 New York Giants team-autographed Riddell $375
1994 New York Giants team-autographed Riddell $325
1992 New York Jets team-autographed Riddell, 47 signatures $350
1992 New York Jets team-autographed Riddell..$375
1993 Philadelphia Eagles team-autographed Riddell..$375
1994 Philadelphia Eagles team-autographed Riddell..$350
1991 Phoenix Cardinals team-autographed Riddell, 41 signatures............................$395
1992 Pittsburgh Steelers team-autographed Riddell, 35 signatures $495
1992 San Diego Chargers team-autographed game-used helmet, 43 signatures.........$395
1994 San Diego Chargers team-autographed Riddell $325
1993 San Francisco 49ers team-autographed Riddell $475
1993 Washington Redskins team-autographed Riddell $375

Autographed mini Riddell helmets

Marcus Allen: Kansas City Chiefs, signed...$95
Troy Aikman: Dallas Cowboys, signed $250
Jerome Bettis: Los Angeles Rams, signed $80
Fred Biletnikoff: Oakland Raiders, signed $95
Drew Bledsoe: New England Patriots, signed $100
Earl Campbell: Houston Oilers, signed $85
Randall Cunningham: Philadelphia Eagles, signed................................$75
Eric Dickerson: Indianapolis Colts, signed..$75

Tony Dorsett: Dallas Cowboys, signed $95
John Elway: Denver Broncos, signed $90
Boomer Esiason: New York Jets, signed $75
Marshall Faulk: Indianapolis Colts, signed $95
Brett Favre: Green Bay Packers, signed $85
Joe Greene: Pittsburgh Steelers, signed $75
Rodney Hampton: New York Giants, signed $85
Paul Hornung: Green Bay Packers, signed $65
Jeff Hostetler: Los Angeles Raiders, signed $90
Michael Irvin: Dallas Cowboys, signed $100
Jim Kelly: Buffalo Bills, signed $125
Bernie Kosar: Miami Dolpins, signed $50
Willie Lanier: Kansas City Chiefs, signed $55
Bob Lilly: Dallas Cowboys, signed $90
Dan Marino: Miami Dolphins, signed $125
Natrone Means: San Diego Chargers, signed $90
Eric Metcalf: Cleveland Browns, signed $90
Rick Mirer: Seattle Seahawks, signed $85
Warren Moon: Houston Oilers, signed $85
Joe Namath: New York Jets, signed $150
Ray Nitschke: Green Bay Packers, signed $55
Erict Rhett: Tampa Bay Buccaneers, signed $55
Jerry Rice: San Francisco 49ers, signed $150
Andre Rison: Atlanta Falcons, signed $75
Barry Sanders: Detroit Lions, signed $125
Gale Sayers: Chicago Bears, signed $85
Sterling Sharpe: Green Bay Packers, signed $100
Don Shula: Miami Dolphins, signed $125
Phil Simms: New York Giants, signed $75
Emmitt Smith: Dallas Cowboys, signed $135
Ken Stabler: Oakland Raiders, signed $75
Lynn Swann: Pittsburgh Steelers, signed $75
Joe Theismann: Washington Redskins, signed $80
Paul Warfield: Miami Dolphins, signed $65
Reggie White: Green Bay Packers, signed $140
Steve Young: San Francisco 49ers, signed $125
1993 Cincinnati Bengals: with 35 signatures $350
1992 Detroit Lions: with 42 signatures $395
1991 Los Angeles Raiders: with 47 signatures $495
1992 Los Angeles Raiders: with 46 signatures $495
1992 New Orleans Saints: with 34 signatures $350
1993 New Orleans Saints: with 57 signatures $350
1993 San Francisco 49ers: with 36 signatures $395

Team-issued USFL Riddells

Note: not used in a game

Arizona Wranglers (Bike) $450
Birmingham Stallions............ $250
Chicago Blitz......................... $250
Los Angeles Express $250
Memphis Showboats $250
Michigan Panthers................. $350
New Jersey Generals $250

Oklahoma Outlaws $250
Orlando Renegades................ $250
Philadelphia Stars $250
Portland Breakers $250
San Antonio Gunslingers........ $250
Tampa Bay Bandits $250
Washington Federals $250

Helmets

1930s Goldsmith black leather football helmet with chin strap.....................$250
1940s MacGregor leather helmet, dark blue, average condition.....................$50
1960s Rawlings face protector, never used, in original box.........................$20
1950s Spalding Norm Van Brocklin kid's football helmet...........................$39

Game-worn shoes

1900s football shoes, profesional quality with stacked leather cleats, perfect
   patina...$120
Hightop football shoes, circa 1940, high quality black leather $55
O.J. Simpson: football shoes, Mint, in the box which pictures Simpson
   five times, includes three other paper items picturing Simpson, plus facsimile
   autograph..$125
Marcus Allen: 1994 Kansas City Chiefs game-used shoes, autographed $495
Edgar Bennett: 1993 Green Bay Packers game-used cleats, autographed $100
Burt Grossman: Nike cleats, autographed.......................................$95
Bill Maas: red/white Converse, autographed....................................$175
Jerry Rice: Nike cleats, autographed $350
Neil Smith: 1992 Nike cleats, used in Pro Bowl, autographed $200
Art Still: white/red Nike cleats, autographed $195
Reggie White: 1993 Green Bay Packers game-used cleats, autographed $225
Barry Word: red/white Champion, autographed...................................$225
Tony Zendejas: Houston Oilers kicking shoe, Puma, autographed $75

Official Wilson Super Bowl footballs

Super Bowl XX: Chicago Bears vs. New England Patriots $64.95
Super Bowl XXI: New York Giants vs. Denver Broncos.....................$59.95
Super Bowl XXII: Washington Redskins vs. Denver Broncos $54.95
Super Bowl XXIII: San Francisco 49ers vs. Cincinnati Bengals $54.95

Footballs

1890s melon-style football, with original lacing and a wonderful patina $285
Early 1900s melon-shaped leather football $225
1920s melon-shaped leather football...$150

Shoulder pads

Johnny Unitas Spalding shoulder pads, red and white, with Spalding logo
   and facsimile autograph $55
Frank Leahy MacGregor/Goldsmith shoulder pads $40
1960s AFL referee jersey, orange with white stripes $600

Uniforms/equipment

1930s kid's uniform, includes tan and black leather Hutch helmet; pair of woolen
   red leggings; well-worn red/white #14 jersey; Wilson shoulder pads; gold canvas
   pants with built-in pads $200
1950s Spalding football jersey #42, blue, no numerals..$49
1960s Rawlings football pants, white..$30
Early Spalding football pants with reeded thigh pads, small tear in the seat $95
Kansas City Chiefs pants, player unknown, autographed by Hall of Famer
   Buck Buchanan $95
Kansas City Chiefs pants, player unknown, autographed by Nick Lowery....................$50
Kansas City Chiefs pants, player unknown, autographed by Hall of Famer
   Bobby Bell $70
Len Dawson early-1970s Kansas City Chiefs practice jersey, NOB $550
1950s MacGregor hip pads, in original box $40
Late-1970s NFL black-and-white referee shirt, with pants, #58................................$225
1960s Rawlings hi-top kangaroo hide football shoes..$49
1940s-50s Rawlings leather football chin straps $10
1950s mouthguard on cardboard placard $10

Basketball items

Game-used shoes

Mark Aguirre: Converse, autographed, game used...$150
Kenny Anderson: white/blue Reebok Instapumps, game used $125
Willie Anderson: white/black Nike Air Flights, game used, autographed $75
B.J. Armstrong: white/red Nike Air Strongs, game used..$150
Stacey Augmon: white/black/red Adidas, game used...$125
Vin Baker: black/white Nike Air Flights, game used $125
Benoit Benjamin: white/green Reeboks, game used, autographed $40
Larry Bird: 1980s Converse, game used, autographed $995
Mookie Blaylock: white/black Nike Air Flights, game used $75

1992 Dream Teamers John Stockton, Chris Mullin and Scottie Pippen wore these shoes.

Muggsy Bogues: black/white Reeboks, game used...$125
Shawn Bradley: Nikes, game used, autographed....................................$350
Dee Brown: black Reebok Pumps, game used, autographed $200
Duane Causwell: black Nikes, game used, autographed $50
Cedric Ceballos: black/blue Adidas, game used, autographed.................$225
Derrick Coleman: Nikes, game used, autographed..................................$295
Derrick Coleman: blue/white British Knights, game used, autographed................$350
Terry Cummings: Pumas, game-used, autographed $135
Walter Davis: Converse, game-used, autographed...............................$175
Vlade Divac: black/white Nike Air Forces, game used, autographed $175
Clyde Drexler: Avias, game used, autographed....................................$225
Chris Dudley: white/black Nike Air Flights, game used autographed.....................$75
Joe Dumars: Adidas, game used, autographed....................................$150
LaPhonso Ellis: black Nikes, game used, autographed............................$150
Pervis Ellison: Nike Airs, game used, autographed $125
Patrick Ewing: 1992 Eclipses, Olympic game used, autographed $895
George Gervin: Nikes, game used, autographed $175
Kendall Gill: 1993-94 Nikes, game used, autographed..........................$250
Harvey Grant: Nikes, game used, autographed....................................$85
Horace Grant: white/red Nikes, game used, autographed......................$225
Horace Grant: black/white Nike Airs, used in the 1995 playoffs $195
A.C. Green: white/purple Asics Tigers, game used, autographed..........................$195
Tom Gugliotta: white/black Reeboks, game used, autographed....................$125
Anfernee Hardaway: black/white Nike Airs, used in the 1995 playoffs................$395
Tim Hardaway: 1992-93 Nikes, game used, autographed $375
Derek Harper: 1993-94 Nikes, game used, autographed.........................$125
Ron Harper: white/red/black Nike Air Solo Flights, game used autographed $125
John Havlicek: one black Converse shoe, game used................................$450
Hersey Hawkins: white/purple Filas, game used....................................$75
Rod Higgins: Ponys, game used, autographed.......................................$75
Grant Hill: 1995 Filas, game used, autographed $595
Lionel Hollins: Nikes, game used, autographed....................................$175
Jeff Hornacek: purple/white Nikes, game used $100
Robert Horry: 1993-94 Nikes, autographed $275
Mark Jackson: LA Techs, game used..$150

Jimmy Jackson: white/blue Nike Air, one shoe, game used, autographed $125
Larry Johnson: Converse, game used, autographed...$625
Eddie Jones: white/black Nike Air Flights, game used, autographed $275
Michael Jordan: 1985-86 Nikes, game used $2,295
Michael Jordan: Nike Airs, used in 1995 playoffs, with #45 on the side $1,995
Shawn Kemp: white/green Reebok Hexalites, autographed $375
Jason Kidd: white/black Nike Airs, game used, autographed $395
Bo Kimble: Adidas, game used...$125
Bernard King: Converse, game used, autographed $120
Stacey King: white/black Nikes, autographed $60
John Koncak: Reeboks, game used, autographed..$185
Tony Kukoc: black/red Nike Airs, used in 1995 playoffs $195
Bob Lanier: Adidas, game used...$395
Grant Long: Nike Airs, game used, autographed..$125
Don MacLean: black/white Adidas, game used, autographed....................................$75
Rick Mahorn: New Balances, game used, autographed $125
Dan Majerle: black Nike Airs, game used, autographed...$195
Karl Malone: LA Techs, game used, autographed..$375
Moses Malone: red/white Nikes, game used autographed $195
Danny Manning: black Reebok Pumps, game used, autographed $175
Donyell Marshall: black Nikes, game used, autographed $175
Jamal Mashburn: white/blue/black Filas, game used from his rookie season,
    autographed..$350
Rodney McCray: Nike Airs, game used, autographed...$75
Derrick McKey: white/green/ Nike Air Forces, autographed....................................$75
Terry Mills: white/black/blue Nike Air Flights, game used, autographed $75
Harold Miner: white/red/black Nike Air Jordans, game used $175
Sidney Moncrief: Nikes, game used, autographed $175
Chris Mullin: Nikes, game used, autographed $595
Dikembe Mutombo: Black Adidas, game used, autographed...................................$395
Johnny Newman: white/black/blue Nike Air Flights, game used autographed $75
Ken Norman: white/red Nike Air Forces, game used, autographed $60
Hakeem Olajuwon: LA Tech Catapults, game used, autographed......................$395
Shaquille O'Neal: 1995 Reeboks, used in the playoffs $1,695
Billy Owens: black Nike Air Flights, game used, autographed $125
Robert Parish: Champions, game used, autographed..$225
Gary Payton: 1993-94 Nikes, game used, autographed..$250
Anthony Peeler: black/white Nike Air Flights, game used $95
Rickey Pierce: white/green Nike Air Flights, game used..$75
Ed Pinckney: black/white Asics, game used, autographed $75
Scottie Pippen: 1994 white/red Nikes, game used, autographed $425
Scottie Pippen: black/white Nike Air Flights, used in the 1995 playoffs $350
Mark Price: black Nike Air FlightS, game used, autographed.................................$225
Kurt Rambis: Asics, game used..$195

Glen Rice: Champions, game used, autographed $175
J.R. Rider: 1994-95 Converse, game used, autographed............................. $400
Mitch Ritchmond: white/blue Nikes, game used, autographed $200
Doc Rivers: Reeboks, game used, autographed $200
Alvin Robertson: white/blue Nike Air Forces, game used, autographed $100
Cliff Robinson: Adidas, game used, autographed... $75
Cliff Robinson: white/red Reeboks, autographed $150
David Robinson: black/white Nike Air Forces, single signed $395
David Robinson: Nike Airs, game used, autographed..................................... $850
David Robinson: white/black Nike Airs, used in the 1995 playoffs....................... $425
Glenn Robinson: white/black Air Jordans, game used................................ $400
Glenn Robinson: black Reeboks, game used, autographed.......................... $450
Dennis Rodman: New Balances, game used, autographed........................... $225
Rodney Rogers: black Nike Air Forces, game used, autographed............................. $95
Tree Rollins: Reeboks, game used, autographed... $100
Danny Schayes: Nike Airs, game used, autographed..................................... $75
Dennis Scott: white/black Nike Air Flights, game used, autographed $125
Malik Sealy: red/white/black Nikes, game used, autographed $50
Rony Seikaly: white/red/black Nike Airs, game used, autographed $95
Brian Shaw: Reebok Pumps, game used, autographed............................... $135
Jack Sikma: Converse, game used, autographed... $100
Lionel Simmons: black/white Nike Airs, game used... $95
Charles Smith: Asics, game used... $150
Steve Smith: 1993-94 Reeboks, game used, autographed $200
Latrell Sprewell: black/white/blue Converse Reacts, with #4 on one shoe for Chris
    Webber and #30 on the other for Billy Owens, autographed with #15 on each $395
John Starks: blue/white Adidas, game used, autographed................................ $250
John Stockton: Nikes, game used, autographed $325
Rod Strickland: Nike Airs, game used $75
Reggie Theus: Converse, game used, autographed $85
Otis Thorpe: red/white Avias, game used, autographed $150
Nick Van Exel: white/black Reebok Blacktops, game used, autographed............. $275
Bill Walton: Adidas, single shoe, game used, personalized autograph $175
Clarence Weatherspoon: Nikes, game used, autographed.......................... $125
Chris Webber: blue/white Nikes, game used, autographed.......................... $550
Dominique Wilkins: black Reeboks, game used, autographed........................ $250
Scott Williams: black Adidas, game used, autographed $75
Scott Williams: white/black Avia, game used, autographed............................... $60
Walt Williams: black/white Nike Air Strongs $95
James Worthy: white/purple Adidas Torsions, game used, autographed................. $225

Brand name shoes

Converse Chuck Taylor shoes, black canvas with flat rubber soles, size 12 1/2, facsimile
    autograph on the heel $70

Trunks/pants

Larry Bird Boston Celtics road shorts, with tags $900
Darryl Dawkins 1988 Detroit Pistons game-used shorts.............................. $145
Patrick Ewing late-1980s New York Knicks warmup pants $75
J.R. Rider 1993-94 Minnesota Timberwolves blue shorts $250
John Stockton 1991-92 Utah Jazz home trunks $245
1955 Marines basketball uniform, military-issued shorts with buckle and a tank top
    jersey, gold with scarlet trim.. $125

Warmups

Nick Anderson: 1991-92 Orlando Magic warmup jacket $350
Paul Arizin: 1950 All-American jacket with pants, NIT............................ $5,000
Rick Barry: early-1970s Golden State Warriors warmup jacket, autographed $2,950
Larry Bird: 1992 Dream Team warmup jacket, NOB, USA patch $2,500
Terry Cummings: 1989 San Antonio Spurs home warmup jacket $375
Adrian Dantley: early-1980s Detroit Pistons warmup $395
Vlade Divac: 1989 Los Angeles Lakers away warmup $300
Julius Erving: 1986 Philadelphia 76ers jacket, with pants $2,500
Rick Fox: 1993-94 Boston Celtics home warmup, complete $425
Hal Greer: 1964 USA World Tour jacket with pants $1,750
Cliff Hagan: 1957 St. Louis Hawks jacket, with World Champions patch,
    and pants.. $5,000
Bob Lanier: 1970s Detroit Pistons jacket with pants.............................. $2,000
Xavier McDaniel: 1993-94 Boston Celtics home warmup, complete,
    autographed $475
Kevin McHale: 1988-89 Boston Celtics home warmup pants $95
Shaquille O'Neal: 1992-93 Orlando Magic warmup jacket $5,500
Larry Nance: 1987-88 Phoenix Suns warmup jacket, NOB $250
Robert Parish: 1988-89 Boston Celtics home warmup pants...................... $95
Robert Parish: mid-1980s Boston Celtics jacket, NOB $650
Gary Payton: 1991-92 Seattle SuperSonics warmup $450
Sam Perkins: 1990-91 Los Angeles Lakers home warmup $300
Scottie Pippen: 1992 Dream Team warmup jacket, NOB, USA patch................. $1,500
David Robinson: 1989 San Antonio Spurs home warmup jacket.................... $1,700
Dan Roundfield: 1986-87 Washington Bullets warmup jacket.................... $125
Reggie Theus: 1987 Sacramento Kings home warmup suit $195

Shooting shirts

Johnny Dawkins 1987-88 Philadelphia 76ers shooting shirt $100
Christian Laettner 1993-94 Minnesota Timberwolves white shooting shirt $475
Clyde Lee early-1970s Golden State Warriors shooting shirt, gold,
    with zipper front... $495
Xavier McDaniel Boston Celtics reversible shooting shirt, autographed $225

Will Perdue 1989 Chicago Bulls shooting shirt, autographed $395
J.R. Rider 1993-94 Minnesota Timberwolves road black shooting shirt $550
John Salley 1988 Detroit Pistons warmup shirt, autographed $200
Orlando Woolridge 1992-93 Philadelphia 76ers game-worn red warmup jacket $250

Basketballs

Buffalo Leather Sporting Goods laced-up leather basketball, excellent condition $145
1940s Nokona laced-up leather basketball $225
1930s laced-up leather basketball $200
Bill Sharman basketball, in box which pictures Sharman and has a facsimile
   autograph $45

Miscellaneous

1940s-50s Spalding basketball jersey $29
1930s Spalding boy's size 26 cotton basketball jersey $15
1940s Spalding knee pad, Mint in box $49
Magic Johnson 1992 Olympic Dream Team hat, autographed $75
David Robinson 1992 Olympic Dream Team hat, autographed $50

Hockey items

Player-signed game-used sticks

Tony Amonte: Easton aluminum, game used, autographed $135
Glenn Anderson: Canadien, game used, cracked/repaired $95
Dave Andreychuk: Koho, game used, uncracked $110
Jason Arnott: 1990s Easton aluminum, autographed $275
Brent Ashton: Canadien, game used, uncracked $50
Donald Audette: Titan, game used $60
Murray Bannerman: Canadien, game used, uncracked, goalie stick, autographed $150
Tom Barrasso: Cooper, game used, goalie stick $125
Andy Bathgate: Northland, game used $800
Ed Belfour: Christian, goalie stick, autographed $255
Ed Belfour: Cooper, goalie stick, autographed $255
Jean Beliveau: 1960s CCM, cracked $700
Brian Bellows: Westar, game used, uncracked, autographed $90
Brian Bellows: Sher-wood, game used $90
Brian Benning: Koho, game used $35
Gary Bergman: Victoriaville, game used $80
Daniel Berthiaume: Sher-wood, game used, goalie stick $40
John Blue: Sher-wood, game used, goalie stick $60
Doug Bodger: Sher-wood, game used $50
Ivan Boldirev: Louisville Slugger, game used, uncracked $100

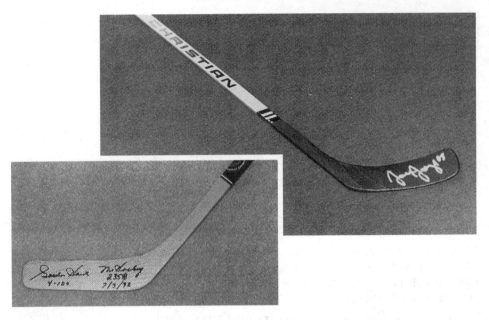

Gordie Howe and Jaromir Jagr signed these hockey sticks.

Peter Bondra: Koho, game used, uncracked...$95
Peter Bondra: Koho, game used, autographed..$80
Radek Bonk: 1995 black Koho Revolution, used in his first NHL game...............$250
Mike Bossy: 1982 Titan, game used $550
Mike Bossy: 1984 Titan, game used, uncracked $375
Philippe Boucher: Koho, game used...$30
Ray Bourque: Sher-wood, game used, uncracked $210
Ray Bourque: Sher-wood, game used, autographed $250
Ray Bourque: Sher-wood, game used $255
Patrick Boutette: Titan, game used $25
Neil Broten: Christian, not game used $45
Neil Broten: Christian, game used aluminum $125
Keith Brown: Canadien, game used, autographed $60
Rob Brown: Koho, game used, uncracked, autographed...$95
Pavel Bure: Easton aluminum, game-used, autographed..$395
Marc Bureau: Sher-wood, game used..$75
Sean Burke: Louisville, game used, autographed...$75
Shawn Burr: Hespeler, game used, autographed $40
Guy Carbonneau: Chimo, game used...$175
Guy Charbonneau: Victoriaville, game used $100
Randy Carlyle: Louisville, game used, autographed...$60
Bob Carpenter: Chimo, uncracked, autographed $75
Bob Carpenter: Victoriaville, game used, uncracked...$60
Bob Carpenter: Victoriaville, game used, autographed $60

Jimmy Carson: Sher-wood, not game used, uncracked, autographed......................$60
Jimmy Carson: Louisville, game used, uncracked, autographed............................$75
Jimmy Carson: Sher-wood, game used..$75
Jon Casey: Christian, game used, uncracked, goalie stick, autographed..................$175
Wayne Cashman: Sher-wood, game used, uncracked, autographed..........................$175
Andrew Cassels: Sher-wood, game used..$60
Jay Caufield: Christian, game used..$20
Paul Cavallini: Koho, game used, uncracked, autographed......................................$50
John Chabot: Sher-wood, game used, uncracked, autographed...............................$50
Chris Chelios: Sher-wood, game used..$125
Gerry Cheevers: early-1970s Louisville Slugger, game used, goalie stick..............$750
Tim Cheveldae: Louisville, game used, uncracked, goalie stick...............................$95
Tim Cheveldae: Hespeler, game used, goalie stick, autographed.............................$75
Dino Ciccarelli: Victoriaville, game used, autographed...$100
Dino Ciccarelli: 1986 Sher-wood, game used, uncracked......................................$125
Bobby Clarke: 1983 Sher-wood, game-used...$375
Jacques Cloutier: Sher-wood, game used, goalie stick..$40
Glen Cochrane: Titan, game used..$25
Paul Coffey: Sher-wood, game used, cracked..$125
Paul Coffey: 1980s Sher-wood, game used...$300
Russ Courtnall: Fontaine, game used..$100
Craig Coxe: Titan, game used, uncracked, autographed...$50
Adam Creighton: Koho, game used, autographed...$100
John Cullen: Koho, game used, uncracked, autographed...$75
Randy Cunneyworth: Bauer, game used...$25
Vincent Damphousse: 1980s Sher-wood, game used, autographed.......................$125
Jeff Daniels: Koho, game used...$20
Matt DelGuidice: Sher-wood, game used, autographed..$20
Alex Delvecchio: Northland, game used...$700
Bob Dillabough: 1966 Northland, game used...$100
Kevin Dineen: Victoriaville, game used, uncracked, autographed...........................$75
Gilbert Dionne: Canadien, game used, autographed..$75
Marcel Dionne: Canadien, white, autographed..$750
Marcel Dionne: 1984 Sher-wood, game used..$350
Paul Di Pietro: Sher-wood, game used...$50
Ken Dryden: Canadien, game used...$1,275
Marv Edwards: Koho, game used, goalie stick...$75
Dave Ellett: Koho, game used, uncracked, autographed..$75
Nelson Emerson: Sher-wood, game used, ...$75
Phil Esposito: Northland, game used, uncracked...$750
Tony Esposito: Northland, game used..$950
Bob Essensa: Victoriaville, game used, goalie stick...$75
Bernie Federko: 1983 Titan, game-used, uncracked..$75
Sergei Fedorov: 1990s Louisville TPS, game used..$375

Sergei Fedorov: Easton aluminum, game used $295
Brent Fedyk: Koho, game used, uncracked, autographed $65
Ray Ferraro: Canadien, game used, uncracked, autographed $75
Stephane Fiset: Sher-wood, game used, goalie stick $85
Mark Fitzpatrick: Victoriaville, game used $75
Theo Fleury: 1993 Titan, game used, uncracked.......................................$145
Mike Foligno: Canadien, game used $25
Ron Francis: Louisville, game used, autographed $175
Grant Fuhr: Sher-wood, game used, uncracked, autographed..................$225
Dave Gagner: Koho, game used, uncracked, autographed $75
Bob Gainey: 1978 Sher-wood, game used, uncracked $150
Bob Gainey: 1980s Koho, game-used..$200
Gerard Gallant: Sher-wood, game used, uncracked, autographed...........$75
Gerard Gallant: Sher-wood, game used $25
Mike Gartner: Victoriaville, game-used, uncracked $275
Martin Gelinas: Sher-wood, game used $45
Greg Gilbert: Sher-wood, game used, autographed................................$55
Clark Gillies: 1982 white Titan, game used $150
Doug Gilmour: Titan, game used, uncracked, autographed....................$295
Doug Gilmour: 1986 Titan, game used $250
Doug Gilmour: 1980s Hespeler, game used, autographed.......................$250
Warren Godfrey: Northland, game used..$270
Michel Goulet: 1986 Titan, game-used, uncracked...............................$95
Dirk Graham: Sher-wood, game used $70
Adam Graves: Sher-wood, game used, uncracked...................................$75
Wayne Gretzky: 1984-85 Titan, game used..$1,250
Wayne Gretzky: 1986 Titan, game used $1,360
Wayne Gretzky: 1992-93 Easton aluminum, game used $1,250
Roman Hamrlik: Sher-wood, game used $70
Craig Hartsburg: Sher-wood, game used, uncracked, autographed $60
Dominik Hasek: white Sher-wood, game used, autographed $300
Kevin Hatcher: Hespeler, game used, uncracked $160
Kevin Hatcher: Koho, game used..$75
Dale Hawerchuk: Louisvllie, autographed, game used, cracked $125
Brian Hayward: Cooper, game used, uncracked, goalie stick, autographed.............$90
Glenn Healy: Cooper, game used $100
Ron Hextall: Sher-wood, game used, goalie stick $150
Bobby Holik: Christian, game used..$60
Tim Horton: 1971 Sher-wood, game used $1,360
Doug Houda: Louisville, game used, uncracked, autographed $60
Phil Housley: Koho, not game used, autographed..................................$45
Gordie Howe: Northland Custom Pro Hockey stick, game used, name and number
    stamped on stick, autographed $1,395
Jim Hrivnak: Victoriaville, game used $60

Charlie Huddy: Sher-wood, game used, uncracked, autographed...........................$750
Mike Hudson: Sher-wood, game used, autographed..$55
Bobby Hull: early-1960s CCM, game used, uncracked, autographed.....................$995
Bobby Hull: 1976 CCM, used in the 1976 Canada Cup, autographed $1,800
Bobby Hull: Northland WHA stick, game used..$1,275
Brett Hull: Easton aluminum, game used $295
Brett Hull: Easton aluminum, game used, autographed by Brett and Bobby Hull....$495
Dale Hunter: Titan, game used, uncracked, autographed..$85
Al Iafrate: Koho, game used, uncracked...$95
Jaromir Jagr: Canadien, game used, uncracked, autographed $195
Jaromir Jagr (Pittsburgh), Canadien, game used, autographed.....................$150-$175
Craig Janney: Sher-wood, game used..$100
Mark Johnson: Sher-wood, game used $25
Curtis Joseph: Louisville Slugger, game used, goalie stick....................................$165
Joe Juneau: white Koho, game used...$150
Valeri Kamensky: Sher-wood, game used $75
Mike Keane: Hespeler, game used $70
Sheldon Kennedy: Hespeler, game used, autographed $60
Dave Keon: early-1970s Sher-wood, game used $400
Dimitri Khristich: Christian, game used, uncracked...$160
Derek King: Victoriaville, game used, autographed..$75
Kelly Kisio: Louisville, game used, autographed..$35
Petr Klima: Koho, game used, uncracked, autographed...$85
Joey Kocur: Easton aluminum, game used...$110
Vladimir Konstantinov: Tackula, game used, autographed $110
Mike Krushelnyski: Sher-wood, game used, uncracked, autographed $65
Mike Krushelnyski: Sher-wood, game used..$30
Bob Kudelski: Sher-wood, game used $90
Tom Kurvers: Sher-wood, game used, uncracked, autographed $60
Jari Kurri: 1980s Koho, game used, autographed...$225
Scott Lachance: Easton, game used..$60
Guy Lafleur: Chimo, game used, uncracked, autographed $350
Pat LaFontaine: Louisville aluminum, game used...$200
Pat LaFontaine: Canadien, game used, uncracked..$235
Rod Langway: Sher-wood, game used, uncracked $110
Rod Langway: Koho, game used, uncracked $125
Rod Langway: Koho, game used $70
Martin Lapointe: Titan, game used, autographed..$75
Igor Larionov: Sher-wood, game used $85
Steve Larmer: Sher-wood, game used $85
Michel Larocque: Titan, game used, goalie stick $200
Reed Larson: Koho, game used, uncracked, autographed $75
Paul Lawless: Canadien, game used, uncracked $50
J.P. LeBlanc: Koho, game used, cracked, autographed...$20

Brian Leetch: 1990s gold Easton aluminum, game used $375
Claude Lemieux: Titan, game used, autographed $85
Jocelyn Lemieux: Titan, game used, autographed...$65
Mario Lemieux: Koho, game used, uncracked...$375
Mario Lemieux: Koho, game used, uncracked, autographed $475
Nicklas Lidstrom: Titan, game used, autographed...$85
Trevor Linden: white Bauer, game used, autographed...$150
Trevor Linden: Canadien Custom Pro, game used..$135
Brett Lindros: 1995 black Bauer, game used, autographed.....................................$250
Eric Lindros: Bauer, game used..$350
Eric Lindros: black Titan, game used in his rookie season.....................................$650
Kevin Lowe: Koho, game used, autographed $80
Paul MacDermid: Christian, game used $30
Al MacInnis: white Sher-wood, game used...$175
John MacLean: Sher-wood, game used, autographed...$60
Rick MacLeish: Koho, game used, uncracked..$145
Pete Mahovlich: late 1970 Sher-wood, game used $200
Frank Mahovlich: 1972 Victoriaville game used $850
Dave Manson: Koho, game used, autographed..$75
Bradley Marsh: Christian, game used $60
Terry Martin: Koho, game used $25
Bryan Maxwell: Sher-wood, game used..$25
Parker McDonald: Northland, game used $275
Shawn McEachern: Easton, game used, aluminum..$175
Bob McGill: Koho, game used, autographed $50
Kirk McLean: 1990s Hespeler, game used, goalie stick..$225
Dave McLlwain: Koho, game used...$30
Mike McNeill: Sher-wood, game used, autographed $40
Marty McSorley: Christian, game used...$95
Mark Messier: Louisville TPS, game used, autographed $325
Mark Messier: 1985 CCM, game used, autographed $400
Mark Messier: Louisville, game used, uncracked $325
Rick Middleton: Sher-wood, game used..$75
Stan Mikita: early-1970s Northland, game used, uncracked....................................$825
Dimitri Mironov: Sher-wood, game used..$45
Mike Modano: 1990s gold Easton aluminum, game used $275
Mike Modano: 1989 white Louisville Slugger, game used, autographed.................$275
Alexander Mogilny: Easton aluminum, game used $275
Alexander Mogilny: Louisvlle, game used, cracked, autographed..........................$200
Andy Moog: Christian, game used, goalie stick $125
Brian Mullen: Canadien, game used, autographed $40
Kirk Muller: Christian, game used, ...$100
Kirk Muller: Sher-wood, game used...$60
Joe Murphy: gold Easton aluminum, game used $125

Larry Murphy: Koho, game used, autographed $80
Troy Murray: Sher-wood, game used, autographed $60
Mats Naslund: Torspo, uncracked, game used, autographed $125
Petr Nedved: Sher-wood, game used, autographed $125
Cam Neely: Canadien Custom Pro, game used $250
Cam Neely: Canadien, game used, uncracked $225
Sergei Nemchinov: Sher-wood, game used, autographed $75
Bernie Nicholls: Sher-wood, game used, autographed $90
Scott Niedermayer: Sher-wood, game used $125
Joe Nieuwendyk: Hespeler, game used $90
James Nill: Louisville, game used, uncracked, autographed $50
Owen Nolan: Easton aluminum, game used $125
Adam Oates: Louisville, game used, uncracked, autographed $145
Adam Oates: Louisville, game used, autographed $125
Mike O'Connell: Louisville, game-used, uncracked, autographed $50
John Ogrodnick: Westar, game used, uncracked $50
Ed Olczyk: Titan, game used $75
Terry O'Reilly: Canadien, game used, uncracked, autographed $110
Terry O'Reilly: Sher-wood, game used $75
Brad Park: Christian, game used, aluminum, uncracked, autographed $295
Brad Park: Christian aluminum, game used $425
Brad Park: Canadien aluminum, game used, autographed $350
Pat Peake: Sher-wood, game used, uncracked, autographed $75
Gilbert Perreault: 1982 Sher-wood, game used, uncracked $345
Michal Pivonka: Victoriaville, game used, uncracked, autographed $75
Michal Pivonka: Sher-wood, game used $30,
Felix Potvin: Koho, game used, uncracked, goalie stick $275
Denis Potvin: Titan, game used, autographed $350
Dave Poulin: Christian, game used, autographed $60
Wayne Presley: Sher-wood, game used, autographed $55
Keith Primeau: Bauer, game used, autographed $100
Keith Primeau: Easton, game used, autographed $130
Bob Probert: Hespeler, game used, uncracked $145
Bob Probert: Hespeler, game used, cracked, autographed $145
Bob Probert: Hespeler, game used $100
Brian Propp: Titan, game used $40
Dan Quinn: Titan, game used $20
Andre Racicot: Sher-wood, game used, autographed $60
Yves Racine: Koho, game used, uncracked, autographed $50
Rob Ramage: Sher-wood, game used $65
Mike Ramsey: Canadien, game used, uncracked $60
Bill Ranford: Christian, game used, uncracked, goalie stick, autographed ... $115
Jean Ratelle: Sher-wood, game-used, uncracked $350
Mark Recchi: Canadien, game used, uncracked, autographed $100

Mark Recchi: Koho, game used, autographed $110
Mark Recchi: Canadien, game used, autographed $150
Henri Richard: late-1960s, Victoriaville, game used $750
Stephane Richer: Christian, game used, autographed $95
Gary Roberts: Sher-wood, game used, autographed $95
Torrie Robertson: Sher-wood, game used, uncracked, autographed......................$50
Larry Robinson: Koho, game used $275
Luc Robitaille: Sher-wood, game used $150
Jeremy Roenick: 1990s gold Easton aluminum, game used $275
Reijo Ruotsalainen: Sher-wood, game used, uncracked, autographed......................$65
Dominic Roussel: black Koho Revolution, game used, goalie stick $85
Patrick Roy: Koho, game used $395
Patrick Roy: 1985-86 Sher-wood $750
Warren Rychel: Fontaine, game used..$60
Joe Sakic: Canadien, game used, cracked, autographed $110
Joe Sakic: white Chimo, game used, autographed $175
Borje Salming: Sher-wood, game used, uncracked..$110
Kjell Samuelsson: Titan, game used, uncracked $50
Geoff Sanderson: Easton, game used $110
Charlie Sands: 1938-39 stick, game-used, personalized autograph.......................$325
Tomas Sandstrom: Sher-wood PMP7000, game used...$60
Tomas Sandstrom: Titan, game used, autographed..$90
Bob Sauve: Titan, game used, uncracked, goalie stick, autographed......................$95
Denis Savard: Canadien, game used, uncracked, autographed $175
Denis Savard: Canadien, game used $150
Serge Savard: 1970s white Canadien, game used..$300
Brad Schlegel: Koho, game used...$20
Mathieu Schneider: Martinville, game used..$70
Al Secord: Canadien, game used, uncracked, autographed...................................$90
Daniel Shank: Sher-wood, game used, uncracked, autographed $50
Jeff Sharples: Titan, game used, uncracked $40
Ray Sheppard: Victoriaville, game used $125
Peter Sidorkiewicz: Louisville, game used, autographed $50
Darryl Sittler: 1983 Sher-wood, game used $340
Doug Smail: Louisville, game used, autographed...$35
Bobby Smith: Sher-wood, game used, uncracked, autographed $75
Bobby Smith: Cooper, game used, autographed $140
Floyd Smith: Northland, game used $175
Greg Smith: Sher-wood, game used $50
Stan Smyl: Sher-wood, game used, uncracked, autographed................................$75
Harold Snepsts: Koho, game used, uncracked, autographed................................$75
Peter Stastny: Christian, game used, autographed $100
Kevin Stevens: Koho, game used, uncracked, autographed $180
Scott Stevens: Christian, game used, autographed $125

Mats Sundin: white Koho Revolution, game used $175
Brian Sutter: Canadien, game used, uncracked, autographed..................................$150
Brian Sutter: Northland, game used, autographed...$60
Darryl Sutter: 1985 CCM, game used, uncracked, autographed.......................$100
Ken Sutton: Christian, game used $25
Petr Svoboda: Koho, game used $40
Kari Takko: Koho, game used, uncracked, goalie stick, autographed.....................$90
Tony Tanti: Titan, game used, uncracked, autographed...$75
Chris Terreri: Sher-wood, game used, autographed...$125
Steve Thomas: Victoriaville, game used..$85
Esa Tikkanen: Sher-wood, game used...$50
Walt Tkaczuk: Sher-wood, game used $250
Rick Tocchet: Koho, game used, uncracked, autographed.....................................$150
John Tonelli: Sher-wood, game used, uncracked, autographed $90
Bryan Trottier: Victoriaville, game used, uncracked, autographed...............$225-$250
Darren Turcotte: Sher-wood, game used, uncracked, autographed........................$80
Pierre Turgeon: Victoriaville, game used, uncracked, autographed $195
John Vanbiesbrouck: Victoriaville, game used, goalie stick, autographed $200
Pat Verbeek: Louisville, game used..$75
Mike Vernon: Koho, game-used goalie stick, uncracked $100
David Volek: Victoriaville, game used..$40
Darcy Wakaluk: Cooper, game used, goalie stick $100
Eric Weinrich: Koho, game used, autographed..$35
Doug Wilson: Canadien, game used $75
Doug Wilson: Sher-wood, game used, uncracked $100
Trent Yawney: Easton, game used, autographed..$125
Paul Ysebaert: Chimo, game used, uncracked, autographed...................................$65
Steve Yzerman: 1989 Louisville TPS, game-used, uncracked, autographed $300
Rick Zombo: Victoriaville, game used, uncracked, autographed..............................$65

Multiple and team-signed sticks

Anaheim Mighty Ducks 1992-93 team-autographed stick...$115
Anaheim Mighty Ducks 1993-94 team-autographed Sher-wood, game used
   by Anatoli Semenov...$135
Boston Bruins 1971-72 team-autographed Northland pro stick, game used
   by Phil Esposito, 18 signatures from the Stanley Cup Champions, including
   John Bucyk, Wayne Cashman, Phil Esposito, Ken Hodge and Bobby Orr...........$1,250
Boston Bruins 1990-91 team-autographed white Titan stick, with 35 signatures,
   including Bob Carpenter, Gord Kluzak, Andy Moog, Chris Nilan, Glen Wesley...........$200
Boston Bruins 1991-92 team-autographed stick, game used by Link Gaetz
   of the San Jose Sharks, with 21 signatures...$200
Boston Bruins 1993-94 team-autographed Moscow Leader stick,
   with 20 signatures...$250
Boston Bruins Ray Bourque model Sher-wood, team signed $135

Equipment

Buffalo Sabres 1974-75 team-signed Victoriaville, game used by Gilbert Perreault, with 20 signatures, including Gerry Desjardins, Danny Gare, Rick Martin, Perreault and Rene Robert..$750
Buffalo Sabres 1991-92 team-autographed white Titan, with 20 signatures $150
Buffalo Sabres 1992-93 team-autographed stick $80
Buffalo Sabres 1993-94 team-autographed stick $80
Calgary Flames 1991-92 team-autographed white Koho, with 27 signatures..............$150
Calgary Flames 1992-93 team-autographed stick $75
Calgary Flames 1993-94 team-autographed stick $75
Chicago Blackhawks 1991-92 team-autographed stick $185
Chicago Blackhawks 1992-93 team-autographed stick $100
Chicago Blackhawks 1993-94 team-autographed stick $100
Chicago Blackhawks 1993-94 team-signed goalie stick...$135
Detroit Red Wings 1975-76 team-autographed stick, game used by Barry
    Saloovaara, with 18 signatures...$150
Detroit Red Wings 1991-92 team-autographed stick $135
Detroit Red Wings 1992-93 team-autographed stick $100
Detroit Red Wings 1993-94 team-autographed Torpso $135
Los Angeles Kings 1992-93 team-autographed stick..$130
Montreal Canadians 1962 team-autographed stick $75
Montreal Canadiens, Guy Lafleur stick, autographed by team $520
Montreal Canadiens 1992-93 team-autographed stick, Stanley Cup Champions.............$125
New Jersey Devils 1989-90 team-autographed stick, 10 signatures, including
    John MacLean and Brendan Shanahan $150
New Jersey Devils 1991-92 team-autographed stick, game used by Jeff Finley
    of the New York Islanders, with 24 signatures $150
New York Islanders 1991-92 team-autographed stick, game used by Randy Hillier
    of the Islanders, 23 signatures $175
Ottawa Senators 1991-92 team-autographed stick..$90
Philadelphia Flyers 1991-92 team-autographed gray Titan, with 24 signatures..........$150
Philadelphia Flyers 1992-93 team-autographed stick $125
Pittsburgh Penguins 1991-92 team-autographed stick, Stanley Cup Champions,
    with 22 signatures...$295
Quebec Nordiques 1991-92 team-autographed stick $60
Quebec Nordiques 1992-93 team-autographed stick $60
Quebec Nordiques 1993-94 team-autographes stick..$60
St. Louis Blues 1991-92 team-autographed stick, game used by Ron Robinson,
    with 20 signatures...$200
St. Louis Blues 1991-92 team-autographed white Koho, with 17 signatures,
    including Brett Hull, Adam Oates..$175
St. Louis Blues 1993-94 team-signed Brett Hull model...$145
San Jose Sharks 1991-92 team-autographed stick..$115
Tampa Bay Lightning 1992-93 team-autographed stick, inaugural year,
    with 15 signatures...$125
Toronto Maple Leafs 1991-92 team-autographed stick $95
Toronto Maple Leafs 1992-93 team-autographed stick $95

Vancouver Canucks 1991-92 team-autographed stick $150
Vancouver Canucks 1993-94 team-autographed stick $115
Washington Capitals 1989-90 team-autographed Koho $150
Washington Capitals 1991-92 team-autographed stick, game used by Bill Berg
    of the New York Islanders, with 25 signatures $175
Winnipeg Jets 1989-90 team-autographed Koho $150
Winnipeg Jets 1991-92 team-autographed stick $75
Winnipeg Jets 1992-93 team-autographed stick $75
Winnipeg Jets 1993-94 team-autographed stick $75
1990-91 All-Star Gretzky stick, team autographed including Hull, Gretzky
    and others $345
All-Star hockey stick, signed by Ray Bourque, Pavel Bure, Chris Chelios, Wayne
    Gretzky, Brett Hull, Jaromir Jagr, Pat LaFontaine, Brian Leetch, Mario Lemieux,
    Eric Lindros, Al MacInnis, Mike Modano, Andy Moog, Cam Neely, Adam Oates,
    Mike Richter, Jeremy Roenick, Patrick Roy, Joe Sakic and Steve Yzerman $450

NHL goal pucks

For a program which ran during the 1972 and 1973 seasons, the NHL labeled pucks
which were used to score goals.
Phil Esposito, dated 12/8/73, on a Boston Bruins puck, in Boston. Numbered
    BB-2-111, meaning Boston Bruins, second season, 111th goal. The NHL
    registration certificate, which is included, indicates the goal was scored against
    Buffalo in the first period by Esposito, with assists from Cashman and Hodge. .... $450.
Guy Lafleur, dated 11/22/72, in Los Angeles, on a Los Angeles Kings puck,
    in Los Angeles. Numbered MC-1-108. .... $400.
Guy Lapointe, dated 1/7/74, in Montreal, on a Montreal Canadiens puck.
    Numbered MC-2-129. .... $300
Jean Ratelle, dated 11/18/73, in New York, on a New York Rangers puck.
    Numbered NYR-2-058. .... $350

Skates/gloves/helmets/equipment

Rod Brind'Amour Easton hockey gloves, game used, autographed $175
Rod Brind'Amour 1994-95 Philadelphia Flyers road helmet, CCM,
    game used $225
Chris Chelios 1990s Chicago Blackhawks helmet, CCM, game used $450
Louie DeBrusk game-used Louisville gloves, name on cuff $120
Kevin Dineen game-used gloves, Philadelphia Flyers black and white $95
Steve Duchesne Los Angeles Kings purple/gold gloves, used in his
    rookie season $125
Ron Francis 1990s Pittsburgh Penguins black gloves, Louisville Slugger,
    game used $200
Grant Fuhr skates, Edmonton Oilers white, Daoust 301, autographed,
    game used $600
Wayne Gretzky autographed game-used helmet, Jofa brand, white, used while
    with Edmonton, #99 stickers, padding and strap $1,650

Equipment

Wayne Gretzky autographed game-used Jofa brand gloves, Edmonton Oilers,
    each glove is autographed $3,750

Wayne Gretzky autographed replica white Jofa helmet... $175

Ron Hextall 1993-94 New York Islanders mask, white with the team logo
    on both sides, #72 on the back plate, game used, autographed............................. $7,500

Gordie Howe 1960s kids' hockey gloves, Easton Trulines.. $50

Bobby Hull store model skates, CCM, late 1960s, facsimile autograph....................... $80

Dennis Hull signature model 1960s Franklin shin guards... $15

Joc Juncau 1993 Boston Bruins gloves, Easton, game used, autographed.................... $275

Uwe Krupp game used gloves, New York Islanders blue and orange CCM,
    name and team logo on cuff $150

Jari Kurri Edmonton Oilers skates, Bauer Custom Supreme 2000, game used,
    autographed $550

Pat Lafontaine 1990s Buffalo Sabres blue and gold gloves, Louisville,
    game used... $450

Eric Lindros Bauer Supreme skates, game used $1,200

Mark Messier mid-1980s blue and orange Edmonton Oilers gloves, Rawlings,
    game used... $1,500

Alexander Mogilny helmet, 1990s Buffalo Sabres white, CCM, #89 on back,
    team logo on both sides, game used.. $500

Alexander Mogilny game-used gloves, 1990s Buffalo Sabres blue and gold,
    Louisville, name on cuff.. $500

Bernie Nichols game-used Edmonton Oilers gloves, name on cuff $100

Adam Oates Bauer game-used skates, number on each blade $350

Gilbert Perreault game-used skates, Bauer 100s $1,500

Mark Recchi CCM hockey gloves, game used, autographed...................................... $235

Mark Recchi 1990s CCM hockey skates, game used... $175

Mark Recchi, Pittsburgh Penguins hockey gloves, Penguins emblem
    on each glove... $400

Mikael Renberg 1994-95 Philadelphia Flyers road helmet, CCM,
    game used.. $375

Mike Richter 1992-93 goalie mask, custom made and painted, game used.............. $2,295

Mike Ridley CCM hockey helmet, game used, autographed...................................... $125

Kevin Stevens 1989-90 Bauer game-used skates... $350

Kevin Stevens Pittsburgh Penguins hockey gloves, game used................................. $500

Keith Tkachuk, 1990s Winnipeg Jets gloves, blue and red, Louisville,
    name on cuff, game used... $450

Rick Tocchet CCM skates, name and number indicated, game used.......................... $245

Jimmy Waite 1992 San Jose Sharks mask, custom made and painted,
    team issued but not used... $2,500

Jay Wells Philadelphia Flyers goalie gloves, game used, Rawlings, autographed $195

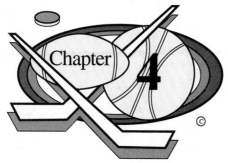

Statues/figurines

Bobbing Head Dolls
Football

Made in Japan from around 1960-70, there are 10 NFL categories known, due to the variations in the dolls. All are boy heads; no mascots were made. Black players exist in the gold round base series dated 1962. There were also college bobbing head dolls made from 1962-68.

I. NFL wood base (1961-62)

All of these dolls, the first NFL dolls to be made, have square bases.

Team	Base Color	Scarcity	Value
1) Baltimore Colts	Blue	Tough	$30-$40
2) Chicago Bears	Black	Scarce	$45-$55
3) Cleveland Browns	Brown	Scarce	$60-$70
4) Dallas Cowboys	Blue	Extremely Rare	$130-$140
5) Detroit Lions	Silver	Common	$20-$30
6) Green Bay Packers	Green	Tough	$45-$55
7) Los Angeles Rams	Black	Tough	$45-$55
8) Minnesota Vikings	Purple	Tough	$55-$65
9) New York Giants	Blue/Red	Scarce	$65-$75
10) Philadelphia Eagles	Green	Tough	$40-$50
11) Pittsburgh Steelers	Gold	Extremely Rare	$100-$125
12) St. Louis Cardinals	Red	Tough	$30-$40
13) San Francisco 49ers	Red	Scarce	$50-$60
14) Washington Redskins	Maroon	Rare	$95-$105

II. NFL square or round ceramic bases (1961-62)

If "NFL" is embossed on the base, add $10-$15 to basic prices. The team names are embossed on the chest; bases are various colors.

Team	Base color	Scarcity	Value
1) Baltimore Colts	Blue	Tough	$30-$40
2) Chicago Bears	Black	Scarce	$45-$55

Statues/figurines

Team	Base color	Scarcity	Value
3) Cleveland Browns	Brown	Scarce	$60-$70
4) Dallas Cowboys	Blue	Extremely Rare	$100-$110
5) Detroit Lions	Silver	Common	$20-$30
6) Green Bay Packers	Green	Tough	$45-$55
7) Los Angeles Rams	Black	Tough	$35-$55
8) Minnesota Vikings	Purple	Tough	$45-$55
9) New York Giants	Blue/Red	Scarce	$65-$75
10) Philadelphia Eagles	Green	Tough	$40-$50
11) Philadelphia Eagles "1960 Champions"	Green/	Scarce	$65-$75
12) Pittsburgh Steelers	Gold	Extremely Rare	$90-$100
13) St. Louis Cardinals	Red	Tough	$30-$40
14) San Francisco 49ers	Red	Tough	$45-$55
15) Washington Redskins	Maroon	Rare	$65-$75

III. NFL "Toes Up," vertical ball, square bases (1962)
The team name is embossed on the chest; the city name is on the base.

Team	Scarcity	Value
1) Baltimore Colts	Scarce	$45-$60
2) Chicago Bears	Scarce	$45-$60
3) Cleveland Browns	Extremely Rare	$90-$110
4) Dallas Cowboys	Extremely Rare	$120-$130
5) Detroit Lions	Scarce	$45-$60
6) Green Bay Packers	Scarce	$45-$60
7) Los Angeles Rams	Scarce	$45-$60
8) Minnesota Vikings	Rare	$50-$65
9) New York Giants	Rare	$50-$65
10) Philadelphia Eagles	Scarce	$50-$75
11) Pittsburgh Steelers	Extremely Rare	$90-$110
12) St. Louis Cardinals	Scarce	$50-$75
13) Washington Redskins	Extremely Rare	$100-$125

IV. NFL "00" series, gold round bases (1966-68)
"00" is on the player's back and on the sleeves, too.

Team	Scarcity	Value
1) Atlanta Falcons	Common	$40-$50
2) Baltimore Colts	Tough	$30-$45
3) Chicago Bears	Tough	$45-$55
4) Cleveland Browns	Rare	$40-$60
5) Dallas Cowboys	Extremely Rare	$75-$100
6) Detroit Lions	Tough	$30-$45
7) Green Bay Packers	Tough	$40-$50
8) Los Angeles Rams	Tough	$35-$45
9) Minnesota Vikings	Common	$40-$50
10) New Orleans Saints	Common	$35-$45
11) New York Giants	Common	$20-$30

Team	Scarcity	Value
12) Philadelphia Eagles	Tough	$45-$60
13) Pittsburgh Steelers	Extremely Rare	$80-$100
14) St. Louis Cardinals	Tough	$40-$50
15) San Francisco 49ers	Rare	$80-$90
16) Washington Redskins	Rare	$85-$100

V. Merger series, gold round bases, modern NFL decals

Some teams appear in home/away uniforms.

Team	Scarcity	Value
1) Atlanta Falcons	Common	$30-$45
2) Baltimore Colts	Common	$30-$45
3) Buffalo Bills	Tough	$50-$75
4) Chicago Bears	Tough	$45-$60
5) Cincinnati Bengals	Common	$20-$30
6) Cleveland Browns	Common	$40-$50
7) Dallas Cowboys	Extremely Rare	$75-$90
8) Denver Broncos	Tough	$50-$75
9) Detroit Lions	Common	$25-$40
10) Green Bay Packers	Tough	$30-$40
11) Houston Oilers	Common	$20-$30
12) Kansas City Chiefs	Common	$20-$30
13) Los Angeles Rams	Common	$25-$45
14) Miami Dolphins	Extremely Rare	$125-$150
15) Minnesota Vikings	Common	$30-$45
16) New England Patriots	Tough	$45-$60
17) New Orleans Saints	Common	$25-$40
18) New York Giants	Common	$25-$40
19) New York Jets	Common	$40-$50
20) Oakland Raiders	Extremely Rare	$80-$100
21) Philadelphia Eagles	Tough	$35-$50
22) Pittsburgh Steelers	Extremely Rare	$75-$100
23) St. Louis Cardinals	Tough	$20-$30
24) San Diego Chargers	Tough	$45-$60
25) San Francisco 49ers	Common	$50-$75
26) Washington Redskins	Extremely Rare	$75-$100

VI. AFL, various colored square and round bases (1961-62)

Enlarged shoulder pads, team name on the chest, some with baggy pants, toes up, and wood bases.

Team	Scarcity	Value
1) Boston Patriots	Extremely Rare	$300-$400
2) Buffalo Bills	Extremely Rare	$225-$325
3) Dallas Texans	Extremely Rare	$400-$500
4) Denver Broncos	Extremely Rare	$300-$400
5) Houston Oilers	Extremely Rare	$350-$450
6) Los Angeles Chargers	Extremely Rare	$500-$600

Statues/figurines

Team	Scarcity	Value
7) New York Titans	Extremely Rare	$450-$550
8) Oakland Raiders (patch over eye)	Extremely Rare	$450-$550

VII. AFL gold round bases, "ear pads" on helmet
Team names on chest, cities on base, AFL decals.

Team	Scarcity	Value
1) Boston Patriots	Rare	$150-$225
2) Buffalo Bills	Rare	$150-$225
3) Denver Broncos	Rare	$125-$200
4) Houston Oilers	Rare	$150-$225
5) Kansas City Chiefs	Rare	$125-$200
6) New York Jets	Rare	$100-$175
7) Oakland Raiders	Extremely Rare	$175-$250
8) San Diego Chargers	Rare	$100-$175

VIII. AFL decals, gold round bases (1966-67)

Team	Scarcity	Value
1) Boston Patriots	Rare	$75-$100
2) Buffalo Bills	Rare	$75-$100
3) Denver Broncos	Rare	$75-$100
4) Houston Oilers	Rare	$50-$75
5) Kansas City Chiefs	Rare	$75-$100
6) New York Jets	Rare	$60-$80
7) Oakland Raiders	Extremely Rare	$125-$150
8) San Diego Chargers	Rare	$60-$80

IX. Black players, gold round bases, toes up, vertical ball (1962)
The team name is embossed on the chest, with the city name on the base. All teams were represented, using NFL decals. These are extremely rare and are generally pursued by advanced collectors. Values are double the high range of category III bobbers.

X. NFL boy and girl kissing dolls, gold round bases (1962)
The team name is embossed on the chest, while the city name is on the base. Each team is represented; the pair was boxed together. The player has a magnet inside the cheek. These are slightly bigger than their 4.5" miniature baseball bobber counterparts. Values are similar to the price ranges for category III statues.

Hockey

Six NHL teams were represented on bobbing head dolls made in 1962. These dolls featured square bases with various colors. Minature versions, each 4 1/2" tall, were also made for the six teams. From 1967-69, gold-based "Gordie Howe" bobbers were also created, each featuring a caricature of the Hall of Famer. The original six teams, plus the Los Angeles Kings and St. Louis Browns, are represented.

1962 bobbers

Team	Scarcity	Value
1) Boston Bruins	Extremely Rare	$350-$450
2) Chicago Blackhawks	Extremely Rare	$200-$250

122

Team	Scarcity	Value
3) Detroit Red Wings	Scarce	$125-$225
4) Montreal Canadiens	Scarce	$75-$100
5) New York Rangers	Rare	$80-$115
6) Toronto Maple Leafs	Scarce	$80-$115
1962 minis		
1) Boston Bruins	Rare	$55-$75
2) Chicago Blackhawks	Rare	$55-$75
3) Detroit Red Wings	Scarce	$25-$50
4) Montreal Canadiens	Scarce	$25-$50
5) New York Rangers	Extremely Rare	$800
6) Toronto Maple Leafs	Scarce	$25-$50
1967-69 bobbers		
1) Boston Bruins	Extremely Rare	$250-$350
2) Chicago Blackhawks	Extremely Rare	$50-$100
3) Detroit Red Wings	Extremely Rare	$125-$150
4) Los Angeles Kings	Extremely Rare	$200-$300
5) Minnesota North Stars	Extremely Rare	$200-$300
6) Montreal Canadiens	Extremely Rare	$175-$200
7) New York Rangers	Extremely Rare	$175-$225
8) Toronto Maple Leafs	Extremely Rare	$200-$225

Basketball

Basketball had the fewest amount of bobbers released. Two teams exist for 1962; three are represented in 1967, with two teams also represented by a black-faced doll. In the late 1960s and early 1970s, an offshoot version of the bobbers were produced. These dolls, called "Little Dribblers," had the head and body as one piece. A ball, underneath the player's hand, is connected to the back of the base by a flat band of metal. If the ball is touched, it bob ups and down, creating an illusion that the doll is dribbling the ball.

1962 bobbers
1) Los Angeles Lakers $325
2) New York Knicks $325

1967 bobbers
1) Los Angeles Lakers $75
2) Los Angeles Lakers black $300
3) San Diego Rockets $150
4) Seattle Sonics $145
5) Seattle Sonics black..$300

Little Dribblers
1) Baltimore Bullets $100
2) Chicago Bulls...$75
3) Detroit Pistons...$75
4) Milwaukee Bucks...$75
5) New York Knicks..$30
6) Philadelphia 76ers $100

Hartland football statues

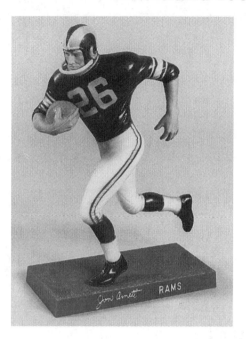 

A running back model and a lineman version were made for each NFL team. Each statue included a sheet of decal numbers which could be applied to the player's jersey. Having the original box in Near Mint to Mint condition adds $75 to the value of the statue. Two specific players - Johnny Unitas and Jon Arnett - were also made.

Team	Running back NM	Lineman EX-MT
Baltimore Colts	$325-$375	$300-$350
Chicago Bears	$250-$300	$225-$275
Cleveland Browns	$275-$325	$250-$300
Dallas Cowboys	$475-$550	$425-$500
Detroit Lions	$275-$325	$275-$325
Green Bay Packers	$225-$275	$200-$250
Los Angeles Rams	$275-$325	$250-$300
Minnesota Vikings	$225-$275	$200-$250
New York Giants	$250-$300	$275-$325
Philadelphia Eagles	$325-$375	$250-$300
Pittsburgh Steelers	$350-$400	$300-$350
St. Louis Cardinals	$325-$375	$300-$350
San Francisco 49ers	$325-$375	$300-$350
Washington Redskins	$475-$550	$425-$500
Johnny Unitas	$325-$350	
Jon Arnett	$225-$250	

Sports, Accessories & Memorabilia

This company, based in Menlo Park, Calif., has primarily issued baseball-related bobbers since 1991, but has tapped into other sports, too. Each doll is 9" tall and features a caricature of a star player in his team's uniform, with his name written at the base of the bobber.

UD represents Upper Deck Authenticated exclusive.

Basketball, 3,000 each

Larry Bird home and away	$44.95 each
Michael Jordan (UD)	$49.95
David Robinson home and away	$44.95 each

Football 5,000 each

Troy Aikman, white uniform	$39.95
Terry Bradshaw	$39.95
Randall Cunningham	$39.95
John Elway	$39.95
Jim Kelly	$39.95
Ronnie Lott LA	$39.95

Ronnie Lott NYJ...$39.95
Ronnie Lott SF $39.95
Dan Marino..$39.95
Art Monk $39.95
Joe Montana KC (UD)...$44.95
Joe Montana SF (UD)...$44.95
Jerry Rice...$39.95
Emmitt Smith, white uniform..$39.95
Roger Staubach..$39.95
Lawrence Taylor..$39.95

Ten NFL players will be featured on bobbers projected to be released in the fall of 1995. In addition to blue-uniformed bobbers for Emmitt Smith and Troy Aikman - who will have different facial features from their previous releases - the others are: Drew Bledsoe, Dave Brown, Marshall Faulk, Brett Favre, Rick Mirer, Barry Sanders, Junior Seau and Steve Young. The release price is $44.95 each. SAM also plans to produce 1,000 generic team bobbers for each of the 30 NFL teams, selling for less than $40 each.

Hockey 3,000 each, projected for fall 1995 release:
Gordie Howe $39.95
Bobby Hull $39.95
Brian Leetch $39.95
Previously produced
Mario Lemieux 5,000 home $44.95
Mario Lemieux 500 away...$44.95

Kenner Starting Lineup Statues

1988 Kenner Basketball Starting Lineups

Note: all prices include the cards

Complete set (85):	$3,500 MT	
Common player:		$15

Atlanta Hawks

Doc Rivers	8,000	$18
Spud Webb(LP)	4,500	$25
Dominique Wilkins(AS)	24,000	$30
Kevin Willis	4,500	$20

Boston Celtics

Danny Ainge	5,000	$22
Larry Bird(AS)	24,000	$60
Dennis Johnson(LP)	4,000	$20
Kevin McHale(AS)	24,000	$25
Robert Parish	6,000	$20

Chicago Bulls

Michael Jordan(AS)	30,000	$45
John Paxson(LP)	4,000	$18
Scottie Pippen	5,000	$40

Cleveland Cavaliers

Brad Daugherty	5,000	$28
Ron Harper	5,000	$16
Mark Price(LP)	3,000	$75
John Williams	3,000	$18

Dallas Mavericks

Mark Aguirre	10,000	$20
Rolando Blackman	8,000	$15
Derek Harper	6,000	$15
Sam Perkins(LP)	4,000	$20

Denver Nuggets

Michael Adams	8,000	$20
Alex English	8,000	$18
Lafayette Lever	5,500	$18
Danny Schayes(LP)	4,500	$15

Detroit Pistons

Adrian Dantley	6,000	$45
Vinnie Johnson(LP)	4,000	$65
Bill Laimbeer	5,000	$30
Isiah Thomas(AS)	24,000	$30

Golden State Warriors

Winston Garland(LP)	4,000	$15
Rod Higgins	5,000	$15
Chris Mullin	6,000	$40
Ralph Sampson	10,000	$15

Houston Rockets

Joe Barry Carroll	6,000	$18
Eric Sleepy Floyd	6,000	$20

Dallas Mavericks

Rodney McCray(LP)	4,000	$18
Akeem Olajuwon(AS)	24,000	$45

Indiana Pacers

Reggie Miller(LP)	4,000	$40
Chuck Person	7,000	$18
Steve Stipanovich	8,000	$15
Wayman Tisdale	6,000	$22

Los Angeles Clippers

Danny Manning(AS)	24,000	$20
Reggie Williams(LP)	4,500	$15

Los Angeles Lakers

Kareem Abdul-Jabbar(AS)	24,000	$35
Michael Cooper(LP)	4,000	$18
Magic Johnson(AS)	24,000	$45
James Worthy	5,000	$25

Milwaukee Bucks

Terry Cummings	8,000	$18
Sidney Moncrief	6,000	$20
Paul Pressey(LP)	5,000	$15
Jack Sikma	6,000	$18

New Jersey Nets

Buck Williams	5,000	$20
Dennis Hopson	4,000	$15

New York Knicks

Mark Jackson	5,500	$22
Patrick Ewing(AP)	24,000	$30
Gerald Wilkins(LP)	5,500	$18

Philadlephia 76ers

Charles Barkley(AS)	24,000	$45
Maurice Cheeks	6,000	$16
Mike Gminski	5,000	$15
Cliff Robinson(LP)	5,000	$28

Phoenix Suns

Tom Chambers	5,500	$18
Armon Gilliam	7,000	$15
Jeff Hornacek(LP)	4,000	$28
Eddie Johnson	6,000	$16

Portland Trailblazers

Clyde Drexler	6,000	$50
Steve Johnson	8,000	$15
Terry Porter(LP)	4,500	$25
Kiki Vandeweghe	8,000	$15

Sacramento Kings

Kenny Smith	10,000	$18
LaSalle Thompson(LP)	5,000	$18
Otis Thorpe	10,000	$22

San Antonio Spurs

Walter Berry	8,000	$18
Johnny Dawkins	8,000	$18
David Greenwood(LP)	4,000	$15
Alvin Robertson	5,500	$15

Seattle Supersonics

Michael Cage	6,000	$18
Dale Ellis	8,000	$20
Xavier McDaniel	6,000	$20
Derrick McKey(LP)	5,000	$25

Utah Jazz

Thurl Bailey	2,800	$135
Mark Eaton (LP)	1,500	$110
Karl Malone	2,800	$450
John Stockton	2,800	$260

Washington Bullets

Bernard King(LP)	10,000	$20
Jeff Malone	10,000	$20
Moses Malone	4,500	$35

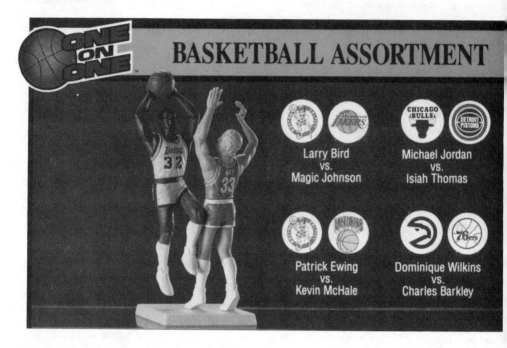

BASKETBALL ASSORTMENT

Larry Bird
vs.
Magic Johnson

Michael Jordan
vs.
Isiah Thomas

Patrick Ewing
vs.
Kevin McHale

Dominique Wilkins
vs.
Charles Barkley

1988-89 Kenner Basketball
Starting Lineups

Slam Dunk white box

Comnplete set (6):		$135
Common player:		$15
1) Larry Bird	5,000	$30
2) Patrick Ewing	3,000	$15
3) Magic Johnson	6,000	$45
4) Michael Jordan	8,000	$50
5) Isiah Thomas	3,000	$15
6) Dominique Wikins	4,000	$25

1989 Kenner Basketball
Starting Lineups

Slam Dunk red box

Complete set (6):		$250
Common player:		$32
1) Larry Bird	1,500	$60
2) Patrick Ewing	1,500	$40
3) Magic Johnson	1,500	$65
4) Michael Jordan	1,500	$65
5) Isiah Thomas	1,500	$40
6) Dominique Wilkins	1,500	$32

1989 Kenner Basketball
Starting Lineups

Complete set (5):	$85
Common player:	$16
1) Del Curry	$16
2) Rex Chapman	$32
3) Kelly Tripucka	$16
4) Ron Harper	$16
5) Larry Nance	$16

1989-90 Kenner Basketball
Starting Lineups

One-On-One

Complete set (4):	$200
Common pair:	$25
1) Michael Jordan vs. Isiah Thomas	$100
2) Larry Bird vs. Magic Johnson	$85
3) Charles Barkley vs. Dominique Wilkins	$40
4) Patrick Ewing vs. Kevin McHale	$25

1990 Kenner Basketball
Starting Lineups

Complete set (17):		$375
Common player:		$15
1) Charles Barkley	8,000	$45
2) Larry Bird	8,000	$50
3) Tom Chambers	5,000	$15
4) Clyde Drexler	5,000	$35
5) Joe Dumars	5,000	$20
6) Patrick Ewing	5,000	$30
7) Magic Johnson	8,000	$35
8) Michael Jordan	15,000	$50
9) Karl Malone	8,000	$25
10) Chris Mullin	5,000	$20
11) David Robinson	16,000	$50
12) Byron Scott	5,000	$15
13) John Stockton	5,000	$30
14) Isiah Thomas	8,000	$20
15) Spud Webb	8,000	$15
16) Dominique Wilkins	8,000	$30
17) James Worthy	8,000	$15

1990 Kenner Basketball Starting Lineups

Basketball Legends
Complete set (4):	$40
Common player:	$10
1) Wilt Chamberlain	$15
2) Julius Erving	$12
3) John Havlicek	$10
4) Oscar Robertson	$12

1991 Kenner Basketball Starting Lineups

Complete set (16):		$280
Common player:		$14
1) Charles Barkley	5,000	$40
2) Larry Bird	5,000	$45
3) Derrick Coleman(LP)	3,500	$28
4) Clyde Drexler	4,000	$22
5) Joe Dumars	4,000	$14
6) Patrick Ewing	5,000	$30
7) Kevin Johnson(LP)	3,500	$25
8) Magic Johnson	6,000	$30
9) Michael Jordan	15,000	$35
10) Michael Jordan (Air)	55,000	$30
11) Reggie Lewis (LP)	3,500	$28
12) David Robinson	13,000	$20
13) Dennis Rodman(LP)	3,500	$20
14) Isiah Thomas	5,000	$14
15) Spud Webb	1,700	$14
16) Dominique Wilkins	4,000	$30

1992 Kenner Basketball Starting Lineups

Olympic Team
Complete set (10):	$75
Common player:	$10
1) Charles Barkley	$12
2) Larry Bird	$15
3) Patrick Ewing	$10
4) Magic Johnson	$15
5) Michael Jordan	$18
6) Karl Malone	$12
7) Chris Mullin	$10
8) Scottie Pippen	$10
9) David Robinson	$12
10) John Stockton	$10

1992 Kenner Basketball Starting Lineups

Complete set (30):	$600
Common player:	$8
1) Charles Barkley	$40
2) Larry Bird	$40
3) Manute Bol	$8
4) Dee Brown	$10
5) Derrick Coleman	$10
6) Vlade Divac	$9
7) Clyde Drexler	$18
8) Joe Dumars	$9
9) Patrick Ewing	$16
10) Tim Hardaway	$22

11) Kevin Johnson	$12
12) Larry Johnson	$55
13) Magic Johnson (purple)	$30
14) Magic Johnson (yellow)	$175
15) Michael Jordan (regular)	$30
16) Michael Jordan (warmup)	$25
17) Dan Majerle	$20
18) Karl Malone	$14
19) Reggie Miller	$15
20) Chris Mullin	$9
21) Dikembe Mutombo	$20
22) Hakeem Olajuwon	$25
23) John Paxson	$12
24) Scottie Pippen	$16
25) Mark Price	$12
26) David Robinson (regular)	$15
27) David Robinson (warmup)	$18
28) Dennis Rodman	$10
29) John Stockton	$10
30) Isiah Thomas	$12

1992-93 Kenner Basketball Starting Lineups

Headliners
Complete set (8):	$200
Common player:	$18
1) Charles Barkley	$40
2) Larry Bird	$45
3) Patrick Ewing	$30
4) Magic Johnson	$35
5) Michael Jordan	$45
6) Dikembe Mutombo	$18
7) Scottie Pippen	$24
8) David Robinson	$20

Statues/figurines

1993 Kenner Basketball Starting Lineups	
Complete set (29):	$500
Common player:	$8
1) Kenny Anderson	$25
2) Stacey Augmon	$20
3) Charles Barkley	$20
4) Brad Daugherty	$8
5) Todd Day	$15
6) Clyde Drexler	$18
7) Sean Elliott	$12
8) Patrick Ewing	$20
9) Horace Grant	$12
10) Tom Gugliotta	$40
11) Tim Hardaway	$12
12) Larry Johnson	$12
13) Michael Jordan	$35
14) Shawn Kemp	$25
15) Christian Laettner	$50
16) Dan Majerle	$8
17) Karl Malone	$12
18) Alonzo Mourning	$60
19) Dikembe Mutombo	$8
20) Shaquille O'Neal	$30
21) Scottie Pippen	$12
22) Terry Porter	$10
23) Mark Price	$9
24) Glen Rice	$18
25) Mitch Richmond	$14
26) David Robinson	$14
27) Detlef Schrempf	$10
28) John Stockton	$12
29) Dominique Wilkins	$15

1994 Kenner Basketball Starting Lineups	
Complete set (26):	$220
Common player:	$10
1) B.J. Armstrong	$11
2) Stacey Augmon	$10
3) Charles Barkley	$12
4) Shawn Bradley	$12
5) Calbert Cheaney	$12
6) Derrick Coleman	$10
7) Sean Elliott	$13
8) LaPhonso Ellis	$10
9) Patrick Ewing	$10
10) Anfernee Hardaway	$20
11) Jim Jackson	$14
12) Larry Johnson	$10
13) Shawn Kemp	$14
14) Karl Malone	$10
15) Jamal Mashburn	$14
16) Harold Miner	$10
17) Alonzo Mourning	$13
18) Chris Mullin	$10
19) Hakeem Olajuwon	$12
20) Shaquille O'Neal	$14
21) Scottie Pippen	$10
22) David Robinson	$10
23) Dennis Rodman	$10
24) Latrell Sprewell	$15
25) Chris Webber	$24
26) Dominique Wilkins	$10

130

1988 Kenner Football Starting Lineups

Complete set (137):	$3,250
Common player:	$18
1) Marcus Allen	$60
1) Marcus Allen	$60
2) Neal Anderson	$18
3) Chip Banks	$30
4) Mark Bavaro	$20
5) Cornelius Bennett	$70
6) Albert Bentley	$18
7) Duane Bickett	$22
8) Todd Blackledge	$18
9) Brian Bosworth	$22
10) Brian Brennan	$18
11) Bill Brooks	$18
12) James Brooks	$18
13) Eddie Brown	$35
14) Joey Browner	$25
15) Aundray Bruce	$18
16) Chris Burkett	$40
17) Keith Byars	$20
18) Scott Campbell	$20
19) Carlos Carson	$18
20) Harry Carson	$28
21) Anthony Carter	$40
22) Gerald Carter	$18
23) Michael Carter	$36
24) Tony Casillas	$18
25) Jeff Chadwick	$18
26) Deron Cherry	$20
27) Ray Childress	$24
28) Todd Christianson	$30
29) Gary Clark	$45
30) Mark Clayton	$32
31) Chris Collinsworth	$40
32) Doug Crosbie	$22
33) Roger Craig	$32
34) Randall Cunningham	$38
35) Jeff Davis	$18
36) Ken Davis	$35
37) Richard Dent	$25
38) Eric Dickerson	$50
39) Floyd Dixon	$20
40) Tony Dorsett	$150
41) Mark Duper	$24
42) Tony Eason	$24
43) Carl Ekern	$18
44) Henry Ellard	$18
45) John Elway	$70
46) Phillip Epps	$22
47) Boomer Esiason	$40
48) Jim Everett	$28
49) Brent Fullwood	$25
50) Mark Gastineau	$18
51) Willie Gault	$40
52) Bob Golic	$18
53) Jerry Gray	$18
54) Darrell Green	$28
55) Jacob Green	$20
56) Roy Green	$26
57) Steve Grogan	$20
58) Ronnie Harmon	$40
59) Bobby Hebert	$20
60) Alonzo Highsmith	$22
61) Drew Hill	$24
62) Earnest Jackson	$18
63) Rickey Jackson	$18
64) Vance Johnson	$22
65) Ed Jones	$28
66) James Jones	$18
67) Rod Jones	$18
68) Rulon Jones	$18
69) Steve Jordan	$24
70) E.J. Junior	$30
71) Jim Kelly	$100
72) Bill Kenney	$24
73) Bernie Kosar	$18
74) Tommy Kramer	$25
75) Dave Krieg	$25
76) Tim Krumrie	$40
77) Mark Lee	$30
78) Ronnie Lippett	$24
79) Louis Lipps	$28
80) Neil Lomax	$22
81) Chuck Long	$18
82) Howie Long	$40
83) Ronnie Lott	$55
84) Kevin Mack	$18

85) Mark Malone	$30	118) Lawrence Taylor	$36
86) Dexter Manley	$20	119) Vinnie Testaverde	$18
87) Dan Marino	$150	120) Andre Tippett	$18
88) Eric Martin	$20	121) Anthony Toney	$22
89) Rueben Mayes	$20	122) Al Toon	$20
90) Jim McMahon	$25	123) Jack Trudeau	$18
91) Freeman McNeil	$18	124) Herschel Walker	$22
92) Karl Mecklenburg	$18	125) Curt Warner	$25
93) Mike Merriweather	$18	126) Dave Waymer	$24
94) Stump Mitchell	$20	127) Charles White	$20
95) Art Monk	$130	128) Danny White	$22
96) Joe Montana	$165	129) Randy White	$35
97) Warren Moon	$65	130) Reggie White	$50
98) Stanley Morgan	$20	131) James Wilder	$18
99) Joe Morris	$18	132) Doug Williams	$24
100) Darrin Nelson	$18	133) Marc Wilson	$60
101) Ozzie Newsome	$22	134) Sammy Winder	$18
102) Ken O'Brien	$18	135) Kellen Winslow	$80
103) John Offerdahl	$22	136) Rod Woodson	$32
104) Christian Okoye	$30	137) Randy Wright	$24
105) Mike Quick	$18		
106) Jerry Rice	$145		

1989 Kenner Football Starting Lineups

107) Gerald Riggs	$18		
108) Reggie Rogers	$18	Complete set (123):	$1,650
109) Mike Rozier	$25	Common player:	$10
110) Jay Schroeder	$30	1) Marcus Allen	$30
111) Mickey Shuler	$18	2) Neal Anderson	$12
112) Phil Simms	$24	3) Carl Banks	$12
113) Mike Singletary	$30	4) Bill Bates	$16
114) Billy Ray Smith	$30	5) Mark Bavaro	$12
115) Bruce Smith	$65	6) Cornelius Bennett	$30
116) J.T. Smith	$25	7) Duane Bickett	$10
117) Troy Stratford	$18		

8) Bennie Blades	$12
9) Bubby Brister	$13
10) Bill Brooks	$10
11) James Brooks	$12
12) Eddie Brown	$12
13) Jerome Brown	$40
14) Tim Brown	$25
15) Joey Browner	$12
16) Kelvin Bryant	$12
17) Jim Burt	$14
18) Keith Byars	$15
19) Dave Cadigan	$12
20) Anthony Carter	$14
21) Michael Carter	$18
22) Chris Chandler	$14
23) Gary Clark	$10
24) Shane Conlan	$35
25) Jimbo Covert	$24
26) Roger Craig	$12
27) Randall Cunningham	$12
28) Richard Dent	$12
29) Hanford Dixon	$10
30) Chris Doleman	$18
31) Tony Dorsett	$65
32) Dave Duerson	$11
33) John Elway	$35
34) Boomer Esiason	$20
35) Jim Everett	$12
36) Thomas Everett	$12
37) Sean Farrell	$12
38) Bill Fralic	$12
39) Irving Fryar	$20
40) David Fulcher	$12
41) Ernest Givins	$15
42) Alex Gordon	$12
43) Charles Haley	$20
44) Bobby Hebert	$24
45) Johnny Hector	$12
46) Drew Hill	$15
47) Dalton Hilliard	$15
48) Bryan Hinkle	$10
49) Michael Irvin	$45
50) Keith Jackson	$20
51) Gary James	$10
52) Sean Jones	$15
53) Jim Kelly	$75
54) Joe Kelly	$10
55) Bernie Kosar	$10
56) Tim Krumrie	$15
57) Louis Lipps	$15
58) Eugene Lockhart	$12
59) James Lofton	$40
60) Neil Lomax	$10
61) Chuck Long	$10
62) Howie Long	$15
63) Ronnie Lott	$42
64) Kevin Mack	$10
65) Pete Mandley	$10
66) Dexter Manley	$12
67) Charles Mann	$10
68) Lionel Manuel	$12
69) Dan Marino	$100
70) Leonard Marshall	$10
71) Eric Martin	$12
72) Rueben Mayes	$10
73) Vann McElroy	$11
74) Dennis McKinnon	$10

75) Jim McMahon	$12
76) Steve McMichael	$18
77) Eric McMillan	$10
78) Freeman McNeil	$10
79) Keith Millard	$12
80) Chris Miller	$20
81) Frank Minnifield	$10
82) Art Monk	$42
83) Joe Montana	$85
84) Warren Moon	$35
85) Joe Morris	$12
86) Anthony Munoz	$22
87) Ricky Nattiel	$10
88) Darrin Nelson	$10
89) Danny Noonan	$10
90) Ken O'Brian (sp)	$40
91) Ken O'Brien	$12
92) Steve Pelluer	$10
93) Mike Quick	$10
94) Andre Reed	$70
95) Jerry Rice	$55
96) Mike Rozier	$15
97) Jay Schroeder	$12
98) John Settle	$10
99) Mickey Shuler	$10
100) Phil Simms	$14
101) Mike Singletary	$14
102) Webster Slaughter	$12
103) Bruce Smith	$40
104) Chris Spielman	$25
105) John Stephens	$10
106) Kelly Stouffer	$16
107) Pat Swilling	$20
108) Lawrence Taylor	$30
109) Vinny Testaverde	$12
110) Thurman Thomas	$70
111) Andre Tippett	$12
112) Anthony Toney	$14
113) Al Toon	$12
114) Garin Veris	$10
115) Herschel Walker	$10
116) Curt Warner	$18
117) Reggie White	$24
118) Doug Williams	$10
119) John Williams	$12
120) Wade Wilson	$14
121) Ickey Woods	$14
122) Rod Woodson	$20
123) Steve Young	$90

1990 Kenner Football Starting Lineups

Complete set (73):	$850
Common player:	$10
1) Troy Aikman	$50
2a) Neal Anderson blue	$10
2b) Neal Anderson white	$10
3) Mark Bavaro	$14
4) Steve Beuerlein	$13
5) Bubby Brister	$14
6) James Brooks	$10
7) Tim Brown	$15
8) Cris Carter	$26
9a) Roger Craig red	$10
9b) Roger Craig white	$10

133

Statues/figurines

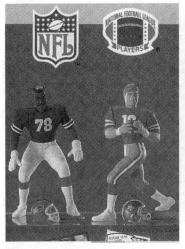

10) Randall Cunningham	$12	50a) Mike Singletary blue	$12
11) Hart Lee Dykes	$10	50b) Mike Singletary white	$12
12a) John Elway orange	$25	51) Webster Slaughter	$10
12b) John Elway white	$25	52) Bruce Smith	$15
13a) Boomer Esiason black	$15	53) John Stephens	$10
13b) Boomer Esiason white	$15	54) John Taylor	$15
14) Jim Everett	$12	55) Thurman Thomas	$35
15) Simon Fletcher	$10	56) Mike Tomczak	$12
16) Doug Flutie	$10	57) Greg Townsend	$10
17) Dennis Gentry	$10	58) Odessa Turner	$10
18) Dan Hampton	$14	59) Herschel Walker	$10
19) Jim Harbaugh	$12	60) Steve Walsh	$18
20) Rodney Holman	$12	61a) Reggie White green	$18
21) Bobby Humphrey	$12	61b) Reggie White white	$18
22) Michael Irvin	$38	62) Wade Wilson	$12
23) Bo Jackson	$18	63) Ickey Woods	$10
24) Keith Jackson	$10	64) Donnell Woolford	$16
25) Vance Johnson	$10	65) Tim Worley	$12
26) Jim Kelly	$18	66) Felix Wright	$10
27) Bernie Kosar	$12		
28) Louis Lipps	$10		
29) Don Majkowski	$12		

1991 Kenner Football Starting Lineups

30) Charles Mann	$10	Complete set (26):	$400
31) Lionel Manuel	$10	Common player:	$10
32) Dan Marino	$60	1) Troy Aikman	$40
33) Tim McGee	$10	2) Flipper Anderson	$10
34) David Meggett	$14	3) Neal Anderson	$14
35) Mike Merriweather	$10	4) James Brooks	$12
36) Eric Metcalf	$12	5) Eddie Brown	$10
37) Keith Millard	$10	6) Mark Carrier	$12
38a) Joe Montana red	$40	7) Boomer Esiason	$10
38b) Joe Montana white	$40	8) James Francis	$18
39) Warren Moon	$25	9) Jeff George	$20
40) Christian Okoye	$12	10) Rodney Hampton	$20
41) Tom Rathman	$12	11) Jim Harbaugh	$20
42) Andre Reed	$18	12) Jeff Hostetler	$18
43) Gerald Riggs	$10	13) Bobby Humphrey	$10
44) Mark Rypien	$18	14) Don Majkowski	$10
45) Barry Sanders	$70	15) Dan Marino	$50
46) Deion Sanders	$38	16) Dave Meggett	$10
47) Ricky Sanders	$12	17) Joe Montana	$28
48) Clyde Simmons	$12	18) Warren Moon	$16
49) Phil Simms	$14		

19) Christian Okoye	$10
20) Jerry Rice	$20
21) Andre Rison	$28
22) Barry Sanders	$15
23) Phil Simms	$10
24) Emmitt Smith	$110
25) Thurman Thomas	$22
26) Herschel Walker	$10

1991 Kenner Football Starting Lineups

Headliners

Complete set (6):	$175
Common player:	$20
1) John Elway	$35
2) Boomer Esiason	$20
3) Dan Marino	$60
4) Joe Montana	$35
5) Jerry Rice	$32
6) Barry Sanders	$30

1992 Kenner Football Starting Lineups

Complete set (26):	$275
Common player:	$10
1) Troy Aikman	$20
2) Earnest Byner	$10
3) Randall Cunningham	$12
4) Rodney Hampton	$10
5) Bobby Hebert	$10
6) Jeff Hostetler	$10
7) Michael Irvin	$16
8) Bo Jackson	$10
9) Haywood Jefferies	$10
10) Seth Joyner	$10
11) Jim Kelly	$14
12) Ronnie Lott	$14
13) Dan Marino	$40
14) Joe Montana	$22
15) Warren Moon	$14
16) Rob Moore	$10
17) Jerry Rice	$16
18) Andre Rison	$14
19) Mark Rypien	$10
20) Barry Sanders	$14
21) Deion Sanders	$16
22) Emmitt Smith	$30
23) Pat Swilling	$10
24) Derrick Thomas	$22
25) Thurman Thomas	$10
26) Steve Young	$25

1992 Kenner Football Starting Lineups

Headliners

Complete set (6):	$100
Common player:	$12
1) Joe Montana	$20
2) Warren Moon	$15
3) Mark Rypien	$12
4) Barry Sanders	$15
5) Emmitt Smith	$40
6) Thurman Thomas	$20

1993 Kenner Football Starting Lineups

Complete set (28):	$220
Common player:	$7
1) Troy Aikman	$15
2) Cornelius Bennett	$7
3) Randall Cunningham	$7
4) Chris Doleman	$7
5) John Elway	$12
6) Barry Foster	$22
7) Michael Irvin	$10
8) Rickey Jackson	$7
9) Cortez Kennedy	$9
10) David Klingler	$18
11) Chip Lohmiller	$12
12) Russell Maryland	$12
13) Anthony Miller	$12
14) Chris Miller	$7
15) Joe Montana	$40
16a) Warren Moon (white)	$10
16b) Warren Moon (blue)	$10
17) Andre Reed	$7
18) Barry Sanders	$10
19) Deion Sanders	$9
20) Junior Seau	$9
21) Sterling Sharpe	$40
22) Emmitt Smith	$15
23) Neil Smith	$8
24) Pete Stoyanovich	$12
25) Ricky Watters	$22
26) Rod Woodson	$8
27) Steve Young	$10

1994 Kenner Football Starting Lineups

Complete set (32):	$325
Common player:	$7
1) Troy Aikman	$14
2) Jerome Bettis	$20
3) Drew Bledsoe	$30
4) Randall Cunningham	$7
5) Boomer Esiason	$7
6) Brett Favre	$30
7) Barry Foster	$9
8) Rodney Hampton	$7
9) Ronnie Harmon	$7
10) Garrison Hearst	$15
11) Raghib Ismail	$15
12) Brent Jones	$8
13) Cortez Kennedy	$7
14) Nick Lowery	$9
15) Dan Marino	$28
16) Eric Metcalf	$10
17) Rick Mirer	$25
18) Joe Montana	$25
19) Ken Norton	$12
20) Jerry Rice	$15
21) Andre Rison	$12
22) Barry Sanders	$14
23) Deion Sanders	$10
24) Junior Seau	$8
25) Phil Simms	$7
26) Emmitt Smith	$14

Statues/figurines

27) Lawrence Taylor	$15	
28) Chris Warren	$8	
29) Lorenxo White	$8	
30) Reggie White	$16	
31) Rod Woodson	$9	
32) Steve Young	$12	

1993 Kenner Hockey Starting Lineups

Complete set American (12):		$400
Complete set Canadian (11):		$275
Common player:		$10
1) Ed Belfour	a$90	c$60
2) Ray Bourque	a$20	c$18
3) Grant Fuhr	a$160	
4) Brett Hull	a$12	c$10
5) Jaromir Jagr	a$22	c$20
6) Pat LaFontaine	a$75	c$40
7) Mario Lemieux	a$18	c$20
8) Eric Lindros	a$36	c$32
9) Mark Messier	a$25	c$22
10) Jeremy Roenick	a$22	c$20
11) Patrick Roy	a$50	c$45
12) Steve Yzerman	a$20	c$20

1994 Kenner Hockey Starting Lineups

Complete set American (20):		$500
Complete set Canadian (13):		$250
Common player:		$12
1) Tom Barrasso	a$55	
2) Ray Bourque	a$22	
3) Pavel Bure	a$25	c$22
4) Sergei Fedorov	a$25	c$22
5) Grant Fuhr		c$70
6) Doug Gilmour	a$25	c$20
7) Brett Hull	a$12	
8) Arturs Irbe	a$60	
9) Pat LaFontaine	a$16	
10) Brian Leetch	a$25	c$25
11) Mario Lemieux	a$12	c$14
12) Eric Lindros	a$18	c$20
13) Jaromir Jagr	a$16	
14) Mark Messier	a$24	
15) Alexander Mogilny	a$20	c$20
16) Adam Oates	a$20	c$20
17) Mike Richter	a$45	c$40
18) Luc Robitaille	a$28	c$24
19) Jeremy Roenick	a$16	
20) Teemu Selanne	a$25	c$22
21) Steve Yzerman	a$15	c$16

Salvino Sports Legends

Many of the sporting world's greatest superstars are honored on hand-signed, limited edition figurines offered by Salvino Inc., of Corona, Calif.

Original artwork is cast by mold makers to ensure an exact reproduction of the original artwork. Every figurine is individually cast by artisans in cold-cast porcelain and inspected for defects. Every casting is then hand-painted by professionals.

The honored athlete personally autographs signature plaques which are permanently mounted to the figurine base. The authenticity of the autograph is guaranteed and endorsed with a certificate of authenticity numbered to match the figurine. * SE equals special edition

Hockey Greats

Paul Coffey 500 home, signed...$275
Paul Coffey 500 away, signed $275
Wayne Gretzky 950 home, signed...$395
Wayne Gretzky 950 away, signed $395
Mario Lemieux 1,000, home, signed...$275
Mario Lemieux 1,000, away, signed $275
Mario Lemieux SE 750, home, signed $285
Mario Lemieux SE 750, away, signed..$285
Luc Robitaille 500 home, signed...$275
Luc Robitaille 500 away, signed $275

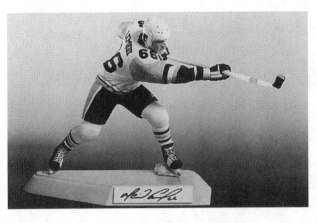 

Football Legends

Jim Brown 1,000, away, signed..$250
Jim Brown SE 300, home, signed $375
Joe Montana 2,500, away, signed...$275
Joe Montana SE 500, home, signed..$375
Joe Namath 2,500, away, signed $275
Joe Namath SE 500, home, signed $375
Joe Montana 1,000 S.F. home, signed...$275
Joe Montana 1,000 S.F. away, signed $275
Joe Montana 450 K.C. home, signed...$275
O.J. Simpson 1,000 home, signed $250
O.J. Simpson 1,000 away, signed..$250

Green Bay Packer Legends
Bart Starr 500, home, signed...$250
Bart Starr 500, away, signed..$250
Paul Hornung 500, away, signed..$250
Paul Hornung 500, home, signed $250
Jim Taylor 500, home, signed $250
Jim Taylor 500, away, signed...$250

Pittsburgh Steelers Greats
Terry Bradshaw, 1,000, home, signed...$275
Terry Bradshaw, 1,000, away, signed $275

Chicago Bears Greats
Gale Sayers 1,000, home, signed...$275
Gale Sayers 1,000, away, signed $275

Basketball Greats

Elgin Baylor 700, home, signed $250
Elgin Baylor SE 300, away, signed $350
Larry Bird 1,000, home, signed..$285
Larry Bird 1,000, away, signed $285
Larry Bird SE 500, away, signed..$375
Larry Bird SE 500, home, signed $375

Michael Jordan SE 368, away	$1,600
Jerry West 700, home, signed	$250
Jerry West SE 300, away, signed	$350

Collegiate Series

O.J. Simpson 1,000, USC away, signed	$275
O.J. Simpson 1,000, USC home, signed	$275
Joe Montana 1,000, Notre Dame home, signed	$275
Joe Montana 1,000, Notre Dame away, signed	$275

Collector Club

Mario Lemieux 6" painted, away, unsigned	$69.95
Joe Montana K.C. away, hand-signed	$275

Dealer Special Series

Joe Namath 368, away, signed	$700
Wayne Gretzky 368, signed	$700

Unsigned Collection

Mario Lemieux 1,200 6" hand-painted figurine	$69.95
Mario Lemieux 2,500 6" cold-cast pewter figurine	$43.95
Mario Lemieux 2,500 8" cold-cast pewter figurine	$99.95
Mario Lemieux 2,500 cold-cast pewter plaque	$24.95
Michael Jordan 5,000 7" home, unsigned	$150
Michael Jordan 5,000 7" away, unsigned	$150
Michael Jordan 2,500 9" home, unsigned	$225
Michael Jordan 2,500 9" away, unsigned	$225
Michael Jordan SP 14" red or white jersey	$1,000
Wayne Gretzky SP after scoring goal #802	$495
Magic Johnson 950, 1995 release	$450
Larry Bird 950, 1995 release	$350

Gartlan statues

Gartlan USA is based in Huntington Beach, Calif., and produces limited-edition ceramic and porcelain sports collectibles, including hand-signed plates and figurines. The larger versions of the statues are about 8 inches tall; the smaller versions are about 5 inches tall. Plates range in size from 10 1/4" diameter, to 8 1/2" to 3 1/4" mini plates. Artist's proofs are signed by the artist and player.

Football

Troy Aikman signed figurine $200
Troy Aikman mini figurine $40
Troy Aikman 10 1/4" signed plate $125
Troy Aikman ceramic three-card set..$50
Joe Montana signed figurine .... $375, or artist's proof $600
Joe Montana mini figurine...$175
Joe Montana mini figurine, unsigned $45
Joe Montana 10 1/4" signed plate ....$150, artist's proof $300
Joe Montana 8 1/2" plate..$100
Joe Montana mini plate $15
Roger Staubach 10 1/4" plate..$100
Roger Staubach mini plate..$10
Roger Staubach ceramic plaque $85
Roger Staubach ceramic card $12
Roger Staubach collector mug..$30

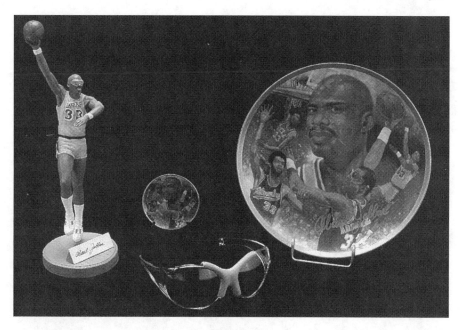

Basketball

Kareem Abdul Jabbar purple uniform figurine $5,000
    artist's proof $500
Kareem Abdul-Jabbar mini figurine...$150
Kareem Abdul-Jabbar 10 1/4" signed plate..$275
Kareem Abdul-Jabbar mini plate..$15
Kareem Abdul-Jabbar signed watch $50
Kareem Abdul-Jabbar/Julius Erving signed watch $89.50
Bob Cousy signed figurine..$150
Bob Cousy mini figurine $40
Bob Cousy 10 1/4" signed plate $100
Magic Johnson signed figurine...$225, artist's proof $1,800
Magic Johnson 10 1/4" signed plate..$375
Magic Johnson mini plate..$15
Shaquille O'Neal signed figurine $200
Shaquille O'Neal 10 1/4" signed plate $125
Shaquille O'Neal ceramic five-card set, signed, artist's proof............ $250, unsigned $80
Shaquille O'Neal Gartlan USA Club kit, 8 1/2" plate and club figurine $70
Isiah Thomas signed figurine $150
Isiah Thomas mini figurine $25
John Wooden signed figurine... $50, artist's proof $175
John Wooden mini figurine..$20
John Wooden 10 1/4" signed plate..$60
John Wooden 8 1/2" unsigned plate...$25
John Wooden mini plate...$10
John Wooden five-piece set, inc. two with autographs...$425

Hockey

Wayne Gretzky signed figurine ....$375/$600
    artist's proof $1,750
Wayne Gretzky mini figurine, unsigned .... $45, signed $295
Wayne Gretzky signed plate.. $150, artist's proof $275
Wayne Gretzky/Gordie Howe signed 10 1/2-inch plate $225
    artist's proof $300
Gordie Howe signed figurine $150
Gordie Howe signed five-inch figurine..$100
Gordie Howe signed 10 1/4-inch plate..$125
Gordie Howe signed 8 1/2-inch plate...$45
Gordie Howe signed 3 1/4-inch plate...$25
Bobby Hull signed figurine $150
Bobby Hull signed mini plate...$27.50
Bobby and Brett Hull signed 10 1/4-inch plate $300
Bobby and Brett Hull signed 8 1/2-inch plate $45
Bobby and Brett Hull signed 3 1/4-inch plate $20
Brett Hull signed figurine...$150
Lanny McDonald signed plate, artist's proof...$200
Lanny McDonald hand-signed plate $125
Lanny McDonald mini plate...$25
Darryl Sittler signed plate, artist's proof..$200
Darryl Sittler hand-signed plate...$125
Darryl Sittler mini plate..$25

Sports Impressions Statues and Plates

Sports Impressions offers a wide variety of players who have been featured on plates and as figurines. Figurine sizes range from 7-8 inches to 5 inches, while plates range from 10 1/4" to 8 1/2" to 4 1/4" mini plates. The company has also produced several player mugs.

Football

- Troy Aikman 8" figurine, unsigned...........$65
- Troy Aikman 10 1/4" gold plate................$75
- Troy Aikman 8 1/2" platinum plate...........$35
- Troy Aikman mini bronze plate $15
- Randall Cunningham 8" figurine.............$125
- Randall Cunningham mini figurine $40
- Randall Cunningham 10 1/4" gold plate $75
- Randall Cunningham 8 1/2" platinum plate ...$35
- Randall Cunningham mini bronze plate $15
- John Elway 8" figurine...........................$125
- John Elway mini figurine $40
- John Elway 10 1/4" gold plate...................$75
- John Elway 8 1/2" platinum plate..............$35
- John Elway mini bronze plate $15
- Boomer Esiason 8" figurine $125
  unsigned $65
- Boomer Esiason mini figurine...................$40
- Boomer Esiason 10 1/4" gold plate...........$65

- Boomer Esiason 8 1/2" platinum plate......$35
- Boomer Esiason mini bronze plate............$15
- Jim Everett mini figurine...........................$40
- Jim Everett 10 1/4" gold plate...................$75
- Jim Everett 8 1/2" platinum plate..............$35
- Jim Everett mini bronze plate....................$15
- Bob Griese 8" figurine...............................$75
- Bob Griese mini figurine............................$40
- Bob Griese 8 1/2" platinum plate..............$35
- Jim Harbaugh mini figurine.......................$40
- Jim Harbaugh 10 1/4" gold plate...............$75
- Jim Harbaugh 8 1/2" platinum plate..........$35
- Jim Harbaugh mini bronze plate................$15
- Jim Kelly 8" figurine, unsigned.................$65
- Jim Kelly mini figurine $40
- Jim Kelly 10 1/4" plate..............................$75
- Jim Kelly 8 1/2" platinum plate.................$35
- Jim Kelly mini bronze plate $15
- Bernie Kosar mini figurine........................$40
- Bernie Kosar 10 1/4" gold plate $75
- Bernie Kosar 8 1/2" platiunum plate $35
- Bernie Kosar mini bronze plate.................$15
- Vince Lombardi 8" figurine $125
- Vince Lombardi 8 1/2" plate $55
- Vince Lombardi mini bronze plate............$20
- Vince Lombardi 8 1/2" platinum plate......$35
- Dan Marino 8" figurine $125
  unsigned $65
- Dan Marino mini figurine..........................$40
- Dan Marino 10 1/4" gold plate..................$75
- Dan Marino 8 1/2" platinum plate.............$35
- Dan Marino mini bronze plate...................$15

- Art Monk mini figurine $40
- Art Monk 8 1/2" platinum plate $35
- Joe Montana 10 1/4" plate.......................$100
- Joe Montana 8 1/2" platinum plate............$60
- Joe Montana mini bronze plate..................$20
- Warren Moon mini figurine........................$40
- Warren Moon 10 1/4" gold plate...............$75
- Warren Moon 8 1/2" platinum plate..........$35
- Warren Moon mini bronze plate................$15
- Christian Okoye mini figurine....................$40
- Christian Okoye 10 1/4" gold plate $75
- Christian Okoye 8 1/2" platinum plate......$35
- Christian Okoye mini bronze plate............$15
- Walter Payton 8" figurine..........................$75
- Walter Payton mini figurine $40
- Walter Payton 10 1/4" gold plate $75
- Walter Payton 8 1/2" platinum plate $35
- Walter Payton mini bronze plate $15
- Jerry Rice 8" figurine, unsigned................$65
- Jerry Rice mini figurine.............................$40
- Jerry Rice 10 1/4" gold plate $75
- Jerry Rice 8 1/2" platinum plate................$35
- Jerry Rice mini bronze plate......................$15
- Mark Rypien mini figurine........................$40
- Mark Rypien 10 1/4" gold plate $75
- Mark Rypien 8 1/2" platinum plate $35
- Mark Rypien mini bronze plate.................$15
- Barry Sanders mini figurine $40
- Barry Sanders 10 1/4" gold plate...............$65
- Barry Sanders 8 1/2" platinum plate $35
- Barry Sanders mini bronze plate $15
- Deion Sanders mini figurine......................$40

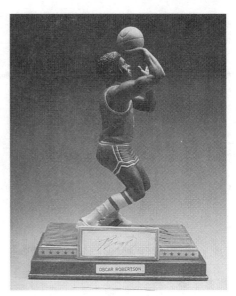

- Deion Sanders 8 1/2" platinum plate.........$35
- Gale Sayers mini figurine.........................$40
- Emmitt Smith 8 1/2" platinum plate..........$35
- Emmitt Smith mini figurine......................$40
- Ken Stabler 8" figurine.............................$75
- Ken Stabler mini figurine.........................$40
- Ken Stabler 8 1/2" platinum plate.............$35
- Lawrence Taylor 8" figurine, unsigned.....$65
- Lawrence Taylor mini figurine..................$40
- Lawrence Taylor 10 1/4" gold plate..........$75
- Lawrence Taylor 8 1/2" platinum plate.....$35
- Lawrence Taylor mini bronze plate...........$15
- Thurman Thomas 10 1/4" gold plate.........$75
- Thurman Thomas 8 1/2" platinum plate.......$35
- Thurman Thomas mini bronze plate..........$15
- Johnny Unitas 8" figurine.........................$75
- Johnny Unitas mini figurine......................$40
- Johnny Unitas 10 1/4" gold plate..............$75
- Johnny Unitas 8 1/2" platinum plate.........$35
- Johnny Unitas mini bronze plate...............$15
- Steve Young mini figurine.........................$40
- Steve Young 8 1/2" platinum plate...........$35

Basketball

- Chicago Bulls 1993 Champions 10 1/4"
  plate..$100
- Chicago Bulls 1993 Champions 8 1/2"
  plate..$40
- Chicago Bulls 1993 Champions mini
  plate..$15

- 1992 Olympic Dream Team 10 1/4"
  gold edition plate, 12 gold signatures $150
- 1992 Olympic Dream Team mug of 10.....$10
- Kenny Anderson 10 1/4" gold plate..........$75
- Kenny Anderson mini plate......................$15
- Charles Barkley 10 1/4" plate..................$150
- Charles Barkley 8 1/2" platinum plate $35
- Charles Barkley mini plate........................$15
- Charles Barkley Dream Team collector
  mug...$10
- Larry Bird 7" figurine..............................$125
- Larry Bird 10 1/4" gold plate .... $100-$200
- Larry Bird 8 1/2" platinum plate,
  two types $35
- Larry Bird mini plate, three types.............$15
- Larry Bird collector mug $10
- Derrick Coleman mini plate $15
- Brad Daugherty mini plate $15
- Clyde Drexler 10 1/4" gold plate..............$75
- Clyde Drexler 8 1/2" platinum plate $35
- Clyde Drexler mini plate, two types..........$15
- Clyde Drexler collector mug $10
- Joe Dumars mini plate $15
- Julius Erving 8" figurine $85
- Julius Erving 8 1/2" platinum plate $35
- Patrick Ewing 10 1/4" gold plate.............$125
- Patrick Ewing 8 1/2" platinum plate $35
- Patrick Ewing mini plate $15
- Tim Hardaway mini plate..........................$15
- Kevin Johnson 10 1/4" gold plate $75
- Kevin Johnson 8 1/2" platinum plate $35
- Kevin Johnson mini plate..........................$15

Statues/figurines

- Magic Johnson 10 1/4" gold plate . $150-$225
- Magic Johnson 8 1/2" platinum plate,
  two types $60
- Magic Johnson mini plate, three types $150
- Magic Johnson collector mug....................$10
- Michael Jordan 10 1/4" gold plate. $150-$225
- Michael Jordan 8 1/2" platinum plate,
  two types $60
- Michael Jordan mini bronze plate,
  two types $25
- Shawn Kemp mini plate $15
- Bernard King 10 1/4" gold plate $75
- Bernard King mini plate $15
- Christian Laettner mini plate $15
- Reggie Lewis mini plate.............................$15
- Dan Majerle 10 1/4" gold plate $75
- Dan Majerle 8 1/2" platinum plate $35
- Karl Malone 10 1/4" gold plate $75
- Karl Malone 8 1/2" platinum plate............$35
- Karl Malone mini plate...............................$15
- Danny Manning mini plate $15
- Kevin McHale 10 1/4" gold plate............$125
- Kevin McHale mini plate $15
- Reggie Miller 10 1/4" gold plate $75
- Reggie Miller mini plate.............................$15
- Chris Mullin 10 1/4" gold plate.................$75
- Chris Mullin 8 1/2" platinum plate............$35
- Chris Mullin mini, two styles $15
- Hakeem Olajuwon 10 1/4" gold plate $75
- Hakeem Olajuwon mini plate.....................$15
- Shaquille O'Neal 10 1/4" gold plate $125
- Shaquille O'Neal mini plate $15
- Shaquille O'Neal collector mug $10
- John Paxson mini plate $15
- Scottie Pippen 10 1/4" gold plate $75
- Scottie Pippen mini plate...........................$15
- Terry Porter mini plate $15
- Mark Price 10 1/4" gold plate $75
- Mark Price mini plate $15
- Mitch Richmond mini plate........................$15
- Oscar Robertson 8" figurine $75
- Oscar Robertson 10 1/4" gold plate...........$75
- Oscar Robertson mini plate $15
- David Robinson 10 1/4" gold plate $75
- David Robinson 8 1/2" platinum plate $35
- David Robinson mini plate, two types $15
- Rony Seikaly 10 1/4" gold plate..............$125
- Rony Seikaly mini plate $15
- Scott Skiles 10 1/4" gold plate $75
- Scott Skiles mini plate................................$15
- John Starks 10 1/4" gold plate...................$75
- Isiah Thomas 10 1/4" gold plate..............$125
- Isiah Thomas 8 1/2" platinum plate...........$35
- Isiah Thomas mini plate $15
- Dominique Wilkins 10 1/4" gold plate....$125
- Dominique Wilkins 8 1/2" platinum
  plate..$50
- Dominique Wilkins mini plate $15
- James Worthy 10 1/4" gold plate $150
- James Worthy mini plate $1

146

Yearbooks/Media guides

Although some exist from the 1950s, it wasn't until the 1960s that what we now consider as yearbooks and media guides were produced by professional teams on a regular basis. The main problem in creating a yearbook checklist is that there is not a general consensus as to whether a certain publication should be considered a yearbook or something else; many teams have labeled their publications with a variety of other names - magazines, roster books, photo albums and sketchbooks.

To be classified as a yearbook, generally a publication must at the very least have photographs of every player on the 25-man roster, plus biographies and player statistics. If, however, a publication has photos, stats and biographies, but is labeled as a media guide, scorecard or program, then it's obviously something other than a yearbook.

Most yearbooks from the 1960s offer collectors an affordable alternative for under $100. Those from the 1940s and 1950s bring the top dollars, depending on scarcity and age, while those which are autographed are even more valuable. Yearbooks should be stored in plastic holders and be kept out of sunlight.

Although there are earlier issues, media guides, as we know them today, debuted in the late 1940s. They are given to radio, television and newspaper beat reporters who cover professional teams throughout the season. They are designed to provide the reporters with almost every imaginable kind of biographical and statistical tidbits to liven up a broadcast or story. Team histories have also been included, contributing to the guides' increases in page size from the 1950s to the 1990s.

The guides are not found on newsstands or bookstores; they are generally available only from the reporters, who sell or give them to memorabilia dealers, or from the teams. In recent years, the teams have given them to season ticket holders or have sold them at the stadiums, by mail or during year-end promotional sales.

The press guide provides far more extensive coverage of the team but, although it does contain profile shots of the players and key people in the organization, lacks the colorful photographs that would appear in a team yearbook.

Football

Atlanta Falcons Media Guides

1966 Randy Johnson	$27
1967 Team helmet	$27
1968 Randy Johnson, Billy Lothridge, Tommy Nobis, others	$27
1969 Four Falcons linemen	$27
1970 Falcons in action	$19
1971 Falcon in action	$16
1972 Bob Berry	$16
1973 Team logos	$16
1974 Bob Lee, offensive line	$13
1975 Marion Campbell	$13
1976 Jim Mitchell	$13
1977 Steve Bartkowski	$13
1978 The new training complex	$13
1979 Falcons defensive line	$12
1980 Falcons in action	$10
1981 Falcons offensive	$9
1982 Three Falcons in action	$9
1983 Team helmet, city skyline	$9
1984 William Andrews, Buddy Curry, B. Johnson	$9
1985 Stacey Bailey, Rick Bryan, Gerald Riggs	$9
1986 Team helmet and falcon	$6
1987 Falcons media equipment	$6
1988 "Putting it all Together"	$6
1989 Chris Miller	$6
1990 25th Anniversary logo	$6
1991	$6
1992	$6
1993	$6
1994	$5

Atlanta Falcons Yearbooks

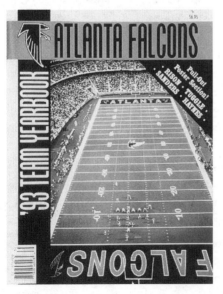

1966 Team logo and 1966	$45
1967 Team logo and 1967	$35
1968 Team logo and 1967	$30
1969 Team logo and 1969	$25
1970	$25
1971	$25
1972	$20
1973 Dave Hampton, team helmet	$20
1974 Tommy Nobis	$20
1975	$15
1976 Steve Bartkowski, others	$15
1977	$15
1992	$8
1993 Georgia Dome field	$8

Baltimore Colts Media Guides
Baltimore Colts

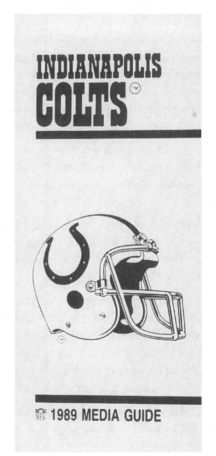

1950 Team logo	$40
1951	$40
1952	$40
1953 Team mascot	$40
1954 Team mascot	$40

1955 Team mascot...$40
1956 Team mascot...$40
1957 Team logo $40
1958 Memorial Stadium $40
1959 Team logo $40
1960 World Champions pennants............................$27
1961 Team helmet, logo $27
1962 Team helmet, logo $27
1963 Colts in action $27
1964 Offensive huddle..$27
1965 Colts offense $27
1966 Colts cheerleaders..$27
1967 Kickoff formation $27
1968 Johnny Unitas $35
1969 Colts sideline $27
1970 Colts offense $13
1971 Super Bowl Trophy..$13
1972 "The Baltimore Colts" $13
1973 Ted Hendricks...$15
1974 Colt in action..$13
1975 Lydell Mitchell $13
1976 Bert Jones...$13
1977 Bert Jones...$13
1978 Bert Jones, Colts in action $13
1979 Team helmet $13
1980 Team helmet $8
1981 Team helmet $8
1982 Championship pennants.....................................$8
1983 Mike Pagel $8

Indianapolis Colts

1984 Colts in action $6
1985 Team helmet, Hoosierdome..............................$6
1986 Team helmet, NFL flag......................................$6
1987 Team helmet $6
1988 Team helmet $6
1989 Team helmet $6
1990 Team helmet $6
1991 ....$6
1992 ....$6
1993 ....$6
1994 ....$6

Baltimore Colts Yearbooks
Baltimore Colts

1953 10th Anniversary helmet....................................$60
1958 Memorial Stadium $45
1959 ....$45
1960 ....$40
1961 Weeb Eubank, Colts sideline...........................$40
1962 Team helmet $40
1963 ....$35
1964 Johnny Unitas $35

Indianapolis Colts

1988 Eric Dickerson $8
1989 ....$8
1991 ....$8
1992 ....$8
1993 10th Celebration logo $8

Buffalo Bills Media Guides

1960 Team logo and 1960..$27
1961 Team mascot and 1961 ....$27
1962 Team mascot and 1962 ....$27
1963 Team mascot and 1963 ....$27
1964 Team logo and 1964..$27
1965 Team logo and 1965..$27
1966 Team picture $27
1967 Bills in action $27
1968 Bills in action $27
1969 John Rauch $27
1970 O.J. Simpson $30
1971 Dennis Shaw $16
1972 Dennis Shaw, O.J. Simpson...............................$20
1973 Bills Stadium...$16
1974 O.J. Simpson $20
1975 Tony Greene...$13
1976 Team helmet...$13
1977 Team logo $13
1978 Chuck Knox $13
1979 20th Anniversary photos....................................$13
1980 Jerry Butler, Joe Ferguson, Jim Haslett $9
1981 Joe Cribbs, Eastern Division Championship
    celebration $9
1982 Team helmet...$9
1983 Buffalo $9
1984 25th Anniversary logo..$9
1985 Past and present team helmets $9
1986 Scott Norwood $6
1987 Team helmet...$6
1988 Cornelius Bennett, Jim Kelly, Bruce Smith,
    others $7
1989 Scott Norwood, others $6
1990 Team helmet and uniform.....................................$6
1991...$6
1992...$6
1993...$6
1994...$6

Buffalo Bills Yearbooks

1965 Buffalo Bills vs. Kansas City Chiefs in action $35
1969 O.J. Simpson $45
1989 Team logo, Bills in action....................................$6
1990...$6
1991...$6
1992...$6
1993...$6

Chicago Bears Media Guides

1934 Name and 1934 ....$70
1935 Beattie Feathers...$70
1936 Jack Manders $70
1937...$70
1938...$70
1939...$70
1940...$50
1941 Bears in action..$50
1942 Bears in action..$50
1943 Bears in action..$50
1944...$50
1945 Team picture $50

Yearbooks/media guides

1946 Name and 1946 .... $50
1947 .... $50
1948 Team mascot $50
1949 Team mascot $50
1950 Team mascot $40
1951 Team mascot $40
1952 Team mascot $40
1953 Team mascot $40
1954 Name and 1954 .... $40
1955 Bears in action $40
1956 Bears in action $40
1957 Bears in action $40
1958 Team mascot $40
1959 Team picture $40
1960 Team mascot $27
1961 Team mascot $27
1962 Bears in action $27
1963 Team mascot and 1963 .... $27
1964 World Champions banner $27
1965 Bears in action $27
1966 Bears action photos $27
1967 Bears in action $27
1968 Team helmet and 1968 .... $27
1969 Golden Anniversary helmets $27
1970 Helmet and 1970 .... $13
1971 Helmet and 1971 .... $13
1972 Helmet and 1972 .... $13
1973 Abe Gibron $13
1974 Helmet and 1974 .... $13
1975 Doug Buffone $13
1976 Helmet and 1976 .... $13
1977 Jack Pardee $13
1978 Team logo and 1978 .... $13
1979 Bears in action $13
1980 George Halas $7
1981 "Home of the Bears" $7
1982 Mike Ditka $7
1983 Mike Ditka, George Halas $7
1984 Walter Payton $9
1985 Bears in action $7
1986 Bears in action $7
1987 Red Grange, Bronko Nagurski, Walter Payton,
    Gale Sayers $7
1988 Team helmet $7
1989 Bears equipment $6
1990 Team helmet $6
1991 .... $6
1992 .... $6
1993 .... $6
1994 .... $6

Chicago Bears Yearbooks

1983 .... $12
1986 Locker with Super Bowl Trophy $10
1987 .... $12
1989 .... $8
1990 .... $8
1991 .... $8
1992 .... $8
1993 Mark Carrier, Richard Dent, Jim Morrissey $8

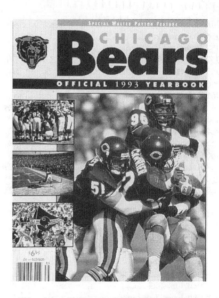

Cincinnati Bengals Media Guides

1968 Paul Brown $27
1969 Riverfront Stadium $27
1970 "Date Book and Media Guide," 1970................$13
1971 "Date Book and Media Guide," 1971................$13
1972 "Date Book and Media Guide," 1972................$13
1973 "Date Book and Media Guide," 1973................$13
1974 ....$13
1975 Bengals in action.............................$13
1976 Ken Anderson $15
1977 Riverfront Stadium $13
1978 Riverfront Stadium $13
1979 Team helmets..................................$13
1980 Tiger, Bengals in action $7
1981 New uniform...................................$7
1982 Ken Anderson, Blair Bush, Dave Lapham,
    Tiger $7
1983 Team helmet $7
1984 Ken Anderson $7
1985 Cris Collinsworth.............................$7
1986 Boomer Esiason................................$7
1987 James Brooks, Eddie Brown, Boomer Esiason,
    others.....................................$6.50/$6
1988 Tiger...$6
1989 Tiger...$6
1990 Tiger...$6
1991 ....$6
1992 ....$6
1993 ....$6
1994 ....$6

Cleveland Browns Media Guides

1949 Team mascot..................................$50
1950 Cleveland Stadium and crowd..................$50
1951 Name and 1951 ....$50
1952 Paul Brown $50
1953 Cartoon Brown................................$45
1954 Media equipment $45
1955 Cartoon reporter.............................$45
1956 Cartoon reporter.............................$45
1957 Coach and player $40
1958 Browns in action $40
1959 Browns in action $40
1960 Team mascot and helmet $27
1961 Team mascot and helmet $27
1962 Jim Brown...................................$30
1963 Jim Brown...................................$30
1964 Jim Brown...................................$30
1965 Team helmet.................................$27
1966 Action pictures.............................$27
1967 Leroy Kelly.................................$27
1968 Team helmet $27
1969 Team helmet $27
1970 Team helmet $13
1971 Team helmet $13
1972 Team helmet $13
1973 Team helmet $13
1974 Team helmet $13
1975 Team helmet $13
1976 Team helmet $13
1977 Team helmet $13
1978 Team helmet $13
1979 Browns in action $13

1980 Sam Rutigliano $6
1981 Brian Sipe..................................$7
1982 Team helmet and Cleveland...................$6
1983 Browns defense in action....................$6
1984 Ozzie Newsome $8
1985 Clay Matthews, Marty Schottenheimer $6
1986 Earnest Byner, Kevin Mack...................$6
1987 Bernie Kosar................................$6
1988 Earnest Byner, Bernie Kosar.................$6
1989 Bernie Kosar................................$6
1990 Reggie Langhorne, Webster Slaughter $6
1991 ....$6
1992 ....$6
1993 ....$6
1994 ....$6

Cleveland Browns Yearbooks

1987 Bernie Kosar $8
1991 ....$8
1992 ....$8
1993 Clay Matthews $8

Dallas Cowboys Media Guides

1960 Team mascot.................................$27
1961 L.G. Dupre $27
1962 Players in uniforms 19, 62 ....$27
1963 Bill Howton................................$27
1964 Team helmet................................$27
1965 Bob Lilly $27
1966 Bob Hayes $27
1967 Don Meredith...............................$27
1968 Don Perkins................................$27
1969 Tom Landry $27
1970 Calvin Hill................................$17
1971 Texas Stadium..............................$13
1972 Tom Landry, Murchison, Tex Schram, trophy.......$13

1973 Mel Renfro..$13
1974 Cornell Green...$13
1975 Roger Staubach..$15
1976 Cliff Harris..$13
1977 Drew Pearson...$13
1978 Harvey Martin, Randy White, two trophies.......$13
1979 20th Anniversary $13
1980 Tony Dorsett $10
1981 Randy White $9
1982 Tom Landry $8
1983 Texas Stadium, Cowboys star...........................$7
1984 25th Anniversary logo $7
1985 Randy White $7
1986 Tony Dorsett, Tom Landry $7
1987 Tony Dorsett, Herschel Walker $6
1988 Cowboys star $6
1989 Jimmy Johnson, Jimmy Jones............................$6
1990 Eugene Lockhart $6
1991 ....$6
1992 ....$6
1993 ....$6
1994 ....$6

Dallas Cowboys Yearbooks

1967 Don Meredith..$45
1968 Bob Hayes...$40
1969 Bob Lilly...$40
1970 Calvin Hill $30
1971 Walt Garrison...$30
1972 Roger Staubach..$30
1973 Tom Landry $25
1991 ....$9
1992 ....$10
1993 Troy Aikman, Super Bowl photos $10

Denver Broncos Media Guides

1960 ....$27
1961 ....$27
1962 ....$27
1963 Team mascot $27
1964 Lionel Taylor...$27
1965 Team mascot $27
1966 Lionel Taylor...$27
1967 Lou Saban $27
1968 Team helmet $27
1969 Team mascot $27
1970 Mike Haffner $13
1971 Rich Jackson, Floyd Little, Lou Saban.............$15
1972 Floyd Little, John Ralston................................$15
1973 Offensive huddle..$15
1974 Team helmet, huddle $13
1975 Otis Armstrong $13
1976 Riley Odoms $15
1977 Orange Crush defense.....................................$13
1978 Mile High Stadium $13
1979 Team helmet $13
1980 Team helmet $7
1981 Broncos uniform #81 ....$7
1982 Dan Reeves $7
1983 Broncos in action $7
1984 John Elway..$8
1985 Bronco silhouette $7

OFFICIAL 1993
TEAM YEARBOOK
DENVER BRONCOS

1986 Broncos in action $6
1987 John Elway..$7
1988 Karl Mecklenburg $6
1989 Football stitching $6
1990 Team headquarters...$6
1991 ....$6
1992 ....$6
1993..$6
1994..$6

Denver Broncos Yearbooks

1974 "The Making of a Contender"..........................$20
1986 Louis Wright $7
1991..$7
1992..$7
1993 John Elway..$8

Detroit Lions Media Guides

1946 Team mascot $50
1947 Name and 1947 ....$50
1948 Bo McMillin $50
1949 a: Lions mascot (40 pgs.)................................$50
    b: Bo McMillin (20 pgs.)...................................$40
1950 Name and 1950 ....$40
1951 a: Doak Walker (48 pgs.).................................$40
    b: Lions mascot (48 pgs.) $40
1952 Name and 1952 ....$40
1953 Mascot, World Champions pennant...................$40
1954 Mascot, World Champions pennant...................$40
1955 Mascot, Western Division Champions banner.......$40
1956 Briggs Stadium $40
1957 Lions in action...$40
1958 Team picture $40
1959 Name and 1959 ....$40
1960 Lions in action...$27
1961 Jim Gibbons $27
1962 Briggs Stadium $27
1963 Lions mascot $27

152

1964 Player in action $27
1965 Team helmet $27
1966 Players with uniform #s 19, 66.........................$27
1967 Team logo $27
1968 Lions in action $27
1969 Lions in action $27
1970 Lions in action $13
1971 Team helmet $13
1972 Team logo $13
1973 Team logo $13
1974 Team logo $13
1975 Lions in action $13
1976 Team helmet $13
1977 Lions in action $13
1978 Lions in action $13
1979 Monte Clark, Gary Danielson...........................$10
1980 Lions in action $10
1981 Billy Sims $10
1982 Lions in action $6
1983 50th Anniversary logo $6
1984 Team helmet $6
1985 James Jones...$6
1986 Ford, Rogers, Thomas, helmet...........................$6
1987 Lion $6
1988 Lion $6
1989 Wayne Fontes $6
1990 Jerry Ball, Eddie Murray, Barry Sanders,
　　 Chris Spielman $7
1991 ....$6
1992 ....$6
1993 ....$6
1994 ....$6

Detroit Lions Yearbooks

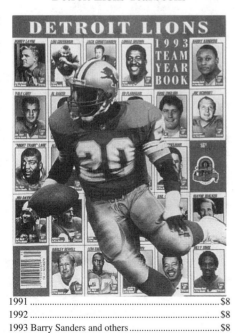

1991 ....$8
1992 ....$8
1993 Barry Sanders and others....................................$8

Green Bay Packers Media Guides

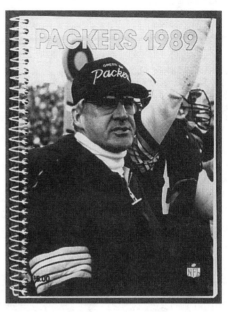

1947 Curly Lambeau, championship teams................$50
1948 Curly Lambeau..$50
1949 "Home of the Packers".......................................$50
1950 Name and 1950 ....$40
1951 State of Wisconsin $40
1952 State of Wisconsin $40
1953 Name and 1953 ....$40
1954 Name and 1954 ....$40
1955 State of Wisconsin $40
1956 State of Wisconsin $40
1957 Green Bay Stadium $40
1958 Green Bay Stadium $40
1959 Vince Lombardi and Stadium $45
1960 Packers in action $27
1961 "West Division Champs 1960".........................$27
1962 ....$27
1963 "World Champions"..$27
1964 Team logo $27
1965 Jim Taylor...$30
1966 Bart Starr...$27
1967 Elijah Pitts..$27
1968 Willie Davis $30
1969 Donny Anderson $25
1970 Packers in action $20
1971 Packers training...$20
1972 John Brockington...$25
1973 Packers defense...$20
1974 John Brockington...$25
1975 Bart Starr...$17
1976 Dave Hanner, Bart Starr......................................$17
1977 Lynn Dickey..$13
1978 Packers entering the field...................................$13
1979 Bart Starr, Vince Lombardi...............................$15
1980 Packers celebrating $6

1981 Mike Douglass	$6
1982 Jan Stenerud	$8
1983 Larry McCarren	$6
1984 Forrest Gregg	$6
1985 Lynn Dickey	$7
1986 Packers defense vs. Miami Dolphins	$6
1987 Mark Lee	$6
1988 Lindy Infante	$6
1989 Lindy Infante	$6
1990 Tim Harris	$6
1991	$6
1992	$6
1993	$6
1994	$6

Green Bay Packer Yearbooks

1960 Paul Hornung, Jerry Kramer	$125
1961 Forrest Gregg	$125
1962 Vince Lombardi	$150
1963 Jim Taylor	$40
1964 Bart Starr	$40
1965 Curly Lambeau, Vince Lombardi	$40
1966 Willie Davis	$35
1967 Packers vs. Kansas City Chiefs	$35
1968 Ray Nitschke	$35
1969 Donny Anderson	$25
1970 Travis Williams	$25
1971 Dan Devine	$25
1972 John Brockington	$25
1973 Chester Marcol, Ron Widby	$25
1974 Jerry Tagge	$20
1975 Bart Starr	$20
1976 Fred Carr	$20
1977 Lynn Dickey	$20
1978 Johnnie Gray	$10
1979 Terdell Middleton, David Whitehurst	$10
1980 Rich Wingo	$10
1981 Gerry Ellis, Eddie Lee Ivery	$10
1982 John Jefferson, James Lofton	$15
1983 Mike Douglass	$10
1984 25th Anniversary, Forrest Gregg	$10
1985 Paul Coffmann	$9
1986 Randy Scott	$6
1987 Randy Wright	$6
1988 Lindy Infante	$6
1989 Tim Harris	$6
1990 Don Majkowski	$6
1991 Sterling Sharpe	$8
1992 Mike Holmgren	$6
1993 Brett Favre	$6
1994 Reggie White	$8

Houston Oilers Media Guides

1960	$27
1961 Team mascot	$27
1962 Ed Husmann, Ivy, Al Jamison	$27
1963 Oilers in action	$27
1964 Sammy Baugh, Oilers in action	$27
1965 Team helmets	$27
1966 Ode Burrell, W.K. Hicks, Bob Talamini	$27
1967 Logo	$27
1968 Astrodome	$27
1969 Astrodome	$27

1970 Oilers artwork	$16
1971 Oilers sculpture	$16
1972 Team helmet	$16
1973 Team helmet	$16
1974 Sid Gillman, Oilers in action	$15
1975 Oilers in action	$13
1976 Cheering fans	$13
1977 Team logo	$13
1978 Oilers in action	$13
1979 20th Anniversary, Oilers in action	$10
1980 Bum Phillips	$10
1981 Oiler in action	$6
1982 Team helmets	$6
1983 Team helmet	$6
1984	$6
1985 Warren Moon, Mike Munchak, Dean Steinkuhler	$8
1986	$6
1987 Ray Childress, Ernest Givins, John Grimsley, Drew Hill	$6
1988 Team helmet, field	$6
1989 Team helmet	$6
1990 Ernest Givins, Drew Hill, Warren Moon	$6
1991	$6
1992	$6
1993	$6
1994	$6

Houston Oilers Yearbooks

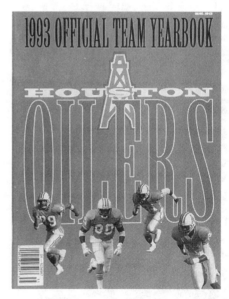

1965 Houston Oilers vs. San Diego Chargers	$40
1968	$30
1970	$30
1990	$8
1991	$8
1992	$8
1993 Curtis Duncan, Ernest Givins, Haywood Jeffires, Webster Slaughter	$8

Kansas City Chiefs Media Guides

1960 .... $27
1961 .... $27
1962 .... $27
1963 Len Dawson, Curtis McClinton, Hank Stram.... $30
1964 Curtis McClinton $27
1965 Len Dawson, Jerry Mays, Hank Stram $30
1966 Chiefs in action $27
1967 Lamar Hunt, Hank Stram, AFL Trophy $27
1968 Chiefs in action $27
1969 Willie Lanier $30
1970 Hank Stram, Chiefs celebrating $13
1971 Ed Podolak $13
1972 Arrowhead Stadium $13
1973 Len Dawson, Otis Taylor, Hank Stram $15
1974 Chiefs in action $13
1975 Team helmet $13
1976 .... $13
1977 Mike Livingston, Paul Wiggin $13
1978 Team helmet and football $13
1979 Chiefs on offense $13
1980 Marv Levy, Chiefs in action $6
1981 Gary Barbaro, Art Still, J.T. Smith $6
1982 Joe Delaney, Jack Rudnay $6
1983 Carlos Carson, John Mackovic $6
1984 25th Anniversary logo $6
1985 John Mackovic, team helmet $6
1986 Stephone Paige $6
1987 Lloyd Burruss, Deron Cherry, Albert Lewis,
     Kevin Ross $6
1988 Albert Lewis, Nick Lowery, Paul Palmer $6
1989 C. Peterson, Marty Schottenheimer $6
1990 Center gripping the ball $6
1991 .... $6
1992 .... $6
1993 .... $6
1994 .... $6

Kansas City Chiefs Yearbooks

1968 .... $40
1969 .... $40
1972 Ed Podolak $20

Oakland/Los Angeles Raiders Media Guides

1960 .... $27
1961 Team mascot $27
1962 .... $27
1963 Bo Roberson $27
1964 Raiders helmet $27
1965 Oakland-Alameda County Stadium $27
1966 Raiders helmet $27
1967 Player in action $27
1968 AFL Champions ring $27
1969 Dan Birdwell $27
1970 Raiders offensive huddle $19
1971 Raiders offense, Daryle Lamonica $16
1972 Team logo and 1972 .... $13
1973 Raiders in action $13
1974 Pre-game huddle $13
1975 Raiders action photos $13

1976 Raider player on the sidelines $13
1977 Super Bowl XI ring $13
1976 Dave Casper in action $13
1979 20th Anniversary memorabilia $13
1980 Raiders third decade $10
1981 Super Bowl XV ring $7

Los Angeles Raiders

1982 Raider player on the sidelines $6
1983 Raiders in action $6
1984 Super Bowl XVIII ring $6
1985 Helmet, three Super Bowl trophies $6
1986 Team logo $6
1987 Matt Millen $6
1988 Van McElroy $6
1989 Team helmet $6
1990 Team helmet $6
1991 .... $6
1992 .... $6
1993 .... $6
1994 .... $6

Los Angeles Rams Media Guides

1945 Bob Waterfield $50
1946 .... $50
1947 Bob Waterfield $50
1948 .... $50
1949 Team logo and 1949 .... $50
1950 Team logo and 1950 .... $40
1951 Team logo and 1951 .... $40
1952 Team logo and 1952 .... $40
1953 Team logo and 1953 .... $40
1954 Team logo and 1954 .... $40
1955 Team logo and 1955 .... $40
1956 Team logo and 1956 .... $40
1957 Team logo and 1957 .... $40
1958 Team logo and 1958 .... $40
1959 Team logo and 1959 .... $40
1960 Team logo and 1960 .... $27
1961 Team logo and 1961 .... $27
1962 Team logo and 1962 .... $27
1963 Team logo and 1963 .... $27
1964 Team logo and 1964 .... $27
1965 Team logo and 1965 .... $27
1966 Team logo and 1966 .... $27
1967 Team logo and 1967 .... $27
1968 Team logo and 1968 .... $27
1969 Team logo and 1969 .... $27
1970 Team logo and 1970 .... $13
1971 Team logo and 1971 .... $13
1972 Team logo and 1972 .... $13
1973 Rams in action $13
1974 Team helmet $13
1975 Team helmet $13
1976 Team helmet $13
1977 Team helmet $13
1978 Past and present team helmets $13
1979 Carroll Rosenbloom $13
1980 Rams in action $13
1981 Ram wearing uniform #81 .... $6
1982 Los Angeles sites $6
1983 Team helmet $6

1984 Rams players entering the field $6
1985 40th Anniversary logo $6
1986 Eric Dickerson $6
1987 .... $6
1988 Rams in action $6
1989 Team helmet, equipment $6
1990 Ram wearing uniform #90 .... $6
1991 .... $6
1992 .... $6
1993 .... $6
1994 .... $6

Los Angeles Rams Yearbooks

1958 Cartoon running back $40
1959 Cartoon mascot on a ram $40
1960 Cartoon ram, helmet $35
1961 Cartoon ram $35
1962 Jon Arnett $35
1963 Dick Bass $35
1983 .... $10
1984 .... $10
1985 .... $10
1989 .... $10
1991 .... $8
1992 .... $8
1993 .... $8

Miami Dolphins Media Guides

1966 George Wilson $27
1967 Dolphins helmet $27
1968 Orange Bowl $27
1969 Jack Clancy, Bob Griese, Karl Noonan $27
1970 Team logo and 1970 .... $13
1971 Bob Griese, Don Shula, Paul Warfield, others .. $15
1972 Garo Yepremian $13
1973 Super Bowl trophy $13
1974 Helmet and Super Bowl trophies $13
1975 Bob Griese, Don Shula $15
1976 Bob Kuechenberg, Jim Langer, Benny Malone. $13
1977 Bob Griese $15
1978 Nat Moore $13
1979 Delvin Williams $13
1980 Vern DenHerder $6
1981 David Woodley $6
1982 Tony Nathan $6
1983 Andra Franklin $6
1984 Dan Marino $10
1985 Mark Clayton, Mark Duper, Dan Marino $8
1986 Joe Robbie, Dwight Stephenson $6
1987 .... $6
1988 Dan Marino $8
1989 Team logo $6
1990 25th Anniversary logo $6
1991 .... $6
1992 .... $6
1993 .... $6
1994 .... $6

Miami Dolphins Yearbooks

1988 .... $10
1993 J.B. Brown, Bryan Cox, David Griggs,
    John Offerdahl, Louis Oliver, Troy Vincent $8

Minnesota Vikings Media Guides

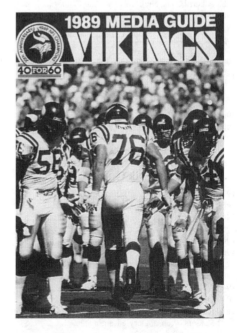

1961 Team logo $27
1962 Team logo $27
1963 Team logo $27

1964 Team logo $27
1965 Team logo $27
1966 Fran Tarkenton..$30
1967 Vikings in action..$27
1968 Joe Kapp $27
1969 Bud Grant..$27
1970 Fred Cox $13
1971 Jim Marshall $15
1972 Alan Page $15
1973 Fan in Viking costume....................................$13
1974 Players during National Anthem $13
1975 Fans cheering..$13
1976 Fran Tarkenton..$15
1977 Team logo $13
1978 Chuck Foreman...$13
1979 Ahmad Rashad..$15
1980 Vikings new offices, stadium $6
1981 Tommy Kramer, Ahmad Rashad, Sammy White $8
1982 Vikings in action..$6
1983 Matt Blair, Johnson, Doug Martin,
     Scott Studwell $6
1984 Les Steckel $6
1985 25th Anniversary logo $6
1986 Jerry Burns...$6
1987 Tommy Kramer, others......................................$6
1988 Joey Browner, Chris Doleman, Keith Millard,
     others $6
1989 Tim Irwin, others $6
1990 30th Anniversary logo $6
1991 ....$6
1992 ....$6
1993 ....$6
1994 ....$6

Minnesota Vikings Yearbooks

1961 Vikings cartoon and referee..............................$55
1975 ....$15
1991 ....$8
1992 ....$8
1993 Artwork by Allen J. Peterson..............................$8

New England Patriots Media Guides
Boston Patriots

1960 ....$40
1961 ....$35
1962 ....$35
1963 Cartoon Patriot, reporters.................................$27
1964 Patriots helmet $27
1965 Gino Cappelletti, Babe April $30
1966 Nick Buoniconti...$30
1967 Jim Nance $27
1968 Team logo $27
1969 Clive Rush $27
1970 Patriots action photos......................................$13

New England Patriots

1971 Foxboro Stadium $13
1972 Julius Adams, Jim Plunkett, Randy Vataha.......$13
1973 Patriots coaching staff.....................................$13
1974 Patriots action photos......................................$13
1975 Patriots fans $13

1976 "Patriots of '76" $13
1977 Chuck Fairbanks $13
1978 Patriot Superhero cartoon $13
1979 Patriots in action $13
1980 Stanley Morgan..$10
1981 Ron Erhardt, action photos $6
1982 Ron Meyer $6
1983 Boston sites $6
1984 Steve Grogan..$6
1985 Patriots helmet $6
1986 Andre Tippett $6
1987 Stanley Morgan $6
1988 Raymond Clayborn $6
1989 Patriots in action $6
1990 Rod Rust $6
1991 ....$6
1992 ....$6
1993 ....$6
1994 ....$6

New England Patriots Yearbooks
Boston Patriots

1965 Gino Cappelletti, Babe Parilli $35
1966 J.D. Garrett, Jim Nance....................................$35
1967 Jim Nance...$35

New England Patriots

1978..$13
1979..$10
1980 Rod Shoate $13
1985 Tony Eason, Craig James, others........................$6
1987..$6
1991..$6

New Orleans Saints Media Guides

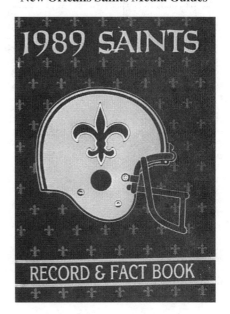

1967 Player in action $27
1968 Band playing in the stadium $27
1969 Saints defense $27
1970 Dan Abramowicz $13
1971 Tom Dempsey 63-yard field goal $15
1972 Jake Kupp, Archie Manning, Jim Strong $13
1973 Bob Pollard $13
1974 Saints defense $13
1975 Saints in action $13
1976 Hank Stram $13
1977 Chuck Muncie, Hank Stram, Superdome $13
1978 Superdome $13
1979 Joe Federspiel, Dick Nolan $13
1980 Saints helmet, uniform $6
1981 Archie Manning, Bum Phillips $7
1982 George Rogers $6
1983 Team logo $6
1984 Bum Phillips $6
1985 Team helmet and Louisiana $6
1986 Team logo, helmet, uniform $6
1987 Rickey Jackson, Rueben Mayes, Jim Mora $6
1988 Team helmet $6
1989 Team helmet $6
1990 Dalton Hilliard $6
1991 .... $6
1992 Superdome crowd $6
1993 .... $6
1994 .... $6

New Orleans Saints Yearbooks

1968 Dan Abramowicz $25
1991 .... $8
1992 .... $8
1993 .... $8

New York Giants Media Guides

1945 Ward Cuff $50
1946 Giants in action $50
1947 Giants in action $50
1948 Team logo $50
1949 1925 Giants $50
1950 Polo Grounds $40
1951 Polo Grounds $40
1952 Radio microphone $40
1953 Steve Owens, others $40
1954 Team logo $40
1955 Team logo $40
1956 Team logo $40
1957 Team logo $40
1958 Team logo $40
1959 Team logo $40
1960 Team logo and 1960 .... $27
1961 Team logo and 1961 .... $27
1962 Team logo and 1962 .... $27
1963 Team logo and 1963 .... $27
1964 Team logo and 1964 .... $27
1965 Team logo and 1965 .... $27
1966 Team mascot and 1966 .... $27
1967 Team helmet and 1967 .... $27
1968 Team helmet and 1968 .... $27
1969 Team helmet and 1969 .... $27
1970 Team helmet and 1970 .... $13

1971 Team helmet and 1971 .... $13
1972 Team helmet and 1972 .... $13
1973 Team helmet and 1973 .... $13
1974 Team logo $13
1975 Team helmet $13
1976 Giants Stadium construction $13
1977 Giants Stadium opening day $13
1978 Giants offensive line $13
1979 Harry Carson $13
1980 Harry Carson, Phil Simms, Lawrence Taylor $15
1981 Phil Simms, offensive line $6
1982 Harry Carson, Lawrence Taylor $8
1983 Harry Carson, Phil Simms, Lawrence Taylor,
      others $8
1984 Giants greats $6
1985 Harry Carson, Phil Simms, Lawrence Taylor,
      others $8
1986 Harry Carson, Phil Simms, Lawrence Taylor,
      others $8
1987 Phil Simms, Super Bowl tickets $6
1988 Gene Banks, Leonard Marshall,
      Lawrence Taylor $7
1989 Giants Stadium, previous homesites $6
1990 Mark Bavaro, Phil Simms, Lawrence Taylor $6
1991 .... $6
1992 .... $6
1993 .... $6
1994 .... $6

New York Giants Yearbooks

1963 .... $95
1964 Y.A. Tittle, Alex Webster $40
1965 Giants offensive line $40
1966 Tucker Frederickson $40
1967 New York Giants vs. St. Louis .... Cardinals $35
1968 Fran Tarkenton $30
1969 Fran Tarkenton $30
1970 Joe Morrison $30
1971 .... $10
1974 .... $25
1975 .... $20
1976 John Mendenhall $20
1986 Phil Simms $10
1987 .... $10
1991 .... $10
1992 .... $8
1993 .... $8

New York Jets Media Guides

1960 .... $27
1961 .... $27
1962 .... $27
1963 .... $27
1964 Team logo and 1964 .... $27
1965 Team logo and 1965 .... $27
1966 Team logo and 1966 .... $27
1967 Team logo and 1967 .... $27
1968 Team logo and 1967 .... $27
1969 Team logo and 1969 .... $27
1970 Team logo and 1970 .... $13
1971 Team logo and 1971 .... $13
1972 Team logo and 1972 .... $13

1973 Team logo and 1973 .... $13
1974 Team logo and 1974 .... $13
1975 Team logo and 1975 .... $13
1976 Team logo and 1976 .... $13
1977 Team logo and 1977 .... $13
1978 Team helmet and logo $13
1979 Jets defensive line.. $13
1980 Marvin Powell, Richard Todd, l
    Statue of Liberty.. $6
1981 Bruce Harper, Marvin Powell............................. $6
1982 Mark Gastineau, others..................................... $6
1983 Freeman McNeil, others $6
1984 25th Anniversary logo $6
1985 Mark Gastineau, Freeman McNeil,
    Joe Namath.. $8
1986 Mark Gastineau, Joe Klecko,
    Freeman McNeil... $6
1987 Don Maynard, Mickey Shuler, Al Toon $6
1988 Al Toon $6
1989 Ernie McMillan, Mickey Shuler, Al Toon.......... $6
1990 Bruce Coslet, Dick Steinberg $6
1991 .... $6
1992 .... $6
1993 .... $6
1994 .... $6

New York Jets Yearbooks

Official 1993 Yearbook

1960 .... $80
1961 "Titans" AFL $70
1962 .... $60
1963 .... $60
1964 Larry Grantham, Wahoo McDaniel,
    Matt Snell.. $60
1965 Matt Snell... $60
1966 Joe Namath $60
1967 New York Jets vs. San Diego Chargers............. $35
1968 Emerson Boozer, Joe Namath........................... $35

1969 Joe Namath.. $75
1970 Don Maynard $20
1971... $15
1972... $15
1973... $15
1974... $15
1975 Jets in action.. $15
1976... $15
1977 Greg Buttle, Clark Gaines, Richard Todd,
    others $15
1978... $15
1979... $15
1980... $15
1981... $15
1982... $15
1983... $15
1986... $10
1987... $10
1988... $10
1989... $10
1990... $10
1991... $8
1992... $8
1993 Player #93 holding helmet $8

Philadelphia Eagles Media Guides

1947 Season schedule $50
1948 $50
1949 Earle Neale... $50
1950 Steve Van Buren $40
1951 Eagle $40
1952 Eagles in action $40
1953 Jim Trimble.. $40
1954 Eagle $40
1955 Eagle $40
1956 Hugh Devore... $40
1957 25th Anniversary eagle $40
1958 L. "Buck" Shaw $40
1959 Eagle, Franklin Field.. $40
1960 Franklin Field.. $27
1961 Eagle wearing a crown....................................... $27
1962 Baby eagle hatching from ball $27
1963 Eagle and goalposts... $27
1964 Franklin Field.. $27
1965 Norm Snead in action.. $27
1966 Tim Brown $27
1967 Harold Wells $27
1968 Norm Snead, offensive line............................... $27
1969 Apollo XI logo $27
1970 Zodiac symbols $13
1971 Eagles history... $13
1972 Eddie Khayat.. $13
1973 Bradley, Roman Gabriel, McCormack $13
1974 Harold Carmichael, Roman Gabriel,
    others $13
1975 Eagles in action $13
1976 Dick Vermiel... $13
1977 Dick Vermiel, action photos $13
1978 Harold Carmichael $13
1979 Harold Carmichael, Wilbert Montqomery........ $13
1980 Dick Vermiel and coaches $6
1981 Team helmet... $6

1982 50th Anniversary logo $6
1983 Marion Campbell...$6
1984 Mike Quick $6
1985 Norman Braman..$6
1986 Buddy Ryan $6
1987 Reggie White $8
1988 Mike Quick $6
1989 Randall Cunningham $7
1990 Randall Cunningham, offensive huddle $7
1991 ....$6
1992 ....$6
1993 ....$6
1994 ....$6

Philadelphia Eagles Yearbooks

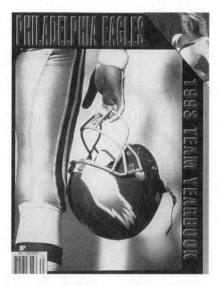

Pittsburgh Steelers Media Guides

1972 Philadelphia Eagles vs. Dallas Cowboys...........$25
1973 Philadelphia Eagles vs. Kansas City Chiefs $20
1974 Harold Carmichael, Roman Gabriel $20
1975 Eagles in action...$20
1976 Dick Vermiel $20
1977 ....$20
1978 ....$20
1979 ....$20
1981 NFC Champions ring...$10
1982 Eagles memorabilia $10
1983 Harold Carmichael, Wilbert Montgomery.........$10
1984 ....$10
1985 ....$10
1986 Mike Quick $10
1987 ....$10
1988 Mike Quick $10
1989 William Frizzell, others $10
1990 Randall Cunningham $10
1991 ....$8
1992 ....$8
1993 Player holding a helmet at his side $8

1947 Name and 1947 ....$50
1948 Cartoon reporters $50
1949 Cartoon reporters $50
1950 Cartoon reporters $40
1951 John P. Michelosen $40
1952 Cartoon steelworker $40
1953 Steeler kicker $40
1954 City of Pittsburgh $40
1955 Steelers in action $40
1956 Steelers in action $40
1957 Brovelli, Elbert Nickel......................................$40
1958 Steelers in action $40
1959 Team mascot and logo $40
1960 Steelers in action $27
1961 Team helmet..$27
1962 Steelers uniform $27
1963 Steelers helmet and 1963 ....$27
1964 Steelers helmet and 1964 ....$27
1965 City of Pittsburgh $27
1966 City of Pittsburgh $27
1967 Steelers in action $27
1968 Team helmet..$27

1969 Three Rivers Stadium $27
1970 Steelers in action..$13
1971 Black and yellow stripes....................................$13
1972 Team helmet $13
1973 Joe Greene $15
1974 Team helmet $13
1975 Terry Bradshaw, Rocky Bleier,
    Franco Harris...$15
1976 Team helmet $13
1977 Team helmet $13
1978 Team helmet $13
1979 Team helmet $13
1980 "Steelers 1980" football.......................................$6
1981 Football $6
1982 50th Anniversary logo $6
1983 Team helmet $6
1984 Franco Harris $8
1985 Team helmet $6
1986 Team helmet $6
1987 Team helmet $6
1988 Chuck Noll..$6
1989 Team helmet, Pittsburgh......................................$6
1990 "Steelers '90" logo...$6
1991 ....$6
1992 ....$6
1993 ....$6
1994 ....$6

Pittsburgh Steelers Yearbooks

1979 Terry Bradshaw $10
1980 ....$10
1990 Bubby Brister, Louis Lipps, Rod Woodson,
    others $6
1991 ....$6
1992 ....$6
1993 ....$6

St. Louis Cardinals Media Guides
Chicago Cardinals

1947 Team logo and 1947 ....$50
1948 Team logo and 1948 ....$50
1949 Team logo and 1949 ....$50
1950 Team logo and 1950 ....$40
1951 Team logo and 1951 ....$40
1952 Team logo and 1952 ....$40
1953 Team logo and 1953 ....$40
1954 Team logo and 1954 ....$40
1955 Team logo and 1955 ....$40
1956 Team logo and 1956 ....$40
1957 Team logo and 1957 ....$40
1958 Team logo and 1958 ....$40
1959 Team logo and 1959 ....$40

St. Louis Cardinals

1960 Team mascot and 1960 ....$27
1961 Team mascot and 1961 ....$27
1962 Team mascot and 1962 ....$27
1963 Charley Johnson, Wally Lemm $27
1964 Bobby Joe Conrad...$27
1965 Jim Bakken $27
1966 Busch Stadium...$27

1967 Larry Wilson $27
1968 Jim Hart, Johnny Roland.....................................$27
1969 Dave Williams $27
1970 Cardinals in action $13
1971 Team helmets $13
1972 Team helmet, St. Louis Arch $13
1973 Jim Bakken..$15
1974 Busch Stadium...$13
1975 Don Coryell, Jim Hart, Terry Metcalf $13
1976 Jim Hart...$15
1977 St. Louis Cardinals vs. Dallas Cowboys...........$13
1978 St. Louis Cardinals greats $13
1979 Cardinals in action $13
1980 Cardinals in action $6
1981 Cardinals in action $6
1982 Stump Mitchell $6
1983 Team helmets..$6
1984 25th Anniversary in St. Louis $6
1985 Team mascot, St. Louis Arch...............................$6
1986 Gene Stallings $6
1987 Cardinals uniform #87 ....$6

Phoenix Cardinals

1988 Neil Lomax, Vai Sikahema, Luis Sharpe,
    others $6
1989 Cardinals in the desert..$6
1990 Cardinals defense $6
1991..$6
1992..$6
1993..$6
1994..$6

St. Louis Cardinals Yearbooks
St. Louis Cardinals

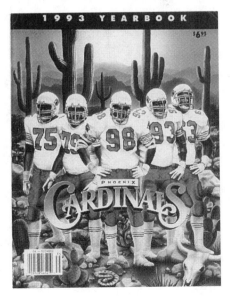

1967 Team Photo $35
1968 .... $35
1969 .... $35
1976 .... $15

Phoenix Cardinals

1988 .... $6
1989 Team helmet in the desert $6
1990 .... $6
1991 .... $6
1992 .... $6
1993 Michael Bankston, Reuben Davis, Mike Jones,
    Keith Rucker, Eric Swann $6

San Diego Chargers Media Guides
Los Angeles Chargers

1960 Team logo and 1960 .... $27

San Diego Chargers

1961 Team logo and 1961 .... $27
1962 Team logo and 1962 .... $27
1963 Team logo and 1963 .... $27
1964 Team logo and 1964 .... $27
1965 Team mascot and 1965 .... $27
1966 Chargers in action $27
1967 Jack Murphy Stadium $27
1968 Chargers in action $27
1969 John Hadl, offensive line $27
1970 Lance Alworth $15
1971 Chargers in action $13
1972 John Hadl $13
1973 Dennis Partee $13
1974 New Chargers uniform $13
1975 Don Woods $13
1976 Dan Fouts $13
1977 Dan Fouts $13
1978 Joe Washington $13
1979 Chargers in action $13
1980 Chargers in action $6
1981 Greg McCrary, Cliff McGee $6
1982 Team airplanes $6
1983 Team helmet $6
1984 25th Anniversary logo $6
1985 Dan Fouts, Charlie Joiner $8
1986 Lionel James, others celebrating $6
1987 Team helmet $6
1988 Team logo $6
1989 Chargers in action $6
1990 Anthony Miller, Leslie O'Neal, Lee Williams $6
1991 .... $6
1992 .... $6
1993 .... $6
1994 .... $6

San Diego Chargers Yearbooks

1989 .... $10
1991 .... $8
1992 .... $8
1993 .... $8

San Francisco 49ers Media Guides

1950 Three cartoon reporters $40
1951 Team mascot $40
1952 Three team mascots $40
1953 Team mascot $40
1954 Team mascot $40
1955 Action shot and team mascot $40
1956 Team mascot $40
1957 Three team mascots $40
1958 .... $40
1959 Team mascot $40
1960 Red Hickey $27
1961 Team mascot $27
1962 Team mascot $27
1963 Team mascot $27
1964 Team mascot $27
1965 Team mascot $27
1966 Team mascot $27
1967 49ers in action $27
1968 Player on the sideline $27
1969 John Brodie, Gary Lewis $27
1970 Frankie Albert, John Brodie $13
1971 Candlestick Park $13
1972 Team helmet, Candlestick Park $13
1973 Dick Nolan $13
1974 Team helmet, Golden Gate Bridge $13
1975 Footballs, team helmet $13
1976 Monte Clark $13
1977 Eddie DeBartolo, K. Meyer, J. Thomas $13
1978 Golden Gate Bridge $13
1979 O.J. Simpson $20
1980 John Ayers, Paul Hofer $6
1981 Joe Montana, Fred Solomon $8
1982 "The Catch," Super Bowl trophy $6
1983 .... $6

1984 Hand holding helmet..$6
1985 Randy Cross, Wendell Tyler................................$6
1986 40th Anniversary logo $6
1987 Joe Montana..$8
1988 Tom Rathman $6
1989 Joe Montana, Jerry Rice $8
1990 Roger Craig...$6
1991 ....$6
1992 ....$6
1993 ....$6
1994 ....$5

San Francisco 49ers Yearbooks

1958 Team mascot shooting guns.............................$50
1963 John Brodie...$40
1982 ....$20
1983 ....$15
1984 ....$15
1985 Bill Walsh, Super Bowl celebration $10
1986 Joe Montana..$15
1987 ....$15
1988 ....$9
1989 3 Super Bowl trophies $9
1990 ....$9
1991 ....$9
1992 ....$9
1993 ....$9

Seattle Seahawks Media Guides

1976 Team helmet $15
1977 Steve Niehaus, Jack Patera, Jim Zorn...............$13
1978 Sherman Smith..$13
1979 Steve Largent, Jim Zorn $13
1980 Jack Patera $6
1981 Steve Largent, seahawk $8
1982 Steve Largent...$8
1983 Chuck Knox, Kingdome $6
1984 Chuck Knox $6
1985 Players entering the field $6
1986 Steve Largent in action $8
1987 Referee signaling a TD $6
1988 Ron Heller, Johnny Holloway $6
1989 Dave Krieg, Steve Largent,
     John L. Williams $6
1990 Uniform #90, equipment......................................$6
1991 ....$6
1992 ....$6
1993 ....$6
1994 ....$6

Seattle Seahawks Yearbooks

1976 Team helmet, NFL pennants..............................$25
1988 Team helmet $8
1989 Team helmet $8
1991 ....$8
1992 ....$8
1993 Cortez Kennedy, Terry Wooden.........................$8

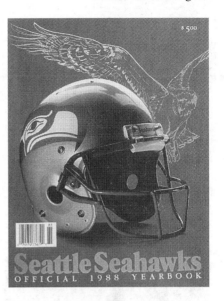

Tampa Bay Buccaneers Media Guides

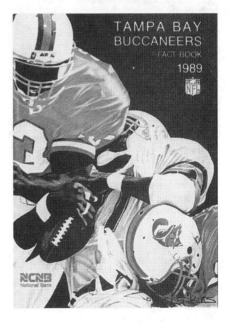

1976 Team helmets..$15
1977 Dave Pear, Lee Roy Selmon $15
1978 John McKay $13
1979 Team helmet, John McKay $13
1980 Jimmy Giles, fans celebrating............................$6
1981 John McKay $6
1982 Hugh Culverhouse, John McKay.........................$6
1983 Buccaneers in action $6

1984 Hugh Green, John McKay, Lee Roy Selmon $8
1985 Leeman Bennett, James Wilder $6
1986 Buccaneers in action $6
1987 .... $6
1988 Don Perkins, Vinny Testaverde $6
1989 Buccaneers in action $6
1990 Mark Carrier $6
1991 .... $6
1992 .... $6
1993 .... $6
1994 .... $6

Tampa Bay Buccaneers Yearbooks

1992 .... $8
1993 Sam Wyche $8

Washington Redskins Media Guides

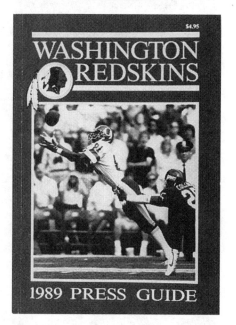

1946 .... $50
1947 Name, Indian mascot $50
1948 Indian mascot and 1948 .... $50
1949 Indian mascot and 1949 .... $50
1950 Indian mascot and 1950 .... $40
1951 Indian mascot and 1951 .... $40
1952 Indian mascot and 1952 .... $40
1953 Indian mascot and 1953 .... $40
1954 Indian mascot and 1954 .... $40
1955 Redskins in action $40
1956 Redskins in action $40
1957 Redskins in action $40
1958 Year and 1958 .... $40
1959 Team helmet, pennant $40
1960 Football and 1960 .... $27
1961 Silver Anniversary $27

1962 Football $27
1963 Capitol building $27
1964 Tomahawk and drum $27
1965 Team helmet $27
1966 Tepee, D.C. Stadium $27
1967 Tepee, D.C. Stadium $27
1968 Tepee, D.C. Stadium $27
1969 Tepee, D.C. Stadium $27
1970 Tepee, D.C. Stadium $13
1971 Tepee, D.C. Stadium $13
1972 Team helmet $13
1973 Team logo, D.C. sites $13
1974 Team helmet, Capitol $13
1975 Pregame huddle $13
1976 Team logo, George Allen $13
1977 Redskins in action $13
1978 Mark Moseley $13
1979 Indian, Redskins in action $13
1980 Team helmet $6
1981 Team logo $6
1982 "Redskins" and helmet $6
1983 Helmet, Super Bowl trophy $8
1984 Joe Theismann $7
1985 John Riggins, Joe Theismann $8
1986 50th Anniversary logo $6
1987 Gary Clark, Art Monk $8
1988 Super Bowl XXII ring $8
1989 Art Monk in action $8
1990 Charles Mann $6
1991 .... $6
1992 .... $6
1993 .... $6
1994 .... $6

Washington Redskins Yearbooks

1973 George Allen, Chris Hanburger $25
1976 .... $20
1977 .... $20
1986 50th Anniversary logo $10
1987 .... $10
1988 Super Bowl action photos $10
1989 Kelvin Bryant, Mark Rypien, Ricky Sanders,
     Doug Williams $8
1990 .... $6
1991 .... $6
1992 .... $6
1993 Redskins defense $6

Basketball

Atlanta Hawks Media Guides

1968-69 Team mascot $75
1969-70 Lou Hudson $25
1970-71 Atlanta skyline, team art $20
1971-72 Richie Guerin, Hawks bench $20
1972-73 Team logo $20
1973-74 Overhead shot of Omni court $20
1974-75 Lou Hudson $20
1975-76 Tom Van Ardsdale $20

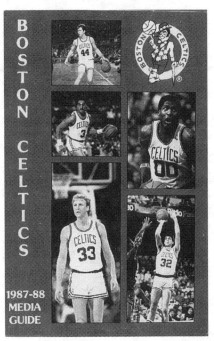

1976-77 John Drew...$15
1977-78 Team logo, artwork $15
1978-79 Team logo, newspaper clips.......................$15
1979-80 Hubie Brown, John Drew, Armond Hill $8
1980-81 Dan Roundfield vs.
    Kareem Abdul-Jabbar $8
1981-82 Action artwork...$8
1982-83 Dan Roundfield $8
1983-84 Action artwork...$8
1984-85 Dominique Wilkins $8
1985-86 Dominique Wilkins $7.50
1986-87 Dominique Wilkins $7.50
1987-88 Dominique Wilkins $7.50
1988-89 Dominique Wilkins $7
1989-90 Moses Malone, Doc Rivers,
    Dominique Wilkins..$6
1990-91 "Let's Run One" $5
1991-92...$5
1992-93...$5
1993-94...$5
1994-95...$9

Atlanta Hawks Yearbooks

1989-90 Moses Malone, Doc Rivers, Dominique
Wilkins...$8.50
1990-91 Dominique Wilkins $7.50
1991-92...$8

Boston Celtics Media Guides

1951-52 Folder report with plain brown cover...... $125-$150
1952-53...$25-$40
1953-54...$25-$40
1954-55 Player photos ....$50-$75

1955-56 Bob Cousy ....$55-$80
1956-57 Player photos ....$50-$75
1957-58 Player photos ....$45-$70
1958-59 Frank Ramsey ....$40-$65
1959-60 Gene Conley..$35-$50
1960-61 Boston Garden ....$30-$45
1961-62 Red Auerbach, five starters ....$40-$60
1962-63 Bob Cousy ....$40-$60
1963-64 Tom Heinsohn ....$35-$50
1964-65 Boston Garden ....$15-$25
1965-66 ....$20-$30
1966-67 Bill Russell ....$25-$45
1967-68 John Havlicek ....$45-$60
1968-69 Red Auerbach, Bill Russell $60
1969-70 Team mascot...$45
1970-71 Dave Cowens, Don Nelson, Jo Jo White,
    others $45
1971-72 Dave Cowens, John Havlicek,
    Jo Jo White...$45
1972-73 Dave Cowens, John Havlicek.......................$45
1973-74 Dave Cowens, John Havlicek,
    Jo Jo White...$35
1974-75 John Havlicek, Paul Silas $30
1975-76 Dave Cowens, John Havlicek.......................$30
1976-77 Championship trophy $25
1977-78 John Havlicek $20
1978-79 Dave Cowens...$20
1979-80 Larry Bird, M.L. Carr $20
1980-81 Red Auerbach, Larry Bird, Bill Fitch...........$15
1981-82 Championship banner, trophy.......................$15
1982-83 Team art, Larry Bird.....................................$15
1983-84 Boston Celtics vs. Atlanta Hawks $15
1984-85 Championship trophy $15

1985-86 Larry Bird $20
1986-87 Larry Bird photos $15
1987-88 Larry Bird, four other starters...................... $15
1988-89 IIistorical tcam photos.............................. $15
1989-90 Red Auerbach $15
1990-91 Team artwork $15
1991-92 .... $10
1992-93 .... $10
1993-94 .... $10
1994-95 .... $10

Boston Celtics Yearbooks

1955-56 through 1973-74: see media guides.
1974-75 Paul Silas ....$25-$35
1975-76 John Havlicek ....$25-$35
1976-77 Jo Jo White ....$20-$30
1977-78 Dave Cowens.......................................$20-$30
1978-79 ....$18-$25
1979-80 ....$18-$25
1980-81 Larry Bird ....$30-$40
1981-82 Larry Bird ....$25-$35
1982-83 Larry Bird, Kevin McHale,
  Robert Parish..$20-$30
1983-84 Robert Parish ....$12-$17
1984-85 Larry Bird vs. Magic Johnson ....$18-$25
1985-86 Larry Bird ....$16-$20
1986-87 Championship banner......................... $14-$17
1987-88 Larry Bird, Kevin McHale,
  Robert Parish..$12-$15
1988-89 Larry Bird ....$10-$15
1989-90 Robert Parish ....$8-$10
1990-91 Larry Bird ....$10-$15
1991-92 .... $10

Charlotte Hornets Media Guides

1988-89 David Stern, G. Shinn, Hornets uniform $25
1989-90 NBA attendance, championship banner $10
1990-91 Gene Little photos $8
1991-92 .... $5
1992-93 .... $5
1993-94 .... $5
1994-95 .... $8

Charlotte Hornets Yearbooks

1993-94 .... $9

Chicago Bulls Media Guides

1966-67 Team logo....................................... $50
1967-68 Team logo....................................... $45
1968-69 Team logo....................................... $35
1969-70 Team logo....................................... $25
1970-71 Team logo....................................... $20
1971-72 Team logo....................................... $20
1972-73 Chet Walker.................................... $20
1973-74 Chet Walker.................................... $20
1974-75 Team logo, action photos $20
1975-76 Team logo, Jerry Sloan.................... $15
1976-77 Team artwork $15
1977-78 Action photos $15
1978-79 Artis Gilmore.................................. $15
1979-80 Artis Gilmore, Jerry Sloan.............. $10

1980-81 Reggie Theus $10
1981-82 Artis Gilmore, David Greenwood $10
1982-83 Rod Thorn, Paul Westhead......................... $10
1983-84 Kcvin Loughery................................. $10
1984-85 Michael Jordan, Orlando Woolridge $10
1985-86 Stan Albeck, Michael Jordan,
  Orlando Woolridge $35
1986-87 Michael Jordan $35
1987-88 Michael Jordan, action photos,
  All-Star Game logo $35
1988-89 Bill Cartwright, Horace Grant,
  Michael Jordan $25
1989-90 Bulls comics $15
1990-91 25th Anniversary artwork $15
1991-92 .... $15
1992-93 .... $15
1993-94 .... $12
1994-95 .... $12

Chicago Bulls Yearbooks

1988-89 .... $10

Cleveland Cavaliers
Media Guides

1970-71 Team logo, year........................... $50
1971-72 Team logo, year........................... $25
1972-73 Team logo, year........................... $25
1973-74 Cavalier artwork $15
1974-75 Team logo, artwork....................... $15
1975-76 Cleveland Coliseum...................... $10
1976-77 Team photo $10
1977-78 Team logo, mascot....................... $10

1978-79 "C'mon Cavaliers"..$10
1979-80 "A New Era...Cavaliers II"..........................$10
1980-81 Team action photos $10
1981-82 Mike Mitchell artwork................................$10
1982-83 Ron Brewer, city skyline............................$10
1983-84 New team logo...$6
1984-85 15th season Cavs basketball cards................$6
1985-86 Team artwork..$6
1986-87 Lenny Wilkens $8
1987-88 Brad Daugherty, Ron Harper,
    Hot Rod Williams $8
1988-89 Cleveland Cavaliers vs. Chicago Bulls $8
1989-90 20th season, Lenny Wilkens, action photos ...$8
1990-91 Team uniform, action photos.........................$8
1991-92 ....$8
1992-93...$8
1993-94...$8
1994-95 ....$8

Cleveland Cavaliers Yearbooks

1992-93...$9

Dallas Mavericks Media Guides

1980-81 Dallas Mavericks uniform...........................$15
1981-82 Dallas Reunion Arena $8
1982-83 Dick Motta..$8
1983-84 Mark Aguirre..$8
1984-85 Rolando Blackman $8
1985-86 Mavericks in action artwork.... ....$10
1986-87 Derek Harper $10
1987-88 James Donaldson, John MacLeod,
    team logo..$10

1988-89 Roy Tarpley...$10
1989-90 Brad Davis, 10th Anniversary $10
1990-91 Rolando Blackman, Derek Harper,
    Fat Lever..$10
1991-92 ....$8
1992-93 ....$8
1993-94 ....$8
1994-95 ....$7

Dallas Mavericks Yearbooks

1980-81 through 1982-83: see media guides.
1987-88 Mark Aguirre .... $7-$10
1988-89 Roy Tarpley... $6-$8

Denver Nuggets Yearbooks

1987-88 ....$10

Denver Nuggets Media Guides
Denver Rockets

1968-69 ....$45
1969-70 Nuggets artwork $35
1970-71 ....$35
1971-72 Ralph Simpson...$35
1972-73 Alex Hannum..$35
1973-74 Team photo...$35

Denver Nuggets

1974-75 Larry Brown, Mack Calvin, Carl Scheer......$20
1975-76 Dan Issel, Doug Moe, Carl Scheer,
    David Thompson $20

Yearbooks/media guides

1976-77 Nuggets in action artwork $20
1977-78 Team logo, year...$15
1978-79 Team mascot..$15
1979-80 David Thompson $8
1980-81 Dan Issel...$8
1981-82 Alex English, Dan Issel, David Thompson $8
1982-83 Team logo...$8
1983-84 10th Anniversary photos $6
1984-85 Nuggest in action artwork $6
1985-86 Alex English, Calvin Natt $8
1986-87 Alex English, team logo $8
1987-88 Alex English, Fat Lever, Calvin Natt.............$8
1988-89 Alex English, Fat Lever, Doug Moe $8
1989-90 Alex English, city skyline $8
1990-91 Bernie Bickerstaff, Carl Scheer....................$8
1991-92 ....$5
1992-93 ....$5
1993-94 ....$8
1994-95 ....$8

Detroit Pistons Media Guides

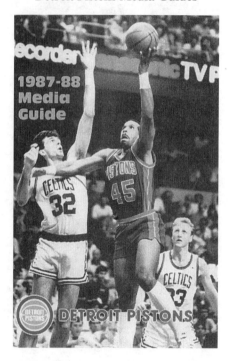

1958-59 ....$100-$125
1960-61 ....$60-$75
1961-62 ....$50-$60
1962-63 ....$50-$60
1963-64 ....$45-$55
1964-65 ....$45-$55
1965-66 ....$45-$55
1967-68 ....$65
1969-70 Happy Hairston...............................$40
1970-71 ....$30
1971-72 ....$25

1972-73 Earl Lloyd.....................................$20
1973-74 ....$20
1974-75 Team logo, ...$15
1975-76 Pistons in action artwork, team logo $10
1976-77 Leon Douglas, Eric Money, Kevin Porter,
    Curtis Rowe..$10
1977-78 Pistons in action artwork $10
1978-79 Pistons in action artwork $10
1979-80 Silverdome, team logo..................................$10
1980-81 ....$10
1981-82 Kent Benson, Isiah Thomas.........................$10
1982-83 ....$8
1983-84 Isiah Thomas, Kelly Tripucka $8
1984-85 Isiah Thomas..$8
1985-86 Bill Laimbeer, Isiah Thomas $8
1986-87 Isiah Thomas..$8
1987-88 Adrian Dantley $8
1988-89 The Palace..$8
1989-90 Championship celebration $6
1990-91 Joe Dumars, Isiah Thomas, trophies.............$6
1991-92 ....$5
1992-93 ....$8
1993-94 ....$8
1994-95 ....$8

Detroit Pistons Yearbooks

1979-80 ....$15
1991-92 ....$9

Warriors Media Guides

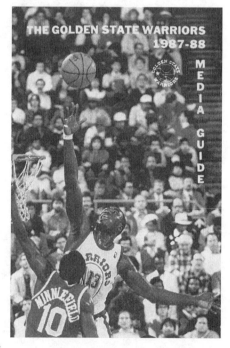

168

San Francisco Warriors

1962-63 ....$50
1963-64 ....$25
1964-65 ....$20
1965-66 ....$75
1966-67 ....$35
1967-68 ....$50
1968-69 Team logo.....................................$40
1969-70 Nate Thurmond...........................$40
1970-71 Nate Thurmond...........................$30

Golden State Warriors

1971-72 Al Attles $20
1972-73 Nate Thurmond...........................$15
1973-74 Nate Thurmond...........................$15
1974-75 Warriors artwork $15
1975-76 NBA Championship trophy........................$15
1976-77 Al Attles $15
1977-78 Warriors in action artwork $15
1978-79 Warriors in action.......................$10
1979-80 Team logos $8
1980-81 Team logo......................................$8
1981-82 Al Attles $8
1982-83 Basketball.......................................$8
1983-84 "Still the Best Game in Town"......................$8
1984-85 Warriors in action artwork $8
1985-86 Sleepy Floyd, Chris Mullin, Purvis Short $8
1986-87 "The New Warriors" $8
1987-88 Larry Smith......................................$8
1988-89 Ralph Sampson...............................$8
1989-90 Chris Mullin $8
1990-91 Warriors in action artwork $8
1991-92 ....$5
1992-93 ....$5
1993-94 ....$5
1994-95 ....$8

Rockets Media Guides
San Diego Rockets

1967-68 Team logo, basketball...................$35
1968-69 Team logo.....................................$35
1969-70 Elvin Hayes $25
1970-71 Elvin Hayes $20

Houston Rockets

1971-72 Rockets in action artwork............$20
1972-73 Rockets in action artwork............$20
1973-74 Mike Newlin, Rudy Tomjanovich...............$10
1974-75 Rudy Tomjanovich $10
1975-76 Mike Newlin...................................$10
1976-77 Calvin Murphy, Tom Nissalke $10
1977-78 John Lucas, Rudy Tomjanovich..................$10
1978-79 Rick Barry, Moses Malone,
  Rudy Tomjanovich....................................$10
1979-80 Moses Malone $10
1980-81 Rockets in action artwork............$10
1981-82 Moses Malone $10
1982-83 Elvin Hayes $10
1983-84 Ralph Sampson $10

1984-85 Bill Fitch, Hakeem Olajuwon,
  Ralph Sampson..$10
1985-86 Rodney McCray, Hakeem Olajuwon,
  Ralph Sampson..$10
1986-87 Hakeem Olajuwon, Robert Reid,
  Ralph Sampson..$10
1987-88 Hakeem Olajuwon $10
1988-89 Don Chaney, Rudy Tomjanovich $10
1989-90 Sleepy Floyd, Hakeem Olajuwon,
  Otis Thorpe..$10
1990-91 20th Anniversary logo $10
1991-92 ....$8
1992-93 ....$8
1993-94 ....$10
1994-95 ....$8

Houston Rockets Yearbooks

1991-92 ....$9
1993-94 ....$10

Indiana Pacers Media Guides

1968-69 Mel Daniels.................................$30
1969-70 Mel Daniels.................................$25
1970-71 Roger Brown................................$20
1971-72 Bob Leonard cartoon $20
1972-73 Mel Daniels, Bob Leonard,
  George McGinnis $20
1973-74 Three ABA trophies....................$20
1974-75 Market Square Arena.................$15
1975-76 Team logo....................................$10
1976-77 Billy Knight $10
1977-78 Bob Leonard, team logo $10

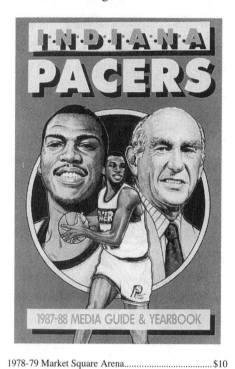

Indiana Pacers Yearbooks

Los Angeles Clippers Media Guides

Buffalo Braves

San Diego Clippers

Los Angeles Clippers

Los Angeles Lakers Media Guides

1975-76 Kareem Abdul-Jabbar.....................................$25
1976-77 Jerry West...$20
1977-78 Laker cheerleader in uniform #1 ....$20
1978-79 Kareem Abdul-Jabbar.....................................$20
1979-80 Kareem Abdul-Jabbar, Magic Johnson $20
1980-81 Kareem Abdul-Jabbar, Magic Johnson $20
1981-82 The Forum, artwork..$12
1982-83 Kareem Abdul-Jabbar, Magic Johnson,
    Norm Nixon $12
1983-84 The Forum $12
1984-85 Kareem Abdul-Jabbar.....................................$12
1985-86 Kareem Abdul-Jabbar,
    championship trophy...$12
1986-87 Chick Hearn...$12
1987-88 Kareem Abdul-Jabbar, Magic Johnson,
    James Worthy, trophy $12
1988-89 Kareem Abdul-Jabbar uniform, locker.........$12
1989-90 Magic Johnson...$12
1990-91 Magic Johnson, Sam Perkins, James Worthy......$12
1991-92 ....$10
1992-93 ....$10
1993-94 ....$10
1994-95 ....$10

Miami Heat Media Guides

1988-89 Team logo..$20
1989-90 Rory Sparrow with a fan $12
1990-91 House with basketball in the driveway.........$12
1991-92 ....$10
1992-93 ....$10
1993-94 ....$8
1994-95 ....$8

Milwaukee Bucks Media Guides

1968-69 Bucks vs. Royals, Wayne Embry $30
1969-70 Team logo..$25
1970-71 Kareem Abdul-Jabbar...................................$25
1971-72 Kareem Abdul-Jabbar...................................$25
1972-73 Kareem Abdul-Jabbar...................................$25
1973-74 Lucius Allen $20
1974-75 Kareem Abdul-Jabbar, city skyline.............$20
1975-76 Milwaukee Bucks vs. Chicago Bulls action .$15
1976-77 Gary Brokaw..$15
1977-78 Brian Winters...$15
1978-79 Marques Johnson artwork..............................$15
1979-80 Five starters artwork $8
1980-81 Team artwork...$8
1981-82 Sidney Moncrief $8
1982-83 Bucks artwork..$8
1983-84 Marques Johnson, Sidney Moncrief,
    Don Nelson..$6
1984-85 Sidney Moncrief $6
1985-86 Paul Pressey...$8
1986-87 Sidney Moncrief, city skyline.........................$8
1987-88 20th anniversary artwork $8
1988-89 Milwaukeee Bucks vs. Houston Rockets $8
1989-90 Del Harris $8
1990-91 Action photos...$8
1991-92 ....$8
1992-93 ....$8
1993-94 ....$8
1994-95 ....$8

Milwaukee Bucks Yearbooks

1991-92 ....$9

Minnesota Timberwolves
Media Guides

1989-90 Team logo..$12
1990-91 Timberwolves basketball.............................$12
1991-92 ....$10
1992-93 ....$10
1993-94 ....$8
1994-95 ....$8

Minnesota Timberwolves
Yearbooks

1989-90 Timberwolves uniform #1 ....$15
1990-91 Five starters...$10
1991-92 ....$7

New Jersey Nets Media Guides
New York Nets

1968-69 Nets in action .... $15-$25
1969-70 .... $10-$20
1970-71 Nets player in action .... $7-$10
1971-72 Rick Barry, others.................................. $8-$12
1972-73 Eastern Division Playoff Champions $30
1973-74 Julius Erving $30
1974-75 Dave DeBusschere, Rowe $20
1975-76 Julius Erving..$20
1976-77 Julius Erving..$15

1987-88
MEDIA GUIDE YEARBOOK

NEW YORK
KNICKERBOCKERS $5.00

Hustle
in the City

1987-88
YEARBOOK

New Jersey Nets

1977-78 State of New Jersey, artwork.........................$15
1978-79 Jordan, Bernard King, John Williamson $15
1979-80 "The Excitement is Building" $10
1980-81 "Up & Coming"...$10
1981-82 "A New Era" logo $10
1982-83 Darryl Dawkins, Mike Gminski....................$6
1983-84 Nets in action artwork $6
1984-85 Darryl Dawkins $6
1985-86 Buck Williams...$10
1986-87 Mike Gminski...$10
1987-88 Mike Gminski, Buck Williams,
        Orlando Woolridge..$10
1988-89 Donaldson, Reed, Buck Williams $10
1989-90 Roy Hinson...$10
1990-91 Nets in action artwork $8
1991-92..$8
1992-93..$8
1993-94..$8
1994-95..$8

New Jersey Nets Yearbooks

1974-75..$25
1975-76 Julius Erving, Bill Melchionni $25
1991-92..$9
1992-93..$9

New York Knicks Media Guides

1956-57..$95
1957-58..$95
1958-59..$75

1959-60..$75
1960-61..$75
1961-62..$75
1962-63..$65
1963-64..$65
1964-65..$35
1965-66..$$35
1966-67 Cartoon player $35
1967-68..$45
1968-69..$45
1969-70 Dave DeBusschere, Willis Reed..................$45
1970-71..$40
1971-72..$25
1972-73..$25
1973-74 Championship trophy $30
1974-75 Bill Bradley uniform....................................$20
1975-76..$15
1976-77..$15
1977-78 Willis Reed $15
1978-79 Earl Monroe, Marvin Webster.....................$10
1979-80 Bill Cartwright..$10
1980-81 Bill Cartwright, Red Holzman,
        Jerome Richardson $10
1981-82 City skyline...$10
1982-83 Hubie Brown...$10
1983-84 Knicks in action..$10
1984-85 Action artwork..$10
1985-86 Bill Cartwright, Patrick Ewing,
        Bernard King, others $10
1986-87 Uniforms, locker...$10
1987-88 Al Bianchi, Rick Pitino................................$10
1988-89 Patrick Ewing, Mark Jackson,
        Charles Oakley $10

1989-90 Patrick Ewing, Mark Jackson, Stu Jackson .. $10
1990-91 Patrick Ewing $10
1991-92 .... $8
1992-93 .... $8
1993-94 .... $8
1994-95 .... $9

New York Knicks Yearbooks

1991-92 .... $8

Orlando Magic Media Guides

1989-90 Magic artwork $20
1990-91 Matt Goukas $15
1991-92 .... $10
1992-93 .... $10
1993-94 .... $10
1994-95 .... $10

Orlando Magic Yearbooks

1991-92 .... $9
1993-94 .... $9

Philadelphia 76ers Media Guides

1966-67 .... $45
1967-68 Wilt Chamberlain, Billy Cunningham $45
1968-69 Hal Greer $45
1969-70 Billy Cunningham, Hal Greer $35
1970-71 Team pictures artwork $20
1971-72 Team mascot $20
1972-73 John Block, Bill Bridges, Fred Carter $20

1973-74 Gene Shue $20
1974-75 Billy Cunningham, Gene Shue $15
1975-76 Harvey Catchings, Billy Cunningham,
    George McGinnis $15
1976-77 Doug Collins, George McGinnis $15
1977-78 Julius Erving $15
1978-79 Doug Collins, Julius Erving, Bobby Jones ... $15
1979-80 Julius Erving $15
1980-81 76ers basketball $15
1981-82 Julius Erving, trophies $15
1982-83 Julius Erving $15
1983-84 Julius Erving, Moses Malone $10
1984-85 Julius Erving $10
1985-86 Moses Malone $10
1986-87 Charles Barkley $10
1987-88 Maurice Cheeks, 25th Anniversary $10
1988-89 Charles Barkley, Maurice Cheeks $10
1989-90 Charles Barkley $10
1990-91 Charles Barkley $10
1991-92 .... $10
1992-93 .... $10
1993-94 .... $10
1994-95 .... $10

Philadelphia 76ers Yearbooks

1992-93 .... $9

Phoenix Suns Media Guides

1968-69 Team logo, year $35
1969-70 Team logo, year $35
1970-71 Team logo, year $20
1971-72 Connie Hawkins $20

Yearbooks/media guides

1972-73 Suns in action $20
1973-74 Charlie Scott, Neil Walk $15
1974-75 Team logo, year $15
1975-76 Team logo, year..$15
1976-77 Alvan Adams...$10
1977-78 Paul Westphal...$10
1978-79 Walter Davis, Ron Lee, Paul Westphal........$10
1979-80 John MacLeod $10
1980-81 Alvan Adams..$8
1981-82 Computer graphics picture $8
1982-83 Basketball...$6
1983-84 Larry Nance...$6
1984-85 Walter Davis...$6
1985-86 "Catch our Fire," team logo $8
1986-87 Suns artwork...$10
1987-88 Suns basketball...$10
1988-89 Tom Chambers, Jeff Hornacek, others.........$10
1989-90 Tom Chambers, Cotton Fitzsimmons,
      Kevin Johnson..$10
1990-91 Suns basketball...$10
1991-92 ....$10
1992-93 ....$10
1993-94 ....$10
1994-95 ....$10

1974-75 Bill Walton $20
1975-76 Lenny Steele $15
1976-77 Bill Walton $15
1977-78 Bill Walton, NBA Champs.............................$15
1978-79 Maurice Lucas $10
1979-80 Jack Ramsey, Bill Walton $10
1980-81 Billy Bates $10
1981-82 Jim Paxson...$10
1982-83 Mychal Thompson...$10
1983-84 Calvin Natt...$10
1984-85 Sam Bowie, Kiki Vandeweghe.......................$10
1985-86 Clyde Drexler $10
1986-87 Kiki Vandeweghe $10
1987-88 Steve Johnson $10
1988-89 Kevin Duckworth $10
1989-90 Rick Adelman, 20th anniversary $10
1990-91 Western Conference Champions $10
1991-92 ....$8
1992-93 ....$8
1993-94 ....$8
1994-95 ....$8

Sacramento Kings Media Guides

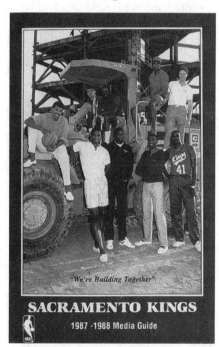

Portland Trailblazers Media Guides

1970-71 Rick Adelman...$25
1971-72 Geoff Petrie $25
1972-73 Sidney Wicks $20
1973-74 Jack McCloskey $20

Cincinnati Royals

1957-58 World wearing a Royals crown $100
1958-59 Basketball wearing a Royals crown...........$100
1959-60 Basketball wearing a Royals crown.............$75
1960-61 Team mascot cartoon....................................$75
1961-62 Team mascot, snake charmer.......................$75
1962-63 Team mascot, with briefcase $75
1963-64 ....$75

174

1964-65 ....$75
1965-66 ....$75
1966-67 ....$75
1967-68 Ed Tucker art $75
1968-69 Oscar Robertson, Wilt Chamberlain $75
1969-70 Bob Cousy $75
1970-71 Nate Archibald, Tom Van Ardsdale,
    Norm Van Lier $25
1971-72 Royals patch $25

Kansas City-Omaha Kings

1972-73 Team logo $35
1973-74 Nate Archibald, Bob Cousy $25
1974-75 Phil Johnson, artwork $20

Kansas City Kings

1975-76 Nate Archibald, Phil Johnson $15
1976-77 Five starters $15
1977-78 Lucius Allen, Otis Birdsong, Tom Burleson $10
1978-79 Team logo $10
1979-80 Team logo, player $8
1980-81 Scott Wedman, Reggie King $8
1981-82 Phil Ford $8
1982-83 Axelson, Fitzsimmons, scoreboard $6
1983-84 Team logo $6
1984-85 Team photo $6

Sacramento Kings

1985-86 Team logo $6
1986-87 Kings fans in crowd $8
1987-88 "We're Building Together" $8
1988-89 Kenny Smith $8
1989-90 Danny Ainge, Rodney McCray,
    Wayman Tisdale $8
1990-91 Anthony Bonner, Lionel Simmons, others $8
1991-92 ....$8
1992-93 ....$8
1993-94 ....$8
1994-95 ....$8

San Antonio Spurs Media Guides

1973-74 Hemisfair Arena $20
1974-75 Team logo $15
1975-76 George Gervin, James Silas, others $15
1976-77 James Silas $10
1977-78 George Gervin $10
1978-79 Billy Paultz $10
1979-80 Team logo $10
1980-81 Stan Albeck $8
1981-82 George Gervin, "Bruise Brothers" $8
1982-83 George Gervin, Artis Gilmore,
    Mike Mitchell $6
1983-84 Artis Gilmore $6
1984-85 Cotton Fitzsimmons $6
1985-86 Mike Mitchell $8
1986-87 Alvin Robertson $8
1987-88 Johnny Moore, Alvin Robertson $8
1988-89 Larry Brown $8
1989-90 Terry Cummings, Sean Elliott,
    David Robinson $10
1990-91 David Robinson $8

1991-92 ....$8
1992-93 ....$8
1993-94 ....$8
1994-95 ....$8

Seattle Supersonics Media Guides

1967-68 Team name, year $35
1968-69 Bob Rule, Tom Meschery, Rod Thorn $30
1969-70 Lenny Wilkens $25
1970-71 Basketball, year $20
1971-72 Sonics in action $20
1972-73 Spencer Haywood $20
1973-74 City skyline $15
1974-75 Fred Brown, Bill Russell, Slick Watts $15
1975-76 Photo montage $10
1976-77 Sonics basketball $10
1977-78 "Great Stuff!" $10
1978-79 John Johnson, Jack Sikma $10
1979-80 Dennis Johnson $8
1980-81 Lonnie Shelton $8
1981-82 Jack Sikma $8
1982-83 Gus Williams $6
1983-84 Fred Brown $6
1984-85 Team logo $6
1985-86 Sonics artwork $10
1986-87 Tom Chambers, Xavier McDaniel $10
1987-88 Bernie Bickerstaff $10
1988-89 Sonics equipment, locker $10
1989-90 Derrick McKey $10
1990-91 K.C. Jones $10

1991-92	$8		1992-93	$8
1992-93	$8		1993-94	$8
1993-94	$8		1994-95	$8
1994-95	$8			

Seattle Supersonics Yearbooks

1993-94 ....$9

Utah Jazz Media Guides
New Orleans Jazz

1974-75 New Orleans scene, logo..............................$20
1975-76 ....$20
1976-77 Pete Maravich..$15
1977-78 ....$10
1978-79 Pete Maravich, Leonard Robinson $10

Utah Jazz

1979-80 Salt Palace $8
1980-81 Adrian Dantley, Tom Nissalke......................$8
1981-82 Adrian Dantley $8
1982-83 Adrian Dantley, Darrell Griffith,
    Frank Layden $8
1983-84 Mark Eaton, Rickey Green $6
1984-85 "A Winning Combination"..............................$6
1985-86 Thurl Bailey, Karl Malone, John Stockton...$10
1986-87 Mark Eaton $10
1987-88 Thurl Bailey, Mark Eaton, Karl Malone $10
1988-89 Karl Malone, 10th Anniversary....................$10
1989-90 Team logo..$10
1990-91 Jerry Sloan photos $10
1991-92 ....$8

Washington Bullets Media Guides
Baltimore Bullets

1964-65 Gus Johnson..$40
1965-66 Media equipment $35
1966-67 Media equipment $35
1967-68 20th anniversary of basketball in Baltimore.$35
1968-69 Bullets in action $35
1969-70 Earl Monroe, Gene Shue, Wes Unseld........$30
1970-71 Wes Unseld...$30
1971-72 Team artwork..$20
1972-73 Bullets in action $20

Washington Bullets

1973-74 K.C. Jones, five starters $20
1974-75 Elvin Hayes..$15
1975-76 Phil Chenier, Elvin Hayes, Wes Unseld.......$15
1976-77 Dick Motta...$10
1977-78 Elvin Hayes, Mitch Kupchak,
    Wes Unseld, others $10
1978-79 "The Fat Lady Sang," NBA Champions $10
1979-80 Championship trophy $8
1980-81 Elvin Hayes, Kevin Porter, Gene Shue,
    Wes Unseld..$8
1981-82 Action photos...$8
1982-83 Greg Ballard, J. Lucas, Jeff Ruland...............$8
1983-84 Rick Mahorn, Jeff Ruland $8
1984-85 Greg Ballard, Rick Mahorn, Jeff Ruland........$8

Bullets
1987-88
Washington Bullets Media Guide

1985-86 Action artwork $8
1986-87 Moses Malone $8
1987-88 Moses Malone, Washington Monument $8
1988-89 Wes Unseld $8
1989-90 Tom Hammonds, Bernard King, Wes Unseld $8
1990-91 Tom Hammonds, Bernard King, Wes Unseld $8
1991-92 .... $8
1992-93 .... $8
1993-94 .... $8
1994-95 .... $8

Washington Bullets Yearbooks

1974-75 See media guides.
1988-89 Wes Unseld .... $7-$10
1989-90 Wes Unseld .... $7-$10

Hockey

Anaheim Mighty Ducks

1993-94 .... $12
1994-95 .... $8

Boston Bruins Media Guides

1946-47 .... $150
1947-48 .... $125
1948-49 .... $100
1949-50 .... $75
1950-51 .... $50
1951-52 Team logo and year $50
1952-53 Bear's head artwork $50
1953-54 Bear's head artwork $50

1954-55 Bear's head artwork $50
1955-56 Bruins name and year $50
1956-57 Bruins name and year $50
1957-58 Bruins name and year $50
1958-59 Bruins name and year $50
1959-60 Bear cartoon $40
1960-61 Bruin cartoon $30
1961-62 Bruins mascot and year $30
1962-63 Wayne Connelly $30
1963-64 John Bucyk $75
1964-65 Gary Dornhofer, Bobby Leiter $50
1965-66 Ed Johnston $50
1966-67 Murray Oliver $45
1967-68 Bobby Orr $60
1968-69 Bruins action vs. Montreal Canadiens $45
1969-70 Esposito, Ken Hodge vs.
    Chicago Blackhawks $45
1970-71 Bruins vs. Chicago Blackhawks $45
1971-72 Pregame anthems with Montreal Canadiens $40
1972-73 Stanley Cup trophy $40
1973-74 50th Anniversary with Esposito, Bobby Orr $30
1974-75 John Bucyk $30
1975-76 Terry O'Reilly $25
1976-77 Don Cherry, Park, Ratelle $25
1977-78 Gerry Cheevers $25
1978-79 Bob Schmautz $15
1979-80 Rick Middleton $15
1980-81 Ray Bourque $12
1981-82 Wayne Cashman $12
1982-83 Steve Kasper with the Selke Trophy $9
1983-84 60th Anniversary, Peter Peeters
    with the Vezina Trophy $9
1984-85 Barry Pederson $9
1985-86 Bruins hockey pucks $9
1986-87 Gord Kluzak $9
1987-88 Ray Bourque with the Norris Trophy $9
1988-89 Cam Neely $9
1989-90 Rejean Lemelin, Andy Moog $9
1990-91 Team artwork $9
1991-92 .... $9
1992-93 .... $9
1993-94 .... $9
1994-95 .... $8

Boston Bruins Yearbooks

1970-71 .... $45
1971-72 .... $45
1972-73 .... $40
1974-75 .... $35
1975-76 .... $30
1976-77 .... $25
1989-90 .... $15

Buffalo Sabres Media Guides

1970-71 Team logo and year $85
1971-72 Action photo $30
1972-73 Roger Crozier $25
1973-74 Gil Perreault $25
1974-75 Richard Martin $20
1975-76 Rene Robert $20
1976-77 Danny Gare $15
1977-78 Gerry Desjardins $15

1978-79 Don Edwards $10
1979-80 Craig Ramsay $9
1980-81 Danny Gare...$9
1981-82 Danny Gare, others...$9
1982-83 Gil Perreault $9
1983-84 Mike Ramsey...$9
1984-85 Tom Barrasso $9
1985-86 Tom Barrasso, Bob Sauve $9
1986-87 Sabres in action $9
1987-88 Team logo and bench $9
1988-89 Tom Barrasso $9
1989-90 Phil Housley $9
1990-91 Pierre Turgeon..$9
1991-92 ....$9
1992-93 ....$9
1993-94 ....$9
1994-95 ....$8

Buffalo Sabres Yearbooks

1974-75...$40
1975-76...$35
1976-77...$20
1978-79...$20
1979-80...$20

Calgary Flames Media Guides
Atlanta Flames

1972-73 Team logo...$45
1973-74 Team logo, Phil Myre...................................$35
1974-75...$30
1975-76 Team logo, photos $20
1976-77 Daniel Bouchard...$20
1977-78 Tom Lysiak, Willi Plett, Eric Vail $20
1978-79 Team uniform, puck, equipment $20
1979-80 Guy Chouinard $20

Calgary Flames

1980-81 Team logo...$20
1981-82 Kent Nilsson...$12
1982-83 Team logo..$6
1983-84 Lanny McDonald..$10
1984-85 Lanny McDonald..$10
1985-86 Goalie gloves a puck $8
1986-87 Campbell Conference trophy........................$9
1987-88 Joe Mullen $9
1988-89 Hakan Loob, Joe Nieuwendyk $9
1989-90 Stanley Cup trophy...$9
1990-91 Al MacInnis, Sergei Makarov $9
1991-92...$9
1992-93 ....$9
1993-94...$9
1994-95...$8

Chicago Blackhawks
Media Guides

1960-61 ....$75
1961-62...$50
1962-63...$45
1963-64...$45
1964-65...$45

1965-66 ....$45
1966-67 ....$45
1967-68 Bobby Hull, Stan Mikita, Arthur Wirtz........$45
1968-69 Bobby Hull, Stan Mikita, William Wirtz $45
1969-70 Team logo and year $30
1970-71 Team mascot, Wales Trophy.......................$30
1971-72 Team logo and year,
    Western Division Champions............................$30
1972-73 Team mascot...$25
1973-74 Team logo, artwork.......................................$25
1974-75 Team artwork..$25
1975-76 50th Anniversary artwork............................$25
1976-77 Team logo and year $15
1977-78 Team logo, artwork.......................................$15
1978-79 Team logo and crossed sticks $15
1979-80 Team logo...$15
1980-81 Tony Esposito, others $12
1981-82 Denis Savard, Darryl Sutter.........................$12
1982-83 Doug Wilson and Norris Trophy $4
1983-84 Celebration photos..$9
1984-85 Denis Savard, Al Secord, others...................$9
1985-86 "Chicago has Fans" slogan $9
1986-87 Robert Murray, Denis Savard, Al Secord......$9
1987-88 Bob Murdock, other coaches........................$9
1988-89 Denis Savard photos and locker $9
1989-90 Celebration photos..$9
1990-91 All-Star Game logo..$9
1991-92...$9
1992-93 Clarence S. Campbell bowl $9
1992-93 ....$9
1993-94 ....$9
1994-95 ....$8

Colorado Rockies Media Guides

1976-77 Team logo...$40
1977-78 Mountains photo, team logo $35
1978-79 Mountains, stream, team logo......................$25
1979-80 Don Cherry $25
1980-81 Lanny McDonald...$30
1981-82 Action photos, team logo.............................$40
    became New Jersey Devils in 1982-83

Dallas North Stars Media Guides
as Minnesota

1967-68 Team logo...$35
1968-69 Cesare Maniago $35
1969-70 Danny Grant, Calder Trophy $35
1970-71 Danny O'Shea $25
1971-72 North Stars vs. Boston Bruins $25
1972-73 Cesare Maniago, Gump Worsley...................$25
1973-74 Dennis Hextall $25
1974-75 Bill Goldsworthy $20
1975-76 North Stars in action $15
1976-77 North Stars vs. Calgary Flames $15
1977-78 Rolie Eriksson, Steve Jensen, Alex Pirus,
    Glen Sharpley...$15
1978-79 North Stars uniforms $15
1979-80 Action artwork...$12
1980-81 Al MacAdam, Steve Payne...........................$12
1981-82 Don Beaupre, others $12
1982-83 Celebrating vs. St. Louis Blues $9

1983-84 John Mariucci artwork...................................$9
1984-85 Neal Broten..$9
1985-86 A. Shaver, action photos...............................$9
1986-87 Neal Broten with trophies...............................$9
1987-88 Dino Ciccarelli $9
1988-89 Celebration photo $9
1989-90 Player in action...$9
1990-91 Brian Bellows, Neal Broten, Jon Casey $9
1991-92...$9
1992-93 ....$9

As Dallas

1993-94...$12
1994-95...$8

Detroit Red Wings Media Guides

1960-61 Cartoon $125
1961-62...$100
1962-63 Team logos $100
1963-64...$100
1964-65...$75
1965-66...$75
1966-67 Roger Crozier, Alex Delvecchio,
   Gordie Howe $75
1967-68...$65
1968-69 Gordie Howe $65
1969-70...$50
1970-71 Gordie Howe $50
1971-72 Alex Delvecchio $30
1972-73 Alex Delvecchio $30
1973-74 Alex Delvecchio, Mickey Redmond $30
1974-75 Alex Delvecchio $20
1975-76 Goalie mask...$20
1976-77 50th Anniversary photos $15
1977-78 Goalie mask, logos $15
1978-79 Action photos with headlines $15
1979-80 Olympia Stadium, Joe Louis Arena $15
1980-81 Red Wings in action $15
1981-82 Reed Larson...$15
1982-83 Team artwork $9
1983-84 Goalie net, team jersey $9
1984-85 Team logo, action photos $9
1985-86 John Ogrodnick $9
1986-87 Jacques Demers, Petr Klima,
   Steve Yzerman $9
1987-88 Jacques Demers, celebration photos.............$9
1988-89 Jacques Demers, Gerard Gallant,
   Steve Yzerman $9
1989-90 Team logo and management...........................$9
1990-91 Shawn Burr, Steve Yzerman $9
1991-92...$9
1992-93 Yves Racine, Paul Ysebaert, others...............$9
1993-94...$9
1994-95...$8

Detroit Red Wings Yearbooks

1968-69 ....$65
1969-70 ....$65

Edmonton Oilers Media Guides

1975-76 Fight vs. Cleveland $50
1976-77 Oilers in action...$40
1977-78 ....$40
1978-79 Dave Dryden, Hamilton.................................$40
1979-80 Dave Dryden, Wayne Gretzky.......................$40
1980-81 Wayne Gretzky, Blair McDonald.................$35
1981-82 Wayne Gretzky, Andy Moog.........................$35
1982-83 Oilers puck...$20
1983-84 Mark Messier, Andy Moog $20
1984-85 Team uniforms, Stanley Cup.........................$20
1985-86 Wayne Gretzky with trophies.......................$25
1986-87 Paul Coffey, Wayne Gretzky
   with trophies..$12
1987-88 Wayne Gretzky, Stanley Cup
   celebration $12
1988-89 10th Anniversary logo $12
1989-90 Team logo $12
1990-91 Mark Messier, trophy $12
1991-92..$12
1992-93 Stanley Cup memorabilia $12
1993-94..$12
1994-95..$8

New England Whalers

1972-73 ....$45
1973-74 Ted Green with WHA trophy $40
1974-75 Al Smith, Hartford Civic Center.................$40

Hartford Whalers

1975-76 Number "5" with Whaler photos $35
1976-77 Rick Ley, Webster, others $35
1977-78 ....$30
1978-79 Gordie Howe..$25
1979-80 Rick Ley $25
1980-81 Dave Keon $10
1981-82 Larry Pleau $10
1982-83 Whalers pucks...$10
1983-84 Ron Francis, Johnson,
   Blaine Stoughton $10
1984-85 Team logo, Greg Millen $10
1985-86 Ron Francis...$10
1986-87 Kevin Dineen, Ron Francis,
   Mike Liut...$10
1987-88 Mike Liut $10
1988-89 Ulf Samuelsson, Dave Tippett.....................$10
1989-90 Kevin Dineen $10
1990-91 Ron Francis...$10
1991-92 ....$10
1992-93 Team jersey...$10
1993-94..$8
1994-95..$8

Los Angeles Kings Media Guides

1966-67 ....$75
1967-68 ....$75
1968-69 Kings artwork $50
1969-70 Gerry Desjardins...$40
1970-71 Team logo $35
1971-72 Bob Pulford...$25
1972-73 Butch Goring $25

1973-74 "Go Kings" artwork.....................................$20
1974-75 Butch Goring $15
1975-76 Marcel Dionne, Bob Pulford, Rogie Vachon$15
1976-77 Butch Goring $15
1977-78 Marcel Dionne, Butch Goring,
   Rogie Vachon...$15
1978-79 Marcel Dionne...$15
1979-80 Marcel Dionne, Butch Goring, Dave Taylor,
Rogie Vachon $15
1980-81 Marcel Dionne, Charlie Simmer,
   Dave Taylor...$15
1981-82 Mario Lessard..$9
1982-83 Steve Bozek $9
1983-84 Marcel Dionne jersey, photos........................$9
1984-85 Pat Quinn, Rogie Vachon $9
1985-86 Marcel Dionne, Bernie Nicholls,
   Dave Taylor, others...$9
1986-87 20th Anniversary logo $9
1987-88 Bernie Nicholls, Luc Robitaille, others $9
1988-89 Wayne Gretzky, Luc Robitaille.......................$9
1989-90 Team logo $9
1990-91 Fan photos, team logo $9
1991-92 ....$9
1992-93 ....$9
1993-94 ....$9
1994-95 ....$8

Montreal Canadiens Media Guides

1953-54 Team logo...$150
1954-55 Team logo...$125
1955-56 Team logo...$75
1956-57 ....$40
1957-58 ....$30
1958-59 ....$25
1959-60 ....$25
1960-61 ....$25
1961-62 ....$125
1962-63 Claude Provost, Henri Richard..................$100
1963-64 ....$45
1964-65 ....$45
1965-66 ....$45
1966-67 ....$45
1967-68 ....$45
1968-69 ....$45
1969-70 ....$45
1970-71 Team artwork $30
1971-72 Team logo...$30
1972-73 Team logo...$30
1973-74 Team artwork $30
1974-75 50th Anniversary artwork.............................$15
1975-76 Scotty Bowman, Guy Lafleur,
   Pollock...$15
1976-77 Yvan Cournoyer, Ken Dryden,
   Guy Lafleur $15
1977-78 Serge Savard..$15
1978-79 Yvan Cournoyer $15
1979-80 Serge Savard..$15
1980-81 Guy Lafleur, Pierre Larouche.......................$15
1981-82 Bob Gainey..$12
1982-83 Guy Lafleur, others..$12
1983-84 Mario Tremblay..$12

1984-85 Guy Carbonneau $12
1985-86 Steve Penney...$12
1986-87 Stanley Cup celebration..................................$12
1987-88 Mats Naslund...$12
1988-89 Mats Nasland, Stephane Richer,
   Patrick Roy, others $12
1989-90 Stanley Cup celebration..................................$12
1990-91 Stephane Richer, Patrick Roy.......................$12
1991-92 ....$12
1992-93 Patrick Roy $12
1993-94 ....$12
1994-95 ....$8

New Jersey Devils Media Guides

1982-83 Devils artwork $20
1983-84 Team in tuxes...$12
1984-85 Mel Bridgman..$12
1985-86 Greg Adams, Tim Higgins,
   Douglas Sulliman $12
1986-87 Kirk Muller...$12
1987-88 Devils' kids' artwork $12
1988-89 Aaron Broten, Kirk Muller $12
1989-90 Sean Burke...$12
1990-91 John MacLean...$12
1991-92 ....$12
1992-93 ....$12
1993-94 ....$12
1994-95 ....$8

New York Islanders Media Guides

1972-73 Team logo...$45
1973-74 Billy Harris $30
1974-75 Syl Apps, Denis Potvin....................................$30
1975-76 ....$30
1976-77 Denis Potvin, Chico Resch $30
1977-78 Ed Westfall..$25
1978-79 Mike Bossy..$25
1979-80 Bryan Trottier $25
1980-81 Stanley Cup Champions $20
1981-82 Stanley Cup Champions $15
1982-83 Bryan Trottier with the Stanley Cup.............$12
1983-84 Denis Potvin, Billy Smith, John Tonelli,
   Bryan Trottier..$12
1984-85 Mike Bossy 400th goal $12
1985-86 Mike Bossy, Brent Sutter, John Tonelli,
   Bryan Trottier..$12
1986-87 Al Arbour, Terry Simpson................................$12
1987-88 ....$12
1988-89 Pat LaFontaine, Bryan Trottier, others $12
1989-90 David Volek...$12
1990-91 Pat LaFontaine $12
1991-92 ....$12
1992-93 "The New Ice Age" $9
1993-94 ....$9
1994-95 ....$8

New York Islanders Media Guides

1972-73 Team logo...$45
1973-74 Billy Harris $30
1974-75 Syl Apps, Denis Potvin....................................$30
1975-76 ....$30

1976-77 Denis Potvin, Chico Resch $30
1977-78 Ed Westfall $25
1978-79 Mike Bossy $25
1979-80 Bryan Trottier $25
1980-81 Stanley Cup Champions $20
1981-82 Stanley Cup Champions $15
1982-83 Bryan Trottier with the Stanley Cup $12
1983-84 Denis Potvin, Billy Smith, John Tonelli,
   Bryan Trottier $12
1984-85 Mike Bossy 400th goal $12
1985-86 Mike Bossy, Brent Sutter, John Tonelli,
   Bryan Trottier $12
1986-87 Al Arbour, Terry Simpson $12
1987-88 .... $12
1988-89 Pat LaFontaine, Bryan Trottier, others $12
1989-90 David Volek $12
1990-91 Pat LaFontaine $12
1991-92 .... $12
1992-93 "The New Ice Age" $9
1993-94 .... $9
1994-95 .... $8

New York Islanders Yearbooks

1972-73 (without poster) $50
1972-73 (with poster) $75
1974-75 .... $40
1975-76 .... $35
1976-77 .... $30
1977-78 .... $30
1978-79 .... $30
1979-80 .... $30
1982-83 .... $30
1985-86 .... $20
1986-87 .... $20
1988-89 .... $20
1989-90 .... $20

New York Rangers Media Guides

1947-48 "Inside the Blue Shirt" $200
1948-49 Buddy O'Connor $175
1949-50 Edgar Laprade $125
1950-51 Chuck Rayner, 25th Anniversary $125
1951-52 Don Raleigh $75
1952-53 .... $50
1953-54 .... $50
1954-55 Muzz Patrick, Ivan Irwin $50
1955-56 .... $40
1956-57 .... $40
1957-58 .... $40
1958-59 .... $40
1959-60 .... $40
1960-61 .... $40
1961-62 .... $40
1962-63 .... $40
1963-64 Jacques Plante $40
1964-65 Rod Gilbert $40
1965-66 Harry Howell vs. Stan Mikita $40
1966-67 Bob Nevin $40
1967-68 Ed Giacomin $40
1968-69 Jean Ratelle $40
1969-70 Arnie Brown vs. Bobby Hull $35
1970-71 Ed Giacomin, Brad Park $35

1971-72 Ed Giacomin, Gilles Villemure $30
1972-73 Vic Hadfield 50th goal $30
1973-74 Ed Giacomin $30
1974-75 Ted Irvine, Brad Park $25
1975-76 50th Anniversary logo $25
1976-77 Rangers jersey artwork $20
1977-78 Phil Esposito, others $20
1978-79 Fred Shero $20
1979-80 John Davidson $15
1980-81 Rangers in action $15
1981-82 Rangers in action $10
1982-83 Rangers in action $6
1983-84 Madison Square Garden $10
1984-85 Team jersey $6
1985-86 Empire State Building $10
1986-87 Statue of Liberty $10
1987-88 Jean-Claude Bergeron, Phil Esposito $10
1988-89 Rangers in action $10
1989-90 Tony Granato, Brian Leetch $10
1990-91 Mike Gartner, Brian Leetch, Bernie Nicholls. $9
1991-92 Brian Leetch, Mike Richter, former Rangers . $9
1992-93 .... $9
1993-94 .... $9
1994-95 .... $8

Seals Media Guides
Oakland Seals

1968-69 Seals in action $35
1969-70 Seals artwork $25
1970-71 Team artwork $20

California Golden Seals

1971-72 Seals artwork $15
1972-73 Seals artwork $10
1973-74 Seals artwork $10
1974-75 .... $10
1975-76 Seals in action $10

Philadelphia Flyers Media Guides

1967-68 Team artwork $35
1968-69 Campbell Trophy $35
1969-70 Flyers artwork $35
1970-71 Team logo, NHL pucks $30
1971-72 TV camera $30
1972-73 Dan Earle, G. Hart $30
1973-74 Flyers artwork $25
1974-75 Stanley Cup artwork $25
1975-76 Trophies $20
1976-77 Bill Barber, Bobby Clarke, Reggie Leach $20
1977-78 Flyers equipment $20
1978-79 Flyers artwork $20
1979-80 Action photos $6
1980-81 Team logo, photos $15
1981-82 Players' faces $15
1982-83 Action photos $6
1983-84 Bobby Clarke $10
1984-85 Brian Propp $10
1985-86 Pelle Lindbergh $10
1986-87 Mark Howe $10
1987-88 Ron Hextall $10
1988-89 Flyers artwork $10

1989-90 Flyers artwork	$10
1990-91 Team equipment	$9
1991-92	$9
1992-93 Eric Lindros, others	$10
1993-94	$9
1994-95	$8

Philadelphia Flyers Yearbooks

1973-74	$20
1974-75	$35
1975-76	$35
1976-77	$35
1978-79	$25
1981-82	$25

Pittsburgh Penguins Media Guides

1968-69 Les Binkley	$40
1969-70 Team artwork	$40
1970-71 Red Kelly	$40
1971-72 Team logo	$35
1972-73 Team logo	$35
1973-74 Ken Schinkel	$20
1974-75 Syl Apps	$15
1975-76 Ron Schock	$20
1976-77 Syl Apps, Jean Pronovost, Pierre Larouche	$20
1977-78 Syl Apps	$20
1978-79 Orest Kindrachuk	$20
1979-80 Randy Carlyle, George Ferguson	$6
1980-81 Rick Kehoe	$15
1981-82 Randy Carlyle, Rick Kehoe	$15
1982-83 Michael Dion	$6
1983-84 Goal celebration	$10
1984-85 Mike Bullard	$10
1985-86 Mario Lemieux	$10
1986-87 Team memorabilia	$10
1987-88 Mario Lemieux	$10
1988-89 Mario Lemieux	$10
1989-90 Tom Barrasso, Rob Brown, Paul Coffey, Mario Lemieux	$10
1990-91 Scotty Bowman, Bob Johnson, Craig Patrick	$9
1991-92	$9
1992-93	$9
1993-94	$9
1994-95	$8

Quebec Nordiques Media Guides

1974-75	$30
1975-76	$25
1976-77 Nordiques fleur-de-lis logo	$25
1977-78	$25
1978-79	$25
1979-80 Nordiques art	$20
1980-81 Nordiques art	$15
1981-82 Anton and Peter Stastny	$15
1982-83 Nordiques art	$12
1983-84 Michel Goulet, Dale Hunter, Anton and Peter Stastny, others	$12
1984-85 Nordiques memorabilia	$10
1985-86 Nordiques art	$10

1986-87 Team logo	$10
1987-88 Nordiques in action	$10
1988-89 Goal celebration	$10
1989-90 Media equipment	$10
1990-91 Guy Lafleur, MichelPetit, Joe Sakic	$10
1991-92	$10
1992-93 Owen Nolan, Joe Sakic, Mats Sundin	$10
1993-94	$10
1994-95	$8

San Jose Sharks Media Guides

1991-92	$15
1992-93 Die cut shark fin	$15
1993-94	$12
1994-95	$8

St. Louis Blues Media Guides

1967-68 Keenan, Martin, Schock, others	$40
1968-69 Glenn Hall	$35
1969-70 Vezina and Campbell trophies	$35
1970-71 Campbell Trophy	$35
1971-72 Team action photos	$35
1972-73 St. Louis Arena	$35
1973-74 Action photos	$30
1974-75 Andy Hebenton, Garry Unger	$25
1975-76 Gratton, Glenn Hall, Eddie Johnston, others	$25
1976-77 Emile Francis	$20
1977-78 Team artwork	$15
1978-79 Team artwork	$15
1979-80 Ed Staniowski	$10
1980-81 Team art	$15
1981-82 Mike Liut	$9
1982-83 Emile Francis	$9
1983-84 Brian Sutter	$9
1984-85 Team jersey	$9
1985-86 Team logo	$9
1986-87 Team memorabilia	$9
1987-88 Team artwork	$9
1988-89 Berry, Micheletti, Brian Sutter	$9
1989-90 Dan Kelly	$9
1990-91 Brett Hull, Rick Meagher	$9
1991-92	$9
1992-93 Brett Hull	$9
1993-94	$9
1994-95	$8

St. Louis Blues Yearbooks

1968-69	$65
1969-70	$50
1970-71	$45

Tampa Bay Lightning Media Guides

1992-93	$15
1993-94	$10
1994-95	$8

Toronto Maple Leafs Media Guides

1962-63 George Armstrong..$75
1963-64 Frank Mahovlich $75
1964-65 Action photos $75
1965-66 Johnny Bower..$75
1966-67 Dave Keon $60
1967-68 Dave Keon $60
1968-69 ....$50
1969-70 Maple Leafs in action $50
1970-71 Maple Leafs artwork $45
1971-72 Maple Leafs artwork $20
1972-73 Maple Leafs Garden, team logo $20
1973-74..$20
1974-75 Team logo..$15
1975-76 Team logo..$15
1976-77 Borje Salming, Darryl Sittler, others............$15
1977-78 Tim Horton, Borge Salming,
    Darryl Sittler, others..$15
1978-79 Darryl Sittler..$15
1979-80 Borje Salming..$15
1980-81 Borje Salming..$15
1981-82 50th Anniversary photos $9
1982-83 Rick Vaive 50th goal $9
1983-84 Gaston Gingras, Rick Vaive,
    Walt Poddubny, others..$9
1984-85 Allen Bester, Rick Vaive..............................$9
1985-86 Maple Leafs in action $9
1986-87 Goal celebration $9
1987-88 Wendell Clark..$9
1988-89 Team logo..$9
1989-90 Vincent Damphousse....................................$9
1990-91 Vincent Damphousse, Gary Leeman,
    Ed Olczyk..$6
1991-92 ....$9
1992-93 ....$9
1993-94 ....$9
1994-95 ....$8

Vancouver Canucks Media Guides

1970-71 Team logo, action photo $60
1971-72 Team logo, action artwork............................$50
1972-73 Team logo..$45
1973-74 Team puck, stick..$25
1974-75 Celebration vs. Chicago Blackhawks...........$20
1975-76 Team artwork $20
1976-77 Action photos $20
1977-78 Don Lever, others $15
1978-79 New team logo..$15
1979-80 Glen Hanlon $15
1980-81 Canucks vs. Minnesota North Stars $9
1981-82 Darcy Rota vs. Capitals................................$9
1982-83 Fans celebrating..$9
1983-84 Action photos $9
1984-85 Team logo..$9
1985-86 Canucks new uniform artwork $9
1986-87 Action photos $9
1987-88 Brian Burke, Bob McCammon, Pat Quinn.....$9
1988-89 Stan Smyl $9
1989-90 Trevor Linden..$9
1990-91 Team jerseys, equipment..............................$9
1991-92 ....$9

Washington Capitals Media Guides

1974-75 Team locker room..$60
1975-76 Ron Low $50
1976-77 Tony White..$25
1977-78 Team artwork..$25
1978-79 Guy Charron $25
1979-80 Ryan Walter..$9
1980-81 Mike Gartner, Dennis Maruk,
    Ryan Walter, others..$20
1981-82 Mike Palmateer..$20
1982-83 Dennis Maruk $9
1983-84 Rod Langway..$12
1984-85 Rod Langway, others......................................$9
1985-86 Bobby Carpenter, Mike Gartner $9
1986-87 Capital building, team puck............................$9
1987-88 Bobby Gould, Larry Murphy..........................$9
1988-89 15th Anniversary, Scott Stevens....................$9
1989-90 Dino Ciccarelli, Russ Courtnall,
    Mike Ridley..$9
1990-91 John Druce, Rod Langway $9
1991-92 ....$9
1992-93 Dale Hunter..$9
1993-94 ....$9
1994-95 ....$8

Winnipeg Jets Media Guides

1972-73 ....$35
1973-74 ....$25
1974-75 ....$25
1975-76 Jets team photos..$25
1976-77 ....$25
1977-78 ....$25
1978-79 WHA Championship trophy........................$25
1979-80 Lars-Erik Sjoberg with WHA trophy $20
1980-81 Dave Christian $20
1981-82 Dave Babych..$15
1982-83 Dale Hawerchuk, Calder Trophy....................$9
1983-84 Dale Hawerchuk, others..............................$15
1984-85 Laurie Boschman, Randy Carlyle,
    Dale Hawerchuk $9
1985-86 Dale Hawerchuk, Jets puck..........................$10
1986-87 Action photos..$10
1987-88 "Lightning on Ice" $10
1988-89 Winnipeg skyline..$10
1989-90 Brent Ashton, Pat Elynuik, others $10
1990-91 "Winnipeg Style"..$10
1991-92 ....$9
1992-93 Troy Murray, Bob Essensa $9
1993-94 ....$9
1994-95 ....$8

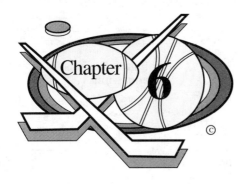

Programs

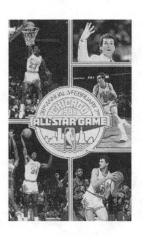

Many people purchase a souvenir program to keep score in when they attend a professional game. Others, however, just purchase the program as reading material, or perhaps to have a player autograph it during pregame warmups or after the game. This increases its value. Although unscored programs are preferred, a scored program, if done neatly, does have intrinsic value; it provides a history of what happened for that particular game, and can trigger fond memories for fans who were there. Programs from games when a record was broken or a significant event happened command premium values, as do those from playoff, championship and all-star games.

Program design and attractiveness add to the value of a program, especially the front cover. Condition is an important factor in determining a program's value. Most collectors want them to be in nice condition, hence it will have a higher value than one which is torn, stained or missing pages. Values given in this guide are for programs in Excellent condition, those which show little wear and tear. Other factors in determining a program's value include scarcity and rarity.

In general, football programs from the 1930s are worth $85-$100, while those from 1940-45 are worth $45-$60; those from 1945-50 are worth $25-$50; those from the 1950s are worth $20-$30; those from the 1960s are worth $15-$35; those from the 1970s are worth $6-$8; those from the 1980s are worth $5-$6; those from the 1990s are worth $5 or less.

In general, NBA game programs from the 1960s are between $20-$25 each, while those from the 1970s bring $10-$20. Special events bring more. Hockey programs from the 1930s can bring between $50-$75, while those from the 1940s are between $40-$50. Programs from the 1960s can bring $25-$35, while those from the 1970s are generally worth $15-$25. Programs from the 1980s are generally up to $15.

Football

AFL Championship programs

- 1960 Houston Oilers vs. Los Angeles Chargers $800
- 1961 San Diego Chargers vs. Houston $300
- 1962 Houston Oilers vs. Dallas Texans $700
- 1963 San Diego Chargers vs. Boston..... $150-$200
- 1964 Buffalo vs. San Diego $250
- 1965 San Diego vs. Buffalo $200
- 1966 Kansas City vs. Buffalo................ $100-$250
- 1967 Oakland vs. Houston $125
- 1968 New York Jets vs. Oakland.................... $200
- 1969 Kansas City vs. New York Jets.............. $295

NFL Championship programs

- 1938 New York vs. Green Bay $2,000
- 1941 Chicago vs. New York $950
- 1942 Washington vs. Chicago......................... $900
- 1943 Washington vs. Chicago................ $700-$900
- 1944 New York Giants vs. Green Bay...$600-$750
- 1945 Cleveland Rams vs. Washington......$600-$1,000
- 1946 New York Giants vs. Chicago Bears...$600-$700

- 1947 Philadelphia vs. Chicago Cardinals........$500
- 1948 Philadelphia vs. Chicago Cardinals........$500
- 1949 Los Angeles Rams vs. Philadelphia $450
- 1950 Cleveland Browns vs. Los Angeles Rams......$350
- 1951 Los Angeles Rams vs. Cleveland Rams ....$250-$350
- 1952 Detroit vs. Cleveland .... $250-$450
- 1953 Cleveland vs. Detroit $450
- 1954 Cleveland vs. Detroit $300
- 1955 Los Angeles Rams vs. Cleveland $250
- 1956 New York Giants vs. Chicago $325
- 1957 Cleveland vs. Detroit .... $295-$450
- 1958 Baltimore vs. New York Giants $400
- 1959 Baltimore vs. New York Giants $350
- 1960 Philadelphia vs. Green Bay $300
- 1961 New York Giants vs. Green Bay .. $175-$250
- 1962 New York Giants vs. Green Bay .. $150-$250
- 1963 New York Giants vs. Chicago $200
- 1964 Cleveland vs. Baltimore $200
- 1965 Cleveland vs. Green Bay .... $125-$200
- 1967 Green Bay vs. Dallas $250

Super Bowl programs

I at Los Angeles, Jan. 15, 1967 (Green Bay Packers vs. Kansas City Chiefs) .... $275-$395
II at Miami, Jan. 14, 1968 (Green Bay Packers vs. Oakland Raiders) .... $350-$400
III at Miami, Jan. 12, 1969 (New York Jets vs. Baltimore Colts) .... $225-$325
IV at New Orleans, Jan. 11, 1970 (Minnesota Vikings vs. Kansas City Chiefs) .... $175-$225
V at Miami, Jan. 17, 1971 (Baltimore Colts vs. Dallas Cowboys) .... $350-$400
VI at New Orleans, Jan. 16, 1972 (Dallas Cowboys vs. Miami Dolphins) .... $125-$200
VII at Los Angeles, Jan. 14, 1973 (Miami Dolphins vs. Washington Redskins) .... $125-$200
VIII at Houston, Jan. 13, 1974 (Minnesota Vikings vs. Miami Dolphins)............................... $125-$200
IX at New Orleans, Jan. 12, 1975 (Pittsburgh Steelers vs. Minnesota Vikings) .... $125-$175
X at Miami, Jan. 18, 1976 (Dallas Cowboys vs. Pittsburgh Steelers) .... $125-$195
XI at Pasadena, Jan. 9, 1977 (Oakland Raiders vs. Minnesota Vikings)................................... $65-$95
XII at New Orleans, Jan. 15, 1978 (Dallas Cowboys vs. Denver Broncos) .... $65-$95
XIII at Miami, Jan. 21, 1979 (Pittsburgh Steelers vs. Dallas Cowboys) .... $65-$95
XIV at Pasadena, Jan. 20, 1980 (Los Angeles Rams vs. Pittsburgh Steelers)........................... $35-$70
XV at New Orleans, Jan. 25, 1981 (Oakland Raiders vs. Philadelphia Eagles)......................... $25-$45
XVI at Pontiac, Jan. 24, 1982 (San Francisco 49ers vs. Cincinnati Bengals) .... $25-$40
XVII at Pasadena, Jan. 30, 1983 (Miami Dolphins vs. Washington Redskins) .... $25-$40
XVIII at Tampa, Jan. 22, 1984 (Washington vs. Los Angeles Raiders)..................................... $25-$35
XIX at Palo Alto, Jan. 20, 1985 (Miami vs. San Francisco).. $20-$30
XX at New Orleans, Jan. 26, 1986 (Chicago Bears vs. New England Patriots).......................... $20-$30
XXI at Pasadena, Jan. 25, 1987 (Denver Broncos vs. New York Giants)................................... $15-$25
XXII at San Diego, Jan. 31, 1988 (Washington Redskins vs. Denver Broncos)......................... $15-$25

Programs

XXIII at Miami, Jan. 22, 1989 (Cincinnati Bengals vs. San Francisco 49ers)...$15-$25
XXIV at New Orleans, Jan. 28, 1990 (San Francisco 49ers vs. Denver Broncos)....................................$15-$25
XXV at Tampa, Jan. 27, 1991 (Buffalo Bills vs. New York Giants) ....$15-$25
XXVI at Minneapolis, Jan. 26, 1992 (Washington Redskins vs. Buffalo Bills) ....$15-$25
XXVII at Pasadena, Jan. 31, 1993 (Buffalo Bills vs. Dallas Cowboys)..$15-$25
XXVIII at Minneapolis, Jan. 1994 (Dallas Cowboys vs. Buffalo Bills) ....$15-$25

Football playoff games

Dec. 22, 1968 1968 NFL Western Conference Championship (Minnesota vs. Baltimore) $50
Dec. 22, 1968 AFL Western Division playoff (Oakland vs. Kansas City)..$50
Dec. 20, 1969 inter-division playoff (New York Jets vs. Kansas City)..$65
Dec. 21, 1969 AFL division playoff (Oakland vs. Houston)...$45
Dec. 27, 1969 Western Conference Championship (Minnesota vs. Los Angeles)............................$40
Dec. 28, 1969 Eastern Conference Championship (Dallas vs. Cleveland)..$75
Dec. 26, 1970 AFC divisional playoff (Baltimore vs. Cincinnati) $40
Dec. 26, 1970 NFC divisional playoff (Dallas vs. Detroit) $40
Dec. 27, 1970 AFC divisional playoff (Oakland vs. Miami)..$40
Dec. 27, 1970 NFC divisional playoff (Minnesota vs. San Francisco) $40
Jan. 3, 1971 NFC Championship (San Francisco vs. Dallas) $75
Dec. 25, 1971 NFC divisional playoff (Minnesota vs. Dallas)..$45
Dec. 25, 1971 AFC divisional playoff (Miami vs. Kansas City)..$125
Dec. 26, 1971 NFC divisional playoff (San Francisco vs. Washington)..$40
Dec. 26, 1971 AFC divisional playoff (Cleveland vs. Baltimore)..$40
Jan. 2, 1972 NFC championship (Dallas vs. San Francisco) $75
Jan. 2, 1972 AFC championship (Baltimore vs. Miami) $75
Dec. 23, 1972 AFC divisional playoff (Pittsburgh vs. Oakland)..$90
Dec. 23, 1972 NFC divisional playoff (San Francisco vs. Dallas)..$65
Dec. 24, 1972 AFC divisional playoff (Miami vs. Cleveland)..$35
Dec. 24, 1972 NFC divisional playoff (Washington vs. Green Bay)..$35
Dec. 31, 1972 NFC divisional playoff (Washington vs. Dallas)..$75
Dec. 31, 1972 AFC divisional playoff (Miami vs. Pittsburgh)...$65
Dec. 22, 1973 AFC divisional playoff (Miami vs. Cincinnati) $35
Dec. 23, 1973 NFC divisional playoff (Los Angeles vs. Dallas) $65
Dec. 23, 1973 AFC divisional playoff (Cincinnati vs. Miami) $35
Dec. 30, 1973 NFC championship (Dallas vs. Minnesota)...$65
Dec. 21, 1974 NFC divisional playoff (Minnesota vs. St. Louis) $35
Dec. 22, 1974 AFC divisional playoff (Pittsburgh vs. Buffalo) $35
Dec. 22, 1974 NFC divisional playoff (Los Angeles vs. Washington) $35
Dec. 29, 1974 NFC championship (Minnesota vs. Los Angeles)..$45
Dec. 29, 1974 AFC championship (Pittsburgh vs. Oakland $65
Jan. 4, 1975 NFC championship (Los Angeles vs. Dallas) $60
Dec. 27, 1975 NFC divisional playoff (Los Angeles vs. St. Louis) $35
Dec. 28, 1975 NFC divisional playoff (Minnesota vs. Dallas)...$75
Dec. 28, 1975 AFC divisional playoff (Cincinnati vs. Oakland)...$35
Jan. 4, 1976 AFC championship (Pittsburgh vs. Oakland)...$65
Dec. 18, 1976 AFC divisional playoff (New England vs. Oakland) $35
Dec. 18, 1976 NFC divisional playoff (Washington vs. Minnesota)..$35
Dec. 19, 1976 AFC divisional playoff (Pittsburgh vs. Baltimore) $35
Dec. 19, 1976 NFC divisional playoff (Los Angeles vs. Dallas) $35
Dec. 26, 1976 NFC championship (Los Angeles vs. Minnesota)..$45
Dec. 24, 1977 AFC divisional playoff (Baltimore vs. Oakland) $35
Dec. 24, 1977 AFC divisional playoff (Pittsburgh vs. Denver)...$25
Dec. 26, 1977 NFC divisional playoff (Chicago vs. Dallas) $25
Dec. 26, 1977 NFC divisional playoff (Minnesota vs. Los Angeles)...$25
Jan. 1, 1978 AFC championship (Oakland vs. Denver) $45

Jan. 1, 1978 NFC championship (Minnesota vs. Dallas)..$45
Dec. 24, 1978 AFC wildcard (Houston vs. Miami)..$25
Dec. 24, 1978 NFC wildcard (Philadelphia vs. Atlanta) $25
Dec. 30, 1978 AFC divisional playoff (Pittsburgh vs. Denver)..$25
Dec. 30, 1978 NFC divisional playoff (Atlanta vs. Dallas)..$25
Dec. 31, 1978 AFC divisional playoff (Houston vs. New England) $25
Dec. 31, 1978 NFC divisional playoff (Minnesota vs. Los Angeles)......................................$25
Jan. 7, 1979 AFC championship (Houston vs. Pittsburgh)..$45
Jan. 7, 1979 NFC championship (Dallas vs. Los Angeles) $45
Dec. 23, 1979 NFC wildcard (Philadelphia vs. Chicago)..$25
Dec. 23, 1979 AFC wildcard (Denver vs. Houston)...$65
Dec. 29, 1979 NFC divisional playoff (Philadelphia vs. Tampa Bay) $25
Dec. 29, 1979 AFC divisional playoff (Houston vs. San Diego) $35
Dec. 30, 1979 NFC divisional playoff (San Francisco vs. Washington)..................................$40
Dec. 30, 1979 AFC divisional playoff (Dallas vs. Los Angeles) $25
Jan. 6, 1980 NFC championship (Los Angeles vs. Tampa Bay) $45
Jan. 6, 1980 AFC championship (Houston vs. Pittsburgh)...$45
Dec. 28, 1980 AFC wildcard (Houston vs. Oakland)...$25
Dec. 28, 1980 NFC wildcard (Los Angeles vs. Dallas)...$25
Jan. 3, 1981 NFC divisional playoff (Philadelphia vs. Minnesota)..$25
Jan. 4, 1981 NFC divisional playoff (Dallas vs. Atlanta)..$25
Dec. 27, 1981 AFC wildcard (Buffalo vs. New York Jets) $35
Jan. 2, 1982 NFC divisional playoff (Tampa Bay vs. Dallas) $25
Jan. 3, 1982 AFC divisional playoff (Buffalo vs. Cincinnati) $35
Jan. 10, 1982 AFC championship (San Diego vs. Cincinnati) $75
Jan. 8, 1983 NFC 1st round (St. Louis vs. Green Bay)..$25
Jan. 9, 1983 AFC 1st round (San Diego vs. Pittsburgh)...$25
Jan. 9, 1983 NFC 1st round (Dallas vs. Tampa Bay) $25
Jan. 15, 1983 AFC 2nd round (Raider vs. New York) $25
Jan. 16, 1983 AFC 2nd round (San Diego vs. Miami) $25
Jan. 23, 1983 AFC championship (Miami vs. New York) $25
Dec. 26, 1983 NFC wildcard (Dallas vs. Los Angeles)..$25
Jan. 1, 1984 NFC divisional playoff (Washington vs. Los Angeles) $25
Dec. 22, 1984 AFC wildcard (Seattle vs. Raiders) $25
Dec. 29, 1984 AFC divisional (Miami vs. Seattle)..$25
Dec. 30, 1984 NFC divisional (Chicago vs. Washington)..$25
Dec. 28, 1985 AFC wildcard (New York Jets vs. New England) $25
Dec. 29, 1985 NFC wildcard (New York Giants vs. San Francisco) $35
Jan. 4, 1986 AFC divisional (Miami vs. Cleveland)..$25
Jan. 4, 1986 NFC divisional (Dallas vs. Los Angeles) $25
Jan. 5, 1986 NFC divisional (Chicago vs. New York) $35
Jan. 12, 1986 NFC championship (Chicago vs. Los Angeles) $45
Jan. 12, 1986 AFC championship (Miami vs. New England) $45
Dec. 28, 1986 AFC wildcard (Miami vs. Seattle)..$25
Dec. 28, 1986 NFC wildcard (Los Angeles vs. Washington)...$25
Jan. 3, 1987 AFC divisional (New York vs. Cleveland) $25
Jan. 3, 1987 NFC divisional (Chicago vs. Washington)...$25
Jan. 11, 1987 NFC championship (New York vs. Washington)...$45
Jan. 11, 1987 AFC championship (Cleveland vs. Denver)..$45
Jan. 3, 1988 NFC wildcard (New Orleans vs. Minnesota)...$20
Jan. 9, 1988 AFC divisional (Cleveland vs. Indianapolis) $25
Jan. 10, 1988 AFC divisional (Denver vs. Houston) $35
Jan. 10, 1988 NFC divisional (Chicago vs. Washington)...$25
Jan. 17, 1988 AFC championship (Denver vs. Cleveland)..$45
Dec. 26, 1988 NFC wildcard (Minnesota vs. Los Angeles) $20

Programs

Dec. 31, 1988 AFC divisional (Cincinnati vs. Seattle)..$20
Dec. 31, 1988 NFC divisional (Chicago vs. Philadelphia)...$20
Jan. 1, 1989 AFC divisional (Buffalo vs. Houston)...$25
Jan. 1, 1989 NFC divisional (San Francisco vs. Minnesota)...$20
Jan. 8, 1989 NFC championship (Chicago vs. San Francisco)...$35
Dec. 31, 1989 NFC wildcard (Philadelphia vs. Los Angeles)..$20
Jan. 6, 1990 AFC divisional (Buffalo vs. Cleveland)...$25
Jan. 7, 1990 NFC divisional (New York vs. Los Angeles)..$25
Jan. 14, 1990 AFC championship (Denver vs. Cleveland)..$40
Jan. 5, 1991 NFC wildcard (Philadelphia vs. Washington)..$20
Jan. 6, 1991 NFC wildcard (New Orleans vs. Chicago)...$20
Jan. 12, 1991 NFC divisional (San Francisco vs. Washington)...$25
Jan. 13, 1991 NFC divisional (Chicago vs. New York)..$25
Dec. 28, 1991 NFC wildcard (Atlanta vs. New Orleans)...$20
Dec. 29, 1991 AFC wildcard (Houston vs. New York)...$20
Dec. 29, 1991 NFC wildcard (Chicago vs. Dallas)..$20
Jan. 5, 1992 AFC divisional (Buffalo vs. Kansas City)..$25
Jan. 12, 1992 AFC championship (Buffalo vs. Denver)...$35
Jan. 3, 1993 NFC wildcard (New Orleans vs. Philadelphia)..$15

Pro Football

Hall of Fame Game

Aug. 11, 1962 New York Giants vs. St. Louis Cardinals...$75
Sept. 7, 1963 Pittsburgh Steelers vs. Cleveland Browns..$60
Sept. 6, 1964 Baltimore Colts vs. Pittsburgh Steelers..$50
Sept. 11, 1965 Detroit Lions vs. Washington Redskins...$50
Sept. 17, 1966 No game was played..$50
Aug. 5, 1967 Cleveland Browns vs. Philadelphia Eagles..$55
Aug. 2, 1968 Dallas Cowboys vs. Chicago Bears...$50
Aug. 12, 1969 Atlanta Falcons vs. Green Bay Packers...$45
Aug. 8, 1970 Minnesota Vikings vs. New Orleans Saints...$45
July 31, 1971 Houston Oilers vs. Los Angeles Rams..$45
July 29, 1972 Kansas City Chiefs vs. New York Giants..$45
July 28, 1973 New England Patriots vs. San Francisco 49ers..$40
1974 issue Buffalo Bills vs. St. Louis Cardinals...$40
Aug. 2, 1975 Washington Redskins vs. Cincinnati Bengals..$40
1976 issue Denver Broncos vs. Detroit Lions...$30
July 30, 1977 Chicago Bears vs. New York Jets...$35
July 29, 1978 Miami Dolphins vs. Philadelphia Eagles...$35
July 28, 1979 Dallas Cowboys vs. Oakland Raiders...$35
Aug. 2, 1980 Green Bay Packers vs. San Diego Chargers..$30
Aug. 1, 1981 Cleveland Browns vs. Atlanta Falcons..$30
Aug. 7, 1982 Minnesota Vikings vs. Baltimore Colts...$30
1983 issue Pittsburgh Steelers vs. New Orleans Saints...$25
July 28, 1984 Tampa Bay Buccaneers vs. Seattle Seahawks...$30
1985 issue New York Giants vs. Houston Oilers...$25
Aug. 2, 1986 New England Patriots vs. St. Louis Cardinals..$25
Aug. 8, 1987 San Francisco 49ers vs. Kansas City Chiefs..$25
July 30, 1988 Cincinnati Bengals vs. Los Angeles Rams..$25
Aug. 5, 1989 Washington Redskins vs. Buffalo Bills..$20
Aug. 4, 1990 Cleveland Brown vs. Chicago Bears..$20
July 27, 1991 Detroit Lions vs. Denver Broncos...$20
Aug. 1, 1992 Philadelphia Eagles vs. New York Jets...$20

Miscellaneous regular season games

Nov. 15, 1942 Green Bay Packers at Chicago Bears..$85

Sept. 13, 1946 Chicago Bears at Philadelphia Eagles $60

Sept. 30, 1946 New York Giants at Boston Yanks..$60

Nov. 11, 1946 Chicago Bears at Los Angeles Rams $60

Aug. 29, 1947 Green Bay Packers at Pittsburgh Steelers..$55

Sept. 17, 1947 Los Angeles Rams at New York Giants, the Gold Cup Football Game.................................$65

Aug. 10, 1949 San Francisco 49ers at Los Angeles Dons, 1st annual charity game.................................$65

Dec. 10, 1950 Green Bay Packers at San Francisco 49ers, Norm Standlee day $35

Dec. 10, 1950 New York Giants at Philadelphia Eagles, Steve Van Buren Day $35

Aug. 28, 1955 Cleveland Browns at San Francisco 49ers, Joe Perry Day $35

Oct. 28, 1956 Green Bay Packers at Baltimore Colts, Johnny Unitas' first start.......................................$35

Sept. 29, 1957 New York Giants at Cleveland Browns, Jim Brown's first game...$50

Sept. 29, 1957 Chicago Bears at Green Bay Packers, new stadium dedication $35

Sept. 23, 1960 St. Louis Cardinals at Los Angeles Rams, St. Louis' first game...

Nov. 13, 1960 Denver Broncos at Dallas Texans, from a first-year contest at the Cotton Bowl....................$75

Aug. 24, 1961, Denver Broncos at New York Titans...$100

Aug. 11, 1962 Dallas Texans at San Diego Chargers...$45

Nov. 23, 1962 Buffalo Bills at Boston Patriots $40

Aug. 3, 1963, Kansas City Chiefs at San Diego Chargers, marks the debut game for the newly-transplanted Dallas
   Texans $50

Sept. 29, 1963 Kansas City Chiefs at San Diego Chargers $50

Oct. 5, 1963 Boston Patriots at New York Jets, Jets first year $40

Sept. 5, 1964 Boston Patriots at Denver Broncos, first annual Elk's Game...$40

Aug. 29, 1970 Los Angeles Rams at San Diego Chargers $15

Oct. 10, 1970 Miami Dolphins at New York Jets..$10

Aug. 6, 1971 Dallas Cowboys at Los Angeles Rams, 26th annual charity game..$12

Oct. 24, 1971 New England Patriots at Dallas Cowboys, first game at Texas Stadium, with ticket stub..........$55

Aug. 23, 1972 Chicago Bears at Green Bay Packers, 23 annual Midwest Game $10

Oct. 29, 1972 Miami Dolphins at Baltimore Colts $15

Aug. 19, 1973 New York Jets at New York Giants, Yale Game..$15

Sept. 23, 1973 Philadelphia Eagles at New York Giants, last game at Yankee Stadium $20

Aug. 9, 1975 Dallas Cowboys at Los Angeles Rams, 30th annual charity game.......................................$12

Oct. 6, 1975 Dallas Cowboys at Detroit Lions, 1st game at Pontiac Stadium..$20

Oct. 3, 1976 Dallas Cowboys at Seattle Seahawks, first year in Seattle $15

Oct. 3, 1976 Tampa Bay Buccaneers at Baltimore Colts, Tampa Bay's first season $15

Nov. 20, 1977 Minnesota Vikings at Chicago Bears, Walter Payton sets rushing record for a game $35

Aug. 11, 1980 New England Patriots at Los Angeles Rams, first game at Anaheim Stadium $20

Aug. 15, 1981 Pittsburgh Steelers at Philadelphia Eagles $15

Aug. 14, 1982 New York Giants at Baltimore Colts, shows HOF Class of 1982 ....$15

Aug. 18, 1984 New York Giants at New York Jets, shows HOF Class of 1984..$15

Oct. 20, 1985 San Francisco 49ers at Detroit Lions, shows Joe Montana..$12

Aug. 9, 1986 New York Jets at Green Bay Packers, shows HOF Class of 1986 ....$15

Oct. 15, 1989 San Francisco 49ers at Dallas Cowboys, shows Joe Montana...$12

Aug. 2, 1991 Cincinnati Bengals at Detroit Lions, shows HOF Class of 1991 ....$12

1989 NFL Toshiba American Bowl, Rams vs. 49ers $25

Jan. 16, 1966 Pro Bowl in Los Angeles...$42

Jan. 19, 1969 Pro Bowl in Los Angeles...$42

Jan. 21, 1973 Pro Bowl in Irving, Texas..$38

Jan. 23, 1978 Pro Bowl in Tampa...$32

Jan. 29, 1979 Pro Bowl game in Los Angeles $8.75

Programs

World Football League programs

- Regular season games are generally worth $10
- Sept. 2, 1974 Birmingham Vulcans vs. Florida Blazers.............$20
- Nov. 21, 1974 Philadelphia Bell at Florida Blazers playoff.............$25
- Nov. 21, 1974 Honolulu at Southern California Sun playoff.............$25
- Nov. 27, 1974 Honolulu at Birmingham Vulcans semi-final.............$25
- Nov. 29, 1974 Florida Blazers at Memphis Southmen semi-final.............$25
- Dec. 5, 1974 Florida Blazers at Birmingham Vulcans, WFL's only championship game......$75
- July 12, 1975 Honolulu Hawaiians vs. Charlotte Hornets.............$20
- Aug. 16, 1975 Honolulu Hawaiians vs. Southern California Sun.............$20
- Aug. 23, 1975 Birmingham Vulcans vs. Charlotte Hornets.............$20
- Sept. 28, 1975 Shreveport Steamer vs. Honolulu Hawaiians.............$20

United States Football League

- July 17, 1983 Michigan vs. Philadelphia, at Denver, Championship Game I.............$30
- July 15, 1984 Arizona vs. Philadelphia, at Tampa, Championship Game II.............$30
- July 14, 1985 Baltimore at Oakland, in New Jersey, Championship Game III.............$30
- Playoff games are generally $10. Regular season programs are generally $5, except for examples, at $25 each: July 9, 1983, Chicago at Philadelphia; July 10, 1973, Oakland at Michigan; July 8, 1984, Los Angeles at Arizona; July 7, 1984, Birmingham at Philadelphia; June 30, 1984, New Jersey at Philadelphia; June 30, 1985, Houston at Birmingham; July 1, 1985, Baltimore at New Jersey; July 7, 1985, Baltimore at Birmingham.

College Bowl Games

Rose Bowl

1929 Georgia Tech vs. California.............$850
1930 Pitt vs. USC.............$485
1931 Alabama vs. Washington State.............$950
1932 Tulane vs. USC.............$395
1933 Pitt vs. USC.............$395
1934 Columbia vs. Stanford.............$495
1935 Alabama vs. California.............$395
1936 SMU vs. Stanford.............$275
1937 Pitt vs. Washington.............$225
1938 Alabama vs. California.............$250
1939 Duke vs. USC.............$250
1940 Tennessee vs. USC.............$225
1941 Nebraska vs. Stanford.............$195
1942 Duke vs. Oregon State.............$1,000
1943 Georgia vs. UCLA.............$135
1944 Washington vs. USC.............$135
1945 Tennessee vs. USC.............$135
1946 Alabama vs. Stanford.............$125
1947 Illinois vs. UCLA.............$125
1948 Michigan vs. USC.............$125
1949 Northwestern vs. California.............$125
1950 Ohio State vs. California.............$95
1951 Michigan vs. California.............$95
1952 Illinois vs. Stanford.............$85
1953 Wisconsin vs. USC.............$85
1954 Michigan State vs. UCLA.............$75
1955 Ohio State vs. USC.............$75
1956 Michigan State vs. UCLA.............$65
1957 Iowa vs. Oregon State.............$65
1958 Ohio State vs. Oregon.............$65
1959 Iowa vs. California.............$65
1960 Wisconsin vs. Washington.............$65
1961 Minnesota vs. Washington.............$65
1962 Minnesota vs. UCLA.............$65
1963 Wisconsin vs. USC.............$75
1964 Illinois vs. Washington.............$65
1965 Michigan vs. Oregon State.............$65
1966 Michigan State vs. UCLA.............$65
1967 Purdue vs. USC.............$65
1968 Indiana vs. USC.............$65
1969 Ohio State vs. USC.............$65
1970 Michigan vs. USC.............$60
1971 Ohio State vs. USC.............$60
1972 Michigan vs. Stanford.............$60
1973 Ohio State vs. USC.............$60
1974 Ohio State vs. USC.............$60
1975 Ohio State vs. USC.............$60
1976 Ohio State vs. UCLA.............$50
1977 Michigan vs. USC.............$45
1978 Michigan vs. Washington.............$45
1979 Michigan vs. USC.............$45
1980 Ohio State vs. USC.............$35
1981 Michigan vs. Washington.............$30
1982 Iowa vs. Washington.............$30
1983 Michigan vs. UCLA.............$30
1984 Illinois vs. UCLA.............$30
1985 Ohio State vs. USC.............$30
1986 Iowa vs. UCLA.............$25
1987 Michigan vs. Arizona State.............$25
1988 Michigan State vs. USC.............$20
1989 Michigan vs. USC.............$20
1990 Michigan vs. USC.............$20
1991 Iowa vs. Washington.............$15
1992 Michigan vs. Washington.............$15
1993 Michigan vs. Washington.............$15
1994 Wisconsin vs. UCLA.............$15

Sugar Bowl
1935 Temple vs. Tulane......................................$850
1936 TCU vs. LSU $500
1937 Santa Clara vs. LSU................................$350
1938 Santa Clara vs. LSU................................$350
1939 Carnegie Tech vs. TCU............................$400
1940 Texas A&M vs. Tulane............................$300
1941 Boston College vs. Tennessee..................$200
1942 Fordham vs. Missouri...............................$200
1943 Tulsa vs. Tennessee $175
1944 Georgia Tech vs. Tulsa.............................$175
1945 Alabama vs. Duke......................................$165
1946 St. Mary's vs. Oklahoma $160
1947 North Carolina vs. Georgia......................$150
1948 Alabama vs. Texas.....................................$145
1949 North Carolina vs. Ohio University...........$125
1950 Oklahoma vs. LSU.....................................$110
1951 Oklahoma vs. Kentucky.............................$95
1952 Maryland vs. Tennessee.............................$95
1953 Georgia Tech vs. Mississippi.....................$95
1954 Georgia Tech vs. West Virginia..................$95
1955 Navy vs. Mississippi..................................$85
1956 Georgia Tech vs. Pittsburgh.......................$85
1957 Baylor vs. Tennessee $85
1958 Texas vs. Mississippi $85
1959 Clemson vs. LSU $85
1960 Mississippi vs. LSU $75
1961 Mississippi vs. Rice $75
1962 Alabama vs. Arkansas.................................$75
1963 Mississippi vs. Arkansas............................$75
1964 Alabama vs. Mississippi $75
1965 LSU vs. Syracuse.......................................$65
1966 Florida vs. Missouri $65
1967 Alabama vs. Nebraska $65
1968 LSU vs. Wyoming $65
1969 Georgia vs. Arkansas $65
1970 Mississippi vs. Arkansas............................$60
1971 Tennessee vs. Air Force.............................$60
1972 Auburn vs. Ohio University........................$60
1973 Ohio University vs. Penn State $60
1974 Alabama vs. Notre Dame............................$60
1975 Florida vs. Nebraska $60
1976 Alabama vs. Penn State..............................$60
1977 Georgia vs. Pittsburgh...............................$50
1978 Alabama vs. Ohio State..............................$50
1979 Alabama vs. Penn State..............................$50
1980 Alabama vs. Arkansas $50
1981 Georgia vs. Notre Dame $45
1982 Georgia vs. Pittsburgh...............................$45
1983 Georgia vs. Penn State $45
1984 Michigan vs. Auburn $40
1985 LSU vs. Nebraska $35

1986 Miami vs. Tennessee $30
1987 LSU vs. Nebraska.......................................$30
1988 Auburn vs. Syracuse...................................$25
1989 FSU vs. Auburn..$20
1990 Miami vs. Alabama $20
1991 Virginia vs. Tennessee $20
1992 Florida vs. Notre Dame $15
1993 Alabama vs. Miami $15
Cotton Bowl
1945 Oklahoma A&M vs. TCU $195
1946 Missouri vs. Texas.....................................$175
1947 Arkansas vs. LSU $200
1948 Penn State vs. SMU...................................$150
1949 Oregon vs. SMU..$135
1950 North Carolina vs. Rice $125
1951 Tennessee vs. Texas $115
1952 Kentucky vs. TCU......................................$95
1953 Tennessee vs. Texas $85
1954 Alabama vs. Rice..$95
1955 Georgia Tech vs. Arkansas.........................$85
1956 Mississippi vs. TCU $85
1957 Syracuse vs. TCU.......................................$85
1958 Navy vs. Rice $75
1959 Air Force vs. TCU $75
1960 Syracuse vs. Texas $70
1961 Duke vs. Arkansas.....................................$70
1962 Mississippi vs. Texas.................................$70
1963 LSU vs. Texas $70
1964 Navy vs. Texas..$70
1965 Arkansas vs. Nebraska $65
1966 LSU vs. Arkansas......................................$65
1967 Georgia vs. Wyoming................................$65
1968 Alabama vs. Texas A&M...........................$65
1969 Tennessee vs. Texas $65
1970 Notre vs. Texas..$125
1971 Notre Dame vs. Texas $125
1972 Penn State vs. Texas..................................$60
1973 Texas vs. Alabama $60
1974 Nebraska vs. Texas....................................$60
1975 Penn State vs. Baylor.................................$60
1976 Georgia vs. Arkansas.................................$50
1977 Maryland vs. Houston $50
1978 Notre Dame vs. Texas $75
1979 Notre Dame vs. Houston $75
1980 Nebraska vs. Houston................................$45
1981 Alabama vs. Baylor $45
1982 Alabama vs. Texas $45
1983 Pittsburgh vs. SMU $45
1984 Georgia vs. Texas......................................$40
1985 Boston College vs. Houston $40
1986 Auburn vs. Texas A&M $35
1987 Ohio State vs. Texas A&M.........................$30

Programs

1988 Notre Dame vs. Texas A&M $25
1989 UCLA vs. Arkansas $20
1990 Tennessee vs. Arkansas $20
1991 Miami vs. Texas...................................... $20
1992 FSU vs. Texas A&M................................. $15
1993 Notre Dame vs. Texas A&M $15

Orange Bowl

1940 Georgia Tech vs. Missouri $275
1941 Mississippi vs. Georgetown $250
1942 TCU vs. Georgia $250
1943 Alabama vs. Boston College..................... $250
1944 LSU vs. Texas.. $225
1945 Georgia Tech vs. Tulsa $200
1946 Holy Cross vs. Miami $175
1947 Tennessee vs. Rice................................... $175
1948 Georgia Tech vs. Kansas........................... $150
1949 Texas vs. Georgia..................................... $100
1950 Santa Clara vs. Kentucky.......................... $100
1951 Clemson vs. Miami $125
1952 Georgia Tech vs. Baylor $100
1953 Alabama vs. Syracuse $100
1954 Oklahoma vs. Maryland............................. $95
1955 Duke vs. Nebraska $125
1956 Maryland vs. Oklahoma............................. $95
1957 Clemson vs. Colorado................................ $95
1958 Duke vs. Oklahoma................................... $95
1959 Syracuse vs. Oklahoma............................. $95
1960 Georgia vs. Missouri................................. $85
1961 Navy vs. Missouri $85
1962 LSU vs. Colorado...................................... $85
1963 Alabama vs. Oklahoma.............................. $85
1964 Auburn vs. Nebraska................................. $75
1965 Texas vs. Alabama.................................... $125
1966 Alabama vs. Nebraska $75
1967 Georgia Tech vs. Florida........................... $75
1968 Oklahoma vs. Tennessee........................... $75
1969 Penn State vs. Kansas $75
1970 Penn State vs. Missouri............................. $60
1971 LSU vs. Nebraska $60
1972 Alabama vs. Nebraska $60
1973 Notre Dame vs. Nebraska $60
1974 Penn State vs. LSU $60
1975 Notre Dame vs. Alabama........................... $60
1976 Michigan vs. Oklahoma $60
1977 Ohio State vs. Colorado $50
1978 Arkansas vs. Oklahoma $50
1979 Nebraska vs. Oklahoma $50
1980 FSU vs. Oklahoma.................................... $45
1981 FSU vs. Oklahoma.................................... $45
1982 Clemson vs. Nebraska............................... $45
1983 LSU vs. Nebraska $45
1984 Miami vs. Nebraska $40

1985 Washington vs. Oklahoma $35
1986 Penn State vs. Oklahoma........................... $35
1987 Arkansas vs. Oklahoma............................. $30
1988 Miami vs. Oklahoma $25
1989 Miami vs. Nebraska.................................. $25
1990 Notre Dame vs. Colorado........................... $15
1991 Colorado vs. Notre Dame $15
1992 Miami vs. Nebraska.................................. $10

Liberty Bowl

1959 Penn State vs. Alabama $95
1960 Penn State vs. Oregon $75
1961 Syracuse vs. Miami $65
1962 Oregon State vs. Villanova........................ $65
1963 Mississippi State vs. N.C. State.................. $65
1964 Utah vs. West Virginia $65
1965 Mississippi vs. Auburn $60
1967 N.C. State vs. Georgia $60
1968 Mississippi vs. Virginia Tech..................... $50
1969 Colorado vs. Alabama $60
1970 Tulane vs. Colorado $50
1971 Tennessee vs. Arkansas............................. $50
1972 Georgia Tech vs. Iowa State....................... $50
1973 N.C. State vs. Kansas $50
1974 Tennessee vs. Maryland $50
1975 USC vs. Texas A&M................................. $50
1976 Alabama vs. UCLA $50
1977 North Carolina vs. Nebraska $75
1978 LSU vs. Missouri..................................... $45
1979 Penn State vs. Tulane $45
1980 Purdue vs. Missouri $45
1981 Ohio State vs. Navy................................. $45
1982 Alabama vs. Illinois................................. $45
1983 Notre Dame vs. Boston College $45
1984 Auburn vs. Arkansas $40
1985 LSU vs. Baylor....................................... $40
1986 Tennessee vs. Minnesota............................ $35
1987 Georgia vs. Arkansas................................ $30
1988 South Carolina vs. Indiana $25
1989 Mississippi vs. Air Force $25
1990 Air Force vs. Ohio State $20
1991 Air Force vs. Mississippi State.................... $20
1992 Air Force vs. Mississippi........................... $15

Fiesta Bowl

1971 Arizona State vs. Florida State $50
1972 Arizona State vs. Missouri $45
1973 Arizona State vs. Pittsburgh $45
1974 Oklahoma State vs. BYU $45
1975 Arizona State vs. Nebraska $45
1976 Oklahoma vs. Wyoming............................. $45
1977 Penn State vs. Arizona State....................... $45
1978 Arkansas vs. UCLA.................................. $45
1979 Pittsburgh vs. Arizona $45
1980 Penn State vs. Ohio State $45
1982 Penn State vs. USC.................................. $40

1983 Arizona State vs. Oklahoma $35
1984 Pittsburgh vs. Ohio State $35
1985 Miami vs. UCLA $35
1986 Michigan vs. Nebraska............................... $35
1987 Penn State vs. Miami $30
1988 Florida State vs. Nebraska $25
1989 Notre Dame vs. West Virginia.................... $20
1990 Florida State vs. Nebraska $15
1991 Louisville vs. Alabama $15
1992 Penn State vs. Tennessee $15
1993 Syracuse vs. Colorado............................... $15
1994 Miami vs. Arizona $15

Holiday Bowl
1978 BYU vs. Navy....................................... $35
1979 BYU vs. Indiana..................................... $30
1980 BYU vs. SMU.. $25
1981 BYU vs. Washington State $25
1982 BYU vs. Ohio State.................................. $25
1983 BYU vs. Missouri $25
1984 BYU vs. Michigan $25
1985 Arkansas vs. Arizona State $20
1986 Iowa vs. San Diego State $20
1987 Iowa vs. Wyoming $20
1988 Oklahoma vs. Wyoming $20
1989 BYU vs. Wyoming................................... $20
1990 BYU vs. Texas A&M $20
1991 Iowa vs. BYU....................................... $15
1992 Hawaii vs. Illinois $15
1993 BYU vs. Ohio State.................................. $15

Hall of Fame Bowl
1977 Maryland vs. Minnesota............................ $45
1978 Texas A&M vs. Iowa State........................ $35
1979 South Carolina vs. Missouri....................... $30
1980 Tulane vs. Arkansas $25
1981 Mississippi State vs. Kansas $25
1982 Air Force at Vanderbilt $25
1984 Wisconsin vs. Kentucky............................ $25
1986 Georgia vs. Boston College $20
1988 Alabama vs. Michigan $20
1989 Syracuse vs. LSU $20
1990 Ohio State vs. Auburn............................... $15
1991 Clemson vs. Illinois $15
1992 Ohio State vs. Syracuse............................. $15

Aloha Bowl
1982 Washington vs. Maryland $35
1983 Washington vs. Penn State......................... $30
1984 Notre Dame vs. SMU................................ $30
1985 Alabama vs. USC.................................... $25
1986 North Carolina vs. Arizona........................ $20
1987 Florida vs. UCLA.................................... $20
1988 Washington State vs. Hawaii $20
1989 Michigan State vs. Hawaii $20
1990 Syracuse vs. Arizona................................ $15
1991 Georgia Tech vs. Stanford $15
1992 Kansas vs. BYU $15

Peach Bowl
1968 LSU vs. Florida State $85
1969 South Carolina vs. West Virginia................ $65
1970 North Carolina vs. Arizona State $65
1971 Georgia Tech vs. Mississippi $55
1972 N.C. State vs. West Virginia $50
1973 Georgia vs. Maryland $50
1974 Vanderbilt vs. Texas Tech........................... $50
1975 N.C. State vs. West Virginia $50
1976 North Carolina vs. Kentucky....................... $50
1977 N.C. State vs. Iowa State........................... $45
1978 Georgia Tech vs. Purdue $45
1979 Clemson vs. Baylor $45
1980 Virginia Tech vs. Miami $65
1981 Florida State vs. North Carolina.................. $40
1982 Tennessee vs. Iowa.................................. $45
1983 Florida State vs. N.C. State $40
1984 Virginia vs. Purdue.................................. $40
1985 Army vs. Illinois..................................... $35
1986 Virginia Tech vs. N.C. State........................ $30
1987 Indiana vs. Tennessee............................... $30
1988 Iowa vs. N.C. State.................................. $25
1989 Syracuse vs. Georgia $20
1990 Auburn vs. Indiana $20
1992 East Carolina vs. N.C. State $15
1993 North Carolina vs. Mississippi State $15

Gator Bowl
1960 Florida vs. Baylor.......................................$100
1961 Penn State vs. Georgia Tech........................$90
1962 Florida vs. Penn State $90
1963 North Carolina vs. Air Force $90
1964 Florida State vs. Oklahoma $90
1965 Georgia Tech vs. Texas Tech $90
1966 Tennessee vs. Syracuse $90
1967 Penn State vs. Florida State $75
1968 Alabama vs. Missouri................................$75
1969 Florida vs. Tennessee $75
1970 Mississippi vs. Auburn $65
1971 North Carolina vs. Georgia $65
1972 Auburn vs. Colorado $65
1973 Tennessee vs. Texas Tech $60
1974 Texas vs. Auburn.....................................$60
1975 Florida vs. Maryland $60
1976 Notre Dame vs. Penn State..........................$60
1977 Clemson vs. Pitt......................................$50
1978 Ohio State vs. Clemson $65
1979 Michigan vs. North Carolina $50
1980 South Carolina vs. Pitt..............................$45
1981 North Carolina vs. Arkansas $40
1982 Florida State vs. West Virginia $40
1983 Florida vs. Iowa......................................$40
1984 South Carolina vs. Oklahoma State.............$35
1985 Florida State vs. Oklahoma $35
1986 Stanford vs. Clemson $35
1987 South Carolina vs. LSU..............................$30

Programs

1988 Georgia vs. Michigan State $25
1989 West Virginia vs. Clemson $20
1990 Michigan vs. Mississippi $20
1991 Oklahoma vs. Virginia $15
Freedom Bowl
1984 Iowa vs. Texas $25
1985 Washington vs. Colorado $20
1986 UCLA vs. BYU $20
1987 Air Force vs. Arizona State $15
1988 Colorado vs. BYU $15
1989 Florida vs. Washington $15
1990 Oregon vs. Colorado State $15
1991 San Diego State vs. Tulsa $15
Sun Bowl
1965 TCU vs. UTEP $65
1966 Wyoming vs. Florida State $65
1967 Mississippi vs. UTEP $65
1968 Auburn vs. Arizona $65
1969 Nebraska vs. Georgia $65
1970 Georgia Tech vs. Texas Tech $60
1971 Iowa State vs. LSU $60
1972 North Carolina vs. Texas Tech $60
1973 Auburn vs. Missouri $60
1974 North Carolina vs. Mississippi State $50
1975 Pitt vs. Kansas $50
1976 Texas A&M vs. Florida $50
1977 Stanford vs. LSU $50
1978 Texas vs. Maryland $45
1979 Texas vs. Washington $45
1980 Mississippi State vs. Nebraska $40
1981 Oklahoma vs. Houston $40
1982 Texas vs. North Carolina $40
1983 Alabama vs. SMU $40
1984 Tennessee vs. Maryland $35
1985 Georgia vs. Arizona $30
1986 Alabama vs. Washington $30
1987 West Virginia vs. Oklahoma State $25
1988 Army vs. Vanderbilt $25
1989 Texas A&M vs. Pitt $20
1990 Michigan State vs. USC $20

Basketball

NBA All-Star Game programs

1951 Boston $600
1952 Boston $500
1953 Fort Wayne $600
1954 New York $550
1955 New York $495
1956 Rochester $495
1957 Boston $325
1958 St. Louis $225
1959 Detroit $195
1960 Philadelphia $225

1961 Syracuse $195
1962 St. Louis $195
1963 Los Angeles $195
1964 Boston $175
1965 St. Louis $175
1966 Cincinnati $75
1967 San Francisco .... $150-$175
1968 New York $90
1969 Baltimore $90
1970 Philadelphia $90
1971 San Diego $90
1972 Los Angeles $90
1973 Chicago $50
1974 Seattle $50
1975 Phoenix $50
1976 Philadelphia $35
1977 Milwaukee $50
1978 Atlanta $50
1979 Detroit $50
1980 Washington $40
1981 Cleveland $40
1982 New Jersey $40
1983 Los Angeles $40
1984 Denver $40
1985 Indiana $40
1986 Dallas $40
1987 Seattle $40
1988 Chicago $25
1989 Houston $25
1990 Miami $25
1991 Charlotte $25
1992 Orlando $25

ABA All-Star Game programs

1968 Indianapolis $195
1969 Louisville $175
1971 Greensboro, N.C. $150
1972 Kentucky $125
1973 Salt Lake City $125
1974 Norfolk, Va. $100
1975 San Antonio $95
1976 Denver $85

NBA Finals programs

1960-61 Syracuse at Boston $225
1962-63 Boston at Los Angeles $195
1963-64 San Francisco at Boston $125
1964-65 Boston at Los Angeles $195
1965-66 Boston at Los Angeles $150
1967-68 Boston at Los Angeles $150
1968-69 Los Angeles at Boston $150
1968-69 Boston at Los Angeles $150
1969-70 Los Angeles at New York $125
1969-70 New York at Los Angeles $150

1971-72 Los Angeles at New York $125
1971-72 New York at Los Angeles $100
1972-73 Los Angeles at New York $100
1973-74 Milwaukee at Boston $100
1974-75 Golden State at Washington $100
1975-76 Phoenix at Boston $100
1976-77 Philadelphia at Portland $100
1978-79 Washington at Seattle $100
1979-80 Philadelphia at Los Angeles $100
1980-81 Houston at Boston $75
1981-82 Philadelphia at Los Angeles $75
1983-84 Boston at Los Angeles $75
1984-85 Boston at Los Angeles $75
1993-94 Houston at New York $25

NBA playoffs programs

1947 Philadelphia at New York $225
1951 Boston at New York $150
1955 Boston at New York $150
1956 Syracuse at Boston $125
1956 Syracuse at Philadelphia $125
1958 Boston at Philadelphia $100
1958 Syracuse at Philadelphia $100
1959 Syracuse at Boston $45
1962 Boston at Philadelphia $45
1962 Los Angeles at Detroit $60
1964 Cincinnati at Philadelphia $45
1965 Philadelphia at Boston $45
1965 Baltimore at Los Angeles $50
1966 St. Louis at Los Angeles $45
1966 Philadelphia at Boston $40
1966 Boston at Philadelphia .... $40-$65
1967 Philadelphia at Boston $40
1967 Los Angeles at San Francisco $40
1967 St. Louis at San Francisco $40
1967 Boston at New York $40
1968 St. Louis at San Francisco $35
1968 San Francisco at Los Angeles $35
1968 Los Angeles at San Francisco $35
1968 Chicago at Los Angeles $35
1968 Los Angeles at Chicago $45
1968 Philadelphia at Boston .... $35-$65
1968 Philadelphia at New York $35
1969 Atlanta at San Diego $45
1969 Boston at Philadelphia $35
1969 Atlanta at Philadelphia $35
1969 Boston at New York $35
1969 Baltimore at New York $35
1969 New York at Baltimore $40
1969 New York at Boston $40
1970 Philadelphia at Milwaukee $35
1970 New York at Philadelphia $35
1970 Milwaukee at Philadelphia $35
1970 Milwaukee at New York $30

1970 Baltimore at New York $30
1970 New York at Baltimore $30
1970 Phoenix at Los Angeles $35
1971 Milwaukee at Los Angeles $40
1971 New York at Baltimore $40
1971 Milwaukee at San Francisco $30
1971 Atlanta at New York $30
1971 Baltimore at New York $30
1972 Chicago at Los Angeles $35
1972 Milwaukee at Golden State $35
1972 New York at Baltimore .... $30-$35
1972 Los Angeles at Milwaukee $35
1972 Boston at Atlanta $35
1972 New York at Boston $35
1972 Baltimore at New York $30
1972 Boston at New York $30
1972 Los Angeles at Chicago $30
1972 Los Angeles at New York $100
1972 New York at Los Angeles $100
1973 Los Angeles at Golden State $35
1973 Milwaukee at Golden State $35
1973 New York at Baltimore $35
1973 New York at Boston $30
1973 Atlanta at Boston $30
1973 Boston at New York $30
1973 Baltimore at New York $30
1973 Chicago at Los Angeles $30
1973 Los Angeles at New York $100
1973 New York at Los Angeles $100
1974 Milwaukee at Los Angeles .... $25-$30
1974 Los Angeles at Milwaukee $30
1974 Chicago at Milwaukee $30
1974 Detroit at Chicago $30
1974 Boston at Buffalo $30
1974 Detroit at Chicago $30
1974 New York at Washington $30
1974 Boston at New York $25
1974 Washington at New York $25
1974 Chicago at Detroit $25
1974 Buffalo at Boston $25
1974 New York at Boston $25
1975 Chicago at Kansas City $25
1975 Seattle at Detroit .... $20-$25
1975 Buffalo at Washington $25
1975 Chicago at Golden State $25
1975 Houston at Boston $25
1975 Boston at Houston $25
1975 Washington at Boston $25
1975 New York at Houston $25
1975 Washington at Buffalo $25
1975 Boston at Washington $25
1975 Houston at Boston $25
1976 Cleveland at Washington $25
1976 Detroit at Golden State $25

1976 Washington at Cleveland $25
1976 Cleveland at Boston $25
1976 Golden State at Detroit...............................$25
1976 Buffalo at Boston ....$20-$25
1976 Boston at Buffalo $25
1976 Boston at Cleveland $25
1976 Philadelphia at Buffalo $25
1976 Buffalo at Philadelphia $25
1976 Detroit at Milwaukee $25
1976 Seattle at Phoenix......................................$25
1977 Los Angeles at Portland $25
1977 Denver at Portland $25
1977 Los Angeles at Golden State......................$25
1977 Washington at Cleveland $25
1977 Portland at Chicago....................................$25
1977 Philadelphia at Boston $25
1977 Washington at Houston...............................$25
1977 Houston at Washington...............................$25
1977 Golden State at Los Angeles.......................$25
1977 San Antonio at Boston $25
1977 Washington at Cleveland $25
1977 Detroit at Golden State...............................$25
1977 Portland at Los Angeles $25
1977 Portland at Denver $25
1978 Philadelphia at New York $20
1978 Cleveland at New York...............................$20
1978 Los Angeles at Seattle................................$20
1978 Seattle at Portland $20
1978 New York at Cleveland...............................$20
1978 Philadelphia at Washington $20
1979 Seattle at Phoenix......................................$20
1979 Phoenix at Seattle......................................$20
1979 Philadelphia at New Jersey $20
1979 Houston at Atlanta $20
1979 Washington at Seattle $75
1980 Milwaukee at Seattle.................................$20
1980 Philadelphia at Boston ....$20-$25
1980 Washington at Philadelphia $20
1980 Philadelphia at Atlanta...............................$20
1980 Houston at Boston......................................$20
1981 Kansas City at Portland..............................$20
1981 Philadelphia at Boston $20
1982 Washington at Boston $20
1982 Philadelphia at Boston $20
1984 Philadelphia at New Jersey Nets................$20
1984 Boston at New York....................................$20
1985 Philadelphia at Boston $20
1986 San Antonio at Los Angeles $20
1988 Detroit at Boston $20
1990 Boston at New York....................................$15
1990 Houston at Los Angeles $15
1994 Houston at New York $25
ABA playoff programs
1969 Indiana at Miami..$45

1970 Los Angeles at Indiana (Finals).................$150
1970 Indiana at Los Angeles (Finals).................$150
1971 New York at Virginia $35
1971 Miami at Kentucky.....................................$30
1972 Indiana at New York (Finals).....................$125
1972 New York at Indiana (Finals).....................$125
1973 Indiana at Kentucky (Finals) $125
1973 Kentucky at Indiana (Finals) $125
1974 New York at Virginia $30
1974 San Diego at Utah......................................$25
1975 Indiana at San Antonio $25
1975 Denver at Indiana $25
1975 Indiana at Kentucky (Finals) $100

Miscellaneous

- 1927-28 Chicago Bruins vs. New York Celtics program: 20-page picture-filled program includes information on Hall of Famers Henry Dehnert, Nat Holman and Joe Lapchick, from a Jan. 1928 game at the Chicago Broadway Armory.................$325
- 1957 Professional Basketball Tour, Boston vs. Major League All-Stars, includes Bob Cousy, Bill Sharman, Bill Russell, Tommy Heinsohn........$50
- 1965 NBA "Invitational Tournament" program and stub: a picture-packed program from this Invitational Classic held in October 1965 at Louisville, Ky. , featuring the Celtics, Royals, 76ers and Hawks $45
- May 5, 1987, Hall of Fame Enshrinement program - signed by the year's five inductees, including Pete Maravich, Walt Frazier, Rick Barry, Bob Wanzer and Bob Houbregs............................$400
- May 10, 1993 Hall of Fame Enshrinement program - signed by 27 Hall of Famers, including Walt Bellamy, Billy Cunningham, Dan Issel, Dick McGuire, Ann Meyers, Calvin Murphy, Bill Walton, Juliana Semenova, Frank Ramsey, Al McGuire, Earl Monroe, Bob Kurland, Clarence Gaines, Ray Meyer, Ed Macauley, Bobby Wanzer, Dolph Schayes, Dave Bing, Harry Gallatin, Lusia Harris, Ben Carnevale, J. Dallas Shirley, John McLendon, Arad McCutchan, Pete Newell, Tom Heinsohn, Walt Frazier and Dave DeBusschere. Package also includes ticket stubs and a Hall of Fame Tribute sheet, one of 2,000 ....$350

Hockey

Stanley Cup Finals programs

1929-30 Montreal/Boston................................$1,500
1930-31 Monteal/Chicago $1,500
1931-32 Toronto/New York Rangers...............$1,200
1932-33 New York Rangers/Toronto...............$1,000
1933-34 Chicago/Detroit....................................$800

1934-35 Montreal/Toronto................................ $800
1935-36 Detroit/Toronto.................................... $700
1936-37 Detroit/New York Rangers................. $700
1937-38 Chicago/Toronto................................. $600
1938-39 Boston/Toronto................................... $600
1939-40 New York Rangers/Toronto $700
1940-41 Boston/Detroit $700
1941-42 Toronto/Detroit................................... $700
1942-43 Detroit/Boston $600
1943-44 Montreal/Chicago............................... $700
1944-45 Toronto/Detroit................................... $500
1945-46 Montreal/Boston $600
1946-47 Toronto/Montreal................................ $500
1947-48 Toronto/Detroit................................... $450
1948-49 Toronto/Detroit................................... $450
1949-50 Detroit/New York Rangers.................. $400
1950-51 Toronto/Montreal................................ $350
1951-52 Detroit/Montreal $350
1952-53 Montreal/Boston $400
1953-54 Detroit/Montreal $275
1954-55 Detroit/Montreal $275
1955-56 Montreal/Boston $300
1957-58 Boston/Montreal $300
1958-59 Montreal/Toronto................................ $300
1959-60 Toronto/Montreal................................ $300
1060-61 Chicago/Detroit $250
1961-62 Toronto/Chicago................................. $200
1962-63 Toronto/Detroit................................... $200
1963-64 Toronto/Detroit................................... $200
1964-65 Chicago/Montreal $250
1965-66 Detroit/Montreal $250
1966-67 Toront/Montreal.................................. $200
1967-68 St. Louis/Montreal $200
1968-69 Montreal/St. Louis $150
1969-70 Boston/St. Louis $125
1970-71 Montreal/Chicago............................... $125
1971-72 Boston/New York Rangers.................. $125
1972-73 Chicago/Montreal $150
1973-74 Philadelphia/Boston............................ $100
1974-75 Philadelphia/Buffalo............................ $100
1975-76 Montreal/Philadelphia $75
1976-77 Montreal/Boston $75
1977-78 Montreal/Boston $75
1978-79 Montreal/New York Rangers................. $75
1979-80 New York Islanders/Philadelphia.......... $75
1980-81 New York Islanders/Minnesota $40
1981-82 New York Islanders/Vancouver $40
1982-83 New York Islanders/Edmonton $45
1983-84 Edmonton/New York Islanders $45
1984-85 Edmonton/Philadelphia $45
1985-86 Montreal/Calgary................................. $45
1986-87 Edmonton/Philadelphia $45
1987-88 Boston/Edmonton $75
1988-89 Calgary/Montreal................................. $45

1990-91 Minnesota/Pittsburgh $45
1991-92 Pittsburgh/Chicago................................ $25
1992-93 Los Angeles/Pittsburgh $25
1993-94 Vancouver/New York Rangers $15

NHL All-Star Game programs

1947-48 Toronto.. $500
1948-49 Chicago .... $300-$350
1949-50 Toronto...................................... $300-$350
1950-51 Detroit .... $225-$250
1951-52 Toronto.. $200
1952-53 Detroit $200
1953-54 Montreal $200
1954-55 Detroit $150
1955-56 Detroit $150
1956-57 Montreal $150
1957-58 Montreal $150
1958-59 Montreal $150
1959-60 Montreal $150
1960-61 Montreal $100
1961-62 Chicago... $75
1962-63 Toronto.. $50
1963-64 Toronto.. $50
1964-65 Toronto.. $50
1965-66 Montreal $75
1966-67 Montreal $75
1967-68 Toronto.. $50
1968-69 Montreal $50
1969-70 St. Louis $50
1970-71 Boston... $35
1971-72 Minnesota.. $35
1972-73 New York... $35
1973-74 Chicago $35
1974-75 Montreal $35
1975-76 Philadelphia.. $30
1976-77 Vancouver $30
1977-78 Buffalo $30
1978-79 New York $50
1979-80 Detroit $30
1980-81 Los Angeles.. $20
1981-82 Washington $20
1982-83 New York $20
1983-84 New Jersey $20
1984-85 Calgary $20
1985-86 Hartford.. $20
1986-87 Quebec $25
1987-88 St. Louis $20
1988-89 Edmonton $20
1989-90 Pittsburgh $15
1990-91 Chicago $10
1991-92 Philadelphia.. $10
1992-93 Montreal $10

Programs

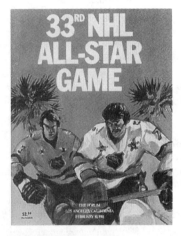

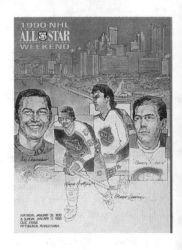

A complete run of NHL All-Star game programs might set you back more than $4,000.

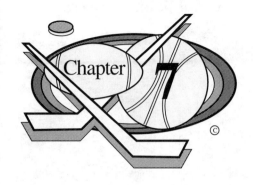

Chapter 7

Periodicals

Sports Illustrated

During the 40 years since its Aug. 16, 1954, debut issue featured an Eddie Mathews' cover, Sports Illustrated has captured some of the sports world's greatest moments on its covers and in its pages.

During that time, more than 2,000 issues have been published, with football subjects leading the way with 490 cover appearances. Baseball, at 405, and basketball, at 300, are second and third. Hockey has been featured 78 times. Boxer Muhammad Ali led all athletes with 32 appearances through 1993, but superstar Michael Jordan caught him early in 1995. Kareem Abdul-Jabbar has 27 appearances to rank third. Magic Johnson, with 21 cover appearances, ranks fifth.

The attractive cover photos are what drive the collectibilty of this magazine. Athletes' first cover issue appearances are especially sought after by those who seek to have them autographed. These issues, especially when autographed, generally command a higher price than subsequent issues with the same player. Generally, a signed Sports Illustrated cover is worth about the value of an unsigned version, plus the value of a signed 8x10 photo. The cover prices listed below are for unsigned versions.

Generally, collectors who seek back issues want them to be in reasonable condition - unripped, uncreased - with the cover attached entirely. But the corners on many issues are often not sharp, especially from the earlier issues.

Old Sports Illustrateds can often be purchased at libraries, flea markets, through hobby publications and mail order houses, at card shops and shows, and at rummage sales. On March 26, 1990, Sports Illustrated issued a supplemental magazine entitled "35 Years of Covers." This magazine features every cover from 1954 through 1989, and offers a worthwhile visual checklist for collectors who are wondering which covers are most appealing.

Key: FB = football, CFB = college football, BB = basketball, CBB = college basketball, H = hockey, FC = first cover, SOY (Sportsman of the Year).

Sports Illustrated Kareem Abdul-Jabbar covers

*Kareem Abdul-Jabbar
began his reign as one of
SI's cover kings under the
name of Lew Alcindor*

April 3, 1967

March 31, 1969

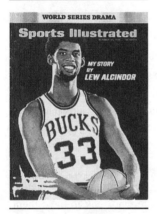

Oct. 27, 1969

February 19, 1973

Oct. 14, 1974

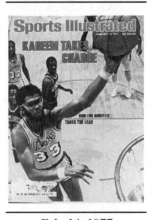

Dec. 23-30, 1985

Feb. 14, 1977

June 22, 1987

1954

09/28/54	CFB	Calvin Jones, Iowa	$15
11/01/54	CFB	Oklahoma Sooners	$15
11/22/54	FB	Y.A. Tittle, 49ers (FC)	$35-$40
12/20/54	CBB	Ken Sears, Santa Clara	$15-$20

1955

09/12/55	CFB	Bud Wilkinson, Oklahoma	$20
10/03/55	FB	Doak Walker, Lions	$30
10/24/55	CFB	Howard Cassady, Ohio State	$25
11/07/55	CFB	Bob Pellegrini, Maryland	$12
11/28/55	CFB	Don Holleder, Army	$15
12/26/55	CFB	Jim Swink, Texas Christian	$12-$14

1956

01/09/56	BB	Bob Cousy, Celtics (FC)	$45
01/23/56	H	Jean Beliveau, Canadiens (FC)	$25
09/24/56	CFB	College Football Preview	$10-$15
10/08/56	FB	Paul Brown, George Ratterman	$20
10/29/56	CFB	Paul Hornung, Notre Dame (FC)	$30-$35
11/05/56	CFB	Yale vs. Dartmouth	$8
11/12/56	CFB	Tom Maentz/Ron Kramer, Michigan	$10
11/26/56	CFB	USC vs. UCLA	$10
12/03/56	FB	Chuck Connerly, Giants	$15-$20

1957

01/21/57	CBB	Johnny Lee, Yale	$10
01/28/57	H	Boston Bruins	$15-$20
02/18/57	CBB	Jim Krebs, SMU	$10
03/18/57	H	Ted Lindsay/Gordie Howe, Red Wings (FC)	$40
09/23/57	CFB	College Football Preview	$15
10/07/57	FB	Ollie Matson, Cardinals	$12
11/04/57	CFB	Bobby Cox, Minnesota	$20
11/18/57	CFB	Oklahoma Sooners	$10
12/09/57	CBB	College Basketball Preview	$20

1958

01/20/58	BB	George Dempsey/Neil Johnston, Warriors	$10
02/17/58	H	Jacques Plante, Canadiens (FC)	$15
09/22/58	CFB	College Football Preview	$12
10/27/58	CFB	Chick Zimmerman, Syracuse	$10
11/24/58	CFB	Dawkins/Walters/Anderson, Army	$15
12/08/58	CBB	College Basketball Preview	$20

1959

01/12/59	H	Andy Bathgate, Rangers	$20
09/21/59	CFB	College Football Preview	$17
10/05/59	FB	Johnny Unitas, Colts (FC)	$30-$35
10/26/59	CFB	George Izo, Notre Dame	$12
11/09/59	CFB	College Football Preview	$12
12/07/59	CBB	College Basketball Preview	$15-$20

1960

01/11/60	CBB	Jerry Lucas, Ohio State	$15-$20
01/25/60	H	USSR Hockey	$5-$8
03/21/60	H	Maurice Richard	$20
09/19/60	CFB	College Football Preview	$12
09/26/60	FB	Jim Brown, Browns	$35
10/03/60	CFB	Bob Schloredt, Washington	$17
10/24/60	FB	Violence in Pro Football	$10
11/14/60	H	Bobby Hull, Blackhawks (FC)	$30
11/28/60	CFB	Joe Bellino, Navy	$7-$10
12/12/60	CBB	College Basketball Preview	$15-$20
12/19/60	FB	Norm Van Brocklin, Eagles	$20

1961

01/16/61	BB	Bob Cousy, Celtics	$25
03/27/61	CBB	John Havlicek, Jerry Lucas, Ohio State	$10-$15
09/18/61	CFB	College Football Preview	$12-$15
09/25/61	FB	Bart Starr, Packers (FC)	$25
10/16/61	CFB	Terry Baker, Oregon State	$12-$15
10/23/61	FB	Jon Arnett/Roy Hord, Rams	$15
10/30/61	BB	Wilt Chamberlain, Dick McGuire	$35
11/20/61	FB	Y.A. Tittle, Giants	$20-$25
11/27/61	CFB	Jimmy Saxton, Texas	$10-$15
12/01/61	FB	Dan Currie, Packers	$8-$12

1962

01/08/62	CBB	Jerry Lucas, Ohio State (SOY)	$20-$25
01/15/62	H	Don Head, Bruins	$10
03/19/62	CBB	UCLA vs. USC	$15
09/10/62	FB	Jim Taylor, Packers (FC)	$20
09/24/62	CFB	College Football Preview	$17
10/08/62	FB	Tommy McDonald, Eagles	$15
10/15/62	CFB	Sonny Gibbs, TCU	$15
10/29/62	FB	Fran Tarkenton, Vikings (FC)	$25
11/19/62	FB	Nick Pietrosante, Lions	$8-$12
11/26/62	CFB	Paul Dietzel, Army	$4-$7
12/10/62	CBB	Cotton Nash, Kentucky	$15
12/17/62	FB	Frank Gifford, Giants	$20-$25

1963

01/07/63	CFB	Terry Baker, Oregon State (SOY)	$17
01/28/63	H	Howie Young, Red Wings	$12
03/18/63	CBB	Larry Singleton, Cincinnati	$15-$20
05/20/63	FB	Paul Hornung, Packers	$20-$25
09/09/63	FB	Pro Football Preview	$17
09/23/63	CFB	George Mira, Miami	$12
10/14/63	FB	Ronnie Bull, Bears	$8-$12
10/21/63	CFB	Duke Carlisle, Texas	$6-$8
10/28/63	BB	Art Heyman, Jerry Lucas	$12-$15

Periodicals

11/04/63	CFB	Jack Cvercko, Northwestern	$6
11/11/63	FB	Violence in Pro Football	$4-$6
11/25/63	FB	Willie Galimore, Bears	$8-$12
12/02/63	CFB	Roger Staubach, Navy (FC)	$35-$45
12/09/63	BB	Frank Ramsey, Celtics	$15
12/16/63	FB	Paul Lowe/Tobin Rote, Chargers	$10-$15

1964

01/06/64	FB	Pete Rozelle, (SOY)	$20
02/03/64	H	Bobby Hull, Blackhawks	$20-$25
03/16/64	H	Gordie Howe, Red Wings	$40-$50
03/30/64	CBB	Walt Hazzard, UCLA	$10-$15
08/17/64	FB	Don Trull, Oilers	$12
09/07/64	FB	Pro Football Preview	$20
09/21/64	CFB	College Football Preview	$15
09/28/64	FB	Tommy Mason, Vikings	$8-$12
10/12/64	CFB	Dick Butkus, Illinois (FC)	$25-$30
10/26/64	BB	Tommy Heinsohn, Celtics	$20
11/02/64	CFB	John Huarte, Notre Dame	$12
11/30/64	FB	Alex Karras, Lions	$10-$15
12/07/64	CBB	Bill Bradley, Princeton	$40
12/14/64	FB	Charley Johnson, Cardinals	$17

1965

01/04/65	FB	Frank Ryan, Browns	$20
01/11/65	CFB	Ernie Koy, Texas	$10
01/25/65	H	Bobby Hull, Blackhawks	$30-$35
02/08/65	BB	Jerry West, Lakers	$25-$30
03/29/65	CBB	Gail Goodrich, UCLA	$15-$20
04/12/65	BB	Wilt Chamberlain, Warriors	$25-$30
07/19/65	FB	Joe Namath, Jets (FC)	$25-$30
08/16/65	FB	Y.A. Tittle, Giants	$20
09/13/65	FB	Fran Tarkenton, Vikings	$25
09/20/65	CFB	Frank Solich, Nebraska	$10-$12
09/27/65	FB	Frank Ryan, Browns	$10-$12
10/11/65	FB	Ken Willard, 49ers	$10
10/18/65	CFB	Tommy Nobis, Texas	$12
10/25/65	BB	Bill Russell, Celtics (FC)	$25
11/01/65	FB	Sonny Randle/Charley Johnson, Cardinals	$10
11/08/65	CFB	Harry Jones, Arkansas	$12
11/29/65	FB	Dennis Gaubatz, Colts	$8
12/06/65	CBB	UCLA Basketball	$15-$20
12/13/65	FB	Lance Alworth, Chargers	$20-$25

1966

01/03/66	CFB	College Bowl Games	$12
01/10/66	FB	Jim Taylor, Packers	$25
01/24/66	CBB	George Peeples, Iowa	$10
01/31/66	H	Stan Mikita, Blackhawks (FC)	$20-$25
02/14/66	BB	Rick Mount, top high school player	$12-$17
03/07/66	CBB	Adolph Rupp, Kentucky	$15-$20
03/28/66	CBB	Texas Western wins NCAA title	$25
04/25/66	H	Chicago vs. Detroit Stanley Cup	$15
05/09/66	BB	John Havlicek, Celtics (FC)	$25-$30
07/25/66	FB	Otto Graham/Edward B. Williams, Browns	$12
08/08/66	FB	Frank Emanuel, Dolphins	$8-$10
08/15/66	CFB	Paul "Bear" Bryant, Alabama (FC)	$25
08/22/66	FB	Paul Hornung/Jim Taylor, Packers	$25-$30
09/12/66	FB	Paul Bukich/Gale Sayers, Bears	$25
09/19/66	CFB	Gary Beban, UCLA	$10-$12
10/03/66	FB	Roman Gabriel, Rams	$12
10/17/66	FB	Joe Namath, Jets	$30

Sports Illustrated
THE SUPER CHAMPION
LOMBARDI OF GREEN BAY

10/24/66	BB	Elgin Baylor, Lakers	$20
10/31/66	FB	Bart Starr, Packers	$25
11/07/66	CFB	Terry Hanratty, Notre Dame	$10-$15
11/21/66	FB	Ross Fichtner, Browns	$8
11/28/66	CFB	Notre Dame vs. Michigan State	$20
12/05/66	BB	Lew Alcindor, UCLA (FC)	$35
12/12/66	FB	Jim Nance, Patriots	$8

1967

01/09/67	FB	Bart Starr, Packers	$25-$30
01/23/67	FB	Max McGee, Packers	$35-$40
01/30/67	H	Rod Gilbert, Rangers	$15-$20
02/13/67	BB	Rick Barry, Warriors	$15
02/27/67	CBB	Walters/Thomforde, Princeton	$8
03/20/67	H	Mikita/Mohns/Wharram, Blackhawks	$20
04/03/67	CBB	Lew Alcindor, UCLA	$25
04/24/67	BB	Rick Barry, Warriors (FC)	$12-$15
07/17/67	FB	Fran Tarkenton, Giants	$20
08/14/67	FB	Jim Taylor/Gary Cuozzo, Saints	$15
09/11/67	CFB	Terry Hanratty, Notre Dame	$8-$10
09/18/67	FB	Tommy Mason, Rams	$12-$15
10/09/67	CFB	Texas vs. USC	$8
10/16/67	CFB	Mike Phipps, Purdue	$8
10/23/67	BB	Pro Basketball Preview	$12
10/30/67	CFB	Tennessee vs. Alabama	$15
11/06/67	FB	Dan Reeves, Cowboys	$15-$20
11/20/67	CFB	Gary Beban, O.J. Simpson (FC)	$25
11/27/67	FB	Jim Hart, Cardinals	$8-$12
12/04/67	CBB	12-foot basket	$10
12/11/67	H	Bobby Orr, Bruins (FC)	$20-$25
12/18/67	FB	Roman Gabriel, Rams	$8-$12

1968

01/08/68	FB	Hewritt Dixon, Chuck Mercein	$10-$12
01/22/68	FB	Vince Lombardi, Packers (FC)	$30-$35
01/29/68	CBB	Lew Alcindor vs. Elvin Hayes	$20-$25

02/12/68	H	Bobby Hull, Blackhawks	$20-$25
03/04/68	CBB	Pete Maravich, LSU	$45-$55
03/18/68	BB	Bill Bradley, Knicks	$20-$30
04/01/68	CBB	UCLA vs. Houston	$15-$20
04/08/68	H	Stanley Cup	$8
04/29/68	BB	Elgin Baylor/Jerry West, Lakers	$12-$15
07/15/68	FB	Ray Nitschke, Packers	$12
08/12/68	FB	Paul Brown, Bengals	$8
09/09/68	CFB	College Football Preview	$12
09/16/68	FB	Don Meredith, Cowboys	$12
10/14/68	CFB	O.J. Simpson, USC	$15
10/28/68	FB	Bob Brown/Forrest Gregg, Packers	$10
11/04/68	BB	Earl Monroe, Bullets	$10-$15
11/11/68	FB	Bruce Jankowski, Ohio State	$7
11/25/68	FB	Earl Morral, Colts	$10
12/02/68	FB	College Basketball Preview	$10-$15
12/09/68	FB	Joe Namath, Jets	$20
12/16/68	FB	Baltimore Colts vs. Green Bay Packers	$8-$10
12/23/68	BB	Bill Russell, Celtics (SOY)	$20

1969

01/06/69	FB	Tom Matte, Colts	$8-$12
01/20/69	FB	Joe Namath, Jets	$50
01/27/69	BB	Wilt Chamberlain, Lakers	$15
02/03/69	H	Bobby Orr, Bruins	$20
02/10/69	CBB	Bud Ogden, Santa Clara	$6
02/24/69	BB	New York Knicks vs. Philadelphia	$8
03/03/69	FB	Vince Lombardi, Redskins	$8-$12
03/24/69	BB	Richie Guerin, Jeff Mullins	$7
03/31/69	CBB	Lew Alcindor, UCLA	$15
04/07/69	H	Red Berenson, Blues	$6-$8
04/28/69	BB	Bill Russell, Celtics	$12
05/12/69	BB	John Havlicek, Celtics	$12
06/16/69	FB	Joe Namath, Jets	$15
07/14/69	FB	O.J. Simpson, Bills	$15
07/28/69	FB	Vince Lombardi, Sonny Jurgensen	$8-$12
08/04/69	BB	Bill Russell, Celtics	$9
08/11/69	FB	Joe Namath, Jets	$15
08/25/69	FB	O.J. Simpson, Bills	$20
09/15/69	FB	Ohio State Buckeyes	$10
09/22/69	FB	Jim Turner, Jets	$10
09/29/69	CFB	Jimmy Jones, USC	$8
10/13/69	CFB	Bruce Kemp, Georgia	$6-$8
10/27/69	BB	Lew Alcindor, Bucks	$15-$20
11/03/69	FB	Minnesota Vikings defense	$10
11/10/69	FB	Steve Owens, Oklahoma	$7
11/24/69	FB	Len Dawson, Chiefs	$10-$12
12/01/69	CBB	Pete Maravich, LSU	$30-$35
12/08/69	BB	Walt Frazier, Knicks	$15
12/15/69	CFB	James Street, Texas	$8

1970

01/05/70	FB	Dave Osborn, Vikings	$6-$8
01/19/70	FB	Len Dawson, Chiefs	$20-$25
01/26/70	BB	Bob Cousy, Royals	$15-$17
02/09/70	FB	Terry Bradshaw, Louisiana Tech	$15
02/16/70	CBB	Tom McMillen, top prep star	$12
03/02/70	H	Eddie Giacomin, Rangers	$8
03/09/70	BB	Lew Alcindor, Bucks	$15
03/16/70	CBB	Collins, Issel, Lanier, Vallely	$7

Sports Illustrated
MARCH 4, 1968   40 CENTS
LSU'S PISTOL PETE—THE HOTTEST SHOT

03/30/70	CBB	UCLA wins NCAA Championship	$10
04/06/70	H	Keith Magnuson, Blackhawks	$10
04/27/70	BB	Lew Alcindor, Willis Reed	$12
05/04/70	H	Bobby Orr, Bruins	$20
05/18/70	BB	Dave DeBusschere, Knicks	$15
07/20/70	FB	Joe Kapp, Vikings	$8
08/10/70	FB	Mike Garrett, Chiefs	$7-$9
08/17/70	FB	Joe Namath, Jets	$10-$15
08/24/70	BB	Rick Barry, Squires	$8-$10
08/31/70	FB	Les Shy, Cowboys	$8
09/14/70	FB	Archie Manning, Mississippi	$15
09/21/70	FB	Dick Butkus, Bears	$20
10/05/70	CFB	Colorado vs. Penn State	$10
10/12/70	FB	Alex Karras, Lions	$10-$12
10/26/70	BB	Oscar Robertson	$10
11/09/70	CFB	Tatum, Theismann, Worster	$8-$12
11/16/70	BB	Calvin Murphy, Rockets	$10
11/23/70	FB	George Blanda, Raiders	$10-$15
11/30/70	CBB	Sidney Wicks, UCLA	$10
12/07/70	FB	Roman Gabriel, Rams	$8-$12
12/14/70	CFB	Steve Worster, Texas	$8
12/21/70	H	Bobby Orr, Bruins (SOY)	$25

1971

01/04/71	CBB	John Roche, South Carolina	$8
01/11/71	CFB	Joe Theismann, Notre Dame	$10
01/18/71	FB	Craig Morton, Cowboys	$10
01/25/71	FB	Jim O'Brien, Jets	$15-$20
02/08/71	BB	Lew Alcindor, Willis Reed	$12
02/15/71	CFB	Jim Plunkett, Stanford	$10
03/29/71	H	Phil and Tony Esposito	$10
04/05/71	CBB	Steve Patterson, UCLA	$7
04/19/71	BB	Willis Reed, Lew Alcindor	$10
04/26/71	H	Montreal vs. Boston	$8
05/10/71	BB	Oscar Robertson, Bucks	$10
05/17/71	CFB	James McAlister, UCLA	$5-$8
07/19/71	FB	George Blanda, Raiders	$12-$15

Periodicals

08/09/71	BB	Mike Peterson, Kansas high school	$7
08/16/71	FB	Calvin Hill, Cowboys	$8
09/13/71	CFB	Tommy Casanova, LSU	$10-$12
09/20/71	FB	John Brodie, 49ers	$12
10/04/71	CFB	Sonny Sixkiller, Washington	$6-$10
10/11/71	FB	Mean Joe Greene, Steelers	$10
10/25/71	BB	Gus Johnson, Dave DeBusschere	$10
11/01/71	FB	Ed Marinaro, Dolphins	$10
11/08/71	FB	Norm Bulaich, Colts	$4-$7
11/22/71	CFB	Oklahoma vs. Nebraska	$10
11/29/71	CBB	Tom Burleson, North Carolina State	$8-$12
12/06/71	CFB	Johnny Musso, Alabama	$7
12/13/71	BB	Gail Goodrich, Lakers	$10-$12

1972

01/03/72	FB	Garo Yepremian, Dolphins	$10
01/10/72	CFB	Nebraska Orange Bowl victory	$8
01/24/72	FB	Duane Thomas, Cowboys	$20
02/07/72	BB	Dave Cowens, Walt Frazier	$10
02/14/72	H	Ken Dryden, Canadiens (FC)	$8
02/21/72	CBB	Allie McGuire, Marquette	$6
03/06/72	CBB	Bill Walton, UCLA (FC)	$10-$12
03/20/72	CBB	NCAA Championship	$8
04/03/72	CBB	Bill Walton, UCLA	$12
04/24/72	BB	Lew Alcindor, Bucks	$8-$10
05/08/72	H	Phil Esposito, Bobby Orr	$20
05/15/72	BB	Wilt Chamberlain, Lakers	$12
06/19/72	H	Bobby Hull, Blackhawks	$15-$20
07/10/72	FB	Johnny Unitas, Colts	$18
07/24/72	FB	Tommy Prothro, Rams	$8
08/07/72	FB	Larry Csonka/Jim Kiick, Dolphins	$12
09/11/72	CFB	Bob Devaney, Nebraska	$8
09/18/72	FB	Walt Garrison, Cowboys	$12-$15
10/02/72	CFB	Greg Pruitt, Oklahoma	$6
10/09/72	FB	Joe Namath, Jets	$12-$15
10/16/72	BB	Wilt Chamberlain, Lakers	$12-$15
10/30/72	CFB	Dave and Don Buckey, Ohio State	$4-$6
11/06/72	FB	Larry Brown, Redskins	$7
11/13/72	BB	John Havlicek, Celtics	$12
11/20/72	CFB	Terry Davis, Alabama	$4-$6
11/27/72	CBB	Walter Luckett, Ohio	$10
12/04/72	FB	Steve Spurrier, 49ers	$8-$12
12/11/72	CBB	Campy Russell, Michigan	$7
12/18/72	FB	Lee Roy Jordan, Cowboys	$10
12/25/72	CBB	John Wooden/B.J. King (SOY)	$15

1973

01/08/73	FB	Mercury Morris, Dolphins	$8-$10
01/15/73	CBB	Doug Collins, Illinois State	$8
01/22/73	FB	Bob Griese, Miami	$15-$20
02/05/73	CBB	Bill Walton, UCLA	$8
02/19/73	BB	Kareem Abdul-Jabbar, Bucks	$7-$9
02/26/73	H	Gilbert Perreault, Sabres	$6-$8
03/26/73	CBB	Bill Walton, UCLA	$8
04/02/73	H	Henri Richard, Canadiens	$9
04/16/73	BB	Earl Monroe, Knicks	$8-$10
05/07/73	BB	Jerry West, Walt Frazier	$12-$15
08/06/73	CFB	John Matuszak, Houston	$4-$8
08/27/73	FB	Duane Thomas, Redskins	$8
09/10/73	CFB	Texas football	$10
09/17/73	FB	Larry Csonka/Bob Griese, Dolphins	$12-$15
10/01/73	CFB	Anthony Davis, USC	$8

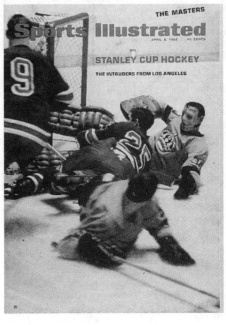

10/08/73	FB	Fran Tarkenton, Vikings	$10
10/15/73	BB	Nate Archibald, Kings	$10
10/29/73	FB	O.J. Simpson, Bills	$15
11/05/73	CFB	Anthony Davis, USC	$8
11/12/73	BB	Pete Maravich, Hawks	$12-$15
11/19/73	H	Phil Esposito, Bruins	$10
11/26/73	CBB	David Thompson, N.C. State	$10
12/03/73	CFB	Bear Bryant, Alabama	$7-$10
12/10/73	CBB	Len Elmore, Bill Walton	$8
12/17/73	FB	Marv Hubbard, Raiders	$6-$8

1974

01/07/74	FB	Fran Tarkenton, Vikings	$8-$12
01/14/74	BB	Julius Erving, Nets (FC)	$25
01/21/74	FB	Larry Csonka, Dolphins	$15-$20
02/18/74	BB	John Havlicek, Celtics	$12
02/25/74	CBB	Bill Walton, UCLA	$10
03/11/74	H	Gordie Howe, Aeros	$10-$15
03/25/74	CBB	Tom Burleson, Bill Walton	$10
04/01/74	CBB	UCLA vs. N.C. State	$12
04/29/74	CFB	Bruce Hardy, Utah	$6
05/06/74	H	Bobby Clarke (FC), Pete Stemkowski	$10
05/20/74	BB	John Havlicek, Celtics	$10-$12
07/29/74	FB	Terry Bradshaw, Steelers	$8-$12
08/05/74	FB	Pro Football Strike	$4-$6
09/09/74	CFB	Archie Griffin, Ohio State	$10
09/16/74	FB	O.J. Simpson, Bills	$15
09/23/74	FB	Joe Gilliam, Steelers	$6-$8
09/30/74	CFB	Tom Clements, Notre Dame	$5-$7
10/14/74	BB	Bill Walton, Kareem Abdul-Jabbar	$8
11/04/74	CFB	Oklahoma Football	$6-$8
11/18/74	FB	Woody Green, Chiefs	$6
11/25/74	H	Ken Dryden, Canadiens	$6
12/02/74	CBB	College Basketball Preview	$10
12/09/74	CFB	Anthony Davis, USC	$6-$10
12/16/74	BB	Rick Barry, Warriors	$10

1975

01/06/75	FB	Franco Harris, Steelers (FC)	$10-$12
01/20/75	FB	Terry Bradshaw, Steelers	$15
02/03/75	CBB	John Laskowski, Indiana	$8
02/10/75	H	Rogie Vachon, Kings	$7
02/17/75	CBB	Dave Meyers, UCLA	$6
03/17/75	CBB	Phil Ford, North Carolina	$7
03/31/75	CBB	Mike Flynn, Kentucky	$6
04/28/74	BB	Garfield Heard, Braves	$6
06/09/75	FB	Rockey Bleier, Steelers	$8
07/28/75	FB	Csonka/Kiick/Warfield, WFL	$12
08/25/75	FB	Bart Starr, Packers	$15
09/08/75	CFB	College Football Preview	$8-$10
09/22/75	FB	Mean Joe Greene, Steelers	$8-$10
09/29/75	CFB	Dan Devine/Rick Slager, Notre Dame	$7
10/27/75	BB	George McGinnis, 76ers	$10
11/10/75	FB	Fran Tarkenton, Vikings	$8-$12
11/17/75	H	Violence in Pro Hockey	$7
11/24/75	CFB	Chuck Muncie, California	$7
12/01/75	CBB	Kent Benson, Indiana	$8
12/08/75	CFB	Bubba Bean, Texas A&M	$6

1976

01/05/76	FB	Preston Pearson, Cowboys	$10
01/12/76	FB	Franco Harris, Steelers	$10
01/26/76	FB	Lynn Swann, Steelers	$15-$20
02/09/76	CBB	Ernie Grunfield/Bernard King, Tennessee	$8-$10
02/23/76	H	Bobby Clarke, Flyers	$7
03/08/76	BB	Bob McAdoo, Braves	$7
03/29/76	CBB	Kent Benson, Indiana	$6
04/05/76	CBB	Scott May, Indiana	$8
05/17/76	BB	Julius Erving, Nets	$15
05/24/76	H	Stanley Cup Playoffs	$8
06/07/76	BB	Alvan Adams, Dave Cowens	$8-$10
08/16/76	FB	Calvin Hill, Redskins	$6
08/23/76	FB	Steve Spurrier, Buccaneers	$10
09/06/76	CFB	Rick Leach, Michigan	$8
09/13/76	FB	Bert Jones, Colts	$10
10/04/76	CFB	Mark Manges, Maryland	$4-$6
10/18/76	FB	Chuck Foreman, Vikings	$6-$8
10/25/76	BB	Dave Cowens, Julius Erving	$12-$15
11/08/76	CFB	Tony Dorsett, Pitt	$8
11/15/76	BB	David Thompson, Nuggets	$8-$10
11/22/76	FB	Walter Payton, Bears	$15-$20
11/29/76	CBB	Rickey Green, Michigan	$10
12/06/76	FB	Rocky Bleier, Steelers	$7
12/13/76	BB	Bill Walton, Trailblazers	$10

1977

01/03/77	FB	Clarence Davis, Raiders	$8-$10
01/10/77	CFB	Tony Dorsett, Pitt	$15
01/17/77	FB	Ken Stabler, Raiders	$15-$18
01/31/77	CBB	Bill Cartwright, San Francisco	$8
02/07/77	H	Guy Lafleur, Canadiens	$7
02/14/77	BB	Kareem Abdul-Jabbar, Lakers	$8
03/21/77	BB	George McGinnis, 76ers	$7
04/04/77	CBB	Butch Lee, Marquette	$8
04/25/77	BB	Sidney Wicks, Celtics	$8
05/09/77	H	Gerry Cheevers, Brad Park	$6
05/23/77	BB	Bill Walton, Kareem Abdul-Jabbar	$12
06/13/77	BB	Bill Walton, Trailblazers	$7
07/25/77	FB	Conrad Dobler, Cardinals	$4-$6
09/05/77	CFB	Ross Browner, Notre Dame	$8
09/19/77	FB	Kenny Stabler, Raiders	$15

10/03/77	CFB	Billy Sims, Oklahoma	$7
10/17/77	FB	Rubin Carter, Broncos	$5
10/31/77	BB	Maurice Lucas, Trailblazers	$8-$10
11/07/77	FB	Semi-Tough, the movie	$4-$6
11/21/77	FB	AFC/NFC rivalry	$5-$7
11/28/77	CBB	Larry Bird, Indiana State (FC)	$35-$50
12/05/77	CFB	Earl Campbell, Texas	$6
12/12/77	H	Bryan Trottier, Islanders	$6

1978

01/02/78	FB	Mark Van Eeghen, Raiders	$6-$8
01/09/78	CFB	Terry Eurick, Notre Dame	$6-$8
01/23/78	FB	Harvey Martin/Randy White, Cowboys	$12
02/13/78	CBB	Sidney Moncrief, Arkansas	$8-$10
02/20/78	BB	Walter Davis, Suns	$8-$10
03/13/78	CBB	Gene Banks, Duke	$6
04/03/78	CBB	Goose Gives, Duke	$8
05/08/78	BB	Elvin Hayes, Bullets	$5-$7
05/22/78	BB	Marvin Webster, Sonics	$6
05/29/78	H	Larry Robinson, Ken Dryden	$6
08/14/78	FB	Brutality in Football	$4
08/21/78	BB	Bill Walton, Trailblazers	$6
09/04/78	FB	Roger Staubach, Cowboys	$12-$15
09/11/78	CFB	Lou Holtz, Arkansas	$10
10/02/78	CFB	Charles White, USC	$5-$7
10/09/78	FB	Terry Bradshaw, Steelers	$7-$8
10/16/78	BB	Marvin Webster, Knicks	$8
11/13/78	CFB	Chuck Fusina, Penn State	$6
11/20/78	CFB	Rick Berns, Nebraska	$6
11/27/78	CBB	Magic Johnson, Michigan State (FC)	$40-$50
12/04/78	FB	Earl Campbell, Houston	$5-$7

1979

01/08/79	CFB	Alabama vs. Penn State	$12-$15
01/15/79	FB	Terry Bradshaw, Steelers	$15
01/22/79	CBB	Ohio State vs. Illinois	$6
01/29/79	FB	Rocky Bleier, Steelers	$12

Periodicals

02/19/79	BB	Moses Malone, Rockets (FC)	$10
03/12/79	CBB	Dudley Bradley, North Carolina	$7
03/26/79	CBB	Larry Bird, Indiana State	$25
04/02/79	CBB	Magic Johnson, Michigan State	$30
04/16/79	H	Denis Potvin, Islanders	$8
05/07/79	BB	Elvin Hayes, Bullets	$7
06/11/79	BB	Gus Williams, Sonics	$6
08/06/79	FB	Ken Stabler, Raiders	$8
08/20/79	FB	John Jefferson, San Diego	$5-$7
09/03/79	FB	Earl Campbell, Houston	$8-$10
09/10/79	CFB	Billy Sims, Charles White	$7
09/24/79	CFB	Vagus Ferguson, Notre Dame	$6
10/01/79	FB	Dewey Selmon, Tampa Bay	$6
10/15/79	BB	Bill Walton, Clippers	$6-$8
11/05/79	FB	Franco Harris, Steelers	$8
11/12/79	CFB	Heismann candidates	$6
11/19/79	BB	Magic Johnson, Lakers	$20
11/26/79	CFB	Art Schlichter, Ohio State	$4-$6
12/03/79	CBB	Indiana Hooisers jersey	$8-$10
12/17/79	CBB	Ralph Sampson, Virginia	$6
12/24/79	FB	Terry Bradshaw, Willie Stargell (SOY)	$10

1980

01/07/80	FB	Ricky Bell, Buccaneers	$5-$7
01/14/80	FB	L.C. Greenwood, Steelers	$6-$7
01/21/80	FB	Gordie Howe, Whalers	$8-$10
01/28/80	FB	John Stallworth, Steelers	$15
03/03/80	H	U.S. Olympic hockey team	$15-$20
03/10/80	H	Jim Craig, Flames	$6
03/17/80	CBB	Albert King, Maryland	$6
03/31/80	CBB	Darrell Griffith, Louisville	$5-$7
04/28/80	BB	Larry Bird, Julius Erving	$15-$20
05/05/80	BB	Kareem Abdul-Jabbar, Lakers	$7-$5
05/26/80	BB	Magic Johnson, Lakers	$15
09/01/80	CFB	Hugh Green, Pitt	$7
09/08/80	FB	Pro Football Preview	$8
09/22/80	FB	Billy Sims, Lions	$4
10/20/80	BB	Paul Westphal, Sonics	$12
11/10/80	FB	L.C. Greenwood, Steelers	$6-$7
11/17/80	CFB	Herschel Walker, Georgia (FC)	$5-$7
12/01/80	CBB	College Basketball Preview	$8
12/08/80	FB	Vince Ferragamo, Rams	$8
12/15/80	BB	Lloyd Free, Warriors	$5
12/22/80	H	U.S. Olympic hockey team (SOY)	$15

1981

01/12/81	FB	Chuck Muncie, San Diego	$4-$6
01/19/81	FB	Mark Van Eeghen, Raiders	$6
01/26/81	CBB	Bobby Knight, Indiana	$7
02/02/81	FB	Rod Martin, Raiders	$10
02/16/81	CBB	Boston College point shaving	$5
02/23/81	H	Bobby Carpenter, high school	$5
03/09/81	BB	Magic Johnson, Lakers	$10
03/23/81	CBB	Rolando Blackman, Kansas State	$4
03/30/81	CBB	Ralph Sampson, Virginia	$5
04/06/81	CBB	Isiah Thomas, Indiana (FC)	$10
05/11/81	BB	Kevin McHale (FC), Maurice Cheeks	$10
07/20/81	FB	Vince Ferragamo, Alouettes	$7
08/03/81	FB	John Hannah, Patriots	$5
08/24/81	FB	Wendell Tyler, Rams	$5
08/31/81	CFB	Herschel Walker, Georgia	$8-$10
09/07/81	FB	Jim Plunkett, Raiders	$8-$10

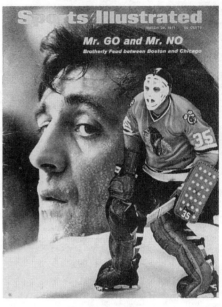

Mr. GO and Mr. NO
Brotherly Feud between Boston and Chicago

10/05/81	FB	Marcus Allen, USC (FC)	$6
10/12/81	H	Wayne Gretzky, Oilers (FC)	$30-$35
10/19/81	CFB	Texas vs. Oklahoma	$4-$6
11/09/81	BB	Larry Bird, Celtics	$20
11/23/81	CFB	Paul "Bear" Bryant, Alabama	$6
11/30/81	CBB	Dean Smith, North Carolina	$10
12/07/81	FB	Tony Dorsett, Cowboys	$7
12/14/81	FB	Cris Collinsworth, Bengals	$7
12/21/81	FB	Earl Cooper, 49ers	$8

1982

01/11/82	CFB	Perry Tuttle, Clemson	$5
01/18/82	FB	Dwight Clark, 49ers	$25-$30
01/25/82	FB	Joe Montana, 49ers (FC)	$25
02/01/82	FB	Earl Cooper, 49ers	$10
02/15/82	FB	Wayne Gretzky, Oilers	$10
02/22/82	BB	Sidney Moncrief, Bucks	$8
03/01/82	FB	Herschel Walker, Georgia	$5-$7
03/22/82	CBB	Patrick Ewing, Georgetown (FC)	$10
03/29/82	CBB	Sam Perkins, North Carolina	$10-$15
04/05/82	CBB	James Worthy, North Carolina	$10-$15
04/26/82	FB	Renaldo Nehemiah, 49ers	$5
05/03/82	BB	Moses Malone, Jack Sikma	$6
05/10/82	FB	Georgia Frontiere/Bert Jones, Rams	$5
05/24/82	BB	Michael Cooper/Magic Johnson, Lakers	$12
05/31/82	BB	Julius Erving, 76ers	$15
08/16/82	FB	Walter Payton, Bears (FC)	$8-$10
08/23/82	FB	Franco Harris, Steelers	$6-$8
08/30/82	FB	Tom Cousineau, Browns	$5
09/13/82	CFB	Wayne Peace, Florida	$5
09/27/82	FB	NFL Strike	$5
10/04/82	CFB	Todd Blackledge, Penn State	$5
11/01/82	BB	Moses Malone, 76ers	$7
11/08/82	CFB	John Elway, Stanford (FC)	$15
11/29/82	CFB	Patrick Ewing, Ralph Sampson	$10
12/06/82	FB	Washington Redskins vs. Philadelphia Eagles	$5

12/13/82	FB	Marcus Allen, Raiders	$7
12/20/82	CBB	Ralph Sampson, Virginia	$7
12/27/82	H	Wayne Gretzky, Oilers (SOY)	$20

1983

01/10/83	CFB	Greg Garrity, Penn State	$6
01/17/83	FB	Chuck Muncie, Chargers	$7
01/24/83	FB	Andra Franklin, Dolphins	$6
01/31/83	FB	Darryl Grant, Redskins	$6
02/07/83	FB	John Riggins, Redskins (FC)	$8-$10
02/21/83	BB	Terry Cummings, Clippers	$8
02/28/83	BB	Julius Erving, 76ers	$15
03/07/83	FB	Herschel Walker, Generals	$7
03/21/83	CBB	Billy Goodwin, St. John's	$5
04/11/83	CBB	N.C. State wins NCAA title	$5
05/02/83	BB	Larry Bird, Celtics	$15
05/09/83	BB	Kareem Abdul-Jabbar, Lakers	$10
05/23/83	H	Billy Smith, Islanders	$5
06/06/83	BB	Moses Malone, 76ers	$8
06/20/83	CFB	Marcus Dupree, Oklahoma	$6
08/01/83	FB	Richard Todd, Jets	$6
08/15/83	FB	John Elway, Broncos	$8-$10
08/29/83	FB	Tony Dorsett, Cowboys	$8
09/05/83	CFB	Mike Rozier, Nebraska	$7
09/26/83	CFB	Doug Flutie, Boston College	$5
10/10/83	FB	Joe Washington, Redskins	$5
10/17/83	FB	Eric Dickerson, Rams	$8
10/31/83	BB	Ralph Sampson, Houston	$5
11/14/83	FB	Dan Marino, Dolphins	$15
11/28/83	CBB	Michael Jordan (FC)/Sam Perkins, North Carolina	$40-$50
12/05/83	CBB	Sam Bowie, Kentucky	$5
12/12/83	FB	Jim Brown, Raiders	$5
12/19/83	FB	John Riggins, Redskins	$5

1984

01/09/84	CFB	Keith Griffin, Miami	$6
01/16/84	FB	Joe Theismann, Redskins	$7
01/23/84	H	Wayne Gretzky, Oilers	$15
01/30/84	FB	Jack Squirek, Redskins	$8-$10
03/05/84	BB	Magic Johnson, Lakers	$10-$15
03/19/84	CBB	Patrick Ewing, Georgetown	$8
03/26/84	CBB	Sam Perkins, North Carolina	$12
04/09/84	CBB	Michael Graham, Georgetown	$5
05/07/84	BB	Bernard King, Knicks	$7
05/14/84	H	Mike Bossy, Islanders	$6-$7
06/04/84	BB	Magic Johnson, Lakers	$10-$12
07/23/84	BB	Michael Jordan, Olympic team	$35-$40
07/30/84	FB	Jack Lambert, Steelers	$7
09/03/84	FB	Joe Theismann, Redskins	$7
09/10/84	FB	Miami Dolphins vs. Washington Redskins	$5
10/01/84	CFB	Jeff Smith, Nebraska	$4
10/08/84	FB	Sammy Winder, Broncos	$5
10/15/84	FB	Walter Payton, Bears	$10-$15
10/29/84	BB	Larry Bird, Bill Russell	$10
11/05/84	CFB	Gerry Faust, Notre Dame	$7
11/12/84	FB	Troubles in the NFL	$5
11/19/84	FB	Mark Duper, Dolphins	$5
11/26/84	CBB	Patrick Ewing, John Thompson, Ronald Reagan	$6
12/03/84	CFB	Doug Flutie, Boston College	$5
12/10/84	BB	Michael Jordan, Bulls	$25-$35
12/17/84	FB	Eric Dickerson, Rams	$7

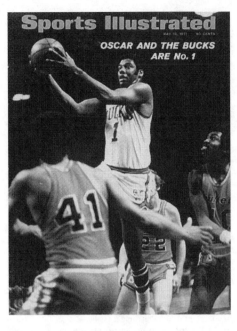

1985

01/07/85	FB	Walter Abercrombie, Steelers	$6
01/14/85	FB	Dan Marino, Dolphins	$12-$15
01/21/85	FB	Dan Marino, Joe Montana	$12-$15
01/28/85	FB	Roger Craig, 49ers	$12
02/04/85	CBB	Walter Berry, St. John's	$7
02/18/85	H	Wayne Gretzky, Oilers	$20
02/25/85	FB	Doug Flutie, Generals	$6
04/01/85	CBB	Patrick Ewing, Dwayne McClain, Chris Mullin	$7
04/08/85	CBB	Ed Pinckney, Villanova	$7
05/13/85	BB	Magic Johnson, Lakers	$15
05/20/85	BB	Patrick Ewing, Knicks	$8
06/10/85	BB	Kareem Abdul-Jabbar, Lakers	$6
06/17/85	BB	Kareem Abdul-Jabbar, Lakers	$6
07/22/85	FB	Howie Long, Raiders	$6
08/12/85	FB	Tony Dorsett, Cowboys	$8
08/26/85	FB	Bernie Kosar, Browns	$7
10/07/85	CFB	Tony Robinson, Tennessee	$5
10/14/85	CFB	Eddie Robinson, Grambling	$5
10/21/85	FB	Jim McMahon, Bears	$7
11/11/85	CFB	Florida vs. Penn State	$6
11/18/85	CBB	Dale Brown, LSU	$5
11/25/85	FB	Danny White, Cowboys	$6-$8
12/02/85	CFB	Heisman Trophy candidates	$15
12/16/85	FB	Marcus Allen, Raiders	$7
12/23/85	BB	Kareem Abdul-Jabbar, Lakers (SOY)	$10

1986

01/13/86	FB	Craig James, Patriots	$6
01/20/86	FB	Jim McMahon, Packers	$8
01/27/86	FB	Mike Singletary, Bears	$7
02/03/86	FB	Chicago Bears vs. New England Patriots	$8
02/17/86	CBB	Danny Manning, Kansas	$9
03/03/86	BB	Larry Bird, Celtics	$15-$20
03/17/86	CBB	Mark Alarie, Duke	$5
03/31/86	CBB	NCAA Final Four	$7

Periodicals

Date	Type	Description	Price
04/07/86	CBB	Pervis Ellison, Louisville	$5
04/28/86	BB	Dominique Wilkins, Hawks	$7-$10
05/19/86	BB	James Worthy, Lakers	$8
05/26/86	BB	Hakeem Olajuwon, Rockets (FC)	$8
06/02/86	H	Canadiens win the Stanley Cup	$6-$8
06/09/86	BB	Larry Bird, Celtics	$15
06/16/86	BB	Kevin McHale, Celtics	$7
06/30/86	BB	Len Bias, Maryland	$5
07/21/86	FB	Jim Kelly, Generals (FC)	$7
08/11/86	FB	"Too Tall" Jones, William Perry	$5
08/18/86	FB	Herschel Walker, Cowboys	$7
09/22/86	CFB	Michigan vs. Notre Dame	$7
09/29/86	FB	Mark Gastineau, Lawrence Taylor	$6-$8
10/13/86	FB	John Elway, Broncos	$5-$7
11/10/86	FB	NFL injuries	$4
11/17/86	BB	Michael Jordan, Bulls	$20
11/24/86	CFB	Vinny Testaverde, Miami	$6-$7
12/08/86	FB	Walter Payton, Bears	$8
12/15/86	FB	Mark Barvarro, Giants	$8
12/22/86	FB	Joe Paterno, Penn State (SOY)	$7

1987

Date	Type	Description	Price
01/05/87	CFB	Brian Bosworth, Oklahoma	$3-$7
01/12/87	FB	Ozzie Newsome, Browns	$4-$7
01/19/87	FB	Rich Karlis, Broncos	$4-$7
01/26/87	FB	Lawrence Taylor, Giants	$8-$10
02/02/87	FB	Phil Simms, Giants	$7-$10
02/23/87	BB	Magic Johnson, Lakers	$6-$9
03/02/87	CBB	J.R. Reid, North Carolina	$7-$8
03/16/87	CBB	Gary McLain, Villanova	$3-$4
03/23/87	CBB	Bobby Knight, Indiana	$7
05/04/87	FB	Julius Erving, 76ers	$7-$10
05/18/87	BB	Isiah Thomas, Pistons	$5-$6
06/01/87	H	Wayne Gretzky, Oilers	$8
06/08/87	BB	Larry Bird, Celtics	$8-$12
06/15/87	BB	Los Angeles Lakers vs. Boston Celtics	$10
06/22/87	BB	Kareem Abdul-Jabbar, Lakers	$10
08/03/87	FB	Vinny Testaverde, Bucanneers	$5
08/24/87	FB	Jim McMahon, Bears	$5
08/31/87	CFB	Tim Brown, Notre Dame	$3-$5
09/21/87	FB	John Elway, Broncos	$5-$6
10/12/87	CFB	Steve Walsh, Miami	$4-$5
11/09/87	FB	Eric Dickerson, Colts	$7
11/16/87	CFB	Rotnei Anderson, Oklahoma	$4
11/23/87	FB	Dexter Manley, Redskins	$4-$5
11/30/87	CFB	Oklahoma vs. Nebraska	$5
12/14/87	FB	Bo Jackson, Raiders	$6-$8
12/28/87-01/04/88	BB	Michael Jordan, Bulls	$15-$20

1988

Date	Type	Description	Price
01/11/88	CFB	Miami vs. Oklahoma	$5-$7
01/18/88	FB	Anthony Carter, Vikings	$5-$6
01/25/88	FB	John Elway, Broncos	$5-$7
02/08/88	FB	Doug Williams, Redskins	$7-$9
02/22/88	BB	Wilt Chamberlain, Bill Russell	$6-$7
03/21/88	BB	Larry Bird, Celtics	$10
03/28/88	CBB	Mark Macon, Temple	$5
04/11/88	CBB	Danny Manning, Kansas	$5
04/18/88	BB	Los Angeles Lakers	$7-$9
05/16/88	BB	Michael Jordan, Bulls	$10
05/23/88	BB	Magic Johnson, Karl Malone	$10
05/30/88	H	Wayne Gretzky, Oilers	$10

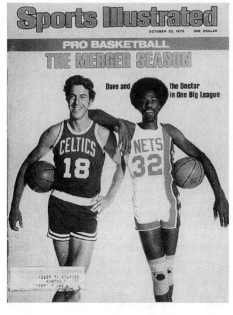

Date	Type	Description	Price
06/27/88	BB	Magic Johnson, Bill Laimbeer	$7-$8
08/01/88	FB	Tony Dorsett, Broncos	$4-$5
08/22/88	H, BB	Wayne Gretzky, Magic Johnson	$10-$15
08/29/88	FB	Bernie Kosar, Browns	$5-$7
09/05/88	CFB	Florida Gators football	$4-$6
09/12/88	FB	Jim McMahon, Bears	$5-$6
10/24/88	CFB	Tony Rice, Notre Dame	$5-$8
11/07/88	BB	Karl Malone, Jazz (FC)	$7-$8
11/14/88	FB	Tom Landry, Chuck Noll	$7-$8
11/21/88	FB	New Orleans Saints vs. Los Angeles Rams	$4-$5
11/28/88	CFB	Rodney Peete, USC	$4
12/05/88	CFB	Tony Rice, Notre Dame	$5
12/12/88	BB	Charles Barkley, 76ers	$10

1989

Date	Type	Description	Price
01/09/89	CFB	Tony Rice, Notre Dame	$5
01/16/89	FB	Ickey Woods, Bengals	$4-$5
01/23/89	BB	Kareem Abdul-Jabbar	$6-$7
01/30/89	FB	Jerry Rice, 49ers (FC)	$9-$12
02/06/89	H	Mario Lemieux, Penguins (FC)	$9-$12
02/13/89	BB	Patrick Ewing, Knicks	$6-$7
02/20/89	CBB	Chris Jackson, LSU	$4-$6
02/27/89	CFB	Charles Thompson, Oklahoma	$6
03/13/89	BB	Michael Jordan, Bulls	$12-$15
03/20/89	FB	Jimmy Johnson, Cowboys	$5-$7
04/10/89	CBB	Glen Rice/Rumeal Robinson, Michigan	$4-$6
04/24/89	CFB	Tony Mandarich, Michigan State	$4-$5
05/15/89	BB	Michael Jordan, Chicago	$10-$12
05/29/89	CBB	Kentucky Wildcats on probation	$3-$4
06/05/89	BB	James Worthy, Lakers	$5-$6
08/07/89	FB	Boomer Esiason, Bengals	$4-$5
08/14/89	BB	Michael Jordan, Bulls	$10-$12
08/21/89	FB	Troy Aikman, Cowboys (FC)	$5-$10
09/04/89	CFB	College Football Preview	$4-$5

09/11/89	FB	Randall Cunningham, Eagles	$4-$8
09/25/89	CFB	Raghib Ismail, Notre Dame	$5
10/02/89	FB	Joe Montana, 49ers	$6-$10
10/23/89	FB	Herschel Walker, Vikings	$4-$5
11/06/89	BB	Joe Dumars, Michael Jordan	$12
11/13/89	FB	Deion Sanders, Falcons	$6-$7
11/20/89	CBB	Rumeal Robinson, Michigan	$5-$6
11/27/89	FB	Heisman Trophy contenders	$4-$8
12/04/89	CFB	Steve McGuire, Miami	$4-$5
12/11/89	BB	Larry Bird, Celtics	$10-$12
12/18/89	F/B/H	Wayne Gretzky, Magic Johnson, Joe Montana	$15

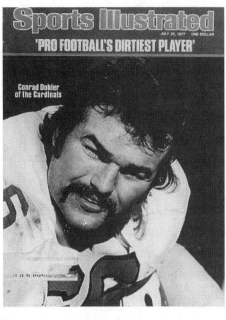

1990

01/08/90	CFB	Scott Erickson, Miami	$4-$5
01/15/90	FB	Jerry Rice, 49ers	$6-$9
01/22/90	FB	John Elway, Broncos	$6-$5
01/29/90	BB	David Robinson, Spurs	$10
02/05/90	FB	Joe Montana, 49ers	$5-$6
03/05/90	CBB	Gary Payton, Oregon State	$3-$4
03/26/90	CBB	Bo Kimble, Loyola-Marymount	$3-$4
04/02/90	CBB	UNLV Runnin' Rebels	$4-$6
04/09/90	CBB	UNLV wins NCAA title	$4-$6
04/23/90	H	Tomas Sandstrom, Kings	$4
04/30/90	FB	Jeff George, Colts	$3-$4
05/21/90	BB	Michael Jordan, Bulls	$12
06/11/90	BB	Isiah Thomas, Pistons	$5-$6
08/06/90	FB	Joe Montana, 49ers	$6-$9
08/27/90	FB	Troy Aikman, Cowboys	$5-$6
09/03/90	CFB	Todd Marinovich, USC	$3-$5
09/10/90	FB	Barry Sanders, Lions (FC)	$4-$6
09/24/90	CFB	Rick Mirer, Notre Dame	$4
10/08/90	FB	O.J. Simpson	$10
10/15/90	FB	Burt Grossman, Chargers	$4-$5
11/05/90	BB	Bill Laimbeer, Pistons	$4-$5
11/12/90	CFB	William Bell, Georgia Tech	$4
11/19/90	CBB	Stacey Augmon/Larry Johnson, UNLV	$6-$7
11/26/90	CFB	Notre Dame vs. Penn State	$4
12/03/90	BB	Magic Johnson, Lakers	$5-$6
12/10/90	CFB	Ty Detmer, BYU	$4-$5
12/17/90	BB	Michael Jordan, Bulls	$10-$15
12/24/90	FB	Joe Montana, 49ers (SOY)	$12

1991

12/31/90- 01/07/91	FB	Kansas City Chiefs receiver	$6
01/14/91	FB	Dan Marino, Dolphins	$8
01/21/91	CBB	Shaquille O'Neal, LSU (FC)	$15
01/28/91	FB	Ottis Anderson, Giants	$4
02/04/91	FB	Everson Walls, Giants	$4
02/11/91	BB	Robert Parish, Celtics	$5
02/18/91	BB	Dream Team (Malone, Barkley, Ewing, M. Johnson, Jordan)	$15
02/25/91	CFB	Rocket Ismail, Notre Dame	$5
03/18/91	H	Brett Hull, Blues	$9
04/01/91	CBB	Mark Randall, Kansas	$4
04/08/91	CBB	Grant Hill, Duke	$7
06/03/91	BB	Michael Jordan, Bulls	$15
06/10/91	BB	Michael Jordan, Magic Johnson	$15
06/17/91	BB	Michael Jordan, Bulls	$15
07/08/91	FB	Lyle Alzado, Raiders	$3
08/12/91	FB	Eric Dickerson, Colts	$5
08/26/91	CFB	David Klingler, Houston	$4
09/02/91	FB	Bruce Smith, Bills	$4

09/23/91	CFB	Desmond Howard, Michigan	$3
10/07/91	FB	Bobby Hebert, Saints	$3
10/14/91	FB	Gary Clark, Redskins	$3
11/11/91	BB	Phil Jackson, Michael Jordan, Scottie Pippen	$12
11/18/91	BB	Magic Johnson, Lakers	$9
11/25/91	CBB	Christian Laettner, Duke	$6
12/02/91	FB	Jim McMahon, Eagles	$6
12/09/91	CFB	Desmond Howard, Michigan	$5
12/16/91	FB	Buffalo Bills defense	$4
12/23/91	BB	Michael Jordan (SOY)	$15

1992

01/20/92	FB	Thurman Thomas, Bills	$4
02/03/92	FB	Mark Rypien, Redskins	$3
02/10/92	BB	Patrick Ewing, Knicks	$3
03/23/92	BB	Larry Bird, Celtics	$6
04/13/92	CBB	Bobby Hurley, Duke	$6
05/11/92	BB	Clyde Drexler, Michael Jordan	$12
05/25/92	BB	Patrick Ewing, Michael Jordan	$6
06/08/92	H	Mario Lemieux, Penguins	$5
06/15/92	BB	Michael Jordan, Bulls	$9
06/22/92	BB	Michael Jordan, Bulls	$9
07/27/92	FB	Joe Montana, 49ers	$4
08/24/92	FB	Deion Sanders, Falcons/Braves	$4
08/31/92	CFB	Miami football player	$3
09/07/92	FB	Jerry Rice, 49ers	$3
09/14/92	FB	Jim Harbaugh, Bears	$3
09/28/92	FB	Tony Mandarich, Packers	$3
10/12/92	FB	Randall Cunningham, Eagles	$3
11/09/92	BB	Charles Barkley, Suns	$5
11/16/92	FB	Jim Everett, Ken Norton	$3
11/30/92	BB	Shaquille O'Neal, Magic	$8
12/07/92	FB	Robert Blackmon, James Campen	$3
12/14/92	BB	Larry Bird, Magic Johnson	$9

1993

01/11/93	CBB	Jim Valvano, NC State	$3
01/18/93	FB	Steve Young, 49ers (FC)	$4

Periodicals

Date	Type	Description	Price
01/25/93	FB	Emmitt Smith, Cowboys (FC)	$5
02/01/93	FB	Super Bowl Preview	$3
02/08/93	FB	Troy Aikman	$6
03/08/93	CBB	Brian Reese, North Carolina	$3
03/15/93	FB	Reggie White, free agent	$3
03/29/93	CBB	Bobby Hurley, Jason Kidd	$4
04/12/93	CBB	Eric Montross, North Carolina	$3
04/19/93	H	Mario Lemieux, Penguins	$4
04/26/93	FB	Joe Montana, 49ers	$4
05/17/93	BB	Hakeem Olajuwon, Rockets	$4
05/31/93	BB	Bill Cartwright, Patrick Ewing	$3
06/07/93	BB	Michael Jordan	$5
06/14/93	H	Los Angeles/Montreal Stanley Cup	$3
06/21/93	BB	Charles Barlely, Michael Jordan	$10
06/28/93	BB	Michael Jordan/Scottie Pippen, Bulls	$10
08/02/93	FB	John Elway, Dan Reeves	$3
08/09/93	BB	Reggie Lewis, Celtics	$3
08/30/93	CFB	Scott Bentley, FSU	$3
09/06/93	FB	Junior Seau, Chargers	$3
09/13/93	FB	Joe Montana, Chiefs	$5
10/04/93	FB	Boomer and Gunnar Esiason, Jets	$3
10/11/93	FB	Chuck Cecil, Cardinals	$3
10/18/93	BB	Michael Jordan, Bulls	$10
10/25/93	FB	Michael Irvin, Cowboys	$4
11/08/93	BB	Alonzo Mourning, Bill Russell	$3
11/22/93	CFB	Jim Flanigan, Notre Dame	$3
11/29/93	CFB	Boston College vs. Notre Dame	$3
12/06/93	FB	Rx for the NFL	$3
12/13/93	CBB	Damon Bailey, Indiana	$3
12/20/93	FB	Don Shula, Dolphins (SOY)	$4

1994

Date	Type	Description
01/10/94	CFB	FSU's #1 football team
01/24/94	FB	Joe Montana, 49ers
01/31/94	FB	Emmitt Smith, Cowboys
02/07/94	FB	Emmitt Smith, Cowboys
03/07/94	BB	David Robinson, Spurs
03/28/94	BB	Boston College vs. North Carolina
04/11/94	CBB	Corliss Williamson, Arkansas
04/25/94	CFB	Dan Wilkinson, Ohio State
05/02/94	BB	Gary Payton, Supersonics
05/16/94	CFB	FSU's tainted title
05/30/94	BB	John Starks, Knicks
06/13/94	H	Mark Messier, Rangers
06/20/94	H/FB	Mark Richter, Patrick Ewing
06/27/94	FB	O.J. Simpson
08/01/94	FB	Troy Aikman, Emmitt Smith, Barry Switzer
08/29/94	CFB	Arizona football
09/12/94	FB	Dan Marino
09/26/94	CFB	Steve McNair, Alcorn State
10/03/94	CFB	Colorado vs. Michigan
10/17/94	FB	Natrone Means, Chargers
10/24/94	CFB	Freddie Scott, Penn State
11/07/94	BB	Charles Barkley, Suns
11/21/94	FB	Ricky Watters
11/28/94	CBB	Felipe Lopez, St. John's
12/05/94	FB	Greg Lloyd
12/12/94	FB	Dallas Cowboys

The Sporting News

The first issue of The Sporting News, then an eight-page newspaper, was published by Alfred Henry Spink of St. Louis in 1886. Although other professional and collegiate sports are covered, baseball has always been TSN's primary attraction. Each weekly issue devotes coverage to every major league team.

In the 1960s, TSN began using color on its covers. During the 1960s and 1970s, the paper's front covers were primarily devoted to baseball players. Collegiate and professional football and basketball covers were secondary. This continued until the 1980s, when the paper began featuring more than one sport on the cover.

Those who collect TSNs, which should have its pages in tact and be in at least Very Good condition, often seek covers which feature one player, members of one team, or superstars. Some people collect issues from an entire memorable season, or try to collect as many issues as possible, for the publication's historical information.

Some collectors have the covers autographed and framed. TSN did not start putting mailing labels on the front cover until the Nov. 28, 1981, issue. However, the labels are positioned so as to not detract from the cover photo.

1964

Date	Type	Description	Price
11/07/64	FB	Ara Parseghian	$15
11/14/64	FB	Dick Butkus	$12-$15
11/21/64	FB	Johnny Unitas	$12-$15
11/28/64	BB	Bob Pettit	$14
12/12/64	FB	Jim Brown	$12-$15
12/19/64	FB	Gino Cappelletti	$10-$12
12/26/64	FB	Jerry Hill, Jim Parker	$10-$12

1965

Date	Type	Description	Price
01/09/65	FB	Don Shula, Johnny Unitas	$14-$18
01/16/65	BB	Red Auerbach	$12
01/23/65	BB	Bill Bradley	$25
01/30/65	BB	Jerry West	$12-$15
02/13/65	BB	Walt Hazzard, Sam Jones	$10
02/20/65	BB	Joe Lapchick	$10
03/06/65	BB	Bill Bradley	$25
03/13/65	BB	Bill Russell	$12-$15
11/13/65	FB	Charlie Johnson	$10
11/20/65	FB	Paul Lowe	$10

Date	Type	Description	Price
11/27/65	FB	Mike Garrett	$10
12/04/65	FB	Don Anderson, Jim Grabowski	$10-$12
12/11/65	FB	All-America Offense	$10
12/18/65	FB	Jim Brown	$15
12/25/65	FB	Gale Sayers	$15

1966

Date	Type	Description	Price
01/01/66	FB	Joe Namath	$20-$25
01/15/66	FB	Green Bay Packers, Vince Lombardi	$15
02/05/66	BB	Cazzie Russell	$10-$12
02/12/66	BB	Guy Rodgers	$10
02/26/66	BB	Wilt Chamberlain	$15
03/12/66	BB	Cazzie Russell	$12
10/29/66	FB	Don Meredith	$12-$15
11/05/66	FB	Terry Hanratty	$10-$12
11/12/66	FB	George Gross, Keith Lincoln	$10
11/19/66	FB	Larry Wilson	$10
11/26/66	FB	Johnny Robinson	$10
12/03/66	FB	Bob Gladieux	$10

Date	Type	Description	Price
12/10/66	FB	Steve Spurrier	$20
12/17/66	BB	Bill Russell	$12-$14
12/24/66	FB	Elijah Pitts	$10
12/31/66	BB	Rick Barry	$12

1967

Date	Type	Description	Price
01/07/67	FB	Bart Starr	$12
01/14/67	FB	Hank Stram	$8-$10
01/21/67	BB	Lew Alcindor	$12-$16
01/28/67	BB	Alex Hannum	$10
02/04/67	BB	Tom & Dick Van Ardsdale	$8-$10
02/11/67	BB	Mendy Rudolph	$12
02/18/67	H	Harry Howell	$8-$12
03/04/67	BB	Bob Cousy	$10-$15
03/11/67	H	Stan Mikita	$10-$15
11/04/67	FB	Len Dawson	$8-$10
11/11/67	FB	Jim Hart	$8-$10
11/18/67	FB	Gary Beban	$8-$10
11/25/67	FB	Fran Tarkenton	$9-$10
12/02/67	FB	Leroy Kelly	$8-$10
12/09/67	BB	Lew Alcindor	$12-$14
12/16/67	FB	Vince Lombardi	$10-$12
12/23/67	FB	Daryle Lamonica	$8-$10
12/30/67	FB	Roman Gabriel	$8-$10

1968

Date	Type	Description	Price
01/06/68	FB	Green Bay Packers	$8-$12
01/13/68	FB	Vince Lombardi, Bart Starr	$10-$12
01/20/68	BB	Wes Unseld	$8-$10
11/27/68	FB	Donny Anderson	$8-$10
02/03/68	H	Phil Esposito	$10-$15
02/10/68	BB	Lenny Wilkins	$8-$10
02/17/68	BB	Don May	$8-$10
02/24/68	BB	Elvin Hayes	$9-$10
09/14/68	FB	Roman Gabriel	$8-$10
10/26/68	FB	Don Meredith	$15
11/02/68	FB	Sonny Jurgensen	$8-$10
11/09/68	FB	Terry Hanratty	$8-$10
11/16/68	FB	Bobby Bell, Willie Lanier, Jerry Lynch	$8-$10
11/23/68	FB	Bart Starr	$9-$10
11/30/68	FB	Earl Morrall	$8-$10
12/07/68	BB	College Basketball Preview	$8-$10
12/14/68	FB	O.J. Simpson	$12-$15
12/21/68	FB	John Hadl	$8-$10
12/28/68	FB	Joe Namath	$15-$20

1969

Date	Type	Description	Price
01/11/69	FB	John Mackey	$8
01/18/69	BB	Elvin Hayes	$8-$9
01/25/69	FB	Joe Namath	$15
02/01/69	H	Norm Ullman	$8
02/08/69	H	Bobby Hull	$10-$15
02/15/69	H	Phil Esposito	$10-$15
02/22/69	H	Gordie Howe	$10-$15
09/20/69	FB	Gale Sayers	$10-$15
11/08/69	FB	Rex Kern	$8
11/15/69	FB	George Allen	$8
11/22/69	FB	Mike Garrett, Robert Holmes, Warren McVea	$8
11/29/69	FB	Mike Phipps	$8
12/06/69	FB	Rick Mount	$8
12/13/69	H	Bobby Orr	$15-$20
12/20/69	FB	Daryle Lamonica	$8-$10
12/17/69	FB	Roman Gabriel	$7-$8

1970

Date	Type	Description	Price
01/10/70	BB	Bill Bradley	$15-$20
01/24/70	H	Rogie Vachon	$7-$8
02/07/70	BB	Lou Hudson	$7-$8
02/14/70	BB	Pete Maravich	$15
02/21/70	H	Tony Esposito	$7-$8
03/07/70	BB	John Vallely	$7-$8
03/14/70	BB	Bill Russell	$8-$9
03/21/70	H	Stan Mikita	$8-$9
03/28/70	BB	Lew Alcindor	$8-$12
09/19/70	FB	Len Dawson	$7-$8
11/07/70	FB	Archie Manning	$8-$10
11/14/70	FB	Bill Munson	$7-$8
11/21/70	FB	Jim Johnson	$7-$8
11/28/70	FB	Joe Thiesmann	$8-$9
12/05/70	FB	Gary Cuozzo	$7-$8
12/12/70	BB	Austin Carr	$7-$8
12/19/70	H	Keith Magnuson	$7-$8
12/26/70	FB	Johnny Robinson	$7-$8

1971

Date	Type	Description	Price
01/02/71	FB	Rex Kern	$5-$7
01/09/71	BB	John Wooden	$5-$8
01/16/71	FB	Johnny Unitas	$7-$9
01/23/71	BB	Dan Issel	$5-$7
01/30/71	FB	Super Bowl V	$6-$7
02/06/71	H	Brad Park	$7
02/13/71	BB	Lew Alcindor	$7-$10
02/20/71	H	Phil Esposito	$7-$9
03/06/71	BB	Pete Maravich	$8-$10
03/13/71	BB	Sidney Wicks	$5-$7
03/20/71	BB	John Havlicek	$7
03/27/71	BB	Mel Daniels	$5-$7
04/03/71	H	Yvan Cournoyer	$5-$7
09/11/71	FB	College Football Preview	$5-$7
11/06/71	FB	Walt Patulski	$5-$7
11/13/71	FB	Billy Kilmer	$5-$7
11/20/71	FB	Terry Beasley, Pat Sullivan	$5-$7
11/27/71	FB	Greg Pruitt	$5-$7
12/04/71	FB	Bob Griese	$5-$8
12/11/71	FB	Otis Taylor	$5-$7
12/25/71	H	Garry Unger	$5-$7

1972

Date	Type	Description	Price
01/01/72	FB	Jerry Tagge	$5-$7
01/15/72	FB	Roger Staubach	$6-$9
01/22/72	BB	Wilt Chamberlain, Gail Goodrich	$6-$8
01/29/72	BB	Artis Gilmore	$5-$7
02/12/72	H	Ted Harris	$5-$7
02/19/72	BB	Dave Cowens	$5-$8
02/26/72	H	Jean Ratelle	$6-$7
03/18/72	BB	Bill Walton	$6-$7
03/25/72	H	Marc Tardif	$6-$7
04/15/74	BB	Kareem Abdul-Jabbar	$6-$9
04/22/72	H	Bobby Hull	$8
05/06/72	H	Gerry Cheevers	$5-$7
09/09/72	FB	Bob Devaney	$5-$7
09/16/72	FB	Len Dawson	$5-$7
10/07/72	FB	Joe Namath	$9-$10
11/11/72	FB	Jerrel Wilson	$5-$7
11/18/72	FB	Larry Csonka	$5-$8
11/25/72	FB	Larry Brown	$5-$7
12/02/72	H	Gilbert Perreault	$5-$7
12/09/72	FB	Terry Bradshaw	$5-$8
12/16/72	BB	Bill Walton	$5-$8
12/23/72	H	Jacques Lemaire	$5-$7
12/30/72	BB	Nate Archibald	$5-$7

1973

Date	Type	Description	Price
01/13/73	FB	Super Bowl VII	$6-$8
01/27/73	BB	Spencer Haywood	$5-$7
02/03/73	BB	Zelmo Beatty	$5-$7
02/10/73	H	Mickey Redmond	$5-$7
02/17/73	BB	UCLA Bruins basketball	$6-$8

Periodicals

Date	Type	Name	Price
02/24/73	BB	George McGinnis	$5-$7
03/10/73	H	Bobby Clarke	$7-$8
03/17/73	BB	Bill Walton, John Wooden	$5-$8
03/24/73	BB	Nate Archibald	$5-$7
03/31/73	BB	Billy Cunningham	$5-$7
04/21/73	H	Phil Esposito	$6-$8
09/15/73	FB	Randy Gradishar, Woody Hayes, John Hicks	$5-$7
11/10/73	FB	John Hadl	$5-$7
11/17/73	FB	Fran Tarkenton	$5-$8
11/24/73	FB	Archie Griffin	$5-$7
12/01/73	FB	Tom Clements	$5-$7
12/08/73	BB	Bill Walton	$5-$8
12/15/73	FB	Bob Lee	$5-$7
12/22/73	FB	O.J. Simpson	$10-$15
12/29/73	FB	Nick Buoniconti	$5-$7

1974

Date	Type	Name	Price
01/05/74	BB	Pete Maravich	$6-$7
01/12/74	BB	Julius Erving	$7-$9
01/19/74	FB	Bob Griese	$4-$6
01/26/74	BB	David Thompson	$4-$6
02/02/74	BB	George Gervin	$4-$6
02/09/74	BB	Kerry & Kim Hughes	$4-$6
02/23/74	BB	Bill Walton	$4-$7
03/09/74	BB	John Shumate	$4-$6
03/16/74	H	Dave Schultz	$4-$6
03/23/74	BB	Bob McAdoo	$4-$6
03/30/74	BB	Rick Barry	$4-$6
09/07/74	FB	Cornelius Green, Archie Griffin	$4-$6
09/21/74	FB	O.J. Simpson	$10-$15
10/05/74	FB	Rod Shoate	$4-$6
10/12/74	FB	Jim Plunkett	$4-$6
11/09/74	FB	Jim Hart	$4-$6
11/16/74	FB	Reggie McKenzie	$4-$6
11/23/74	FB	Dennis Franklin	$4-$6
11/30/74	FB	George Blanda	$5-$6
12/07/74	FB	Ken Anderson	$4-$6
12/14/74	BB	Monty Towe	$4-$6
12/21/74	FB	Marv Hubbard	$4-$6
12/28/74	BB	Rick Barry	$5-$6

1975

Date	Type	Name	Price
01/11/75	BB	Bob McAdoo	$4-$6
01/18/75	FB	Terry Bradshaw, Fran Tarkenton	$5-$7
01/25/75	BB	Swen Nater	$4-$6
02/01/75	H	Guy Lafleur	$4-$6
02/08/75	BB	Steve Green	$4-$6
02/15/75	BB	Walt Frazier	$5-$6
03/01/75	BB	Adrian Dantley	$5-$6
03/15/75	BB	Julius Erving	$7-$9
03/22/75	BB	Dave Cowens	$4-$6
03/29/75	BB	George McGinnis	$4-$6
04/05/75	H	Rogie Vachon	$4-$6
04/19/75	BB	Elvin Hayes	$4-$6
09/13/75	FB	Archie Griffin	$4-$6
09/27/75	FB	Terry Bradshaw	$5-$7
10/25/75	BB	Rick Barry	$4-$7
11/01/75	FB	Roger Staubach	$5-$7
11/08/75	FB	Pete Johnson	$4-$6
11/15/75	FB	Curly Culp	$4-$6
11/22/75	FB	Lynn Swann	$5-$7
11/29/75	FB	Fran Tarkenton	$5-$7
12/06/75	FB	Jim Bakken	$4-$6
12/13/75	BB	Richard Washington	$4-$6
12/20/75	FB	Bert Jones	$4-$6
12/27/75	FB	Ray Guy	$4-$6

1976

Date	Type	Name	Price
01/03/76	FB	John Sciarra	$4-$6
01/10/76	FB	Archie Griffin	$4-$6
01/17/76	BB	Adrian Dantley	$4-$6
01/24/76	FB	Franco Harris	$5-$7
01/31/76	BB	Scott May	$4-$6
02/07/76	BB	Alvan Adams	$4-$6
02/14/76	BB	Kareem Abdul-Jabbar	$6-$8
02/21/76	BB	John Lucas	$4-$6
02/28/76	BB	George McGinnis	$4-$6
03/13/76	BB	David Thompson	$4-$6
03/20/76	BB	Jim Cleamons, Bill Fitch, Bobby Smith, Dick Snyder	$4-$6
03/27/76	BB	Phil Smith	$4-$6
04/03/76	BB	John Havlicek	$5-$7
09/04/76	FB	Tony Dorsett	$6-$7
09/11/76	FB	Jack Lambert	$4-$6
10/02/76	FB	Rick Leach	$5-$6
10/09/76	FB	Billy Kilmer	$4-$6
10/30/76	BB	JoJo White	$4-$6
11/06/76	FB	Steve Grogan	$4-$6
11/13/76	FB	Ricky Bell	$4-$6
11/20/76	FB	Conrad Dobler	$4-$6
11/27/76	FB	Wally Chambers	$4-$6
12/04/76	BB	Marques Johnson	$4-$6
12/11/76	FB	Dave Casper	$4-$6
12/18/76	FB	Isaac Curtis	$4-$6
12/25/76	FB	Bert Jones	$4-$6

1977

Date	Type	Name	Price
01/01/77	FB	Tony Dorsett	$6-$7
01/08/77	BB	David Thompson	$5-$7
01/15/77	FB	Ken Stabler	$5-$7
01/22/77	BB	Bill Walton	$5-$7
01/29/77	BB	Rudy Tomjanovich	$4-$6
02/05/77	BB	Rick Robey	$4-$6
02/12/77	BB	Julius Erving	$6-$9
02/19/77	BB	Pete Maravich	$7-$8
02/26/77	BB	Billy Knight	$4-$7
03/12/77	BB	Paul Westphal	$4-$6
03/19/77	BB	Elvin Hayes	$4-$6
09/10/77	FB	Ross Browner	$4-$6
09/17/77	FB	Tony Dorsett	$5-$7
10/29/77	BB	Pete Maravich	$8-$10
11/05/77	FB	Earl Campbell	$7-$10
11/12/77	FB	Craig Morton	$4-$6
11/19/77	FB	Walter Payton	$9-$12
11/26/77	FB	Drew Pearson	$4-$6
12/03/77	BB	Reggie Theus	$4-$6
12/10/77	FB	Jack Ham	$4-$6
12/17/77	FB	Pat Haden	$4-$6
12/24/77	FB	Bob Griese	$4-$6
12/31/77	FB	"Bear" Bryant, Woody Hayes	$6

1978

Date	Type	Name	Price
01/14/78	BB	Butch Lee	$4-$5
01/21/78	FB	Craig Morton, Roger Staubach	$5-$6
01/28/78	BB	Dave Twardzik	$4-$6
02/05/78	BB	Jack Givens	$4-$5
02/12/78	BB	Julius Erving	$6-$7
02/19/78	BB	Walter Davis	$5
02/26/78	BB	Larry Bird	$12-$15
03/11/78	BB	David Greenwood, Roy Hamilton	$4-$5
03/18/78	BB	David Thompson	$4-$5
03/25/78	BB	Kareem Abdul-Jabbar	$6
04/01/78	BB	Bernard King	$4-$5
09/02/78	FB	Roger Staubach	$4-$6
09/09/78	FB	Joe Montana	$10-$15
10/07/78	FB	Chuck Fusina	$5
10/14/78	BB	Elvin Hayes	$4-$5
11/04/78	FB	Joe Theismann	$4-$6
11/11/78	FB	Billy Sims	$4-$5
11/18/78	FB	Jack Thompson	$4-$5
11/25/78	FB	Terry Bradshaw	$5-$6
12/02/78	BB	Mike Gminski	$4-$5

Date	Type	Description	Price
12/09/78	FB	Earl Campbell	$6
12/16/78	FB	Steve Grogan	$4-$5
12/23/78	FB	Matt Bahr	$4-$5
12/30/78	FB	Jeff Rutledge	$4-$5

1979

Date	Type	Description	Price
01/13/79	BB	Kelly Tripucka	$4-$5
01/20/79	BB	Walter Davis, Paul Westphal	$4-$5
01/27/79	FB	Franco Harris	$4-$6
02/03/79	BB	Moses Malone	$4-$6
02/10/79	BB	George Gervin	$4-$5
02/17/79	BB	Darrell Griffith	$4-$5
02/24/79	BB	John Drew	$4-$5
03/10/79	BB	Lloyd Free, Randy Smith	$4-$5
03/17/79	BB	Larry Bird	$10-$15
03/24/79	BB	Phil Ford	$4-$5
03/31/79	BB	Magic Johnson	$15-$17
04/14/79	BB	Bobby Dandridge	$4-$5
07/14/79	FB	Terry Bradshaw	$5-$6
09/01/79	FB	Walter Payton	$7-$10
09/08/79	FB	Mark Hermann	$4-$5
10/13/79	BB	Dennis Johnson	$4-$5
10/27/79	FB	Wilbert Montgomery	$4-$6
11/03/79	FB	Art Schlichter	$4-$5
11/10/79	FB	Paul McDonald	$4-$5
11/17/79	FB	Dan Fouts	$4-$5
11/24/79	FB	Lee Roy Selmon	$4-$5
12/01/79	BB	Mike Gminski, Darrell Griffith, Mike O'Koren	$4-$5
12/08/79	FB	Ottis Anderson	$4-$5
12/15/79	FB	John Stallworth	$4-$5
12/22/79	FB	Brian Sipe	$4-$5

1980

Date	Type	Description	Price
01/19/80	BB	Kyle Macy	$4-$5
01/26/80	FB	Jack Lambert, Jack Youngblood	$4-$5
02/02/80	BB/FB	Billy Cunningham, Lynn Swann	$4-$6
02/09/80	BB	Larry Bird	$10-$15
02/16/80	BB	Joe Barry Carroll	$4-$5
02/23/80	BB	Truck Robinson	$4-$5
03/01/80	BB	Mark Aguirre, Ray Meyer	$4-$5
03/15/80	BB	Magic Johnson	$15
03/22/80	BB	Darrell Griffith	$4-$5
03/29/80	BB	Joe Barry Carroll	$4-$5
04/05/80	H	Bobby Clarke, Guy Lafleur	$4-$5
05/03/80	FB	Billy Sims, Marc Wilson	$4-$5
07/19/80	FB	Franco Harris	$4-$6
09/06/80	FB	Ken Stabler	$4-$5
09/13/80	FB	Hugh Green, Major Oglivie	$4-$5
09/27/80	FB	Walter Payton	$6-$8
10/11/80	BB	Kareem Abdul-Jabbar, Magic Johnson	$12-$15
10/18/80	FB	Ron Jaworski	$4-$5
11/08/80	FB	John Jefferson	$6-$8
11/15/80	FB	"Bear" Bryant, Vince Ferragamo	$5-$6
11/22/80	FB	Herschel Walker	$5-$6
11/29/80	FB	Conrad Dobler	$4-$5
12/06/80	BB	Albert King	$4-$5
12/13/80	FB	Steve Bartkowski	$4-$5
12/20/80	FB	Joe Cribbs, Billy Sims	$4-$5
12/27/80	FB	Earl Campbell	$6

1981

Date	Type	Description	Price
01/03/81	FB	Bob Crable, Herschel Walker	$5-$6
01/17/81	FB	Tommy Kramer, Jerry Robinson	$4-$5
01/24/81	FB	Wilbert Montgomery, Jim Plunkett	$4-$5
01/31/81	FB	Bill Bergey, Ted Hendricks	$4-$5
02/07/81	FB	Jim Plunkett	$4-$5
02/14/81	BB	Steve Johnson, Ralph Sampson	$4-$5
02/21/81	BB	NBA Headaches	$4-$5

Date	Type	Description	Price
02/28/81	H	Mike Bossy, Denis Potvin, Bryan Trottier	$4-$5
03/14/81	BB	Joe Barry Carroll, Lloyd Free, Bernard King	$4-$5
03/21/81	BB	Mark Aguirre	$4-$5
04/04/81	BB	Jeff Lamp, Isiah Thomas	$5-$6
05/02/81	FB	Bum Phillips	$4-$5
07/11/81	FB	Tony Dorsett	$4-$6
08/01/81	FB	Hugh Green, E.J. Junior, Lawrence Taylor	$6-$8
09/05/81	FB	Anthony Carter	$4-$5
09/12/81	FB	Kellen Winslow	$4-$5
09/26/81	FB	David Woodley	$4-$5
10/10/81	FB	Nolan Cromwell	$4-$6
10/17/81	FB	Ed Jones, Harvey Martin	$6-$8
10/24/81	FB	Leeman Bennett, Chuck Knox, Dick Vermiel	$4-$5
11/07/81	BB	Larry Bird, Cedric Maxwell	$8-$10
11/14/81	FB	Tommy Kramer	$4-$5
11/21/81	FB	Fred Dean, Joe Montana	$15
11/28/81	FB	Dan Marino	$15
12/05/81	BB	Denny Crum, Jerry Eaves, Derek Smith	$4-$5
12/12/81	FB	Ken Anderson	$4-$5
12/19/81	FB	Marcus Allen	$5
12/26/81	FB	Mark Gastineau, Joe Klecko	$5

1982

Date	Type	Description	Price
01/02/82	FB	Herschel Walker	$4-$5
01/09/82	H	Wayne Gretzky	$15
01/16/82	FB	Dan Fouts, Doug Wilkerson	$4
01/23/82	FB	Ken Anderson, Pete Johnson, Ronnie Lott	$4
01/30/82	FB	Ken Anderson, Joe Montana, Joe Namath, Don Shula, John Stallworth	$12
02/06/82	FB	Eddie Edwards, Joe Montana	$12
02/13/82	BB	Sam Perkins	$4-$6
02/20/82	BB	Isiah Thomas	$4-$6
02/27/80	BB	Moses Malone	$4-$5
03/13/82	H	Mike Bossy, Guy Lafleur, Billy Smith, Bryan Trottier	$5-$7
03/20/82	BB	Ralph Sampson	$4
04/03/82	BB	Eric Floyd, Rodney McCray, Sam Perkins, Lynden Rose	$4
04/26/82	FB	Ron Meyer, Kenneth Sims	$4
07/19/82	FB	Mike Ditka, Frank Kush	$4
08/16/82	FB	Vince Ferragamo, Bert Jones	$4
08/30/82	FB	Herschel Walker	$4-$5
09/06/82	FB	Randy White	$4-$5
09/13/82	FB	Marcus Allen	$5
09/27/82	FB	John Elway	$5-$7
10/04/82	FB	Todd Blackledge	$4-$5
11/01/82	BB	Julius Erving, Moses Malone	$5-$6
11/08/82	FB	Pitt football team	$4
11/15/82	FB	Gerry Faust	$4
11/29/82	FB	Neil Lomax, Jim Stuckey	$4
12/06/82	FB	Terry Bradshaw	$4-$5
12/13/82	FB	Herschel Walker	$4-$5
12/20/82	FB	Ken Stabler	$4
12/27/82	FB	James Brooks, Bruce Harper	$4

1983

Date	Type	Description	Price
01/10/83	FB	Mark Moseley, John Riggins, Joe Theismann	$5-$6
01/17/83	FB	Tom Landry, Don Shula	$5-$7
01/24/83	FB	Joe Jacoby, Freeman McNeil, John Riggins	$4-$6
01/31/83	FB	Bob Brudzinski, A.J. Duhe, Dexter Manley	$4-$6
02/07/83	FB	Ross Grimm, John Riggins	$5-$6

Date	Type	Description	Price
02/14/83	BB	Wayman Tisdale	$4
02/21/83	H	Wayne Gretzky, Pete Peeters	$15
02/28/83	BB	Maurice Cheeks, Sidney Moncrief, Jim Paxson	$4
03/14/83	BB	Stewart Granger, Dirk Minniefield, Jon Sundvold	$4
03/28/83	BB	Michael Jordan	$15-$20
04/25/83	FB	John Elway	$5-$6
05/30/83	BB	Kareem Abdul-Jabbar, Moses Malone	$5
08/15/83	FB	Franco Harris, Jack Lambert	$4-$5
08/29/83	FB	Blair Kiel	$4
09/05/83	FB	Lam Jones, Richard Todd, Wesley Walker	$4
09/19/83	FB	Walter Payton	$5-$7
10/17/83	FB	Lyle Alzado, Ted Hendricks	$4
10/31/83	BB	Ralph Sampson	$4
11/14/83	FB	Eric Dickerson	$4
11/21/83	FB	Mike Rozier	$4
11/28/83	BB	Akeem Olajuwon	$5-$6
12/05/83	FB	Dan Marino, Tony Nathan	$12
12/12/83	FB	Roy Green	$4-$6
12/19/83	FB	Mike Rozier	$4
12/26/83	FB	John Riggins	$4-$6

1984

Date	Type	Description	Price
01/09/84	FB	Doug Betters, Dave Krieg	$4
01/16/84	FB	Willie Harper, Lawrence Pillars, John Riggins	$4
01/23/84	BB	Mark Aguirre	$4-$5
02/06/84	H	U.S. Olympic hockey team	$5
02/13/84	BB	Michael Jordan/Sam Perkins, UNC	$15
02/20/84	BB	Larry Bird, Robert Parish	$12
02/27/84	FB	Mike Rozier	$4
03/12/84	BB	Patrick Ewing	$5
03/19/84	H	Bob Bourne, Billy Smith, Bryan Trottier	$4-$7
03/26/84	BB	Michael Jordan	$15
04/16/84	BB	Kareem Abdul-Jabbar	$4-$5
06/04/84	FB	USFL cartoon	$4
07/16/84	FB	Warren Moon	$5-$8
08/27/84	FB	University of Texas	$4
09/03/84	FB	Ed Jones, Tom Landry, Danny White	$4-$5
10/29/84	BB	Michael Jordan	$15
11/05/84	FB	Dan Marino	$10
11/12/84	FB	Doug Flutie	$4
11/19/84	FB	Mark Gastineau	$4-$5
11/26/84	FB/BB	Robbie Bosco, Wayman Tisdale	$4
12/03/84	FB	Denver Broncos/Seattle Seahawks	$4
12/10/84	FB	Eric Dickerson	$4
12/17/84	FB	Roger Craig, Bill Walsh	$6-$8

1985

Date	Type	Description	Price
01/14/85	FB	Mark Clayton	$4
01/21/85	FB	Joe Montana	$12
01/28/85	FB	Joe Montana, Wendell Tyler	$12
02/04/85	H	Wayne Gretzky	$12
02/18/85	BB	Chris Mullin	$5-$6
02/25/85	BB	Larry Bird, Derek Smith	$10
03/11/85	BB	Akeem Olajuwon, Ralph Sampson	$8
03/18/85	H	Bob Carpenter, Dave Christian, Rod Langway	$4
04/01/85	BB	Patrick Ewing	$5-$6
05/06/85	BB	Magic Johnson, James Worthy	$12
06/03/85	FB	Anderson, Bryant, Kelly, Walker	$5
07/22/85	FB	Foot kicking a football	$4
08/05/85	FB	Joe Namath, O.J. Simpson, Roger Staubach	$5
08/26/85	FB	Bo Jackson	$5
09/02/85	FB	Curt Warner	$4
09/23/85	FB	Neil Lomax	$4
10/21/85	BB	Kareem Abdul-Jabbar, Julius Erving	$5-$6
10/28/85	FB	Jim McMahon	$8
11/11/85	FB	Chuck Long	$4
11/18/85	FB	Nolan Cromwell, Gary Green, LeRoy Irvin, Johnnie Johnson	$4
11/25/85	FB	Gerry Faust	$4
12/02/85	FB	Freeman McNeil, Lawrence Taylor	$5-$6
12/16/85	FB	Allen, Craig, Payton, Wilder	$5-$8
12/23/85	FB	Iowa, Miami, Oklahoma, Penn State helmets	$4

1986

Date	Type	Description	Price
01/13/86	FB	Dan Marino	$8
01/20/86	FB	Richard Dent	$4
01/27/86	BB	Akeem Olajuwon	$6
02/03/86	FB	Dan Hampton	$6
02/24/86	BB	Charles Barkley, Johnny Dawkins, Duane Ferrell, Kenny Smith	$4
03/10/86	FB/BB	Manute Bol, Doug Flutie, Herschel Walker, Spud Webb	$4
03/17/86	BB	Danny Manning, Kenny Walker	$4
03/31/86	BB	Larry Bird, Magic Johnson	$12
04/14/86	H	Paul Coffey, Wayne Gretzky, Jari Kurri	$8
06/16/86	BB	Bill Walton	$4
06/30/86	BB	Len Bias	$6
07/21/86	FB	Dieter Brock	$4
08/04/86	BB/FB	Bill Bradley, Jack Kemp	$6
08/11/86	FB	Frank Rothman, Pete Rozelle	$4
09/08/86	FB	Jay Schroeder	$4
09/15/86	FB	Herschel Walker	$5
09/22/86	FB	Lou Holtz	$4
10/06/86	H/FB	Patrick Roy, Vinny Testaverde	$4
10/20/86	FB	John Elway, Pete Rozelle	$6
11/10/86	FB	Jim McMahon	$6
11/17/86	FB	Lawrence Taylor	$8
11/24/86	FB	Eric Dickerson	$5
12/01/86	FB	Vinny Testaverde	$4
12/08/86	FB	Joe Montana	$8
12/15/86	FB	Jerry Rice	$5
12/22/86	FB	Bernie Kosar	$6

1987

Date	Type	Description	Price
01/05/87	BB	Larry Bird	$10
01/12/87	FB	Penn State football	$4
01/19/87	FB	Jim Burt, Leonard Marshall	$4
01/26/87	FB	John Elway	$5
02/02/87	FB	Phil McConkey	$4
02/09/87	BB	Los Angeles Clippers	$4
02/16/87	BB	Bobby Knight	$4
02/23/87	BB	David Robinson	$10
03/09/87	BB	Steve Alford	$4
03/16/87	BB	Tito Horford, J.R. Reid	$4
03/23/87	BB	Julius Erving, Michael Jordan	$8
04/27/87	BB	Magic Johnson	$8
06/22/87	BB	Kareem Abdul-Jabbar	$7
08/17/87	FB	Len Dawson, Joe Greene, Jim McMahon	$5
09/14/87	FB	Jamelle Holieway	$4
09/21/87	FB	Brian Bosworth, Vinny Testaverde	$4
09/28/87	FB	Baltimore: Life After Football	$4
10/12/87	H	Wayne Gretzky	$8
11/09/87	FB	Gaston Green, Danny White	$4
11/23/87	FB	Ozzie Newsome, Walter Payton, D. Sanders	$5
11/30/87	FB	Emmitt Smith	$10
12/07/87	FB/H	Bo Jackson, Pat LaFontaine	$5

12/14/87	BB/FB	George Bell, Manute Bol,	
		Tim Brown	$5
12/21/87	FB	Bobby Hebert, T. Richmond	$4

1988

01/04/88	FB	Jerry Rice	$10
01/11/88	FB	Jimmy Johnson	$5
01/18/88	FB	Joe Bostic, William Perry,	
		Doug Williams	$4
01/25/88	FB	John Elway, Doug Williams	$6
02/08/88	FB	Rulon Jones, Raleigh McKenzie,	
		Doug Williams	$4
02/15/88	H	Ron Hextall	$4
02/22/88	BB	Charles Barkley, Magic Johnson	$8
02/29/88	BB	Danny Ferry, J.R. Reid	$4
03/14/88	H	Paul Coffey, Mario Lemieux	$6
03/21/88	BB	Danny Ainge	$4
03/28/88	BB	Hersey Hawkins	$4
04/04/88	BB	Stacey King	$4
04/11/88	BB	Larry Brown	$4
04/25/88	BB	Pat Riley	$5
05/23/88	BB	Larry Bird, Dennis Johnson	$7
07/04/88	BB	Magic Johnson	$7
07/11/88	BB	Danny Manning	$5
07/18/88	FB	Tony Dorsett	$5
08/15/88	FB	Darryl Stingley	$4
09/12/88	FB	Jack Cooke, Bobby Beathard,	
		Joe Gibbs	$4
09/19/88	FB	Cornelius Bennett	$5
09/26/88	FB	Michael Irvin	$8
11/07/88	BB	Larry Bird, Magic Johnson	$8
11/14/88	FB	Dick Shultz, Vinny Testaverde,	
		Broderick Thomas	$4
11/21/88	FB	Boomer Esiason	$6
11/28/88	FB	Lou Holtz, Tom Landry,	
		Chuck Noll	$5
12/05/88	FB	Notre Dame football	$4
12/12/88	FB	Neil Lomax, J.T. Smith	$4
12/19/88	FB	Barry Sanders	$8

1989

01/09/89	FB	Neal Anderson	$4
01/16/89	FB	Boomer Esiason, Joe Montana	$7
01/30/89	FB	David Fulcher, Jerry Rice	$6
02/06/89	H	Wayne Gretzky	$7
02/13/89	FB/BB	Marcus Allen, Nick Anderson,	
		Karl Malone	$6
02/20/89	H/BB	Wayne Gretzky, Chris Jackson	$7
02/27/89	BB	Sean Elliott, Pervis Ellison,	
		Danny Ferry, Stacey King	$5
03/13/89	BB	Stacey King	$
03/20/89	BB	Charles Barkley, Michael Jordan	$8
03/27/89	BB	Stacey King, Chris Mullin	$4
04/17/89	FB	Troy Aikman	$6
04/24/89	BB	Terry Cummings	$4
05/01/89	BB/FB	Kareem Abdul-Jabbar,	
		Barry Sanders	$7
05/29/89	BB	Dennis Rodman, Isiah Thomas	$6
06/26/89	BB	John Edwards, A.C. Green,	
		John Salley	$4
07/03/89	FB	Neil Lomax, Barry Switzer	$4
07/10/89	BB	Pervis Ellison, David Stern	$4
08/28/89	FB	Lou Holtz	$4
09/11/89	FB	Bo Schembechler, Marty	
		Schottenheimer	$4
09/25/89	FB	Notre Dame vs. Michigan	$4
10/02/89	FB	Tim Krumrie, Jim McMahon	$6
10/09/89	FB/H	Randall Cunningham, Mario	
		Lemieux, Reggie White	$6

11/13/89	FB	Phil Simms, Emmitt Smith	$7
12/04/89	FB	D. Dawkins, Todd Marinovich	$4
12/18/89	FB	Steve Largent	$5

1990

01/01/90	BB	Joe Montana	$8
01/15/90	BB/FB	Patrick Ewing, Barry Sanders,	
		Phil Simms	$6
01/22/90	FB	John Elway, Joe Montana	$8
02/05/90	FB	Joe Montana	$8
02/12/90	FB	Paul Tagliabue	$4
02/19/90	H/BB	Brett Hull, Alonzo Mourning	$6
02/26/90	BB	Chris Jackson, Isiah Thomas	$5
03/26/90	BB	Charles Barkley, Dennis Scott	$5
04/02/90	BB	Alaa Abdelnaby	$4
04/16/90	FB	Blair Thomas	$4
04/23/90	BB	David Robinson	$7
05/14/90	BB	Mark Jackson, Magic Johnson	$6
05/28/90	BB	Michael Jordan	$8
06/25/90	BB	Bill Laimbeer	$5
07/16/90	BB	Mouse Davis, Lyle Alzado	$4
08/27/90	FB	John Elway	$6
09/03/90	FB	Roger Craig	$5
09/17/90	FB	Jeff George	$4
11/12/90	FB	Warren Moon	$6
11/19/90	BB	Paul Westhead, Olando Woolridge	$4
11/26/90	H	Wayne Grezky	$7
12/03/90	FB	Joe Montana, Lawrence Taylor	$8
12/10/90	BB/FB	Clyde Drexler, Boomer Esiason	$5
12/24/90	B/F/H	Norm Ellenberger, Bobby Knight,	
		Pete Peeters, Jerry Rice	$5

1991

01/14/91	BB/H	George Ackles, Ed Belfour	$3
01/21/91	H/FB	Brett Hull, Buddy Ryan, J. Williams	$4
01/28/91	FB	Scott Radecic, Darryl Talley	$3
02/04/91	FB	James Lofton, Everson Walls,	
		P. Williams	$4
02/11/91	BB	Kevin Johnson, Magic Johnson	$6
02/18/91	BB	Sam Perkins, Rick Pitino	$4
02/25/91	BB	Bernard King, L. Robinson	$4
03/04/91	BB	Michael Jordan, Scottie Pippen	$7
03/11/91	H/BB	Wayne Gretzky, Doc Rivers	$7
03/25/91	BB	Richmond Spiders basketball team	$3
04/08/91	BB	Christian Laettner	$4
04/29/91	BB	Portland Trailblazers	$4
06/03/91	H	Mario Lemieux	$6
06/10/91	BB	Magic Johnson, Michael Jordan	$7
06/24/91	BB	Michael Jordan	$7
07/15/91	FB	Roger Craig, Ronnie Lott	$5
07/22/91	BB	Michael Jordan	$7
08/19/91	FB	Herschel Walker	$5
08/26/91	FB	David Klingler	$3
09/09/91	FB	Randall Cunningham	$5
09/16/91	FB	Jackie Sherrill	$3
09/23/91	FB	Don Shula	$5
09/30/91	H/FB	Rocket Ismail, Wayne Gretzky	$5
10/07/91	FB	Sam Mills	$3
10/21/91	FB	Jim Mora	$3
10/28/91	FB	Ray Handley, Jeff Hostetler	$4
11/04/91	FB/BB	Ty Detmer, Clyde Drexler	$4
11/18/91	BB	Magic Johnson	$6
12/02/91	FB	Tom Rathman	$4
12/09/91	BB/FB	Kevin Loughery, Derrick Thomas	$4
12/23/91	FB	Steve Emtman, Gino Torretta	$3
12/30/91	FB	Mark Rypien	$4

1992

01/06/92	BB	Michael Jordan	$6
01/13/92	FB/BB	John Elway, Tim Hardaway	$5

Sport Magazine has been publishing since 1946, featuring athletes from all major sports

01/20/92	FB/H	Ron Hextall, Billy Smith,	
		Jeff Wright	$4
01/27/92	BB/FB	Kenny Smith, Thurman Thomas	$4
02/03/92	H/FB	B. Edwards, Alexander Mogilny,	
		Andre Reed	$4
02/10/92	BB	Jerry Tarkanian	$4
02/17/92	H/BB	Wayne Gretzky, Michael Jordan,	
		Alonzo Mourning	$6
02/24/92	BB	Charles Barkley	$6
03/02/92	FB	Sam Wyche	$3
03/09/92	BB	Christian Laettner	$3
03/16/92	BB	Dennis Rodman	$3
03/23/92	H/BB	Mark Messier, Shaquille O'Neal	$5
03/30/92	BB	Jim Jackson	$3
04/13/92	BB	Christian Laettner	$3
04/27/92	BB	Scottie Pippen	$5
05/04/92	FB	Steve Emtman	$3
05/11/92	BB	John Bagley	$3
05/18/92	BB	Clyde Drexler	$5
06/01/92	FB/BB	Chris Miller, Terry Porter	$4
06/08/92	BB	Scottie Pippen	$5
06/15/92	BB	Michael Jordan	$6
06/22/92	BB	Chicago Bulls	$6
06/29/92	FB	Mark Rypien	$4
07/13/92	FB	Eric Dickerson	$4
07/20/92	BB	Charles Barkley, Patrick Ewing	$5
07/27/92	FB	Jeff George	$3
08/24/92	FB	Bill Walsh	$3
08/31/92	BB	Larry Bird	$6
09/07/92	FB	Randall Cunningham	$4
09/14/92	FB	Minnesota Vikings	$3
09/21/92	FB	Paul Tagliabue	$3
09/28/92	FB	Dave Krieg	$3
10/05/92	H	Eric Lindros	$5
10/19/92	FB	Don Majkowski	$3
10/26/92	FB	Dan Marino	$6
11/09/92	BB/FB	Frank Boyles, Robert Parish	$4
11/16/92	FB	Jimmy Johnson, Gino Torretta	$3
11/23/92	FB	Football helmet	$3
11/30/92	FB/BB	Elvis Grbac, Jamal Mashburn	$4
12/07/92	FB/BB	Bill Bidwell, Dennis Rodman	$3
12/14/92	FB	Dick Butkus, Mike Singletary	$5
12/21/92	FB	Paul Tagliabue	$3
12/28/92	FB	Mike Kryzyewski	$3
1993			
01/11/93	FB	Steve Young	$5
01/18/93	BB	Charles Barkley,	
		Othella Harrington	$4

01/25/93	H/FB	Mario Lemiuex, Emmitt Smith	$5
02/08/93	FB	Dallas Cowboy dynasty	$4
02/15/93	BB	Chris Mullin, Shaquille O'Neal	$5
03/08/93	BB	Kentucky vs. Indiana	$3
03/15/93	BB	Shawn Kemp	$5
03/22/93	BB	Thomas Hill, Eric Montross	$3
03/29/93	BB	John Lucas	$3
04/12/93	BB	Eric Montross, Chris Webber	$5
04/26/93	H	Mario Lemieux	$4
05/03/93	BB	Danny Ainge, Charles Barkley,	
		Kevin Johnson	$4
05/10/93	FB	Bobby Beathard, Darrien Gordon	$3
05/24/93	BB	Hakeem Olajuwon vs. 76ers	$4
06/07/93	BB	Charles Barkley, Oliver Miller	$5
06/21/93	BB	Charles Barkley, Scottie Pippen	$5
06/28/93	BB	Danny Ainge, Michael Jordan	$6
07/12/93	FB	Reggie White	$5
08/23/93	FB	Gene Stallings	$3
09/06/93	FB	Joe Montana	$5
09/13/93	FB	John Elway	$4
09/27/93	FB	Rick Mirer	$3
10/04/93	FB	Junior Seau	$3
10/18/93	BB	Michael Jordan	$6
11/08/93	BB	Shaquille O'Neal	$6
11/15/93	FB	Phil Simms	$4
11/22/93	FB	John Covington	$3
11/29/93	BB	Eric Montross	$3
12/06/93	FB	Richard Dent, Ken Ruettgers	$4
12/13/93	FB	Charlie Ward	$3
12/20/93	FB	Jerry Rice	$5
1994			
01/10/94	FB	Scott Bentley, Dan Kannel	
01/17/94	FB	Warren Moon	
01/24/94	BB	Chris Webber	
01/31/94	FB	Thurman Thomas	
02/07/94	FB	Emmitt Smith	
02/21/94	BB	Donyell Marshall	
03/21/94	BB	Corliss Williamson	
03/28/94	BB	Charles Barkley	
04/11/94	BB	Christian Laettner, Corliss Williamson	
04/25/94	BB	Danny Manning	
05/09/94	BB	Shaquille O'Neal	
05/16/94	H	Mark Messier	
05/23/94	BB	Charles Oakley, Scottie Pippen	
06/13/94	H	Hakeem Olajuwon	
06/20/94	BB	Patrick Ewing	
06/27/94	FB	O.J. Simpson	

07/18/94	FB	Dan Marino
08/29/94	FB	Rohan Marley
09/05/94	FB	Emmitt Smith, Thurman Thomas
09/12/94	FB	Emmitt Smith
09/19/94	FB	Steve Young
10/03/94	H	Mike Keenan
10/10/94	FB	Fuzzy Thurston
10/17/94	FB	Natrone Means
10/24/94	FB	Ronnie Lott
11/21/94	FB	Jerry Rice
11/28/94	BB	Felipe Lopez
12/05/94	FB	Charles Haley
12/12/94	H/F/B	Scotty Bowman, Eddie Robinson, Lenny Wilkens
12/19/94	FB	Emmitt Smith
12/26/94	BB	Vernon Maxwell, Reggie Miller

Sport Magazine

Oct. 1946	FB	Glen Davis, Doc Blanchard .... $75-$95
Nov. 1946	FB	College football .... $75-$95
Dec. 1946	FB	Tom Harmon .... $75-$95
Jan. 1947	BB	Andy Phillips .... $18-$25
March 1947	FB	Alex Groza .... $25-$30
Oct. 1947	FB	Harry Gilmer .... $16-$22
Nov. 1947	FB	Johnny Lujack .... $20-$22
Dec. 1947	FB	Charlie Trippi .... $20-$22
Jan. 1948	BB	Ralph Beard .... $14-$18
Feb. 1948	H	Frank Brimsek .... $14-$18
Nov. 1948	FB	Doak Walker .... $20-$25
Dec. 1948	FB	Johnny Lujack .... $20-$22
Jan. 1949	BB	Ed Macauley .... $15-$18
March 1949	BB	Ralph Beard .... $15-$18
Nov. 1949	FB	Charlie Justice .... $15-$18
Dec. 1949	FB	Johnny Lujack, Sid Luckman .... $20-$25
March 1950	BB	George Mikan .... $20-$22
Jan. 1951	BB	Basketball $12
Feb. 1951	BB	Nat Holman $12
Nov. 1951	BB	Bill McColl $12
Dec. 1951	FB	Johnny Lujack .... $12-$15
Dec. 1952	FB	John Olszewski .... $10-$12
March 1953	BB	Bob Cousy .... $15-$18
Dec. 1953	FB	Michigan football .... $10-$12
Jan. 1954	FB	Eddie LeBaron $12
Nov. 1954	FB	Larry Morris $10
Dec. 1954	FB	Army football .... $10-$12
Nov. 1955	FB	Eddie Erdelatz $10
Jan. 1956	FB	Doak Walker $10
Nov. 1956	FB	Paul Hornung .... $10-$15
Jan. 1957	BB	Wilt Chamberlain .... $11-$15
Feb. 1957	H	Jacques Plante $12
Dec. 1957	FB	Chicago Bears $8
Dec. 1958	FB	Johnny Unitas .... $9-$15
Jan. 1959	H	Maurice "Rocket" Richard .... $10-$12
Dec. 1959	FB	Johnny Unitas $10
Jan. 1960	BB	Bob Cousy .... $10-$15
Dec. 1960	FB	Johnny Unitas .... $8-$10
Jan. 1961	FB	Bobby Layne .... $8-$12
March 1961	BB	Oscar Robertson .... $10-$15
Nov. 1961	FB	Paul Hornung $10
Dec. 1961	FB	Sam Huff .... $8-$9
Jan. 1962	FB	Jim Brown .... $10-$12
March 1962	BB	Wilt Chamberlain .... $10-$12
Nov. 1962	FB	Tommy Davis, Jim Taylor $8
Dec. 1962	FB	Jim Brown, Johnny Unitas .... $8-$10
Jan. 1963	FB	Paul Hornung .... $6-$8

March 1963	BB	Bob Cousy .... $7-$9
April 1963	BB	Wilt Chamberlain .... $7-$10
Dec. 1963	FB	Del Shafner $7
Jan. 1964	FB	Jim Taylor $8
April 1964	BB	Oscar Robertson .... $7-$9
Dec. 1964	FB	Jim Brown .... $9-$10
Jan. 1965	FB	Johnny Unitas .... $6-$9
March 1965	BB	Jerry West .... $8-$9
Nov. 1965	FB	Tommy Mason, Johnny Unitas .... $6-$8
Dec. 1965	FB	Sonny Jurgensen, Fran Tarkenton .... $7-$9
Jan. 1966	FB	Charley Johnson .... $5-$6
March 1966	BB	Bill Russell .... $7-$10
April 1966	FB	Paul Hornung .... $7-$11
June 1966	FB	Joe Namath .... $10-$15
Nov. 1966	FB	John Brodie .... $6-$7
Dec. 1966	FB	Gale Sayers .... $7-$10
Jan. 1967	FB	Don Meredith .... $6-$8
March 1967	BB	Wilt Chamberlain .... $6-$9
April 1967	BB	Lew Alcindor .... $8-$10
Oct. 1967	FB	Johnny Unitas .... $6-$8
Nov. 1967	FB	Joe Namath .... $9-$10
Dec. 1967	FB	Bart Starr .... $6-$8
Jan. 1967	FB	Mike Garrett $5
March 1968	BB	Lew Alcindor .... $6-$9
April 1968	H	Bobby Hull .... $6-$9
Oct. 1968	FB	Fran Tarkenton .... $5-$6
Nov. 1968	FB	Don Meredith $5
Dec. 1968	FB	O.J. Simpson .... $10-$15
Jan. 1969	FB	Deacon Jones .... $4-$6
Feb. 1969	B/F	John Havlicek, O.J. Simpson ...... $10-$15
March 1969	BB	Elgin Baylor, Wilt Chamberlain, Jerry West .... $7-$10
Aug. 1969	FB	O.J. Simpson .... $10-$15
Oct. 1969	FB	Sonny Jurgensen $5
Nov. 1969	FB	Gale Sayers .... $7-$9
Dec. 1969	FB	O.J. Simpson .... $10-$15
Jan. 1970	FB	Calvin Hill $7
Feb. 1970	BB	Lew Alcindor .... $7-$9
March 1970	BB	Jerry West .... $7-$8
April 1970	BB	Willis Reed $7
July 1970	FB	Bart Starr, Johnny Unitas $7
Oct. 1970	FB	Top quarterbacks .... $6-$9
Nov. 1970	FB	Dick Butkus .... $6-$7
Dec. 1970	FB	Roman Gabriel .... $4-$6
Jan. 1971	FB	Larry Brown, Mike Lucci .... $4-$6
Feb. 1971	BB	Dave Bing, Dave DeBusschere ...... $5-$6
March 1971	BB	Pete Maravich .... $10-$15
April 1971	BB	John Havlicek .... $6-$9
Nov. 1971	FB	Ken Willard $5
Dec. 1971	FB	Bob Griese .... $6-$7
Jan. 1972	FB	Larry Brown $5
Feb. 1972	BB	Spencer Haywood $5
March 1972	BB	Wilt Chamberlain .... $5-$7
April 1972	H	Bobby Orr .... $12-$15
May 1972	H	Bobby Hull .... $7-$8
July 1972	FB	Joe Namath .... $8-$9
Oct. 1972	FB	Jim Plunkett .... $6-$7
Nov. 1972	FB	Otis Taylor .... $5-$6
Dec. 1972	FB	Fran Tarkenton .... $5-$6
Jan. 1973	FB	Merlin Olsen .... $4-$5
Feb. 1973	BB	Rick Barry $5
March 1973	H	Ken Dryden .... $4-$5
April 1973	BB	Oscar Robertson $7
May 1973	BB	Dave Cowens .... $5-$6
Nov. 1973	FB	Franco Harris $7
Dec. 1973	FB	Joe Namath .... $8-$10
Jan. 1974	FB	Manny Fernandez, Larry Little .... $6-$8
Feb. 1974	BB	Kareem Abdul-Jabbar .... $7-$9

March 1974	BB	Basketball coaches	$5-$6	Dec. 1984	BB	Patrick Ewing, Chris Mullin	$15
April 1974	BB	Dave DeBusschere	$5-$6	Jan. 1985	FB	Dan Marino	$15
Aug. 1974	FB	Larry Csonka	$8-$12	Aug. 1985	FB	Joe Montana	$15
Nov. 1974	FB	Joe Namath	$9	Sept. 1985	FB	Maryland football	$4-$6
Dec. 1974	FB	O.J. Simpson	$10-$15	Oct. 1985	FB	Dan Marino	$15
Jan. 1975	FB	Fran Tarkenton	$5-$8	Nov. 1985	FB	Marcus Allen, Lawrence Taylor	$10
March 1975	FB	Julius Erving	$10	Dec. 1985	BB	Patrick Ewing	$10
April 1975	BB	Rick Barry	$5-$6	Jan. 1986	FB	Jim McMahon	$15
Oct. 1975	FB	James Harris	$4-$6	Feb. 1986	FB	William Perry	$3-$5
Nov. 1975	FB	Joe Namath	$6-$10	Aug. 1986	FB	Howie Long	$3-$5
Dec. 1975	FB	Joe Greene	$6-$9	Sept. 1986	FB	Jim Harbaugh	$3-$5
Jan. 1976	FB	Super Bowl preview	$6-$7	Oct. 1986	FB	Dan Marino	$12
Feb. 1976	FB	Fran Tarkenton	$6-$7	Nov. 1986	BB	Pervis Ellison	$3-$5
March 1976	BB	George McGinnis	$4-$5	Jan. 1987	FB	John Elway	$7-$10
Sept. 1976	FB	Franco Harris	$5-$7	Feb. 1987	FB	Marcus Allen, Joe Montana	$8-$10
Oct. 1976	FB	Bert Jones	$4-$6	May 1987	BB	Dominique Wilkins	$3-$5
Nov. 1976	FB	O.J. Simpson	$10-$15	Aug. 1987	FB	Roger Craig	$3-$5
Jan. 1977	FB	Roger Staubach	$7-$8	Sept. 1987	FB	Lawrence Taylor	$5-$7
Feb. 1977	BB	Julius Erving	$8-$12	Oct. 1987	FB	Jim Kelly	$4-$7
March 1977	FB	Joe Namath	$8-$9	Nov. 1987	BB	Larry Bird	$6-$8
April 1977	BB	Bill Walton	$4-$6	Jan. 1988	FB	Boomer Esiason	$4-$5
Nov. 1977	BB	Earl Monroe	$6-$7	Feb. 1988	FB	NFL coaches	$3-$5
Dec. 1977	FB	Ken Stabler	$6-$7	May 1988	BB	Isiah Thomas	$4-$5
Jan. 1978	FB	Tony Dorsett	$7-$8	Aug. 1988	FB	Los Angeles Raiders	$3-$5
Feb. 1978	BB	Kareem Abdul-Jabbar	$7-$8	Sept. 1988	FB	Troy Aikman	$10
March 1978	BB	Maurice Lucas	$4-$6	Oct. 1988	FB	Cornelius Bennett	$3-$5
June 1978	BB	Julius Erving	$8-$12	Nov. 1988	BB	Michael Jordan	$12
Sept. 1978	BB	Cliff Branch	$5-$7	Dec. 1988	BB	Stacey King	$3-$5
Nov. 1978	FB	O.J. Simpson	$10-$15	Jan. 1989	FB	Dennis Gentry	$3-$5
Dec. 1978	FB	Jack Lambert	$5-$8	May 1989	BB	Magic Johnson	$5-$6
Jan. 1979	FB	Harvey Martin	$4-$6	Aug. 1989	FB	Troy Aikman, Randall Cunningham, Joe Montana	$10
Feb. 1979	BB	Julius Erving	$10-$12			
March 1979	BB	John Drew	$4-$6	Sept. 1989	FB	College football preview	$10
Sept. 1979	FB	Tony Dorsett	$7	Nov. 1989	BB	Larry Bird, Magic Johnson, Michael Jordan	$10
Nov. 1979	FB	Oakland Raiders	$6-$8			
Dec. 1979	FB	Pat Haden	$4-$5	Dec. 1989	BB	College basketball preview	$3-$5
Jan. 1980	FB	Jack Ham	$5-$6	Jan. 1990	FB	Jim Everett	$4-$5
Feb. 1980	BB	Magic Johnson	$10-$15	June 1990	M	Gretzky, Jordan, Montana, Stockton	$10
March 1980	BB	Larry Bird	$10-$15			
Aug. 1980	FB	Terry Bradshaw	$6-$8	Aug. 1990	FB	Willie Anderson, Bobby Humphrey	$6-$8
Oct. 1980	FB	Earl Campbell	$5-$6			
Nov. 1980	FB	Lee Roy Selmon	$4-$6	Sept. 1990	FB	Roger Craig, John Elway, Jim Everett, Bo Jackson	$6-$8
Dec. 1980	FB	Football's special teams	$4-$6			
Jan. 1981	FB	Billy Sims	$4-$6	Oct. 1990	M	Wayne Gretzky, Michael Jordan, Karl Malone, Joe Montana, Jerry Rice, Reggie White	$5-$6
Feb. 1981	FB	Danny White	$4-$6			
March 1981	BB	Kelly Tripuka	$4-$6			
Aug. 1981	FB	Jim Plunkett	$4-$6	Nov. 1990	FB	Joe Montana	$10
Sept. 1981	FB	Earl Campbell	$5-$7	Dec. 1990	FB	Flipper Anderson, Randall Cunningham, Bobby Humphrey, Ronnie Lott, Mike Singletary, Lawrence Taylor	$5-$7
Oct. 1981	FB	Doug Plank	$4-$6			
Nov. 1981	FB	Lester Hayes	$5-$6			
Dec. 1981	FB	Steve Bartkowski	$4-$6			
Jan. 1982	FB	Tony Dorsett	$5-$7	Jan. 1991	BB	Michael Jordan	$10
Feb. 1982	BB	Magic Johnson	$8-$12	July 1991	M	Jumbo Elliott, Bernard King, Joe Montana	$9
Aug. 1982	FB	Joe Montana	$20			
Sept. 1982	FB	Herschel Walker	$5-$6	Aug. 1991	FB	Ronnie Lott	$7
Oct. 1982	FB	Los Angeles Rams	$4-$6	Sept. 1991	FB	Marcus Allen, Jim Everett, Bobby Humphrey, Joe Montana	$7
Nov. 1982	FB	Lawrence Taylor	$8-$12			
Dec. 1982	BB	Patrick Ewing	$6-$10			
Feb. 1983	FB	Tony Dorsett	$5-$7	Oct. 1991	FB	Bo Jackson	$8
Aug. 1983	FB	Marcus Allen	$5-$6	Nov. 1991	BB	Charles Barkley, Clyde Drexler, Magic Johnson, Michael Jordan, David Robinson	$10
Sept. 1983	FB	Marcus Dupree	$4-$6			
Oct. 1983	FB	Mark Gastineau	$4-$6			
Nov. 1983	FB	Franco Harris	$5-$6	Dec. 1991	BB	Michael Jordan	$10
Dec. 1983	FB	Lyle Alzado	$5-$6	Jan. 1992	FB	Jim Kelly	$8
Jan. 1984	FB	Dan Marino	$20	Feb. 1992	BB	Charles Barkley	$10
May 1984	H	Wayne Gretzky	$15	June 1992	BB	Magic Johnson, Michael Jordan, Scottie Pippen	$15
Aug. 1984	FB	Eric Dickerson	$4-$6			
Oct. 1984	FB	Walter Payton	$6	July 1992	FB	Troy Aikman	$10
Nov. 1984	FB	Betting on football	$4-$6	Aug. 1992	FB	Steve Emtman, Jerry Rice, Mark Rypien	$8

Sept. 1992	FB	John Elway, Warren Moon, Barry Sanders, Thurman Thomas $8
Oct. 1992	BB	Larry Johnson...$8
Nov. 1992	M	Reggie Lewis, Pete Rose..................$8
Dec. 1992	F/B	Rocket Ismail, Rod Woodson/ Jason Kidd $6
Jan. 1993	M	Magic Johnson, Michael Jordan, Jerry Rice, Barry Sanders, Thurman Thomas.........................$8
Feb. 1993	BB	Charles Barkley.............................$10
May 1993	BB	Patrick Ewing, Michael Jordan $12
June 1993	BB	Charles Barkley, Patrick Ewing, Michael Jordan, David Robinson $10
July 1993	FB	Troy Aikman $10
Aug. 1993	FB	Troy Aikman, Joe Montana, Reggie White, Steve Young $10
Sept. 1993	FB	Joe Montana $10
Oct. 1993	FB	Troy Aikman, Randall Cunningham, Dan Marino, Steve Young $10
Nov. 1993	BB	Charles Barkley, Patrick Ewing, Michael Jordan, Shaquille O'Neal............................$10
Dec. 1993	BB	Michael Jordan................................$10
Jan. 1994	M	Charles Barkley, Michael Jordan, Junior Seau, Emmitt Smith, Steve Young
Feb. 1994	FB	Troy Aikman, Joe Montana, Jerry Rice
May 1994	BB	Patrick Ewing, Hakeem Olajuwon
June 1994	BB	Scottie Pippen
July 1994	FB	Emmitt Smith
Aug. 1994	FB	Dan Marino
Sept. 1994	FB	NFL's 75th anniversary
Oct. 1994	FB	Troy Aikman, John Elway, Boomer Esiason, Dan Marino, Joe Montana
Nov. 1994	BB	Charles Barkley, Patrick Ewing, Michael Jordan, Hakeem Olajuwon
Dec. 1994	BB	Shaquille O'Neal

Inside Sports

May 1980	BB	Magic Johnson .... $12-$15
Sept. 1980	FB	Art Schlichter, Ken Stabler............$7-$10
Oct. 1980	FB	Howard Cosell, Frank Gifford, Don Meredith...................... $5-$10
Dec. 1980	F/B	"Bear" Bryant, Ray Meyer........ $5-$7
July 1981	FB	Joe Namath.............................. $7-$15
Sept. 1981	FB	Herschel Walker...................... $4-$7
Oct. 1981	FB	John Matuszek.......................... $5-$7
Nov. 1981	FB	Tony Dorsett .... $7-$10
Dec. 1981	FB	Terry Bradshaw........................ $7-$10
Jan. 1982	FB	Randy White .... $4-$7
Aug. 1982	FB	Joe Montana .... 10-$15
Sept. 1982	FB	Kellen Winslow........................ $5-$7
Oct. 1982	FB	Jack Lambert .... $5-$7
Nov. 1982	FB	Ed "Too Tall" Jones.................. $5-$7
Oct. 1983	FB	John Riggins.............................$7
Nov. 1983	FB	Lawrence Taylor $7
Jan. 1984	FB	Ken Stabler...................................$7
Sept. 1984	FB	Danny White $7
Oct. 1984	FB	Walter Payton................................$15
Nov. 1984	FB	Joe Theismann...............................$7
Dec. 1984	FB	Marcus Allen, Eric Dickerson $7

Jan. 1985	FB	Joe Montana $10
Aug. 1985	FB	NFL ratings $7
Sept. 1985	FB	NFL & college football preview.........$15
Oct. 1985	FB	Mark Gastineau $7
Nov. 1985	BB	Patrick Ewing, Michael Jordan...........$25
Dec. 1985	FB	College All-Americans $7
Jan. 1986	FB	Jim McMahon $10
June 1986	BB	Larry Bird, Magic Johnson $10
July 1986	FB	Walter Payton...............................$12
Aug. 1986	FB	Football ratings...............................$12
Sept. 1986	FB	NFL & college football preview.........$12
Oct. 1986	FB	Football's best players $12
Nov. 1986	BB	Larry Bird, Julius Erving, Magic Johnson, Michael Jordan...$15
Dec. 1986	BB	Steve Alford, David Robinson...........$10
Jan. 1987	FB	NFL playoffs...................................$10
June 1987	BB	Michael Jordan...............................$12
July 1987	FB	Jim McMahon, Phil Simms............$10
Aug. 1987	FB	Football ratings $12
Sept. 1987	FB	NFL and college football preview...$7
Oct. 1987	FB	Football's best players $7
Nov. 1987	BB	NBA and college basketball preview...$7
Dec. 1987	BB	Basketball ratings............................$12
May 1988	BB	Patrick Ewing, Magic Johnson $12
July 1988	FB	100 football questions $12
Aug. 1988	FB	Football ratings $7
Sept. 1988	FB	Bernie Kosar, Rodney Peete, Phil Simms, S. Smith...................$7
Oct. 1988	FB	NFL defenses $7
Nov. 1988	BB	Larry Bird, Magic Johnson, Michael Jordan...............................$12
Dec. 1988	F/B	Mark Jackson, Magic Johnson............$7
May 1989	BB	NBA playoff preview......................$5
July 1989	FB	Joe Montana, Jerry Rice, Jimmy Johnson $6
Aug. 1989	FB	Troy Aikman, Mike Singletary........$6
Sept. 1989	FB	Randall Cunningham, Warren Moon...................................$5
Oct. 1989	BB	Michael Jordan...................... $7-$10
Nov. 1989	BB	Magic Johnson, Michael Jordan..................................... $7-$10
Dec. 1989	BB	Akeem Olajuwon $8
Jan. 1990	FB	Randall Cunningham, John Elway, Boomer Esiason, Jim Everett, Bernie Kosar, Dan Marino, Joe Montana, Phil Simms ...... $5-$7
Feb. 1990	M	Wayne Gretzky, Bo Jackson, Michael Jordan, Mario Lemieux, Karl Malone, Warren Moon, Jerry Rice, others $10
May 1990	BB	Michael Jordan...............................$10
June 1990	M	Wayne Gretzky, Magic Johnson, Joe Montana, others $10
July 1990	FB	Joe Montana, Bill Walsh $10
Aug. 1990	FB	Jeff George, Lou Holtz, Bernie Kosar, Phil Simms .... $5-$6
Sept. 1990	FB	Craig Erickson, Boomer Esiason, Jim Everett, Raghib Ismail ....$5-$6
Oct. 1990	M	Ray Bourque, Brett Hull, Michael Jordan, Al MacInnis, Mark Messier, Bernie Nicholls, Joel Otto $6
Nov. 1990	BB	Tom Chambers, Larry Johnson, Michael Jordan, Alonzo Mourning .... $5-$7

Periodicals

Dec. 1990	BB	Charles Barkely, Joe Dumars, Patrick Ewing, Magic Johnson, Michael Jordan............................$10
Jan. 1991	FB	Bo Jackson, Joe Montana, Mike Singletary, Lawrence Taylor $8
April 1991	M	Wayne Gretzky, Brett Hull, Michael Jordan, Joe Montana, David Robinson, Lawrence Taylor, others ....$
May 1991	BB	Larry Bird, Clyde Drexler, Magic Johnson, Michael Jordan.................................. $8-$10
June 1991	FB	Bo Jackson................................$7
July 1991	FB	Boomer Esiason, Jeff Hostetler, Jim Kelly, Dan Marino, Joe Montana .... $6-$8
Aug. 1991	FB	Elvis Grbac, Amp Lee, Phil Simms, Derrick Thomas $5
Sept. 1991	FB	Joe Montana ....$8-$10
Oct. 1991	BB	Michael Jordan.........................$10
Nov. 1991	BB	Calbert Cheaney, Clyde Drexler, Michael Jordan, Christian Laettner .... $5-$7
Dec. 1991	BB	Charles Barkley, Larry Bird, Magic Johnson, Michael Jordan, Karl Malone, Hakeem Olajuwon, David Robinson.......$8-$10
Jan. 1992	FB	Steve DeBerg, John Elway, Bobby Hebert, Jim Kelly, Warren Moon, Mark Rypien ......$5-$7
May 1992	BB	Michael Jordan, Karl Malone...........$8
June 1992	BB	Dream Tream - Charles Barkley, Larry Bird, Chuck Daly, Patrick Ewing, Magic Johnson, Michael Jordan, Mike Krzyzewski, Karl Malone $10
July 1992	FB	Barry Sanders, Thurman Thomas $7
Aug. 1992	FB	Randall Cunningham, Eric Dickerson, Desmond Howard, Mark Rypien .... $5-$6
Sept. 1992	FB	Randall Cunningham, Mark Rypien $6
Oct. 1992	M	Bobby Hurley, Michael Jordan, Mario Lemieux $7
Nov. 1992	BB	Clyde Drexler, Michael Jordan, Shaquille O'Neal, Pat Riley.........$8
Dec. 1992	BB	Wilt Chamberlain, Michael Jordan.....................................$7-$8
Jan. 1993	FB	Troy Aikman, Randall Cunningham, Steve Young..........$8
Feb. 1993	BB	Charles Barkley, Patrick Ewing, Michael Jordan, Karl Malone, Shaquille O'Neal, Scottie Pippen, David Robinson, John Stockton.............................$8
May 1993	BB	Charles Barkley, Clyde Drexler, Patrick Ewing, Shawn Kemp, Michael Jordan, Shaquille O'Neal, Mark Price................ $5-$7
June 1993	BB	Shaquille O'Neal.............................$8
July 1993	FB	Mike Ditka, Warren Moon, Bill Parcells, Deion Sanders, Emmitt Smith, Rod Woodson .... $5-$7
Aug. 1993	FB	Joe Montana, Tamarick Vanover, Tyrone Wheatley, Reggie White............................$6
Sept. 1993	FB	Troy Aikman, Jim Kelly, Dan Marino, Warren Moon, Joe Montana, Steve Young $6

Oct. 1993	BB	Shaquille O'Neal...............................$8
Nov. 1993	BB	Charles Barkley, Michael Jordan......... $7
Dec. 1993	BB	Larry Johnson, Shawn Kemp, Christian Laettner, Shaquille O'Neal, Isiah Thomas, James Worthy......................................$6
Jan. 1994	FB	Troy Aikman, Jim Kelly, Joe Montana, Barry Sanders, Phil Simms, Wade Wilson
Feb. 1994	BB	Charles Barkley, Clyde Drexler, Patrick Ewing, Shawn Kemp, Larry Johnson, Mark Price
April 1994	BB	Jason Kidd, Eric Montross, Glenn Robinson, Jalen Rose, Corliss Williamson
June 1994	M	Wayne Grezky, Joe Montana, Isiah Thomas
July 1994	FB	Jimmy Johnson, Jerry Jones, Emmitt Smith, Barry Switzer, Thurman Thomas
Aug. 1994	FB	Dan Marino, Joe Montana, Emmitt Smith, Steve Young
Sept. 1994	FB	Drew Bledsoe, Randall Cunningham, Boomer Esiason, Dan Marino, Barry Sanders, Thurman Thomas
Oct. 1994	FB	Al Davis, Jimmy Johnson, Dan Marino, Ken Norton, Jerry Rice, Buddy Ryan, Steve Young
Nov. 1994	BB	Charles Barkley, Patrick Ewing, Reggie Miller, Hakeem Olajuwon, Shaquille O'Neal, Scottie Pippen
Dec. 1994	BB	Charles Barkley, Larry Johnson, Michael Jordan, Shaquille O'Neal, Pat Riley

Football magazines

AFL Yearbook

1960 Handoff artwork	....$50
1961	....$45
1962 Pro Bowl photo	....$30
1963	....$25
1964 Kansas City Chiefs vs. Houston Oilers	....................$20
1965 George Blanda	....$25
1966 Action photos	....$20
1967	....$15
1968 AFL autograph handbook	................................$15
1969 Matt Snell	....$20

All-Pro Football (Maco Magazine)

1957 Scrambling quarterback	...................................$45
1958	....$35
1959 Johnny Unitas	....$45
1960	....$25
1961 Kyle Rote	....$20
1962 Y.A. Tittle	....$20
1963 Bart Starr	....$25
1964 Johnny Unitas	....$20
1965 Fran Tarkenton	....$25
1966 Frank Ryan	....$15

1967 Carroll Dale $10
1968 ....$12
1969 Joe Namath $25
1970 Hank Stram $12
1971 ....$10
1972 ....$10
1973 Fran Tarkenton $15
1974 Fran Tarkenton $15

Athlon's Pro Football

1983 John Riggins $15
1984 Brian Sipe $12
All other covers $12
1985 All covers $12
1986 All covers $12
1987 Bernie Kosar $13
All other covers $10
1988 Bernie Kosar $10
All other covers $8
1989 All covers $10
1990 Eric Metcalf $8
All other covers $8

Complete Sports
AFL & NFL Yearbook

1964 Jim Brown $30
1965 Charlie Hennigan, Johnny Morris $25
1966 Jim Brown, Jack Kemp $30
1967 Gale Sayers $25
1968 Roman Gabriel $15
1969 Sonny Jurgensen, Matt Snell $15
1970 Curley Culp $12
1971 Dick Butkus $18
1972 Larry Csonka, Jim Plunkett $15
1973 ....$12
1974 ....$12
1975 ....$13
1976 ....$14

Cord Sportfacts'
Pro Football Guide

1969 John Mackey $17
1970 ....$17
1971 ....$15
1972 Joe Namath $25
1973 Larry Brown $12
1974 Larry Csonka $15
1975 Franco Harris $18
1976 Franco Harris $18
1977 ....$15
1978 ....$15
1979 ....$15
1980 ....$12
1981 Jack Lambert $15

Cord Sportfacts'
Pro Football Report

1969 Sonny Jurgensen $20
1970 ....$15
1971 Ron Johnson $12
1972 Dick Butkus $18
1973 Larry Csonka $18
1974 O.J. Simpson $25

Dell Sports' Pro Football Preview

1958 Bobby Layne $80
1959 Johnny Unitas $75
1960 Charlie Conerly, Don Meredith $60
1961 Paul Hornung $55
1962 Jim Brown, Jim Taylor $60
1963 Y.A. Tittle $45
1964 Jim Brown $55
1965 Joe Namath, Johnny Unitas $55
1966 Gale Sayers $35
1967 Bart Starr $35
1968 Donny Anderson $30
1969 Leroy Kelly $30
1970 Johnny Unitas $25
1971 Joe Namath $30
1972 Roger Staubach $30
1973 Bob Griese $20
1974 Larry Csonka $20

Fawcett's Pro Football

1961 Paul Hornung $30
1962 Jim Taylor $25
1963 Jim Taylor $20

Football Digest
Simons Publishing

1947 Johnny Lujack .... $35-$70
1948 Chuck Bednarik .... $25-$40
1949 Sammy Baugh .... $30-$55
1950 Gordon Soltau .... $25-$40
1951 Fred Benners, Sonny Gandee .... $25-$40
1952 Hugh McElhenny .... $25-$40

Digest Publishing Corp.

Dec. 1967 Don Perkins $30
Feb. 1968 ....$25
April 1968 Bart Starr $30
Aug. 1968 Bobby Bell $25
Oct. 1968 Leroy Kelly $20
Nov. 1968 Dave Parks $15
Dec. 1968 Noland Smith $15

Century Publishing Co.

Sept. 1971 Gene Washington .... $50-$60
Oct. 1971 Sonny Jurgensen .... $10-$12
Nov. 1971 Greg Landry .... $7-$12
Dec. 1971 Dick Gordon .... $7-$12
Jan. 1972 John Brodie .... $10-$12
Feb. 1972 Dave Osborn .... $10-$12
March 1972 John Brockington .... $7-$8
April 1972 Duane Thomas .... $10-$12
May 1972 Fran Tarkenton .... $10-$12
July 1972 Daryle Lamonica .... $7-$8
Sept. 1972 Dick Butkus .... $10-$12
Oct. 1972 Len Dawson .... $10-$12
Nov. 1972 Joe Namath .... $15-$20
Dec. 1972 Mercury Morris .... $10-$12
Jan. 1973 Larry Brown, Dick Butkus, Tommy
  Nobis .... $10-$12
Feb. 1973 Terry Bradshaw .... $10-$12
March 1973 John Brockingion .... $7-$8
April 1973 Bob Griese .... $10-$12

221

Periodicals

May 1973 Norm Snead .... $7-$8
July 1973 O.J. Simpson .... $15-$20
Aug. 1973 Larry Csonka .... $10-$12
Sept. 1973 Mean Joe Greene .... $10-$12
Nov. 1973 Bobby Douglass .... $7-$8
Dec. 1973 Daryle Lamonica .... $7-$8
Jan. 1974 Chuck Foreman .... $10-$12
Feb. 1974 John Hadl .... $7-$8
March 1974 O.J Simpson .... $15-$20
April 1974 Larry Csonka .... $10-$12
May 1974 Calvin Hill .... $10-$12
July 1974 Archie Manning .... $15-$16
Sept. 1974 Bob Griese, John Hadl .... $10-$12
Oct. 1974 Roger Staubach .... $10-$12
Nov. 1974 Fran Tarkenton .... $10-$12
Dec. 1974 John Brockingion .... $7-$8
Jan. 1975 Ken Stabler .... $7-$8
Feb. 1975 Jim Hart .... $7-$8
March 1975 Ken Stabler .... $7-$8
April 1975 Franco Harris, Chuck Noll .... $10-$12
May 1975 Ken Anderson .... $7-$8
July 1975 Otis Armstrong .... $7-$8
Sept. 1975 Terry Bradshaw .... $10-$12
Oct. 1975 Jim Plunkett .... $10-$12
Nov. 1975 Wally Chambers .... $7-$8
Dec. 1975 Joe Namath .... $15-$20
Jan. 1976 Mercury Morris .... $10-$12
Feb. 1976 Jeff Siemon .... $7-$8
March 1976 O.J. Simpson .... $15-$20
April 1976 Lynn Swann .... $10-$12
May 1976 Dan Pastorini .... $7-$8
July 1976 Bert Jones .... $7-$8
Sept. 1976 Jack Lambert, Roger Staubach .... $10-$12
Oct. 1976 Roger Staubach .... $10-$12
Nov. 1976 Terry Metcalf .... $7-$8
Dec. 1976 Billy Kilmer .... $7-$8
Jan. 1977 Fran Tarkenton .... $10-$12
Feb. 1977 Jim Langer .... $10-$12
March 1977 Ken Stabler .... $10-$12
April 1977 Clarence Davis .... $10-$12
May 1977 Steve Grogan .... $7-$8
July 1977 Greg Pruitt .... $7-$8
Sept. 1977 Joe Namath .... $15-$20
Oct. 1977 Terry Bradshaw, Ken Stabler .... $10-$12
Nov. 1977 Walter Payton .... $15-$20
Dec. 1977 Ken Anderson .... $7-$8
Jan. 1978 Steve Bartkowski, Jack Youngblood .... $7-$8
Feb. 1978 Bert Jones .... $7-$8
March 1978 Tony Dorsett .... $15-$16
April 1978 Craig Morton, Randy White .... $10-$12
May 1978 Jim Zorn .... $7-$8
July 1978 Roger Staubach .... $10-$12
Sept. 1978 Chuck Foreman .... $8-$10
Oct. 1978 Ron Jaworski .... $7-$8
Nov. 1978 O.J. Simpson .... $10-$15
Dec. 1978 Franco Harris .... $10-$12
Jan. 1979 Pat Haden .... $7-$8
Feb. 1979 Don Shula .... $10-$12
March 1979 Earl Campbell .... $10-$12
April 1979 Terry Bradshaw .... $10-$12
May 1979 Archie Manning .... $15-$16
July 1979 Craig Morton .... $10-$12
Sept. 1979 Steve Grogan .... $7-$8
Oct. 1979 Bill Bergey .... $10-$12
Nov. 1979 Dan Fouts .... $10-$12
Dec. 1979 David Whitehurst .... $7-$8
Jan. 1980 Larry Csonka .... $8-$10
Feb. 1980 Terry Bradshaw .... $10-$12
March 1980 Dan Fouts .... $8-$10
April 1980 Lynn Swann .... $5-$7

May 1980 Lee Roy Selmon .... $5-$7
July 1980 Vince Ferragamo .... $5-$7
Sept. 1980 Ken Stabler .... $7-$8
Oct. 1980 Harry Carson .... $8-$10
Nov. 1980 Walter Payton .... $12-$15
Dec. 1980 Russ Francis .... $5-$7
Jan. 1981 Wilbert Montgomery .... $5-$7
Feb. 1981 Bert Jones .... $5-$7
March 1981 Brian Sipe .... $8-$10
April 1981 Billy Sims .... $10-$12
May 1981 Steve Bartkowski .... $5-$7
July 1981 Joe Ferguson .... $5-$7
Sept. 1981 Jim Plunkett .... $7-$8
Oct. 1981 Tommy Kramer .... $5-$7
Nov. 1981 O.J. Anderson .... $7-$8
Dec. 1981 Dan White .... $8-$10
Jan. 1982 David Woodley .... $8-$10
Feb. 1982 Ron Jaworski .... $5-$7
March 1982 George Rogers .... $5-$7
April 1982 Ken Anderson .... $5-$7
May 1982 Joe Montana .... $15-$20
July 1982 Joe Theismann .... $8-$10
Sept. 1982 Bert Jones .... $5-$7
Oct. 1982 Joe Klecko .... $6-$10
Nov. 1982 Terry Bradshaw .... $8-$10
Dec. 1982 Joe Montana, Bill Walsh .... $20-$25
Jan. 1983 Dan Fouts $8
Feb. 1983 William Andrews .... $5-$7
March 1983 Randy White $8
April 1983 Marcus Allen $10
May 1983 John Riggins $8
July 1983 Herschel Walker .... $8-$10
Sept. 1983 Lawrence Taylor .... $10-$15
Oct. 1983 Doug Williams $6
Nov. 1983 Kellen Winslow $5
Dec. 1983 Lynn Dickey .... $5-$7
Jan. 1984 Brian Sipe .... $6-$10
Feb. 1984 Danny White $8
March 1984 Eric Dickerson .... $7-$8
April 1984 Joe Theismann $6
May 1984 Dan Marino $15
July 1984 Curt Warner $8
Sept. 1984 Marcus Allen .... $6-$7
Oct. 1984 Franco Harris $8
Nov. 1984 John Elway .... $8-$10
Dec. 1984 Billy Sims $5
Jan. 1985 Tony Dorsett $8
Feb. 1985 Joe Montana .... $15-$20
March 1985 Walter Payton .... $12-$15
April 1985 Dan Marino .... $15-$20
May 1985 Eric Dickerson .... $7-$8
July 1985 Doug Flutie $5
Sept. 1985 Dave Krieg .... $5-$7
Oct. 1985 Danny White .... $5-$7
Nov. 1985 Mark Gastineau $5
Dec. 1965 Neil Lomax $5
Jan. 1986 Howie Long $6
Feb. 1986 Jim McMahon .... $5-$8
March 1986 Dieter Brock $5
April 1986 Marcus Allen $6
May 1986 Tony Eason, Otis Wilson $8
July 1986 Joe Morris $5
Sept. 1986 Jim McMahon $5
Oct. 1986 Louis Lipps $5
Nov. 1986 James Lofton .... $5-$7
Dec. 1986 Dan Fouts $6
Jan. 1987 Herschel Walker $6
Feb. 1987 Walter Paylon $10
March 1987 Jay Schroeder $5
April 1987 Lawrence Taylor $8

May 1987 Phil Simms $8
July 1987 Dan Marino...$10
Sept. 1987 Bernie Kosar...................................... $5-$7
Oct. 1987 Tommy Kramer $5
Nov. 1987 Tony Eason...$5
Dec. 1987 Curt Warner $5
Jan. 1988 Joe Montana...$10
Feb. 1988 Walter Payton $10
March 1988 Eric Dickerson $6
April 1988 Jerry Rice $8
May 1988 Doug Williams...$8
July 1988 John Elway $6
Sept. 1988 Phil Simms $5
Oct. 1988 Morten Andersen $5
Nov. 1988 Cornelius Bennett, Shane Conlan....................$6
Dec. 1988 Chris Doleman $5
Jan. 1989 Brian Bosworth $5
Feb. 1989 Mike Singletary .... $6-$7
March 1989 Keith Jackson $6
April 1989 Boomer Esiason $6
May 1989 Troy Aikman $8
July 1989 Warren Moon...$5
Sept. 1989 Jim Everett $5
Oct. 1989 Vinny Testaverde...$5
Nov. 1989 Jim Kelly $6
Dec. 1989 Lawrence Taylor $6
Jan. 1990 Roger Craig...$3
Feb. 1990 John Elway $3
March 1990 Barry Sanders...$4
April 1990 Joe Montana...$6
May 1990 Keith McCants $3
July 1990 Christian Okoye $3
Sept. 1990 James Brooks $3
Oct. 1990 Bill Fralic...$3
Nov. 1990 Randall Cunningham..$3
Dec. 1990 Bo Jackson $5
1991-1995 are .... $3-$5

Football Forecast
(Fawcett Publishing)

1962 Y.A. Tittle $25
1963 Bart Starr $20

Game Plan Pro Football

1971 George Banda..$18
1972 Roger Staubach $20
1973 Larry Csonka $15
1974 Fran Tarkenton $14
1975 Franco Harris $17
1976 Roger Staubach $17
1977 Walter Payton $20
1978 ....$15
1979 Archie Manning..$10
1980 Joe Ferguson...$10
1981 Ricky Bell..$8
1982 ....$10
1983 Richard Todd...$8
1984 ....$10
1985 John Elway $15
1986 Phil Simms $10
1987 Jim Everett, John Elway, Phil Simms $12
1988 ....$10
1989 ....$7
1990 Dan Marino $10

Goal Post Pro Football

1975 O.J. Simpson $25
1976 Chuck Foreman, Fran Tarkenton $12
1977 Lawrence McCutcheon $10
1978 ....$12
1979 Brian Sipe $8

Inside Football
(Sport Magazine)

1961 Ernie Davis, Johnny Unitas.....................................$30
1962 Jim Taylor $25
1963 Jim Brown, George Mira $20
1964 Roger Staubach $25
1965 Joe Namath $25
1966..$20
1967 Terry Hanratty $20
1968..$15
1969 Sonny Jurgensen, Vince Lombardi $15

Kickoff

1956 Jim Swink (TCU) $30
1957 Walt Lowalczyk (Michigan State) $25
1958 Bob Anderson (Army) $20
1959 Billy Cannon (LSU) $20
1960 Alan Ameche..$20
1961 ....$15
1962 George Mira (Miami) $15
1963 George Mira, Roger Staubach..................................$25

Popular Library

1964..$10
1965 Floyd Little, Tommy Nobis......................................$15
1966..$10
1967 Terry Hanratty (Notre Dame)...................................$20
1968 O.J. Simpson (USC)...$25
1969 Rex Kern (Ohio State), O.J. Simpson (USC)...........$25
1970 ....$10
1971 Ed Marinaro (Cornell)...$10
1972 John Hufnagel (Penn State) $10
1973 A. Davis (USC) $12
1974 Archie Griffin..$15

Lindy's Pro Football

1987 Boomer Esiason, Bernie Kosar $8
Phil Simms, Al Toon...$7
1988 Tommy Kramer, Randy Wright................................$6
1989 Boomer Esiason, Bernie Kosar $7
1990 Boomer Esiason, Eric Metcalf $6

NFL Yearbook

1953 Quarterback and team logos....................................$75
1954 Player in 3-point stance $60
1955 Wide receiver $50
1956 ....$40
1957 ....$35
1958 ....$30
1959 Black-and-white cartoon $25
1960 Ball carrier...$25
1961 ....$20
1962 ....$20

1963 .... $20
1964 .... $15
1965 .... $15
1966 Fran Tarkenton $20
1967 Donny Anderson $20
1968 Now "NFL autograph handbook" $15
1969 Roman Gabriel $10

Official NFL Annuals
Pro Football Yearbook

1979 Earl Campbell, Tony Dorsett, Walter Payton $12
1980 Terry Bradshaw, Dan Fouts, Walter Payton $12

NFL Team Book

1986 Wiliam Perry $7

Preview

1989 Joe Montana $10

Petersen's Football

1956 Ron Waller .... $35-$60
1957 Frank Gifford .... $25-$40
1958 Jon Arnett, Tom Wilson .... $25-$40
1959 Lenny Moore .... $25-$40
1960 Pro Bowl scene .... $25-$30
1961 Bill Anderson .... $20-$30
1962 Jim Brown $45
1963 Y.A. Tittle .... $25-$35
1964 Jim Brown, George Halas .... $25-$35
1970 Roman Gabriel .... $15-$20
1971 George Blanda, John Brodie, Bart Starr .... $15-$20
1972 Washington Redskins vs. Los Angeles
Rams .... $15-$20
1973 Larry Brown, Larry Csonka, Bob Greise,
Jim Kiick .... $15-$20
1974 O.J. Simpson .... $15-$25
1975 Jack Lambert, Dwight White .... $12-$16
1976 Bert Jones .... $12-$16
1977 John Madden, Ken Stabler .... $12-$16
1978 Ed "Too Tall" Jones, Roger Staubach.......... $12-$16
1979 Terry Bradshaw .... $12-$16
1980 Vince Ferragamo, Pat Haden .... $10-$12
1981 Jim Plunkett, O.J. Simpson, Johnny Unitas ..... $10-$12
1982 Joe Montana .... $15-$20
1983 Joe Theismann, John Riggins.......... $10-$12
1984 Wendell Tyler.................................. $10-$12
1985 Calvin Muhammad .... $10-$12
1986 Walter Payton .... $12-$15
1987 Warren Moon, Herschel Walker ..... $10-$12
1988 .... $8
1989 .... $7
1990 Joe Montana $20

Pro Football Annual
(Reliance Publishing)

1979 Terry Bradshaw, Earl Campbell $17
1980 Terry Bradshaw, Earl Campbell $15
1981 Earl Campbell, Jim Plunkett, Billy Sims.......... $10
1982 Dan Fouts, Joe Montana...................... $15
1983 Marcus Allen, John Riggins $12

Pro Football Annual
(Sport Magazine)

1964 Jim Brown $35
1965 Johnny Unitas $30
1966 .... $25
1967 Bart Starr $25
1968 Sonny Jurgensen, Johnny Unitas............. $20
1969 Joe Namath, Gale Sayers........................ $25
1970 Roman Gabriel, Joe Namath $20
1971 Joe Namath $20

Pro Football Illustrated
(Elbak Publishing)

1941 New York Giants...................................... $200
1942 Ball carrier in action $175
1943 Sammy Baugh $175
1944 Over-the-shoulder catch $140
1945 Ball carrier in action $140
1946 Wilbur Moore $125
1947 Pat Harder.. $125
1948 Bosh Pritchard $100
1949 Clyde Goodknight $100
1950 Fred Gehrke... $75
1951 Billy Vessels.. $75

(Becomes) Sports Review

1952 Action shot $75
1953 Leon Hart, Perry Lowell........................... $65
1954 UCLA vs. USC... $65
1955 Notre Dame vs. Texas $65
1956 Ted Kress (Michigan)................................ $65
1957 Hugh McElhenny, Clendon Thomas....... $60
1958 Blanche Martin, Sam Williams $60
1959 Jeff Langston, Donald Norton $50
1960 Johnny Unitas.. $60
1961 Baltimore Colts vs. New York Giants...... $60
1962 Baltimore Colts vs. Chicago Bears $60
1965 Johnny Unitas.. $60

Pro Football Illustrated
(Complete Sports)

1961 Johnny Unitas.. $35
1962 Paul Hornung.. $30
1963 Jim Brown $35
1964 Jim Brown $35
1967 Joe Namath, Johnny Unitas $30
1968 Joe Namath $30
1969 Roman Gabriel, Joe Namath $25
1970 Gale Sayers, Leroy Kelly $20
1971 John Brodie, Joe Namath $25
1972 Joe Namath, Fran Tarkenton $25
1973 Larry Csonka $20
1974 O.J. Simpson $25
1975 O.J. Simpson, Chuck Foreman.................. $20
1976 Ken Anderson, Fran Tarkenton $15
1977 .... $12
1978 .... $12
1980 O.J. Anderson $15
1981 Billy Sims.. $12
1983 Tony Dorsett, Freeman McNeil $15

224

(New Publisher)
Lexington Library

1985 John Elway, Dan Marino, Joe Montana $15
1986 Jim McMahon $10
1987 John Elway, Dan Marino, Phil Simms $12
1988 Herschel Walker $8
1989 Boomer Esiason $8
1990 Joe Montana $10

Pro Football Stars
(Whitestone Publishing)

1957 Frank Gifford $75
1960 Johnny Unitas $45
1961 Jim Brown $50
1962 Bart Starr $40
1963 Jim Taylor $35
1964 Paul Hornung $30

(Becomes) Pro & College Football

1965 ....$30
1968 Joe Namath $35
1969 Cleveland Browns vs. New York Giants $20
1970 Leroy Kelly $15

Pro Football Weekly

11/17/67 Bart Starr $25
11/24/67 Mike Farr $8
10/05/67 Bart Starr $12
10/12/67 Cowboys, Packers $12
10/19/67 Johnny Unitas $15
10/26/67 Don Maynard $10
11/02/67 Colts vs. Vikings $8
11/09/67 B. Thompson $8
11/16/67 John Mackey, Willie Wood $8
11/23/67 Walter Johnson, Elijah Pitts $8
11/30/67 Jerry Logan, Ron Porter $8
12/07/67 Vince Lombardi, Bart Starr $12
12/14/67 Joe Morrison $10
12/21/67 George Allen, Paul Warfield $8
12/28/67 Deacon Jones, Johnny Unitas $10
01/04/68 Bob Jeter, Vince Lombardi $10
11/11/68 Packers, Raiders $10
11/18/68 Daryle Lamonica, Bart Starr $10
11/25/68 Green Bay Packers Champions $17
Feb. 1968 Roman Gabriel, Les Josephson $8
March 1968 Joe Namath $15
April 1968 Jack Concannon $8
May 1968 Don Meredith $12
June 1968 Len Dawson $10
July 1968 Ray Nitschke $10
Aug. 1968 George Halas, Vince Lombardi $10
08/15/68 Bears, Cowboys $7
08/22/68 Tucker Frederickson, Bart Starr $10
08/29/68 Leroy Kelly $8
09/05/68 Chargers, Rams $7
09/12/68 Len Dawson, Otis Taylor $8
09/19/68 Dennis Partee $7
09/26/68 Otto Graham, Gale Sayers $10
10/03/68 Lee Roy Caffey $8
10/10/68 Charlie Taylor $7
10/17/68 Hewritt Dixon $7
10/24/68 Ray Nitschke, Dave Robinson $7

10/31/68 O.J. Simpson $15
11/07/68 Mike Garrett $7
11/14/68 Ray Nitschke $8
11/21/68 Johnny Unitas $10
11/28/68 Ben Davidson $8
12/05/68 Bruce Gossett, Ed Meador $7
12/12/68 Don Meredith $10
12/19/68 Bart Starr, Johnny Unitas $12
12/16/68 Len Dawson, Jacky Lee $8
01/02/69 Lindsey, Don Meredith $10
01/09/69 Joe Namath $12
01/16/69 Joe Namath $12
01/23/69 New York Jets champions $17
01/30/69 Jim Kiick, Ken Willard $8
02/13/69 O.J. Simpson $12
12/20/69 Vince Lombardi $12
April 1969 Gale Sayers $9
May 1969 Paul Brown $7
June 1969 Pete Rozelle $7
July 1969 Billy Kilmer $7
08/14/69 Sonny Jurgenseon, Vince Lombardi $8
08/21/69 Joe Namath, Fran Tarkenton $10
08/28/69 O.J. Simpson $15
09/04/69 Browns vs. Chargers $7
09/11/69 Ed Meador, Ron Smith $7
09/18/69 Kansas City Chiefs $7
09/25/69 Pete Beathard, Tom Keating $7
10/02/69 John Brodie $8
10/09/69 Lance Alworth $8
10/16/69 Joe Kapp $7
10/23/69 Tommy Hart $7
10/30/69 Bob Griese $9
11/06/69 Fran Tarkenton $9
11/13/69 Roman Gabriel $7
11/20/69 Jim Marshall $7
11/27/69 Dick Butkus $9
12/04/69 Chiefs, Raiders $7
12/11/69 Maxie Baughan, Sonny Jurgensen $7
12/18/69 Rams, Vikings $7
12/25/69 Daryle Lamonica $7
01/01/70 Joe Namath $9
01/08/70 Leroy Kelly, Craig Morton $7
01/15/70 Len Dawson, Joe Kapp $7
01/22/70 Len Dawson, Chiefs champs $12
01/29/70 Terry Bradshaw $9
Feb. 1970 Mike McCoy, Steve Owens $7
March 1970 Bruce Gossett, Johnny Unitas $8
April 1970 Vince Lombardi, Hank Stram $9
May 1970 Allie Sherman $7
June 1970 Joe Kapp $7
July 1970 Lance Alworth, Dick Butkus $9
Aug. 1970 Jim Otis $7
08/15/70 Jan Stenerud $7
08/22/70 Joe Kapp, Joe Namath $9
08/29/70 Roman Gabriel, Calvin Hill $6
09/05/70 Walt Garrison, Don Shula $7
09/12/70 Paul Guidry $7
09/19/70 Vince Lombardi $10
09/26/70 Les Josephson $6
10/03/70 Bill Munson $6
10/10/70 Bob Griese $8
10/17/70 Ray Nitschke $7
10/24/70 Kermit Alexander, Joe Kapp $6
10/31/70 Bill Nelsen, Bob Brown $6
11/07/70 George Blanda, Landry $8
11/14/70 Lance Alworth $8
11/21/70 Rick Dempsey $6
11/28/70 Mike Phillips $6
12/05/70 Bart Starr $9

Periodicals

12/12/70 John Hadl $6
12/19/70 Fred Cox $6
12/26/70 Browns, Cowboys $8
01/02/71 John Brodie, Daryle Lamonica $7
01/09/71 Alan Page $7
01/16/71 Johnny Unitas, Duane Thomas $8
01/23/71 Craig Morton, Johnny Unitas $7
01/30/71 Chuck Howley $7
02/13/71 Mike Curtis, MacArthur Lane $6
02/20/71 Archie Manning, Jim Plunkett $6
April 1971 Don Meredith, Dan Reeves $8
May 1971 Gale Sayers $8
June 1971 Johnny Unitas $8
July 1971 Joe Namath $9
Aug. 1971 Jim Plunkett $6
08/14/71 Eddie Hinton $7
08/21/71 Joe Namath $10
08/28/71 Willie Lanier $7
09/04/71 J. Reynolds $7
09/11/71 Tody Smith $7
09/18/71 Emmitt Thomas $7
09/25/71 Carl Eller $7
10/02/71 Dan Devine $7
10/09/71 Dick Butkus, Kent Nix $9
10/16/71 Ken Anderson $7
10/23/71 Jerry Sherk $7
10/30/71 Archie Manning $8
11/06/71 Bill Nelsen $7
11/13/71 George Blanda $9
11/20/71 John Brockington, Dick Butkus $8
11/27/71 Len Dawson, Otis Taylor $7
12/04/71 Pettis Norman $7
12/11/71 Bob Gresham $7
12/18/71 Tom Dempsey $7
12/25/71 George Blanda $8
01/01/72 Charlie Durkee $7
01/08/72 Don Nottingham, Johnny Unitas $8
01/15/72 John Brodie, Johnny Unitas $9
01/22/72 Bob Griese, Roger Staubach $9
01/29/72 Roger Staubach $15
Feb. 1972 John Reaves $7
March 1972 Alan Page, Fran Tarkenton $9
April 1972 Who is the best QB? $7
May 1972 Willie Ellison $7
June 1972 Alan Page $8
July 1972 49ers, Lions, Bears $7
Aug. 1972 Calvin Hill $8
08/12/72 Ron Johnson $6
08/19/72 Daryle Lamonica $7
08/26/72 Roger Staubach $8
09/02/72 Billy Kilmer $8
09/09/72 Mike Lucci $7
09/16/72 Jim Lynch $6
09/23/72 Len Dawson, Otis Taylor $8
09/30/72 Joe Greene $8
10/07/72 Joe Namath $9
10/14/72 John Brockington, Vern Vandy $6
10/21/72 Leroy Kelly $6
10/28/72 Bob Griese $8
11/04/72 Mel Farr $7
11/11/72 Dan Pastorini $6
11/18/72 Steve Spurrier $6
11/25/72 Dick Butkus $8
12/02/72 Earl Morrall $7
12/09/72 John Mackey, Dan Pastorini $6
12/16/72 Tom Landry $8
12/23/72 Ken Willard $6
12/30/72 Roman Gabriel $6
01/06/73 Larry Brown $6

01/13/73 L.C. Greenwood $7
01/20/73 George Allen, Don Shula $7
01/27/73 Larry Csonka, Bob Griese, Dolphins champs $15
Feb. 1973 O.J. Simpson $9
March 1973 John Matuszak $8
April 1973 McCafferty $6
May 1973 Don Shula $7
June 1973 O.J. Simpson $9
July 1973 Dick Butkus $8
Aug. 1973 John McKay, Don Shula $7
08/11/73 49ers, Patriots $6
08/18/73 Calvin Hill $6
08/25/73 B. Brunet $6
09/01/73 Johnny Unitas $9
09/08/73 John Riggins $8
09/15/73 Jim Files $6
09/22/73 Sonny Jurgensen, Billy Kilmer $7
09/29/73 O.J. Simpson $10
10/06/73 Redskins, Cardinals $6
10/13/73 Rams, 49ers $6
10/20/73 Ed Podolak $6
10/27/73 Terry Bradshaw $8
11/03/73 Rich McGeorge $7
11/10/73 Gene Hickerson $6
11/17/73 Bobby Douglass $6
11/24/73 Daryle Lamonica $7
12/01/73 John Madden $7
12/08/73 Greg Pruitt $6
12/15/73 Pete Athas $6
12/22/73 Cowboys, Redskins $9
12/29/73 Terry Bradshaw, O.J. Simpson $9
01/05/74 Mercury Morris $6
01/12/74 Bob Hayes $8
01/19/74 Bob Griese, Fran Tarkenton $9
01/26/74 Larry Csonka, Dolphins champs $12
Feb. 1974 Garo Yepremian $7
March 1974 Joe Theismann $9
April 1974 Bob Griese $9
May 1974 Larry Csonka, Jim Kiick $7
June 1974 Paul Warfield $7
July 1974 Dallas Cowboys $8
Aug. 1974 Jake Scott $6
08/10/74 M. Botts $6
08/17/74 Charlie Napper $7
08/24/74 J. Johnson $6
08/31/74 Ken Stabler $7
09/07/74 Don Strock $6
09/14/74 R. Moscati $6
09/21/74 Chuck Knox, Don Shula $7
09/28/74 Jim Plunkett $5
10/05/74 Emerson Boozer $7
10/12/74 Chester Marcol $6
10/19/74 Charlie Johnson $6
10/26/74 Sonny Jurgensen $7
11/02/74 O.J. Simpson $9
11/09/74 Larry Csonka $8
11/16/74 Dave Osborn $6
11/23/74 Ken Anderson $6
11/30/74 O.J. Simpson $9
12/07/74 Duane Thomas $6
12/14/74 J. Kenworth $6
12/21/74 Joe Namath $9
12/28/74 Ken Grandberry $6
01/04/75 Art Thoms $6
01/11/75 Dave Osborn $6
01/18/75 George Blanda, Joe Greene $8
01/25/75 Joe Greene, Steelers champs $12
Feb. 1975 Joe Greene, Jim Hart $7

March 1975 Walter Payton $8
April 1975 Ken Stabler $7
May 1975 Joe Greene, L.C. Greenwood $7
June 1975 Raiders vs. Colts $6
July 1975 Joe Namath $9
Aug. 1975 Virgil Livers $6
08/12/75 Terry Bradshaw..$8
08/19/75 MacArthur Lane...$6
08/26/75 Merlin Olsen $7
09/02/75 New Orleans Saints Superdome........................$7
09/09/75 Cullen Bryant $6
09/16/75 Roman Gabriel $6
09/23/75 Lawrence McCutcheon $6
09/30/75 Archie Manning $7
10/07/75 Gary Huff $6
10/14/75 Norm Snead...$6
10/21/75 Essex Johnson $6
10/28/75 O.J. Simpson $9
11/04/75 Rocky Bleier $6
11/11/75 Don Hardeman $6
11/18/75 Robert Miller..$6
11/25/75 Pat Sullivan $6
12/02/75 George Blanda..$8
12/09/75 Boobie Clark $6
12/16/75 Billy Kilmer $8
12/23/75 Bert Jones $7
12/30/75 Lydell Mitchell..$6
01/06/76 Ron Jaworski...$7
01/13/76 Dave Edwards $7
01/20/76 Tom Landry...$7
01/27/76 L.C. Greenwood, Steelers champs $12
Feb. 1976 Joe Namath...$9
March 1976 John Riggins $7
April 1976 John Hadl $6
May 1976 Lee Roy Selmon..$6
June 1976 Kenny Stabler..$8
July 1976 Texas A&M $6
Aug. 1976 Steelers, college season $6
08/09/76 Jets, Cardinals $7
08/16/76 Mike Livingston $6
08/23/76 Walter Payton..$8
08/30/76 Chiefs, Redskins...$6
09/06/76 R. Davis..$6
09/13/76 Richard Todd...$7
09/20/76 Mike Thomas $6
09/27/76 Joe Greene...$7
10/04/76 Haskel Stanback $6
10/11/76 Billy Kilmer $7
10/18/76 Craig Clemons...$6
10/25/76 Hugh McKinnis $6
11/01/76 John Hicks...$6
11/08/76 Chip Myers $6
11/15/76 Rocky Bleier $6
11/22/76 Lynn Dickey...$6
11/29/76 Carlos Brown $6
12/06/76 Roger Staubach $7
12/13/76 Jack Lambert $7
12/20/76 Gordon Bell..$6
12/27/76 Ken Stabler...$7
Jan. 1977 Wally Hilgenberg, Ken Stabler...........................$7
Feb. 1977 John Madden $11
March 1977 Fran Tarkenton...$8
April 1977 Ron Jaworski...$7
May 1977 Bears, 49ers..$6
June 1977 Ricky Bell $6
July 1977 Steelers, Vikings...$6
08/15/77 Dan Pastorini, Mike Phipps $6
Aug. 1977 Chuck Noll $6
08/15/77 Greg Latta $6
08/22/77 Henry Marshall $6

08/29/77 Ron East $6
09/05/77 Tony Reed, Eckern...$6
09/12/77 Lawrence McCutcheon $6
09/19/77 Bert Jones $6
09/26/77 Preston Pearson $7
10/03/77 David Lewis $6
10/10/77 Pat Leahy...$6
10/17/77 Tom MacLeod $6
10/24/77 Don McCauley $6
10/31/77 John James $6
11/07/77 Don Hardeman $6
11/14/77 O.J. Simpson $8
11/21/77 Walter Payton...$8
11/28/77 Walter Payton...$8
12/05/77 Terry Bradshaw, Joe Klecko $8
12/12/77 Delvin Williams $6
12/19/77 Rocky Bleier $6
12/26/77 Larry Csonka..$8
01/02/78 John Matuszak..$8
Jan. 1978 Cowboys, Broncos $7
Feb. 1978 Ed Jones, Cowboys champs $12
March 1978 Ken Houston, Greg Pruitt...............................$6
April 1978 Terry Metcalf $6
May 1978 John Dutton, B. Williams..................................$6
June 1978 Earl Campbell $7
July 1978 Bob Griese, Roger Staubach...............................$8
07/15/78 Coy Bacon...$7
08/07/78 Steve Schubert..$6
08/14/78 Craig Colquitt...$5
10/02/78 Richard Todd..$5
10/09/78 Tony Galbreath $5
10/16/78 Bubba Bean $5
10/23/78 Lawrence McCutcheon $5
10/30/78 Joe Pisarcik $5
11/06/78 T. Daykin $5
11/13/78 Joe Federspiel...$5
11/27/78 Don Macek...$5
12/04/78 Rick Kane $5
12/11/78 Joe Theismann $7
12/18/78 Dexter Bussey $5
12/25/78 Ricky Thompson...$5
01/01/79 Bum Phillips, Don Shula....................................$6
01/08/78 Jack Dolbin $5
01/15/78 Terry Bradshaw, Roger Staubach $8

Profile

1974 O.J. Simpson $25
1975 Ken Stabler...$17

Prolog Official NFL Annual

1971 Logo and 1971 (hardcover)......................................$25
Logo and 1971 (paperback)...$20
1972 Miami vs. Dallas (hardcover)...................................$15
Miami vs. Dallas (paperback)..$15
1973 Larry Brown (hardcover)..$20
Larry Brown (paperpack) $15
1974 Mercury Morris $15
1975 Terry Bradshaw, Franco Harris..................................$15
1976 Fran Tarkenton $15
1977 Bert Jones $15
1978 Walter Payton..$15
1979 Terry Bradshaw $15
1980 Jack Youngblood $15
1981 Jim Plunkett...$15
1982 Joe Montana..$20
1983 Freeman McNeil...$15
1984 Eric Dickerson...$15
1985 Walter Payton...$20

Joe Montana $20
1986 Marcus Allen $15
Joe Morris...$15
Mike Singletary $15
1987 Phil Simms $15
Walter Payton...$20
1988 Anthony Carter, Bernie Kosar, Jim McMahon $10
Jerry Rice...$15
1989 Tim Brown, Joe Montana, J.L. Williams $10
1990 Bo Jackson, Joe Montana, Lawrence Taylor...........$15

The Sporting News AFL Guide

1962 Dick Harris .... $75-$100
1963 Charlie Hennigan............................. $65-$90
1964 Curtis McClinton .... $40-$75
1965 Tobin Rote .... $40-$60
1966 Buck Buchanan, Paul Lowe .... $30-$60
1967 Bobby Burnett, Jack Kemp .... $35-$60
1968 George Blanda, Dayle Lamonica, Jim Nance,
  George Sauer...................................... $20-$55
1969 Matt Snell .... $20-$35
1970 Lance Alworth................................. $20-$30

The Sporting News Football Guide

1970 Hank Stram..$45
1971 Jim Bakken..................................... $35-$40
1972 Roger Staubach .... $35-$40
1973 Mercury Morris .... $32-$35
1974 Larry Csonka .... $32-$35
1975 Franco Harris................................... $28-$35
1976 Lynn Swann..................................... $25-$30
1977 Ken Stabler...................................... $25-$30
1978 Roger Staubach .... $25-$30
1979 Terry Bradshaw .... $25-$30
1980 John Stallworth, Lynn Swann .... $20-$25
1981 Billy Sims.. $20-$25
1982 Ken Anderson................................... $20-$25
1983 Mark Moseley .... $20-$25
1984 Eric Dickerson................................. $20-$25
1985 Dan Marino $25
1986 Marcus Allen .... $15-$20
1987 Phil Simms .... $15-$20
1988 John Elway .... $15-$20
1989 Steve Largent................................... $15-$20
1990 Joe Montana .... $15-$20
1991 Warren Moon $15

The Sporting News Football Record & Rule Book

1945 Wide receiver $40
1946 A.A. Stagg...$35
1947 Pop Warner...$35
1948 Frank Leahy..$30
1949 Sammy Baugh $30
1950 Earle "Greasy" Neale $25

The Sporting News Football Register

1966 St. Louis defense .... $45-$60
1967 Curt McClinton .... $35-$45
1968 George Mira .... $35-$45
1969 Bart Starr $40

1970 Roman Gabriel $30
1971 Sonny Jurgensen.....................................$30
1972 Philadelphia Eagles vs. St. Louis Cardinals............$30
1973 Terry Bradshaw $30
1974 O.J. Simpson $40
1975 Ken Stabler $25
1976 Fran Tarkenton .... $20-$25
19T7 Bert Jones .... $15-$20
1978 Walter Payton.................................. $25-$30
1979 Earl Campbell.................................. $20-$25
1980 Dan Fouts .... $15-$20
1981 Brian Sipe .... $15-$20
1982 George Rogers .... $15-$20
1983 Marcus Allen .... $15-$20
1984 Dan Marino $20
1985 Walter Payton................................... $15-$20
1986 Eddie Brown .... $10-$15
1987 Rueben Mayes .... $10-$15
1988 Jerry Rice...$15
1989 Boomer Esiason................................ $10-$15
1990 Barry Sanders $15

The Sporting News Pro Yearbook

1981 Brian Sipe..$20
1982 Kellen Winslow.......................................$15
1983 John Riggins $15
1984 Ken Anderson, Tom Cousineau $20
All other covers $15
1985 Dan Marino, Joe Montana.......................$35
1986 Jim McMahon $15
All other covers $12
1987 Boomer Esiason, Bernie Kosar $15
All other covers $12
1988 Eric Dickerson.......................................$10
All other covers $10
1989 Reggie Williams $8
All other covers $10
1990 All covers $8

The Sporting News Super Bowl Book

1981 Jim Plunkett...$15
1982 Joe Montana $20
1983 Russ Grimm, John Riggins......................$15
1984 Raiders blocking Redskins punt $10
1985 Joe Montana $20
1986 Dan Hampton $10
1987 Mark Bavaro, Phil McConkey $10
1988 Doug Williams $10
1989 Jerry Rice...$10
1990 Joe Montana $10
1991 Jeff Hostetler $10

Sports All Stars (Maco Magazine)

1958 Rams running back..................................$35
1959 ....$30
1960 Johnny Unitas...$35
1961 ....$20
1962...$25
1963 Jim Taylor $20
1964 Jim Brown $25
1965 Charley Johnson $15
1966 Dick Butkus...$25
1967 Gale Sayers..$25

All others $20
1968 Johnny Unitas $25
1968 Roman Gabriel $15
All others $12
1969 Fran Tarkenton $15
1969 Leroy Kelly $14
All others $12
1970 Don Maynard.......................................$15
1971 ....$12
1972 Jim Plunkett...$12
1973 Mercury Morris $10
1974 Roger Staubach $15
1975 Terry Bradshaw $15
1976 Terry Bradshaw $15
1977 ....$12
1978 ....$12
1979 Ken Anderson......................................$10

Sports Quarterly

1968 Donny Anderson $15
1969 Joe Namath $20
1970 Sonny Jurgensen...................................$17
1971 ....$12
1972 Oakland Raiders vs. Los Angeles Rams $15
1973 Larry Csonka, Bob Griese, Jim Kiick $15
1974 O.J Simpson $25
1975 Minnesota Vikings vs. Pittsburgh Steelers.........$15
1976 Lynn Swann..$20
1977 ....$12
1978 Lyle Alzado $12
1979 Terry Bradshaw $15

Sports Review

1967 Bart Starr $25
1968 Bart Starr, Johnny Unitas $20
1969 Joe Namath $25
1970 Joe Kapp $15
1971 Baltimore Colts vs. Dallas Cowboys.........$15
1972...$15
1973 Billy Kilmer..$15

Sports Stars
Of Pro & College Football

1972 Jim Plunkett...$17
1973 Bob Griese..$15
1974 Larry Csonka $18
1975 Ken Stabler...$15

Sports Stars Of Pro Football

1968 Bart Starr $25
1969 Joe Namath $30
1970...$15
1971...$15
1972 Joe Namath $25
1973 Larry Brown $15
1974 Bob Griese..$18
1975 Terry Bradshaw $20

Sports Today

1971 Joe Namath...$25
1972 Roger Staubach $20
1973 Joe Namath...$20
1974 O.J. Simpson $25

Street & Smith's College Football

1940 Center hiking the ball ....$175-$250
1941 Frankie Albert (Stanford)..............$75-$150
1942 Alan Cameron (Navy) ....$75-$150
1943 Steve Juzwik....................................$75-$150
1944 Bob Kelly (Notre Dame) ....$75-$150
1945 Bob Jenkins (Navy)..........................$65-$100
1946 John Ferraro (USC).........................$65-$100
1947 George Connor (Notre Dame).......$65-$100
1948 Jack Cloud (William & Mary) ......$65-$100
1949 Charley Justice (North Carolina)...$65-$100
1950 Leon Heath (Oklahoma)..................$50-$85
1951 Bob Smith (Texas A&M) ....$50-$85
1952 Johnny Olszewskj (California).........$50-$85
1953 "Ike" Eisenhauer (Navy) ....$75-$100
1954 Ralph Guglielmi (Notre Dame).......$50-$85
1955 Howard Cassidy (Ohio State) ....$75-$100
1956 Jim Swink (TCU) ....$50-$85
1957 Clendon Thomas, Oklahoma..........$75-$100
1958 Bob White (Ohio State).....................$50-$85
1959 Brennan, Izo, Kuharich (Notre Dame) ....$50-$85
1960 Rich Mayo (Air Force) ....$40-$60
1961 Ronnie Bull (Baylor)..........................$40-$60
1962 Jay Wilkinson (Duke).........................$40-$60
1963 Tom Myers (Northwestern) ....$35-$60
    Pete Beathard, Hal Bedsole (USC) ......$40-$60
    Paul Martha (Pitt).................................$40-$60
1964 Roger Staubach (Navy) ....$50-$75
    Dick Butkus (Illinois)...........................$40-$60
    Craig Morton (Californa) ....$35-$60
1965 Roger Bird (Kentucky).......................$35-$45
    Phil Sheridan (Notre Dame).................$35-$45
    Ray Handley (Stanford) ....$35-$45
1966 Steve Spurrier (Florida) ....$35-$50
    Bob Griese (Purdue) ....$45-$60
    Gary Beban (UCLA)..............................$35-$45
1967 Ted Hendricks (Miami) ....$30-$45
    Terry Hanratty (Notre Dame)...............$30-$45
    Ron Drake (USC)..................................$30-$45
1968 O.J. Simpson (USC)............................$50-$60
    Chris Gilbert (Texas)............................$30-$45
    Larry Smith (Florida) ....$30-$45
1969 Rex Kern (Ohio State)........................$30-$35
    Billy Main ....$25-$30
    Steve Kiner (Tennessee).........................$30-$45
1970 Jim Plunkett (Stanford) ....$35-$45
    Archie Manning (Mississippi)..............$40-$45
    Steve Worster (Texas)............................$30-$35
1971 Pat Sullivan (Auburn).........................$25-$30
    Joe Ferguson (Arkansas) ....$25-$30
    Sonny Sixkiller (Washington)...............$25-$30
1972 Brad Van Pelt (Michigan State) ....$25-$30
    John Hufnagel (Penn State)..................$20-$25
    Pete Adams (USC) ....$25-$30
1973 Champ Henson (Ohio State) ....$20-$25
    Kermit Johnson (UCLA).......................$20-$25
    Wayne Wheeler (Alabama)....................$20-$25
1974 Tom Clements (Notre Dame).............$20-$25
    Pat Haden (USC)...................................$20-$25
    Brad Davis (LSU).................................$20-$25
1975 Archie Griffin (Ohio State) ....$20-$25
    Richard Todd (Alabama).......................$20-$25
    John Sciarra (UCLA) ....$25-$30
1976 Tony Dorsett (Pittsburgh) ....$28-$32
    Rob Lytle (Michigan) ....$20-$24
    Ricky Bell (USC) ....$20-$24
1977 Guy Benjamin (Stanford) ....$20-$24
    Ken MacAfee (Notre Dame)..................$20-$24
    Ben Zambiasi (Georgia).........................$20-$24

1978 Rick Leach (Michigan)..................................... $20-$24
   Jack Thompson (Washington State)...................... $20-$24
   Jeff Rutledge (Alabama) .... $20-$24
1979 Charles White (USC) .... $20-$24
   Mark Herrmann (Purdue)..................................... $20-$24
   Jeff Pyburn (Georgia)... $20-$24
1980 Art Schlichter (Ohio State) $20
   Rich Campbell (California)................................... $20
   Scott Woerner (Georgia) $20
1981 Bear Bryant, Herschel Walker.......................... $18
   Anthony Carter, Bob Crable.................................. $15
   Dan Marino, Joe Morris $30
   John Elway (Stanford).. $25
1982 Herschel Walker (Georgia) $25
   John Elway (Stanford).. $20
   Dan Marino, Curt Warner $25
   Tony Eason, Marcus Marek $15
1983 Mike Rozier (Nebraska) $15
   Jacque Robinson (Washington)............................. $15
   Kenny Jackson (Penn State) $15
   Marcus Dupree (Oklahoma)................................. $15
1984 Bo Jackson (Auburn)....................................... $30
   Doug Flutie (Boston College) $15
   Jack Trudeau (Illinois) $15
1985 Keith Byars (Ohio State) .... $10-$15
   D.J. Dozier (Penn State)....................................... $15
   Robbie Bosco (Brigham Young)........................... $10-$15
   Jeff Wickersham (LSU).. $10
1986 Vinny Testaverde (Miami) .... $10-$15
   Lorenzo White (Michigan State)......................... $10-$15
   D.J. Dozier, Joe Paterno .... $10-$15
   UCLA Bruins $12
1987 Tim Brown (Notre Dame) $15
   Gaston Green (UCLA) $10
   Kerwin Bell (Florida)... $15
   Gordie Lockbaum (Holy Cross) $12
   Joe Paterno (Penn State)...................................... $12
   Jamelle Holieway (Oklahoma)............................. $10
1968 Troy Aikman, Rodney Peete $15
   Bobby Humphrey (Alabama) $10
   Steve Taylor (Nebraska) $10
   Todd Ellis (South Carolina) $10
   Mike Power (Boston College).............................. $10
1989 Emmitt Smith (Florida) $20
   Mark Carrier (USC)... $10
   Tony Rice (Notre Dame)...................................... $15
   Troy Taylor (California)....................................... $10
   Major Harris (West Virginia)............................... $10
   Demetrius Brown (Michigan) $10
   Bill Musgrave (Oregon) $10
   Mike Gundy (Oklahoma State) $10
1990 50th Anniversary $10

Street & Smith's Pro Football

1963 Y.A. Tittle $90
   Milt Plum... $60-$90
   Roman Gabriel .... $60-$90
1964 Bart Starr .... $40-$60
   Jim Katcavage .... $40-$60
   Terry Baker .... $40-$60
1965 Johnny Unitas $75
   Frank Ryan .... $40-$60
   Dick Bass... $40-$60
1966 J. Hillebrand, R. LaLonde .... $40-$60
   Ken Willard .... $40-$60
   Charley Johnson .... $40-$60
1967 Mike Rabold, Gale Sayers.............................. $35-$60
   Dick Bass... $35-$45
   Tony Lorick, Bob Vogel .... $35-$45

1968 Don Meredith .... $35-$55
   Norm Snead .... $35-$45
   Hewritt Dixon.. $35-$45
1969 Joe Namath .... $45-$75
   John Brodie.. $35-$45
   Jack Concannon, George Seals .... $35-$45
1970 Joe Namath .... $40-$75
   Roman Gabriel .... $30-$40
   Joe Kapp.. $30-$35
1971 Ralph Neely, Duane Thomas .... $25-$30
   Earl Morrall .... $25-$30
   John Brodie, Ken Willard..................................... $25-$30
1972 Roger Staubach, Duane Thomas .... $25-$35
   Bob Griese .... $25-$30
   John Hadl... $25-$30
1973 Larry Csonka .... $25-$30
   Chester Marcol .... $25-$30
   Steve Spurrier .... $35-$40
1974 Roger Staubach .... $25-$35
   O.J. Simpson .... $30-$40
   Jim Bertelsen .... $25-$30
1975 Franco Harris .... $20-$30
   Jim Hart... $20-$25
   Lawrence McCutcheon .... $20-$25
1976 Roger Staubach .... $25-$30
   Terry Bradshaw .... $25-$30
   Ken Stabler .... $20-$25
1977 Walter Payton .... $30-$40
   Bert Jones .... $20-$25
   John Cappelletti .... $20-$25
1978 Tony Dorsett.. $20
   Bob Griese .... $20-$28
   Mark VanEeghen .... $20-$25
1979 Roger Staubach .... $25-$30
   Terry Bradshaw .... $20-$25
   Jim Zorn .... $20-$25
1980 Walter Payton .... $25-$30
   Terry Bradshaw .... $15-$20
   Dan Fouts $15
1981 Tommy Kramer, Brian Sipe $15
   Jim Plunkett, Jim Zorn $15
   Steve Bartkowski, Earl Campbell $15
   Joe Ferguson, Ron Jaworski.................................. $15
1982 Joe Montana $30
   Lawrence Taylor .... $15-$20
   Tony Dorsett.. $15-$20
   Ken Anderson .... $12-$15
1983 Marcus Allen $20
   Joe Theismann .... $12-$15
   Ken Anderson .... $12-$15
   A.J. Duhe .... $12-$15
1984 Walter Payton .... $20-$25
   Dan Marino $25
   Marcus Allen $20
   John Riggins .... $12-$15
1985 Joe Montana .... $18-$20
   Walter Payton .... $12-$15
   Dan Marino $15
   Phil Simms $12
1986 Dan Marino .... $15-$18
   Eric Dickerson .... $10-$12
   Mike Singletary .... $10-$12
   Joe Morris.. $10-$12
1987 Dan Marino $15
   Tony Dorsett.. $10
   John Elway... $10-$12
   Phil Simms .... $10-$12
   Bernie Kosar.. $10-$12
1988 Jerry Rice.. $15

Warren Moon $10
John Offerdahl $8
Doug Williams $8
Anthony Carter $8
Ozzie Newsome $10
1989 Boomer Esiason $10
Jim Everett $10
Roger Craig $10
Jim Kelly .... $10-$12
Randall Cunningham $10
Mike Singletary .... $10-$12
Herschel Walker $10
Morten Andersen $10
1990 Joe Montana .... $14-$18
1991 Lawrence Taylor $12
1992 Lawrence Taylor $12
Randall Cunningham $10
1993 Phil Simms $10

Touchdown All-Pro

1964 Ron Bull $40
1967 Fran Tarkenton $30
1968 Donny Anderson, Daryle Lamonica.......$25
1969 Joe Namath $30
1970 Roman Gabriel, Calvin Hill $15
1971 Mike Curtis, Fran Tarkenton $20
1972 Calvin Hill $17
1973 Larry Brown $17
1974 O.J. Simpson $25

True Football Yearbook

1950 Punter in action.....................................$75
1951 Kyle Rote...$70
1952 Otto Graham $65
1953 ....$60
1963 Herb Adderly $25
1964 Jim Brown $30
1965 Johnny Unitas $30
1966..$15
1967 Bart Starr $18
1968 John Unitas $18
1969 Earl Morrall $12
1970 Len Dawson $15
1971 Tom Nowatzke $10
1972 Alan Page, Roger Staubach $20
1978 Roger Staubach $18
1979 Earl Campbell..$15
1980 Mean Joe Greene $15
1981 Jim Plunkett..$12

Woodward's Football Yearbook

1949 Dan Foldberg .... $35-$75
1950 Bobby Williams............................. $25-$40
1951 Bob Smith..................................... $25-$40
1952 Harry Agganis .... $25-$40
1953 Bob Burkhart .... $25-$40
1954 Ralph Gugliemi .... $25-$40
1955 George Welsh .... $25-$40
1956 Tommy McDonald .... $25-$40
1957 Bobby Cox...................................... $25-$40
1958 Bob Reifsnyder .... $25-$40
1959 Bob Anderson................................. $25-$40
1960 Bob Schloredt .... $20-$30
1961 Joe Romig.. $20-$30

Pocket Pro Football Annuals Complete Handbook Of Pro Football (Lancer Books)

1971 Fran Tarkenton $15
1972 Roger Staubach $20
1973 Bob Griese $15
1974 O.J. Simpson $20
1975 Mean Joe Greene $15
1976 Terry Bradshaw $15
1977 Ken Stabler $15
1978 Walter Payton $15
1979 Pittsburgh Steelers $12
1980 Lynn Swann..$12
1981 Jim Plunkett..$10
1982 Joe Montana $20
1983 John Riggins Joe Theismann...................$10
1984 Marcus Allen $10
1985 Joe Montana $18
1986 Jim McMahon $10
1987 Phil Simms $10
1968 Bo Jackson..$10
1989 Jerry Rice..$15
1990 Terry Bradshaw, Joe Montana $10

NFL Report

1972 Jim Plunkett (Signet)..............................$15
1973 Terry Bradshaw, Franco Harris (Signet) $20
1974 Larry Csonka (Signet) $15
1975 Lawrence McCutcheon (Dell)...................$10
1976 Franco Harris (Dell) $15
19T7 Ken Stabler (Dell)...................................$12
1978 Mark Van Eeghen (Dell)..........................$8
1979 Tony Dorsett (Dell) $15
1980 Earl Campbell (Dell) $12
1981 Wilbert Montgomery (Dell) $7
1982 Kellen Winslow (Dell).............................$9
1983 James Lofton (Dell)..................................$8
1984 Todd Christensen (Dell) $7
1987 Eric Dickerson (Signet)............................$8
1988 John Elway (Signet) $10

Pro Football (Ballantine Books)

1976 Lynn Swann..$15
1977 O.J. Simpson $25

Pro Football Almanac (Fawcett Gold Medal Books)

1964 Jim Brown $30
1965 Bill Brown, Fran Tarkenton $20

Pro Football Handbook (Pocket Books)

1960 Johnny Unitas...$35
1961 Sonny Jurgensen.....................................$30
1962 Football action.......................................$25
1963 Cleats and ball $20
1964 Ball carrier..$15

1965 Jim Brown	$30
1966	$15
1967 Ball bursting through paper	$35
1968 White helmet	$10
1969 Jets wool cap on a football	$10

(Becomes) The Pocket Book Of Pro Football

1974 O.J. Simpson	$25
1975 Mean Joe Greene	$15
1976 Terry Bradshaw	$15
1977 Ken Stabler	$12
1978 Walter Payton	$15
1979 Terry Bradshaw	$15
1980 Earl Campbell	$12

Basketball magazines

All-Pro Basketball Stars

1976 Rick Barry	$8
1977 John Havlicek	$10
1978 Julius Erving	$12
1979 David Thompson	$7.50
1981 Larry Bird, Julius Erving	$20
1982 Julius Erving	$10

Basketball Annual (Complete Sports)

1970-71 Lew Alcindor	$20
1971-72 Pete Maravich	$15
1972-73	$10
1973-74 Bill Walton	$10
1974-75 David Thompson	$7.50
1975-76 Rick Barry	$7.50
1976-77	$7.50

(Published By) Tiger Press

1977-78	$15
1978-79 Artis Gilmore	$15
1979-80 Mike Gminski, Mike O'Koren, Kelly Tripucka	$15
1980-81 Mark Aguirre, Rod Foster, Kelly Tripucka	$15
1981-82 John Bagley, John Paxson, Ralph Sampson	$15
1982-83 Ralph Sampson	$15
1983-84	$12
1984-85	$12
1985-86	$12
1986-87 David Robinson	$17.50
1987-88 Charles Barkley, Magic Johnson, Michael Jordan	$20
1988-89 Magic Johnson, Isiah Thomas	$15
1989-90	$10
1990-91	$10

Basketball Digest

Nov. 1973	Artis Gilmore	$45
Dec. 1973	Jerry West	$15
Jan. 1974	Norm Van Lier	$10
Feb. 1974	Kareem Abdul-Jabbar	$12

March 1974	Walt Frazier	$12
April 1974	Dave DeBusschere	$12
Nov. 1974	John Havlicek	$12
Dec. 1974	Bob McAdoo	$10
Jan. 1975	Bob Lanier	$10
Feb. 1975	Bill Walton	$12
March 1975	Nate Thurmond	$10
April 1975	Rick Barry	$10
Nov. 1975	Kareem Abdul-Jabbar	$12
Dec. 1975	Walt Frazier	$12
Jan. 1976	Pete Maravich	$15
Feb. 1976	Julius Erving	$15
March 1976	Elvin Hayes	$10
April 1976	Dave Cowens	$10
Nov. 1976	Bob McAdoo	$10
Dec. 1976	Julius Erving, David Thompson	$15
Jan. 1977	Artis Gilmore	$10
Feb. 1977	George McGinnis	$10
March 1977	Earl Monroe	$10
April 1977	Bill Walton	$10
May 1977	Jo Jo White	$10
June 1977	Kareem Abdul-Jabbar	$10
Nov. 1977	Maurice Lucas	$10
Dec. 1977	Rick Barry	$10
Jan. 1978	Darryl Dawkins, Moses Malone	$10
Feb. 1978	Alvan Adams	$10
March 1978	Dan Issel	$10
April 1978	Dave Cowens	$10
May 1978	Bob Lanier	$10
June 1978	Bill Walton	$10
Nov. 1978	Marvin Webster	$10
Dec. 1978	George Gervin	$10
Jan. 1979	David Thompson	$10
Feb. 1979	Pete Maravich	$15
March 1979	Bob McAdoo	$10
April 1979	Elvin Hayes	$10
May 1979	Artis Gilmore	$10
June 1979	Moses Malone	$10
Nov. 1979	Dennis Johnson	$10
Dec. 1979	Kareem Abdul-Jabbar	$10
Jan. 1980	Paul Westphal	$10
Feb. 1980	Julius Erving	$15
March 1980	Larry Bird	$20
April 1980	Marques Johnson	$8
May 1980	Lloyd Free	$8
June 1980	Julius Erving, Magic Johnson	$25
Nov. 1980	Magic Johnson	$20
Dec. 1980	Phil Ford	$8
Jan. 1981	Bill Cartwright	$10
Feb. 1981	Walter Davis	$8
March 1981	Darryl Dawkins	$8
April 1981	Adrian Dantley, Darrell Griffith	$8
May 1981	George Gervin	$8
June 1981	Julius Erving	$15
Nov. 1981	Larry Bird	$15
Dec. 1981	Moses Malone	$10
Jan. 1982	Joe Barry Carroll	$8
Feb. 1982	Isiah Thomas	$10
March 1982	Reggie Theus	$8
April 1982	Sidney Moncrief	$8
May 1982	Alex English	$8
June 1982	Kareem Abdul-Jabbar	$20
Nov. 1982	Magic Johnson	$20
Dec. 1982	Buck Williams	$8
Jan. 1983	Robert Parish	$10
Feb. 1983	Kelly Tripucka	$8
March 1983	Gus Williams	$8
April 1983	Bernard King	$10
May 1983	Artis Gilmore	$10
June 1983	Moses Malone	$10

Nov. 1983	Julius Erving	$15
Dec. 1983	Kiki Vandeweghe	$8
Jan. 1984	Larry Bird	$15
Feb. 1984	Mark Aguirre	$10
March 1984	Maurice Lucas	$8
April 1984	Jim Paxson	$8
May 1984	Magic Johnson	$15
June/July 1984	Ralph Sampson	$8
Nov. 1984	Larry Bird	$15
Dec. 1984	Jack Sikma	$10
Jan. 1985	Bernard King	$7
Feb. 1985	Isiah Thomas	$8
March 1985	Jeff Ruland	$4
April 1985	Hakeem Olajuwon	$8
May 1985	Kareem Abdul-Jabbar	$7
June/July 1985	Michael Jordan	$15
Nov. 1985	Patrick Ewing	$10
Dec. 1985	Rolando Blackman	$4
Jan. 1986	Kevin McHale	$7
Feb. 1986	Dominique Wilkins	$7
March 1986	Ralph Sampson	$5
April 1986	Charles Barkley	$8
May 1986	Magic Johnson	$8
June/July 1986	Larry Bird	$8
Nov. 1986	Hakeem Olajuwon	$8
Dec. 1986	Xavier McDaniel	$4
Jan. 1987	Michael Jordan	$10
Feb. 1987	Moses Malone	$6
March 1987	Terry Cummings	$4
April 1987	Julius Erving	$6
May 1987	Kevin McHale, Kevin Willis	$6
June/July 1987	Magic Johnson	$8
Nov. 1987	Larry Bird	$7
Dec. 1987	Isiah Thomas	$5
Jan. 1988	Karl Malone	$5
Feb. 1988	Charles Barkley	$6
March 1988	Rolando Blackman, Derek Harper	$4
April 1988	Michael Jordan	$8
May 1988	Adrian Dantley	$5
June/July 1988	Magic Johnson	$7
Nov. 1988	Larry Bird	$8
Dec. 1988	Kevin Duckworth	$4
Jan. 1989	Moses Malone, Reggie Theus	$4
Feb. 1989	Kareem Abdul-Jabbar	$6
March 1989	Brad Daugherty, Patrick Ewing	$5
April 1989	Michael Adams	$4
May 1989	Karl Malone,Hakeem Olajuwon	$5
June/July 1989	Michael Jordan	$6
Nov. 1989	Joe Dumars	$4
Dec. 1989	Chris Mullin	$4
Jan. 1990	Patrick Ewing, Michael Jordan, Trent Tucker	$6
Feb. 1990	Dennis Rodman	$4
March 1990	Charles Barkley	$6
April 1990	Terry Porter	$4
May 1990	Michael Jordan	$6
June/July 1990	David Robinson	$7.50
Nov. 1990	Kevin Johnson	$4
Dec. 1990	Mark Price	$4
Jan. 1991	Charles Smith	$3
Feb. 1991	Bill Laimbeer	$3
March 1991	Hakeem Olajuwon, David Robinson	$6
April 1991	Kevin McHale, Brian Shaw	$4
May 1991	Clyde Drexler	$4
June/July 1991	Michael Jordan	$7

Basketball Forecast

1985-86 Larry Bird, Michael Jordan	$12
1986-87 Patrick Ewing, Hakeem Olajuwon	$8

1987-88 Magic Johnson	$9
1988-89 Michael Jordan	$10
1989-90 Magic Johnson	$7.50

Basketball News Yearbook

1973 Archibald, Cunninghan, Russell	$15
1974 Julius Erving	$15
1975 Walt Frazier, John Havlicek	$13
1976 Rick Barry	$12
1977 Julius Erving	$15
1978 Pete Maravich, Willis Reed, Bill Walton	$15
1979 Nancy Lieberman, Wes Unseld, Bill Walton	$10
1980 Jack Sikma	$12
1981 Larry Bird	$17

Basketball Scene

1979-80	$10
1980-81 Larry Bird, Magic Johnson	$15
1981-82	$10
1982-83	$8
1983-84	$7.50
1984-85	$7.50
1985-86 Patrick Ewing	$8
1986-87 Larry Bird, Michael Jordan, Hakeem Olajuwon, Dominique Wilkins	$8
1987-88	$6
1988-89	$6
1989-90	$5
1990-91	$4
1991-92 Larry Bird, Magic Johnson, Michael Jordan	$4

Basketball Sports Stars (Hewfred)

1969 Lew Alcindor, Bill Bradley, Earl Monroe	$20
1970 Lew Alcindor	$15
1971 Jerry West	$13-$15
1972 Pete Maravich	$20
1973 Wilt Chamberlain	$13-$15
1974 Walt Frazier	$15
1975 Dave Cowens, John Havlicek	$15
1976 Rick Barry	$15

Basketball Weekly

12/04/67 Lew Alcindor, Will NBA Survive?	$25
12/11/67 Butch Van Breda Kolff	$15
12/21/67 Walter Kennedy, No War With ABA	$15
12/31/67 Dave Bing, College holiday tournaments	$15
01/08/68 Calvin Murphy, UCLA wins 42nd straight	$15
01/15/68 Doug Moe, First ABA All-Star game	$15
01/22/68 Houston (Elvin Hayes) vs. UCLA	$15
01/29/68 Houston (Elvin Hayes) vs. UCLA	$15
02/05/68 Wilt Chamberlain, NBA expansion	$15
02/12/68 Dean Smith, NCAA conference races	$15
02/19/68 Dave Bing, 76ers won't lose Hannum	$15
02/26/68 Clark, Miller, Scott, NCAA tournament	$15
03/11/68 NCAA All-Americans	$15
03/18/68 Howard, Nelson, Kentucky, UNC as dark horses	$15
03/25/68 Elvin Hayes, Can Houston do it again?	$15
04/30/68 Wilt Chamberlain, Bill Russell, All-NBA team	$15
11/01/68 Wilt Chamberlain, Jerry West	$17
12/02/68 John Wooden, UCLA preseason #1	$15
12/12/68 Rick Barry, Earl Monroe, Wes Unseld	$15

Periodicals

12/23/68 Steve Patterson, UCLA after Lew Alcindor $15
12/30/68 Charlie Scott, NCAA holiday tournaments........$15
01/06/69 Wilt Chamberlain $17
01/13/69 Oscar Robertson, NBA All-Stars $15
01/20/69 Kevin Loughery, Bullets as most improved
team $15
02/03/69 NBA referees...$15
02/10/69 Who's #2 behind UCLA? $15
02/17/69 LaSalle on NCAA probation.............................$15
02/24/69 NCAA basketball upsets $15
03/03/69 Scouting reports, Lew Alcindor $15
03/10/69 NCAA All-Americans.......................................$15
03/17/69 John Wooden, Who will challenge UCLA?......$15
04/01/69 Lew Alcindor, UCLA shoots for #3...................$15
05/01/69 All-NBA Team...$15
11/22/69 Rick Barry, Spencer Haywood, NBA vs.
ABA $13
12/08/69 Charlie Scott, Many try to succeed UCLA $13
12/19/69 Bill Bradley, Willis Reed, Kentucky #1 ....$13
12/29/69 M. Hauer, College holiday tournaments $13
01/05/70 Dan Issel, Pratt, Steele, Kentucky is #1 ....$13
01/12/70 Hall, Taylor, Kentucky #1, UCLA #2...............$13
01/19/70 Lew Alcindor, Jerry West, NBA All-Stars $13
01/26/70 Walter Kennedy, No merger for the NBA,
ABA $13
02/02/70 Pistol Pete Maravich $16
02/09/70 Charlie Scott, ABA makes "war plans" $13
02/16/70 Bob Lanier, St. Bonaventure............................$13
02/23/70 Rick Mount $13
03/02/70 Kentucky, UCLA tied in poll...........................$13
03/09/70 Dan Issel, NCAA All-Americans......................$13
03/16/70 Adolph Rupp, NCAA tournament preview........$13
03/23/70 J. Williams, UCLA shoots for 4th title $13
04/06/70 Pro basketball war continues............................$13
05/10/70 Wilt Chamberlain, Willis Reed, Lakers vs.
Knicks $13
11/23/70 Red Holzman, NBA vs. ABA $12
11/30/70 UCLA is preseason #1 ....$12
12/10/70 Frank Ramsey, ABA/NBA merger gap
widens $12
12/21/70 Larry Costello, Bucks set record pace $12
01/04/71 McGuire, Kraft, College holiday
tournaments..$12
01/11/71 Pistons are for real...$12
01/18/71 Wilt Chamberlain, Jerry West, NBA All-Star
game...$12
01/25/71 Mel Daniels, Dan Issel, ABA All-Star
game...$12
02/01/71 Sidney Wicks, UCLA $12
02/08/71 Bing, McGlocklin, #2 USC vs. #1 UCLA $12
02/15/71 John Wooden, UCLA is #1 ....$12
02/22/71 Parity in the ABA...$12
02/29/71 Who can beat UCLA?.......................................$12
03/01/71 Who's the #1 Pick?...$12
03/08/71 NCAA All-Americans.......................................$12
03/15/71 Al McGuire, NCAA tournament.......................$12
03/22/71 Adolph Rupp, Kentucky $12
05/15/71 Italy attracts U.S. players $12
11/23/71 ABA/NBA start new seasons.............................$12
11/30/71 USC becomes new #1 ....$12
12/10/71 Wilt Chamberlain..$10
12/21/71 UCLA is #1 ....$10
01/11/72 Jim Chones, Marquette.....................................$10
01/18/72 Kareem Abdul-Jabbar, Walt Frazier,
Jerry West, NBA All-Star game $10
01/25/72 Ivy League, UCLA is #1 ....$10
02/01/72 Gilmore, Issel, Simpson, ABA All-Star
game...$10
02/08/72 Denny Crum, ABA draft....................................$10

02/15/72 Proposed division after merger $10
02/22/72 UCLA favored again...$10
02/29/72 Jim McDaniels $10
03/07/72 Julius Erving to jump leagues? $10
03/14/72 Bill Walton $10
03/21/72 Bill Walton $10
03/28/72 Adolph Rupp's last game?.................................$10
05/15/72 Jerry West $10
11/21/72 Jim Chones, NBA-ABA war continues $10
12/05/72 Doug Collins, Illinois State...............................$10
12/12/72 Dave Cowens $10
12/19/72 Joe B. Hall, Kentucky.......................................$10
12/26/72 Phil Sellers, David Thompson $10
01/04/73 Kareem Abdul-Jabbar, Wilt Chamberlain $10
01/18/73 Dwight Lamar, SW Louisiana State $10
01/25/73 Walt Frazier, Jerry West, NBA All-Star
game..$10
02/01/73 Bill Walton, UCLA Eyes #61 ....$10
02/08/73 ABA All-Star game, Julius Erving $10
02/15/73 S. Mitchell, The Big Eight $10
02/22/73 Larry Brown $10
03/01/73 Ed Ratleff, Long Beach State............................$10
03/08/73 Phil Chenier, Archie Clark $10
03/15/73 Kenon, Ratleff, Walton, NCAA
All-Americans..$10
03/22/73 Bill Walton $10
03/29/73 John Wooden, Meet Me in St. Louis $10
05/15/73 Kareem Abdul-Jabbar, Nate Archibald,
Julius Erving $10
11/21/73 Bill Russell with the Sonics $10
12/12/73 Marvin Barnes, Providence................................$8
12/19/73 Geoff Petrie, Sidney Wicks $8
12/26/73 David Thompson, N.C. State $5
01/02/74 Wilt Chamberlain...$10
01/09/74 Kent Benson, Scott May, Indiana $8
01/16/74 Kareem Abdul-Jabbar, NBA All-Star
game...$8
01/23/74 Cazzie Russell, Michigan leads Big 10...............$8
01/30/74 Mel Daniels $8
02/06/74 Larry Fogle, Canisius $8
02/13/74 Dave DeBusschere, Jerry West........................$10
02/20/74 Referee Ed Rush...$8
02/27/74 Bill Walton $8
03/06/74 James Jones, Willie Wise....................................$8
03/13/74 Marvin Barnes, Bill Walton, NCAA
All-Americans..$8
03/20/74 Bill Walton $8
03/27/74 David Thompson $8
05/15/74 Julius Erving $8
11/21/74 The ABA $8
12/01/74 L. Dunbar, NCAA preview $8
12/26/74 End of an Era, Wilt Chamberlain......................$8
01/02/75 John Drew, NBA Rookies...................................$8
01/09/75 Hubie Brown $8
01/16/75 Marvin Webster, Morgan State.........................$8
01/23/75 Denny Crum, Louisville....................................$8
01/30/75 Moses Malone $8
02/06/75 30-second clock in NCAA $8
02/13/75 Bob McAdoo..$8
02/20/75 N.C. State $8
02/27/75 Dave Bing, Norm Van Lier...............................$8
03/06/75 Wes Unseld $8
03/12/75 Mack Calvin $8
03/20/75 Adrian Dantley, NCAA All-Americans...............$8
03/27/75 David Thompson $8
04/03/75 Kentucky vs. Louisville $8
05/15/75 Julius Erving $8
06/19/75 Golden State, Kentucky champions $8

234

1975-76 issues

#1 Thompson, Webster $7
#2 Scott May, Indiana $7
#3 Death of the NBA? $7
#4 Charlie Scott $7
#5 John Wooden UCLA $7
#6 Rick Barry, Curtis Rowe $7
#7 George McGinnis $7
#8 Kansas State, NC State $7
#9 Norm Van Lier $7
#10 Artis Gilmore $7
#11 Marquette basketball $7
#12 Kareem Abdul-Jabbar $7
#13 Robert Parish, Centenary $7
#14 Phil Chenier, Elvin Hayes $7
#15 Ford, King, May, NCAA $7
#16 Scott May, Indiana $7
#17 Kent Benson, Bernard Toone $7
#18 Indiana winners $7
#19 Olympic issue $7

1976-77 issues

11/25/76 All-Time ABA team: Rick Barry,
  Julius Erving $7
12/09/76 Al McGuire, Marquette #1 ....$7
12/23/76 Albert King $7
12/30/76 Jim Chones, Campy Russell............................$7
01/06/77 Larry O'Brien $7
01/13/77 Jack Givens, Kentucky....................................$7
01/20/77 Bob Lanier...$7
01/27/77 Julius Erving, George McGinnis.....................$7
02/03/77 Jerry West $7
02/10/77 Cincinnati Bearcats $7
02/17/77 College/Pros TV ratings $7
02/24/77 David Thompson $7
03/03/77 Ricky Green, Michigan $7
03/10/77 University of San Francisco.............................$7
03/17/77 David Thompson, NCAA All-Americans...........$7
03/31/77 The Final Four...$7
04/14/77 Al McGuire, Marquette champions $7
11/30/77 Kareem-Abdul Jabbar, Bill Walton $7
12/14/77 Dean Smith..$7
12/21/77 Prep basketball $7
12/28/77 Adolph Rupp $7
01/05/78 Al McGuire $6
01/12/78 Larry Bird, Indiana State.................................$8
01/09/78 Portland Trailblazers $6
01/26/78 Kyle Macy, Kentucky $6
02/02/78 Artis Gilmore $6
02/09/78 Sidney Moncrief, Arkansas.............................$6
02/16/78 NBA mid-season report $6
02/23/78 Kareem Abdul-Jabbar $6
03/02/78 Marques Johnson..$6
03/09/78 NCAA All-Americans: Larry Bird, Phil Ford,
  others $7
03/16/78 Butch Lee $6
03/23/78 Ted Owens $6
03/30/78 Mike Phillips, Kentucky $6
04/15/78 Kentucky's NCAA Championship.....................$6
11/29/78 Bill Walton $6
12/13/78 David Greenwood, UCLA $6
12/20/78 DeMetha Prep Coach Wooten..........................$6
12/27/78 Gene Barlow $6
01/04/79 John Havlicek $6
01/11/79 George Gervin $6
01/25/79 Elvin Hayes $6
02/01/79 Jack Ramsey..$6
02/08/79 Duke University $6

02/15/79 Phil Ford..$6
02/22/79 Digger Phelps $6
03/01/79 Jim Boeheim, Syracuse $6
03/08/79 NCAA All-Americans: Larry Bird, Magic
  Johnson, others $7
03/15/79 Larry Bird..$7
03/22/79 Dean Smith..$6
03/29/79 Larry Bird, Magic Johnson, NCAA
  tournament $7
04/15/79 Dick Motta $6
06/15/79 Class of '83, Ralph Sampson............................$7
11/28/79 Kareem Abdul-Jabbar, Julius Erving, John
  Havlicek $6
12/12/79 Ohio State is #1 ....$6
12/12/79 Prep stars $6
12/26/79 Doug Collins, Julius Erving $6
01/03/80 Ray Meyer..$6
01/10/80 Larry Brown $6
01/17/80 Hubie Brown, John Drew.................................$6
01/24/80 Darrell Griffith $6
01/31/80 Moses Malone $6
02/07/80 Larry Bird..$7
02/14/80 Danny Ainge $6
02/21/80 Dennis Johnson, Gus Williams $6
02/28/80 Frank McGuire $6
03/07/80 NCAA All-Americans: Mark Aguirre,
  others $6
03/14/80 Mark Aguirre..$6
03/21/80 Denny Crum $6
03/28/80 NCAA Final Four $6
04/15/80 NBA Playoffs $6
11/28/80 NCAA Preview $6
12/12/80 Walter Davis $6
12/26/80 Magic Johnson $7
01/08/81 Albert King, Maryland.....................................$5
01/15/81 New York Knicks $5
01/22/81 Oregon State...$5
12/29/81 Ray Meyer..$5
02/05/81 Marques Johnson $5
02/12/81 David Thompson $5
02/26/81 Billy Cunningham $5
03/05/81 Durand Macklin, LSU $5
03/12/81 Larry Bird, Robert Parish $6
03/19/81 NCAA All-Americans: Ralph Sampson,
  Isiah Thomas $5
03/26/81 Ralph Miller, Oregon State $5
04/02/81 Ralph Sampson $5
04/15/81 Paul Westhead $5
06/15/81 Patrick Ewing, Georgetown $5
11/20/81 Otis Birdsong, Mitch Kupchak $5
11/27/81 Larry Farmer, UCLA $5
12/04/81 Billy Thompson, Camden $5
12/19/81 Adrian Dantley $5
12/26/81 Wes Unseld $7
01/07/82 Antoine Carr, Wichita State $5
01/21/82 Scooter McCray, Rodney McCray......................$5
01/28/82 Julius Erving, Darryl Dawkins $7
02/04/82 Sleepy Floyd, Georgetown $5
02/11/82 Bill Fitch $5
02/18/82 Michael Cooper, Kevin McHale $5
02/25/82 Steve Stipanovich, Missouri $5
03/04/82 James Worthy, North Carolina $5
03/11/82 George Gervin $5
03/18/82 Dominique Wilkins, James Worthy, NCAA
  All-Americans $5
03/25/82 Ralph Sampson, Virginia $5
04/01/82 Dana Kirk $5
05/08/82 NCAA Final Four $8
05/15/82 Julius Erving, Magic Johnson $7

235

Periodicals

06/15/82 Norm Nixon $5
11/14/82 Moses Malone $6
11/21/82 Patrick Ewing, Sam Perkins, Ralph Sampson $7
12/09/82 Reggie Williams $5
12/23/82 Gus Williams $5
01/03/83 Dean Smith, North Carolina $5
01/13/83 Rollie Massimino, Villanova $5
01/20/83 UCLA vs. Jackson Wright $5
01/27/83 Kareem Abdul-Jabbar, Robert Parish $5
02/03/83 Melvin Turpin, Kentucky $5
02/10/83 Julius Erving, Moses Malone $7
02/17/83 Marques Johnson $5
02/24/83 Larry Brown, Buck Williams $5
03/03/83 Ralph Sampson, others $5
03/10/83 Maurice Lucas $5
03/17/83 Troy Taylor, Randy Wittman, Indiana $5
03/24/83 Michael Jordan, NCAA All-Americans $8
03/31/83 Ralph Sampson $5
04/07/83 Guy Lewis $5
04/14/83 Derrick Floyd $5
05/15/83 Moses Malone $5
11/14/83 New NBA coaches $5
11/28/83 Patrick Ewing, Georgetown $6
12/12/83 Denny Crum, Jack Sikma $4
12/19/83 Adrian Dantley, NCAA coaches $4
01/03/84 World Free, others $4
01/16/84 Julius Erving $6
01/23/84 Ralph Sampson, Steve Stipanovich $4
01/30/84 Michael Cage $4
02/06/84 Isiah Thomas, Kelly Tripucka $4
02/13/84 Terry Holland, Othell Wilson $4
02/20/84 Wayman Tisdale $4
02/27/84 Kevin McHale, Mark Price $4
03/05/84 Magic Johnson, Isiah Thomas $4
03/12/84 Michael Jordan, Sam Perkins $6
03/19/84 Michael Jordan, Chris Mullin, NCAA
    All-Americans $6
03/26/84 NCAA tournament $5
04/02/84 Billy Tubbs, Oklahoma $5
04/09/84 Hakeem Olajuwon, Final Four $5
05/21/84 Moses Malone $5
06/18/84 Kareem Abdul-Jabbar, Robert Parish $6
11/12/84 Magic Johnson, David Stern $5
11/26/84 Chris Mullin, Wayman Tisdale, Pearl
    Washington $4
12/10/84 High school basketball $4
12/17/84 Patrick Ewing, Georgetown $6
12/31/84 Larry Bird $5
01/14/85 Orlando Woolridge $4
01/21/85 Hakeem Olajuwon $5
01/28/85 Dominique Wilkins $5
02/04/85 James Worthy $5
02/11/85 Danny Manning, Kansas $4
02/18/85 Kareem Abdul-Jabbar, Julius Erving $5
02/25/85 Ed Pickney, Villanova $4
03/04/85 John Williams $4
03/11/85 Terry Cummings, Danny Ferry, Larry
    Nance $4
03/18/85 Patrick Ewing, Chris Mullin, NCAA
    All-Americans $5
03/25/85 Patrick Ewing $5
04/01/85 Bill Frieder $5
04/08/85 Patrick Ewing, Keith Lee, Chris Mullin,
    Ed Pickney $5
05/20/85 Larry Bird, Robert Parish $5
06/24/85 Chris Mullin, Wayman Tisdale $4
11/11/85 Dave DeBusschere, Patrick Ewing, David
    Stern $5
11/25/85 Brad Daugherty, Dean Smith $4

11/16/85 J.R. Reid $4
01/06/86 Kareem Abdul-Jabbar $5
01/20/86 M. Martin, J. McCaffrey $4
01/27/86 Reggie Lewis $4
02/03/86 Julius Erving, Geroge Gervin $5
02/10/86 Dana Kirk, others $4
02/17/86 Magic Johnson, Guy Lewis, Olden Polynice ... $4
02/24/86 Manute Bol, Rick Pitino, Spud Webb $4
03/03/86 Hakeem Olajuwon, Ron Harper $5
03/10/86 Mark Alarie, Johnny Dawkins $4
03/17/86 NCAA All-Americans: Brad Daugherty,
    others $4
03/24/86 Walter Berry $4
03/31/86 Mike Krzyzewski $5
04/07/86 NCAA Final Four coaches $4
04/21/86 High School All-Americans: J.R. Reid,
    others $4
05/19/86 Larry Bird $5
06/23/86 NBA draft preview: Len Bias, others $4
12/01/86 Rex Chapman, Kentucky $4
12/21/86 Alonzo Mourning, Billy Owens, others $5
01/04/88 Bobby Knight, Dick Vitale $4
01/11/88 David Robinson $5
01/25/88 Pete Maravich $4
02/01/88 Walt Hazzard, Michael Ray Richardson $4
02/08/88 NBA All-Stars: Magic Johnson, Michael
    Jordan $5
02/15/88 Michael Jordan, Billy Packer, Malik Sealy $5
02/22/88 Michael Smith $3
03/29/88 John Chaney $3
03/07/88 Hersey Hawkins, others $3
03/14/88 Bobby Hurley, others $3
03/21/88 NCAA All-Americans: Sean Elliott,
    Danny Manning $3
03/28/88 Danny Manning $3
04/04/88 Lute Olson $3
04/11/88 NCAA Final Four picks $3
05/02/88 Alonzo Mourning, Billy Owens $4
05/16/88 Mark Jackson, Michael Jordan, Pat Riley ... $4
06/20/88 NBA draft: Danny Manning, Rony Seikaly $3
11/15/88 Danny Manning $3
12/06/88 Duke #1, Danny Ferry, Mike Krzyzewski $3
12/20/88 Kenny Anderson $3
01/03/89 Michael Jordan, Jerry Tarkanian $5
01/10/89 Jerry West $3
01/24/89 Randy White, Louisiana Tech $2
01/31/89 Tom Hammonds, Dominique Wilkins $2
02/07/89 Brad Daugherty, Ron Harper, others $1.50
02/14/89 NBA All-Stars: Hakeem Olajuwon $2
02/21/89 Mookie Blaylock, Stacey King $1.50
02/28/89 Terry Cummings $1
03/07/89 Chris Jackson $1.25
03/14/89 Tom Chambers, Kevin Johnson $1.75
03/21/89 Lute Olson $1
03/27/89 NCAA All-Americans: Sean Elliott, Stacey
    King, others $1.25
04/03/89 Sean Elliott $1.25
04/10/89 Final Four preview $1.25
05/29/89 Michigan's Glen Rice, Rumeal Robinson ... $1.50
05/16/89 Can Los Angeles win three in a row? $1.25
06/20/89 Draft preview: Sean Elliott, Danny Ferry,
    others $1.50
11/14/89 Isiah Thomas $1.75
12/05/89 Todd Day, Lee Mayberry, Arkansas #1 ... $1.50
12/19/89 Shawn Bradley, Eric Montross $2
01/02/90 Basketball cards $1.25
01/10/90 Chuck Daley $1.25
01/23/90 Gary Payton, others $1.25
01/30/90 Alonzo Mourning $2

02/13/90 Doug Smith, NBA All-Stars $1.75
02/20/90 Karl Malone $2
02/27/90 Georgia Tech's Dennis Scott, Bobby
 Cremins $1.50
03/06/90 Charles Barkley $3
03/13/90 Chris Smith, University of Connecticut..........$1.50
03/20/90 Hakeem Olajuwon, others..............................$1.75
03/26/90 NCAA All-Americans: Derrick Coleman,
 Gary Payton, others...$2
04/02/90 Lionel Simmons $1.75
04/09/90 Leather, Anderson, others $2
05/01/90 UNLV'S Stacey Augmon, Larry Johnson,
 Jerry Tarkanian...$2.75
05/15/90 NBA playoffs preview $1.25
06/01/90 Draft preview: Derrick Coleman,
 Dennis Scott...$1.50
11/13/90 Michael Jordan $3
11/27/90 Arizona's Sean Rooks, Ed Stokes, Brian
 Williams $1.50
12/10/90 Chris Webber $2.50
15/17/90 Paul Westhead..$1
01/14/91 Shaquille O'Neal $4
02/04/91 Denny Crum, Rick Pitino.......................................$1
02/11/91 Bernard King $1.25
02/18/91 Stacey Augmon, Lee Mayberry $1.50
02/25/91 Michael Jordan $3
03/04/91 Calbert Cheaney, Jim Jackson $1.75
03/11/91 Maurice Cheeks, Alex English, Moses
 Malone $1.25
03/18/91 Terry Dehere, David Booth, others.................$1.25
03/25/91 NCAA All-Americans: Larry Johnson,
 Shaquille O'Neal $3
04/01/91 Larry Johnson...$2
04/08/91 Final Four Preview $1.25
04/29/91 Chris Webber $1.75
05/13/91 Michael Jordan, playoff preview $2.50
07/08/91 Larry Johnson, Dikembe Mutombo,
 Billy Owens...$2
11/19/91 Clyde Drexler...$2
12/03/91 UCLA's Don MacLean, Gerald Madkins,
 Darrick Martin...$1.75
01/07/92 Mike Krzyzewski $2
03/10/92 LaPhonso Ellis $2
05/12/92 Michael Jordan $4
07/06/92 Magic Johnson $3
11/17/92 Patrick Ewing, NBA preview.............................$3

Basketball's Best

1951-52 Harry Boykoff..$60
1952-53 George Mikan $75
1953-54 Bob Cousy, George Mikan, Dolph Schayes $75
1954-55 Bob Cousy, George Mikan, Dolph Schayes $75
1955-56 Red Rocha..$30
1956-57 Hand palming a basketball..................................$25
1957-58 Bob Cousy..$45
1958-59 Tom Heinsohn, Bill Russell.................................$45
1959-60 Frank Ramsey $20
1960-61 Elgin Baylor $25
1961-62 Wilt Chamberlain $30
1962-63 Elgin Baylor, Wilt Chamberlain, Jerry West......$30
1963-64 Jerry West $25
1964-65 Wilt Chamberlain $25
1965-66 Elgin Baylor $20
1966-67 Rick Barry $15
1967-68 Wilt Chamberlain, Bill Russell $20
1968-69 John Havlicek, Bailey Howell $15
1969-70 Lew Alcindor, Willis Reed $35
1970-71 Wilt Chamberlain, Willis Reed $15
1971-72 Lew Alcindor, Willis Reed $15
1972-73 Lew Alcindor, Wilt Chamberlain $20

Complete Sports Basketball

1961-62 Bill Russell...$25
1962-63...$25
1963-64 Jerry West $25

(Becomes) Pro Basketball Illustrated

1964-65 Oscar Robertson $20
1965-66 Wilt Chamberlain $20
1966-67 Bill Russell...$15
1967-68 Bill Bradley $15
1968-69 Baylor, Chamberlain, West.................................$15
1969-70 Lew Alcindor $15
1970-71 Lew Alcindor $15
1971-72 Lew Alcindor $15
1972-73 John Havlicek...$15
1973-74 Dave Cowens $15
1974-75 Julius Erving $20
1975-76 Bob McAdoo $15
1976-77 Julius Erving $20
1977-78 Julius Erving $20
1978-79...$10
1979-80 Larry Bird, Magic Johnson $20

(Published by) Lexington Library

1980-81...$15
1981-82...$10
1982-83...$10
1983-84 Julius Erving $15
1984-85...$10
1985-86 Larry Bird, Michael Jordan.................................$12
1986-87 Magic Johnson $10
1987-88 Michael Jordan...$10
1988-89...$8
1989-90 Michael Jordan...$10
1990-91...$8

Cord Sportfacts
Pro Basketball Guide

1972 Lew Alcindor...$15
1973 Kareem Abdul-Jabbar, Jerry West $15
1974 Walt Frazier..$15
1975 Kareem Abdul-Jabbar, Dave Cowens $15
1976 Rick Barry $15

Courtside

March 1989 Kelly Tripucka $4
April 1989 Hakeem Olajuwon $7
May 1989 Kiki Vandeweghe...$4.50
Nov. 1989 David Robinson, Season preview......................$8
Dec. 1989 Magic Johnson $10
Jan. 1990 Tom Chambers $4
Feb. 1990 Mr. and Mrs. Bill Laimbeer $3
March 1990 Alexander Volkov...$3
April 1990 Sherman Douglas..$3
May 1990 Magic Johnson, Isiah Thomas...........................$8
Nov. 1990 Terry Cummings, Dennis Rodman,
 Season preview $4
Dec. 1990 Moses Malone, Alvin Robertson $4
Jan. 1991 Reggie Lewis $4.50
Feb. 1991 Mr. and Mrs. Sarunas Marciulionis..................$3

Periodicals

March 1991 Patrick Ewing, Moses Malone $4.50
May 1991 Joe Dumars, Jerome Kersey, Dan Majerle,
  Scottie Pippen $6
Dec. 1991 Kevin McHale, David Robinson, Season
  preview... $5

Dell Basketball Woodward's 1951

1950 Don Logfran, University of San Francisco $45
1951 Bob Zawoluk, St. John's $40
1952 .... $30
1953 .... $25
1954 Bob Cousy $45
1955 Tom Gola, LaSalle $40
1956 Tom Heinsohn, Hot Rod Hundley, Bill Russell $40
1957 Wilt Chamberlain, Hot Rod Hundley,
  Bob Pettit... $40
1958 Wilt Chamberlain $40
1959 Connie Hawkins, Oscar Robertson,
  Jerry West $40
1960 Wilt Chamberlain, Jerry West $35
1961 Jerry Lucas, Ohio State $35
1962 Wilt Chamberlain, Bill Russell $35
1963 Oscar Robertson $35
1964 Barry Kramer, NYU $30
1965 Bill Bradley $30
1966 Cazzie Russell $30
1967 Bill Russell $30
1968 Lew Alcindor.. $30

Fast Break
(Popular Library)

1969 Dave Bing, Jerry West $15
1970 Lew Alcindor, John Havlicek, Bill Russell,
  Jerry West $15

(Becomes) Basketball's
All-Pro Annual

1971 Lew Alcindor, Pete Maravich, Rick Mount,
  Willis Reed.. $15
1972... $10
1973 Wilt Chamberlain, Kareem Abdul-Jabbarr $15
1974... $10
1975 John Havlicek $10

Game Plan College
Basketball Yearbook

1977-78 Phil Ford, North Carolina $20
1978-79 Larry Bird, David Greenwood,
  Magic Johnson $30
1980-81 Kyle Macy $20
1981-82 Albert King $20
1982-83 Sleepy Floyd $20
1983-84 Sam Perkins $20
1984-85 Keith Lee $20
1985-86 Wayman Tisdale $20
1987-88 Charles Smith, Pitt $20
1988-89 .... $15
1989-90 Jim Boeheim, Derrick Coleman, Billy
  Owens.. $15
1990-91.. $15

Game Plan Pro
Basketball Yearbook

1977-78 Julius Erving $25
1978-79 Doug Collins $20
1986-87 Mark Price, Kenny Smith $12
1987-88 David Robinson $15
1988-89 .... $10
1989-90 .... $10
1990-91 .... $10

Hoop Basketball Yearbook

1985-86 Patrick Ewing.. $15
1986-87 Charles Barkley, Larry Bird.............................. $12
1987-88 Magic Johnson, Kevin McHale.......................... $12
1988-89.. $10
1989-90.. $10
1990-91.. $10

Hoop NBA Today Edition

Nov. 1984 Larry Bird.. $12
Dec. 1984 Bernard King.. $6
Jan. 1985 Michael Jordan... $15
Feb. 1985 Reggie Theus.. $5
March 1985 Kareem Abdul-Jabbar, Bill Walton $7.50
April 1985 Isiah Thomas... $7
May 1985 Larry Bird... $8
July 1985 Kareem Abdul-Jabbar, Larry Bird.................... $8
Nov. 1985 Patrick Ewing.. $7
Dec. 1985 Julius Erving $7.50
Jan. 1986 Terry Cummings.. $5
Feb. 1986 Rolando Blackman, Detlef Schrempf,
  others $4.50
March 1986 Derek Smith $4
April 1986 Dominique Wilkins.. $6
May 1986 Magic Johnson.. $12
June 1986 Larry Bird... $8
Nov. 1986 Hall of Fame special edition....................... $7.50
Dec. 1986 Larry Bird, Moses Malone.......................... $7.50
Jan. 1987 Michael Jordan... $10
Feb. 1987 Hakeem Olajuwon....................................... $7.50
March 1987 Kiki Vandeweghe $4
April 1987 .... $4
May 1987 Julius Erving $8
June 1987 Trophy ball, shoe and towel........................... $4
July 1987 Magic Johnson.. $8
Dec. 1987 Michael Jordan $10
Jan. 1988 Kareem Adbul-Jabbar $6
Feb. 1988 Buck Williams.. $4
March 1988 Karl Malone $5
April 1988 Isiah Thomas... $5
May 1988 Charles Barkley.. $6
June 1988 Championship trophy...................................... $4
July 1988 Kareem Abdul-Jabbar, Magic Johnson,
  James Worthy... $7
Dec. 1988 Danny Manning $4
Jan. 1989 Moses Malone, Reggie Theus,
  Dominique Wilkins.. $4.50
Feb. 1989 Roy Tarpley.. $4
March 1989 Chris Mullin.. $5
April 1989 Larry Nance $4
May 1989 Kareem Abdul-Jabbar, Bill Laimbeer............... $5
June 1989 Trophy and ball.. $4
July 1989 Isiah Thomas.. $4.50
Dec. 1989 David Robinson $7.50
Jan. 1990 Mark Aquirre $4
Feb. 1990 Karl Malone... $4

March 1990 Kevin Johnson..$4.50
April 1990 Patrick Ewing...$4
May 1990 Fat Lever..$3.50
June 1990 Trophy and basketballs $3
July 1990 Bill Laimbeer, Dennis Rodman, Buck
   Williams...$3.50
Dec. 1990 Jerome Kersey, Buck Williams $3
Jan. 1991 Charles Barkley, Larry Bird..............................$6
Feb. 1991..$4
March 1991 Michael Jordan, Dennis Rodman,
   John Salley...$7.50
April 1991 Shawn Kemp..$6
May 1991 Karl Malone, Mychal Thompson....................$4
June 1991 Isiah Thomas..$4
July 1991 Michael Jordan with trophy.........................$7.50
Dec. 1991 Michael Jordan..$6

Inside Basketball
(Sport Magazine)

1964 Wilt Chamberlain, Bill Russell $20
1965 Oscar Robertson $20
1966 Bill Russell $15
1967 Lew Alcindor, Wilt Chamberlain...........................$15
1968 Lew Alcindor..$15
1969 Lew Alcindor..$15
1970 Pete Maravich, Rick Mount, Calvin Murphy..........$15
1971 Walt Frazier, Jerry West..$15

Petersen's Pro Basketball

1978-79 Elvin Hayes...$20
1979-80 Kareem Abdul-Jabbar, Dennis Johnson.............$20
1980-81 Magic Johnson $20
1982-86 Not published
1987-88 Sleepy Floyd, Magic Johnson...........................$20
   Tom Chambers, Clyde Drexler, Xavier McDaniel $12
   Mark Aguirre, Hakeem Olajuwon $15
   Charles Barkley, Dominique Wilkins $15
   Charles Barkley, Moses Malone $15
   Larry Bid, Patrick Ewing $15
   Michael Jordan, Isiah Thomas $15
   Larry Bird, Magic Johnson $15
1988-89 Magic Johnson, Michael Jordan $12
   Magic Johnson, Ralph Sampson $8
   Clyde Drexler, Dale Ellis $6
   Hakeem Olajuwon, Roy Tarpley $7.50
   Michael Jordan, Dominique Wilkins $7.50
   Larry Bird, Patrick Ewing $7.50
   Terry Cummings, Isiah Thomas $6
   Alex English, Karl Malone $6
1989-90 Magic Johnson, Chris Mullin.............................$7
   Charles Barkley, Kelly Tripucka....................................$7
   Magic Johnson, Michael Jordan $10
   Dale Ellis, Karl Malone..$6
   Michael Jordan, Moses Malone $7.50
   Ron Harper, Isiah Thomas $6
   Adrian Dantley, Hakeem Olajuwon $6
   Robert Parish, Patrick Ewing $6
1990-91 Magic Johnson, Michael Jordan $12
   Clyde Drexler, Magic Johnson.......................................$9
   Tom Chambers, Karl Malone..$6
   Hakeem Olajuwon, David Robinson...............................$8
   Rony Seikaly, Dominique Wilkins..................................$6
   Larry Bird, Patrick Ewing $8
   Charles Barkley, Muggsy Bogues $7.50
   Michael Jordan, Isiah Thomas $10

Popular Library
Basketball Yearbook

1960 Jerry West..$25
1961 Jerry Lucas..$25
1962 Jerry Lucas..$25
1963 Ron Bonham, Cincinnati $25
1964 Gary Bradds, Ohio State...$20
1965 Bill Bradley, Oscar Robertson...............................$20
1966 Cazzie Russell, Jerry West $15
1967 Lew Alcindor..$15
1966 Lew Alcindor, Rick Barry, Bill Bradey.................$15
1969 Lew Alcindor, Elvin Hayes, John Havlicek.........$15
1970 Walt Frazier, Rick Mount.......................................$15
1971 Lew Alcindor, Willis Reed.......................................$15
1972 Lew Alcindor, Tom McMillen $15
1973 Bill Walton $15
1974 Bill Walton $15
1975 Dave Cowens, John Havlicek..................................$12
1976 Rick Barry $15
1977 Julius Erving $20
1978 Bill Walton $15
1979 Bill Walton $15
1980 Larry Bird $20
1981 Kareem Abdul-Jabbar, Magic Johnson $15

Pro Basketball Almanac

1968 Wilt Chamberlain, Bill Russell...........................$18
1969 Wilt Chamberlain, Bill Russell...........................$15
1970 John Havlicek $15
1971 Pete Maravich...$20
1972 Lew Alcindor, Willis Reed....................................$15

The Sporting News College
& Pro Yearbook

1982-83 Kareem Abdul-Jabbar, Patrick Ewing,
   Ralph Sampson...$20
1983-84 Kareem Abdul-Jabbar, Michael Jordan,
   Keith Lee...$35
1984-85 Ralph Sampson, Wayman Tisdale $20
   Steve Alford, Dallas Comegys, Bobby Knight $20
   Larry Bird, Patrick Ewing $25
   Patrick Ewing, Magic Johnson......................................$20
   Keith Lee, James Worthy $20
1985-86 Mark Price, Kenny Walker $15
   Magic Johnson, Mark Price..$20
   Michael Jordan, David Rivers..$35
   Kevin McHale, Pearl Washington..................................$20
1986-87 Charles Barkley, Reggie Miller $25
   Steve Alford, Danny Manning $12
   Charles Barkley, Pervis Ellison.....................................$25
   Charles Barkley, David Robinson..................................$15
1988-89 Mark Aquirre, Magic Johnson, Isiah Thomas $15

The Sporting News
College Yearbook

1987-88 Rex Chapman...$6
   Fennis Denbo $5
   David Rivers...$5
   Rony Seikaly $6
   Danny Manning...$7.50

1988-89 Mookie Blaylock, Stacey King $6
   Danny Ferry...$6
   Patrick Ewing, Alonzo Mourning $12
   B.J. Armstrong $7
   Dyron Nix, Dwayne Schintzius.....................................$5
   Sean Elliott, Todd Lichti $7
1989-90 Chris Jackson $5
   Greg Anthony, Stacey Augmon, Jerry Tarkanian $7
   Derrick Coleman, Billy Owens, others $8
   Rumeal Robinson $5
   Chris Corchiani, Rodney Monroe $5
1990-91 Kenny Anderson, Rodney Monroe $7.50
   Shaquille O'Neal, Allan Houston $15
   Stacey Augmon, Larry Johnson, Chris Mills.................$7
   Eric Anderson, Jimmy Jackson, Steve Smith.................$6
   Jim Calhoun, Billy Owens, Chris Smith $6
   Alonzo Mourning, Billy Owens $8
   Todd Day, Lee Mayberry, Shaquille O'Neal.................$15
   Henry Iba, Mark Randall, Doug Smith $4
1990-91 Alonzo Mourning, Billy Owens $15
The Sporting News Official ABA Guide
1968-69 Rick Barry...$75
1969-70 Warren Armstrong, Mel Daniels.....................$45
1970-71 Official ABA ball..$50
1971-72 Mel Daniels, Julius Keye $45
1972-73 Artis Gilmore $45
1973-74 Billy Cunningham...$45
1975-76 Artis Gilmore $40

The Sporting News
Official NBA Guide

1958-59 Bob Pettit $75
1959-60 Bill Russell...$60
1960-61 Referee artwork..$50
1961-62 Bob Pettit $50
1962-63 Tom Heinsohn..$50
1963-64 Hawks vs. Royals $25
1964-65 John Havlicek..$45
1965-66 Bill Russell, Jerry West....................................$45
1966-67 Gene Wiley, Los Angeles Lakers $25
1967-68 Wilt Chamberlain, Nate Thurmond...................$35
1968-69 Oscar Robertson, Jerry West.............................$30
1969-70 Team logos $30
1970-71 Wilt Chamberlain, Willis Reed.........................$25
1971-72 Lew Alcindor, Wes Unseld...............................$25
1972-73 Wilt Chamberlain...$25
1973-74 Willis Reed...$25
1974-75 John Havlicek..$25
1975-76 Rick Barry .... $16-$20
1976-77 Jo Jo White... $16-$20
1977-78 Bill Walton... $17-$20
1978-79 Wes Unseld... $15-$20
1979-80 Elvin Hayes .... $16-$20
1980-81 Larry Bird, Magic Johnson $45
1981-82 Cedric Maxwell..$20
1982-83 Magic Johnson $25
1983-84 Kareem Abdul-Jabbar, Julius Erving $20
1984-85 Larry Bird...$25
1985-86 Larry Bird, Michael Jordan $30
1986-87 Larry Bird...$25
1987-88 Magic Johnson $25
1988-89 Michael Jordan $30
1989-90 Joe Dumars...$20
1990-91 Isiah Thomas...$20

The Sporting News
Official NBA Register

1980-81 Kareem Abdul-Jabbar $20
1981-82 Julius Erving $20
1982-83 Moses Malone..$20
1983-84 Moses Malone..$20
1984-85 Kareem Abdul-Jabbar, Ralph Sampson $20
1985-86 Kareem Abdul-Jabbar, Robert Parish $20
1986-87 Larry Bird, Hakeem Olajuwon, Bill Walton.......$20
1987-88 Michael Jordan $20
1988-89 James Worthy...$20
1989-90 Karl Malone...$20
1990-91 Patrick Ewing, David Robinson.........................$20

The Sporting News
Pro Basketball Yearbook

1987-88 Magic Johnson $15
   Dominique Wilkins $8
   Ralph Sampson...$5
   Michael Jordon $15
   Larry Bird $15
1988-89 Kevin McHale $10
   Mark Aguirre, Magic Johnson, Isiah Thomas...............$10
1989-90 Mark Jackson $5
   Joe Dumars $7.50
   Robert Parish $7.50
   Michael Jordan $12
   Hakeem Olajuwon $12
   Karl Malone...$10
1990-91 Larry Bird, Patrick Ewing, Karl Malone $8
   Magic Johnson, Michael Jordan...................................$10
   Magic Johnson, David Robinson $8
   Michael Jordan, Bill Laimbeer......................................$8
   Hakeem Olajuwon, David Robinson...............................$8

Sports Quarterly
Pro Basketball Special

1968-69 Bill Bradley...$15
1969-70 Lew Alcindor, Bob Cousy $15
1970-71 Pete Maravich, Willis Reed $15
1971-72 Lew Alcindor $15
1972-73 Walt Frazier $15
1973-74 Wilt Chamberlain...$8
1974-75 Julius Erving, John Havlicek $15
1975-76 Rick Barry $15
1976-77 Alvan Adams, JoJo White................................$15
1977-78 Julius Erving, Bill Walton................................$15

Street & Smith's Basketball

1957 Charlie Tyra, Louisville $125
1958 Tommy Kearns, North Carolina...........................$100
1970-71 Lew Alcindor, Willis Reed $40
   Austin Carr, Rudy Tomjanovich $40
   Wes Unseld, Jerry West $40
1971-72 Kareem Abdul-Jabbar, Willis Reed $40
1972-73 Kareem Abdul-Jabbar, Dave Cowens.................$40
   Gail Goodrich, John McGlockin $30
   Bill Walton $40
1973-74 John Havlicek, Pete Maravich $40
   Oscar Robertson, Jerry West...$40
   Gail Goodrich...$30
1974-75 Julius Erving $35

1974-75 Dave Cowens, Kareem Abdul-Jabbar $35
1975-76 Julius Erving $35
    Adrian Dantley, Marques Johnson $35
    Rick Barry, Paul Silas $35
1976-77 John Havlicek $30
    Pete Maravich $30
    Alvan Adams, Dave Cowens, Paul Westphal $30
1977-78 Melvin Bennett, Julius Erving $25
1977-78 Bill Walton $30
1978-79 Kyle Macy $20
    Kareem Abdul-Jabbar $25
    Gene Banks, Kelly Tripucka $25
1979-80 Gene Banks, Mike O'Koren $20
    Darnell Valentine $20
    Bill Walton $25
1980-81 Larry Bird, Julius Erving $25
    Sam Bowie, Julius Erving, Al Wood $20
1981-82 Sam Bowie $15
    Rod Foster, John Paxson $15
    Kareem Abdul-Jabbar, Magic Johnson $30
    Rod Foster, Moses Malone $20
    Larry Bird $30
1982-83 Sam Perkins $20
    John Paxson $20
    Larry Bird, Julius Erving, Patrick Ewing $30
1983-84 Patrick Ewing $15
    Bobby Knight $15
    A.C. Green $15
1984-85 Chris Mullin $15
    Milt Wagner $5
    Wayman Tisdale $15
    Magic Johnson $20
1985-86 Pearl Washington $10
    Danny Manning $15
    James Worthy $15
1986-87 Kenny Smith $10
    Michael Jordan $30
    Hakeem Olajuwon $15
    Larry Bird, David Robinson $20
1987-88 Larry Bird $20
    Magic Johnson $20
    Bob Knight, Keith Smart $15
    Dominique Wilkins $15
    Hakeem Olajuwon $15
    J.R. Reid $10
1988-89 Sherman Douglas, Mark Macon $10
    Danny Ferry $5
    Stacey King $5
    Tom Hammonds $5
    (Pro) Larry Bird, Magic Johnson, Michael Jordan $30
1989-90 Hank Gathers $15
    Rumeal Robinson $12
    Alonzo Mourning $15
    Chris Jackson $12
    Patrick Ewing $20
    (Pro) Isiah Thomas $15
    (Pro) Karl Malone $15
    (Pro) Michael Jordan $25
1990-91 Doug Smith $10
    Chris Smith $5
    Steve Smith $7
    Kenny Anderson, Bobby Hurley $15
    Don MacLean, Harold Miner $7
    Larry Johnson $10
    (Pro) Michael Jordan $20
1991-92 Shaquille O'Neal $15
1991-92 Michael Jordan $20
1991-92 Terry DeHere, Alonzo Mourning $12
1993-94 Shaquille O'Neal $12

Vitale's Basketball

1983-84 Michael Jordan, North Carolina $35
    Moses Malone $10
    Magic Johnson $35
1985-86 Kareem Abdul-Jabbar $15
    Mark Price, Kenny Smith $10
    Michael Jordan $20
    Patrick Ewing, Bernard King $15
1986-87 David Robinson, Navy $20
    Larry Bird, Magic Johnson $20
    Dominique Wilkins $12
    Kenny Smith, North Carolina $8
    Kareem Abdul-Jabbar, Ralph Sampson $12
    James Blackmon, Pervis Ellison $7
    Steve Alford, Danny Manning $8
1987-88 Derrick Coleman, J.R. Reid $12
    Larry Bird $15
    James Worthy $10
    Dominique Wilkins $10
    Xavier McDaniel, Kiki Vandeweghe $7
    Derrick Chievous, Danny Manning $7
    Bob Knight, Everette Stephens $6
    Isiah Thomas $10
    Michael Jordan $12
    Moses Malone $8
    Rex Chapman, Charles Smith $5
    Mark Aguirre, Rodney McCray $6
1988-89 Mark Jackson $5
    Sherman Douglas, John Thompson $7
    Michael Jordan, Isiah Thomas $15
    Danny Ferry, J.R. Reid $6
    B.J. Armstrong, Stacey King $6
    Pervis Ellison, Dwayne Schintzius $5
    Sean Elliott, Todd Lichti $6
    James Worthy $7.50
1989-90 Magic Johnson, Jerry Tarkanian $12
    Joe Dumars, Rumeal Robinson $7.50
    Patrick Ewing, Alonzo Mourning $10
    Michael Jordan, Kendall Gill $10
    Kevin Johnson, Lute Olson $7
    Chris Jackson, Hakeem Olajuwon $8
    Chris Mullin, John Stockton $8
    Rex Chapman, Scott Williams $4
1990-91 Charles Oakley, Billy Owens $6
    Larry Bird, Magic Johnson $10
    Kenny Anderson, Rodney Monroe $7
    Michael Jordan, Doug Smith $10
    Reggie Miller, LaBradford Smith $7.50
    Tom Chambers, Buck Williams $5
    Steve Smith, Isiah Thomas $7
    Shaquille O'Neal, David Robinson $10

Basketball Stars Of...

1961   Wilt Chamberlain $20
1962   Bob Cousy $20
1963   Duquesne vs. Bradley $20
1964   Wilt Chamberlain $20
1965   Bill Russell $20
1966   Bill Russell $20
1967   Willis Reed, Bill Russell $15
1968   Wilt Chamberlain $15
1969   Willis Reed $15
1970   Lew Alcindor $15
1971   Willis Reed $15
1972   Lew Alcindor $15
1973   Jerry West $15
1974   Dave Cowens, Walt Frazier $15
1975   Kareem Abdul-Jabbar, Dave Cowens,
    John Havlicek $15

The Complete Handbook Of Pro Basketball

1975	Julius Erving, John Havlicek	$15
1976	Jerry West	$10
1977	Julius Erving	$15
1978	Bill Walton	$10
1979	Elvin Hayes	$7.50
1980	Dennis Johnson	$6
1981	Magic Johnson	$20
1982	Larry Bird, Julius Erving	$20
1983	Julius Erving, Magic Johnson	$20
1984	Kareem Abdul-Jabbar, Moses Malone	$10
1985	Larry Bird	$15
1986	Patrick Ewing	$10
1987	Larry Bird	$10
1988	Magic Johnson	$12
1989	Magic Johnson, Isiah Thomas	$15
1990	Kareem Abdul-Jabbar, Joe Dumars, Magic Johnson, James Worthy	$10
1991	Michael Jordan, Bill Laimbeer	$8

Hockey Magazines

Action Sports Hockey

Jan. 1972 Dave Keon $12
Feb. 1972 Keith Magnuson $7
March 1972 Jean Ratelle $8
April 1972 Frank and Pete Mahovlich $10
May 1972 Bobby Hull $12
Oct. 1972 Brad Park $12
Nov. 1972 Bobby Orr $12
Dec. 1972 Marcel Dionne $8
Jan. 1973 Bobby Clarke $8
Feb. 1973 Garry Unger $7
March 1973 Bobby Hull $10
April 1973 ...... $7
May 1973 Jacques Lemaire $7
Nov. 1973 Bobby Clarke $8
Dec. 1973 Brad Park $9
Jan. 1974 Tony Esposito $7
Feb. 1974 Paul Henderson $6
March 1974 Phil Esposito $7
April 1974 Bobby Orr $8
May 1974 Yvan Cournoyer $7
Dec. 1974 Bobby Clarke $8
Jan. 1975 ...... $6
Feb. 1975 Derek Sanderson $6
March 1975 Bobby Orr, Brad Park $8
April 1975 New York Rangers vs. Montreal Canadiens $5
May 1975 ...... $5
Dec. 1975 Guy Lafleur $7
Jan. 1976 ...... $5
Feb. 1976 Denis Potvin $5
March 1976 Phil Esposito, Brad Park $7
April 1976 ...... $5
May 1976 Philadelphia Flyers vs. USSR $4
Nov. 1976 Guy Lafleur, Reggie Leach $6.50
Jan. 1977 Darryl Sittler $5
Feb. 1977 Bobby Orr, Denis Potvin $5
March 1977 Ken Dryden, Pete McNab $5
April 1977 ...... $5
May 1977 Bobby Clarke, Brad Park $5
Nov. 1977 Guy Lafleur $6
Jan. 1978 Borje Salming $5

Feb. 1978 Gil Perreault $6
March 1978 Larry Robinson $5
April 1978 Gordie Howe, Mike Palmateer $7
Nov. 1978 Tiger Williams $5
Jan. 1979 Guy Lafleur $6
Feb. 1979 Ken Dryden $5
March 1979 Borje Salming $5
April 1979 Terry O'Reilly $5
Nov. 1979 Guy Lafleur $5
Jan. 1980 Ulf Nilsson $4
Feb. 1980 Darryl Sittler $5
March 1980 Chicago Blackhawks vs. New York Islanders $4
April 1980 Marcel Dionne $5

Complete Handbook Of Pro Hockey

1971-72 Chicago Blackhawks vs. Boston Bruins $12
1972-73 New York Rangers vs. Boston Bruins $8
1973-74 New York Rangers vs. Montreal Canadiens $8
1974-75 Bobby Clarke $10
1975-76 ...... $7
1976-77 Paul Newman in the movie Slapshot $10
1977-78 Guy Lafleur $10
1978-79 Montreal Canadiens vs. Boston Bruins $7
1979-80 Bob Gainey $8
1980-81 New York Islanders with the Stanley Cup $7
1981-82 Wayne Merrick $5
1982-83 Wayne Gretzky $12
1983-84 Billy Smith $5
1984-85 Wayne Gretzky, Edmonton Oilers with Stanley Cup $10
1985-86 Wayne Gretzky $10
1986-87 Philadelphia Flyers vs. Calgary Flames $4
1987-88 Ron Hextall $4

Cord Sportfacts Hockey Guide

1969-70 Norm Ullman $15
1970-71 Bobby Orr $20
1971-72 Bobby Orr $20
1972-73 Bobby Orr $20
1973-74 Frank Mahovlich $10

Hockey Blueline Magazine

Oct. 1954 Gordie Howe $200
Nov. 1954 Maurice Richard $100
Dec. 1954 Al Rollins $80
Jan. 1955 Milt Schmidt $80
Feb. 1955 Jim Thomson $60
March 1955 Jean Beliveau $80
April 1955 Bob Goldham $60
May 1955 Edgar Laprade $50
June 1955 Bill Quackenbush $80
Oct. 1955 Toe Blake $80
Nov. 1955 Tony Leswick $50
Dec. 1955 Jacques Plante $80
Jan. 1956 Ted Lindsay $75
March 1956 Gil Mayer $50
April 1956 Jean Beliveau $80
May 1956 Toe Blake, Bernie Geoffrion, Dickie Moore, Jacques Plante $75
Sept. 1956 Maurice Richard $80
Oct. 1956 Gordie Howe $100
Nov. 1956 Maurice Richard $80

Dec. 1956 Ted Sloan $50
Jan. 1957 Ted Lindsay $50
Feb. 1957 Doug Mohns...$50
March 1957 Jean Beliveau $75
April 1957 Gump Worsley...$60
May 1957 Gordie Howe...$80
Nov. 1957 Ed Litzenberger $40
Dec. 1957 Bernie Geoffrion $50
Jan. 1958 Lou Fontinato...$40
Feb. 1958 Don McKenney $30
March 1958 Andy Bathgate $50
April 1958 Frank Mahovlich..$50
May 1958 Maurice Richard..$45
Oct. 1958 Henri Richard..$45
Nov. 1958 Fleming Mackell...$30
Nov. 1958 Bill Gadsby..$45
Jan. 1959 Dickie Duff $50
Feb. 1959 Andy Bathgate...$45
March 1959 Hockey fights $40
April 1959 Jean Beliveau $50
May 1959 Andy Bathgate, Jean Beliveau, Jacques
  Plante, others $50

Hockey Digest

Nov. 1972 Bobby Orr... $45-$60
Dec. 1972 Ken Dryden... $20-$24
Jan. 1973 Minnesota North Stars vs. New York
  Rangers.. $12-$16
June 1973 Keith Magnuson.................................... $10-$12
March 1973 Brad Park .... $12-$16
April 1973 Derek Sanderson $10
May 1973 Garry Unger .... $10-$12
June 1973 Phil Esposito .... $12-$16
Nov. 1973 Rick MacLeish .... $10-$12
Dec. 1973 Henri Richard.. $10-$12
Jan. 1974 Bobby Hull... $15-$20
Feb. 1974 Mickey Redmond .... $10-$12
March 1974 Gil Perreault.. $10-$12
April 1974 Steve Vickers .... $10-$12
May 1974 Tony Esposito .... $10-$12
June 1974 Tom Lysiak .... $10-$12
Nov. 1974 Dave Schultz... $10-$12
Dec. 1974 Mike Walton .... $10-$12
Jan. 1975 Bobby Orr.. $15-$20
Feb. 1975 Stan Mikita.. $12-$16
March 1975 Marcel Dionne .... $10-$12
April 1975 Rick Martin .... $10-$12
May 1975 Derek Sanderson .... $10-$16
June 1975 Guy Lafleur .... $10-$12
Nov. 1975 Bobby Clarke... $10-$12
Dec. 1975 Gil Perreault.. $10-$12
Jan. 1976 Denis Potvin... $8-$10
Feb. 1976 Bobby Hull .... $12-$16
March 1976 Bobby Sheehan .... $8-$10
April 1976 Garry Unger .... $8-$10
May 1976 Jean Ratelle .... $8-$10
June 1976 Ken Dryden... $10-$12
Nov. 1976 Bobby Orr.. $15-$20
Dec. 1976 Phil Esposito .... $12-$16
Jan. 1977 Larry Robinson, Guy Lafleur................... $10-$12
Feb. 1977 Dave Schultz...$8
March 1977 Peter McNab .... $8-$10
April 1977 Steve Shutt .... $8-$10
May 1977 Borje Salming .... $8-$10
June 1977 Glenn Resch .... $8-$10
Nov. 1977 Serge Savard .... $10-$12
Dec. 1977 Willi Plett .... $8-$10

Jan. 1978 Rick MacLeish...$12
Feb. 1978 Wayne Cashman...$8
March 1978 Mike Bossy $12
April 1978 Rick Martin .... $8-$10
May 1978 Darryl Sittler .... $10-$12
June 1978 Guy Lafleur .... $10-$12
Nov. 1978 Terry O'Reilly.. $8-$12
Dec. 1978 Anders Hedberg, Ulf Nilsson.................... $8-$10
Jan. 1979 Danny Gare... $8-$10
Feb. 1979 Dale McCourt... $8-$10
March 1979 Clark Gillies .... $8-$10
April 1979 New York Rangers vs. Philadelphia
  Flyers...$8
May 1979 Ken Dryden, Bryan Trottier.................... $10-$12
June 1979 Guy Lafleur .... $10-$12
Nov. 1979 New York Rangers vs. Montreal
  Canadiens .... $8-$10
Dec. 1979 Marcel Dionne .... $10-$12
Jan. 1980 Bobby Clarke...$8
Feb. 1980 New York Islanders vs. Edmonton
  Oilers .... $5-$7
March 1980 Phil Esposito .... $8-$10
April 1980 Gil Perreault...$6
May 1980 Wayne Gretzky .... $25-$40
June 1980 Tony Esposito .... $6-$10
Nov. 1980 New York Islanders with the Stanley
  Cup $5
Dec. 1980 Ray Bourque .... $5-$7
Jan. 1981 Clark Gillies .... $5-$7
Feb. 1981 Philadelphia Flyers vs. St. Louis Blues.............$5
March 1981 Mike Bossy $8
April 1981 Phil Esposito, Bob Gainey $6
May 1981 Charlie Simmer .... $5-$7
June 1981 Denis Savard .... $5-$7
Nov. 1981 Wayne Gretzky .... $25-$30
Dec. 1981 Bryan Trottier .... $6-$10
Jan. 1982 Rick Kehoe.. $5-$7
Feb. 1982 Reed Larson.. $5-$7
March 1982 Bobby Smith .... $5-$7
April 1982 Normand Leveille .... $5-$7
May 1982 Wayne Gretzky .... $25-$30
June 1982 Mark Acton .... $5-$7
Nov. 1982 Bryan Trottier.. $6-$10
Dec. 1982 Doug Wilson $5
Jan. 1983 Bobby Carpenter .... $4-$5
Feb. 1983 Peter Stastny $5
March 1983 Denis Savard $5
April 1983 Dino Ciccarelli .... $4-$5
May 1983 Pete Peeters .... $4-$5
June 1983 Wayne Gretzky $20
Nov. 1983 Billy Smith $5
Dec. 1983 Barry Pederson .... $5-$7
Jan. 1984 Phil Housley...$5
Feb. 1984 Mark Pavelich .... $5-$7
March 1984 Richard Brodeur..$5
April 1984 Larry Robinson $5
May 1984 Wayne Gretzky .... $20-$25
June 1984 Denis Potvin .... $5-$7
Nov. 1984 Mark Messier...$6
Dec. 1984 Tom Barrasso .... $4-$5
Jan. 1985 Michel Goulet $5
Feb. 1985 Dino Ciccarelli $5
March 1985 Herb Brooks .... $4-$5
April 1985 Tim Kerr $5
May 1985 Mike Bossy $8
June 1985 Wayne Gretzky $20
Nov. 1985 Paul Coffey $5
Dec. 1985 Pelle Lindbergh..$8
Jan. 1986 Rod Langway..$5

Periodicals

Feb.1986 Marcel Dionne..$6
March 1986 Mario Lemieux $25
April 1986 Barry Pederson.....................................$5
May 1986 Kelly Hrudey...$5
June 1986 Wayne Gretzky......................................$5
Nov. 1986 Patrick Roy..$8
Dec. 1986 John Vanbiesbrouck..............................$5
Jan. 1987 Wendel Clark $5
Feb. 1987 Bernie Federko $5
March 1987 Mark Howe $8
April 1987 Scott Stevens..$5
May 1987 Mike Bossy $8
June 1987 Wayne Gretzky $20
Nov. 1987 Ron Hextall...$5
Dec. 1987 Glen Hanlon $5
Jan. 1988 Dale Hawerchuk.....................................$6
Feb. 1988 Mario Lemieux......................................$20
March 1988 Kevin Dineen $5
April 1988 Denis Potvin..$5
May 1988 Montreal Canadiens vs. Boston Bruins..............$5
June 1988 Grant Fuhr...$5
Nov. 1988 Wayne Gretzky......................................$15
Dec. 1988 Sean Burke...$5
Jan. 1989 Mike Keenan $5
Feb. 1989 Al MacInnis $5
March 1989 Cam Neely $5
April 1989 Brian Leetch..$5
May 1989 Steve Yzerman $5
June 1989 Mario Lemieux..$15
Nov. 1989 Joe Mullen..$5
Dec. 1989 Wayne Gretzky.......................................$15
Jan. 1990 Chris Chelios..$3
Feb. 1990 Kevin Hatcher, Mick Vukota $3
March 1990 Sergei Makarov $4
April 1990 Doug Wilson $3
May 1990 Philadelphia Flyers vs. New York
  Rangers $3
June 1990 Ray Bourque $4
Nov. 1990 Mark Messier...$4
Dec. 1990 John Druce $3
Jan. 1991 Jon Casey $3
Feb. 1991 Dale Hawerchuk.......................................$4
March 1991 Brett Hull...$5
April 1991 John Vanbiesbrouck................................$3
May 1991 Chris Chelios...$3
June 1991 Wayne Gretzky $10
Nov. 1991 Mario Lemieux..$8
Dec. 1991 Stephane Richer $3
to date ....$3-$5 each

Hockey Illustrated

Nov. 1962 Jacques Plante..$60
Dec. 1962 Andy Bathgate $35
Jan. 1963 Jean Beliveau $35
Feb. 1963 Bobby Hull $45
March 1963 Gordie Howe $50
Nov. 1963 ....$30
Dec. 1963 Dave Keon, Terry Sawchuck $25
Jan. 1964 Boom Boom Geoffrion $25
Feb. 1964 Henri Richard $20
March 1964 Glenn Hall, Elmer Vasko.....................$20
April 1964 Bobby Hull...$40
Nov. 1964 ....$20
Dec. 1964 Johnny Bower, Marcel Pronovost..........$20
Jan. 1965 Jean Beliveau $20
Feb. 1965 Dave Keon $20

March 1965 Montreal Canadiens vs. Chicago
  Blackhawks $18
April 1965 Bobby Hull...$35
Nov. 1965 Jean Beliveau $20
Dec. 1965 Bobby Hull, Frank Mahovlich, Henri
  Richard $20
Jan. 1966 Gordie Howe $45
Feb. 1966 Johnny Bower, Bobby Hull...............$20
March 1966 Henri Richard.......................................$18
April 1966 Jean Beliveau $20
Nov. 1966 Henri Richard $18
Dec. 1966 Bobby Hull, Gordie Howe $45
Jan. 1967 Bobby Hull..$25
Feb. 1967 Jean Beliveau...$20
March 1967 Bobby Rousseau $18
April 1967 Dave Keon, Henri Richard.............$18
Nov. 1967 Bobby Hull...$25
Dec. 1967 Henri Richard $18
Jan. 1968 Ed Giacomin $18
Feb. 1968 Bobby Hull..$20
March 1968 Gordie Howe $30
April 1968 Frank Mahovlich $20
May 1968 Bobby Hull $20
Nov. 1968 Jean Beliveau $20
Dec. 1968 Bobby Hull..$20
Jan. 1969 Rod Gilbert...$18
Feb. 1969 Gordie Howe $30
March 1969 Bobby Orr $30
April 1969 Bobby Hull..$20
May 1969 Jean Beliveau $20
Nov. 1969 ....$20
Dec. 1969 Gordie Howe $30
Jan. 1970 Bobby Hull...$18
Feb. 1970 Stan Mikita $15
March 1970 Alex Delvecchio $15
April 1970 Bobby Orr $20
May 1970 Ed Giacomin $15
Nov. 1970 Bobby Orr $20
Dec. 1970 Tony Esposito $15
Jan. 1971 Gordie Howe $20
Feb. 1971 Keith Magnuson $12
March 1971 Jean Beliveau, Yvan Cournoyer $15
April 1971 Brad Park, Ed Westfall $15
May 1971 Derek Sanderson $15
Nov. 1971 Ken Dryden $15
Dec. 1971 Phil Esposito $18
Jan. 1972 Gil Perreault...$15
Feb. 1972 Dennis Hull $12
March 1972 Garry Unger $12
April 1972 Rod Gilbert, Vic Hadfield, Jean Ratelle $12
May 1972 Gump Worsley $15
June 1972 John McKenzie $10
Nov. 1972 Walt Tkaczuk $15
Dec. 1972 Phil Esposito $15
Jan. 1973 Marcel Dionne $15
Feb. 1973 Paul Henderson $10
March 1973 Dennis Hull $12
April 1973 Derek Sanderson $15
May 1973 Rick Martin, Gil Perreault...............$12
June 1973 Bobby Orr $15
Nov. 1973 ....$10
Dec. 1973 ....$10
Jan. 1974 Yvan Cournoyer, Rene Robert...............$10
Feb. 1974 Doug Favell, Bobby Orr..........................$12
March 1974 Rod Gilbert, Bobby Hull, Dave Schultz $12
April 1974 Tony Esposito $12
May 1974 Gil Perreault, Norm Ullman...............$12
June 1974 Rick Martin, Brad Park, Henri Richard $12
Jan. 1975 Bobby Orr $15

Feb. 1975 Ken Dryden $12
March 1975 Bobby Clarke $12
April 1975 Phil Esposito $12
May 1975 RogieVachon..$12
Jan. 1976 Bobby Orr $15
Feb. 1976 Guy Lafleur $12
March 1976 Tony Esposito $12
April 1976 Ken Dryden...$12
May 1976 Bobby Clarke, Guy Lafleur...........................$12
Jan. 1977 Denis Potvin..$10
Feb. 1977 Darryl Sittler...$10
March 1977 Larry Robinson $10
April 1977 Bernie Parent..$10
May 1977 Guy Lafleur $10
Jan. 1978 Rick Martin $10
Feb. 1978 Ken Dryden $10
March 1978 Bobby Clarke $12
April 1978 Rogie Vachon $10
May 1978 Guy Lafleur $10
Jan. 1979 Jacques Lemaire $10
Feb. 1979 Darryl Sittler...$10
March 1979 Marcel Dionne $10
April 1979 Bryan Trottier $10
Jan. 1980 Mike Palmateer $8
Feb. 1980 Real Cloutier $8
March 1980 Reggie Leach $8
April 1980 Anders Hedberg $8
Jan. 1981 Jim Schoenfeld...$8
Feb. 1981 Bobby Smith...$7.50
March 1981 Borje Salming $7.50
April 1981 Mike Bossy $5
Feb. 1984 Kent Nilsson $5
Feb. 1985 Mark Messier...$7
March. 1985 Brent Sutter...$5
May 1985 Mike Bossy, Wayne Gretzky, Kent
    Nilsson...$5
Feb. 1986 Paul Coffey, Rick Vaive....................................$5
Feb. 1987 Wendel Clark..$5
Feb. 1989 Wayne Gretzky, Denis Savard $5
April 1989 Wayne Gretzky, Brian Leetch.........................$5

Hockey Illustrated Yearbook

1961-62 Bernie Geoffrion $30
1962-63 ....$20
1963-64...$20
1964-65 Eddie Shack $20
1965-66 ....$18
1966-67...$15
1967-68...$15
1968-69...$15
1969-70...$12
1970-71...$12
1971-72...$15
1972-73...$10
1973-74 Bobby Clarke $12
1974-75 Bernie Parent..$10
1975-76 Bobby Clarke $10
1976-77 Ken Dryden $10
1977-78 Guy Lafleur $10
1978-79 Mike Bossy $8
1979-80 Guy Lafleur $8
1980-81 Wayne Gretzky $18
1981-82..$8
1982-83 Wayne Gretzky $15
1983-84 Wayne Gretzky $10
1986-87 Wayne Gretzky $10

Hockey News Yearbook

1982-83 Wayne Gretzky $12
1983-84 Wayne Gretzky, Pete Peeters...........................$10
1984-85...$7.50
1985-86...$7.50
1986-87 Paul Coffey, Wayne Gretzky, Claude
    Lemieux..$10
1987-88..$7
1988-89 Mario Lemieux..$8
1989-90 Wayne Gretzky, Mario Lemieux,
    Al MacInnis..$8
1990-91..$5

Hockey Pictorial

Oct. 1955 Jean Beliveau, others $100
Nov. 1955 Red Kelly, others...$80
Dec. 1955 Leo Labine $70
Jan. 1956 Tod Sloan, others $60
Feb. 1956 Andy Bathgate...$70
March 1956 Henri and Maurice Richard..........................$75
April 1956 Glenn Hall...$60
May 1956 Henri Richard, Stanley Cup $70
Oct. 1956 Jean Beliveau, Gordie Howe, Ted
    Lindsay...$80
Nov. 1956 Gordie Howe, Norm Ullman, Gump
    Worsley...$65
Dec. 1956 Jean Beliveau..$60
Jan. 1957 Leo Labine $40
Feb. 1957 Gordie Howe, Ted Lindsay $65
March 1957 Doug Harvey...$55
April 1957 Doug Harvey, Gordie Howe, Ted
    Lindsay...$55
May 1957 Henri Richard..$50
Oct. 1957 Rocket Richard $50
Nov. 1957 Bill Gadsby $50
Dec. 1957 Gordie Howe $70
Jan. 1958 Real Chevrefils...$30
Feb. 1958 Camille Henry $30
March 1958 Ed Chadwick..$30
April 1958 Henri Richard...$40
May 1958 Allan Stanley...$40
Oct. 1958 Frank Mahovlich...$40
Nov. 1958 Ed Litzenberger $30
Dec. 1958 Norm Ullman $32
Jan. 1959 Andy Bathgate...$35
Feb. 1959 Doug Mohns...$30
March 1959 Tom Johnson $30
April 1959 Glenn Hall..$30
May 1959 Montreal Canadiens, Stanley Cup $30
Oct. 1959 Dickie Moore...$30
Nov. 1959 Bobby Hull..$55
Dec. 1959 Alex Delvecchio $32
Jan. 1960 Carl Brewer $25
Feb. 1960 Vic Stasiuk $25
March 1960 "Kid Hockey Flourishes" $20
April 1960 Jean Beliveau..$35
Sept. 1960 Bob Pulford...$20
Oct. 1960 Dean Prentice...$22
Nov. 1960 Billy Hay...$20
Dec. 1960 Don McKenney..$20
Jan. 1961 Murray Oliver...$20
Feb. 1961 Ralph Backstrom $22
March 1961 Bobby Hull..$40
April 1961 Frank Mahovlich...$28
Sept. 1961 Bernie Geoffrion $28
Oct. 1961 Dave Keon $24
Nov. 1961 Doug Mohns $22

Periodicals

Dec. 1961 Jean Beliveau, Glenn Hall, others....................$24
Jan. 1962 Bernie Geoffrion, Glenn Hall, Andre
    Pronovost, others.......................................$24
Feb. 1962 Carl Brewer $20
March 1962 Boston, Detroit, Montreal, Toronto $20
April 1962 Red Kelly, Jacques Plante, Bob Pulford........$20
Sept. 1962 Toronto Maple Leafs vs. Boston Bruins $20
Oct. 1962 Henri Richard $20
Nov. 1962 Chicago Blackhawks vs. Montreal
    Canadiens $20
Dec. 1962 Chicago Blackhawks vs. Toronto
    Maple Leafs..$20
Jan. 1963 Gordie Howe....................................$35
Feb. 1963 Stan Mikita $30
March 1963 Don Simmons $20
April 1963 Bobby Hull....................................$28
Sept. 1963 Johnny Bower, Bobby Hull......................$25
Oct. 1963 Jacques Plante.................................$24
Nov. 1963 Gordie Howe $40
Dec. 1963 Chicago Blackhawks bench $20
Jan. 1964 Leo Boivin, Milt Schmidt $24
Feb. 1964 Jean Beliveau..................................$24
March 1964 Pierre Pilote.................................$20
April 1964 Jacques Laperriere $16
Sept. 1964 Charlie Hodge.................................$16
Oct. 1964 All-Star Game..................................$18
Nov. 1964 ....$15
Dec. 1964 Harry Howell $18
Jan. 1965 Elmer Vasko....................................$16
Feb. 1965 Toronto vs. Montreal...........................$16
March 1965 New York Rangers..............................$18
April 1965 Ron Ellis, Charlie Hodge......................$16
May 1965 Gordie Howe, Norm Ullman........................$25
Oct. 1965 Frank Mahovlich, Henri Richard.................$20
Nov. 1965 Rod Gilbert $22
Dec. 1965 Bill Gadsby, Gordie Howe.......................$27
Jan. 1966 Frank Mahovlich................................$22
Feb. 1966 Stan Mikita $25
March 1966 Roger Crozier.................................$18
April 1966 Glenn Hall, Bobby Hull, Stan Mikita,
    Pierre Pilote..$25
May 1966...$15
Oct. 1966 Montreal Canadiens goalies $20
Nov. 1966 Bob Pulford $15
Dec. 1966 Alex Delvecchio, Gordie Howe...................$24
Jan. 1967 Gerry Cheevers $18
Feb. 1967 Ed Giacomin....................................$18
March 1967 Bobby Rousseau $14
April 1967 Bobby Hull....................................$24
Oct. 1967 NHL expansion..................................$20
Nov. 1967 Bobby Orr......................................$30
Dec. 1967 Hank Bassen, Terry Crisp, Jim
    Roberts $15
Jan. 1968 Cesare Maniago, Bob Woytowich $14
Feb. 1968 Stan Mikita $20
March 1968 Paul Henderson, Bruce MacGregor,
    Norm Ullman..$15
April 1968 Stanley Cup...................................$15
Oct. 1968 St. Louis Blues................................$20
Nov. 1968 Claude Ruel $14
Dec. 1968 Wren Blair, Wayne Connelly.....................$12
Jan. 1969 Gump Worsley...................................$15
Feb. 1969 Stan Mikita $18
March 1969 Gordie Howe, Brad Park........................$20
April 1969 J.C. Tremblay.................................$12
Nov. 1969 Montreal Canadiens vs. St. Louis Blues.........$20
Dec. 1969 Ken Hodge $15
Jan. 1970..$12
Feb. 1970 Yvan Cournoyer.................................$14
March 1970 Bobby Orr $20
April 1970 Mike Laughton, Juha Widing $13

May 1970 St. Louis Blues.................................$13
Nov. 1970 Carol Vadnais..................................$15
Dec. 1970 Tony Esposito..................................$14
Jan. 1971 Roger Crozier..................................$13
Feb. 1971 Phil Esposito..................................$21
March 1971 Keith Magnuson $10
April 1971 Bobby Orr $20
May 1971 Ken Dryden......................................$18
Nov. 1971 Chicago Blackhawks vs. Montreal
    Canadiens $15
Dec. 1971 Norm Ullman....................................$14
Jan. 1972 Bill White.....................................$10
Feb. 1972 Frank Mahovlich, Jacques Plante................$14
March 1972 Carol Vadnais $10
April 1972 Tony Esposito, Bobby Hull, Pete
    Mahovlich..$14
May 1972 Rod Gilbert.....................................$14
Nov. 1972 1972-73 Preview................................$15
Dec. 1972 Brad Park $16
Jan. 1973 Jim Neilson, Gilles Villemure..................$12
Feb. 1973 Richard Martin, Gil Perreault..................$16
March 1973 Dan Awrey, Phil Esposito......................$16
April 1973 Ken Dryden, Murray Oliver, Dean
    Prentice...$14
May 1973 Bobby Orr $18
Nov. 1973 Gil Perreault $14
Dec. 1973 Jim Neilson, Steve Vickers.....................$12
Jan. 1974 Bobby Orr $18
Feb. 1974 Dave Keon......................................$14
March 1974 Richard Martin................................$14
April 1974 Tony Esposito.................................$12
May 1974 Frank Mahovlich.................................$12
Nov. 1974 Phil Esposito..................................$16
Dec. 1974 Denis Potvin...................................$12
Jan. 1975 Bobby Orr......................................$15
Feb. 1975 Gary Smith $10
March 1975 Phil Russell..................................$10
April 1975 Danny Grant...................................$10
May 1975 Ken Dryden......................................$12
Nov. 1975 Rod Gilbert....................................$12
Dec. 1975 Stan Mikita....................................$12
Jan. 1976 Bobby Clarke...................................$15
Feb. 1976 Phil Esposito..................................$12
March 1976 Rogie Vachon $10
April 1976 Gerry Cheevers $10
May 1976 Bobby Clarke $15
Nov. 1976 Bobby Clarke...................................$15
Dec. 1976 Phil Esposito..................................$12
Jan. 1977 Brad Park $12
Feb. 1977 Don Murdoch $10
March 1977 Marcel Dionne $12
April 1977 Steve Shutt $10
May 1977 Reggie Leach $10
June 1977 Guy Lafleur....................................$14
Oct. 1977 Larry Robinson $12
Nov. 1977 Lanny McDonald $10
Dec. 1977 Denis Potvin...................................$10
Jan. 1978 Guy LaPointe, Richard Martin...................$10
Feb. 1978 Bryan Trottier $10
March 1978 Keith Magnuson $10
April 1978 Gil Perreault $10
May 1978 Guy Lafleur.....................................$10
Oct. 1978 Guy Lafleur....................................$12
Nov. 1978 Terry O'Reilly.................................$10
Dec. 1978 Bobby Orr, Brad Park, Borje Salming...........$12
Jan. 1979 Anders Hedberg, Glenn Resch, Joe
    Watson...$10
Feb. 1979 Dale McCourt, Larry Robinson, Vladislav
    Tretiak..$10
March 1979 Tony Esposito, Tom Lysiak, Gary
    Sargent, Rogie Vachon................................$10
April 1979 Mike Bossy, Garry Unger $12

May 1979 Stan Mikita, Denis Potvin $12
Oct. 1979 1979-80 Preview $12
Nov. 1979 Darryl Sittler $10
Dec. 1979 Mike Milbury $10
Jan. 1980 Don Edwards $8
Feb. 1980 Mark Howe $10
March 1980 Brian Propp $8
April 1980 Brian Sutter $8

Hockey Times

Nov. 1970 Gordie Howe, Bobby Orr $20
Dec. 1970 Ken Hodge $10
Jan. 1971 Boston Bruins vs. Chicago Blackhawks $8
Feb. 1971 Bobby Orr $15
March 1971 St. Louis Blues vs. Boston Bruins $8
April 1971 Boston Bruins with the Stanley Cup $10
May 1971 Eddie Johnston $8
June 1971 Montreal Canadiens with the Stanley Cup $10
July 1971 Jean Beliveau $12
Aug. 1971 Tony Esposito, Gordie Howe $12
Sept. 1971 Bobby Orr $12
Oct. 1971 Bobby Orr $12
Nov. 1971 Phil Esposito $12
Dec. 1971 Derek Sanderson $8
Jan. 1972 Reggie Leach $8
Feb. 1972 Ken Hodge, Bobby Hull, Bobby Orr $15
March 1972 Montreal Canadiens vs. Boston Bruins $10
April 1972 Ken Dryden $10
May 1972 Bobby Orr $12
June 1972 Bobby Orr $12
July 1972 Boston Bruins executives $7
Aug. 1972 Eddie Johnston $7
Sept. 1972 Bobby Orr $12
Oct. 1972 John Bucyk $10
Nov. 1972 Bobby Orr $12
Dec. 1972 Tony Esposito $8
Jan. 1973 Boston Bruins artwork $7
Feb. 1973 Fred Stanfield $7
March 1973 Bobby Orr $10
April 1973 Bobby Orr $10
May 1973 Ted Green $7
June 1973 .... $7
July 1973 .... $7
Aug. 1973 .... $7
Sept. 1973 .... $7

Hockey Today (Published By CAHA)

1977-78 Darryl Sittler $18
1978-79 Guy Lafleur $15
1979-80 .... $12
1980-81 Bobby Smith $10
1981-82 .... $12
1982-83 .... $12
1983-84 Wayne Gretzky, James Patrick, Bryan Trottier $15
1984-85 .... $8
1985-86 Lanny McDonald $7
1986-87 .... $7
1987-88 Wayne Gretzky, Mario Lemieux $12
1988-89 Scan Burke $6
1989-90 Wayne Gretzky, Gordie Howe $10
1990-91 Eric Lindros, Mark Messier, Mike Ricci $8

Hockey World

May 1966 Jean Beliveau $60
Oct. 1966 Boom Boom Geoffrion $35
Nov. 1966 Bobby Hull, Stan Mikita, Billy Reay $35
Jan. 1967 Bruce MacGregor, Norm Ullman, Gump Worsley $25
Feb. 1967 Rod Gilbert, Phil Goyette, Don Marshall $22
March 1967 Yvan Cournoyer $22
April 1967 Bobby Hull, Bobby Orr $35
May 1967 Henri Richard $25
Oct. 1967 Glenn Hall $20
Nov. 1967 Eddie Johnston, Dave Keon $20
Dec. 1967 New York Rangers vs. Toronto Maple Leafs $18
Jan. 1968 Bobby and Dennis Hull $25
Feb. 1968 Eddie Shack $18
March 1968 Bernie Parent $18
April 1968 Doug Favell, Bobby Hull, Bobby Orr, Ed Vam Impe $22
May 1968 Jean Beliveau, Bobby Hull, Stan Mikita, Bobby Orr $24
Oct. 1968 1968-69 Preview $22
Nov. 1968 Bobby Orr $35
Dec. 1968 Stan Mikita $25
Jan. 1969 Bob Nevin $20
Feb. 1969 Red Berenson $20
March 1969 All-Star Game $20
April 1969 Stanley Cup playoffs $22
Oct. 1969 1969-70 Preview $22
Nov. 1969 Ed Giacomin $20
Dec. 1969 Phil Esposito, Bill Flett $20
Jan. 1970 Keith Magnuson, Danny O'Shea $14
Feb. 1970 Gary Smith $10
March 1970 Tony Esposito $18
April 1970 Bobby Hull, Bobby Orr $25
May 1970 Stanley Cup playoffs $20
Oct. 1970 1970-71 Preview $17
Nov. 1970 Jacques Plante $17
Dec. 1970 Vic Hadfield, Jean Ratelle $14
Jan. 1971 Garry Unger $14
Feb. 1971 Dennis Hull $14
March 1971 Gil Perreault $14
April 1971 Stanley Cup playoffs $17
May 1971 Gerry Cheevers, Jean Ratelle $17
Oct. 1971 Garry Unger $12
Nov. 1971 Gerry Cheevers $14
Dec. 1971 Gil Perreault $12
Jan. 1972 John Bucyk $12
March 1972 Doug Favell $12
April 1972 Stanley Cup playoffs $15
May 1972 Walter Tkaczuk $14
Jan. 1972 Minnesota North Stars in action $15
Nov. 1972 Ken Dryden $14
Dec. 1972 Dunc Wilson $10
Jan. 1973 Yvan Cournoyer, Eddie Johnston $12
March 1973 Bobby Orr $20
April 1973 Stanley Cup playoffs $17
May 1973 Keith Magnuson $14
Oct. 1973 1973-74 Preview $17
Nov. 1973 Tony Esposito $14
Dec. 1973 Rick MacLeish $14
Jan. 1974 Stan Mikita $14
March 1974 Bill Goldsworthy $14
April 1974 Syl Apps $12
May 1974 Bobby Orr $20
Oct. 1974 Bobby Clarke $15
Nov. 1974 Darryl Sittler $12
Dec. 1974 Garry Unger $10
Jan. 1975 Dick Redmond $10
March 1975 Tom Lysiak $10

Periodicals

April 1975 Dennis Hextall $10
May 1975 Phil Esposito $12
Oct. 1975 Bernie Parent $12
Nov. 1975 Bobby Orr..$15
Jan. 1976 Phil Esposito $14
Feb. 1976 Danny Gare $10
March 1976 Darryl Sittler $10
April 1976 Tony Esposito $10
May 1976 Stanley Cup playoffs...............................$14

Inside Hockey

Nov. 1987 Dale Hawerchuk $5
Jan. 1988 Mark Messier $6
March 1988 Scott Stevens $4
May 1988 Stephane Richer $4
Oct. 1988 Sean Burke...$4
Nov. 1988 Hockey violence $3
Jan. 1989 Mats Nashlund, Larry Robinson $4
Feb. 1989 Glenn Anderson......................................$3
April 1989 Claude Lemieux $3
May 1989 25 People You Should Know $6
Oct. 1989 Darryl Sittler..$3
Nov. 1989 Wayne Gretzky....................................$7.50
Dec. 1989 Trevor Linden $4
Jan. 1990 Paul Coffey, Mike Ricci $4.50
Feb. 1990 Tomas Sandstrom $3
April 1990 Hockey fighting $5
May 1990 Doug Gilmour, Mark Messier,
    Adam Oates $5
Oct. 1990 Ray Bourque, Brett Hull...........................$7.50
Nov. 1990 Eric Lindros (Canada) $10
Kirk Muller (United States)......................................$5
Jan. 1991 Esa Tikkanen $5
Feb. 1991 Chris Chelios $5
April 1991 Theoren Fleury..$4
May 1991 Don Cherry (Canada)................................$3
Brett Hull (United States)..$5
Oct. 1991 Ed Belfour, Dave Gagner, Mark Recchi.......$5
Nov. 1991 Mario Lemieux $6
Dec. 1991 Joe Sakic $5
Jan. 1992 Pavel Bure $5
Feb. 1992 Sergei Fedorov $5
April 1992 Jeremy Roenick $5
Sept. 1992 Mario Lemieux, Mark Messier,
    Patrick Roy $5
Nov. 1992 Eric Lindros...$5
Dec. 1992 Patrick Roy $5
Feb. 1993 Ron Hextall $5
April 1993 Doug Gilmour $5

Official NHL Guide

1932-33 Howie Morenz $450
1933-34...$400
1934-35...$300
1935-36 Action artwork $250
1936-37...$200
1937-38...$200
1938-39...$200
1939-40...$200
1940-41...$200
1941-42...$150
1942-43...$150
1943-44...$150
1944-45...$150
1945-46 Action artwork $150
1946-47 Elmer Lach...$150
1947-48 Max Bentley..$150
1948-49 Maurice Richard...$175

1949-50 Buddy O'Connor..$125
1950-51 Sid Abel $100
1951-52 Chuck Rayner..$100
1952-53 NHL logo $100
1953-54 NHL logo $100
1954-55 NHL logo $100
1955-56 NHL logo $100
1956-57 NHL logo $100
1957-58 NHL logo $100
1958-59 NHL logo $100
1959-60 NHL logo $100
1960-61 NHL logo $80
1961-62 NHL logo $80
1962-63 NHL logo $80
1963-64 NHL logo $80
1964-65 NHL logo $80
1965-66 NHL logo $60
1966-67 50th Anniversary NHL logo $60
1967-68 NHL logo $60
1968-69 NHL logo $60
1969-70 Phil Esposito, Serge Savard, Gump
    Worsley $50
1970-71 Clarence Campbell, Gordie Howe $35
1971-72 John Bucyk, Phil Esposito, Bernie Geoffrion,
    Bobby Hull, Maurice Richard $30
1972-73 Phil Esposito, Gump Worsley.........................$25
1973-74 Bobby Clarke, Yvan Cournoyer, Phil Esposito,
    Bobby Orr..$30
1974-75 Bobby Clarke, Phil Esposito $30
1975-76 Ken Dryden, Ed Westfall..............................$20
1976-77 Curt Bennett, Garry Unger............................$17
1977-78 Clarence Campbell $16
1978-79 Bob Gainey, the Selke Trophy.......................$16
1979-80 NHL team logos $15
1980-81 Wayne Gretzky $30
1981-82 Mike Liut $12
1982-83 Wayne Gretzky $25
1983-84 New York Islanders $12

(Becomes) Official NHL
Guide & Record Book

1984-85 Gretzky, Oilers, with Stanley Cup $20
1985-86 Paul Coffey, Wayne Gretzky $16
1986-87 Bob Gainey, Larry Robinson $10
1987-88 Michel Goulet, Wayne Gretzky, Gordie
    Howe $15
1988-89 Wayne Gretzky, Mario Lemieux $15
1989-90 Lanny McDonald, Stanley Cup........................$8
1990-91 Ray Bourque, Brett Hull, Mark Messier.............$7

Official NHL Record Book

1948-49 Bill Durnan..$70
1949-50..$70
1950-51 Terry Sawchuck $50
1951-52..$50
1952-53..$50
1953-54..$50
1954-55..$50
1955-56..$50
1956-57..$50
1957-58 Jean Beliveau, Bill Gadsby, Gordie Howe,
    others $50
1958-59 Andy Bathgate, Glenn Hall, Gordie Howe,
    others $50
1959-60..$50

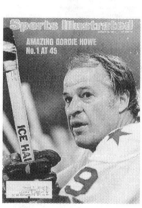

1960-61 Bernie Geoffrion, Gordie Howe, Bobby Hull,
others $45
1961-62...$36
1962-63...$36
1963-64 Jean Beliveau, Gordie Howe, Stan Mikita,
others $45
1964-65...$36
1965-66 John Bucyk, Jean Beliveau, Gordie Howe,
Bobby Hull, others $36
1966-67...$30
1967-68...$30
1968-69...$30
1969-70...$30
1970-71...$20
1971-72...$20
1972-73...$20
1973-74...$20
1974-75...$16
1975-76...$16
1976-77...$16
1977-78...$16
1978-79...$16
1979-80...$16
1980-81...$10
1981-82...$10
1982-83 NHL logo and year..$10
1983-84 Wayne Gretzky $20

(Becomes) Official NHL Guide & Record Book

Popular Library's Face-Off Hockey Yearbook

1969-70 Bobby Orr $25
1970-71 Bobby Orr, Chicago Blackhawks $20
1971-72 Ken Dryden, Phil Esposito...............................$20

Proudfoot's Pro Hockey

1968-69 Chicago Blackhawks vs. Montreal
Canadiens $21
1969-70 Hockey skate..$14
1970-71 Hockey cartoon $14
1971-72 Hockey cartoon $14
1972-73 Hockey cartoon $14
1973-74 Hockey cartoon $14
1974-75 Bernie Parent..$17
1975-76 Hockey cartoon $14
1976-77 ....$14
1977-78 Guy Lafleur...$17
1978-79..$14

1979-80...$12
1980-81...$12
1981-82 Dino Ciccarelli $14
1982-83 Mike Bossy $14
1983-84...$12
1984-85 Wayne Gretzky $20
1985-86 Bobby Carpenter $10

Rinkside

Nov. 1989 Calgary Flames.............................$5
Dec. 1989 Tom Barrasso................................$4
Jan. 1990 Mario Lemieux................................$7
Feb. 1990 Kevin Dineen..................................$3
March 1990 Bob Kudelski $3
April 1990 Don Beaupre $3
Nov. 1990 Paul Cavallini $3
Dec. 1990 Luc Robitaille $4
Jan. 1991 Doug Wilson $3
Feb. 1991 Bobby Holik.....................................$3
March 1991 Jimmy Carson $4
April 1991 Playoff Preview................................$3

The Sporting News
Hockey Yearbook

1990-91 Pat LaFontaine, Brian Leetch $7
  Brett Hull, Mike Keenan $7
  Wayne Gretzky, Mario Lemieux...................$10
  Ray Bourque, Patrick Roy.............................$7
  Mark Messier, Patrick Roy............................$7

The Sporting News NHL Guide

1967-68 Detroit goalie .... $125-$175
1968-69 Johnny Bower, Bobby Hull....................... $60-$90
1969-70 Bobby Orr.............................. $50-$75
1970-71 Gordie Howe............................ $40-$60
1971-72 Phil Esposito .... $40-$60
1972-73 Bobby Orr.............................. $45-$60
1973-74 Yvan Cournoyer........................ $35-$45
1974-75 Bernie Parent........................... $35-$45
1975-76 Bobby Clarke .... $25-$40
1976-77 Ken Dryden .... $20-$40
1977-78 Guy Lafleur.................................$40
1978-79 Larry Robinson, Canadiens with the
  Stanley Cup .... $25-$35
1979-80 Bob Gainey .... $25-$35
1980-81 Denis Potvin............................ $20-$30
1981-82 Mike Bossy .... $15-$25
1982-83 Wayne Gretzky .... $30-$40
1983-84 Wayne Gretzky .... $30-$35
1984-85 Wayne Gretzky .... $30-$35
1985-86 Paul Coffey, Wayne Gretzky, Jari Kurri.............$30-$35
1986-87 Claude Lemieux .... $25-$30
1987-88 Ron Hextall............................. $20-$30
1988-89 Mario Lemieux.............................$25
1989-90..$15
1990-91..$10

The Sporting News
NHL Registers

1972-73 Rick Martin .... $35-$40
1973-74 Bobby Clarke $30
1974-75 Stan Mikita .... $20-$30
1975-76 Rick Martin, Gil Perreault, Rene Robert ....$25-$30
1976-77 Marcel Dionne .... $20-$25
1977-78 Borje Salming $25
1978-79 Denis Potvin.................................$25

1979-80 Bryan Trottier.............................. $20-$25
1980-81 Wayne Gretzky .... $30-$40
1981-82 Mike Liut $15
1982-83 Mike Bossy .... $10-$15
1983-84 Pete Peeters .... $15-$20
1984-85 Ron Langway $15
1985-86 Tim Kerr, New York Islanders .... $15-$20
1986-87 Mario Lemieux..............................$25
1987-88 Wayne Gretzky $25
1988-89 Grant Fuhr............................... $10-$15
1989-90..$10
1990-91..$8

Sports Extra Hockey

Jan. 1972 Bobby Orr $12
March 1972 Phil Esposito $12
May 1972 Ed Giacomin, Gilles Villemure.............$10
Dec. 1972 Bobby Hull...............................$12
Feb. 1973 Vic Hadfield, Bobby Orr, Montreal
  Canadiens $10
April 1973 Bobby Orr, Brad Park $10
Dec. 1973 Tony and Phil Esposito, Gordie Howe $7
Jan. 1974 Walt Tkaczuck, Chicago Blackhawks $6
March 1974 Phil Esposito $8
Nov. 1974 Bobby Clarke, Bobby Orr $8
March 1975 Bobby Clarke, Bobby Orr, Gil Perreault $6

Sports Quarterly
Inside Hockey

1967-68 Jean Beliveau, Bobby Hull, Stan Mikita,
  Rogie Vachon, others .... $20-$25
1968-69 .... $15-$20
1969-70.. $12-$15
1970-71.. $10-$12
1971-72 Ken Dryden, Brad Park, Henri Richard...........$12-$15
1972-73 Yvan Cournoyer, Bobby Orr, Jean
  Ratelle .... $12-$15
1973-74 Yvan Cournoyer, Phil Esposito,
  Redmond .... $10-$12
1974-75... $8-$10
1975-76... $8-$10
1976-77.. $6-$8
1977-78.. $6-$8
1978-79.. $6-$8
1979-80 Mike Bossy, Guy Lafleur................. $8-$10
1980-81 Wayne Gretzky, Billy Smith..................... $12-$15

Sports Special Hockey

Dec. 1968 Bobby Hull................................ $20-$25
Feb. 1969 Gordie Howe .... $15-$20
May 1969 Jean Beliveau .... $12-$16
Dec. 1969 Bobby Orr .... $15-$20
April 1970 Ed Giacomin .... $10-$12
Dec. 1970 Bobby Hull, Bobby Orr .... $15-$20
Feb. 1971 Bobby Hull .... $12-$16
April 1971 Stan Mikita.............................. $15-$20
Dec. 1971 Ken Dryden.............................. $12-$16
Feb. 1972 Bobby Hull .... $12-$16
April 1972 Jean Ratelle............................ $10-$12
Dec. 1972 Jean Ratelle .... $10-$12
Feb. 1973 Derek Sanderson .... $8-$10
April 1973 Phil Esposito .... $10-$12
Dec. 1973 Bobby Clarke, Yvan Cournoyer, Bobby
  Hull.. $12-$16
Jan. 1974 Bobby Orr, Gil Perreault .... $10-$12
March 1974 Bobby Clarke .... $8-$10
Jan. 1974 Phil Esposito, Gordie Howe, Bernie
  Parent... $10-$12
March 1975 Phil Esposito .... $8-$10

Tom Harmon and Vince Lombardi have appeared on Time magazine covers.

Other Magazines

* Note: this is a representative sample of non-sport magazines which have featured athletes on the cover. Any additions to the lists in this chapter are welcome. Please contact the editor at the address given at the front of the book.

Life Magazine

10/11/37 USC football captain Chuck Williams...............$25
10/24/38 Sid Luckman $30
01/15/40 USC basketball (Ralph Vaughn).......................$25
11/11/40 Tom Harmon, Michigan....................................$30
11/17/41 Texas football..$10
01/22/45 St. John's basketball (Bill Kotsores) $15
10/22/45 Ohio State football (Paul Sarringhaus) $15
09/16/46 Army's Blanchard & Davis $30
09/29/47 Johnny Lujack $25
09/27/48 Doak Walker $25
10/03/49 College football roundup $20
12/05/60 Pro football kickoff $10
11/17/61 Minnesota Vikings $10
12/10/65 Tommy Nobis $10
10/14/66 Cleveland Browns vs. Green Bay Packers.........$12
12/13/68 Dennis Gaubatz $13
06/20/69 Joe Namath..$15
12/03/71 Pro football's most violent players......................$8
01/14/72 Tom Landry, Roger Staubach $20
03/24/72 Kareem Abdul-Jabbar, Wilt Chamberlain $15
10/06/72 Pro football, Bob Lilly $10
11/03/72 Joe Namath..$10

Newsweek

12/07/53 Notre Dame's Frank Leahy...............................$15
11/01/71 George Allen $10

Time

01/17/72 Super Bowl VI (Bob Griese, Roger
  Staubach)..$15
02/24/75 Bernie Parent..$8
01/10/77 Super Bowl XI (Oakland vs. Minnesota)............$8
01/16/78 Super Bowl XII (Dallas vs. Denver)...................$8
09/29/80 Alabama's Bear Bryant.......................................$5
01/25/82 Joe Montana $20
03/16/85 Larry Bird, Wayne Gretzky $20
01/27/86 Walter Payton, William Perry...........................$15

Colliers

11/14/42 Cover has a referee, inside has Jim Thorpe
  article..$12
10/12/42 Cover is play action, inside has football
  article..$12

Look

09/14/48 Doak Walker $14
09/12/50 Bob Williams of Notre Dame $10

Saturday Evening Post

09/21/68 Fran Tarkenton..$8
Nov. 1974 Roosevelt Grier and his needlepoint $7

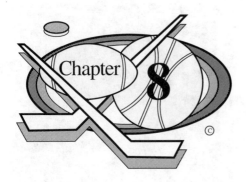

Books

Having a book's original dust jacket adds to its value.

The outlook for books as collectibles is very good; prices of quality used sports books are still relatively low. However, prices have been rising, and, as more and more collectors discover this overlooked area of the memorabilia hobby, prices will escalate accordingly. For lovers of sports literature and for investors, there is no better time than now to buy quality sports books.

Four main factors determine the value of a used sports book: scarcity, desirability, condition, and edition. Generally, scarcity adds to the value of a book, but not significantly unless the book is considered desirable in the first place. In other words, hundreds of fairly hard-to-find sports books are not particularly valuable because there is no demand for them. However, desirable books that are scarce always command premium prices.

Desirability is ultimately in the eye of the reader/buyer, but the author, the subject, the degree of originality, and the overall quality or "readability" of the book are the main factors that determine a book's standing with collectors. Sports card collectors should have little trouble understanding that condition greatly affects the value of books. Torn or missing pages, coffee cup rings on the cover, general wear and tear on the spine - such defects definitely reduce any book's value.

Two particularly important aspects of condition to be aware of are: 1) "ex libre" books, i.e. discards from libraries, are considered damaged goods and are shunned by collecting purists; and 2) a lack of a dust jacket (if issued) significantly reduces the value of a book, sometimes up to 50 percent or more. Closely related to condition is the matter of a book's edition. To be worth top dollar a book should be a first printing of a first edition.

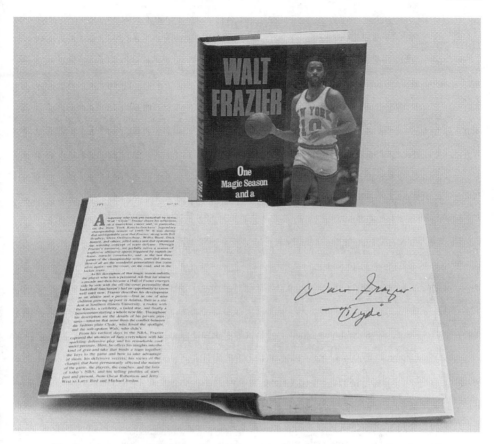

Having the author or main character autograph a book increases its value.

Two other influences on value are worth noting. First, although an autograph normally lessons the value of a premier sports card, it enhances a sports book, whether the book is signed by the author or the subject(s), or both. Second, a biography is not necessarily valuable because the subject is a superstar. It often depends on scarcity; a hard-to-find biography of a lesser player could be considered more valuable.

Of course, there is no guarantee that any sports book will appreciate dramatically, so the average collector would be well advised to collect books he enjoys for his own sake.

Because there are so many sports books, with a few hundred new ones published annually, most collectors should consider specializing. Four common approaches to specialization are collecting by quality, team, genre (e.g., record books, fiction, picture books, general histories), or topic.

Finally, there is a wide variety of sources for used sports books. The top sources, ranging from the least to the most productive, are: garage sales, card shows, library sales, antiquarian book sales, hobby periodicals (such as Sports Collectors Digest), used book stores, and used baseball book dealers who issue mail-order catalogs. Remaindered books at cut-rate prices can also be found in new-book book stores, but these offerings will always be recently published books that either didn't sell well or were over-printed.

Included among the list below are some of the best sports books ever published, books which would form the foundation of any worthy collections. While not truly rare, first editions of many of these titles are becoming quite scarce. Because there is no comprehensive used sports book price guide, it is difficult to state exact values for these books with any certainty.

SC means soft cover, HC means hard cover

Football

Hard covers

About Three Bricks Shy of a Load, by Roy Blount Jr. (1974), HC, with dust jacket $12
Against the Grain, by Eugene "Mercury" Morris and Steve Fiffer (1988), HC 278 pages, with dust jacket $18
Always on the Run, by Larry Csonka and Jim Kiick with Dave Anderson (1973), HC 225 pages,
   with dust jacket $20
A Matter of Style, by Joe Namath with Bob Oates Jr. (1973) HC 196 pages, with dust jacket................$35
The Art of Quarterbacking, by Kenny Anderson with Jack Clancy (1984), HC 220 pages, dust jacket of Anderson $18
Audibles, by Joe Montana and Bob Raissman (1986), HC 205 pages, with dust jacket..................$18
The Best of the Athletic Boys - The White Man's Impact on Jim Thorpe, by Jack Newcombe, HC 250 pages,
   with dust jacket of Jim Thorpe...$25
Best Plays of the Year, by Robert Riger (1962), HC, dust jacket of Jim Taylor.....................$25
Blanda: Alive and Kicking, by Wells Twombley, HC 305 pages, with dust jacket $12.95
Bo Knows Bo, Bo Jackson and Dick Schaap (1990), HC 218 pages, with dust jacket................$15
Bootlegger's Boy, by Barry Switzer (1990), HC 416 pages, with dust jacket.....................$7.95
Born to Referee, My Life on the Gridiron, by Jerry Markbreit with Alan Steinberg (1988), HC 272 pages,
   with dust jacket $18
Born to Run, the O.J. Simpson Story, by Larry Fox, HC 173 pages, with dust jacket $25
The Boz: Confessions of a Modern Anti-Hero, by Brian Bosworth with Rick Reilly (1988), HC 252 pages,
   with dust jacket $12.50
Brian Piccolo: A Short Season, by Jeannie Morris (1971), HC 159 pages, basis for the movie "Brian's Song" $10
Broadway Joe and his Super Jets, by Larry Fox (1969), HC 255 pages, 1968-69 New York Jets season $20
Broken Patterns, the Education of a Quarterback, by Fran Tarkenton and Brock Yates (1971), HC 191 pages,
   with dust jacket $12.50
Bud: The Other Side of the Glacier, by Bill McGrane (1986), HC 175 pages, with dust jacket, Bud Grant............$30
Building a Champion, by Bill Walsh with Glenn Dickey (1990), HC 272 pages, with dust jacket $18.95
Calling the Shots, by Mike Singletary with Armen Keteyian (1984), HC 231 pages, with dust jacket...............$25
Coach: A Season With Lombardi, by Tom Dowling (1970), HC 333 pages, with dust jacket................$25
Coaching: The Way of A Winner, by Knute Rockne (1929), HC $65
Dennis Byrd, Rise and Walk, by Dennis Byrd with Michael D'Orso (1993), HC 258 pages, with dust jacket...........$20
Distant Replay, by Jerry Kramer with Dick Schaap (1985), HC 236 pages, with dust jacket $15
Ditka, An Autobiography, by Mike Ditka with Don Pierson (1986), HC 271 pages, with dust jacket $15
Ditka: Monster of the Midway, by Armen Keteyian (1992), HC 346 pages, with dust jacket $20
Earl Campbell: The Driving Force, by Sam Blair (1980), HC 175 pages, with dust jacket................$6.95
The End of Autumn, by Michael Oriard (1982), HC, former Kansas City Chiefs/Notre Dame player reflects
   on his football career...$15
Even Big Guys Cry, by Alex Karras with Herb Gluck (1977), HC 246 pages, with dust jacket $25
Fatso, Football When Men Were Really Men, Arthur J. Donovan Jr. and Bob Drury (1987), HC 228 pages,
   with dust jacket $14
Fighting Back, by Rocky Bleier with Terry O'Neil (1975), HC 224 pages, with dust jacket of Bleier.................$25
Football and the Single Man, by Paul Hornung (1965), HC 252 pages, with dust jacket $14.95
Frank Gifford: The Golden Year 1956, by William Wallace, HC 130 pages, with dust jacket................$18.95
Great Pass Receivers of the NFL, by Dave Anderson (1966), HC...........................$20
The Green Bay Packers, by Arch Ward (1946), HC 240 pages, with dust jacket $18.95
The Green Bay Packers: Pro Football's Pioneer Team, by Chuck Johnson (1961), HC 170 pages,
   with dust jacket $17.95
Halas on Halas, by George Halas (1979), HC 351 pages, with dust jacket $45
Happy To Be Alive, by Darryl Stingley with Mark Mulvoy (1983), HC 237 pages, with dust jacket $25
Hard Nose: The 1986 New York Giants, by Jim Burt (1987), HC, with dust jacket $25
Hard Knox: The Life of an NFL Coach, by Chuck Knox and Bill Plaschke (1988), HC 274 pages $25
Hearing the Noise: My Life in the NFL, by Preston Pearson (1985), HC 303 pages, with dust jacket $30
Heart of a Lion, the Wild and Woolly Life of Bobby Layne, by Bob St. John (1991), HC 207 pages,
   with dust jacket $19.95
Hey! Wait a Minute (I Wrote a Book), by John Madden with Dave Anderson (1984), HC 241 pages,
   with dust jacket $35
The Hundred Yard Lie: The Corruption of College Football, by Rick Telander (1989), HC 223 pages,
   with dust jacket $8.95
I Can't Wait Until Tomorrow Cause I Get Better Looking Every Day, by Joe Namath with Dick Schaap
   (1969), HC 280 pages...$30
I Am Third, by Gale Sayers with Al Silverman (1970), HC 238 pages, with dust jacket $45

I'm Still Scrambling, by Randall Cunningham with Steve Wartenberg (1993), HC 231 pages, with dust jacket...............$20

Inside Football, by George Allen (1970), HC 452 pages, with dust jacket...$15.95

Inside Pro Football, by J. King (1958), HC 216 pages...$10.95

Inside the Pressure Cooker, by Gilman (1974), HC, with dust jacket, about the New York Jets...............$30

Instant Replay: The Green Bay Diary of Jerry Kramer, by Dick Schaap (1968), HC 287 pages,
with dust jacket of Kramer..$25

In the Pocket: My Life As A QB, Earl Morrall (1969), HC, with dust jacket...$30

Iron Men: Bucko, Crazylegs and the Boys Recall the Golden Days of Pro Football, by Stuart Leuthner
(1988), HC 324 pages, with dust jacket...$8.95

Jerry Kramer's Farewell to Football, by Dick Schaap (1969), HC 200 pages , with dust jacket of Kramer...........$25

The Jim Plunkett Story, by Jim Plunkett and Dave Newhouse (1981), HC 256 pages, with dust jacket $30

Knute Rockne: Man Builder, by Harry Stuhldreher (1931), HC 335 pages, with dust jacket......................$60

The Last Season of Weeb Ewbank, by Paul Zimmerman (1974), HC 326 pages, with dust jacket...............$25

Little Men of the NFL, by Bob Rubin (1974), HC, Fran Tarkenton cover...$20

Lombardi: Winning Is the Only Thing, by Jerry Kramer (1971), HC 177 pages, with dust jacket............$35

Looking Deep, by Terry Bradshaw with Buddy Martin (1989), HC 204 pages $35

LT, Living on the Edge, by Lawrence Taylor with David Falkner, HC 225 pages, with dust jacket,
autographed..$125

The Man Inside, (Tom) Landry, by Bob St. John (1979), HC 250 pages, with dust jacket $11

McMahon!, by Jim McMahon and Bob Verdi (1986), HC 223 pages, with dust jacket.............................$35

Mean Joe Greene and the Steelers Front Four, by Larry Fox (1975), HC 241 pages, with dust jacket $30

Mean on Sunday, the Autobiography of Ray Nitschke, with Robert W. Wells (1973), HC 302 pages,
with dust jacket $15

The Miami Dolphins, by Morris McLemore (1972), HC 344 pages, with dust jacket................................$20

My Greatest Day in Football, by Murray Goodman and Leonard Lewin, HC 210 pages............................$10

My Life with the Redskins, by Corinne Griffith, HC 238 pages, with dust jacket.....................................$11.95

My Story (And I'm Sticking to It), by Alex Hawkins (1989), HC 264 pages, with dust jacket $18.95

My Sunday Best, by J. Fleischer, HC 202 pages...$10

The New York Giants, by Al Derogatis (1964), HC...$25

Nose to Nose: Survival in the Trenches of the NFL, by Joe Klecko and Joe Fields with Greg Logan (1989),
HC 287 pages, with dust jacket...$25

Nothing to Kick About: The Autobiography of a Modern Immigrant, by Pete Gogolack with Joseph Carter
(1973), HC 274 pages, with dust jacket...$7.95

Off My Chest, by Jimmy Brown with Myron Cope (1964), HC 230 pages, with dust jacket.................$17.95

The $1 League, by Jim Byrne (1986), HC 352 pages, history of the USFL...$12.50

One Giant League, by Jeff Hostetler with Ed Fitzgerald (1991), HC 236 pages, with dust jacket...........$25

Once a Cowboy, by Walt Garrison with John Tullius (1988), HC 212 pages, with dust jacket $35

One Knee Equals Two Feet, by John Madden and Dave Anderson (1986), HC 227 pages, with dust jacket $14

Open Field, by John Brodie with James D. Houston (1974), HC 230 pages, with dust jacket $13.95

Out of Control, by Thomas "Hollywood" Henderson and Peter Knobler (1987), HC 304 pages...............$10

Over the Hill to the Super Bowl, by Owens (1973), HC, with dust jacket, about the 1973 Redskins $35

Packer Dynasty, Phil Bengston with Todd Hunt (1968), HC 278 pages, with dust jacket $35

Paper Lion, by George Plimpton (1966), HC 362 pages, with dust jacket...$45

Pittsburgh Steelers - Great Teams, Great Years, by Ray Didinger (1974), dust jacket of Terry Bradshaw $20

The Players, by Tex Maule (1967), HC 238 pages..$20

Quarterbacks Have all the Fun, by Dick Schaap (1974), HC 260 pages, with dust jacket.........................$18

The Red Grange Story, by Red Grange (1953), HC 178 pages, with dust jacket $19.95

Roger Craig: Strictly Business, by Garry Niver (1992), HC 209 pages, with dust jacket..........................$35

Roger Staubach: A Special Kind of QB, by Sullivan (1974, 3rd ed.), HC $25

Rosey: The Gentle Giant, by Rosey Grier with Dennis Baker (1986), HC 301 pages, with dust jacket........$30

Running Tough: Memoirs of a Football Maverick, by Tony Dorsett and Harvey Frommer (1989),
HC 225 pages, with dust jacket...$7.95

Seven Days to Sunday, by Asinoff (1968), HC, with dust jacket..$35

Simms To McConkey: Blood, Sweat and Gatorade, by Phil McConkey and Phil Simms (1987), HC 243 pages,
with dust jacket $6.95

Singletary on Singletary, by Mike Singletary and Jerry Jenkins (1991), HC 220 pages............................$30

Starr - My Life in Football, by Bart Starr with Murray Olderman (1987), HC 224 pages, with dust jacket $13

Steelers, Team of the Decade, by Lou Sahadi (1979), HC, with dust jacket $45

Super Bowl: Of Men, Myths and Moments, by Marty Ralbovsky (1971), HC 208 pages, with dust jacket.........$12.95

Tarkenton, by Jim Klobuchar and Fran Tarkenton (1976), HC 274 pages, with dust jacket.......................$15

Books

Terry Bradshaw, Man of Steel, by Terry Bradshaw with David Diles (1979), HC (303 pages),
  with dust jacket $30
The Whole Ten Yards, by Frank Gifford and Harry Waters (1993), HC 285 pages $7.50
The Winning Edge, by Don Shula (1973), HC, with dust jacket..$30
They Call It A Game, by Bernie Parrish (1971), HC 317 pages..$9.95
They Call Me Assassin, by Jack Tatum with Bill Kushner (1979), HC 251 pages........................$15
They Call Me Dirty, by Conrad Dobler and Vic Carucci (1988), HC 288 pages, with dust jacket $15
They're Playing My Game, by Hank Stram with Lou Sahadi (1986), HC 166 pages, with dust jacket $4.95
Tom Landry, by Tom Landry and Gregg Lewis (1990), HC 302 pages $7.50
Total Impact, Straight Talk from Football's Hardest Hitter, by Ronnie Lott with Jill Lieber (1991), HC 305 pages,
  with dust jacket $19.50
Vikes, Mikes and Something on the Backside, by Ahmad Rashad with Peter Bodo (1988), HC, (278 pages)
  with dust jacket $25
Vince, A Personal Biography of Vince Lombardi, by Michael O'Brien (1987), HC 457 pages, with dust jacket............$22
Weeb Ewbank's The Football Way, by Lud Duroska (1967), HC, with dust jacket of Joe Namath $20
When the Grass was Real (Ten Best Years of Pro Football), by Bob Carroll (1993), HC 303 pages,
  with dust jacket $27.50
Y.A. Tittle: I Pass, by Don Smith (1964), HC 300 pages, with dust jacket..$35

Soft covers

1975 All-Pro Football Stars, by J. Brondfield (1975), SC, Ken Stabler cover $7
1976 All-Pro Football Stars, by J. Brondfield (1976), SC, Fran Tarkenton cover $7
The Cincinnati Bengals and the Magic of Paul Brown, by D. Forbes (1973) SC......................................$15
1975 Complete Handbook of Pro Football, by Zander Hollander (1975), SC, Joe Greene cover $9
1979 Complete Handbook of Pro Football, by Zander Hollander (1979), SC $7
Football Stars of 1964, by Barry Goetthrer (1964), SC..$10
Football Stars of 1968, by Barry Stainback (1968), SC..$7
Football Stars of 1973, by Hal Bock and Ben Olan (1973), SC..$6
Gifford on Courage, by C. Mangel (Frank Gifford), SC..$12
I Can't Wait Until Tomorrow Cause I Get Better Looking Every Day, by Joe Namath with Dick Schaap
  (1969), SC...$15
Instant Replay: The Green Bay Diary of Jerry Kramer, by Dick Schaap (1969), SC $12
Joe Namath, by John Devaney (1972), SC $12
Len Dawson: Super Bowl Quarterback, by Larry Bortstein (1970), SC $12
The Miami Dolphins: Football's Greatest Team, by A. Levine (1973), SC...$10
1967 Official Pro Football Record Book, by Complete Sports Publications (1967), SC, Bart Starr cover $10
1968 Official Pro Football Record Book, by Complete Sports Publications (1968), SC, Joe Namath cover $10
O.J. Simpson: Football's Greatest Runner, by John Devaney (1974), SC..$6
Pro Football 1967, by Jack Zanger (1967), SC $10
Pro Football 1971, by Jack Zanger (1971), SC $8
Sports Focus Football New York Giants, 1975, SC $12
Sports Focus Football Washington Redskins, 1975, SC $12
Super Bowl: Pro Football's Greatest Games, by S. Gelman (1975), SC, Terry Bradshaw cover....................$6
Super Joe: The Joe Namath Story, by Larry Bortstein (1969), SC...$10
Winning Football, by Bart Starr (1968), SC...$10

Basketball

Hard covers

Against the World, by Kerry Eggers and Dwight Jaynes (1993), HC, recaps the Portland Trailblazer's
  1991-92 season..$12.50
A Season Inside: One Year in College Basketball, by John Feinstein, HC 462 pages, with dust jacket............$9.95
A Season On The Brink: A Year with Bob Knight and the Indiana Hoosiers, by John Feinstein (1986),
  HC 311 pages, with dust jacket..$8.95
A View From Above, by Wilt Chamberlain (1991), HC 290 pages, with dust jacket of Chamberlain,
  autographed...$30
A View From the Bench, Red Holzman with Leonard Lewin (1980), HC 288 pages, with dust jacket....................$25
A View From the Rim: Willis Reed on basketball, by Willis Reed and Phil Pepe (1971), HC 208 pages $20
Bill Bradley: One to Remember, by Halter (1975), HC, with dust jacket..$35
Bill Walton, Nothing but Net, by Bill Walton with Gene Wojciechowski (1994), HC 257 pages,
  with dust jacket $22.95

Bird: The Making of An American Sports Legend, by Lee Daniel Levine (1988), HC 342 pages $35
The Cockroach Basketball League, by Charles Rosen (1992), HC...$18
Cousy on the Celtic Mystique, by Bob Cousy with Bob Ryan (1988), HC 202 pages $20
Drive, the Story of My Life, Larry Bird with Bob Ryan (1989), HC 260 pages, with dust jacket..................$25
Forty-Eight Minutes, A Night in the Life of the NBA, by Bob Ryan and Terry Pluto (1987), 356 pages.................$20
Foul! The Connie Hawkins Story, by David Wolf (1972), HC 400 pages, with dust jacket $35
The Franchise, by Cameron Stauth (1990), HC 365 pages, with dust jacket......................................$19.95
George McGinnis: Basketball Superstar, by James Haskins, HC 128 pages, with dust jacket....................$7.95
Giant Steps, by Kareem Abdul-Jabbar and Peter Knobler (1983), HC 324 pages, with dust jacket $18
Go Up For Glory, by Bill Russell and William McSweeney (1966), HC 224 pages $25
Hang Time, Days & Dreams with Michael Jordan, by Bob Greene (1992), HC 406 pages, with dust jacket.......$30
Heir to a Dream, by Pete Maravich and Darrel Campbell (1987), HC 234 pages $27.50
Holzman's Basketball: Winning Strategy and Tactics, by Red Holzman (1973), HC 242 pages,
    with dust jacket $16.95
Hondo, Celtic Man In Motion, by Bob Ryan (1977), HC, biography of John Havlicek, autographed....................$40
In the Land of the Giants, My Life in Basketball, by Tyrone "Muggsy" Bogues and David Levine (1994),
    HC 233 pages, with dust jacket...$19.95
The Jordan Rules, by Sam Smith (1992), HC 333 pages, with dust jacket....................................$20
John Wooden: They Call Me Coach, by Jack Tobin (1973), HC 190 pages, with dust jacket...................$45
Kareem, by Kareem Abdul-Jabbar with Mignon McCrthy (1990), HC, 233 pages, with dust jacket $12
The Killer Instinct, by Bob Cousy with Jim Devaney (1975), HC 212 pages, with dust jacket $35
Krazy about the Knicks, by Marv Albert (1971), HC, with dust jacket...$35
The Last Loud Roar, Bob Cousy with Ed Linn (1964), HC 271 pages, with dust jacket $45
Life on the Run, by Bill Bradley (1976), HC 229 pages, with dust jacket....................................$25
Loose Balls, by Terry Pluto (1990), HC 450 pages, traces the history of the ABA, Julius Erving cover $25
Magic's Touch, by Earvin "Magic" Johnson Jr. and Roy S. Johnson, HC 236 pages.............................$20
Mr. Basketball, by George Mikan and Bill Carlson (1951), HC, inscribed inside...............................$65
Mr. Clutch: The Jerry West story, by Jerry West and Bill Libby (1969), HC 238 pages, with dust jacket.......$35
My Life, by Earvin "Magic" Johnson with William Novak (1992), HC 331 pages $10
Obsession - Timberwolves Stalk the NBA, by Bill Heller (1989), HC, traces startup of the Minnesota Timberwolves
    basketball team..$10
One Basketball and Glory, by Newt Oliver (1969), HC, the Bevo Francis story $15
The Open Man: A championship diary, by Dave DeBusschere with Paul Zimmerman and Dick Schaap (1970),
    HC 267 pages, with dust jacket..$25
Pistol Pete Maravich, the making of a basketball star, by Bill Gutman (1972), HC 192 pages $25
Rebound: K.C. Jones Autobiography, by Jack Warner (1986), HC 190 pages, with dust jacket of K.C. Jones ...$15
Red on Red, Red Holzman and Harvey Frommer (1987), HC 206 pages, with dust jacket $18
Second Wind, the Memoirs of an opinionated man, by Bill Russell with Taylor Branch (1979, HC 265 pages....$25
Shaq Attaq!, by Shaquille O'Neal with Jack McCallum (1993), HC, with dust jacket $12.50
Show Time - Inside the Lakers' Breakthrough Season, by Pat Riley (1988), HC 259 pages, with dust jacket $22
Stand Tall, the Lew Alcindor Story, by Phil Pepe (1970), HC 206 pages, with dust jacket $25
Tall Tales - Glory Years of the NBA, by Terry Pluto (1992), HC 397 pages, with dust jacket $25
24 Seconds to Shoot: Informal History of the NBA, by Leonard Koppett (1968), HC, with dust jacket...........$35
Unfinished Business, by Jack McCallum (1992), HC, recaps the 1990-91 Celtics season.....................$20
The View From Section III, by Mike Shatzkin (1970), HC , with dust jacket, recaps the Knicks' 1969-70 season.......$35
Vitale, by Dick Vitale (1988), HC 334 pages, with dust jacket $9.95
Walt Frazier: One Magic Season and a Basketball Life, by Walt Frazier and Neil Offen (1988), HC 259 pages,
    with dust jacket $15
The Walton Gang, by Bill Libby (1974), HC 288 pages, with dust jacket......................................$12.95
Willis Reed, The Knicks Take Charge Man, by Larry Fox (1970), HC, with dust jacket.......................$30
Wilt, by Wilt Chamberlain and David Shaw (1973), HC 310 pages..$35
The Winner Within, A Life Plan for Team Players, by Pat Riley (1993), HC 272 pages, with dust jacket $30

Soft covers

Basketball Stars of 1970, by Lou Sabin (1970), SC, Lew Alcindor cover $10
Basketball Stars of 1975, by Hal Bock and Ben Olan (1974), SC..$6
Big A: The Story of Lew Alcindor, by Joel Cohen (1971), SC..$12
John Wooden: They Call Me Coach, by Jack Tobin (1972), SC..$6
Loose Balls, by Terry Pluto (1990), SC , traces the history of the ABA, Julius Erving cover $15
Michael Jordan/Magic Johnson, by Richard Brenner (1989), SC..$6
Pete Maravich: Basketball Magician, by Lou Sabin (1973), SC $10

Books

Pro Basketball 1976-77, by Ballantine (1976), SC, Jo Jo White cover...$7
Red Auerbach, Basketball: For the Player, the Fan, and the Coach (1953) SC $20
Second Wind, by Bill Russell (1991), SC $10
Shaq!, by Bill Dunn (1993), SC, reviews Shaquille O'Neal's rookie season, done by the staff at the Orlando Sentinel
    newspaper..$10
Wilt Chamberlain, by George Sullivan (1967)..$6

Hockey

Andy Bathgate's Hockey Secrets, by Andy Bathgate (1964), HC 158 pages, with dust jacket...............................$4.95
A Spin of the Wheel: Birth of the Buffalo Sabres, by R. Brewitt (1975), HC 197 pages, with dust jacket $22.95
Bernie! Bernie! Bernie!, by Bernie Parent with Bill Fleischman and Sonny Schwartz (1975), HC 272 pages,
    with dust jacket $19.95
Bobby Clarke, by Edward Dolan and Richard Lyttle (1977), HC 94 pages $16.95
Bobby Clarke and the Ferocious Flyers, by Stan Fischler (1974), HC 213 pages, with dust jacket........................$35
Bobby Orr and the Big Bad Bruins, by Stan Fischler (1969), HC 273 pages, with dust jacket $17.95
Bobby Orr: Lightning On Ice, by Howard Liss (1975), HC 96 pages, with dust jacket.......................................$17.50
Bobby Orr: My Game, by Bobby Orr and Mark Mulvoy (1974), HC 235 pages, with dust jacket........................$19.95
Cowboy on Ice, by Phil Lorange (1975), HC, biography of Howie Young, autographed.......................................$30
Cyclone Taylor: A Hockey Legend, by Eric Whitehead (1977), HC 205 pages, with dust jacket........................$9.95
Eddie: A Goalie's Story, by H. Delano (1976), biography of Eddie Giacomin, HC 319 pages, with
    dust jacket $17.95
Face-Off at the Summit, by Ken Dryden (1973), HC 207 pages, with dust jacket...$14.95
The Fastest Sport, by Gerald Eskenazi (1974), HC..$15
The Flying Frenchmen, Hockey's Greatest Dynasty, by Maurice "Rocket" Richard and Stan Fischler (1971),
    HC 340 pages, with dust jacket...$20
The Game, by Ken Dryden (1983), HC 248 pages...$12.50
Garry Unger and the battling Blues, by Stan Fischler (1976), HC 213 pages...$15
Goaltender, by Gerry Cheevers (1971), HC 211 pages, with dust jacket...$17.95
Gordie Howe, by Stan Fischler (1967), HC..$15
Gordie Howe: Number 9, by Jim Vipond (1968), HC 157 pages, with dust jacket, autographed $125
Great Upsets of Stanley Cup Hockey, by John Devaney (1976), HC 96 pages, Bobby Orr on dust jacket $9.95
Gretzky, An Autobiography, by Wayne Gretzky with Rick Reilly (1990), HC 258 pages $25
The Hammer, by Dave Schultz with Stan Fischler (1981), HC 208 pages $10
High Stick, by Ted Green (1971), HC 211 pages, with dust jacket..$17.95
Hockey In My Blood, by Johnny Bucyk with Russ Conway (1972), HC 197 pages, with dust jacket...................$17.95
Hockey Is A Battle, by Punch Imlach (1969), HC 203 pages, with dust jacket..$16.95
Hockey Is My Game, by Bobby Hull (1967), HC 212 pages, with dust jacket $25
Hockey Is My Life, by Phil Esposito with Gerald Eskenazi (1972), HC 207 pages, with dust jacket.....................$14.95
I Play to Win, by Stan Mikita (1969), HC 223 pages $20
Larinov, by Igor Larinov, Jim Taylor and Leonid Reizer (1990), HC, saga of Russian player pursuing
    NHL career *$10*
The Men in the Nets, by J. Hunt (1967), HC 133 pages, with dust jacket..$10.95
Mr. Hockey: The World of Gordie Howe (1975), HC 197 pages, with dust jacket..$18.95
My Three Hockey Players, by Colleen Howe (1972), HC 192 pages, with dust jacket $14.95
None Against! by Keith Magnuson (1973), HC 179 pages, with dust jacket $12.95
Orr on Ice, by Bobby Orr (1970) with Dick Grace, HC 176 pages, with dust jacket, autographed $45
Play the Man, by Brad Park with Stan Fischler (1971), HC 211 pages, with dust jacket $17.95
Power Play: The Story of the Toronto Maple Leafs, by Stan Fischler (1972), HC 272 pages,
    with dust jacket $18.95
Rocket Richard, by Andy O'Brien (1969), HC 134 pages, with dust jacket $17.95
Strength Down Centre, by Hugh Hood (1970), HC 192 pages, biography of Jean Beliveau.................................$27.50
They Call Me Gump, by Lorne "Gump" Worsley with Tim Moriarity (1975), HC 176 pages,
    with dust jacket $20
Those Were the Days, by Stan Fischler (1976), HC 337 pages, with dust jacket $14.95
We Love You Bruins: Boston's Gashouse Gang from Eddie Shore to Bobby Orr, by John Devaney,
    HC 183 pages, Bobby Orr cover...$20

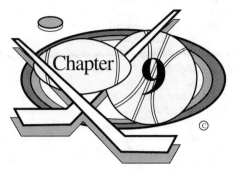

Chapter 9

Commemoratives

Gateway Stamp Co.

Gateway Stamp Co., of Florissant, Mo., has been producing its full-color "silk" commemorative cachets since 1977. The company has covered all the primary sports, with baseball as its main subject.

The limited-edition envelopes are postmarked on the historic dates by the United States Postal service, which only dates items submitted before midnight. Gateway has employees who track a player's progress toward a milestone accomplishment; they also follow the player, with a determined number of stamped cachets to be postmarked, until the event has occurred. When the event has happened, the employee has the post office in that city hand-cancel the envelopes. Whenever possible, Gateway also incorporates philatelic cancellations on the envelopes.

The cachets feature gold borders, biographical information and full-color silk cachets, which are actual event photos, publicity photos, or artists' renditions. A primary attraction of the cachets is that Gateway has designed the envelopes to be autographed, and obtains the signatures of the players represented on them.

Values of the covers are determined by condition (cleanliness, crispness of corners, centering, positioning of copy, clarity of postmarks) and autographs - quality and player represented. In the following checklist, based on Mint condition, the values are for unsigned cachets, unless they were issued autographed.

GS53 Super Sunday: Postmarked Jan. 20, 1980, Pasadena, Calif., featuring artwork by Scott Forst. 2,000 issued, some autographed by Cullen Bryant, L.C. Greenwood, John Stallworth or Wendell Tyler: ....$25.

GS54 Los Angeles Rams: Postmarked Jan. 20, 1980, Pasadena, Calif. 2,000 issued, featuring photo of Vince Ferragamo and Rich Saul. Some autographed by Vince Ferragamo, Rich Saul, Cullen Bryant or Wendell Tyler: ....$20.

GS55 Pittsburgh Steelers: Postmarked Jan. 20, 1980, Pasadena, Calif. 2,000 issued, featuring photo of Franco Harris and Fred Dryer. Some autographed by Franco Harris, L.C. Greenwood or John Stallworth: ....$30.

GS73 New Orleans: Postmarked Jan. 25, 1981, New Orleans, La., site of the 1981 Super Bowl between the Oakland Raiders and Philadelphia Eagles. 2,000 issued: ....$20.

GS74 Oakland: Postmarked Jan. 25, 1981, New Orleans, La., site of the 1981 Super Bowl between Oakland and Philadelphia. 2,000 issued: ....$20.

GS75 Philadelphia: Postmarked Jan. 25, 1981, New Orleans, La., site of the 1981 Super Bowl between Oakland and Philadelphia. 2,000 issued: ....$20.

GS97 Bear Bryant: Postmarked Dec. 29, 1982, Memphis, Tenn., upon Bryant's last collegiate game, a victory for an all-time record of 323 wins. Bryant photo. 2,000 issued: ....$50.

GS98 Wayne Gretzky 77 Goals: Postmarked Feb. 24, 1982, Buffalo, N.Y., as Gretzky broke Phil Esposito's all-time single-season goal scoring record. 500 issued, autographed: ....$350.

GS120 Wayne Gretzky Points Record: Postmarked Dec. 5, 1982, Edmonton, Alberta, Canada, as Gretzky scored a point in his 29th consecutive game, a new single season record. 2,000 issued with Gretzky action photo, autographed: ....$250.

GS165 Jim Thorpe First Day of Issue: Postmarked "First Day of Issue" May 24, 1984, Broken Arrow, Okla. 3,500 issued. Bill Perry artwork. 50 hand-cancellations: ....Undetermined.

GS182 Walter Payton Rushing Record: Postmarked Oct. 7, 1984, Chicago, Ill. 1,500 issued, autographed: ....$50.

GS188 Eric Dickerson Single-Season Rushing Record: Postmarked Dec. 9, 1984, Anaheim, Calif. 1,500 issued, autographed: ....$30.

GS189 Dan Marino Passing Record: Postmarked Dec. 18, 1984, commemorating Marino's single-season record of 5,000 yards passing. 1,000 issued: ....$35.

GS193 Super Bowl, Palo Alto: Postmarked Jan. 20, 1985, Palo Alto, Calif., with pictorial Super Bowl XIX postmark. 1,100 issued with Scott Forst artwork. Issued autographed by various players or Bill Walsh: ....$15.

GS194 Super Bowl Dolphins: Postmarked Jan. 20, 1985, Palo Alto, Calif., with pictorial Super Bowl XIX postmark. 1,100 issued, autographed by Dan Marino: ....$25.

GS195 Super Bowl 49ers: Postmarked Jan. 20, 1985, Palo Alto, Calif., with pictorial Super Bowl XIX postmark. 1,100 issued autographed by Joe Montana, with action photo: ....$50.

GS209 Roger Staubach Hall of Fame Induction: Postmarked Aug. 3, 1985, Canton, Ohio, with a special Hall of Fame Induction Day postmark. 1,500 issued, autographed. Bill Perry artwork: ....$25.

GS210 O.J. Simpson Hall of Fame Induction: Postmarked Aug. 3, 1985, Canton, Ohio. 1,000 issued, autographed. Bill Perry artwork: ....$50.

GS211 Joe Namath Hall of Fame Induction: Postmarked Aug. 3, 1985, Canton, Ohio. 1,500 issued, autographed. Bill Perry artwork: ....$50.

GS222 Eddie Robinson Coaching Record: Postmarked Oct. 5, 1985, Dallas, Texas, as Grambling University's Robinson passed Paul "Bear" Bryant as the winningest coach in college football history. 1,000 issued, autographed: ....$20.

GS237 1986 Super Bowl, Superdome: Postmarked Jan. 26, 1986, New Orleans, La., with large U.S.P.S. pictorial Super Bowl XX cancellation. Stadium artwork by Scott Forst. 800 issued unautographed or autographed by Mike Singletary or Richard Dent: ....$15.

GS238 1986 Super Bowl, Chicago Offense: Postmarked Jan. 26, 1986, New Orleans, La., with large pictorial Super Bowl XX postmark. 800 issued picturing Jim McMahon, 500 autographed: ....$20.

GS239 1986 Super Bowl, Chicago Defense: Postmarked Jan. 26, 1986, New Orleans, La., with large pictorial Super Bowl XX cancellation. 800 issued picturing William "Refrigerator" Perry. 500 autographed by Perry, 300 autographed by Richard Dent: ....$20.

GS290 Paul Hornung Hall of Fame Induction: Postmarked Aug. 3, 1986, Canton, Ohio, with pictorial philatelic postmark. 1,000 issued, autographed. Bill Perry artwork: ....$20.

GS317 1987 Super Bowl, Pasadena: Postmarked Jan. 25, 1987, Pasadena, Calif., with large Super Bowl XXI U.S.P.S. cancellation. Vince Lombardi trophy artwork by Scott Forst. 800 issued with various New York Giants autographs, including Jim Burt, Harry Carson and Lawrence Taylor: ....$15.

GS318 1987 Super Bowl, New York: Postmarked Jan. 25, 1987, Pasadena, Calif., with large Super Bowl XXI cancellation. 800 issued picturing Phil Simms, autographed by Simms or Simms and Joe Morris: ....$35.

GS319 1987 Super Bowl, Denver: Postmarked Jan. 25, 1987, Pasadena, Calif., with large Super Bowl XXI cancellation. 800 issued picturing John Elway and Bobby Humphrey. Autographed by Elway: ....$30.

GS378 1988 Super Bowl, Jack Murphy Stadium: Postmarked Jan. 31, 1988, San Diego, Calif., with large U.S.P.S. pictorial Super Bowl XXII cancellation. 800 issued with Scott Forst stadium artwork. 500 autographed by Art Monk: ....$15.

GS379 1988 Super Bowl, Washington: Postmarked Jan. 31, 1988, San Diego, Calif., with large Super Bowl XXII cancellation. 800 issued, autographed, picturing Doug Williams: ....$20.

GS380 1988 Super Bowl, Denver: Postmarked Jan. 31, 1988, San Diego, Calif., with large Super Bowl XXII cancellation. 800 issued, autographed, picturing John Elway: ....$25.

GS390 Mike Ditka, Hall of Famer: Postmarked July 30, 1988, Canton, Ohio, on Ditka's induction into the Football Hall of Fame. 1,000 issued, autographed. Bill Perry artwork: ....$30.

GS391 Fred Biletnikoff, Hall of Famer: Postmarked July 30, 1988, Canton, Ohio, on Biletnikoff's induction into Football Hall of Fame. 600 issued, autographed. Bill Perry artwork: ....$25.

GS419 1989 Super Bowl, Miami: Postmarked Jan. 22, 1989, Opa Locka, Fla. 650 issued, bearing Scott Forst artwork of Joe Robbie Stadium. 300 autographed by Ickey Woods, 100 autographed by Jerry Rice, Ronnie Lott and Roger Craig: ....$15.

GS420 1989 Super Bowl, San Francisco: Postmarked Jan. 22, 1989, Opa Locka, Fla. 650 issued, autographed, picturing Joe Montana: ....$125.

GS451 Terry Bradshaw Hall of Fame Induction: Postmarked Aug. 22, 1989, Canton, Ohio, with large pictorial Hall of Fame postmark. 1,000 issued, autographed, featuring Bill Perry artwork: ....$25.

GS464 Mario Lemieux Pittsburgh: Postmarked Jan. 21, 1990, Pittsburgh, Pa., upon the 1990 NHL All-Star Game. 500 issued, autographed, picturing Lemieux in action, with Wayne Gretzky in the background: .... $65.

GS467 1990 Super Bowl, Superdome: Postmarked Jan. 28, 1990, New Orleans, La., with special philatelic Super Bowl XXIV postmark. 800 issued featuring Scott Forst Superdome stadium artwork. 100 autographed by Jerry Rice: ....$15.

GS468 1990 Super Bowl, San Francisco: Postmarked Jan. 28, 1990, New Orleans, La. 800 issued, autographed, bearing action photo of Joe Montana. All bear Super Bowl XXIV postmarks, while 500 have "Montana" statehood anniversary postage stamps: ....$50.

GS469 1990 Super Bowl, Denver: Postmarked Jan. 28, 1990, New Orleans, La., with Super Bowl XXIV philatelic postmark. 800 issued, autographed, with John Elway photo: ....$25.

GS483 Tom Landry Hall of Fame Induction: Postmarked Aug. 8, 1990, Canton, Ohio, with pictorial Hall of Fame postmark. 1,200 issued, autographed, featuring Bill Perry artwork: .... $20.

GS484 Bob Griese Hall of Induction: Postmarked Aug. 8, 1990, with pictorial Hall of Fame postmark. 1,000 issued, autographed, featuring Bill Perry artwork: ....$20.

GS538 Basketball First Day of Issue: Postmarked Aug. 28, 1991, Springfield, Mass., "First Day of Issue" on the 29-cent commemorative basketball postage stamp. 1,000 issued, 50 hand-cancellations acquired: ....$30.

GS539 Larry Bird: Postmarked Aug. 28, 1991, Springfield, Mass., on the 29-cent basketball stamp. 500 issued, autographed: ....$65.

Z Silk Cachets

Historic Limited Editions, in New Canaan, Conn., captures sporting events on a silk-cacheted philatelic cover which features an original painting of the player or event. These silk cachets are then applied by hand to envelopes which have been stamped and postmarked by the post office in the corresponding city where the event occurred. Generally, 200 to 600 covers are produced per event, depending on the player and/or event involved and potential demand by collectors. The covers are suitable for autographing, although the company has offered a limited number already signed by certain players.

Basketball

Shaquille O'Neal Rookie of the Year NBA 1992-93, May 6, 1993, New York, N.Y. $12

Hockey

Phil Esposito named general manager $5
Wayne Gretzky 1993 Playoffs.................$18
Wayne Gretzky record in March 1994 ....$10
Stanley Cup 1983 - set of two..................$15
Stanley Cup 1994......................................$5

Football

Fred Biletnikoff 1988 Football Hall of Fame
....$15
Mike Ditka 1988 Football Hall of Fame....$6
Jack Ham 1988 Football Hall of Fame $6

Alan Page 1988 Football Hall of Fame..... $6
Super Bowl XXIII $10
Super Bowl 17.. $5
Super Bowl 18, set of two $15
Super Bowl 20.. $6
Super Bowl 21.. $6
Super Bowl 28, Emmitt Smith $5

black-and-whites

Mel Blount Hall of Fame induction $6
Terry Bradshaw Hall of Fame induction... $6
Art Shell Hall of Fame induction $6
Willie Wood Hall of Fame induction........ $6

Wild Horse cachets

These limited-edition individually hand-painted cachets are signed and numbered by the artist, Warren Reed. The majority of those created are baseball related, but football, basketball and hockey are represented, too.

Player/theme	Date	# issued	Issue Price	Value
Kareem Abdul-Jabbar, 700 double figures	March 9, 1990	55	$31.95	$100
Ottis Anderson, Super Bowl	Jan. 27, 1991	65	$24.95	$24.95
Buffalo Bills/New York Giants Super Bowl	Jan. 27, 1991	65	$24.95	$24.95
Terry Bradshaw, NFL Hall of Fame Induction	Aug. 5, 1989	30	$24.95	$50
Wilt Chamberlain, 100th point game anniversary	March 2, 1991	111	$34.95	$34.95
Wilt Chamberlain/Bill Russell	April 21, 1990	50	$24.95	$75
Mean Joe Greene, Hall of Fame Induction	Aug. 8, 1987	35	$24.95	$45
Wayne Grezky	Feb. 1, 1980	50	$24.95	$80
Wayne Grezky	Feb. 1, 1980	129	$24.95	$50
Jack Ham, NFL Hall of Fame Induction	July 30, 1988	35	$24.95	$40
Brett Hull, 50-50 Club	Feb. 1, 1980	50	$24.95	$50
Brett Hull/Bobby Hull	Feb. 1, 1980	65	$24.95	$50
Magic Johnson, NBA MVP	May 18, 1987	54	$34.95	$75
Magic Johnson, unforgettable	Aug. 28, 1991	158	$24.95	$24.95
Magic Johnson/Larry Bird	Jan. 27, 1991	55	$24.95	$60
Kevin Johnson, 1991 All-Star	Feb. 10, 1991	56	$24.95	$50
Michael Jordan, Stamp Expo	Feb. 16, 1990	40	$24.95	$75
Michael Jordan, Chicago vs. Miami	Jan. 25, 1991	55	$24.95	$75
Michael Jordan, NBA Champs	June 2, 1991	125	$24.95	$45
Joe Montana, 1990 Super Bowl	Jan. 28, 1990	50	$24.95	$100
Jerry Rice, 1990 Super Bowl	Jan. 28, 1990	50	$24.95	$75
David Robinson, Mr. Robinson	Dec. 21, 1990	40	$24.95	$75
O.J. Simpson, hologram	Sept. 9, 1990	60	$31.95	$60
Mike Singletary, Chicago Bears	Aug. 4, 1990	51	$24.95	$24.95
Doug Williams, 1988 Super Bowl	Jan. 31, 1988	30	$24.95	$60

1989 Goal Line Hall of Fame

These postcard-size cards (4" by 6") feature full-color action paintings of inductees into the Pro Football Hall of Fame. The cards were part of an art series done by artist Gary Thomas and were offered by subscription. Each set was packaged in a custom box and was given a serial number (Set No. x of 5,000), which appears on each card, too. The back of the card is white and uses black ink. The player's name, college, position, biographical information, years he played, teams he played with and the year he was inducted are all listed, as well as a set and card number. A Football Hall of Fame logo is also given. Each of the first five series contains 30 cards; series 6 has 25. However, a card for Johnny Unitas (#174) was never issued. Series I was issued in 1989; a new series has followed each year since then. The cards are numbered alphabetically within each series.

		MT	NM	EX
Complete Set (175):		400.00	300.00	160.00
Common Player:		2.00	1.50	.80
1	Lance Alworth	6.00	4.50	2.50
2	Morris (Red) Badgro	2.50	2.00	1.00
3	Cliff Battles	2.50	2.00	1.00
4	Mel Blount	2.50	2.00	1.00
5	Terry Bradshaw	10.00	7.50	4.00
6	Jim Brown	12.00	9.00	4.75
7	George Connor	2.50	2.00	1.00
8	Turk Edwards	2.50	2.00	1.00
9	Tom Fears	2.50	2.00	1.00
10	Frank Gifford	10.00	7.50	4.00
11	Otto Graham	6.00	4.50	2.50
12	Red Grange	5.00	3.75	2.00
13	George Halas	4.00	3.00	1.50
14	Clarke Hinkle	2.50	2.00	1.00
15	Robert (Cal) Hubbard	2.50	2.00	1.00
16	Sam Huff	2.50	2.00	1.00
17	Frank (Bruiser) Kinard	2.50	2.00	1.00
18	Dick (Night Train) Lane	2.50	2.00	1.00
19	Sid Luckman	6.00	4.50	2.50
20	Bobby Mitchell	2.50	2.00	1.00
21	Merlin Olsen	4.00	3.00	1.50
22	Jim Parker	2.50	2.00	1.00
23	Joe Perry	3.00	2.25	1.25
24	Pete Rozelle	3.00	2.25	1.25
25	Art Shell	3.00	2.25	1.25
26	Fran Tarkenton	9.00	6.75	3.50
27	Jim Thorpe	6.00	4.50	2.50
28	Paul Warfield	3.00	2.25	1.25
29	Larry Wilson	2.50	2.00	1.00
30	Willie Wood	2.50	2.00	1.00
31	Doug Atkins	2.00	1.50	.80
32	Bobby Bell	2.00	1.50	.80
33	Raymond Berry	3.00	2.25	1.25
34	Paul Brown	2.00	1.50	.80
35	Guy Chamberlin	2.00	1.50	.80
36	Earl (Dutch) Clark	2.00	1.50	.80
37	Jimmy Conzelman	2.00	1.50	.80
38	Len Dawson	3.00	2.25	1.25
39	Mike Ditka	8.00	6.00	3.25
40	Dan Fortmann	2.00	1.50	.80
41	Frank Gatski	2.00	1.50	.80
42	Bill George	2.00	1.50	.80
43	Elroy Hirsch	3.00	2.25	1.25
44	Paul Hornung	4.00	3.00	1.50
45	John Henry Johnson	2.00	1.50	.80
46	Walt Kiesling	2.00	1.50	.80
47	Yale Lary	2.00	1.50	.80
48	Bobby Layne	3.00	2.25	1.25
49	Tuffy Leemans	2.00	1.50	.80
50	Geo. Preston Marshall	2.00	1.50	.80
51	George McAfee	2.00	1.50	.80
52	Wayne Millner	2.00	1.50	.80
53	Bronko Nagurski	4.00	3.00	1.50
54	Joe Namath	12.00	9.00	4.75
55	Ray Nitschke	3.00	2.25	1.25
56	Jim Ringo	2.00	1.50	.80
57	Art Rooney	2.00	1.50	.80
58	Joe Stydahar	2.00	1.50	.80
59	Charley Taylor	2.00	1.50	.80
60	Charlie Trippi	2.00	1.50	.80
61	Fred Biletnikoff	3.00	2.25	1.25
62	Buck Buchanan	2.00	1.50	.80
63	Dick Butkus	6.00	4.50	2.50
64	Earl Campbell	8.00	6.00	3.25
65	Tony Canadeo	2.00	1.50	.80
66	Art Donovan	3.00	2.25	1.25
67	Ray Flaherty	2.00	1.50	.80
68	Forrest Gregg	2.50	2.00	1.00
69	Lou Groza	3.00	2.25	1.25
70	John Hannah	2.00	1.50	.80
71	Don Hutson	2.50	2.00	1.00
72	David (Deacon) Jones	2.00	1.50	.80
73	Stan Jones	2.00	1.50	.80
74	Sonny Jurgensen	3.00	2.25	1.25
75	Vince Lombardi	3.00	2.25	1.25
76	Tim Mara	2.00	1.50	.80
77	Ollie Matson	2.00	1.50	.80
78	Mike McCormack	2.00	1.50	.80
79	John (Blood) McNally	2.00	1.50	.80
80	Marion Motley	2.00	1.50	.80
81	George Musso	2.00	1.50	.80
82	Earle (Greasy) Neale	2.00	1.50	.80
83	Clarence (Ace) Parker	2.00	1.50	.80
84	Pete Pihos	2.00	1.50	.80

Commemoratives

#	Name				#	Name			
85	Tex Schramm	2.00	1.50	.80	133	Tom Landry	4.00	3.00	1.50
86	Roger Staubach	12.00	9.00	4.75	134	Willie Lanier	2.00	1.50	.80
87	Jan Stenerud	2.00	1.50	.80	135	Larry Little	2.00	1.50	.80
88	Y.A. Tittle	3.00	2.25	1.25	136	Don Maynard	3.00	2.25	1.25
89	Clyde (Bulldog) Turner	2.00	1.50	.80	137	Lenny Moore	3.00	2.25	1.25
90	Steve Van Buren	2.00	1.50	.80	138	Chuck Noll	3.00	2.25	1.25
91	Herb Adderley	2.00	1.50	.80	139	Jim Otto	2.00	1.50	.80
92	Lem Barney	2.00	1.50	.80	140	Walter Payton	10.00	7.50	4.00
93	Sammy Baugh	5.00	3.75	2.00	141	Hugh (Shorty) Ray	2.00	1.50	.80
94	Chuck Bednarik	3.00	2.25	1.25	142	Andy Robustelli	2.00	1.50	.80
95	Charles W. Bidwill	2.00	1.50	.80	143	Bob St. Clair	2.00	1.50	.80
96	Willie Brown	2.00	1.50	.80	144	Joe Schmidt	3.00	2.25	1.25
97	Al Davis	4.00	3.00	1.50	145	Jim Taylor	3.00	2.25	1.25
98	Bill Dudley	2.00	1.50	.80	146	Doak Walker	3.00	2.25	1.25
99	Weeb Ewbank	2.00	1.50	.80	147	Bill Walsh	3.00	2.25	1.25
100	Len Ford	2.00	1.50	.80	148	Bob Waterfield	3.00	2.25	1.25
101	Sid Gillman	2.00	1.50	.80	149	Arnie Weinmeister	2.00	1.50	.80
102	Jack Ham	2.00	1.50	.80	150	Bill Willis	2.00	1.50	.80
103	Mel Hein	2.00	1.50	.80	151	Roosevelt Brown	2.00	1.50	.80
104	Bill Hewitt	2.00	1.50	.80	152	Jack Christiansen	2.00	1.50	.80
105	Dante Lavelli	2.00	1.50	.80	153	Willie Davis	3.00	2.25	1.25
106	Bob Lilly	3.00	2.25	1.25	154	Tony Dorsett	6.00	4.50	2.50
107	John Mackey	2.00	1.50	.80	155	Bud Grant	2.00	1.50	.80
108	Hugh McElhenny	3.00	2.25	1.25	156	Joe Greene	5.00	3.75	2.00
109	Mike Michalske	2.00	1.50	.80	157	Joe Guyon	2.00	1.50	.80
110	Ron Mix	2.00	1.50	.80	158	Franco Harris	4.00	3.00	1.50
111	Leo Nomenllini	2.00	1.50	.80	159	Ted Hendricks	2.00	1.50	.80
112	Steve Owen	2.00	1.50	.80	160	Arnie Herber	2.00	1.50	.80
113	Alan Page	2.50	2.00	1.00	161	Jimmy Johnson	2.00	1.50	.80
114	Dan Reeves	2.00	1.50	.80	162	Leroy Kelly	2.00	1.50	.80
115	John Riggins	3.00	2.25	1.25	163	Curly Lambeau	2.00	1.50	.80
116	Gale Sayers	6.00	4.50	2.50	164	Jim Langer	2.00	1.50	.80
117	Ken Strong	2.00	1.50	.80	165	Link Lyman	2.00	1.50	.80
118	Gene Upshaw	3.00	2.25	1.25	166	Gino Marchetti	3.00	2.25	1.25
119	Norm Van Brocklin	4.00	3.00	1.50	167	Ernie Nevers	3.00	2.25	1.25
120	Alex Wojciechowicz	2.00	1.50	.80	168	O.J. Simpson	12.00	9.00	4.75
121	Bert Bell	2.00	1.50	.80	169	Jackie Smith	2.00	1.50	.80
122	George Blanda	4.00	3.00	1.50	170	Bart Starr	6.00	4.50	2.50
123	Joe Carr	2.00	1.50	.80	171	Ernie Stautner	2.50	2.00	1.00
124	Larry Csonka	4.00	3.00	1.50	172	George Trafton	2.00	1.50	.80
125	John (Paddy) Driscoll	2.00	1.50	.80	173	Emien Tunnell	2.00	1.50	.80
126	Dan Fouts	3.00	2.25	1.25	174	Johnny Unitas (not issued)			
127	Bob Griese	4.00	3.00	1.50	175	Randy White			
128	Ed Healy	2.00	1.50	.80	176	Jim Finks			
129	Wilbur (Fats) Henry	2.00	1.50	.80	177	Henry Jordan			
130	Ken Houston	2.00	1.50	.80	178	Steve Largent			
131	Lamar Hunt	2.00	1.50	.80	179	Lee Roy Selmon			
132	Jack Lambert	2.50	2.00	1.00	180	Kellen Winslow			

1992 Centercourt Hall of Fame

Artist Ron Lewis's work is featured in this set which includes NBA Hall of Fame players, coaches and referees. Each card is 3 1/2" by 5 1/2" and has a colorful posed drawing. The back, similar to a postcard, has the year of induction, the set number (out 10,000), Lewis' signature, the Hall of Fame logo, and the name of the producer (Forgotten Heroes). The set was available through the mail from the producer and was also sold at the Hall of Fame. It is updated annually.

		MT	NM	EX
	Complete Set (52):	75.00	56.00	30.00
	Common Player:	2.00	1.50	.80
1	George Mikan	5.00	3.75	2.00
2	Bill Bradley	4.00	3.00	1.50
3	Bob Wanzer	2.00	1.50	.80
4	Ed McCauley	2.50	2.00	1.00
5	Harry Gallatan	2.00	1.50	.80
6	Willie "Pop" Gates	3.00	2.25	1.25
7	Bobby Knight	4.00	3.00	1.50
8	Dolph Schayes	3.00	2.25	1.25
9	Bob Pettit	3.00	2.25	1.25
10	Walt Frazier	3.00	2.25	1.25
11	Elvin Hayes	3.00	2.25	1.25
12	Paul Arizin	2.50	2.00	1.00
13	Phogg Allen	2.00	1.50	.80
14	Oscar Robertson	4.00	3.00	1.50
15	John Wooden	3.00	2.25	1.25
16	Red Holzman	2.50	2.00	1.00
17	Jack Twyman	2.00	1.50	.80
18	Dean Smith	3.00	2.25	1.25
19	John Nucatola	2.00	1.50	.80
20	Elgin Baylor	3.00	2.25	1.25
21	Dave Bing	3.00	2.25	1.25
22	Lester Harrison	2.00	1.50	.80
23	Joe Lapchick	2.50	2.00	1.00
24	Rick Barry	3.00	2.25	1.25
25	Lou Carnesecca	3.00	2.25	1.25
26	Checklist	2.00	1.50	.80
27	Red Auerbach	3.00	2.25	1.25
28	Dave DeBusschere	2.50	2.00	1.00
29	Clarence Gaines	3.00	2.25	1.25
30	Tom Gola	2.00	1.50	.80
31	Hal Greer	2.00	1.50	.80
32	Luisa-Harris Stewart	3.00	2.25	1.25
33	K.C. Jones	2.50	2.00	1.00
34	Sam Jones	2.00	1.50	.80
35	Bob Davies	2.00	1.50	.80
36	Harry Litwack	2.00	1.50	.80
37	Clyde Lovelette	2.50	2.00	1.00
38	Slater Martin	2.00	1.50	.80
39	Al McGuire	3.00	2.25	1.25
40	Ray Meyer	3.00	2.25	1.25
41	Earl Monroe	3.00	2.25	1.25
42	Andy Phillip	2.00	1.50	.80
43	Jim Pollard	2.00	1.50	.80
44	Bill Sharman	3.00	2.25	1.25
45	J. Dallas Shirley	3.50	2.75	1.50
46	Nate Thurmond	2.00	1.50	.80
47	Stan Watts	3.00	2.25	1.25
48	Bobby McDermott	2.00	1.50	.80
49	Clair F. Bee	2.50	2.00	1.00
50	Willis Reed	3.00	2.25	1.25
51	Larry O'Brien	3.50	2.75	1.50
52	Checklist	2.00	1.50	.80

1983 Hall of Fame Postcards

These 4 x6 postcards, issued in series, feature full-color artwork by artist Carlton McDiarmid. They were produced by the Hockey Hall of Fame and Cartophilium. Each player's name and year he was inducted into the Hall are on the back. Career achievements are also listed, in French and English.

	MT	NM	EX
Complete set (240):	$200.00	$150.00	$80.00
Common player:	$1.00	.70	.40
Series 1			
1) Sid Abel	$1.50	$1.25	.70
2) Punch Broadbent	$1.00	.70	.40
3) Clarence Campbell	$1.25	.90	.50
4) Neil Colville	$1.00	.70	.40
5) Charlie Conacher	$2.50	$2.00	$1.00
6) Mervyn "Red" Dutton	$1.00	.70	.40
7) Foster Hewitt	$1.50	$1.25	.70
8) Fred Hume	$1.00	.70	.40
9) Mickey Ion	$1.00	.70	.40
10) Ernest "Moose" Johnson	$1.00	.70	.40
11) Bill Mosienko	$1.00	.70	.40
12) Maurice Richard	$6.00	$4.50	$2.50
13) Barney Stanley	$1.00	.70	.40
14) Lord Stanley	$1.25	.90	.50
15) Cyclone Taylor	$1.50	$1.25	.70
16) Tiny Thompson	$1.00	.70	.40

Commemoratives

Series 2

1) Dan Bain	$1.00	.70	.40
2) Hobey Baker	$1.25	.90	.50
3) Frank Calder	$1.25	.90	.50
4) Frank Foyston	$1.00	.70	.40
5) James Hendy	$1.00	.70	.40
6) Gordie Howe	$7.50	$5.75	$3.00
7) Harry Lumley	$1.25	.90	.50
8) Reg Noble	$1.00	.70	.40
9) Frank Patrick	$1.25	.90	.50
10) Harvey Pulford	$1.00	.70	.40
11) Ken Reardon	$1.25	.90	.50
12) Bullet Joe Simpson	$1.00	.70	.40
13) Conn Smythe	$1.50	$1.25	.70
14) Red Storey	$1.00	.70	.40
15) Lloyd Turner	$1.00	.70	.40
16) Georges Vezina	$4.00	$3.00	$1.50

Series 3

1) Jean Beliveau	$4.00	$3.00	$1.50
2) Max Bentley	$1.25	.90	.50
3) King Clancy	$2.50	$2.00	$1.00
4) Babe Dye	$1.00	.70	.40
5) Eddie Goodfellow	$1.00	.70	.40
6) Charles Hay	$1.00	.70	.40
7) Percy Lesueur	$1.00	.70	.40
8) Tommy Lockhart	$1.00	.70	.40
9) Jack Marshall	$1.00	.70	.40
10) Lester Patrick	$2.00	$1.50	.80
11) Bill Quackenbush	$1.00	.70	.40
12) Frank Selke	$1.50	$1.25	.70
13) Cooper Smeaton	$1.00	.70	.40
14) Hooley Smith	$1.00	.70	.40
15) Capt. J.T. Sutherland	$1.00	.70	.40
16) Fred Whitcroft	$1.00	.70	.40

Series 4

1) Charles F. Adams	$1.00	.70	.40
2) Russell Bowie	$1.00	.70	.40
3) Frank Frederickson	$1.00	.70	.40
4) Billy Glimour	$1.00	.70	.40
5) Ivan "Ching" Johnson	$1.25	.90	.50
6) Tom Johnson	$1.25	.90	.50
7) Aurel Joliat	$2.50	$2.00	$1.00
8) Duke Keats	$1.00	.70	.40
9) Red Kelly	$1.50	$1.25	.70
10) Frank McGee	$1.00	.70	.40
11) James D. Norris	$1.25	.90	.50
12) Philip D. Ross	$1.00	.70	.40
13) Terry Sawchuk	$2.50	$2.00	$1.00
14) Babe Siebert	$1.50	$1.25	.70
15) Anatoli V. Tarasov	$1.25	.90	.50
16) Roy Worters	$1.25	.90	.50

Series 5

1) T. Franklin Ahearn	$1.00	.70	.40
2) Harold E. Ballard	$2.50	$2.00	$1.00
3) Billy Burch	$1.00	.70	.40
4) Bill Chadwick	$1.00	.70	.40
5) Sprague Cleghorn	$1.25	.90	.50
6) Rusty Crawford	$1.00	.70	.40
7) Alex Delvecchio	$1.50	$1.25	.70
8) George S. Dudley	$1.00	.70	.40

9) Ted Kennedy	$1.50	$1.25	.70
10) Newsy Lalonde	$2.00	$1.50	.80
11) Billy McGimsie	$1.00	.70	.40
12) Frank Nighbor	$1.00	.70	.40
13) Bobby Orr	$6.00	$4.50	$2.50
14) Sen. Donart Raymond	$1.00	.70	.40
15) Art Ross	$2.00	$1.50	.80
16) Jack Walker	$1.00	.70	.40

Series 6

1) Doug Bentley	$1.25	.90	.50
2) Walter A. Brown	$1.00	.70	.40
3) Dit Clapper	$1.25	.90	.50
4) Hap Day	$1.00	.70	.40
5) Frank Dilio	$1.00	.70	.40
6) Bobby Hewitson	$1.00	.70	.40
7) Harry Howell	$1.00	.70	.40
8) Paul Loicq	$1.00	.70	.40
9) Sylvio Mantha	$1.00	.70	.40
10) Jacques Plante	$2.50	$2.00	$1.00
11) George Richardson	$1.00	.70	.40
12) Nels Stewart	$1.50	$1.25	.70
13) Hod Stuart	$1.00	.70	.40
14) Harry Trihey	$1.00	.70	.40
15) Marty Walsh	$1.00	.70	.40
16) Arthur M. Wirtz	$1.25	.90	.50

Series 7

1) Toe Blake	$1.50	$1.25	.70
2) Frank Boucher	$1.00	.70	.40
3) Turk Broda	$2.00	$1.50	.80
4) Harry Cameron	$1.00	.70	.40
5) Leo Dandurand	$1.00	.70	.40
6) Joe Hall	$1.00	.70	.40
7) George Hay	$1.00	.70	.40
8) William A. Hewitt	$1.00	.70	.40
9) Bouse Hutton	$1.00	.70	.40
10) Dick Irvin	$1.25	.90	.50
11) Henri Richard	$2.00	$1.50	.80
12) John Ross Robertson	$1.00	.70	.40
13) Frank D. Smith	$1.00	.70	.40
14) Allan Stanley	$1.00	.70	.40
15) Norm Ullman	$1.00	.70	.40
16) Harry Watson	$1.00	.70	.40

Series 8

1) Clint Benedict	$1.50	$1.25	.70
2) Dickie Boon	$1.00	.70	.40
3) Gordie Drillon	$1.25	.90	.50
4) Bill Gadsby	$1.00	.70	.40
5) Rod Gilbert	$1.25	.90	.50
6) Moose Goheen	$1.00	.70	.40
7) T.P. Gorman	$1.00	.70	.40
8) Glenn Hall	$1.50	$1.25	.70
9) Red Horner	$1.00	.70	.40
10) Gen. J.R. Kilpatrick	$1.00	.70	.40
11) Robert Lebel	$1.00	.70	.40
12) Howie Morenz	$4.00	$3.00	$1.50
13) Fred Scanlan	$1.00	.70	.40
14) Tommy Smith	$1.00	.70	.40
15) Fred C. Waghorne	$1.00	.70	.40
16) Cooney Weiland	$1.00	.70	.40

Series 9

1) Weston Adams	$1.00	.70	.40
2) Sir Montagu Allan	$1.00	.70	.40
3) Frank Brimsek	$1.25	.90	.50
4) Angus Campbell	$1.25	.90	.50
5) Bill Cook	$1.00	.70	.40
6) Tom Dunderdale	$1.00	.70	.40
7) Emile Francis	$1.00	.70	.40
8) Charlie Gardiner	$1.00	.70	.40
9) Elmer Lach	$1.00	.70	.40
10) Frank Mahovlich	$2.00	$1.50	.80
11) Didier Pitre	$1.00	.70	.40
12) Joe Primeau	$1.50	$1.25	.70
13) Frank Rankin	$1.00	.70	.40
14) Ernie Russell	$1.25	.90	.50
15) Thayer Tutt	$1.00	.70	.40
16) Harry Westwick	$1.00	.70	.40

Series 10

1) Jack Adams	$1.00	.70	.40
2) J.F. "Bunny" Ahearne	$1.00	.70	.40
3) J.P. Bickell	$1.00	.70	.40
4) Johnny Bucyk	$1.50	$1.25	.70
5) Art Coulter	$1.00	.70	.40
6) C.G. Drinkwater	$1.00	.70	.40
7) George Hainsworth	$1.25	.90	.50
8) Tim Horton	$2.50	$2.00	$1.00
9) Maj. F. McLaughlin	$1.00	.70	.40
10) Dickie Moore	$1.50	$1.25	.70
11) Pierre Pilot	$1.00	.70	.40
12) Claude C. Robinson	$1.00	.70	.40
13) Sweeney Schriner	$1.00	.70	.40
14) Oliver Seibert	$1.00	.70	.40
15) Alfred Smith	$1.00	.70	.40
16) Phat Wilson	$1.25	.90	.50

Series 11

1) Yvan Cournoyer	$1.25	.90	.50
2) Scotty Davidson	$1.00	.70	.40
3) Cy Denneny	$1.00	.70	.40
4) Bill Durnan	$1.25	.90	.50
5) Shorty Green	$1.00	.70	.40
6) Riley Hern	$1.00	.70	.40
7) Bryan Hextall	$1.00	.70	.40
8) W.M. (Bill) Jennings	$1.00	.70	.40
9) Gordon W. Juckes	$1.00	.70	.40
10) Paddy Moran	$1.00	.70	.40
11) James Norris	$1.00	.70	.40
12) Harry Oliver	$1.00	.70	.40
13) Sam Pollack	$1.00	.70	.40
14) Marcel Pronovost	$1.00	.70	.40
15) Jack Ruttan	$1.00	.70	.40
16) Earl Seibert	$1.00	.70	.40

Series 12

1) George "Buck" Boucher	$1.00	.70	.40
2) George V. Brown	$1.00	.70	.40
3) Arthur F. Farrell	$1.00	.70	.40
4) Herb Gardiner	$1.00	.70	.40
5) Si Griffis	$1.00	.70	.40
6) Hap Holmes	$1.00	.70	.40
7) Harry Hyland	$1.00	.70	.40
8) Tommy Ivan	$1.00	.70	.40

9) Jack Laviolette	$1.00	.70	.40
10) Ted Lindsay	$1.50	$1.25	.70
11) Francis Nelson	$1.00	.70	.40
12) William M. Northey	$1.00	.70	.40
13) Babe Pratt	$1.00	.70	.40
14) Chuck Rayner	$1.25	.90	.50
15) Milt Rodden	$1.00	.70	.40
16) Milt Schmidt	$1.50	$1.25	.70

Series 13

1) Butch Bouchard	$1.00	.70	.40
2) Jack Butterfield	$1.00	.70	.40
3) Joseph Cattarinich	$1.00	.70	.40
4) Alex Connell	$1.25	.90	.50
5) Bill Cowley	$1.00	.70	.40
6) Chaucer Elliott	$1.00	.70	.40
7) Jimmy Gardner	$1.00	.70	.40
8) Boom Boom Geoffrion	$2.50	$2.00	$1.00
9) Tom Hooper	$1.00	.70	.40
10) Syd Howe	$1.00	.70	.40
11) Harvey "Busher" Jackson	$1.25	.90	.50
12) Al Leader	$1.00	.70	.40
13) Steamer Maxwell	$1.00	.70	.40
14) Blair Russell	$1.00	.70	.40
15) William W. Wirtz	$1.00	.70	.40
16) Gump Worsley	$1.50	$1.25	.70

Series 14

1) George Armstrong	$1.25	.90	.50
2) Ace Bailey	$1.00	.70	.40
3) Jack Darragh	$1.00	.70	.40
4) Ken Dryden	$2.50	$2.00	$1.00
5) Eddie Gerard	$1.00	.70	.40
6) Jack Gibson	$1.00	.70	.40
7) Hugh Lehman	$1.00	.70	.40
8) Mickey MacKay	$1.00	.70	.40
9) Joe Malone	$1.25	.90	.50
10) Bruce A. Norris	$1.00	.70	.40
11) J. Ambrose O'Brien	$1.00	.70	.40
12) Lynn Patrick	$1.00	.70	.40
13) Tommy Phillips	$1.00	.70	.40
14) Allan W. Pickard	$1.00	.70	.40
15) Jack Stewart	$1.00	.70	.40
16) Frank Udvari	$1.00	.70	.40

Series 15

1) Syl Apps	$1.25	.90	.50
2) John G. Ashley	$1.00	.70	.40
3) Marty Barry	$1.00	.70	.40
4) Andy Bathgate	$1.25	.90	.50
5) Johnny Bower	$1.25	.90	.50
6) Frank Buckland	$1.00	.70	.40
7) Jimmy Dunn	$1.00	.70	.40
8) Michael Grant	$1.00	.70	.40
9) Doug Harvey	$2.00	$1.50	.80
10) George McNamara	$1.00	.70	.40
11) Stan Mikita	$2.00	$1.50	.80
12) Sen. H. de M. Molson	$1.00	.70	.40
13) Gordon Roberts	$1.00	.70	.40
14) Eddie Shore	$3.00	$2.25	$1.25
15) Bruce Stuart	$1.00	.70	.40
16) Carl P. Voss	$1.00	.70	.40

Hockey Hall of Fame

The Legends of Hockey Collectors

Series 1, 2, 3 and 4

Hockey Legends Inc., in association with the Hockey Hall of Fame, has released a series of limited-edition postcards featuring the work of sports artists Doug West and Michael Taylor. They have an exclusive agreement with the Hall to produce the 3" by 5" postcards for a Legends of Hockey set.

Each card front has a full-color action shot against a posed shot of the player. The back has the player's career statistics, biography and individual serial number (1 of 10,000). Each of the first four series was selling for $80, with a duration of the project to be 16 series. Collectors were able to retain exclusive rights to their serial number throughout the project.

Several players were participating in an autograph program run through the mail by Legends of Hockey/ Diamond Connection, based in Center Line, Mich. Those players are indicated by an *.

A specially-designed storage binder was also created to store the post cards. The Legends of Hockey logo is embossed in gold on the front.

The original 17" by 10 1/2" artwork used for several postcards was also available. They include: Hobey Baker ($700), Jean Beliveau ($2,400), Johnny Bower ($1,400), Cecil Dye ($800), Foster Hewitt ($900), Tim Horton ($900), Teeder Kennedy ($1,100), Frank Mahovlich ($1,300), Brad Park ($1,100), Lester Patrick ($1,000), Jacques Plante ($1,300), Eddie Shore ($700), Harry Sinden ($700), Conn Smythe ($800) and Gump Worsley ($900).

Series 1

Sid Abel*, Hobey Baker, King Clancy, Bobby Clarke*, Charlie Conacher, Phil Esposito*, Emile Francis*, Bernie Geoffrion*, Foster Hewitt, Harry Lumley*, Stan Mikita*, Bobby Orr, Jacques Plante, Maurice Richard*, Conn Smythe, Norm Ullman*, Lord Stanley

Series 2

Jack Adams, Ace Bailey, Johnny Bower*, Frank Calder, Ed Giacomin*, Bryan Hextall, Tim Horton, Punch Imlach, Tommy Ivan*, Duke Keats, Ted Lindsay*, Lanny McDonald*, Bill Mosienko, Babe Pratt, Earl Seibert, Harry Sinden*, Georges Vezina, Gump Worsley*

Series 3

Sir Montagu Allan, Jean Beliveau*, Marcel Dionne*, Woody Dumart* Cecil Dye, Tony Esposito*, Hap Holmes, Syd Howe, Ivan Johnson, Red Kelly*, Elmer Lach, Frank Mahovlich, Harold Oliver, Brad Park*, Frank Patrick, Milt Schmidt*, Red Storey*, Jack Walker

Series 4

Bill Barber*, Bill Gadsby*, Rod Gilbert*, Harry Howell*, Red Horner*, Dick Irvin, Aurel Joliat, Ted Kennedy*, Dave Keon*, Joe Malone, Fred Maxwell, Howie Morenz, Lester Patrick, Eddie Shore, Daryl Sittler*, Hoolie Smith, Clint Smith*, Allan Stanley*

Chapter 10

Pins

This run of 23 Super Bowl pin is worth between $6,000-$8,000.

Press pins are distributed to members of the media by the host team for a particular sporting event, usually a playoff or all-star game. The lapel pins provide reporters legitimate access to cover the game. Generally, there are fewer all-star game pins available to collectors, because fewer reporters cover these games compared to a Super Bowl or Stanley Cup Finals series. There are two types of hockey pins - all-star games and Stanley Cup finals, which are in the shape of the Stanley Cup. The all-star pins go for about $200 each, while those for the Stanley Cup Finals are in the $150 range. The big-ticket pins are the Super Bowl pins; a pin from Super Bowl I can cost almost $1,500, while a run of pins for the first 23 would set someone back between $6,000-$8,000.

Super Bowl pins

I at Los Angeles, Jan. 15, 1967 (Green Bay Packers vs. Kansas City Chiefs) $1,450
II at Miami, Jan. 14, 1968 (Green Bay Packers vs. Oakland Raiders) $1,250
III at Miami, Jan. 12, 1969 (New York Jets vs. Baltimore Colts) $850
IV at New Orleans, Jan. 11, 1970 (Minnesota Vikings vs. Kansas City Chiefs) ....patch$85
V at Miami, Jan. 17, 1971 (Baltimore Colts vs. Dallas Cowboys ....patch$90
VI at New Orleans, Jan. 16, 1972 (Dallas Cowboys vs. Miami Dolphins) $400
VII at Los Angeles, Jan. 14, 1973 (Miami Dolphins vs. Washington Redskins) $375
VIII at Houston, Jan. 13, 1974 (Minnesota Vikings vs. Miami Dolphins)...$375
IX at New Orleans, Jan. 12, 1975 (Pittsburgh Steelers vs. Minnesota Vikings) $285
X at Miami, Jan. 18, 1976 (Dallas Cowboys vs. Pittsburgh Steelers)......................................$325-$350
XI at Pasadena, Jan. 9, 1977 (Oakland Raiders vs. Minnesota Vikings)..$250
XII at New Orleans, Jan. 15, 1978 (Dallas Cowboys vs. Denver Broncos) ....$275-$295
XIII at Miami, Jan. 21, 1979 (Pittsburgh Steelers vs. Dallas Cowboys) $200
XIV at Pasadena, Jan. 20, 1980 (Los Angeles Rams vs. Pittsburgh Steelers).....................................$200
XV at New Orleans, Jan. 25, 1981 (Oakland Raiders vs. Philadelphia Eagles)...................................$175
XVI at Pontiac, Jan. 24, 1982 (San Francisco 49ers vs. Cincinnati Bengals) $150
XVII at Pasadena, Jan. 30, 1983 (Miami Dolphins vs. Washington Redskins) $150
XVIII at Tampa, Jan. 22, 1984 (Washington vs. Los Angeles Raiders).......................................$140-$150
XIX at Palo Alto, Jan. 20, 1985 (Miami vs. San Francisco)...$130-$175
XX at New Orleans, Jan. 26, 1986 (Chicago Bears vs. New England Patriots)..........................$135-$175
XXI at Pasadena, Jan. 25, 1987 (Denver Broncos vs. New York Giants)....................................$120-$135
XXII at San Diego, Jan. 31, 1988 (Washington Redskins vs. Denver Broncos)...................$125-$135
XXIII at Miami, Jan. 22, 1989 (Cincinnati Bengals vs. San Francisco 49ers)............................$125-$135
XXIV at New Orleans, Jan. 28, 1990 (San Francisco 49ers vs. Denver Broncos)...............................$125
XXV at Tampa, Jan. 27, 1991 (Buffalo Bills vs. New York Giants) ....$95-$110
XXVI at Minneapolis, Jan. 26, 1992 (Washington Redskins vs. Buffalo Bills) ....$100-$125
XXVII at Pasadena, Jan. 31, 1993 (Buffalo Bills vs. Dallas Cowboys)...$95
XXVIII at Minneapolis, Jan. 29, 1994 (Buffalo Bills vs. Dallas Cowboys) $125

NFL Championship pins

1936 Green Bay Packers vs. Boston Shamrocks $600
1937 Washington Redskins vs. Chicago Bears...$600
1938 New York Giants vs. Green Bay Packers $600
1941 Chicago Bears vs. New York Giants $800
1944 New York Giants vs. Green Bay Packers $700
1945 Cleveland Rams vs. Washington Redskins...$600
1946 New York Giants vs. Chicago Bears $600
1947 All American F.C. New York Yankees vs. Cleveland Browns $800
1947 Chicago Cardinals vs. Philadelphia Eagles..$600
1949 All American F.C. Browns vs. San Francisco $800
1959 NFL Championship game $495
1962 NFL Championship game $325

NFL Draft pins

1987	$185	1991	$175
1988	$165	1992	$165
1990	$160	1993	$135

NBA/NCAA basketball press pins

1970 New York Knicks	$195	1992 NCAA Final Four at Minnesota	$165
1979 NCAA Final Four at Salt Lake City	$250	1993 NCAA Final Four at New Orleans	$95
1990 NCAA Final Four at Denver	$155	1994 NCAA Final Four at Charlotte	$125

1970-72 Montreal Canadiens pins

These metal pins, measuring 1 3/4" in diameter, feature a black-and-white picture of a Canadiens player. The player's name is below the picture. The back has a metal clasp. The pins are not dated, but were apparently issued between 1970-72 because Bobby Rousseau last played for the team in 1969-70, while three players made their NHL debuts in 1971-72.

	NM	EX	VG
Complete set (17):	100.00	50.00	30.00
Common player:	4.00	2.00	1.25
1. Jean Beliveau	15.00	7.50	4.50
2. Yvan Cournoyer	7.50	3.75	2.25
3. Ken Dryden	25.00	12.50	7.50
4. John Ferguson	4.00	2.00	1.25
5. Terry Harper	4.00	2.00	1.25
6. Guy Lafleur	25.00	12.50	7.50
7. Jacques Laperriere	5.00	2.50	1.50
8. Guy Lapointe	5.00	2.50	1.50
9. Jacques Lemaire	7.50	3.75	2.25
10. Frank Mahovlich	10.00	5.00	3.00
11. Peter Mahovlich	5.00	2.50	1.50
12. Herni Richard	7.50	3.75	2.25
13. Bobby Rousseau	5.00	2.50	1.50
14. Claude Ruel	4.00	2.00	1.25
15. Serge Savard	5.00	2.50	1.50
16. J.C. Tremblay	4.00	2.00	1.25
17. Rogatien Vachon	6.00	3.00	1.75

Action Packed Badge of Honor pins

Action Packed produced football pins in 1994, featuring the 25 members of the Quarterback Club. Each pin has a metal base with an embossed photo on it with gold foil stamping. Four pins were included in each pack, but only one could be seen through the package window. In addition, 24-karat gold leaf pins were randomly inserted in packs. The suggested retail price for a pack of four pins was $9.95. The players featured are: Troy Aikman, Drew Bledsoe, Bubby Brister, Randall Cunningham, John Elway, Boomer Esiason, Jim Everett, Brett Farve, Jim Harbaugh, Jeff Hostetler, Michael Irvin, Jim Kelly, David Klingler, Bernie Kosar, Dan Marino, Rick Mirer, Chris Miller, Warren Moon, Neil O'Donnell, Jerry Rice, Mark Rypien, Barry Sanders, Phil Simms, Emmitt Smith and Steve Young.

In 1995, the company also produced a 52-pin set of hockey players. The pins also had 24-karat gold leaf versions made, which were available by sending in seven proofs of purchase and $4.95. The players featured are: Dave Andreychuk, Ed Belfour, Ray Bourque, Rod Brind'Amour, Martin Brodeur, Pavel Bure, Chris Chelios, Wendel Clark, Paul Coffey, Vincent Damphousse, Sergei Fedorov, Theoren Fleury, Ron Francis, Doug Gilmour, Adam Graves, Wayne Gretzky, Dominik Hasek, Brett Hull, Arturs Irbe, Jaromir Jagr, Curtis Joseph, Jari Kurri, Pat LaFontaine, Brian Leetch, Trevor Linden, Eric Lindros, Al MacInnis, Mark Messier, Mike Modano, Alexander Mogilny, Cam Neely, Joe Nieuwendyk, Adam Oates, Felix Potvin, Mark Recchi, Robert Reichel, Mikael Renberg, Mike Richter, Jeremy Roenick, Patrick Roy, Joe Sakic, Geoff Sanderson, Teemu Selanne, Brendan Shanahan, Kevin Stevens, Scott Stevens, Steve Thomas, Keith Tkachuk, Pierre Turgeon, John Vanbiesbrouck, Alexei Yashin and Steve Yzerman.

NFL Throwback-style pins

National Football League 75th Anniversary pins were produced in 1994 by Pinnacle Brands. The die-struck pins use a "throwback style" to commemorate the beginnings of each of 12 teams. There were 30,000 of each team made, along with 100,000 of a Super Bowl pin. Each package shows the pin and includes a design that captures the team logo with the NFL's 75th anniversary logo. The teams featured are: Dallas Cowboys, Miami Dolphins, Kansas City Chiefs, San Francisco 49ers, Los Angeles Raiders, New York Giants, Green Bay Packers, Philadelphia Eagles, Chicago Bears, Pittsburgh Steelers, Buffalo Bills and Washington Redskins.

 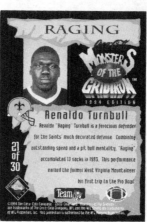 

Coca-Cola "Monsters of the Gridiron" pins

Coca-Cola and Score Board's Classic Games distributed these 30 pins in card packs available within Coke products during a six-week period around Halloween 1994. Each card transforms the player's on-field persona into a bizarre, supernatural creature. The label pins, featuring a Monsters shot of the player and his nickname, were a subset titled "Pinheads." One pin, a tattoo, an instant win game card, and two player cards were in every pack. Carolina Panthers and Jacksonville Jaguar pins were also produced; they were available as instant-win card redemptions.

The players featured are: 1) Eric "The Red" Swann, 2) Jessie "Tarantula" Tuggle, 3) Cornelius "Big Bear" Bennett, 4) Chris "Zorro" Zorich, 5) Dan "Big Daddy" Wilkinson, 6) Eric "Bad Bone" Turner, 7) Emmitt "Lone Star Sherriff" Smith, 8) Steve "The Bandit" Atwater, 9) Pat "Chillin'" Swilling, 10) Sean "Ghost" Jones, 11) Ray "Scarecrow" Childress, 12) Marshall "The Missle" Faulk, 13) Derrick "Attack Cat" Thomas, 14) Chester "Renegade Raider" McGlockton, 15) Shane "The Barbarian" Conlan, 16) Marco "Cobra" Coleman, 17) John "Runaway Train" Randle, 18) Bruce "The Pile Driver" Armstrong, 19) Renaldo "Raging" Turnbull, 20) John "Jumbo" Elliot, 21) Ronnie "The Rattler" Lott, 22) Randall "Rocket Man" Cunningham, 23) Neil "Knight Raider" O'Donnell, 24) Junior "Stealth" Seau, 25) Ken "Commando" Norton Jr., 26) Cortez "Tex Rex" Kennedy, 27) Hardy "Hyena" Nickerson, 28) Ken "Jackhammer" Harvey, 29) Jacksonville Jaguars mascot, 30) Carolina Panthers mascot.

Chapter 11

Ticket stubs/schedules

Ticket stubs do not command high prices unless they are from Super Bowl, championship, All-Star or playoff games, or from a game in which a significant achievement or record occurred. Generally, the stubs are in either Poor or Fair condition, because they have been bent and are worn, or Very Good to Excellent because they have been preserved. Full, unused tickets are worth more money than stubs, and are generally for seats which went unsold for a playoff game, or one in which a milestone occurred.

If you search through the scrapbooks, wallets and shoe boxes of memorabilia long enough, inevitably you'll find an annual schedule or two for a favorite team of yesteryear. Schedules, or skeds for short, offer collectors an inexpensive alternative to the big-ticket items which anchor any fan's collection. The limits are endless.

Although the most common form is a pocket schedule, skeds come in all shapes and sizes and for all sports. Collegiate sports such as basketball, football and hockey often utilize sked-cards, which are usually a single piece of paper or tagboard stock with artwork on one side and a game schedule on the back. Professional sports teams generally use folded skeds, similar to sked-cards, but with multiple panels separated by folds. These types of schedules are commonly provided by the major league teams' ticket offices. Other schedule varieties include matchbook covers, schedule cups, ticket brochures, decals, magnets, rulers, napkins, place mats, stickers, key chains, plastic coin purses and poster skeds.

The easiest way to begin or add to a schedule collection is to contact professional teams for ticket information. You'll usually get a response, especially if you send a self-addressed stamped envelope, which means the team isn't paying postage and already has a pre-addressed envelope to send back. When mailing to Canada, remember that any SASEs sent to these teams require Canadian postage.

Because schedules are primarily advertising pieces through which the sponsors can reach a wide, varying target audience, the sponsors themselves can be a source for schedules. Other possible sources can be found by determining who advertises in the team's yearbook and programs. Radio and television sponsors, and stations which carry the broadcasts, also often produce skeds, as may those who advertise on the television and radio broadcasts.

Off-the-wall skeds can be found in a variety of locations, such as restaurants, which often offer matchbook schedules, liquor stores, sporting goods stores, museums, banks and credit unions, motels and hotels, and ticket offices. When traveling, remember to check gas stations, convenience stores, and kiosks which are located along interstate rest stops. Another way to obtain schedules is by trading, searching for prospective partners in classified ads in hobby publications such as Sports Collectors Digest and sked newsletters.

If the conventional shoe box or scrapbook is not used for displaying schedules, many pocket schedules will fit into eight- or nine-pocket baseball card plastic sheets which are held together in an album. These sheets protect the skeds from getting dinged and folded. Oversized schedules may fit into 5-by-7 inch, dollar bill-sized, or postcard-sized plastic sheets.

Condition is not a critical factor in determining a schedule's value, but it is important. It's more valuable if it isn't damaged, ripped or torn, or marked on. Schedules for defunct teams carry a slight premium value compared to other schedules of the same year, as do localized, scarcer schedules and those featuring team or player photos. Eamples include a 1968-69 Houston Mavericks schedule at $12; a 1979-80 Los Angeles Lakers schedule, from Magic Johnson's first year, at $35; and a 1989-90 Boston Celtics schedule, featuring Larry Bird vs. Michael Jordan, at $8. In general, schedules before 1970 are worth more than $10, while those in the 1970s and 1980s fall between $5-$10, while 1990s schedules are less than $5

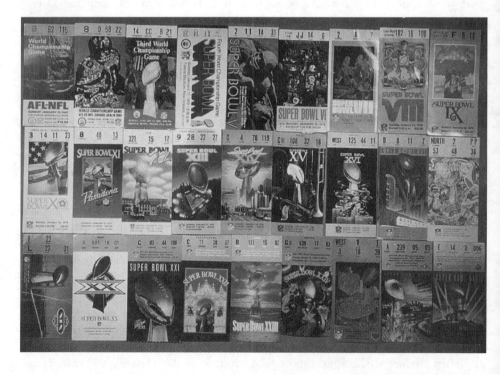

Super Bowl tickets are the cream of the crop for ticket collectors.

Pro Football ticket stubs

It's best if you can get a Super Bowl ticket as a full ticket.

Super Bowl tickets	fulls	stubs
I at Los Angeles, Jan. 15, 1967 (Green Bay Packers vs. Kansas City Chiefs)	NA	$400-$600
II at Miami, Jan. 14, 1968 (Green Bay Packers vs. Oakland Raiders)	NA	$500-$700
III at Miami, Jan. 12, 1969 (New York Jets vs. Baltimore Colts)	NA	$350-$500
IV at New Orleans, Jan. 11, 1970		
(Minnesota Vikings vs. Kansas City Chiefs)	NA	$300-$475
V at Miami, Jan. 17, 1971 (Baltimore Colts vs. Dallas Cowboys	NA	$250-$350
VI at New Orleans, Jan. 16, 1972 (Dallas Cowboys vs. Miami Dolphins)	NA	$150-$250
VII at Los Angeles, Jan. 14, 1973		
(Miami Dolphins vs. Washington Redskins)	$550-$650	$150-$225
VIII at Houston, Jan. 13, 1974 (Minnesota Vikings vs. Miami Dolphins)	$450-$550	$150-$200
IX at New Orleans, Jan. 12, 1975		
(Pittsburgh Steelers vs. Minnesota Vikings)	$400-$500	$175-$225
X at Miami, Jan. 18, 1976 (Dallas Cowboys vs. Pittsburgh Steelers)	$300-$400	$150-$175
XI at Pasadena, Jan. 9, 1977 (Oakland Raiders vs. Minnesota Vikings)	$300-$400	$100-$150
XII at New Orleans, Jan. 15, 1978 (Dallas Cowboys vs. Denver Broncos)	$300-$400	$125-$175
XIII at Miami, Jan. 21, 1979 (Pittsburgh Steelers vs. Dallas Cowboys)	$500-$600	$125-$175
XIV at Pasadena, Jan. 20, 1980		
(Los Angeles Rams vs. Pittsburgh Steelers)	$300-$400	$75-$125
XV at New Orleans, Jan. 25, 1981		
(Oakland Raiders vs. Philadelphia Eagles)	$300-$400	$75-$125
XVI at Pontiac, Jan. 24, 1982 (San Francisco 49ers vs. Cincinnati Bengals)	$350-$500	$100-$150
XVII at Pasadena, Jan. 30, 1983		
(Miami Dolphins vs. Washington Redskins)	$300-$450	$100-$150
XVIII at Tampa, Jan. 22, 1984 (Washington vs. Los Angeles Raiders)	$300-$450	$100-$150
XIX at Palo Alto, Jan. 20, 1985 (Miami vs. San Francisco)	$300-$400	$100-$150

XX at New Orleans, Jan. 26, 1986		
(Chicago Bears vs. New England Patriots)	$300-$400	$100-$150
XXI at Pasadena, Jan. 25, 1987 (Denver Broncos vs. New York Giants)	$300-$450	$100-$150
XXII at San Diego, Jan. 31, 1988		
(Washington Redskins vs. Denver Broncos)	$225-$400	$50-$100
XXIII at Miami, Jan. 22, 1989		
(Cincinnati Bengals vs. San Francisco 49ers)	$250-$400	$50-$100
XXIV at New Orleans, Jan. 28, 1990		
(San Francisco 49ers vs. Denver Broncos)	$235-$350	$50-$100
XXV at Tampa, Jan. 27, 1991 (Buffalo Bills vs. New York Giants)	$225-$350	$50-$100
XXVI at Minneapolis, Jan. 26, 1992		
(Washington Redskins vs. Buffalo Bills)	$200-$350	$100-$150
XXVII at Pasadena, Jan. 31, 1993 (Buffalo Bills vs. Dallas Cowboys)	$225-$350	$50-$100
XXVIII at Minneapolis, Jan. 30, 1994 (Buffalo Bills vs. Dallas Cowboys)	$295-$400	$60-$110

Football ticket stubs

- 1947 Rose Bowl game stub.............. $65
- 1949 NFL Championship game, Philadelphia vs. Los Angeles Rams $375
- 1958 Rose Bowl game stub.............. $25
- 1960 Rose Bowl game stub.............. $20
- 1961 Minnesota Vikings ticket from team's first season $50
- 1963 NFL Championship game stub, Chicago vs. New York Giants......... $100
- 1971 Sugar Bowl full $60
- 1972 Miami Dolphins stub, from the team's perfect 17-0 season $25
- 1975 Minnesota Vikings/Dallas Cowboys "Hail Mary" pass playoff game $95
- 1975 WFL full tickets $10
- 1983 AFC Championship game stub, Raiders vs. Seattle $35
- 1983 USFL Championship game stub....$50
- 1986 Sun Bowl full $25
- 1988 Hula Bowl full......................... $25
- 1991 NFC Championship game, New York Giants phantom ticket, full....... $35

NBA/NCAA basketball stubs

- 1950 Minneapolis Lakers vs. College All-Stars stub..................................... $35
- Feb. 21, 1960 Minneapolis Lakers vs. St. Louis Hawks at the Los Angeles Sports Arena, despite being team's last year in Minnesota....................................... $125

- 1963 NBA All-Star Game, in Los Angeles... $225
- 1965 Los Angeles Lakers home playoff tickets..$95 each
- Oct. 30, 1968 Los Angeles Stars vs. New Orleans Blues, full............................ $75
- 1969 NBA All-Star Game, in Baltimore $100
- 1970 NBA All-Star Game, in Philadelphia $150
- 1971 NCAA Final Four, in Houston.....$175
- 1974 NCAA Final Four, in Greensboro, N.C... $125
- 1980 NBA All-Star Game, in Washington...................................... $45
- 1982 NBA All-Star Game, in New Jersey $75
- 1984 NBA All-Star Game, in Denver$75
- 1985 Boston Celtics playoff game full for a skybox $20
- 1988 NBA All-Star Game, in Chicago.... .... $35
- 1988 NCAA Final Four, in Kansas City $40
- 1991 NBA All-Star Game, in Charlotte $30

NHL ticket stubs

- 1972 All-Star game, in Minnesota..... $35
- 1980 All-Star game, in Detroit, full.. $75
- 1993 All-Star game, in Montreal....... $20
- Wayne Gretzky's 802nd goal stub... $150

Medallions/discs

Football

1976 Buckman Discs

These discs, each measuring 3 3/8" in diameter, were produced by Michael Schechter Associates for distribution at various Buckman's Ice Cream Village outlets in Rochester, N.Y. The Buckman's and MSA logos appear on the disc back; a black-and-white closeup shot of the player is on the front. The disc is rimmed by a colored band which includes biographical information. The player's name, team and position are also featured on the front, which has four stars at the top of the disc, above the player photo.

		NM	EX	VG
Complete Set (20):		20.00	10.00	6.00
Common Player:		.60	.30	.20
(1)	Otis Armstrong	.75	.40	.25
(2)	Steve Bartkowski	.60	.30	.20
(3)	Terry Bradshaw	4.00	2.00	1.25
(4)	Doug Buffone	.60	.30	.20
(5)	Wally Chambers	.60	.30	.20
(6)	Chuck Foreman	.75	.40	.25
(7)	Roman Gabriel	1.00	.50	.30
(8)	Mel Gray	.60	.30	.20
(9)	Franco Harris	4.00	2.00	1.25
(10)	James Harris	.60	.30	.20
(11)	Jim Hart	.80	.40	.25
(12)	Gary Huff	.60	.30	.20
(13)	Bill Kilmer	.85	.45	.25
(14)	Terry Metcalf	.60	.30	.20
(15)	Jim Otis	.60	.30	.20
(16)	Jim Plunkett	1.00	.50	.30
(17)	Greg Pruitt	.65	.35	.20
(18)	Roger Staubach	5.00	2.50	1.50
(19)	Jan Stenerud	1.50	.70	.45
(20)	Roger Wehrli	.60	.30	.20

1976 Crane Discs

These circular cards measure 3 3/8" in diameter and were produced by Michael Schechter Associates, as noted by the MSA letters on the card back. Each card front has a black- and-white mug shot of a player, along with his team, name and position. The card has a colored border with the word "Crane" at the top, representing Crane Potato Chips, which offered the cards as a mail-in offer. The Crane logo appears on the card

back, but there are a few other sponsors which may also appear on the back; these are slightly more valuable than their Crane counterparts. The cards are unnumbered.

		NM	EX	VG
Complete Set (30):		15.00	7.50	4.50
Common Player:		.10	.05	.03
(1)	Ken Anderson	.50	.25	.15
(2)	Otis Armstrong	.15	.08	.05
(3)	Steve Bartkowski	.35	.20	.11
(4)	Terry Bradshaw	2.00	1.00	.60
(5)	John Brockington	.25	.13	.08
(6)	Doug Buffone	.10	.05	.03
(7)	Wally Chambers	.10	.05	.03
(8)	Isaac Curtis	.25	.13	.08
(9)	Chuck Foreman	.20	.10	.06
(10)	Roman Gabriel	.75	.40	.25
(11)	Mel Gray	.15	.08	.05
(12)	Joe Greene	.65	.35	.20
(13)	James Harris	.25	.13	.08
(14)	Jim Hart	.25	.13	.08
(15)	Billy Kilmer	.25	.13	.08
(16)	Greg Landry	.25	.13	.08
(17)	Ed Marinaro	.50	.25	.15
(18)	Lawrence McCutcheon	.25	.13	.08
(19)	Terry Metcalf	.15	.08	.05
(20)	Lydell Mitchell	.25	.13	.08
(21)	Jim Otis	.15	.08	.05
(22)	Alan Page	.35	.20	.11
(23)	Walter Payton	10.00	5.00	3.00
(24)	Greg Pruitt	.40	.20	.12
(25)	Charlie Sanders	.25	.13	.08
(26)	Ron Shanklin	.25	.13	.08
(27)	Roger Staubach	2.00	1.00	.60
(28)	Jan Stenerud	.40	.20	.12
(29)	Charley Taylor	.40	.20	.12
(30)	Roger Wehrli	.25	.13	.08

1989 King B Discs

These red-bordered discs, which feature 24 NFL stars, were included in specially-marked cans of King B beef jerky, one per can. The front has a color head shot of the player, along with the King B logo. "1st Annual Collectors Edition" is also written on the front. The back includes the King B and NFLPA logos, plus biographical informations and 1988 and career statistics. A ring of stars runs along the border. The cards, produced by Michael Schechter Associates, are numbered 1 of 24, etc., on the back.

Medallions/discs

		MT	NM	EX
	Complete Set (24):	50.00	37.00	20.00
	Common Player:	1.00	.70	.40
1	Chris Miller	2.50	2.00	1.00
2	Shane Conlan	1.25	.90	.50
3	Richard Dent	1.75	1.25	.70
4	Boomer Esiason	1.75	1.25	.70
5	Frank Minnifield	1.00	.70	.40
6	Herschel Walker	2.00	1.50	.80
7	Karl Mecklenburg	1.50	1.25	.60
8	Mike Cofer	1.00	.70	.40
9	Warren Moon	3.00	2.25	1.25
10	Chris Chandler	1.50	1.25	.60
11	Deron Cherry	1.00	.70	.40
12	Bo Jackson	2.00	1.50	.80
13	Jim Everett	1.50	1.25	.60
14	Dan Marino	12.00	9.00	4.75
15	Anthony Carter	1.25	.90	.50
16	Andre Tippett	1.50	1.25	.60
17	Bobby Hebert	1.50	1.25	.60
18	Phil Simms	1.75	1.25	.70
19	Al Toon	1.50	1.25	.60
20	Gary Anderson	1.50	1.25	.60
21	Joe Montana	14.00	10.50	5.50
22	Dave Krieg	1.50	1.25	.60
23	Randall Cunningham	2.50	2.00	1.00
24	Bubby Brister	1.00	.70	.40

1990 King B Discs

Once again, these discs were available in specially-marked cans of King B beef jerky, one per can. The front has a color mug shot of the player, surrounded by a red border with a yellow background. The year 1990 appears at the bottom of the card in green; the King B logo is underneath the year. Each card back is numbered (1 of 24, etc.) and has a border of stars around it. Biographical information and a comment about the player's accomplishments are also given on the back, along with the King B and NFLPA logos.

		MT	NM	EX
	Complete Set (24):	45.00	34.00	18.00
	Common Player:	1.00	.70	.40
1	Jim Everett	2.00	1.50	.80
2	Marcus Allen	2.00	1.50	.80
3	Brian Blades	1.50	1.25	.60
4	Bubby Brister	1.00	.70	.40
5	Mark Carrier	1.50	1.25	.60
6	Steve Jordan	1.00	.70	.40
7	Barry Sanders	7.00	5.25	2.75
8	Ronnie Lott	2.00	1.50	.80
9	Howie Long	2.00	1.50	.80
10	Steve Atwater	1.50	1.25	.60
11	Dan Marino	8.00	6.00	3.25
12	Boomer Esiason	2.00	1.50	.80
13	Dalton Hilliard	1.00	.70	.40
14	Phil Simms	2.50	2.00	1.00
15	Jim Kelly	3.00	2.25	1.25
16	Mike Singletary	1.50	1.25	.60
17	John Stephens	1.50	1.25	.60
18	Christian Okoye	1.50	1.25	.60
19	Art Monk	2.00	1.50	.80
20	Chris Miller	2.50	2.00	1.00
21	Roger Craig	2.00	1.50	.80
22	Duane Bickett	1.00	.70	.40
23	Don Majkowski	1.00	.70	.40
24	Eric Metcalf	2.50	2.00	1.00

1991 King B Discs

Specially-marked cans of King B beef jerky each contained a disc featuring one of 24 NFL stars. The front has a color mug shot of the player surrounded by a purple border. His name, team and position are printed in gold. The King B logo and 1991 are printed at the bottom of the disc.

The back is numbered 1 of 24, etc., and includes 1990 and career statistics, plus brief biographical information, all in red ink. A ring of stars comprises the border. An NFLPA and King B logo are also included on the back. The discs were produced by Michael Schechter Associates.

		MT	NM	EX
	Complete Set (24):	35.00	26.00	14.00
	Common Player:	1.00	.70	.40
1	Mark Rypien	1.25	.90	.50
2	Art Monk	2.00	1.50	.80
3	Sean Jones	1.00	.70	.40
4	Bubby Brister	1.00	.70	.40
5	Warren Moon	3.00	2.25	1.25
6	Andre Rison	2.00	1.50	.80
7	Emmitt Smith	9.00	6.75	3.50
8	Mervyn Fernandez	1.00	.70	.40
9	Rickey Jackson	1.00	.70	.40
10	Bruce Armstrong	1.00	.70	.40
11	Neal Anderson	1.25	.90	.50
12	Christian Okoye	1.00	.70	.40
13	Thurman Thomas	3.00	2.25	1.25
14	Bruce Smith	1.25	.90	.50
15	Jeff Hostetler	1.50	1.25	.60
16	Barry Sanders	6.00	4.50	2.50
17	Andre Reed	1.25	.90	.50
18	Derrick Thomas	2.50	2.00	1.00
19	Jim Everett	1.25	.90	.50
20	Boomer Esiason	1.50	1.25	.60
21	Merril Hoge	1.00	.70	.40
22	Steve Atwater	1.25	.90	.50
23	Dan Marino	8.00	6.00	3.25
24	Mark Collins	1.00	.70	.40

1992 King B Discs

This fourth annual collectors' edition features 24 NFL stars on discs available in specially-marked cans of King B beef jerky. The front of each disc, which is black with a yellow border, has a color mug shot of the player. His name, team and position are written in white at the top of the card. A yellow King B logo and the year, 1992, are at the bottom. The back is numbered 1 of 24, etc., and includes 1991 and career statistics, plus brief biographical information. King B and NFLPA logos also appear. An alternating ring of white and black stars runs along the border of the back. Michael Schechter Associates again produced the set.

		MT	NM	EX
	Complete Set (24):	30.00	22.00	12.00
	Common Player:	1.00	.70	.40
1	Derrick Thomas	2.00	1.50	.80
2	Wilber Marshall	1.50	1.25	.60
3	Andre Rison	2.00	1.50	.80
4	Thurman Thomas	2.50	2.00	1.00
5	Emmitt Smith	8.00	6.00	3.25
6	Charles Mann	1.00	.70	.40
7	Michael Irvin	3.00	2.25	1.25
8	Jim Everett	1.50	1.25	.60
9	Gary Anderson	1.00	.70	.40
10	Trace Armstrong	1.00	.70	.40
11	John Elway	3.50	2.75	1.50
12	Chip Lohmiller	1.00	.70	.40
13	Bobby Hebert	1.00	.70	.40
14	Cornelius Bennett	1.25	.90	.50
15	Chris Miller	1.50	1.25	.60
16	Warren Moon	2.00	1.50	.80
17	Charles Haley	1.50	1.25	.60
18	Mark Rypien	1.00	.70	.40
19	Darrell Green	1.25	.90	.50
20	Barry Sanders	5.00	3.75	2.00
21	Rodney Hampton	2.50	2.00	1.00
22	Shane Conlan	1.00	.70	.40
23	Jerry Ball	1.00	.70	.40
24	Morten Andersen	1.50	1.25	.60

1993 King B Discs

These 2 3/8" discs were included one per specially-marked cans of King B beef jerky. Twenty-four NFL stars are featured. The front of the card uses a green football field motif and features a color mug shot of the player. A black panel at the top includes the player's name, team and position, written in orange and white letters. A blue King B logo and the year appear at the bottom of the disc. The back is numbered and uses black ink to present brief biographical information, plus a brief career summary. King B and NFLPA logos are also included on the back, which has black and white stars along the rim. Each disc, produced by Michael Schechter Associates, measures 2 3/8". An uncut sheet, measuring 17 1/4" by 12 3/4", was also issued.

		MT	NM	EX
Complete Set (24):		30.00	22.00	12.00
Common Player:		1.00	.70	.40
1	Luis Sharpe	1.00	.70	.40
2	Erik McMillan	1.00	.70	.40
3	Chris Doleman	1.25	.90	.50
4	Cortez Kennedy	1.50	1.25	.60
5	Howie Long	1.25	.90	.50
6	Bill Romanowski	1.00	.70	.40
7	Andre Tippett	1.00	.70	.40
8	Simon Fletcher	1.50	1.25	.60
9	Derrick Thomas	2.00	1.50	.80
10	Rodney Peete	1.00	.70	.40
11	Ronnie Lott	1.50	1.25	.60
12	Duane Bickett	1.00	.70	.40
13	Steve Walsh	1.25	.90	.50
14	Stan Humphries	1.50	1.25	.60
15	Jeff George	2.75	2.00	1.00
16	Jay Novacek	2.00	1.50	.80
17	Andre Reed	2.00	1.50	.80
18	Andre Rison	2.00	1.50	.80
19	Emmitt Smith	8.00	6.00	3.25
20	Neal Anderson	1.00	.70	.40
21	Ricky Sanders	1.25	.90	.50
22	Thurman Thomas	2.50	2.00	1.00
23	Lorenzo White	1.00	.70	.40
24	Barry Foster	2.50	2.00	1.00

1981 Michael Schechter Associates Test Discs

These discs, produced by Michael Schecter Associates, were included in specially-marked packages of bread. The front shows a head shot of the player, but team logos have been airbrushed off the helmets. An NFLPA logo appears on the card front, along with the player's name, team, position and biographical information. Four stars appear at the top of the card. The unnumbered cards have blank backs. Holsum and Gardner's are among the brands of bread which included the cards inside packages. These two companies also made different posters which were intended to be used to display the discs.

		MT	NM	EX
Complete Set (32):		175.00	131.00	70.00
Common Player:		2.50	2.00	1.00
(1)	Ken Anderson	4.00	3.00	1.50
(2)	Ottis Anderson	6.00	4.50	2.50
(3)	Steve Bartkowski	3.00	2.25	1.25
(4)	Ricky Bell	3.00	2.25	1.25
(5)	Terry Bradshaw	17.50	13.00	7.00
(6)	Harold Carmichael	3.00	2.25	1.25
(7)	Joe Cribbs	2.50	2.00	1.00
(8)	Gary Danielson	2.50	2.00	1.00
(9)	Lynn Dickey	2.50	2.00	1.00
(10)	Dan Doornink	2.50	2.00	1.00
(11)	Vince Evans	3.00	2.25	1.25
(12)	Joe Ferguson	3.00	2.25	1.25
(13)	Vagas Ferguson	2.50	2.00	1.00
(14)	Dan Fouts	8.00	6.00	3.25
(15)	Steve Fuller	2.50	2.00	1.00
(16)	Archie Griffin	3.00	2.25	1.25
(17)	Steve Grogan	3.00	2.25	1.25
(18)	Bruce Harper	2.50	2.00	1.00
(19)	Jim Hart	3.00	2.25	1.25
(20)	Jim Jensen	2.50	2.00	1.00
(21)	Bert Jones	3.00	2.25	1.25
(22)	Archie Manning	4.00	3.00	1.50
(23)	Ted McKnight	2.50	2.00	1.00
(24)	Joe Montana	85.00	64.00	34.00
(25)	Craig Morton	3.00	2.25	1.25
(26)	Robert Newhouse	3.00	2.25	1.25
(27)	Phil Simms	9.00	6.75	3.50
(28)	Billy Taylor	2.50	2.00	1.00
(29)	Joe Theismann	5.00	3.75	2.00
(30)	Mark Van Eeghen	2.50	2.00	1.00
(31)	Delvin Williams	2.50	2.00	1.00
(32)	Tim Wilson	2.50	2.00	1.00

1990 Michael Schechter Associates Superstars

These unnumbered cards, produced by Michael Schechter Associates, were included two per box of Ralston Purina's Staff and Food Club Frosted Flakes cereal. Each card front has a color closeup shot of the player, with "Superstars" written at the top, and the player's name and team at the bottom. Three footballs are in different corners; an NFLPA logo is in the fourth corner. The card back also has the NFLPA logo, plus biographical information and statistics.

		MT	NM	EX
Complete Set (12):		15.00	11.00	6.00
Common Player:		.75	.60	.30
(1)	Carl Banks	.75	.60	.30
(2)	Cornelius Bennett	.75	.60	.30
(3)	Roger Craig	1.50	1.25	.60
(4)	Jim Everett	1.00	.70	.40
(5)	Bo Jackson	2.00	1.50	.80
(6)	Ronnie Lott	1.50	1.25	.60
(7)	Don Majkowski	.75	.60	.30
(8)	Dan Marino	8.00	6.00	3.25
(9)	Karl Mecklenburg	.75	.60	.30
(10)	Christian Okoye	.75	.60	.30
(11)	Mike Singletary	1.00	.70	.40
(12)	Herschel Walker	1.00	.70	.40

1976 Pepsi Discs

This set was regionally produced in the Cincinnati area; hence the majority of the discs feature members of the Cincinnati Bengals (#s 21-40). The remaining discs feature top NFL stars. The cards are valued with the tab in tact; this is how they are commonly found. The tab was used to hang the disc from a bottle included in six packs of Pepsi products. Each disc is 3 1/2" in diameter and features a player photo, biographical information and 1975 statistics on the front. Discs 1, 5, 7, 8 and 14 are reportedly scarcer than the others because they were short-printed. A free, personalized T-shirt was also offered to those who sent in 200 capliners which read "Pepsi Players." The shirt would picture either Ken Anderson or Archie Griffin, with the collector's first name. It would say "To my buddy xxxx, Best Wishes, Ken Anderson."

		NM	EX	VG
	Complete Set (40):	90.00	45.00	27.00
	Common Player:	.50	.25	.15
1	Steve Bartkowski	22.00	11.00	6.50
2	Lydell Mitchell	1.00	.50	.30
3	Wally Chambers	.50	.25	.15
4	Doug Buffone	.50	.25	.15
5	Jerry Sherk	20.00	10.00	6.00
6	Drew Pearson	1.00	.50	.30
7	Otis Armstrong	22.00	11.00	6.50
8	Charlie Sanders	20.00	10.00	6.00
9	John Brockington	.75	.40	.25
10	Curley Culp	.75	.40	.25
11	Jan Stenerud	1.50	.70	.45
12	Lawrence McCutcheon	.75	.40	.25
13	Chuck Foreman	1.00	.50	.30
14	Bob Pollard	20.00	10.00	6.00
15	Ed Marinaro	10.00	5.00	3.00
16	Jack Lambert	5.00	2.50	1.50
17	Terry Metcalf	.75	.40	.25
18	Mel Gray	.75	.40	.25
19	Russ Washington	.50	.25	.15
20	Charley Taylor	2.00	1.00	.60
21	Ken Anderson	2.50	1.25	.70
22	Bob Brown	.50	.25	.15
23	Ron Carpenter	.50	.25	.15
24	Tom Casanova	1.25	.60	.40
25	Boobie Clark	1.00	.50	.30
26	Isaac Curtis	1.00	.50	.30
27	Lenvil Elliott	.50	.25	.15
28	Stan Fritts	.50	.25	.15
29	Vernon Holland	.50	.25	.15
30	Bob Johnson	1.00	.50	.30
31	Ken Johnson	.50	.25	.15
32	Bill Kollar	.50	.25	.15
33	Jim LeClair	.75	.40	.25
34	Chip Myers	.50	.25	.15
35	Lemar Parrish	.75	.40	.25
36	Rob Pritchard	.50	.25	.15
37	Bob Trumpy	1.00	.50	.30
38	Sherman White	.50	.25	.15
39	Archie Griffin	1.00	.50	.30
40	John Shinners	.50	.25	.15

1962 Salada Coins

These coins, featuring 154 pro football players, are color-coded according to the team the player plays for; each team has a specific rim color. The fronts feature a color head-and-shoulders shot of the player without his helmet on. The backs are numbered and contain advertising for Salada Tea and Junket brand desserts. Brief biographical information, including the collegiate school the player attended, is also given. Each coin measures 1 1/2" diameter. The set can sometimes be found as a complete set in its own custom box. Double- and triple-printed coins are indicated by (DP) and (TP) and are easier to find than the others.

		NM	EX	VG
	Complete Set (154):	3000.	1500.	900.00
	Common Player DP:	8.00	4.00	2.50
	Common Player SP:	25.00	12.50	7.50
1	Johnny Unitas	175.00	87.00	52.00
2	Lenny Moore	80.00	40.00	24.00
3	Jim Parker	50.00	25.00	15.00
4	Gino Marchetti	60.00	30.00	18.00
5	Dick Szymanski	25.00	12.50	7.50
6	Alex Sandusky	25.00	12.50	7.50
7	Raymond Berry	90.00	45.00	27.00
8	Jimmy Orr	30.00	15.00	9.00
9	Ordell Braase	25.00	12.50	7.50
10	Bill Pellington	25.00	12.50	7.50
11	Bob Boyd	25.00	12.50	7.50
12	Paul Hornung (DP)	25.00	12.50	7.50
13	Jim Taylor (DP)	20.00	10.00	6.00
14	Henry Jordan (DP)	8.00	4.00	2.50
15	Dan Currie (DP)	8.00	4.00	2.50
16	Bill Forester (DP)	8.00	4.00	2.50
17	Dave Hanner (DP)	8.00	4.00	2.50
18	Bart Starr (DP)	30.00	15.00	9.00
19	Max McGee (DP)	7.50	3.75	2.25
20	Jerry Kramer (DP)	9.00	4.50	2.75
21	Forrest Gregg (DP)	15.00	7.50	4.50
22	Jim Ringo (DP)	15.00	7.50	4.50
23	Billy Kilmer	50.00	25.00	15.00
24	Charlie Krueger	25.00	12.50	7.50
25	Bob St. Clair	50.00	25.00	15.00
26	Abe Woodson	25.00	12.50	7.50
27	Jimmy Johnson	65.00	32.00	19.50
28	Matt Hazeltine	25.00	12.50	7.50
29	Bruce Bosley	25.00	12.50	7.50
30	Dan Conners	25.00	12.50	7.50
31	John Brodie	80.00	40.00	24.00
32	J.D. Smith	25.00	12.50	7.50
33	Monty Stickles	25.00	12.50	7.50
34	Johnny Morris (DP)	9.00	4.50	2.75
35	Stan Jones (DP)	15.00	7.50	4.50
36	J.C. Caroline (DP)	8.00	4.00	2.50
37	Richie Petitbon (DP)	9.00	4.50	2.75
38	Joe Fortunato (DP)	9.00	4.50	2.75
39	Larry Morris (DP)	6.00	3.00	1.75
40	Doug Atkins (DP)	12.00	6.00	3.50
41	Billy Wade (DP)	7.50	3.75	2.25
42	Rick Casares (DP)	9.00	4.50	2.75
43	Willie Galimore (DP)	9.00	4.50	2.75
44	Angelo Coia (DP)	8.00	4.00	2.50
45	Ollie Matson	65.00	32.00	19.50
46	Carroll Dale	30.00	15.00	9.00
47	Ed Meador	30.00	15.00	9.00
48	Jon Arnett	35.00	17.50	10.50
49	Joe Marconi	25.00	12.50	7.50
50	John LoVetere	25.00	12.50	7.50
51	Red Phillips	25.00	12.50	7.50
52	Zeke Bratkowski	35.00	17.50	10.50

53	Dick Bass	30.00	15.00	9.00
54	Les Richter	30.00	15.00	9.00
55	Art Hunter (DP)	8.00	4.00	2.50
56	Jim Brown (TP)	60.00	30.00	18.00
57	Mike McCormack (DP)	12.00	6.00	3.50
58	Bob Gain (DP)	8.00	4.00	2.50
59	Paul Wiggin (DP)	7.50	3.75	2.25
60	Jim Houston (DP)	7.50	3.75	2.25
61	Ray Renfro (DP)	7.50	3.75	2.25
62	Galen Fiss (DP)	8.00	4.00	2.50
63	J.R. Smith (DP)	8.00	4.00	2.50
64	John Morrow (DP)	8.00	4.00	2.50
65	Gene Hickerson (DP)	8.00	4.00	2.50
66	Jim Ninowski (DP)	7.50	3.75	2.25
67	Tom Tracy	30.00	15.00	9.00
68	Buddy Dial	30.00	15.00	9.00
69	Mike Sandusky	30.00	15.00	9.00
70	Lou Michaels	30.00	15.00	9.00
71	Preston Carpenter	25.00	12.50	7.50
72	John Reger	25.00	12.50	7.50
73	John Henry Johnson	65.00	32.00	19.50
74	Gene Lipscomb	40.00	20.00	12.00
75	Mike Henry	30.00	15.00	9.00
76	George Tarasovic	25.00	12.50	7.50
77	Bobby Layne	70.00	35.00	21.00
78	Harley Sewell (DP)	8.00	4.00	2.50
79	Darris McCord (DP)	8.00	4.00	2.50
80	Yale Lary (DP)	12.00	6.00	3.50
81	Jim Gibbons (DP)	8.00	4.00	2.50
82	Gail Codgill (DP)	8.00	4.00	2.50
83	Nick Pietrosante (DP)	9.00	4.50	2.75
84	Alex Karras (DP)	15.00	7.50	4.50
85	Dick Lane (DP)	12.00	6.00	3.50
86	Joe Schmidt (DP)	15.00	7.50	4.50
87	John Gordy (DP)	8.00	4.00	2.50
88	Milt Plum (DP)	7.50	3.75	2.25
89	Andy Stynchula	25.00	12.50	7.50
90	Bob Toneff	25.00	12.50	7.50
91	Bill Anderson	30.00	15.00	9.00
92	Sam Horner	25.00	12.50	7.50
93	Norm Snead	30.00	15.00	9.00
94	Bobby Mitchell	60.00	30.00	18.00
95	Billy Barnes	25.00	12.50	7.50
96	Rod Breedlove	25.00	12.50	7.50
97	Fred Hageman	25.00	12.50	7.50
98	Vince Promuto	25.00	12.50	7.50
99	Joe Rutgens	25.00	12.50	7.50
100	Maxie Baughan (DP)	9.00	4.50	2.75
101	Pete Retzlaff (DP)	7.50	3.75	2.25
102	Tom Brookshier (DP)	9.00	4.50	2.75
103	Sonny Jurgensen (DP)	25.00	12.50	7.50
104	Ed Khayat (DP)	6.00	3.00	1.75
105	Chucl Bednarik (DP)	15.00	7.50	4.50
106	Tommy McDonald (DP)	9.00	4.50	2.75
107	Bobby Walston (DP)	8.00	4.00	2.50
108	Ted Dean (DP)	8.00	4.00	2.50
109	Clarence Peaks (DP)	8.00	4.00	2.50
110	Jimmy Carr (DP)	8.00	4.00	2.50
111	Sam Huff (DP)	15.00	7.50	4.50
112	Erich Barnes (DP)	7.50	3.75	2.25
113	Del Shofner (DP)	9.00	4.50	2.75
114	Bob Gaiters (DP)	8.00	4.00	2.50
115	Alex Webster (DP)	9.00	4.50	2.75
116	Dick Modzelewski (DP)	7.50	3.75	2.25
117	Jim Katcavage (DP)	7.50	3.75	2.25
118	Roosevelt Brown (DP)	15.00	7.50	4.50
119	Y.A. Tittle (DP)	25.00	12.50	7.50
120	Andy Robustelli (DP)	12.00	6.00	3.50
121	Dick Lynch (DP)	7.50	3.75	2.25
122	Don Webb (DP)	8.00	4.00	2.50
123	Larry Eisenhauer (DP)	8.00	4.00	2.50
124	Babe Parilli (DP)	7.50	3.75	2.25
125	Charles Long (DP)	8.00	4.00	2.50
126	Billy Lott (DP)	8.00	4.00	2.50
127	Harry Jacobs (DP)	8.00	4.00	2.50
128	Bob Dee (DP)	8.00	4.00	2.50
129	Ron Burton (DP)	7.50	3.75	2.25
130	Jim Colclough (TP)	3.00	1.50	.90

131	Gino Cappelletti (DP)	9.00	4.50	2.75
132	Tommy Addison (DP)	8.00	4.00	2.50
133	Larry Grantham (DP)	7.50	3.75	2.25
134	Dick Christy (DP)	8.00	4.00	2.50
135	Bill Mathis (DP)	7.50	3.75	2.25
136	Butch Songin (DP)	8.00	4.00	2.50
137	Dainard Paulson (DP)	8.00	4.00	2.50
138	Roger Ellis (DP)	8.00	4.00	2.50
139	Mike Hudock (DP)	8.00	4.00	2.50
140	Don Maynard (DP)	20.00	10.00	6.00
141	Al Dorow (DP)	7.50	3.75	2.25
142	Jack Klotz (DP)	8.00	4.00	2.50
143	Lee Riley (DP)	8.00	4.00	2.50
144	Bill Atkins (DP)	8.00	4.00	2.50
145	Art Baker (DP)	8.00	4.00	2.50
146	Stew Barber (DP)	8.00	4.00	2.50
147	Glen Bass (DP)	8.00	4.00	2.50
148	Al Bemiller (DP)	8.00	4.00	2.50
149	Richie Lucas (DP)	7.50	3.75	2.25
150	Archie Matsos (DP)	8.00	4.00	2.50
151	Warren Rabb (DP)	8.00	4.00	2.50
152	Ken Rice (DP)	8.00	4.00	2.50
153	Billy Shaw (DP)	7.50	3.75	2.25
154	Laverne Torczon (DP)	8.00	4.00	2.50

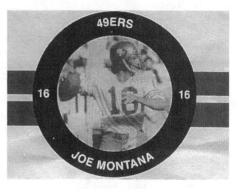

1983 7-11 Discs

These discs were available at participating 7-Eleven stores in 1983. Each disc, which is numbered on the back as "x of Fifteen," has a portrait and an action picture on the front. The player's team name is at the top of the disc, while his name is at the bottom. His jersey number is on each side. The disc back has the player's career totals, pro honors, a Slurpee logo and the year, 1983.

		MT	NM	EX
Complete Set (15):		30.00	22.00	12.00
Common Player:		1.00	.70	.40
1	Franco Harris	5.00	3.75	2.00
2	Dan Fouts	3.00	2.25	1.25
3	Lee Roy Selmon	1.25	.90	.50
4	Nolan Cromwell	1.25	.90	.50
5	Marcus Allen	5.00	3.75	2.00
6	Joe Montana	10.00	7.50	4.00
7	Kellen Winslow	2.00	1.50	.80
8	Hugh Green	1.00	.70	.40
9	Ted Hendricks	2.00	1.50	.80
10	Danny White	1.50	1.25	.60
11	Wes Chandler	1.00	.70	.40
12	Jimmie Giles	1.00	.70	.40
13	Jack Youngblood	2.00	1.50	.80
14	Lester Hayes	1.00	.70	.40
15	Vince Ferragamo	1.00	.70	.40

1984 7-11 Discs

These discs, available at participating 7-Eleven stores, were available in two regions, East and West, as indicated by the card number prefix. The disc has a diameter of 1 3/4" and is designed like the previous year's issue, except the year on the back is 1984.

		MT	NM	EX
Complete Set (40):		60.00	45.00	24.00
Common Player:		.75	.60	.30
1E	Franco Harris	3.00	2.25	1.25
2E	Lawrence Taylor	2.00	1.50	.80
3E	Mark Gastineau	.75	.60	.30
4E	Lee Roy Selmon	1.00	.70	.40
5E	Ken Anderson	1.50	1.25	.60
6E	Walter Payton	4.00	3.00	1.50
7E	Ken Stabler	1.50	1.25	.60
8E	Marcus Allen	2.00	1.50	.80
9E	Fred Smerlas	.75	.60	.30
10E	Ozzie Newsome	1.25	.90	.50
11E	Steve Bartkowski	1.00	.70	.40
12E	Tony Dorsett	2.00	1.50	.80
13E	John Riggins	1.50	1.25	.60
14E	Billy Sims	.75	.60	.30
15E	Dan Marino	9.00	6.75	3.50
16E	Tony Collins	.75	.60	.30
17E	Curtis Dickey	.75	.60	.30
18E	Ron Jaworski	.75	.60	.30
19E	William Andrews	.75	.60	.30
20E	Joe Theismann	1.50	1.25	.60
1W	Franco Harris	2.00	1.50	.80
2W	Joe Montana	10.00	7.50	4.00
3W	Matt Blair	.75	.60	.30
4W	Warren Moon	6.00	4.50	2.50
5W	Marcus Allen	2.00	1.50	.80
6W	John Riggins	1.50	1.25	.60
7W	Walter Payton	4.00	3.00	1.50
8W	Vince Ferragamo	.75	.60	.30
9W	Billy Sims	.75	.60	.30
10W	Ken Anderson	1.25	.90	.50
11W	Lynn Dickey	.75	.60	.30
12W	Tony Dorsett	2.00	1.50	.80
13W	Bill Kenney	.75	.60	.30
14W	Ottis Anderson	1.00	.70	.40
15W	Dan Fouts	1.50	1.25	.60
16W	Eric Dickerson	3.00	2.25	1.25
17W	John Elway	6.00	4.50	2.50
18W	Ozzie Newsome	1.25	.90	.50
19W	Curt Warner	1.00	.70	.40
20W	Joe Theismann	1.50	1.25	.60

1978 Slim Jim discs

Specially-marked packages of Slim Jim products contained a pair of these Superstar trading discs, with each disc featuring an NFL star from 1978. The discs, which came in 3" by 5 3/4" panels of two discs each, always have the same two players paired together. Prices below reflect the panels intact. The individual discs are 2 3/8" in diameter and came in three colors - yellow, red or brown, with black lettering. Each disc front says "Slim Jim Collection" around the top of the disc, with a player mug shot in the center. His name is below the photo, with biographical information, an NFL logo and a MSA designation at the bottom. The pairs are unnumbered; each disc is perforated.

	NM	EX	VG
Complete set (35)	300.00	225.00	125.00
Common pair:	7.50	5.75	3.00
1. Lyle Alzado/Archie Manning	15.00	11.00	6.00
2. Bill Bergey/John Riggins	15.00	11.00	6.00
3. Fred Biletnikoff/ Dan Dierdorf	15.00	11.00	6.00
4. John Cappelletti/Bob Chandler	7.50	5.75	3.00
5. Tommy Casanova/Darryl Stingley	7.50	5.75	3.00
6. Billy Joe DuPree/Nat Moore	7.50	5.75	3.00
7. John Dutton/Paul Krause	7.50	5.75	3.00
8. Leon Gray/Richard Kaster	7.50	5.75	3.00
9. Mel Gray/Claude Humphrey	7.50	5.75	3.00
10. Joe Greene/Dexter Bussey	12.00	9.00	4.75
11. Jack Gregory/Billy Johnson	7.50	5.75	3.00
12. Steve Grogan/Jerome Barkum	7.50	5.75	3.00
13. John Hannah/Isaac Curtis	10.00	7.50	4.00
14. Jim Hart/Otis Sistrunk	7.50	5.75	3.00
15. Tommy Hart/Ron Howard	7.50	5.75	3.00
16. Wilbur Jackson/Riley Odoms	7.50	5.75	3.00
17. Ron Jaworski/Mike Thomas	10.00	7.50	4.00
18. Larry Little/Isiah Robertson	10.00	7.50	4.00
19. Ron McDole/Willie Buchanon	7.50	5.75	3.00
20. Lydell Mitchell/Glen Edwards	7.50	5.75	3.00
21. Robert Newhouse/Glenn Doughty	7.50	5.75	3.00
22. Alan Page/Fred Carr	10.00	7.50	4.00
23. Walter Payton/Larry Csonka	45.00	34.00	18.00
24. Greg Pruitt/Doug Buffone	7.50	5.75	3.00
25. Ahmad Rashad/Jeff Van Note	12.00	9.00	4.75
26. Golden Richards/Rocky Bleier	10.00	7.50	4.00
27. Clarence Scott/Joe DeLamielleure	7.50	5.75	3.00
28. Lee Roy Selmon/Charlie Sanders	10.00	7.50	4.00
29. Bruce Taylor/Otis Armstrong	7.50	5.75	3.00
30. Emmitt Thomas/Elvin Bethea	7.50	5.75	3.00
31. Brad Van Pelt/Ted Washington	7.50	5.75	3.00
32. Gene Washington/Charlie Joiner	12.00	9.00	4.75
33. Clarence Williams/Lemar Parrish	7.50	5.75	3.00
34. Roger Wehrli/Gene Upshaw	10.00	7.50	4.00
35. Don Woods/Ron Jessie	7.50	5.75	3.00

1976 Chicago Bears Coke discs

These unnumbered discs, featuring 22 Chicago Bears players, were produced by Michael Schecter Associates (MSA) for Coca-Cola products in the Chicago area. Each disc had a hang tab to hang around a pop bottle; frequently the discs can be found with the tabs sill intact, which is what the prices below reflect. Each disc measures 3 3/8" in diameter, but with the hang tab still intact, it measures 5 1/4". The front has a head shot of the player, with his team name and helmet on the left, and his name on the right side. His position is listed below the head shot. Biographical information runs along the outer rim of the disc, which says Coca-Cola at the top. The back has a Coca-Cola logo and the phrase "Coke adds life to...halftime fun." Two color versions were made for Doug Plank and Craig Clemens discs; the complete set price reflects these variations.

	NM	EX	VG
Complete set (24):	50.00	37.00	20.00
Common player:	1.25	.90	.50
1. Lionel Antoine	1.25	.90	.50
2. Bob Avellini	2.00	1.50	.80
3. Waymond Bryant	1.50	1.25	.60
4. Doug Bufone	2.00	1.50	.80
5. Wally Chambers	2.00	1.50	.80
6a. Craig Clemens yellow	1.25	.90	.50
6b. Craig Clemens orange	1.25	.90	.50
7. Allan Ellis	1.25	.90	.50
8. Roland Harper	2.00	1.50	.80
9. Mike Hartenstine	1.25	.90	.50
10. Noah Jackson	1.50	1.25	.60
11. Virgil Livers	1.25	.90	.50
12. Jim Osborne	1.25	.90	.50

13. Bob Parsons	1.25	.90	.50
14. Walter Payton	25.00	18.50	10.00
15. Dan Peiffer	1.25	.90	.50
16a. Doug Plank yellow	1.50	1.25	.60
16b. Doug Plank green	1.50	1.25	.60
17. Bo Rather	1.50	1.25	.60
18. Don Rives	1.25	.90	.50
19. Jeff Sevy	1.25	.90	.50
20. Ron Shanklin	1.50	1.25	.60
21. Revie Sorey	1.50	1.25	.60
22. Roger Stillwell	1.25	.90	.50

1989 Minnesota Vikings Taystee discs

These numbered white-bordered discs, featuring players from the Minnesota Vikings, were inserted in specially-marked Taystee products in Minnesota. Each measures 2 3/4" in diameter and has a color mug shot of the player on the front. The words "1st Annual Collector's Edition," player name and team are below the photo. A Taystee logo is at the top. The back has biographical and statistical information, plus a card number.

	MT	NM	EX
Complete set (12):	5.00	3.75	2.00
Common player:	.50	.40	.20
1. Anthony Carter	1.00	.70	.40
2. Chris Doleman	.75	.60	.30
3. Joey Browner	.75	.60	.30
4. Steve Jordan	.75	.60	.30
5. Scott Studwell	.50	.40	.20
6. Wade Wilson	.75	.60	.30
7. Kirk Lowdermilk	.50	.40	.20
8. Tommy Kramer	.75	.60	.30
9. Keith Millard	.75	.60	.30
10. Rick Fenney	.50	.40	.20
11. Gary Zimmerman	.50	.40	.20
12. Darrin Nelson	.50	.40	.20

Basketball

1976 Buckman Discs

These unnumbered discs, featuring 20 NBA stars of the time, were distributed through Buckman's Ice Cream Village in Rochester, N.Y., which is indicated on the card backs. Each disc has a black-and-white drawing on the front, along with a facsimile autograph, and measures 3 3/8" in diameter. Biographical and statistical info runs along the card, too.

		NM	EX	VG
Complete Set (20):		65.00	32.00	19.50
Common Player:		1.00	.50	.30
(1)	Nate Archibald	5.00	2.50	1.50
(2)	Rick Barry	8.00	4.00	2.50
(3)	Tom Boerwinkle	1.00	.50	.30
(4)	Bill Bradley	10.00	5.00	3.00
(5)	Dave Cowens	5.00	2.50	1.50
(6)	Bob Dandridge	1.00	.50	.30
(7)	Walt Frazier	5.00	2.50	1.50
(8)	Gail Goodrich	4.00	2.00	1.25
(9)	John Havlicek	8.00	4.00	2.50
(10)	Connie Hawkins	5.00	2.50	1.50
(11)	Lou Hudson	1.50	.70	.45
(12)	Kareem Abdul-Jabbar	15.00	7.50	4.50
(13)	Sam Lacey	1.00	.50	.30
(14)	Bob Lanier	5.00	2.50	1.50
(15)	Bob Love	1.50	.70	.45
(16)	Bob McAdoo	2.50	1.25	.70
(17)	Earl Monroe	4.00	2.00	1.25
(18)	Jerry Sloan	1.50	.70	.45
(19)	Norm Van Lier	1.75	.90	.50
(20)	Jo Jo White	1.50	.70	.45

1975 Carvel Discs

These discs, similar to the 1976 Buckman Discs, measure 3 3/8" in diameter and have different colored borders for each player. The discs, unnumbered and blank backed, have black-and-white drawings on the front, plus biographical and statistical info. One of five different colors was used for the border. Some white border discs exist, too; they come in two versions - with or without Carvel at the top. These discs are scarcer than the regular colored ones. A poster was also produced to display all 36 discs.

		NM	EX	VG
Complete Set (36):		150.00	75.00	45.00
Common Player:		1.00	.50	.30
(1)	Nate Archibald	6.00	3.00	1.75
(2)	Bill Bradley	12.00	6.00	3.50
(3)	Don Chaney	3.00	1.50	.90
(4)	Dave Cowens	6.00	3.00	1.75
(5)	Bob Dandridge	1.50	.70	.45
(6)	Ernie DiGregorio	2.50	1.25	.70
(7)	Walt Frazier	6.00	3.00	1.75
(8)	John Gianelli	1.00	.50	.30
(9)	Gail Goodrich	4.00	2.00	1.25
(10)	Happy Hairston	1.50	.70	.45
(11)	John Havlicek	12.00	6.00	3.50
(12)	Spencer Haywood	2.00	1.00	.60
(13)	Garfield Heard	1.00	.50	.30
(14)	Lou Hudson	2.00	1.00	.60
(15)	Kareem Abdul-Jabbar	25.00	12.50	7.50
(16)	Phil Jackson	5.00	2.50	1.50
(17)	Sam Lacey	1.00	.50	.30
(18)	Bob Lanier	5.00	2.50	1.50
(19)	Bob Love	2.00	1.00	.60
(20)	Bob McAdoo	3.00	1.50	.90
(21)	Jim McMillian	1.50	.70	.45
(22)	Dean Meminger	1.00	.50	.30
(23)	Earl Monroe	6.00	3.00	1.75
(24)	Don Nelson	3.00	1.50	.90
(25)	Jim Price	1.00	.50	.30
(26)	Clifford Ray	1.00	.50	.30
(27)	Charlie Scott	1.50	.70	.45
(28)	Paul Silas	3.00	1.50	.90
(29)	Jerry Sloan	2.00	1.00	.60
(30)	Randy Smith	1.50	.70	.45
(31)	Dick Van Arsdale	2.00	1.00	.60
(32)	Norm Van Lier	2.00	1.00	.60
(33)	Chet Walker	2.00	1.00	.60
(34)	Paul Westphal	5.00	2.50	1.50
(35)	Jo Jo White	2.50	1.25	.70
(36)	Hawthorne Wingo	4.00	2.00	1.25

1976 Crane Discs

These cards, issued by Crane Potato Chips, has a picture of the company logo on the front to distinguish it from similar discs which have been made. The fronts have a posed photo of the player, a biography, statistics and an NBA license logo. Backs have a picture of the Crane logo and say Crane Potato Chips. Cards are unnumbered and measure about 3 1/2" in diameter.

		NM	EX	VG
Complete Set (20):		210.00	105.00	63.00
Common Player:		6.00	3.00	1.75
(1)	Nate Archibald	12.00	6.00	3.50
(2)	Rick Barry	20.00	10.00	6.00
(3)	Tom Boerwinkle	6.00	3.00	1.75
(4)	Bill Bradley	25.00	12.50	7.50
(5)	Dave Cowens	15.00	7.50	4.50
(6)	Bob Dandridge	6.00	3.00	1.75
(7)	Walt Frazier	15.00	7.50	4.50
(8)	Gail Goodrich	12.00	6.00	3.50
(9)	John Havlicek	20.00	10.00	6.00
(10)	Connie Hawkins	10.00	5.00	3.00
(11)	Lou Hudson	6.00	3.00	1.75
(12)	Kareem Abdul-Jabbar	30.00	15.00	9.00
(13)	Sam Lacey (spelled Lacy)	6.00	3.00	1.75
(14)	Bob Lanier	10.00	5.00	3.00
(15)	Bob Love	8.00	4.00	2.50
(16)	Bob McAdoo	10.00	5.00	3.00
(17)	Earl Monroe	12.00	6.00	3.50
(18)	Jerry Sloan	6.00	3.00	1.75
(19)	Norm Van Lier	7.50	3.75	2.25
(20)	Jo Jo White	8.00	4.00	2.50

Hockey

1973 Mac's Milk

These discs, which each measures 3" in diameter, feature caricatures of NHL stars of the time. Each disc, which is unnumbered, is actually a sticker, using a circular border on the front in red, purple, green, blue or black. The player's name is also on the front. The back is blank. Mac's Milk is not identified on the discs as being a sponsor.

		NM	EX	VG
Complete Set (30):		150.00	75.00	45.00
Common Player:		3.00	1.50	.90
1	Gary Bergman	3.00	1.50	.90
2	John Bucyk	7.50	3.75	2.25
3	Wayne Cashman	4.00	2.00	1.25
4	Bobby Clarke	14.00	7.00	4.25
5	Yvan Cournoyer	8.00	4.00	2.50
6	Ron Ellis	3.00	1.50	.90
7	Rod Gilbert	6.00	3.00	1.75
8	Brian Glennie	3.00	1.50	.90
9	Paul Henderson	4.00	2.00	1.25
10	Eddie Johnston	4.00	2.00	1.25
11	Rick Kehoe	3.50	1.75	1.00
12	Orland Kurtenbach	3.00	1.50	.90
13	Guy Lapointe	7.50	3.75	2.25
14	Jacques Lemaire	7.50	3.75	2.25
15	Frank Mahovlich	10.00	5.00	3.00
16	Pete Mahovlich	4.00	2.00	1.25
17	Richard Martin	4.00	2.00	1.25
18	Jim McKenny	3.00	1.50	.90
19	Bobby Orr	35.00	17.50	10.50
20	Jean Paul Parise	3.00	1.50	.90
21	Brad Park	6.00	3.00	1.75
22	Jacques Plante	13.00	6.50	4.00
23	Jean Ratelle	7.50	3.75	2.25
24	Mickey Redmond	5.00	2.50	1.50
25	Serge Savard	7.00	3.50	2.00
26	Darryl Sittler	8.00	4.00	2.50
27	Pat Stapleton	3.00	1.50	.90
28	Dale Tallon	3.00	1.50	.90
29	Norm Ullman	6.00	3.00	1.75
30	Bill White	3.00	1.50	.90

1960 Shirriff Hockey Coins

These 1 3/8" diameter colored plastic coins feature players from all six NHL teams (Toronto, Montreal, Detroit, Chicago, New York and Boston) at that time. They were used as premiums in Shirriff's Foods dessert products. The coins are numbered on the front and include the player's name. Each gas a color profile of the featured player. The back has an imprint which says "Shirriff Lushus Jelly & Puddings Pat. Pend." and says "Save 120 Hockey Coins" in English and French around the rim. The set was also issued in limited quantities as a factory set in a black box.

		NM	EX	VG
Complete Set (120):		400.00	200.00	120.00
Common Player:		2.50	1.25	.70
1	Johnny Bower	8.00	4.00	2.50
2	Dick Duff	3.50	1.75	1.00
3	Carl Brewer	3.50	1.75	1.00
4	Red Kelly	7.50	3.75	2.25
5	Tim Horton	8.00	4.00	2.50
6	Allan Stanley	5.00	2.50	1.50
7	Bob Baun	3.50	1.75	1.00
8	Billy Harris	2.50	1.25	.70
9	George Armstrong	6.00	3.00	1.75
10	Ron Stewart	2.50	1.25	.70
11	Bert Olmstead	5.00	2.50	1.50
12	Frank Mahovlich	12.00	6.00	3.50
13	Bob Pulford	5.00	2.50	1.50
14	Garry Edmundson	2.50	1.25	.70
15	Johnny Wilson	2.50	1.25	.70
16	Larry Regan	2.50	1.25	.70
17	Gerry James	3.50	1.75	1.00
18	Rudy Migay	2.50	1.25	.70
19	Gerry Ehman	2.50	1.25	.70
20	Punch Imlach	3.50	1.75	1.00
21	Jacques Plante	14.00	7.00	4.25
22	Dickie Moore	7.50	3.75	2.25
23	Don Marshall	2.50	1.25	.70
24	Al Langlois	2.50	1.25	.70
25	Tom Johnson	5.00	2.50	1.50
26	Doug Harvey	9.00	4.50	2.75
27	Phil Goyette	2.50	1.25	.70
28	Bernie Geoffrion	14.00	7.00	4.25
29	Marcel Bonin	2.50	1.25	.70
30	Jean Beliveau	16.00	8.00	4.75
31	Ralph Backstrom	3.50	1.75	1.00
32	Andre Pronovost	2.50	1.25	.70
33	Claude Provost	3.50	1.75	1.00
34	Henri Richard	8.00	4.00	2.50
35	Jean-Guy Talbot	3.50	1.75	1.00
36	J.C. Tremblay	3.50	1.75	1.00
37	Bob Turner	2.50	1.25	.70
38	Bill Hicke	2.50	1.25	.70
39	Charlie Hodge	3.50	1.75	1.00
40	Toe Blake	5.00	2.50	1.50
41	Terry Sawchuk	14.00	7.00	4.25
42	Gordie Howe	40.00	20.00	12.00
43	John McKenzie	2.50	1.25	.70
44	Alex Delvecchio	7.50	3.75	2.25
45	Norm Ullman	6.00	3.00	1.75
46	Jack McIntyre	2.50	1.25	.70
47	Barry Cullen	3.50	1.75	1.00
48	Val Fonteyne	2.50	1.25	.70

49	Warren Godfrey	2.50	1.25	.70
50	Peter Goegan	2.50	1.25	.70
51	Gerry Melnyk (error)	2.50	1.25	.70
52	Marc Reaume	2.50	1.25	.70
53	Gary Aldcorn	2.50	1.25	.70
54	Len Lunde	2.50	1.25	.70
55	Murray Oliver	2.50	1.25	.70
56	Marcel Pronovost	5.00	2.50	1.50
57	Howie Glover	2.50	1.25	.70
58	Gerry Odrowski	2.50	1.25	.70
59	Parker MacDonald	2.50	1.25	.70
60	Sid Abel	5.00	2.50	1.50
61	Glenn Hall	9.00	4.50	2.75
62	Ed Litzenberger	2.50	1.25	.70
63	Bobby Hull	28.00	14.00	8.50
64	Tod Sloan	2.50	1.25	.70
65	Murray Balfour	2.50	1.25	.70
66	Pierre Pilote	5.00	2.50	1.50
67	Al Arbour	5.00	2.50	1.50
68	Earl Balfour	2.50	1.25	.70
69	Eric Nesterenko	3.50	1.75	1.00
70	Kenny Wharram	3.50	1.75	1.00
71	Stan Mikita	14.00	7.00	4.25
72	Ab McDonald	2.50	1.25	.70
73	Elmer Vasko	2.50	1.25	.70
74	Dollard St. Laurent	2.50	1.25	.70
75	Ron Murphy	2.50	1.25	.70
76	Jack Evans	2.50	1.25	.70
77	Billy Hay	2.50	1.25	.70
78	Reggie Fleming	2.50	1.25	.70
79	Cecil Hoekstra	2.50	1.25	.70
80	Tommy Ivan	3.50	1.75	1.00
81	Jack McCartan	3.50	1.75	1.00
82	Red Sullivan	2.50	1.25	.70
83	Camille Henry	3.50	1.75	1.00
84	Larry Popein	2.50	1.25	.70
85	John Hanna	2.50	1.25	.70
86	Harry Howell	5.00	2.50	1.50
87	Eddie Shack	5.00	2.50	1.50
88	Irv Spencer	2.50	1.25	.70
89	Andy Bathgate	6.00	3.00	1.75
90	Bill Gadsby	5.00	2.50	1.50
91	Andy Hebenton	2.50	1.25	.70
92	Earl Ingarfield, Sr.	2.50	1.25	.70
93	Don Johns	2.50	1.25	.70
94	Dave Balon	2.50	1.25	.70
95	Jim Morrison	2.50	1.25	.70
96	Ken Schinkel	2.50	1.25	.70
97	Louie Fontinato	2.50	1.25	.70
98	Ted Hampson	2.50	1.25	.70
99	Brian Cullen	3.50	1.75	1.00
100	Alf Pike	2.50	1.25	.70
101	Don Simmons	2.50	1.25	.70
102	Fern Flaman	5.00	2.50	1.50
103	Vic Stasiuk	2.50	1.25	.70
104	John Bucyk	8.00	4.00	2.50
105	Bronco Horvath	2.50	1.25	.70
106	Doug Mohns	3.50	1.75	1.00
107	Leo Boivin	5.00	2.50	1.50
108	Don McKenney	2.50	1.25	.70
109	John-Guy Gendron	2.50	1.25	.70
110	Jerry Toppazzini	2.50	1.25	.70
111	Dick Meissner	2.50	1.25	.70
112	Aut Erickson	2.50	1.25	.70
113	Jim Bartlett	2.50	1.25	.70
114	Orval Tessier	3.50	1.75	1.00
115	Billy Carter	2.50	1.25	.70
116	Dallas Smith	3.50	1.75	1.00
117	Leo Labine	2.50	1.25	.70
118	Bob Armstrong	2.50	1.25	.70
119	Bruce Gamble	2.50	1.25	.70
120	Milt Schmidt	4.00	2.00	1.25

1961 Shirriff/Salada
Hockey Coins

These coins follow the same format as those issued the previous year; the only difference is that Salada Foods also produced the coins in 1961. So, Shirriff and Salada versions of each coin could be found. There is no difference in value for the two types. The front is also a bit different; in addition to a color profile shot and coin number, these coins add the year to the front (1961-62). The coins measure 1 3/8" in diameter and once again feature players from the six NHL teams at that time. Shirriff also produced team shield holders to display the coins in; this was the only year this was done, and the shields are not considered part of the complete set.

		NM	EX	VG
Complete Set (120):		375.00	187.00	112.00
Common Player:		2.50	1.25	.70
1	Cliff Pennington	2.50	1.25	.70
2	Dallas Smith	3.50	1.75	1.00
3	Andre Pronovost	2.50	1.25	.70
4	Charlie Burns	2.50	1.25	.70
5	Leo Boivin	5.00	2.50	1.50
6	Don McKenney	2.50	1.25	.70
7	John Bucyk	6.00	3.00	1.75
8	Murray Oliver	2.50	1.25	.70
9	Jerry Toppazzini	2.50	1.25	.70
10	Doug Mohns	3.50	1.75	1.00
11	Don Head	2.50	1.25	.70
12	Bob Armstrong	2.50	1.25	.70
13	Pat Stapleton	3.50	1.75	1.00
14	Orland Kurtenbach	3.50	1.75	1.00
15	Dick Meissner	2.50	1.25	.70
16	Ted Green	3.50	1.75	1.00
17	Tom Williams	2.50	1.25	.70
18	Aut Erickson	2.50	1.25	.70
19	Phil Watson	5.00	2.50	1.50
20	Ed Chadwick	3.50	1.75	1.00
----	Team Shield (Brown)	50.00	25.00	15.00
21	Wayne Hillman	2.50	1.25	.70
22	Stan Mikita	10.00	5.00	3.00
23	Eric Nesterenko	3.50	1.75	1.00
24	Reggie Fleming	2.50	1.25	.70
25	Bobby Hull	22.00	11.00	6.50
26	Elmer Vasko	2.50	1.25	.70
27	Pierre Pilote	5.00	2.50	1.50
28	Chico Maki	3.50	1.75	1.00
29	Glenn Hall	9.00	4.50	2.75
30	Murray Balfour	2.50	1.25	.70
31	Bronco Horvath	2.50	1.25	.70
32	Kenny Wharram	3.50	1.75	1.00
33	Ab McDonald	2.50	1.25	.70
34	Billy Hay	2.50	1.25	.70
35	Dollard St. Laurent	2.50	1.25	.70
36	Ron Murphy	2.50	1.25	.70
37	Bob Turner	2.50	1.25	.70
38	(Gerry Melnyk) (error)	2.50	1.25	.70
39	Jack Evans	2.50	1.25	.70
40	Rudy Pilous	5.00	2.50	1.50
----	Team Shield (Yellow)	50.00	25.00	15.00
41	Johnny Bower	7.50	3.75	2.25
42	Allan Stanley	6.00	3.00	1.75
43	Frank Mahovlich	8.00	4.00	2.50
44	Tim Horton	9.00	4.50	2.75
45	Carl Brewer	3.50	1.75	1.00
46	Bob Pulford	5.00	2.50	1.50
47	Bob Nevin	3.50	1.75	1.00
48	Eddie Shack	6.00	3.00	1.75
49	Red Kelly	6.00	3.00	1.75

50	Bob Baun	3.50	1.75	1.00
51	George Armstrong	6.00	3.00	1.75
52	Bert Olmstead	5.00	2.50	1.50
53	Dick Duff	3.50	1.75	1.00
54	Billy Harris	3.50	1.75	1.00
55	Larry Keenan	2.50	1.25	.70
56	John MacMillan	2.50	1.25	.70
57	Punch Imlach	3.50	1.75	1.00
58	Dave Keon	5.00	2.50	1.50
59	Larry Hillman	2.50	1.25	.70
60	Al Arbour	5.00	2.50	1.50
----	Team Shield (Light Blue)	50.00	25.00	15.00
61	Sid Abel	5.00	2.50	1.50
62	Warren Godfrey	2.50	1.25	.70
63	Vic Stasiuk	2.50	1.25	.70
64	Leo Labine	2.50	1.25	.70
65	Howie Glover	2.50	1.25	.70
66	Gordie Howe	45.00	22.00	13.50
67	Val Fonteyne	2.50	1.25	.70
68	Marcel Pronovost	5.00	2.50	1.50
69	Parker MacDonald	2.50	1.25	.70
70	Alex Delvecchio	7.50	3.75	2.25
71	Ed Litzenberger	2.50	1.25	.70
72	Al Johnson	2.50	1.25	.70
73	Bruce MacGregor	2.50	1.25	.70
74	Howie Young	2.50	1.25	.70
75	Peter Goegan	2.50	1.25	.70
76	Norm Ullman	6.00	3.00	1.75
77	Terry Sawchuk	17.00	8.50	5.00
78	Gerry Odrowski	2.50	1.25	.70
79	Bill Gadsby	5.00	2.50	1.50
80	Hank Bassen	2.50	1.25	.70
----	Team Shield (Red)	50.00	25.00	15.00
81	Doug Harvey	7.00	3.50	2.00
82	Earl Ingarfield, Sr.	2.50	1.25	.70
83	Pat Hannigan	2.50	1.25	.70
84	Dean Prentice	3.50	1.75	1.00
85	Gump Worsley	10.00	5.00	3.00
86	Irv Spencer	2.50	1.25	.70
87	Camille Henry	3.50	1.75	1.00
88	Andy Bathgate	4.00	2.00	1.25
89	Harry Howell	5.00	2.50	1.50
90	Andy Hebenton	2.50	1.25	.70
91	Red Sullivan	2.50	1.25	.70
92	Ted Hampson	2.50	1.25	.70
93	Jean-Guy Gendron	2.50	1.25	.70
94	Al Langlois	2.50	1.25	.70
95	Larry Cahan	2.50	1.25	.70
96	Bob Cunningham	2.50	1.25	.70
97	Vic Hadfield	3.50	1.75	1.00
98	Jean Ratelle	9.00	4.50	2.75
99	Ken Schinkel	2.50	1.25	.70
100	Johnny Wilson	2.50	1.25	.70
----	Team Shield (Dark Blue)	50.00	25.00	15.00
101	Toe Blake	5.00	2.50	1.50
102	Jean Beliveau	16.00	8.00	4.75
103	Don Marshall	2.50	1.25	.70
104	Bernie Geoffrion	10.00	5.00	3.00
105	Claude Provost	3.50	1.75	1.00
106	Tom Johnson	5.00	2.50	1.50
107	Dickie Moore	7.50	3.75	2.25
108	Bill Hicke	2.50	1.25	.70
109	Jean-Guy Talbot	3.50	1.75	1.00
110	Henri Richard	9.00	4.50	2.75
111	Louie Fontinato	2.50	1.25	.70
112	Gilles Tremblay	2.50	1.25	.70
113	Jacques Plante	14.00	7.00	4.25
114	Ralph Backstrom	3.50	1.75	1.00
115	Marcel Bonin	2.50	1.25	.70
116	Phil Goyette	2.50	1.25	.70
117	Bobby Rousseau	3.50	1.75	1.00
118	J.C. Tremblay	3.50	1.75	1.00
119	Al MacNeil	2.50	1.25	.70
120	Jean Gauthier	2.50	1.25	.70
----	Team Shield (White)	50.00	25.00	15.00

1962 Shirriff Hockey Coins

These coins are difficult to find well-centered and un-scratched because Shirriff made them out of metal this year. The coins measure 1 1/2" in diameter and feature a color profile shot of the player on the front, along with his name and coin number. The back, written in French and English, has the player's name, biographical information and a short list of the player's accomplishments. Twelve All-Stars, six Trophy winners and players from Montreal (20) and Toronto (22) comprise the set.

		NM	EX	VG
Complete Set (60):		325.00	162.00	97.00
Common Player:		3.50	1.75	1.00
1	Johnny Bower	8.00	4.00	2.50
2	Allan Stanley	7.50	3.75	2.25
3	Frank Mahovlich	14.00	7.00	4.25
4	Tim Horton	10.00	5.00	3.00
5	Carl Brewer	6.00	3.00	1.75
6	Bob Pulford	6.00	3.00	1.75
7	Bob Nevin	4.50	2.25	1.25
8	Eddie Shack	7.50	3.75	2.25
9	Red Kelly	8.00	4.00	2.50
10	George Armstrong	7.50	3.75	2.25
11	Bert Olmstead	6.00	3.00	1.75
12	Dick Duff	4.50	2.25	1.25
13	Billy Harris	3.50	1.75	1.00
14	John MacMillan	3.50	1.75	1.00
15	Punch Imlach	4.50	2.25	1.25
16	Dave Keon	6.00	3.00	1.75
17	Larry Hillman	3.50	1.75	1.00
18	Ed Litzenberger	3.50	1.75	1.00
19	Bob Baun	4.50	2.25	1.25
20	Al Arbour	6.00	3.00	1.75
21	Ron Stewart	3.50	1.75	1.00
22	Don Simmons	3.50	1.75	1.00
23	Louie Fontinato	3.50	1.75	1.00
24	Gilles Tremblay	3.50	1.75	1.00
25	Jacques Plante	14.00	7.00	4.25
26	Ralph Backstrom	4.50	2.25	1.25
27	Marcel Bonin	3.50	1.75	1.00
28	Phil Goyette	3.50	1.75	1.00
29	Bobby Rousseau	4.50	2.25	1.25
30	J.C. Tremblay	4.50	2.25	1.25
31	Toe Blake	7.50	3.75	2.25
32	Jean Beliveau	16.00	8.00	4.75
33	Don Marshall	3.50	1.75	1.00
34	Bernie Geoffrion	14.00	7.00	4.25
35	Claude Provost	4.50	2.25	1.25
36	Tom Johnson	7.50	3.75	2.25
37	Dickie Moore	7.00	3.50	2.00
38	Bill Hicke	3.50	1.75	1.00
39	Jean-Guy Talbot	4.50	2.25	1.25
40	Al MacNeil	3.50	1.75	1.00
41	Henri Richard	10.00	5.00	3.00
42	Red Berenson	4.50	2.25	1.25
43	Jacques Plante	12.00	6.00	3.50
44	Jean-Guy Talbot	4.50	2.25	1.25
45	Doug Harvey	7.50	3.75	2.25
46	Stan Mikita	9.00	4.50	2.75
47	Bobby Hull	20.00	10.00	6.00
48	Andy Bathgate	7.50	3.75	2.25
49	Glenn Hall	9.00	4.50	2.75
50	Pierre Pilote	7.50	3.75	2.25
51	Carl Brewer	6.00	3.00	1.75
52	Dave Keon	7.50	3.75	2.25

		NM	EX	VG
53	Frank Mahovlich	9.00	4.50	2.75
54	Gordie Howe	32.00	16.00	9.50
55	Byng Trophy: (Dave Keon)	6.00	3.00	1.75
56	Calder Trophy: (Bobby Rousseau)	4.50	2.25	1.25
57	Art Ross Trophy: (Bobby Hull)	18.00	9.00	5.50
58	Vezina Trophy/Hart Trophy: with mask (Jacques Plante)	12.00	6.00	3.50
59	Vezina Trophy/Hart Trophy: without mask (Jacques Plante)	12.00	6.00	3.50
60	Norris Trophy: (Doug Harvey)	6.00	3.00	1.75

1968 Shirriff Hockey Coins

These coins, measuring 1 3/8" in diameter, are once again plastic. A color player profile, player name and abbreviation with coin number appear on each front. This set numbers the coins within each team, not as a complete set. The back, in French and English, has a Shirriff imprint on it and instructs collectors to save the hockey coins. The teams are checklisted alphabetically - Boston, Chicago, Detroit, Los Angeles, Minnesota, Montreal, New York, Oakland, Philadelphia, Pittsburgh, St. Louis and Toronto. Some teams have players who share a number; they are listed with the number and an A or B. Higher numbers within each team were short-printed. They are scarcer and more valuable.

		NM	EX	VG
Complete Set (176):		5000.	2500.	1500.
Common Player:		4.00	2.00	1.25
1	Eddie Shack	7.50	3.75	2.25
2	Ed Westfall	5.00	2.50	1.50
3	Don Awrey	4.00	2.00	1.25
4	Gerry Cheevers	10.00	5.00	3.00
5	Bobby Orr	100.00	50.00	30.00
6	John Bucyk	10.00	5.00	3.00
7	Derek Sanderson	7.50	3.75	2.25
8	Phil Esposito	20.00	10.00	6.00
9	Fred Stanfield	4.00	2.00	1.25
10	Ken Hodge, Sr.	5.00	2.50	1.50
11	John McKenzie	4.00	2.00	1.25
12	Ted Green	5.00	2.50	1.50
13	Dallas Smith	75.00	37.00	22.00
14	Gary Doak	75.00	37.00	22.00
15	Glen Sather	100.00	50.00	30.00
16	Tom Williams	75.00	37.00	22.00
1	Bobby Hull	50.00	25.00	15.00
2	Pat Stapleton	4.00	2.00	1.25
3	Wayne Maki	4.00	2.00	1.25
4	Denis DeJordy	5.00	2.50	1.50
5	Kenny Wharram	4.00	2.00	1.25
6	Pit Martin	4.00	2.00	1.25
7	Chico Maki	4.00	2.00	1.25
8	Doug Mohns	5.00	2.50	1.50
9	Stan Mikita	17.50	8.75	5.25
10	Doug Jarrett	4.00	2.00	1.25
11A	(Dennis Hull) (small portrait)	100.00	50.00	30.00
11B	(Dennis Hull) (large portrait)	25.00	12.50	7.50
12	Matt Ravlich	4.00	2.00	1.25
13	Dave Dryden	75.00	37.00	22.00
14	Eric Nesterenko	75.00	37.00	22.00
15	Gilles Marotte	75.00	37.00	22.00
16	Jim Pappin	75.00	37.00	22.00
1	Gary Bergman	4.00	2.00	1.25
2	Roger Crozier	5.00	2.50	1.50
3	Pete Mahovlich	5.00	2.50	1.50
4	Alex Delvecchio	7.50	3.75	2.25

5	Dean Prentice	5.00	2.50	1.50
6	Kent Douglas	4.00	2.00	1.25
7	Roy Edwards	4.00	2.00	1.25
8	Bruce MacGregor	4.00	2.00	1.25
9	Garry Unger	4.00	2.00	1.25
10	Pete Stemkowski	4.00	2.00	1.25
11	Gordie Howe	4.00	2.00	1.25
12	Frank Mahovlich	4.00	2.00	1.25
13	Bob Baun	4.00	2.00	1.25
14	Brian Conacher	4.00	2.00	1.25
15	Jimmy Watson	4.00	2.00	1.25
16	Nick Libett	4.00	2.00	1.25
1	Real Lemieux	4.00	2.00	1.25
2	Ted Irvine	4.00	2.00	1.25
3	Bob Wall	4.00	2.00	1.25
4	Bill White	4.00	2.00	1.25
5	Gord Labossiere	4.00	2.00	1.25
6	Eddie Joyal	4.00	2.00	1.25
7	Lowell MacDonald	4.00	2.00	1.25
8	Bill Flett	4.00	2.00	1.25
9	Wayne Rutledge	4.00	2.00	1.25
10	Dave Amadio	4.00	2.00	1.25
11	Skip Krake	4.00	2.00	1.25
12	Doug Robinson	4.00	2.00	1.25
1	Wayne Connelly	4.00	2.00	1.25
2	Bob Woytowich	4.00	2.00	1.25
3	Andre Boudrias	4.00	2.00	1.25
4	Bill Goldsworthy	4.00	2.00	1.25
5	Cesare Maniago	4.00	2.00	1.25
6	Milan Marcetta	4.00	2.00	1.25
7A	Bill Collins	4.00	2.00	1.25
7B	Claude Larose	4.00	2.00	1.25
8	Parker MacDonald	4.00	2.00	1.25
9	Ray Cullen	4.00	2.00	1.25
10	Mike McMahon	4.00	2.00	1.25
11	Bob McCord	4.00	2.00	1.25
12	Larry Hillman	4.00	2.00	1.25
1	Gump Worsley	4.00	2.00	1.25
2	Rogatien Vachon	4.00	2.00	1.25
3	Ted Harris	4.00	2.00	1.25
4	Jacques Laperriere	4.00	2.00	1.25
5	J.C. Tremblay	4.00	2.00	1.25
6	Jean Beliveau	4.00	2.00	1.25
7	Gilles Tremblay	4.00	2.00	1.25
8	Ralph Backstrom	4.00	2.00	1.25
9	Bobby Rousseau	4.00	2.00	1.25
10	John Ferguson	4.00	2.00	1.25
11	Dick Duff	4.00	2.00	1.25
12	Terry Harper	4.00	2.00	1.25
13	Yvan Cournoyer	4.00	2.00	1.25
14	Jacques Lemaire	4.00	2.00	1.25
15	Henri Richard	4.00	2.00	1.25
16	Claude Provost	4.00	2.00	1.25
17	Serge Savard	4.00	2.00	1.25
18	Mickey Redmond	4.00	2.00	1.25
1	Rod Seiling	4.00	2.00	1.25
2	Jean Ratelle	4.00	2.00	1.25
3	Ed Giacomin	4.00	2.00	1.25
4	Reggie Fleming	4.00	2.00	1.25
5	Phil Goyette	4.00	2.00	1.25
6	Arnie Brown	4.00	2.00	1.25
7	Don Marshall	4.00	2.00	1.25
8	Orland Kurtenbach	4.00	2.00	1.25
9	Bob Nevin	4.00	2.00	1.25
10	Rod Gilbert	4.00	2.00	1.25
11	Harry Howell	4.00	2.00	1.25
12	Jim Neilson	4.00	2.00	1.25
13	Vic Hadfield	4.00	2.00	1.25
14	Larry Jeffrey	4.00	2.00	1.25
15	Dave Balon	4.00	2.00	1.25
16	Ron Stewart	4.00	2.00	1.25
1	Gerry Ehman	4.00	2.00	1.25
2	John Brenneman	4.00	2.00	1.25

3	Ted Hampson	4.00	2.00	1.25
4	Billy Harris	4.00	2.00	1.25
5A	George Swarbrick	4.00	2.00	1.25
5B	Carol Vadnais	4.00	2.00	1.25
6	Gary Smith	4.00	2.00	1.25
7	Charlie Hodge	4.00	2.00	1.25
8	Bert Marshall	4.00	2.00	1.25
9	Bill Hicke	4.00	2.00	1.25
10	Tracy Pratt	4.00	2.00	1.25
11	Gary Jarrett	4.00	2.00	1.25
12	Howie Young	4.00	2.00	1.25
1	Bernie Parent	4.00	2.00	1.25
2	John Miszuk	4.00	2.00	1.25
3A	Ed Hoekstra	4.00	2.00	1.25
3B	Allan Stanley	4.00	2.00	1.25
4	Gary Dornhoefer	4.00	2.00	1.25
5	Doug Favell	4.00	2.00	1.25
6	Andre Lacroix	4.00	2.00	1.25
7	Brit Selby	4.00	2.00	1.25
8	Don Blackburn	4.00	2.00	1.25
9	Leon Rochefort	4.00	2.00	1.25
10	Forbes Kennedy	4.00	2.00	1.25
11	Claude Laforge	4.00	2.00	1.25
12	Pat Hannigan	4.00	2.00	1.25
1	Ken Schinkel	4.00	2.00	1.25
2	Earl Ingarfield, Sr.	4.00	2.00	1.25
3	Val Fonteyne	4.00	2.00	1.25
4	Noel Price	4.00	2.00	1.25
5	Andy Bathgate	4.00	2.00	1.25
6	Les Binkley	4.00	2.00	1.25
7	Leo Boivin	4.00	2.00	1.25
8	Paul Andrea	4.00	2.00	1.25
9	Dunc McCallum	4.00	2.00	1.25
10	Keith McCrearty	4.00	2.00	1.25
11	Lou Angotti	4.00	2.00	1.25
12	Wally Boyer	4.00	2.00	1.25
1	Ron Schock	4.00	2.00	1.25
2	Bob Plager	4.00	2.00	1.25
3	Al Arbour	4.00	2.00	1.25
4	Red Berenson	4.00	2.00	1.25
5	Glenn Hall	4.00	2.00	1.25
6	Jim Roberts	4.00	2.00	1.25
7	Noel Picard	4.00	2.00	1.25
8	Barclay Plager	4.00	2.00	1.25
9	Larry Keenan	4.00	2.00	1.25
10	Terry Crisp	4.00	2.00	1.25
11	Gary Sabourin	4.00	2.00	1.25
12	Ab McDonald	4.00	2.00	1.25
1	George Armstrong	4.00	2.00	1.25
2	Wayne Carleton	4.00	2.00	1.25
3	Paul Henderson	4.00	2.00	1.25
4	Bob Pulford	4.00	2.00	1.25
5	Mike Walton	4.00	2.00	1.25
6	Johnny Bower	4.00	2.00	1.25
7	Ron Ellis	4.00	2.00	1.25
8	Mike Pelyk	4.00	2.00	1.25
9	Murray Oliver	4.00	2.00	1.25
10	Norm Ullman	4.00	2.00	1.25
11	Dave Keon	4.00	2.00	1.25
12	Floyd Smith	4.00	2.00	1.25
13	Marcel Pronovost	4.00	2.00	1.25
14	Tim Horton	4.00	2.00	1.25
15	Bruce Gamble	4.00	2.00	1.25
16	Jim McKenny	4.00	2.00	1.25
17	Mike Byers	4.00	2.00	1.25
18	Pierre Pilote	4.00	2.00	1.25

1984 7-11 Sticker Discs

These discs, which measure 2" in diameter, were produced by 7-Eleven. Each has adhesive backing and features a mug shot which alternates with a team logo when the disc is tilted. The player's name and number is incorporated into the colored border. The discs are unnumbered and are checklisted below alphabetically by team, then by player. A paper checklist sheet was also produced.

		MT	NM	EX
Complete Set (60):		65.00	49.00	26.00
Common Player:		1.00	.70	.40
1	Raymond Bourque	4.00	3.00	1.50
2	Rick Middleton	1.50	1.25	.60
3	Tom Barrasso	3.00	2.25	1.25
4	Gilbert Perreault	2.00	1.50	.80
5	Rejean Lemelin	1.00	.70	.40
6	Lanny McDonald	2.50	2.00	1.00
7	Paul Reinhart	1.00	.70	.40
8	Doug Risebrough	1.00	.70	.40
9	Denis Savard	2.50	2.00	1.00
10	Alan Secord	1.00	.70	.40
11	Dave Williams	1.25	.90	.50
12	Steve Yzerman	5.00	3.75	2.00
13	Glenn Anderson	1.50	1.25	.60
14	Paul Coffey	5.00	3.75	2.00
15	Wayne Gretzky	14.00	10.50	5.50
16	Charles Huddy	1.00	.70	.40
17	Pat Hughes	1.00	.70	.40
18	Jari Kurri	2.50	2.00	1.00
19	Kevin Lowe	1.25	.90	.50
20	Mark Messier	6.00	4.50	2.50
21	Ron Francis	2.00	1.50	.80
22	Sylvain Turgeon	1.25	.90	.50
23	Marcel Dionne	2.00	1.50	.80
24	David Taylor	1.25	.90	.50
25	Brian Bellows	1.50	1.25	.60
26	Dino Ciccarelli	1.50	1.25	.60
27	Harold Snepsts	1.25	.90	.50
28	Bob Gainey	2.00	1.50	.80
29	Larry Robinson	2.50	2.00	1.00
30	Mel Bridgman	1.00	.70	.40
31	Glenn Resch	1.50	1.25	.60
32	Mike Bossy	3.00	2.25	1.25
33	Bryan Trottier	2.50	2.00	1.00
34	Barry Beck	1.00	.70	.40
35	Donald Maloney	1.00	.70	.40
36	Tim Kerr	1.25	.90	.50
37	Darryl Sittler	2.50	2.00	1.00
38	Mike Bullard	1.00	.70	.40
39	Rick Kehoe	1.25	.90	.50
40	Michel Goulet	2.50	2.00	1.00
41	Peter Stastny	2.00	1.50	.80
42	Bernie Federko	1.50	1.25	.60
43	Rob Ramage	1.25	.90	.50
44	John Anderson	1.00	.70	.40
45	Bill Derlago	1.00	.70	.40
46	Gary Nylund	1.00	.70	.40
47	Richard Vaive	1.25	.90	.50
48	Richard Brodeur	1.25	.90	.50
49	Gary Lupul	1.00	.70	.40
50	Darcy Rota	1.00	.70	.40
51	Stanley Smyl	1.25	.90	.50
52	Tony Tanti	1.25	.90	.50
53	Michael Gartner	2.50	2.00	1.00
54	Rod Langway	1.50	1.25	.60
55	Scott Arniel	1.00	.70	.40
56	David Babych	1.25	.90	.50
57	Laurie Boschman	1.00	.70	.40
58	Dale Hawerchuk	1.50	1.25	.60
59	Paul MacLean	1.00	.70	.40
60	Brian Mullen	1.25	.90	.50

Chicagoland Processing Enviromint medallions

This company's medallions, featuring a wide variety of professional athletes and teams, are officially licensed by their respective entities (NBA, NHL, NFL). The one-troy ounce medallions are made from silver extracted from recycled film; the company has annually kept an estimated 12 million pounds of scrap from landfills. Bronze and 24k gold versions are also sometimes made; the 24k gold select medallions are pure silver medallions with an overlay of 24-karat gold on select areas.

Enviromint does not produce medallions from any non-precious metal material. Limited-edition medallions are created only to commemorate events or special occasions. This limits the variety of coins produced and makes them more valuable.

All Enviromint issues are individually numbered and accompanied by a certificate of authenticity. There are never any second editions. Once an edition is sold out (s/o), the original dies are retired from production. The company, located in Mt. Prospect, Ill., has been producing silver medallions since 1985.

In addition to football, basketball and hockey, Enviromint has minted medallions licensed by Major League Baseball, the National Collegiate Athletic Association, Paramount Pictures, Warner Bros., Winterland Productions, Carolco Licensing, Curtis Licensing, Determined Productions, MCA Records and Apple Records. Non-sport events commemorated by the company have included Batman's 50th anniversary, Star Trek's 25th anniversary and the history of the Beattles. The medallions generally have an initial release price of $29.95.

1994-95 National Basketball Association releases

Atlanta Hawks 1994 Central Division Champs regular and 24k

Boston Garden/Fleet Center Old/New 1995 regular and 24k

Boston Celtics Final Game at the Boston Garden 1995 regular and 24k

Boston Celtics/Boston Garden 1995 two-piece silver set and two-piece 24k set

Houston Rockets 1995 World Champions double clutch city, 24k and one-ounce gold

Houston Rockets 1995 World Champions three-piece proof set, three-piece silver set and three-piece 24k set

Houston Rockets 1994-95 two-piece Back-to-Back silver set and Back-to-Back 24k set

Houston Rockets 1995 Western Conference Champs regular and 24k

Houston Rockets 1994 World Champions regular, 24k and one-ounce gold

Houston Rockets 1994 World Champions three-piece set and three-piece 24k set

289

Medallions/discs

Houston Rockets 1994 World Champions/Hakeem Olajuwon MVP, two-piece set

Houston Rockets 1994 Western Conference Champs regular and 24k

Houston Rockets 1994 Midwestern Division Champs regular and 24k

New York Knicks 1994 Eastern Conference Champs regular and 24k

New York Knicks 1994 Atlantic Division Champs regular and 24k

Orlando Magic 1995 Eastern Conference Champs regular and 24k

Orlando Magic 1995 Eastern Conference Champs three-piece set

Seattle Supersonics 1994 Pacific Division Champs regular and 24k

Toronto Raptors New Franchise regular and 24k

Toronto Raptors Inaugural Season

Vancouver Grizzlies New Franchise regular and 24k

Raptors/Grizzlies two-piece silver set and 24k set

1995 NBA All-Star Game, Phoenix

All-NBA Team five-piece silver set and five-piece 24k set

1994 NBA releases

Medallion	Year	Mintage	Issue Price	Value
1994 NBA All-Star Game	1994	5,000	$29.95	$29.95
1994 USA Basketball	1994	team set silver (83/at $595/so) and 24k set		
		(17/at $875/so)		

1993 NBA releases

Medallion	Year	Mintage	Issue Price	Value
Chicago Bulls Consecutive Champs (three-piece set)	1993	1,000 s/o	$125	$175
Chicago Bulls World Champs (three-piece set)	1993	500	$125	$125
1993 Chicago Bulls NBA World Champs	1993	25,000	$29.95	$29.95
1993 Chicago Bulls NBA World Champs	1993	193	$849.95	$849.95
1993 Chicago Bulls Eastern Conference Champs	1993	10,000	$29.95	$29.95
1993 Chicago Bulls Central Division Champs	1993	5,000	$29.95	$29.95
1993 Houston Rockets Midwest Division Champs	1993	5,000	$29.95	$29.95
1993 NBA All-Star Game	1993	5,000	$29.95	$29.95
1994 NBA All-Star Game - Minnesota Timberwolves	1993	5,000	$29.95	$29.95
1993 New York Knicks Atlantic Division Champs	1993	42	$29.95	$75
1993 Phoenix Suns Western Conference Champs	1993	10,000	$29.95	$29.95
1993 Phoenix Suns Pacific Division Champs	1993	5,000	$29.95	$29.95
1993 USA Basketball Team	Undetermined			

1992 NBA releases

Medallion	Year	Mintage	Issue Price	Value
All 27 NBA basic team commemoratives	1992	1,000 each	$29.95	$29.95
Atlanta Hawks 25th Anniversary	1992	5,000	$29.95	$29.95
Basketball Tournament of Americas	1992	5,000	$29.95	$29.95
1992 Boston Celtics Atlantic Division Champs	1992	5,000	$29.95	$29.95
1992 Chicago Bulls NBA World Championship	1992	25,000	$29.95	$29.95
1992 Chicago Bulls Central Division Champs	1992	1,053 s/o	$29.95	$39.95

1992 Chicago Bulls Eastern Conference Champs	1992	1,543 s/o	$29.95	$39.95
Chicago Bulls Back-to-Back Champs	1992	1,000	$82.95	$82.95
Complete Eastern/Western Conference (27-piece matched set)	1992	100	$899	$899
Denver Nuggets 25th Anniversary	1992	5,000	$29.95	$29.95
Indiana Pacers 25th Anniversary	1992	5,000	$29.95	$29.95
1992 NBA All-Star Game	1992	10,000	$29.95	$29.95
Phoenix Suns 25th Anniversary	1992	5,000	$29.95	$29.95
1992 Portland Trailblazers Western Conference Champs	1992	10,000	$29.95	$29.95
1992 Portland Trailblazers Pacific Division Champs	1992	5,000	$29.95	$29.95
Seattle Supersonics 25th Anniversary	1992	xxx	$29.95	$29.95
USA Basketball (10-coin set)	1992	250 s/o	$425	$495
USA Basketball (12-coin set)	1992	750 s/o	$510	$695
USA Basketball (two 6-piece sets)	1992	475 s/o	$515	$595
1992 Utah Jazz Midwest Division	1992	5,000	$29.95	$29.95
1992 World Championship (three-piece set)	1992	500	$125	$125

1991 NBA releases

Medallion	Year	Mintage	Issue Price	Value
1991 Chicago Bulls NBA World Championship	1991	25,000	$29.95	$29.95
1991 Chicago Bulls Central Division Champs	1991	1,500 s/o	$29.95	$35
1991 Chicago Bulls Eastern Conference Champs	1991	1,500 s/o	$29.95	$49
Chicago Bulls 25th Anniversary	1991	5,000	$29.95	$29.95

NBA Players

Medallion	Year	Mintage	Issue Price	Value
Charles Barkley - 1993 NBA MVP	1993	15,000	$29.95	$29.95
USA Charles Barkley	1992	$2,750 s/o	$29.95	$49.95
USA Larry Bird	1992	5,150 s/o	$29.95	$60

Medallions/discs

USA Derrick Coleman	1994	silver (45 s/o) and 24k (5 at $49.95 each, s/o)		
Derrick Coleman - 1991 Rookie of the Year	1992	15,000	$29.95	$29.95
Clyde Drexler - 1995 Houston Rockets regular and 24k				
USA Clyde Drexler	1992	2,950 s/o	$29.95	$45
USA Joe Dumars	1994	silver (45 s/o) and 24k (5 at $49.95 each, s/o)		
Patrick Ewing - New York Knicks	1995	regular and 24k		
USA Patrick Ewing	1992	2,500 s/o	$29.95	$49.95
Anfernee Hardaway	1995	All-NBA Team regular and 24k		
USA Tim Hardaway	1994	silver (95 s/o) and 24k (5 at $49.95 each, s/o)		
Grant Hill/Jason Kidd	1995	two-piece silver rookie set and two-piece 24k rookie set		
Grant Hill -1995 co-rookie of the year regular and 24k				
USA Kevin Johnson	1994	silver (75 s/o) and 24k (20 at $49.95 each, s/o)		
USA Larry Johnson	1994	silver (55 s/o) and 24k (20 at $49.95 each, s/o)		
Larry Johnson - 1992 Rookie of the Year	1992	15,000	$29.95	$29.95
USA Magic Johnson	1992	5,000 s/o	$29.95	$55
Magic Johnson - All-Time Assists	1991	3,583	$29.95	$29.95
USA Michael Jordan	1992	7,500 s/o	$29.95	$75
Michael Jordan - 1992 MVP	1992	3,905 s/o	$29.95	$85
Michael Jordan - 1991 MVP	1991	13,299 s/o	$29.95	$75
USA Shawn Kemp	1994	silver (60 s/o) and 24k (14 at $49.95 each, s/o)		
Jason Kidd - 1995 co-rookie of the year regular and 24k				
USA Christian Laettner	1992	2,600 s/o	$29.95	$32.50
Jim Les - 3-Point Field Goal Percentage	1991	15,000	$29.95	$29.95
USA Dan Majerle	1994	silver (76 s/o) and 24k (30 at $49.95 each, s/o)		
Karl Malone -1995 All-NBA Team regular and 24k				
USA Karl Malone	1992	2,450 s/o	$29.95	$49.95
Reggie Miller - Indiana Pacers	1995	regular and 24k		
USA Reggie Miller	1994	silver (75 s/o) and 24k (20 at $49.95 each, s/o)		
Reggie Miller-Free Throw Percentage	1991	15,000	$29.95	$29.95
USA Chris Mullin	1992	2,500 s/o	$29.95	$42.50
USA Alonzo Mourning	1994	silver (55 s/o) and 24k (20 at $49.95 each, s/o)		
Hakeem Olajuwon - 1994 NBA MVP	1994	regular and 24k (125 at $49.95 each, now $65 and s/o)		
Hakeem Olajuwon - Blocked Shots	1992	144 (s/o)	$29.95	$125
USA Shaquille O'Neal	1994	silver (507 s/o) and 24k (215 at $49.95 each, s/o)		
Shaquille O'Neal - 1992 1st Round Draft Pick	1993	15,000	$29.95	$29.95
Shaquille O'Neal/Chris Webber (two-piece set)	1993	1,000	$82.95	$82.95
Scottie Pippen - All-NBA Team	1995	regular and 24k		
USA Scottie Pippen	1992	3,100 s/o	$29.95	$49.95
USA Mark Price	1994	silver (74 s/o) and 24k (5 at $49.95 each, s/o)		
David Robinson - All-NBA Team regular and 24k				

David Robinson - San Antonio Spurs	1994	regular		
USA David Robinson	1992	2,750 s/o	$29.95	$49.95
David Robinson - Rebounding Champ	1991	15,000 s/o	$29.95	$39.50
Glenn Robinson - Milwaukee Bucks	1995	two-piece silver set and two-piece 24k set		
Glenn Robinson - 1994 1st Round Draft Pick	1994	regular and 24k		
USA Steve Smith	1994	silver (45 s/o) and 24k (5 at $49.95 each, s/o)		
John Stockton - NBA Assists All-Time Leader	1995	regular and 24k		
John Stockton - All-NBA Team	1995	regular and 24k		
John Stockton - 1994 NBA Assists	1994	75 (s/o)	$29.95	
USA John Stockton	1992	2,500 s/o	$29.95	$42.50
John Stockton - Assists	1992	15,000	$29.95	$29.95
Isiah Thomas	1994	silver (45 s/o) and 24k (20 at $49.95 each, s/o)		
Chris Webber - Washington Bullets	1994	regular		
Chris Webber - 1993 1st Round Draft Pick	1993	1,255 (s/o)	$29.95	$29.95
Buck Williams - Field Goal Percentage	1991	15,000	$29.95	$29.95
USA Dominique Wilkins	1994	silver (50 s/o) and 24k (5 at $49.95 each, s/o)		

National Hockey League 1994-95 releases

Boston Bruins Final Game at the Boston Garden	1995	regular and 24k
Boston Bruins/Boston Garden	1995	two-piece silver and two-piece 24k
Detroit Red Wings 1995 Western Conference Champs	1995	regular and 24k
Detroit Red Wings 1995 Western Conference Champs	1995	three-piece set
New Jersey Devils 1995 Eastern Conference Champs	1995	regular and 24k
New Jersey Devils 1995 Eastern Conference Champs	1995	three-piece proof set
New Jersey Devils 1995 Stanley Cup Champs	1995	regular, 24k and one-ounce
New Jersey Devils 1995 Stanley Cup Champs	1995	three-piece proof set, three-piece regular and three-piece 24k

Medallions/discs

1994 NHL releases

Calgary Flames 1994 Pacific Division Champs	1994	regular and 24k
Detroit Red Wings 1994 Central Division Champs	1994	regular and 24k
New York Rangers 1994 Atlantic Division Champs	1994	regular and 24k
New York Rangers 1994 Eastern Conference Champs	1994	regular and 24k
New York Rangers 1994 Stanley Cup Champs	1994	regular, 24k and one-ounce gold
New York Rangers 1994 Stanley Cup Champs	1994	three-piece regular set and three-piece 24k set
Opening Night - Fleet Center (Boston Bruins)	1994	regular and 24k
Pittsburgh Penguins Northeast Division Champs	1994	regular and 24k
St. Louis Blues - Kiel Center Inaugural Season 1994-95	1994	regular
Vancouver Canucks 1994 Western Conference Champs	1994	regular and 24k

1993 NHL releases

Medallion	Year	Mintage	Issue Price	Value
1993 Adams Division Playoff Champion Montreal Canadiens	1993	5,000	$29.95	$29.95
1993 Adams Division - Boston Bruins	1993	5,000	$29.95	$29.95
1993 Campbell Conference - Los Angeles Kings	1993	10,000	$29.95	$29.95
Dallas Stars Inaugural	1993	5,000	$29.95	$29.95
Ducks/Panthers Inaugural (two-piece set)	1993	500	$82.95	$82.95
Florida Panthers - Inaugural Season	1993	1,500	$29.95	$29.95
Mighty Ducks of Anaheim - Inaugural Season	1993	1,500 s/o	$29.95	$55
NHL 45th New York Rangers All-Star Game	1993	5,000	$29.95	$29.95
NHL 44th Montreal Canadiens All-Star Game	1993	5,000	$29.95	$29.95
1993 Norris Division Playoff Champion Toronto Maple Leafs	1993	5,000	$29.95	$29.95
1993 Norris Division - Chicago Blackhawks	1993	5,000	$29.95	$29.95
1993 Patrick Division Playoff Champion New York Islanders	1993	5,000	$29.95	$29.95
1993 Patrick Division - Pittsburgh Penguins	1993	211 (s/o)	$29.95	xxx
San Jose Sharks New Arena Inaugural	1993	5,000	$29.95	$29.95
1993 Smythe Division Playoff Champion Los Angeles Kings	1993	5,000	$29.95	$29.95
1993 Smythe Division - Vancouver Canucks	1993	5,000	$29.95	$29.95
1993 Stanley Cup - Montreal Canadiens	1993	25,000	$29.95	$29.95
1993 Stanley Cup set (three-pieces)	1993	500	$125	$125
1993 Stanley Cup Centennial	1993	500	$125	$125
1993 Wales Conference - Montreal Canadiens	1993	10,000	$29.95	$29.95

1992 NHL releases

Medallion	Year	Mintage	Issue Price	Value
All 24 NHL basic team commemoratives	1992	1,000 each	$29.95	$29.95
Complete Wales/Campbell Conference (24-piece set)	1992	100	$899	$899
1992 Adams Division - Montreal Canadiens	1992	5,000	$29.95	$29.95
1992 Campbell Conference - Chicago Blackhawks	1992	10,000	$29.95	$29.95
1992 Norris Division - Detroit Red Wings	1992	31 (s/o)	$29.95	$55
Ottawa Senators - Inaugural	1992	5,000	$29.95	$29.95
1992 Patrick Division - New York Rangers	1992	366 (s/o)	$29.95	xxx
Pittsburgh Penguins Back-to-Back Champs (two piece set)	1992	1,000	$82.95	$82.95

Medallion	Year	Mintage	Issue Price	Value
Pittsburgh Penguins 25th Anniversary	1992	5,000	$29.95	$29.95
1992 Smythe Division - Vancouver Canucks	1992	378 s/o	$29.95	$55
1992 Stanley Cup set (three-pieces)	1992	500	$29.95	$29.95
1992 Stanley Cup - Pittsburgh Penguins	1992	25,000	$29.95	$29.95
St. Louis Blues 25th Anniversary	1992	5,000	$29.95	$29.95
Tampa Bay Lightning - Inaugural	1992	5,000	$29.95	$29.95
1992 Wales Conference - Pittsburgh Penguins	1992	10,000	$29.95	$29.95

1991 NHL releases

Medallion	Year	Mintage	Issue Price	Value
1991 Adams Division - Boston Bruins	1991	300 s/o	$29.95	$75
1991 Campbell Conference - Minnesota North Stars	1991	800 s/o	$29.95	$29.95
Labatt-Coupe Canada Cup - Canada	1991	10,000 s/o	$29.95	$50
Labatt-Coupe Canada Cup - Czechoslovakia	1991	1,000 s/o	$29.95	$50
Labatt-Coupe Canada Cup - Finland	1991	1,000 s/o	$29.95	$50
Labatt-Coupe Canada Cup - Sweden	1991	1,000 s/o	$29.95	$50
Labatt-Coupe Canada Cup - United States	1991	10,000	$29.95	$29.95
Labatt-Coupe Canada Cup - U.S.S.R.	1991	1,000 s/o	$29.95	$100
Los Angeles Kings 25th Anniversary	1991	5,000	$29.95	$29.95
NHL 43rd Philadelphia Flyers All-Star Game	1991	xxx	$29.95	$29.95
1991 Norris Division Playoffs - Minnesota North Stars	1991	900	$29.95	$29.95
1991 Norris Division - Chicago Blackhawks	1991	300 s/o	$29.95	$75
1991 Patrick Division - Pittsburgh Penguins	1991	3,525 s/o	$29.95	$55
San Jose Sharks Inaugural Year	1991	10,000	$29.95	$29.95
1991 Smythe Division - Los Angeles Kings	1991	5,000	$29.95	$29.95
1991 Stanley Cup - Pittsburgh Penguins	1991	25,000	$29.95	$29.95
1991 Wales Conference - Pittsburgh Penguins	1991	3,000 s/o	$29.95	$55

1990 NHL releases

Medallion	Year	Mintage	Issue Price	Value
NHL 42nd Chicago Blackhawks All-Star Game	1990	1,500 s/o	$29.95	$49.50
1990 Norris Division - Chicago Blackhawks	1990	500 s/o	$29.95	$60
1990 Patrick Division - New York Rangers	1990	300 s/o	$29.95	$55
1990 Stanley Cup - Edmonton Oilers	1990	5,000	$29.95	$29.95

1989 NHL releases

Medallion	Year	Mintage	Issue Price	Value
1989 Campbell Conference - Calgary Flames	1989	5,000 s/o	$29.95	$75
NHL 41st Annual All-Star Game	1989	500 s/o	$29.95	$49.50
1989 Stanley Cup - Calgary Flames	1989	5,000 s/o	$29.95	$29.95
1989 Wales Conference - Montreal Canadiens	1989	300 s/o	$29.95	$75

1988 NHL releases

Medallion	Year	Mintage	Issue Price	Value
1988 Campbell Conference - Edmonton Oilers	1988	300 s/o	$29.95	$70
1988 Norris Division - Detroit Red Wings	1988	400 s/o	$29.95	$60

Medallions/discs

1988 Patrick Division - New Jersey Devils	1988	500 s/o	$29.95	$50
1988 Stanley Cup - Edmonton Oilers	1988	5,000	$29.95	$29.95
1988 Wales Conference - Boston Bruins	1988	300 s/o	$29.95	$55

NHL Players

Medallion	Year	Mintage	Issue Price	Value
Dave Andreychuk - Toronto Maple Leafs	1995	regular, 24k and bronze		
Ed Belfour - Chicago Blackhawks	1995	24k gold select set (500)		
Ed Belfour - Vezina and Calder trophies	1991	5,000	$29.95	$29.95
Ray Bourque - Boston Bruins	1995	24k gold select set (500)		
Ray Bourque - Norris Trophy	1991	5,000	$29.95	$29.95
Pavel Bure - Vancouver Canucks	1994	24k gold select set (125 at $49.95 each, s/o)		
Pavel Bure - Vancouver Canucks	1992	5,000	$29.95	$29.95
Guy Charbonneau - Montreal Canadians	1993	5,000	$29.95	$29.95
Chris Chelios - Chicago Blackhawks	1995	regular, 24k and bronze		
Wendel Clark - Toronto Maple Leafs	1995	regular, 24k and bronze		
Paul Coffey - Detroit Red Wings	1995	regular		
Paul Coffey - Detroit Red Wings	1995	24k gold select set (500)		
Paul Coffey - Los Angeles Kings	1992	4,250	$29.95	$29.95
Paul Coffey - Leading Defenseman, Penguins	1991	750 s/o	$29.95	$55
Sergei Fedorov - Detroit Red Wings	1995	regular, 24k and bronze		
Grant Fuhr - Toronto Maple Leafs	1995	24k gold select set (500)		
Grant Fuhr - Vezina Trophy	1992	5,000	$29.95	$29.95
Doug Gilmour - Toronto Maple Leafs	1995	24k gold select set (500)		
Doug Gilmour - Toronto Maple Leafs, Most Goals	1993	5,000	$29.95	$29.95
Wayne Gretzky - All-Time Goals	1994	one-ounce silver (25,000), one-ounce gold (199) and 1/4-ounce gold (1,851)		
Wayne Gretzky - All-Time Goals	1994	24k gold select (5,000), bronze (50,000)		
Wayne Gretzky - All-Time Goals	1994	two-piece set (802)		
Wayne Gretzky - All-Time Goals	1994	three-piece set (999)		
Wayne Gretzky - All-Time Goals	1994	1/2-pound (1,851)		
Wayne Gretzky - All-Time Points	1994	regular and one-ounce pure gold (99)		
Wayne Gretzky - Canadian Edition	1989	18,510 s/o	$29.95	$85
Wayne Gretzky - Domestic Edition	1989	10,893 s/o	$29.95	$55
Brett Hull/Bobby Hull	1995	24k gold select (500)		
Brett Hull/Bobby Hull - Father/Son Commemorative	1991	15,000	$29.95	$29.95
Jaromir Jagr - Pittsburgh Penguins	1995	24k gold select (500)		
Jaromir Jagr - Pittsburgh Penguins	1992	5,000	$29.95	$29.95
Jari Kurri - Los Angeles Kings	1995	regular, 24k and bronze		
Pat LaFontaine - New York Islanders	1993	5,000	$29.95	$29.95
Steve Larmer - New York Rangers	1995	regular and 24k gold select (500)		
Steve Larmer - Chicago Blackhawks	1992	5,000	$29.95	$29.95
Brian Leetch - New York Rangers	1994	regular, 24k (125 at $49.95, now $65 and s/o) and bronze		
Brian Leetch - 1994 Conn Smythe Trophy	1994	24k and bronze		
Mario Lemieux - 1992 Conn Smythe Trophy	1992	5,000	$29.95	$29.95
Mario Lemieux - 1992 Conn Smythe Trophy		heirloom 24k		
Mario Lemieux - Conn Smythe Trophy	1991	5,000 s/o	$29.95	$60
Mario Lemieux - 1991 Conn Smythe Trophy		heirloom 24k		

Eric Lindros - Philadelphia Flyers	1994	regular, 24k (125 at $49.95 each, s/o) and bronze		
Al MacInnis - Calgary Flames, Norris Trophy	1993	5,000	$29.95	$29.95
Mark Messier - New York Rangers	1995	24k (500)		
Mark Messier - Hart, Conn, Smythe, Pearson	1992	5,000	$29.95	$29.95
Adam Oates - Boston Bruins	1995	regular, 24k and bronze		
Felix Potvin - Toronto Maple Leafs	1994	regular, 24k (125 at $49.95 each, now and s/o) and bronze		$55
Mike Richter - New York Rangers	1995	regular, 24k and bronze		
Luc Robitaille - Los Angeles Kings	1993	5,000	$29.95	$29.95
Patrick Roy - Montreal Canadiens	1994	24k gold select (125 at $49.95 each, s/o)		
Patrick Roy - 1993 Conn Smythe Trophy	1993	5,000	$29.95	$29.95
Patrick Roy - Montreal Canadiens	1992	5,000	$29.95	$29.95
Joe Sakic - Quebec Nordiques	1995	24k gold select (500)		
Joe Sakic - Quebec Nordiques, Team Scoring	1993	5,000	$29.95	$29.95
Teemu Selanne - Winnipeg Jets	1995	24k gold select (500)		
Teemu Selanne - 1993 Calder Trophy	1993	5,000	$29.95	$29.95
John Vanbiesbrouck - Florida Panthers	1995	regular, 24k and bronze		
Steve Yzerman - Detroit Red Wings	1995	24k gold select (500)		
Steve Yzerman - Detroit Red Wings	1992	5,000	$29.95	$29.95

National Football League 1994-95 releases

Buffalo Bills 35th Anniversary regular and 24k (100 at $135 each, s/o)

Carolina Panthers Inaugural Season regular and 24k

Carolina Panthers flip coin 24k

Chicago Bears coin-art regular and 24k

Chicago Bears Super Bowl XX Champs heirloom

Chicago Bears Super Bowl XX/Walter Payton Rushing Record two-piece heirloom 24k set

Chicago Bears 75th Anniversary regular and 24k

Chicago Bears/Mike Ditka/Walter Payton three-piece 24k gold set

Medallions/discs

Dallas Cowboys 1994 NFC Eastern Division regular and 24k

Green Bay Packers 1994 NFC Wild Card regular and 24k

Jacksonville Jaguars coin-art regular and 24k

Jacksonville Jaguars Inaugural Season regular and 24k

Jacksonville Jaguars flip coin 24k

Jacksonville Jaguars Franchise/new logo

Jaguars/Panthers inaugural season two-piece silver set and two-piece 24k set

Jaguars/Panthers flip coin 24k

Jaguars/Panthers matched two-piece set

New Jaguars/Panthers matched two-piece set

Miami Dolphins 1994 AFC Eastern Division regular and 24k

Minnesota Vikings 1994 NFC Central Division regular and 24k

Monday Night Football 25th Anniversary regular and 24k

Pittsburgh Steelers 1994 AFC Central Division regular and 24k

San Diego Chargers AFC/Super Bowl XXIX two-piece regular set and two-piece 24k set

San Diego Chargers 1994 AFC Champions regular and 24k (1,000 at $49.95 each, s/o)

San Diego Chargers 1994 AFC Western Division regular and 24k

San Francisco 49ers NFC/Super Bowl XXIX two-piece regular set and two-piece 24k set

San Francisco 49ers 1994 NFC Champions regular and 24k

San Francisco 49ers 1994 NFC Western Division regular and 24k

Super Bowl XXIX/Joe Robbie Stadium commemorative regular and 24k

Super Bowl XXIX Champions - San Francisco 49ers regular, 24k and one-ounce

Super Bowl XXIX Champions - San Francisco 49ers three-piece set regular and three-piece 24k set

Super Bowl XXVIII Champions - Dallas Cowboys three-piece set (500)

Super Bowl XXVIII Champions - Dallas Cowboys regular, one-ounce gold (194) and 24k gold select

1993 NFL releases

Medallion	Year	Mintage	Issue Price	Value
Buffalo Bills 1993 AFC Champions	1993	xxx	xxx	xxx
Buffalo Bills 1993 AFC Western Division	1993	xxx	xxx	xxx
Carolina Panthers Franchise	1993	xxx	$29.95	$29.95
Dallas Cowboys Super Bowl XXVII Champs	1993	25,000	$29.95	$29.95
Dallas Cowboys 1993 NFC Champions	1993	xxx	xxx	xxx
Dallas Cowboys 1993 NFC Eastern Division	1993	265 s/o	$29.95	xxx
Detroit Lions 1993 NFC Central Division	1993	xxx	xxx	xxx
Green Bay Packers 75th Anniversary	1993	5,000	$29.95	$29.95
Green Bay Packers/Bart Starr (two-piece set)	1993	500 s/o	$82.95	$82.95
Houston Oilers 1993 AFC Eastern Division	1993	xxx	xxx	xxx
Jacksonville Jaguars Franchise	1993	1,922 s/o	$29.95	$29.95
Kansas City Chiefs 1993 AFC Western Division	1993	xxx	xxx	xxx
San Francisco 49ers 1993 NFC Western Division	1993	89 s/o	$29.95	xxx
Super Bowl XXVII (three-piece set)	1993	500	$125	$125

1992 NFL releases

Medallion	Year	Mintage	Issue Price	Value
All 28 NFL basic team commemoratives	1992	1,000 each	$29.95	$29.95
Complete 28-piece AFC/NFC matched set	1992	100	$899	$899
100th Anniversary of Professional Football	1992	1,000	$29.95	$29.95
1992 Buffalo Bills AFC Champions	1992	2,050 s/o	$29.95	$35
1992 Dallas Cowboys NFC Champions	1992	1,644 s/o	$29.95	$35
1992 Dallas Cowboys NFC Eastern Division	1992	499 s/o	$29.95	$45
1992 Miami Dolphins AFC Eastern Division	1992	180 s/o	$29.95	xxx
1992 Minnesota Vikings NFC Central Division	1992	139 s/o	$29.95	xxx
1992 Pittsburgh Steelers AFC Central Division	1992	330 s/o	$29.95	$35
1992 San Diego Chargers AFC Western Division	1992	574 s/o	$29.95	xxx
1992 San Francisco 49ers NFC Western Division	1992	118 s/o	$29.95	$55
1992 Washington Redskins NFC Champions	1992	10,000	$29.95	$29.95

1991 NFL releases

Medallion	Year	Mintage	Issue Price	Value
1991 Buffalo Bills AFC Champions	1991	10,000 s/o	$29.95	$55
1991 Buffalo Bills AFC Eastern Division	1991	5,000 s/o	$29.95	$40
1991 Denver Broncos AFC Western Division	1991	5,000	$29.95	$29.95
1991 Detroit Lions NFC Central Division	1991	5,000	$29.95	$29.95
1991 Houston Oilers AFC Central Division	1991	300 s/o	$29.95	xxx
1991 New Orleans Saints NFC Western Division	1991	5,000	$29.95	$29.95
1991 Washington Redskins NFC Eastern Division	1991	5,000	$29.95	$29.95
Washington Redskins Super Bowl XXVI Champs	1991	25,000	$29.95	$29.95

1990 NFL releases

Medallion	Year	Mintage	Issue Price	Value
1990 Buffalo Bills AFC Champions	1990	2,800 s/o	$29.95	$85
1990 Buffalo Bills AFC East Division	1990	1,400 s/o	$29.95	$65
1990 Chicago Bears NFC Central Division	1990	5,000 s/o	$29.95	$50
Chicago Bears 70th Anniversary	1990	7,500 s/o	$29.95	$34.95
1990 Cincinnati Bengals AFC Central Division	1990	5,000	$29.95	$29.95
1990 Los Angeles Raiders AFC Western Division	1990	5,000	$29.95	$29.95
New York Giants Super Bowl XXV Champions	1990	10,000	$29.95	$29.95
1990 New York Giants 1990 NFC Champions	1990	1,400 s/o	$29.95	$50
1990 New York Giants NFC Eastern Division	1990	5,000	$29.95	$29.95
1990 San Francisco 49ers NFC Western Division	1990	5,000 s/o	$29.95	$45

1989 NFL releases

Medallion	Year	Mintage	Issue Price	Value
1989 Buffalo Bills AFC Eastern Division	1989	2,000 s/o	$29.95	$225
1989 Cleveland Browns AFC Central Division	1989	3,400 s/o	$29.95	$50
1989 Denver Broncos AFC Champions	1989	10,000 s/o	$29.95	$29.95

Medallions/discs

1989 Denver Broncos AFC Western Division	1989	5,000 s/o	$29.95	$29.95
1989 Minnesota Vikings NFC Central Division	1989	5,000 s/o	$29.95	$29.95
1989 New York Giants NFC Eastern Division	1989	5,000 s/o	$29.95	$34.50
San Francisco 49ers Super Bowl XXIV Champions	1989	10,000	$29.95	$29.95
1989 San Francisco 49ers NFC Champions	1989	10,000 s/o	$29.95	$45
1989 San Francisco 49ers NFC Western Division	1989	5,000 s/o	$29.95	$45

1988 NFL releases

Medallion	Year	Mintage	Issue Price	Value
1988 Buffalo Bills AFC Eastern Division	1988	1,800 s/o	$29.95	$350
1988 Chicago Bears NFC Central Division	1988	900 s/o	$29.95	$75
1988 Cincinnati Bengals AFC Champions	1988	1,400 s/o	$29.95	$40
1988 Cincinnati Bengals AFC Central Division	1988	900 s/o	$29.95	$55
1988 Philadelphia Eagles NFC Eastern Division	1988	300	$29.95	$70
San Francisco 49ers Super Bowl XXIII Champions	1988	10,000	xxx	xxx
1988 San Francisco 49ers NFC Champions	1988	1,300 s/o	$29.95	$55
1988 San Francisco 49ers NFC Western Division	1988	100 s/o	$29.95	$150
1988 Seattle Seahawks AFC Western Division	1988	700 s/o	$29.95	$65

1987 NFL releases

Medallion	Year	Mintage	Issue Price	Value
1987 Chicago Bears NFC Central Division	1987	500 s/o	$29.95	$75
1987 Cleveland Browns AFC Central Division	1987	2,400 s/o	$29.95	$75
1987 Denver Broncos AFC Champions	1987	3,100 s/o	$29.95	$35
1987 Denver Broncos AFC Western Division	1987	900 s/o	$29.95	$75
Houston Oilers 1987 AFC Playoff Wild Card	1987	100 s/o	$29.95	$225
1987 Indianapolis Colts AFC Eastern Division	1987	700 s/o	$29.95	$50
Minnesota Vikings 1987 NFC Playoff Wild Card	1987	1,300	$29.95	$40
New Orleans Saints 1987 NFC Playoff Wild Card	1987	500 s/o	$29.95	$55
1987 San Francisco 49ers NFC Western Division	1987	500 s/o	$29.95	$55
Seattle Seahawks 1987 AFC Playoff Wild Card	1987	100 s/o	$29.95	$250
Washington Redskins Super Bowl XXII Champs	1987	7,200	$29.95	$29.95
1987 Washington Redskins NFC Champions	1987	2,000 s/o	$29.95	$45
1987 Washington Redskins NFC Eastern Division	1987	1,500	$29.95	$45

1986 NFL releases

Medallion	Year	Mintage	Issue Price	Value
1986 Cleveland Browns AFC Central Division	1986	4,450 s/o	$29.95	$50
Dallas Cowboys NFL Champs 1971 and 1977	1986	1,200 s/o	$29.95	$45
1986 Denver Broncos AFC Champions	1986	4,250	$29.95	$50
New York Giants Super Bowl XXI Champions	1986	10,000 s/o	$29.95	$55
1986 New York Giants NFC Champions	1986	4,500	$29.95	$45
Pittsburgh Steelers Super Bowls IX, X, XIII and XIV	1986	800 s/o	$29.95	$175
Washington Redskins 50th Anniversary	1986	586 s/o	$29.95	$250

1985 NFL releases

Medallion	Year	Mintage	Issue Price	Value
Chicago Bears Super Bowl XX Champions	1985	8,918	$29.95	$125
1985 Chicago Bears NFC Champions	1985	7,000 s/o	$29.95	$55
1985 New England Patriots AFC Champions	1985	4,000 s/o	$29.95	$45

NFL Players

Medallion	Year	Mintage	Issue Price	Value
Troy Aikman - Dallas Cowboys	1992	2,386 s/o	$29.95	$40
Troy Aikman - Dallas Cowboys (#2) and 24k				
Marcus Allen - Kansas City Chiefs regular and 24k				
Jerome Bettis - Los Angeles Rams regular and 24k				
Mark Carrier - 1990 Defensive Rookie of the Year		35 s/o	$29.95	$45
Randall Cunningham - Philadelphia Eagles regular and 24k				
Mike Ditka - 1988 NFL Hall of Fame	1988	15,000	$29.95	$29.95
Mike Ditka - Chicago Bears regular				
John Elway - Denver Broncos	1992	1,144 s/o	$29.95	$40
John Elway - Denver Broncos (#2) regular and 24k				
Boomer Esiason - New York Jets	1993	30 s/o	$29.95	$65
Boomer Esiason - Cincinnati Bengals	1990	624 s/o	$29.95	$50
Brett Favre - Green Bay Packers regular and 24k				
Brett Favre, Sterling Sharpe, Reggie White three-piece silver set (100 s/o at $125) and three-piece 24k set				
Dan Hampton - 4-Time Pro Bowl	1990	1,551	$29.95	$35
Michael Irvin - Dallas Cowboys	1992	1,393 s/o	$29.95	$35
Michael Irvin - Dallas Cowboys (#2) regular				
Bo Jackson - Baseball/Football	1990	15,000 s/o	$29.95	$29.95
Jim Kelly - Buffalo Bills	1992	1,640 s/o	$29.95	$40
Jim Kelly - Buffalo Bills (#2) regular and 24k				
Jim Kelly/Buffalo Bills 35th Anniversary two-piece silver set and two-piece 24k set				
Bernie Kosar - Cleveland Browns	1990	1,065 s/o	$29.95	$40
Bernie Kosar - Miami Dolphins regular				
Tom Landry	1988	4,083 s/o	$29.95	xxx
Vince Lombardi - 1971 NFL Hall of Fame	1987	2,535 s/o	$29.95	$50
Dan Marino - Miami Dolphins	1992	1,710 s/o	$29.95	$40
Dan Marino - Miami Dolphins (#2) regular and 24k				
Art Monk - All-Time NFL Receptions	1992	1,178 s/o	$29.95	$35
Joe Montana - Retirement regular and 24k				
Joe Montana - Retirement two-piece card and coin set				
Joe Montana - Retirement one-ounce gold				
Joe Montana - Kansas City Chiefs	1993	7,000	$29.95	$29.95
Joe Montana - Kansas City Chiefs (#2) 1994 regular and 24k				
Joe Montana - K.C. 1-ounce pure gold	1993	100	$850	$850
Joe Montana - card/medallion (two-piece set)	1993	367	$120	$120

Medallions/discs

Joe Montana - Player of the Decade, 49ers	1990	8,000 s/o	$29.95	$65
Joe Montana/Marcus Allen two-piece silver set and two-piece 24k set				
Warren Moon - Minnesota Vikings regular and 24k				
Warren Moon - 1991 AFC Player of the Year	1991	702 s/o	$29.95	$55
Neil O'Donnell -Pittsburgh Steelers regular				
Walter Payton two-piece matched set				
Walter Payton 24k gold select				
Walter Payton - 1993 Hall of Fame	1993	16,726	$39.95	$34.95
Walter Payton - 1993 Hall of Fame Gold	1993	110	$850	$850
Walter Payton - All-Time Leading Rusher	1987	16,726 s/o	$29.95	$45
Walter Payton - commemorative card set	1987	16,726 s/o	$34.34	$65
Jerry Rice - 101 Touchdowns	1992	336 s/o	$29.95	$60
Jerry Rice - San Francisco 49ers/127 touchdowns regular (900 s/o) and 24k				
Jerry Rice/Steve Young two-piece silver set and two-piece 24k set				
Barry Sanders - 1989 Rookie of the Year	1992	1,307 s/o	$29.95	$40
Barry Sanders - Detroit Lions (#2) regular and 24k				
Deion Sanders - San Francisco 49ers regular and 24k				
Sterling Sharpe - Green Bay Packers regular and 24k				
Mike Singletary - Retirement	1992	681 s/o	$29.95	$45
Emmitt Smith - Dallas Cowboys	1992	2,191 s/o	$29.95	$40
Emmitt Smith - Dallas Cowboys (#2) regular (900 s/o) and 24k				
Emmitt Smith, Troy Aikman, Michael Irvin (three-piece set)	1992	710 s/o	$125	$145
Emmitt Smith, Troy Aikman, Michael Irvin three-piece set (#2) and 24k set				
Bart Starr - Green Bay Packers	1993	5,000	$29.95	$29.95
Lawrence Taylor - Defensive Player of the Decade	1990	2,238	$29.95	$45
Reggie White - Green Bay Packers regular and 24k				
Steve Young - San Francisco 49ers regular and 24k				
Steve Young - Super Bowl XXIX MVP regular and 24k				

## Chapter 13

Stamps/stickers

Football

1992 Diamond Stickers

Each of these stickers features a color action photo framed by the player's corresponding team colors bordered in white. The player's team is at the top; his name and card number are at the bottom. The back is horizontal and uses purple ink to provide statistics and a biography. A card number is also included. Each sticker is 1 15/16" by 2 15/16" and could be pasted in a 36-page album produced by Diamond Publishing, which also made the stickers. The stickers were sold in packs of six. Cornelius Bennett, Mark Carrier, Chris Miller and Rob Moore each signed 200 stickers, which were randomly inserted in the packs.

		MT	NM	EX
Complete Set (160):		15.00	11.00	6.00
Common Player:		.10	.08	.04
1	Super Bowl XXVI logo	.10	.08	.04
	(Top portion)			
2	Super Bowl XXVI logo	.10	.08	.04
	(Bottom portion)			
3	Jim Kelly	.30	.25	.12
4	Thurman Thomas	.30	.25	.12
5	Andre Reed	.20	.15	.08
6	James Lofton	.15	.11	.06
7	Cornelius Bennett	.15	.11	.06
8	Boomer Esiason	.15	.11	.06
9	Harold Green	.20	.15	.08
10	Anthony Munoz	.15	.11	.06
11	Mitchell Price	.10	.08	.04
12	Louis Billups	.10	.08	.04
13	Bernie Kosar	.20	.15	.08
14	Eric Metcalf	.15	.11	.06
15	Michael Dean Perry	.15	.11	.06
16	Van Waiters	.10	.08	.04
17	Brian Brennan	.12	.09	.05
18	John Elway	.50	.40	.20
19	Gaston Green	.10	.08	.04
20	Vance Johnson	.12	.09	.05
21	Dennis Smith	.10	.08	.04
22	Clarence Kay	.10	.08	.04
23	Warren Moon	.20	.15	.08
24	Haywood Jeffires	.20	.15	.08
25	Cris Dishman	.10	.08	.04
26	Bubba McDowell	.10	.08	.04
27	Ray Childress	.10	.08	.04
28	Eric Dickerson	.20	.15	.08
29	Jesse Hester	.10	.08	.04
30	Clarence Verdin	.10	.08	.04
31	Bill Brooks	.10	.08	.04
32	Albert Bentley	.10	.08	.04
33	Christian Okoye	.10	.08	.04
34	Derrick Thomas	.25	.20	.10
35	Dino Hackett	.10	.08	.04
36	Deron Cherry	.10	.08	.04
37	Bill Maas	.10	.08	.04
38	Todd Marinovich	.12	.09	.05
39	Roger Craig	.15	.11	.06
40	Greg Townsend	.10	.08	.04
41	Ronnie Lott	.15	.11	.06
42	Howie Long	.15	.11	.06
43	Dan Marino	1.25	.90	.50
44	Mark Clayton	.15	.11	.06
45	Sammie Smith	.10	.08	.04
46	Jim Jensen	.15	.11	.06
47	Reggie Roby	.10	.08	.04
48	Brent Williams	.10	.08	.04
49	Andre Tippett	.10	.08	.04
50	John Stephens	.15	.11	.06
51	Johnny Rembert	.10	.08	.04
52	Irving Fryar	.20	.15	.08
53	Ken O'Brien	.10	.08	.04
54	Al Toon	.15	.11	.06
55	Brad Baxter	.20	.15	.08
56	James Hasty	.10	.08	.04
57	Rob Moore	.25	.20	.10
58	Neil O'Donnell	.35	.25	.14
59	Bubby Brister	.10	.08	.04
60	Louis Lipps	.10	.08	.04
61	Merril Hoge	.10	.08	.04
62	Gary Anderson	.10	.08	.04
63	John Friesz	.20	.15	.08
64	Junior Seau	.25	.20	.10
65	Leslie O'Neal	.15	.11	.06
66	Rod Bernstine	.15	.11	.06
67	Burt Grossman	.10	.08	.04
68	Brian Blades	.15	.11	.06
69	Cortez Kennedy	.25	.20	.10
70	Dave Wyman	.10	.08	.04
71	John L. Williams	.15	.11	.06
72	Robert Blackmon	.10	.08	.04
73	Checklist 33-48	.15	.11	.06
	(Jim Kelly)			
74	Checklist 49-64	.15	.11	.06
	(Ronnie Lott)			
75	Jerry Rice, Andre Reed	.30	.25	.12
76	Jay Novacek, Dennis Smith	.15	.11	.06
77	Mark Rypien, Jim Kelly	.20	.15	.08
78	Pat Swilling,	.15	.11	.06
	Derrick Thomas			

79	Deion Sanders, Cris Dishman	.15	.11	.06
80	Mel Gray, Gaston Green	.12	.09	.05
81	Earnest Byner, Christian Okoye	.10	.08	.04
82	Eric Allen, Ronnie Lott	.15	.11	.06
83	Mike Singletary, Junior Seau	.15	.11	.06
84	Andre Rison, Haywood Jeffires	.20	.15	.08
85	Checklist 65-80 (Steve Young)	.20	.15	.08
86	Checlist 81-96 (Pat Swilling)	.10	.08	.04
87	Chris Miller	.15	.11	.06
88	Andre Rison	.25	.20	.10
89	Deion Sanders	.25	.20	.10
90	Michael Haynes	.20	.15	.08
91	Tim Green	.10	.08	.04
92	Jim Harbaugh	.20	.15	.08
93	Mark Carrier	.15	.11	.06
94	Mike Singletary	.15	.11	.06
95	William Perry	.15	.11	.06
96	Donnell Woolford	.10	.08	.04
97	Troy Aikman	1.00	.70	.40
98	Michael Irvin	.35	.25	.14
99	Russell Maryland	.25	.20	.10
100	Jay Novacek	.20	.15	.08
101	Ken Norton Jr.	.15	.11	.06
102	Mel Gray	.12	.09	.05
103	Bennie Blades	.10	.08	.04
104	Rodney Peete	.15	.11	.06
105	Brett Perriman	.10	.08	.04
106	William White	.10	.08	.04
107	Vai Sikahema	.10	.08	.04
108	Vince Workman	.15	.11	.06
109	Jeff Query	.15	.11	.06
110	Sterling Sharpe	.40	.30	.15
111	Tony Mandarich	.10	.08	.04
112	Jim Everett	.15	.11	.06
113	Flipper Anderson	.15	.11	.06
114	Robert Delpino	.15	.11	.06
115	Darryl Henley	.10	.08	.04
116	Henry Ellard	.15	.11	.06
117	Wade Wilson	.15	.11	.06
118	Anthony Carter	.15	.11	.06
119	Chris Doleman	.15	.11	.06
120	Cris Carter	.20	.15	.08
121	Henry Thomas	.10	.08	.04
122	Steve Walsh	.15	.11	.06
123	Pat Swilling	.15	.11	.06
124	Dalton Hilliard	.15	.11	.06
125	Floyd Turner	.15	.11	.06
126	Craig Heyward	.20	.15	.08
127	Jeff Hostetler	.20	.15	.08
128	Phil Simms	.20	.15	.08
129	Lawrence Taylor	.25	.20	.10
130	Mark Ingram	.15	.11	.06
131	Leonard Marshall	.10	.08	.04
132	Randall Cunningham	.25	.20	.10
133	Eric Allen	.10	.08	.04
134	Keith Byars	.15	.11	.06
135	Fred Barnett	.20	.15	.08
136	Wes Hopkins	.12	.09	.05
137	Ernie Jones	.15	.11	.06
138	Johnny Johnson	.30	.25	.12
139	Anthony Thompson	.15	.11	.06
140	Timm Rosenbach	.15	.11	.06
141	Randal Hill	.25	.20	.10
142	Steve Young	.35	.25	.14
143	Jerry Rice	.50	.40	.20
144	Tom Rathman	.15	.11	.06
145	Charles Haley	.15	.11	.06
146	John Taylor	.15	.11	.06
147	Vinny Testaverde	.20	.15	.08
148	Gary Anderson	.15	.11	.06
149	Broderick Thomas	.10	.08	.04
150	Mark Carrier	.15	.11	.06

151	Ian Beckles	.10	.08	.04
152	Mark Rypien	.15	.11	.06
153	Earnest Byner	.10	.08	.04
154	Gary Clark	.15	.11	.06
155	Monte Coleman	.10	.08	.04
156	Ricky Ervins	.15	.11	.06
157	Earnest Byner	.12	.09	.05
158	Jim Kelly, Fred Stokes, James Geathers	.15	.11	.06
159	Checklist 129-144 (Mark Rypien)	.10	.08	.04
160	Mark Rypien	.15	.11	.06

1969 Glendale Stamps

These unnumbered stamps, which measure 1 13/16" by 3 15/16", feature a color player photo on the front; the back has his name, team and instructions on how to apply the stamp to the corresponding album which was produced. "Dampen strip and affix in ablum" is on the back. The album measures 9" by 12" and is arranged alphabetically by team city.

		NM	EX	VG
Complete Set (312):		200.00	100.00	60.00
Common Player:		.25	.13	.08
(1)	Bob Berry	.40	.20	.12
(2)	Clark Miller	.25	.13	.08
(3)	Jim Butler	.25	.13	.08
(4)	Junior Coffey	.25	.13	.08
(5)	Paul Flatley	.40	.20	.12
(6)	Randy Johnson	.45	.25	.14
(7)	Charlie Bryant	.25	.13	.08
(8)	Billy Lothridge	.25	.13	.08
(9)	Tommy Nobis	2.00	1.00	.60
(10)	Claude Humphrey	.40	.20	.12
(11)	Ken Reaves	.25	.13	.08
(12)	Jerry Simmons	.40	.20	.12
(13)	Mike Curtis	.75	.40	.25
(14)	Dennis Gaubatz	.25	.13	.08
(15)	Jerry Logan	.25	.13	.08
(16)	Lenny Lyles	.25	.13	.08
(17)	John Mackey	2.00	1.00	.60
(18)	Tom Matte	.50	.25	.15
(19)	Lou Michaels	.35	.20	.11
(20)	Jimmy Orr	.50	.25	.15
(21)	Willie Richardson	.35	.20	.11
(22)	Don Shinnick	.25	.13	.08
(23)	Dan Sullivan	.25	.13	.08
(24)	Johnny Unitas	15.00	7.50	4.50
(25)	Houston Antwine	.25	.13	.08
(26)	John Bramlett	.25	.13	.08
(27)	Aaron Marsh	.25	.13	.08
(28)	R.C. Gamble	.25	.13	.08
(29)	Gino Cappelletti	.75	.40	.25
(30)	John Charles	.25	.13	.08
(31)	Larry Eisenhauer	.35	.20	.11
(32)	Jon Morris	.25	.13	.08
(33)	Jim Nance	.50	.25	.15
(34)	Len St. Jean	.25	.13	.08
(35)	Mike Taliaferro	.25	.13	.08
(36)	Jim Whalen	.25	.13	.08
(37)	Stew Barber	.35	.20	.11
(38)	Al Bemiller	.25	.13	.08
(39)	George (Butch) Byrd	.35	.20	.11
(40)	Booker Edgerson	.25	.13	.08
(41)	Harry Jacobs	.35	.20	.11
(42)	Jack Kemp	18.00	9.00	5.50
(43)	Ron McDole	.35	.20	.11
(44)	Joe O'Donnell	.25	.13	.08
(45)	John Pitts	.25	.13	.08
(46)	George Saimes	.35	.20	.11
(47)	Mike Stratton	.35	.20	.11
(48)	O.J. Simpson	35.00	17.50	10.50
(49)	Ronnie Bull	.35	.20	.11
(50)	Dick Butkus	8.00	4.00	2.50
(51)	Jim Cadile	.25	.13	.08
(52)	Jack Concannon	.35	.20	.11

(53)	Dick Evey	.25	.13	.08		(131)	Bart Starr	10.00	5.00	3.00
(54)	Bennie McRae	.25	.13	.08		(132)	Willie Wood	1.50	.70	.45
(55)	Ed O'Bradovich	.25	.13	.08		(133)	Pete Beathard	.75	.40	.25
(56)	Brian Piccolo	10.00	5.00	3.00		(134)	Jim Beirne	.25	.13	.08
(57)	Mike Pyle	.25	.13	.08		(135)	Garland Boyette	.25	.13	.08
(58)	Gale Sayers	10.00	5.00	3.00		(136)	Woody Campbell	.25	.13	.08
(59)	Dick Gordon	.35	.20	.11		(137)	Miller Farr	.25	.13	.08
(60)	Roosevelt Taylor	.35	.20	.11		(138)	Hoyle Granger	.25	.13	.08
(61)	Al Beauchamp	.25	.13	.08		(139)	Mac Haik	.25	.13	.08
(62)	Dave Middendorf	.25	.13	.08		(140)	Ken Houston	3.00	1.50	.90
(63)	Harry Gunner	.25	.13	.08		(141)	Bobby Maples	.35	.20	.11
(64)	Bobby Hunt	.25	.13	.08		(142)	Alvin Reed	.25	.13	.08
(65)	Bob Johnson	.40	.20	.12		(143)	Don Trull	.35	.20	.11
(66)	Charley King	.25	.13	.08		(144)	George Webster	.50	.25	.15
(67)	Andy Rice	.25	.13	.08		(145)	Bobby Bell	2.00	1.00	.60
(68)	Paul Robinson	.35	.20	.11		(146)	Aaron Brown	.25	.13	.08
(69)	Bill Staley	.25	.13	.08		(147)	Buck Buchanan	2.00	1.00	.60
(70)	Pat Matson	.25	.13	.08		(148)	Len Dawson	5.00	2.50	1.50
(71)	Bob Trumpy	2.00	1.00	.60		(149)	Mike Garrett	.50	.25	.15
(72)	Sam Wyche	5.00	2.50	1.50		(150)	Robert Holmes	.35	.20	.11
(73)	Erich Barnes	.35	.20	.11		(151)	Willie Lanier	3.00	1.50	.90
(74)	Gary Collins	.35	.20	.11		(152)	Frank Pitts	.25	.13	.08
(75)	Ben Davis	.25	.13	.08		(153)	Johnny Robinson	.75	.40	.25
(76)	John Demarie	.25	.13	.08		(154)	Jan Stenerud	3.00	1.50	.90
(77)	Gene Hickerson	.35	.20	.11		(155)	Otis Taylor	.75	.40	.25
(78)	Jim Houston	.35	.20	.11		(156)	Jim Tyrer	.50	.25	.15
(79)	Ernie Kellerman	.25	.13	.08		(157)	Dick Bass	.35	.20	.11
(80)	Leroy Kelly	3.00	1.50	.90		(158)	Maxie Baughan	.50	.25	.15
(81)	Dale Lindsey	.25	.13	.08		(159)	Rich Petitbon	.50	.25	.15
(82)	Bill Nelsen	.75	.40	.25		(160)	Roger Brown	.35	.20	.11
(83)	Jim Kanicki	.25	.13	.08		(161)	Roman Gabriel	1.50	.70	.45
(84)	Dick Schafrath	.35	.20	.11		(162)	Bruce Gossett	.25	.13	.08
(85)	George Andrie	.75	.40	.25		(163)	David (Deacon) Jones	1.50	.70	.45
(86)	Mike Clark	.25	.13	.08		(164)	Tom Mack	1.25	.60	.40
(87)	Cornell Green	.50	.25	.15		(165)	Tommy Mason	.50	.25	.15
(88)	Bob Hayes	1.50	.70	.45		(166)	Ed Meador	.35	.20	.11
(89)	Chuck Howley	.75	.40	.25		(167)	Merlin Olsen	3.00	1.50	.90
(90)	Lee Roy Jordan	1.25	.60	.40		(168)	Pat Studstill	.35	.20	.11
(91)	Bob Lilly	3.00	1.50	.90		(169)	Jack Clancy	.25	.13	.08
(92)	Craig Morton	1.00	.50	.30		(170)	Maxie Williams	.25	.13	.08
(93)	John Niland	.25	.13	.08		(171)	Larry Csonka	10.00	5.00	3.00
(94)	Dan Reeves	5.00	2.50	1.50		(172)	Jimmy Warren	.25	.13	.08
(95)	Mel Renfro	1.00	.50	.30		(173)	Norm Evans	.35	.20	.11
(96)	Lance Rentzel	.50	.25	.15		(174)	Rick Norton	.25	.13	.08
(97)	Tom Beer	.25	.13	.08		(175)	Bob Griese	7.50	3.75	2.25
(98)	Billy Van Heusen	.25	.13	.08		(176)	Howard Twilley	.50	.25	.15
(99)	Mike Current	.25	.13	.08		(177)	Billy Neighbors	.35	.20	.11
(100)	Al Denson	.25	.13	.08		(178)	Nick Buoniconti	1.25	.60	.40
(101)	Pete Duranko	.25	.13	.08		(179)	Tom Goode	.25	.13	.08
(102)	George Goeddeke	.25	.13	.08		(180)	Dick Westmoreland	.25	.13	.08
(103)	John Huard	.25	.13	.08		(181)	Grady Alderman	.25	.13	.08
(104)	Richard Jackson	.25	.13	.08		(182)	Bill Brown	.75	.40	.25
(105)	Pete Jaquess	.35	.20	.11		(183)	Fred Cox	.35	.20	.11
(106)	Fran Lynch	.25	.13	.08		(184)	Clint Jones	.35	.20	.11
(107)	Floyd Little	2.00	1.00	.60		(185)	Joe Kapp	1.00	.50	.30
(108)	Steve Tensi	.50	.25	.15		(186)	Paul Krause	1.00	.50	.30
(109)	Lem Barney	3.00	1.50	.90		(187)	Gary Larsen	.25	.13	.08
(110)	Nick Eddy	.50	.25	.15		(188)	Jim Marshall	1.50	.70	.45
(111)	Mel Farr	.75	.40	.25		(189)	Dave Osborn	.25	.13	.08
(112)	Ed Flanagan	.25	.13	.08		(190)	Alan Page	4.00	2.00	1.25
(113)	Larry Hand	.25	.13	.08		(191)	Mike Tingelhoff	.75	.40	.25
(114)	Alex Karras	2.50	1.25	.70		(192)	Roy Winston	.35	.20	.11
(115)	Dick LeBeau	.35	.20	.11		(193)	Dan Abramowicz	.50	.25	.15
(116)	Mike Lucci	.35	.20	.11		(194)	Doug Atkins	1.50	.70	.45
(117)	Earl McCullouch	.35	.20	.11		(195)	Bo Burris	.25	.13	.08
(118)	Bill Munson	.40	.20	.12		(196)	John Douglas	.25	.13	.08
(119)	Jerry Rush	.25	.13	.08		(197)	Don Shy	.25	.13	.08
(120)	Wayne Walker	.35	.20	.11		(198)	Bill Kilmer	.75	.40	.25
(121)	Herb Adderley	2.00	1.00	.60		(199)	Tony Lorick	.25	.13	.08
(122)	Donny Anderson	.50	.25	.15		(200)	David Parks	.50	.25	.15
(123)	Lee Roy Caffey	.25	.13	.08		(201)	Dave Rowe	.25	.13	.08
(124)	Carroll Dale	.35	.20	.11		(202)	Monty Stickles	.25	.13	.08
(125)	Willie Davis	1.50	.70	.45		(203)	Steve Stonebreaker	.35	.20	.11
(126)	Boyd Dowler	.35	.20	.11		(204)	Del Williams	.25	.13	.08
(127)	Marv Fleming	.50	.25	.15		(205)	Pete Case	.25	.13	.08
(128)	Bob Jeter	.35	.20	.11		(206)	Tommy Crutcher	.35	.20	.11
(129)	Henry Jordan	.35	.20	.11		(207)	Scott Eaton	.25	.13	.08
(130)	Dave Robinson	.35	.20	.11		(208)	Tucker Frederickson	.75	.40	.25

(209)	Peter Gogolak	.35	.20	.11
(210)	Homer Jones	.35	.20	.11
(211)	Ernie Koy	.35	.20	.11
(212)	Carl (Spider) Lockhart	.35	.20	.11
(213)	Bruce Maher	.25	.13	.08
(214)	Aaron Thomas	.35	.20	.11
(215)	Fran Tarkenton	12.00	6.00	3.50
(216)	Jim Katcavage	.35	.20	.11
(217)	Al Atkinson	.25	.13	.08
(218)	Emerson Boozer	.35	.20	.11
(219)	John Elliott	.25	.13	.08
(220)	Dave Herman	.25	.13	.08
(221)	Winston Hill	.35	.20	.11
(222)	Jim Hudson	.25	.13	.08
(223)	Pete Lammons	.35	.20	.11
(224)	Gerry Philbin	.35	.20	.11
(225)	George Sauer	.50	.25	.15
(226)	Joe Namath	20.00	10.00	6.00
(227)	Matt Snell	.50	.25	.15
(228)	Jim Turner	.35	.20	.11
(229)	Fred Biletnikoff	3.00	1.50	.90
(230)	Willie Brown	1.50	.70	.45
(231)	Billy Cannon	.50	.25	.15
(232)	Dan Conners	.25	.13	.08
(233)	Ben Davidson	.75	.40	.25
(234)	Hewritt Dixon	.35	.20	.11
(235)	Daryle Lamonica	1.00	.50	.30
(236)	Ike Lassiter	.25	.13	.08
(237)	Ken McCloughan	.25	.13	.08
(238)	Jim Otto	1.50	.70	.45
(239)	Harry Schuh	.25	.13	.08
(240)	Gene Upshaw	3.00	1.50	.90
(241)	Gary Ballman	.35	.20	.11
(242)	Joe Carollo	.25	.13	.08
(243)	Dave Lloyd	.25	.13	.08
(244)	Fred Hill	.25	.13	.08
(245)	Al Nelson	.25	.13	.08
(246)	Joe Scarpati	.25	.13	.08
(247)	Sam Baker	.35	.20	.11
(248)	Fred Brown	.25	.13	.08
(249)	Floyd Peters	.50	.25	.15
(250)	Nate Ramsey	.25	.13	.08
(251)	Norman Snead	.50	.25	.15
(252)	Tom Woodeshick	.25	.13	.08
(253)	John Hilton	.25	.13	.08
(254)	Kent Nix	.25	.13	.08
(255)	Paul Martha	.50	.25	.15
(256)	Ben McGee	.25	.13	.08
(257)	Andy Russell	.50	.25	.15
(258)	Dick Shiner	.25	.13	.08
(259)	J.R. Wilburn	.25	.13	.08
(260)	Marv Woodson	.25	.13	.08
(261)	Earl Gros	.25	.13	.08
(262)	Dick Hoak	.50	.25	.15
(263)	Roy Jefferson	.50	.25	.15
(264)	Larry Gagner	.25	.13	.08
(265)	Johnny Roland	.75	.40	.25
(266)	Jackie Smith	3.00	1.50	.90
(267)	Jim Bakken	.50	.25	.15
(268)	Don Brumm	.25	.13	.08
(269)	Bob DeMarco	.35	.20	.11
(270)	Irv Goode	.25	.13	.08
(271)	Ken Gray	.35	.20	.11
(272)	Charlie Johnson	1.00	.50	.30
(273)	Ernie McMillan	.35	.20	.11
(274)	Larry Stallings	.35	.20	.11
(275)	Jerry Stovall	.50	.25	.15
(276)	Larry Wilson	1.50	.70	.45
(277)	Chuck Allen	.25	.13	.08
(278)	Lance Alworth	3.00	1.50	.90
(279)	Kenny Graham	.25	.13	.08
(280)	Steve DeLong	.35	.20	.11
(281)	Willie Frazier	.35	.20	.11
(282)	Gary Garrison	.35	.20	.11
(283)	Sam Gruniesen	.25	.13	.08
(284)	John Hadl	.75	.40	.25
(285)	Brad Hubbert	.25	.13	.08
(286)	Ron Mix	2.00	1.00	.60
(287)	Dick Post	.35	.20	.11
(288)	Walt Sweeney	.35	.20	.11
(289)	Kermit Alexander	.50	.25	.15
(290)	Ed Beard	.25	.13	.08
(291)	Bruce Bosley	.35	.20	.11
(292)	John Brodie	3.00	1.50	.90
(293)	Stan Hindman	.25	.13	.08
(294)	Jim Johnson	1.50	.70	.45
(295)	Charlie Krueger	.35	.20	.11
(296)	Clifton McNeil	.35	.20	.11
(297)	Gary Lewis	.25	.13	.08
(298)	Howard Mudd	.25	.13	.08
(299)	Dave Wilcox	.50	.25	.15
(300)	Ken Willard	.50	.25	.15
(301)	Charlie Gogolak	.35	.20	.11
(302)	Len Hauss	.50	.25	.15
(303)	Sonny Jurgensen	3.50	1.75	1.00
(304)	Carl Kammerer	.25	.13	.08
(305)	Walt Rock	.25	.13	.08
(306)	Ray Schoenke	.25	.13	.08
(307)	Chris Hanburger	.75	.40	.25
(308)	Tom Brown	.50	.25	.15
(309)	Sam Huff	2.00	1.00	.60
(310)	Bob Long	.25	.13	.08
(311)	Vince Promuto	.25	.13	.08
(312)	Pat Richter	.50	.25	.15

1972 NFLPA Iron Ons

These 35 cards were created as cloth patches to be ironed onto clothes. Hence, the backs are blank. The front of the card has a full color head shot of the player, with his name and 1972 NFLPA copyright at the bottom. The player's name is above the photo, which is framed by a black border. The cards, which were sold through vending machines, measure 2 1/4" by 3 1/2" and are unnumbered.

		NM	EX	VG
Complete Set (35):		175.00	87.00	52.00
Common Player:		2.00	1.00	.60
(1)	Donny Anderson	2.00	1.00	.60
(2)	George Blanda	7.50	3.75	2.25
(3)	Terry Bradshaw	20.00	10.00	6.00
(4)	john Brockington	2.00	1.00	.60
(5)	John Brodie	5.00	2.50	1.50
(6)	Dick Butkus	10.00	5.00	3.00
(7)	Larry Csonka	10.00	5.00	3.00
(8)	Mike Curtis	2.00	1.00	.60
(9)	Len Dawson	6.00	3.00	1.75
(10)	Carl Eller	3.00	1.50	.90
(11)	Mike Garrett	2.00	1.00	.60
(12)	Joe Greene	8.00	4.00	2.50
(13)	Bob Griese	9.00	4.50	2.75
(14)	Dick Gordon	2.00	1.00	.60
(15)	John Hadl	3.00	1.50	.90
(16)	Bob Hayes	3.00	1.50	.90
(17)	Ron Johnson	2.00	1.00	.60
(18)	Deacon Jones	3.00	1.50	.90
(19)	Sonny Jurgensen	6.00	3.00	1.75
(20)	Leroy Kelly	3.00	1.50	.90
(21)	Jim Kiick	2.50	1.25	.70
(22)	Greg Landry	2.00	1.00	.60
(23)	Floyd Little	3.00	1.50	.90
(24)	Mike Lucci	2.00	1.00	.60
(25)	Archie Manning	5.00	2.50	1.50
(26)	Joe Namath	35.00	17.50	10.50
(27)	Tommy Nobis	3.00	1.50	.90
(28)	Alan Page	3.00	1.50	.90
(29)	Jim Plunkett	4.00	2.00	1.25
(30)	Gale Sayers	10.00	5.00	3.00
(31)	O.J. Simpson	35.00	17.50	10.50
(32)	Roger Staubach	30.00	15.00	9.00
(33)	Duane Thomas	2.00	1.00	.60
(34)	Johnny Unitas	25.00	12.50	7.50
(35)	Paul Warfield	5.00	2.50	1.50

1972 NFLPA Vinyl Stickers

These stickers feature 20 of the NFL's stars and were sold through vending machines. Each sticker is 2 3/4" by 4 3/4" and is copyrighted on the front by the NFLPA. Each player's head appears on a caricature drawing of him in a football uniform; the outline of his body is what can actually be used as a sticker. Consequently, the backs are blank. The stickers are unnumbered.

		NM	EX	VG
Complete Set (20):		90.00	45.00	27.00
Common Player:		2.00	1.00	.60
(1)	Donny Anderson	2.00	1.00	.60
(2)	George Blanda	5.00	2.50	1.50
(3)	Terry Bradshaw	17.00	8.50	5.00
(4)	John Brockington	2.00	1.00	.60
(5)	John Brodie	4.00	2.00	1.25
(6)	Dick Butkus	8.00	4.00	2.50
(7)	Dick Gordon	2.00	1.00	.60
(8)	Joe Greene	5.00	2.50	1.50
(9)	John Hadl	2.00	1.00	.60
(10)	Bob Hayes	3.00	1.50	.90
(11)	Ron Johnson	9.00	4.50	2.75
(12)	Floyd Little	3.00	1.50	.90
(13)	Joe Namath	25.00	12.50	7.50
(14)	Tommy Nobis	3.00	1.50	.90
(15)	Alan Page	13.00	6.50	4.00
(16)	Jim Plunkett	5.00	2.50	1.50
(17)	Gale Sayers	10.00	5.00	3.00
(18)	Roger Staubach	22.00	11.00	6.50
(19)	Johnny Unitas	18.00	9.00	5.50
(20)	Paul Warfield	4.00	2.00	1.25

1972 NFLPA
Wonderful World Stamps

These numbered stamps, which each measure 1 15/16" by 2 7/8", feature stars from each team in the NFL. The front of each stamp has a color photo of the player; the back has player's name, a stamp number and a place for it to be glued so it can be put into an accompanying album. The 30-page 9 1/2" by 13 1/4" album traces the history of pro football in the United States and provides short biographies of the players who are featured on the stamps. The NFLPA sponsored the album, which is titled "The Wonderful World of Pro Football USA." Stamps which are listed in the checklist with an A were issued in 1971.

		NM	EX	VG
Complete Set (390):		275.00	137.00	82.00
Common Player:		.35	.20	.11
1	Bob Berry	.50	.25	.15
2	Greg Brezina	.35	.20	.11
3	Ken Burrow	.35	.20	.11
4	Jim Butler	.40	.20	.12
5	Wes Chesson	.35	.20	.11
6	Claude Humphrey	.50	.25	.15
7	George Kunz	1.00	.50	.30
8	Tom McCauley	.35	.20	.11
9	Jim Mitchell	.50	.25	.15
10	Tommy Nobis	3.00	1.50	.90
11	Ken Reaves	.35	.20	.11
12	Bill Sandeman	.35	.20	.11
13	John Small	.35	.20	.11
14	Harmon Wages	.35	.20	.11
15	John Zook	.50	.25	.15
16	Norm Bulaich	.60	.30	.20
17	Bill Curry	.75	.40	.25
18	Mike Curtis	.75	.40	.25
19	Ted Hendricks	3.00	1.50	.90
20	Roy Hilton	.35	.20	.11
21	Eddie Hinton	.35	.20	.11
22	David Lee	.35	.20	.11
23	Jerry Logan	.35	.20	.11
24	John Mackey	2.00	1.00	.60
25	Tom Matte	.75	.40	.25
26	Jim O'Brien	.50	.25	.15
27	Glenn Ressler	.35	.20	.11
28	Johnny Unitas	15.00	7.50	4.50
29	Bob Vogel	.50	.25	.15
30	Rick Volk	.50	.25	.15
31	Paul Costa	.35	.20	.11
32	Jim Dunaway	.50	.25	.15
33	Paul Guidry	.35	.20	.11
34	Jim Harris	.35	.20	.11
35	Robert James	.35	.20	.11
36	Mike McBath	.35	.20	.11
37	Haven Moses	1.00	.50	.30
38	Wayne Patrick	.35	.20	.11
39	John Pitts	.35	.20	.11
40	Jim Reilly	.35	.20	.11
41	Pete Richardson	.35	.20	.11
42	Dennis Shaw	.50	.25	.15
43	O.J. Simpson	25.00	12.50	7.50
44	Mike Stratton	.50	.25	.15
45	Bob Tatarek	.35	.20	.11
46	Dick Butkus	8.00	4.00	2.50
47	Jim Cadile	.35	.20	.11
48	Jack Concannon	.50	.25	.15
49	Bobby Douglass	.75	.40	.25
50	George Farmer	.50	.25	.15
51	Dick Gordon	.50	.25	.15
52	Bobby Joe Green	.35	.20	.11
53	Ed O'Bradovich	.35	.20	.11
54A	Bob Hyland	.35	.20	.11
54B	Mac Percival	.35	.20	.11
55A	Ed O'Bradovich	.50	.25	.15
55B	Gale Sayers	9.00	4.50	2.75
56A	Mac Percival	.35	.20	.11
56B	George Seals	.35	.20	.11
57	Jim Seymour	.35	.20	.11
58A	George Seals	.35	.20	.11
58B	Ron Smith	.50	.25	.15
59	Bill Staley	.35	.20	.11
60	Cecil Turner	.40	.20	.12
61	Al Beauchamp	.45	.25	.14
62	Virgil Carter	.50	.25	.15
63	Vernon Holland	.35	.20	.11
64	Bob Johnson	.50	.25	.15
65	Ron Lamb	.35	.20	.11
66	Dave Lewis	.35	.20	.11
67	Rufus Mayes	.50	.25	.15
68	Horst Muhlmann	.35	.20	.11
69	Lemar Parrish	.75	.40	.25
70	Jess Phillips	.35	.20	.11
71	Mike Reid	2.00	1.00	.60
72	Ken Riley	1.00	.50	.30
73	Paul Robinson	.50	.25	.15
74	Bob Trumpy	2.25	1.25	.70
75	Fred Willis	.35	.20	.11
76	Don Cockroft	.50	.25	.15
77	Gary Collins	.50	.25	.15
78	Gene Hickerson	.50	.25	.15

No.	Name				No.	Name			
79	Fair Hooker	.75	.40	.25	156	John Charles	.35	.20	.11
80	Jim Houston	.50	.25	.15	157	Lynn Dickey	.75	.40	.25
81	Walter Johnson	.50	.25	.15	158	Elbert Drungo	.35	.20	.11
82	Joe Jones	.35	.20	.11	159	Gene Ferguson	.35	.20	.11
83	Leroy Kelly	3.00	1.50	.90	160	Charlie Johnson	.75	.40	.25
84	Milt Morin	.50	.25	.15	161	Charlie Joyner	3.00	1.50	.90
85	Reece Morrison	.35	.20	.11	162	Dan Patorini	.75	.40	.25
86	Bill Nelsen	.50	.25	.15	163	Ron Pritchard	.35	.20	.11
87	Mike Phipps	.75	.40	.25	164	Walt Suggs	.35	.20	.11
88	Bo Scott	.50	.25	.15	165	Mike Tilleman	.35	.20	.11
89	Jerry Sherk	.50	.25	.15	166	Bobby Bell	3.00	1.50	.90
90	Ron Snidow	.35	.20	.11	167	Aaron Brown	.50	.25	.15
91	Herb Adderley	3.00	1.50	.90	168	Buck Buchanan	2.00	1.00	.60
92	George Andrie	.75	.40	.25	169	Ed Buddle	.75	.40	.25
93	Mike Clark	.35	.20	.11	170	Curley Culp	1.00	.50	.30
94	Dave Edwards	.50	.25	.15	171	Len Dawson	6.00	3.00	1.75
95	Walt Garrison	1.50	.70	.45	172	Willie Lanier	2.50	1.25	.70
96	Cornell Green	.75	.40	.25	173	Jim Lynch	.50	.25	.15
97	Bob Hayes	2.00	1.00	.60	174	Jim Marsalis	.50	.25	.15
98	Calvin Hill	2.00	1.00	.60	175	Mo Moorman	.35	.20	.11
99	Chuck Howley	.75	.40	.25	176	Ed Podolak	.50	.25	.15
100	Lee Roy Jordan	2.50	1.25	.70	177	Johnny Robinson	.75	.40	.25
101	Dave Manders	.50	.25	.15	178	Jan Stenerud	2.00	1.00	.60
102	Craig Morton	1.25	.60	.40	179	Otis Taylor	1.50	.70	.45
103	Ralph Neely	.50	.25	.15	180	Jim Tyrer	.75	.40	.25
104	Mel Renfro	1.00	.50	.30	181	Kermit Alexander	.50	.25	.15
105	Roger Staubach	30.00	15.00	9.00	182	Coy Bacon	.35	.20	.11
106	Bobby Anderson	.75	.40	.25	183	Dick Buzin	.35	.20	.11
107	Sam Brunelli	.35	.20	.11	184	Roman Gabriel	1.00	.50	.30
108	Dave Costa	.35	.20	.11	185	Gene Howard	.35	.20	.11
109	Mike Current	.35	.20	.11	186	Ken Iman	.35	.20	.11
110	Pete Duranko	.35	.20	.11	187	Les Josephson	.50	.25	.15
111	George Goeddeke	.35	.20	.11	188	Marlin McKeever	.50	.25	.15
112	Cornell Gordon	.35	.20	.11	189	Merlin Olsen	4.00	2.00	1.25
113	Don Horn	.50	.25	.15	190A	Richie Petitbon	.75	.40	.25
114	Rich Jackson	.35	.20	.11	190B	Phil Olsen	.35	.20	.11
115	Larry Kaminski	.35	.20	.11	191	David Ray	.35	.20	.11
116	Floyd Little	1.50	.70	.45	192	Lance Rentzel	.75	.40	.25
117	Marv Montgomery	.35	.20	.11	193	Isiah Robertson	.50	.25	.15
118	Steve Ramsey	.50	.25	.15	194	Larry Smith	.35	.20	.11
119	Paul Smith	.50	.25	.15	195	Jack Snow	.75	.40	.25
120	Billy Thompson	.75	.40	.25	196	Nick Buoniconti	2.00	1.00	.60
121	Lem Barney	3.00	1.50	.90	197	Doug Crusan	.35	.20	.11
122	Nick Eddy	.50	.25	.15	198	Larry Csonka	8.00	4.00	2.50
123	Mel Farr	.75	.40	.25	199	Bob DeMarco	.50	.25	.15
124	Ed Flanagan	.35	.20	.11	200	Marv Fleming	.50	.25	.15
125	Larry Hand	.35	.20	.11	201	Bob Griese	10.00	5.00	3.00
126	Greg Landry	.75	.40	.25	202	Jim Klick	1.00	.50	.30
127	Dick LeBeau	.50	.25	.15	203	Bob Kuechenberg	1.00	.50	.30
128	Mike Lucci	.50	.25	.15	204	Mercury Morris	1.25	.60	.40
129	Earl McCullouch	.50	.25	.15	205A	Jim Riley	.35	.20	.11
130	Bill Munson	.75	.40	.25	205B	John Richardson	.35	.20	.11
131	Wayne Rasmussen	.35	.20	.11	206	Jim Riley	.35	.20	.11
132	Joe Robb	.35	.20	.11	207	Jake Scott	.75	.40	.25
133	Jerry Rush	.35	.20	.11	208	Howard Twilley	.75	.40	.25
134	Altie Taylor	.50	.25	.15	209	Paul Warfield	5.00	2.50	1.50
135	Wayne Walker	.50	.25	.15	210	Garo Yepremian	.75	.40	.25
136	Ken Bowman	.35	.20	.11	211	Grady Alderman	.50	.25	.15
137	John Brockington	.75	.40	.25	212	John Beasley	.35	.20	.11
138	Fred Carr	.50	.25	.15	213	John Henderson	.35	.20	.11
139	Carroll Dale	.50	.25	.15	214	Wally Hilgenberg	.50	.25	.15
140	Ken Ellis	.35	.20	.11	215	Clinton Jones	.50	.25	.15
141	Gale Gillingham	.50	.25	.15	216	Karl Kassulke	.35	.20	.11
142	Dave Hampton	.50	.25	.15	217	Paul Krause	1.25	.60	.40
143	Doug Hart	.35	.20	.11	218	Dave Osborn	.50	.25	.15
144A	John Hilton	.35	.20	.11	219	Alan Page	2.00	1.00	.60
144B	MacArthur Lane	.35	.20	.11	220	Ed Sharockman	.35	.20	.11
145	Mike McCoy	.50	.25	.15	221	Fran Tarkenton	10.00	5.00	3.00
146	Ray Nitschke	2.50	1.25	.70	222	Mick Tingelhoff	.75	.40	.25
147	Frank Patrick	.35	.20	.11	223	Charlie West	.35	.20	.11
148	Francis Peay	.35	.20	.11	224	Lonnie Warwick	.35	.20	.11
149	Dave Robinson	.75	.40	.25	225	Gene Washington	.75	.40	.25
150	Bart Starr	9.00	4.50	2.75	226	Hank Barton	.35	.20	.11
151	Bob Atkins	.35	.20	.11	227A	Larry Carwell	.35	.20	.11
152	Elvin Bethea	.75	.40	.25	227B	Ron Berger	.35	.20	.11
153	Garland Boyette	.35	.20	.11	228	Larry Carwell	.35	.20	.11
154	ken Burrough	.75	.40	.25	229A	Carl Garrett	.50	.25	.15
155	Woody Campbell	.35	.20	.11	229B	Jim Cheyunski	.50	.25	.15

230A	Jim Hunt	.35	.20	.11		300A	Warren Wells	.50	.25	.15
230B	Carl Garrett	.50	.25	.15		300B	Gene Upshaw	3.00	1.50	.90
231	Rickie Harris	.35	.20	.11		301	Rick Arrington	.35	.20	.11
232	Daryl Johnson	.35	.20	.11		302	Gary Ballman	.50	.25	.15
233	Steve Kiner	.35	.20	.11		303	Lee Bouggess	.35	.20	.11
234	Jon Morris	.35	.20	.11		304	Bill Bradley	.75	.40	.25
235	Jim Nance	.75	.40	.25		305A	Richard Harris	.35	.20	.11
236	Tom Neville	.35	.20	.11		305B	Happy Feller	.75	.40	.25
237	Jim Plunkett	4.00	2.00	1.25		306A	Ben Hawkins	.35	.20	.11
238	Ron Sellers	.50	.25	.15		306B	Richard Harris	.35	.20	.11
239	Len St. Jean	.35	.20	.11		307	Ben Hawkins	.35	.20	.11
240A	Gerald Warren	.35	.20	.11		308	Harold Jackson	1.50	.70	.45
240B	Don Webb	.35	.20	.11		309	Pete Liske	.75	.40	.25
241	Dan Abramowicz	.75	.40	.25		310	Al Nelson	.35	.20	.11
242A	Tony Baker	.35	.20	.11		311	Gary Pettigrew	.35	.20	.11
242B	Dick Absher	.35	.20	.11		312	Tim Rossovich	.75	.40	.25
243	Leo Carroll	.35	.20	.11		313	Tom Woodeshick	.50	.25	.15
244	Jim Duncan	.35	.20	.11		314	Adrian Young	.50	.25	.15
245	Al Dodd	.35	.20	.11		315	Steve Zabel	.50	.25	.15
246	Jim Flanigan	.35	.20	.11		316	Chuck Allen	.35	.20	.11
247	Hoyle Granger	.35	.20	.11		317	Warren Bankston	.50	.25	.15
248	Edd Hargett	.75	.40	.25		318	Chuck Beatty	.35	.20	.11
249	Glen Ray Hines	.35	.20	.11		319	Terry Bradshaw	20.00	10.00	6.00
250	Hugo Hollas	.35	.20	.11		320	John Fuqua	.50	.25	.15
251	Jake Kupp	.35	.20	.11		321	Terry Hanratty	1.00	.50	.30
252	Dave Long	.35	.20	.11		322	Ray Mansfield	.35	.20	.11
253	Mike Morgan	.35	.20	.11		323	Ben McGee	.35	.20	.11
254	Tom Roussel	.35	.20	.11		324	John Rowser	.35	.20	.11
255	Del Williams	.35	.20	.11		325	Andy Russell	1.00	.50	.30
256	Otto Brown	.35	.20	.11		326	Ron Shanklin	.50	.25	.15
257	Bobby Duhon	.50	.25	.15		327	Dave Smith	.35	.20	.11
258	Scott Eaton	.35	.20	.11		328	Bruce Van Dyke	.35	.20	.11
259	Jim Flies	.35	.20	.11		329	Lloyd Voss	.35	.20	.11
260	Tucker Fredrickson	.75	.40	.25		330	Bobby Walden	.35	.20	.11
261A	Don Herrmann	.35	.20	.11		331	Donny Anderson	.75	.40	.25
261B	Pete Gogolak	.50	.25	.15		332	Jim Bakken	.75	.40	.25
262	Bob Grim	.50	.25	.15		333	Pete Beathard	.75	.40	.25
263	Don Herrmann	.35	.20	.11		334A	Mel Gray	2.00	1.00	.60
264A	Ernie Koy	.75	.40	.25		334B	Miller Farr	.50	.25	.15
264B	Ron Johnson	1.00	.50	.30		335A	Jim Hart	1.00	.50	.30
265A	Spider Lockhart	.50	.25	.15		335B	Mel Gray	1.00	.50	.30
265B	Jim Kanicki	.35	.20	.11		336	Jim Hart	1.00	.50	.30
266	Spider Lockhart	.50	.25	.15		337A	Chuck Latourette	.35	.20	.11
267	Joe Morrison	.75	.40	.25		337B	Rol Krueger	.35	.20	.11
268	Bob Tucker	2.00	1.00	.60		338	Chuck Latourette	.35	.20	.11
269	Willie Williams	.35	.20	.11		339A	Bob Reynolds	.35	.20	.11
270	Willie Young	.35	.20	.11		339B	Ernie McMillan	.50	.25	.15
271	Al Atkinson	.35	.20	.11		340	Bob Reynolds	.35	.20	.11
272	Ralph Baker	.35	.20	.11		341	Jackie Smith	3.50	1.75	1.00
273	Emerson Boozer	.75	.40	.25		342	Larry Stallings	.50	.25	.15
274	John Elliott	.35	.20	.11		343	Chuck Walker	.35	.20	.11
275	Dave Herman	.35	.20	.11		344	Roger Wehrli	.75	.40	.25
276A	Dave Herman	.35	.20	.11		345	Larry Wilson	2.00	1.00	.60
276B	Winston Hill	.50	.25	.15		346	Bob Babich	.35	.20	.11
277	Gus Hollomon	.35	.20	.11		347	Pete Barnes	.35	.20	.11
278	Bob Howfield	.35	.20	.11		348A	Marty Domres	.50	.25	.15
279	Pete Lammons	.50	.25	.15		348B	Steve DeLong	.50	.25	.15
280	Joe Namath	22.00	11.00	6.50		349	Marty Domres	.50	.25	.15
	(numbered 281)					350	Gary Garrison	.50	.25	.15
281	Gerry Philbin	.50	.25	.15		351A	Walker Gillette	.35	.20	.11
282	Matt Snell	.75	.40	.25		351B	John Hadl	1.25	.60	.40
283	Steve Tannen	.35	.20	.11		352	Kevin Hardy	.35	.20	.11
284	Earlie Thomas	.35	.20	.11		353	Bob Howard	.35	.20	.11
285	Al Woodall	.50	.25	.15		354A	Jim Hill	.35	.20	.11
286	Fred Biletnikoff	4.00	2.00	1.25		354B	Deacon Jones	1.75	.90	.50
287	George Blanda	6.00	3.00	1.75		355	Terry Owens	.75	.40	.25
288	Willie Brown	3.00	1.50	.90		356	Dennis Partee	.35	.20	.11
289	Ray Chester	1.00	.50	.30		357A	Dennis Partee	.35	.20	.11
290	Tony Cline	.35	.20	.11		357B	Jeff Queen	.35	.20	.11
291	Dan Conners	.35	.20	.11		358	Jim Tolbert	.35	.20	.11
292	Ben Davidson	1.50	.70	.45		359	Russ Washington	.35	.20	.11
293	Hewritt Dixon	.50	.25	.15		360	Doug Wilkerson	.35	.20	.11
294	Tom Keating	.50	.25	.15		361	John Brodie	3.50	1.75	1.00
295	Daryle Lamonica	1.50	.70	.45		362	Doug Cunningham	.35	.20	.11
296	Gus Otto	.35	.20	.11		363	Bruce Gossett	.35	.20	.11
297	Jim Otto	3.00	1.50	.90		364	Stan Hindman	.35	.20	.11
298	Rod Sherman	.35	.20	.11		365	John Isenbarger	.50	.25	.15
299	Bubba Smith	.35	.20	.11		366	Charlie Krueger	.50	.25	.15

367	Frank Nunley	.35	.20	.11	29	Reggie Williams	.10	.08	.04
368	Woody Peoples	.35	.20	.11	30	Carl Zander	.05	.04	.02
369	Len Rohde	.35	.20	.11	31	Uniform	.05	.04	.02
370	Steve Spurrier	6.50	3.25	2.00	32	Browns Helmet	.05	.04	.02
371	Gene Washington	1.00	.50	.30	33	Browns Action	.15	.11	.06
372	Dave Wilcox	.75	.40	.25	34	Earnest Byner	.10	.08	.04
373	Ken Willard	1.00	.50	.30	35	Hanford Dixon	.05	.04	.02
374	Bob Windsor	.50	.25	.15	36	Bob Golic	.10	.08	.04
375	Dick Witcher	.50	.25	.15	37	Mike Johnson	.05	.04	.02
376	Verlon Biggs	.75	.40	.25	38	Bernie Kosar	.30	.25	.12
377	Larry Brown	3.00	1.50	.90	39	Kevin Mack	.10	.08	.04
378	Speedy Duncan	.50	.25	.15	40	Browns	.05	.04	.02
379	Chris Hanburger	1.00	.50	.30	41	Clay Matthews	.15	.11	.06
380	Charlie Harraway	.50	.25	.15	42	Gerald McNeil	.05	.04	.02
381	Sonny Jurgensen	5.00	2.50	1.50	43	Frank Minnifield	.05	.04	.02
382	Bill Kilmer	1.50	.70	.45	44	Ozzie Newsome	.15	.11	.06
383	Tommy Mason	.50	.25	.15	45	Cody Risien	.05	.04	.02
384	Ron McDole	.50	.25	.15	46	Uniform	.05	.04	.02
385	Brig Owens	.35	.20	.11	47	Broncos Helmet	.05	.04	.02
386	Jack Pardee	2.00	1.00	.60	48	Broncos Action	.05	.04	.02
387	Myron Pottios	1.00	.50	.30	49	Keith Bishop	.05	.04	.02
388	Jerry Smith	.50	.25	.15	50	Tony Dorsett	.35	.25	.14
389	Diron Talbert	.50	.25	.15	51	John Elway	1.25	.90	.50
390	Charley Taylor	4.00	2.00	1.25	52	Simon Fletcher	.25	.20	.10

1988 Panini Stickers

These stickers, which each measure 2 1/8" by 2 3/4", were made to be stored in a special collector's album which was produced. John Elway is featured on the cover of the album, which has the stickers arranged on pages according to the way they are numbered. The sticker number appears on both sides of the sticker. The front of the sticker has a closeup shot of the player, between two team color-coded bars. His team's name is above the photo; his name is below the photo. The stickers were sold in packs which also included one of three types of foil stickers - team name stickers, team helmet stickers, and team uniform stickers. Each team name sticker was produced with a player sticker, listed in . Backs for the team name stickers had a referee signal, while helmet foils had a stadium shot and uniform foils had a mascot cartoon on the back.

		MT	NM	EX
Complete Set:		35.00	26.00	14.00
Common Player:		.05	.04	.02
1	Super Bowl XXII Program Cover	.15	.11	.06
2	Bills Helmet	.05	.04	.02
3	Bills Action	.05	.04	.02
4	Cornelius Bennett	.50	.40	.20
5	Chris Burkett	.05	.04	.02
6	Derrick Burroughs	.05	.04	.02
7	Shane Conlan	.25	.20	.10
8	Ronnie Harmon	.25	.20	.10
9	Jim Kelly	.80	.60	.30
10	Buffalo Bills	.05	.04	.02
11	Mark Kelso	.05	.04	.02
12	Nate Odomes	.05	.04	.02
13	Andre Reed	.25	.20	.10
14	Fred Smerlas	.05	.04	.02
15	Bruce Smith	.25	.20	.10
16	Uniform	.05	.04	.02
17	Bengals Helmet	.05	.04	.02
18	Bengals Action	.05	.04	.02
19	Jim Breech	.05	.04	.02
20	James Brooks	.10	.08	.04
21	Eddie Brown	.10	.08	.04
22	Cris Collinsworth	.10	.08	.04
23	Boomer Esiason	.20	.15	.08
24	Rodney Holman	.10	.08	.04
25	Bengals	.05	.04	.02
26	Larry Kinnebrew	.05	.04	.02
27	Tim Krumrie	.05	.04	.02
28	Anthony Munoz	.15	.11	.06

53	Mark Jackson	.10	.08	.04
54	Vance Johnson	.10	.08	.04
55	Broncos	.05	.04	.02
56	Rulon Jones	.05	.04	.02
57	Rick Karlis	.05	.04	.02
58	Karl Mecklenburg	.10	.08	.04
59	Ricky Nattiel	.10	.08	.04
60	Sammy Winder	.05	.04	.02
61	Uniform	.05	.04	.02
62	Oilers Helmet	.05	.04	.02
63	Oilers Action	.25	.20	.10
64	Keith Bostic	.05	.04	.02
65	Steve Brown	.05	.04	.02
66	Ray Childress	.15	.11	.06
67	Jeff Donaldson	.05	.04	.02
68	John Grimsley	.05	.04	.02
69	Robert Lyles	.05	.04	.02
70	Oilers	.05	.04	.02
71	Drew Hill	.10	.08	.04
72	Warren Moon	.85	.60	.35
73	Mike Munchak	.15	.11	.06
74	Mike Rozier	.10	.08	.04
75	Johnny Meads	.05	.04	.02
76	Uniform	.05	.04	.02
77	Colts Helmet	.05	.04	.02
78	Colts Action	.15	.11	.06
79	Albert Bentley	.10	.08	.04
80	Dean Biasucci	.05	.04	.02
81	Duane Bickett	.15	.11	.06
82	Bill Brooks	.15	.11	.06
83	Johnny Cooks	.05	.04	.02
84	Eric Dickerson	.40	.30	.15
85	Colts	.05	.04	.02
86	Ray Donaldson	.05	.04	.02
87	Chris Hinton	.10	.08	.04
88	Cliff Odom	.05	.04	.02
89	Barry Krauss	.10	.08	.04
90	Jack Trudeau	.15	.11	.06
91	Uniform	.05	.04	.02
92	Chiefs Helmet	.05	.04	.02
93	Chiefs Action	.05	.04	.02
94	Carlos Carson	.05	.04	.02
95	Deron Cherry	.10	.08	.04
96	Dino Hackett	.05	.04	.02
97	Bill Kenney	.05	.04	.02
98	Albert Lewis	.10	.08	.04
99	Nick Lowery	.10	.08	.04
100	Chiefs	.05	.04	.02
101	Bill Maas	.05	.04	.02
102	Christian Okoye	.15	.11	.06
103	Stephone Paige	.10	.08	.04
104	Paul Palmer	.05	.04	.02
105	Kevin Ross	.05	.04	.02
106	Uniform	.05	.04	.02

#	Name				#	Name			
107	Raiders Helmet	.05	.04	.02	185	Chip Banks	.10	.08	.04
108	Raiders Action	.25	.20	.10	186	Martin Bayless	.05	.04	.02
109	Marcus Allen	.35	.25	.14	187	Chuck Ehin	.05	.04	.02
110	Todd Christensen	.15	.11	.06	188	Venice Glenn	.05	.04	.02
111	Mike Haynes	.15	.11	.06	189	Lionel James	.05	.04	.02
112	Bo Jackson	.60	.45	.25	190	Chargers	.05	.04	.02
113	James Lofton	.20	.15	.08	191	Mark Malone	.05	.04	.02
114	Howie Long	.15	.11	.06	192	Ralf Mojsiejenko	.05	.04	.02
115	Raiders	.05	.04	.02	193	Billy Ray Smith	.10	.08	.04
116	Rod Martin	.05	.04	.02	194	Lee Williams	.15	.11	.06
117	Vann McElroy	.05	.04	.02	195	Kellen Winslow	.15	.11	.06
118	Bill Pickel	.05	.04	.02	196	Uniform	.05	.04	.02
119	Don Mosebar	.05	.04	.02	197	Seahawks Helmet	.05	.04	.02
120	Stacey Toran	.05	.04	.02	198	Seahawks Action	.10	.08	.04
121	Uniform	.05	.04	.02	199	Eugene Robinson	.05	.04	.02
122	Dolphins Helmet	.05	.04	.02	200	Jeff Bryant	.05	.04	.02
123	Dolphins Action	.05	.04	.02	201	Ray Butler	.05	.04	.02
124	John Bosa	.05	.04	.02	202	Jacob Green	.10	.08	.04
125	Mark Clayton	.15	.11	.06	203	Norm Johnson	.10	.08	.04
126	Mark Duper	.10	.08	.04	204	Dave Krieg	.10	.08	.04
127	Lorenzo Hampton	.05	.04	.02	205	Seahawks	.05	.04	.02
128	William Judson	.05	.04	.02	206	Steve Largent	.75	.60	.30
129	Dan Marino	2.50	2.00	1.00	207	Joe Nash	.05	.04	.02
130	Dolphins	.05	.04	.02	208	Curt Warner	.10	.08	.04
131	John Offerdahl	.10	.08	.04	209	Bobby Joe Edmonds	.10	.08	.04
132	Reggie Roby	.05	.04	.02	210	Daryl Turner	.05	.04	.02
133	Jackie Shipp	.05	.04	.02	211	Uniform	.05	.04	.02
134	Dwight Stephenson	.10	.08	.04	212	AFC Logo	.05	.04	.02
135	Troy Stradford	.10	.08	.04	213	Bernie Kosar	.35	.25	.14
136	Uniform	.05	.04	.02	214	Curt Warner	.10	.08	.04
137	Patriots Helmet	.05	.04	.02	215	Jerry Rice, Steve Largent	1.25	.90	.50
138	Patriots Action	.05	.04	.02	216	Mark Bavaro, Anthony Munoz	.15	.11	.06
139	Bruce Armstron	.05	.04	.02	217	Gary Zimmerman, Bill Fralic	.10	.08	.04
140	Raymond Clayborn	.05	.04	.02	218	Dwight Stephenson, Mike Munchak	.10	.08	.04
141	Reggie Dupard	.05	.04	.02	219	Joe Montana	3.00	2.25	1.25
142	Steve Grogan	.10	.08	.04	220	Charles White, Eric Dickerson	.40	.30	.15
143	Craig James	.25	.20	.10	221	Morten Andersen, Vai Sikahema	.10	.08	.04
144	Ronnie Lippett	.05	.04	.02	222	Bruce Smith, Reggie White	.30	.25	.12
145	Patriots	.05	.04	.02	223	Michael Carter, Steve McMichael	.10	.08	.04
146	Fred Marion	.05	.04	.02	224	Jim Arnold	.05	.04	.02
147	Stanley Morgan	.15	.11	.06	225	Carl Banks, Andre Tippett	.10	.08	.04
148	Mosi Tatupu	.05	.04	.02	226	Barry Wilburn, Mike Singletary	.10	.08	.04
149	Andre Tippett	.10	.08	.04	227	Hanford Dixon, Frank Minnifield	.05	.04	.02
150	Garin Veris	.05	.04	.02	228	Ronnie Lott, Joey Browner	.15	.11	.06
151	Uniform	.05	.04	.02	229	NFC Logo	.05	.04	.02
152	Jets Helmet	.05	.04	.02	230	Gary Clark	.15	.11	.06
153	Jets Action	.05	.04	.02	231	Richard Dent	.15	.11	.06
154	Bob Crable	.05	.04	.02	232	Falcons Helmet	.05	.04	.02
155	Mark Gastineau	.10	.08	.04	233	Falcons Action	.05	.04	.02
156	Pat Leahy	.05	.04	.02	234	Rick Bryan	.10	.08	.04
157	Johnny Hector	.10	.08	.04	235	Bobby Butler	.05	.04	.02
158	Marty Lyons	.10	.08	.04	236	Tony Casillas	.15	.11	.06
159	Freeman McNeil	.15	.11	.06	237	Floyd Dixon	.05	.04	.02
160	Jets	.05	.04	.02	238	Rick Donnelly	.05	.04	.02
161	Ken O'Brien	.10	.08	.04	239	Bill Fralic	.10	.08	.04
162	Mickey Shuler	.05	.04	.02	240	Falcons	.05	.04	.02
163	Al Toon	.10	.08	.04	241	Mike Gann	.05	.04	.02
164	Roger Vick	.05	.04	.02	242	Chris Miller	.40	.30	.15
165	Wesley Walker	.10	.08	.04	243	Robert Moore	.05	.04	.02
166	Uniform	.05	.04	.02	244	John Rade	.05	.04	.02
167	Steelers Helmet	.05	.04	.02	245	Gerald Riggs	.10	.08	.04
168	Steelers Action	.05	.04	.02	246	Uniform	.05	.04	.02
169	Walter Abercrombie	.05	.04	.02	247	Bears Helmet	.05	.04	.02
170	Gary Anderson	.05	.04	.02	248	Bears Action	.15	.11	.06
171	Todd Blackledge	.05	.04	.02	249	Neal Anderson	.30	.25	.12
172	Thomas Everett	.15	.11	.06	250	Jim Covert	.10	.08	.04
173	Delton Hall	.05	.04	.02	251	Richard Dent	.15	.11	.06
174	Bryan Hinkle	.05	.04	.02	252	Dave Duerson	.05	.04	.02
175	Steelers	.05	.04	.02	253	Dennis Gentry	.05	.04	.02
176	Earnest Jackson	.10	.08	.04	254	Jay Hilgenberg	.10	.08	.04
177	Louis Lipps	.10	.08	.04					
178	David Little	.05	.04	.02					
179	Mike Merriweather	.10	.08	.04					
180	Mike Webster	.15	.11	.06					
181	Uniform	.05	.04	.02					
182	Chargers Helmet	.05	.04	.02					
183	Chargers Action	.05	.04	.02					
184	Gary Anderson	.15	.11	.06					

255	Bears	.05	.04	.02
256	Jim McMahon	.20	.15	.08
257	Steve McMichael	.10	.08	.04
258	Matt Suhey	.05	.04	.02
259	Mike Singletary	.20	.15	.08
260	Otis Wilson	.10	.08	.04
261	Uniform	.05	.04	.02
262	Cowboys Helmet	.05	.04	.02
263	Cowboys Action	.15	.11	.06
264	Bill Bates	.10	.08	.04
265	Doug Crosbie	.05	.04	.02
266	Ron Francis	.05	.04	.02
267	Jim Jeffcoat	.15	.11	.06
268	Ed Too Tall Jones	.20	.15	.08
269	Eugene Lockhart	.05	.04	.02
270	Cowboys	.05	.04	.02
271	Danny Noonan	.05	.04	.02
272	Steve Pelluer	.10	.08	.04
273	Herschel Walker	.10	.08	.04
274	Everson Walls	.20	.15	.08
275	Randy White	.05	.04	.02
276	Uniform	.05	.04	.02
277	Lions Helmet	.05	.04	.02
278	Lions Action	.05	.04	.02
279	Jim Arnold	.10	.08	.04
280	Jerry Ball	.05	.04	.02
281	Michael Cofer	.05	.04	.02
282	Keith Ferguson	.05	.04	.02
283	Dennis Gibson	.05	.04	.02
284	James Griffin	.05	.04	.02
285	Lions	.05	.04	.02
286	James Jones	.10	.08	.04
287	Chuck Long	.10	.08	.04
288	Pete Mandley	.05	.04	.02
289	Eddie Murray	.05	.04	.02
290	Garry James	.05	.04	.02
291	Uniform	.05	.04	.02
292	Packers Helmet	.05	.04	.02
293	Packers Action	.05	.04	.02
294	John Anderson	.05	.04	.02
295	Dave Brown	.10	.08	.04
296	Alphonso Carreker	.05	.04	.02
297	Kenneth Davis	.20	.15	.08
298	Phillip Epps	.05	.04	.02
299	Brent Fullwood	.05	.04	.02
300	Packers	.05	.04	.02
301	Tim Harris	.15	.11	.06
302	Johnny Holland	.10	.08	.04
303	Mark Murphy	.05	.04	.02
304	Brian Noble	.05	.04	.02
305	Walter Stanley	.10	.08	.04
306	Uniform	.05	.04	.02
307	Rams Helmet	.05	.04	.02
308	Rams Action	.05	.04	.02
309	Jim Collins	.05	.04	.02
310	Henry Ellard	.15	.11	.06
311	Jim Everett	.30	.25	.12
312	Jerry Gray	.05	.04	.02
313	LeRoy Irvin	.05	.04	.02
314	Mike Lansford	.05	.04	.02
315	Los Angeles Rams	.05	.04	.02
316	Mel Owens	.05	.04	.02
317	Jackie Slater	.10	.08	.04
318	Doug Smith	.05	.04	.02
319	Charles White	.10	.08	.04
320	Mike Wilcher	.05	.04	.02
321	Uniform	.05	.04	.02
322	Vikings Helmet	.05	.04	.02
323	Vikings Action	.05	.04	.02
324	Joey Browner	.10	.08	.04
325	Anthony Carter	.15	.11	.06
326	Chris Doleman	.15	.11	.06
327	D.J. Dozier	.10	.08	.04
328	Steve Jordan	.10	.08	.04
329	Tommy Kramer	.10	.08	.04
330	Vikings	.05	.04	.02
331	Darrin Nelson	.10	.08	.04
332	Jesse Solomon	.10	.08	.04
333	Scott Studwell	.10	.08	.04
334	Wade Wilson	.35	.25	.14
335	Gary Zimmerman	.05	.04	.02
336	Uniform	.05	.04	.02
337	Saints Helmet	.05	.04	.02
338	Saints Action	.15	.11	.06
339	Morten Andersen	.10	.08	.04
340	Bruce Clark	.05	.04	.02
341	Brad Edelman	.05	.04	.02
342	Bobby Hebert	.15	.11	.06
343	Dalton Hilliard	.10	.08	.04
344	Rickey Jackson	.15	.11	.06
345	Saints	.05	.04	.02
346	Vaughan Johnson	.10	.08	.04
347	Rueben Mayes	.10	.08	.04
348	Sam Mills	.10	.08	.04
349	Lionel Manuel	.35	.25	.14
350	Dave Waymer	.05	.04	.02
351	Uniform	.05	.04	.02
352	Giants Helmet	.05	.04	.02
353	Giants Action	.05	.04	.02
354	Carl Banks	.15	.11	.06
355	Mark Bavaro	.15	.11	.06
356	Jim Burt	.05	.04	.02
357	Harry Carson	.10	.08	.04
358	Terry Kinard	.05	.04	.02
359	Lionel Manuel	.05	.04	.02
360	Giants	.05	.04	.02
361	Leonard Marshall	.10	.08	.04
362	George Martin	.05	.04	.02
363	Joe Morris	.10	.08	.04
364	Phil Simms	.50	.40	.20
365	George Adams	.05	.04	.02
366	Uniform	.05	.04	.02
367	Eagles Helmet	.05	.04	.02
368	Eagles Action	.25	.20	.10
369	Jerome Brown	.30	.25	.12
370	Keith Byars	.15	.11	.06
371	Randall Cunningham	.40	.30	.15
372	Terry Hoage	.05	.04	.02
373	Seth Joyner	.20	.15	.08
374	Mike Quick	.15	.11	.06
375	Eagles	.05	.04	.02
376	Clyde Simmons	.20	.15	.08
377	Anthony Toney	.05	.04	.02
378	Andre Waters	.10	.08	.04
379	Reggie White	.35	.25	.14
380	Roynell Young	.05	.04	.02
381	Uniform	.05	.04	.02
382	Cardinals Helmet	.05	.04	.02
383	Cardinals Action	.05	.04	.02
384	Robert Awalt	.05	.04	.02
385	Roy Green	.15	.11	.06
386	Neil Lomax	.10	.08	.04
387	Stump Mitchell	.10	.08	.04
388	Niko Noga	.06	.05	.02
389	Freddie Joe Nunn	.05	.04	.02
390	Cardinals	.05	.04	.02
391	Luis Sharpe	.10	.08	.04
392	Vai Sikahema	.10	.08	.04
393	J.T. Smith	.10	.08	.04
394	Leonard Smith	.05	.04	.02
395	Lonnie Young	.05	.04	.02
396	Uniform	.05	.04	.02
397	49ers Helmet	.05	.04	.02
398	49ers Action	1.50	1.25	.60
399	Dwaine Board	.05	.04	.02
400	Michael Carter	.10	.08	.04
401	Roger Craig	.25	.20	.10
402	Jeff Fuller	.05	.04	.02
403	Don Griffin	.05	.04	.02
404	Ronnie Lott	.20	.15	.08
405	49ers	.05	.04	.02
406	Joe Montana	3.00	2.25	1.25
407	Tom Rathman	.25	.20	.10
408	Jerry Rice	1.50	1.25	.60
409	Keena Turner	.05	.04	.02
410	Michael Walter	.05	.04	.02

No.	Player	MT	NM	EX
411	Uniform	.05	.04	.02
412	Bucs Helmet	.05	.04	.02
413	Bucs Action	.05	.04	.02
414	Mark Carrier	.25	.20	.10
415	Gerald Carter	.05	.04	.02
416	Ron Holmes	.10	.08	.04
417	Rod Jones	.05	.04	.02
418	Calvin Magee	.05	.04	.02
419	Ervin Randle	.05	.04	.02
420	Buccaneers	.05	.04	.02
421	Donald Igwebuike	.05	.04	.02
422	Vinny Testaverde	.25	.20	.10
423	Jackie Walker	.05	.04	.02
424	Chris Washington	.05	.04	.02
425	James Wilder	.10	.08	.04
426	Uniform	.05	.04	.02
427	Redskins Helmet	.05	.04	.02
428	Redskins Action	.10	.08	.04
429	Gary Clark	.15	.11	.06
430	Monte Coleman	.05	.04	.02
431	Darrell Green	.10	.08	.04
432	Charles Mann	.10	.08	.04
433	Kelvin Bryant	.10	.08	.04
434	Art Monk	.25	.20	.10
435	Redskins	.05	.04	.02
436	Ricky Sanders	.15	.11	.06
437	Jay Schroeder	.15	.11	.06
438	Alvin Walton	.05	.04	.02
439	Barry Wilburn	.10	.08	.04
440	Doug Williams	.10	.08	.04
441	Uniform	.05	.04	.02
442	Super Bowl Action	.05	.04	.02
443	Super Bowl Action	.05	.04	.02
444	Doug Williams (Super Bowl MVP)	.15	.11	.06
445	Super Bowl Action	.05	.04	.02
446	Super Bowl Action	.05	.04	.02
447	Super Bowl Action	.05	.04	.02
----	Panini Album (John Elway on cover)	2.00	1.50	.80

1989 Panini Stickers

These 1989 stickers from Panini are slightly larger than those issued in 1988, measuring 1 15/16" by 3."

No.	Player	MT	NM	EX
	Complete Set (416):	30.00	22.00	12.00
	Common Player:	.05	.04	.02
1	SB XXIII Program	.10	.08	.04
2	SB XXIII Program	.05	.04	.02
3	Floyd Dixon	.05	.04	.02
4	Tony Casillas	.10	.08	.04
5	Bill Fralic	.10	.08	.04
6	Aundray Bruce	.05	.04	.02
7	Scott Case	.05	.04	.02
8	Rick Donnelly	.05	.04	.02
9	Atlanta logo	.05	.04	.02
10	Helmet	.05	.04	.02
11	Marcus Cotton	.05	.04	.02
12	Chris Miller	.25	.20	.10
13	Robert Moore	.05	.04	.02
14	Bobby Butler	.05	.04	.02
15	Rick Bryan	.05	.04	.02
16	John Settle	.10	.08	.04
17	Jim McMahon	.15	.11	.06
18	Neal Anderson	.15	.11	.06
19	Dave Duerson	.05	.04	.02
20	Steve McMichael	.05	.04	.02
21	Jay Hilgenberg	.05	.04	.02
22	Dennis McKinnon	.05	.04	.02
23	Chicago logo	.05	.04	.02
24	Helmet	.05	.04	.02
25	Richard Dent	.15	.11	.06
26	Dennis Gentry	.05	.04	.02
27	Mike Singletary	.15	.11	.06
28	Vestee Jackson	.05	.04	.02
29	Mike Tomczak	.15	.11	.06
30	Dan Hampton	.15	.11	.06
31	Michael Irvin	1.75	1.25	.70
32	Eugene Lockhart	.10	.08	.04
33	Herschel Walker	.30	.25	.12
34	Kelvin Martin	.15	.11	.06
35	Jim Jeffcoat	.10	.08	.04
36	Everson Walls	.10	.08	.04
37	Dallas logo	.05	.04	.02
38	Helmet	.05	.04	.02
39	Danny Noonan	.05	.04	.02
40	Ray Alexander	.05	.04	.02
41	Garry Cobb	.05	.04	.02
42	Ed Too Tall Jones	.15	.11	.06
43	Kevin Brooks	.05	.04	.02
44	Bill Bates	.10	.08	.04
45	Detroit logo	.05	.04	.02
46	Chuck Long	.10	.08	.04
47	Jim Arnold	.05	.04	.02
48	Michael Cofer	.05	.04	.02
49	Eddie Murray	.05	.04	.02
50	Keith Ferguson	.05	.04	.02
51	Pete Mandley	.05	.04	.02
52	Helmet	.05	.04	.02
53	Jerry Ball	.05	.04	.02
54	Bennie Blades	.15	.11	.06
55	Dennis Gibson	.05	.04	.02
56	Chris Spielman	.15	.11	.06
57	Eric Williams	.05	.04	.02
58	Lomas Brown	.05	.04	.02
59	Johnny Holland	.10	.08	.04
60	Tim Harris	.15	.11	.06
61	Mark Murphy	.05	.04	.02
62	Walter Stanley	.10	.08	.04
63	Brent Fullwood	.05	.04	.02
64	Ken Ruettgers	.10	.08	.04
65	Green Bay logo	.05	.04	.02
66	Helmet	.05	.04	.02
67	John Anderson	.05	.04	.02
68	Brian Noble	.05	.04	.02
69	Sterling Sharpe	1.50	1.25	.60
70	Keith Woodside	.10	.08	.04
71	Mark Lee	.05	.04	.02
72	Don Majkowski	.15	.11	.06
73	Aaron Cox	.10	.08	.04
74	LeRoy Irvin	.05	.04	.02
75	Jim Everett	.15	.11	.06
76	Mike Lansford	.05	.04	.02
77	Mike Wilcher	.05	.04	.02
78	Henry Ellard	.10	.08	.04
79	Rams helmet	.05	.04	.02
80	Jerry Gray	.05	.04	.02
81	Doug Smith	.05	.04	.02
82	Tom Newberry	.10	.08	.04
83	Jackie Slater	.10	.08	.04
84	Greg Bell	.10	.08	.04
85	Kevin Greene	.10	.08	.04
86	Chris Doleman	.10	.08	.04
87	Steve Jordan	.10	.08	.04
88	Jesse Solomon	.05	.04	.02
89	Randall McDaniel	.05	.04	.02
90	Hassan Jones	.10	.08	.04
91	Joey Browner	.10	.08	.04
92	Vikings logo	.05	.04	.02
93	Helmet	.05	.04	.02
94	Anthony Carter	.10	.08	.04
95	Gary Zimmerman	.05	.04	.02
96	Wade Wilson	.15	.11	.06
97	Scott Studwell	.10	.08	.04
98	Keith Millard	.10	.08	.04
99	Carl Lee	.10	.08	.04
100	Morten Andersen	.10	.08	.04
101	Bobby Hebert	.15	.11	.06
102	Rueben Mayes	.10	.08	.04
103	Sam Mills	.10	.08	.04
104	Vaughan Johnson	.10	.08	.04
105	Pat Swilling	.15	.11	.06
106	Saints logo	.05	.04	.02
107	Helmet	.05	.04	.02

#	Name				#	Name			
108	Brad Edelman	.05	.04	.02	186	Mark May	.05	.04	.02
109	Craig Heyward	.15	.11	.06	187	Darrell Green	.10	.08	.04
110	Eric Martin	.10	.08	.04	188	Jim Lachey	.10	.08	.04
111	Dalton Hilliard	.10	.08	.04	189	Doug Williams	.10	.08	.04
112	Lonzell Hill	.05	.04	.02	190	Helmet	.05	.04	.02
113	Rickey Jackson	.10	.08	.04	191	Redskins logo	.05	.04	.02
114	Erik Howard	.05	.04	.02	192	Kelvin Bryant	.05	.04	.02
115	Phil Simms	.35	.25	.14	193	Charles Mann	.05	.04	.02
116	Leonard Marshall	.10	.08	.04	194	Alvin Walton	.05	.04	.02
117	Joe Morris	.10	.08	.04	195	Art Monk	.20	.15	.08
118	Bart Oates	.10	.08	.04	196	Barry Wilburn	.05	.04	.02
119	Mark Bavaro	.10	.08	.04	197	Mark Rypien	.25	.20	.10
120	Giants logo	.05	.04	.02	198	NFC logo	.05	.04	.02
121	Helmet	.05	.04	.02	199	Scott Case	.05	.04	.02
122	Terry Kinard	.05	.04	.02	200	Herschel Walker	.30	.25	.12
123	Carl Banks	.10	.08	.04	201	Herschel Walker,	.25	.20	.10
124	Lionel Manuel	.05	.04	.02		Roger Craig			
125	Stephen Baker	.15	.11	.06	202	Henry Ellard, Jerry Rice	.65	.50	.25
126	Pepper Johnson	.10	.08	.04	203	Bruce Matthews,	.05	.04	.02
127	Jim Burt	.05	.04	.02		Tom Newberry			
128	Cris Carter	.35	.25	.14	204	Gary Zimmerman,	.10	.08	.04
129	Mike Quick	.10	.08	.04		Anthony Munoz			
130	Terry Hoage	.05	.04	.02	205	Boomer Esiason	.15	.11	.06
131	Keith Jackson	.80	.60	.30	206	Jay Hilgenberg	.10	.08	.04
132	Clyde Simmons	.15	.11	.06	207	Keith Jackson	.25	.20	.10
133	Eric Allen	.05	.04	.02	208	Reggie White, Bruce Smith	.25	.20	.10
134	Eagles logo	.05	.04	.02	209	Keith Millard,	.10	.08	.04
135	Helmet	.05	.04	.02		Tim Krumrie			
136	Randall Cunningham	.40	.30	.15	210	Carl Lee, Frank Minnifield	.05	.04	.02
137	Mike Pitts	.05	.04	.02	211	Joey Browner,	.10	.08	.04
138	Keith Byars	.10	.08	.04		Deron Cherry			
139	Seth Joyner	.15	.11	.06	212	Shane Conlan	.10	.08	.04
140	Jerome Brown	.15	.11	.06	213	Mike Singletary	.15	.11	.06
141	Reggie White	.30	.25	.12	214	Cornelius Bennett	.15	.11	.06
142	Jay Novacek	.30	.25	.12	215	AFC logo	.05	.04	.02
143	Neil Lomax	.10	.08	.04	216	Boomer Esiason	.25	.20	.10
144	Ken Harvey	.10	.08	.04	217	Erik McMillan	.10	.08	.04
145	Freddie Joe Nunn	.05	.04	.02	218	Jim Kelly	.60	.45	.25
146	Robert Awalt	.05	.04	.02	219	Cornelius Bennett	.15	.11	.06
147	Niko Noga	.05	.04	.02	220	Fred Smerlas	.10	.08	.04
148	Phoenix logo	.05	.04	.02	221	Shane Conlan	.10	.08	.04
149	Helmet	.05	.04	.02	222	Scott Norwood	.05	.04	.02
150	Tim McDonald	.25	.20	.10	223	Mark Kelso	.05	.04	.02
151	Roy Green	.10	.08	.04	224	Bills logo	.05	.04	.02
152	Stump Mitchell	.10	.08	.04	225	Helmet	.05	.04	.02
153	J.T. Smith	.10	.08	.04	226	Thurman Thomas	1.50	1.25	.60
154	Luis Sharpe	.05	.04	.02	227	Pete Metzelaars	.05	.04	.02
155	Vai Sikhema	.10	.08	.04	228	Bruce Smith	.25	.20	.10
156	Jeff Fuller	.05	.04	.02	229	Art Still	.10	.08	.04
157	Joe Montana	3.00	2.25	1.25	230	Kent Hull	.10	.08	.04
158	Harris Barton	.05	.04	.02	231	Andre Reed	.25	.20	.10
159	Michael Carter	.10	.08	.04	232	Tim Krumrie	.05	.04	.02
160	Jeff Fuller	.05	.04	.02	233	Boomer Esiason	.25	.20	.10
161	Jerry Rice	2.00	1.50	.80	234	Ickey Woods	.10	.08	.04
162	49ers logo	.05	.04	.02	235	Eric Thomas	.10	.08	.04
163	Helmet	.05	.04	.02	236	Rodney Holman	.10	.08	.04
164	Tom Rathman	.15	.11	.06	237	Jim Skow	.05	.04	.02
165	Roger Craig	.20	.15	.08	238	Bengals helmet	.05	.04	.02
166	Ronnie Lott	.30	.25	.12	239	James Brooks	.10	.08	.04
167	Charles Haley	.15	.11	.06	240	David Fulcher	.10	.08	.04
168	John Taylor	.50	.40	.20	241	Carl Zander	.05	.04	.02
169	Michael Walter	.05	.04	.02	242	Eddie Brown	.10	.08	.04
170	Ron Hall	.05	.04	.02	243	Max Montoya	.05	.04	.02
171	Ervin Randle	.05	.04	.02	244	Anthony Munoz	.15	.11	.06
172	James Wilder	.10	.08	.04	245	Felix Wright	.05	.04	.02
173	Ron Holmes	.05	.04	.02	246	Clay Matthews	.15	.11	.06
174	Mark Carrier	.15	.11	.06	247	Hanford Dixon	.05	.04	.02
175	William Howard	.05	.04	.02	248	Ozzie Newsome	.15	.11	.06
176	Tampa Bay logo	.05	.04	.02	249	Bernie Kosar	.25	.20	.10
177	Helmet	.05	.04	.02	250	Kevin Mack	.10	.08	.04
178	Lars Tate	.05	.04	.02	251	Bengals Helmet	.05	.04	.02
179	Vinny Testaverde	.20	.15	.08	252	Brian Brennan	.05	.04	.02
180	Paul Gruber	.15	.11	.06	253	Reggie Langhorne	.05	.04	.02
181	Bruce Hill	.10	.08	.04	254	Cody Risien	.05	.04	.02
182	Reuben Davis	.05	.04	.02	255	Webster Slaughter	.15	.11	.06
183	Ricky Reynolds	.05	.04	.02	256	Mike Johnson	.05	.04	.02
184	Ricky Sanders	.15	.11	.06	257	Frank Minnifield	.05	.04	.02
185	Gary Clark	.15	.11	.06	258	Mike Horan	.05	.04	.02

#	Name				#	Name			
259	Dennis Smith	.10	.08	.04	337	Mark Brown	.05	.04	.02
260	Ricky Nattiel	.05	.04	.02	338	Mark Duper	.10	.08	.04
261	Karl Mecklenburg	.10	.08	.04	339	Troy Stradford	.05	.04	.02
262	Keith Bishop	.05	.04	.02	340	T.J. Turner	.05	.04	.02
263	John Elway	1.50	1.25	.60	341	Mark Clayton	.15	.11	.06
264	Broncos helmet	.05	.04	.02	342	Patriots logo	.05	.04	.02
265	Broncos logo	.05	.04	.02	343	Johnny Rembert	.05	.04	.02
266	Simon Fletcher	.15	.11	.06	344	Garin Veris	.05	.04	.02
267	Vance Johnson	.10	.08	.04	345	Stanley Morgan	.10	.08	.04
268	Tony Dorsett	.35	.25	.14	346	John Stephens	.15	.11	.06
269	Greg Kragen	.10	.08	.04	347	Fred Marion	.05	.04	.02
270	Mike Harden	.05	.04	.02	348	Irving Fryar	.15	.11	.06
271	Mark Jackson	.05	.04	.02	349	Helmet	.05	.04	.02
272	Warren Moon	.75	.60	.30	350	Andre Tippett	.10	.08	.04
273	Mike Rozier	.10	.08	.04	351	Roland James	.05	.04	.02
274	Houston logo	.05	.04	.02	352	Brent Williams	.05	.04	.02
275	Allen Pinkett	.10	.08	.04	353	Raymond Clayborn	.05	.04	.02
276	Tony Zendejas	.05	.04	.02	354	Tony Eason	.10	.08	.04
277	Alonzo Highsmith	.10	.08	.04	355	Bruce Armstrong	.05	.04	.02
278	Johnny Meads	.05	.04	.02	356	Jets logo	.05	.04	.02
279	Helmet	.05	.04	.02	357	Marty Lyons	.10	.08	.04
280	Mike Munchak	.10	.08	.04	358	Bobby Humphrey	.05	.04	.02
281	John Grimsley	.05	.04	.02	359	Pat Leahy	.05	.04	.02
282	Ernest Givins	.15	.11	.06	360	Mickey Shuler	.10	.08	.04
283	Drew Hill	.10	.08	.04	361	James Hasty	.05	.04	.02
284	Bruce Matthews	.10	.08	.04	362	Ken O'Brien	.10	.08	.04
285	Ray Childress	.10	.08	.04	363	Helmet	.05	.04	.02
286	Colts logo	.05	.04	.02	364	Alex Gordon	.05	.04	.02
287	Chris Hinton	.10	.08	.04	365	Al Toon	.10	.08	.04
288	Clarence Verdin	.10	.08	.04	366	Erik McMillan	.10	.08	.04
289	Jon Hand	.15	.11	.06	367	Johnny Hector	.10	.08	.04
290	Chris Chandler	.15	.11	.06	368	Wesley Walker	.10	.08	.04
291	Eugene Daniel	.05	.04	.02	369	Freeman McNeil	.10	.08	.04
292	Dean Biasucci	.05	.04	.02	370	Steelers logo	.05	.04	.02
293	Helmet	.05	.04	.02	371	Gary Anderson	.05	.04	.02
294	Duane Bickett	.10	.08	.04	372	Rodney Carter	.05	.04	.02
295	Rohn Stark	.05	.04	.02	373	Merril Hoge	.10	.08	.04
296	Albert Bentley	.10	.08	.04	374	David Little	.05	.04	.02
297	Bill Brooks	.10	.08	.04	375	Bubby Brister	.15	.11	.06
298	O'Brien Alston	.05	.04	.02	376	Thomas Everett	.10	.08	.04
299	Ray Donaldson	.05	.04	.02	377	Helmet	.05	.04	.02
300	Carlos Carson	.05	.04	.02	378	Rod Woodson	.40	.30	.15
301	Lloyd Burruss	.05	.04	.02	379	Bryan Hinkle	.05	.04	.02
302	Steve DeBerg	.15	.11	.06	380	Tunch Ilkin	.05	.04	.02
303	Irv Eatman	.05	.04	.02	381	Aaron Jones	.05	.04	.02
304	Dino Hackett	.05	.04	.02	382	Louis Lipps	.10	.08	.04
305	Albert Lewis	.10	.08	.04	383	Warren Williams	.05	.04	.02
306	Chiefs helmet	.05	.04	.02	384	Anthony Miller	.75	.60	.30
307	Chiefs logo	.05	.04	.02	385	Gary Anderson	.15	.11	.06
308	Deron Cherry	.10	.08	.04	386	Lee Williams	.10	.08	.04
309	Paul Palmer	.05	.04	.02	387	Lionel James	.10	.08	.04
310	Neil Smith	.40	.30	.15	388	Gary Plummer	.05	.04	.02
311	Christian Okoye	.10	.08	.04	389	Gill Byrd	.10	.08	.04
312	Stephone Paige	.10	.08	.04	390	Chargers helmet	.05	.04	.02
313	Bill Maas	.05	.04	.02	391	Ralf Mojsiejenko	.05	.04	.02
314	Marcus Allen	.40	.30	.15	392	Rod Bernstine	.25	.20	.10
315	Vann McElroy	.05	.04	.02	393	Keith Browner	.05	.04	.02
316	Mervyn Fernandez	.10	.08	.04	394	Billy Ray Smith	.10	.08	.04
317	Bill Pickel	.05	.04	.02	395	Leslie O'Neal	.15	.11	.06
318	Greg Townsend	.10	.08	.04	396	Jamie Holland	.05	.04	.02
319	Tim Brown	1.25	.90	.50	397	Tony Woods	.10	.08	.04
320	Raiders logo	.05	.04	.02	398	Bruce Scholtz	.05	.04	.02
321	Helmet	.05	.04	.02	399	Joe Nash	.05	.04	.02
322	James Lofton	.15	.11	.06	400	Curt Warner	.10	.08	.04
323	Willie Gault	.10	.08	.04	401	John L. Williams	.10	.08	.04
324	Jay Schroeder	.10	.08	.04	402	Bryan Millard	.05	.04	.02
325	Matt Millen	.05	.04	.02	403	Seahawks logo	.05	.04	.02
326	Howie Long	.10	.08	.04	404	Helmet	.05	.04	.02
327	Bo Jackson	.50	.40	.20	405	Steve Largent	.30	.25	.12
328	Lorenzo Hampton	.05	.04	.02	406	Norm Johnson	.10	.08	.04
329	Jarvis Williams	.05	.04	.02	407	Jacob Green	.10	.08	.04
330	Jim C. Jensen	.05	.04	.02	408	Dave Krieg	.10	.08	.04
331	Dan Marino	2.50	2.00	1.00	409	Paul Moyer	.05	.04	.02
332	John Offerdahl	.10	.08	.04	410	Brian Blades	.50	.40	.20
333	Brian Sochia	.05	.04	.02	411	SB XXIII	.05	.04	.02
334	Miami logo	.05	.04	.02	412	Jerry Rice	1.50	1.25	.60
335	Helmet	.05	.04	.02	413	SB XXIII	.10	.08	.04
336	Ferrell Edmunds	.05	.04	.02	414	SB XXIII	.10	.08	.04

		MT	NM	EX
415	SB XXIII	.10	.08	.04
416	SB XXIII	.10	.08	.04
----	Panini Album	4.00	3.00	1.50
	(Joe Montana on conver)			

1990 Panini Stickers

These stickers were intended to be stored in an album titled "The Hitters." Ronnie Lott, Mike Single-tary and Lawrence Taylor are featured on the album cover. The stickers measure 1 7/8" by 2 15/16" and have a color action photo on the front, using a design distinctly different from those used the two years before.

		MT	NM	EX
	Complete Set (396):	20.00	15.00	8.00
	Common Player:	.05	.04	.02
1	Super Bowl XXIV	.15	.11	.06
	Program Cover (top)			
2	Super Bowl XXIV	.10	.08	.04
	Program Cover (bottom)			
3	Bills Crest	.05	.04	.02
4	Thurman Thomas	.50	.40	.20
5	Nate Odomes	.05	.04	.02
6	Jim Kelly	.45	.35	.20
7	Cornelius Bennett	.20	.15	.08
8	Scott Norwood	.05	.04	.02
9	Mark Kelso	.05	.04	.02
10	Kent Hull	.05	.04	.02
11	Jim Ritcher	.05	.04	.02
12	Darryl Talley	.10	.08	.04
13	Bruce Smith	.15	.11	.06
14	Shane Conlan	.10	.08	.04
15	Andre Reed	.15	.11	.06
16	Jason Buck	.05	.04	.02
17	David Fulcher	.10	.08	.04
18	Jim Skow	.05	.04	.02
19	Anthony Munoz	.15	.11	.06
20	Eric Thomas	.05	.04	.02
21	Eric Ball	.05	.04	.02
22	Tim Krumrie	.05	.04	.02
23	James Brooks	.10	.08	.04
24	Bengals Crest	.05	.04	.02
25	Rodney Holman	.05	.04	.02
26	Boomer Esiason	.25	.20	.10
27	Eddie Brown	.10	.08	.04
28	Tim McGee	.10	.08	.04
29	Browns Crest	.05	.04	.02
30	Mike Johnson	.05	.04	.02
31	David Grayson	.05	.04	.02
32	Thane Gash	.05	.04	.02
33	Robert Banks	.05	.04	.02
34	Eric Metcalf	.20	.15	.08
35	Kevin Mack	.10	.08	.04
36	Reggie Langhorne	.05	.04	.02
37	Webster Slaughter	.10	.08	.04
38	Felix Wright	.05	.04	.02
39	Bernie Kosar	.25	.20	.10
40	Frank Minnifield	.05	.04	.02
41	Clay Matthews	.15	.11	.06
42	Vance Johnson	.10	.08	.04
43	Ron Holmes	.05	.04	.02
44	Melvin Bratton	.10	.08	.04
45	Greg Kragen	.05	.04	.02
46	Karl Mecklenburg	.10	.08	.04
47	Dennis Smith	.10	.08	.04
48	Bobby Humphrey	.10	.08	.04
49	Simon Fletcher	.10	.08	.04
50	Broncos Crest	.05	.04	.02
51	Michael Brooks	.05	.04	.02
52	Steve Atwater	.10	.08	.04
53	John Elway	.80	.60	.30
54	David Treadwell	.05	.04	.02
55	Oilers Crest	.05	.04	.02
56	Bubba McDowell	.05	.04	.02
57	Ray Childress	.10	.08	.04
58	Bruce Matthews	.05	.04	.02
59	Allen Pinkett	.10	.08	.04
60	Warren Moon	.55	.40	.20
61	John Grimsley	.05	.04	.02
62	Alonzo Highsmith	.10	.08	.04
63	Mike Munchak	.10	.08	.04
64	Ernest Givins	.10	.08	.04
65	Johnny Meads	.05	.04	.02
66	Drew Hill	.10	.08	.04
67	William Fuller	.05	.04	.02
68	Duane Bickett	.10	.08	.04
69	Jack Trudeau	.10	.08	.04
70	Jon Hand	.10	.08	.04
71	Chris Hinton	.10	.08	.04
72	Bill Brooks	.10	.08	.04
73	Donnell Thompson	.05	.04	.02
74	Jeff Herrod	.05	.04	.02
75	Andre Rison	.25	.20	.10
76	Colts Crest	.05	.04	.02
77	Chris Chandler	.10	.08	.04
78	Ray Donaldson	.05	.04	.02
79	Albert Bentley	.10	.08	.04
80	Keith Taylor	.05	.04	.02
81	Chiefs Crest	.05	.04	.02
82	Leonard Griffin	.05	.04	.02
83	Dino Hackett	.05	.04	.02
84	Christian Okoye	.10	.08	.04
85	Chris Martin	.10	.08	.04
86	John Alt	.05	.04	.02
87	Kevin Ross	.05	.04	.02
88	Steve DeBerg	.10	.08	.04
89	Albert Lewis	.10	.08	.04
90	Stephone Paige	.10	.08	.04
91	Derrick Thomas	.40	.30	.15
92	Neil Smith	.15	.11	.06
93	Pete Mandley	.05	.04	.02
94	Howie Long	.10	.08	.04
95	Greg Townsend	.05	.04	.02
96	Mervyn Fernandez	.10	.08	.04
97	Scott Davis	.05	.04	.02
98	Steve Beuerlein	.40	.30	.15
99	Mike Dyal	.05	.04	.02
100	Willie Gault	.10	.08	.04
101	Eddie Anderson	.05	.04	.02
102	Raiders Crest	.05	.04	.02
103	Trey McDaniel	.05	.04	.02
104	Bo Jackson	.30	.25	.12
105	Steve Wisniewski	.05	.04	.02
106	Steve Smith	.10	.08	.04
107	Dolphins Crest	.05	.04	.02
108	Mark Clayton	.15	.11	.06
109	Louis Oliver	.10	.08	.04
110	Jarvis Williams	.05	.04	.02
111	Ferrell Edmunds	.05	.04	.02
112	Jeff Cross	.05	.04	.02
113	John Offerdahl	.10	.08	.04
114	Brian Sochia	.05	.04	.02
115	Dan Marino	2.00	1.50	.80
116	Jim C. Jensen	.05	.04	.02
117	Sammie Smith	.05	.04	.02
118	Reggie Roby	.05	.04	.02

119	Roy Foster	.05	.04	.02
120	Bruce Armstrong	.05	.04	.02
121	Steve Grogan	.10	.08	.04
122	Hart Lee Dykes	.05	.04	.02
123	Andre Tippett	.10	.08	.04
124	Johnny Rembert	.05	.04	.02
125	Ed Reynolds	.05	.04	.02
126	Cedric Jones	.05	.04	.02
127	Vincent Brown	.05	.04	.02
128	Patriots Crest	.05	.04	.02
129	Brent Williams	.05	.04	.02
130	John Stephens	.10	.08	.04
131	Eric Sievers	.05	.04	.02
132	Maurice Hurst	.05	.04	.02
133	Jets Crest	.05	.04	.02
134	Johnny Hector	.10	.08	.04
135	Eric McMillan	.05	.04	.02
136	Jeff Lageman	.05	.04	.02
137	Al Toon	.10	.08	.04
138	James Hasty	.05	.04	.02
139	Kyle Clifton	.05	.04	.02
140	Ken O'Brien	.10	.08	.04
141	Jim Sweeney	.05	.04	.02
142	Jo Jo Townsell	.10	.08	.04
143	Dennis Byrd	.20	.15	.08
144	Mickey Shuler	.10	.08	.04
145	Alex Gordon	.05	.04	.02
146	Keith Willis	.05	.04	.02
147	Louis Lipps	.10	.08	.04
148	David Little	.05	.04	.02
149	Greg Lloyd	.10	.08	.04
150	Carnell Lake	.05	.04	.02
151	Tim Worley	.10	.08	.04
152	Dwayne Woodruff	.05	.04	.02
153	Gerald Williams	.05	.04	.02
154	Steelers Crest	.05	.04	.02
155	Merril Hoge	.10	.08	.04
156	Bubby Brister	.10	.08	.04
157	Tunch Ilkin	.05	.04	.02
158	Rod Woodson	.15	.11	.06
159	Charger Crest	.05	.04	.02
160	Leslie O'Neal	.10	.08	.04
161	Billy Ray Smith	.05	.04	.02
162	Marion Butts	.15	.11	.06
163	Lee Williams	.10	.08	.04
164	Gill Byrd	.10	.08	.04
165	Jim McMahon	.15	.11	.06
166	Courtney Hall	.05	.04	.02
167	Burt Grossman	.15	.11	.06
168	Gary Plummer	.05	.04	.02
169	Anthony Miller	.40	.30	.15
170	Billy Joe Tolliver	.15	.11	.06
171	Venice Glenn	.05	.04	.02
172	Andy Heck	.05	.04	.02
173	Brian Blades	.15	.11	.06
174	Bryan Millard	.05	.04	.02
175	Tony Woods	.05	.04	.02
176	Rufus Porter	.05	.04	.02
177	Dave Wyman	.05	.04	.02
178	John L. Williams	.10	.08	.04
179	Jacob Green	.05	.04	.02
180	Seahawks Crest	.05	.04	.02
181	Eugene Robinson	.05	.04	.02
182	Jeff Bryant	.05	.04	.02
183	Dave Krieg	.10	.08	.04
184	Joe Nash	.05	.04	.02
185	Christian Okoye	.05	.04	.02
186	Felix Wright	.05	.04	.02
187	Rod Woodson	.10	.08	.04
188	Barry Sanders, Christian Okoye	.75	.60	.30
189	Jerry Rice, Sterling Sharpe	1.00	.70	.40
190	Bruce Matthews	.05	.04	.02
191	Jay Hilgenberg	.05	.04	.02
192	Tom Newbury	.05	.04	.02
193	Anthony Munoz	.10	.08	.04
194	Jim Lachey	.05	.04	.02
195	Keith Jackson	.15	.11	.06
196	Joe Montana	1.50	1.25	.60
197	David Fulcher, Ronnie Lott	.10	.08	.04
198	Albert Lewis, Eric Allen	.05	.04	.02
199	Reggie White	.20	.15	.08
200	Keith Millard	.05	.04	.02
201	Chris Doleman	.05	.04	.02
202	Mike Singletary	.15	.11	.06
203	Tim Harris	.05	.04	.02
204	Lawrence Taylor	.20	.15	.08
205	Rich Camarrilo	.05	.04	.02
206	Sterling Sharpe	.25	.20	.10
207	Chris Doleman	.05	.04	.02
208	Barry Sanders	.55	.40	.20
209	Falcons Crest	.05	.04	.02
210	Michael Haynes	.30	.25	.12
211	Scott Case	.05	.04	.02
212	Marcus Cotton	.05	.04	.02
213	Chris Miller	.15	.11	.06
214	Keith Jones	.05	.04	.02
215	Tim Green	.05	.04	.02
216	Deion Sanders	.50	.40	.20
217	Shawn Collins	.10	.08	.04
218	John Settle	.05	.04	.02
219	Bill Fralic	.05	.04	.02
220	Aundray Bruce	.05	.04	.02
221	Jessie Tuggle	.05	.04	.02
222	James Thornton	.05	.04	.02
223	Dennis Gentry	.05	.04	.02
224	Richard Dent	.15	.11	.06
225	Jay Hilgenberg	.05	.04	.02
226	Steve McMichael	.05	.04	.02
227	Brad Muster	.10	.08	.04
228	Donnell Woodford	.05	.04	.02
229	Mike Singletary	.15	.11	.06
230	Bears Crest	.05	.04	.02
231	Mark Bortz	.05	.04	.02
232	Kevin Butler	.05	.04	.02
233	Neal Anderson	.10	.08	.04
234	Trace Armstrong	.05	.04	.02
235	Cowboys Crest	.05	.04	.02
236	Mark Tuinei	.10	.08	.04
237	Tony Tolbert	.05	.04	.02
238	Eugene Lockhart	.10	.08	.04
239	Daryl Johnston	.25	.20	.10
240	Troy Aikman	3.00	2.25	1.25
241	Jim Jeffcoat	.10	.08	.04
242	James Dixon	.05	.04	.02
243	Jesse Solomon	.05	.04	.02
244	Ken Norton	.25	.20	.10
245	Kelvin Martin	.05	.04	.02
246	Danny Noonan	.05	.04	.02
247	Michael Irvin	.50	.40	.20
248	Eric Williams	.05	.04	.02
249	Richard Johnson	.05	.04	.02
250	Michael Cofer	.05	.04	.02
251	Chris Spielman	.10	.08	.04
252	Rodney Peete	.20	.15	.08
253	Bennie Blades	.10	.08	.04
254	Jerry Ball	.05	.04	.02
255	Eddie Murray	.08	.06	.03
256	Lions Crest	.05	.04	.02
257	Barry Sanders	1.75	1.25	.70
258	Jerry Holmes	.05	.04	.02
259	Dennis Gibson	.05	.04	.02
260	Lomas Brown	.05	.04	.02
261	Packers Crest	.05	.04	.02
262	Dave Brown	.05	.04	.02
263	Mark Murphy	.05	.04	.02
264	Perry Kemp	.05	.04	.02
265	Don Majkowski	.10	.08	.04
266	Chris Jacke	.05	.04	.02
267	Keith Woodside	.10	.08	.04
268	Tony Mandarich	.05	.04	.02
269	Robert Brown	.05	.04	.02
270	Sterling Sharpe	.75	.60	.30
271	Tim Harris	.10	.08	.04
272	Brent Fullwood	.05	.04	.02
273	Brian Noble	.05	.04	.02

274	Alvin Wright	.05	.04	.02
275	Flipper Anderson	.10	.08	.04
276	Jackie Slater	.10	.08	.04
277	Kevin Greene	.10	.08	.04
278	Pete Holohan	.05	.04	.02
279	Tom Newberry	.05	.04	.02
280	Jerry Gray	.05	.04	.02
281	henry Ellard	.10	.08	.04
282	Rams Crest	.05	.04	.02
283	LeRoy Irvin	.05	.04	.02
284	Jim Everett	.15	.11	.06
285	Greg Bell	.10	.08	.04
286	Doug Smith	.05	.04	.02
287	Vikings Crest	.05	.04	.02
288	Joey Browner	.10	.08	.04
289	Wade Wilson	.15	.11	.06
290	Chris Doleman	.10	.08	.04
291	Al Noga	.05	.04	.02
292	Herschel Walker	.20	.15	.08
293	Henry Thomas	.10	.08	.04
294	Steve Jordan	.10	.08	.04
295	Anthony Carter	.10	.08	.04
296	Keith Millard	.10	.08	.04
297	Carl Lee	.05	.04	.02
298	Randall McDaniel	.05	.04	.02
299	Gary Zimmerman	.05	.04	.02
300	Morten Andersen	.05	.04	.02
301	Rickey Jackson	.10	.08	.04
302	Sam Mills	.05	.04	.02
303	Hoby Brenner	.05	.04	.02
304	Dalton Hilliard	.05	.04	.02
305	Robert Massey	.05	.04	.02
306	John Fourcade	.10	.08	.04
307	Lonzell Hill	.05	.04	.02
308	Saints Crest	.05	.04	.02
309	Jim Dombrowski	.05	.04	.02
310	Pat Swilling	.15	.11	.06
311	Vaughan Johnson	.05	.04	.02
312	Eric Martin	.10	.08	.04
313	Giants Crest	.05	.04	.02
314	Ottis Anderson	.10	.08	.04
315	Myron Guyton	.05	.04	.02
316	Terry Kinard	.05	.04	.02
317	Mark Bavaro	.10	.08	.04
318	Phil Simms	.25	.20	.10
319	Lawrence Taylor	.30	.25	.12
320	Odessa Turner	.05	.04	.02
321	Erik Howard	.05	.04	.02
322	Mark Collins	.05	.04	.02
323	Dave Meggett	.15	.11	.06
324	Leonard Marshall	.05	.04	.02
325	Carl Banks	.10	.08	.04
326	Anthony Toney	.05	.04	.02
327	Seth Joyner	.15	.11	.06
328	Cris Carter	.20	.15	.08
329	Eric Allen	.05	.04	.02
330	Keith Jackson	.20	.15	.08
331	Clyde Simmons	.10	.08	.04
332	Byron Evans	.05	.04	.02
333	Keith Byars	.10	.08	.04
334	Eagles Crest	.05	.04	.02
335	Reggie White	.25	.20	.10
336	Izel Jenkins	.05	.04	.02
337	Jerome Brown	.15	.11	.06
338	David Alexander	.05	.04	.02
339	Cardinals Crest	.05	.04	.02
340	Rich Camarillo	.05	.04	.02
341	Ken Harvey	.05	.04	.02
342	Luis Sharpe	.05	.04	.02
343	Timm Rosenbach	.10	.08	.04
344	Tim McDonald	.15	.11	.06
345	Vai Sikahema	.05	.04	.02
346	Freddie Joe Nunn	.05	.04	.02
347	Ernie Jones	.05	.04	.02
348	J.T. Smith	.10	.08	.04
349	Eric Hill	.05	.04	.02
350	Roy Green	.10	.08	.04
351	Anthony Bell	.05	.04	.02
352	Kevin Fagan	.05	.04	.02
353	Roger Craig	.15	.11	.06
354	Ronnie Lott	.20	.15	.08
355	Mike Cofer	.05	.04	.02
356	John Taylor	.20	.15	.08
357	Joe Montana	3.00	2.25	1.25
358	Charles Haley	.10	.08	.04
359	Guy McIntyre	.05	.04	.02
360	49ers Crest	.05	.04	.02
361	Pierce Holt	.15	.11	.06
362	Tom Rathman	.15	.11	.06
363	Jerry Rice	1.50	1.25	.60
364	Michael Carter	.10	.08	.04
365	Buccaneers Crest	.05	.04	.02
366	Lars Tate	.05	.04	.02
367	Paul Gruber	.10	.08	.04
368	Winston Moss	.05	.04	.02
369	Reuben Davis	.05	.04	.02
370	Mark Robinson	.05	.04	.02
371	Bruce Hill	.05	.04	.02
372	Kevin Murphy	.05	.04	.02
373	Ricky Reynolds	.05	.04	.02
374	Harry Hamilton	.05	.04	.02
375	Vinny Testaverde	.15	.11	.06
376	Mark Carrier	.15	.11	.06
377	Ervin Randle	.05	.04	.02
378	Ricky Sanders	.10	.08	.04
379	Charles Mann	.10	.08	.04
380	Jim Lachey	.10	.08	.04
381	Wilber Marshall	.10	.08	.04
382	A.J. Johnson	.05	.04	.02
383	Darrell Green	.10	.08	.04
384	Mark Rypien	.15	.11	.06
385	Gerald Riggs	.10	.08	.04
386	Redskins Crest	.05	.04	.02
387	Alvin Walton	.05	.04	.02
388	Art Monk	.15	.11	.06
389	Gary Clark	.15	.11	.06
390	Earnest Byner	.10	.08	.04
391	SB XXIV Action (Jerry Rice)	.75	.60	.30
392	SB XXIV Action (49er Offensive Line)	.15	.11	.06
393	SB XXIV Action (Tom Rathman)	.25	.20	.10
394	SB XXIV Action (Chet Brooks)	.10	.08	.04
395	SB XXIV Action (John Elway)	1.00	.70	.40
396	SB XXIV Action (Joe Montana)	3.00	2.25	1.25
----	Panin Album	2.00	1.50	.80

1972 Sunoco Stamps

22 Zeke Moore LCB
Houston Oilers

Each NFL team is represented by 24 players in this 624-stamp set - 12 offensive and 12 defensive players have been chosen. The stamps measure 1 5/8" by 2 3/8" and were given away in perforated sheets of

318

nine at participating Sun Oil Co. gas stations. Each stamp, featuring an oval with a player photo inside against a corresponding team color-coded background, is unnumbered. Two albums were issued to hold the stamps - a 56-page "NFL Action '72" album and a 128-page album. The albums had specific spots for each sticker, as indicated by a square providing the player's name, age, height, weight and college he attended. There were 16 additional perforated sheets inside the album, too. The stamps could be placed inside the album by using the tabs which were provided with the album, instead of licking them.

		NM	EX	VG
	Complete Set (624):	125.00	62.00	37.00
	Common Player:	.10	.05	.03
(1)	Ken Burrow	.15	.08	.05
(2)	Bill Sandeman	.10	.05	.03
(3)	Andy Maurer	.10	.05	.03
(4)	Jeff Van Note	.20	.10	.06
(5)	Malcolm Snider	.10	.05	.03
(6)	George Kunz	.25	.13	.08
(7)	Jim Mitchell	.10	.05	.03
(8)	Wes Chesson	.10	.05	.03
(9)	Bob Berry	.20	.10	.06
(10)	Dick Shiner	.10	.05	.03
(11)	Jim Butler	.10	.05	.03
(12)	Art Malone	.10	.05	.03
(13)	Claude Humphrey	.25	.13	.08
(14)	John Small	.10	.05	.03
(15)	Glen Condren	.10	.05	.03
(16)	John Zook	.20	.10	.06
(17)	Don Hansen	.10	.05	.03
(18)	Tommy Nobis	1.25	.60	.40
(19)	Greg Brezina	.20	.10	.06
(20)	Ken Reaves	.10	.05	.03
(21)	Tom Hayes	.10	.05	.03
(22)	Tom McCauley	.10	.05	.03
(23)	Bill Bell	.15	.08	.05
(24)	Bill Lothridge	.20	.10	.06
(25)	Ed Hinton	.10	.05	.03
(26)	Bob Vogel	.10	.05	.03
(27)	Glenn Ressler	.10	.05	.03
(28)	Bill Curry	.30	.15	.09
(29)	John Williams	.10	.05	.03
(30)	Dan Sullivan	.10	.05	.03
(31)	Tom Mitchell	.10	.05	.03
(32)	John Mackey	1.50	.70	.45
(33)	Ray Perkins	2.00	1.00	.60
(34)	John Unitas	6.00	3.00	1.75
(35)	Tom Matte	.30	.15	.09
(36)	Norm Bulaich	.25	.13	.08
(37)	Bubba Smith	1.00	.50	.30
(38)	Bill Newsome	.10	.05	.03
(39)	Fred Miller	.10	.05	.03
(40)	Roy Hinton	.10	.05	.03
(41)	Ray May	.10	.05	.03
(42)	Ted Hendricks	1.50	.70	.45
(43)	Charlie Stukes	.10	.05	.03
(44)	Rex Kern	.30	.15	.09
(45)	Jerry Logan	.10	.05	.03
(46)	Rick Volk	.20	.10	.06
(47)	David Lee	.15	.08	.05
(48)	Jim O'Brien	.25	.13	.08
(49)	J.D. Hill	.20	.10	.06
(50)	Willie Young	.10	.05	.03
(51)	Jim Reilly	.10	.05	.03
(52)	Bruce Jarvis	.15	.08	.05
(53)	Levert Carr	.10	.05	.03
(54)	Donnie Green	.10	.05	.03
(55)	Jan White	.20	.10	.06
(56)	Marlin Briscoe	.40	.20	.12
(57)	Dennis Shaw	.15	.08	.05
(58)	O.J. Simpson	12.00	6.00	3.50
(59)	Wayne Patrick	.10	.05	.03
(60)	John Leypoldt	.10	.05	.03
(61)	Al Cowlings	.75	.40	.25
(62)	Jim Dunaway	.20	.10	.06
(63)	Bob Tatarek	.10	.05	.03
(64)	Cal Snowden	.10	.05	.03
(65)	Paul Guidry	.10	.05	.03
(66)	Edgar Chandler	.20	.10	.06
(67)	Al Andrews	.10	.05	.03
(68)	Robert James	.10	.05	.03
(69)	Alvin Wyatt	.10	.05	.03
(70)	John Pitts	.10	.05	.03
(71)	Pete Richardson	.15	.08	.05
(72)	Spike Jones	.10	.05	.03
(73)	Dick Gordon	.20	.10	.06
(74)	Randy Jackson	.10	.05	.03
(75)	Glen Holloway	.10	.05	.03
(76)	Rick Coady	.10	.05	.03
(77)	Jim Cadile	.10	.05	.03
(78)	Steve Wright	.10	.05	.03
(79)	Bob Wallace	.10	.05	.03
(80)	George Farmer	.15	.08	.05
(81)	Bobby Douglass	.40	.20	.12
(82)	Don Shy	.10	.05	.03
(83)	Cyril Pinder	.10	.05	.03
(84)	Mac Percival	.10	.05	.03
(85)	Willie Holman	.10	.05	.03
(86)	George Seals	.15	.08	.05
(87)	Bill Staley	.10	.05	.03
(88)	Ed O'Bradovich	.20	.10	.06
(89)	Doug Buffone	.10	.05	.03
(90)	Dick Butkus	3.00	1.50	.90
(91)	Ross Brupbacher	.20	.10	.06
(92)	Charlie Ford	.10	.05	.03
(93)	Joe Taylor	.10	.05	.03
(94)	Ron Smith	.20	.10	.06
(95)	Jerry Moore	.10	.05	.03
(96)	Bobby Joe Green	.15	.08	.05
(97)	Chip Myers	.10	.05	.03
(98)	Rufus Mayes	.10	.05	.03
(99)	Howard Fest	.10	.05	.03
(100)	Bob Johnson	.30	.15	.09
(101)	Pat Matson	.10	.05	.03
(102)	Vern Holland	.10	.05	.03
(103)	Bruce Coslet	.75	.40	.25
(104)	Bob Trumpy	1.00	.50	.30
(105)	Virgil Carter	.20	.10	.06
(106)	Fred Willis	.10	.05	.03
(107)	Jess Phillips	.10	.05	.03
(108)	Horst Muhlmann	.15	.08	.05
(109)	Royce Berry	.10	.05	.03
(110)	Mike Reid	.50	.25	.15
(111)	Steve Chomyszak	.10	.05	.03
(112)	Ron Carpenter	.10	.05	.03
(113)	Al Beauchamp	.15	.08	.05
(114)	Bill Bergey	.50	.25	.15
(115)	Ken Avery	.10	.05	.03
(116)	Lemar Parrish	.40	.20	.12
(117)	Ken Riley	.40	.20	.12
(118)	Sandy Durko	.10	.05	.03
(119)	Dave Lewis	.10	.05	.03
(120)	Paul Robinson	.20	.10	.06
(121)	Fair Hooker	.20	.10	.06
(122)	Doug Dieken	.10	.05	.03
(123)	John Demarie	.10	.05	.03
(124)	Jim Copeland	.10	.05	.03
(125)	Gene Hickerson	.10	.05	.03
(126)	Bob McKay	.10	.05	.03
(127)	Milt Morin	.20	.10	.06
(128)	Frank Pitts	.10	.05	.03
(129)	Mike Phipps	.50	.25	.15
(130)	Leroy Kelly	1.50	.70	.45
(131)	Bo Scott	.20	.10	.06
(132)	Don Cockroft	.10	.05	.03
(133)	Ron Snidow	.10	.05	.03
(134)	Walter Johnson	.10	.05	.03
(135)	Jerry Sherk	.30	.15	.09
(136)	Jack Gregory	.10	.05	.03
(137)	Jim Houston	.10	.05	.03
(138)	Dale Lindsey	.10	.05	.03
(139)	Bill Andrews	.25	.13	.08

(140)	Clarence Scott	.20	.10	.06	(218)	Francis Peay	.10	.05	.03
(141)	Ernie Kellerman	.10	.05	.03	(219)	Bill Lueck	.10	.05	.03
(142)	Walt Sumner	.10	.05	.03	(220)	Ken Bowman	.10	.05	.03
(143)	Mike Howell	.10	.05	.03	(221)	Gale Gillingham	.20	.10	.06
(144)	Reece Morrison	.10	.05	.03	(222)	Dick Himes	.10	.05	.03
(145)	Bob Hayes	1.00	.50	.30	(223)	Rich McGeorge	.10	.05	.03
(146)	Ralph Neely	.20	.10	.06	(224)	Carroll Dale	.20	.10	.06
(147)	John Niland	.10	.05	.03	(225)	Bart Starr	3.50	1.75	1.00
(148)	Dave Manders	.20	.10	.06	(226)	Scott Hunter	.30	.15	.09
(149)	Blaine Nye	.10	.05	.03	(227)	John Brockington	.30	.15	.09
(150)	Rayfield Wright	.20	.10	.06	(228)	Dave Hampton	.20	.10	.06
(151)	Billy Truax	.10	.05	.03	(229)	Clarence Williams	.10	.05	.03
(152)	Lance Alworth	3.00	1.50	.90	(230)	Mike McCoy	.20	.10	.06
(153)	Roger Staubach	10.00	5.00	3.00	(231)	Bob Brown	.20	.10	.06
(154)	Duane Thomas	.50	.25	.15	(232)	Alden Roche	.10	.05	.03
(155)	Walt Garrison	.30	.15	.09	(233)	Dave Robinson	.25	.13	.08
(156)	Mike Clark	.10	.05	.03	(234)	Jim Carter	.20	.10	.06
(157)	Larry Cole	.10	.05	.03	(235)	Fred Carr	.20	.10	.06
(158)	Jethro Pugh	.20	.10	.06	(236)	Ken Ellis	.15	.08	.05
(159)	Bob Lilly	2.00	1.00	.60	(237)	Doug Hart	.10	.05	.03
(160)	George Andrie	.20	.10	.06	(238)	Al Randolph	.10	.05	.03
(161)	Dave Edwards	.10	.05	.03	(239)	Al Matthews	.10	.05	.03
(162)	Lee Roy Jordan	.90	.45	.25	(240)	Tim Webster	.10	.05	.03
(163)	Chuck Howley	.30	.15	.09	(241)	Jim Beirne	.10	.05	.03
(164)	Herb Adderley	1.00	.50	.30	(242)	Bob Young	.10	.05	.03
(165)	Mel Renfro	.75	.40	.25	(243)	Elbert Drungo	.10	.05	.03
(166)	Cornell Green	.30	.15	.09	(244)	Sam Walton	.20	.10	.06
(167)	Cliff Harris	.20	.10	.06	(245)	Alvin Reed	.10	.05	.03
(168)	Ron Widby	.10	.05	.03	(246)	Charlie Joiner	1.50	.70	.45
(169)	Jerry Simmons	.10	.05	.03	(247)	Dan Pastorini	.30	.15	.09
(170)	Roger Shoals	.10	.05	.03	(248)	Charlie Johnson	.30	.15	.09
(171)	Larron Jackson	.10	.05	.03	(249)	Lynn Dickey	.40	.20	.12
(172)	George Goeddeke	.10	.05	.03	(250)	Woody Campbell	.10	.05	.03
(173)	Mike Schnitker	.10	.05	.03	(251)	Robert Holmes	.20	.10	.06
(174)	Mike Current	.10	.05	.03	(252)	Mark Moseley	.30	.15	.09
(175)	Billy Masters	.15	.08	.05	(253)	Pat Holmes	.10	.05	.03
(176)	Jack Gehrke	.10	.05	.03	(254)	Mike Tilleman	.10	.05	.03
(177)	Don Horn	.20	.10	.06	(255)	Leo Brooks	.10	.05	.03
(178)	Floyd Little	1.00	.50	.30	(256)	Elvin Bethea	.30	.15	.09
(179)	Bobby Anderson	.30	.15	.09	(257)	George Webster	.30	.15	.09
(180)	Jim Turner	.20	.10	.06	(258)	Garland Boyette	.10	.05	.03
(181)	Rich Jackson	.10	.05	.03	(259)	Ron Pritchard	.15	.08	.05
(182)	Paul Smith	.10	.05	.03	(260)	Zeke Moore	.10	.05	.03
(183)	Dave Costa	.10	.05	.03	(261)	Willie Alexander	.10	.05	.03
(184)	Lyle Alzado	1.00	.50	.30	(262)	Ken Houston	1.00	.50	.30
(185)	Olen Underwood	.10	.05	.03	(263)	John Charles	.10	.05	.03
(186)	Fred Forsberg	.10	.05	.03	(264)	Linzy Cole	.10	.05	.03
(187)	Chip Myrtle	.10	.05	.03	(265)	Elmo Wright	.25	.13	.08
(188)	Leroy Mitchell	.10	.05	.03	(266)	Jim Tyrer	.20	.10	.06
(189)	Billy Thompson	.20	.10	.06	(267)	Ed Buddle	.20	.10	.06
(190)	Charlie Greer	.10	.05	.03	(268)	Jack Rudnay	.10	.05	.03
(191)	George Saimes	.20	.10	.06	(269)	Mo Moorman	.10	.05	.03
(192)	Billy Van Heusen	.10	.05	.03	(270)	Dave Hill	.10	.05	.03
(193)	Earl McCullouch	.20	.10	.06	(271)	Morris Stroud	.10	.05	.03
(194)	Jim Yarbrough	.10	.05	.03	(272)	Otis Taylor	.40	.20	.12
(195)	Chuck Walton	.15	.08	.05	(273)	Len Dawson	3.00	1.50	.90
(196)	Ed Flanagan	.10	.05	.03	(274)	Ed Podolak	.30	.15	.09
(197)	Frank Gallagher	.10	.05	.03	(275)	Wendell Hayes	.10	.05	.03
(198)	Rockne Freitas	.10	.05	.03	(276)	Jan Stenerud	1.25	.60	.40
(199)	Charlie Sanders	.25	.13	.08	(277)	Marvin Upshaw	.10	.05	.03
(200)	Larry Walton	.10	.05	.03	(278)	Curley Culp	.30	.15	.09
(201)	Greg Landry	.40	.20	.12	(279)	Buck Buchanan	1.00	.50	.30
(202)	Altie Taylor	.20	.10	.06	(280)	Aaron Brown	.10	.05	.03
(203)	Steve Owens	.40	.20	.12	(281)	Bobby Bell	1.25	.60	.40
(204)	Errol Mann	.10	.05	.03	(282)	Willie Lanier	1.50	.70	.45
(205)	Joe Robb	.10	.05	.03	(283)	Jim Lynch	.20	.10	.06
(206)	Dick Evey	.10	.05	.03	(284)	Jim Marsalis	.20	.10	.06
(207)	Jerry Rush	.10	.05	.03	(285)	Emmitt Thomas	.20	.10	.06
(208)	Larry Hand	.15	.08	.05	(286)	Jim Kearney	.10	.05	.03
(209)	Paul Naumoff	.20	.10	.06	(287)	Johnny Robinson	.40	.20	.12
(210)	Mike Lucci	.20	.10	.06	(288)	Jerrel Wilson	.10	.05	.03
(211)	Wayne Walker	.10	.05	.03	(289)	Jack Snow	.35	.20	.11
(212)	Lem Barney	1.00	.50	.30	(290)	Charlie Cowan	.10	.05	.03
(213)	Dick LeBeau	.20	.10	.06	(291)	Tom Mack	.50	.25	.15
(214)	Mike Weger	.10	.05	.03	(292)	Ken Iman	.10	.05	.03
(215)	Wayne Rasmussen	.10	.05	.03	(293)	Joe Scibelli	.10	.05	.03
(216)	Herman Weaver	.10	.05	.03	(294)	Harry Schuh	.10	.05	.03
(217)	John Spilis	.10	.05	.03	(295)	Rob Klein	.20	.10	.06

320

(296)	Lance Rentzel	.35	.20	.11	(374)	Dave Rowe	.10	.05	.03
(297)	Roman Gabriel	.60	.30	.20	(375)	Julius Adams	.20	.10	.06
(298)	Les Josephson	.20	.10	.06	(376)	Dennis Wirgowski	.10	.05	.03
(299)	Willie Ellison	.20	.10	.06	(377)	Ed Weisacosky	.10	.05	.03
(300)	David Ray	.10	.05	.03	(378)	Jim Cheyunski	.10	.05	.03
(301)	Jack Youngblood	1.25	.60	.40	(379)	Steve Kiner	.10	.05	.03
(302)	Merlin Olsen	1.75	.90	.50	(380)	Larry Carwell	.10	.05	.03
(303)	Phil Olsen	.10	.05	.03	(381)	John Outlaw	.10	.05	.03
(304)	Coy Bacon	.10	.05	.03	(382)	Rickie Harris	.10	.05	.03
(305)	Jim Purnell	.10	.05	.03	(383)	Don Webb	.10	.05	.03
(306)	Marlin McKeever	.20	.10	.06	(384)	Tom Janik	.10	.05	.03
(307)	Isiah Robertson	.30	.15	.09	(385)	Al Dodd	.20	.10	.06
(308)	Jim Nettles	.10	.05	.03	(386)	Don Morrison	.10	.05	.03
(309)	Gene Howard	.10	.05	.03	(387)	Jake Kupp	.10	.05	.03
(310)	Kermit Alexander	.20	.10	.06	(388)	John Didion	.10	.05	.03
(311)	Dave Elmendorf	.10	.05	.03	(389)	Del Williams	.10	.05	.03
(312)	Pat Studstill	.20	.10	.06	(390)	Glen Ray Hines	.10	.05	.03
(313)	Paul Warfield	1.50	.70	.45	(391)	Dave Parks	.20	.10	.06
(314)	Doug Crusan	.10	.05	.03	(392)	Dan Abramowicz	.40	.20	.12
(315)	Bob Kuechenberg	.50	.25	.15	(393)	Archie Manning	2.00	1.00	.60
(316)	Bob DeMarco	.20	.10	.06	(394)	Bob Gresham	.10	.05	.03
(317)	Larry Little	1.00	.50	.30	(395)	Virgil Robinson	.10	.05	.03
(318)	Norm Evans	.20	.10	.06	(396)	Charlie Durkee	.10	.05	.03
(319)	Marv Fleming	.20	.10	.06	(397)	Richard Neal	.10	.05	.03
(320)	Howard Twilley	.30	.15	.09	(398)	Bob Pollard	.10	.05	.03
(321)	Bob Griese	2.50	1.25	.70	(399)	Dave Long	.10	.05	.03
(322)	Jim Klick	.60	.30	.20	(400)	Joe Owens	.10	.05	.03
(323)	Larry Csonka	2.00	1.00	.60	(401)	Carl Cunningham	.10	.05	.03
(324)	Garo Yepremian	.30	.15	.09	(402)	Jim Flanigan	.15	.08	.05
(325)	Jim Riley	.10	.05	.03	(403)	Wayne Colman	.10	.05	.03
(326)	Manny Fernandez	.30	.15	.09	(404)	D'Artagnan Martin	.10	.05	.03
(327)	Bob Heinz	.10	.05	.03	(405)	Delles Howell	.10	.05	.03
(328)	Bill Stanfill	.30	.15	.09	(406)	Hugo Hollas	.10	.05	.03
(329)	Doug Swift	.10	.05	.03	(407)	Doug Wyatt	.10	.05	.03
(330)	Nick Buoniconti	1.00	.50	.30	(408)	Julian Fagan	.10	.05	.03
(331)	Mike Kolen	.10	.05	.03	(409)	Don Hermann	.10	.05	.03
(332)	Tim Foley	.30	.15	.09	(410)	Willie Young	.10	.05	.03
(333)	Curtis Johnson	.10	.05	.03	(411)	Bob Hyland	.10	.05	.03
(334)	Dick Anderson	.40	.20	.12	(412)	Greg Larson	.10	.05	.03
(335)	Jake Scott	.50	.25	.15	(413)	Doug Van Horn	.10	.05	.03
(336)	Larry Seiple	.10	.05	.03	(414)	Charlie Harper	.10	.05	.03
(337)	Gene Washington	.20	.10	.06	(415)	Bob Tucker	.25	.13	.08
(338)	Grady Alderman	.10	.05	.03	(416)	Joe Morrison	.20	.10	.06
(339)	Ed White	.25	.13	.08	(417)	Randy Johnson	.20	.10	.06
(340)	Mick Tingelhoff	.20	.10	.06	(418)	Tucker Frederickson	.30	.15	.09
(341)	Milt Sunde	.10	.05	.03	(419)	ROn Johnson	.30	.15	.09
(342)	Ron Yary	.50	.25	.15	(420)	Pete Gogolak	.20	.10	.06
(343)	John Beasley	.10	.05	.03	(421)	Henry Reed	.10	.05	.03
(344)	John Henderson	.10	.05	.03	(422)	Jim Kanicki	.10	.05	.03
(345)	Fran Tarkenton	4.00	2.00	1.25	(423)	Roland Lakes	.10	.05	.03
(346)	Clint Jones	.20	.10	.06	(424)	John Douglas	.10	.05	.03
(347)	Dave Osborn	.20	.10	.06	(425)	Ron Hornsby	.10	.05	.03
(348)	Fred Cox	.20	.10	.06	(426)	Jim Files	.10	.05	.03
(349)	Carl Eller	.50	.25	.15	(427)	Willie Williams	.10	.05	.03
(350)	Gary Larsen	.10	.05	.03	(428)	Otto Brown	.10	.05	.03
(351)	Alan Page	1.00	.50	.30	(429)	Scott Eaton	.10	.05	.03
(352)	Jim Marshall	1.00	.50	.30	(430)	Carl Lockhart	.20	.10	.06
(353)	Roy Winston	.20	.10	.06	(431)	Tom Blanchard	.20	.10	.06
(354)	Lonnie Warwick	.10	.05	.03	(432)	Rocky Thompson	.20	.10	.06
(355)	Wally Hilgenberg	.10	.05	.03	(433)	Rich Caster	.30	.15	.09
(356)	Bobby Bryant	.15	.08	.05	(434)	Randy Rasmussen	.10	.05	.03
(357)	Ed Sharockman	.10	.05	.03	(435)	John Schmitt	.10	.05	.03
(358)	Charlie West	.10	.05	.03	(436)	Dave Herman	.20	.10	.06
(359)	Paul Krause	.60	.30	.20	(437)	Winston Hill	.20	.10	.06
(360)	Bob Lee	.20	.10	.06	(438)	Pete Lammons	.20	.10	.06
(361)	Randy Vataha	.40	.20	.12	(439)	Don Maynard	2.00	1.00	.60
(362)	Mike Montler	.10	.05	.03	(440)	Joe Namath	10.00	5.00	3.00
(363)	Halvor Hagen	.10	.05	.03	(441)	Emerson Boozer	.30	.15	.09
(364)	Jon Morris	.10	.05	.03	(442)	John Riggins	4.00	2.00	1.25
(365)	Len St. Jean	.10	.05	.03	(443)	George Nock	.10	.05	.03
(366)	Tom Neville	.10	.05	.03	(444)	Bobby Howfield	.10	.05	.03
(367)	Tom Beer	.15	.08	.05	(445)	Gerry Philbin	.10	.05	.03
(368)	Ron Sellers	.20	.10	.06	(446)	John Little	.10	.05	.03
(369)	Jim Plunkett	1.00	.50	.30	(447)	Chuck Hinton	.10	.05	.03
(370)	Carl Garrett	.20	.10	.06	(448)	Mark Lomas	.10	.05	.03
(371)	Jim Nance	.30	.15	.09	(449)	Ralph Baker	.10	.05	.03
(372)	Charlie Gogolak	.20	.10	.06	(450)	Al Atkinson	.10	.05	.03
(373)	Ike Lassiter	.10	.05	.03	(451)	Larry Grantham	.20	.10	.06

Stamps/stickers

(452)	John Dockery	.10	.05	.03
(453)	Earlie Thomas	.10	.05	.03
(454)	Phil Wise	.10	.05	.03
(455)	W.K. Hicks	.10	.05	.03
(456)	Steve O'Neal	.15	.08	.05
(457)	Drew Buie	.10	.05	.03
(458)	Art Shell	2.00	1.00	.60
(459)	Gene Upshaw	2.00	1.00	.60
(460)	Jim Otto	.75	.40	.25
(461)	Geprge Buehler	.10	.05	.03
(462)	Bob Brown	.40	.20	.12
(463)	Ray Chester	.40	.20	.12
(464)	Fred Biletnikoff	2.00	1.00	.60
(465)	Daryle Lamonica	.60	.30	.20
(466)	Marv Hubbard	.20	.10	.06
(467)	Clarence Davis	.20	.10	.06
(468)	George Blanda	2.00	1.00	.60
(469)	Tony Cline	.10	.05	.03
(470)	Art Thoms	.10	.05	.03
(471)	Tom Keating	.20	.10	.06
(472)	Ben Davidson	1.00	.50	.30
(473)	Phil Villapiano	.40	.20	.12
(474)	Dan Conners	.10	.05	.03
(475)	Duane Benson	.10	.05	.03
(476)	Nemiah Wilson	.10	.05	.03
(477)	Willie Brown	1.00	.50	.30
(478)	George Atkinson	.20	.10	.06
(479)	Jack Tatum	.40	.20	.12
(480)	Jerry DePoyster	.10	.05	.03
(481)	Harold Jackson	.50	.25	.15
(482)	Wade Key	.10	.05	.03
(483)	Henry Allison	.10	.05	.03
(484)	Mike Evans	.10	.05	.03
(485)	Steve Smith	.20	.10	.06
(486)	Harold Carmichael	1.25	.60	.40
(487)	Ben Hawkins	.20	.10	.06
(488)	Pete Liske	.40	.20	.12
(489)	Rick Arrington	.10	.05	.03
(490)	Lee Bouggess	.10	.05	.03
(491)	Tom Woodeshick	.20	.10	.06
(492)	Tom Dempsey	.50	.25	.15
(493)	Richard Harris	.20	.10	.06
(494)	Don Hultz	.10	.05	.03
(495)	Ernie Calloway	.15	.08	.05
(496)	Mel Tom	.10	.05	.03
(497)	Steve Zabel	.20	.10	.06
(498)	Tim Rossovich	.20	.10	.06
(499)	Ron Porter	.10	.05	.03
(500)	Al Nelson	.10	.05	.03
(501)	Nate Ramsey	.10	.05	.03
(502)	Leroy Keyes	.40	.20	.12
(503)	Bill Bradley	.50	.25	.15
(504)	Tom McNeill	.10	.05	.03
(505)	Dave Smith	.10	.05	.03
(506)	Jon Kolb	.10	.05	.03
(507)	Gerry Mullins	.10	.05	.03
(508)	Ray Mansfield	.10	.05	.03
(509)	Bruce Van Dyke	.10	.05	.03
(510)	John Brown	.10	.05	.03
(511)	Ron Shanklin	.30	.15	.09
(512)	Terry Bradshaw	7.50	3.75	2.25
(513)	Terry Hanratty	.40	.20	.12
(514)	Preston Pearson	.40	.20	.12
(515)	John Fuqua	.20	.10	.06
(516)	Roy Gerela	.10	.05	.03
(517)	L.C. Greenwood	.75	.40	.25
(518)	Joe Greene	2.50	1.25	.70
(519)	Lloyd Voss	.10	.05	.03
(520)	Dwight White	.20	.10	.06
(521)	Jack Ham	2.50	1.25	.70
(522)	Chuck Allen	.10	.05	.03
(523)	Brian Stenger	.10	.05	.03
(524)	Andy Russell	.75	.40	.25
(525)	John Rowser	.10	.05	.03
(526)	Mel Blount	2.00	1.00	.60
(527)	Mike Wagner	.20	.10	.06
(528)	Bobby Walden	.10	.05	.03
(529)	Mel Gray	.30	.15	.09
(530)	Bob Reynolds	.10	.05	.03
(531)	Dan Dierdorf	.60	.30	.20
(532)	Wayne Mulligan	.10	.05	.03
(533)	Clyde Williams	.10	.05	.03
(534)	Ernie McMillan	.10	.05	.03
(535)	Jackie Smith	1.00	.50	.30
(536)	John Gilliam	.20	.10	.06
(537)	Jim Hart	.50	.25	.15
(538)	Pete Beathard	.40	.20	.12
(539)	Johnny Roland	.30	.15	.09
(540)	Jim Bakken	.30	.15	.09
(541)	Ron Yankowski	.10	.05	.03
(542)	Fred Heron	.15	.08	.05
(543)	Bob Rowe	.10	.05	.03
(544)	Chuck Walker	.10	.05	.03
(545)	Larry Stallings	.20	.10	.06
(546)	Jamie Rivers	.10	.05	.03
(547)	Mike McGill	.10	.05	.03
(548)	Miller Farr	.10	.05	.03
(549)	Roger Wehrli	.30	.15	.09
(550)	Larry Willingham	.10	.05	.03
(551)	Larry Wilson	1.00	.50	.30
(552)	Chuck Latourette	.10	.05	.03
(553)	Billy Parks	.20	.10	.06
(554)	Terry Owens	.25	.13	.08
(555)	Doug Wilkerson	.10	.05	.03
(556)	Carl Mauck	.10	.05	.03
(557)	Walt Sweeney	.10	.05	.03
(558)	Russ Washington	.10	.05	.03
(559)	Pettis Norman	.20	.10	.06
(560)	Gary Garrison	.20	.10	.06
(561)	John Hadl	.60	.30	.20
(562)	Mike Montgomery	.10	.05	.03
(563)	Mike Garrett	.30	.15	.09
(564)	Dennis Partee	.10	.05	.03
(565)	Deacon Jones	1.00	.50	.30
(566)	Ron East	.10	.05	.03
(567)	Kevin Hardy	.10	.05	.03
(568)	Steve DeLong	.20	.10	.06
(569)	Rick Redman	.10	.05	.03
(570)	Bob Babich	.15	.08	.05
(571)	Pete Barnes	.10	.05	.03
(572)	Bob Howard	.10	.05	.03
(573)	Joe Beauchamp	.10	.05	.03
(574)	Bryant Salter	.10	.05	.03
(575)	Chris Fletcher	.10	.05	.03
(576)	Jerry LeVias	.20	.10	.06
(577)	Dick Witcher	.10	.05	.03
(578)	Len Rohde	.12	.06	.04
(579)	Randy Beisler	.10	.05	.03
(580)	Forrest Blue	.20	.10	.06
(581)	Woody Peoples	.10	.05	.03
(582)	Cas Banaszek	.10	.05	.03
(583)	Ted Kwalick	.40	.20	.12
(584)	Gene Washington	.50	.25	.15
(585)	John Brodie	1.25	.60	.40
(586)	Ken Willard	.40	.20	.12
(587)	Vic Washington	.20	.10	.06
(588)	Bruce Gossett	.10	.05	.03
(589)	Tommy Hart	.15	.08	.05
(590)	Charlie Krueger	.20	.10	.06
(591)	Earl Edwards	.10	.05	.03
(592)	Cedric Hardman	.20	.10	.06
(593)	Dave Wilcox	.25	.13	.08
(594)	Frank Nunley	.10	.05	.03
(595)	Skip Vanderbundt	.10	.05	.03
(596)	Jimmy Johnson	.60	.30	.20
(597)	Bruce Taylor	.30	.15	.09
(598)	Mel Phillips	.10	.05	.03
(599)	Rosey Taylor	.20	.10	.06
(600)	Steve Spurrier	2.50	1.25	.70
(601)	Charley Taylor	1.50	.70	.45
(602)	Jim Snowden	.10	.05	.03
(603)	Ray Schoenke	.10	.05	.03
(604)	Len Hauss	.20	.10	.06
(605)	John Wilbur	.10	.05	.03
(606)	Walt Rock	.10	.05	.03
(607)	Jerry Smith	.20	.10	.06

(608)	Roy Jefferson	.20	.10	.06
(609)	Bill Kilmer	1.00	.50	.30
(610)	Larry Brown	1.00	.50	.30
(611)	Charlie Harraway	.20	.10	.06
(612)	Curt Knight	.10	.05	.03
(613)	Ron McDole	.10	.05	.03
(614)	Manuel Sistrunk	.10	.05	.03
(615)	Diron Talbert	.20	.10	.06
(616)	Verlon Biggs	.10	.05	.03
(617)	Jack Pardee	.75	.40	.25
(618)	Myron Pottios	.20	.10	.06
(619)	Chris Hanburger	.50	.25	.15
(620)	Pat Fischer	.20	.10	.06
(621)	Mike Bass	.10	.05	.03
(622)	Richie Petitbon	.20	.10	.06
(623)	Brig Owens	.10	.05	.03
(624)	Mike Bragg	.15	.08	.05

1972 Sunoco Stamps Update

These unnumbered 1 5/8" by 2 3/8" stamps are identical to the 1972 Sunoco stamps, but were not listed in the album which was produced to house the stamps. They were issued as team sheets later in the year.

		NM	EX	VG
	Complete Set (82):	75.00	37.00	22.00
	Common Player:	1.00	.50	.30
(1)	Clarence Ellis	1.00	.50	.30
(2)	Dave Hampton	1.50	.70	.45
(3)	Dennis Havig	1.00	.50	.30
(4)	John James	1.00	.50	.30
(5)	Joe Profit	1.00	.50	.30
(6)	Lonnie Hepburn	1.00	.50	.30
(7)	Dennis Nelson	1.00	.50	.30
(8)	Mike McBath	1.00	.50	.30
(9)	Walt Patulski	1.00	.50	.30
(10)	Bob Asher	1.00	.50	.30
(11)	Steve DeLong	1.00	.50	.30
(12)	Tony McGee	1.00	.50	.30
(13)	James Osborne	1.00	.50	.30
(14)	Jim Seymour	1.00	.50	.30
(15)	Tommy Casanova	1.50	.70	.45
(16)	Neil Craig	1.00	.50	.30
(17)	Essex Johnson	1.25	.60	.40
(18)	Sherman White	1.00	.50	.30
(19)	Bob Briggs	1.00	.50	.30
(20)	Thom Darden	1.25	.60	.40
(21)	Marv Bateman	1.00	.50	.30
(22)	Toni Fritsch	1.00	.50	.30
(23)	Calvin Hill	3.00	1.50	.90
(24)	Pat Toomay	1.25	.60	.40
(25)	Pete Duranko	1.00	.50	.30
(26)	Marv Montgomery	1.00	.50	.30
(27)	Rod Sherman	1.00	.50	.30
(28)	Bob Kowalkowski	1.00	.50	.30
(29)	Jim Mitchell	1.00	.50	.30
(30)	Larry Woods	1.00	.50	.30
(31)	Willie Buchanon	1.50	.70	.45
(32)	Leland Glass	1.00	.50	.30
(33)	MacArthur Lane	1.50	.70	.45
(34)	Chester Marcol	1.00	.50	.30
(35)	Ron Widby	1.00	.50	.30
(36)	Ken Burrough	1.50	.70	.45
(37)	Calvin Hunt	1.00	.50	.30
(38)	Ron Saul	1.00	.50	.30
(39)	Greg Simpson	1.00	.50	.30
(40)	Mike Sensibaugh	1.00	.50	.30
(41)	Dave Chapple	1.00	.50	.30
(42)	Jim Langer	6.00	3.00	1.75
(43)	Mike Eischeid	1.00	.50	.30
(44)	John Gilliam	1.25	.60	.40
(45)	Ron Acks	1.00	.50	.30
(46)	Bob Gladieux	1.00	.50	.30
(47)	Honoe Jackson	1.00	.50	.30
(48)	Reggie Rucker	1.50	.70	.45
(49)	Pat Studsill	1.00	.50	.30

(50)	Bob Windsor	1.00	.50	.30
(51)	Joe Federspiel	1.00	.50	.30
(52)	Bob Newland	4.00	2.00	1.25
(53)	Pete Athas	1.00	.50	.30
(54)	Charlie Evans	1.00	.50	.30
(55)	Jack Gregory	1.00	.50	.30
(56)	John Mendenhall	1.00	.50	.30
(57)	Ed Bell	1.00	.50	.30
(58)	John Elliott	1.00	.50	.30
(59)	Chris Farasopoulos	1.00	.50	.30
(60)	Bob Svihus	1.00	.50	.30
(61)	Steve Tannen	1.00	.50	.30
(62)	Cliff Branch	3.00	1.50	.90
(63)	Gus Otto	1.00	.50	.30
(64)	Otis Sistrunk	1.25	.60	.40
(65)	Charlie Smith	1.00	.50	.30
(66)	John Reaves	1.00	.50	.30
(67)	Larry Watkins	1.00	.50	.30
(68)	Henry Davis	1.00	.50	.30
(69)	Ben McGee	1.00	.50	.30
(70)	Donny Anderson	1.25	.60	.40
(71)	Walker Gillette	1.00	.50	.30
(72)	Martin Imhoff	1.00	.50	.30
(73)	Bobby Moore	8.00	4.00	2.50
	(aka Ahmad Rashad)			
(74)	Norm Thompson	1.00	.50	.30
(75)	Lionel Aldridge	1.00	.50	.30
(76)	Dave Costa	1.00	.50	.30
(77)	Cid Edwards	1.00	.50	.30
(78)	Tim Rossovich	1.00	.50	.30
(79)	Dave Williams	1.00	.50	.30
(80)	Johnny Fuller	1.00	.50	.30
(81)	Terry Hermeling	1.00	.50	.30
(82)	Paul Laaveg	1.00	.50	.30

1981 Topps Red Border Stickers

These stickers came in their own little containers and measure 1 15/16" by 2 9/16". Each of the 28 NFL teams is represented in the set, which features red borders on the front, framing a color photo. The player's name and position are also listed. The sticker back has the sticker number, player name, position and team, biographical information and instructions on how to apply the sticker.

		MT	NM	EX
	Complete Set (28):	20.00	15.00	8.00
	Common Player:	.40	.30	.15
1	Steve Bartkowski	1.00	.70	.40
2	Bert Jones	1.00	.70	.40
3	Joe Cribbs	.60	.45	.25
4	Walter Payton	5.00	3.75	2.00
5	Ross Browner	.40	.30	.15
6	Brian Sipe	.75	.60	.30
7	Tony Dorsett	2.50	2.00	1.00
8	Randy Gradishar	.60	.45	.25
9	Billy Sims	1.00	.70	.40
10	Mike Lofton	1.75	1.25	.70
11	Mike Barber	.40	.30	.15
12	Art Still	.40	.30	.15
13	Jack Youngblood	.75	.60	.30
14	Dave Woodley	.50	.40	.20
15	Ahmad Rashad	1.25	.90	.50
16	Russ Francis	.50	.40	.20
17	Archie Manning	.75	.60	.30
18	Dave Jennings	.40	.30	.15
19	Richard Todd	.50	.40	.20
20	Lester Hayes	.60	.45	.25
21	Ron Jaworski	.50	.40	.20
22	Franco Harris	2.00	1.50	.80
23	Ottis Anderson	1.00	.70	.40
24	John Jefferson	.50	.40	.20
25	Freddie Solomon	.40	.30	.15
26	Steve Largent	3.50	2.75	1.50
27	Lee Roy Selmon	.75	.60	.30
28	Art Monk	8.00	6.00	3.25

1981 Topps Stickers

These stickers, which measure 1 15/16" by 2 9/16", are numbered alphabetically by teams within divisions. The front has a color photo with a white frame, plus the sticker number. That number is also on the back, along with the player's name, position, team and instructions on how to apply the sticker. A sticker album, iwas also made available as a mail-in offer. The album cover features a Buffalo Bills player.

		MT	NM	EX
	Complete Set (262):	25.00	18.50	10.00
	Common Player:	.05	.04	.02
1	AFC Passing Leader (Brian Sipe)	.10	.08	.04
2	AFC Passing Yardage Leader (Dan Fouts)	.50	.40	.20
3	AFC Receiving Yardage Leader (John Jefferson)	.08	.06	.03
4	AFC Kickoff Return Yardage Leader (Bruce Harper)	.05	.04	.02
5	AFC Punt Return Yardage Leader (J.T. Smith)	.05	.04	.02
6	AFC Punting Leader (Luke Prestidge)	.05	.04	.02
7	AFC Interceptions Leader (Lester Hayes)	.05	.04	.02
8	AFC Sacks Leader (Gary Johnson)	.05	.04	.02
9	Bert Jones	.15	.11	.06
10	Fred Cook	.05	.04	.02
11	Roger Carr	.10	.08	.04
12	Greg Landry	.08	.06	.03
13	Raymond Butler	.08	.06	.03
14	Bruce Laird	.05	.04	.02
15	Ed Simonini	.05	.04	.02
16	Curtis Dickey	.10	.08	.04
17	Joe Cribbs	.10	.08	.04
18	Joe Ferguson	.15	.11	.06
19	Ben Williams	.05	.04	.02
20	Jerry Butler	.08	.06	.03
21	Roland Hooks	.05	.04	.02
22	Fred Smerlas	.08	.06	.03
23	Frank Lewis	.05	.04	.02
24	Mark Brammer	.05	.04	.02
25	Dave Woodley	.08	.06	.03
26	Nat Moore	.10	.08	.04
27	Uwe Von Schamann	.05	.04	.02
28	Vern Den Herder	.05	.04	.02
29	Tony Nathan	.10	.08	.04
30	Duriel Harris	.08	.06	.03
31	Don McNeal	.05	.04	.02
32	Delvin Williams	.05	.04	.02
33	Stanley Morgan	.15	.11	.06
34	John Hannah	.15	.11	.06
35	Horace Ivory	.05	.04	.02
36	Steve Nelson	.05	.04	.02
37	Steve Grogan	.15	.11	.06
38	Vagas Ferguson	.10	.08	.04
39	John Smith	.05	.04	.02
40	Mike Haynes	.12	.09	.05
41	Mark Gastineau	.15	.11	.06
42	Wesley Walker	.15	.11	.06
43	Joe Klecko	.10	.08	.04
44	Chris Ward	.05	.04	.02
45	Johnny Lam Jones	.08	.06	.03
46	Marvin Powell	.08	.06	.03
47	Richard Todd	.15	.11	.06
48	Greg Buttle	.08	.06	.03
49	Eddie Edwards	.05	.04	.02
50	Dan Ross	.08	.06	.03
51	Ken Anderson	.50	.40	.20
52	Ross Browner	.08	.06	.03
53	Don Bass	.08	.06	.03
54	Jim LeClair	.05	.04	.02
55	Pete Johnson	.08	.06	.03
56	Anthony Munoz	1.25	.90	.50
57	Brian Sipe	.12	.09	.05
58	Mike Pruitt	.10	.08	.04
59	Greg Pruitt	.15	.11	.06
60	Thom Darden	.05	.04	.02
61	Ozzie Newsome	.40	.30	.15
62	Dave Logan	.05	.04	.02
63	Lyle Alzado	.15	.11	.06
64	Reggie Rucker	.08	.06	.03
65	Robert Brazile	.08	.06	.03
66	Mike Barber	.08	.06	.03
67	Carl Roaches	.10	.08	.04
68	Ken Stabler	.30	.25	.12
69	Gregg Bingham	.08	.06	.03
70	Mike Renfro	.08	.06	.03
71	Leon Gray	.05	.04	.02
72	Rob Carpenter	.10	.08	.04
73	Franco Harris	.50	.40	.20
74	Jack Lambert	.30	.25	.12
75	Jim Smith	.05	.04	.02
76	Mike Webster	.15	.11	.06
77	Sidney Thornton	.05	.04	.02
78	Joe Greene	.40	.30	.15
79	John Stallworth	.20	.15	.08
80	Tyrone McGriff	.05	.04	.02
81	Randy Gradishar	.12	.09	.05
82	Haven Moses	.08	.06	.03
83	Riley Odoms	.10	.08	.04
84	Matt Robinson	.05	.04	.02
85	Craig Morton	.12	.09	.05
86	Rulon Jones	.05	.04	.02
87	Rick Upchurch	.10	.08	.04
88	Jim Jensen	.05	.04	.02
89	Art Still	.12	.09	.05
90	J.T. Smith	.12	.09	.05
91	Steve Fuller	.05	.04	.02
92	Gary Barbaro	.05	.04	.02
93	Ted McKnight	.05	.04	.02
94	Bob Grupp	.05	.04	.02
95	Henry Marshall	.05	.04	.02
96	Mike Williams	.05	.04	.02
97	Jim Plunkett	.25	.20	.10
98	Lester Hayes	.12	.09	.05
99	Cliff Branch	.20	.15	.08
100	John Matuszak	.10	.08	.04
101	Matt Millen	.10	.08	.04
102	Kenny King	.05	.04	.02
103	Ray Guy	.15	.11	.06
104	Ted Hendricks	.20	.15	.08
105	John Jefferson	.12	.09	.05
106	Fred Dean	.12	.09	.05
107	Dan Fouts	.35	.25	.14
108	Charlie Joiner	.25	.20	.10
109	Kellen Winslow	1.25	.90	.50
110	Gary Johnson	.08	.06	.03
111	Mike Thomas	.05	.04	.02
112	Louie Kelcher	.12	.09	.05
113	Jim Zorn	.12	.09	.05
114	Terry Beeson	.05	.04	.02
115	Jacob Green	.35	.25	.14
116	Steve Largent	1.25	.90	.50
117	Dan Doornink	.05	.04	.02
118	Manu Tuiasosopo	.05	.04	.02
119	John Sawyer	.05	.04	.02
120	Jim Jodat	.05	.04	.02
121	Walter Payton (All-Pro)	2.00	1.50	.80
122	Brian Sipe (All-Pro)	.25	.20	.10
123	Joe Cribbs (All-Pro)	.25	.20	.10
124	James Lofton (All-Pro)	.60	.45	.25
125	John Jefferson (All-Pro)	.25	.20	.10
126	Leon Gray (All-Pro)	.15	.11	.06
127	Joe DeLamielleure (All-Pro)	.20	.15	.08
128	Mike Webster (All-Pro)	.30	.25	.12
129	John Hannah (All-Pro)	.30	.25	.12
130	Mike Kenn (All-Pro)	.20	.15	.08
131	Kellen Winslow (All-Pro)	1.50	1.25	.60
132	Lee Roy Selmon (All-Pro)	.30	.25	.12

133	Randy White (All-Pro)	.30	.25	.12
134	Gary Johnson (All-Pro)	.15	.11	.06
135	Art Still (All-Pro)	.20	.15	.08
136	Robert Brazile (All-Pro)	.20	.15	.08
137	Nolan Cromwell (All-Pro)	.20	.15	.08
138	Ted Hendricks (All-Pro)	.50	.40	.20
139	Lester Hayes (All-Pro)	.25	.20	.10
140	Randy Gradishar (All-Pro)	.35	.25	.14
141	Lemar Parrish (All-Pro)	.20	.15	.08
142	Donnie Shell (All-Pro)	.20	.15	.08
143	NFC Passing Leader (Ron Jaworski)	.12	.09	.05
144	NFC Passing Leader (Archie Manning)	.20	.15	.08
145	NFC Rushing Yardage Leader (Walter Payton)	.75	.60	.30
146	NFC Rushing Touchdowns Leader (Billy Sims)	.25	.20	.10
147	NFC Receiving Yardage Leader (James Lofton)	.25	.20	.10
148	NFC Punting Leader (Dave Jennings)	.05	.04	.02
149	NFC Interceptions Leader (Nolan Cromwell)	.08	.06	.03
150	NFC Sacks Leader (Al (Bubba) Baker)	.08	.06	.03
151	Tony Dorsett	.50	.40	.20
152	Harvey Martin	.15	.11	.06
153	Danny White	.25	.20	.10
154	Pat Donovan	.05	.04	.02
155	Drew Pearson	.15	.11	.06
156	Robert Newhouse	.10	.08	.04
157	Randy White	.40	.30	.15
158	Butch Johnson	.10	.08	.04
159	Dave Jennings	.05	.04	.02
160	Brad Van Pelt	.05	.04	.02
161	Phil Simms	.40	.30	.15
162	Mike Friede	.05	.04	.02
163	Billy Taylor	.08	.06	.03
164	Gary Jeter	.08	.06	.03
165	George Martin	.05	.04	.02
166	Earnest Gray	.05	.04	.02
167	Ron Jaworski	.15	.11	.06
168	Bill Bergey	.10	.08	.04
169	Wilbert Montgomery	.08	.06	.03
170	Charlie Smith	.05	.04	.02
171	Jerry Robinson	.08	.06	.03
172	Herman Edwards	.05	.04	.02
173	Harold Carmichael	.15	.11	.06
174	Claude Humphrey	.10	.08	.04
175	Ottis Anderson	.30	.25	.12
176	Jim Hart	.15	.11	.06
177	Pat Tilley	.08	.06	.03
178	Rush Brown	.05	.04	.02
179	Tom Brahaney	.05	.04	.02
180	Dan Dierdorf	.25	.20	.10
181	Wayne Morris	.05	.04	.02
182	Doug Marsh	.05	.04	.02
183	Art Monk	3.00	2.25	1.25
184	Clarence Harmon	.05	.04	.02
185	Lemar Parrish	.12	.09	.05
186	Joe Theismann	.35	.25	.14
187	Joe Lavender	.05	.04	.02
188	Wilbur Jackson	.05	.04	.02
189	Dave Butz	.05	.04	.02
190	Coy Bacon	.05	.04	.02
191	Walter Payton	1.50	1.25	.60
192	Alan Page	.15	.11	.06
193	Vince Evans	.20	.15	.08
194	Roland Harper	.08	.06	.03
195	Dan Hampton	.80	.60	.30
196	Gary Fencik	.08	.06	.03
197	Mike Hartenstine	.05	.04	.02
198	Robin Earl	.05	.04	.02
199	Billy Sims	.25	.20	.10
200	Leonard Thompson	.05	.04	.02
201	Jeff Komlo	.08	.06	.03
202	Al (Bubba) Baker	.10	.08	.04

203	Ed Murray	.15	.11	.06
204	Dexter Bussey	.05	.04	.02
205	Tom Ginn	.05	.04	.02
206	Freddie Scott	.08	.06	.03
207	James Lofton	.50	.40	.20
208	Mike Butler	.05	.04	.02
209	Lynn Dickey	.12	.09	.05
210	Gerry Ellis	.05	.04	.02
211	Edd Lee Ivery	.10	.08	.04
212	Ezra Johnson	.05	.04	.02
213	Paul Coffman	.08	.06	.03
214	Aundra Thompson	.05	.04	.02
215	Ahmad Rashad	.25	.20	.10
216	Tommy Kramer	.08	.06	.03
217	Matt Blair	.08	.06	.03
218	Sammie White	.08	.06	.03
219	Ted Brown	.08	.06	.03
220	Joe Senser	.08	.06	.03
221	Rickey Young	.08	.06	.03
222	Randy Holloway	.05	.04	.02
223	Lee Roy Selmon	.15	.11	.06
224	Doug Williams	.10	.08	.04
225	Ricky Bell	.10	.08	.04
226	David Lewis	.05	.04	.02
227	Gordon Jones	.08	.06	.03
228	Dewey Selmon	.08	.06	.03
229	Jimmie Giles	.10	.08	.04
230	Mike Washington	.05	.04	.02
231	William Andrews	.15	.11	.06
232	Jeff Van Note	.08	.06	.03
233	Steve Bartkowski	.15	.11	.06
234	Junior Miller	.08	.06	.03
235	Lynn Cain	.08	.06	.03
236	Joel Williams	.05	.04	.02
237	Alfred Jenkins	.08	.06	.03
238	Kenny Johnson	.05	.04	.02
239	Jack Youngblood	.20	.15	.08
240	Elvis Peacock	.08	.06	.03
241	Cullen Bryant	.10	.08	.04
242	Dennis Harrah	.05	.04	.02
243	Billy Waddy	.05	.04	.02
244	Nolan Cromwell	.10	.08	.04
245	Doug France	.05	.04	.02
246	Johnnie Johnson	.08	.06	.03
247	Archie Manning	.25	.20	.10
248	Tony Galbreath	.10	.08	.04
249	Wes Chandler	.15	.11	.06
250	Stan Brock	.05	.04	.02
251	Ike Harris	.05	.04	.02
252	Russell Erxleben	.05	.04	.02
253	Jimmy Rogers	.05	.04	.02
254	Tom Myers	.05	.04	.02
255	Dwight Clark	.75	.60	.30
256	Earl Cooper	.05	.04	.02
257	Steve DeBerg	.25	.20	.10
258	Randy Cross	.10	.08	.04
259	Freddie Solomon	.08	.06	.03
260	Jim Miller	.05	.04	.02
261	Charley Young	.08	.06	.03
262	Bobby Leopold	.05	.04	.02

1982 Topps "Comming Soon" Stickers

These stickers were inserted in 1992 Topps football card packs. They are 1 15/16" by 2 9/16", making them the same size as Topps' regular 1982 stickers. They also share the same card numbers, which is why the set is skip-numbered. The card number is on the back, along with the words "Coming Soon!" The fronts of the stickers are gold-bordered foil stickers.

		MT	NM	EX
Complete Set (16):		5.00	3.75	2.00
Common Player:		.10	.08	.04
5	MVP Super Bowl XVI (Joe Montana)	2.00	1.50	.80
6	NFC Championship	.10	.08	.04

9	Super Bowl XVI	1.50	1.25	.60
	(Joe Montana)			
71	Tommy Kramer	.30	.25	.12
73	George Rogers	.30	.25	.12
75	Tom Skladany	.10	.08	.04
139	Nolan Cromwell	.30	.25	.12
143	Jack Lambert	.50	.40	.20
144	Lawrence Taylor	1.75	1.25	.70
150	Billy Sims	.40	.30	.15
154	Ken Anderson	.50	.40	.20
159	John Hannah	.40	.30	.15
160	Anthony Munoz	.75	.60	.30
220	Ken Anderson	.50	.40	.20
221	Dan Fouts	.50	.40	.20
222	Frank Lewis	.10	.08	.04

1982 Topps Stickers

263

TERRY BRADSHAW
Pittsburgh Steelers

TO COLLECT YOUR STICKERS . . .
Ask your dealer for the
TOPPS Football Sticker ALBUM

IT'S **Topps** FOR SPORTS
© 1982 TOPPS CHEWING GUM, INC.
MADE IN ITALY

These stickers follow the same format as the 1981 stickers, complete with an album featuring Joe Montana on the cover. However, these stickers have yellow borders and a 1982 copyright date on the back. Foil stickers were also produced again (#s 1-10, 70-77, 139-160, 220-227). Stickers 1 and two combine as a puzzle to form a picture of the San Francisco 49ers; 3 and 4 show Super Bowl theme art.

		MT	NM	EX
Complete Set (288):		30.00	22.00	12.00
Common Player"		.05	.04	.02
1	Super Bowl XVI	.35	.25	.14
	(49er Team)			
2	Super Bowl XVI	.15	.11	.06
	(49er Team)			
3	Super Bowl XVI	.15	.11	.06
	(Theme Art Trophy)			
4	Super Bowl XVI	.15	.11	.06
	(Theme Art Trophy)			
5	MVP Super Bowl XVI	3.50	2.75	1.50
	(Joe Montana)			
6	1981 NFC Champions	.15	.11	.06
	49ers			
7	1981 AFC Champions	.25	.20	.10
	(Ken Anderson)			
8	Super Bowl XVI	.25	.20	.10
	(Ken Anderson)			
9	Super Bowl XVI	3.00	2.25	1.25
	(Joe Montana)			
10	Super Bowl XVI	.15	.11	.06
	(line blocking)			
11	Steve Bartkowski	.15	.11	.06
12	William Andrews	.10	.08	.04
13	Lynn Cain	.08	.06	.03
14	Wallace Francis	.08	.06	.03
15	Alfred Jackson	.08	.06	.03
16	Alfred Jenkins	.10	.08	.04
17	Mike Kenn	.08	.06	.03
18	Junior Miller	.10	.08	.04
19	Vince Evans	.10	.08	.04

20	Walter Payton	1.25	.90	.50
21	Dave Williams	.05	.04	.02
22	Brian Baschnagel	.05	.04	.02
23	Rickey Watts	.05	.04	.02
24	Ken Margerum	.08	.06	.03
25	Revie Sorey	.05	.04	.02
26	Gary Fencik	.05	.04	.02
27	Matt Suhey	.05	.04	.02
28	Danny White	.20	.15	.08
29	Tony Dorsett	.50	.40	.20
30	Drew Pearson	.25	.20	.10
31	Rafael Septien	.08	.06	.03
32	pat Donovan	.05	.04	.02
33	Herbert Scott	.05	.04	.02
34	Ed Too Tall Jones	.20	.15	.08
35	Randy White	.25	.20	.10
36	Tony Hill	.08	.06	.03
37	Eric Hipple	.08	.06	.03
38	Billy Sims	.25	.20	.10
39	Dexter Bussey	.05	.04	.02
40	Freddie Scott	.08	.06	.03
41	David Hill	.05	.04	.02
42	Ed Murray	.10	.08	.04
43	Tom Skladany	.05	.04	.02
44	Doug English	.08	.06	.03
45	Al (Bubba) Baker	.12	.09	.05
46	Lynn Dickey	.12	.09	.05
47	Gerry Ellis	.05	.04	.02
48	Harlan Huckleby	.05	.04	.02
49	James Lofton	.40	.30	.15
50	John Jefferson	.08	.06	.03
51	Paul Coffman	.05	.04	.02
52	Jan Stenerud	.20	.15	.08
53	Rich Wingo	.05	.04	.02
54	Wendell Tyler	.10	.08	.04
55	Preston Dennard	.05	.04	.02
56	Billy Waddy	.05	.04	.02
57	Frank Corral	.05	.04	.02
58	Jack Youngblood	.15	.11	.06
59	Pat Thomas	.05	.04	.02
60	Rod Perry	.08	.06	.03
61	Nolan Cromwell	.10	.08	.04
62	Tommy Kramer	.10	.08	.04
63	Rickey Young	.08	.06	.03
64	Ted Brown	.05	.04	.02
65	Ahmad Rashad	.25	.20	.10
66	Sammie White	.08	.06	.03
67	Joe Senser	.05	.04	.02
68	Ron Yary	.08	.06	.03
69	Matt Blair	.08	.06	.03
70	NFC Passing Leader	3.50	2.75	1.50
	(Joe Montana)			
71	NFC Passing Yardage	.20	.15	.08
	Leader (Tommy Kramer)			
72	NFC Receiving Yardage	.15	.11	.06
	Leader (Alfred Jenkins)			
73	NFC Rushing Yardage	.25	.20	.10
	Leader (George Rogers)			
74	NFC Rushing Touchdowns	.30	.25	.12
	Leader (Wendell Tyler)			
75	NFC Punting Leader	.15	.11	.06
	(Tom Skladany)			
76	NFC Interceptions Leader	.35	.25	.14
	(Everson Walls)			
77	MFC Sacks Leader	.15	.11	.06
	(Curtis Greer)			
78	Archie Manning	.25	.20	.10
79	Dave Waymer	.05	.04	.02
80	George Rogers	.20	.15	.08
81	Jack Holmes	.05	.04	.02
82	Toussaint Tyler	.05	.04	.02
83	Wayne Wilson	.05	.04	.02
84	Russell Erxleben	.05	.04	.02
85	Elois Grooms	.05	.04	.02
86	Phil Simms	.20	.15	.08
87	Scott Brunner	.10	.08	.04
88	Rob Carpenter	.08	.06	.03
89	Johnny Perkins	.05	.04	.02

#	Player				#	Player			
90	Dave Jennings	.05	.04	.02	168	Nesby Glasgow	.05	.04	.02
91	harry Carson	.12	.09	.05	169	Joe Ferguson	.08	.06	.03
92	Lawrence Taylor	2.50	2.00	1.00	170	Joe Cribbs	.08	.06	.03
93	Beasley Reece	.05	.04	.02	171	jerry Butler	.08	.06	.03
94	Mark Haynes	.05	.04	.02	172	Frank Lewis	.08	.06	.03
95	Ron Jaworski	.12	.09	.05	173	Mark Brammer	.05	.04	.02
96	Wilbert Montgomery	.08	.06	.03	174	Fred Smerlas	.10	.08	.04
97	Hubert Oliver	.05	.04	.02	175	Jim Haslett	.05	.04	.02
98	Harold Carmichael	.10	.08	.04	176	Charles Alexander	.05	.04	.02
99	Jerry Robinson	.08	.06	.03	177	Bill Simpson	.05	.04	.02
100	Stan Walters	.05	.04	.02	178	Ken Anderson	.20	.15	.08
101	Charlie Johnson	.05	.04	.02	179	Charles Alexander	.05	.04	.02
102	Roynell Young	.05	.04	.02	180	Pete Johnson	.05	.04	.02
103	Tony Franklin	.05	.04	.02	181	Isaac Curtis	.05	.04	.02
104	Neil Lomax	.15	.11	.06	182	Cris Collinsworth	.50	.40	.20
105	Jim Hart	.15	.11	.06	183	Pat McInally	.08	.06	.03
106	Ottis Anderson	.20	.15	.08	184	Anthony Munoz	.50	.40	.20
107	Stump Mitchell	.12	.09	.05	185	Louis Breeden	.05	.04	.02
108	Pat Tilley	.08	.06	.03	186	Jim Breech	.10	.08	.04
109	Rush Brown	.05	.04	.02	187	Brian Sipe	.10	.08	.04
110	E.J. Junior	.05	.04	.02	188	Charles White	.10	.08	.04
111	Ken Greene	.05	.04	.02	189	Mike Pruitt	.08	.06	.03
112	Mel Gray	.08	.06	.03	190	Reggie Rucker	.12	.09	.05
113	Joe Montana	2.50	2.00	1.00	191	Dave Logan	.05	.04	.02
114	Ricky Patton	.05	.04	.02	192	Ozzie Newsome	.30	.25	.12
115	Earl Cooper	.05	.04	.02	193	Dick Ambrose	.05	.04	.02
116	Dwight Clark	.25	.20	.10	194	Joe DeLamielleure	.05	.04	.02
117	Freddie Solomon	.08	.06	.03	195	Ricky Feacher	.05	.04	.02
118	Randy Cross	.10	.08	.04	196	Craig Morton	.12	.09	.05
119	Fred Dean	.08	.06	.03	197	Dave Preston	.05	.04	.02
120	Ronnie Lott	1.75	1.25	.70	198	Rick Parros	.05	.04	.02
121	Dwight Hicks	.08	.06	.03	199	Rick Upchurch	.08	.06	.03
122	Doug Williams	.15	.11	.06	200	Steve Watson	.10	.08	.04
123	Jerry Eckwood	.08	.06	.03	201	Riley Odoms	.08	.06	.03
124	James Owens	.08	.06	.03	202	Randy Gradishar	.10	.08	.04
125	Kevin House	.08	.06	.03	203	Steve Foley	.05	.04	.02
126	Jimmie Giles	.05	.04	.02	204	Ken Stabler	.30	.25	.12
127	Charley Hannah	.05	.04	.02	205	Gifford Nielsen	.08	.06	.03
128	Lee Roy Selmon	.15	.11	.06	206	Tim Wilson	.05	.04	.02
129	Hugh Green	.12	.09	.05	207	Ken Burrough	.10	.08	.04
130	Joe Theismann	.30	.25	.12	208	Mike Renfro	.10	.08	.04
131	Joe Washington	.08	.06	.03	209	Greg Stemrick	.05	.04	.02
132	John Riggins	.25	.20	.10	210	Robert Brazile	.08	.06	.03
133	Art Monk	.50	.40	.20	211	Gregg Bingham	.08	.06	.03
134	Ricky Thompson	.05	.04	.02	212	Steve Fuller	.08	.06	.03
135	Don Warren	.08	.06	.03	213	Bill Kenney	.08	.06	.03
136	Perry Brooks	.05	.04	.02	214	Joe Delaney	.20	.15	.08
137	Mike Nelms	.05	.04	.02	215	Henry Marshall	.05	.04	.02
138	Mark Moseley	.05	.04	.02	216	Nick Lowery	.10	.08	.04
139	Nolan Cromwell (All-Pro)	.20	.15	.08	217	Art Still	.08	.06	.03
140	Dwight Hicks (All-Pro)	.15	.11	.06	218	Gary Green	.05	.04	.02
141	Ronnie Lott (All-Pro)	2.00	1.50	.80	219	Gary Barbaro	.05	.04	.02
142	Harry Carson (All-Pro)	.20	.15	.08	220	AFC PAssing Leader (Ken Anderson)	.35	.25	.14
143	Jack Lambert (All-Pro)	.40	.30	.15	221	AFC PAssing Yardage Leader (Dan Fouts)	.50	.40	.20
144	Lawrence Taylor (All-Pro)	2.50	2.00	1.00	222	AFC Receiving Yardage Leader (Frank Lewis)	.20	.15	.08
145	Mel Blount (All-Pro)	.30	.25	.12	223	AFC Kickoff Return Yardage Leader (James Brooks)	.75	.60	.30
146	Joe Klecko (All-Pro)	.15	.11	.06	224	AFC Rushing Touchdowns Leader (Chuck Muncie)	.20	.15	.08
147	Randy White (All-Pro)	.35	.25	.14	225	AFC Punting Leader (Pat McInally)	.20	.15	.08
148	Doug English (All-Pro)	.10	.08	.04	226	AFC Interceptions Leader (John Harris)	.20	.15	.08
149	Fred Dean (All-Pro)	.20	.15	.08	227	AFC Sacks Leader (Joe Klecko)	.20	.15	.08
150	Billy Sims (All-Pro)	.25	.20	.10	228	Dave Woodley	.08	.06	.03
151	Tony Dorsett (All-Pro)	.75	.60	.30	229	Tony Nathan	.08	.06	.03
152	James Lofton (All-Pro)	.75	.60	.30	230	Andra Franklin	.05	.04	.02
153	Alfred Jenkins (All-Pro)	.20	.15	.08	231	Nat Moore	.08	.06	.03
154	Ken Anderson (All-Pro)	.35	.25	.14	232	Duriel Harris	.08	.06	.03
155	Kellen Winslow (All-Pro)	.50	.40	.20	233	Uwe Von Schamann	.05	.04	.02
156	Marvin Powell (All-Pro)	.10	.08	.04	234	Bob Baumhower	.10	.08	.04
157	Randy Cross (All-Pro)	.20	.15	.08	235	Glenn Blackwood	.10	.08	.04
158	Mike Webster (All-Pro)	.30	.25	.12	236	Tommy Vigorito	.05	.04	.02
159	John Hannah (All-Pro)	.30	.25	.12					
160	Anthony Munoz (All-Pro)	1.25	.90	.50					
161	Curtis Dickey	.08	.06	.03					
162	Randy McMillan	.08	.06	.03					
163	Roger Carr	.08	.06	.03					
164	Raymond Butler	.05	.04	.02					
165	Reese McCall	.05	.04	.02					
166	Ed Simonini	.05	.04	.02					
167	Herb Oliver	.05	.04	.02					

237	Steve Grogan	.12	.09	.05
238	Matt Cavanaugh	.08	.06	.03
239	Tony Collins	.08	.06	.03
240	Vagas Ferguson	.10	.08	.04
241	John Smith	.05	.04	.02
242	Stanley Morgan	.10	.08	.04
243	John Hannah	.15	.11	.06
244	Steve Nelson	.05	.04	.02
245	Don Hasselback	.05	.04	.02
246	Richard Todd	.12	.09	.05
247	Bruce Harper	.05	.04	.02
248	Wesley Walker	.12	.09	.05
249	Jerome Barkum	.08	.06	.03
250	Marvin Powell	.08	.06	.03
251	Mark Gastineau	.15	.11	.06
252	Joe Klecko	.08	.06	.03
253	Darrol Ray	.05	.04	.02
254	Marty Lyons	.08	.06	.03
255	Marc Wilson	.10	.08	.04
256	Kenny King	.08	.06	.03
257	Mark Van Eeghen	.08	.06	.03
258	Cliff Branch	.12	.09	.05
259	Bob Chandler	.08	.06	.03
260	Ray Guy	.15	.11	.06
261	Ted Hendricks	.20	.15	.08
262	Lester Hayes	.20	.15	.08
263	Terry Bradshaw	.60	.45	.25
264	Franco Harris	.35	.25	.14
265	John Stallworth	.15	.11	.06
266	Jim Smith	.05	.04	.02
267	Mike Webster	.12	.09	.05
268	Jack Lambert	.20	.15	.08
269	Mel Blount	.15	.11	.06
270	Donnie Shell	.12	.09	.05
271	Bennie Cunningham	.08	.06	.03
272	Dan Fouts	.40	.30	.15
273	Chuck Muncie	.10	.08	.04
274	james Brooks	.65	.50	.25
275	Charlie Joiner	.20	.15	.08
276	Wes Chandler	.12	.09	.05
277	Kellen Winslow	.25	.20	.10
278	Doug Wilkerson	.05	.04	.02
279	Gary Johnson	.08	.06	.03
280	Rolf Benirschke	.08	.06	.03
281	Jim Zorn	.12	.09	.05
282	Theotis Brown	.08	.06	.03
283	Dan Doornink	.05	.04	.02
284	Steve Largent	1.25	.90	.50
285	Sam McCullum	.08	.06	.03
286	Efren Herrera	.05	.04	.02
287	Manu Tuiasosopo	.05	.04	.02
288	John Harris	.05	.04	.02

1983 Topps Sticker Boxes

These boxes contained 35 stickers inside, but also had two 2 1/2" by 3 1/2" on them; an offensive player and defensive player were on each box. The cards are not numbered, and there was no issue for #10, but the box is numbered with a tab. The prices below are for an uncut box.

		MT	NM	EX
Complete Set (12):		10.00	7.50	4.00
Common Player:		.75	.60	.30
1	Pat Donovan, Mark Gastineau	.75	.60	.30
2	Wes Chandler, Nolan Cromwell	1.25	.90	.50
3	Marvin Powell, Ed Too Tall Jones	1.25	.90	.50
4	Ken Anderson, Tony Peters	1.25	.90	.50
5	Freeman McNeil, Lawrence Taylor	2.00	1.50	.80
6	Mark Moseley, Dave Jennings	.75	.60	.30
7	Dwight Clark, Mark Haynes	1.50	1.25	.60

8	Jeff Van Note, Harry Carson	.75	.60	.30
9	Tony Dorsett, Hugh Green	2.00	1.50	.80
11	Randy Cross, Gary Johnson	1.00	.70	.40
12	Kellen Winslow, Lester Hayes	1.25	.90	.50
13	John Hannah, Randy White	2.00	1.50	.80

1983 Topps Sticker Inserts

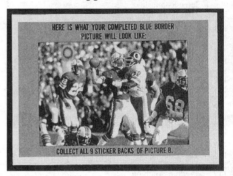

These 33 different inserts, which came in each wax pack of 1983 Topps football cards, pictured an NFL star on the front and a piece to one of three different puzzles on the backs. A gold plaque at the bottom of the card identifies the player.

		MT	NM	EX
Complete Set:		20.00	15.00	8.00
Common Player:		.35	.25	.14
1	Marcus Allen	5.00	3.75	2.00
2	Ken Anderson	.50	.40	.20
3	Ottis Anderson	.35	.25	.14
4	William Andrews	.35	.25	.14
5	Terry Bradshaw	1.25	.90	.50
6	Wes Chandler	.35	.25	.14
7	Dwight Clark	.50	.40	.20
8	Cris Collinsworth	.35	.25	.14
9	Joe Cribbs	.35	.25	.14
10	Nolan Cromwell	.35	.25	.14
11	Tony Dorsett	1.50	1.25	.60
12	Dan Fouts	1.00	.70	.40
13	Mark Gastineau	.35	.25	.14
14	Jimmie Giles	.35	.25	.14
15	Franco Harris	1.00	.70	.40
16	Ted Hendricks	.60	.45	.25
17	Tony Hill	.35	.25	.14
18	John Jefferson	.35	.25	.14
19	James Lofton	1.00	.70	.40
20	Freeman McNeil	.50	.40	.20
21	Joe Montana	6.00	4.50	2.50
22	Mark Moseley	.35	.25	.14
23	Ozzie Newsome	1.00	.70	.40
24	Walter Payton	3.00	2.25	1.25
25	John Riggins	1.00	.70	.40
26	Billy Sims	.35	.25	.14
27	John Stallworth	.50	.40	.20
28	Lawrence Taylor	3.00	2.25	1.25
29	Joe Theismann	1.25	.90	.50
30	Richard Todd	.35	.25	.14
31	Wesley Walker	.35	.25	.14
32	Danny White	.35	.25	.14
33	Kellen Winslow	.50	.40	.20

1983 Topps Stickers

These stickers are similar to those issued in previous years, but can be identified by the rounded frame around the picture on the front and the reference on the back to the 1983 sticker album which was produced. Once again, Topps included foil stickers in the set (#s 1-4, 73-80, 143-152 and 264-271. Foil stickers 1-2 are right and left sides of Franco Harris; 3 and 4 portray Walter Payton.

		MT	NM	EX
	Complete Set (330):	30.00	22.00	12.00
	Common Player:	.05	.04	.02
1	Franco Harris	.50	.40	.20
2	Franco Harris	.50	.40	.20
3	Walter Payton	1.25	.90	.50
4	Walter Payton	1.25	.90	.50
5	John Riggins	.35	.25	.14
6	Tony Dorsett	.40	.30	.15
7	Mark Van Eeghen	.05	.04	.02
8	Chuck Muncie	.08	.06	.03
9	Wilbert Montgomery	.08	.06	.03
10	Greg Pruitt	.08	.06	.03
11	Sam Cunningham	.10	.08	.04
12	Ottis Anderson	.20	.15	.08
13	Mike Pruitt	.08	.06	.03
14	Dexter Bussey	.05	.04	.02
15	Mike Pagel	.05	.04	.02
16	Curtis Dickey	.08	.06	.03
17	Randy McMillan	.08	.06	.03
18	Raymond Butler	.05	.04	.02
19	Nesby Glasgow	.05	.04	.02
20	Zachary Dixon	.05	.04	.02
21	Matt Bouza	.05	.04	.02
22	Johnie Cooks	.05	.04	.02
23	Curtis Brown	.05	.04	.02
24	Joe Cribbs	.10	.08	.04
25	Rossevelt Leaks	.08	.06	.03
26	Jerry Butler	.08	.06	.03
27	Frank Lewis	.08	.06	.03
28	Fred Smerlas	.05	.04	.02
29	Ben Williams	.05	.04	.02
30	Joe Ferguson	.15	.11	.06
31	Isaac Curtis	.08	.06	.03
32	Cris Collinsworth	.15	.11	.06
33	Anthony Munoz	.20	.15	.08
34	Max Montoya	.05	.04	.02
35	Ross Browner	.08	.06	.03
36	Reggie Williams	.10	.08	.04
37	Ken Riley	.10	.08	.04
38	Pete Johnson	.08	.06	.03
39	Ken Anderson	.20	.15	.08
40	Charles White	.10	.08	.04
41	Dave Logan	.05	.04	.02
42	Doug Dieken	.05	.04	.02
43	Ozzie Newsome	.20	.15	.08
44	Tom Cousineau	.05	.04	.02
45	Bob Golic	.08	.06	.03
46	Brian Sipe	.10	.08	.04
47	Paul McDonald	.05	.04	.02
48	Mike Pruitt	.10	.08	.04
49	Luke Prestridge	.05	.04	.02
50	Randy Gradishar	.10	.08	.04
51	Rulon Jones	.05	.04	.02
52	Rick Parros	.05	.04	.02
53	Steve DeBerg	.15	.11	.06
54	Tom Jackson	.10	.08	.04
55	Rick Upchurch	.08	.06	.03
56	Steve Watson	.08	.06	.03
57	Robert Brazile	.10	.08	.04
58	Willie Tullis	.05	.04	.02
59	Archie Manning	.15	.11	.06
60	Gifford Nielsen	.08	.06	.03
61	Harold Bailey	.05	.04	.02
62	Carl Roaches	.08	.06	.03
63	Gregg Bingham	.05	.04	.02
64	Daryl Hunt	.05	.04	.02
65	Gary Green	.05	.04	.02
66	Gary Barbaro	.08	.06	.03
67	Bill Kenney	.08	.06	.03
68	Joe Delaney	.10	.08	.04
69	Henry Marshall	.05	.04	.02
70	Nick Lowery	.10	.08	.04
71	Jeff Gossett	.05	.04	.02
72	Art Still	.10	.08	.04
73	AFC Passing Leader (Ken Anderson)	.40	.30	.15
74	AFC PAssing Yardage Leader (Dan Fouts)	.50	.40	.20
75	AFC Receiving Yardage Leader (Wes Chandler)	.25	.20	.10
76	AFC Kickoff Return Yardage Leader (James Brooks)	.40	.30	.15
77	AFC Punt Return Yardage Leader (Rick Upchurch)	.30	.25	.12
78	AFC Punting Leader (Luke Prestridge)	.15	.11	.06
79	AFC Sacks Leader (Jesse Baker)	.15	.11	.06
80	AFC Rushing Yardage Leader (Freeman McNeil)	.30	.25	.12
81	Ray Guy	.15	.11	.06
82	Jim Plunkett	.15	.11	.06
83	Lester Hayes	.08	.06	.03
84	Kenny King	.05	.04	.02
85	Cliff Branch	.12	.09	.05
86	Todd Christensen	.12	.09	.05
87	Lyle Alzado	.15	.11	.06
88	Ted Hendricks	.20	.15	.08
89	Rod Martin	.10	.08	.04
90	Dave Woodley	.10	.08	.04
91	Ed Newman	.05	.04	.02
92	Earnie Rhone	.05	.04	.02
93	Don McNeal	.05	.04	.02
94	Glenn Blackwood	.08	.06	.03
95	Andra Franklin	.08	.06	.03
96	Nat Moore	.12	.09	.05
97	Lyle Blackwood	.08	.06	.03
98	A.J. Duhe	.10	.08	.04
99	Tony Collins	.08	.06	.03
100	Stanley Morgan	.10	.08	.04
101	Pete Brock	.05	.04	.02
102	Steve Nelson	.05	.04	.02
103	Steve Grogan	.15	.11	.06
104	Mark Van Eeghen	.08	.06	.03
105	Don Hasselbeck	.05	.04	.02
106	John Hannah	.15	.11	.06
107	Mike Haynes	.15	.11	.06
108	Wesley Walker	.10	.08	.04
109	Marvin Powell	.05	.04	.02
110	Joe Klecko	.08	.06	.03
111	Bobby Jackson	.05	.04	.02
112	Richard Todd	.10	.08	.04
113	Lance Mehl	.08	.06	.03
114	Johnny Lam Jones	.10	.08	.04
115	Mark Gastineau	.10	.08	.04
116	Freeman McNeil	.15	.11	.06
117	Franco Harris	.30	.25	.12
118	Mike Webster	.15	.11	.06
119	Mel Blount	.15	.11	.06
120	Donnie Shell	.10	.08	.04
121	Terry Bradshaw	.75	.60	.30
122	John Stallworth	.12	.09	.05
123	Jack Lambert	.25	.20	.10
124	Dwayne Woodruff	.05	.04	.02
125	Bennie Cunningham	.05	.04	.02
126	Charlie Joiner	.20	.15	.08
127	Kellen Winslow	.20	.15	.08
128	Rolf Benirschke	.05	.04	.02
129	Louis Kelcher	.08	.06	.03
130	Chuck Muncie	.08	.06	.03
131	Wes Chandler	.10	.08	.04
132	Gary Johnson	.08	.06	.03
133	James Brooks	.15	.11	.06
134	Dan Fouts	.35	.25	.14
135	Jacob Green	.10	.08	.04
136	Michael Jackson	.05	.04	.02
137	Jim Zorn	.12	.09	.05
138	Sherman Smith	.08	.06	.03
139	Keith Simpson	.05	.04	.02

329

Stamps/stickers

140	Steve Largent	1.25	.90	.50		218	Emery Moorehead	.05	.04	.02
141	John Harris	.08	.06	.03		219	Mike Hartenstine	.05	.04	.02
142	Jeff West	.08	.06	.03		220	Danny White	.20	.15	.08
143	Ken Anderson (top)	.45	.35	.20		221	Drew Pearson	.10	.08	.04
144	Ken Anderson (bottom)	.45	.35	.20		222	Rafael Septien	.05	.04	.02
145	Tony Dorsett (top)	.40	.30	.15		223	Ed Too Tall Jones	.15	.11	.06
146	Tony Dorsett (bottom)	.40	.30	.15		224	Everson Walls	.10	.08	.04
147	Dan Fouts (top)	.40	.30	.15		225	Randy White	.20	.15	.08
148	Dan Fouts (bottom)	.40	.30	.15		226	Harvey Martin	.10	.08	.04
149	Joe Montana (top)	2.00	1.50	.80		227	Tony Hill	.08	.06	.03
150	Joe Montana (bottom)	2.00	1.50	.80		228	John Jefferson	.30	.25	.12
151	Mark Moseley (top)	.15	.11	.06		229	Billy Sims	.20	.15	.08
152	Mark Moseley (bottom)	.15	.11	.06		230	Leonard Thompson	.05	.04	.02
153	Richard Todd	.10	.08	.04		231	Ed Murray	.05	.04	.02
154	Butch Johnson	.10	.08	.04		232	Doug English	.05	.04	.02
155	Bill (Gary) Hogeboom	.08	.06	.03		233	Ken Fantetti	.05	.04	.02
156	A.J. Duhe	.08	.06	.03		234	Tom Skladany	.05	.04	.02
157	Kurt Sohn	.05	.04	.02		235	Freddie Scott	.05	.04	.02
158	Drew Pearson	.10	.08	.04		236	Eric Hipple	.08	.06	.03
159	John Riggins	.35	.25	.14		237	David Hill	.05	.04	.02
160	Pat Donovan	.05	.04	.02		238	John Jefferson	.08	.06	.03
161	John Hannah	.15	.11	.06		239	Paul Coffman	.05	.04	.02
162	Jeff Van Note	.10	.08	.04		240	Ezra Johnson	.05	.04	.02
163	Randy Cross	.10	.08	.04		241	Mike Douglass	.05	.04	.02
164	Marvin Powell	.08	.06	.03		242	Mark Lee	.08	.06	.03
165	Kellen Winslow	.25	.20	.10		243	John Anderson	.10	.08	.04
166	Dwight Clark	.20	.15	.08		244	Jan Stenerud	.15	.11	.06
167	Wes Chandler	.08	.06	.03		245	Lynn Dickey	.10	.08	.04
168	Tony Dorsett	.40	.30	.15		246	James Lofton	.30	.25	.12
169	Freeman McNeil	.12	.09	.05		247	Vince Ferragamo	.12	.09	.05
170	Ken Anderson	.25	.20	.10		248	Preston Dennard	.05	.04	.02
171	Mark Moseley	.05	.04	.02		249	Jack Youngblood	.15	.11	.06
172	Mark Gastineau	.08	.06	.03		250	Mike Guman	.05	.04	.02
173	Gary Johnson	.05	.04	.02		251	LeRoy Irvin	.08	.06	.03
174	Randy White	.30	.25	.12		252	Mike Lansford	.05	.04	.02
175	Ed Too Tall Jones	.12	.09	.05		253	Kent Hill	.05	.04	.02
176	Hugh Green	.08	.06	.03		254	Nolan Cromwell	.05	.04	.02
177	Harry Carson	.10	.08	.04		255	Doug Martin	.05	.04	.02
178	Lawrence Taylor	.30	.25	.12		256	Greg Coleman	.05	.04	.02
179	Lester Hayes	.08	.06	.03		257	Ted Brown	.05	.04	.02
180	Mark Haynes	.05	.04	.02		258	Mark Mullaney	.05	.04	.02
181	Dave Jennings	.05	.04	.02		259	Joe Senser	.08	.06	.03
182	Nolan Cromwell	.08	.06	.03		260	Randy Holloway	.05	.04	.02
183	Tony Peters	.05	.04	.02		261	Matt Blair	.08	.06	.03
184	Jimmy Cefalo	.05	.04	.02		262	Sammie White	.10	.08	.04
185	A.J. Duhe	.08	.06	.03		263	Tommy Kramer	.10	.08	.04
186	John Riggins	.35	.25	.14		264	NFC Passing Leader	.40	.30	.15
187	Charlie Brown	.05	.04	.02			(Joe Theismann)			
188	Mike Nelms	.05	.04	.02		265	NFC Passing Yardage	1.50	1.25	.60
189	Mark Murphy	.05	.04	.02			Leader (Joe Montana)			
190	Fulton Walker	.05	.04	.02		266	NFC Receiving Yardage	.25	.20	.10
191	Marcus Allen	2.50	2.00	1.00			Leader (Dwight Clark)			
192	Chip Banks	.08	.06	.03		267	NFC Kickoff Return	.10	.08	.04
193	Charlie Brown	.05	.04	.02			Yardage Leader			
194	Bob Crable	.05	.04	.02			(Mike Nelms)			
195	Vernon Dean	.05	.04	.02		268	NFC Punting Leader	.10	.08	.04
196	Jim McMahon	.75	.60	.30			(Carl Birdsong)			
197	James Robbins	.08	.06	.03		269	NFC Interceptions Leader	.20	.15	.08
198	Luis Sharpe	.08	.06	.03			(Everson Walls)			
199	Rohn Stark	.05	.04	.02		270	NFC Sacks Leader	.15	.11	.06
200	Lester Williams	.05	.04	.02			(Doug Martin)			
201	Leo Wisniewski	.05	.04	.02		271	NFC Rushing Yardage	.40	.30	.15
202	Butch Woolfolk	.10	.08	.04			Leader (Tony Dorsett)			
203	Mike Kenn	.10	.08	.04		272	Russell Erxleben	.05	.04	.02
204	R.C. Thielemann	.05	.04	.02		273	Stan Brock	.05	.04	.02
205	Buddy Curry	.05	.04	.02		274	Jeff Groth	.05	.04	.02
206	Steve Bartkowski	.12	.09	.05		275	Bruce Clark	.05	.04	.02
207	Alfred Jenkins	.08	.06	.03		276	Ken Stabler	.30	.25	.12
208	Don Smith	.05	.04	.02		277	George Rogers	.10	.08	.04
209	Alfred Jenkins	.08	.06	.03		278	Derland Moore	.08	.06	.03
210	Fulton Kuykendall	.05	.04	.02		279	Wayne Wilson	.05	.04	.02
211	William Andrews	.10	.08	.04		280	Lawrence Taylor	.35	.25	.14
212	Gary Fencik	.08	.06	.03		281	Harry Carson	.10	.08	.04
213	Walter Payton	1.50	1.25	.60		282	Brian Kelley	.05	.04	.02
214	Mike Singletary	1.50	1.25	.60		283	Brad Van Pit	.05	.04	.02
215	Otis Wilson	.08	.06	.03		284	Earnest Gray	.05	.04	.02
216	Matt Suhey	.05	.04	.02		285	Dave Jennings	.05	.04	.02
217	Dan Hampton	.20	.15	.08		286	Rob Carpenter	.05	.04	.02

287	Scott Brunner	.05	.04	.02
288	Ron Jaworski	.15	.11	.06
289	Jerry Robinson	.08	.06	.03
290	Frank LeMaster	.05	.04	.02
291	Wilbert Montgomery	.08	.06	.03
292	Tony Franklin	.05	.04	.02
293	Harold Carmichael	.15	.11	.06
294	John Spagnola	.05	.04	.02
295	Herman Edwards	.05	.04	.02
296	Ottis Anderson	.15	.11	.06
297	Carl Birdsong	.05	.04	.02
298	Doug Marsh	.05	.04	.02
299	Neil Lomax	.12	.09	.05
300	Rush Brown	.05	.04	.02
301	Pat Tilley	.08	.06	.03
302	Wayne Morris	.08	.06	.03
303	Dan Dierdorf	.20	.15	.08
304	Roy Green	.30	.25	.12
305	Joe Montana	1.75	1.25	.70
306	Randy Cross	.10	.08	.04
307	Freddie Solomon	.08	.06	.03
308	Jack Reynolds	.10	.08	.04
309	Ronnie Lott	.50	.40	.20
310	Renaldo Nehemiah	.15	.11	.06
311	Russ Francis	.08	.06	.03
312	Dwight Clark	.20	.15	.08
313	Doug Williams	.12	.09	.05
314	Bill Capece	.05	.04	.02
315	Mike Washington	.05	.04	.02
316	Hugh Green	.10	.08	.04
317	Kevin House	.08	.06	.03
318	Lee Roy Selmon	.12	.09	.05
319	Neal Colzie	.10	.08	.04
320	Jimmie Giles	.08	.06	.03
321	Cedric Brown	.05	.04	.02
322	Tony Peters	.05	.04	.02
323	Neal Olkewicz	.05	.04	.02
324	Dexter Manley	.05	.04	.02
325	Joe Theismann	.30	.25	.12
326	Rich Milot	.05	.04	.02
327	Mark Moseley	.08	.06	.03
328	Art Monk	.40	.30	.15
329	Mike Nelms	.08	.06	.03
330	John Riggins	.35	.25	.14

1984 Topps Stickers

Topps has followed its same format for these stickers, except some of the stickers come in pairs, which are listed in . Those without are full stickers, comprising the entire card. An album, featuring Charlie Joiner on the front and Dan Fouts on the back, was also issued, as were foil stickers.

		MT	NM	EX
	Complete Set (283):	25.00	18.50	10.00
	Common Player:	.05	.04	.02
1	Super Bowl XVIII	.35	.25	.14
	(Plunkett/Allen)			
2	Super Bowl XVIII	.15	.11	.06
	(Plunkett/Allen)			
3	Super Bowl XVIII	.15	.11	.06
	(Plunkett/Allen)			
4	Super Bowl XVIII	.15	.11	.06
	(Plunkett/Allen)			
5	Marcus Allen	.75	.60	.30
	(Super Bowl MVP)			
6	Walter Payton	1.00	.70	.40
7	Mike Richardson (157)	.03	.02	.01
8	Jim McMahon (158)	.10	.08	.04
9	Mike Hartenstine (159)	.05	.04	.02
10	Mike Singletary	.20	.15	.08
11	Willie Gault	.10	.08	.04
12	Terry Schmidt (162)	.05	.04	.02
13	Emery Moorehead (163)	.05	.04	.02
14	Leslie Frazier (164)	.06	.05	.02
15	Jack Thompson (165)	.05	.04	.02
16	Booker Reese (166)	.05	.04	.02

17	James Wilder (166)	.05	.04	.02
18	Lee Roy Selmon (167)	.08	.06	.03
19	Hugh Green	.06	.05	.02
20	Gerald Carter (170)	.05	.04	.02
21	Steve Wilson (171)	.05	.04	.02
22	Michael Morton (172)	.05	.04	.02
23	Kevin House	.05	.04	.02
24	Ottis Anderson	.12	.09	.05
25	Lionel Washington (175)	.08	.06	.03
26	Pat Tilley (176)	.05	.04	.02
27	Curtis Greer (177)	.05	.04	.02
28	Roy Green	.08	.06	.03
29	Carl Bridsong	.05	.04	.02
30	Neil Lomax (180)	.06	.05	.02
31	Lee Nelson (181)	.05	.04	.02
32	Stump Mitchell (182)	.04	.03	.02
33	Tony Hill (183)	.05	.04	.02
34	Everson Walls (184)	.05	.04	.02
35	Danny White (185)	.08	.06	.03
36	Tony Dorsett	.40	.30	.15
37	Ed Too Tall Jones	.12	.09	.05
38	Rafael Septien (188)	.05	.04	.02
39	Doug Crosbie (189)	.05	.04	.02
40	Drew Pearson (190)	.06	.05	.02
41	Randy White	.20	.15	.08
42	Ron Jaworski	.10	.08	.04
43	Anthony Griggs (193)	.05	.04	.02
44	Hubert Oliver (194)	.05	.04	.02
45	Wilbert Montgomery (195)	.05	.04	.02
46	Dennis Harrison	.05	.04	.02
47	Mike Quick	.08	.06	.03
48	Jerry Robinson (198)	.04	.03	.02
49	Michael Williams (199)	.05	.04	.02
50	Herman Edwards (200)	.05	.04	.02
51	Steve Bartkowski (201)	.06	.05	.02
52	Mick Luckhurst (202)	.05	.04	.02
53	Mike Pitts (203)	.05	.04	.02
54	William Andrews	.10	.08	.04
55	R.C. Thielemann	.05	.04	.02
56	Buddy Curry (206)	.05	.04	.02
57	Billy Johnson (207)	.04	.03	.02
58	Ralph Giacomaro (208)	.05	.04	.02
59	Mike Kenn	.08	.06	.03
60	Joe Montana	1.50	1.25	.60
61	Fred Dean (211)	.05	.04	.02
62	Dwight Clark (212)	.10	.08	.04
63	Wendell Tyler (213)	.05	.04	.02
64	Dwight Hicks	.05	.04	.02
65	Ronnie Lott	.25	.20	.10
66	Roger Craig (216)	.40	.30	.15
67	Fred Solomon (217)	.05	.04	.02
68	Ray Wersching (218)	.05	.04	.02
69	Brad Van Pelt (219)	.05	.04	.02
70	Butch Woolfolk (220)	.05	.04	.02
71	Terry Kinard (221)	.05	.04	.02
72	Lawrence Taylor	.35	.25	.14
73	Aji Haji-Sheikh	.05	.04	.02
74	Mark Haynes (224)	.05	.04	.02
75	Rob Carpenter (225)	.05	.04	.02
76	Earnest Gray (226)	.05	.04	.02
77	Harry Carson	.10	.08	.04
78	Billy Sims	.15	.11	.06
79	Ed Murray (229)	.05	.04	.02
80	William Gay (230)	.05	.04	.02
81	Leonard Thompson (231)	.05	.04	.02
82	Doug English	.08	.06	.03
83	Eric Hipple	.08	.06	.03
84	Ken Fantetti (234)	.05	.04	.02
85	Bruce McNorton (235)	.05	.04	.02
86	James Jones (236)	.05	.04	.02
87	Lynn Dickey (237)	.06	.05	.02
88	Ezra Johnson (238)	.05	.04	.02
89	Jan Stenerud (239)	.08	.06	.03
90	James Lofton	.20	.15	.08
91	Larry McCarren	.05	.04	.02
92	John Jefferson (242)	.05	.04	.02
93	Mike Douglass (243)	.05	.04	.02
94	Gerry Ellis (244)	.05	.04	.02

#	Name				#	Name			
95	Paul Coffman	.05	.04	.02	160	Anthony Munoz	.20	.15	.08
96	Eric Dickerson	1.00	.70	.40	161	Cris Collinsworth	.15	.11	.06
97	Jackie Slater (247)	.20	.15	.08	162	Charles Alexander (12)	.05	.04	.02
98	Carl Ekern (248)	.05	.04	.02	163	Ray Horton (13)	.10	.08	.04
99	Vince Ferragamo (249)	.06	.05	.02	164	Steve Keider (14)	.05	.04	.02
100	Kent Hill	.05	.04	.02	165	Ben Williams (15)	.05	.04	.02
101	Nolan Cromwell	.08	.06	.03	166	Frank Lewis (16)	.08	.06	.03
102	Jack Youngblood (252)	.10	.08	.04	167	Roosevelt Leaks (17)	.05	.04	.02
103	John Misko (253)	.05	.04	.02	168	Joe Ferguson	.08	.06	.03
104	Mike Barber (254)	.07	.05	.03	169	Fred Smerlas	.08	.06	.03
105	Jeff Bostic (255)	.05	.04	.02	170	Joe Danelo (20)	.05	.04	.02
106	Mark Murphy (256)	.05	.04	.02	171	Chris Keating (21)	.05	.04	.02
107	Joe Jacoby (257)	.05	.04	.02	172	Jerry Butler (22)	.05	.04	.02
108	John Riggins	.25	.20	.10	173	Eugene Marve	.05	.04	.02
109	Joe Theismann	.30	.25	.12	174	Louis Wright	.08	.06	.03
110	Russ Grimm (260)	.05	.04	.02	175	Barney Chavous (25)	.10	.08	.04
111	Neal Olkewicz (261)	.07	.05	.03	176	Zack Thomas (26)	.05	.04	.02
112	Charlie Brown (262)	.05	.04	.02	177	Luke Prestridge (27)	.05	.04	.02
113	Dave Butz	.08	.06	.03	178	Steve Watson	.08	.06	.03
114	George Rogers	.10	.08	.04	179	John Elway	2.00	1.50	.80
115	Jim Kovach (265)	.05	.04	.02	180	Steve Foley (30)	.05	.04	.02
116	Dave Wilson (266)	.05	.04	.02	181	Sammy Winder (31)	.10	.08	.04
117	Johnnie Poe (267)	.05	.04	.02	182	Rick Upchurch (32)	.05	.04	.02
118	Russell Erxleben	.05	.04	.02	183	Bobby Jones (33)	.08	.06	.03
119	Rickey Jackson	.50	.40	.20	184	Matt Bahr (34)	.05	.04	.02
120	Jeff Groth (270)	.05	.04	.02	185	Doug Dieken (35)	.05	.04	.02
121	Richard Todd (271)	.06	.05	.02	186	Mike Pruitt	.08	.06	.03
122	Wayne Wilson (272)	.05	.04	.02	187	Chip Banks	.10	.08	.04
123	Steve Dils (273)	.05	.04	.02	188	Tom Cousineau (38)	.05	.04	.02
124	Benny Ricardo (274)	.05	.04	.02	189	Paul McDonald (39)	.05	.04	.02
125	John Turner (275)	.05	.04	.02	190	Clay Matthews (40)	.08	.06	.03
126	Ted Brown	.05	.04	.02	191	Ozzie Newsome	.20	.15	.08
127	Greg Coleman	.05	.04	.02	192	Dan Fouts	.40	.30	.15
128	Darrin Nelson (278)	.05	.04	.02	193	Chuck Muncie (43)	.05	.04	.02
129	Scott Studwell (279)	.06	.05	.02	194	Linden King (44)	.05	.04	.02
130	Tommy Kramer (280)	.06	.05	.02	195	Charlie Joiner (45)	.08	.06	.03
131	Doug Martin	.05	.04	.02	196	Wes Chandler	.08	.06	.03
132	Nolan Cromwell (145, All-Pro)	.10	.08	.04	197	Kellen Winslow	.20	.15	.08
					198	James Brooks (48)	.10	.08	.04
133	Carl Birdsong (145, All-Pro)	.10	.08	.04	199	Mike Green (49)	.05	.04	.02
					200	Rolf Benirschke (58)	.05	.04	.02
134	Deron Cherry (146, All-Pro)	.20	.15	.08	201	Henry Marshall (51)	.05	.04	.02
					202	Nick Lowery (52)	.06	.05	.02
135	Ronnie Lott (147, All-Pro)	.30	.25	.12	203	Jerry Blanton (53)	.05	.04	.02
136	Lester Hayes (148, All-Pro)	.10	.08	.04	204	Bill Kenney	.08	.06	.03
137	Lawrence Taylor (149, All-Pro)	.30	.25	.12	205	Carlos Carson	.08	.06	.03
					206	Billy Jackson (56)	.05	.04	.02
138	Jack Lambert (150, All-Pro)	.20	.15	.08	207	Art Still (57)	.05	.04	.02
					208	Theotis Brown (58)	.05	.04	.02
139	Chip Banks (151, All-Pro)	.10	.08	.04	209	Deron Cherry	.25	.20	.10
140	Lee Roy Selmon (152, All-Pro)	.15	.11	.06	210	Curtis Dickey	.08	.06	.03
					211	Nesby Glasgow (61)	.05	.04	.02
141	Fred Smerlas (153, All-Pro)	.10	.08	.04	212	Mike Pagel (62)	.05	.04	.02
					213	Ray Donaldson (63)	.05	.04	.02
142	Doug English (154, All-Pro)	.10	.08	.04	214	Raul Allegre	.05	.04	.02
					215	Chris Hinton	.30	.25	.12
143	Doug Betters (155, All-Pro)	.10	.08	.04	216	Rohn Stark (66)	.08	.06	.03
					217	Randy McMillan (67)	.08	.06	.03
144	Dan Marino (132, All-Pro)	3.00	2.25	1.25	218	Vernon Maxwell (68)	.05	.04	.02
145	Ali Haji-Sheikh (133, All-Pro)	.10	.08	.04	219	A.J. Duhe (69)	.10	.08	.04
					220	Andra Franklin (70)	.05	.04	.02
146	Eric Dickerson (134, All-Pro)	.65	.50	.25	221	Ed Newman (71)	.05	.04	.02
					222	Dan Marino	4.00	3.00	1.50
147	Curt Warner (135, All-Pro)	.15	.11	.06	223	Doug Betters	.08	.06	.03
148	James Lofton (136, All-Pro)	.25	.20	.10	224	Bob Baumhower (74)	.05	.04	.02
					225	Reggie Roby (75)	.08	.06	.03
149	Todd Christensen (All-Pro)	.15	.11	.06	226	Dwight Stephenson (76)	.08	.06	.03
150	Cris Collinsworth (All-Pro)	.20	.15	.08	227	Mark Duper	.40	.30	.15
151	Mike Kenn (139, All-Pro)	.10	.08	.04	228	Mark Gastineau	.15	.11	.06
152	Russ Grimm (140, All-Pro)	.10	.08	.04	229	Freeman McNeil (79)	.08	.06	.03
153	Jeff Bostic (141, All-Pro)	.10	.08	.04	230	Bruce Harper (80)	.05	.04	.02
154	John Hannah (142, All-Pro)	.15	.11	.06	231	Wesley Walker (81)	.06	.05	.02
155	Anthony Munoz (143, All-Pro)	.20	.15	.08	232	Marvin Powell	.08	.06	.03
					233	Joe Klecko	.08	.06	.03
156	Ken Anderson	.35	.25	.14	234	Johnny Lam Jones (84)	.05	.04	.02
157	Pete Johnson (7)	.05	.04	.02	235	Lance Mehl (85)	.05	.04	.02
158	Reggie Williams (8)	.06	.05	.02	236	Pat Ryan (86)	.05	.04	.02
159	Isaac Curtis (9)	.05	.04	.02	237	Florian Kempf (87)	.05	.04	.02

		MT	NM	EX
238	Carl Roaches (88)	.05	.04	.02
239	Gregg Bigham (89)	.05	.04	.02
240	Tim Smith	.05	.04	.02
241	Jesse Baker	.05	.04	.02
242	Doug France (92)	.08	.06	.03
243	Chris Dressel (93)	.05	.04	.02
244	Willie Tullis (94)	.05	.04	.02
245	Robert Brazile	.08	.06	.03
246	Tony Collins	.08	.06	.03
247	Brian Holloway (97)	.05	.04	.02
248	Stanley Morgan (98)	.06	.05	.02
249	Rick Sanford (99)	.05	.04	.02
250	John Hannah	.15	.11	.06
251	Rich Camarillo	.08	.06	.03
252	Andre Tippett (102)	.08	.06	.03
253	Steve Grogan (103)	.08	.06	.03
254	Clayton Weishuhn (104)	.05	.04	.02
255	Jim Plunkett (105)	.08	.06	.03
256	Rod Martin (106)	.08	.06	.03
257	Lester Hayes (107)	.05	.04	.02
258	Marcus Allen	.50	.40	.20
259	Todd Chistensen	.10	.08	.04
260	Ted Hendricks (110)	.08	.06	.03
261	Greg Pruitt (111)	.05	.04	.02
262	Howie Long (112)	.50	.40	.20
263	Vann McElroy	.05	.04	.02
264	Curt Warner	.25	.20	.10
265	Jacob Green (115)	.06	.05	.02
266	Bruce Scholtz (116)	.05	.04	.02
267	Steve Largent (117)	.50	.40	.20
268	Kenny Easley	.08	.06	.03
269	Dave Krieg	.35	.25	.14
270	Dave Brown (120)	.05	.04	.02
271	Zachary Dixon (121)	.05	.04	.02
272	Norm Johnson (122)	.05	.04	.02
273	Terry Bradshaw (123)	.30	.25	.12
274	Keith Willis (124)	.05	.04	.02
275	Gary Anderson (125)	.05	.04	.02
276	Franco Harris	.35	.25	.14
277	Mike Webster	.15	.11	.06
278	Calvin Sweeney (128)	.05	.04	.02
279	Rick Woods (129)	.05	.04	.02
280	Bennie Cunningham (130)	.08	.06	.03
281	Jack Lambert	.15	.11	.06
282	Curt Warner (283)	.35	.25	.14
283	Todd Christensen (282)	.15	.11	.06

1985 Topps "Coming Soon" Stickers

These stickers say "Coming Soon" on the backs and share identical card numbers with their counterparts in Topps' regular 1985 sticker set; thus, the checklist is skip-numbered. These stickers, which were random inserts in 1985 Topps football packs, measure 2 1/8" by 3" each but, unlike many of the regular stickers, feature only one player per sticker. The stickers have a colored photo on the front with a color frame and white border surrounding it.

		MT	NM	EX
	Complete Set (30):	5.00	3.75	2.00
	Common Player:	.08	.06	.03
6	Ken Anderson	.30	.25	.12
15	Greg Bell	.15	.11	.06
24	John Elway	.75	.60	.30
33	Ozzie Newsome	.25	.20	.10
42	Charlie Joiner	.25	.20	.10
51	Bill Kenney	.15	.11	.06
60	Randy McMillan	.08	.06	.03
69	Dan Marino	2.00	1.50	.80
77	Mark Clayton	.50	.40	.20
78	Mark Gastineau	.08	.06	.03
87	Warren Moon	2.00	1.50	.80
96	Tony Eason	.15	.11	.06
105	Marcus Allen	.50	.40	.20
114	Steve Largent	.60	.45	.25
123	John Stallworth	.20	.15	.08

		MT	NM	EX
156	Walter Payton	1.00	.70	.40
165	James Wilder	.12	.09	.05
174	Neil Lomax	.15	.11	.06
183	Tony Dorsett	.35	.25	.14
192	Mike Quick	.15	.11	.06
201	William Andrews	.10	.08	.04
210	Joe Montana	2.50	2.00	1.00
214	Dwight Clark	.35	.25	.14
219	Lawrence Taylor	.35	.16	.04
228	Billy Sims	.15	.11	.06
237	James Lofton	.30	.25	.12
246	Eric Dickerson	.50	.40	.20
255	John Riggins	.25	.20	.10
268	George Rogers	.12	.09	.05
281	Tommy Kramer	.08	.06	.03

1985 Topps Stickers

These stickers are different than those issued in previous years, because no foil stickers were produced. However, there were stickers issued in pairs on some cards; they are noted as being partners by the which follows the player's name in the checklist. Charlie Joiner, Art Monk, Joe Montana, Dan Marino, Walter Payton and Eric Dickerson are all featured on the album cover; the 49ers team is on the back.

		MT	NM	EX
	Complete Set (285):	20.00	15.00	8.00
	Common Player:	.05	.04	.02
1	Super Bowl XIX	1.50	1.25	.60
2	Super Bowl XIX	1.00	.70	.40
3	Super Bowl XIX	.10	.08	.04
4	Super Bowl XIX	.10	.08	.04
5	Super Bow XIX	.08	.06	.03
6	Ken Anderson	.30	.25	.12
7	M.L. Harris (157)	.05	.04	.02
8	Eddie Edwards (157)	.05	.04	.02
9	Louis Breeden (159)	.05	.04	.02
10	Larry Kinnebrew	.05	.04	.02
11	Isaac Curtis (161)	.06	.05	.02
12	James Brooks (162)	.12	.09	.05
13	Jim Breech (163)	.05	.04	.02
14	Boomer Esiason (164)	.75	.60	.30
15	Greg Bell	.10	.08	.04
16	Fred Smerlas (166)	.05	.04	.02
17	Joe Ferguson (167)	.06	.05	.02
18	Ken Johnson (168)	.05	.04	.02
19	Darryl Talley (169)	.25	.20	.10
20	Preston Dennard (170)	.05	.04	.02
21	Charles Romes (171)	.05	.04	.02
22	Jim Haslett (172)	.05	.04	.02
23	Byron Franklin	.05	.04	.02
24	John Elway	1.25	.90	.50
25	Rulon Jones (175)	.05	.04	.02
26	Butch Johnson (176)	.05	.04	.02
27	Rick Karlis (177)	.05	.04	.02
28	Sammy Winder	.05	.04	.02
29	Tom Jackson (179)	.10	.08	.04
30	Mike Harden (180)	.05	.04	.02
31	Steve Watson (181)	.05	.04	.02
32	Steve Foley (182)	.05	.04	.02
33	Ozzie Newsome	.25	.20	.10
34	Al Gross (184)	.05	.04	.02
35	Paul McDonald (185)	.05	.04	.02
36	Matt Bahr (186)	.07	.05	.03
37	Charles White (187)	.06	.05	.02
38	Don Rogers (188)	.05	.04	.02
39	Mike Pruitt (189)	.05	.04	.02
40	Reggie Camp (190)	.05	.04	.02
41	Boyce Green	.05	.04	.02
42	Charlie Joiner	.20	.15	.08
43	Dan Fouts (193)	.25	.20	.10
44	Keith Ferguson (194)	.05	.04	.02
45	Pete Holohan (195)	.05	.04	.02
46	Earnest Jackson	.08	.06	.03

Stamps/stickers

47	Wes Chandler (197)	.06	.05	.02		123	John Stallworth	.12	.09	.05
48	Gill Byrd (198)	.15	.11	.06		124	Donnie Shell (274)	.05	.04	.02
49	Kellen Winslow (199)	.15	.11	.06		125	Gary Anderson (275)	.05	.04	.02
50	Billy Ray Smith (200)	.06	.05	.02		126	Mark Malone (276)	.05	.04	.02
51	Bill Kenney	.08	.06	.03		127	Sam Washington (277)	.05	.04	.02
52	Herman Heard (202)	.05	.04	.02		128	Frank Pollard (278)	.05	.04	.02
53	Art Still (203)	.05	.04	.02		129	Mike Merriweather (279)	.10	.08	.04
54	Nick Lowery (204)	.05	.04	.02		130	Walter Abercrombie (280)	.05	.04	.02
55	Deron Cherry (205)	.08	.06	.03		131	Louis Lipps	.30	.25	.12
56	Jenry Marshall (206)	.05	.04	.02		132	Mark Clayton (144)	.35	.25	.14
57	Mike Bell (207)	.05	.04	.02		133	Randy Cross (145)	.06	.05	.02
58	Todd Blackledge (208)	.05	.04	.02		134	Eric Dickerson (146)	.35	.25	.14
59	Carlos Carson	.08	.06	.03		135	John Hannah (147)	.10	.08	.04
60	Randy McMillan	.05	.04	.02		136	Mike Kenn (148)	.05	.04	.02
61	Donnell Thompson (211)	.05	.04	.02		137	Dan Marino (149)	1.50	1.25	.60
62	Raymond Butler (212)	.05	.04	.02		138	Art Monk (151)	.15	.11	.06
63	Ray Donaldson (213)	.05	.04	.02		139	Anthony Munoz (151)	.10	.08	.04
64	Art Schlichter	.15	.11	.06		140	Ozzie Newsome (152)	.10	.08	.04
65	Rohn Stark (215)	.05	.04	.02		141	Walter Payton (153)	.40	.30	.15
66	Johnie Cooks (216)	.05	.04	.02		142	Jan Stenerud (154)	.08	.06	.03
67	Mike Pagel (217)	.05	.04	.02		143	Dwight Stephenson (155)	.05	.04	.02
68	Eugene Daniel (218)	.05	.04	.02		144	Todd Bell (132)	.05	.04	.02
69	Dan Marino	2.00	1.50	.80		145	Richard Dent (133)	.50	.40	.20
70	Pete Johnson (220)	.05	.04	.02		146	Kenny Easley (134)	.05	.04	.02
71	Tony Nathan (221)	.05	.04	.02		147	Mark Gastineau (135)	.06	.05	.02
72	Glenn Blackwood (222)	.05	.04	.02		148	Dan Hampton (136)	.10	.08	.04
73	Woody Bennett (223)	.05	.04	.02		149	Mark Haynes (137)	.05	.04	.02
74	Dwight Stephenson (224)	.05	.04	.02		150	Mike Haynes (138)	.06	.05	.02
75	Mark Duper (225)	.10	.08	.04		151	E.J. Junior (139)	.05	.04	.02
76	Doug Betters (226)	.05	.04	.02		152	Rod Martin (140)	.10	.08	.04
77	Mark Clayton	.50	.40	.20		153	Steve Nelson (141)	.05	.04	.02
78	Mark Gastineau	.08	.06	.03		154	Reggie Roby (142)	.05	.04	.02
79	Johnny Lam Jones (229)	.05	.04	.02		155	Lawrence Taylor (143)	.15	.11	.06
80	Mickey Shuler (230)	.05	.04	.02		156	Walter Payton	.60	.45	.25
81	Tony Paige (231)	.15	.11	.06		157	Dan Hampton (7)	.08	.06	.03
82	Freeman McNeil	.15	.11	.06		158	Willie Gault (8)	.06	.05	.02
83	Russell Carter (233)	.06	.05	.02		159	Matt Suhey (9)	.05	.04	.02
84	Wesley Walker (234)	.06	.05	.02		160	Richard Dent	1.00	.70	.40
85	Bruce Harper (235)	.15	.11	.06		161	Mike Singletary (11)	.10	.08	.04
86	Ken O'Brien (236)	1.75	1.25	.70		162	Gary Fencik (12)	.05	.04	.02
87	Warren Moon	.05	.04	.02		163	Jim McMahon (13)	.10	.08	.04
88	Jesse Baker (238)	.05	.04	.02		164	Bob Thomas (14)	.05	.04	.02
89	Carl Roaches (239)	.05	.04	.02		165	James Wilder	.08	.06	.03
90	Carter Hartwig (240)	.05	.04	.02		166	Steve DeBerg (16)	.08	.06	.03
91	Larry Moriarty (241)	.05	.04	.02		167	Mark Cotney (17)	.05	.04	.02
92	Robert Brazile (242)	.05	.04	.02		168	Adger Armstrong (18)	.05	.04	.02
93	Oliver Luck (243)	.05	.04	.02		169	Gerald Carter (19)	.05	.04	.02
94	Willie Tullis (244)	.05	.04	.02		170	David Logari (20)	.05	.04	.02
95	Tim Smith	.05	.04	.02		171	Hugh Green (21)	.05	.04	.02
96	Tony Eason	.12	.09	.05		172	Lee Roy Selmon (22)	.06	.05	.02
97	Stanley Morgan (247)	.10	.08	.04		173	Kevin House	.10	.08	.04
98	Mosi Tatupu (248)	.05	.04	.02		174	Neil Lomax	.12	.09	.05
99	Raymond Clayborn (249)	.08	.06	.03		175	Ottis Anderson (25)	.10	.08	.04
100	Andre Tippett	.10	.08	.04		176	Al (Bubba) Baker (26)	.05	.04	.02
101	Craig James (251)	.15	.11	.06		177	E.J. Junior (27)	.08	.06	.03
102	Derrick Ramsey (252)	.05	.04	.02		178	Roy Green	.10	.08	.04
103	Tony Collins (253)	.05	.04	.02		179	Pat Tilley (29)	.05	.04	.02
104	Tony Franklin (254)	.05	.04	.02		180	Stump Mitchell (30)	.05	.04	.02
105	Marcus Allen	.40	.30	.15		181	Lionel Washington (31)	.05	.04	.02
106	Chris Bahr (256)	.05	.04	.02		182	Curtis Greer (32)	.05	.04	.02
107	Marc Wilson (257)	.05	.04	.02		183	Tony Dorsett	.25	.20	.10
108	Howie Long (258)	.10	.08	.04		184	Gary Hogeboom (34)	.06	.05	.02
109	Bill Pickel (259)	.05	.04	.02		185	Jim Jeffcoat (35)	.06	.05	.02
110	Mike Haynes (260)	.08	.06	.03		186	Danny White (36)	.08	.06	.03
111	Malcolm Barnwell (261)	.05	.04	.02		187	Michael Downs (37)	.05	.04	.02
112	Rod Martin (262)	.05	.04	.02		188	Doug Cosbie (38)	.08	.06	.03
113	Todd Christensen	.10	.08	.04		189	Tony Hill (39)	.05	.04	.02
114	Steve Largent	.75	.60	.30		190	Rafael Septein (40)	.05	.04	.02
115	Curt Warner (265)	.08	.06	.03		191	Randy White	.15	.11	.06
116	Kenny Easley (266)	.05	.04	.02		192	Mike Quick	.08	.06	.03
117	Jacob Green (267)	.05	.04	.02		193	Ray Ellis (43)	.05	.04	.02
118	Daryl Turner	.08	.06	.03		194	John Spagnola (44)	.05	.04	.02
119	Norm Johnson (269)	.05	.04	.02		195	Dennis Harrison (45)	.05	.04	.02
120	Dave Krieg (270)	.10	.08	.04		196	Wilbert Montgomery	.08	.06	.03
121	Eric Lane (271)	.05	.04	.02		197	Greg Brown (47)	.05	.04	.02
122	Jeff Bryant (272)	.05	.04	.02		198	Ron Jaworski (48)	.08	.06	.03

199	Paul McFadden (49)	.05	.04	.02
200	Wes Hopkins (50)	.05	.04	.02
201	William Andrews	.10	.08	.04
202	Mike Pitts (52)	.05	.04	.02
203	Steve Bartkowski (53)	.08	.06	.03
204	Gerald Riggs (54)	.08	.06	.03
205	Alfred Jackson (55)	.05	.04	.02
206	Don Smith (56)	.05	.04	.02
207	Mike Kenn (57)	.05	.04	.02
208	Kenny Johnson (58)	.05	.04	.02
209	Stacey Bailey	.05	.04	.02
210	Joe Montana	1.25	.90	.50
211	Wendell Tyler (61)	.05	.04	.02
212	Keena Turner (62)	.08	.06	.03
213	Ray Wersching (63)	.05	.04	.02
214	Dwight Clark	.15	.11	.06
215	Dwaine Board (65)	.05	.04	.02
216	Roger Craig (66)	.15	.11	.06
217	Ronnie Lott (67)	.15	.11	.06
218	Freddie Solomon (68)	.08	.06	.03
219	Lawrence Taylor	.25	.20	.10
220	Zeke Mowatt (70)	.05	.04	.02
221	Harry Carson (71)	.06	.05	.02
222	Rob Carpenter (72)	.05	.04	.02
223	Bobby Johnson (73)	.05	.04	.02
224	Joe Morris (74)	.07	.05	.03
225	Mark Haynes (75)	.05	.04	.02
226	Lionel Manuel (76)	.05	.04	.02
227	Phil Simms	.15	.11	.06
228	Billy Simms	.12	.09	.05
229	Leonard Thompson (79)	.03	.02	.01
230	James Jones (80)	.05	.04	.02
231	Ed Murray (81)	.05	.04	.02
232	William Gay	.05	.04	.02
233	Gary Danielson (83)	.05	.04	.02
234	Curtis Green (84)	.05	.04	.02
235	Bobby Watkins (85)	.05	.04	.02
236	Doug English (86)	.05	.04	.02
237	James Lofton	.20	.15	.08
238	Eddie Lee Ivery (88)	.06	.05	.02
239	Mike Douglas (89)	.05	.04	.02
240	Gerry Ellis (90)	.05	.04	.02
241	Tim Lewis (91)	.08	.06	.03
242	Paul Coffman (92)	.05	.04	.02
243	Tom Flynn (93)	.05	.04	.02
244	Ezra Johnson (94)	.05	.04	.02
245	Lynn Dickey	.08	.06	.03
246	Eric Dickerson	.60	.45	.25
247	Jack Youngblood (97)	.08	.06	.03
248	Doug Smith (98)	.05	.04	.02
249	Jeff Kemp (99)	.05	.04	.02
250	Kent Hill	.05	.04	.02
251	Mike Lansford (101)	.05	.04	.02
252	Henry Ellard (102)	.35	.25	.14
253	LeRoy Irvin (103)	.06	.05	.02
254	Ron Brown (104)	.20	.15	.08
255	John Riggins	.06	.05	.02
256	Dexter Manley (106)	.10	.08	.04
257	Darrell Green (107)	.15	.11	.06
258	Joe Theismann (108)	.05	.04	.02
259	Mark Moseley (109)	.05	.04	.02
260	Clint Didier (110)	.05	.04	.02
261	Vernon Dean (111)	.05	.04	.02
262	Calvin Muhammad (112)	.05	.04	.02
263	Art Monk	.20	.15	.08
264	Bruce Clark	.08	.06	.03
265	Hoby Brenner (115)	.05	.04	.02
266	Dave Wilson (116)	.06	.05	.02
267	Hokie Gajan (117)	.05	.04	.02
268	George Rogers	.10	.08	.04
269	Rickey Jackson (119)	.08	.06	.03
270	Brian Hansen (120)	.04	.03	.02
271	Dave Waymer (121)	.05	.04	.02
272	Richard Todd (122)	.05	.04	.02
273	Jan Stenerud	.15	.11	.06
274	Ted Brown (124)	.05	.04	.02

275	Leo Lewis (125)	.05	.04	.02
276	Scott Studwell (126)	.05	.04	.02
277	Alfred Anderson (127)	.05	.04	.02
278	Rufus Bess (128)	.05	.04	.02
279	Darrin Nelson (129)	.05	.04	.02
280	Greg Coleman (130)	.05	.04	.02
281	Tommy Kramer	.08	.06	.03
282	Joe Montana (283)	1.25	.90	.50
283	Dan Marino (282)	1.00	.70	.40
284	Brian Hansen (285)	.05	.04	.02
285	Jim Arnold (284)	.05	.04	.02

1986 Topps Stickers

Topps included foil stickers in its sticker set again in 1986, and followed the format it used for previous issues. The stickers use a shadow box for the frame on the front, around a color photo. A card number appears on both sides. The back has its information printed in brown ink against a white background. Some stickers were issued in pairs, as indicated by the after the player's name in the checklist. The All-Pro players are foil stickers (#s 132-143), as are #s 282-285. The Chicago Bears are featured on the covers of the corresponding album which was issued to hold the stickers; Walter Payton is on the front.

		MT	NM	EX
Complete Set (285):		20.00	15.00	8.00
Common Player:		.05	.04	.02
1	Walter Payton (left)	.60	.45	.25
2	Walter Payton (right)	.60	.45	.25
3	Richard Dent (left)	.10	.08	.04
4	Richard Dent (right)	.10	.08	.04
5	Richard Dent	.40	.30	.15
	(Super Bowl MVP)			
6	Walter Payton	1.00	.70	.40
7	William Perry	.12	.09	.05
8	Jim McMahon (158)	.10	.08	.04
9	Richard Dent (159)	.10	.08	.04
10	Jim Covert (160)	.05	.04	.02
11	Dan Hampton (161)	.08	.06	.03
12	Mike Singletary (162)	.08	.06	.03
13	Jay Hilgenberg (163)	.06	.05	.02
14	Otis Wilson (164)	.04	.03	.02
15	Jimmie Giles	.05	.04	.02
16	Kevin House (166)	.03	.02	.01
17	Jeremiah Castille (167)	.03	.02	.01
18	James Wilder	.05	.04	.02
19	Donald Igwebuike (169)	.05	.04	.02
20	David Logan (170)	.05	.04	.02
21	Jeff Davis (171)	.05	.04	.02
22	Frank Garcia (172)	.05	.04	.02
23	Steve Young (173)	1.00	.70	.40
24	Stump Mitchell	.08	.06	.03
25	E.J. Junior	.08	.06	.03
26	J.T. Smith (176)	.05	.04	.02
27	Pat Tilley (177)	.05	.04	.02

335

Stamps/stickers

28	Neil Lomax (178)	.06	.05	.02
29	Leonard Smith (179)	.05	.04	.02
30	Ottis Anderson (180)	.08	.06	.03
31	Curtis Greer (181)	.05	.04	.02
32	Roy Green (182)	.06	.05	.02
33	Tony Dorsett	.30	.25	.12
34	Tony Hill (184)	.05	.04	.02
35	Doug Cosbie (185)	.06	.05	.02
36	Everson Walls	.08	.06	.03
37	Randy White (187)	.10	.08	.04
38	Rafael Septein (188)	.05	.04	.02
39	Mike Renfro (189)	.05	.04	.02
40	Danny White (190)	.06	.05	.02
41	Ed Too Tall Jones (191)	.10	.08	.04
42	Earnest Jackson	.08	.06	.03
43	Mike Quick	.08	.06	.03
44	Wes Hopkins (194)	.05	.04	.02
45	Reggie White (195)	.75	.60	.30
46	Greg Brown (196)	.05	.04	.02
47	Paul McFadden (197)	.05	.04	.02
48	John Spagnola (198)	.05	.04	.02
49	Ran Jaworski (199)	.05	.04	.02
50	Herman Hunter (200)	.05	.04	.02
51	Gerald Riggs	.10	.08	.04
52	Mike Pitts (202)	.05	.04	.02
53	Buddy Curry (203)	.05	.04	.02
54	Billy Johnson	.12	.09	.05
55	Rick Donnelly (205)	.05	.04	.02
56	Rick Bryan (206)	.08	.06	.03
57	Bobby Butler (207)	.05	.04	.02
58	Mike Luckhurst (208)	.05	.04	.02
59	Mike Kenn (209)	.05	.04	.02
60	Roger Craig	.25	.20	.10
61	Joe Montana	1.75	1.25	.70
62	Michael Carter (212)	.10	.08	.04
63	Eric Wright (213)	.05	.04	.02
64	Dwight Clark (214)	.10	.08	.04
65	Ronnie Lott (215)	.12	.09	.05
66	Carlton Williamson (216)	.05	.04	.02
67	Wendell Tyler (217)	.08	.06	.03
68	Dwaine Board (218)	.05	.04	.02
69	Joe Morris	.12	.09	.05
70	Leonard Marshall (220)	.05	.04	.02
71	Lionel Manuel (221)	.05	.04	.02
72	Harry Carson	.10	.08	.04
73	Phil Simms (223)	.10	.08	.04
74	Sean Landeta (224)	.05	.04	.02
75	Lawrence Taylor (225)	.15	.11	.06
76	Elvis Patterson (226)	.05	.04	.02
77	George Adams (227)	.05	.04	.02
78	James Jones	.08	.06	.03
79	Leonard Thompson	.05	.04	.02
80	William Graham (230)	.05	.04	.02
81	Mark Nichols (231)	.05	.04	.02
82	William Gay (232)	.05	.04	.02
83	Jimmy Williams (233)	.05	.04	.02
84	Billy Sims (234)	.12	.09	.05
85	Bobby Watkins (235)	.05	.04	.02
86	Ed Murray (236)	.05	.04	.02
87	James Lofton	.25	.20	.10
88	Jessie Clark (238)	.05	.04	.02
89	Tim Lewis (239)	.05	.04	.02
90	Eddie Lee Ivery	.08	.06	.03
91	Phillip Epps (241)	.05	.04	.02
92	Ezra Johnson (242)	.05	.04	.02
93	Mike Douglass (243)	.05	.04	.02
94	Paul Coffman (244)	.05	.04	.02
95	Randy Scott (245)	.03	.02	.01
96	Eric Dickerson	.45	.35	.20
97	Dale Hatcher	.05	.04	.02
98	Ron Brown (248)	.06	.05	.02
99	LeRoy Irvin (249)	.05	.04	.02
100	Ken Hill (250)	.05	.04	.02
101	Dennis Harrah (251)	.05	.04	.02
102	Jackie Slater (252)	.08	.06	.03
103	Mike Wilcher (253)	.05	.04	.02
104	Doug Smith (254)	.05	.04	.02
105	Art Monk	.25	.20	.10
106	Joe Jacoby (256)	.05	.04	.02
107	Russ Grimm (257)	.05	.04	.02
108	George Rogers	.10	.08	.04
109	Dexter Manley (259)	.05	.04	.02
110	Jay Schroeder (260)	.12	.09	.05
111	Gary Calrk (261)	.50	.40	.20
112	Curtis Jordan (262)	.05	.04	.02
113	Charles Mann (263)	.08	.06	.03
114	Morten Andersen	.08	.06	.03
115	Rickey Jackson	.10	.08	.04
116	Glen Redd (266)	.05	.04	.02
117	Bobby Hebert (267)	.20	.15	.08
118	Hoby Brenner (268)	.05	.04	.02
119	Brian Hansen (269)	.05	.04	.02
120	Dave Waymer (270)	.05	.04	.02
121	Bruce Clark (271)	.05	.04	.02
122	Wayne Wilson (272)	.05	.04	.02
123	Joey Browner	.25	.20	.10
124	Darrin Nelson (274)	.08	.06	.03
125	Keith Millard (275)	.15	.11	.06
126	Anthony Carter	.35	.25	.14
127	Buster Rhymes (277)	.04	.03	.02
128	Steve Jordan (278)	.20	.15	.08
129	Greg Coleman (279)	.05	.04	.02
130	Ted Brown (280)	.05	.04	.02
131	John Turner (281)	.05	.04	.02
132	Harry Carson (144, All-Pro)	.20	.15	.08
133	Deron Cherry (145, All-Pro)	.10	.08	.04
134	Richard Dent (146, All-Pro)	.20	.15	.08
135	Mike Haynes (147, All-Pro)	.12	.09	.05
136	Wes Hopkins (148, All-Pro)	.10	.08	.04
q				
137	Joe Klecko (149, All-Pro)	.10	.08	.04
138	Leonard Marshall (150, All-Pro)	.10	.08	.04
139	Karl Mecklenburg (151, All-Pro)	.12	.09	.05
140	Rohn Stark (152, All-Pro)	.10	.08	.04
141	Lawrence Taylor (153, All-Pro)	.25	.20	.10
142	Andre Tippett (154, All-Pro)	.12	.09	.05
143	Everson Walls (155, All-Pro)	.12	.09	.05
144	Marcus Allen (132, All-Pro)	.35	.25	.14
145	Gary Anderson (133, All-Pro)	.10	.08	.04
146	Doug Cosbie (134, All-Pro)	.15	.11	.06
147	Jim Covert (135, All-Pro)	.15	.11	.06
148	John Hannah (136, All-Pro)	.15	.11	.06
149	Jay Hilgenberg (137, All-Pro)	.12	.09	.05
150	Ken Hil (138, All-Pro)	.10	.08	.04
151	Brian Holloway (139, All-Pro)	.10	.08	.04
152	Steve Largent (140, All-Pro)	.75	.60	.30
153	Dan Marino (141, All-Pro)	1.50	1.25	.60
154	Art Monk (142, All-Pro)	.25	.20	.10
155	Walter Payton (143, All-Pro)	.75	.60	.30
156	Anthony Munoz	.15	.11	.06
157	Boomer Esiason	.40	.30	.15
158	Cris Collinsworth (8)	.06	.05	.02
159	Eddie Edwards (9)	.05	.04	.02
160	James Griffin (10)	.05	.04	.02
161	Jim Breech (11)	.05	.04	.02
162	Eddie Brown (12)	.05	.04	.02
163	Ross Browner (13)	.05	.04	.02
164	James Brooks (14)	.07	.05	.03

165	Greg Bell	.08	.06	.03
166	Jerry Butler (16)	.05	.04	.02
167	Don Wilson (17)	.05	.04	.02
168	Andre Reed	.75	.60	.30
169	Jim Haslett (19)	.05	.04	.02
170	Bruce Mathison (20)	.05	.04	.02
171	Bruce Smith (21)	.40	.30	.15
172	Joe Cribbs (22)	.05	.04	.02
173	Charles Romes (23)	.05	.04	.02
174	Karl Mecklenburg	.08	.06	.03
175	Rulon Jones	.05	.04	.02
176	John Elway (26)	.40	.30	.15
177	Sammy Winder (27)	.10	.08	.04
178	Louis Wright (28)	.05	.04	.02
179	Steve Watson (29)	.05	.04	.02
180	Dennis Smith (30)	.05	.04	.02
181	Mike Harden (31)	.05	.04	.02
182	Vance Johnson (32)	.10	.08	.04
183	Kevin Mack	.10	.08	.04
184	Chip Banks (34)	.05	.04	.02
185	Bob Golic (35)	.05	.04	.02
186	Earnest Byner	.35	.25	.14
187	Ozzie Newsome (37)	.12	.09	.05
188	Bernie Kosar (38)	.60	.45	.25
189	Don Rogers (39)	.05	.04	.02
190	Al Gross (40)	.05	.04	.02
191	Clarence Weathers (41)	.08	.06	.03
192	Lionel James	.08	.06	.03
193	Dan Fouts	.40	.30	.15
194	Wes Chandler (44)	.06	.05	.02
195	Kellen Winslow (45)	.10	.08	.04
196	Gary Anderson (46)	.07	.05	.03
197	Charlie Joiner (47)	.08	.06	.03
198	Ralf Mojsiejenko (48)	.05	.04	.02
199	Bob Thomas (49)	.05	.04	.02
200	Tim Spencer (50)	.05	.04	.02
201	Deron Cherry	.10	.08	.04
202	Bill Maas (52)	.05	.04	.02
203	Herman Heard (53)	.05	.04	.02
204	Carlos Carson	.08	.06	.03
205	Nick Lowery (55)	.08	.06	.03
206	Bill Kenney (56)	.05	.04	.02
207	Albert Lewis (57)	.25	.20	.10
208	Art Still (58)	.05	.04	.02
209	Stephone Paige (59)	.25	.20	.10
210	Rohn Stark	.05	.04	.02
211	Chris Hinton	.10	.08	.04
212	Albert Bentley (62)	.10	.08	.04
213	Eugene Daniel (63)	.05	.04	.02
214	Pat Beach (64)	.05	.04	.02
215	Cliff Odom (65)	.05	.04	.02
216	Duane Bickett (66)	.20	.15	.08
217	George Wonsley (67)	.05	.04	.02
218	Randy McMillan (68)	.05	.04	.02
219	Dan Marino	1.50	1.25	.60
220	Dwight Stephenson (70)	.08	.06	.03
221	Roy Foster (71)	.05	.04	.02
222	Mark Clayton	.20	.15	.08
223	Mark Duper (73)	.10	.08	.04
224	Fuad Reveiz (74)	.05	.04	.02
225	Reggie Roby (75)	.05	.04	.02
226	Tony Nathan (76)	.05	.04	.02
227	Ron Davenport (77)	.05	.04	.02
228	Freeman McNeil	.10	.08	.04
229	Joe Klecko	.08	.06	.03
230	Mark Gastineau (80)	.05	.04	.02
231	Ken O'Brien (81)	.06	.05	.02
232	Lance Mehl (82)	.05	.04	.02
233	Al Toon (83)	.20	.15	.08
234	Mickey Shuler (84)	.05	.04	.02
235	Pat Leahy (85)	.05	.04	.02
236	Wesley Walker (86)	.06	.05	.02
237	Drew Hill	.10	.08	.04
238	Warren Moon (88)	.40	.30	.15
239	Mike Rozier (89)	.10	.08	.04
240	Mike Munchak	.10	.08	.04
241	Tim Smith (91)	.05	.04	.02

242	Butch Woolfolk (92)	.05	.04	.02
243	Willie Drewrey (93)	.05	.04	.02
244	Keith Bostic (94)	.05	.04	.02
245	Jesse Baker (95)	.05	.04	.02
246	Craig James	.15	.11	.06
247	John Hannah	.12	.09	.05
248	Tony Eason (98)	.06	.05	.02
249	Andre Tippett (99)	.06	.05	.02
250	Tony Collins (100)	.05	.04	.02
251	Brian Holloway (101)	.05	.04	.02
252	Irving Fryar (102)	.10	.08	.04
253	Raymond Clayborn (103)	.05	.04	.02
254	Steve Nelson (104)	.05	.04	.02
255	Marcus Allen	.25	.20	.10
256	Mike Haynes (106)	.08	.06	.03
257	Todd Christensen (107)	.06	.05	.02
258	Howie Long	.12	.09	.05
259	Lester Hayes (109)	.05	.04	.02
260	Rod Martin (110)	.08	.06	.03
261	Dokie Williams (111)	.08	.06	.03
262	Chris Bahr (112)	.05	.04	.02
263	Bill Pickel (113)	.05	.04	.02
264	Curt Warner	.10	.08	.04
265	Steve Largent	.60	.45	.25
266	Fredd Young (116)	.06	.05	.02
267	Dave Krieg (117)	.08	.06	.03
268	Daryl Turner (118)	.05	.04	.02
269	John Harris (119)	.05	.04	.02
270	Randy Edwards (120)	.05	.04	.02
271	Kenny Easley (121)	.05	.04	.02
272	Jacob Green (122)	.05	.04	.02
273	Gary Anderson	.05	.04	.02
274	Mike Webster (124)	.07	.05	.03
275	Walter Abercombie (125)	.08	.06	.03
276	Louis Lipps	.10	.08	.04
277	Frank Pollard (127)	.05	.04	.02
278	Mike Merriweather (128)	.05	.04	.02
279	Mark Malone (129)	.05	.04	.02
280	Donnie Shell (130)	.08	.06	.03
281	John Stallworth (131)	.06	.05	.02
282	Marcus Allen (284)	.50	.40	.20
283	Ken O'Brien (285)	.15	.11	.06
284	Kevin Butler (282)	.15	.11	.06
285	Roger Craig (283)	.35	.25	.14

1987 Topps Stickers

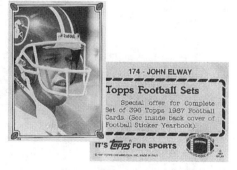

Each of these stickers is 2 1/8" by 3" and features a new design element from previous years' issues - four footballs are included in the frame around the picture on the front, one for each corner. A sticker number appears on both sides. All-Pro foils were again produced, as were stickers in pairs; they are matched up as indicated by the number in player's name in the checklist. The backs have red ink on a white background. The album cover this time features artwork devoted to the New York Giants.

Stamps/stickers

	MT	NM	EX
Complete Set (285):	15.00	11.00	6.00
Common Player:	.05	.04	.02
1 Phil Simms	.40	.30	.15
(Super Bowl MVP)			
2 Super Bowl XXI	.15	.11	.06
(upper left)			
3 Super Bowl XXI	.15	.11	.06
(upper right)			
4 Super Bowl XXI	.15	.11	.06
(lower left)			
5 Super Bowl XXI	.15	.11	.06
(lower right)			
6 Mike Singletary	.12	.09	.05
7 Jim Covert (156)	.50	.40	.20
8 Willie Gault (157)	.06	.05	.02
9 Jim McMahon (158)	.08	.06	.03
10 Doug Flutie (159)	.35	.25	.14
11 Richard Dent (160)	.08	.06	.03
12 Kevin Butler (161)	.05	.04	.02
13 Wilber Marshall (162)	.08	.06	.03
14 Walter Payton	.60	.45	.25
15 Calvin Magee	.05	.04	.02
16 David Logan (165)	.05	.04	.02
17 Jeff Davis (166)	.05	.04	.02
18 Gerald Carter (167)	.05	.04	.02
19 James Wilder	.05	.04	.02
20 Chris Washington (168)	.05	.04	.02
21 Phil Freeman (169)	.05	.04	.02
22 Frank Garcia (170)	.05	.04	.02
23 Donald Igwebuike (171)	.05	.04	.02
24 Al (bubba) Baker (175)	.08	.06	.03
25 Vai Sikhema (176)	.05	.04	.02
26 Leonard Smith (177)	.05	.04	.02
27 Ron Wolgley (178)	.05	.04	.02
28 J.T. Smith	.08	.06	.03
29 Roy Green (179)	.06	.05	.02
30 Cedric Mack (180)	.05	.04	.02
31 Neil Lomax (181)	.06	.05	.02
32 Stump Mitchell	.08	.06	.03
33 Herschel Walker	.50	.40	.20
34 Danny White (184)	.06	.05	.02
35 Michael Downs (185)	.05	.04	.02
36 Randy White (186)	.08	.06	.03
37 Eugene Lockhart (188)	.05	.04	.02
38 Mike Sherrard (189)	.20	.15	.08
39 Jim Jeffcoat (190)	.05	.04	.02
40 Tony Hill (191)	.06	.05	.02
41 Tony Dorsett	.35	.25	.14
42 Keith Byars (192)	.30	.25	.12
43 Andre Waters (193)	.06	.05	.02
44 Kenny Jackson (194)	.05	.04	.02
45 John Teltschik (195)	.05	.04	.02
46 Roynell Young (196)	.05	.04	.02
47 Randall Cunningham (197)	.60	.45	.25
48 Mike Reichenbach (198)	.05	.04	.02
49 Reggie White	.40	.30	.15
50 Mike Quick	.08	.06	.03
51 Bill Fralic (201)	.05	.04	.02
52 Sylvester Stamps (202)	.05	.04	.02
53 Bret Clark (203)	.05	.04	.02
54 William Andrews (204)	.05	.04	.02
55 Buddy Curry (205)	.05	.04	.02
56 Dave Archer (206)	.10	.08	.04
57 Rick Bryan (207)	.05	.04	.02
58 Gerald Riggs	.12	.09	.05
59 Charlie Brown	.05	.04	.02
60 Joe Montana	2.00	1.50	.80
61 Jerry Rice	1.50	1.25	.60
62 Carlton Williamson (212)	.05	.04	.02
63 Roger Craig (213)	.12	.09	.05
64 Ronnie Lott (214)	.15	.11	.06
65 Dwight Clark (215)	.15	.11	.06
66 Jeff Stover (216)	.05	.04	.02
67 Charles Haley (217)	.20	.15	.08
68 Ray Wersching (218)	.05	.04	.02
69 Lawrence Taylor	.30	.25	.12
70 Joe Morris	.12	.09	.05
71 Carl Banks (221)	.10	.08	.04
72 Mark Bavaro (222)	.06	.05	.02
73 Harry Carson (223)	.05	.04	.02
74 Phil Simms (224)	.10	.08	.04
75 Jim Burt (225)	.05	.04	.02
76 Brad Benson (226)	.05	.04	.02
77 Leonard Marshall (227)	.05	.04	.02
78 Jeff Chadwick	.05	.04	.02
79 Devon Mitchell (228)	.05	.04	.02
80 Chuck Long (229)	.06	.05	.02
81 Demetrious Johnson (230)	.05	.04	.02
82 Herman Hunter (231)	.05	.04	.02
83 Kieth Ferguson (232)	.05	.04	.02
84 Gary James (233)	.05	.04	.02
85 Leonard Thompson (234)	.05	.04	.02
86 James Jones	.08	.06	.03
87 Kenneth Davis	.35	.25	.14
88 Brian Noble (237)	.07	.05	.03
89 Al Del Greco (238)	.05	.04	.02
90 Mark Lee (239)	.05	.04	.02
91 Randy Wright	.05	.04	.02
92 Tim Harris (240)	.25	.20	.10
93 Phillip Epps (241)	.05	.04	.02
94 Walter Stanley (242)	.10	.08	.04
95 Eddie Lee Ivery (243)	.05	.04	.02
96 Doug Smith (247)	.05	.04	.02
97 Jerry Gray (248)	.05	.04	.02
98 Jim Everett (250)	.05	.04	.02
99 Jim Everett (250)	.60	.45	.25
100 Jackie Slater (251)	.06	.05	.02
101 Vince Newsome (252)	.10	.08	.04
102 LeRoy Irvin (253)	.10	.08	.04
103 Henry Ellard	.10	.08	.04
104 Eric Dickerson	.60	.45	.25
105 George Rogers (256)	.06	.05	.02
106 Darrell Green (257)	.07	.05	.03
107 Art Monk (258)	.10	.08	.04
108 Neal Olkewicz (260)	.05	.04	.02
109 Russ Grimm (261)	.05	.04	.02
110 Dexter Manley (262)	.05	.04	.02
111 Kelvin Bryant (263)	.05	.04	.02
112 Jay Schroeder	.15	.11	.06
113 Gary Clark	.15	.11	.06
114 Rickey Jackson	.08	.06	.03
115 Eric Martin (264)	.07	.05	.03
116 Dave Waymer (265)	.05	.04	.02
117 Morten Andersen (266)	.06	.05	.02
118 Bruce Clark (167)	.08	.06	.03
119 Hoby Brenner (269)	.07	.05	.03
120 Brian Hansen (270)	.05	.04	.02
121 Dave Wilson (271)	.05	.04	.02
122 Rueben Mayes	.10	.08	.04
123 Tommy Kramer	.08	.06	.03
124 Mark Malone (124)	.05	.04	.02
125 Anthony Carter (275)	.10	.08	.04
126 Keith Millard (276)	.08	.06	.03
127 Steve Jordan	.12	.09	.05
128 Chuck Nelson (277)	.06	.05	.02
129 Issiac Holt (278)	.05	.04	.02
130 Darrin Nelson (279)	.05	.04	.02
131 Gary Zimmerman (280)	.05	.04	.02
132 Mark Bavaro	.10	.08	.04
(146, All-Pro)			
133 Jim Covert (147, All-Pro)	.10	.08	.04
134 Eric Dickerson	.35	.25	.14
(148, All-Pro)			
135 Bill Fralic (149, All-Pro)	.10	.08	.04
136 Tony Franklin	.10	.08	.04
(150, All-Pro)			
137 Dennis Harrah	.10	.08	.04
(151, All-Pro)			
138 Dan Marino (152, All-Pro)	1.25	.90	.50
139 Joe Morris (153, All-Pro)	.25	.20	.10
140 Jerry Rice (154, All-Pro)	1.00	.70	.40
141 Cody Risien (155, All-Pro)	.10	.08	.04
142 Dwight Stephenson	.12	.09	.05
(282, All-Pro)			
143 Al Toon (283, All-Pro)	.20	.15	.08

144	Deron Cherry (284, All-Pro)	.12	.09	.05
145	Hanford Dixon (285, All-Pro)	.10	.08	.04
146	Darrell Green (132, All-Pro)	.15	.11	.06
147	Ronnie Lott (133, All-Pro)	.20	.15	.08
148	Bill Maas (134, All-Pro)	.10	.08	.04
149	Dexter Manley (135, All-Pro)	.10	.08	.04
150	Karl Mecklenburg (136, All-Pro)	.12	.09	.05
151	Mike Singletary (137, All-Pro)	.20	.15	.08
152	Rohn Stark (138, All-Pro)	.10	.08	.04
153	Lawrence Taylor (139, All-Pro)	.30	.25	.12
154	Andre Tippett (140, All-Pro)	.12	.09	.05
155	Reggie White (141, All-Pro)	.35	.25	.14
156	Boomer Esiason (7)	.15	.11	.06
157	Anthony Munoz (8)	.12	.09	.05
158	Tim McGee (9)	.20	.15	.08
159	Max Montoya (10)	.05	.04	.02
160	Jim Breech (11)	.05	.04	.02
161	Tim Krumrie (12)	.05	.04	.02
162	Eddie Brown (13)	.06	.05	.02
163	James Brooks	.10	.08	.04
164	Cris Collinsworth	.12	.09	.05
165	Charles Romes (16)	.05	.04	.02
166	Robb Riddick (17)	.05	.04	.02
167	Eugene Marve (18)	.05	.04	.02
168	Chris Burkett (20)	.10	.08	.04
169	Bruce Smith (21)	.12	.09	.05
170	Greg Bell (22)	.05	.04	.02
171	Pete Metzelaars (23)	.05	.04	.02
172	Jim Kelly	1.50	1.25	.60
173	Andre Reed	.30	.25	.12
174	John Elway	.60	.45	.25
175	Mike Harden (24)	.05	.04	.02
176	Gerald Willhite (25)	.05	.04	.02
177	Rulon Jones (26)	.05	.04	.02
178	Ricky Hunley (27)	.05	.04	.02
179	Mark Jackson (29)	.05	.04	.02
180	Rich Karlis (30)	.05	.04	.02
181	Sammy Winder (31)	.08	.06	.03
182	Karl Mecklenburg	.08	.06	.03
183	Bernie Kosar	.35	.25	.14
184	Kevin Mack (34)	.05	.04	.02
185	Bob Golic (35)	.08	.06	.03
186	Ozzie Newsome (36)	.08	.06	.03
187	Brian Brennan	.05	.04	.02
188	Gerald McNeil (37)	.05	.04	.02
189	Hanford Dixon (38)	.05	.04	.02
190	Cody Risien (39)	.05	.04	.02
191	Chris Rockins (40)	.05	.04	.02
192	Gill Byrd (42)	.05	.04	.02
193	Kellen Winslow (43)	.08	.06	.03
194	Billy Ray Smith (44)	.05	.04	.02
195	Wes Chandler (45)	.08	.06	.03
196	Leslie O'Neal (46)	.25	.20	.10
197	Ralf Mojsiejenko (47)	.05	.04	.02
198	Lee Williams (48)	.20	.15	.08
199	Gary Anderson	.08	.06	.03
200	Dan Fouts	.30	.25	.12
201	Stephone Paige (51)	.08	.06	.03
202	Irv Eatman (52)	.05	.04	.02
203	Bill Kenney (53)	.05	.04	.02
204	Dino Hackett (54)	.08	.06	.03
205	Carlos Carson (55)	.05	.04	.02
206	Art Still (56)	.06	.05	.02
207	Lloyd Burruss (57)	.05	.04	.02
208	Deron Cherry	.08	.06	.03
209	Bill Maas	.05	.04	.02
210	Gary Hogeboom	.08	.06	.03
211	Rohn Stark	.05	.04	.02
212	Cliff Odom (62)	.05	.04	.02
213	Randy McMillan (63)	.05	.04	.02
214	Chris Hinton (64)	.05	.04	.02
215	Matt Bouza (65)	.05	.04	.02
216	Ray Donaldson (66)	.05	.04	.02
217	Bill Brooks (67)	.08	.06	.03
218	Jack Trudeau (68)	.06	.05	.02
219	Mark Duper	.15	.11	.06
220	Dan Marino	1.50	1.25	.60
221	Dwight Stephenson (71)	.08	.06	.03
222	Mark Clayton (72)	.10	.08	.04
223	Roy Foster (73)	.05	.04	.02
224	John Offerdahl (74)	.20	.15	.08
225	Lorenzo Hampton (75)	.05	.04	.02
226	Reggie Roby (76)	.05	.04	.02
227	Tony Nathan (77)	.08	.06	.03
228	Johnny Hector (79)	.08	.06	.03
229	Wesley Walker (80)	.06	.05	.02
230	Mark Gastineau (81)	.10	.08	.04
231	Ken O'Brien (82)	.05	.04	.02
232	Dave Jennings (83)	.05	.04	.02
233	Mickey Shuler (84)	.05	.04	.02
234	Joe Klecko (85)	.05	.04	.02
235	Freeman McNeil	.10	.08	.04
236	Al Toon	.08	.06	.03
237	Warren Moon (88)	.35	.25	.14
238	Dean Steinkuhler (89)	.08	.06	.03
239	Mike Rozier (90)	.06	.05	.02
240	Ray Childress (92)	.08	.06	.03
241	Tony Zendejas (93)	.05	.04	.02
242	John Grimsley (94)	.05	.04	.02
243	Jesse Baker (95)	.05	.04	.02
244	Ernest Givins	.50	.40	.20
245	Drew Hill	.10	.08	.04
246	Tony Franklin	.05	.04	.02
247	Steve Grogan (96)	.06	.05	.02
248	Garin Veris (97)	.05	.04	.02
249	Stanley Morgan (98)	.06	.05	.02
250	Fred Morgan (98)	.05	.04	.02
251	Raymond Clayborn (100)	.07	.05	.03
252	Mosi Tatupu (101)	.05	.04	.02
253	Tony Eason (102)	.05	.04	.02
254	Andre Tippett	.08	.06	.03
255	Todd Christensen	.08	.06	.03
256	Howie Long (105)	.06	.05	.02
257	Marcus Allen (106)	.12	.09	.05
258	Vann McElroy (107)	.05	.04	.02
259	Dokie Williams	.05	.04	.02
260	Mike Haynes (108)	.08	.06	.03
261	Sean Jones	.10	.08	.04
262	Jim Plunkett (110)	.07	.05	.03
263	Chris Bahr (111)	.05	.04	.02
264	Dave Krieg (115)	.08	.06	.03
265	Jacob Green (116)	.05	.04	.02
266	Norm Johnson (117)	.05	.04	.02
267	Fredd Young (118)	.05	.04	.02
268	Steve Largent	.50	.40	.20
269	Dave Brown (119)	.05	.04	.02
270	Kenny Easley (120)	.05	.04	.02
271	Bobby Joe Edmonds (121)	.05	.04	.02
272	Curt Warner	.15	.11	.06
273	Mike Merriweather	.08	.06	.03
274	Mark Malone (124)	.05	.04	.02
275	Bryan Hinkle (125)	.05	.04	.02
276	Earnest jackson (126)	.05	.04	.02
277	Keith Willis (128)	.05	.04	.02
278	Walter Abercrombie (129)	.06	.05	.02
279	Donnie Shell (130)	.08	.06	.03
280	John Stallworth (131)	.06	.05	.02
281	Louis Lipps	.10	.08	.04
282	Eric Dickerson (142)	.30	.25	.12
283	Dan Marino (143)	1.00	.70	.40
284	Tony Franklin (144)	.08	.06	.03
285	Todd Christensen	.12	.09	.05

1988 Topps Sticker Backs

These cards were left after collectors would remove the 1988 Topps stickers from their card. Each card measures 2 1/8" by 3" and features a prominent offensive player. The sticker has "Superstar" written at the top, above the color player photo. His name and card number appear at the bottom in a stat box, using 1 of 67, etc..

		MT	NM	EX
Complete Set (67):		5.00	3.75	2.00
Common Player:		.05	.04	.02
1	Doug Williams	.10	.08	.04
2	Gary Clark	.15	.11	.06
3	John Elway	.50	.40	.20
4	Sammy Winder	.05	.04	.02
5	Vance Johnson	.07	.05	.03
6	Joe Montana	1.50	1.25	.60
7	Roger Craig	.15	.11	.06
8	Jerry Rice	1.00	.70	.40
9	Rueben Mayes	.10	.08	.04
10	Eric Martin	.10	.08	.04
11	Neal Anderson	.30	.25	.12
12	Willie Gault	.10	.08	.04
13	Bernie Kosar	.25	.20	.10
14	Kevin Mack	.05	.04	.02
15	Webster Slaughter	.15	.11	.06
16	Warren Moon	.40	.30	.15
17	Mike Rozier	.10	.08	.04
18	Drew Hill	.10	.08	.04
19	Eric Dickerson	.30	.25	.12
20	Bill Brooks	.05	.04	.02
21	Curt Warner	.15	.11	.06
22	Steve Largent	.40	.30	.15
23	Darrin Nelson	.05	.04	.02
24	Anthony Carter	.15	.11	.06
25	Earnest Jackson	.05	.04	.02
26	Weegie Thompson	.05	.04	.02
27	Stephen Starring	.05	.04	.02
28	Stanley Morgan	.10	.08	.04
29	Dan Marino	1.50	1.25	.60
30	Troy Stadford	.10	.08	.04
31	Mark Clayton	.15	.11	.06
32	Curtis Adams	.05	.04	.02
33	Kellen Winslow	.15	.11	.06
34	Jim Kelly	.60	.45	.25
35	Ronnie Harmon	.25	.20	.10
36	Chris Burkett	.05	.04	.02
37	Randall Cunningham	.35	.25	.14
38	Anthony Toney	.05	.04	.02
39	Mike Quick	.10	.08	.04
40	Neil Lomax	.10	.08	.04
41	Stump Mitchell	.10	.08	.04
42	J.T. Smith	.05	.04	.02
43	Herschel Walker	.25	.20	.10
44	Herschel Walker	.25	.20	.10
45	Joe Morris	.12	.09	.05
46	Mark Bavaro	.10	.08	.04
47	Charles White	.15	.11	.06
48	Henry Ellard	.10	.08	.04
49	Ken O'Brien	.10	.08	.04
50	Freeman McNeil	.10	.08	.04
51	Al Toon	.12	.09	.05
52	Kenneth Davis	.10	.08	.04
53	Walter Stanley	.05	.04	.02
54	Marcus Allen	.30	.25	.12
55	James Lofton	.25	.20	.10
56	Boomer Esiason	.20	.15	.08
57	Larry Kinnebrew	.05	.04	.02
58	Eddie Brown	.10	.08	.04
59	James Wilder	.07	.05	.03
60	Gerald Carter	.05	.04	.02
61	Christian Okoye	.20	.15	.08
62	Carlos Carson	.05	.04	.02
63	James Jones	.05	.04	.02
64	Pete Mandley	.05	.04	.02
65	Gerald Riggs	.10	.08	.04
66	Floyd Dixon	.05	.04	.02
67	Checklist Card	.10	.08	.04

1988 Topps Stickers

These stickers can be distinguished from Topps' previous efforts by the two frames used on the front to border the color photograph. An inner frame of yellow footballs is adjacent to an outer red frame of the picture. Each sticker measures 2 1/8" by 3" and is numbered on both sides. All-Pro stickers were produced as foil stickers again, and pairs of stickers were also made, as indicated by . Stickers 2-5 form a puzzle of Doug Williams featured in action during Super Bowl XXII. Williams is also featured on the back of the album cover which was produced to hold the stickers; the Redskins in action are featured on the front.

		MT	NM	EX
Complete Set (285):		15.00	11.00	6.00
Common Player:		.05	.04	.02
1	Doug Williams	.20	.15	.08
	(Super Bowl XXII MVP)			
2	Super Bowl XXII	.08	.06	.03
3	Super Bowl XXII	.08	.06	.03
4	Super Bowl XXII	.08	.06	.03
5	Super Bowl XXII	.08	.06	.03
6	Neal Anderson (234)	.25	.20	.10
7	Willie Gault (224)	.08	.06	.03
8	Dennis Gentry (219)	.05	.04	.02
9	Dave Duerson (197)	.05	.04	.02
10	Steve McMichael (266)	.05	.04	.02
11	Dennis McKinnon (230)	.05	.04	.02
12	Mike Singletary (209)	.08	.06	.03
13	Jim McMahon	.12	.09	.05
14	Richard Dent	.10	.08	.04
15	Vinny Testaverde (167)	.20	.15	.08

16	Gerald Carter (187)	.05	.04	.02
17	Jeff Smith (185)	.05	.04	.02
18	Chris Washington (212)	.05	.04	.02
19	Bobby Futrell (231)	.05	.04	.02
20	Calvin Magee (182)	.05	.04	.02
21	Ron Holmes (169)	.05	.04	.02
22	Ervin Randle	.05	.04	.02
23	James Wilder	.08	.06	.03
24	Neil Lomax	.08	.06	.03
25	Robert Awalt (161)	.05	.04	.02
26	Leonard Smith (177)	.05	.04	.02
27	Stump Mitchell (178)	.05	.04	.02
28	Vai Sikahema (280)	.06	.05	.02
29	Freddie Joe Nunn (222)	.05	.04	.02
30	Earl Ferrell (223)	.05	.04	.02
31	Roy Green (157)	.10	.08	.04
32	J.T. Smith	.10	.08	.04
33	Michael Downs	.05	.04	.02
34	Herschel Walker	.30	.25	.12
35	Roger Ruzek (269)	.05	.04	.02
36	Ed Too Tall Jones (245)	.07	.05	.03
37	Everson Walls (252)	.05	.04	.02
38	Bill Bates (213)	.05	.04	.02
39	Doug Cosbie (179)	.05	.04	.02
40	Eugene Lockhart (186)	.05	.04	.02
41	Danny White (205)	.07	.05	.03
42	Randall Cunningham	.40	.30	.15
43	Reggie White	.30	.25	.12
44	Anthony Toney (256)	.05	.04	.02
45	Mike Quick (248)	.08	.06	.03
46	John Spagnola (235)	.05	.04	.02
47	Clyde Simmons (275)	.20	.15	.08
48	Andre Waters (261)	.05	.04	.02
49	Keith Byars (265)	.08	.06	.03
50	Jerome Brown (240)	.15	.11	.06
51	John Rade	.05	.04	.02
52	Rick Donnelly	.05	.04	.02
53	Scott Campbell (160)	.05	.04	.02
54	Floyd Dixon (246)	.05	.04	.02
55	Gerald Riggs (236)	.06	.05	.02
56	Bill Fralic (267)	.08	.06	.03
57	Mike Gann (165)	.05	.04	.02
58	Tony Casillas (168)	.15	.11	.06
59	Rick Bryan (257)	.05	.04	.02
60	Jerry Rice	1.00	.70	.40
61	Ronnie Lott	.25	.20	.10
62	Ray Wersching (220)	.05	.04	.02
63	Charles Haley (281)	.06	.05	.02
64	Joe Montana (190)	.75	.60	.30
65	Joe Cribbs (221)	.05	.04	.02
66	Mike Wilson (203)	.05	.04	.02
67	Roger Craig (251)	.12	.09	.05
68	Michael Walter (162)	.05	.04	.02
69	Mark Bavaro	.08	.06	.03
70	Carl Banks	.10	.08	.04
71	George Adams (274)	.03	.02	.01
72	Phil Simms (216)	.15	.11	.06
73	Lawrence Taylor (181)	.12	.09	.05
74	Joe Morris (198)	.06	.05	.02
75	Lionel Manuel (204)	.05	.04	.02
76	Sean Landeta (210)	.05	.04	.02
77	Harry Carson (159)	.05	.04	.02
78	Chuck Long (166)	.05	.04	.02
79	James Jones (159)	.08	.06	.03
80	Gary James (158)	.05	.04	.02
81	Gary Lee (176)	.05	.04	.02
82	Jim Arnold (260)	.05	.04	.02
83	Dennis Gibson (232)	.05	.04	.02
84	Mike Cofer (242)	.05	.04	.02
85	Pete Mandley	.05	.04	.02
86	James Griffin	.05	.04	.02
87	Randy Wright (206)	.05	.04	.02
88	Phillip Epps (191)	.05	.04	.02
89	Brian Noble (249)	.05	.04	.02

90	Johnny Holland (258)	.10	.08	.04
91	Dave Brown (156)	.05	.04	.02
92	Brent Fullwood (207)	.05	.04	.02
93	Kenneth Davis (194)	.08	.06	.03
94	Tim Harris	.15	.11	.06
95	Walter Stanley	.08	.06	.03
96	Charles White	.15	.11	.06
97	Jackie Slater	.08	.06	.03
98	Jim Everett (271)	.12	.09	.05
99	Mike Lansford (200)	.05	.04	.02
100	Henry Ellard (199)	.06	.05	.02
101	Dale Hatcher (170)	.05	.04	.02
102	Jim Collins (268)	.05	.04	.02
103	Jerry Gray (214)	.05	.04	.02
104	LeRoy Irvin (276)	.05	.04	.02
105	Darrell Green	.12	.09	.05
106	Doug Williams	.10	.08	.04
107	Gary Clark (247)	.10	.08	.04
108	Charles Mann (171)	.10	.08	.04
109	Art Monk (270)	.12	.09	.05
110	Barry Wilburn (196)	.05	.04	.02
111	Alvin Walton (188)	.05	.04	.02
112	Dexter Manley (233)	.05	.04	.02
113	Kelvin Bryant (180)	.04	.03	.02
114	Morten Andersen	.10	.08	.04
115	Rueben Mayes (244)	.06	.05	.02
116	Brian Hansen (279)	.05	.04	.02
117	Dalton Hilliard (241)	.10	.08	.04
118	Rickey Jackson (195)	.06	.05	.02
119	Eric Martin (189)	.06	.05	.02
120	Mel Gray (278)	.05	.04	.02
121	Bobby Hebert (215)	.08	.06	.03
122	Pat Swilling	.40	.30	.15
123	Anthony Carter	.12	.09	.05
124	Wade Wilson (225)	.20	.15	.08
125	Darrin Nelson (250)	.05	.04	.02
126	D.J. Dozier (239)	.06	.05	.02
127	Chris Doleman	.30	.25	.12
128	Henry Thomas (255)	.05	.04	.02
129	Jesse Solomon (211)	.05	.04	.02
130	Neal Guggemos (243)	.05	.04	.02
131	Joey Browner (208)	.06	.05	.02
132	Carl Banks (152, All-Pro)	.10	.08	.04
133	Joey Browner (145, All-Pro)	.10	.08	.04
134	Hanford Dixon (149, All-Pro)	.10	.08	.04
135	Rick Donnelly (147, All-Pro)	.10	.08	.04
136	Kenny Easley (155, All-Pro)	.15	.11	.06
137	Darrell Green (151, All-Pro)	.15	.11	.06
138	Bill Maas (148, All-Pro)	.10	.08	.04
139	Mike Singletary (153, All-Pro)	.15	.11	.06
140	Bruce Smith (154, All-Pro)	.20	.15	.08
141	Andre Tippett (146, All-Pro)	.10	.08	.04
142	Reggie White (150, All-Pro)	.20	.15	.08
143	Fredd Young (144, All-Pro)	.10	.08	.04
144	Morten Andersen (143, All-Pro)	.10	.08	.04
145	Mark Bavaro (133, All-Pro)	.10	.08	.04
146	Eric Dickerson (141, All-Pro)	.30	.25	.12
147	John Elway (134, All-Pro)	.75	.60	.30
148	Bill Fralic (138, All-Pro)	.10	.08	.04
149	Mike Munchak (135, All-Pro)	.10	.08	.04

150	Anthony Munoz (142, All-Pro)	.15	.11	.06
151	Jerry Rice (137, All-Pro)	1.00	.70	.40
152	Jackie Slater (132, All-Pro)	.12	.09	.05
153	J.T. Smith (139, All-Pro)	.10	.08	.04
154	Dwight Stephenson (140, All-Pro)	.12	.09	.05
155	Charles White (136, All-Pro)	.12	.09	.05
156	Larry Kinnebrew (91)	.05	.04	.02
157	Stanford Jennings (31)	.05	.04	.02
158	Eddie Brown (80)	.05	.04	.02
159	Scott Fulhage (77)	.05	.04	.02
160	Boomer Esiason (53)	.12	.09	.05
161	Tim Krumrie (25)	.05	.04	.02
162	Anthony Munoz (68)	.08	.06	.03
163	Jim Breech	.05	.04	.02
164	Reggie Williams	.08	.06	.03
165	Andre Reed (57)	.20	.15	.08
166	Cornelius Bennett (78)	.30	.25	.12
167	Ronnie Harmon (15)	.15	.11	.06
168	Shane Conlan (58)	.15	.11	.06
169	Chris Burkett (21)	.06	.05	.02
170	Mark Kelso (101)	.08	.06	.03
171	Robb Riddick (108)	.05	.04	.02
172	Bruce Smith	.15	.11	.06
173	Jim Kelly	.60	.45	.25
174	Jim Ryan	.05	.04	.02
175	John Elway	.60	.45	.25
176	Sammy Winder (81)	.05	.04	.02
177	Karl Mecklenburg (26)	.05	.04	.02
178	Mark Haynes (27)	.05	.04	.02
179	Rulon Jones (39)	.05	.04	.02
180	Ricky Nattiel (113)	.08	.06	.03
181	Vance Johnson (73)	.05	.04	.02
182	Mike Harden (20)	.05	.04	.02
183	Frank Minnifield	.05	.04	.02
184	Bernie Kosar	.25	.20	.10
185	Earnest Byner (17)	.12	.09	.05
186	Webster Slaughter (40)	.15	.11	.06
187	Brian Brennan (16)	.05	.04	.02
188	Carl Hairston (111)	.05	.04	.02
189	Mike Johnson (119)	.05	.04	.02
190	Clay Matthews (64)	.06	.05	.02
191	Kevin Mack (88)	.06	.05	.02
192	Kellen Winslow	.12	.09	.05
193	Billy Ray Smith	.08	.06	.03
194	Gary Anderson (93)	.06	.05	.02
195	Chip Banks (118)	.05	.04	.02
196	Elvis Patterson (110)	.05	.04	.02
197	Lee Williams (9)	.07	.05	.03
198	Curtis Adams (74)	.05	.04	.02
199	Vencie Glenn (100)	.05	.04	.02
200	Ralf Mojsiejenko (99)	.05	.04	.02
201	Carlos Carson	.05	.04	.02
202	Bill Maas	.05	.04	.02
203	Christian Okoye (66)	.15	.11	.06
204	Deron Cherry (75)	.08	.06	.03
205	Doni Hackett (41)	.05	.04	.02
206	Mike Bell (87)	.05	.04	.02
207	Stephone Paige (92)	.06	.05	.02
208	Bill Kenney (131)	.06	.05	.02
209	Paul Palmer (12)	.05	.04	.02
210	Jack Trudeau (76)	.06	.05	.02
211	Albert Bentley (129)	.06	.05	.02
212	Bill Brooks (18)	.06	.05	.02
213	Dean Biasucci (38)	.05	.04	.02
214	Cliff Odom (103)	.05	.04	.02
215	Barry Krauss (121)	.05	.04	.02
216	Mike Prior (72)	.06	.05	.02
217	Eric Dickerson	.35	.25	.14
218	Duane Bickett	.08	.06	.03
219	Dwight Stephenson (8)	.08	.06	.03
220	John Offerdahl (62)	.10	.08	.04
221	Troy Stradford (65)	.06	.05	.02
222	John Bosa (29)	.04	.03	.02
223	Jackie Shipp (30)	.05	.04	.02
224	Paul Lankford (7)	.05	.04	.02
225	Mark Duper (124)	.08	.06	.03
226	Dan Marino	1.50	1.25	.60
227	Mark Clayton	.15	.11	.06
228	Bob Crable	.05	.04	.02
229	Al Toon	.08	.06	.03
230	Freeman McNeil (11)	.06	.05	.02
231	Johnny Hector (19)	.05	.04	.02
232	Pat Leahy (83)	.05	.04	.02
233	Ken O'Brien (112)	.05	.04	.02
234	Alex Gordon (6)	.05	.04	.02
235	Harry Hamilton (46)	.05	.04	.02
236	Mickey Shuler (55)	.05	.04	.02
237	Mike Rozier	.08	.06	.03
238	Al Smith	.15	.11	.06
239	Ernest Givins (126)	.15	.11	.06
240	Warren Moon (50)	.25	.20	.10
241	Drew Hill (117)	.10	.08	.04
242	Alonzo Highsmith (84)	.15	.11	.06
243	Mike Munchak (130)	.06	.05	.02
244	Keith Bostic (115)	.05	.04	.02
245	Sean Jones (36)	.08	.06	.03
246	Stanley Morgan (54)	.06	.05	.02
247	Garin Veris (107)	.05	.04	.02
248	Stephen Starring (45)	.05	.04	.02
249	Steve Grogan (89)	.06	.05	.02
250	Irving Fryar (125)	.10	.08	.04
251	Rich Camarillo (67)	.05	.04	.02
252	Ronnie Lippett (37)	.05	.04	.02
253	Andre Tippett	.08	.06	.03
254	Fred Marion	.05	.04	.02
255	Howie Long (128)	.10	.08	.04
256	James Lofton (44)	.12	.09	.05
257	Vance Mueller (59)	.05	.04	.02
258	Jerry Robinson (90)	.05	.04	.02
259	Todd Christensen (79)	.06	.05	.02
260	Vann McElroy (82)	.05	.04	.02
261	Greg Townsend (48)	.10	.08	.04
262	Bo Jackson	.85	.60	.35
263	Marcus Allen	.30	.25	.12
264	Curt Warner	.08	.06	.03
265	Jacob Green (49)	.06	.05	.02
266	Norm Johnson (10)	.05	.04	.02
267	Briwn Bosworth (56)	.05	.04	.02
268	Bobby Joe Edmonds (102)	.05	.04	.02
269	Dave Krieg (35)	.07	.05	.03
270	Kenny Easley (109)	.06	.05	.02
271	Steve Largent (98)	.30	.25	.12
272	Fredd Young	.05	.04	.02
273	David Little	.05	.04	.02
274	Frank Pollard (71)	.05	.04	.02
275	Dwight Stone (47)	.08	.06	.03
276	Mike Merriweather (104)	.06	.05	.02
277	Earnest Jackson	.05	.04	.02
278	Delton Hall (120)	.05	.04	.02
279	Gary Anderson (116)	.05	.04	.02
280	Harry Newsome (28)	.08	.06	.03
281	Dwyane Woodruff (63)	.05	.04	.02
282	J.T. Smith (283)	.05	.04	.02
283	Charles White (282)	.05	.04	.02
284	Reggie White (285)	.15	.11	.06
285	Morten Andersen (284)	.10	.08	.04

1964 Wheaties Stamps

These unnumbered stamps, which measure 2 1/2" by 2 3/4", were created to be stored in an accompanying stamp album titled "Pro Bowl Football Player Stamp Album." Each stamp has a color photo of the player, plus his facsimile signature, bordered by a white frame. The stamps were in panels of 12 inside the album and were perforated so they could be put on the corresponding spot within the album. Two stickers were attached to the inside front cover. Four team logo stamps and 70 players are represented on the stamps, but there were no spots in the album for the logo stamps or those for Y.A. Tittle or Joe Schmidt.

		NM	EX	VG
Complete Set (74):		250.00	125.00	75.00
Common Player:		2.00	1.00	.60
(1)	Herb Adderley	6.00	3.00	1.75
(2)	Grady Alderman	2.00	1.00	.60
(3)	Doug Atkins	4.00	2.00	1.25
(4)	Sam Baker	2.00	1.00	.60
(5)	Erich Barnes	2.00	1.00	.60
(6)	Terry Barr	2.00	1.00	.60
(7)	Dick Bass	2.00	1.00	.60
(8)	Maxie Baughan	3.00	1.50	.90
(9)	Raymond Berry	6.00	3.00	1.75
(10)	Charley Bradshaw	2.50	1.25	.70
(11)	Jim Brown	35.00	17.50	10.50
(12)	Roger Brown	2.50	1.25	.70
(13)	Timmy Brown	3.00	1.50	.90
(14)	Gail Cogdill	2.00	1.00	.60
(15)	Tommy Davis	2.00	1.00	.60
(16)	Willie Davis	6.00	3.00	1.75
(17)	Bob DeMarco	2.00	1.00	.60
(18)	Darrell Dess	2.00	1.00	.60
(19)	Buddy Dial	3.00	1.50	.90
(20)	Mike Ditka	18.00	9.00	5.50
(21)	Galen Fiss	2.00	1.00	.60
(22)	Lee Folkins	2.00	1.00	.60
(23)	Joe Fortunato	2.00	1.00	.60
(24)	Bill Glass	3.00	1.50	.90
(25)	John Gordy	2.00	1.00	.60
(26)	Ken Gray	2.50	1.25	.70
(27)	Forrest Gregg	5.00	2.50	1.50
(28)	Rip Hawkins	2.00	1.00	.60
(29)	Charlie Johnson	3.00	1.50	.90
(30)	John Henry Johnson	5.00	2.50	1.50
(31)	Henry Jordan	3.00	1.50	.90
(32)	Jim Katcavage	2.00	1.00	.60
(33)	Jerry Kramer	5.00	2.50	1.50
(34)	Joe Krupa	2.00	1.00	.60
(35)	John LoVetere	2.00	1.00	.60
(36)	Dick Lynch	3.00	1.50	.90
(37)	Gino Marchetti	5.00	2.50	1.50
(38)	Joe Marconi	2.00	1.00	.60
(39)	Tommy Mason	3.00	1.50	.90
(40)	Dale Meinert	2.00	1.00	.60
(41)	Lou Michaels	2.00	1.00	.60
(42)	Minnesota Vikings Emblem	3.00	1.50	.90
(43)	Bobby Mitchell	6.00	3.00	1.75
(44)	John Morrow	2.00	1.00	.60
(45)	New York Giants Emblem	3.00	1.50	.90
(46)	Merlin Olsen	10.00	5.00	3.00
(47)	Jack Pardee	4.00	2.00	1.25
(48)	Jim Parker	4.00	2.00	1.25
(49)	Bernie Parrish	2.00	1.00	.60
(50)	Don Perkins	3.00	1.50	.90
(51)	Richie Petitbon	2.00	1.00	.60
(52)	Vince Promuto	2.00	1.00	.60
(53)	Myron Pottios	2.00	1.00	.60
(54)	Mike Pyle	2.00	1.00	.60
(55)	Pete Retzlaff	3.00	1.50	.90
(56)	Jim Ringo	5.00	2.50	1.50
(57)	Joe Rutgens	2.00	1.00	.60
(58)	St. Louis Cardinals Emblem	3.00	1.50	.90
(59)	San Francisco 49ers Emblem	3.00	1.50	.90
(60)	Dick Schafrath	2.00	1.00	.60
(61)	Joe Schmidt	6.00	3.00	1.75
(62)	Del Shofner	3.00	1.50	.90
(63)	Norm Snead	3.00	1.50	.90
(64)	Bart Starr	15.00	7.50	4.50
(65)	Jim Taylor	6.00	3.00	1.75
(66)	Roosevelt Taylor	2.00	1.00	.60
(67)	Clendon Thomas	2.00	1.00	.60
(68)	Y.A. Tittle	12.50	6.25	3.75
(69)	John Unitas	18.00	9.00	5.50
(70)	Bill Wade	3.00	1.50	.90
(71)	Wayne Walker	2.00	1.00	.60
(72)	Jesse Whittenton	2.00	1.00	.60
(73)	Larry Wilson	5.00	2.50	1.50
(74)	Abe Woodson	2.00	1.00	.60

1987 Wheaties

Specially-marked boxes of Wheaties cereal each contained one of these 5" by 7" posters. The posters, which were wrapped in cellophane, were produced by Starline Inc. with the cooperation of the NFLPA and organizational efforts of Michael Schechter Associates. Each front has a color action photo, with the player's name, team, position and uniform number listed in a white box at the bottom. "Wheaties" is written in a banner in the upper left corner. The poster back is numbered and includes biographical information and career summary notes.

		MT	NM	EX
Complete Set (26):		130.00	97.00	52.00
Common Player:		2.50	2.00	1.00
1	Tony Dorsett	5.00	3.75	2.00
2	Herschel Walker	5.00	3.75	2.00
3	Marcus Allen	5.00	3.75	2.00
4	Eric Dickerson	6.00	4.50	2.50
5	Walter Payton	12.00	9.00	4.75
6	Phil Simms	4.00	3.00	1.50
7	Tommy Kramer	2.50	2.00	1.00
8	Joe Morris	2.50	2.00	1.00
9	Roger Craig	4.00	3.00	1.50
10	Curt Warner	3.50	2.75	1.50
11	Andre Tippett	2.50	2.00	1.00
12	Joe Montana	20.00	15.00	8.00
13	Jim McMahon	3.00	2.25	1.25
14	Bernie Kosar	25.00	18.50	10.00
15	Jay Schroeder	2.50	2.00	1.00
16	Al Toon	2.50	2.00	1.00
17	Mark Gastineau	2.50	2.00	1.00
18	Kenny Easley	2.50	2.00	1.00
19	Howie Long	2.50	2.00	1.00
20	Dan Marino	15.00	11.00	6.00
21	Karl Mecklenburg	3.25	2.50	1.25
22	John Elway	10.00	7.50	4.00
23	Boomer Esiason	5.00	3.75	2.00
24	Dan Fouts	4.00	3.00	1.50
25	Jim Kelly	10.00	7.50	4.00
26	Louis Lipps	3.00	2.25	1.25

Basketball

1986 Fleer Stickers

These stickers were put one per pack in the Fleer basketball packs. The front shows an action photo; red, white and blue backs have information about the player's career. Stickers are listed in alphabetical order and are standard size.

		MT	NM	EX
Complete Set (11):		145.00	109.00	58.00
Common Player:		2.00	1.50	.80
1	Kareem Abdul Jabbar	4.00	3.00	1.50
2	Larry Bird	17.00	12.50	6.75
3	Adrian Dantley	2.00	1.50	.80
4	Alex English	2.00	1.50	.80
5	Julius Erving	6.00	4.50	2.50
6	Patrick Ewing	13.00	9.75	5.25
7	Magic Johnson	10.00	7.50	4.00
8	Michael Jordan	100.00	75.00	40.00
9	Hakeem Olajuwon	22.00	16.50	8.75
10	Isiah Thomas	5.00	3.75	2.00
11	Dominique Wilkins	8.00	6.00	3.25

1987 Fleer Stickers

Fleer's 11-card insert stickers were once again included one per pack of basketball cards. Stickers, attached to heavy white cardboard stock, show an action photo on the front and text of each player on the back. The NBA's superstars are once again featured. Fronts are red, white, blue and yellow; backs are red, white and blue. Stickers are standard size and are numbered 1 of 11, etc..

		MT	NM	EX
Complete Set (11):		55.00	41.00	22.00
Common Player:		1.00	.70	.40
1	Magic Johnson	8.00	6.00	3.25
2	Michael Jordan	40.00	30.00	16.00

3	Hakeem Olajuwon	12.00	9.00	4.75
4	Larry Bird	12.00	9.00	4.75
5	Kevin McHale	1.50	1.25	.60
6	Charles Barkley	10.00	7.50	4.00
7	Dominique Wilkins	5.00	3.75	2.00
8	Kareem Abdul-Jabbar	3.00	2.25	1.25
9	Mark Aguirre	.35	.25	.14
10	Chuck Person	1.00	.70	.40
11	Alex English	.35	.25	.14

1988 Fleer Stickers

These stickers are on heavy white cardboard stock with a color action photo of the player. Backs contain personal career data. Backs are baby blue, red and white; the backs are pink and blue. The standard size stickers were issued one per pack of Fleer cards. Cards are numbered 1 of 11, etc..

		MT	NM	EX
Complete Set (11):		28.00	21.00	11.00
Common Player:		.35	.25	.14
1	Mark Aguirre	.35	.25	.14
2	Larry Bird	4.00	3.00	1.50
3	Clyde Drexler	1.50	1.25	.60
4	Alex English	.35	.25	.14
5	Patrick Ewing	2.00	1.50	.80
6	Magic Johnson	3.00	2.25	1.25
7	Michael Jordan	16.00	12.00	6.50
8	Karl Malone	1.50	1.25	.60
9	Kevin McHale	1.00	.70	.40
10	Isiah Thomas	1.00	.70	.40
11	Dominique Wilkins	1.50	1.25	.60

1989 Fleer Stickers

With 11 stickers in all, these All-Star stickers were inserted one per pack in 1989-90 Fleer wax packs. Fronts show action shots of the players, surrounded by a blue and purple star design, plus "Fleer '89 All-Stars." This design is also used for the card backs, which are numbered.

		MT	NM	EX
	Complete Set (11):	7.00	5.25	2.75
	Common Player:	.20	.15	.08
1	Karl Malone	.75	.60	.30
2	Hakeem Olajuwon	1.00	.70	.40
3	Michael Jordan	5.00	3.75	2.00
4	Charles Barkley	1.00	.70	.40
5	Magic Johnson	1.00	.70	.40
6	Isiah Thomas	.40	.30	.15
7	Patrick Ewing	.75	.60	.30
8	Dale Ellis	.50	.40	.20
9	Chris Mullin	.40	.30	.15
10	Larry Bird	1.50	1.25	.60
11	Tom Chambers	.50	.40	.20

1988-89 Panini European Stickers

These 2" by 2 5/8" stickers were designed to be stored in an accompanying album which was produced. The stickers are numbered on the back; the front has a color posed photo with a white border. The album is 9" by 12". Stickers were distributed throughout Europe and were produced by Edizioni Panini S.P.A. Modena. The sticker backs say "Panini Basket NBA/89" and provide instructions on how to put the stickers in the album. Stickers 1-2 form a puzzle.

		MT	NM	EX
	Complete Set (292):	225.00	169.00	90.00
	Common Player:	.25	.20	.10
1	NBA Official Licensed Product Logo	.25	.20	.10
2	NBA Official Licensed Product Logo	.25	.20	.10
3	Boston Celtics Logo	.25	.20	.10
4	Jimmy Rodgers	.25	.20	.10
5	Dennis Johnson	.75	.60	.30
6	Brian Shaw	.75	.60	.30
7	Danny Ainge	1.00	.70	.40
8	Larry Bird	15.00	11.00	6.00
9	Kevin McHale	1.00	.70	.40
10	Robert Parish	1.00	.70	.40
11	Robert Parish	1.00	.70	.40
12	Celtics Jersey	.25	.20	.10
13	Charlotte Hornets Logo	.25	.20	.10
14	Dick Harter	.25	.20	.10
15	Rex Chapman	.50	.40	.20
16	Tyrone Bogues	1.50	1.25	.60
17	Kelly Tripucka	.25	.20	.10
18	Robert Reid	.25	.20	.10
19	Kurt Rambis	.50	.40	.20
20	Dave Hoppen	.25	.20	.10
21	Tyrone Bogues	1.50	1.25	.60
22	Hornets Jersey	.25	.20	.10
23	New Jersey Nets Logo	.25	.20	.10
24	Willis Reed	.50	.40	.20
25	John Bagley	.25	.20	.10
26	Dennis Hopson	.25	.20	.10
27	Mike McGee	.25	.20	.10
28	Roy Hinson	.25	.20	.10
29	Buck Williams	.50	.40	.20
30	Joe Barry Carroll	.25	.20	.10
31	Roy Hinson	.25	.20	.10
32	Nets Jersey	.25	.20	.10
33	New York Knicks Logo	.25	.20	.10
34	Rick Pitino	.75	.60	.30
35	Mark Jackson	.75	.60	.30
36	Trent Tucker	.25	.20	.10
37	Johnny Newman	.25	.20	.10
38	Gerald Wilkins	.25	.20	.10
39	Charles Oakley	1.25	.90	.50
40	Patrick Ewing	10.00	7.50	4.00
41	Gerald Wilkins	.25	.20	.10
42	Knicks Jersey	.25	.20	.10
43	Philadelphia 76ers Logo	.25	.20	.10
44	Jim Lynam	.25	.20	.10
45	Maurice Cheeks	.50	.40	.20
46	Hersey Hawkins	1.00	.70	.40
47	Ron Anderson	.25	.20	.10
48	Charles Barkley	15.00	11.00	6.00
49	Cliff Robinson	.25	.20	.10
50	Mike Gminski	.25	.20	.10
51	Hersey Hawkins	1.00	.70	.40
52	76ers Jersey	.25	.20	.10
53	Washington Bullets Logo	.25	.20	.10
54	Wes Unseld	.75	.60	.30
55	Jeff Malone	.25	.20	.10
56	Darrell Walker	.25	.20	.10
57	Bernard King	1.00	.70	.40
58	Terry Catledge	.25	.20	.10
59	John Williams	.25	.20	.10
60	Dave Feitl	.25	.20	.10
61	Jeff Malone	.30	.25	.12
62	Bullets Jersey	.25	.20	.10
63	Atlanta Hawks Logo	.25	.20	.10
64	Mike Fratello	.50	.40	.20
65	Doc Rivers	.50	.40	.20
66	Spud Webb	.50	.40	.20
67	Reggie Theus	.50	.40	.20
68	Dominique Wilkins	7.50	5.75	3.00
69	Kevin Willis	1.50	1.25	.60
70	Moses Malone	2.00	1.50	.80
71	Reggie Theus	.50	.40	.20
72	Hawks Jersey	.25	.20	.10
73	Chicago Bulls Logo	.25	.20	.10
74	Doug Collins	.50	.40	.20
75	Craig Hodges	.25	.20	.10
76	Michael Jordan	35.00	26.00	14.00
77	Scottie Pippen	25.00	18.50	10.00
78	Horace Grant	5.00	3.75	2.00
79	Brad Sellers	.25	.20	.10
80	Bill Cartwright	.50	.40	.20
81	Brad Sellers	.25	.20	.10
82	Bulls Jersey	.25	.20	.10
83	Cleveland Cavaliers Logo	.25	.20	.10
84	Lenny Wilkins	.75	.60	.30
85	Mark Price	5.00	3.75	2.00
86	Ron Harper	1.00	.70	.40
87	Hot Rod Williams	.75	.60	.30
88	Mike Sanders	.25	.20	.10
89	Larry Nance	.75	.60	.30
90	Brad Daugherty	1.50	1.25	.60
91	Mike Sanders	.25	.20	.10
92	Cavaliers Jersey	.25	.20	.10
93	Detroit Pistons Logo	.25	.20	.10
94	Chuck Daly	.50	.40	.20
95	Isiah Thomas	2.50	2.00	1.00
96	Joe Dumars	2.00	1.50	.80
97	Dennis Rodman	5.00	3.75	2.00
98	Adrian Dantley	.50	.40	.20
99	John Salley	.30	.25	.12
100	Bill Laimbeer	.50	.40	.20
101	Dennis Rodman	7.50	5.75	3.00
102	Pistons Jersey	.25	.20	.10
103	Indiana Pacers Logo	.25	.20	.10
104	Dick Versace	.25	.20	.10
105	Vern Fleming	.25	.20	.10
106	Reggie Miller	14.00	10.50	5.50
107	Chuck Person	.50	.40	.20
108	Herb Williams	.25	.20	.10
109	Steve Stipanovich	.25	.20	.10
110	Rik Smits	1.00	.70	.40
111	Chuck Person	.50	.40	.20
112	Pacers Jersey	.25	.20	.10
113	Milwaukee Bucks Logo	.25	.20	.10
114	Del Harris	.25	.20	.10
115	Sidney Moncrief	.75	.60	.30
116	Jay Humphries	.25	.20	.10
117	Paul Pressey	.25	.20	.10
118	Ricky Pierce	.30	.25	.12
119	Terry Cummings	.75	.60	.30
120	Jack Sikma	.50	.40	.20

Stamps/stickers

121	Jay Humphries	.25	.20	.10
122	Bucks Jersey	.25	.20	.10
123	Dallas Mavericks Logo	.25	.20	.10
124	John MacLeod	.25	.20	.10
125	Derek Harper	.50	.40	.20
126	Rolando Blackman	.50	.40	.20
127	Detlef Schrempf	1.00	.70	.40
128	Mark Aguirre	.50	.40	.20
129	Sam Perkins	.50	.40	.20
130	James Donaldson	.25	.20	.10
131	Sam Perkins	.50	.40	.20
132	Mavericks Jersey	.25	.20	.10
133	Denver Nuggets Logo	.25	.20	.10
134	Doug Moe	.50	.40	.20
135	Walter Davis	.75	.60	.30
136	Michael Adams	.50	.40	.20
137	Fat Lever	.50	.40	.20
138	Alex English	.75	.60	.30
139	Wayne Cooper	.25	.20	.10
140	Dan Schayes	.25	.20	.10
141	Fat Lever	.50	.40	.20
142	Nuggets Jersey	.25	.20	.10
143	Houston Rockets Logo	.25	.20	.10
144	Don Chaney	.50	.40	.20
145	Sleepy Floyd	.50	.40	.20
146	Mike Woodson	.25	.20	.10
147	Purvis Short	.25	.20	.10
148	Buck Johnson	.25	.20	.10
149	Otis Thorpe	1.00	.70	.40
150	Hakeem Olajuwon	15.00	11.00	6.00
151	Otis Thorpe	1.25	.90	.50
152	Rockets Jersey	.25	.20	.10
153	Miami Heat Logo	.25	.20	.10
154	Ron Rothstein	.25	.20	.10
155	Jon Sundvold	.25	.20	.10
156	Kevin Edwards	.25	.20	.10
157	Grant Long	.25	.20	.10
158	Billy Thompson	.25	.20	.10
159	Dwayne Washington	.25	.20	.10
160	Rony Seikaly	1.00	.70	.40
161	Rony Seikaly	1.00	.70	.40
162	Heat Jersey	.25	.20	.10
163	San Antonio Spurs Logo	.25	.20	.10
164	Larry Brown	.50	.40	.20
165	Johnny Dawkins	.25	.20	.10
166	Alvin Robertson	.25	.20	.10
167	Willie Anderson	.50	.40	.20
168	Albert King	.25	.20	.10
169	Greg Anderson	.25	.20	.10
170	Frank Brickowski	.25	.20	.10
171	Willie Anderson	.50	.40	.20
172	Spurs Jersey	.25	.20	.10
173	Utah Jazz Logo	.25	.20	.10
174	Jerry Sloan	.50	.40	.20
175	John Stockton	10.00	7.50	4.00
176	Darrell Griffith	.50	.40	.20
177	Marc Iavaroni	.25	.20	.10
178	Thurl Bailey	.25	.20	.10
179	Karl Malone	7.50	5.75	3.00
180	Mark Eaton	.50	.40	.20
181	Thurl Bailey	.25	.20	.10
182	Jazz Jersey	.25	.20	.10
183	Golden State Warriors Logo	.25	.20	.10
184	Don Nelson	.50	.40	.20
185	Mitch Richmond	4.00	3.00	1.50
186	Winston Garland	.25	.20	.10
187	Larry Smith	.25	.20	.10
188	Chris Mullin	2.00	1.50	.80
189	Ralph Sampson	.50	.40	.20
190	Manute Bol	.50	.40	.20
191	Ralph Sampson	.50	.40	.20
192	Warriors Jersey	.25	.20	.10
193	Los Angeles Clippers Logo	.25	.20	.10
194	Don Casey	.25	.20	.10
195	Gary Grant	.50	.40	.20
196	Quintin Dailey	.25	.20	.10
197	Norm Nixon	.50	.40	.20
198	Ken Norman	.50	.40	.20
199	Danny Manning	4.00	3.00	1.50
200	Benoit Benjamin	.25	.20	.10
201	Ken Norman	.50	.40	.20
202	Clippers Jersey	.25	.20	.10
203	Los Angeles Lakers Logo	.25	.20	.10
204	Pat Riley	.75	.60	.30
205	Magic Johnson	12.00	9.00	4.75
206	Byron Scott	.50	.40	.20
207	James Worthy	1.00	.70	.40
208	A.C. Green	.75	.60	.30
209	Mychal Thompson	.25	.20	.10
210	Kareem Abdul-Jabbar	5.00	3.75	2.00
211	Byron Scott	.50	.40	.20
212	Lakers Jersey	.25	.20	.10
213	Phoenix Suns Logo	.25	.20	.10
214	Cotton Fitzsimmons	.25	.20	.10
215	Kevin Johnson	4.00	3.00	1.50
216	Dan Majerle	4.00	3.00	1.50
217	Eddie Johnson	.25	.20	.10
218	Armon Gilliam	.30	.25	.12
219	Tom Chambers	.50	.40	.20
220	Mark West	.25	.20	.10
221	Kevin Johnson	4.00	3.00	1.50
222	Suns Jersey	.25	.20	.10
223	Portland Trail Blazers Logo	.25	.20	.10
224	Mike Schuler	.25	.20	.10
225	Terry Porter	.25	.20	.10
226	Clyde Drexler	3.00	2.25	1.25
227	Jerome Kersey	.25	.20	.10
228	Kiki Vandeweghe	.50	.40	.20
229	Steve Johnson	.25	.20	.10
230	Kevin Duckworth	.50	.40	.20
231	Jerome Kersey	.25	.20	.10
232	Trail Blazers Jersey	.25	.20	.10
233	Sacremento Kings Logo	.25	.20	.10
234	Jerry Reynolds	.25	.20	.10
235	Kenny Smith	1.50	1.25	.60
236	Rodney McCray	.25	.20	.10
237	Derek Smith	.25	.20	.10
238	Ed Pickney	.25	.20	.10
239	Jim Petersen	.25	.20	.10
240	LaSalle Thompson	.25	.20	.10
241	Kenny Smith	1.50	1.25	.60
242	Kings Jersey	.25	.20	.10
243	Seattle Supersonics Logo	.25	.20	.10
244	Bernie Bickerstaff	.25	.20	.10
245	Nate McMillan	.25	.20	.10
246	Dale Ellis	.50	.40	.20
247	Xavier McDaniel	.50	.40	.20
248	Derrick McKey	.50	.40	.20
249	Michael Cage	.25	.20	.10
250	Alton Lister	.25	.20	.10
251	Xavier McDaniel	.50	.40	.20
252	Supersonics Jersey	.25	.20	.10
253	All-Star Game	.25	.20	.10
254	All-Star Game	.25	.20	.10
255	All-Star Game	.25	.20	.10
256	All-Star Game	.25	.20	.10
257	All-Star Game	.25	.20	.10
258	All-Star Game	.25	.20	.10
259	Lenny Wilkins	.50	.40	.20
260	Isiah Thomas	1.25	.90	.50
261	Michael Jordan	15.00	11.00	6.00
262	Dominique Wilkins	3.00	2.25	1.25
263	Charles Barkley	7.50	5.75	3.00
264	Moses Malone	.75	.60	.30
265	Mark Jackson	.50	.40	.20
266	Mark Price	1.50	1.25	.60
267	Larry Nance	.50	.40	.20
268	Terry Cummings	.50	.40	.20
269	Kevin McHale	.75	.60	.30
270	Brad Daugherty	.75	.60	.30
271	Patrick Ewing	5.00	3.75	2.00
272	Pat Riley	.50	.40	.20
273	John Stockton	5.00	3.75	2.00
274	Dale Ellis	.50	.40	.20
275	Alex English	.50	.40	.20
276	Karl Malone	5.00	3.75	2.00

		MT	NM	EX
277	Hakeem Olajuwon	7.50	5.75	3.00
278	Kareem Abdul-Jabbar	3.00	2.25	1.25
279	Clyde Drexler	1.50	1.25	.60
280	Chris Mullin	1.00	.70	.40
281	James Worthy	.50	.40	.20
282	Tom Chambers	.50	.40	.20
283	Kevin Duckworth	.50	.40	.20
284	Mark Eaton	.50	.40	.20
285	Michael Jordan	15.00	11.00	6.00
286	Mark Jackson	.75	.60	.30
287	Charles Barkley	7.50	5.75	3.00
288	Jack Sikma	.25	.20	.10
289	Michael Cage	.25	.20	.10
290	Mark Eaton	.25	.20	.10
291	John Stockton	4.50	3.50	1.75
292	Doug Moe	.25	.20	.10
NNO	Panini Album	10.00	7.50	4.00

1989-90 Panini European Stickers

These 2 1/8" by 3" stickers were produced by Edizioni Panini S.P.A. - Modena and were distributed throughout Europe. Each front has a color action photo of the player, with his name, team name and sticker number at the bottom. The back says "Panini Basket NBA 90" and offers directions on how to apply the sticker to a corresponding album which was produced. An NBA action photo can be formed from stickers for Ken Norman and #s 268-272.

		MT	NM	EX
Complete Set (272):		200.00	150.00	80.00
Common Player:		1.50	1.25	.60
1	Boston Celtics	1.50	1.25	.60
2	Dennis Johnson	2.00	1.50	.80
3	Reggie Lewis	7.00	5.25	2.75
4	Kelvin Upshaw	1.50	1.25	.60
5	Kevin Gamble	1.50	1.25	.60
6	Larry Bird	7.50	5.75	3.00
7	Ed Pinckney	1.50	1.25	.60
8	Kevin McHale	3.00	2.25	1.25
9	Robert Parish	3.00	2.25	1.25
10	Miami Heat	1.50	1.25	.60
11	Jon Sundvold	1.50	1.25	.60
12	Rory Sparrow	1.50	1.25	.60
13	Dwayne Washington	1.50	1.25	.60
14	Billy Thompson	1.50	1.25	.60
15	Grant Long	2.00	1.50	.80
16	Kevin Edwards	1.50	1.25	.60
17	Pat Cummings	1.50	1.25	.60
18	Rony Seikaly	2.00	1.50	.80
19	New Jersey Nets	1.50	1.25	.60
20	Dennis Hopson	1.50	1.25	.60
21	Lester Conner	1.50	1.25	.60
22	Chris Morris	1.50	1.25	.60
23	Charles Shackleford	1.50	1.25	.60
24	Purvis Short	1.50	1.25	.60
25	Roy Hinson	1.50	1.25	.60
26	Sam Bowie	1.50	1.25	.60
27	Joe Barry Carroll	1.50	1.25	.60
28	New York Knicks	1.50	1.25	.60
29	Mark Jackson	2.00	1.50	.80
30	Rod Strickland	2.00	1.50	.80
31	Gerald Wilkins	1.50	1.25	.60
32	Trent Tucker	1.50	1.25	.60
33	Johnny Newman	1.50	1.25	.60
34	Kenny Walker	1.50	1.25	.60
35	Charles Oakley	2.00	1.50	.80
36	Patrick Ewing	6.00	4.50	2.50
37	Philadelphia 76ers	1.50	1.25	.60
38	Scott Brooks	1.50	1.25	.60
39	Johnny Dawkins	1.50	1.25	.60
40	Hersey Hawkins	2.00	1.50	.80
41	Derek Smith	1.50	1.25	.60
42	Ron Anderson	1.50	1.25	.60
43	Charles Barkley	10.00	7.50	4.00
44	Rick Mahorn	1.50	1.25	.60
45	Mike Gminski	1.50	1.25	.60
46	Washington Bullets	1.50	1.25	.60
47	Steve Colter	1.50	1.25	.60
48	Jeff Malone	2.00	1.50	.80
49	Ledell Eackles	1.50	1.25	.60
50	Darrell Walker	1.50	1.25	.60
51	Bernard King	4.00	3.00	1.50
52	Charles Jones	1.50	1.25	.60
53	Mark Alarie	1.50	1.25	.60
54	Harvey Grant	2.00	1.50	.80
55	Atlanta Hawks	1.50	1.25	.60
56	Spud Webb	3.00	2.25	1.25
57	Doc Rivers	2.00	1.50	.80
58	John Battle	1.50	1.25	.60
59	Dominique Wilkins	7.00	5.25	2.75
60	Cliff Levingston	2.50	2.00	1.00
61	Jon Koncak	1.50	1.25	.60
62	Antoine Carr	1.50	1.25	.60
63	Moses Malone	4.00	3.00	1.50
64	Chicago Bulls	1.50	1.25	.60
65	Craig Hodges	1.50	1.25	.60
66	John Paxson	2.00	1.50	.80
67	Michael Jordan	20.00	15.00	8.00
68	Scottie Pippen	15.00	11.00	6.00
69	Charles Davis	1.50	1.25	.60
70	Horace Grant	5.00	3.75	2.00
71	Will Perdue	1.50	1.25	.60
72	Bill Cartwright	1.50	1.25	.60
73	Cleveland Cavaliers	1.50	1.25	.60
74	Mark Price	5.00	3.75	2.00
75	Craig Ehlo	2.00	1.50	.80
76	Chris Dudley	1.50	1.25	.60
77	Randolph Keys	1.50	1.25	.60
78	Larry Nance	2.00	1.50	.80
79	John Williams	1.50	1.25	.60
80	Paul Mokeski	1.50	1.25	.60
81	Wayne Rollins	2.00	1.50	.80
82	Detroit Pistons	1.50	1.25	.60
83	Isiah Thomas	5.00	3.75	2.00
84	Vinnie Johnson	2.00	1.50	.80
85	Joe Dumars	4.00	3.00	1.50
86	Mark Aguirre	4.00	3.00	1.50
87	Dennis Rodman	5.00	3.75	2.00
88	John Salley	1.50	1.25	.60
89	James Edwards	1.50	1.25	.60
90	Bill Laimbeer	1.50	1.25	.60
91	Indiana Pacers	1.50	1.25	.60
92	Reggie Miller	5.00	3.75	2.00
93	Vern Fleming	1.50	1.25	.60
94	Randy Wittman	1.50	1.25	.60
95	Chuck Person	2.00	1.50	.80
96	Mike Sanders	1.50	1.25	.60
97	Rickey Green	1.50	1.25	.60
98	LaSalle Thompson	1.50	1.25	.60
99	Rik Smits	2.00	1.50	.80
100	Milwaukee Bucks	1.50	1.25	.60
101	Jay Humphries	1.50	1.25	.60
102	Ricky Pierce	1.50	1.25	.60
103	Paul Pressey	1.50	1.25	.60
104	Alvin Robertson	1.50	1.25	.60
105	Tony Brown	1.50	1.25	.60
106	Fred Roberts	1.50	1.25	.60
107	Randy Breuer	1.50	1.25	.60
108	Jack Sikma	2.00	1.50	.80
109	Orlando Magic	1.50	1.25	.60
110	Sam Vincent	1.50	1.25	.60
111	Reggie Theus	2.00	1.50	.80
112	Scott Skiles	2.00	1.50	.80
113	Otis Smith	1.50	1.25	.60
114	Sidney Green	1.50	1.25	.60
115	Nick Anderson	5.00	3.75	2.00
116	Terry Catledge	1.50	1.25	.60
117	Mark Acres	1.50	1.25	.60
118	Charlotte Hornets	1.50	1.25	.60
119	Muggsy Bogues	1.50	1.25	.60
120	Dell Curry	1.50	1.25	.60
121	Rex Chapman	1.50	1.25	.60
122	Kelly Tripucka	1.50	1.25	.60
123	Jerry Sichting	1.50	1.25	.60

124	Brian Rowsom	1.50	1.25	.60
125	J.R. Reid	1.50	1.25	.60
126	Stuart Gray	1.50	1.25	.60
127	Dallas Mavericks	1.50	1.25	.60
128	Brad Davis	1.50	1.25	.60
129	Derek Harper	1.50	1.25	.60
130	Rolando Blackman	1.50	1.25	.60
131	Adrian Dantley	2.00	1.50	.80
132	Herb Williams	1.50	1.25	.60
133	Bill Wennington	1.50	1.25	.60
134	Sam Perkins	1.50	1.25	.60
135	James Donaldson	1.50	1.25	.60
136	Denver Nuggets	1.50	1.25	.60
137	Walter Davis	3.00	2.25	1.25
138	Michael Adams	1.50	1.25	.60
139	Fat Lever	1.50	1.25	.60
140	Alex English	3.00	2.25	1.25
141	Todd Lichti	1.50	1.25	.60
142	Jerome Lane	1.50	1.25	.60
143	Tim Kempton	1.50	1.25	.60
144	Blair Rasmussen	1.50	1.25	.60
145	Houston Rockets	1.50	1.25	.60
146	Eric Floyd	1.50	1.25	.60
147	Mike Woodson	1.50	1.25	.60
148	Derrick Chievous	1.50	1.25	.60
149	John Lucas	1.50	1.25	.60
150	Buck Johnson	1.50	1.25	.60
151	Otis Thorpe	3.00	2.25	1.25
152	Larry Smith	1.50	1.25	.60
153	Hakeem Olajuwon	7.50	5.75	3.00
154	Minnesota Timberwolves	1.50	1.25	.60
155	Pooh Richardson	3.00	2.25	1.25
156	Sidney Lowe	1.50	1.25	.60
157	Doug West	1.50	1.25	.60
158	Adrian Branch	1.50	1.25	.60
159	Tony Campbell	1.50	1.25	.60
160	David Rivers	1.50	1.25	.60
161	Steve Johnson	1.50	1.25	.60
162	Brad Lohaus	1.50	1.25	.60
163	San Antonio Spurs	1.50	1.25	.60
164	Maurice Cheeks	1.50	1.25	.60
165	Vernon Maxwell	1.50	1.25	.60
166	Zarko Paspali	1.50	1.25	.60
167	Sean Elliott	3.00	2.25	1.25
168	Terry Cummings	3.00	2.25	1.25
169	Frank Brickowski	1.50	1.25	.60
170	Willie Anderson	1.50	1.25	.60
171	David Robinson	25.00	18.50	10.00
172	Utah Jazz	1.50	1.25	.60
173	John Stockton	10.00	7.50	4.00
174	Darrell Griffith	1.50	1.25	.60
175	Bobby Hansen	1.50	1.25	.60
176	Karl Malone	10.00	7.50	4.00
177	Mike Brown	1.50	1.25	.60
178	Thurl Bailey	1.50	1.25	.60
179	Eric Leckner	1.50	1.25	.60
180	Mark Eaton	1.50	1.25	.60
181	Golden State Warriors	1.50	1.25	.60
182	Winston Garland	1.50	1.25	.60
183	Mitch Richmond	4.00	3.00	1.50
184	Sarunas Marciulionis	1.50	1.25	.60
185	Terry Teagle	1.50	1.25	.60
186	Chris Mullin	6.00	4.50	2.50
187	Rod Higgins	1.50	1.25	.60
188	Uwe Blab	1.50	1.25	.60
189	Manute Bol	1.50	1.25	.60
190	Los Angeles Clippers	1.50	1.25	.60
191	Gary Grant	1.50	1.25	.60
192	Ron Harper	2.00	1.50	.80
193	Ken Norman	3.50	2.75	1.50
194	Charles Smith	2.00	1.50	.80
195	Danny Manning	4.00	3.00	1.50
196	Joe Wolf	1.50	1.25	.60
197	Benoit Benjamin	1.50	1.25	.60
198	Ken Bannister	1.50	1.25	.60
199	Los Angeles Lakers	1.50	1.25	.60
200	Magic Johnson	10.00	7.50	4.00
201	Byron Scott	1.50	1.25	.60
202	Michael Cooper	1.50	1.25	.60
203	Orlando Woolridge	2.00	1.50	.80
204	James Worthy	4.00	3.00	1.50
205	A.C. Green	1.50	1.25	.60
206	Vlade Divac	3.00	2.25	1.25
207	Mychal Thompson	1.50	1.25	.60
208	Phoenix Suns	1.50	1.25	.60
209	Kevin Johnson	5.00	3.75	2.00
210	Jeff Hornacek	5.00	3.75	2.00
211	Greg Grant	1.50	1.25	.60
212	Dan Majerle	5.00	3.75	2.00
213	Tim Perry	1.50	1.25	.60
214	Eddie Johnson	1.50	1.25	.60
215	Tom Chambers	2.00	1.50	.80
216	Andrew Lang	1.50	1.25	.60
217	Portland Trailblazers	1.50	1.25	.60
218	Clyde Drexler	8.00	6.00	3.25
219	Terry Porter	7.00	5.25	2.75
220	Drazen Petrovic	5.00	3.75	2.00
221	Jerome Kersey	2.00	1.50	.80
222	Mark Bryant	1.50	1.25	.60
223	Danny Young	1.50	1.25	.60
224	Wayne Cooper	1.50	1.25	.60
225	Kevin Duckworth	1.50	1.25	.60
226	Sacramento Kings	1.50	1.25	.60
227	Danny Ainge	3.00	2.25	1.25
228	Michael Jackson	1.50	1.25	.60
229	Vinny Del Negro	1.50	1.25	.60
230	Kenny Smith	1.50	1.25	.60
231	Harold Pressley	1.50	1.25	.60
232	Rodney McCray	1.50	1.25	.60
233	Wayman Tisdale	2.00	1.50	.80
234	Greg Kite	1.50	1.25	.60
235	Seattle Supersonics	1.50	1.25	.60
236	Sedale Threatt	1.50	1.25	.60
237	Avery Johnson	1.50	1.25	.60
238	Nate McMillan	1.50	1.25	.60
239	Dale Ellis	2.00	1.50	.80
240	Xavier McDaniel	2.00	1.50	.80
241	Derrick McKey	1.50	1.25	.60
242	Michael Cage	1.50	1.25	.60
243	Olden Polynice	1.50	1.25	.60
244	Charles Barkley (AS)	7.00	5.25	2.75
245	Larry Bird (AS)	6.00	4.50	2.50
246	Tom Chambers (AS)	2.00	1.50	.80
247	Adrian Dantley (AS)	3.00	2.25	1.25
248	Clyde Drexler (AS)	4.00	3.00	1.50
249	Joe Dumars (AS)	3.00	2.25	1.25
250	Dale Ellis (AS)	2.00	1.50	.80
251	Patrick Ewing (AS)	5.00	3.75	2.00
252	A.C. Green (AS)	2.00	1.50	.80
253	Magic Johnson (AS)	7.00	5.25	2.75
254	Michael Jordan (AS)	15.00	11.00	6.00
255	Bill Laimbeer (AS)	2.00	1.50	.80
256	Jeff Malone (AS)	2.00	1.50	.80
257	Karl Malone (AS)	6.00	4.50	2.50
258	Moses Malone (AS)	3.00	2.25	1.25
259	Xavier McDaniel (AS)	3.00	2.25	1.25
260	Hakeem Olajuwon (AS)	6.00	4.50	2.50
261	Robert Parish (AS)	3.00	2.25	1.25
262	Mark Price (AS)	4.00	3.00	1.50
263	Jack Sikma (AS)	2.00	1.50	.80
264	John Stockton (AS)	4.00	3.00	1.50
265	Isiah Thomas	4.00	3.00	1.50
266	Dominique Wilkins	4.00	3.00	1.50
267	James Worthy	3.00	2.25	1.25
268	NBA Action (Ken Norman)	1.50	1.25	.60
269	NBA Action (Ken Norman)	1.50	1.25	.60
270	NBA Action (Ken Norman)	1.50	1.25	.60
271	NBA Action (Ken Norman)	1.50	1.25	.60
272	NBA Action (Ken Norman)	1.50	1.25	.60

1990-91 Panini Stickers

These stickers each measure 1 7/8' by 2 15/16" and were produced by Panini. The stickers were issued as sheets of three rows of four, included in a package which also contained an album. Each front has an action photo against a white background. The player's name and team are at the bottom. The back has an NBA licensing logo, sticker number, and Panini logo. The last 18 in the set use letters instead of numbers.

	MT	NM	EX
Complete Set (180):	7.50	5.75	3.00
Common Player (1-162):	.03	.02	.01
Common Player (I-R):	.05	.04	.02
1 Magic Johnson	.60	.45	.25
2 Mychal Thompson	.03	.02	.01
3 Vlade Divac	.07	.05	.03
4 Byron Scott	.05	.04	.02
5 James Worthy	.10	.08	.04
6 A.C. Green	.05	.04	.02
7 Jerome Kersey	.05	.04	.02
8 Clyde Drexler	.25	.20	.10
9 Buck Williams	.07	.05	.03
10 Kevin Duckworth	.05	.04	.02
11 Terry Porter	.07	.05	.03
12 Cliff Robinson	.10	.08	.04
13 Tom Chambers	.07	.05	.03
14 Dan Majerle	.15	.11	.06
15 Mark West	.03	.02	.01
16 Kevin Johnson	.15	.11	.06
17 Jeff Hornacek	.10	.08	.04
18 Kurt Rambis	.05	.04	.02
19 Nate McMillan	.03	.02	.01
20 Shawn Kemp	.50	.40	.20
21 Dale Ellis	.03	.02	.01
22 Michael Cage	.03	.02	.01
23 Xavier McDaniel	.05	.04	.02
24 Derrick McKey	.03	.02	.01
25 Manute Bol	.05	.04	.02
26 Chris Mullin	.15	.11	.06
27 Terry Teagle	.03	.02	.01
28 Tim Hardaway	.35	.25	.14
29 Sarunas Marciulionis	.07	.05	.03
30 Mitch Richmond	.15	.11	.06
31 Gary Grant	.03	.02	.01
32 Danny Manning	.15	.11	.06
33 Benoit Benjamin	.03	.02	.01
34 Ron Harper	.07	.05	.03
35 Ken Norman	.05	.04	.02
36 Charles Smith	.05	.04	.02
37 Harold Pressley	.03	.02	.01
38 Antoine Carr	.03	.02	.01
39 Danny Ainge	.10	.08	.04
40 Wayman Tisdale	.05	.04	.02
41 Ralph Sampson	.03	.02	.01
42 Vinny Del Negro	.03	.02	.01
43 David Robinson	.50	.40	.20
44 Sean Elliott	.10	.08	.04
45 Terry Cummings	.07	.05	.03
46 Willie Anderson	.05	.04	.02
47 Rod Strickland	.10	.08	.04
48 Frank Brickowski	.03	.02	.01
49 Karl Malone	.03	.02	.01
50 Darrell Griffith	.03	.02	.01
51 John Stockton	.25	.20	.10
52 Blue Edwards	.05	.04	.02
53 Mark Eaton	.05	.04	.02
54 Thurl Bailey	.03	.02	.01
55 Rolando Blackman	.05	.04	.02
56 Sam Perkins	.05	.04	.02
57 James Donaldson	.03	.02	.01
58 Herb Williams	.03	.02	.01
59 Roy Tarpley	.05	.04	.02
60 Derek Harper	.05	.04	.02
61 Michael Adams	.05	.04	.02
62 Blair Rasmussen	.03	.02	.01
63 Jerome Lane	.03	.02	.01
64 Walter Davis	.07	.05	.03
65 Todd Lichti	.05	.04	.02
66 Joe Barry Carroll	.03	.02	.01
67 Vernon Maxwell	.05	.04	.02
68 Otis Thorpe	.07	.05	.03
69 Hakeem Olajuwon	.60	.45	.25
70 Buck Johnson	.03	.02	.01
71 Sleepy Floyd	.03	.02	.01
72 Mitchell Wiggins	.03	.02	.01
73 Tony Campbell	.03	.02	.01
74 Tod Murphy	.03	.02	.01
75 Tyrone Corbin	.03	.02	.01
76 Sam Mitchell	.03	.02	.01
77 Randy Breuer	.03	.02	.01
78 Pooh Richardson	.07	.05	.03
79 Rex Chapman	.05	.04	.02
80 Dell Curry	.05	.04	.02
81 Tyrone Bogues	.05	.04	.02
82 J.R. Reid	.05	.04	.02
83 Armon Gilliam	.03	.02	.01
84 Kelly Tripucka	.03	.02	.01
85 Dennis Rodman	.15	.11	.06
86 Joe Dumars	.15	.11	.06
87 Isiah Thomas	.20	.15	.08
88 Bill Laimbeer	.05	.04	.02
89 Vinnie Johnson	.03	.02	.01
90 James Edwards	.03	.02	.01
91 Michael Jordan	1.00	.70	.40
92 Stacey King	.03	.02	.01
93 Scottie Pippen	.50	.40	.20
94 John Paxson	.07	.05	.03
95 Horace Grant	.15	.11	.06
96 Craig Hodges	.03	.02	.01
97 Brad Lohaus	.03	.02	.01
98 Jack Sikma	.05	.04	.02
99 Ricky Pierce	.05	.04	.02
100 Greg Anderson	.03	.02	.01
101 Alvin Robertson	.03	.02	.01
102 Jay Humphries	.03	.02	.01
103 Mark Price	.15	.11	.06
104 Winston Bennett	.03	.02	.01
105 Brad Daugherty	.10	.08	.04
106 Craig Ehlo	.05	.04	.02
107 Larry Nance	.07	.05	.03
108 Hot Rod Williams	.05	.04	.02
109 Rik Smits	.07	.05	.03
110 Chuck Person	.05	.04	.02
111 Reggie Miller	.15	.11	.06
112 LaSalle Thompson	.03	.02	.01
113 Detlef Schrempf	.10	.08	.04
114 Vern Fleming	.05	.04	.02
115 Moses Malone	.10	.08	.04
116 Doc Rivers	.05	.04	.02
117 Dominique Wilkins	.30	.25	.12
118 Spud Webb	.10	.08	.04
119 Kevin Willis	.10	.08	.04
120 Kenny Smith	.05	.04	.02
121 Otis Smith	.03	.02	.01
122 Sidney Green	.03	.02	.01
123 Nick Anderson	.10	.08	.04
124 Scott Skiles	.05	.04	.02
125 Jerry Reynolds	.03	.02	.01
126 Terry Catledge	.03	.02	.01
127 Charles Barkley	.60	.45	.25
128 Ron Anderson	.03	.02	.01
129 Hersey Hawkins	.07	.05	.03
130 Mike Gminski	.03	.02	.01
131 Johnny Dawkins	.03	.02	.01
132 Rick Mahorn	.03	.02	.01
133 Michael Smith	.03	.02	.01
134 Reggie Lewis	.10	.08	.04
135 Larry Bird	1.00	.70	.40
136 Kevin McHale	.10	.08	.04
137 Joe Kleine	.03	.02	.01
138 Robert Parish	.10	.08	.04
139 Robert Parish	.07	.05	.03
140 Patrick Ewing	.50	.40	.20
141 Charles Oakley	.10	.08	.04
142 Gerald Wilkins	.05	.04	.02
143 Kenny Walker	.03	.02	.01
144 Mark Jackson	.07	.05	.03
145 Mark Alarie	.03	.02	.01
146 John Williams	.03	.02	.01
147 Darrell Walker	.03	.02	.01

		MT	NM	EX
148	Bernard King	.10	.08	.04
149	Harvey Grant	.05	.04	.02
150	Ledell Eackles	.03	.02	.01
151	Glen Rice	.10	.08	.04
152	Kevin Edwards	.03	.02	.01
153	Tellis Frank	.03	.02	.01
154	Rony Seikaly	.07	.05	.03
155	Billy Thompson	.05	.04	.02
156	Sherman Douglas	.05	.04	.02
157	Roy Hinson	.03	.02	.01
158	Chris Morris	.03	.02	.01
159	Lester Conner	.03	.02	.01
160	Sam Bowie	.05	.04	.02
161	Purvis Short	.03	.02	.01
162	Mookie Blaylock	.07	.05	.03
A	John Stockton	.15	.11	.06
B	Magic Johnson	.30	.25	.12
C	A.C. Green	.10	.08	.04
D	Hakeem Olajuwon	.30	.25	.12
E	James Worthy	.10	.08	.04
F	Isiah Thomas	.15	.11	.06
G	Michael Jordan	.75	.60	.30
H	Larry Bird	.50	.40	.20
I	Patrick Ewing	.30	.25	.12
J	Charles Barkley	.30	.25	.12
K	Michael Jordan	.75	.60	.30
L	Larry Bird	.50	.40	.20
M	Hakeem Olajuwon	.30	.25	.12
N	NBA Finals	.05	.04	.02
O	NBA Finals	.05	.04	.02
P	NBA Finals	.05	.04	.02
Q	NBA Finals	.05	.04	.02
R	NBA Finals	.05	.04	.02
NNO	Panini Album	1.00	.70	.40

1991-92 Panini Stickers

These 1 3/4" by 2 11/16" stickers were sold in packs of six, with 100 packs included in each box. The front has a color action photo, with the player's name and biological information running along the left side of the sticker. The player's team name is above the photo; his 1990-91 season and career statistics are below the picture. The sticker back has a number, the Panini logo, an NBA logo and a notation that an album was made to hold the stickers.

		MT	NM	EX
	Complete Set (192):	25.00	18.50	10.00
	Common Player:	.05	.04	.02
1	NBA Official Licensed Product Logo	.05	.04	.02
2	1991 NBA Finals Logo	.05	.04	.02
3	Chris Mullin	.25	.20	.10
4	Mitch Richmond	.20	.15	.08
5	Alton Lister	.05	.04	.02
6	Tim Hardaway	.30	.25	.12
7	Tom Tolbert	.05	.04	.02
8	Rod Higgins	.05	.04	.02
9	Charles Smith	.07	.05	.03
10	Ron Harper	.07	.05	.03
11	Olden Polynice	.05	.04	.02
12	Ken Norman	.05	.04	.02
13	Gary Grant	.05	.04	.02
14	Danny Manning	.15	.11	.06
15	Sam Perkins	.07	.05	.03
16	Vlade Divac	.10	.08	.04
17	James Worthy	.10	.08	.04
18	Magic Johnson	1.50	1.25	.60
19	A.C. Green	.07	.05	.03
20	Byron Scott	.05	.04	.02
21	Kevin Johnson	.25	.20	.10
22	Mark West	.05	.04	.02
23	Dan Majerle	.30	.25	.12
24	Jeff Hornacek	.20	.15	.08
25	Xavier McDaniel	.07	.05	.03
26	Tom Chambers	.07	.05	.03
27	Terry Porter	.07	.05	.03
28	Kevin Duckworth	.05	.04	.02
29	Clyde Drexler	.20	.15	.08
30	Jerome Kersey	.05	.04	.02
31	Buck Williams	.07	.05	.03
32	Danny Ainge	.15	.11	.06
33	Wayman Tisdale	.07	.05	.03
34	Antoine Carr	.05	.04	.02
35	Lionel Simmons	.07	.05	.03
36	Travis Mays	.05	.04	.02
37	Rory Sparrow	.05	.04	.02
38	Duane Causwell	.05	.04	.02
39	Benoit Benjamin	.05	.04	.02
40	Michael Cage	.05	.04	.02
41	Derrick McKey	.07	.05	.03
42	Shawn Kemp	1.00	.70	.40
43	Gary Payton	.25	.20	.10
44	Ricky Pierce	.07	.05	.03
45	Derek Harper	.10	.08	.04
46	James Donaldson	.05	.04	.02
47	Randy White	.05	.04	.02
48	Rodney McCray	.05	.04	.02
49	Alex English	.10	.08	.04
50	Rolando Blackman	.07	.05	.03
51	Orlando Woolridge	.07	.05	.03
52	Todd Lichti	.05	.04	.02
53	Chris Jackson	.10	.08	.04
54	Blair Rasmussen	.05	.04	.02
55	Reggie Williams	.07	.05	.03
56	Marcus Liberty	.05	.04	.02
57	Hakeem Olajuwon	1.50	1.25	.60
58	Kenny Smith	.10	.08	.04
59	Vernon Maxwell	.07	.05	.03
60	Otis Thorpe	.10	.08	.04
61	Buck Johnson	.05	.04	.02
62	Larry Smith	.05	.04	.02
63	Pooh Richardson	.05	.04	.02
64	Felton Spencer	.05	.04	.02
65	Tod Murphy	.05	.04	.02
66	Tyrone Corbin	.05	.04	.02
67	Tony Campbell	.05	.04	.02
68	Sam Mitchell	.05	.04	.02
69	Dennis Scott	.07	.05	.03
70	Nick Anderson	.10	.08	.04
71	Terry Catledge	.07	.05	.03
72	Scott Skiles	.07	.05	.03
73	Otis Smith	.05	.04	.02
74	Greg Kite	.05	.04	.02
75	Terry Cummings	.07	.05	.03
76	Rod Strickland	.10	.08	.04
77	David Robinson	1.50	1.25	.60
78	Willie Anderson	.05	.04	.02
79	Sean Elliott	.10	.08	.04
80	Paul Pressey	.05	.04	.02
81	John Stockton	.50	.40	.20
82	Jeff Malone	.07	.05	.03
83	Mark Eaton	.07	.05	.03
84	Thurl Bailey	.05	.04	.02
85	Karl Malone	.75	.60	.30
86	Blue Edwards	.07	.05	.03
87	Kevin Johnson	.25	.20	.10
88	'91 Western Division All-Stars	.10	.08	.04
89	NBA All-Star Weekend Logo	.05	.04	.02
90	Magic Johnson	.60	.45	.25
91	Karl Malone	.40	.30	.15
92	David Robinson	.60	.45	.25
93	Chris Mullin	.20	.15	.08
94	Charles Barkley	.60	.45	.25
95	'91 Eastern Division All-Stars	.10	.08	.04
96	Michael Jordan	1.50	1.25	.60
97	Isiah Thomas	.20	.15	.08
98	Charles Barkley	.60	.45	.25
99	Patrick Ewing	.40	.30	.15
100	Larry Bird	.60	.45	.25
101	Dominique Wilkins	.40	.30	.15
102	Kevin Willis	.15	.11	.06

103	John Battle	.05	.04	.02
104	Doc Rivers	.10	.08	.04
105	Spud Webb	.10	.08	.04
106	Moses Malone	.15	.11	.06
107	J.R. Reid	.05	.04	.02
108	Johnny Newman	.07	.05	.03
109	Rex Chapman	.05	.04	.02
110	Muggsy Bogues	.10	.08	.04
111	Mike Gminski	.05	.04	.02
112	Kendall Gill	.25	.20	.10
113	Scottie Pippen	.60	.45	.25
114	Bill Cartwright	.10	.08	.04
115	John Paxson	.07	.05	.03
116	Michael Jordan	5.00	3.75	2.00
117	Horace Grant	.25	.20	.10
118	B.J. Armstrong	.25	.20	.10
119	Brad Daugherty	.15	.11	.06
120	Larry Nance	.10	.08	.04
121	Hot Rod Williams	.07	.05	.03
122	Craig Ehlo	.07	.05	.03
123	Darnell Valentine	.05	.04	.02
124	Danny Ferry	.05	.04	.02
125	Isiah Thomas	.25	.20	.10
126	James Edwards	.05	.04	.02
127	Bill Laimbeer	.07	.05	.03
128	Vinnie Johnson	.05	.04	.02
129	Joe Dumars	.25	.20	.10
130	Dennis Rodman	.15	.11	.06
131	Reggie Miller	.25	.20	.10
132	Detlef Schrempf	.15	.11	.06
133	Chuck Person	.10	.08	.04
134	LaSalle Thompson	.07	.05	.03
135	Vern Fleming	.07	.05	.03
136	Rik Smits	.07	.05	.03
137	Dale Ellis	.07	.05	.03
138	Frank Brickowski	.05	.04	.02
139	Jay Humphries	.05	.04	.02
140	Jack Sikma	.10	.08	.04
141	Fred Roberts	.05	.04	.02
142	Alvin Robertson	.05	.04	.02
143	Robert Parish	.15	.11	.06
144	Kevin McHale	.15	.11	.06
145	Kevin Gamble	.07	.05	.03
146	Larry Bird	2.00	1.50	.80
147	Reggie Lewis	.25	.20	.10
148	Brian Shaw	.07	.05	.03
149	Sherman Douglas	.07	.05	.03
150	Rony Seikaly	.07	.05	.03
151	Glen Rice	.20	.15	.08
152	Grant Long	.07	.05	.03
153	Billy Thompson	.05	.04	.02
154	Willie Burton	.05	.04	.02
155	Reggie Theus	.07	.05	.03
156	Sam Bowie	.05	.04	.02
157	Derrick Coleman	.50	.40	.20
158	Drazen Petrovic	.25	.20	.10
159	Mookie Blaylock	.15	.11	.06
160	Chris Morris	.05	.04	.02
161	Gerald Wilkins	.07	.05	.03
162	Charles Oakley	.10	.08	.04
163	Patrick Ewing	1.00	.70	.40
164	Kiki Vandeweghe	.07	.05	.03
165	Maurice Cheeks	.07	.05	.03
166	John Starks	.25	.20	.10
167	Hersey Hawkins	.10	.08	.04
168	Rick Mahorn	.07	.05	.03
169	Charles Barkley	1.50	1.25	.60
170	Rickey Green	.05	.04	.02
171	Ron Anderson	.05	.04	.02
172	Armon Gilliam	.05	.04	.02
173	Bernard King	.10	.08	.04
174	Ledell Eackles	.05	.04	.02
175	John Williams	.05	.04	.02
176	Darrell Walker	.05	.04	.02
177	Haywoode Workman	.05	.04	.02
178	Harvey Grant	.07	.05	.03
179	Derrick Coleman (ART)	.50	.40	.20
180	Dee Brown (ART)	.15	.11	.06

181	Lionel Simmons (ART)	.10	.08	.04
182	Felton Spencer (ART)	.05	.04	.02
183	Dennis Scott (ART)	.10	.08	.04
184	Gary Payton (ART)	.20	.15	.08
185	Travis Mays (ART)	.05	.04	.02
186	Kendall Gill (ART)	.25	.20	.10
187	All-NBA First Team	.50	.40	.20
188	Charles Barkley (AS)	.50	.40	.20
189	Patrick Ewing (AS)	.50	.40	.20
190	Michael Jordan (AS)	1.50	1.25	.60
191	Karl Malone (AS)	.40	.30	.15
192	Magic Johnson (AS)	.50	.40	.20
NNO	Panini Album	2.50	2.00	1.00

1992-93 Panini Stickers

These stickers feature full-color action photos on the front, bordered by a white frame. The player's name and team are listed at the top of the card, in a team color- coded bar. The sticker back has a number, Panini and NBA logos, and information about the corresponding album which was produced to hold the set. The stickers are 1 3/4" by 2 11/16".

		MT	NM	EX
Complete Set (192):		20.00	15.00	8.00
Common Player:		.05	.04	.02
1	Shaquille O'Neal	7.50	5.75	3.00
2	Tracy Murray	.05	.04	.02
3	Robert Horry	.20	.15	.08
4	Bryant Stith	.10	.08	.04
5	Randy Woods	.07	.05	.03
6	Adam Keefe	.07	.05	.03
7	Byron Houston	.07	.05	.03
8	Duane Cooper	.07	.05	.03
9	Western Playoffs (Action Scene Left)	.05	.04	.02
10	Western Playoffs (Action Scene Right)	.05	.04	.02
11	Clyde Drexler	.25	.20	.10
12	Michael Jordan	1.50	1.25	.60
13	Eastern Playoffs (Action Scene Left)	.05	.04	.02
14	Eastern Playoffs (Action Scene Right)	.05	.04	.02
15	Chicago Bulls Logo	.05	.04	.02
16	1992 NBA Finals (Michael Jordan) (Action Scene Upper Left)	.50	.40	.20
17	1992 NBA Finals (Michael Jordan) (Action Scene Upper Right)	.50	.40	.20
18	1992 NBA Finals (Michael Jordan) (Action Scene Lower Left)	.50	.40	.20
19	1992 NBA Finals (Michael Jordan) (Action Scene Lower Right)	.50	.40	.20
20	Michael Jordan (MVP)	1.50	1.25	.60
21	Tim Hardaway	.20	.15	.08
22	Chris Mullin	.20	.15	.08
23	Billy Owens	.20	.15	.08
24	Sarunas Marciulionis	.05	.04	.02
25	Jeff Grayer	.05	.04	.02
26	Tyrone Hill	.07	.05	.03
27	Danny Manning	.10	.08	.04
28	Ron Harper	.07	.05	.03
29	Ken Norman	.07	.05	.03
30	Charles Smith	.07	.05	.03
31	Gary Grant	.05	.04	.02
32	Doc Rivers	.07	.05	.03
33	James Worthy	.10	.08	.04
34	Sam Perkins	.07	.05	.03
35	Byron Scott	.07	.05	.03
36	Sedale Threatt	.05	.04	.02
37	Elden Campbell	.05	.04	.02
38	A.C. Green	.07	.05	.03

Stamps/stickers

No.	Player				No.	Player			
39	Charles Barkley	.75	.60	.30	117	Paul Graham	.05	.04	.02
40	Kevin Johnson	.20	.15	.08	118	Dominique Wilkins	.50	.40	.20
41	Tom Chambers	.07	.05	.03	119	Kevin Willis	.15	.11	.06
42	Dan Majerle	.20	.15	.08	120	Duane Ferrell	.05	.04	.02
43	Mark West	.05	.04	.02	121	Tyrone Bogues	.07	.05	.03
44	Danny Ainge	.15	.11	.06	122	Kendall Gill	.15	.11	.06
45	Buck Williams	.07	.05	.03	123	Dell Curry	.07	.05	.03
46	Clyde Drexler	.15	.11	.06	124	Larry Johnson	.75	.60	.30
47	Jerome Kersey	.07	.05	.03	125	Johnny Newman	.07	.05	.03
48	Terry Porter	.07	.05	.03	126	J.R. Reid	.05	.04	.02
49	Cliff Robinson	.07	.05	.03	127	Scottie Pippen	.75	.60	.30
50	Kevin Duckworth	.05	.04	.02	128	Michael Jordan	2.50	2.00	1.00
51	Mitch Richmond	.25	.20	.10	129	Bill Cartwright	.07	.05	.03
52	Lionel Simmons	.07	.05	.03	130	Horace Grant	.15	.11	.06
53	Wayman Tisdale	.07	.05	.03	131	John Paxson	.07	.05	.03
54	Spud Webb	.07	.05	.03	132	B.J. Armstrong	.15	.11	.06
55	Duane Causwell	.05	.04	.02	133	Mark Price	.20	.15	.08
56	Jim Les	.05	.04	.02	134	Brad Daugherty	.10	.08	.04
57	Eddie Johnson	.07	.05	.03	135	Larry Nance	.07	.05	.03
58	Ricky Pierce	.07	.05	.03	136	Craig Ehlo	.07	.05	.03
59	Shawn Kemp	.60	.45	.25	137	Hot Rod Williams	.07	.05	.03
60	Benoit Benjamin	.05	.04	.02	138	Terrell Brandon	.05	.04	.02
61	Gary Payton	.20	.15	.08	139	Joe Dumars	.15	.11	.06
62	Dana Barros	.05	.04	.02	140	Isiah Thomas	.15	.11	.06
63	Herb Williams	.05	.04	.02	141	Dennis Rodman	.15	.11	.06
64	Doug Smith	.05	.04	.02	142	Orlando Woolridge	.07	.05	.03
65	Terry Davis	.05	.04	.02	143	John Salley	.20	.15	.08
66	Derek Harper	.07	.05	.03	144	Bill Laimbeer	.10	.08	.04
67	Mike Iuzzolino	.05	.04	.02	145	Reggie Miller	.07	.05	.03
68	Rodney McCray	.05	.04	.02	146	Detlef Schrempf	.05	.04	.02
69	Greg Anderson	.05	.04	.02	147	Chuck Person	.05	.04	.02
70	Reggie Williams	.05	.04	.02	148	Michael Williams	.05	.04	.02
71	Dikembe Mutombo	.25	.20	.10	149	Rik Smits	.07	.05	.03
72	Mark Macon	.05	.04	.02	150	Vern Fleming	.05	.04	.02
73	Winston Garland	.05	.04	.02	151	Lester Conner	.05	.04	.02
74	Chris Jackson	.07	.05	.03	152	Nick Anderson	.15	.11	.06
75	Otis Thorpe	.10	.08	.04	153	Scott Skiles	.07	.05	.03
76	Hakeem Olajuwon	.75	.60	.30	154	Terry Catledge	.05	.04	.02
77	Vernon Maxwell	.07	.05	.03	155	Jerry Reynolds	.05	.04	.02
78	Kenny Smith	.07	.05	.03	156	Dennis Scott	.07	.05	.03
79	Avery Johnson	.05	.04	.02	157	Rick Fox	.07	.05	.03
80	Sleepy Floyd	.05	.04	.02	158	Reggie Lewis	.15	.11	.06
81	Pooh Richardson	.05	.04	.02	159	Robert Parish	.15	.11	.06
82	Tony Campbell	.05	.04	.02	160	Kevin Gamble	.05	.04	.02
83	Thurl Bailey	.05	.04	.02	161	Kevin McHale	.15	.11	.06
84	Doug West	.07	.05	.03	162	John Bagley	.05	.04	.02
85	Gerald Glass	.05	.04	.02	163	Steve Smith	.15	.11	.06
86	Felton Spencer	.05	.04	.02	164	Glen Rice	.15	.11	.06
87	David Robinson	.60	.45	.25	165	Grant Long	.05	.04	.02
88	Terry Cummings	.07	.05	.03	166	Rony Seikaly	.07	.05	.03
89	Sidney Green	.05	.04	.02	167	Bimbo Coles	.05	.04	.02
90	Sean Elliott	.07	.05	.03	168	Willie Burton	.05	.04	.02
91	Willie Anderson	.05	.04	.02	169	Derrick Coleman	.50	.40	.20
92	Antoine Carr	.05	.04	.02	170	Drazen Petrovic	.15	.11	.06
93	Clyde Drexler (FF)	.20	.15	.08	171	Sam Bowie	.07	.05	.03
94	Patrick Ewing (FF)	.40	.30	.15	172	Chris Morris	.05	.04	.02
95	Magic Johnson (FF)	.50	.40	.20	173	Mookie Blaylock	.10	.08	.04
96	Scottie Pippen (FF)	.35	.25	.14	174	Chris Dudley	.05	.04	.02
97	John Stockton (FF)	.25	.20	.10	175	Patrick Ewing	.60	.45	.25
98	Tim Hardaway (FF)	.25	.20	.10	176	Mark Jackson	.10	.08	.04
99	David Robinson (FF)	.40	.30	.15	177	Xavier McDaniel	.05	.04	.02
100	Karl Malone (FF)	.25	.20	.10	178	John Starks	.25	.20	.10
101	Chris Mullin (FF)	.15	.11	.06	179	Charles Oakley	.10	.08	.04
102	Michael Jordan (FF)	2.00	1.50	.80	180	Rolando Blackman	.07	.05	.03
103	Mark Eaton	.05	.04	.02	181	Hersey Hawkins	.10	.08	.04
104	Karl Malone	.40	.30	.15	182	Johnny Dawkins	.05	.04	.02
105	Jeff Malone	.05	.04	.02	183	Armon Gilliam	.05	.04	.02
106	John Stockton	.30	.25	.12	184	Jeff Hornacek	.10	.08	.04
107	David Benoit	.05	.04	.02	185	Tim Perry	.05	.04	.02
108	Jay Humphries	.05	.04	.02	186	Andrew Lang	.05	.04	.02
109	Alvin Robertson	.05	.04	.02	187	Pervis Ellison	.07	.05	.03
110	Moses Malone	.10	.08	.04	188	Michael Adams	.05	.04	.02
111	Sam Vincent	.05	.04	.02	189	Harvey Grant	.05	.04	.02
112	Frank Brickowski	.05	.04	.02	190	Ledell Eackles	.05	.04	.02
113	Fred Roberts	.05	.04	.02	191	A.J. English	.05	.04	.02
114	Blue Edwards	.05	.04	.02	192	David Wingate	.05	.04	.02
115	Stacey Augmon	.10	.08	.04	193	Panini Album	1.50	1.25	.60
116	Rumeal Robinson	.05	.04	.02					

1993-94 Panini Stickers

These stickers once again feature team color-coded backgrounds framed by a black border. A color action photo is in the center of the sticker, with the player's team name above it and the player's name at the bottom. A team logo also appears on the front. The stickers are 2 3/8" by 3 3/8" and are numbered on the back. An NBA logo, Panini logo and information about the corresponding album which was produced to hold the stickers is also given. Six stickers (A-F) at the end of the checklist were part of an NBA honor roll picture which was featured in the middle of the album.

		MT	NM	EX
Complete Set (253):		20.00	15.00	8.00
Common Player (1-247):		.05	.04	.02
Common Player (A-F):		.25	.20	.10
1	John Paxson	.07	.05	.03
	(top part of photo)			
2	John Paxson	.07	.05	.03
	(bottom part of photo)			
3	Charles Barkley	.50	.40	.20
	(top part of photo)			
4	Charles Barkley	.50	.40	.20
	(bottom part of photo)			
5	Victor Alexander	.05	.04	.02
6	Chris Gatling	.05	.04	.02
7	Tim Hardaway	.25	.20	.10
8	Warriors Team Logo	.05	.04	.02
9	Tyrone Hill	.07	.05	.03
10	Sarunas Marciulionis	.05	.04	.02
11	Chris Mullin	.25	.20	.10
12	Billy Owens	.15	.11	.06
13	Latrell Sprewell	.50	.40	.20
14	Gary Grant	.05	.04	.02
15	Ron Harper	.07	.05	.03
16	Mark Jackson	.07	.05	.03
17	Clippers Team Logo	.05	.04	.02
18	Danny Manning	.15	.11	.06
19	Ken Norman	.07	.05	.03
20	Stanley Roberts	.05	.04	.02
21	Loy Vaught	.05	.04	.02
22	John Williams	.05	.04	.02
23	Sam Bowie	.07	.05	.03
24	Elden Campbell	.05	.04	.02
25	Vlade Divac	.10	.08	.04
26	Lakers Team Logo	.05	.04	.02
27	A.C. Green	.07	.05	.03
28	Anthony Peeler	.10	.08	.04
29	Doug Christie	.07	.05	.03
30	Sedale Threatt	.05	.04	.02
31	James Worthy	.15	.11	.06
32	Danny Ainge	.15	.11	.06
33	Charles Barkley	.75	.60	.30
34	Cedric Ceballos	.15	.11	.06
35	Suns Team Logo	.05	.04	.02
36	Tom Chambers	.07	.05	.03
37	Richard Dumas	.05	.04	.02
38	Kevin Johnson	.25	.20	.10
39	Dan Majerle	.25	.20	.10
40	Oliver Miller	.07	.05	.03
41	Clyde Drexler	.25	.20	.10
42	Mario Elie	.07	.05	.03
43	Harvey Grant	.05	.04	.02
44	Trailblazers Team Logo	.05	.04	.02
45	Jerome Kersey	.07	.05	.03
46	Terry Porter	.07	.05	.03
47	Cliff Robinson	.07	.05	.03
48	Rod Strickland	.10	.08	.04
49	Buck Williams	.07	.05	.03
50	Anthony Bonner	.07	.05	.03
51	Duane Causwell	.07	.05	.03
52	Kurt Rambis	.07	.05	.03
53	Kings Team Logo	.05	.04	.02
54	Mitch Richmond	.25	.20	.10
55	Lionel Simmons	.10	.08	.04
56	Wayman Tisdale	.10	.08	.04
57	Spud Webb	.10	.08	.04
58	Walt Williams	.10	.08	.04
59	Dana Barros	.15	.11	.06
60	Eddie Johnson	.07	.05	.03
61	Shawn Kemp	.75	.60	.30
62	Supersonics Team Logo	.05	.04	.02
63	Derrick McKey	.07	.05	.03
64	Nate McMillian	.07	.05	.03
65	Gary Payton	.15	.11	.06
66	Sam Perkins	.07	.05	.03
67	Ricky Pierce	.07	.05	.03
68	Terry Davis	.07	.05	.03
69	Derek Harper	.07	.05	.03
70	Donald Hodge	.05	.04	.02
71	Mavericks Team Logo	.05	.04	.02
72	Mike Iuzzolino	.05	.04	.02
73	Jim Jackson	.25	.20	.10
74	Sean Rooks	.07	.05	.03
75	Doug Smith	.07	.05	.03
76	Randy White	.05	.04	.02
77	LaPhonso Ellis	.10	.08	.04
78	Scott Hastings	.05	.04	.02
79	Mahmoud Abdul-Rauf	.15	.11	.06
80	Nuggets Team Logo	.05	.04	.02
81	Marcus Liberty	.05	.04	.02
82	Mark Macon	.07	.05	.03
83	Dikembe Mutombo	.60	.45	.25
84	Robert Pack	.10	.08	.04
85	Reggie Williams	.07	.05	.03
86	Scott Brooks	.05	.04	.02
87	Sleepy Floyd	.07	.05	.03
88	Carl Herrera	.05	.04	.02
89	Rockets Team Logo	.05	.04	.02
90	Robert Horry	.25	.20	.10
91	Vernon Maxwell	.10	.08	.04
92	Hakeem Olajuwon	.75	.60	.30
93	Kenny Smith	.07	.05	.03
94	Otis Thorpe	.10	.08	.04
95	Thurl Bailey	.05	.04	.02
96	Chris Smith	.05	.04	.02
97	Mike Brown	.05	.04	.02
98	Timberwolves Team Logo	.05	.04	.02
99	Christian Laettner	.25	.20	.10
100	Luc Longley	.07	.05	.03
101	Chuck Person	.07	.05	.03
102	Doug West	.05	.04	.02
103	Michael Williams	.05	.04	.02
104	Willie Anderson	.05	.04	.02
105	Antoine Carr	.05	.04	.02
106	Terry Cummings	.07	.05	.03
107	Spurs Team Logo	.05	.04	.02
108	Sean Elliott	.10	.08	.04
109	Dale Ellis	.05	.04	.02
110	Avery Johnson	.05	.04	.02
111	J.R. Reid	.07	.05	.03
112	David Robinson	.75	.60	.30
113	David Benoit	.05	.04	.02
114	Tyrone Corbin	.05	.04	.02
115	Mark Eaton	.07	.05	.03
116	Jazz Team Logo	.05	.04	.02
117	Jay Humphries	.07	.05	.03
118	Jeff Malone	.07	.05	.03
119	Karl Malone	.50	.40	.20
120	Felton Spencer	.07	.05	.03
121	John Stockton	.40	.30	.15
122	Anthony Avent	.05	.04	.02
123	Frank Brickowski	.05	.04	.02
124	Todd Day	.10	.08	.04
125	Bucks Team Logo	.05	.04	.02
126	Blue Edwards	.07	.05	.03
127	Brad Lohaus	.05	.04	.02
128	Moses Malone	.20	.15	.08
129	Lee Mayberry	.07	.05	.03

130	Eric Murdock	.15	.11	.06
131	Stacey Augmon	.25	.20	.10
132	Mookie Blaylock	.20	.15	.08
133	Duane Ferrell	.07	.05	.03
134	Hawks Team Logo	.05	.04	.02
135	Steve Henson	.05	.04	.02
136	Adam Keefe	.07	.05	.03
137	Jon Koncak	.05	.04	.02
138	Dominique Wilkins	.50	.40	.20
139	Kevin Willis	.15	.11	.06
140	Tyrone Bogues	.10	.08	.04
141	Dell Curry	.07	.05	.03
142	Kenny Gattison	.05	.04	.02
143	Hornets Team Logo	.05	.04	.02
144	Kendall Gill	.15	.11	.06
145	Larry Johnson	1.00	.70	.40
146	Alonzo Mourning	2.00	1.50	.80
147	Johnny Newman	.07	.05	.03
148	David Wingate	.05	.04	.02
149	B.J. Armstrong	.15	.11	.06
150	Bill Cartwright	.07	.05	.03
151	Horace Grant	.15	.11	.06
152	Bulls Team Logo	.05	.04	.02
153	Stacey King	.05	.04	.02
154	John Paxson	.07	.05	.03
155	Will Perdue	.05	.04	.02
156	Scottie Pippen	.60	.45	.25
157	Scott Williams	.07	.05	.03
158	Terrell Brandon	.05	.04	.02
159	Brad Daugherty	.15	.11	.06
160	Craig Ehlo	.10	.08	.04
161	Cavaliers Team Logo	.05	.04	.02
162	Danny Ferry	.07	.05	.03
163	Larry Nance	.07	.05	.03
164	Mark Price	.20	.15	.08
165	Gerald Wilkins	.07	.05	.03
166	Hot Rod Williams	.07	.05	.03
167	Mark Aguirre	.10	.08	.04
168	Joe Dumars	.25	.20	.10
169	Bill Laimbeer	.10	.08	.04
170	Pistons Team Logo	.05	.04	.02
171	Terry Mills	.07	.05	.03
172	Olden Polynice	.07	.05	.03
173	Alvin Robertson	.07	.05	.03
174	Dennis Rodman	.20	.15	.08
175	Isiah Thomas	.25	.20	.10
176	Dale Davis	.15	.11	.06
177	Vern Fleming	.07	.05	.03
178	Reggie Miller	.25	.20	.10
179	Pacers Team Logo	.05	.04	.02
180	Pooh Richardson	.07	.05	.03
181	Detlef Schrempf	.15	.11	.06
182	Malik Sealy	.07	.05	.03
183	Rik Smits	.10	.08	.04
184	LaSalle Thompson	.05	.04	.02
185	Nick Anderson	.10	.08	.04
186	Anthony Bowie	.05	.04	.02
187	Shaquille O'Neal	4.00	3.00	1.50
188	Magic Team Logo	.05	.04	.02
189	Donald Royal	.05	.04	.02
190	Dennis Scott	.07	.05	.03
191	Scott Skiles	.07	.05	.03
192	Tom Tolbert	.05	.04	.02
193	Jeff Turner	.05	.04	.02
194	Alaa Abdelnaby	.05	.04	.02
195	Dee Brown	.10	.08	.04
196	Sherman Douglas	.10	.08	.04
197	Celtics Team Logo	.05	.04	.02
198	Rick Fox	.07	.05	.03
199	Kevin Gamble	.07	.05	.03
200	Xavier McDaniel	.10	.08	.04
201	Robert Parish	.15	.11	.06
202	Lorenzo Williams	.05	.04	.02
203	Bimbo Coles	.05	.04	.02
204	Matt Geiger	.05	.04	.02
205	Harold Miner	.15	.11	.06

206	Heat Team Logo	.05	.04	.02
207	Glen Rice	.15	.11	.06
208	John Sailey	.07	.05	.03
209	Rony Seikaly	.10	.08	.04
210	Brian Shaw	.07	.05	.03
211	Steve Smith	.15	.11	.06
212	Rafael Addison	.05	.04	.02
213	Kenny Anderson	.25	.20	.10
214	Benoit Benjamin	.05	.04	.02
215	Nets Team Logo	.05	.04	.02
216	Derrick Coleman	.50	.40	.20
217	Chris Dudley	.07	.05	.03
218	Rick Mahorn	.07	.05	.03
219	Chris Morris	.07	.05	.03
220	Rumeal Robinson	.07	.05	.03
221	Greg Anthony	.07	.05	.03
222	Rolando Blackman	.07	.05	.03
223	Patrick Ewing	.60	.45	.25
224	Knicks Team Logo	.05	.04	.02
225	Anthony Mason	.10	.08	.04
226	Charles Oakley	.15	.11	.06
227	Doc Rivers	.10	.08	.04
228	Charles Smith	.07	.05	.03
229	John Starks	.10	.08	.04
230	Ron Anderson	.05	.04	.02
231	Johnny Dawkins	.07	.05	.03
232	Armon Gilliam	.07	.05	.03
233	76ers Team Logo	.05	.04	.02
234	Hersey Hawkins	.07	.05	.03
235	Jeff Hornacek	.10	.08	.04
236	Andrew Lang	.07	.05	.03
237	Tim Perry	.07	.05	.03
238	Clarence Weatherspoon	.25	.20	.10
239	Michael Adams	.07	.05	.03
240	Rex Chapman	.07	.05	.03
241	Kevin Duckworth	.07	.05	.03
242	Bullets Team Logo	.05	.04	.02
243	Pervis Ellison	.10	.08	.04
244	Tom Gugliotta	.30	.25	.12
245	Don MacLean	.20	.15	.08
246	Brent Price	.05	.04	.02
247	LaBradford Smith	.07	.05	.03
A	Charles Barkley (MVP)	1.25	.90	.50
B	Mahmoud Abdul-Rauf	.25	.20	.10
	(Most Improved Player)			
C	Shaquille O'Neal (ROY)	2.50	2.00	1.00
D	Hakeem Olajuwon	1.25	.90	.50
	(Defensive POY)			
E	John Stockton	.50	.40	.20
	(Court Vision)			
F	Cliff Robinson	.25	.20	.10
	(Sixth Man Award)			
NNO	Panini Album	1.00	.70	.40

1979 Quaker Iron-Ons

This set, officially licensed by the NBA, is sponsored by Quaker Oats and features posed photos on the fronts of the iron-on cards. The front tells how to iron the photo onto clothing; backs are blank. Cards measure 4 3/8" by 6 1/8".

		NM	EX	VG
Complete Set (8):		100.00	50.00	30.00
Common Player:		9.00	4.50	2.75
(1)	Kareem Abdul-Jabbar	25.00	12.50	7.50
(2)	Rick Barry	15.00	7.50	4.50
(3)	Julius Erving	20.00	10.00	6.00
(4)	George Gervin	15.00	7.50	4.50
(5)	Elvin Hayes	18.00	9.00	5.50
(6)	Maurice Lucas	9.00	4.50	2.75
(7)	David Thompson	15.00	7.50	4.50
(8)	Paul Westphal	9.00	4.50	2.75

1971 Topps Stickers

These stickers, which were card-size and included three players per sticker (very similar to the 1980-81 cards), showed ABA and NBA players, plus three logo stickers. Each has a black border. Because of the black borders and the flimsiness of the stickers, it's difficult to find these in Mint condition.

		NM	EX	VG
Complete Set:		500.00	250.00	150.00
Common Player:		7.50	3.75	2.25
1	Lou Hudson	7.50	3.75	2.25
2	Bob Rule	7.50	3.75	2.25
3	Calvin Murphy	7.50	3.75	2.25
4	Walt Wesley	7.50	3.75	2.25
5	Jo Jo White	7.50	3.75	2.25
6	Bob Dandridge	7.50	3.75	2.25
7	Nate Thurmond	20.00	10.00	6.00
8	Earl Monroe	20.00	10.00	6.00
9	Spencer Haywood	20.00	10.00	6.00
10	Dave DeBusschere	20.00	10.00	6.00
11	Bob Lanier	20.00	10.00	6.00
12	Tom Van Arsdale	20.00	10.00	6.00
13	Hal Greer	20.00	10.00	6.00
14	Johnny Green	20.00	10.00	6.00
15	Elvin Hayes	20.00	10.00	6.00
16	Jimmy Walker	7.50	3.75	2.25
17	Don May	7.50	3.75	2.25
18	Archie Clark	7.50	3.75	2.25
19	Happy Hairston	7.50	3.75	2.25
20	Leroy Ellis	7.50	3.75	2.25
21	Jerry Sloan	7.50	3.75	2.25
22	Pete Maravich	75.00	27.50	22.50
23	Bob Kauffman	75.00	27.50	22.50
24	John Havlicek	75.00	27.50	22.50
25	Walt Frazier	20.00	10.00	6.00
26	Dick Van Ardsdale	20.00	10.00	6.00
27	Dave Bing	20.00	10.00	6.00
28	Bob Love	7.50	3.75	2.25
29	Ron Williams	7.50	3.75	2.25
30	Dave Cowens	7.50	3.75	2.25
31	Jerry West	60.00	30.00	18.00
32	Willis Reed	60.00	30.00	18.00
33	Chet Walker	60.00	30.00	18.00
34	Oscar Robertson	50.00	25.00	14.00
35	Wes Unseld	50.00	25.00	14.00
36	Bobby Smith	50.00	25.00	14.00
37	Connie Hawkins	100.00	50.00	30.00
38	Jeff Mullins	100.00	50.00	30.00
39	Lew Alcindor	100.00	50.00	30.00
40	Billy Cunningham	25.00	12.50	7.50
41	Walt Bellamy	25.00	12.50	7.50
42	Geoff Petrie	25.00	12.50	7.50
43	Wilt Chamberlain	75.00	37.50	22.50
44	Gus Johnson	75.00	37.50	22.50
45	Norm Van Lier	75.00	37.50	22.50

Stamps/stickers before 1981 are priced Near Mint (NM), Excellent (EX), and Very Good (VG). Stamps/stickers 1981 to present are priced Mint (MT), Near Mint (NM), and Excellent (EX).

Grading Guide

Mint (MT): A perfect card. Well-centered with all corners sharp and square. No creases, stains, edge nicks, surface marks, yellowing or fading.

Near Mint (NM): A nearly perfect card. At first glance, a NM card appears to be perfect. May be slightly off-center. No surface marks, creases or loss of gloss.

Excellent (EX): Corners are still fairly sharp with only moderate wear. Borders may be off-center. No creases or stains on fronts or backs, but may show slight loss of surface luster.

Very Good (VG): Shows obvious handling. May have rounded corners, minor creases, major gum or wax stains. No major creases, tape marks, writing, etc.

Good (G): A well-worn card, but exhibits no intentional damage. May have major or multiple creases. Corners may be rounded.

Hockey

1970 Colgate Stamps

These sheets of stamps were offered as premiums through various sizes of Colgate toothpaste products. Colgate offered three sheets, each featuring 31 of the 1" by 1 1/4" stamps. Each colored stamp has a white border and includes a facsimile autograph of the player pictured. His name and number, given in a star, are also incuded. The stamp back is blank.

		NM	EX	VG
Complete Set (93):		110.00	55.00	33.00
Common Player:		.75	.40	.25
1	Walt McKechnie	.75	.40	.25
2	Bob Pulford	1.50	.70	.45
3	Mike Walton	1.00	.50	.30
4	Alex Delvecchio	2.00	1.00	.60
5	Tom Williams	.75	.40	.25
6	Derek Sanderson	2.00	1.00	.60
7	Garry Unger	1.25	.60	.40
8	Lou Angotti	.75	.40	.25
9	Ted Hampson	.75	.40	.25
10	Phil Goyette	.75	.40	.25
11	Juha Widing	.75	.40	.25
12	Norm Ullman	2.00	1.00	.60
13	Garry Monahan	.75	.40	.25
14	Henri Richard	4.00	2.00	1.25
15	Ray Cullen	1.00	.50	.30

355

16	Danny O'Shea	.75	.40	.25
17	Marc Tardif	1.00	.50	.30
18	Jude Drouin	.75	.40	.25
19	Charlie Burns	.75	.40	.25
20	Gerry Meehan	1.00	.50	.30
21	Ralph Backstrom	1.00	.50	.30
22	Frank St. Marseille	.75	.40	.25
23	Orland Kurtenbach	1.00	.50	.30
24	Red Berenson	1.00	.50	.30
25	Jean Ratelle	2.00	1.00	.60
26	Syl Apps Jr.	1.00	.50	.30
27	Don Marshall	.75	.40	.25
28	Gilbert Perreault	5.00	2.50	1.50
29	Andre Lacroix	1.00	.50	.30
30	Jacques Lemaire	2.00	1.00	.60
31	Pit Martin	1.00	.50	.30
32	Dennis Hull	1.25	.60	.40
33	Dave Balon	.75	.40	.25
34	Keith McCreary	.75	.40	.25
35	Bobby Rousseau	1.00	.50	.30
36	Danny Grant	1.00	.50	.30
37	Brit Selby	.75	.40	.25
38	Bob Nevin	.75	.40	.25
39	Rosaire Paiement	.75	.40	.25
40	Gary Dornhoefer	1.00	.50	.30
41	Eddie Shack	1.50	.70	.45
42	Ron Schock	.75	.40	.25
43	Jim Pappin	1.00	.50	.30
44	Mickey Redmond	1.25	.60	.40
45	Vic Hadfield	1.25	.60	.40
46	John Bucyk	2.50	1.25	.70
47	Gordie Howe	30.00	15.00	9.00
48	Ron C. Anderson	.75	.40	.25
49	Gary Jarrett	.75	.40	.25
50	Jean Pronovost	1.00	.50	.30
51	Simon Nolet	.75	.40	.25
52	Bill Goldsworthy	1.25	.60	.40
53	Rod Gilbert	2.00	1.00	.60
54	Ron Ellis	1.00	.50	.30
55	Mike Byers	.75	.40	.25
56	Norm Ferguson	.75	.40	.25
57	Gary Sabourin	.75	.40	.25
58	Tim Ecclestone	.75	.40	.25
59	John McKenzie	.75	.40	.25
60	Yvan Cournoyer	3.00	1.50	.90
61	Ken Schinkel	.75	.40	.25
62	Ken Hodge Sr.	1.25	.60	.40
63	Cesare Maniago	1.00	.50	.30
64	J.C. Tremblay	1.00	.50	.30
65	Gilles Marotte	1.00	.50	.30
66	Bob Baun	1.00	.50	.30
67	Gerry Desjardins	1.00	.50	.30
68	Charlie Hodge	1.25	.60	.40
69	Matt Ravlich	.75	.40	.25
70	Ed Giacomin	2.00	1.00	.60
71	Gerry Cheevers	3.00	1.50	.90
72	Pat Quinn	1.25	.60	.40
73	Gary Bergman	1.00	.50	.30
74	Serge Savard	2.00	1.00	.60
75	Les Binkley	1.00	.50	.30
76	Arnie Brown	.75	.40	.25
77	!at Stapleton	1.00	.50	.30
78	Ed Van Impe	.75	.40	.25
79	Jim Dorey	.75	.40	.25
80	Dave Dryden	1.00	.50	.30
81	Dale Tallon	1.00	.50	.30
82	Bruce Gamble	.75	.40	.25
83	Roger Crozier	1.00	.50	.30
84	Denis DeJordy	1.00	.50	.30
85	Rogatien Vachon	2.00	1.00	.60
86	Carol Vadnais	.75	.40	.25
87	Bobby Orr	25.00	12.50	7.50
88	Noel Picard	.75	.40	.25
89	Gilles Villemure	1.00	.50	.30
90	Gary Smith	1.00	.50	.30
91	Doug Favell	1.00	.50	.30
92	Ernie Wakely	.75	.40	.25
93	Bernie Parent	2.00	1.00	.60

1971 Eddie Sargent Promotions

These stickers were issued on 7 3/4" by 9 3/4" sheets of 16 - one player from each of the 14 NHL teams is featured, plus two series stickers. Each sticker is in color, with a white border, and measures 1 7/8" by 2 1/2". The player's name, team and sticker number are listed on the front. Card backs are blank. "1971 NHLPA PRINTED IN USA" is also on each card.

		NM	EX	VG
	Complete Set:	45.00	22.00	13.50
	Common Player:	.50	.25	.15
2	Ed Westfall	1.00	.50	.30
3	John McKenzie	2.00	1.00	.60
5	Ted Green	.50	.25	.15
18	Ron Anderson	.50	.25	.15
19	Gilbert Perreault	12.00	6.00	3.50
22	Kevin O'Shea	.50	.25	.15
34	Bobby Hull	14.00	7.00	4.25
35	Cliff Koroll	.50	.25	.15
38	Lou Angotti	.50	.25	.15
50	Bob Wall	.50	.25	.15
51	Red Berenson	.50	.25	.15
54	Gary Bergman	.50	.25	.15
66	Bob Pulford	1.50	.70	.45
67	Bill Flett	.50	.25	.15
70	Gilles Marotte	.50	.25	.15
82	Jude Drouin	.50	.25	.15
83	Jean Paul Parise	.50	.25	.15
86	Bill Goldsworthy	.50	.25	.15
98	Guy LaPointe	1.00	.50	.30
99	Peter Mahovlich	1.50	.70	.45
102	Yvan Cournoyer	4.00	2.00	1.25
114	Jean Ratelle	3.00	1.50	.90
115	Peter Stemkowski	1.00	.50	.30
118	Dale Rolfe	.50	.25	.15
130	Tommy Williams	.50	.25	.15
131	Wayne Carleton	.50	.25	.15
134	Bert Marshall	.50	.25	.15
146	Wayne Hillman	.50	.25	.15
147	Brent Hughes	.50	.25	.15
150	Ed Van Impe	.50	.25	.15
162	Ken Schinkel	.50	.25	.15
163	Val Fonteyne	.50	.25	.15
166	Les Binkley	.50	.25	.15
178	Garry Unger	.50	.25	.15
179	Terry Crisp	1.00	.50	.30
182	Barclay Plager	.50	.25	.15
194	Jim McKenny	.50	.25	.15
195	Rick Ley	.50	.25	.15
198	Bill MacMillan	.50	.25	.15
210	Danny Johnson	.50	.25	.15
211	Murray Hall	.50	.25	.15
214	Gary Doak	2.00	1.00	.60

1972 Eddie Sargent Promotions Stickers

Each of these sheets of 16 feature 14 players from one team, plus two series number stickers. Each four-color sticker is 1 7/8" by 2 1/2" and is similar to the 1971-72 stickers (name, team and sticker number), except the back indicates the stickers were produced by the National Hockey League Players' Association, Sports Album Inc., and Eddie Sargent Promotions Ltd. Two albums with different covers, featuring Bobby Orr or Paul Henderson, were also available.

		NM	EX	VG
	Complete Set:	130.00	65.00	39.00
	Common Player:	.50	.25	.15
1	Lucien Grenier	.50	.25	.15
2	Phil Myre (Goalie)	.60	.30	.20
3	Ernie Hicke	.50	.25	.15

#	Player				#	Player			
4	Keith McCreary	.50	.25	.15	79	Gary Bergman	.60	.30	.20
5	Billy MacMillan	.60	.30	.20	80	Guy Charron	.50	.25	.15
6	Pat Quinn	.75	.40	.25	81	Leon Rochefort	.50	.25	.15
7	William Plager	.60	.30	.20	82	Larry Johnston	.50	.25	.15
8	Noel Price	.50	.25	.15	83	Andy Brown (Goalie)	.50	.25	.15
9	Bobby Leiter	.50	.25	.15	84	Henry Boucha	.60	.30	.20
10	Randy Manery	.50	.25	.15	85	Paul Curtis	.50	.25	.15
11	Bob Paradise	.50	.25	.15	86	Jim Stanfield	.50	.25	.15
12	Larry Romanchych	.50	.25	.15	87	Rogatien Vachon (Goalie)	1.50	.70	.45
13	Lew Morrison	.50	.25	.15	88	Ralph Backstrom	.60	.30	.20
14	Dan Bouchard (Goalie)	.60	.30	.20	89	Gilles Marotte	.60	.30	.20
15	Fred Stanfield	.50	.25	.15	90	Harry Howell	1.00	.50	.30
16	John Bucyk	3.00	1.50	.90	91	Real Lemieux	.50	.25	.15
17	Bobby Orr	35.00	17.50	10.50	92	Butch Goring	.75	.40	.25
18	Wayne Cashman	.60	.30	.20	93	Juha Widing	.50	.25	.15
19	Dallas Smith	.60	.30	.20	94	Mike Corrigan	.50	.25	.15
20	Eddie Johnston (Goalie)	.75	.40	.25	95	Larry Brown	.50	.25	.15
21	Phil Esposito	5.00	2.50	1.50	96	Terry Harper	.60	.30	.20
22	Ken Hodge, Sr.	.75	.40	.25	97	Serge Bernier	.50	.25	.15
23	Don Awrey	.50	.25	.15	98	Bob Berry	.60	.30	.20
24	Mike Walton	.60	.30	.20	99	Tom Reid	.60	.30	.20
25	Carol Vadnais	.60	.30	.20	100	Jude Drouin	.50	.25	.15
26	Doug Roberts	.50	.25	.15	101	Jean Paul Parise	.60	.30	.20
27	Don Marcotte	.50	.25	.15	102	Doug Mohns	.60	.30	.20
28	Garnet Bailey	.50	.25	.15	103	Danny Grant	.60	.30	.20
29	Gerry Meehan	.60	.30	.20	104	Bill Goldsworthy	.75	.40	.25
30	Tracy Pratt	.50	.25	.15	105	Gump Worsley (Goalie)	3.00	1.50	.90
31	Gilbert Perreault	3.00	1.50	.90	106	Charlie Burns	.50	.25	.15
32	Roger Crozier (Goalie)	.60	.30	.20	107	Murray Oliver	.50	.25	.15
33	Don Luce	.50	.25	.15	108	Barry Gibbs	.50	.25	.15
34	Dave Dryden (Goalie)	.60	.30	.20	109	Ted Harris	.60	.30	.20
35	Richard Martin	1.00	.50	.30	110	Cesare Maniago (Goalie)	.60	.30	.20
36	Jim Lorentz	.50	.25	.15	111	Lou Nanne	.60	.30	.20
37	Tim Horton	3.00	1.50	.90	112	Bob Nevin	.60	.30	.20
38	Craig Ramsey	.50	.25	.15	113	Guy Lapointe	1.00	.50	.30
39	Larry Hillman	.50	.25	.15	114	Pete Mahovlich	.75	.40	.25
40	Steve Atkinson	.50	.25	.15	115	Jacques Lamaire	2.50	1.25	.70
41	Jim Schoenfeld	.75	.40	.25	116	Pierre Bouchard	.60	.30	.20
42	Rene Robert	.75	.40	.25	117	Yvan Cournoyer	2.00	1.00	.60
43	Walt McKechnie	.50	.25	.15	118	Marc Tardif	.60	.30	.20
44	Marshall Johnston	.50	.25	.15	119	Henri Richard	4.00	2.00	1.25
45	Joey Johnston	.50	.25	.15	120	Frank Mahovlich	4.00	2.00	1.25
46	Dick Redmond	.50	.25	.15	121	Jacques Laperriere	1.50	.70	.45
47	Bert Marshall	.50	.25	.15	122	Claude Larose	.60	.30	.20
48	Gary Croteau	.50	.25	.15	123	Serge Savard	2.00	1.00	.60
49	Marv Edwards (Goalie)	.50	.25	.15	124	Ken Dryden (Goalie)	12.00	6.00	3.50
50	Gilles Meloche (Goalie)	.60	.30	.20	125	Rejean Houle	.60	.30	.20
51	Ivan Boldirev	.50	.25	.15	126	Jim Roberts	.60	.30	.20
52	Stan Gilbertson	.50	.25	.15	127	Ed Westfall	.75	.40	.25
53	Pete Laframboise	.50	.25	.15	128	Terry Crisp	.60	.30	.20
54	Reggie Leach	1.00	.50	.30	129	Gerry Desjardins (Goalie)	.60	.30	.20
55	Craig Patrick	1.00	.50	.30	130	Error (Denis DeJordy) (Goalie)	.60	.30	.20
56	Bob Stewart	.50	.25	.15	131	Billy Harris	.60	.30	.20
57	Keith Magnuson	.75	.40	.25	132	Brian Spencer	.75	.40	.25
58	Doug Jarrett	.50	.25	.15	133	Germain Gagnon	.50	.25	.15
59	Cliff Koroll	.50	.25	.15	134	Dave Hudson	.50	.25	.15
60	Chico Maki	.60	.30	.20	135	Lorne Henning	.60	.30	.20
61	Gary Smith (Goalie)	.60	.30	.20	136	Brian Marchinko	.50	.25	.15
62	Bill White	.60	.30	.20	137	Tom Miller	.50	.25	.15
63	Stan Mikita	5.00	2.50	1.50	138	Gerrry Hart	.50	.25	.15
64	Jim Pappin	.60	.30	.20	139	Bryan Lefley	.50	.25	.15
65	Lou Angotti	.50	.25	.15	140	Jim Mair	.50	.25	.15
66	Tony Esposito (Goalie)	3.00	1.50	.90	141	Rod Gilbert	2.00	1.00	.60
67	Dennis Hull	1.00	.50	.30	142	Jean Ratelle	2.00	1.00	.60
68	Pit Martin	.60	.30	.20	143	Pete Stemkowski	.60	.30	.20
69	Pat Stapleton	.60	.30	.20	144	Brad Park	2.00	1.00	.60
70	Dan Maloney	.60	.30	.20	145	Bobby Rousseau	.60	.30	.20
71	Bill Collins	.50	.25	.15	146	Dale Rolfe	.60	.30	.20
72	Arnie Brown	.50	.25	.15	147	Ed Giacomin (Goalie)	2.00	1.00	.60
73	Red Berenson	.75	.40	.25	148	Rod Seiling	.50	.25	.15
74	Mickey Redmond	1.00	.50	.30	149	Walt Tkaczuk	.60	.30	.20
75	Nick Libett	.60	.30	.20	150	Bill Fairbairn	.50	.25	.15
76	Alex Delvecchio	2.00	1.00	.60	151	Vic Hadfield	.60	.30	.20
77	Ron Stackhouse	.50	.25	.15	152	Ted Irvine	.50	.25	.15
78	Tim Ecclestone	.50	.25	.15					

153	Bruce MacGregor	.50	.25	.15
154	Jim Neilson	.50	.25	.15
155	Brent Hughes	.50	.25	.15
156	Wayne Hillman	.50	.25	.15
157	Doug Favell (Goalie)	.60	.30	.20
158	Simon Nolet	.50	.25	.15
159	Joe Watson	.50	.25	.15
160	Ed Van Impe	.50	.25	.15
161	Gary Dornhoefer	.60	.30	.20
162	Bobby Clarke	3.50	1.75	1.00
163	Bob Kelly	.60	.30	.20
164	Bill Flett	.50	.25	.15
165	Rick Foley	.50	.25	.15
166	Ross Lonsberry	.50	.25	.15
167	Rick MacLeish	.75	.40	.25
168	Bill Clement	.75	.40	.25
169	Syl Apps, Jr.	.60	.30	.20
170	Ken Schinkel	.50	.25	.15
171	Nick Harbaruk	.50	.25	.15
172	Bryan Watson	.60	.30	.20
173	Bryan Hextall, Jr.	.60	.30	.20
174	Roy Edwards (Goalie)	.50	.25	.15
175	Jim Rutherford (Goalie)	.75	.40	.25
176	Jean Pronovost	.60	.30	.20
177	Rick Kessell	.50	.25	.15
178	Greg Polis	.50	.25	.15
179	Ron Schock	.50	.25	.15
180	Duane Rupp	.50	.25	.15
181	Darryl Edestrand	.50	.25	.15
182	Dave Burrows	.50	.25	.15
183	Gary Sabourin	.50	.25	.15
184	Garry Unger	.75	.40	.25
185	Noel Picard	.50	.25	.15
186	Bob Plager	.75	.40	.25
187	Barclay Plager	.75	.40	.25
188	Frank St. Marseille	.50	.25	.15
189	Danny O'Shea	.50	.25	.15
190	Kevin O'Shea	.50	.25	.15
191	Wayne Stephenson (Goalie)	.60	.30	.20
192	Chris Evans	.50	.25	.15
193	Jacques Caron (Goalie)	.50	.25	.15
194	Andre Dupont	.60	.30	.20
195	Mike Murphy	.50	.25	.15
196	Jack Egers	.50	.25	.15
197	Norm Ullman	2.00	1.00	.60
198	Jim McKenny	.50	.25	.15
199	Bob Baun	.75	.40	.25
200	Mike Pelyk	.50	.25	.15
201	Ron Ellis	.60	.30	.20
202	Garry Monahan	.50	.25	.15
203	Paul Henderson	1.00	.50	.30
204	Darryl Sittler	2.50	1.25	.70
205	Brian Glennie	.50	.25	.15
206	Dave Keon	2.00	1.00	.60
207	Jacques Plante (Goalie)	3.00	1.50	.90
208	Pierre Jarry	.50	.25	.15
209	Rick Kehoe	.75	.40	.25
210	Denis Dupere	.50	.25	.15
211	Dale Tallon	.60	.30	.20
212	Murray Hall (Goalie)	.50	.25	.15
213	Dunc Wilson (Goalie)	.60	.30	.20
214	Andre Boudrias	.50	.25	.15
215	Orland Kurtenbach	.60	.30	.20
216	Wayne Maki	.50	.25	.15
217	Barry Wilkins	.50	.25	.15
218	Richard Lemieux	.50	.25	.15
219	Bobby Schmautz	.50	.25	.15
220	Dave Balon	.50	.25	.15
221	Bobby Lalonde	.50	.25	.15
222	Jocelyn Guevremont	.60	.30	.20
223	Gregg Boddy	.50	.25	.15
224	Dennis Kearns	.50	.25	.15

1988 Esso All-Star Stickers

These 2 1/8" by 3 1/4" stickers feature 48 all-star caliber players. Each sticker has a color photo, player name, team logo, and facsimile autograph on the front. Each bilingual back has a checklist. A checklist card was also made; although it indicates there are 53 players in the set, there are five photographs of players already in the album, so they can't be collected (Pierre Pilot, Ed Giacomin, Bernie Parent, Al MacInnis and Rick Middleton). Stickers are unnumbered, so the players are listed below alphabetically. A 32-page album was also issued, in French and English versions.

		MT	NM	EX
Complete Set (48):		15.00	11.00	6.00
Common Player:		.25	.20	.10
(1)	Jean Béliveau	.75	.60	.30
(2)	Mike Bossy	.75	.60	.30
(3)	Raymond Bourque	.75	.60	.30
(4)	Johnny Bower	.35	.25	.14
(5)	Bobby Clarke	.50	.40	.20
(6)	Paul Coffey	.75	.60	.30
(7)	Yvan Cournoyer	.35	.25	.14
(8)	Marcel Dionne	.50	.40	.20
(9)	Ken Dryden	.75	.60	.30
(10)	Phil Esposito	.75	.60	.30
(11)	Tony Esposito	.50	.40	.20
(12)	Grant Fuhr	.35	.25	.14
(13)	Clark Gillies	.25	.20	.10
(14)	Michel Goulet	.35	.25	.14
(15)	Wayne Gretzky	4.00	3.00	1.50
(16)	Dale Hawerchuk	.35	.25	.14
(17)	Ron Hextall	.25	.20	.10
(18)	Gordie Howe	1.50	1.25	.60
(19)	Mark Howe	.25	.20	.10
(20)	Bobby Hull	1.00	.70	.40
(21)	Tim Kerr	.25	.20	.10
(22)	Jari Kurri	.35	.25	.14
(23)	Guy Lafleur	.75	.60	.30
(24)	Rod Langway	.25	.20	.10
(25)	Jacques Laperriere	.25	.20	.10
(26)	Guy Lapointe	.35	.25	.14
(27)	Mario Lemieux	1.75	1.25	.70
(28)	Frank Mahovlich	.50	.40	.20
(29)	Lanny McDonald	.35	.25	.14
(30)	Mark Messier	1.00	.70	.40
(31)	Stan Mikita	.50	.40	.20
(32)	Mats Naslund	.25	.20	.10
(33)	Bobby Orr	2.00	1.50	.80
(34)	Brad Park	.35	.25	.14
(35)	Gilbert Perreault	.35	.25	.14
(36)	Denis Potvin	.35	.25	.14
(37)	Larry Robinson	.35	.25	.14
(38)	Luc Robitaille	.75	.60	.30
(39)	Borje Salming	.25	.20	.10
(40)	Denis Savard	.35	.25	.14
(41)	Serge Savard	.35	.25	.14

(42)	Steve Shutt	.25	.20	.10
(43)	Darryl Sittler	.35	.25	.14
(44)	Billy Smith	.35	.25	.14
(45)	John Tonelli	.25	.20	.10
(46)	Bryan Trottier	.35	.25	.14
(47)	Norm Ullman	.35	.25	.14
(48)	Gump Worsley	.50	.40	.20
Esso	NHL All-Star Collection	2.50	2.00	1.00

1988 Frito-Lay Stickers

These stickers feature a color action photo on the front, along with the player's name and uniform number, all bordered by a white frame. The back has the NHLPA and NHL logos, but no sticker number. A poster was made to display these stickers; it was available as a mail-in offer from Frito Lay, which included stickers one per specially-marked bags of Ruffle's, Doritos, O'Grady's, Cheetos, Tostitos, Fritos, Lays, Dulac and Chester Popcorn snack products. Each sticker was in a small cello pack; the stickers were 1 3/8" by 1 3/4".

		MT	NM	EX
	Complete Set:	22.00	16.50	8.75
	Common Player:	.35	.25	.14
1	Glenn Anderson	.50	.40	.20
2	Tom Barrasso (Goalie)	.50	.40	.20
3	Brian Bellows	.35	.25	.14
4	Raymond Bourque	1.25	.90	.50
5	Neal Broten	.35	.25	.14
6	Sean Burke (Goalie)	.35	.25	.14
7	Wendel Clark	.75	.60	.30
8	Paul Coffey	1.00	.70	.40
9	Kevin Dineen	.35	.25	.14
10	Marcel Dionne	.75	.60	.30
11	Bernie Federko	.35	.25	.14
12	Michael Foligno	.35	.25	.14
13	Ron Francis	.50	.40	.20
14	Mike Gartner	.75	.60	.30
15	Douglas Gilmour	2.00	1.50	.80
16	Michel Goulet	.50	.40	.20
17	Dale Hawerchuk	.50	.40	.20
18	Ron Hextall	.50	.40	.20
19	Pat LaFontaine	1.25	.90	.50
20	Mario Lemieux	3.50	2.75	1.50
21	Al MacInnis	.75	.60	.30
22	Andrew McBain	.35	.25	.14
23	Mark Messier	1.75	1.25	.70
24	Kirk Muller	.75	.60	.30
25	Troy Murray	.35	.25	.14
26	Mats Naslund	.35	.25	.14
27	Cam Neely	1.25	.90	.50
28	Bernie Nicholls	.50	.40	.20
29	Joe Nieuwendyk	1.25	.90	.50
30	Ed Olczyk	.35	.25	.14
31	James Patrick	.35	.25	.14
32	Barry Pederson	.35	.25	.14
33	David Poulin	.35	.25	.14
34	Bob Probert	.75	.60	.30
35	Stephane J.J. Richer	.50	.40	.20
36	Luc Robitaille	1.00	.70	.40
37	Denis Savard	.50	.40	.20
38	Peter Stastny	.50	.40	.20
39	Scott Stevens	.50	.40	.20
40	Tony Tanti	.35	.25	.14
41	Bryan Trottier	.75	.60	.30
42	Steve Yzerman	1.50	1.25	.60

1990 Kraft Stickers

These bilingual sticker sheets each feature two NHL stars in their All-Star uniforms, plus four team logos. The sheets were available in packages of Kraft Singles sold in Canada. Each sticker measures 4 1/2" by 2 3/4" and has a white background. The back is also white and has an order form, in English and French, for a sticker album. The sticker number is on the front.

		MT	NM	EX
	Complete Set (6):	12.00	9.00	4.75
	Common Player:	2.00	1.50	.80
1	Paul Reinhart, Mike McPhee	2.00	1.50	.80
2	Wayne Gretzky, Rick Tocchet	6.00	4.50	2.50
3	Paul Coffey, Steve Yzerman	3.00	2.25	1.25
4	Mike Vernon, Raymond Bourque (Goalie)	3.00	2.25	1.25
5	Jari Kurri, Mario Lemieux	3.00	2.25	1.25
6	Kevin Lowe, Sean Burke (Goalie)	2.00	1.50	.80

1973 Letraset Action Replay Transfers

Letraset, in England, issued these action transfers in Canada. Each replay card is 5 1/4" by 6 1/4" and has a front scene showing Danny O'Shea (Hawks) facing off against Jean Ratelle (Rangers). The back side has a series of arm signals used by hockey referees - it's titled "Know Your Signals." The inside unfolds to show a 5" by 4 1/2" action scene, with a description of the play and spots for head shot transfers to be applied. The center of the photo is filled in by the player action transfers supplied on a separate sheet; the players could be transfered onto the scene by rubbing them over the spot.

		NM	EX	VG
	Complete Set (24):	100.00	50.00	30.00
	Common Player:	4.00	2.00	1.25
1	Rogatien Vachon, David Keon, Gilles Marotte	6.00	3.00	1.75
2	Ken Dryden, Chiko Maki, Jacques Laperriere	14.00	7.00	4.25
3	Gary Dornhoefer, Roger Crozier, Tracy Pratt	4.00	2.00	1.25
4	Walt Tkaczuk, Gump Worsley, Vic Hadfield	6.00	3.00	1.75
5	Dallas Smith, Bobby Orr, Walt McKechnie	20.00	10.00	6.00
6	Ab MacDonald, Gary Sabourin, Garry Unger	4.00	2.00	1.25
7	Jim Rutherford, Orland Kurtenbach, Bob Woytowich	4.00	2.00	1.25
8	Gerry Cheevers, Frank Mahovlich, Don Awrey	9.00	4.50	2.75
9	Tim Ecclestone, Bob Baun, Jacques Plante	6.00	3.00	1.75
10	Stan Mikita, Ed Giacomin, Jim Pappin	9.00	4.50	2.75
11	Doug Favell, Danny Grant, Ed Van Impe	4.00	2.00	1.25
12	Ernie Wakley, Barclay Plager, Gary Croteau	4.00	2.00	1.25
13	Unknown	6.00	3.00	1.75
14	Jean Ratelle, Rod Gilbert, Jim Roberts	6.00	3.00	1.75
15	Jacques Lemaire, Henri Richard, Yvan Cournoyer	12.00	6.00	3.50
16	George Gardiner, Dennis Hull, Lou Angotti	4.00	2.00	1.25
17	Ed Johnston, Norm Ullman, Bobby Orr	30.00	15.00	9.00
18	Gilles Meloche, Wayne Carleton, Dick Redmond	4.00	2.00	1.25
19	Al Smith, Gary Bergman, Stan Gilbertson	4.00	2.00	1.25
20	Dunc Wilson, Brad Park, Dale Tallon	6.00	3.00	1.75
21	Jude Drouin, Doug Favell, Barry Ashbee	4.00	2.00	1.25

22	Ron Ellis, Ken Dryden, Paul Henderson	15.00	7.50	4.50
23	Gary Edwards, Jean Pronovost, Ron Schock	4.00	2.00	1.25
24	Cesare Maniago, Chris Bordeleau, Ted Harris	4.00	2.00	1.25

1974 Loblaws NHL Action Players

These action stamps, each measuring 1 11/16 by 2 1/4", feature a full-color action photo on the front with a white border. The player's jersey number, name and position are under the photo, followed by his team name at the bottom of the card. The stamps, unnumbered, were given out in strips of seven at participating grocery stores throughout North America, including Loblaw's IGA, A&P and Acme. Strips which are left in tact are worth about 50 percent more than the total of the seven stamps combined. An album was also produced to hold the stamps; it included 20 stamps with it. The stamps are listed below alphabetically by team, then alphabetically by player name.

		NM	EX	VG
	Complete Set (324):	225.00	112.00	67.00
	Common Player:	.25	.13	.08
1	Curt Bennett	.25	.13	.08
2	Dan Bouchard	.50	.25	.15
3	Arnie Brown	.25	.13	.08
4	Jerry Byers	.25	.13	.08
5	Rey Comeau	.25	.13	.08
6	Fred (Buster) Harvey	.25	.13	.08
7	Bobby Leiter	.25	.13	.08
8	Jean Lemieux	.25	.13	.08
9	Tom Lysiak	.25	.13	.08
10	Randy Manery	.25	.13	.08
11	Keith McCreary	.25	.13	.08
12	Bob J. Murray	.25	.13	.08
13	Phil Myre	.50	.25	.15
14	Noel Price	.25	.13	.08
15	Pat Quinn	.25	.13	.08
16	Jacques Richard	.25	.13	.08
17	Larry Romanchych	.25	.13	.08
18	Eric Vail	.25	.13	.08
19	Ross Brooks	.25	.13	.08
20	John Bucyk	1.00	.50	.30
21	Wayne Cashman	.40	.20	.12
22	Darryl Edestrand	.25	.13	.08
23	Phil Esposito	2.50	1.25	.70
24	Dave Forbes	.25	.13	.08
25	Gilles Gilbert	.50	.25	.15
26	Ken Hodge, Sr.	.25	.13	.08
27	Don Marcotte	.25	.13	.08
28	Walt McKechnie	.25	.13	.08
29	Terry O'Reilly	.25	.13	.08
30	Bobby Orr	22.00	11.00	6.50
31	Andre Savard	.25	.13	.08
32	Bobby Schmautz	.25	.13	.08
33	Gregg Sheppard	.25	.13	.08
34	Al Sims	.25	.13	.08
35	Dallas Smith	.25	.13	.08
36	Carol Vadnais	.25	.13	.08
37	Gary Bromley	.25	.13	.08
38	Larry Carriere	.25	.13	.08
39	Roger Crozier	.50	.25	.15
40	Rick Dudley	.25	.13	.08
41	Lee Fogolin	.50	.25	.15
42	Norm Gratton	.25	.13	.08
43	Jerry Korab	.25	.13	.08
44	Jim Lorentz	.25	.13	.08
45	Don Luce	.40	.20	.12
46	Richard Martin	.40	.20	.12
47	Gerry Meehan	.25	.13	.08
48	Larry Mickey	.25	.13	.08
49	Gilbert Perreault	2.50	1.25	.70
50	Craig Ramsay	.25	.13	.08
51	Rene Robert	.30	.15	.09
52	Mike Robitaille	.25	.13	.08
53	Jim Schoenfeld	.40	.20	.12
54	Brian Spencer	.25	.13	.08
55	Bruce Affleck	.25	.13	.08
56	Mike Christie	.25	.13	.08
57	Len Frig	.25	.13	.08
58	Stan Gilbertson	.25	.13	.08
59	Rick Hampton	.25	.13	.08
60	David Hrechkosy	.25	.13	.08
61	Ron Huston	.25	.13	.08
62	Joseph Johnston	.25	.13	.08
63	Wayne King	.25	.13	.08
64	Al MacAdam	.40	.20	.12
65	Ted McAneely	.25	.13	.08
66	Gilles Meloche	.50	.25	.15
67	Jim Neilson	.25	.13	.08
68	Larry Patey	.25	.13	.08
69	Craig Patrick	.25	.13	.08
70	Robert Stewart	.25	.13	.08
71	Stanley Weir	.25	.13	.08
72	Larry Wright	.25	.13	.08
73	Ivan Boldirev	.25	.13	.08
74	J.P. Bordeleau	.25	.13	.08
75	Tony Esposito	3.00	1.50	.90
76	Germain Gagnon	.25	.13	.08
77	Dennis Hull	.25	.13	.08
78	Doug Jarrett	.25	.13	.08
79	Cliff Koroll	.25	.13	.08
80	Keith Magnuson	.25	.13	.08
81	Chico Maki	.25	.13	.08
82	John Marks	.25	.13	.08
83	Pit Martin	.25	.13	.08
84	Stan Mikita	5.00	2.50	1.50
85	Jim Pappin	.40	.20	.12
86	Dick Redmond	.30	.15	.09
87	Darcy Rota	.25	.13	.08
88	Phil Russell	.25	.13	.08
89	Dale Tallon	.25	.13	.08
90	Bill White	.30	.15	.09
91	Red Berenson	.25	.13	.08
92	Thommie Bergman	.25	.13	.08
93	Guy Charron	.25	.13	.08
94	Marcel Dionne	3.00	1.50	.90
95	Danny Grant	.30	.15	.09
96	Doug Grant	.25	.13	.08
97	Jean Hamel	.25	.13	.08
98	Bill Hogaboam	.25	.13	.08
99	Pierre Jarry	.25	.13	.08
100	Nick Libett	.25	.13	.08
101	Bill Lochead	.25	.13	.08
102	Jack Lynch	.25	.13	.08
103	Henry Hawk	.25	.13	.08
104	Nelson Pyatt	.25	.13	.08
105	Mickey Redmond	.30	.15	.09
106	Doug Roberts	.25	.13	.08
107	Jim Rutherford	.25	.13	.08
108	Bryan Watson	.25	.13	.08
109	Robin Burns	.25	.13	.08
110	Gary Coalter	.25	.13	.08
111	Gary Croteau	.25	.13	.08
112	Chris Evans	.25	.13	.08
113	Ed Gilbert	.25	.13	.08
114	Doug Horbul	.25	.13	.08
115	Dave Hudson	.25	.13	.08
116	Brent Hughes	.25	.13	.08
117	Bryan Lefley	.25	.13	.08
118	Richard Lemieux	.25	.13	.08
119	Pete McDuffe	.25	.13	.08
120	Simon Nolet	.25	.13	.08
121	Dennis Patterson	.25	.13	.08
122	Michel Plasse	.25	.13	.08
123	Lynn Powis	.25	.13	.08
124	Randy Rota	.25	.13	.08
125	Ted Snell	.25	.13	.08
126	John Wright	.25	.13	.08
127	Bob Berry	.25	.13	.08
128	Gene Carr	.25	.13	.08
129	Mike Corrigan	.25	.13	.08

130	Gary Edwards	.50	.25	.15
131	Butch Goring	.75	.40	.25
132	Terry Harper	.25	.13	.08
133	Dave Hutchison	.25	.13	.08
134	Sheldon Kannegiesser	.25	.13	.08
135	Neil Komadoski	.25	.13	.08
136	Don Kozak	.25	.13	.08
137	Dan Maloney	.30	.15	.09
138	Bob Murdoch	.25	.13	.08
139	Mike Murphy	.30	.15	.09
140	Bob Nevin	.25	.13	.08
141	Frank St. Marseille	.25	.13	.08
142	Rogatien Vachon	2.50	1.25	.70
143	Juha Widing	.25	.13	.08
144	Tom Williams	.25	.13	.08
145	Chris Ahrens	.25	.13	.08
146	Fred Barrett	.25	.13	.08
147	Gary Bergman	.25	.13	.08
148	Henry Boucha	.25	.13	.08
149	Jude Drouin	.25	.13	.08
150	Blake Dunlop	.25	.13	.08
151	Barry Gibbs	.25	.13	.08
152	Bill Goldsworthy	.25	.13	.08
153	Dennis Hextall	.25	.13	.08
154	Cesare Maniago	1.00	.50	.30
155	Don Martineau	.25	.13	.08
156	Lou Nanne	.40	.20	.12
157	Dennis O'Brien	.25	.13	.08
158	Murray Oliver	.25	.13	.08
159	Jean Paul Parise	.25	.13	.08
160	Tom Reid	.25	.13	.08
161	Fern Rivard	.25	.13	.08
162	Fred Stanfield	.25	.13	.08
163	Pierre Bouchard	.25	.13	.08
164	Yvan Cournoyer	3.00	1.50	.90
165	Ken Dryden	15.00	7.50	4.50
166	Guy Lafleur	12.00	6.00	3.50
167	Yvon Lambert	.25	.13	.08
168	Jacques Laperriere	.50	.25	.15
169	Guy Lapointe	.50	.25	.15
170	Michel Larocque	.25	.13	.08
171	Claude Larose	.25	.13	.08
172	Chuck Lefley	.25	.13	.08
173	Jacques Lamaire	.50	.25	.15
174	Pete Mahovlich	.25	.13	.08
175	Henri Richard	1.50	.70	.45
176	Jim Roberts	.25	.13	.08
177	Larry Robinson	2.50	1.25	.70
178	Serge Savard	.50	.25	.15
179	Steve Shutt	.50	.25	.15
180	Murray Wilson	.25	.13	.08
181	Craig Cameron	.25	.13	.08
182	Clark Gillies	.50	.25	.15
183	Billy Harris	.25	.13	.08
184	Gerry Hart	.25	.13	.08
185	Lorne Henning	.25	.13	.08
186	Ernie Hicke	.25	.13	.08
187	Garry Howatt	.25	.13	.08
188	Dave Lewis	.25	.13	.08
189	Billy MacMillan	.25	.13	.08
190	Bert Marshall	.25	.13	.08
191	Bob Nystrom	.40	.20	.12
192	Denis Potvin	7.00	3.50	2.00
193	Jean Potvin	.25	.13	.08
194	Glenn Resch	1.00	.50	.30
195	Doug Rombough	.25	.13	.08
196	Billy Smith	1.00	.50	.30
197	Ralph Stewart	.25	.13	.08
198	Ed Westfall	.25	.13	.08
199	Jerry Butler	.25	.13	.08
200	Bill Fairbairn	.25	.13	.08
201	Ed Giacomin	2.00	1.00	.60
202	Rod Gilbert	.40	.20	.12
203	Ron Harris	.25	.13	.08
204	Ted Irvine	.25	.13	.08
205	Gilles Marotte	.25	.13	.08
206	Brad Park	1.50	.70	.45
207	Greg Polis	.25	.13	.08
208	Jean Ratelle	.40	.20	.12
209	Dale Rolfe	.25	.13	.08
210	Bobby Rousseau	.25	.13	.08
211	Derek Sanderson	1.00	.50	.30
212	Rod Seiling	.25	.13	.08
213	Pete Stemkowski	.30	.15	.09
214	Walt Tkaczuk	.30	.15	.09
215	Steve Vickers	.25	.13	.08
216	Gilles Villemure	.75	.40	.25
217	Bill Barber	.75	.40	.25
218	Tom Bladon	.25	.13	.08
219	Bobby Clarke	7.00	3.50	2.00
220	Bill Clement	.25	.13	.08
221	Terry Crisp	.30	.15	.09
222	Gary Dornhoefer	.30	.15	.09
223	Andre Dupont	.25	.13	.08
224	Bob Kelly	.25	.13	.08
225	Orest Kindrachuk	.25	.13	.08
226	Reggie Leach	.40	.20	.12
227	Ross Lonsberry	.25	.13	.08
228	Rick MacLeish	.25	.13	.08
229	Bernie Parent	5.00	2.50	1.50
230	Don Saleski	.25	.13	.08
231	Dave Schultz	.50	.25	.15
232	Ed Van Impe	.25	.13	.08
233	Jimmy Watson	.30	.15	.09
234	Joe Watson	.30	.15	.09
235	Syl Apps, Sr.	.25	.13	.08
236	Chuck Arnason	.25	.13	.08
237	Wayne Bianchin	.25	.13	.08
238	Dave Burrows	.25	.13	.08
239	Denis Herron	.60	.30	.20
240	Ron Schock	.25	.13	.08
241	Nelson Debenedet	.25	.13	.08
242	Ab DeMarco	.25	.13	.08
243	Steve Durbano	.25	.13	.08
244	Vic Hadfield	.75	.40	.25
245	Bob Johnson	.25	.13	.08
246	Rick Kehoe	.30	.15	.09
247	Bob Kelly	.25	.13	.08
248	Bobby Lalonde	.25	.13	.08
249	Lowell MacDonald	.25	.13	.08
250	Bob Paradise	.25	.13	.08
251	Jean Pronovost	.25	.13	.08
252	Ron Stackhouse	.25	.13	.08
253	Don Awrey	.25	.13	.08
254	Ace Bailey	.30	.15	.09
255	Bill Collins	.25	.13	.08
256	John Davidson	.75	.40	.25
257	Dave Gardner	.25	.13	.08
258	Bob Gassoff	.25	.13	.08
259	Larry Giroux	.25	.13	.08
260	Eddie Johnston	1.00	.50	.30
261	Wayne Merrick	.25	.13	.08
262	Brian Ogilvie	.25	.13	.08
263	Barclay Plager	.25	.13	.08
264	Bob Plager	.25	.13	.08
265	Pierre Plante	.25	.13	.08
266	Phil Roberto	.25	.13	.08
267	Larry Sacharuk	.25	.13	.08
268	Floyd Thomson	.25	.13	.08
269	Garry Unger	.50	.25	.15
270	Rick Wilson	.25	.13	.08
271	Willie Brossart	.25	.13	.08
272	Tim Ecclestone	.25	.13	.08
273	Ron Ellis	.30	.15	.09
274	Doug Favell	.60	.30	.20
275	Bill Flett	.25	.13	.08
276	Brian Glennie	.25	.13	.08
277	Inge Hammarstrom	.30	.15	.09
278	Dave Keon	.75	.40	.25
279	Lanny McDonald	3.50	1.75	1.00
280	Jim McKenny	.25	.13	.08
281	Bob Neely	.25	.13	.08
282	Gary Sabourin	.25	.13	.08
283	Borje Salming	.75	.40	.25
284	Darryl Sittler	3.00	1.50	.90
285	Errol Thompson	.25	.13	.08

286	Ian Turnbull	.25	.13	.08
287	Norm Ullman	.75	.40	.25
288	Dunc Wilson	.25	.13	.08
289	Gregg Boddy	.25	.13	.08
290	Paulin Bordeleau	.25	.13	.08
291	Andre Boudrias	.25	.13	.08
292	Bob Dailey	.25	.13	.08
293	Dave Dunn	.25	.13	.08
294	John Gould	.25	.13	.08
295	Jocelyn Guevremont	.30	.15	.09
296	Dennis Kearns	.40	.20	.12
297	Don Lever	.25	.13	.08
298	Ken Lockett	.25	.13	.08
299	Bryan McSheffrey	.25	.13	.08
300	Chris Oddleifson	.25	.13	.08
301	Gerry O'Flaherty	.25	.13	.08
302	Tracy Pratt	.25	.13	.08
303	Gary Smith	.25	.13	.08
304	Dennis Ververgaert	.25	.13	.08
305	Jim Wiley	.25	.13	.08
306	Barry Wilkins	.25	.13	.08
307	Ron H. Anderson	.25	.13	.08
308	Steve Atkinson	.25	.13	.08
309	Mike Bloom	.25	.13	.08
310	Gord Brooks	.25	.13	.08
311	Bob Collyard	.25	.13	.08
312	Jack Egers	.25	.13	.08
313	Lawrence Fullan	.25	.13	.08
314	Bob Gryp	.25	.13	.08
315	Jim Hrycuik	.25	.13	.08
316	Greg Joly	.30	.15	.09
317	Dave Kryskow	.25	.13	.08
318	Peter Laframboise	.25	.13	.08
319	Ron Low	.50	.25	.15
320	Joe Lundrigan	.25	.13	.08
321	Mike Marson	.25	.13	.08
322	Bill Mikkelson	.25	.13	.08
323	Doug Mohns	.25	.13	.08
324	Lew Morrison	.25	.13	.08

1982 McDonald's Stickers

These stickers, measuring 1 15/16" by 2 1/2" each, were issued in Canada only in the province of Quebec. Each front has a color action photo bordered by a red frame. The player's name is included in the blade of a hockey stick which runs along the right side. A McDonald's logo rests under the blade. A sticker number appears on the front and back. The back also has the player's name, position, team and instructions on how to apply the sticker - this is all in French and English. A McDonald's logo is also featured prominently on the card back. All-Star stickers are gold foils. A sticker album was also produced for the set.

		MT	NM	EX
Complete Set (36):		30.00	22.00	12.00
Common Player:		.50	.40	.20
1	Dan Bouchard	.50	.40	.20
2	Richard Brodeur	.60	.45	.25
3	Gilles Meloche	.40	.30	.15
4	Billy Smith	1.00	.70	.40
5	Richard Wamsley	.40	.30	.15
6	Mike Bossy	1.50	1.25	.60
7	Dino Ciccarelli	.75	.60	.30
8	Guy Lafleur	1.25	.90	.50
9	Rick Middleton	.60	.45	.25
10	Marian Stastny	.50	.40	.20
11	Bill Barber	.60	.45	.25
12	Bob Gainey	.75	.60	.30
13	Clark Gillies	.60	.45	.25
14	Michel Goulet	.75	.60	.30
15	Mark Messier	3.00	2.25	1.25
16	Billy Smith	.60	.45	.25
17	Larry Robinson	.60	.45	.25
18	Denis Potvin	.60	.45	.25

19	Michel Goulet	.60	.45	.25
20	Wayne Gretzky	4.00	3.00	1.50
21	Mike Bossy	.75	.60	.30
22	Wayne Gretzky	7.00	5.25	2.75
23	Denis Savard	.75	.60	.30
24	Peter Stastny	.75	.60	.30
25	Bryan Trottier	1.00	.70	.40
26	Douglas Wickenheiser	.50	.40	.20
27	Barry Beck	.50	.40	.20
28	Raymond Bourque	1.50	1.25	.60
29	Brian Engblom	.50	.40	.20
30	Craig Hartsburg	.50	.40	.20
31	Mark Howe	.60	.45	.25
32	Rod Langway	.60	.45	.25
33	Denis Potvin	.75	.60	.30
34	Larry Robinson	1.00	.70	.40
35	Norman Rochefort	.40	.30	.15
36	Douglas Wilson	.60	.45	.25

1968 O-Pee-Chee Stickers

These adhesive-backed stickers were included in 1968-69 O-Pee-Chee packs, one per pack. The sticker, in the form of a puck, measures 2 1/2" by 3 1/2" and is perforated so it could be pushed out. Application instructions are given on the front of the card, but keeping the sticker intact is recommended. The front has a card number; the puck has a color mug shot of the featured player, and lists his team and position. The stickers were printed in Canada.

		NM	EX	VG
Complete Set (22):		275.00	137.00	82.00
Common Player:		3.00	1.50	.90
1	Stan Mikita	11.00	5.50	3.25
2	Frank Mahovlich	11.00	5.50	3.25
3	Bobby Hull	30.00	15.00	9.00
4	Bobby Orr	50.00	25.00	15.00
5	Phil Esposito	17.00	8.50	5.00
6	Gump Worsley	10.00	5.00	3.00
7	Jean Beliveau	17.00	8.50	5.00
8	Elmer Vasko	3.00	1.50	.90
9	Rod Gilbert	7.50	3.75	2.25
10	Roger Crozier	3.00	1.50	.90
11	Lou Angotti	3.00	1.50	.90
12	Charlie Hodge	3.00	1.50	.90
13	Glenn Hall	10.00	5.00	3.00
14	Doug Harvey	10.00	5.00	3.00
15	Jacques Plante	14.00	7.00	4.25
16	Allan Stanley	8.00	4.00	2.50
17	Johnny Bower	9.00	4.50	2.75
18	Tim Horton	10.00	5.00	3.00
19	Dave Keon	11.00	5.50	3.25
20	Terry Sawchuk	14.00	7.00	4.25
21	Henri Richard	10.00	5.00	3.00
22	Gordie Howe (700th Goal)	55.00	27.00	16.50

Values for recent stamps/stickers are listed in Mint (MT), Near Mint (NM), reflecting the fact that many stamps/stickers from recent years have been preserved in top condition. Recent cards and sets in less than Excellent condition have little collector interest.

1969 O-Pee-Chee Mini Stickers

These adhesive-backed stickers were inserts in 1969-70 O-Pee- Chee Series II packs. The color cards are 2 1/2" by 3 1/2" but each features four smaller cards each measuring 1" by 1 1/2". The mini cards are perforated so they could be fastened to small team album which were also produced. The mini card has a mug shot of the player and his team and position are also listed. The cards are unnumbered.

		NM	EX	VG
Complete Set (72):		800.00	400.00	240.00
Common Player:		30.00	15.00	9.00
1	Bob Baun, Ken Schinkel, Tim Horton, Bernie Parent	40.00	20.00	12.00
2	Les Binkley, Ken Hodge, Sr., Reggin Fleming, Jacques Laperriere	30.00	15.00	9.00
3	Yvan Cournoyer, Jim Neilson, Gary Sabourin, John Miszuk	30.00	15.00	9.00
4	Bruce Gamble, Carol Vadnais, Frank Mahovlich, Larry Hillman	45.00	22.00	13.50
5	Ed Giacomin, Jean Beliveau, Eddie Joyal, Leo Bolvin	50.00	25.00	15.00
6	Phil Goyette, Doug Jarrett, Ted Green, Bill Hicke	30.00	15.00	9.00
7	Ted Hampson, Carl Brewer, Denis DeJordy, Leon Rochefort	30.00	15.00	9.00
8	Charlie Hodge, Pat Quinn, Derek Sanderson, Duane Rupp	30.00	15.00	9.00
9	Earl Engarfield, Jim Roberts, Gump Worsley, Bobby Hull	100.00	50.00	30.00
10	Andre Lacroix, Bob Wall, Serge Savard, Roger Crozier	30.00	15.00	9.00
11	Cesare Maniago, Bobby Orr, Dave Keon, Jean-Guy Gendron	200.00	100.00	60.00
12	Keith McCreary, Claude Larose, Rod Gilbert, Gerry Cheevers	45.00	22.00	13.50
13	Stan Mikita, Al Arbour, Rod Seiling, Ron Schock	45.00	22.00	13.50
14	Doug Mohns, Bob Woytowich, Gordie Howe, Gerry Desjardins	150.00	75.00	45.00
15	Bob Nevin, Jacques Plante, Mike Walton, Ray Cullen	45.00	22.00	13.50
16	Bob Pulford, Henri Richard, Red Berenson, Eddie Shack	50.00	25.00	15.00
17	Pat Stapleton, Danny Grant, Bert Marshall, Jean Ratelle	30.00	15.00	9.00
18	Ed Van Impe, Dale Rolfe, Alex Delvecchio, Phil Esposito	65.00	32.00	19.50

1969 O-Pee-Chee Mini Stickers Albums

These team booklets were designed to hold the 1969-70 O-Pee-Chee four-in-one stickers. The booklets, which measure 2 1/2" by 3 1/2", are light green and have four pages in them to hold six team stickers. A booklet was made for each of the 12 NHL teams; player statistics are given for the corresponding stickers.

		NM	EX	VG
Complete Set (12):		75.00	37.00	22.00
Common Player:		7.50	3.75	2.25
1	Boston Bruins	10.00	5.00	3.00
2	Chicago Black Hawks	10.00	5.00	3.00
3	Detroit Red Wings	10.00	5.00	3.00
4	Los Angeles Kings	7.50	3.75	2.25
5	Minnesota North Stars	7.50	3.75	2.25
6	Montreal Canadiens	10.00	5.00	3.00
7	New York Rangers	10.00	5.00	3.00
8	Oakland Seals	7.50	3.75	2.25
9	Philadelphia Flyers	10.00	5.00	3.00
10	Pittsburgh Penguins	7.50	3.75	2.25
11	St. Louis Blues	7.50	3.75	2.25
12	Toronto Maple Leafs	10.00	5.00	3.00

1969 O-Pee-Chee Stamps

These stickers were made to be applied to the backs of the corresponding cards in the 1969-70 O-Pee-Chee hockey cards. The stamps were included in Series I 1969-70 O-Pee-Chee packs. The stamps were produced in pairs; it is recommended that collectors keep them intact, and not apply them to the cards because that will devalue them. Stickers that are kept together are generally twice the value of the individually listed values. The front of the sticker has a black-and-white photo of the featured player, plus a red cartoon hockey player. Each stamp is 1 1/2" by 1 1/4" and is unnumbered; they are checklisted alphabetically. The stickers were made for the regular O-Pee-Chee cards numbered 6, 10, 12, 20, 24, 27, 30, 33, 37, 42, 51 61, 62, 70, 76, 82, 86, 89, 98, 99, 108, 110, 114, 125 and 130.

		NM	EX	VG
Complete Set (26):		100.00	50.00	30.00
Common Player:		2.00	1.00	.60
(1)	Jean Beliveau	10.00	5.00	3.00
(2)	Red Berenson	2.00	1.00	.60
(3)	Les Binkley	2.00	1.00	.60
(4)	Yvan Cournoyer			
(5)	Ray Cullen	2.00	1.00	.60
(6)	Gerry Desiardins	2.00	1.00	.60
(7)	Phil Esposito	10.00	5.00	3.00
(8)	Ed Giacomin	5.00	2.50	1.50
(9)	Rod Gilbert	5.00	2.50	1.50
(10)	Danny Grant	2.00	1.00	.60
(11)	Glenn Hall	6.00	3.00	1.75
(12)	Ted Hampson	2.00	1.00	.60
(13)	Ken Hodge, Sr.	2.50	1.25	.70
(14)	Gordie Howe	25.00	12.50	7.50
(15)	Bobby Hull	12.50	6.25	3.75
(16)	Eddie Joyal	2.00	1.00	.60
(17)	Dave Keon	6.00	3.00	1.75
(18)	Andre Lacroix	2.00	1.00	.60
(19)	Frank Mahovlich	8.00	4.00	2.50
(20)	Keith McCreary	2.00	1.00	.60
(21)	Stan Mikita	8.00	4.00	2.50
(22)	Bobby Orr	25.00	12.50	7.50
(23)	Bernie Parent	7.50	3.75	2.25
(24)	Jean Ratelle	5.00	2.50	1.50
(25)	Norm Ullman	5.00	2.50	1.50
(26)	Carol Vadnais	2.00	1.00	.60

1970 O-Pee-Chee Stickers

These 2 1/2" by 3 1/2" stickers were inserts in 1970-71 O-Pee- Chee packs. Each unnumbered peel-off sticker has a color photo on the front, with an oval frame. The player's name and team name are also included on the front.

		NM	EX	VG
Complete Set (33):		250.00	125.00	75.00
Common Player:		2.50	1.25	.70
1	Jean Beliveau	15.00	7.50	4.50
2	Red Berenson	2.50	1.25	.70
3	Wayne Carleton	2.50	1.25	.70
4	Tim Ecclestone	2.50	1.25	.70
5	Ron Ellis	2.50	1.25	.70
6	Phil Esposito	17.00	8.50	5.00

7	Tony Esposito	15.00	7.50	4.50
8	Bill Flett	3.50	1.75	1.00
9	Ed Giacomin	4.50	2.25	1.25
10	Rod Gilbert	5.00	2.50	1.50
11	Danny Grant	2.50	1.25	.70
12	Bill Hicke	2.50	1.25	.70
13	Gordie Howe	40.00	20.00	12.00
14	Bobby Hull	30.00	15.00	9.00
15	Earl Engarfield	3.50	1.75	1.00
16	Eddie Joyal	2.50	1.25	.70
17	Dave Keon	5.00	2.50	1.50
18	Andre Lacroix	2.50	1.25	.70
19	Jacques Laperriere	3.50	1.75	1.00
20	Jacques Lemaire	4.50	2.25	1.25
21	Frank Mahovlich	10.00	5.00	3.00
22	Keith McCreary	2.50	1.25	.70
23	Stan Mikita	10.00	5.00	3.00
24	Bobby Orr	50.00	25.00	15.00
25	Jean Paul Parise	4.00	2.00	1.25
26	Jean Ratelle	4.00	2.00	1.25
27	Derek Sanderson	2.50	1.25	.70
28	Frank St. Marseille	2.50	1.25	.70
29	Ron Schock	2.50	1.25	.70
30	Garry Unger	2.50	1.25	.70
31	Carol Vadnais	2.50	1.25	.70
32	Ed Van Impe	2.50	1.25	.70
33	Bob Woytowich	2.50	1.25	.70

1972 O-Pee-Chee Player Stickers

These 1972-73 O-Pee-Chee Series I inserts feature cardboard player crest stickers which were designed to be popped out from the card. This is not recommended. The front numbered and does include application instructions on it in French and English. The crest sticker is in color and features a closeup shot of the player, his name, position and team. The adhesive-back back is blank.

		NM	EX	VG
Complete Set (22):		85.00	42.00	25.00
Common Player:		2.00	1.00	.60
1	Pat Quinn	2.50	1.25	.70
2	Phil Esposito	10.00	5.00	3.00
3	Bobby Orr	35.00	17.50	10.50
4	Richard Martin	2.50	1.25	.70
5	Stan Mikita	8.00	4.00	2.50
6	Bill White	2.00	1.00	.60
7	Red Berenson	2.50	1.25	.70
8	Gary Bergman	2.00	1.00	.60
9	Gary Edwards	2.00	1.00	.60
10	Bill Goldsworthy	2.50	1.25	.70
11	Jacques Laperriere	2.50	1.25	.70
12	Ken Dryden	13.00	6.50	4.00
13	Ed Westfall	2.50	1.25	.70
14	Walt Tkaczuk	2.50	1.25	.70
15	Brad Park	5.00	2.50	1.50
16	Doug Favell	2.00	1.00	.60
17	Eddie Shack	3.00	1.50	.90
18	Jacques Caron	2.00	1.00	.60
19	Paul Henderson	2.50	1.25	.70
20	Jim Harrison	2.00	1.00	.60
21	Dale Tallon	2.00	1.00	.60
22	Orland Kurtenbach	2.50	1.25	.70

1981 O-Pee-Chee Stickers

These stickers, which each measure 2" by 2 1/2", are bilingual, presenting information on the back in French and English. The front has a full-color action photo, framed by a inner colored border and an outer white border. A sticker number appears in the lower left corner. The back also has a sticker number, along with the player's name, team, a 1981 O-Pee-Chee copyright date, and information about an album offered through the mail. Instructions are also given on how to apply the stickers to the album. Stickers were also available through a mail-in offer. Several stickers in the set are foils, to honor significant events and stars. Their numbers are: 1-6, 19, 27-28, 144-157, 251, 254, 257, 260, 262 and 265.

		MT	NM	EX
Complete Set (269):		35.00	26.00	14.00
Common Player:		.05	.04	.02
1	The Stanley Cup	.25	.20	.10
2	The Stanley Cup	.15	.11	.06
3	The Stanley Cup	.15	.11	.06
4	The Stanley Cup	.15	.11	.06
5	The Stanley Cup	.15	.11	.06
6	The Stanley Cup	.15	.11	.06
7	Oiler vs. Islanders	.05	.04	.02
8	Oiler vs. Islanders	.05	.04	.02
9	Oiler vs. Islanders	.05	.04	.02
10	Oiler vs. Islanders	.05	.04	.02
11	Jari Kurri	1.25	.90	.50
12	Pat Riggin	.05	.04	.02
13	Flames vs. Flyers	.05	.04	.02
14	Flames vs. Flyers	.05	.04	.02
15	Flames vs. Flyers	.05	.04	.02
16	Flames vs. Flyers	.05	.04	.02
17	Stanley Cup Winners 1980/81 NY Islander	.05	.04	.02
18	Stanley Cup Winners 1980/81 NY Islander	.05	.04	.02
19	Conn Smythe Trophy MVP-Finals	.20	.15	.08
20	Most Valuable Player (Butch Goring)	.05	.04	.02
21	North Stars vs. Islanders	.05	.04	.02
22	Steve Payne	.05	.04	.02
23	North Stars vs. Islanders	.05	.04	.02
24	North Stars vs. Islanders	.05	.04	.02
25	North Stars vs. Islanders	.05	.04	.02
26	North Stars vs. Islanders	.05	.04	.02
27	Prince of Wales Trophy	.15	.11	.06
28	Prince of Wales Trophy	.15	.11	.06
29	Guy Lafleur	.35	.25	.14
30	Bob Gainey	.20	.15	.08
31	Larry Robinson	.20	.15	.08
32	Steve Shutt	.15	.11	.06
33	Brian Engblom	.05	.04	.02
34	Doug Jarvis	.05	.04	.02
35	Yvon Lambert	.05	.04	.02
36	Mark Napier	.05	.04	.02
37	Rejean Houle	.05	.04	.02
38	Pierre Larouche	.07	.05	.03
39	Rod Langway	.15	.11	.06
40	Richard Sevigny	.05	.04	.02
41	Guy Lafleur	.35	.25	.14
42	Larry Robinson	.20	.15	.08
43	Bob Gainey	.20	.15	.08
44	Steve Shutt	.15	.11	.06
45	Rick Middleton	.10	.08	.04
46	Peter McNab	.05	.04	.02
47	Rogatien Vachon	.25	.20	.10
48	Brad Park	.20	.15	.08
49	Raymond Bourque	.75	.60	.30
50	Terry O'Reilly	.07	.05	.03
51	Stephen Kasper	.07	.05	.03
52	Dwight Foster	.05	.04	.02
53	Danny Gare	.05	.04	.02
54	Andre Savard	.07	.05	.03
55	Don Edwards	.07	.05	.03
56	Bob Sauve	.07	.05	.03
57	Anthony McKegney	.05	.04	.02
58	John Van Boxmeer	.05	.04	.02
59	Derek Smith	.05	.04	.02
60	Gilbert Perreault	.20	.15	.08
61	Mike Rogers	.05	.04	.02
62	Mark Howe	.12	.09	.05
63	Blaine Stoughton	.05	.04	.02
64	Rick Ley	.05	.04	.02
65	Jordy Douglas	.05	.04	.02
66	Al Sims	.05	.04	.02

67	Norm Barnes	.05	.04	.02	145	Mark Howe	.30	.25	.12
68	John Garrett	.05	.04	.02	146	Donald Beaupre	.40	.30	.15
69	Peter Stastny	1.25	.90	.50	147	Marcel Dionne	.50	.40	.20
70	Anton Stastny	.07	.05	.03	148	Larry Robinson	.45	.35	.20
71	Jacques Richard	.05	.04	.02	149	David Taylor	.25	.20	.10
72	Robbie Ftorek	.07	.05	.03	150	Mike Bossy	.75	.60	.30
73	Dan Bouchard	.05	.04	.02	151	Denis Potvin	.50	.40	.20
74	Real Cloutier	.05	.04	.02	152	Bryan Trottier	.50	.40	.20
75	Michel Goulet	.75	.60	.30	153	Michael Liut	.25	.20	.10
76	Marc Tardif	.07	.05	.03	154	George (Rob) Ramage	.20	.15	.08
77	Capitals vs. Maple Leafs	.05	.04	.02	155	Bill Barber	.30	.25	.12
78	Capitals vs. Maple Leafs	.05	.04	.02	156	Campbell Bowl	.15	.11	.06
79	Capitals vs. Maple Leafs	.05	.04	.02	157	Campbell Bowl	.15	.11	.06
80	Capitals vs. Maple Leafs	.05	.04	.02	158	Mike Bossy	.40	.30	.15
81	Whalers vs. Capitals	.05	.04	.02	159	Denis Potvin	.25	.20	.10
82	Whalers vs. Capitals	.05	.04	.02	160	Bryan Trottier	.25	.20	.10
83	Canadiens vs. Capitals	.05	.04	.02	161	Billy Smith	.15	.11	.06
84	Dan Bouchard	.05	.04	.02	162	Anders Kallur	.05	.04	.02
85	North Stars vs. Capitals	.05	.04	.02	163	Bob Bourne	.05	.04	.02
86	North Stars vs. Capitals	.05	.04	.02	164	Clark Gillies	.07	.05	.03
87	Bruins vs. Capitals	.05	.04	.02	165	Ken Morrow	.07	.05	.03
88	Robert Smith	.25	.20	.10	166	Anders Hedberg	.07	.05	.03
89	Donald Beaupre	.15	.11	.06	167	Ronald Greschner	.07	.05	.03
90	Al MacAdam	.05	.04	.02	168	Barry Beck	.07	.05	.03
91	Craig Hartsburg	.05	.04	.02	169	Eddie Johnstone	.05	.04	.02
92	Steve Payne	.05	.04	.02	170	Donald Maloney	.05	.04	.02
93	Gilles Meloche	.07	.05	.03	171	Ron Duguay	.07	.05	.03
94	Tim Young	.05	.04	.02	172	Ulf Nilsson	.07	.05	.03
95	Tom McCarthy	.05	.04	.02	173	Dave Maloney	.07	.05	.03
96	Wilf Paiement	.05	.04	.02	174	Bill Barber	.15	.11	.06
97	Darryl Sittler	.20	.15	.08	175	Behn Wilson	.05	.04	.02
98	Borje Salming	.15	.11	.06	176	Ken Linseman	.07	.05	.03
99	Bill Derlago	.05	.04	.02	177	Peter Peeters	.15	.11	.06
100	Ian Turnbull	.05	.04	.02	178	Bobby Clarke	.25	.20	.10
101	Richard Vaive	.10	.08	.04	179	Paul Holmgren	.07	.05	.03
102	Dan Maloney	.05	.04	.02	180	Brian Propp	.15	.11	.06
103	Laurie Boschman	.05	.04	.02	181	Reggie Leach	.07	.05	.03
104	Pat Hickey	.05	.04	.02	182	Rick Kehoe	.07	.05	.03
105	Michel Larocque	.07	.05	.03	183	Randy Carlyle	.07	.05	.03
106	Jiri Crha	.05	.04	.02	184	George Ferguson	.05	.04	.02
107	John Anderson	.07	.05	.03	185	Peter Lee	.05	.04	.02
108	Bill Derlago	.05	.04	.02	186	Rod Schutt	.05	.04	.02
109	Darryl Sittler	.20	.15	.08	187	Paul Gardner	.05	.04	.02
110	Wilf Paiement	.05	.04	.02	188	Ron Stackhouse	.05	.04	.02
111	Borje Salming	.15	.11	.06	189	Mario Faubert	.05	.04	.02
112	Denis Savard	1.25	.90	.50	190	Michael Gartner	1.00	.70	.40
113	Tony Esposito	.25	.20	.10	191	Dennis Maruk	.07	.05	.03
114	Tom Lysiak	.05	.04	.02	192	Ryan Walter	.07	.05	.03
115	Keith Brown	.10	.08	.04	193	Richard Green	.05	.04	.02
116	Glen Sharpley	.05	.04	.02	194	Mike Palmateer	.07	.05	.03
117	Terry Ruskowski	.07	.05	.03	195	Bob Kelly	.07	.05	.03
118	Reg Kerr	.05	.04	.02	196	Jean Pronovost	.07	.05	.03
119	Bob Murray	.05	.04	.02	197	Al Hangsleben	.05	.04	.02
120	Dale McCourt	.05	.04	.02	198	Flames vs. Capitals	.05	.04	.02
121	John Ogrodnick	.10	.08	.04	199	Oilers vs. Islanders	.05	.04	.02
122	Mike Foligno	.07	.05	.03	200	Oilers vs. Islanders	.05	.04	.02
123	Gilles Gilbert	.07	.05	.03	201	Oilers vs. Islanders	.05	.04	.02
124	Reed Larson	.05	.04	.02	202	Oilers vs. Islanders	.05	.04	.02
125	Vaclav Nedomansky	.05	.04	.02	203	Rangers vs. Islanders	.05	.04	.02
126	Willie Huber	.05	.04	.02	204	Rangers vs. Islanders	.05	.04	.02
127	James Korn	.05	.04	.02	205	Flyers vs. Capitals	.05	.04	.12
128	Bernie Federko	.15	.11	.06	206	Flyers vs. Capitals	.05	.04	.02
129	Michael Liut	.15	.11	.06	207	Rangers vs. Capitals	.05	.04	.02
130	Wayne Babych	.05	.04	.02	208	Canadiens vs. Capitals	.05	.04	.02
131	Blake Dunlop	.05	.04	.02	209	Wayne Gretzky	6.00	4.50	2.50
132	Mike Zuke	.05	.04	.02	210	Mark Messier	2.50	2.00	1.00
133	Brian Sutter	.15	.11	.06	211	Jari Kurri	1.25	.90	.50
134	Rick Lapointe	.05	.04	.02	212	Brett Callighen	.05	.04	.02
135	Jorgen Pettersson	.05	.04	.02	213	Matti Hagman	.05	.04	.02
136	Dave Christian	.15	.11	.06	214	Risto Siltanen	.05	.04	.02
137	David Babych	.07	.05	.03	215	Lee Fogolin	.05	.04	.02
138	Morris Lukowich	.05	.04	.02	216	Ed Mio	.07	.05	.03
139	Norm Dupont	.05	.04	.02	217	Glenn Anderson	.60	.45	.25
140	Ronald Wilson	.05	.04	.02	218	Karl Nilsson	.07	.05	.03
141	Danny Geoffrion	.05	.04	.02	219	Guy Chouinard	.07	.05	.03
142	Barry Long	.05	.04	.02	220	Eric Vail	.07	.05	.03
143	Pierre Hamel	.05	.04	.02	221	Pat Riggin	.10	.08	.04
144	Charlie Simmer	.25	.20	.10	222	Willi Plett	.05	.04	.02

223	Pekka Rautakallio	.05	.04	.02	
224	Paul Reinhart	.07	.05	.03	
225	Bradley Marsh	.07	.05	.03	
226	Phil Russell	.05	.04	.02	
227	Lanny McDonald	.20	.15	.08	
228	Merlin Malinowski	.05	.04	.02	
229	George (Rob) Ramage	.15	.11	.06	
230	Glenn Resch	.12	.09	.05	
231	Ron Delorme	.05	.04	.02	
232	Lucien DeBlois	.05	.04	.02	
233	Paul Gagne	.05	.04	.02	
234	Joel Quenneville	.05	.04	.02	
235	Marcel Dionne	.25	.20	.10	
236	Charlie Simmer	.12	.09	.05	
237	David Taylor	.12	.09	.05	
238	Mario Lessard	.07	.05	.03	
239	Lawrence Murphy	.60	.45	.25	
240	Jerry Korab	.05	.04	.02	
241	Mike Murphy	.05	.04	.02	
242	Billy Harris	.05	.04	.02	
243	Thomas Gradin	.07	.05	.03	
244	Per-Olov Brasar	.05	.04	.02	
245	Glen Hanlon	.07	.05	.03	
246	Chris Oddleifson	.05	.04	.02	
247	David Williams	.07	.05	.03	
248	Kevin McCarthy	.05	.04	.02	
249	Dennis Kearns	.05	.04	.02	
250	Harold Snepsts	.07	.05	.03	
251	Art Ross Trophy, Most Points	.20	.15	.08	
252	Art Ross Trophy Winner: (Wayne Gretzky)	6.00	4.50	2.50	
253	Most Goals: (Mike Bossy)	.50	.40	.20	
254	Norris Trophy, Best Defenseman	.20	.15	.08	
255	James Norris Trophy Winner: (Randy Carlyle)	.07	.05	.03	
256	Vezina Trophy Winner: (Richard Sevigny)	.07	.05	.03	
257	Vezina Trophy Goal Tending - Team	.20	.15	.08	
258	Vezina Trophy Winner: (Denis Herron)	.07	.05	.03	
259	Vezina Trophy Winner: (Michel Larocque)	.07	.05	.03	
260	Lady Byng Trophy, Sportsmanship	.20	.15	.08	
261	Lady Byng Trophy Winner (Rick Kehoe)	.07	.05	.03	
262	Calder Trophy, Rookie of the Year	.20	.15	.08	
263	Calder Trophy Winner: (Peter Stastny)	1.25	.90	.50	
264	Hart Trophy Winner: (Wayne Gretzky)	6.00	4.50	2.50	
265	Hart Trophy, Most Valuable Player	.20	.15	.08	
266	Charlie Simmer	.15	.11	.06	
267	Marcel Dionne	.25	.20	.10	
268	David Taylor	.12	.09	.05	
269	Bob Gainey	.20	.15	.08	

1982 O-Pee-Chee Stickers

These stickers are similar to the Topps stickers issued the same year, except there are a few differences on the backs. Each front has a full-color action photo, with a number in the lower right corner. A number also appears on the back, which is bilingual and gives information about how to order an O-Pee-Chee album made to hold them. The stickers have a 1982 Topps Chewing Gum Inc. copyright and measure 2" by 2 1/2". Foils were also made for numbers 2, 44-45, 159-170, 238-239, 248, 250, 255, 260-261 and 263.

		MT	NM	EX
	Complete Set (263):	35.00	26.00	14.00
	Common Player:	.05	.04	.02
1	Conn Smythe Trophy: (Mike Bossy)	.40	.30	.15
2	Conn Smythe Trophy	.20	.15	.08
3	1981/82 Stanley Cup Winners: Islanders	.05	.04	.02
4	1981/82 Stanley Cup Winners: Islanders	.05	.04	.02
5	Stanley Cup Finals	.05	.04	.02
6	Stanley Cup Finals	.05	.04	.02
7	Richard Brodeur	.07	.05	.03
8	Victory	.05	.04	.02
9	Stanley Cup Finals	.05	.04	.02
10	Stanley Cup Finals	.05	.04	.02
11	Stanley Cup Playoffs	.05	.04	.02
12	Stanley Cup Playoffs	.05	.04	.02
13	Stanley Cup Playoffs	.05	.04	.02
14	Tom Lysiak	.05	.04	.02
15	Peter Stastny	.40	.30	.15
16	Stanley Cup Playoffs	.05	.04	.02
17	Stanley Cup Playoffs	.05	.04	.02
18	Stanley Cup Playoffs	.05	.04	.02
19	Peter Stastny	.40	.30	.15
20	Marian Stastny	.05	.04	.02
21	Marc Tardif	.05	.04	.02
22	Wilf Paiement	.05	.04	.02
23	Real Cloutier	.05	.04	.02
24	Anton Stastny	.07	.05	.03
25	Michel Goulet	.25	.20	.10
26	Dale Hunter	.20	.15	.08
27	Dan Bouchard	.05	.04	.02
28	Guy Lafleur	.30	.25	.12
29	Guy Lafleur	.30	.25	.12
30	Mario Tremblay	.05	.04	.02
31	Larry Robinson	.20	.15	.08
32	Steve Shutt	.15	.11	.06
33	Steve Shutt	.15	.11	.06
34	Rod Langway	.10	.08	.04
35	Pierre Mondou	.05	.04	.02
36	Bob Gainey	.15	.11	.06
37	Rick Wamsley	.07	.05	.03
38	Mark Napier	.05	.04	.02
39	Mark Napier	.05	.04	.02
40	Doug Jarvis	.07	.05	.03
41	Denis Heron	.07	.05	.03
42	Keith Acton	.05	.04	.02
43	Keith Acton	.05	.04	.02
44	Prince of Wales Trophy	.15	.11	.06
45	Prince of Wales Trophy	.15	.11	.06
46	Denis Potvin	.25	.20	.10
47	Bryan Trottier	.25	.20	.10
48	Bryan Trottier	.25	.20	.10
49	John Tonelli	.07	.05	.03
50	Mike Bossy	.40	.30	.15
51	Mike Bossy	.40	.30	.15
52	Duane Sutter	.10	.08	.04
53	Bob Bourne	.05	.04	.02
54	Clark Gillies	.07	.05	.03
55	Clark Gillies	.07	.05	.03
56	Brent Sutter	.25	.20	.10
57	Anders Kallur	.05	.04	.02
58	Ken Morrow	.07	.05	.03
59	Bob Nystrom	.05	.04	.02
60	Billy Smith	.20	.15	.08
61	Billy Smith	.20	.15	.08
62	Richard Vaive	.07	.05	.03
63	Richard Vaive	.07	.05	.03
64	Jim Benning	.05	.04	.02
65	Miroslav Frycer	.05	.04	.02
66	Terry Martin	.05	.04	.02
67	Bill Derlago	.05	.04	.02
68	Bill Derlago	.05	.04	.02
69	Rocky Saganiuk	.05	.04	.02
70	Vince Tremblay	.05	.04	.02
71	Bob Manno	.05	.04	.02
72	Dan Maloney	.07	.05	.03

#	Name				#	Name			
73	John Anderson	.05	.04	.02	151	Dennis Maruk	.07	.05	.03
74	John Anderson	.05	.04	.02	152	Ryan Walter	.07	.05	.03
75	Borje Salming	.10	.08	.04	153	Michael Gartner	.50	.40	.20
76	Borje Salming	.10	.08	.04	154	Robert Carpenter	.30	.25	.12
77	Michel Larocque	.07	.05	.03	155	Chris Valentine	.05	.04	.02
78	Rick Middleton	.10	.08	.04	156	Richard Green	.07	.05	.03
79	Rick Middleton	.10	.08	.04	157	Bengt-Aka Gustafsson	.05	.04	.02
80	Keith Crowder	.05	.04	.02	158	Dave Parro	.05	.04	.02
81	Stephen Kasper	.07	.05	.03	159	Mark Messier	1.50	1.25	.60
82	Brad Park	.15	.11	.06	160	Paul Coffey	1.50	1.25	.60
83	Peter McNab	.05	.04	.02	161	Grant Fuhr	1.50	1.25	.60
84	Peter McNab	.05	.04	.02	162	Wayne Gretzky	6.00	4.50	2.50
85	Terry O'Reilly	.07	.05	.03	163	Douglas Wilson, Jr.	.35	.25	.14
86	Raymond Bourque	.50	.40	.20	164	David Taylor	.25	.20	.10
87	Raymond Bourque	.50	.40	.20	165	Mike Bossy	.75	.60	.30
88	Tom Fergus	.05	.04	.02	166	Raymond Bourque	.75	.60	.30
89	Michael O'Connell	.05	.04	.02	167	Peter Stastny	.75	.60	.30
90	Byron (Brad) McCrimmon	.07	.05	.03	168	Michel Dion	.20	.15	.08
91	Don Marcotte	.05	.04	.02	169	Larry Robinson	.35	.25	.14
92	Barry Pederson	.07	.05	.03	170	Bill Barber	.30	.25	.12
93	Barry Pederson	.07	.05	.03	171	Denis Savard	.40	.30	.15
94	Mark Messier	1.25	.90	.50	172	Douglas Wilson, Jr.	.15	.11	.06
95	Grant Fuhr	1.25	.90	.50	173	Grant Mulvey	.07	.05	.03
96	Kevin Lowe	.35	.25	.14	174	Tom Lysiak	.07	.05	.03
97	Wayne Gretzky	5.00	3.75	2.00	175	Alan Secord	.07	.05	.03
98	Wayne Gretzky	5.00	3.75	2.00	176	Reg Kerr	.05	.04	.02
99	Glenn Anderson	.20	.15	.08	177	Tim Higgins	.05	.04	.02
100	Glenn Anderson	.20	.15	.08	178	Terry Ruskowski	.07	.05	.03
101	Dave Lumley	.05	.04	.02	179	John Ogrodnick	.07	.05	.03
102	Dave Hunter	.05	.04	.02	180	Reed Larson	.05	.04	.02
103	Matti Hagman	.05	.04	.02	181	Bob Sauve	.07	.05	.03
104	Paul Coffey	1.25	.90	.50	182	Mark Osborne	.05	.04	.02
105	Paul Coffey	1.25	.90	.50	183	Jim Schoenfeld	.07	.05	.03
106	Lee Fogolin	.05	.04	.02	184	Danny Gare	.07	.05	.03
107	Ron Low	.07	.05	.03	185	Willie Huber	.05	.04	.02
108	Jari Kurri	.50	.40	.20	186	Walt McKechnie	.05	.04	.02
109	Jari Kurri	.50	.40	.20	187	Paul Woods	.05	.04	.02
110	Bill Barber	.15	.11	.06	188	Robert Smith	.12	.09	.05
111	Brian Propp	.10	.08	.04	189	Dino Ciccarelli	.50	.40	.20
112	Ken Linseman	.07	.05	.03	190	Neal Broten	.25	.20	.10
113	Ron Flockhart	.07	.05	.03	191	Steve Payne	.07	.05	.03
114	Darryl Sittler	.15	.11	.06	192	Craig Hartsburg	.05	.04	.02
115	Bobby Clarke	.30	.25	.12	193	Donald Beaupre	.12	.09	.05
116	Paul Holmgren	.07	.05	.03	194	Steve Christoff	.07	.05	.03
117	Peter Peeters	.10	.08	.04	195	Gilles Meloche	.07	.05	.03
118	Gilbert Perreault	.20	.15	.08	196	Michael Liut	.10	.08	.04
119	Dale McCourt	.05	.04	.02	197	Bernie Federko	.12	.09	.05
120	Mike Foligno	.05	.04	.02	198	Brian Sutter	.12	.09	.05
121	John Van Boxmeer	.05	.04	.02	199	Blake Dunlop	.05	.04	.02
122	Anthony McKegney	.07	.05	.03	200	Joe Mullen	1.50	1.25	.60
123	Ric Seiling	.05	.04	.02	201	Wayne Babych	.05	.04	.02
124	Don Edwards	.07	.05	.03	202	Jorgen Pettersson	.05	.04	.02
125	Yvon Lambert	.05	.04	.02	203	Perry Turnbull	.05	.04	.02
126	Blaine Stoughton	.07	.05	.03	204	Dale Hawerchuk	2.00	1.50	.80
127	Pierre Larouche	.07	.05	.03	205	Morris Lukowich	.05	.04	.02
128	Douglas Sulliman	.05	.04	.02	206	Dave Christian	.07	.05	.03
129	Ron Francis	1.25	.90	.50	207	David Babych	.07	.05	.03
130	Greg Millen	.07	.05	.03	208	Paul MacLean	.10	.08	.04
131	Mark Howe	.10	.08	.04	209	Willy Lindstrom	.05	.04	.02
132	Christopher Kotsopoulos	.05	.04	.02	210	Ed Staniowski	.05	.04	.02
133	Garry Howatt	.05	.04	.02	211	Doug Soetaert	.05	.04	.02
134	Ron Duguay	.07	.05	.03	212	Lucien DeBlois	.05	.04	.02
135	Barry Beck	.07	.05	.03	213	Mel Bridgman	.05	.04	.02
136	Mike Rogers	.05	.04	.02	214	Lanny McDonald	.20	.15	.08
137	Donald Maloney	.05	.04	.02	215	Guy Chouinard	.05	.04	.02
138	Mark Pavelich	.07	.05	.03	216	James Peplinski	.07	.05	.03
139	Eddie Johnstone	.05	.04	.02	217	Kent Nilsson	.07	.05	.03
140	Dave Maloney	.05	.04	.02	218	Pekka Rautakallio	.07	.05	.03
141	Stephan Weeks	.07	.05	.03	219	Paul Reinhart	.07	.05	.03
142	Ed Mio	.07	.05	.03	220	Kevin LaVallee	.05	.04	.02
143	Rick Kehoe	.07	.05	.03	221	Ken Houston	.05	.04	.02
144	Randy Carlyle	.07	.05	.03	222	Glenn Resch	.12	.09	.05
145	Paul Gardner	.05	.04	.02	223	George (Rob) Ramage	.07	.05	.03
146	Michel Dion	.07	.05	.03	224	Don Lever	.05	.04	.02
147	Rick MacLeish	.10	.08	.04	225	Bob MacMillan	.05	.04	.02
148	Pat Boutette	.05	.04	.02	226	Steve Tambellini	.05	.04	.02
149	Mike Bullard	.07	.05	.03	227	Brent Ashton	.05	.04	.02
150	George Ferguson	.05	.04	.02	228	Bob Lorimer	.05	.04	.02

		MT	NM	EX
229	Merlin Malinowski	.05	.04	.02
230	Marcel Dionne	.25	.20	.10
231	David Taylor	.10	.08	.04
232	Lawrence Murphy	.25	.20	.10
233	Steve Bozek	.05	.04	.02
234	Greg Terrion	.05	.04	.02
235	Jim Fox	.05	.04	.02
236	Marion Lessard	.07	.05	.03
237	Charlie Simmer	.12	.09	.05
238	Campbell Bowl	.15	.11	.06
239	Campbell Bowl	.15	.11	.06
240	Thomas Gradin	.07	.05	.03
241	Ivan Boldirev	.05	.04	.02
242	Stanley Smyl	.07	.05	.03
243	Harold Snepsts	.07	.05	.03
244	Curt Fraser	.05	.04	.02
245	Lars Molin	.05	.04	.02
246	Kevin McCarthy	.05	.04	.02
247	Richard Brodeur	.07	.05	.03
248	Calder Trophy	.15	.11	.06
249	Calder Trophy Winner: Rookie of the Yea (Dale Hawerchuk)	1.25	.90	.50
250	Vezina Trophy	.15	.11	.06
251	Vezina Trophy: Most Valuable Goalie (Billy Smith)	.12	.09	.05
252	William Jennings Trophy Winners: (Denis Heron, Rick Gamsley)	.07	.05	.03
253	Frank J. Selke Trophy Winner: (Stephen Kasper)	.07	.05	.03
254	Norris Trophy Winner: (Douglas Wilson, Jr.)	.15	.11	.06
255	Norris Trophy	.20	.15	.08
256	Art Ross Trophy Winner: (Wayne Gretzky)	3.00	2.25	1.25
257	Wayne Gretzky	3.00	2.25	1.25
258	Wayne Gretzky	3.00	2.25	1.25
259	Wayne Gretzky	3.00	2.25	1.25
260	Hart Trophy	.15	.11	.06
261	Art Ross Trophy	.15	.11	.06
262	Lady Byng Trophy Winner: Sportmanship (Rick Middleton)	.10	.08	.04
263	Lady Byng Trophy	.20	.15	.08

1983 O-Pee-Chee Stickers

These cards are once again similar to the Topps stickers of the same year, except for differences on the backs. The front has a full-color action photo, bordered by a white frame. The sticker number appears in the lower left corner. The back is bilingual and includes the sticker number and player's name in the center. Information about how to order an album to hold the stickers is also presented above and below the name and number; above material is in English, while that below is in French. "1983 Season Saison" is at the bottom of the sticker, along with instructions on how to apply the sticker and a 1983 O-Pee-Chee copyright. Foils were numbers 1-4, 15, 22-24, 299-300, 304-305, 308-311, 314-315 and 319-330. All-Stars are stickers 160-171. The stickers measure 1 15/16" by 2 9/16".

		MT	NM	EX
Complete Set (330):		30.00	22.00	12.00
Common Player:		.05	.04	.02
1	Marcel Dionne	.40	.30	.15
2	Guy Lafleur	.60	.45	.25
3	Darryl Sittler	.35	.25	.14
4	Gilbert Perreault	.35	.25	.14
5	Bill Barber	.15	.11	.06
6	Steve Shutt	.15	.11	.06
7	Wayne Gretzky	4.50	3.50	1.75
8	Lanny McDonald	.20	.15	.08
9	Reggie Leach	.07	.05	.03
10	Mike Bossy	.40	.30	.15
11	Rick Kehoe	.07	.05	.03
12	Bobby Clarke	.30	.25	.12
13	Butch Goring	.07	.05	.03
14	Rick Middleton	.10	.08	.04
15	Conn Smythe Trophy	.20	.15	.08
16	Conn Smythe Trophy Winner: MVP Finals (Billy Smith)	.15	.11	.06
17	Lee Fogolin	.05	.04	.02
18	Stanley Cup Finals	.05	.04	.02
19	Stanley Cup Finals	.05	.04	.02
20	Stanley Cup Finals	.05	.04	.02
21	Stanley Cup Finals	.05	.04	.02
22	Stanley Cup	.15	.11	.06
23	Stanley Cup	.15	.11	.06
24	Stanley Cup	.15	.11	.06
25	Richard Vaive	.07	.05	.03
26	Richard Vaive	.07	.05	.03
27	Billy Harris	.05	.04	.02
28	Dan Daoust	.05	.04	.02
29	Dan Daoust	.05	.04	.02
30	John Anderson	.05	.04	.02
31	John Anderson	.05	.04	.02
32	Peter Ihnacak	.05	.04	.02
33	Borje Salming	.10	.08	.04
34	Borje Salming	.10	.08	.04
35	Bill Derlago	.05	.04	.02
36	Rick St. Croix	.05	.04	.02
37	Greg Terrion	.05	.04	.02
38	Miroslav Frycer	.05	.04	.02
39	Mike Palmateer	.07	.05	.03
40	Gaston Gingras	.05	.04	.02
41	Peter Peeters	.07	.05	.03
42	Peter Peeters	.07	.05	.03
43	Michael Krushelnyski	.07	.05	.03
44	Rick Middleton	.10	.08	.04
45	Rick Middleton	.10	.08	.04
46	Raymond Bourque	.50	.40	.20
47	Raymond Bourque	.50	.40	.20
48	Brad Park	.20	.15	.08
49	Barry Pederson	.07	.05	.03
50	Barry Pederson	.07	.05	.03
51	Peter McNab	.05	.04	.02
52	Michael O'Connell	.05	.04	.02
53	Stephen Kasper	.07	.05	.03
54	Marty Howe	.05	.04	.02
55	Tom Fergus	.05	.04	.02
56	Keith Crowder	.05	.04	.02
57	Steve Shutt	.15	.11	.06
58	Guy Lafleur	.30	.25	.12
59	Guy Lafleur	.30	.25	.12
60	Larry Robinson	.20	.15	.08
61	Larry Robinson	.20	.15	.08
62	Ryan Walter	.07	.05	.03
63	Ryan Walter	.07	.05	.03
64	Mark Napier	.07	.05	.03
65	Mark Napier	.07	.05	.03
66	Bob Gainey	.15	.11	.06
67	Douglas Wickenheiser	.05	.04	.02
68	Pierre Mondou	.05	.04	.02
69	Mario Tremblay	.05	.04	.02
70	Gilbert Delorme	.05	.04	.02
71	Mats Naslund	.25	.20	.10
72	Rick Wamsley	.07	.05	.03
73	Ken Morrow	.07	.05	.03
74	John Tonelli	.07	.05	.03
75	John Tonelli	.07	.05	.03
76	Bryan Trottier	.25	.20	.10
77	Bryan Trottier	.25	.20	.10
78	Mike Bossy	.40	.30	.15
79	Mike Bossy	.40	.30	.15
80	Bob Bourne	.05	.04	.02
81	Denis Potvin	.20	.15	.08
82	Denis Potvin	.20	.15	.08
83	Dave Langevin	.05	.04	.02
84	Clark Gillies	.07	.05	.03
85	Bob Nystrom	.07	.05	.03
86	Billy Smith	.15	.11	.06

87	Tomas Jonsson	.05	.04	.02	165	Douglas Wilson, Jr.	.10	.08	.04
88	Rolland Melanson	.07	.05	.03	166	Michel Goulet	.15	.11	.06
89	Wayne Gretzky	4.00	3.00	1.50	167	Peter Stastny	.20	.15	.08
90	Wayne Gretzky	4.00	3.00	1.50	168	Marian Stastny	.05	.04	.02
91	Willy Lindstrom	.07	.05	.03	169	Denis Potvin	.15	.11	.06
92	Glenn Anderson	.15	.11	.06	170	Peter Peeters	.07	.05	.03
93	Glenn Anderson	.15	.11	.06	171	Mark Howe	.07	.05	.03
94	Paul Coffey	.60	.45	.25	172	Luc Dufour	.05	.04	.02
95	Paul Coffey	.60	.45	.25	173	Raymond Bourque	.50	.40	.20
96	Charles Huddy	.05	.04	.02	174	Bob Bourne	.05	.04	.02
97	Mark Messier	1.50	1.25	.60	175	Denis Potvin	.15	.11	.06
98	Mark Messier	1.50	1.25	.60	176	Mike Bossy	.35	.25	.14
99	Andrew Moog	.60	.45	.25	177	Butch Goring	.07	.05	.03
100	Lee Fogolin	.05	.04	.02	178	Brad Park	.20	.15	.08
101	Kevin Lowe	.15	.11	.06	179	James (Murray) Brumwell	.05	.04	.02
102	Ken Linseman	.05	.04	.02	180	Guy Carbonneau	.50	.40	.20
103	Tom Roulston	.05	.04	.02	181	Lindsay Carson	.05	.04	.02
104	Jari Kurri	.35	.25	.14	182	Luc Dufour	.05	.04	.02
105	Darryl Sutter	.07	.05	.03	183	Robert Froese	.15	.11	.06
106	Denis Savard	.20	.15	.08	184	Mats Hallin	.05	.04	.02
107	Denis Savard	.20	.15	.08	185	Gordon Kluzak	.07	.05	.03
108	Steve Larmer	.75	.60	.30	186	Jeff Larmer	.05	.04	.02
109	Bob Murray	.05	.04	.02	187	Milan Novy	.05	.04	.02
110	Tom Lysiak	.07	.05	.03	188	Scott Stevens	1.00	.70	.40
111	Alan Secord	.07	.05	.03	189	Bob Sullivan	.05	.04	.02
112	Douglas Wilson, Jr.	.15	.11	.06	190	Mark Taylor	.05	.04	.02
113	Murray Bannerman	.07	.05	.03	191	Darryl Sittler	.20	.15	.08
114	Gordan Roberts	.07	.05	.03	192	Ron Flockhart	.05	.04	.02
115	Tom McCarthy	.05	.04	.02	193	Byron (Brad) McCrimmon	.07	.05	.03
116	Robert Smith	.15	.11	.06	194	Bill Barber	.15	.11	.06
117	Craig Hartsburg	.05	.04	.02	195	Mark Howe	.10	.08	.04
118	Dino Ciccarelli	.35	.25	.14	196	Mark Howe	.10	.08	.04
119	Dino Ciccarelli	.35	.25	.14	197	Pelle Lindbergh	.75	.60	.30
120	Neal Broten	.15	.11	.06	198	Bobby Clarke	.30	.25	.12
121	Steve Payne	.05	.04	.02	199	Brian Propp	.10	.08	.04
122	Donald Beaupre	.10	.08	.04	200	Ken Houston	.05	.04	.02
123	Jorgen Pettersson	.05	.04	.02	201	Rod Langway	.10	.08	.04
124	Perry Turnbull	.05	.04	.02	202	Al Jensen	.07	.05	.03
125	Bernie Federko	.15	.11	.06	203	Brian Engblom	.05	.04	.02
126	Mike Crombeen	.05	.04	.02	204	Dennis Maruk	.07	.05	.03
127	Brian Sutter	.10	.08	.04	205	Dennis Maruk	.07	.05	.03
128	Brian Sutter	.10	.08	.04	206	Robert Carpenter	.10	.08	.04
129	Michael Liut	.07	.05	.03	207	Michael Gartner	.30	.25	.12
130	George (Rob) Ramage	.07	.05	.03	208	Doug Jarvis	.07	.05	.03
131	Blake Dunlop	.05	.04	.02	209	Ed Mio	.07	.05	.03
132	Ivan Boldirev	.05	.04	.02	210	Barry Beck	.07	.05	.03
133	Dwight Foster	.05	.04	.02	211	Dave Maloney	.07	.05	.03
134	Reed Larson	.05	.04	.02	212	Donald Maloney	.05	.04	.02
135	Danny Gare	.07	.05	.03	213	Mark Pavelich	.07	.05	.03
136	Jim Schoenfeld	.07	.05	.03	214	Mark Pavelich	.07	.05	.03
137	John Ogrodnick	.07	.05	.03	215	Anders Hedberg	.07	.05	.03
138	John Ogrodnick	.07	.05	.03	216	Reijo Ruotsalainen	.05	.04	.02
139	Willie Huber	.05	.04	.02	217	Mike Rogers	.07	.05	.03
140	Greg Smith	.05	.04	.02	218	Don Lever	.05	.04	.02
141	Eddy Beers	.05	.04	.02	219	Steve Tambellini	.05	.04	.02
142	Brian Bellows	.75	.60	.30	220	Bob MacMillan	.05	.04	.02
143	Jiri Bubla	.05	.04	.02	221	Hector Marini	.05	.04	.02
144	Daryl Evans	.05	.04	.02	222	Glenn Resch	.12	.09	.05
145	Randall Gregg	.07	.05	.03	223	Glenn Resch	.12	.09	.05
146	James Jackson	.05	.04	.02	224	Carol Vadnais	.05	.04	.02
147	Corrado Micalef	.05	.04	.02	225	Joel Quenneville	.05	.04	.02
148	Brian Mullen	.25	.20	.10	226	Aaron Broten	.05	.04	.02
149	Frank Nigro, Jr.	.05	.04	.02	227	Randy Carlyle	.07	.05	.03
150	Walter Poddubny	.07	.05	.03	228	Douglas Shedden	.05	.04	.02
151	Jaroslav Pouzar	.05	.04	.02	229	Greg Malone	.05	.04	.02
152	Patrik Sundstrom	.15	.11	.06	230	Paul Gardner	.05	.04	.02
153	Denis Savard	.20	.15	.08	231	Rick Kehoe	.07	.05	.03
154	Dave Hunter	.05	.04	.02	232	Rick Kehoe	.07	.05	.03
155	Andrew Moog	.60	.45	.25	233	Pat Boutette	.05	.04	.02
156	Alan Secord	.07	.05	.03	234	Michel Dion	.07	.05	.03
157	Mark Messier	1.50	1.25	.60	235	Mike Bullard	.07	.05	.03
158	Glenn Anderson	.15	.11	.06	236	Dale McCourt	.05	.04	.02
159	Jaroslav Pouzar	.05	.04	.02	237	Mike Foligno	.07	.05	.03
160	Alan Secord	.05	.04	.02	238	Phil Housley	1.50	1.25	.60
161	Wayne Gretzky	2.50	2.00	1.00	239	Anthony McKegney	.05	.04	.02
162	Lanny McDonald	.15	.11	.06	240	Gilbert Perreault	.15	.11	.06
163	David Babych	.07	.05	.03	241	Gilbert Perreault	.15	.11	.06
164	Murray Bannerman	.07	.05	.03	242	Bob Sauve	.07	.05	.03

243	Michael Ramsey	.07	.05	.03
244	John Van Boxmeer	.05	.04	.02
245	Dan Bouchard	.07	.05	.03
246	Real Cloutier	.05	.04	.02
247	Marc Tardif	.07	.05	.03
248	Randy Moller	.05	.04	.02
249	Michel Goulet	.20	.15	.08
250	Michel Goulet	.20	.15	.08
251	Marian Stastny	.07	.05	.03
252	Anton Stastny	.07	.05	.03
253	Peter Stastny	.30	.25	.12
254	Mark Johnson	.07	.05	.03
255	Ron Francis	.30	.25	.12
256	Douglas Sulliman	.05	.04	.02
257	Risto Siltanen	.05	.04	.02
258	Blaine Stoughton	.07	.05	.03
259	Blaine Stoughton	.07	.05	.03
260	Ray Neufeld	.05	.04	.02
261	Pierre Lacroix	.05	.04	.02
262	Greg Millen	.07	.05	.03
263	Lanny McDonald	.20	.15	.08
264	Paul Reinhart	.07	.05	.03
265	Mel Bridgman	.07	.05	.03
266	Rejean Lemelin	.10	.08	.04
267	Kent Nilsson	.07	.05	.03
268	Kent Nilsson	.07	.05	.03
269	Doug Risebrough	.07	.05	.03
270	Kari Eloranta	.05	.04	.02
271	Phil Russell	.05	.04	.02
272	Darcy Rota	.05	.04	.02
273	Thomas Gradin	.07	.05	.03
274	Stanley Smyl	.07	.05	.03
275	John Garrett	.07	.05	.03
276	Richard Brodeur	.07	.05	.03
277	Richard Brodeur	.07	.05	.03
278	Doug Halward	.05	.04	.02
279	Kevin McCarthy	.05	.04	.02
280	Rick Lanz	.05	.04	.02
281	Morris Lukowich	.05	.04	.02
282	Dale Hawerchuk	.50	.40	.20
283	Paul MacLean	.07	.05	.03
284	Lucien DeBlois	.05	.04	.02
285	David Babych	.07	.05	.03
286	David Babych	.07	.05	.03
287	Douglas Small	.07	.05	.03
288	Doug Soetaert	.05	.04	.02
289	Thomas Steen	.10	.08	.04
290	Charlie Simmer	.10	.08	.04
291	Terry Ruskowski	.07	.05	.03
292	Bernie Nicholls	.75	.60	.30
293	Jim Fox	.05	.04	.02
294	Marcel Dionne	.25	.20	.10
295	Marcel Dionne	.25	.20	.10
296	Gary Laskoski	.05	.04	.02
297	Jerry Korab	.05	.04	.02
298	Lawrence Murphy	.25	.20	.10
299	Hart Trophy	.20	.15	.08
300	Hart Trophy	.20	.15	.08
301	Hart Trophy Winner: MVP (Wayne Gretzky)	3.00	2.25	1.25
302	Frank J. Selke Trophy Winner: (Bobby Clarke)	.30	.25	.12
303	Bill Masterton Trophy Winner: (Lanny McDonald)	.20	.15	.08
304	Lady Byng Trophy	.15	.11	.06
305	Lady Byng Trophy	.15	.11	.06
306	Lady Byng Trophy Winner : Sportsmanship (Mike Bossy)	.35	.25	.14
307	Art Ross Trophy Winner: (Wayne Gretzky)	3.00	2.25	1.25
308	Art Ross Trophy	.20	.15	.08
309	Art Ross Trophy	.20	.15	.08
310	Calder Trophy	.15	.11	.06
311	Calder Trophy	.15	.11	.06
312	Calder Trophy Winner: Rookie of the Year (Steve Larmer)	.50	.40	.20
313	Norris Trophy Winner: Best Defenseman (Rod Langway)	.07	.05	.03
314	Norris Trophy	.15	.11	.06
315	Norris Trophy	.15	.11	.06
316	Wm. Jennings Trophy Winner: Goal Tending (Billy Smith)	.15	.11	.06
317	Wm. Jennings Trophy Winner: Goal Tending (Roland Melanson)	.07	.05	.03
318	Vezina Trophy Winner: MV Goalie (Peter Peeters)	.07	.05	.03
319	Vezina Trophy	.15	.11	.06
320	Vezina Trophy	.15	.11	.06
321	Mike Bossy	.50	.40	.20
322	Mike Bossy	.50	.40	.20
323	Marcel Dionne	.40	.30	.15
324	Marcel Dionne	.40	.30	.15
325	Wayne Gretzky	3.00	2.25	1.25
326	Wayne Gretzky	3.00	2.25	1.25
327	Pat Hughes	.15	.11	.06
328	Pat Hughes	.15	.11	.06
329	Rick Middleton	.25	.20	.10
330	Rick Middleton	.25	.20	.10

1984 O-Pee-Chee Stickers

These stickers, each 1 7/8" by 2 15/16", added a different wrinkle to the fronts; a shadow box appears along the left and bottom sides of the sticker, while the number moved to the upper right corner. A full-color action photo is also on the front. The back has information in French and English about how to order through the mail an album which was made for the stickers. The player's name and sticker number are in the center of the sticker. "1984 Season Saison" is written at the bottom of the sticker, along with a 1984 O-Pee-Chee copyright. Some stickers were issued in pairs, as indicated by the . These were all foil stickers, as were numbers 134-145.

		MT	NM	EX
Complete Set (292):		30.00	22.00	12.00
Common Player:		.05	.04	.02
1	The Stanley Cup (Islanders vs. Oilers)	.07	.05	.03
2	The Stanley Cup (Islanders vs. Oilers)	.05	.04	.02
3	The Stanley Cup (Islanders vs. Oilers)	.05	.04	.02
4	The Stanley Cup (Islanders vs. Oilers)	.05	.04	.02
5	Conn Smythe Trophy Winner: MVP - Finals (Mark Messier)	.50	.40	.20
6	Toronto Maple Leafs Logo (23)	.10	.08	.04
7	Borje Salming	.07	.05	.03
8	Borje Salming	.07	.05	.03
9	Dan Daoust	.05	.04	.02
10	Dan Daoust	.05	.04	.02
11	Richard Vaive	.07	.05	.03
12	Richard Vaive	.07	.05	.03
13	Dale McCourt	.05	.04	.02
14	Bill Derlago	.05	.04	.02
15	Gary Nylund	.07	.05	.03
16	Gary Nylund	.07	.05	.03
17	James Korn	.05	.04	.02
18	John Anderson	.05	.04	.02
19	Greg Terrion	.05	.04	.02
20	Allan Bester	.05	.04	.02
21	Jim Benning	.05	.04	.02
22	Mike Palmateer	.07	.05	.03

370

23	Chicago Blackhawks Logo (6)	.10	.08	.04
24	Denis Savard	.20	.15	.08
25	Denis Savard	.20	.15	.08
26	Bob Murray	.05	.04	.02
27	Douglas Wilson, Jr.	.12	.09	.05
28	Keith Brown	.07	.05	.03
29	Steve Larmer	.40	.30	.15
30	Darryl Sutter	.07	.05	.03
31	Tom Lysiak	.07	.05	.03
32	Murray Bannerman	.07	.05	.03
33	Detroit Red Wings Team Logo (43)	.10	.08	.04
34	John Ogrodnick	.07	.05	.03
35	John Ogrodnick	.07	.05	.03
36	Reed Larson	.05	.04	.02
37	Steve Yzerman	5.00	3.75	2.00
38	Brad Park	.15	.11	.06
39	Ivan Boldirev	.05	.04	.02
40	Kelly Kisio	.07	.05	.03
41	Gregory Stefan	.07	.05	.03
42	Ron Duguay	.07	.05	.03
43	Minnesota North Stars Team Logo (33)	.10	.08	.04
44	Brian Bellows	.35	.25	.14
45	Brian Bellows	.35	.25	.14
46	Neal Broten	.12	.09	.05
47	Dino Ciccarelli	.20	.15	.08
48	Dennis Maruk	.07	.05	.03
49	Steve Payne	.05	.04	.02
50	Gilles Meloche	.05	.04	.02
51	Gilles Meloche	.07	.05	.03
52	Tom McCarthy	.05	.04	.02
53	St. Louis Blues Logo (67)	.10	.08	.04
54	Bernie Federko	.12	.09	.05
55	Bernie Federko	.12	.09	.05
56	Brian Sutter	.10	.08	.04
57	Michael Liut	.07	.05	.03
58	Douglas Wickenheiser	.05	.04	.02
59	Jorgen Pettersson	.05	.04	.02
60	Douglas Gilmour	5.00	3.75	2.00
61	Joe Mullen	.25	.20	.10
62	George (Rob) Ramage	.07	.05	.03
63	4 categories (Wayne Gretzky) (64)	1.25	.90	.50
64	Game Winning Goals (Michel Goulet) (63)	.15	.11	.06
65	Goals Against Average (Pat Riggins) (66)	.10	.08	.04
66	Leading Defenseman (Denis Potvin) (65)	.20	.15	.08
67	New Jersey Devils Team Logo (53)	.10	.08	.04
68	Glenn Resch	.10	.08	.04
69	Glenn Resch	.10	.08	.04
70	Don Lever	.05	.04	.02
71	Mel Bridgman	.07	.05	.03
72	Bob MacMillan	.05	.04	.02
73	Patrick Verbeek	.60	.45	.25
74	Joe Cirella	.07	.05	.03
75	Phil Russell	.05	.04	.02
76	Jan Ludvig	.05	.04	.02
77	New York Islanders Logo (94)	.10	.08	.04
78	Denis Potvin	.20	.15	.08
79	Denis Potvin	.20	.15	.08
80	John Tonelli	.07	.05	.03
81	John Tonelli	.07	.05	.03
82	Mike Bossy	.40	.30	.15
83	Mike Bossy	.40	.30	.15
84	Butch Goring	.07	.05	.03
85	Bob Nystrom	.05	.04	.02
86	Bryan Trottier	.25	.20	.10
87	Bryan Trottier	.25	.20	.10
88	Brent Sutter	.07	.05	.03
89	Bob Bourne	.05	.04	.02
90	Gregory Gilbert	.07	.05	.03
91	Billy Smith	.15	.11	.06
92	Ronald Melanson	.07	.05	.03
93	Ken Morrow	.07	.05	.03
94	New York Rangers Logo (77)	.10	.08	.04
95	Donald Maloney	.05	.04	.02
96	Donald Maloney	.05	.04	.02
97	Mark Pavelich	.05	.04	.02
98	Glen Hanlon	.07	.05	.03
99	Mike Rogers	.07	.05	.03
100	Barry Beck	.07	.05	.03
101	Reijo Ruotsalainen	.05	.04	.02
102	Anders Hedberg	.07	.05	.03
103	Pierre Larouche	.07	.05	.03
104	Philadelphia Flyers Logo (114)	.10	.08	.04
105	Tim Kerr	.12	.09	.05
106	Tim Kerr	.12	.09	.05
107	Ronald Sutter	.10	.08	.04
108	Darryl Sittler	.15	.11	.06
109	Mark Howe	.10	.08	.04
110	David Poulin	.12	.09	.05
111	Richard Sutter	.10	.08	.04
112	Brian Propp	.10	.08	.04
113	Robert Froese	.08	.06	.03
114	Pittsburgh Penguins Logo (104)	.05	.04	.02
115	Ron Flockhart	.05	.04	.02
116	Ron Flockhart	.05	.04	.02
117	Rick Kehoe	.07	.05	.03
118	Mike Bullard	.07	.05	.03
119	Kevin McCarthy	.05	.04	.02
120	Douglas Shedden	.05	.04	.02
121	Mark Taylor	.05	.04	.02
122	Denis Herron	.07	.05	.03
123	Tom Roulston	.05	.04	.02
124	Washington Capitals Logo (146)	.10	.08	.04
125	Rod Langway	.07	.05	.03
126	Rod Langway	.07	.05	.03
127	Lawrence Murphy	.15	.11	.06
128	Al Jensen	.07	.05	.03
129	Doug Jarvis	.07	.05	.03
130	Bengt-ake Gustafsson	.05	.04	.02
131	Michael Gartner	.25	.20	.10
132	Robert Carpenter	.10	.08	.04
133	Dave Christian	.07	.05	.03
134	Paul Coffey	.75	.60	.30
135	Murray Bannerman	.15	.11	.06
136	George (Rob) Ramage	.15	.11	.06
137	John Ogrodnick	.15	.11	.06
138	Wayne Gretzky	2.50	2.00	1.00
139	Richard Vaive	.15	.11	.06
140	Michel Goulet	.35	.25	.14
141	Peter Stastny	.50	.40	.20
142	Rick Middleton	.25	.20	.10
143	Raymond Bourque	.75	.60	.30
144	Peter Peeters	.20	.15	.08
145	Denis Potvin	.40	.30	.15
146	Montreal Canadiens Logo (124)	.10	.08	.04
147	Larry Robinson	.15	.11	.06
148	Larry Robinson	.15	.11	.06
149	Guy Lafleur	.25	.20	.10
150	Guy Lafleur	.25	.20	.10
151	Robert Smith	.10	.08	.04
152	Robert Smith	.10	.08	.04
153	Bob Gainey	.15	.11	.06
154	Craig Ludwig	.05	.04	.02
155	Mats Naslund	.07	.05	.03
156	Mats Naslund	.07	.05	.03
157	Rick Wamsley	.07	.05	.03
158	Jean Hamel	.05	.04	.02
159	Ryan Walter	.07	.05	.03
160	Guy Carbonneau	.20	.15	.08
161	Mario Tremblay	.05	.04	.02
162	Pierre Mondou	.05	.04	.02
163	Quebec Nordiques Logo (180)	.10	.08	.04

164	Peter Stastny	.20	.15	.08
165	Peter Stastny	.20	.15	.08
166	Mario Marois	.05	.04	.02
167	Mario Marois	.05	.04	.02
168	Michel Goulet	.15	.11	.06
169	Michel Goulet	.15	.11	.06
170	Andre Savard	.05	.04	.02
171	Anthony McKegney	.05	.04	.02
172	Dan Bouchard	.05	.04	.02
173	Dan Bouchard	.05	.04	.02
174	Randy Moller	.05	.04	.02
175	Wilf Paiement	.07	.05	.03
176	Normand Rochefort	.05	.04	.02
177	Marian Stastny	.07	.05	.03
178	Anton Stastny	.07	.05	.03
179	Dale Hunter	.15	.11	.06
180	Boston Bruins Logo (163)	.10	.08	.04
181	Rick Middleton	.10	.08	.04
182	Rick Middleton	.10	.08	.04
183	Raymond Bourque	.40	.30	.15
184	Peter Peeters	.07	.05	.03
185	Michael O'Connell	.05	.04	.02
186	Gord Kluzak	.07	.05	.03
187	Barry Pederson	.07	.05	.03
188	Michael Krushelnyski	.07	.05	.03
189	Tom Fergus	.07	.05	.03
190	Hartford Whalers Logo (190)	.10	.08	.04
191	Sylvain Turgeon	.07	.05	.03
192	Sylvain Turgeon	.07	.05	.03
193	Mark Johnson	.07	.05	.03
194	Greg Malone	.05	.04	.02
195	Mike Zuke	.05	.04	.02
196	Ron Francis	.25	.20	.10
197	Bob Crawford	.05	.04	.02
198	Greg Millen	.07	.05	.03
199	Ray Neufeld	.05	.04	.02
200	Buffalo Sabres Logo (190)	.10	.08	.04
201	Gilbert Perreault	.15	.11	.06
202	Gilbert Perreault	.15	.11	.06
203	Phil Housley	.35	.25	.14
204	Phil Housley	.35	.25	.14
205	Tom Barrasso	1.25	.90	.50
206	Tom Barrasso	1.25	.90	.50
207	Larry Playfair	.05	.04	.02
208	Bob Sauve	.07	.05	.03
209	David Andreychuk	1.50	1.25	.60
210	David Andreychuk	1.50	1.25	.60
211	Michael Ramsey	.05	.04	.02
212	Mike Foligno	.07	.05	.03
213	Lindy Ruff	.05	.04	.02
214	Bill Hajt	.05	.04	.02
215	Craig Ramsay	.05	.04	.02
216	Ric Seiling	.05	.04	.02
217	Hart Trophy (224)	.10	.08	.04
218	Vezina Trophy (223)	.10	.08	.04
219	Jennings Trophy (221)	.10	.08	.04
220	Calder Trophy (225)	.10	.08	.04
221	Art Ross Trophy (219)	.10	.08	.04
222	Norris Trophy (283)	.10	.08	.04
223	Masterton Trophy (218)	.10	.08	.04
224	Selke Trophy (217)	.10	.08	.04
225	Lady Byng Trophy (220)	.10	.08	.04
226	Hart Trophy Winner: (Wayne Gretzky) (227)	1.00	.70	.40
227	Vezina Trophy Winner: (Tom Barrasso) (226)	.50	.40	.20
228	Calder Trophy Winner: (Tom Barrasso) (229)	.50	.40	.20
229	Art Ross Trophy Winner: (Wayne Gretzky) (228)	1.00	.70	.40
230	Norris Trophy Winner: (Rod Langway) (231)	.05	.04	.02
231	Bill Masterton Trophy Winner: (Brad Park) (230)	.10	.08	.04
232	William Jennings Trophy Winner: (Al Jensen) (233)	.05	.04	.02
233	William Jennings Trophy Winner: (Pat Riggin) (232)	.05	.04	.02
234	Frank J. Selke Trophy Winner: (Doug Jarvis) (235)	.05	.04	.02
235	Lady Byng Trophy Winner: (Mike Bossy) (234)	.15	.11	.06
236	Calgary Flames Logo (246)	.10	.08	.04
237	Lanny McDonald	.20	.15	.08
238	Lanny McDonald	.20	.15	.08
239	Steve Tambellini	.07	.05	.03
240	Rejean Lemelin	.07	.05	.03
241	Doug Risebrough	.07	.05	.03
242	Hakan Loob	.05	.04	.02
243	Eddy Beers	.05	.04	.02
244	Mike Eaves	.07	.05	.03
245	Kent Nilsson	.10	.08	.04
246	Edmonton Oilers Logo (236)	.10	.08	.04
247	Glenn Anderson	.15	.11	.06
248	Glenn Anderson	.15	.11	.06
249	Jari Kurri	.30	.25	.12
250	Jari Kurri	.30	.25	.12
251	Paul Coffey	.50	.40	.20
252	Paul Coffey	.50	.40	.20
253	Kevin Lowe	.15	.11	.06
254	Lee Fogolin	.05	.04	.02
255	Wayne Gretzky	2.00	1.50	.80
256	Wayne Gretzky	2.00	1.50	.80
257	Randall Gregg	.07	.05	.03
258	Charles Huddy	.07	.05	.03
259	Grant Fuhr	.35	.25	.14
260	Willy Lindstrom	.05	.04	.02
261	Mark Messier	.75	.60	.30
262	Andrew Moog	.35	.25	.14
263	Los Angeles Kings Logo (273)	.25	.20	.10
264	Marcel Dionne	.25	.20	.10
265	Marcel Dionne	.25	.20	.10
266	Charlie Simmer	.10	.08	.04
267	David Taylor	.10	.08	.04
268	Jim Fox	.05	.04	.02
269	Bernie Nicholls	.40	.30	.15
270	Terry Ruskowski	.07	.05	.03
271	Brian Engblom	.05	.04	.02
272	Mark Hardy	.05	.04	.02
273	Vancouver Canucks Logo (263)	.10	.08	.04
274	Tony Tanti	.07	.05	.03
275	Tony Tanti	.07	.05	.03
276	Rick Lanz	.05	.04	.02
277	Richard Brodeur	.07	.05	.03
278	Doug Halward	.05	.04	.02
279	Patrik Sundstrom	.07	.05	.03
280	Darcy Rota	.05	.04	.02
281	Stanley Smyl	.07	.05	.03
282	Thomas Gradin	.07	.05	.03
283	Winnipeg Jets Logo (222)	.10	.08	.04
284	Dale Hawerchuk	.35	.25	.14
285	Dale Hawerchuk	.35	.25	.14
286	Scott Arniel	.05	.04	.02
287	David Babych	.07	.05	.03
288	Laurie Boschman	.07	.05	.03
289	Paul MacLean	.07	.05	.03
290	Lucien DeBlois	.05	.04	.02
291	Randy Carlyle	.07	.05	.03
292	Thomas Steen	.10	.08	.04

1985 O-Pee-Chee Stickers

Once again, these stickers, measuring 2 1/8" by 3", feature a full color action photo on the front, with a distinct color border and a number in the lower left corner. The back is in French, and includes a promotional mail-in offer from O-Pee-Chee, plus the player's name and sticker number. Stickers which were issued as pairs are indicated by . Foil stickers were numbers 54-56, 113-124, 194-197 and 203-207. An album was also produced.

		MT	NM	EX
	Complete Set (255):	30.00	22.00	12.00
	Common Player:	.03	.02	.01
1	Stanley Cup Final	.07	.05	.03
2	Stanley Cup Final	.05	.04	.02
3	Stanley Cup Final	.05	.04	.02
4	Stanley Cup Final	.05	.04	.02
5	Conn Smythe Trophy Winner (Wayne Gretzky)	2.50	2.00	1.00
6	Richard Vaive	.07	.05	.03
7	Bill Derlago	.05	.04	.02
8	Rick St. Croix (136)	.03	.02	.01
9	Tim Bernhardt (137)	.03	.02	.01
10	John Anderson (138)	.03	.02	.01
11	Dan Daoust (139)	.03	.02	.01
12	Borje Salming	.07	.05	.03
13	Al Iafrate (143)	.60	.45	.25
14	Gary Nylund (144)	.03	.02	.01
15	Robert McGill (145)	.03	.02	.01
16	Jim Benning (146)	.03	.02	.01
17	Robert (Stewart) Gavin (148)	.03	.02	.01
18	Greg Terrion (149)	.03	.02	.01
19	Peter Ihnacak (150)	.03	.02	.01
20	Russ Courtnall (151)	.60	.45	.25
21	Miroslav Frycer	.05	.04	.02
22	Denis Savard	.15	.11	.06
23	Darryl Sutter (153)	1.00	.70	.40
24	Curt Fraser	.03	.02	.01
25	Douglas Wilson, Jr.	.10	.08	.04
26	Ed Olczyk (154)	.30	.25	.12
27	Murray Bannerman (155)	.03	.02	.01
28	Steve Larmer (158)	.12	.09	.05
29	Troy Murray (159)	.07	.05	.03
30	Steve Yzerman	2.00	1.50	.80
31	Gregory Stefan (161)	.05	.04	.02
32	Ron Duguay (162)	.05	.04	.02
33	Reed Larson (163)	.03	.02	.01
34	Ivan Boldirev (164)	.03	.02	.01
35	Darryl Sittler (166)	.05	.04	.02
36	Darryl Sittler (167)	.10	.08	.04
37	John Ogrodnick	.07	.05	.03
38	Keith Acton	.05	.04	.02
39	Dino Ciccarelli (168)	.10	.08	.04
40	Neal Broten (169)	.05	.04	.02
41	Brian Bellows	.25	.20	.10
42	Steve Payne (170)	.03	.02	.01
43	Gordon Roberts (171)	.03	.02	.01
44	Harold Snepsts (175)	.05	.04	.02
45	Anthony McKegney (176)	.03	.02	.01
46	Brian Sutter	.10	.08	.04
47	Joe Mullen (177)	.10	.08	.04
48	Douglas Gilmour (178)	1.00	.70	.40
49	Tim Bothwell (180)	.03	.02	.01
50	Mark Johnson (181)	.03	.02	.01
51	Greg Millen (182)	.05	.04	.02
52	Douglas Wickenheiser (183)	.03	.02	.01
53	Bernie Federko	.10	.08	.04
54	4 categories (Wayne Gretzky) (197)	1.00	.70	.40
55	Goals against average (Tom Barrasso) (203)	.25	.20	.10
56	Leading defenseman (Paul Coffey) (204)	.40	.30	.15
57	Mel Bridgman	.05	.04	.02
58	Phil Russell (184)	.03	.02	.01
59	Dave Lewis (185)	.03	.02	.01
60	Paul Gagne (186)	.03	.02	.01
61	Glenn Resch (187)	.07	.05	.03
62	Aaron Broten (189)	.03	.02	.01
63	Dave Pichette (190)	.03	.02	.01
64	Kirk Muller	1.25	.90	.50
65	Bryan Trottier	.20	.15	.08
66	Mike Bossy	.30	.25	.12
67	Bob Bourne (191)	.03	.02	.01
68	Clark Gillies (192)	.05	.04	.02
69	Bob Nystrom (193)	.03	.02	.01
70	Denis Potvin (198)	.10	.08	.04
71	Brent Sutter	.07	.05	.03
72	Duane Sutter (199)	.05	.04	.02
73	Patrick Flatley (200)	.05	.04	.02
74	Pat LaFontaine (201)	1.00	.70	.40
75	Gregory Gilbert (202)	.03	.02	.01
76	Billy Smith (209)	.07	.05	.03
77	Gord Lane (210)	.03	.02	.01
78	Tomas Jonsson (211)	.03	.02	.01
79	Kelly Hrudey (212)	.50	.40	.20
80	John Tonelli	.07	.05	.03
81	Reijo Ruotsalainen	.05	.04	.02
82	Barry Beck (213)	.05	.04	.02
83	James Patrick (214)	.15	.11	.06
84	Mark Pavelich	.05	.04	.02
85	Pierre Larouche	.07	.05	.03
86	Mike Rogers (219)	.03	.02	.01
87	Glen Hanlon (220)	.05	.04	.02
88	John Vanbiesbrouck (221)	.75	.60	.30
89	David Poulin	.07	.05	.03
90	Brian Propp (223)	.07	.05	.03
91	Pelle Lindbergh (224)	1.50	1.25	.60
92	Byron (Brad) McCrimmon (225)	.05	.04	.02
93	Mark Howe (226)	.07	.05	.03
94	Peter Zezel (227)	.25	.20	.10
95	Murray Craven (228)	.05	.04	.02
96	Tim Kerr	.07	.05	.03
97	Mario Lemieux	7.50	5.75	3.00
98	Maurice Mantha (229)	.03	.02	.01
99	Doug Bodger (230)	.05	.04	.02
100	Warren Young	.07	.05	.03
101	John Chabot (233)	.03	.02	.01
102	Douglas Shedden (234)	.03	.02	.01
103	Wayne Babych (236)	.03	.02	.01
104	Mike Bullard (237)	.03	.02	.01
105	Rod Langway	.07	.05	.03
106	Pat Riggin (238)	.05	.04	.02
107	Scott Stevens (239)	.20	.15	.08
108	Alan Haworth (241)	.03	.02	.01
109	Doug Jarvis (242)	.03	.02	.01
110	Dave Christian (243)	.05	.04	.02
111	Michael Gartner (244)	.12	.09	.05
112	Robert Carpenter	.07	.05	.03
113	Rod Langway	.15	.11	.06
114	Tom Barrasso	.25	.20	.10
115	Raymond Bourque	.50	.40	.20
116	John Tonelli	.15	.11	.06
117	Brent Sutter	.15	.11	.06
118	Mike Bossy	.45	.35	.20
119	John Ogrodnick	.15	.11	.06
120	Wayne Gretzky	2.00	1.50	.80
121	Jari Kurri	.45	.35	.20
122	Douglas Wilson, Jr.	.25	.20	.10
123	Andrew Moog	.40	.30	.15
124	Paul Coffey	.50	.40	.20
125	Chris Chelios	.60	.45	.25
126	Steve Penney	.07	.05	.03
127	Christopher Nilan (245)	.05	.04	.02
128	Ron Flockhart (246)	.03	.02	.01
129	Tom Kurvers (249)	.03	.02	.01
130	Craig Ludwig (250)	.03	.02	.01
131	Mats Naslund	.10	.08	.04
132	Robert Smith (252)	.07	.05	.03
133	Pierre Mondou (253)	.03	.02	.01
134	Mario Tremblay (254)	.03	.02	.01
135	Guy Carbonneau (255)	.07	.05	.03
136	Doug Soetaert (8)	.03	.02	.01
137	Mark Hunter (9)	.03	.02	.01
138	Bob Gainey (10)	.07	.05	.03
139	Petr Svoboda (11)	.10	.08	.04
140	Larry Robinson	.12	.09	.05
141	Michel Goulet	.15	.11	.06
142	Bruce Bell	.05	.04	.02
143	Dan Bouchard (13)	.03	.02	.01
144	Mario Marois (14)	.03	.02	.01
145	Randy Moller (15)	.03	.02	.01
146	Mario Gosselin (16)	.03	.02	.01
147	Anton Stastny	.05	.04	.02

148	Normand Rochefort (17)	.03	.02	.01
149	Alain Cote (18)	.03	.02	.01
150	Paul Gillis (19)	.03	.02	.01
151	Dale Hunter (20)	.07	.05	.03
152	Wilf Paiement (23)	.03	.02	.01
153	Brent Ashton (24)	.03	.02	.01
154	Brad Maxwell (26)	.03	.02	.01
155	Jenn F. Sauve (27)	.03	.02	.01
156	Peter Stastny	.03	.02	.01
157	Raymond Bourque	.35	.25	.14
158	Charlie Simmer (28)	.07	.05	.03
159	Rick Middleton (29)	.07	.05	.03
160	Peter Peeters	.07	.05	.03
161	Michael O'Connell (31)	.03	.02	.01
162	Terry O'Reilly (32)	.05	.04	.02
163	Keith Crowder (33)	.03	.02	.01
164	Tom Fergus (34)	.03	.02	.01
165	Sylvain Turgeon	.07	.05	.03
166	Greg Malone (35)	.03	.02	.01
167	Bob Crawford (36)	.03	.02	.01
168	Kevin Dineen (39)	.30	.25	.12
169	Michael Liut	.07	.05	.03
170	Joel Quenneville (42)	.03	.02	.01
171	Ray Neufeld (43)	.03	.02	.01
172	Ron Francis	.20	.15	.08
173	Phil Housley	.25	.20	.10
174	Mike Foligno	.05	.04	.02
175	Craig Ramsay (44)	.03	.02	.01
176	Bill Hajt (45)	.03	.02	.01
177	Dave Maloney (47)	.03	.02	.01
178	Brent Peterson (48)	.03	.02	.01
179	Tom Barasso	.25	.20	.10
180	Michael Ramsey (49)	.03	.02	.01
181	Bob Sauve (50)	.05	.04	.02
182	Ric Seiling (51)	.03	.02	.01
183	Paul Cyr (52)	.03	.02	.01
184	John Tucker (58)	.03	.02	.01
185	Gilles Hamel (59)	.03	.02	.01
186	Mal Davis (60)	.03	.02	.01
187	David Andreychuk (61)	.35	.25	.14
188	Gilbert Perreault	.15	.11	.06
189	William Jennings Trophy Winner: (Tom Barrasso) (62)	.25	.20	.10
190	William Jennings Trophy Winner: (Bob Sauve) (63)	.05	.04	.02
191	Norris Trophy Winner: (Paul Coffey) (67)	.25	.20	.10
192	Frank J. Selke Trophy Winner: (Craig Ramsay) (68)	.03	.02	.01
193	Vezina Trophy Winner: (Pelle Lindbergh) (69)	1.50	1.25	.60
194	Jennings Trophy (205)	.10	.08	.04
195	Norris Trophy (206)	.10	.08	.04
196	Selke Trophy (207)	.10	.08	.04
197	Vezina Trophy (54)	.10	.08	.04
198	Hart Trophy Winner: (Wayne Gretzky) (70)	1.00	.70	.40
199	Calder Trophy Winner: (Mario Lemieux) (72)	3.00	2.25	1.25
200	Bill Masterton Trophy Winner: (Anders Hedberg) (73)	.05	.04	.02
201	Lady Byng Trophy Winner: (Jari Kurri) (74)	.15	.11	.06
202	Art Ross Trophy Winner: (Wayne Gretzky) (75)	1.00	.70	.40
203	Hart Trophy (55)	.10	.08	.04
204	Calder Trophy (56)	.10	.08	.04
205	Masterton Trophy (194)	.10	.08	.04
206	Lady Byng Trophy (195)	.10	.08	.04
207	Art Ross Trophy (196)	.10	.08	.04
208	Kent Nilsson	.07	.05	.03
209	Paul Reinhart (76)	.05	.04	.02
210	Rejean Lemelin (77)	.05	.04	.02
211	Al MacInnis (78)	2.00	1.50	.80
212	Jamie Macoun (79)	.05	.04	.02
213	Carey Wilson (82)	.07	.05	.03

214	Eddy Beers (83)	.03	.02	.01
215	Lanny McDonald	.15	.11	.06
216	Charles Huddy	.05	.04	.02
217	Paul Coffey	.40	.30	.15
218	Lee Fogolin (85)	.03	.02	.01
219	Kevin Lowe (86)	.07	.05	.03
220	Andrew Moog (87)	.20	.15	.08
221	Grant Fuhr (88)	.20	.15	.08
222	Wayne Gretzky	2.00	1.50	.80
223	Michael Krushelnyski (90)	.05	.04	.02
224	Billy Carroll (91)	.03	.02	.01
225	Randall Gregg (92)	.05	.04	.02
226	Willy Lindstrom (93)	.03	.02	.01
227	Glenn Anderson (94)	.07	.05	.03
228	Mark Messier (95)	.30	.25	.12
229	Pat Hughes (98)	.03	.02	.01
230	Kevin McClelland (99)	.03	.02	.01
231	Jari Kurri	.25	.20	.10
232	Bernie Nicholls	.25	.20	.10
233	Brian Engblom (101)	.03	.02	.01
234	Mark Hardy (102)	.03	.02	.01
235	Marcel Dionne	.25	.20	.10
236	Jim Fox (103)	.03	.02	.01
237	Terry Ruskowski (104)	.05	.04	.02
238	David Taylor (106)	.05	.04	.02
239	Bob Janecyk (107)	.05	.04	.02
240	Thomas Gradin	.07	.05	.03
241	Patrik Sundstrom (108)	.05	.04	.02
242	Al MacAdam (109)	.03	.02	.01
243	Doug Halward (110)	.03	.02	.01
244	Peter McNab (211)	.03	.02	.01
245	Tony Tanti (127)	.05	.04	.02
246	Moe Lemay (128)	.03	.02	.01
247	Stanley Smyl	.05	.04	.02
248	Dale Hawerchuk	.30	.25	.12
249	David Babych (129)	.05	.04	.02
250	Paul MacLean (130)	.05	.04	.02
251	Randy Carlyle	.05	.04	.02
252	Robert Picard (132)	.03	.02	.01
253	Thomas Steen (133)	.05	.04	.02
254	Laurie Boschman (134)	.03	.02	.01
255	Douglas Small (135)	.05	.04	.02

1986 O-Pee-Chee Stickers

These stickers, measuring 2 1/8" by 3", once again were issued as foils and in pairs, as noted in . Each sticker front has a color action photo on it, with a sticker number in the lower left corner. The right border of the photo forms a hockey stick. The back is in French and includes the player's name and sticker number, plus a 1986 O-Pee-Chee copyright and mail-in promotional offer. An album to hold the stickers was once again issued. Foil stickers are numbers 5, 112-135 and 182-185.

		MT	NM	EX
	Complete Set (255):	30.00	22.00	12.00
	Common Player:	.03	.02	.01
1	Stanley Cup Finals	.25	.20	.10
2	Stanley Cup Finals	.15	.11	.06
3	Stanley Cup Finals	.15	.11	.06
4	Stanley Cup Finals	.15	.11	.06
5	Patrick Roy (Conn Smythe Trophy Winner, M.V.P.)	9.00	6.75	3.50
6	Chris Chelios (151)	.20	.15	.08
7	Guy Carbonneau (152)	.10	.08	.04
8	Larry Robinson	.15	.11	.06
9	Mario Tremblay (154)	.03	.02	.01
10	Tom Kurvers (155)	.03	.02	.01
11	Mats Naslund	.07	.05	.03
12	Bob Gainey	.12	.09	.05
13	Robert Smith	.07	.05	.03
14	Craig Ludwig (156)	.03	.02	.01
15	Michael McPhee (157)	.05	.04	.02
16	Doug Soetaert (159)	.03	.02	.01
17	Petr Svoboda (160)	.05	.04	.02
18	Kjell Dahlin	.10	.08	.04

19	Patrick Roy	6.00	4.50	2.50
20	Alain Cote (161)	.03	.02	.01
21	Mario Gosselin (162)	.03	.02	.01
22	Michel Goulet	.15	.11	.06
23	Jenn F. Sauve (163)	.03	.02	.01
24	Paul Gillis (164)	.03	.02	.01
25	Brent Ashton	.05	.04	.02
26	Peter Stastny	.20	.15	.08
27	Anton Stastny	.05	.04	.02
28	Gilbert Delorme (167)	.03	.02	.01
29	Risto Siltanen (168)	.03	.02	.01
30	Robert Picard (170)	.03	.02	.01
31	David Shaw (171)	.05	.04	.02
32	Dale Hunter	.07	.05	.03
33	Clint Malarchuk	.07	.05	.03
34	Raymond Bourque	.35	.25	.14
35	Rick Middleton (172)	.07	.05	.03
36	Charlie Simmer (173)	.05	.04	.02
37	Keith Crowder	.05	.04	.02
38	Barry Pederson (175)	.05	.04	.02
39	Reed Larson (176)	.03	.02	.01
40	Stephen Kasper (177)	.05	.04	.02
41	Pat Riggin (178)	.05	.04	.02
42	Mike Foligno	.05	.04	.02
43	Gilbert Perreault (179)	.10	.08	.04
44	Michael Ramsey (180)	.05	.04	.02
45	Tom Barrasso (186)	.15	.11	.06
46	Brian Engblom (187)	.03	.02	.01
47	Phil Housley (188)	.15	.11	.06
48	John Tucker (189)	.05	.04	.02
49	David Andreychuk	.25	.20	.10
50	David Babych	.07	.05	.03
51	Ron Francis (190)	.07	.05	.03
52	Michael Liut (191)	.07	.05	.03
53	Sylvain Turgeon	.07	.05	.03
54	John Anderson (192)	.03	.02	.01
55	Joel Quenneville (193)	.03	.02	.01
56	Kevin Dineen (194)	.07	.05	.03
57	Ray Ferraro (195)	.15	.11	.06
58	Action	.15	.11	.06
59	Action	.05	.04	.02
60	Action	.05	.04	.02
61	Action	.05	.04	.02
62	Action	.05	.04	.02
63	Action	.05	.04	.02
64	Action	.05	.04	.02
65	Action	.05	.04	.02
66	Andrew Moog (197)	.15	.11	.06
67	Grant Fuhr (198)	.15	.11	.06
68	Paul Coffey	.35	.25	.14
69	Charles Huddy (199)	.05	.04	.02
70	Kevin Lowe (200)	.07	.05	.03
71	Lee Fogolin	.05	.04	.02
72	Wayne Gretzky	1.50	1.25	.60
73	Jari Kurri	.25	.20	.10
74	Michael Krushelnyski (201)	.05	.04	.02
75	Mark Napier (202)	.05	.04	.02
76	Craig MacTavish (204)	.15	.11	.06
77	Kevin McClelland (205)	.03	.02	.01
78	Glenn Anderson	.15	.11	.06
79	Mark Messier	.50	.40	.20
80	Lanny McDonald	.15	.11	.06
81	John Tonelli (207)	.05	.04	.02
82	Joe Mullen (208)	.12	.09	.05
83	Rejean Lemelin	.07	.05	.03
84	James Peplinski (212)	.03	.02	.01
85	Jamie Macoun (213)	.03	.02	.01
86	Al MacInnis (214)	.50	.40	.20
87	Dan Quinn (215)	.05	.04	.02
88	Marcel Dionne	.20	.15	.08
89	Jim Fox (219)	.03	.02	.01
90	David Taylor (220)	.05	.04	.02
91	Bob Janecyk (222)	.05	.04	.02
92	Gordon (Jay) Wells (223)	.03	.02	.01
93	Bryan Erikson (224)	.03	.02	.01
94	David Williams (225)	.05	.04	.02
95	Bernie Nicholls	.25	.20	.10
96	Stanley Smyl	.05	.04	.02
97	Doug Halward (227)	.03	.02	.01
98	Richard Brodeur (228)	.05	.04	.02
99	Tony Tanti	.07	.05	.03
100	Brent Peterson (229)	.03	.02	.01
101	Patrik Sundstrom (230)	.05	.04	.02
102	Doug Lidster (231)	.05	.04	.02
103	Petri Skriko (232)	.05	.04	.02
104	Dale Hawerchuk	.25	.20	.10
105	Bill Derlago (234)	.03	.02	.01
106	Ray Neufeld (235)	.03	.02	.01
107	Randy Carlyle (237)	.03	.02	.01
108	Paul MacLean (238)	.05	.04	.02
109	Brian Mullen (242)	.05	.04	.02
110	Thomas Steen (243)	.05	.04	.02
111	Laurie Boschman	.05	.04	.02
112	Paul Coffey (126)	.30	.25	.12
113	Michel Goulet (127)	.20	.15	.08
114	John Vanbiesbrouck (128)	.25	.20	.10
115	Wayne Gretzky (129)	1.00	.70	.40
116	Mark Howe (130)	.12	.09	.05
117	Mike Bossy (131)	.20	.15	.08
118	Jari Kurri (132)	.15	.11	.06
119	Raymond Bourque (133)	.25	.20	.10
120	Mario Lemieux (134)	1.50	1.25	.60
121	Grant Fuhr (135)	.20	.15	.08
122	Mats Naslund (182)	.10	.08	.04
123	Larry Robinson (183)	.15	.11	.06
124	Chris Cichocki (184)	.10	.08	.04
125	Wendel Clark (185)	1.00	.70	.40
126	Kjell Dahlin (112)	.12	.09	.05
127	Per-Erik Eklund (113)	.12	.09	.05
128	Jim Johnson (114)	.10	.08	.04
129	Petr Klima (115)	.25	.20	.10
130	Joel Otto (116)	.15	.11	.06
131	Mike Ridley (117)	.30	.25	.12
132	Patrick Roy (118)	4.00	3.00	1.50
133	David Shaw (119)	.12	.09	.05
134	Gary Suter (120)	.35	.25	.14
135	Steve Thomas (121)	.20	.15	.08
136	Borje Salming (244)	.07	.05	.03
137	Gary Nylund (245)	.05	.04	.02
138	Richard Vaive	.07	.05	.03
139	Don Edwards (249)	.05	.04	.02
140	Steve Thomas (250)	.05	.04	.02
141	Wendel Clark	1.00	.70	.40
142	Miroslav Frycer	.05	.04	.02
143	Tom Fergus	.05	.04	.02
144	Marian Stastny (252)	.03	.02	.01
145	Brad Maxwell (253)	.03	.02	.01
146	Dan Daoust (254)	.03	.02	.01
147	Greg Terrion (255)	.03	.02	.01
148	Al Iafrate	.40	.30	.15
149	Russ Courtnall	.30	.25	.12
150	Denis Savard	.15	.11	.06
151	Darryl Sutter (6)	.05	.04	.02
152	Bob Sauve (7)	.05	.04	.02
153	Douglas Wilson, Jr.	.12	.09	.05
154	Troy Murray (9)	.05	.04	.02
155	Alan Secord (10)	.05	.04	.02
156	Ed Olczyk (14)	.12	.09	.05
157	Steve Larmer (15)	.12	.09	.05
158	John Ogrodnick	.07	.05	.03
159	Danny Gare (16)	.05	.04	.02
160	Michael O'Connell (160)	.05	.04	.02
161	Steve Yzerman (20)	.75	.60	.30
162	Petr Klima (21)	.15	.11	.06
163	Kelly Kisio (23)	.05	.04	.02
164	Douglas Shedden (24)	.03	.02	.01
165	Gregory Stefan	.07	.05	.03
166	Neal Broten	.07	.05	.03
167	Brian Bellows (28)	.10	.08	.04
168	Scott Bjugstad (29)	.03	.02	.01
169	Dino Ciccarelli	.12	.09	.05
170	Dennis Maruk (30)	.05	.04	.02
171	Dirk Graham (31)	.25	.20	.10
172	Curt Giles (35)	.03	.02	.01
173	Craig Hartsburg (36)	.03	.02	.01
174	Bernie Federko	.10	.08	.04

175	Brian Sutter (38)	.05	.04	.02
176	Ron Flockhart (39)	.03	.02	.01
177	Douglas Gilmour (40)	.75	.60	.30
178	Charlie Bourgeois (41))	.03	.02	.01
179	Rick Wamsley (43)	.05	.04	.02
180	George (Rob) Ramage (44)	.05	.04	.02
181	Mark Hunter	.05	.04	.02
182	Robert Froese (122)	.05	.04	.02
183	Wayne Gretzky (123)	1.00	.70	.40
184	Mark Howe (124)	.12	.09	.05
185	Jari Kurri (125)	.20	.15	.08
186	William Jennings Trophy: (Robert Froese) (45)	.05	.04	.02
187	William Jennings Trophy: (Darren Jensen) (46)	.05	.04	.02
188	Norris Trophy: (Paul Coffey) (47)	.20	.15	.08
189	Frank J. Selke Trophy: (Troy Murray) (48)	.07	.05	.03
190	Vezina Trophy: (John Vanbiesbrouck) (51)	.30	.25	.12
191	Art Ross Trophy: (Wayne Gretzky) (52)	1.00	.70	.40
192	Calder Trophy: (Gary Suter) (54)	.10	.08	.04
193	Bill Masterton Trophy: (Robert Froese) (55)	.07	.05	.03
194	Lady Byng Trophy: (Mike Bossy) (56)	.15	.11	.06
195	Art Ross Trophy: (Wayne Gretzky) (57)	1.00	.70	.40
196	Gregory Adams	.05	.04	.02
197	Dave Lewis (66)	.03	.02	.01
198	Joe Cirella (67)	.05	.04	.02
199	Rich Preston (69)	.03	.02	.01
200	Mark Johnson (70)	.05	.04	.02
201	Kirk Muller (74)	.25	.20	.10
202	Patrick Verbeek (75)	.12	.09	.05
203	Mel Bridgman	.05	.04	.02
204	Bob Nystrom (76)	.03	.02	.01
205	Clark Gillies (77)	.05	.04	.02
206	Pat LaFontaine	.75	.60	.30
207	Patrick Flatley (81)	.03	.02	.01
208	Bob Bourne (82)	.03	.02	.01
209	Denis Potvin	.15	.11	.06
210	Duane Sutter	.07	.05	.03
211	Brent Sutter	.07	.05	.03
212	Kelly Hrudey (84)	.15	.11	.06
213	Billy Smith (85)	.07	.05	.03
214	Tomas Jonsson (86)	.05	.04	.02
215	Ken Morrow (87)	.03	.02	.01
216	Bryan Trottier	.20	.15	.08
217	Mike Bossy	.30	.25	.12
218	John Vanbiesbrouck	.40	.30	.15
219	Bob Brooke (89)	.03	.02	.01
220	James Patrick (90)	.05	.04	.02
221	Mike Ridley	.35	.25	.14
222	Ronald Greschner (91)	.05	.04	.02
223	Thomas Laidlaw (92)	.03	.02	.01
224	Larry Melnyk (93)	.03	.02	.01
225	Reijo Ruotsalainen (94)	.03	.02	.01
226	Terry Ruskowski	.07	.05	.03
227	Willy Lindstrom (97)	.03	.02	.01
228	Mike Bullard (98)	.03	.02	.01
229	Roberto Romano (100)	.03	.02	.01
230	John Chabot (101)	.03	.02	.01
231	Maurice Mantha (102)	.03	.02	.01
232	Doug Bodger (103)	.05	.04	.02
233	Mario Lemieux	4.00	3.00	1.50
234	Glenn Resch (105)	.07	.05	.03
235	Bradley Marsh (106)	.05	.04	.02
236	Robert Froese	.07	.05	.03
237	Doug Crossman (107)	.03	.02	.01
238	Ilkka Sinisalo (108)	.03	.02	.01
239	Brian Propp	.07	.05	.03
240	Tim Kerr	.07	.05	.03
241	David Poulin	.07	.05	.03
242	Richard Sutter (109)	.05	.04	.02

243	Ronald Sutter (110)	.05	.04	.02
244	Murray Craven (136)	.05	.04	.02
245	Peter Zezel (137)	.10	.08	.04
246	Mark Howe	.07	.05	.03
247	Byron (Brad) McCrimmon	.07	.05	.03
248	Dave Christian	.07	.05	.03
249	Rod Langway (139)	.07	.05	.03
250	Robert Carpenter (140)	.07	.05	.03
251	Michael Gartner	.15	.11	.06
252	Al Jensen (144)	.05	.04	.02
253	Craig Laughlin (145)	.03	.02	.01
254	Scott Stevens (146)	.12	.09	.05
255	Alan Haworth (147)	.03	.02	.01

1987 O-Pee-Chee Stickers

These stickers, each measuring 2 1/8" by 3", have a color action photo on the front, with a card number in the lower left corner. The right photo border forms an hockey stick, with a puck next to the blade. The back is in French and includes the player's name and sticker number, plus a mail-in offer from O-Pee-Chee. Some stickers were made in pairs, as indicated by . This set does not have any foils, but an album was produced again.

		MT	NM	EX
Complete Set (255):		20.00	15.00	8.00
Common Player:		.05	.04	.02
1	Ron Hextall	.20	.15	.08
2	Stanley Cup Action	.05	.04	.02
3	Stanley Cup Action	.05	.04	.02
4	Stanley Cup Action	.05	.04	.02
5	Stanley Cup Action	.05	.04	.02
6	Mats Naslund	.07	.05	.03
7	Guy Carbonneau (146)	.07	.05	.03
8	Gaston Gingras (147)	.03	.02	.01
9	Chris Chelios	.20	.15	.08
10	Robert Smith	.07	.05	.03
11	Richard Green (149)	.03	.02	.01
12	Bob Gainey (150)	.07	.05	.03
13	Patrick Roy	2.00	1.50	.80
14	Kjell Dahlin (153)	.05	.04	.02
15	Christopher Nilan (154)	.05	.04	.02
16	Larry Robinson	.12	.09	.05
17	Ryan Walter (157)	.05	.04	.02
18	Petr Svoboda (158)	.05	.04	.02
19	Claude Lemieux	.75	.60	.30
20	George (Rob) Ramage (160)	.05	.04	.02
21	Mark Hunter (161)	.03	.02	.01
22	Rick Wamsley (163)	.05	.04	.02
23	Greg Palawski (164)	.03	.02	.01
24	Bernie Federko	.07	.05	.03
25	Ron Flockhart (166)	.03	.02	.01
26	Tim Bothwell (167)	.03	.02	.01
27	Douglas Gilmour	.60	.45	.25
28	Kelly Kisio (168))	.05	.04	.02
29	Donald Maloney (169)	.03	.02	.01
30	James Patrick (171)	.05	.04	.02
31	Willie Huber (172)	.03	.02	.01
32	Walter Poddubny	.05	.04	.02
33	John Vanbiesbrouck (178)	.15	.11	.06
34	Marcel Dionne (179)	.12	.09	.05
35	Tomas Sandstrom	.15	.11	.06
36	Joe Mullen	.15	.11	.06
37	Mike Bullard (180)	.03	.02	.01
38	Neil Sheehy (181)	.03	.02	.01
39	Paul Reinhart	.05	.04	.02
40	Al MacInnis	.40	.30	.15
41	Michael Vernon (182)	.20	.15	.08
42	Joel Otto (183)	.05	.04	.02
43	Lanny McDonald	.15	.11	.06
44	Hakan Loob (184)	.05	.04	.02
45	Carey Wilson (185)	.03	.02	.01
46	James Peplinski	.05	.04	.02
47	John Tonelli (186)	.05	.04	.02
48	Jamie Macoun (187)	.03	.02	.01
49	Gary Suter	.15	.11	.06

50	Dennis Maruk (189)	.05	.04	.02
51	Donald Beaupre (190)	.05	.04	.02
52	Neal Broten (193)	.05	.04	.02
53	Brian Bellows (194)	.10	.08	.04
54	Craig Hartsburg	.05	.04	.02
55	Gordon Roberts (196)	.03	.02	.01
56	Steve Payne (197)	.03	.02	.01
57	Dino Ciccarelli	.12	.09	.05
58	Patrick Verbeek (199)	.07	.05	.03
59	Douglas Sulliman (200)	.03	.02	.01
60	Bruce Driver (202)	.03	.02	.01
61	Joe Cirella (203)	.05	.04	.02
62	Aaron Broten	.05	.04	.02
63	Alain Chevrier (204)	.05	.04	.02
64	Mark Johnson (205)	.05	.04	.02
65	Kirk Muller	.25	.20	.10
66A	Jim Sandlak	.05	.04	.02
66B	Stephen Kasper	.05	.04	.02
67	Raymond Bourque	.05	.04	.02
68	Calgary vs. Boston	.05	.04	.02
69	Murray Craven	.05	.04	.02
70	Boston Bruins	.05	.04	.02
71	New York Islanders	.05	.04	.02
72	Sean Burke	.05	.04	.02
73	Patrick Roy	.05	.04	.02
74	Alan Secord (207)	.05	.04	.02
75	Bob Sauve (208)	.05	.04	.02
76	Ed Olczyk (210)	.07	.05	.03
77	Douglas Wilson, Jr. (211)	.07	.05	.03
78	Denis Savard	.15	.11	.06
79	Troy Murray (212)	.05	.04	.02
80	Gary Nylund (213)	.05	.04	.02
81	Steve Larmer	.15	.11	.06
82	Jari Kurri	.20	.15	.08
83	Esa Tikkanen (215)	.50	.40	.20
84	Kevin Lowe (216)	.07	.05	.03
85	Grant Fuhr	.20	.15	.08
86	Wayne Gretzky	1.25	.90	.50
87	Charles Huddy (219)	.05	.04	.02
88	Kent Nilsson (220)	.05	.04	.02
89	Paul Coffey	.25	.20	.10
90	Michael Krushelnyski (223)	.05	.04	.02
91	Craig MacTavish (224)	.07	.05	.03
92	Mark Messier	.30	.25	.12
93	Andrew Moog (226)	.12	.09	.05
94	Randall Gregg (227)	.05	.04	.02
95	Glenn Anderson	.12	.09	.05
96	Peter Zezel (229)	.05	.04	.02
97	Brian Propp (230)	.07	.05	.03
98	David Poulin (232)	.05	.04	.02
99	Byron (Brad) McCrimmon (233)	.05	.04	.02
100	Mark Howe	.07	.05	.03
101	Ron Hextall (234)	.15	.11	.06
102	Ronald Sutter (235)	.05	.04	.02
103	Tim Kerr	.07	.05	.03
104	Petr Klima (237)	.10	.08	.04
105	Adam Oates (238)	1.25	.90	.50
106	Gerard Gallant (240)	.07	.05	.03
107	Michael O'Connell (241)	.03	.02	.01
108	Brent Ashton	.05	.04	.02
109	Glen Hanlon (242)	.05	.04	.02
110	Harold Snepsts (243)	.03	.02	.01
111	Steve Yzerman	.60	.45	.25
112	Mark Howe (124)	.07	.05	.03
113	Michel Goulet (125)	.07	.05	.03
114	Ron Hextall (126)	.15	.11	.06
115	Wayne Gretzky (127)	.75	.60	.30
116	Raymond Bourque (128)	.15	.11	.06
117	Jari Kurri (129)	.12	.09	.05
118	Dino Ciccarelli (130)	.07	.05	.03
119	Lawrence Murphy (131)	.10	.08	.04
120	Mario Lemieux (132)	.75	.60	.30
121	Michael Liut (133)	.05	.04	.02
122	Luc Robitaille (134)	1.50	1.25	.60
123	Al MacInnis (135)	.20	.15	.08
124	Brian Benning (112)	.03	.02	.01
125	Shawn Burr (113)	.03	.02	.01
126	Jimmy Carson (114)	.25	.20	.10
127	Shayne Corson (115)	.20	.15	.08
128	Vincent Damphousse (116)	.35	.25	.14
129	Ron Hextall (117)	.15	.11	.06
130	Jason Lafreniere (118)	.03	.02	.01
131	Ken Leiter (119)	.03	.02	.01
132	Allen Pedersen (120)	.03	.02	.01
133	Luc Robitaille (121)	1.50	1.25	.60
134	Christian Ruuttu (122)	.07	.05	.03
135	Jim Sandlak (123)	.03	.02	.01
136	Keith Crowder (245)	.03	.02	.01
137	Charlie Simmer (246)	.05	.04	.02
138	Rick Middleton (248)	.05	.04	.02
139	Doug Keans (249)	.05	.04	.02
140	Raymond Bourque	.25	.20	.10
141	Tom McCarthy (250)	.03	.02	.01
142	Reed Larson (251)	.03	.02	.01
143	Cam Neely	.75	.60	.30
144	Christian Ruuttu (253)	.05	.04	.02
145	John Tucker (254)	.05	.04	.02
146	Steve Dykstra (7)	.03	.02	.01
147	David Andreychuk (8)	.15	.11	.06
148	Tom Barrasso	.15	.11	.06
149	Michael Ramsey (11)	.03	.02	.01
150	Mike Foligno (12)	.03	.02	.01
151	Phil Housley	.15	.11	.06
152	Wendel Clark	.25	.20	.10
153	Greg Terrion (14)	.03	.02	.01
154	Steve Thomas (15)	.05	.04	.02
155	Richard Vaive	.05	.04	.02
156	Russ Courtnall	.30	.25	.12
157	Rick Lanz (17)	.03	.02	.01
158	Miroslav Frycer (18)	.03	.02	.01
159	Tom Fergus (20)	.05	.04	.02
160	Al Iafrate (21)	.20	.15	.08
161	Gary Leeman	.05	.04	.02
162	Allan Bester	.05	.04	.02
163	Todd Gill (22)	.03	.02	.01
164	Ken Wregget (23)	.10	.08	.04
165	Borje Salming	.07	.05	.03
166	Craig Simpson (25)	.20	.15	.08
167	Terry Ruskowski (26)	.05	.04	.02
168	Gilles Meloche (28)	.05	.04	.02
169	John Chabot (29)	.03	.02	.01
170	Mario Lemieux	2.00	1.50	.80
171	Maurice Mantha (30)	.03	.02	.01
172	Jim Johnson (31)	.03	.02	.01
173	Dan Quinn	.05	.04	.02
174	Wayne Gretzky (176)	.75	.60	.30
175	Brian Hayward (177)	.07	.05	.03
176	Mark Howe (174)	.07	.05	.03
177	Luc Robitaille (175)	1.50	1.25	.60
178	Raymond Bourque (33)	.15	.11	.06
179	David Poulin (34)	.05	.04	.02
180	Hart Trophy Winner: (Wayne Gretzky) (37)	.75	.60	.30
181	Ross Trophy Winner: (Wayne Gretzky) (38)	.75	.60	.30
182	Ron Hextall (41)	.15	.11	.06
183	Doug Jarvis (42)	.03	.02	.01
184	Brian Hayward (44)	.07	.05	.03
185	Patrick Roy (45)	1.00	.70	.40
186	Joe Mullen (47)	.15	.11	.06
187	Luc Robitaille (48)	1.50	1.25	.60
188	Barry Pederson	.07	.05	.03
189	Richard Brodeur (50)	.05	.04	.02
190	Dave Richter (51)	.03	.02	.01
191	Doug Lidster	.05	.04	.02
192	Petri Skriko	.08	.06	.03
193	Richard Sutter (52)	.05	.04	.02
194	Jim Sandiak (53)	.07	.05	.03
195	Tony Tanti	.07	.05	.03
196	Michel Petit (55)	.05	.04	.02
197	Jim Benning (56)	.03	.02	.01
198	Stanley Smyl	.05	.04	.02
199	Brent Peterson (58)	.03	.02	.01
200	Garth Butcher (59)	.20	.15	.08
201	Patrik Sundstrom	.07	.05	.03

		MT	NM	EX
202	Kevin Dineen (60)	.07	.05	.03
203	Sylvain Turgeon (61)	.05	.04	.02
204	John Anderson (63)	.03	.02	.01
205	Ulf Samuelsson (64)	.25	.20	.10
206	Ron Francis	.15	.11	.06
207	Doug Jarvis (74)	.03	.02	.01
208	David Babych (75)	.03	.02	.01
209	Michael Liut	.07	.05	.03
210	Jimmy Carson (76)	.25	.20	.10
211	Larry Playfair (77)	.03	.02	.01
212	Gordon (Jay) Wells (79)	.03	.02	.01
213	Roland Melanson (80)	.05	.04	.02
214	Bernie Nicholls	.20	.15	.08
215	David Taylor (83)	.05	.04	.02
216	Jim Fox (84)	.03	.02	.01
217	Luc Robitaille	2.50	2.00	1.00
218	John Ogrodnick	.07	.05	.03
219	Jason Lafreniere (87)	.03	.02	.01
220	Mike Hough (88)	.03	.02	.01
221	Paul Gillis	.05	.04	.02
222	Peter Stastny	.20	.15	.08
223	David Shaw (90)	.03	.02	.01
224	Bill Derlago (91)	.03	.02	.01
225	Michel Goulet	.15	.11	.06
226	Douglas Shedden (93)	.03	.02	.01
227	Basil McRae (94)	.03	.02	.01
228	Anton Stastny	.05	.04	.02
229	Randy Moller (96)	.03	.02	.01
230	Robert Picard (97)	.03	.02	.01
231	Mario Gosselin	.07	.05	.03
232	Lawrence Murphy (98)	.07	.05	.03
233	Scott Stevens (99)	.10	.08	.04
234	Mike Ridley (101)	.07	.05	.03
235	Dave Christian (102)	.05	.04	.02
236	Rod Langway	.07	.05	.03
237	Robert Gould (104)	.03	.02	.01
238	Bob Mason (105)	.03	.02	.01
239	Michael Gartner	.20	.15	.08
240	Bryan Trottier (106)	.12	.09	.05
241	Brent Sutter (107)	.07	.05	.03
242	Kelly Hrudey (109)	.10	.08	.04
243	Pat LaFontaine (110)	.40	.30	.15
244	Mike Bossy	.35	.25	.14
245	Patrick Flatley (136)	.05	.04	.02
246	Ken Morrow (137)	.03	.02	.01
247	Denis Potvin	.15	.11	.06
248	Randy Carlyle (138)	.05	.04	.02
249	Daniel Berthiaume (139)	.03	.02	.01
250	Mario Marois (141)	.03	.02	.01
251	Dave Ellett (142)	.07	.05	.03
252	Paul MacLean	.06	.05	.02
253	Gilles Hamel (144)	.03	.02	.01
254	Douglas Small (145)	.03	.02	.01
255	Dale Hawerchuk	.25	.20	.10

1988 O-Pee-Chee Stickers

These stickers measure 2 1/2" by 3 1/2". Each front has a color action photo on it, along with a sticker number in a square in the lower right corner. The right and bottom borders of the photo have a shadow-boxed frame. The player's name is not on the sticker; they are listed in the corresponding sticker album which was produced. The set does not have any foils in it, but some stickers are in pairs, as noted by . The back is done in one of three ways - trivia questions and answers, Future Stars cards, or various promotional offers. The are bilingual.

		MT	NM	EX
	Complete Set (270):	20.00	15.00	8.00
	Common Player:	.03	.02	.01
1	Conn Smythe Trophy Winner (Wayne Gretzky)	1.25	.90	.50
2	Oilers vs. Bruins	.05	.04	.02
3	Oilers vs. Bruins	.05	.04	.02
4	Oilers vs. Bruins	.05	.04	.02
5	Oilers vs. Bruins	.05	.04	.02

6	Douglas Wilson, Jr. (135)	.07	.05	.03
7	Dirk Graham (136)	.05	.04	.02
8	Darren Pang (137)	.05	.04	.02
9	Richard Vaive (138)	.05	.04	.02
10	Troy Murray (139)	.05	.04	.02
11	Brian Noonan (140)	.05	.04	.02
12	Steve Larmer	.12	.09	.05
13	Denis Savard	.12	.09	.05
14	Mark Hunter (141)	.03	.02	.01
15	Brian Sutter (142)	.05	.04	.02
16	Brett Hull (145)	2.00	1.50	.80
17	Anthony McKegney (146)	.03	.02	.01
18	Brian Benning (151)	.03	.02	.01
19	Anthony Hrkac (152)	.05	.04	.02
20	Douglas Gilmour	.50	.40	.20
21	Bernie Federko	.07	.05	.03
22	Cam Neely	.35	.25	.14
23	Raymond Bourque	.30	.25	.12
24	Rejean Lemelin (153)	.05	.04	.02
25	Gordon Kluzak (154)	.03	.02	.01
26	Rick Middleton (155)	.07	.05	.03
27	Stephen Kasper (156)	.05	.04	.02
28	Robert Sweeney (168)	.03	.02	.01
29	Randy Burridge (169)	.05	.04	.02
30	Whalers vs. Bruins	.05	.04	.02
31	Canadiens vs. Bruins	.05	.04	.02
32	Canadiens vs. Bruins	.05	.04	.02
33	Blues vs. Devils	.05	.04	.02
34	Canadiens vs. Bruins	.05	.04	.02
35	Canadiens vs. Bruins	.05	.04	.02
36	Canadiens vs. Bruins	.05	.04	.02
37	Canadiens vs. Bruins	.05	.04	.02
38	Canadiens vs. Bruins	.05	.04	.02
39	Larry Robinson (170)	.07	.05	.03
40	Ryan Walter (171)	.03	.02	.01
41	Guy Carbonneau (172)	.07	.05	.03
42	Bob Gainey (173)	.07	.05	.03
43	Claude Lemieux (176)	.15	.11	.06
44	Petr Svoboda (177)	.05	.04	.02
45	Patrick Roy	1.00	.70	.40
46	Robert Smith	.07	.05	.03
47	Michael McPhee (182)	.05	.04	.02
48	Craig Ludwig (183)	.03	.02	.01
49	Stephane J.J. Richer (182)	.30	.25	.12
50	Mats Naslund	.07	.05	.03
51	Chris Chelios	.15	.11	.06
52	Brian Hayward	.07	.05	.03
53	Larry Melnyk (184)	.03	.02	.01
54	Garth Butcher (185)	.07	.05	.03
55	Kirk McLean (186)	.50	.40	.20
56	Douglas Wickenheiser (187)	.03	.02	.01
57	Richard Sutter (190)	.05	.04	.02
58	Jim Benning (191)	.03	.02	.01
59	Tony Tanti	.05	.04	.02
60	Stanley Smyl	.05	.04	.02
61	David Saunders (196)	.03	.02	.01
62	Steve Tambellini (197)	.03	.02	.01
63	Doug Lidster	.05	.04	.02
64	Petri Skriko	.05	.04	.02
65	Barry Pederson	.05	.04	.02
66	Gregory Adams	.07	.05	.03
67	Michael Gartner	.20	.15	.08
68	Scott Stevens	.15	.11	.06
69	Rod Langway (198)	.05	.04	.02
70	Dave Christian (199)	.05	.04	.02
71	Lawrence Murphy (200)	.10	.08	.04
72	Clint Malarchuk (201)	.05	.04	.02
73	Dale Hunter (204)	.07	.05	.03
74	Mike Ridley (205)	.05	.04	.02
75	Kirk Muller	.25	.20	.10
76	Aaron Broten	.05	.04	.02
77	Bruce Driver (206)	.03	.02	.01
78	John MacLean (207)	.15	.11	.06
79	Joe Cirella (208)	.05	.04	.02
80	Doug Brown (209)	.05	.04	.02
81	Patrick Verbeek (210)	.07	.05	.03
82	Sean Burke (211)	.25	.20	.10
83	Joel Otto (212)	.05	.04	.02

84	George (Rob) Ramage (213)	.05	.04	.02
85	Lanny McDonald (215)	.10	.08	.04
86	Michael Vernon (216)	.15	.11	.06
87	John Tonelli (217)	.05	.04	.02
88	James Peplinski (218)	.03	.02	.01
89	Gary Suter	.10	.08	.04
90	Joe Nieuwendyk	1.25	.90	.50
91	Eric Nattress (219)	.03	.02	.01
92	Al MacInnis (220)	.20	.15	.08
93	Mike Bullard	.05	.04	.02
94	Hakan Loob	.07	.05	.03
95	Joe Mullen	.12	.09	.05
96	Byron (Brad) McCrimmon	.07	.05	.03
97	Brian Propp (221)	.05	.04	.02
98	Murray Craven (222)	.05	.04	.02
99	Rick Tocchet (225)	.40	.30	.15
100	Doug Crossman (226)	.03	.02	.01
101	Bradley Marsh (233)	.05	.04	.02
102	Peter Zezel (234)	.05	.04	.02
103	Ron Hextall	.15	.11	.06
104	Mark Howe	.10	.08	.04
105	Brent Sutter (235)	.05	.04	.02
106	Alan Kerr (236)	.03	.02	.01
107	Randy Wood (237)	.03	.02	.01
108	Mikko Makela (238)	.03	.02	.01
109	Kelly Hrudey (241)	.07	.05	.03
110	Steve Konroyd (242)	.03	.02	.01
111	Pat LaFontaine	.40	.30	.15
112	Bryan Trottier	.20	.15	.08
113	Gary Suter (243)	.05	.04	.02
114	Luc Robitaille (244)	.50	.40	.20
115	Patrick Roy (245)	.50	.40	.20
116	Mario Lemieux (246)	.75	.60	.30
117	Raymond Bourque (247)	.15	.11	.06
118	Hakan Loob (248)	.05	.04	.02
119	Mike Bullard (249)	.03	.02	.01
120	Byron (Brad) McCrimmon (250)	.05	.04	.02
121	Wayne Gretzky (251)	1.00	.70	.40
122	Grant Fuhr (252)	.15	.11	.06
123	Craig Simpson (255)	.10	.08	.04
124	Mark Howe (256)	.05	.04	.02
125	Joe Nieuwendyk (257)	.50	.40	.20
126	Ray Sheppard (258)	.25	.20	.10
127	Brett Hull (259)	2.00	1.50	.80
128	Ulf Dahlen (260)	.10	.08	.04
129	Anthony Hrkac (265)	.05	.04	.02
130	Robert Sweeney (266)	.05	.04	.02
131	Rob Brown (267)	.10	.08	.04
132	Lain Duncan (268)	.03	.02	.01
133	Pierre Turgeon (269)	.75	.60	.30
134	Calle Johansson (270)	.05	.04	.02
135	Darren Pang (6)	.05	.04	.02
136	Kirk McLean (7)	.50	.40	.20
137	Douglas Small (8)	.05	.04	.02
138	Thomas Steen (9)	.05	.04	.02
139	Laurie Boschman (10)	.03	.02	.01
140	Lain Duncan (11)	.03	.02	.01
141	Ray Neufeld (14)	.03	.02	.01
142	Mario Marois (15)	.03	.02	.01
143	Dale Hawerchuk	.15	.11	.06
144	Paul MacLean	.05	.04	.02
145	James Kyte (16)	.03	.02	.01
146	Eldon Reddick (17)	.05	.04	.02
147	Andrew McBain	.05	.04	.02
148	Randy Carlyle	.07	.05	.03
149	Daniel Berthiaume	.07	.05	.03
150	Dave Ellett	.07	.05	.03
151	Roland Melanson (18)	.03	.02	.01
152	Steve Duchesne (19)	.15	.11	.06
153	Robert Carpenter (24)	.05	.04	.02
154	Jim Fox (25)	.03	.02	.01
155	David Taylor (26)	.05	.04	.02
156	Bernie Nicholls (27)	.15	.11	.06
157	Luc Robitaille	.75	.60	.30
158	Jimmy Carson	.15	.11	.06
159	Bruins vs. Canadiens	.05	.04	.02
160	Nordiques vs. Devils	.05	.04	.02
161	Nordiques vs. Devils	.05	.04	.02
162	North Stars vs. Devils	.05	.04	.02
163	Oilers vs. Devils	.05	.04	.02
164	Oilers vs. Devils	.05	.04	.02
165	Oilers vs. Devils	.05	.04	.02
166	Oilers vs. Devils	.05	.04	.02
167	Bruins vs. Canadiens	.05	.04	.02
168	Mark Osborne (28)	.03	.02	.01
169	Dan Daoust (29)	.03	.02	.01
170	Tom Fergus (39)	.03	.02	.01
171	Vincent Damphousse (40)	.20	.15	.08
172	Wendel Clark (41)	.25	.20	.10
173	Luke Richardson (42)	.05	.04	.02
174	Borje Salming	.07	.05	.03
175	Russ Courtnall	.12	.09	.05
176	Rick Lanz (43)	.03	.02	.01
177	Ken Wregget (44)	.07	.05	.03
178	Gary Leeman	.07	.05	.03
179	Alan Secord	.07	.05	.03
180	Al Iafrate	.15	.11	.06
181	Ed Olczyk	.10	.08	.04
182	Normand Rochefort (47)	.03	.02	.01
183	Lane Lambert (48)	.03	.02	.01
184	Tommy Albelin (53)	.03	.02	.01
185	Jason Lafreniere (54)	.03	.02	.01
186	Alain Cote (55)	.03	.02	.01
187	Gaetan Duchesne (56)	.03	.02	.01
188	Michel Goulet	.15	.11	.06
189	Peter Stastny	.20	.15	.08
190	Jeff Jackson (57)	.03	.02	.01
191	Mike Eagles (58)	.03	.02	.01
192	Jeff Brown	.40	.30	.15
193	Mario Gosselin	.07	.05	.03
194	Anton Stastny	.05	.04	.02
195	Alan Haworth	.05	.04	.02
196	Donald Beaupre (61)	.07	.05	.03
197	Brian MacLellan (62)	.03	.02	.01
198	Brian Lawton (69)	.03	.02	.01
199	Craig Hartsburg (70)	.03	.02	.01
200	Maurice Mantha (71)	.03	.02	.01
201	Neal Broten (72)	.05	.04	.02
202	Dino Ciccarelli	.15	.11	.06
203	Brian Bellows	.15	.11	.06
204	Mario Lemieux (73)	.75	.60	.30
205	Joe Nieuwendyk (74)	.50	.40	.20
206	Byron (Brad) McCrimmon (77)	.05	.04	.02
207	Peter Peeters (78)	.05	.04	.02
208	Norris Trophy Winner: (Raymond Bourque) (79)	.12	.09	.05
209	Frank J. Selke Trophy Winner: (Guy Carbonneau) (80)	.05	.04	.02
210	Hart Trophy Winner: (Mario Lemieux) (81)	.75	.60	.30
211	Art Ross Trophy Winner: (Mario Lemieux) (82)	.75	.60	.30
212	Vezina Trophy Winner: (Grant Fuhr) (83)	.10	.08	.04
213	Bill Masterton Trophy Winner: (Bob Bourne) (84)	.03	.02	.01
214	William Jennings Trophy Winner: (Brian Hayward)	.35	.25	.14
215	Lady Byng Trophy Winner: (Mats Naslund) (85)	.05	.04	.02
216	Calder Trophy Winner: (Joe Nieuwendyk) (86)	.50	.40	.20
217	Craig MacTavish (87)	.03	.02	.01
218	Chris Joseph (88)	.03	.02	.01
219	Kevin Lowe (91)	.05	.04	.02
220	Esa Tikkanen (92)	.25	.20	.10
221	Charles Huddy (97)	.03	.02	.01
222	Geoff Courtnall (98)	.50	.40	.20
223	Grant Fuhr	.15	.11	.06
224	Wayne Gretzky	1.50	1.25	.60
225	James (Steve) Smith (99)	.25	.20	.10
226	Michael Krushelnyski (100)	.05	.04	.02
227	Jari Kurri	.12	.09	.05

228	Craig Simpson	.12	.09	.05
229	Glenn Anderson	.12	.09	.05
230	Mark Messier	.40	.30	.15
231	Randy Cunneyworth	.05	.04	.02
232	Mario Lemieux	1.50	1.25	.60
233	Paul Coffey (101)	.15	.11	.06
234	Doug Bodger (102)	.05	.04	.02
235	Dave Hunter (105)	.03	.02	.01
236	Dan Quinn (106)	.03	.02	.01
237	Rob Brown (107)	.10	.08	.04
238	Gilles Meloche (108)	.05	.04	.02
239	Kelly Kisio	.05	.04	.02
240	Walter Poddubny	.05	.04	.02
241	John Vanbiesbrouck (109)	.15	.11	.06
242	Tomas Sandstrom (110)	.10	.08	.04
243	David Shaw (113)	.05	.04	.02
244	Marcel Dionne (114)	.12	.09	.05
245	Christopher Nilan (115)	.05	.04	.02
246	James Patrick (116)	.05	.04	.02
247	Bob Probert (117)	.50	.40	.20
248	Michael O'Connell (118)	.03	.02	.01
249	Jeff Sharples (119)	.03	.02	.01
250	Brent Ashton (120)	.03	.02	.01
251	Petr Klima (121)	.05	.04	.02
252	Gregory Stefan (122)	.05	.04	.02
253	Steve Yzerman	.50	.40	.20
254	Gerald Gallant	.10	.08	.04
255	Phil Housley (123)	.10	.08	.04
256	Christian Ruuttu (124)	.03	.02	.01
257	Mike Foligno (125)	.03	.02	.01
258	Scott Arniel (126)	.03	.02	.01
259	Tom Barrasso (127)	.10	.08	.04
260	Michael Ramsey (128)	.03	.02	.01
261	David Andreychuk	.20	.15	.08
262	Ray Sheppard	.35	.25	.14
263	Michael Liut	.07	.05	.03
264	Ron Francis	.12	.09	.05
265	Ulf Samuelsson (129)	.10	.08	.04
266	Carey Wilson (130)	.03	.02	.01
267	Dave Babych (131)	.05	.04	.02
268	Ray Ferraro (132)	.05	.04	.02
269	Kevin Dineen (133)	.05	.04	.02
270	John Anderson (134)	.03	.02	.01

1989 O-Pee-Chee Stickers

These stickers add a fourth option for how the back is designed. In addition to the various promotional offers, Future Stars cards and trivia questions and answers, a new set, titled All-Stars, also appears. Each sticker has a number in a white square in the lower right corner on the front, plus either an action photo, team photo or trophy. Team photos consist of more than one sticker combination; other half-size stickers are also in pairs, as noted in . Each regular sticker measures 2 1/8" by 3". An album was also issued for the stickers.

		MT	NM	EX
	Complete Set (270):	20.00	15.00	8.00
	Common Player:	.03	.02	.01
1	Calgary Flames vs. Montreal Canadiens	.07	.05	.03
2	Calgary Flames vs. Montreal Canadiens	.05	.04	.02
3	Calgary Flames vs. Montreal Canadiens	.05	.04	.02
4	Calgary Flames vs. Montreal Canadiens	.05	.04	.02
5	Conn Smythe Trophy Winner (Al MacInnis)	.20	.15	.08
6	Calgary Flames vs. Montreal Canadiens	.05	.04	.02
7	Calgary Flames vs. Montreal Canadiens	.05	.04	.02
8	Calgary Flames vs. Montreal Canadiens	.05	.04	.02
9	Calgary Flames vs. Montreal Canadiens	.05	.04	.02
10	Darren Pang (150)	.03	.02	.01
11	Troy Murray (151)	.05	.04	.02
12	Dirk Graham (152)	.05	.04	.02
13	Dave Manson (153)	.10	.08	.04
14	Douglas Wilson, Jr. (156)	.07	.05	.03
15	Steve Thomas (157)	.05	.04	.02
16	Denis Savard	.12	.09	.05
17	Steve Larmer	.12	.09	.05
18	Paul MacLean (158)	.05	.04	.02
19	Paul Cavallini (159)	.05	.04	.02
20	Cliff Ronning (160)	.20	.15	.08
21	Gaston Gingras (161)	.03	.02	.01
22	Brett Hull	.75	.60	.30
23	Peter Zezel	.07	.05	.03
24	Brian Benning (162)	.05	.04	.02
25	Anthony Hrkac (163)	.03	.02	.01
26	Ken Linseman (164)	.03	.02	.01
27	Glen Wesley (165)	.07	.05	.03
28	Randy Burridge (166)	.05	.04	.02
29	Craig Janney (167)	.40	.30	.15
30	Andrew Moog (170)	.12	.09	.05
31	Robert Joyce (171)	.05	.04	.02
32	Raymond Bourque	.25	.20	.10
33	Cam Neely	.30	.25	.12
34	Sean Burke (174)	.12	.09	.05
35	Pat Elynuik (175)	.10	.08	.04
36	Tony Granato (176)	.10	.08	.04
37	Benoit Hogue (177)	.15	.11	.06
38	Craig Janney (180)	.40	.30	.15
39	Brian Leetch (181)	.75	.60	.30
40	Trevor Linden (184)	.60	.45	.25
41	Joe Sakic (185)	.75	.60	.30
42	Peter Sidorkiewicz (188)	.05	.04	.02
43	David Volek (189)	.07	.05	.03
44	Scott Young (190)	.05	.04	.02
45	Zarley Zalapski (191)	.10	.08	.04
46	Mats Naslund	.05	.04	.02
47	Robert Smith	.07	.05	.03
48	Guy Carbonneau (194)	.05	.04	.02
49	Shayne Corson (195)	.07	.05	.03
50	Brian Hayward	.07	.05	.03
51	Stephane J.J. Richer	.15	.11	.06
52	Claude Lemieux (196)	.10	.08	.04
53	Russ Courtnall (197)	.07	.05	.03
54	Petr Svoboda (198)	.05	.04	.02
55	Larry Robinson (199)	.07	.05	.03
56	Chris Chelios	.15	.11	.06
57	Patrick Roy	.75	.60	.30
58	Bob Gainey (200)	.07	.05	.03
59	Michael McPhee (201)	.05	.04	.02
60	Barry Pederson	.05	.04	.02
61	Trevor Linden	1.00	.70	.40
62	Richard Sutter (204)	.05	.04	.02
63	Brian Bradley (205)	.12	.09	.05
64	Kirk McLean	.35	.25	.14
65	Paul Reinhart	.05	.04	.02

380

66	Robert Nordmark (206)	.03	.02	.01
67	Steve Bozek (207)	.03	.02	.01
68	Stanley Smyl (208)	.05	.04	.02
69	Doug Lidster (209)	.03	.02	.01
70	Petri Skriko	.05	.04	.02
71	Tony Tanti	.05	.04	.02
72	Garth Butcher (210)	.07	.05	.03
73	Larry Melnvk (212)	.03	.02	.01
74	Kelly Miller (213)	.07	.05	.03
75	Dino Ciccarelli (214)	.07	.05	.03
76	Scott Stevens (215)	.10	.08	.04
77	Rod Langway (216)	.05	.04	.02
78	Dave Christian (219)	.05	.04	.02
79	Stephen Leach (220)	.07	.05	.03
80	Geoff Courtnall	.30	.25	.12
81	Mike Ridley	.07	.05	.03
82	Patrik Sundstrom (223)	.05	.04	.02
83	Kirk Muller (224)	.10	.08	.04
84	Tom Kurvers (225)	.03	.02	.01
85	Walter Poddubny (226)	.03	.02	.01
86	Sean Burke	.15	.11	.06
87	John MacLean	.15	.11	.06
88	Aaron Broten (229)	.03	.02	.01
89	Brendan Shanahan (230)	.35	.25	.14
90	Joe Mullen	.12	.09	.05
91	Byron (Brad) McCrimmon	.07	.05	.03
92	Lanny McDonald (231)	.10	.08	.04
93	Rick Wamsley (232)	.05	.04	.02
94	Michael Vernon	.15	.11	.06
95	Al MacInnis	.20	.15	.08
96	Joel Otto (233)	.03	.02	.01
97	Jiri Hrdina (234)	.03	.02	.01
98	Gary Roberts (235)	.30	.25	.12
99	James Peplinski (236)	.03	.02	.01
100	Gary Suter	.10	.08	.04
101	Joe Nieuwendyk	.25	.20	.10
102	Colin Patterson (239)	.03	.02	.01
103	Douglas Gilmour (240)	.30	.25	.12
104	Mike Bullard (241)	.03	.02	.01
105	Per-Erik Eklund (242)	.05	.04	.02
106	Brian Propp (245)	.05	.04	.02
107	Ronald Sutter (246)	.05	.04	.02
108	Rick Tocchet (247)	.12	.09	.05
109	Mark Howe (248)	.07	.05	.03
110	Tim Kerr	.07	.05	.03
111	Ron Hextall	.12	.09	.05
112	Mikko Makela (249)	.03	.02	.01
113	David Volek (250)	.03	.02	.01
114	Gary Nylund (251)	.03	.02	.01
115	Brent Sutter (252)	.05	.04	.02
116	Derek King (255)	.20	.15	.08
117	Gerald Diduck (256)	.03	.02	.01
118	Bryan Trottier	.15	.11	.06
119	Pat LaFontaine	.35	.25	.14
120	St. Louis Blues vs. Boston Bruins	.05	.04	.02
121	St. Louis Blues vs. Boston Bruins	.05	.04	.02
122	New York Rangers vs. Boston Bruins	.05	.04	.02
123	New York Rangers vs. Boston Bruins	.05	.04	.02
124	Chicago Black Hawks	.05	.04	.02
125	Boston Bruins vs. Montreal Canadiens	.12	.09	.05
126	New Jersey Devils vs. Boston Bruins	.05	.04	.02
127	Calgary Flames vs. New Jersey Devils	.05	.04	.02
128	Montreal Canadiens vs. Philly Flyers	.05	.04	.02
129	Philadelphia Flyers vs. Edmonton Oilers	.05	.04	.02
130	Vancouver Canucks vs. Boston Bruins	.05	.04	.02
131	Vancouvers Canucks vs. Boston Bruins	.05	.04	.02
132	Minnesota North Stars vs. Boston Bruins	.05	.04	.02
133	Minnesota North Stars vs. Boston Bruins	.05	.04	.02
134	Dale Hawerchuk	.15	.11	.06
135	Andrew McBain	.05	.04	.02
136	Lain Duncan (257)	.03	.02	.01
137	Eldon Reddick (258)	.07	.05	.03
138	Brent Ashton	.05	.04	.02
139	Dave Ellett	.05	.04	.02
140	James Kyte (259)	.03	.02	.01
141	Dougals Small (260)	.05	.04	.02
142	Pat Elynuik (263)	.10	.08	.04
143	Randy Carlyle (264)	.05	.04	.02
144	Thomas Steen	.07	.05	.03
145	Hannu Jarvenpaa	.05	.04	.02
146	Peter Taglianetti (265)	.03	.02	.01
147	Laurie Boschman (266)	.03	.02	.01
148	Luc Robitaille (267)	.25	.20	.10
149	Kelly Hrudey (268)	.07	.05	.03
150	Steve Duchesne (10)	.07	.05	.03
151	David Taylor (11)	.05	.04	.02
152	Stephen Kasper (12)	.05	.04	.02
153	Michael Krushelnyski (13)	.05	.04	.02
154	Wayne Gretzky	1.00	.70	.40
155	Bernie Nicholls	.15	.11	.06
156	Chris Chelios (14)	.10	.08	.04
157	Gerard Gallant (15)	.05	.04	.02
158	Mario Lemieux (18)	.50	.40	.20
159	Al MacInnis (19)	.12	.09	.05
160	Joe Mullen (20)	.07	.05	.03
161	Patrick Roy (21)	.35	.25	.14
162	Raymond Bourque (24)	.15	.11	.06
163	Rob Brown (25)	.05	.04	.02
164	Geoff Courtnall (26)	.10	.08	.04
165	Steve Duchesne (27)	.07	.05	.03
166	Wayne Gretzky (28)	.50	.40	.20
167	Michael Vernon (29)	.10	.08	.04
168	Gary Leeman	.05	.04	.02
169	Allan Bester	.05	.04	.02
170	David Reid (30)	.05	.04	.02
171	Craig Laughlin (31)	.03	.02	.01
172	Ed Olczyk	.07	.05	.03
173	Tom Fergus	.05	.04	.02
174	Mark Osborne (34)	.03	.02	.01
175	Bradley Marsh (35)	.05	.04	.02
176	Daniel Marois (36)	.05	.04	.02
177	Dan Daoust (37)	.03	.02	.01
178	Al Iafrate	.15	.11	.06
179	Vincent Damphousse	.20	.15	.08
180	Christopher Kotsopoulos (38)	.03	.02	.01
181	Derek Laxdal (39)	.03	.02	.01
182	Peter Stastny	.15	.11	.06
183	Paul Gillis	.05	.04	.02
184	Jeff Jackson (40)	.03	.02	.01
185	Mario Marois (41)	.03	.02	.01
186	Michel Goulet	.12	.09	.05
187	Joe Sakic	1.50	1.25	.60
188	Bob Mason (42)	.03	.02	.01
189	Marc Fortier (43)	.03	.02	.01
190	Robert Picard (44)	.03	.02	.01
191	Steve Finn (45)	.03	.02	.01
192	Iiro Jarvi	.05	.04	.02
193	Jeff Brown	.12	.09	.05
194	Gaetan Duchesne (48)	.03	.02	.01
195	Randy Moller (49)	.03	.02	.01
196	Michael Gartner (52)	.10	.08	.04
197	Jon Casey (53)	.20	.15	.08
198	Marc Habscheid (54)	.03	.02	.01
199	Lawrence Murphy (55)	.08	.06	.03
200	Neal Broten (58)	.05	.04	.02
201	Dave Archibald (59)	.03	.02	.01
202	Neal Broten	.05	.04	.02
203	Dave Gagner	.25	.20	.10
204	Vezina Trophy (62)	.03	.02	.01
205	Jennings Trophy (63)	.03	.02	.01

206	Selke Trophy (66)	.03	.02	.01
207	Masterton Trophy (67)	.03	.02	.01
208	Art Ross Trophy (Mario Lemieux) (68)	.50	.40	.20
209	Hart Trophy (Wayne Gretzky) (69)	.60	.45	.25
210	Vezina Trophy (Patrick Roy) (72)	.35	.25	.14
211	William Jennings Trophy: (Patrick Roy)	.20	.15	.08
212	Norris Trophy: (Chris Chelios) (73)	.10	.08	.04
213	Frank J. Selke Trophy (Guy Carbonneau) (74)	.05	.04	.02
214	Lady Byng Trophy: (Joe Mullen) (75)	.05	.04	.02
215	Calder Trophy: (Brian Leetch) (76)	.40	.30	.15
216	Masterton Trophy: (Tim Kerr) (77)	.03	.02	.01
217	Craig Simpson	.10	.08	.04
218	Glenn Anderson	.10	.08	.04
219	Esa Tikkanen (78)	.07	.05	.03
220	Charles Huddy (79)	.05	.04	.02
221	Jari Kurri	.15	.11	.06
222	Jimmy Carson	.07	.05	.03
223	James (Steve) Smith (82)	.07	.05	.03
224	Kevin Lowe (83)	.07	.05	.03
225	Chris Joseph (84)	.03	.02	.01
226	Craig MacTavish (85)	.05	.04	.02
227	Mark Messier	.40	.30	.15
228	Grant Fuhr	.15	.11	.06
229	Craig Muni (88)	.03	.02	.01
230	Bill Ranford (89)	.35	.25	.14
231	John Cullen (92)	.20	.15	.08
232	Zarley Zalapski (93)	.07	.05	.03
233	Bob Errey (96)	.03	.02	.01
234	Dan Quinn (97)	.03	.02	.01
235	Tom Barrasso (98)	.07	.05	.03
236	Rob Brown (99)	.05	.04	.02
237	Paul Coffey	.20	.15	.08
238	Mario Lemieux	1.00	.70	.40
239	Carey Wilson (102)	.03	.02	.01
240	Brian Leetch (103)	.75	.60	.30
241	Tony Granato (104)	.10	.08	.04
242	James Patrick (105)	.05	.04	.02
243	Brian Mullen	.07	.05	.03
244	Tomas Sandstrom	.10	.08	.04
245	Guy Lafleur (106)	.15	.11	.06
246	John Vanbiesbrouck (107)	.10	.08	.04
247	Bernie Federko (108)	.05	.04	.02
248	Gregory Stefan (109)	.05	.04	.02
249	Michael O'Connell (112)	.03	.02	.01
250	David Barr (113)	.03	.02	.01
251	Lee Norwood (114)	.03	.02	.01
252	Shawn Burr (115)	.03	.02	.01
253	Gerard Gallant	.05	.04	.02
254	Steve Yzerman	.40	.30	.15
255	Christian Ruuttu (116)	.03	.02	.01
256	Richard Vaive (117)	.03	.02	.01
257	Doug Bodger (136)	.03	.02	.01
258	David Andreychuk (137)	.10	.08	.04
259	Ray Sheppard (140)	.07	.05	.03
260	Mike Foligno (141)	.03	.02	.01
261	Phil Housley	.12	.09	.05
262	Pierre Turgeon	.50	.40	.20
263	Ray Ferraro (142)	.07	.05	.03
264	Scott Young (143)	.05	.04	.02
265	David Babych (146)	.05	.04	.02
266	Paul MacDermid (147)	.03	.02	.01
267	Michael Liut (148)	.05	.04	.02
268	Dave Tippett (149)	.03	.02	.01
269	Ron Francis	.10	.08	.04
270	Kevin Dineen	.07	.05	.03

1987 Panini Stickers

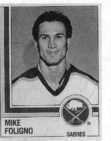 

These stickers, numbered only on the back, have a full-color photo of the player on the front, with his name, team name and team logo at the bottom of the card. The back says "Hockey '87" at the top, and has the card number in a black circle, flanked by NHL and NHLPA logos. The back is bilingual and has biographical information, a Panini logo and information about ordering an album which was produced to hold the stickers. The stickers are 2 1/8" by 2 11/16." Team logos are foil stickers. Stickers were made available through the album, too, which is why some prices are lower than expected.

		MT	NM	EX
Complete Set (396):		32.00	24.00	13.00
Common Player:		.05	.04	.02
1	Stanley Cup	.10	.08	.04
2	Boston Bruins "Action Player"	.05	.04	.02
3	Boston Bruins Team Logo	.05	.04	.02
4	Doug Keans	.05	.04	.02
5	Bill Ranford	.75	.60	.30
6	Raymond Bourque	.30	.25	.12
7	Reed Larson	.05	.04	.02
8	Mike Milbury	.08	.06	.03
9	Michael Thelven	.05	.04	.02
10	Cam Neely	.35	.25	.14
11	Charlie Simmer	.08	.06	.03
12	Rick Middleton	.08	.06	.03
13	Tom McCarthy	.05	.04	.02
14	Keith Crowder	.05	.04	.02
15	Stephen Kasper	.05	.04	.02
16	Ken Linseman	.05	.04	.02
17	Dwight Foster	.05	.04	.02
18	Jay Miller	.05	.04	.02
19	Buffalo Sabres "Action Player"	.05	.04	.02
20	Buffalo Sabres Team Logo	.05	.04	.02
21	Jacques Cloutier	.08	.06	.03
22	Tom Barrasso	.20	.15	.08
23	Daren Puppa	.25	.20	.10
24	Phil Housley	.25	.20	.10
25	Michael Ramsey	.05	.04	.02
26	Bill Hajt	.05	.04	.02
27	David Andreychuk	.35	.25	.14
28	Christian Ruuttu	.10	.08	.04
29	Mike Foligno	.05	.04	.02
30	John Tucker	.05	.04	.02
31	Adam Creighton	.15	.11	.06
32	Wilf Paiement	.05	.04	.02
33	Paul Cyr	.05	.04	.02
34	Clark Gillies	.08	.06	.03
35	Lindy Ruff	.05	.04	.02
36	Hartford Whalers "Action Player"	.05	.04	.02
37	Hartford Whalers Team Logo	.05	.04	.02

38	Mike Liut	.08	.06	.03
39	Stephen Weeks	.08	.06	.03
40	David Babych	.08	.06	.03
41	Ulf Samuelsson	.25	.20	.10
42	Dana Murzyn	.05	.04	.02
43	Ron Francis	.15	.11	.06
44	Kevin Dineen	.10	.08	.04
45	John Anderson	.05	.04	.02
46	Ray Ferraro	.15	.11	.06
47	Dean Evason	.05	.04	.02
48	Paul Lawless	.05	.04	.02
49	Robert (Stewart) Gavin	.05	.04	.02
50	Sylvain Turgeon	.08	.06	.03
51	Dave Tippett	.05	.04	.02
52	Doug Jarvis	.08	.06	.03
53	Montreal Canadiens "Action Player"	.05	.04	.02
54	Montreal Canadiens Team Logo	.05	.04	.02
55	Brian Hayward	.10	.08	.04
56	Patrick Roy	1.50	1.25	.60
57	Larry Robinson	.15	.11	.06
58	Chris Chelios	.15	.11	.06
59	Craig Ludwig	.05	.04	.02
60	Richard Green	.05	.04	.02
61	Mats Naslund	.08	.06	.03
62	Robert Smith	.08	.06	.03
63	Claude Lemieux	.30	.25	.12
64	Guy Carbonneau	.10	.08	.04
65	Stephane J.J. Richer	.75	.60	.30
66	Michael McPhee	.10	.08	.04
67	Brian Skrudland	.08	.06	.03
68	Christopher Nilan	.08	.06	.03
69	Bob Gainey	.15	.11	.06
70	New Jersey Devils "Action Player"	.05	.04	.02
71	New Jersey Devils Team Logo	.05	.04	.02
72	Craig Billington	.15	.11	.06
73	Alain Chevrier	.08	.06	.03
74	Bruce Driver	.10	.08	.04
75	Joe Cirella	.08	.06	.03
76	Ken Daneyko	.08	.06	.03
77	Craig Wolanin	.05	.04	.02
78	Aaron Broten	.05	.04	.02
79	Kirk Muller	.25	.20	.10
80	John MacLean	.25	.20	.10
81	Patick Verbeek	.15	.11	.06
82	Douglas Sulliman	.05	.04	.02
83	Mark Johnson	.08	.06	.03
84	Greg Adams	.08	.06	.03
85	Claude Loiselle	.05	.04	.02
86	Andy Brickley	.08	.06	.03
87	New York Islanders "Action Player"	.05	.04	.02
88	New York Islander Team Logo	.05	.04	.02
89	Billy Smith	.15	.11	.06
90	Kelly Hrudey	.25	.20	.10
91	Denis Potvin	.15	.11	.06
92	Tomas Jonsson	.05	.04	.02
93	Ken Leiter	.05	.04	.02
94	Ken Morrow	.08	.06	.03
95	Brian Curran	.05	.04	.02
96	Bryan Trottier	.20	.15	.08
97	Mike Bossy	.30	.25	.12
98	Pat LaFontaine	.50	.40	.20
99	Brent Sutter	.10	.08	.04
100	Mikko Makela	.05	.04	.02
101	Patrick Flatley	.05	.04	.02
102	Duane Sutter	.08	.06	.03
103	Richard Kromm	.05	.04	.02
104	New York Rangers "Action Player"	.05	.04	.02
105	New York Rangers Team Logo	.05	.04	.02
106	John Vanbiesbrouck	.35	.25	.14
107	James Patrick	.08	.06	.03
108	Ronald Greschner	.08	.06	.03
109	Willie Huber	.05	.04	.02
110	Curt Giles	.05	.04	.02
111	Larry Melnyk	.05	.04	.02
112	Walter Poddubny	.08	.06	.03
113	Marcel Dionne	.25	.20	.10
114	Tomas Sandstrom	.15	.11	.06
115	Kelly Kisio	.08	.06	.03
116	Pierre Larouche	.08	.06	.03
117	Donald Maloney	.05	.04	.02
118	Anthony McKegney	.05	.04	.02
119	Ron Duguay	.08	.06	.03
120	Jan Erixon	.08	.06	.03
121	Philadelphia Flyers "Action Player"	.05	.04	.02
122	Philadelphia Flyers Team Logo	.05	.04	.02
123	Ron Hextall	.20	.15	.08
124	Mark Howe	.10	.08	.04
125	Doug Crossman	.08	.06	.03
126	Byron (Brad) McCrimmon	.08	.06	.03
127	Bradley Marsh	.08	.06	.03
128	Tim Kerr	.08	.06	.03
129	Peter Zezel	.08	.06	.03
130	David Poulin	.08	.06	.03
131	Brian Propp	.08	.06	.03
132	Per-Erik Eklund	.08	.06	.03
133	Murray Craven	.08	.06	.03
134	Rick Tocchet	.75	.60	.30
135	Derrick Smith	.08	.06	.03
136	Ilkka Sinisalo	.08	.06	.03
137	Ronald Sutter	.08	.06	.03
138	Pittsburgh Penguins "Action Player"	.05	.04	.02
139	Pittsburgh Penguins Team Logo	.05	.04	.02
140	Gilles Meloche	.08	.06	.03
141	Doug Bodger	.08	.06	.03
142	Maurice Mantha	.05	.04	.02
143	Jim Johnson	.05	.04	.02
144	Rod Buskas	.05	.04	.02
145	Randy Hillier	.05	.04	.02
146	Mario Lemieux	2.00	1.50	.80
147	Dan Quinn	.05	.04	.02
148	Randy Cunneyworth	.05	.04	.02
149	Craig Simpson	.25	.20	.10
150	Terry Ruskowski	.08	.06	.03
151	John Chabot	.05	.04	.02
152	Bob Errey	.05	.04	.02
153	Dan Frawley	.05	.04	.02
154	David Hannan	.05	.04	.02
155	Quebec Nordiques "Action Player"	.05	.04	.02
156	Quebec Nordiques Team Logo	.05	.04	.02
157	Mario Gosselin	.08	.06	.03
158	Clint Malarchuk	.10	.08	.04
159	Risto Siltanen	.05	.04	.02
160	Robert Picard	.05	.04	.02
161	Normand Rochefort	.05	.04	.02
162	Randy Moller	.05	.04	.02
163	Michel Goulet	.15	.11	.06
164	Peter Stastny	.20	.15	.08
165	John Ogrodnick	.08	.06	.03
166	Anton Stastny	.08	.06	.03
167	Paul Gillis	.05	.04	.02
168	Dale Hunter	.12	.09	.05
169	Alain Cote	.05	.04	.02
170	Mike Eagles	.05	.04	.02
171	Jason Lafreniere	.05	.04	.02
172	Washington Capitals "Action Player"	.05	.04	.02
173	Washington Capitals Team Logo	.05	.04	.02
174	Peter Peeters	.08	.06	.03
175	Bob Mason	.08	.06	.03
176	Lawrence Murphy	.20	.15	.08
177	Scott Stevens	.20	.15	.08

178	Rod Langway	.10	.08	.04
179	Kevin Hatcher	.50	.40	.20
180	Michael Gartner	.20	.15	.08
181	Mike Ridley	.12	.09	.05
182	Craig Laughlin	.05	.04	.02
183	Gaetan Duchesne	.05	.04	.02
184	Dave Christian	.08	.06	.03
185	Greg Adams	.08	.06	.03
186	Kelly Miller	.08	.06	.03
187	Alan Haworth	.05	.04	.02
188	Lou Franceschetti	.05	.04	.02
189	Stanley Cup	.08	.06	.03
190	Stanley Cup	.08	.06	.03
191	Ron Hextall	.35	.25	.14
192	Wayne Gretzky	3.00	2.25	1.25
193	Brian Propp	.10	.08	.04
194	Mark Messier	1.00	.70	.40
195	Skates Through Oilers Defence (Mark Messier)	.10	.08	.04
196	Skates Through Oilers Defence (Mark Messier)	.10	.08	.04
197	Hoists The Stanley Cup for the 3rd Time (Gretzky)	.75	.60	.30
198	Hoists The Stanley Cup for the 3rd Time (Gretzky)	.75	.60	.30
199	Hoists The Stanley Cup for the 3rd Time (Gretzky)	.75	.60	.30
200	Hoists The Stanley Cup for the 3rd Time (Gretzky)	.75	.60	.30
201	Calgary Flames "Action Player"	.05	.04	.02
202	Calgary Flames Team Logo	.05	.04	.02
203	Mike Vernon	.40	.30	.15
204	Rejean Lemelin	.08	.06	.03
205	Allan MacInnis	.25	.20	.10
206	Paul Reinhart	.08	.06	.03
207	Gary Suter	.12	.09	.05
208	Jamie Macoun	.05	.04	.02
209	Neil Sheehy	.05	.04	.02
210	Joe Mullen	.15	.11	.06
211	Carey Wilson	.05	.04	.02
212	Joel Otto	.05	.04	.02
213	James Peplinski	.08	.06	.03
214	Hakan Loob	.08	.06	.03
215	Lanny McDonald	.20	.15	.08
216	Timothy Hunter	.05	.04	.02
217	Gary Roberts	.50	.40	.20
218	Chicago Black Hawks "Action Player"	.05	.04	.02
219	Chicago Black Hawks Team Logo	.05	.04	.02
220	Bob Sauve	.08	.06	.03
221	Murray Bannerman	.05	.04	.02
222	Douglas Wilson	.10	.08	.04
223	Rob Murray	.05	.04	.02
224	Gary Nylund	.05	.04	.02
225	Denis Savard	.15	.11	.06
226	Steve Larmer	.15	.11	.06
227	Troy Murray	.10	.08	.04
228	Wayne Presley	.05	.04	.02
229	Alan Secord	.08	.06	.03
230	Ed Olczyk	.10	.08	.04
231	Curt Fraser	.05	.04	.02
232	Bill Watson	.05	.04	.02
233	Keith Brown	.08	.06	.03
234	Darryl Sutter	.08	.06	.03
235	Detroit Red Wings "Action Player"	.05	.04	.02
236	Detroit Red Wings Team Logo	.05	.04	.02
237	Gregory Stefan	.08	.06	.03
238	Glen Hanlon	.08	.06	.03
239	Darren Veitch	.08	.06	.03
240	Mike O'Connell	.05	.04	.02
241	Harold Snepsts	.08	.06	.03
242	Dave Lewis	.05	.04	.02
243	Steve Yzerman	.60	.45	.25
244	Brent Ashton	.05	.04	.02
245	Gerard Gallant	.12	.09	.05
246	Petr Klima	.10	.08	.04
247	Shawn Burr	.08	.06	.03
248	Adam Oates	2.00	1.50	.80
249	Mel Bridgman	.08	.06	.03
250	Tim Higgins	.05	.04	.02
251	Joey Kocur	.15	.11	.06
252	Edmonton Oilers "Action Player"	.05	.04	.02
253	Edmonton Oilers Team Logo	.05	.04	.02
254	Grant Fuhr	.20	.15	.08
255	Andrew Moog	.20	.15	.08
256	Paul Coffey	.30	.25	.12
257	Kevin Lowe	.08	.06	.03
258	Craig Muni	.05	.04	.02
259	James (Steve) Smith	.30	.25	.12
260	Charles Huddy	.08	.06	.03
261	Wayne Gretzky	3.00	2.25	1.25
262	Jari Kurri	.20	.15	.08
263	Mark Messier	.50	.40	.20
264	Esa Tikkanen	.75	.60	.30
265	Glenn Anderson	.12	.09	.05
266	Michael Krusheinyski	.08	.06	.03
267	Craig MacTavish	.10	.08	.04
268	Dave Hunter	.05	.04	.02
269	Los Angeles King "Action Player"	.05	.04	.02
270	Los Angeles Kings Team Logo	.05	.04	.02
271	Roland Melanson	.08	.06	.03
272	Darren Eliot	.05	.04	.02
273	Grant Ledyard	.05	.04	.02
274	Gordon (Jay) Wells	.05	.04	.02
275	Mark Hardy	.05	.04	.02
276	Edward (Dean) Kennedy	.05	.04	.02
277	Luc Robitaille	2.00	1.50	.80
278	Bernie Nicholls	.20	.15	.08
279	Jimmy Carson	.30	.25	.12
280	David Taylor	.08	.06	.03
281	Jim Fox	.05	.04	.02
282	Bryan Erickson	.05	.04	.02
283	David Williams	.08	.06	.03
284	Sean McKenna	.05	.04	.02
285	Phil Sykes	.05	.04	.02
286	Minnesota North Stars "Action Player"	.05	.04	.02
287	Minnesota North Stars Team Logo	.05	.04	.02
288	Kari Takko	.08	.06	.03
289	Donald Beaupre	.08	.06	.03
290	Craig Hartsburg	.05	.04	.02
291	Ronald Wilson	.05	.04	.02
292	Frantisek Musil	.10	.08	.04
293	Dino Ciccarelli	.15	.11	.06
294	Brian MacLellan	.05	.04	.02
295	Dirk Graham	.10	.08	.04
296	Brian Bellows	.10	.08	.04
297	Neal Broten	.08	.06	.03
298	Dennis Maruk	.08	.06	.03
299	Keith Acton	.05	.04	.02
300	Brian Lawton	.08	.06	.03
301	Bob Brooke	.05	.04	.02
302	Willi Plett	.05	.04	.02
303	St. Louis Blues "Action Player"	.05	.04	.02
304	St. Louis Blues Team Logo	.05	.04	.02
305	Richard Wamsley	.08	.06	.03
306	George (Rob) Ramage	.08	.06	.03
307	Eric Nattress	.05	.04	.02
308	Bruce Bell	.05	.04	.02
309	Charlie Bourgeois	.05	.04	.02
310	Jim Pavese	.05	.04	.02
311	Douglas Gilmour	.60	.45	.25
312	Bernie Federko	.10	.08	.04
313	Mark Hunter	.05	.04	.02
314	Gregory Paslawski	.05	.04	.02
315	Gino Cavallini	.08	.06	.03
316	Richard Meagher	.08	.06	.03

317	Ron Flockhart	.05	.04	.02
318	Douglas Wickenheiser	.05	.04	.02
319	Jocelyn Lemieux	.06	.05	.02
320	Toronto Maple Leafs "Action Player"	.05	.04	.02
321	Toronto Maple Leafs Team Logo	.05	.04	.02
322	Ken Wregget	.15	.11	.06
323	Allan Bester	.08	.06	.03
324	Todd Gill	.05	.04	.02
325	Al Iafrate	.25	.20	.10
326	Borje Salming	.10	.08	.04
327	Russell Courtnall	.35	.25	.14
328	Richard Vaive	.08	.06	.03
329	Steve Thomas	.10	.08	.04
330	Wendel Clark	.75	.60	.30
331	Gary Leeman	.08	.06	.03
332	Tom Fergus	.05	.04	.02
333	Vincent Damphousse	.60	.45	.25
334	Peter Ihnacak	.05	.04	.02
335	Brad Smith	.05	.04	.02
336	Miroslav Ihnacak	.05	.04	.02
337	Vancouver Canucks "Action Player"	.05	.04	.02
338	Vancouver Canucks Team Logo	.05	.04	.02
339	Frank Caprice	.05	.04	.02
340	Richard Brodeur	.08	.06	.03
341	Doug Lidster	.05	.04	.02
342	Michel Petit	.05	.04	.02
343	Garth Butcher	.15	.11	.06
344	Dave Richter	.05	.04	.02
345	Tony Tanti	.08	.06	.03
346	Barry Pederson	.08	.06	.03
347	Petri Skriko	.08	.06	.03
348	Patrik Sundstrom	.08	.06	.03
349	Stanley Smyl	.08	.06	.03
350	Richard Sutter	.08	.06	.03
351	Steve Tambellini	.05	.04	.02
352	Jim Sandlak	.10	.08	.04
353	Dave Lowry	.05	.04	.02
354	Winnipeg Jets "Action Player"	.05	.04	.02
355	Winnipeg Jets Team Logo	.05	.04	.02
356	Daniel Berthiaume	.10	.08	.04
357	Eldon Reddick	.25	.20	.10
358	Dave Ellett	.10	.08	.04
359	Mario Marois	.05	.04	.02
360	Randy Carlyle	.08	.06	.03
361	Fredrick Olausson	.25	.20	.10
362	James Kyte	.05	.04	.02
363	Dale Hawerchuk	.20	.15	.08
364	Paul MacLean	.08	.06	.03
365	Thomas Steen	.10	.08	.04
366	Gilles Hamel	.05	.04	.02
367	Douglas Smail	.05	.04	.02
368	Laurie Boschman	.05	.04	.02
369	Ray Neufeld	.05	.04	.02
370	Andrew McBain	.05	.04	.02
371	Wayne Gretzky	1.50	1.25	.60
372	Hart Memorial Trophy	.05	.04	.02
373	Wayne Gretzky	1.50	1.25	.60
374	Art Ross Trophy	.05	.04	.02
375	William M. Jennings Trophy	.05	.04	.02
376A	Brian Hayward	.08	.06	.03
376B	Patrick Roy	.75	.60	.30
377	Vezina Trophy	.05	.04	.02
378	Ron Hextall	.20	.15	—
379	Luc Robitaille	1.50	1.25	.60
380	Calder Memorial Trophy	.05	.04	.02
381	Raymond Bourque	.15	.11	.06
382	James Norris Memorial Trophy	.05	.04	.02
383	Lady Byng Memorial Trophy	.05	.04	.02
384	Joe Mullen	.12	.09	.05
385	Frank J. Selke Trophy	.05	.04	.02
386	David Poulin	.07	.05	.03
387	Doug Jarvis	.05	.04	.02
388	Bill Masterton Memorial Trophy	.05	.04	.02
389	Wayne Gretzky	1.50	1.25	.60
390	Emery Edge Award	.05	.04	.02
391	Philadelphia Flyers Team Photo	.10	.08	.04
392	Philadelphia Flyers Team Photo	.10	.08	.04
393	Prince of Wales Trophy	.05	.04	.02
394	Clarence S. Campbell Bowl	.05	.04	.02
395	Edmonton Oilers Team Photo	.15	.11	.06
396	Edmonton Oilers Team Photo	.15	.11	.06

1988 Panini Stickers

Panini increased its sticker set in 1988-89 to 408. Once again, the sticker number is only on the back, which is bilingual and says there is an album available to hold the stickers. Panini, NHL and NHLPA logos are also on the back, as is the word Hockey, with the O in hockey has 88/89 in it. The front has a mug shot of the player on one side, with his name and team name underneath it. An action photo is on the other side. A continuous colored frame borders both pictures. Team stickers come in pairs, which must be put together to form the entire picture. Values for some stars may seem lower than expected, due to the fact the album offered them via the mail. Stickers measure 2 1/8" by 2 11/16."

		MT	NM	EX
Complete Set (408):		28.00	21.00	11.00
Common Player:		.05	.04	.02
1	Road to the Cup Stanley Cup Draw	.10	.08	.04
2	Calgary Flames Team Logo	.05	.04	.02
3	Calgary Flames Uniform	.05	.04	.02
4	Mike Vernon	.15	.11	.06
5	Al MacInnis	.20	.15	.08
6	Byron (Brad) McCrimmon	.08	.06	.03
7	Gary Suter	.10	.08	.04
8	Mike Bullard	.05	.04	.02
9	Hakan Loob	.08	.06	.03
10	Lanny McDonald	.15	.11	.06
11	Joe Mullen	.15	.11	.06
12	Joe Nieuwendyk	.75	.60	.30
13	Joe Otto	.08	.06	.03
14	James Peplinski	.05	.04	.02
15	Gary Roberts	.30	.25	.12
16	Calgary Flames Team Photo	.05	.04	.02
17	Calgary Flames Team Photo	.05	.04	.02
18	Chicago Black Hawks Team Logo	.05	.04	.02
19	Chicago Black Hawks Uniform	.05	.04	.02
20	Bob Mason	.05	.04	.02
21	Darren Pang	.05	.04	.02
22	Rob Murray	.05	.04	.02
23	Gary Nylund	.05	.04	.02
24	Douglas Wilson	.10	.08	.04
25	Dirk Graham	.08	.06	.03
26	Steve Larmer	.12	.09	.05
27	Troy Murray	.08	.06	.03
28	Brian Noonan	.10	.08	.04
29	Denis Savard	.12	.09	.05
30	Steve Thomas	.08	.06	.03
31	Richard Vaive	.08	.06	.03
32	Chicago Black Hawks Team	.05	.04	.02
33	Chicago Black Hawks Team	.05	.04	.02
34	Detroit Red Wings Team Logo	.05	.04	.02
35	Detroit Red Wings Uniform	.05	.04	.02
36	Glen Hanon	.08	.06	.03
37	Gregory Stefan	.08	.06	.03
38	Jeff Sharples	.05	.04	.02

39	Darren Veitch	.05	.04	.02
40	Brent Ashton	.05	.04	.02
41	Shawn Burr	.05	.04	.02
42	John Chabot	.05	.04	.02
43	Gerard Gallant	.08	.06	.03
44	Petr Klima	.08	.06	.03
45	Adam Oates	.50	.40	.20
46	Bob Probert	.40	.30	.15
47	Steve Yzerman	.50	.40	.20
48	Detroit Red Wings Team Photo	.05	.04	.02
49	Detroit Red Wings Team Photo	.05	.04	.02
50	Edmonton Oilers Team Logo	.05	.04	.02
51	Edmonton Oilers Uniform	.05	.04	.02
52	Grant Fuhr	.15	.11	.06
53	Charles Huddy	.08	.06	.03
54	Kevin Lowe	.08	.06	.03
55	James (Steve) Smith	.25	.20	.10
56	Jeff Beukeboom	.05	.04	.02
57	Glenn Anderson	.12	.09	.05
58	Wayne Gretzky	1.50	1.25	.60
59	Jari Kurri	.15	.11	.06
60	Craig MacTavish	.10	.08	.04
61	Mark Messier	.75	.60	.30
62	Craig Simpson	.12	.09	.05
63	Esa Tikkanen	.15	.11	.06
64	Edmonton Oilers Team Photo	.05	.04	.02
65	Edmonton Oilers Team Photo	.05	.04	.02
66	Los Angeles Kings Team Logo	.05	.04	.02
67	Los Angeles Kings Uniform	.05	.04	.02
68	Glenn Healy	.08	.06	.03
69	Roland Melanson	.08	.06	.03
70	Steve Duchesne	.30	.25	.12
71	Thomas Laidlaw	.05	.04	.02
72	Gordon (Jay) Wells	.05	.04	.02
73	Mike Allison	.05	.04	.02
74	Robert Carpenter	.08	.06	.03
75	Jimmy Carson	.12	.09	.05
76	Jim Fox	.05	.04	.02
77	Bernie Nicholls	.15	.11	.06
78	Luc Robitaille	.60	.45	.25
79	David Taylor	.10	.08	.04
80	Los Angeles Kings Team Photo	.05	.04	.02
81	Los Angeles Kings Team Photo	.05	.04	.02
82	Minnesota North Stars Team Logo	.05	.04	.02
83	Minnesota North Stars Uniform	.05	.04	.02
84	Donald Beaupre	.10	.08	.04
85	Kari Takko	.08	.06	.03
86	Craig Hartsburg	.05	.04	.02
87	Frantisek Musil	.08	.06	.03
88	Dave Archibald	.05	.04	.02
89	Brian Bellows	.10	.08	.04
90	Scott Bjugstad	.05	.04	.02
91	Bob Brooke	.05	.04	.02
92	Neal Broten	.08	.06	.03
93	Dino Ciccarelli	.15	.11	.06
94	Brian Lawton	.05	.04	.02
95	Brian MacLellan	.05	.04	.02
96	Minnesota North Stars Team Photo	.05	.04	.02
97	Minnesota North Stars Team Photo	.05	.04	.02
98	St. Louis Blues Team Logo	.05	.04	.02
99	St. Louis Blues Uniform	.05	.04	.02
100	Greg Millen	.08	.06	.03
101	Brian Benning	.05	.04	.02
102	Gordon Roberts	.05	.04	.02
103	Gino Cavallini	.08	.06	.03
104	Bernie Federko	.10	.08	.04
105	Douglas Gilmour	.50	.40	.20
106	Anthony Hrkac	.08	.06	.03
107	Brett Hull	3.00	2.25	1.25
108	Mark Hunter	.05	.04	.02
109	Anthony McKegney	.05	.04	.02
110	Richard Meagher	.05	.04	.02
111	Brian Sutter	.08	.06	.03
112	St. Louis Blues Team Photo	.05	.04	.02
113	St. Louis Blues Team Photo	.05	.04	.02
114	Toronto Maple Leafs Team Logo	.05	.04	.02
115	Toronto Maple Leafs Uniform	.05	.04	.02
116	Allan Bester	.05	.04	.02
117	Ken Wregget	.08	.06	.03
118	Al Iafrate	.15	.11	.06
119	Luke Richardson	.05	.04	.02
120	Borje Salming	.10	.08	.04
121	Wendel Clark	.25	.20	.10
122	Russ Courtnall	.15	.11	.06
123	Vincent Damphousse	.35	.25	.14
124	Dan Daoust	.05	.04	.02
125	Gary Leeman	.08	.06	.03
126	Ed Olczyk	.08	.06	.03
127	Mark Osborne	.05	.04	.02
128	Toronto Maple Leafs Team Photo	.05	.04	.02
129	Toronto Maple Leafs Team Photo	.05	.04	.02
130	Vancouver Canucks Team Logo	.05	.04	.02
131	Vancouver Canucks Uniform	.05	.04	.02
132	Kirk McLean	.50	.40	.20
133	Jim Benning	.05	.04	.02
134	Garth Butcher	.10	.08	.04
135	Doug Lidster	.05	.04	.02
136	Greg Adams	.08	.06	.03
137	David Bruce	.08	.06	.03
138	Barry Pederson	.05	.04	.02
139	Jim Sandlak	.08	.06	.03
140	Petri Skriko	.08	.06	.03
141	Stanley Smyl	.05	.04	.02
142	Richard Sutter	.08	.06	.03
143	Tony Tanti	.08	.06	.03
144	Vancouver Canucks Team Photo	.05	.04	.02
145	Vancouver Canucks Team Photo	.05	.04	.02
146	Winnipeg Jets Team Logo	.05	.04	.02
147	Winnipeg Jets Uniform	.05	.04	.02
148	Daniel Berhiaume	.10	.08	.04
149	Randy Carlyle	.08	.06	.03
150	Dave Ellett	.08	.06	.03
151	Mario Marois	.05	.04	.02
152	Peter Taglianetti	.05	.04	.02
153	Laurie Boschman	.05	.04	.02
154	Iain Duncan	.05	.04	.02
155	Dale Hawerchuk	.15	.11	.06
156	Paul MacLean	.08	.06	.03
157	Andrew McBain	.05	.04	.02
158	Douglas Smail	.08	.06	.03
159	Thomas Steen	.08	.06	.03
160	Winnipeg Jets Team Photo	.05	.04	.02
161	Winnipeg Jets Team Photo	.05	.04	.02
162	Prince of Wales Trophy	.05	.04	.02
163	Washington Defeats Flyers	.05	.04	.02
164	Boston Beat Montreal	.05	.04	.02
165	Devils Skate Past The Capitals	.05	.04	.02
166	Bruins Were Victorious Over New Jersey	.05	.04	.02
167	Bruins Were Victorious Over New Jersey	.05	.04	.02
168	Calgary Too Much For Kings	.05	.04	.02
169	Clarence S. Campbell Bowl	.05	.04	.02
170	Edmonton Put Out Flames	.05	.04	.02
171	Detroit Defeat St. Louis	.05	.04	.02

172	Oilers Overpowered Detroit	.05	.04	.02
173	Oilers Overpowered Detroit	.05	.04	.02
174	Edmonton Celebrate a Victory in Game 1	.05	.04	.02
175	Game 2, Oilers Eyed Another Victory	.05	.04	.02
176	Stanley Cup	.08	.06	.03
177	Stanley Cup	.08	.06	.03
178	Gretzky & Teammates Take 3-0 Lead (Gretzky)	.08	.06	.03
179	Gretzky & Teammates Take 3-0 Lead (Gretzky)	.08	.06	.03
180	Gretzky & Teammates Take 3-0 Lead (Gretzky)	.08	.06	.03
181	M.V.P. (Wayne Gretzky)	1.50	1.25	.60
182	Conn Smythe Trophy	.05	.04	.02
183	Edmonton Oilers Celebrate 4th Stanley	.08	.06	.03
184	Edmonton Oilers Celebrate 4th Stanley	.08	.06	.03
185	Edmonton Oilers Celebrate 4th Stanley	.08	.06	.03
186	Edmonton Oilers Celebrate 4th Stanley	.08	.06	.03
187	Calgary Flames Action	.05	.04	.02
188	Grant Fuhr	.15	.11	.06
189	New Jersey Devils Action	.05	.04	.02
190	Marcel Dionne	.15	.11	.06
191	Bruins Action	.05	.04	.02
192	Washington Capitals Action	.05	.04	.02
193	Wayne Gretzky	1.50	1.25	.60
194	Winnipeg Jets	.08	.06	.03
195	Boston Bruins	.05	.04	.02
196	St. Louis Blues	.05	.04	.02
197	Philadelphia Flyers vs Wash. Capitals	.05	.04	.02
198	New York Islanders	.05	.04	.02
199	Calgary Flames	.05	.04	.02
200	Pittsburgh Penguins	.05	.04	.02
201	Boston Bruins Team Logo	.05	.04	.02
202	Boston Bruins Uniform	.05	.04	.02
203	Rejean Lemelin	.08	.06	.03
204	Raymond Bourque	.25	.20	.10
205	Gordon Kluzak	.05	.04	.02
206	Michael Thelven	.05	.04	.02
207	Glen Wesley	.12	.09	.05
208	Randy Burridge	.15	.11	.06
209	Keith Crowder	.05	.04	.02
210	Stephen Kasper	.08	.06	.03
211	Ken Linseman	.05	.04	.02
212	Jay Miller	.05	.04	.02
213	Cam Neely	.30	.25	.12
214	Robert Sweeney	.05	.04	.02
215	Boston Bruins Team Photo	.05	.04	.02
216	Boston Bruins Team Photo	.05	.04	.02
217	Buffalo Sabres Team Logo	.05	.04	.02
218	Buffalo Sabres Uniform	.05	.04	.02
219	Tom Barrasso	.20	.15	.08
220	Phil Housley	.20	.15	.08
221	(Calle Johansson)	.05	.04	.02
222	Michael Ramsey	.05	.04	.02
223	David Andreychuk	.25	.20	.10
224	Scott Arniel	.05	.04	.02
225	Adam Creighton	.10	.08	.04
226	Mike Foligno	.05	.04	.02
227	Christian Ruuttu	.05	.04	.02
228	Ray Sheppard	.20	.15	.08
229	John Tucker	.05	.04	.02
230	Pierre Turgeon	1.00	.70	.40
231	Buffalo Sabres Team Photo	.05	.04	.02
232	Buffalo Sabres Team Photo	.05	.04	.02
233	Hartford Whalers Team Logo	.05	.04	.02
234	Hartford Whalers Uniform	.05	.04	.02
235	Mike Liut	.08	.06	.03
236	David Babych	.08	.06	.03
237	Sylvain Cote	.05	.04	.02
238	Ulf Samuelsson	.15	.11	.06
239	John Anderson	.05	.04	.02
240	Kevin Dineen	.10	.08	.04
241	Ray Ferraro	.08	.06	.03
242	Ron Francis	.12	.09	.05
243	Paul MacDermid	.05	.04	.02
244	Dave Tippett	.05	.04	.02
245	Sylvain Turgeon	.08	.06	.03
246	Carey Wilson	.05	.04	.02
247	Hartford Whalers Team Photo	.05	.04	.02
248	Hartford Whalers Team Photo	.05	.04	.02
249	Montreal Canadiens Team Logo	.05	.04	.02
250	Montreal Canadiens Uniform	.05	.04	.02
251	Brian Hayward	.08	.06	.03
252	Patrick Roy	1.00	.70	.40
253	Chris Chelios	.15	.11	.06
254	Craig Ludwig	.05	.04	.02
255	Petr Svoboda	.08	.06	.03
256	Guy Carbonneau	.10	.08	.04
257	Claude Lemieux	.25	.20	.10
258	Michael McPhee	.08	.06	.03
259	Mats Naslund	.08	.06	.03
260	Stephane J.J. Richer	.15	.11	.06
261	Robert Smith	.08	.06	.03
262	Ryan Walter	.08	.06	.03
263	Montreal Canadiens Team Photo	.05	.04	.02
264	Montreal Canadiens Team Photo	.05	.04	.02
265	New Jersey Devils Team Logo	.05	.04	.02
266	New Jersey Devils Uniform	.05	.04	.02
267	Sean Burke	.20	.15	.08
268	Joe Cirella	.08	.06	.03
269	Bruce Driver	.08	.06	.03
270	Craig Wolanin	.05	.04	.02
271	Aaron Broten	.05	.04	.02
272	Doug Brown	.05	.04	.02
273	Claude Loiselle	.05	.04	.02
274	John MacLean	.15	.11	.06
275	Kirk Muller	.25	.20	.10
276	Brendan Shanahan	1.25	.90	.50
277	Patrik Sundstrom	.08	.06	.03
278	Patrick Verbeek	.10	.08	.04
279	New Jersey Devils Team Photo	.05	.04	.02
280	New Jersey Devils Team Photo	.05	.04	.02
281	New York Islanders Team Logo	.05	.04	.02
282	New York Islanders Uniform	.05	.04	.02
283	Kelly Hrudey	.12	.09	.05
284	Stephen Konroyd	.05	.04	.02
285	Ken Morrow	.08	.06	.03
286	Patrick Flatley	.08	.06	.03
287	Gregory Gilbert	.05	.04	.02
288	Alan Kerr	.05	.04	.02
289	Derek King	.30	.25	.12
290	Pat LaFontaine	.50	.40	.20
291	Mikko Makela	.05	.04	.02
292	Brent Sutter	.08	.06	.03
293	Bryan Trottier	.20	.15	.08
294	Randy Wood	.08	.06	.03
295	New York Islanders Team	.05	.04	.02
296	New York Islanders Team	.05	.04	.02
297	New York Rangers Team Logo	.05	.04	.02
298	New York Rangers Uniform	.05	.04	.02
299	Robert Froese	.08	.06	.03
300	John Vanbiesbrouck	.25	.20	.10
301	Brian Leetch	1.75	1.25	.70
302	Norm Maciver	.08	.06	.03
303	James Patrick	.08	.06	.03
304	Michel Petit	.08	.06	.03
305	Ulf Dahlen	.08	.06	.03

306	Jan Erixon	.08	.06	.03
307	Kelly Kisio	.08	.06	.03
308	Donald Maloney	.05	.04	.02
309	Walter Poddubny	.05	.04	.02
310	Tomas Sandstrom	.10	.08	.04
311	New York Rangers Team Photo	.05	.04	.02
312	New York Rangers Team Photo	.05	.04	.02
313	Philadelphia Flyers Team Logo	.05	.04	.02
314	Philadelphia Flyers Uniform	.05	.04	.02
315	Ron Hextall	.15	.11	.06
316	Mark Howe	.10	.08	.04
317	Kerry Huffman	.05	.04	.02
318	Kjell Samuelsson	.08	.06	.03
319	David Brown	.05	.04	.02
320	Murray Craven	.08	.06	.03
321	Tim Kerr	.08	.06	.03
322	Scott Mellanby	.08	.06	.03
323	David Poulin	.08	.06	.03
324	Brian Propp	.08	.06	.03
325	Ilkka Sinisalo	.05	.04	.02
326	Rick Tocchet	.25	.20	.10
327	Philadelphia Flyers Team Photo	.05	.04	.02
328	Philadelphia Flyers Team Photo	.05	.04	.02
329	Pittsburgh Penguins Team Logo	.05	.04	.02
330	Pittsburgh Penguins Uniform	.05	.04	.02
331	Frank Pietrangelo	.20	.15	.08
332	Doug Bodger	.08	.06	.03
333	Paul Coffey	.30	.25	.12
334	Jim Johnson	.05	.04	.02
335	Ville Siren	.05	.04	.02
336	Rob Brown	.12	.09	.05
337	Randy Cunneyworth	.05	.04	.02
338	Dan Frawley	.05	.04	.02
339	Dave Hunter	.05	.04	.02
340	Mario Lemieux	1.50	1.25	.60
341	Troy Loney	.05	.04	.02
342	Dan Quinn	.05	.04	.02
343	Pittsburgh Penguins Team Photo	.05	.04	.02
344	Pittsburgh Penguins Team Photo	.05	.04	.02
345	Quebec Nordiques Team Logo	.05	.04	.02
346	Quebec Nordiques Uniform	.05	.04	.02
347	Marion Gosselin	.05	.04	.02
348	Tommy Albelin	.05	.04	.02
349	Jeff Brown	.30	.25	.12
350	Steven Finn	.05	.04	.02
351	Randy Moller	.05	.04	.02
352	Alain Cote	.05	.04	.02
353	Gaetan Duchesne	.05	.04	.02
354	Mike Eagles	.05	.04	.02
355	Michel Goulet	.12	.09	.05
356	Lane Lambert	.05	.04	.02
357	Anton Stastny	.05	.04	.02
358	Peter Stastny	.15	.11	.06
359	Quebec Nordiques Team Photo	.05	.04	.02
360	Quebec Nordiques Team Photo	.05	.04	.02
361	Washington Capitals Team Logo	.05	.04	.02
362	Washington Capitals Uniform	.05	.04	.02
363	Clint Malarchuk	.08	.06	.03
364	Peter Peeters	.08	.06	.03
365	Kevin Hatcher	.25	.20	.10
366	Rod Langway	.08	.06	.03
367	Lawrence Murphy	.10	.08	.04
368	Scott Stevens	.12	.09	.05
369	Dave Christian	.08	.06	.03
370	Michael Gartner	.15	.11	.06

371	Bengt-ake Gustafsson	.05	.04	.02
372	Dale Hunter	.10	.08	.04
373	Kelly Miller	.08	.06	.03
374	Mike Ridley	.10	.08	.04
375	Washington Capitals Team Photo	.05	.04	.02
376	Washington Capitals Team Photo	.05	.04	.02
377	Hockey Rink	.05	.04	.02
378	Hockey Rink	.05	.04	.02
379	Cross-checking	.05	.04	.02
380	Elbowing	.05	.04	.02
381	High-sticking	.05	.04	.02
382	Holding	.05	.04	.02
383	Hooking	.05	.04	.02
384	Interference	.05	.04	.02
385	Spearing	.05	.04	.02
386	Tripping	.05	.04	.02
387	Boarding	.05	.04	.02
388	Charging	.05	.04	.02
389	Delayed Calling of Penalty	.05	.04	.02
390	Kneeing	.05	.04	.02
391	Misconduct	.05	.04	.02
392	Roughing	.05	.04	.02
393	Slashing	.05	.04	.02
394	Unsportsmanlike Conduct	.05	.04	.02
395	Wash-out	.05	.04	.02
396	Icing	.05	.04	.02
397	Off-side	.05	.04	.02
398	Wash-out	.05	.04	.02
399	Bill Masterson Memorial Cup: (Bob Borne)	.05	.04	.02
400	Hart Memorial Trophy: (Mario Lemieux)	.75	.60	.30
401	Art Ross Trophy: (Mario Lemieux)	.75	.60	.30
402	William M. Jennings Trophy: (Brian Hayward, Patrick Roy)	.25	.20	.10
403	Vezina Trophy: (Grant Fuhr)	.12	.09	.05
404	Calder Memorial Trophy: (Joe Nieuwendyk)	.25	.20	.10
405	James Norris Memorial Trophy: (Raymond Bourque)	.15	.11	.06
406	Lady Byng Memorial Trophy: (Mats Naslund)	.08	.06	.03
407	Frank J. Selke Trophy: (Guy Carbonneau)	.05	.04	.02
408	Emery Edge Award: (Byron (Brad) McCrimmon)	.05	.04	.02

1989 Panini Stickers

Each 1989-90 sticker has a full-color photo on the front, with the player's name above the photo. A hockey stick runs along the right border, with the blade at the base of the photo. A hockey puck is at the end of the stick; the team name is in the center of the blade. The back has "Hockey '89-'90" at the top, with a sticker number below, flanked by NHL and NHLPA logos. Information about trading double stickers so one could complete the entire album is written in French and English. The stickers measure 1 7/8" by 3". Some team stickers come in pairs which have to be matched up to form an entire picture.

		MT	NM	EX
	Complete Set (384):	22.00	16.50	8.75
	Common Player:	.05	.04	.02
1	NHL Logo	.08	.06	.03
2	Playoff schedule	.05	.04	.02
3	Calgary Flames vs Chicago Black Hawks	.05	.04	.02
4	Calgary Flames vs Vancouver Canucks	.05	.04	.02
5	Los Angeles Kings vs Edmonton Oilers	.05	.04	.02

6	Mike Vernon	.08	.06	.03
7	Mike Vernon	.08	.06	.03
8	Boston Bruins vs Buffalo Sabres	.05	.04	.02
9	Montreal Canadiens vs Boston Bruins	.05	.04	.02
10	Philadelphia Flyers score	.05	.04	.02
11	Mont. Canadiens vs Philadelphia Flyers	.05	.04	.02
12	Mont. Canadiens vs Philadelphia Flyers	.05	.04	.02
13	Montreal Canadiens vs Calgary Flames	.05	.04	.02
14	Celebration: Montreal Canadiens	.05	.04	.02
15	Montreal Canadiens vs Calgary Flames	.05	.04	.02
16	Montreal Canadiens vs Calgary Flames	.05	.04	.02
17	Celebration: Calgary Flames	.05	.04	.02
18	Calgary Flames vs Montreal Canadiens	.05	.04	.02
19	Calgary Flames vs Montreal Canadiens	.05	.04	.02
20	Conn Smythe Trophy: (Al MacInnis)	.15	.11	.06
21	Calgary Flames	.05	.04	.02
22	Calgary Flames	.05	.04	.02
23	Calgary Flames	.05	.04	.02
24	Calgary Flames	.05	.04	.02
25	Stanley Cup	.08	.06	.03
26	Calgary Flames Logo	.05	.04	.02
27	Joe Mullen	.10	.08	.04
28	Douglas Gilmour	.50	.40	.20
29	Joe Nieuwendyk	.15	.11	.06
30	Gary Suter	.08	.06	.03
31	Calgary Flames Team Photo	.05	.04	.02
32	Al MacInnis	.15	.11	.06
33	Byron (Brad) McCrimmon	.08	.06	.03
34	Mike Vernon	.10	.08	.04
35	Gary Roberts	.15	.11	.06
36	Colin Patterson	.05	.04	.02
37	James Peplinski	.08	.06	.03
38	Jamie Macoun	.05	.04	.02
39	Lanny McDonald	.15	.11	.06
40	Saddledome	.05	.04	.02
41	Chicago Black Hawks Logo	.05	.04	.02
42	Darren Pang	.08	.06	.03
43	Steve Larmer	.12	.09	.05
44	Dirk Graham	.08	.06	.03
45	Douglas Wilson	.10	.08	.04
46	Chicago Black Hawks vs Edmonton Oilers	.50	.40	.20
47	Dave Manson	.15	.11	.06
48	Troy Murray	.08	.06	.03
49	Denis Savard	.12	.09	.05
50	Steve Thomas	.08	.06	.03
51	Adam Creighton	.08	.06	.03
52	Wayne Presley	.05	.04	.02
53	Trent Yawney	.08	.06	.03
54	Alain Chevrier	.08	.06	.03
55	Chicago Stadium	.05	.04	.02
56	Detroit Red Wings Logo	.05	.04	.02
57	Steve Yzerman	.40	.30	.15
58	Gerard Gallant	.08	.06	.03
59	Gregory Stefan	.08	.06	.03
60	David Barr	.05	.04	.02
61	Detroit Red Wings Team Photo	.05	.04	.02
62	Steve Chiasson	.08	.06	.03
63	Shawn Burr	.08	.06	.03
64	Richard Zombo	.08	.06	.03
65	Glen Hanlon	.08	.06	.03
66	Jeff Sharples	.08	.06	.03
67	Joey Kocur	.05	.04	.02
68	Lee Norwood	.05	.04	.02
69	Mike O'Connell	.05	.04	.02
70	Joe Louis Arena	.05	.04	.02
71	Edmonton Oilers Logo	.05	.04	.02
72	Jimmy Carson	.10	.08	.04
73	Jari Kurri	.15	.11	.06
74	Mark Messier	.60	.45	.25
75	Craig Simpson	.08	.06	.03
76	Edmonton Oilers vs Philadelphia Flyers	.05	.04	.02
77	Glenn Anderson	.10	.08	.04
78	Craig MacTavish	.08	.06	.03
79	Kevin Lowe	.08	.06	.03
80	Craig Muni	.05	.04	.02
81	Bill Ranford	.25	.20	.10
82	Charles Huddy	.08	.06	.03
83	James (Steve) Smith	.12	.09	.05
84	Normand Lacombe	.05	.04	.02
85	Northlands Coliseum	.05	.04	.02
86	Los Angeles Kings Logo	.05	.04	.02
87	Wayne Gretzky	1.00	.70	.40
88	Bernie Nicholls	.15	.11	.06
89	Kelly Hrudey	.12	.09	.05
90	John Tonelli	.08	.06	.03
91	Edmonton Oilers vs Los Angeles Kings	.05	.04	.02
92	Stephen Kasper	.05	.04	.02
93	Steve Duchesne	.08	.06	.03
94	Michael Krushelnyski	.08	.06	.03
95	Luc Robitaille	.35	.25	.14
96	Ron Duguay	.08	.06	.03
97	Glenn Healy	.08	.06	.03
98	David Taylor	.08	.06	.03
99	Martin McSorley	.25	.20	.10
100	The Great Western Forum	.05	.04	.02
101	Minnesota North Stars Logo	.05	.04	.02
102	Kari Takko	.08	.06	.03
103	Dave Gagner	.20	.15	.08
104	Michael Gartner	.15	.11	.06
105	Brian Bellows	.10	.08	.04
106	Minnesota North Stars Team Photo	.05	.04	.02
107	Neal Broten	.08	.06	.03
108	Lawrence Murphy	.10	.08	.04
109	Basil McRae	.05	.04	.02
110	Perry Berezan	.05	.04	.02
111	Shawn Chambers	.05	.04	.02
112	Curt Giles	.05	.04	.02
113	Robert (Stewart) Gavin	.05	.04	.02
114	Jon Casey	.25	.20	.10
115	Metropolitan Sports Center	.05	.04	.02
116	St. Louis Blues Logo	.05	.04	.02
117	Brett Hull	.05	.04	.02
118	Peter Zezel	.05	.04	.02
119	Anthony Hrkac	.25	.20	.10
120	Vincent Riendeau	.05	.04	.02
121	St. Louis Blues vs New York Islanders	.25	.20	.10
122	Cliff Ronning	.08	.06	.03
123	Gino Cavallini	.05	.04	.02
124	Brian Benning	.05	.04	.02
125	Richard Meagher	.05	.04	.02
126	Steve Tuttle	.05	.04	.02
127	Paul Cavallini	.05	.04	.02
128	Tom Tilley	.08	.06	.03
129	Greg Millen	.05	.04	.02
130	St. Louis Arena	.05	.04	.02
131	Toronto Maple Leafs Logo	.10	.08	.04
132	Ed Olczyk	.08	.06	.03
133	Gary Leeman	.20	.15	.08
134	Vincent Damphousse	.05	.04	.02
135	Tom Fergus	.05	.04	.02
136	Toronto Maple Leafs Team Photo	.08	.06	.03
137	Daniel Marois	.05	.04	.02
138	Mark Osborne	.05	.04	.02
139	Allan Bester	.15	.11	.06
140	Al Iafrate	.08	.06	.03
141	Bradley Marsh	.05	.04	.02
142	Luke Richardson	.08	.06	.03
143	Todd Gill	.20	.15	.08

Stamps/stickers

144	Wendel Clark	.05	.04	.02
145	Maple Leaf Gardens	.05	.04	.02
146	Vancouver Canucks Logo	.05	.04	.02
147	Petri Skriko	.05	.04	.02
148	Trevor Linden	.60	.45	.25
149	Tony Tanti	.08	.06	.03
150	Stephen Weeks	.08	.06	.03
151	Vancouver Canucks vs New York Islanders	.05	.04	.02
152	Brian Bradley	.20	.15	.08
153	Barry Pederson	.08	.06	.03
154	Greg Adams	.08	.06	.03
155	Kirk McLean	.25	.20	.10
156	Jim Sandlak	.08	.06	.03
157	Richard Sutter	.08	.06	.03
158	Garth Butcher	.08	.06	.03
159	Stanley Smyl	.05	.04	.02
160	Pacific Coliseum	.05	.04	.02
161	Winnipeg Jets Logo	.05	.04	.02
162	Dale Hawerchuk	.15	.11	.06
163	Thomas Steen	.08	.06	.03
164	Brent Ashton	.05	.04	.02
165	Pat Elynuik	.10	.08	.04
166	Winnipeg Jets vs New York Islanders	.05	.04	.02
167	Dave Ellett	.08	.06	.03
168	Randy Carlyle	.08	.06	.03
169	Laurie Boschman	.05	.04	.02
170	Iain Duncan	.05	.04	.02
171	Douglas Smail	.08	.06	.03
172	Teppo Numminen	.10	.08	.04
173	Bob Essensa	.25	.20	.10
174	Peter Taglianetti	.05	.04	.02
175	Winnipeg Arena	.05	.04	.02
176	Steve Duchesne	.08	.06	.03
177	Luc Robitaille	.25	.20	.10
178	Mike Vernon	.10	.08	.04
179	Wayne Gretzky	.60	.45	.25
180	Kevin Lowe	.08	.06	.03
181	Jari Kurri	.15	.11	.06
182	Cam Neely	.20	.15	.08
183	Paul Coffey	.15	.11	.06
184	Mario Lemieux	.40	.30	.15
185	Sean Burke	.08	.06	.03
186	Rob Brown	.05	.04	.02
187	Raymond Bourque	.15	.11	.06
188	Boston Bruins Logo	.05	.04	.02
189	Greg Hawgood	.05	.04	.02
190	Ken Linseman	.05	.04	.02
191	Andrew Moog	.12	.09	.05
192	Cam Neely	.30	.25	.12
193	Boston Bruins vs Philadelphia Flyers	.05	.04	.02
194	Andy Brickley	.08	.06	.03
195	Rejean Lemelin	.08	.06	.03
196	Robert Carpenter	.08	.06	.03
197	Randy Burridge	.08	.06	.03
198	Craig Janney	.40	.30	.15
199	Bob Joyce	.05	.04	.02
200	Glen Wesley	.10	.08	.04
201	Raymond Bourque	.15	.11	.06
202	Boston Garden	.05	.04	.02
203	Buffalo Sabres Logo	.05	.04	.02
204	Pierre Turgeon	.40	.30	.15
205	Phil Housley	.12	.09	.05
206	Richard Viave	.08	.06	.03
207	Christian Ruuttu	.08	.06	.03
208	Philadelphia Flyers v Buffalo Sabres	.05	.04	.02
209	Doug Bodger	.05	.04	.02
210	Mike Foligno	.05	.04	.02
211	Ray Sheppard	.20	.15	.08
212	John Tucker	.05	.04	.02
213	Scott Arniel	.05	.04	.02
214	Daren Puppa	.10	.08	.04
215	David Andreychuk	.20	.15	.08
216	Uwe Krupp	.05	.04	.02
217	Memorial Auditorium	.05	.04	.02
218	Hartford Whalers Logo	.05	.04	.02
219	Kevin Dineen	.08	.06	.03
220	Peter Sidorkiewicz	.08	.06	.03
221	Ron Francis	.10	.08	.04
222	Ray Ferraro	.10	.08	.04
223	New York Islanders vs Hartford Whalers	.05	.04	.02
224	Scott Young	.08	.06	.03
225	David Babych	.08	.06	.03
226	Dave Tippett	.05	.04	.02
227	Paul MacDermid	.05	.04	.02
228	Ulf Samuelsson	.12	.09	.05
229	Sylvain Cote	.05	.04	.02
230	Jody Hull	.05	.04	.02
231	Donald Maloney	.05	.04	.02
232	Hartford Civic Center	.05	.04	.02
233	Montreal Canadiens Logo	.05	.04	.02
234	Mats Naslund	.08	.06	.03
235	Patrick Roy	.60	.45	.25
236	Robert Smith	.08	.06	.03
237	Chris Chelios	.15	.11	.06
238	Calgary Flames vs Montreal Canadiens	.05	.04	.02
239	Stephane J.J. Richer	.15	.11	.06
240	Claude Lemieux	.15	.11	.06
241	Guy Carbonneau	.10	.08	.04
242	Shayne Corson	.15	.11	.06
243	Michael McPhee	.08	.06	.03
244	Petr Svoboda	.08	.06	.03
245	Larry Robinson	.15	.11	.06
246	Brian Hayward	.08	.06	.03
247	Montreal Forum	.08	.06	.03
248	New Jersey Devils Logo	.05	.04	.02
249	John MacLean	.12	.09	.05
250	Patrik Sundstrom	.08	.06	.03
251	Kirk Muller	.15	.11	.06
252	Tom Kurvers	.05	.04	.02
253	Boston Bruins vs New Jersey Devils act	.05	.04	.02
254	Aaron Broten	.05	.04	.02
255	Brendan Shanahan	.50	.40	.20
256	Sean Burke	.12	.09	.05
257	Tommy Albelin	.05	.04	.02
258	Ken Daneyko	.08	.06	.03
259	Randy Velischek	.05	.04	.02
260	Mark Johnson	.05	.04	.02
261	James Korn	.05	.04	.02
262	Brendan Byrne Arena	.05	.04	.02
263	New York Islanders Logo	.05	.04	.02
264	Pat LaFontaine	.50	.40	.20
265	Mark Fitzpatrick	.25	.20	.10
266	Brent Sutter	.08	.06	.03
267	David Volek	.05	.04	.02
268	New York Islanders vs New York Rangers	.05	.04	.02
269	Bryan Trottier	.15	.11	.06
270	Mikko Makela	.05	.04	.02
271	Derek King	.15	.11	.06
272	Patrick Flatley	.05	.04	.02
273	Jeff Norton	.08	.06	.03
274	Gerald Diduck	.05	.04	.02
275	Alan Kerr	.05	.04	.02
276	Jeff Hackett	.20	.15	.08
277	Nassau Veterans Memorial Coliseum	.05	.04	.02
278	New York Rangers Logo	.05	.04	.02
279	Brian Leetch	.60	.45	.25
280	Carey Wilson	.05	.04	.02
281	Tomas Sandstrom	.10	.08	.04
282	John Vanbiesbrouck	.20	.15	.08
283	Edmonton Oilers vs New York Rangers	.05	.04	.02
284	Robert Froese	.08	.06	.03
285	Tony Granato	.10	.08	.04
286	Brian Mullen	.08	.06	.03
287	Kelly Kisio	.08	.06	.03
288	Ulf Dahlen	.08	.06	.03
289	James Patrick	.08	.06	.03

290	John Ogrodnick	.08	.06	.03
291	Michel Petit	.08	.06	.03
292	Madison Square Garden	.05	.04	.02
293	Philadelphia Flyers Logo	.05	.04	.02
294	Tim Kerr	.08	.06	.03
295	Rick Tocchet	.15	.11	.06
296	Per-Erik Eklund	.08	.06	.03
297	Terry Carkner	.08	.06	.03
298	Philadelphia Flyers vs Mont. Canadiens	.05	.04	.02
299	Ronald Sutter	.08	.06	.03
300	Mark Howe	.08	.06	.03
301	Keith Acton	.05	.04	.02
302	Ron Hextall	.10	.08	.04
303	Gordon Murphy	.05	.04	.02
304	Derrick Smith	.05	.04	.02
305	David Poulin	.05	.04	.02
306	Brian Propp	.08	.06	.03
307	The Spectrum	.05	.04	.02
308	Pittsburgh Penguins Logo	.05	.04	.02
309	Mario Lemieux	.75	.60	.30
310	Rob Brown	.08	.06	.03
311	Paul Coffey	.20	.15	.08
312	Tom Barrasso	.15	.11	.06
313	Pitts. Penguins vs Philadelphia Flyers	.05	.04	.02
314	Dan Quinn	.05	.04	.02
315	Bob Errey	.05	.04	.02
316	John Cullen	.20	.15	.08
317	Phil Bourque	.05	.04	.02
318	Zarley Zalapski	.08	.06	.03
319	Troy Loney	.08	.06	.03
320	Jim Johnson	.05	.04	.02
321	Kevin Stevens	1.00	.70	.40
322	Civic Arena	.05	.04	.02
323	Quebec Nordiques Logo	.05	.04	.02
324	Peter Stastny	.15	.11	.06
325	Jeff Brown	.10	.08	.04
326	Michel Goulet	.10	.08	.04
327	Joe Sakic	1.25	.90	.50
328	Philadelphia Flyers vs Quebec Nordiques	.05	.04	.02
329	Iiro Jarvi	.05	.04	.02
330	Paul Gillis	.05	.04	.02
331	Randy Moller	.20	.15	.08
332	Ron Tugnutt	.05	.04	.02
333	Robert Picard	.08	.06	.03
334	Curtis Leschyshyn	.05	.04	.02
335	Marc Fortier	.05	.04	.02
336	Mario Marois	.05	.04	.02
337	Le Colisee	.05	.04	.02
338	Washington Capitals Logo	.08	.06	.03
339	Mike Ridley	.15	.11	.06
340	Geoff Courtnall	.10	.08	.04
341	Scott Stevens	.10	.08	.04
342	Dino Ciccarelli	.05	.04	.02
343	Washington Capitals vs Calgary Flames	.05	.04	.02
344	Bob Mason	.08	.06	.03
345	Dave Christian	.08	.06	.03
346	Dale Hunter	.15	.11	.06
347	Kevin Hatcher	.08	.06	.03
348	Kelly Miller	.08	.06	.03
349	Stephen Leach	.08	.06	.03
350	Rod Langway	.05	.04	.02
351	Robert Rouse	.05	.04	.02
352	Capital Centre	.05	.04	.02
353	Calgary Flames	.05	.04	.02
354	Edmonton Oilers	.05	.04	.02
355	Winnipeg Jets	.05	.04	.02
356	Toronto Maple Leafs	.05	.04	.02
357	Buffalo Sabres	.05	.04	.02
358	Montreal Canadiens	.05	.04	.02
359	Quebec Nordiques	.05	.04	.02
360	New Jersey Devils	.05	.04	.02
361	Boston Bruins	.05	.04	.02
362	Hartford Whalers	.05	.04	.02
363	Vancouver Canucks	.05	.04	.02

364	Minnesota North Stars	.05	.04	.02
365	Los Angeles Kings	.05	.04	.02
366	St. Louis Blues	.05	.04	.02
367	Chicago Black Hawks	.05	.04	.02
368	Detroit Red Wings	.05	.04	.02
369	Pittsburgh Penguins	.05	.04	.02
370	Washington Capitals	.05	.04	.02
371	Philadelphia Flyers	.05	.04	.02
372	New York Rangers	.05	.04	.02
373	New York Islanders	.05	.04	.02
374	Wayne Gretzky	.75	.60	.30
375	Mario Lemieux	.50	.40	.20
376	Patrick Roy, Brian Hayward	.25	.20	.10
377	Tim Kerr	.08	.06	.03
378	Brian Leetch	.40	.30	.15
379	Chris Chelios	.10	.08	.04
380	Joe Mullen	.08	.06	.03
381	Guy Carbonneau	.08	.06	.03
382	Bryan Trottier	.15	.11	.06
383	Patrick Roy	.35	.25	.14
384	Joe Mullen	.08	.06	.03

1990 Panini Stickers

These stickers have full-color action photos on the front, with a team-colored triangle in the upper left corner of the photo which gives the team name. The player's name is below the picture. The sticker number is on the back, as is information, in French and English, about the album which was produced to hold the stickers. "Hockey '90-'91" is also included on the sticker back. Conference and team logo stickers are foils. Each sticker measures 2 1/16" by 2 15/16."

		MT	NM	EX
Complete Set (351):		18.00	13.50	7.25
Common Player:		.05	.04	.02
1	Prince of Wales Conference	.08	.06	.03
2	Clarence Campbell Conference	.05	.04	.02
3	Stanley Cup	.08	.06	.03
4	David Poulin	.05	.04	.02
5	Brian Propp	.08	.06	.03
6	Glen Wesley	.08	.06	.03
7	Robert Carpenter	.08	.06	.03
8	John Carter	.05	.04	.02
9	Cam Neely	.20	.15	.08
10	Greg Hawgood	.05	.04	.02
11	Andrew Moog	.12	.09	.05
12	Boston Bruins logo	.05	.04	.02
13	Rejean Lemelin	.08	.06	.03
14	Craig Janney	.15	.11	.06
15	Robert Sweeney	.05	.04	.02
16	Andy Brickley	.05	.04	.02
17	Raymond Bourque	.15	.11	.06
18	Dave Christian	.08	.06	.03
19	Dave Snuggerud	.05	.04	.02
20	Christian Ruuttu	.05	.04	.02
21	Phil Housley	.12	.09	.05
22	Uwe Krupp	.05	.04	.02
23	Richard Vaive	.08	.06	.03
24	Michael Ramsey	.05	.04	.02
25	Mike Foligno	.05	.04	.02
26	Clint Malarchuk	.08	.06	.03
27	Buffalo Sabres logo	.05	.04	.02
28	Pierre Turgeon	.40	.30	.15
29	David Andreychuk	.15	.11	.06
30	Scott Arniel	.05	.04	.02
31	Daren Puppa	.08	.06	.03
32	Mike Hartman	.05	.04	.02
33	Doug Bodger	.08	.06	.03
34	Scott Young	.08	.06	.03
35	Todd Krygier	.08	.06	.03
36	Patrick Verbeek	.08	.06	.03
37	Dave Tippett	.05	.04	.02
38	Peter Sidorkiewicz	.08	.06	.03
39	Ron Francis	.10	.08	.04
40	David Babych	.08	.06	.03

Stamps/stickers

41	Randy Ladouceur	.05	.04	.02		120	Tim Kerr	.08	.06	.03
42	Hartford Whalers logo	.05	.04	.02		121	Rick Tocchet	.12	.09	.05
43	Kevin Dineen	.08	.06	.03		122	Mark Howe	.08	.06	.03
44	Dean Evason	.08	.06	.03		123	Ilkka Sinisalo	.05	.04	.02
45	Ray Ferraro	.08	.06	.03		124	Tony Tanti	.05	.04	.02
46	Mike Tomiak	.05	.04	.02		125	John Cullen	.08	.06	.03
47	Bo-Mikael Andersson	.05	.04	.02		126	Zarley Zalapski	.08	.06	.03
48	Brad Shaw	.05	.04	.02		127	Wendell Young	.08	.06	.03
49	Chris Chelios	.12	.09	.05		128	Rob Brown	.08	.06	.03
50	Petr Svoboda	.05	.04	.02		129	Phil Bourque	.05	.04	.02
51	Patrick Roy	.50	.40	.20		130	Mark Recchi	.60	.45	.25
52	Robert Smith	.08	.06	.03		131	Kevin Stevens	.60	.45	.25
53	Stephane J.J. Richer	.10	.08	.04		132	Pittsburgh Penguins logo	.05	.04	.02
54	Shayne Corson	.10	.08	.04		133	Bob Errey	.05	.04	.02
55	Brian Skrudland	.05	.04	.02		134	Tom Barrasso	.12	.09	.05
56	Russ Courtnall	.10	.08	.04		135	Paul Coffey	.15	.11	.06
57	Montreal Canadiens logo	.05	.04	.02		136	Mario Lemieux	.75	.60	.30
58	Guy Carbonneau	.08	.06	.03		137	Randy Hillier	.05	.04	.02
59	Sylvain Lefebvre	.08	.06	.03		138	Troy Loney	.05	.04	.02
60	Mathieu Schneider	.12	.09	.05		139	Joe Sakic	.35	.25	.14
61	Brian Hayward	.08	.06	.03		140	Lucien DeBlois	.05	.04	.02
62	Mats Naslund	.08	.06	.03		141	Joe Cirella	.05	.04	.02
63	Michael McPhee	.08	.06	.03		142	Ron Tugnutt	.12	.09	.05
64	Brendan Shanahan	.40	.30	.15		143	Paul Gillis	.05	.04	.02
65	Patrik Sundstrom	.08	.06	.03		144	Bryan Fogarty	.08	.06	.03
66	Mark Johnson	.05	.04	.02		145	Guy Lafleur	.15	.11	.06
67	Doug Brown	.05	.04	.02		146	Anthony Hrkac	.05	.04	.02
68	Chris Terreri	.25	.20	.10		147	Quebec Nordiques logo	.05	.04	.02
69	Bruce Driver	.05	.04	.02		148	Michel Petit	.05	.04	.02
70	Peter Stastny	.12	.09	.05		149	Anthony McKegney	.05	.04	.02
71	Sylvain Turgeon	.08	.06	.03		150	Curtis Leschyshyn	.05	.04	.02
72	New Jersey Devils logo	.05	.04	.02		151	Claude Loiselle	.05	.04	.02
73	Kirk Muller	.15	.11	.06		152	Mario Brunetta	.05	.04	.02
74	John MacLean	.12	.09	.05		153	Marc Fortier	.05	.04	.02
75	Viacheslav Fetisov	.20	.15	.08		154	Michal Pivonka	.10	.08	.04
76	Tommy Albelin	.05	.04	.02		155	Scott Stevens	.10	.08	.04
77	Sean Burke	.10	.08	.04		156	Kelly Miller	.08	.06	.03
78	Janne Ojanen	.05	.04	.02		157	John Tucker	.05	.04	.02
79	Randy Wood	.05	.04	.02		158	Donald Beaupre	.08	.06	.03
80	Gary Nylund	.05	.04	.02		159	Geoff Courtnall	.10	.08	.04
81	Pat LaFontaine	.30	.25	.12		160	Alan May	.05	.04	.02
82	Patrick Flatley	.05	.04	.02		161	Dino Ciccarelli	.10	.08	.04
83	Bryan Trottier	.15	.11	.06		162	Washington Capitals logo	.05	.04	.02
84	Donald Maloney	.05	.04	.02		163	Mike Ridley	.08	.06	.03
85	Gerald Diduck	.05	.04	.02		164	Robert Rouse	.05	.04	.02
87	Mark Fitzpatrick	.10	.08	.04		165	Mike Liut	.08	.06	.03
88	Glenn Healy	.08	.06	.03		166	Stephen Leach	.08	.06	.03
89	Alan Kerr	.05	.04	.02		167	Kevin Hatcher	.12	.09	.05
90	Brent Sutter	.08	.06	.03		168	Dale Hunter	.10	.08	.04
91	Doug Crossman	.05	.04	.02		169	Prince of Wales Trophy	.05	.04	.02
92	Hubie McDonough	.05	.04	.02		170	Clarence Campbell Trophy	.05	.04	.02
93	Jeff Norton	.08	.06	.03		171	Stanley Cup Championship	.08	.06	.03
94	Kelly Kisio	.08	.06	.03		172	Doug Gilmour	.40	.30	.15
95	Brian Leetch	.35	.25	.14		173	Byron (Brad) McCrimmon	.08	.06	.03
96	Brian Mullen	.08	.06	.03		174	Joe Nieuwendyk	.15	.11	.06
97	James Patrick	.08	.06	.03		175	Mike Vernon	.12	.09	.05
98	Mike Richter	.50	.40	.20		176	Theoren Fleury	.20	.15	.08
99	John Ogrodnick	.08	.06	.03		177	Gary Suter	.08	.06	.03
100	Troy Mallette	.05	.04	.02		178	Jamie Macoun	.05	.04	.02
101	Mark Janssens	.05	.04	.02		179	Gary Roberts	.12	.09	.05
102	New York Rangers logo	.05	.04	.02		180	Calgary Flames logo	.05	.04	.02
103	Michael Gartner	.15	.11	.06		181	Paul Ranheim	.08	.06	.03
104	Jan Erixon	.05	.04	.02		182	Jiri Hrdina	.05	.04	.02
105	Carey Wilson	.05	.04	.02		183	Joe Mullen	.10	.08	.04
106	Bernie Nicholls	.10	.08	.04		184	Sergei Makarov	.20	.15	.08
107	Darren Turcotte	.10	.08	.04		185	Allan MacInnis	.15	.11	.06
108	John Vanbiesbrouck	.15	.11	.06		186	Richard Wamsley	.08	.06	.03
109	Ronald Sutter	.08	.06	.03		187	Trent Yawney	.05	.04	.02
110	Kjell Samuelsson	.05	.04	.02		188	Greg Millen	.08	.06	.03
111	Ken Linseman	.05	.04	.02		189	Douglas Wilson	.08	.06	.03
112	Ken Wregget	.08	.06	.03		190	Jocelyn Lemieux	.05	.04	.02
113	Per-Erik Eklund	.08	.06	.03		191	Dirk Graham	.08	.06	.03
114	Terry Carkner	.05	.04	.02		192	Keith Brown	.05	.04	.02
115	Gordon Murphy	.05	.04	.02		193	Adam Creighton	.08	.06	.03
116	Murray Craven	.05	.04	.02		194	Steve Larmer	.10	.08	.04
117	Philadelphia Flyers logo	.05	.04	.02		195	Chicago Black Hawks logo	.05	.04	.02
118	Ron Hextall	.10	.08	.04		196	Gregory Gilbert	.05	.04	.02
119	Mike Bullard	.05	.04	.02		197	Jacques Cloutier	.05	.04	.02

198	Denis Savard	.10	.08	.04
199	Dave Manson	.08	.06	.03
200	Troy Murray	.08	.06	.03
201	Jeremy Roenick	1.50	1.25	.60
202	Lee Norwood	.05	.04	.02
203	Glen Hanlon	.08	.06	.03
204	Marc Habscheid	.05	.04	.02
205	Gerard Gallant	.08	.06	.03
206	Richard Zombo	.05	.04	.02
207	Steve Chiasson	.08	.06	.03
208	Steve Yzerman	.40	.30	.15
209	Bernie Federko	.10	.08	.04
210	Detroit Red Wings logo	.05	.04	.02
211	Joey Kocur	.08	.06	.03
212	Tim Cheveldae	.25	.20	.10
213	Shawn Burr	.05	.04	.02
214	Jimmy Carson	.08	.06	.03
215	Mike O'Connell	.05	.04	.02
216	John Chabot	.05	.04	.02
217	Craig Muni	.05	.04	.02
218	Bill Ranford	.15	.11	.06
219	Mark Messier	.50	.40	.20
220	Craig MacTavish	.08	.06	.03
221	Charles Huddy	.05	.04	.02
222	Jari Kurri	.15	.11	.06
223	Esa Tikkanen	.10	.08	.04
224	Kevin Lowe	.08	.06	.03
225	Edmonton Oilers logo	.06	.05	.02
226	James (Steve) Smith	.10	.08	.04
227	Glenn Anderson	.10	.08	.04
228	Petr Klima	.08	.06	.03
229	Craig Simpson	.08	.06	.03
230	Grant Fuhr	.12	.09	.05
231	Randall Gregg	.05	.04	.02
232	Bob Kudelski	.10	.08	.04
233	Luc Robitaille	.20	.15	.08
234	Martin McSorley	.20	.15	.08
235	John Tonelli	.08	.06	.03
236	David Taylor	.08	.06	.03
237	Mikko Makela	.05	.04	.02
238	Stephen Kasper	.05	.04	.02
239	Tony Granato	.10	.08	.04
240	Los Angeles Kings logo	.05	.04	.02
241	Steve Duchesne	.08	.06	.03
242	Wayne Gretzky	1.00	.70	.40
243	Tomas Sandstrom	.10	.08	.04
244	Larry Robinson	.10	.08	.04
245	Michael Krushelnyski	.08	.06	.03
246	Kelly Hrudey	.10	.08	.04
247	Aaron Broten	.05	.04	.02
248	Dave Gagner	.10	.08	.04
249	Basil McRae	.05	.04	.02
250	Curt Giles	.05	.04	.02
251	Lawrence Murphy	.10	.08	.04
252	Shawn Chambers	.05	.04	.02
253	Michael Modano	.50	.40	.20
254	Jon Casey	.10	.08	.04
255	Minnesota North Stars logo	.05	.04	.02
256	Gaetan Duchesne	.05	.04	.02
257	Brian Bellows	.10	.08	.04
258	Frantisek Musil	.05	.04	.02
259	Don Barber	.05	.04	.02
260	Robert (Stewart) Gavin	.05	.04	.02
261	Neal Broten	.08	.06	.03
262	Brett Hull	.60	.45	.25
263	Sergio Momesso	.08	.06	.03
264	Peter Zezel	.05	.04	.02
265	Gino Cavallini	.05	.04	.02
266	Rod Brind'Amour	.25	.20	.10
267	Mike Lalor	.05	.04	.02
268	Vincent Riendeau	.12	.09	.05
269	Gordon Roberts	.05	.04	.02
270	St. Louis Blues logo	.05	.04	.02
271	Paul MacLean	.05	.04	.02
272	Curtis Joseph	.50	.40	.20
273	Richard Meagher	.05	.04	.02
274	Jeff Brown	.10	.08	.04
275	Adam Oates	.20	.15	.08
276	Paul Cavallini	.05	.04	.02
277	Bradley Marsh	.08	.06	.03
278	Mark Osborne	.05	.04	.02
279	Gary Leeman	.08	.06	.03
280	George (Rob) Ramage	.08	.06	.03
281	Jeff Reese	.08	.06	.03
282	Tom Fergus	.05	.04	.02
283	Ed Olczyk	.08	.06	.03
284	Daniel Marois	.05	.04	.02
285	Toronto Maple Leafs logo	.05	.04	.02
286	Wendel Clark	.20	.15	.08
287	Tom Kurvers	.05	.04	.02
288	Gilles Thibaudeau	.05	.04	.02
289	Lou Franceschetti	.05	.04	.02
290	Al Iafrate	.15	.11	.06
291	Vincent Damphousse	.12	.09	.05
292	Stanley Smyl	.05	.04	.02
293	Paul Reinhart	.05	.04	.02
294	Igor Larionov	.15	.11	.06
295	Doug Lidster	.05	.04	.02
296	Kirk McLean	.20	.15	.08
297	Andrew McBain	.05	.04	.02
298	Petri Skriko	.05	.04	.02
299	Trevor Linden	.30	.25	.12
300	Vancouver Canucks logo	.05	.04	.02
301	Steve Bozek	.05	.04	.02
302	Brian Bradley	.12	.09	.05
303	Greg Adams	.08	.06	.03
304	Vladimir Krutov	.05	.04	.02
305	Dan Quinn	.05	.04	.02
306	Jim Sandlak	.08	.06	.03
307	Teppo Numminen	.05	.04	.02
308	Douglas Smail	.05	.04	.02
309	Gregory Paslawski	.05	.04	.02
310	Dave Ellett	.08	.06	.03
311	Bob Essensa	.12	.09	.05
312	Pat Elynuik	.08	.06	.03
313	Paul Fenton	.05	.04	.02
314	Randy Carlyle	.08	.06	.03
315	Winnipeg Jets logo	.05	.04	.02
316	Thomas Steen	.08	.06	.03
317	Dale Hawerchuk	.12	.09	.05
318	Fredrick Olausson	.08	.06	.03
319	Dave McLlwain	.05	.04	.02
320	Laurie Boschman	.05	.04	.02
321	Brent Ashton	.05	.04	.02
322	Raymond Bourque	.15	.11	.06
323	Patrick Roy	.50	.40	.20
324	Paul Coffey	.15	.11	.06
325	Brian Propp	.08	.06	.03
326	Mario Lemieux	.75	.60	.30
327	Cam Neely	.20	.15	.08
328	Al MacInnis	.15	.11	.06
329	Mike Vernon	.10	.08	.04
330	Kevin Lowe	.08	.06	.03
331	Luc Robitaille	.20	.15	.08
332	Wayne Gretzky	1.00	.70	.40
333	Brett Hull	.50	.40	.20
334	Sergei Makarov	.15	.11	.06
335	Alexei Kasatonov	.10	.08	.04
336	Igor Larionov	.15	.11	.06
337	Vladimir Krutov	.05	.04	.02
338	Alexander Mogilny	.75	.60	.30
339	Viacheslav Fetisov	.15	.11	.06
340	Michael Modano	.75	.60	.30
341	Mark Recchi	.50	.40	.20
342	Paul Ranheim	.08	.06	.03
343	Rod Brind'Amour	.30	.25	.12
344	Brad Shaw	.05	.04	.02
345	Mike Richter	.40	.30	.15
346	Hart Memorial Trophy	.08	.06	.03
347	Art Ross Trophy	.08	.06	.03
348	Calder Memorial Trophy	.08	.06	.03
349	Lady Byng Memorial Trophy	.08	.06	.03
350	James Norris Memorial Trophy	.08	.06	.03
351	Vezina Trophy	.08	.06	.03

1991 Panini Stickers

Once again, these stickers feature color action photos on the fronts, and offered an album to hold them in. The photo on the front is framed around three sides by a colored border. The player's name and team run vertically inside the right border. Biographical information and statistics from the 1990-91 are below the photo. A sticker number is on the back, along with "Hockey '91-'92" and information, in French and English, about trading double stickers to fill in your sticker album. The stickers measure 1 7/8" by 2 7/8". The team logos and NHL 75th anniversary logo are foils.

		MT	NM	EX
	Complete Set (344):	15.00	11.00	6.00
	Common Player:	.05	.04	.02
1	NHL Logo	.08	.06	.03
2	NHLPA Logo	.05	.04	.02
3	NHL 75th Anniversary Logo	.05	.04	.02
4	NHL 75th Anniversary Logo	.05	.04	.02
5	Clarence Campbell Conference Logo	.05	.04	.02
6	Prince of Wales Conference Logo	.05	.04	.02
7	Stanley Cup Championship Logo	.05	.04	.02
8	Steve Larmer	.10	.08	.04
9	Ed Belfour	.40	.30	.15
10	Chris Chelios	.12	.09	.05
11	Michel Goulet	.10	.08	.04
12	Jeremy Roenick	.60	.45	.25
13	Adam Creighton	.08	.06	.03
14	Steve Thomas	.08	.06	.03
15	Dave Manson	.08	.06	.03
16	Dirk Graham	.08	.06	.03
17	Troy Murray	.08	.06	.03
18	Douglas Wilson	.08	.06	.03
19	Wayne Presley	.05	.04	.02
20	Jocelyn Lemieux	.05	.04	.02
21	Keith Brown	.05	.04	.02
22	Curtis Joseph	.25	.20	.10
23	Jeff Brown	.10	.08	.04
24	Gino Cavallini	.05	.04	.02
25	Brett Hull	.40	.30	.15
26	Scott Stevens	.10	.08	.04
27	Dan Quinn	.05	.04	.02
28	Garth Butcher	.08	.06	.03
29	Bob Bassen	.05	.04	.02
30	Rod Brind'Amour	.15	.11	.06
31	Adam Oates	.15	.11	.06
32	Dave Lowry	.05	.04	.02
33	Richard Sutter	.08	.06	.03
34	Ronald Wilson	.05	.04	.02
35	Paul Cavallini	.05	.04	.02
36	Trevor Linden	.20	.15	.08
37	Troy Gamble	.15	.11	.06
38	Geoff Courtnall	.08	.06	.03
39	Greg Adams	.08	.06	.03
40	Doug Lidster	.05	.04	.02
41	Dave Capuano	.05	.04	.02
42	Igor Larionov	.10	.08	.04
43	Tom Kurvers	.05	.04	.02
44	Sergio Momesso	.08	.06	.03
45	Kirk McLean	.15	.11	.06
46	Cliff Ronning	.10	.08	.04
47	Robert Kron	.08	.06	.03
48	Steve Bozek	.05	.04	.02
49	Petr Nedved	.40	.30	.15
50	Al MacInnis	.15	.11	.06
51	Theoren Fleury	.12	.09	.05
52	Gary Roberts	.10	.08	.04
53	Joe Nieuwendyk	.10	.08	.04
54	Paul Ranheim	.05	.04	.02
55	Mike Vernon	.10	.08	.04
56	Carey Wilson	.05	.04	.02
57	Gary Suter	.08	.06	.03
58	Sergei Makarov	.15	.11	.06
59	Douglas Gilmour	.40	.30	.15
60	Joel Otto	.08	.06	.03
61	Jamie Macoun	.05	.04	.02
62	Stephane Matteau	.08	.06	.03
63	Robert Reichel	.25	.20	.10
64	Ed Olczyk	.08	.06	.03
65	Phil Housley	.10	.08	.04
66	Pat Elynuik	.08	.06	.03
67	Fredrik Olausson	.08	.06	.03
68	Thomas Steen	.08	.06	.03
69	Paul MacDermid	.05	.04	.02
70	Brent Ashton	.05	.04	.02
71	Teppo Numminen	.05	.04	.02
72	Danton Cole	.05	.04	.02
73	Dave McLlwain	.05	.04	.02
74	Scott Arniel	.05	.04	.02
75	Bob Essensa	.08	.06	.03
76	Randy Carlyle	.08	.06	.03
77	Mark Osborne	.05	.04	.02
78	Wayne Gretzky	1.00	.70	.40
79	Tomas Sandstrom	.10	.08	.04
80	Steve Duchesne	.08	.06	.03
81	Kelly Hrudey	.10	.08	.04
82	Larry Robinson	.10	.08	.04
83	Tony Granato	.08	.06	.03
84	Martin McSorley	.15	.11	.06
85	Todd Elik	.08	.06	.03
86	Rob Blake	.20	.15	.08
87	Bob Kudelski	.08	.06	.03
88	Stephen Kasper	.05	.04	.02
89	David Taylor	.08	.06	.03
90	John Tonelli	.08	.06	.03
91	Luc Robitaille	.20	.15	.08
92	Vincent Damphousse	.12	.09	.05
93	Brian Bradley	.10	.08	.04
94	Dave Ellett	.08	.06	.03
95	Daniel Marois	.05	.04	.02
96	George (Rob) Ramage	.08	.06	.03
97	Michael Krushelnyski	.08	.06	.03
98	Michel Petit	.05	.04	.02
99	Peter Ing	.08	.06	.03
100	Lucien DeBlois	.05	.04	.02
101	Robert Rouse	.05	.04	.02
102	Wendel Clark	.15	.11	.06
103	Peter Zezel	.08	.06	.03
104	David Reid	.05	.04	.02
105	Aaron Broten	.05	.04	.02
106	Brian Hayward	.08	.06	.03
107	Neal Broten	.08	.06	.03
108	Brian Bellows	.08	.06	.03
109	Mark Timordi	.10	.08	.04
110	Ulf Dahlen	.08	.06	.03
111	Douglas Smail	.08	.06	.03
112	Dave Gagner	.08	.06	.03
113	Robert Smith	.08	.06	.03
114	Brian Glynn	.05	.04	.02
115	Brian Propp	.08	.06	.03
116	Michael Modano	.35	.25	.14
117	Gaetan Duchesne	.05	.04	.02
118	Jon Casey	.10	.08	.04
119	Basil McRae	.05	.04	.02
120	Glenn Anderson	.10	.08	.04
121	James (Steve) Smith	.10	.08	.04
122	Adam Graves	.25	.20	.10
123	Esa Tikkanen	.10	.08	.04
124	Mark Messier	.50	.40	.20
125	Bill Ranford	.15	.11	.06
126	Petr Klima	.08	.06	.03
127	Anatoli Semenov	.10	.08	.04
128	Martin Gelinas	.10	.08	.04
129	Charles Huddy	.05	.04	.02
130	Craig Simpson	.08	.06	.03
131	Kevin Lowe	.08	.06	.03
132	Craig MacTavish	.08	.06	.03
133	Craig Muni	.05	.04	.02
134	Steve Yzerman	.35	.25	.14
135	Shawn Burr	.05	.04	.02

#	Player				#	Player			
136	Tim Cheveldae	.15	.11	.06	214	Lee Norwood	.05	.04	.02
137	Richard Zombo	.05	.04	.02	215	Laurie Boschman	.05	.04	.02
138	Marc Habscheid	.05	.04	.02	216	Alexei Kasatonov	.08	.06	.03
139	Jimmy Carson	.08	.06	.03	217	Patrik Sundstrom	.08	.06	.03
140	Brent Fedyk	.08	.06	.03	218	Ken Daneyko	.08	.06	.03
141	Yves Racine	.05	.04	.02	219	Kirk Muller	.12	.09	.05
142	Gerard Gallant	.08	.06	.03	220	Peter Stastny	.12	.09	.05
143	Steve Chiasson	.08	.06	.03	221	Chris Terreri	.10	.08	.04
144	Johan Garpenlov	.12	.09	.05	222	Brendan Shanahan	.20	.15	.08
145	Sergei Fedorov	.75	.60	.30	223	Eric Weinrich	.08	.06	.03
146	Bob Probert	.12	.09	.05	224	Claude Lemieux	.10	.08	.04
147	Richard Green	.05	.04	.02	225	Bruce Driver	.08	.06	.03
148	Chicago Black Hawks	.05	.04	.02	226	Tim Kerr	.08	.06	.03
149	Detroit Red Wings	.05	.04	.02	227	Ron Hextall	.10	.08	.04
150	Minnesota North Stars	.05	.04	.02	228	Per-Erik Eklund	.08	.06	.03
151	St. Louis Blues	.05	.04	.02	229	Rick Tocchet	.10	.08	.04
152	Toronto Maple Leafs	.05	.04	.02	230	Gordon Murphy	.05	.04	.02
153	Calgary Flames	.05	.04	.02	231	Mike Ricci	.30	.25	.12
154	Edmonton Oilers	.05	.04	.02	232	Derrick Smith	.05	.04	.02
155	Los Angeles Kings	.05	.04	.02	233	Ronald Sutter	.08	.06	.03
156	San Jose Sharks	.25	.20	.10	234	Murray Craven	.05	.04	.02
157	Vancouver Canucks	.05	.04	.02	235	Terry Carkner	.05	.04	.02
158	Winnipeg Jets	.05	.04	.02	236	Ken Wregget	.08	.06	.03
159	Boston Bruins	.05	.04	.02	237	Keith Acton	.05	.04	.02
160	Buffalo Sabres	.05	.04	.02	238	Scott Mellanby	.05	.04	.02
161	Hartford Whalers	.05	.04	.02	239	Kjell Samuelsson	.05	.04	.02
162	Montreal Canadiens	.08	.06	.03	240	Jeff Hackett	.08	.06	.03
163	Quebec Nordiques	.05	.04	.02	241	David Volek	.05	.04	.02
164	New Jersey Devils	.05	.04	.02	242	Craig Ludwig	.05	.04	.02
165	New York Islanders	.05	.04	.02	243	Pat LaFontaine	.35	.25	.14
166	New York Rangers	.05	.04	.02	244	Randy Wood	.05	.04	.02
167	Philadelphia Flyers	.05	.04	.02	245	Patrick Flatley	.05	.04	.02
168	Pittsburgh Penguins	.05	.04	.02	246	Brent Sutter	.08	.06	.03
169	Washington Capitals	.05	.04	.02	247	Derek King	.10	.08	.04
170	Craig Janney	.12	.09	.05	248	Jeff Norton	.08	.06	.03
171	Raymond Bourque	.15	.11	.06	249	Glenn Healy	.08	.06	.03
172	Rejean Lemelin	.08	.06	.03	250	Ray Ferraro	.08	.06	.03
173	Dave Christian	.08	.06	.03	251	Gary Nylund	.05	.04	.02
174	Randy Burridge	.08	.06	.03	252	Joe Reekie	.05	.04	.02
175	Garry Galley	.08	.06	.03	253	David Chyzowski	.05	.04	.02
176	Cam Neely	.20	.15	.08	254	Mike Hough	.05	.04	.02
177	Robert Sweeney	.05	.04	.02	255	Mats Sundin	.35	.25	.14
178	Kenneth Hodge, Jr.	.08	.06	.03	256	Curtis Leschyshyn	.08	.06	.03
179	Andrew Moog	.12	.09	.05	257	Joe Sakic	.30	.25	.12
180	Don Sweeney	.05	.04	.02	258	Stephane Fiset	.15	.11	.06
181	Robert Carpenter	.08	.06	.03	259	Bryan Fogarty	.08	.06	.03
182	Glen Wesley	.08	.06	.03	260	Alexei Gusarov	.08	.06	.03
183	Christopher Nilan	.08	.06	.03	261	Steven Finn	.05	.04	.02
184	Patrick Roy	.35	.25	.14	262	Everett Sanipass	.05	.04	.02
185	Petr Svoboda	.08	.06	.03	263	Stephane Morin	.08	.06	.03
186	Russ Courtnall	.08	.06	.03	264	Craig Wolanin	.05	.04	.02
187	Denis Savard	.10	.08	.04	265	Randy Velischek	.05	.04	.02
188	Michael McPhee	.08	.06	.03	266	Owen Nolan	.25	.20	.10
189	Eric Desjardins	.08	.06	.03	267	Ron Tugnutt	.10	.08	.04
190	Mike Keane	.08	.06	.03	268	Mario Lemieux	.50	.40	.20
191	Stephan Lebeau	.15	.11	.06	269	Kevin Stevens	.25	.20	.10
192	Jean-Jacques Daigneault	.08	.06	.03	270	Lawrence Murphy	.10	.08	.04
193	Stephane J.J. Richer	.10	.08	.04	271	Tom Barrasso	.10	.08	.04
194	Brian Skrudland	.05	.04	.02	272	Phil Bourque	.05	.04	.02
195	Mathieu Schneider	.10	.08	.04	273	Scott Young	.08	.06	.03
196	Shayne Corson	.08	.06	.03	274	Paul Stanton	.05	.04	.02
197	Guy Carbonneau	.08	.06	.03	275	Jaromir Jagr	.75	.60	.30
198	Kevin Hatcher	.10	.08	.04	276	Paul Coffey	.15	.11	.06
199	Mike Ridley	.08	.06	.03	277	Ulf Samuelsson	.08	.06	.03
200	John Druce	.05	.04	.02	278	Joe Mullen	.08	.06	.03
201	Donald Beaupre	.08	.06	.03	279	Bob Errey	.05	.04	.02
202	Kelly Miller	.08	.06	.03	280	Mark Recchi	.30	.25	.12
203	Dale Hunter	.08	.06	.03	281	Ron Francis	.10	.08	.04
204	Nick Kypreos	.05	.04	.02	282	John Vanbiesbrouck	.15	.11	.06
205	Calle Johansson	.05	.04	.02	283	Jan Erixon	.05	.04	.02
206	Michal Pivonka	.15	.11	.06	284	Brian Leetch	.30	.25	.12
207	Dino Ciccarelli	.10	.08	.04	285	Darren Turcotte	.08	.06	.03
208	Al Iafrate	.12	.09	.05	286	Ray Sheppard	.08	.06	.03
209	Rod Langway	.08	.06	.03	287	James Patrick	.08	.06	.03
210	Mikhail Tatarinov	.10	.08	.04	288	Bernie Nicholls	.10	.08	.04
211	Stephen Leach	.08	.06	.03	289	Brian Mullen	.08	.06	.03
212	Sean Burke	.10	.08	.04	290	Mike Richter	.35	.25	.14
213	John MacLean	.08	.06	.03	291	Kelly Kisio	.08	.06	.03

292	Michael Gartner	.12	.09	.05
293	John Ogrodnick	.08	.06	.03
294	David Shaw	.08	.06	.03
295	Troy Mallette	.05	.04	.02
296	Dale Hawerchuk	.12	.09	.05
297	Richard Vaive	.08	.06	.03
298	Daren Puppa	.08	.06	.03
299	Michael Ramsey	.08	.06	.03
300	Benoit Hogue	.10	.08	.04
301	Clint Malarchuk	.08	.06	.03
302	Mikko Makela	.05	.04	.02
303	Pierre Turgeon	.35	.25	.14
304	Alexander Mogilny	.40	.30	.15
305	Uwe Krupp	.08	.06	.03
306	Christian Ruuttu	.05	.04	.02
307	Doug Bodger	.08	.06	.03
308	Dave Snuggerud	.05	.04	.02
309	David Andreychuk	.15	.11	.06
310	Peter Sidorkiewicz	.08	.06	.03
311	Brad Shaw	.08	.06	.03
312	Dean Evason	.05	.04	.02
313	Patrick Verbeek	.08	.06	.03
314	John Cullen	.10	.08	.04
315	Rob Brown	.08	.06	.03
316	Robert Holik	.20	.15	.08
317	Todd Krygier	.08	.06	.03
318	Adam Burt	.05	.04	.02
319	Mike Tomlak	.05	.04	.02
320	Randy Cunneyworth	.05	.04	.02
321	Paul Cyr	.05	.04	.02
322	Zarley Zalapski	.08	.06	.03
323	Kevin Dineen	.08	.06	.03
324	Luc Robitaille	.20	.15	.08
325	Brett Hull	.40	.30	.15
326	All-Star Game Logo	.08	.06	.03
327	Wayne Gretzky	.75	.60	.30
328	Mike Vernon	.10	.08	.04
329	Chris Chelios	.10	.08	.04
330	Al MacInnis	.10	.08	.04
331	Rick Tocchet	.10	.08	.04
332	Cam Neely	.15	.11	.06
333	Patrick Roy	.35	.25	.14
334	Joe Sakic	.25	.20	.10
335	Raymond Bourque	.15	.11	.06
336	Paul Coffey	.15	.11	.06
337	Ed Belfour	.30	.25	.12
338	Mike Ricci	.25	.20	.10
339	Rob Blake	.12	.09	.05
340	Sergei Fedorov	.75	.60	.30
341	Kenneth Hodge, Jr.	.08	.06	.03
342	Robert Holik	.15	.11	.06
343	Robert Reichel	.15	.11	.06
344	Jaromir Jagr	.60	.45	.25

1992 Panini Insert English

These stickers, randomly inserted in English and French versions of 1992-93 Panini stickers, feature a star from each NHL team, excpet the two new expansion teams. The "Ice Breaker" cards have a silver metallic background, with a color action photo. The player's name is in a triangle at the bottom of the card. Statistics and biographical information run vertically along the right side of the card. Each sticker measures 2 1/2" by 3 1/2". Both versions have equal values.

		MT	NM	EX
Complete Set (22):		10.00	7.50	4.00
Common Player:		.35	.25	.14
A	Igor Kravchuk	.35	.25	.14
B	Nelson Emerson	.50	.40	.20
C	Pavel Bure	4.00	3.00	1.50
D	Tomas Forslund	.35	.25	.14
E	Luciano Borsato	.35	.25	.14
F	Darryl Sydor	.50	.40	.20
G	Felix Potvin	1.50	1.25	.60
H	Derian Hatcher	.50	.40	.20
I	Joseph Beranek	.40	.30	.15

J	Nicklas Lidstrom	.75	.60	.30
K	Pat Falloon	.75	.60	.30
L	Joseph Juneau	1.00	.70	.40
M	Gilbert Dionne	.75	.60	.30
N	Dimitri Khristich	.50	.40	.20
O	Kevin Todd	.50	.40	.20
P	Eric Lindros	6.00	4.50	2.50
Q	Scott Lachance	.50	.40	.20
R	Valeri Kamensky	.50	.40	.20
S	Jarimir Jagr	1.50	1.25	.60
T	Anthony Amonte	.75	.60	.30
U	Donald Audette	.50	.40	.20
V	Geoff Sanderson	1.25	.90	.50

1992 Panini Stickers English

These stickers, which included an insert set, have color action photos on the front, along with statistics running along the right side of the card. A sticker number is in the lower right corner, inside a hockey puck. A team logo is in the lower left corner, while the player's name is in the upper left corner. "Hockey 1992-1993" is in the upper right corner. The back features "Slap-Shot" game trivia questions and answers, which accompany the game that is included in the sticker album. Panini issued an identical French version of the sticker set, except the stickers were written in French. This set is the same value as the English set. Both sets also had "Ice-Breaker" stickers (22) randomly inserted in the packs. They feature a star from each NHL team. Both sets of stickers measure 2 1/2" by 3 1/2".

		MT	NM	EX
Complete Set (308):		30.00	22.00	12.00
Common Player:		.05	.04	.02
1	Stanley Cup	.08	.06	.03
2	Chicago Black Hawks Logo	.05	.04	.02
3	Ed Belfour	.30	.25	.12
4	Jeremy Roenick	.50	.40	.20
5	Steve Larmer	.10	.08	.04
6	Michel Goulet	.10	.08	.04
7	Dirk Graham	.08	.06	.03
8	Jocelyn Lemieux	.05	.04	.02
9	Brian Noonan	.08	.06	.03
10	Rob Brown	.08	.06	.03
11	Chris Chelios	.10	.08	.04
12	Steve Smith	.08	.06	.03
13	Keith Brown	.05	.04	.02
14	St. Louis Blues Logo	.05	.04	.02
15	Curtis Joseph	.20	.15	.08
16	Brett Hull	.40	.30	.15
17	Brendan Shanahan	.20	.15	.08
18	Ronald Wilson	.05	.04	.02
19	Richard Sutter	.08	.06	.03
20	Ronald Sutter	.08	.06	.03
21	Dave Lowry	.05	.04	.02
22	Craig Janney	.15	.11	.06
23	Paul Cavallini	.05	.04	.02

24	Garth Butcher	.08	.06	.03
25	Jeff Brown	.10	.08	.04
26	Vancouver Canucks Logo	.05	.04	.02
27	Kirk McLean	.12	.09	.05
28	Trevor Linden	.15	.11	.06
29	Geoff Courtnall	.08	.06	.03
30	Cliff Ronning	.08	.06	.03
31	Petr Nedved	.25	.20	.10
32	Igor Larionov	.10	.08	.04
33	Robert Kron	.08	.06	.03
34	Jim Sandlak	.08	.06	.03
35	David Babych	.08	.06	.03
36	Jyrki Lumme	.08	.06	.03
37	Doug Lidster	.05	.04	.02
38	Calgary Flames Logo	.05	.04	.02
39	Michael Vernon	.10	.08	.04
40	Joe Nieuwendyk	.10	.08	.04
41	Gary Leeman	.05	.04	.02
42	Robert Reichel	.10	.08	.04
43	Joel Otto	.05	.04	.02
44	Paul Ranheim	.05	.04	.02
45	Gary Roberts	.10	.08	.04
46	Theoren Fleury	.12	.09	.05
47	Sergei Makarov	.15	.11	.06
48	Gary Suter	.08	.06	.03
49	Allan MacInnis	.12	.09	.05
50	Winnipeg Jets Logo	.05	.04	.02
51	Bob Essensa	.10	.08	.04
52	Teppo Numminen	.05	.04	.02
53	Thomas Steen	.08	.06	.03
54	Pat Elynuik	.08	.06	.03
55	Ed Olczyk	.08	.06	.03
56	Danton Cole	.05	.04	.02
57	Troy Murray	.08	.06	.03
58	Darrin Shannon	.08	.06	.03
59	Russell Romaniuk	.05	.04	.02
60	Error (Fredrick Olausson) (Fredrik on Card))	.08	.06	.03
61	Phil Housley	.10	.08	.04
62	Los Angeles King Logo	.05	.04	.02
63	Kelly Hrudey	.10	.08	.04
64	Wayne Gretzky	.75	.60	.30
65	Luc Robitaille	.20	.15	.08
66	Jari Kurri	.12	.09	.05
67	Tomas Sandstrom	.10	.08	.04
68	Tony Granato	.08	.06	.03
69	Bob Kudelski	.08	.06	.03
70	Corey Millen	.15	.11	.06
71	Robert Blake	.10	.08	.04
72	Paul Coffey	.15	.11	.06
73	Martin McSorley	.15	.11	.06
74	Toronto Maple Leafs Logo	.05	.04	.02
75	Grant Fuhr	.10	.08	.04
76	Glenn Anderson	.10	.08	.04
77	Douglas Gilmour	.35	.25	.14
78	Michael Krushelnyski	.08	.06	.03
79	Wendel Clark	.15	.11	.06
80	Rob Pearson	.12	.09	.05
81	Peter Zezel	.08	.06	.03
82	Todd Gill	.05	.04	.02
83	David Ellett	.08	.06	.03
84	Mike Foligno	.05	.04	.02
85	Ken Baumgartner	.05	.04	.02
86	Minnesota North Stars Logo	.05	.04	.02
87	Jon Casey	.10	.08	.04
88	Brian Bellows	.10	.08	.04
89	Neal Broten	.08	.06	.03
90	Dave Gagner	.08	.06	.03
91	Michael Modano	.30	.25	.12
92	Ulf Dahlen	.05	.04	.02
93	Brian Propp	.08	.06	.03
94	Jim Johnson	.05	.04	.02
95	Mike Craig	.08	.06	.03
96	Bobby Smith	.08	.06	.03
97	Mark Tinordi	.08	.06	.03
98	Edmonton Oilers Logo	.05	.04	.02
99	Bill Ranford	.10	.08	.04
100	Joe Murphy	.08	.06	.03
101	Craig MacTavish	.08	.06	.03
102	Craig Simpson	.08	.06	.03
103	Esa Tikkanen	.10	.08	.04
104	Vincent Damphousse	.12	.09	.05
105	Petr Klima	.08	.06	.03
106	Martin Gelinas	.08	.06	.03
107	Kevin Lowe	.08	.06	.03
108	Dave Manson	.08	.06	.03
109	Bernie Nicholls	.10	.08	.04
110	Detroit Red Wings Logo	.05	.04	.02
111	Tim Cheveldae	.12	.09	.05
112	Steve Yzerman	.35	.25	.14
113	Sergei Fedorov	.50	.40	.20
114	Jimmy Carson	.10	.08	.04
115	Kevin Miller	.08	.06	.03
116	Gerard Gallant	.05	.04	.02
117	Keith Primeau	.15	.11	.06
118	Paul Ysebaert	.10	.08	.04
119	Yves Racine	.05	.04	.02
120	Steve Chiasson	.08	.06	.03
121	Ray Sheppard	.10	.08	.04
122	San Jose Sharks Logo	.15	.11	.06
123	Jeff Hackett	.10	.08	.04
124	Kelly Kisio	.08	.06	.03
125	Brian Mullen	.08	.06	.03
126	David Bruce	.08	.06	.03
127	Rob Zettler	.08	.06	.03
128	Neil Wilkinson	.08	.06	.03
129	Douglas Wilson	.08	.06	.03
130	Jeff Odgers	.05	.04	.02
131	Dean Evason	.05	.04	.02
132	Brian Lawton	.05	.04	.02
133	Dale Craigwell	.08	.06	.03
134	Boston Bruins Logo	.05	.04	.02
135	Andrew Moog	.10	.08	.04
136	Adam Oates	.15	.11	.06
137	David Poulin	.05	.04	.02
138	Vladimir Ruzicka	.08	.06	.03
139	Jeff Lazaro	.05	.04	.02
140	Robert Carpenter	.08	.06	.03
141	Peter Douris	.05	.04	.02
142	Glen Murray	.10	.08	.04
143	Cam Neely	.15	.11	.06
144	Raymond Bourque	.12	.09	.05
145	Glen Wesley	.08	.06	.03
146	Montreal Canadiens Logo	.05	.04	.02
147	Patrick Roy	.30	.25	.12
148	Kirk Muller	.12	.09	.05
149	Guy Carbonneau	.08	.06	.03
150	Shayne Corson	.08	.06	.03
151	Stephan Lebeau	.08	.06	.03
152	Dennis Savard	.10	.08	.04
153	Brent Gilchrist	.05	.04	.02
154	Russell Courtnall	.08	.06	.03
155	Patrice Brisebois	.08	.06	.03
156	Eric Desjardins	.08	.06	.03
157	Mathieu Schneider	.10	.08	.04
158	Washington Capitals Logo	.05	.04	.02
159	Donald Beaupre	.08	.06	.03
160	Dino Ciccarelli	.10	.08	.04
161	Michal Pivonka	.10	.08	.04
162	Mike Ridley	.08	.06	.03
163	Randy Burridge	.08	.06	.03
164	Peter Bondra	.08	.06	.03
165	Dale Hunter	.08	.06	.03
166	Kelly Miller	.08	.06	.03
167	Kevin Hatcher	.10	.08	.04
168	Al Iafrate	.12	.09	.05
169	Rod Langway	.08	.06	.03
170	New Jersey Devils Logo	.05	.04	.02
171	Chris Terreri	.08	.06	.03
172	Claude Lemieux	.10	.08	.04
173	Stephane Richer	.10	.08	.04
174	Peter Stastny	.10	.08	.04
175	Zdeno Giger	.05	.04	.02
176	Alexander Semak	.15	.11	.06
177	Valeri Zelepukin	.10	.08	.04
178	Bruce Driver	.08	.06	.03

179	Scott Niedermayer	.25	.20	.10
180	Alexei Kasatonov	.12	.09	.05
181	Scott Stevens	.10	.08	.04
182	Philadelphia Flyers Logo	.05	.04	.02
183	Dominic Roussel	.15	.11	.06
184	Mike Ricci	.15	.11	.06
185	Mark Reechi	.25	.20	.10
186	Kevin Dineen	.08	.06	.03
187	Rod Brind'Amour	.12	.09	.05
188	Mark Pederson	.05	.04	.02
189	Per-Erik (Pelle) Eklund	.08	.06	.03
190	Terry Carkner	.05	.04	.02
191	Mark Howe	.08	.06	.03
192	Steve Duchesne	.08	.06	.03
193	Andrei Lomakin	.08	.06	.03
194	New York Islanders Logo	.05	.04	.02
195	Mark Fitzpatrick	.10	.08	.04
196	Pierre Turgeon	.25	.20	.10
197	Benoit Hogue	.10	.08	.04
198	Ray Ferraro	.10	.08	.04
199	Derek King	.10	.08	.04
200	David Volek	.05	.04	.02
201	Patrick Flatley	.05	.04	.02
202	Uwe Krupp	.05	.04	.02
203	Steve Thomas	.08	.06	.03
204	Adam Creighton	.05	.04	.02
205	Jeff Norton	.05	.04	.02
206	Quebec Nordiques Logo	.05	.04	.02
207	Stephane Fiset	.10	.08	.04
208	Mikhail Tatarinov	.08	.06	.03
209	Joe Sakic	.25	.20	.10
210	Owen Nolan	.20	.15	.08
211	Mike Hough	.05	.04	.02
212	Mats Sundin	.25	.20	.10
213	Claude Lapointe	.10	.08	.04
214	Stephane Morin	.08	.06	.03
215	Alexei Gusarov	.08	.06	.03
216	Steven Finn	.05	.04	.02
217	Curtis Leschyshyn	.08	.06	.03
218	Pittsburgh Penguins Logo	.05	.04	.02
219	Tom Barasso	.10	.08	.04
220	Mario Lemieux	.50	.40	.20
221	Kevin Stevens	.25	.20	.10
222	Shawn McEachern	.20	.15	.08
223	Joe Mullen	.10	.08	.04
224	Ronald Francis	.10	.08	.04
225	Phillippe Bourque	.05	.04	.02
226	Rick Tocchet	.10	.08	.04
227	Bryan Trottier	.12	.09	.05
228	Lawrence (Larry) Murphy	.10	.08	.04
229	Ulf Samuelsson	.08	.06	.03
230	New York Rangers Logo	.05	.04	.02
231	Mike Richter	.30	.25	.12
232	John Vanbiesbrouck	.15	.11	.06
233	Mark Messier	.40	.30	.15
234	Sergei Nemchinov	.10	.08	.04
235	Darren Turcotte	.10	.08	.04
236	Doug Weight	.10	.08	.04
237	Michael Gartner	.12	.09	.05
238	Adam Graves	.25	.20	.10
239	Brian Leetch	.20	.15	.08
240	James Patrick	.05	.04	.02
241	Jan Erixon	.05	.04	.02
242	Buffalo Sabres Logo	.05	.04	.02
243	Tom Draper	.10	.08	.04
244	Grant Ledyard	.05	.04	.02
245	Doug Bodger	.05	.04	.02
246	Pat LaFontaine	.35	.25	.14
247	Dale Hawerchuk	.12	.09	.05
248	Alexander Mogilny	.35	.25	.14
249	David Andreychuk	.15	.11	.06
250	Christian Ruuttu	.05	.04	.02
251	Randy Wood	.05	.04	.02
252	Brad May	.08	.06	.03
253	Michael Ramsey	.05	.04	.02
254	Hartford Whalers Logo	.05	.04	.02
255	Kay Whitmore	.10	.08	.04
256	Patrick Verbeek	.08	.06	.03
257	John Cullen	.08	.06	.03
258	Bo Mikael Andersson	.08	.06	.03
259	Yvon Corriveau	.05	.04	.02
260	Randy Cunneyworth	.08	.06	.03
261	Robert Holik	.10	.08	.04
262	Murray Craven	.05	.04	.02
263	Zarley Zalapski	.08	.06	.03
264	Adam Burt	.05	.04	.02
265	Brad Shaw	.05	.04	.02
266	Tampa Bay Lightning Logo	.08	.06	.03
267	Tampa Bay Lightning Jersey	.08	.06	.03
268	Ottawa Senators Logo	.05	.04	.02
269	Ottawa Senators Jersey	.05	.04	.02
270	Anthony Amonto	.20	.15	.08
271	Pavel Bure	1.25	.90	.50
272	Gilbert Dionne	.25	.20	.10
273	Pat Falloon	.25	.20	.10
274	Nicklas Lidstrom	.20	.15	.08
275	Kevin Todd	.10	.08	.04
276	Prince of Wales Conference Logo	.05	.04	.02
277	Patrick Roy	.25	.20	.10
278	Paul Coffey	.12	.09	.05
279	Raymond Bourque	.12	.09	.05
280	Mario Lemieux	.35	.25	.14
281	Kevin Stevens	.20	.15	.08
282	Jaromir Jagr	.30	.25	.12
283	Clarence Campbell Conference Logo	.05	.04	.02
284	Ed Belfour	.20	.15	.08
285	Allan MacInnis	.10	.08	.04
286	Chris Chelios	.10	.08	.04
287	Wayne Gretzky	.60	.45	.25
288	Luc Robitaille	.15	.11	.06
289	Brett Hull	.25	.20	.10
290	Pavel Bure	.75	.60	.30
291	Sergei Fedorov	.50	.40	.20
292	Dominik Hasek	.15	.11	.06
293	Robert Holik	.10	.08	.04
294	Jaromir Jagr	.30	.25	.12
295	Valeri Kamensky	.15	.11	.06
296	Alexander Semak	.15	.11	.06
297	Igor Kravchuk	.10	.08	.04
298	Nicklas Lidstrom	.15	.11	.06
299	Alexander Mogilny	.25	.20	.10
300	Petr Nedved	.20	.15	.08
301	Robert Reichel	.12	.09	.05
302	Mats Sundin	.15	.11	.06
303	Calder Trophy	.05	.04	.02
304	Hart Trophy	.05	.04	.02
305	Lady Byng Trophy	.05	.04	.02
306	Norris Trophy	.05	.04	.02
307	Frank J. Selke Trophy	.05	.04	.02
308	Vezina Trophy	.05	.04	.02

1960 Topps Stamps

These 1960-61 Topps inserts feature players from the Boston Bruins, New York Rangers, Chicago Blackhawks and all-time greats. The stickers are unnumbered and are grouped below by teams. The front of the stamp is blue and white and includes the player's name, team and position. The back is blank. Each stamp is 1 3/8" by 1 7/8".

		NM	EX	VG
	Complete Set (52):	1200.	600.00	360.00
	Common Player:	15.00	7.50	4.50
1	Leo Boivin	30.00	15.00	9.00
2	John Bucyk	40.00	20.00	12.00
3	Charlie Burns	30.00	15.00	9.00
4	Don McKenney	17.50	8.75	5.25
5	Doug Mohns	17.50	8.75	5.25
6	Murray Oliver	15.00	7.50	4.50
7	Andre Pronovost	15.00	7.50	4.50
8	Dallas Smith	17.50	8.75	5.25
9	Andy Bathgate	35.00	17.50	10.50
10	Doug Harvey	40.00	20.00	12.00

11	Andy Hebenton	15.00	7.50	4.50
12	Camille Henry	15.00	7.50	4.50
13	Harry Howell	30.00	15.00	9.00
14	Al Langlois	15.00	7.50	4.50
15	Dean Prentice	17.50	8.75	5.25
16	Gump Worsley	45.00	22.00	13.50
17	Murray Balfour	15.00	7.50	4.50
18	Jack Evans	15.00	7.50	4.50
19	Glenn Hall	50.00	25.00	15.00
20	Billy Hay	17.50	8.75	5.25
21	Bronco Horvath	15.00	7.50	4.50
22	Bobby Hull	100.00	50.00	30.00
23	Stan Mikita	100.00	50.00	30.00
24	Ron Murphy	15.00	7.50	4.50
25	Pierre Pilote	30.00	15.00	9.00
26	Elmer Vasko	15.00	7.50	4.50
27	Richard Boon	17.50	8.75	5.25
28	Frank Boucher	17.50	8.75	5.25
29	Francis (King) Clancy	50.00	25.00	15.00
30	Dit Clapper	25.00	12.50	7.50
31	Spague Cleghorn	17.50	8.75	5.25
32	Alex Connell	17.50	8.75	5.25
33	Bill Cook	17.50	8.75	5.25
34	Cy Denneny	17.50	8.75	5.25
35	Frank Frederickson	15.00	7.50	4.50
36	Chuck Gardiner	17.50	8.75	5.25
37	Herb Gardiner	15.00	7.50	4.50
38	Eddie Gerard	15.00	7.50	4.50
39	Frank (Moose) Goheen	15.00	7.50	4.50
40	George Hay	17.50	8.75	5.25
41	Dick Irvin	15.00	7.50	4.50
42	Ernest (Moose) Johnson	17.50	8.75	5.25
43	Edouard Lalonde	30.00	15.00	9.00
44	Hugh Lehman	15.00	7.50	4.50
45	Joe Malone	30.00	15.00	9.00
46	Paddy Moran	25.00	12.50	7.50
47	Howie Morenz	75.00	37.00	22.00
48	Frank Nighbor	17.50	8.75	5.25
49	Art Ross	35.00	17.50	10.50
50	Nels Stewart	35.00	17.50	10.50
51	Fred Taylor	40.00	20.00	12.00
52	Georges Vezina	60.00	30.00	18.00

1982 Topps Stickers

See 1982 O-Pee-Chee Stickers.

1983 Topps Stickers

See 1983 O-Pee-Chee Stickers.

1985 Topps Stickers

These standard-size stickers were inserted in 1985-86 Topps hockey wax packs. They feature 12 All-Stars and 21 team helmet stickers. The All-Star stickers have a full-color action photo on the front, with "All-Star" and an NHL logo at the top of the card. The player's name an position are below the photo. The front has a white border. The back is in red and blue ink and lists the player's statistics from the All-Star game in 1985. The team stickers have numbers, pucks and logos on them. The backs have a promotional offer.

		MT	NM	EX
	Complete Set (33):	18.00	13.50	7.25
	Common Player:	.25	.20	.10
	Common Team:	.15	.11	.06
1	John Ogrodick	.25	.20	.10
2	Wayne Gretzky	8.00	6.00	3.25
3	Jari Kurri	.60	.45	.25
4	Paul Coffey	1.00	.70	.40
5	Raymond Bourque	1.25	.90	.50
6	Pelle Lindbergh	4.00	3.00	1.50
7	John Tonelli	.25	.20	.10
8	Dale Hawerchuk	.60	.45	.25
9	Mike Bossy	1.00	.70	.40
10	Rod Langway	.30	.25	.12

11	Douglas Wilson	.30	.25	.12
12	Tom Barrasso	.60	.45	.25
13	Toronto Maple Leafs	.15	.11	.06
14	Buffalo Sabres	.15	.11	.06
15	Detroit Red Wings	.15	.11	.06
16	Pittsburgh Penguins	.15	.11	.06
17	New York Rangers	.15	.11	.06
18	Calgary Flames	.15	.11	.06
19	Winnipeg Jets	.15	.11	.06
20	Quebec Nordiques	.15	.11	.06
21	Chicago Black Hawks	.15	.11	.06
22	Los Angeles Kings	.15	.11	.06
23	Montreal Canadiens	.15	.11	.06
24	Vancouver Canucks	.15	.11	.06
25	Hartford Whalers	.15	.11	.06
26	Philadelphia Flyers	.15	.11	.06
27	New Jersey Devils	.15	.11	.06
28	St. Louis Blues	.15	.11	.06
29	Minnesota North Stars	.15	.11	.06
30	Washington Capitals	.15	.11	.06
31	Boston Bruins	.15	.11	.06
32	New York Islanders	.15	.11	.06
33	Edmonton Oilers	.15	.11	.06

1986 Topps Stickers

These stickers were issued as inserts in 1986-87 Topps wax packs. They feature 12 All-Stars and 21 team logo stickers. Each sticker is standard size. Each All-Star sticker has a color action photo of the player, along with his name and All-Star below the photo. The left side of the sticker has stars running vertically along it, with an NHL logo at the bottom, in the lower left corner. The back lists the player's name, position and team, and indicates the player was a 1985-86 All-Star team selection. A sticker number is also included.

		MT	NM	EX
	Complete Set (33):	20.00	15.00	8.00
	Common Player:	.35	.25	.14
	Common Team:	.15	.11	.06
1	John Vanbiesbrouck	2.00	1.50	.80
2	Michel Goulet	.50	.40	.20
3	Wayne Gretzky	7.50	5.75	3.00
4	Mike Bossy	1.00	.70	.40
5	Paul Coffey	1.00	.70	.40
6	Mark Howe	.35	.25	.14
7	Bob Froese	.35	.25	.14
8	Mats Naslund	.35	.25	.14
9	Mario Lemieux	7.50	5.75	3.00
10	Jari Kurri	.75	.60	.30
11	Raymond Bourque	.75	.60	.30
12	Larry Robinson	.50	.40	.20
13	Toronto Maple Leafs	.15	.11	.06
14	Buffalo Sabres	.15	.11	.06
15	Detroit Red Wings	.15	.11	.06
16	Pittsburgh Penguins	.15	.11	.06
17	New York Rangers	.15	.11	.06
18	Calgary Flames	.15	.11	.06
19	Winnipeg Jets	.15	.11	.06
20	Quebec Nordiques	.15	.11	.06
21	Chicago Black Hawks	.15	.11	.06
22	Los Angeles Kings	.15	.11	.06
23	Montreal Canadiens	.15	.11	.06
24	Vancouver Canucks	.15	.11	.06
25	Hartford Whalers	.15	.11	.06
26	Philadelphia Flyers	.15	.11	.06
27	New Jersey Devils	.15	.11	.06
28	St. Louis Blues	.15	.11	.06
29	Minnesota North Stars	.15	.11	.06
30	Washington Capitals	.15	.11	.06
31	Boston Bruins	.15	.11	.06
32	New York Islanders	.15	.11	.06
33	Edmonton Oliers	.15	.11	.06

1987 Topps Stickers

These stickers were inserted in 1987-88 Topps hockey wax packs. Twelve All-Stars and 21 team logo sticker are represented in the set. The stickers are standard size. Team logo stickers have combinations of team logos, pucks and numbers. The All-Star stickers have an All-Star banner at the top. A color picture is in the center of the card, with the player's name below, written in a hockey blade which extends from the left side of the card. An NHL logo is in the lower right corner. The back has the player's name, team name, position and an indication that he was an All-Star selection in 1986-87. A sticker number is also included. The backs are done in blue and red.

		MT	NM	EX
Complete Set (33):		17.00	12.50	6.75
Common Player:		.25	.20	.10
Common Team:		.15	.11	.06
1	Raymond Bourque	1.00	.70	.40
2	Ron Hextall	.50	.40	.20
3	Mark Howe	.25	.20	.10
4	Jari Kurri	.75	.60	.30
5	Wayne Gretzky	5.00	3.75	2.00
6	Michel Goulet	.50	.40	.20
7	Lawrence Murphy	.50	.40	.20
8	Michael Liut	.25	.20	.10
9	Al MacInnis	.75	.60	.30
10	Tim Kerr	.25	.20	.10
11	Mario Lemieux	5.00	3.75	2.00
12	Luc Robitaille	5.00	3.75	2.00
13	Toronto Maple Leafs	.15	.11	.06
14	Buffalo Sabres	.15	.11	.06
15	Detroit Red Wings	.15	.11	.06
16	Pittsburgh Penguins	.15	.11	.06
17	New York Rangers	.15	.11	.06
18	Calgary Flames	.15	.11	.06
19	Winnipeg Jets	.15	.11	.06
20	Quebec Nordiques	.15	.11	.06
21	Chicago Black Hawks	.15	.11	.06
22	Los Angeles Kings	.15	.11	.06
23	Montreal Canadiens	.15	.11	.06
24	Vancouver Canucks	.15	.11	.06
25	Hartford Whalers	.15	.11	.06
26	Philadelphia Flyers	.15	.11	.06
27	New Jersey Devils	.15	.11	.06
28	St. Louis Blues	.15	.11	.06
29	Minnesota North Stars	.15	.11	.06
30	Washington Capitals	.15	.11	.06
31	Boston Bruins	.15	.11	.06
32	New York Islanders	.15	.11	.06
33	Edmonton Oilers	.15	.11	.06

1988 Topps Stickers

Once again, Topps inserted these stickers in 1988-89 hockey wax packs. As usual, the standard-size stickers feature All-Stars and team logos. The front has an All-Star banner pinned to the top of the card, next to an NHL logo. The player's name is below the banner; a photo comprised the rest of the sticker front, which also has a Topps' logo in the lower left corner. The back lists the player's name, position, team and which All-Star team he was selected to. A sticker number is also included. Backs are done in red and blue.

		MT	NM	EX
Complete Set: (33)		12.00	9.00	4.75
Common Player:		.25	.20	.10
Common Team:		.15	.11	.06
1	Luc Robitaille	1.25	.90	.50
2	Mario Lemieux	4.50	3.50	1.75
3	Hakan Loob	.25	.20	.10
4	Scott Stevens	.50	.40	.20
5	Raymond Bourque	.75	.60	.30
6	Grant Fuhr	.50	.40	.20
7	Michel Goulet	.50	.40	.20
8	Wayne Gretzky	4.50	3.50	1.75
9	Cam Neely	.75	.60	.30
10	Bryon (Brad) McCrimmon	.25	.20	.10
11	Gary Suter	.25	.20	.10
12	Patrick Roy	2.00	1.50	.80
13	Toronto Maple Leafs	.15	.11	.06
14	Bufflo Sabres	.15	.11	.06
15	Detroit Red Wings	.15	.11	.06
16	Pittsburgh Penguins	.15	.11	.06
17	New York Rangers	.15	.11	.06
18	Calgary Flames	.15	.11	.06
19	Winnipeg Jets	.15	.11	.06
20	Quebec Nordiques	.15	.11	.06
21	Chicago Black Hawks	.15	.11	.06
22	Los Angeles Kings	.15	.11	.06
23	Montreal Canadiens	.15	.11	.06
24	Vancouver Canucks	.15	.11	.06
25	Hartford Whalers	.15	.11	.06
26	Philadelphia Flyers	.15	.11	.06
27	New Jersey Devils	.15	.11	.06
28	St. Louis Blues	.15	.11	.06
29	Minnesota North Stars	.15	.11	.06
30	Washington Capitals	.15	.11	.06
31	Boston Bruins	.15	.11	.06
32	New York Islanders	.15	.11	.06
33	Edmonton Oilers	.15	.11	.06

1989 Topps Stickers

These standard-size stickers once again feature 21 team logo stickers and 12 All-Stars. They were random inserts in 1989-90 Topps hockey wax packs, one per pack. Each All-Star sticker says "NHL All Star" along the right side. A color action photo is in the center, with the player's name, position and NHL logo below. A Topps logo is in the upper left corner. The back is red and blue and includes the player's name, position, team name and which All-Star team he was named to. A sticker number also appears on the back.

		MT	NM	EX
Complete Set (33):		10.00	7.50	4.00
Common Player:		.25	.20	.10
Common Team:		.10	.08	.04
1	Chris Chelios	.50	.40	.20
2	Gerard Gallant	.25	.20	.10
3	Mario Lemieux	4.00	3.00	1.50
4	Al MacInnis	.60	.45	.25
5	Joe Mullen	.25	.20	.10
6	Patrick Roy	1.50	1.25	.60
7	Raymond Bourque	.75	.60	.30
8	Rob Brown	.25	.20	.10
9	Geoff Courtnall	.25	.20	.10
10	Steve Duchesne	.25	.20	.10
11	Wayne Gretzky	4.00	3.00	1.50
12	Michael Vernon	.25	.20	.10
13	Toronto Maple Leafs	.15	.11	.06
14	Buffalo Sabres	.15	.11	.06
15	Detroit Red Wings	.15	.11	.06
16	Pittsburgh Penguins	.15	.11	.06
17	New York Rangers	.15	.11	.06
18	Calgary Flames	.15	.11	.06
19	Winnipeg Jets	.15	.11	.06
20	Quebec Nordiques	.15	.11	.06
21	Chicago Black Hawks	.15	.11	.06
22	Los Angeles Kings	.15	.11	.06
23	Montreal Canadiens	.15	.11	.06
24	Vancouver Canucks	.15	.11	.06
25	Hartford Whalers	.15	.11	.06
26	Philadelphia Flyers	.15	.11	.06
27	New Jersey Devils	.10	.08	.04
28	St. Louis Blues	.10	.08	.04
29	Minnesota North Stars	.10	.08	.04
30	Washington Capitals	.10	.08	.04
31	Boston Bruins	.10	.08	.04
32	New York Islanders	.10	.08	.04
33	Edmonton Oilers	.10	.08	.04

Pennants

Since almost every kid who had a felt pennant tacked it up on his bedroom wall, it's unusual to find a vintage pennant in well-preserved, investment grade condition. Most, measuring 12x30, have pin holes in them and can be purchased for less than $50. Today's versions, often available at stadiums and arenas, are made in large quantities, so look for 1950s and before models, and concentrate on pennants for popular teams, championship teams, teams which no longer exist, or those which commemorate a specific event. Some of the best places to find several pennants would be at larger card shows or through sports memorabilia auctions. Sometimes a pennant or two will turn up in an antique shop, too. Although it probably isn't going to offer big returns as an investment piece, a pennant can still add a nice decorative touch to any memorabilia display.

Basketball pennants

Baltimore Bullets late 1960s pennant $55
Boston Celtics 1960s, green on white...$55
Boston Celtics 1983-84 world champions pennant, with player names on a scroll $30
Buffalo Braves, black/light blue on white $55
Chicago Bulls pennant signed by 12 of the 1990-91 world champions, including
  Bill Cartwright, Michael Jordan and Scottie Pippen..$250
Dallas Mavericks 1991-92 team autographed pennant...$60
Harlem Globetrotters pennant, 1970s, shows three players holding basketballs
  in betweeen the letters $80

Pennants

Houston Rockets 1994-95 NBA Champions $5
Kansas City Kings 1970s pennant, 12x30, red/white/blue $25
Los Angeles Clippers 1986-87 autographed team pennant, signed by 10 players,
    including Elgin Baylor and Norm Nixon $50
Milwaukee Bucks 1960s pennant, buck's head with basketball in the antlers,
    green on white $65
New York Knicks late 1950s, player dunking, orange/blue on white $95
New York Knicks 1960s, large basketball, blue on orange..............................$55
New York Knicks 1969 pennant, 12x30, white/orange/blue.............................$45
New York Nets, ABA logo, red and light blue on white.................................$55
Philadelphia 76ers 1960s pennant, red letters with a basketball player in action....$25
Philadelphia 76ers 1982-83 World Championship pennant, 12x30, red/white/blue $60
Philadelphia 76ers 1984-85 pennant, 12x20, red/white/blue with players' names.....$45
Portland Trailblazers 1991-92 team autographed pennant $70
Sacramento Kings 1986-87 autographed team pennant, signed by 11 players,
    including Reggie Theus and Otis Thorpe...$50
San Antonio Spurs 1986-87 autographed team pennant, signed by 11 players,
    including Artis Gilmore...$50
San Antonio Spurs 1991-92 team autographed pennant..................................$65
San Diego Rockets NBA, gold on green felt $75
Utah Jazz 1991-92 team autographed pennant $60
Washington Bullets 1986-87 autographed team pennant, signed by nine players,
    including Manute Bol and Jeff Malone $50
38th All-Star Game in Chicago, 1988...$10
40th All-Star Game in Miami, 1990 ....$10
1994-95 NBA Finals pennants signed by Hakeem Olajuwon or Patrick Ewing $75
1985 autographed Boston Celtics mini banner, green and white, commemorates
    the championships from 1957-84, signed by 10 players, including John Havlicek,
    Kevin McHale and Robert Parish $15
Charles Barkley autographed Phoenix Suns pennant $50
David Robinson 12x30 caricature pennant, autographed $40
James Worthy 12x30 caricature pennant, autographed $30

Hockey pennants

Atlanta Flames red on white $45
Boston Bruins 1970s pennant with player names $65
Boston Bruins 1980s pennant $5
Chicago Blackhawks 1960s pennant, red and white on black $65
Chicago Blackhawks 1970 Indian head, multi-colored on black $55
Chicago Blackhawks 1985-86 pennant...$5
Detroit Red Wings 1969 pennant, white on red...$45
Montreal Canadiens 1991-92 autographed team pennant (16 signatures)...............$80
Montreal Canadiens 1993-94 autographed team pennant.................................$95
New York Rangers mid-1950s pennant, white on green, crossed hockey stick
    and puck $100
New York Rangers 1980s pennant $5
New York Rangers 1994-95 Stanley Cup Champions $5
New York Islanders 1980s pennant $5
Philadelphia Flyers 1980s pennant, 12x30, lists players $30
Pittsburgh Penguins 1970s pennant, blue with a Penguins logo in a circle............$25

Football pennants

Atlanta Falcons 1967 pennant..$10
Atlanta Falcons 1970s pennant $10
Baltimore Colts 1980s pennant 12x30, blue with white letters and helmet.............................$30
Baltimore\Indy Colts 1983 autographed pennant with 45 autographs,
    modern helmet design on blue felt $145
Buffalo Bills 1967 pennant, 12x30, blue/red/white $70
Buffalo Bills early 1980s white with updated logo $35
Chicago Bears black with orange print and orange bear on it $125
Chicago Bears mid-1950s, runner with ball, orange on blue...$65
Chicago Bears mid-1960s, bear on dark blue $45
Chicago Bears 1960s pennant, 12x30, shows a helmet $60
Chicago Bears Super Bowl XX Champs $10
Cincinnati Bengals 1967 helmet, orange/black on white...$45
Cincinnati Bengals 1981 AFC Champions, autographed by nine players,
    including Ken Anderson, Anthony Munoz $15
Cincinnati Bengals AFC Champions Super Bowl XVI Jan. 24, 1982..$15
Cleveland Browns late-1940s Brownie tossing football, orange on white..................................$125
Cleveland Browns late-1950s kicker, stadium, brown $85
Cleveland Browns mid-1960s pennant, player kicking the football over stadium,
    multi-colored on brown $75
Dallas Cowboys 1960s, player kicking football, white on blue $95
Dallas Cowboys 1960s...$75
Dallas Cowboys 1970s...$25
Dallas Cowboys Super Bowl XIII, Jan. 21, 1979, NFC Champs, Orange Bowl pictured...........$50
Denver Broncos 1984 AFC West Champs $10
Denver Broncos Super Bowl 21 ....$10
Denver Broncos 1988 Super Bowl Champs $10
Denver Broncos 1993 team pennant, autographed $95
Detroit Lions early-1950s, runner with lion, gray on blue $85
Detroit Lions mid-1960s runner with lion, multi-colored on blue...$65
Detroit Lions 1967 helmet pennant, silver on blue..$45
Green Bay Packers 1940s, gold/green with player running the ball...$125
Green Bay Packers 1950s pennant, player running on state of Wisconsin,
    multi-colored on green $95
Green Bay Packers 1960s pennant, 12x30, shows helmet..$50
Green Bay Packers 1967 helmet pennant, gold and white on green...$55
Green Bay Packers Super Bowl II, gold on green $250
Kansas City Chiefs AFL helmet pennant...$45
Kansas City Chiefs 1960s Indian in headdress, multi-colored on red $75
Kansas City Chiefs Super Bowl IV in New Orleans, AFL logo, gold on red $165
Los Angeles Rams 1960s ram's head in circle, white on gold $45
Los Angeles Rams 1970s pennant, 12x30, white/blue/gold...$20
Los Angeles Raiders Super Bowl XVII Champions..$20
Los Angeles Raiders Super Bowl XVII Champions, 12x30, white with black letters $40
"Mean Joe" Greene 1981 football pennant, says "One for the Thumb in '81,"
    cartoon shows him wearing four Super Bowl rings $25
Miami Dolphins early 1970s...$40
Miami Dolphins World Champions 1972, white and teal on orange $55
Miami Dolphins World Champions 1973..$50
Miami Dolphins Super Bowl VIII pennant...$50
Minnesota Vikings 1967 helmet, purple/yellow on white $55
Minnesota Vikings Super Bowl VIII pennant...$50
Minnesota Vikings Super Bowl IX at New Orleans, NFC Champions.......................................$55
Minnesota Vikings 1970s pennant, 12x30, shows helmet..$25
New England Patriots 1985 AFC Champs Super Bowl XX...$12
New York Giants 1930s pennant, player kicking a ball, white on gray $150

Pennants

New York Giants 1940s pennant, white on dark blue, runner with ball $165
New York Giants 1962 team picture pennant $145
New York Giants early-1960s, quarterback in Yankee Stadium,
    white/pink on blue $65
New York Giants late 1970s pennant, quarterback throwing a football,
    red and blue on white $35
New York Giants 1987 Super Bowl XXI pennant, 12x30, with team photo $25
New York Giants Super Bowl XXI Champs $45
New York Giants 1990-91 Super Bowl Champions, signed by 30 players,
    including Ottis Anderson, Phil Simms and Lawrence Taylor $225
New York Jets 1967 pennant, 12x30, green and white $75
New York Jets 1960s pennant, multi-colored runner on green felt $85
New York Jets AFL helmet 1968 World Champs $125
Oakland Raiders helmet 1967, silver/white on black $50
Oakland Raiders 1970s pennant $40
Oakland Raiders mid-1970s helmet pennant $45
Oakland Raiders Super Bowl XI Champions $55
Oakland Raiders 1970s pennant, 12x30, black/silver/white $40
Philadelphia Eagles 1960s pennant $25
Philadelphia Eagles 1960 NFL Champions $125
Philadelphia Eagles 1967 white helmet, green wings $55
Philadelphia Eagles 1967 pennant, 12x30, shows helmet $60
Philadelphia Eagles Super Bowl 15 .... $10
Philadelphia Eagles Super Bowl XV pennant, 12x30, NFC Champions $20
Philadelphia Stars 1984 USFL Champs $30
Pittsburgh Steelers 1950s gold on black $75
Pittsburgh Steelers Super Bowl XIII pennant, black and gold with a team photo $65
Pittsburgh Steelers 1974 World Champions pennant, commemorates the team's
    Super Bowl victory $55
Pittsburgh Steelers 1970s pennant, 12x30, gold/black/white $45
Pittsburgh Steelers World Champions 1974, white/black on gold $30
Pittsburgh Steelers Super Bowl IX, New Orleans, Jan. 12, 1975, AFC Champs $45
Pittsburgh Steelers Super Bowl X, Miami, Jan. 18, 1976, AFC Champs $45
Pittsburgh Steelers Super Bowl XIII Champs picture pennant $50
Pittsburgh Steelers Super Bowl XIV, Jan. 20, 1980, pictures the Rose Bowl $45
St. Louis Cardinals 1980s pennant, 12x30, red and white $30
San Diego Chargers 1967 helmet pennant, lightning bolts on white helmet, on blue ... $45
San Diego Chargers 1970s pennant $15
San Francisco 49ers 1960s pennant, 12x30, shows a helmet, red/white/gold $40
San Francisco 49ers 1967 helmet, gold/white on red $55
San Francisco 49ers Super Bowl 23 .... $10
San Francisco 49ers Super Bowl XXIII World Champions $15
Washington Redskins 1960s helmet pennant, yellow helmet/maroon R $50
Washington Redskins 1960s Indian in white circle on maroon $95
Washington Redskins 1960s pennant, 12x30, helmet design with arrow,
    yellow and red $175
Washington Redskins 1970s pennant, 12x30, Indian head on helmet $30
Washington Redskins Super Bowl 17 .... $10
Washington Redskins Super Bowl 18 .... $10

USFL pennants

    Birmingham Stallions, Boston Breakers, Chicago Blitz, Denver Gold, Houston Gamblers, Jacksonville Bulls, L.A. Express, Memphis Showboats, New Jersey Generals, New Orleans Breakers, Oakland Invaders, Philadelphia Stars, Pittsburgh Maulers, San Antonio Gunslingers, Tampa Bay Bandits, Washington Federals ...... $20-$40 each.

World Football League pennants

    Birmingham Vulcans, Charlotte Hornets, Chicago Wind, Jacksonville Express, Memphis Grizzlies, Portland Thunder, San Antonio Wings .... $20 each

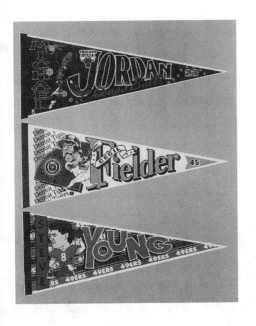

1992 Win Craft player pennants

Basketball (25)

1. Charles Barkley..............................$5
2. Larry Bird......................................$8
3. Derrick Coleman...........................$3
4. Vlade Divac $3
5. Clyde Drexler................................$4
6. Joe Dumars....................................$3
7. Kevin Johnson...............................$3
8. Larry Johnson (two).............. $5 each
9. Michael Jordan............................$10
10. Shawn Kemp.................................$4
11. Bo Kimble....................................$3
12. Karl Malone $4
13. Danny Manning $3
14. Reggie Miller $3
15. Chris Mullin $4
16. Shaquille O'Neal...........................$6
17. Scottie Pippen $4
18. Mark Price....................................$3
19. Pooh Richardson $3
20. David Robinson $5
21. John Stockton...............................$4
22. Isiah Thomas................................$3
23. Dominique Wilkins.....................$4
24. James Worthy................................$3

Football (26)

1. Troy Aikman $6
2. Morten Andersen...........................$3
3. Neal Anderson...............................$3
4. Bubby Brister $3
5. Randall Cunningham.....................$4
6. John Elway $4
7. Boomer Esiason $3
8. Jim Everett $3
9. Jim Harbaugh $3
10. Jim Kelly.....................................$5
11. Bernie Kosar.................................$3
12. Howie Long..................................$3
13. Dan Marino $5
14. Art Monk $4
15. Joe Montana $7
16. Warren Moon $4
17. Christian Okoye $3
18. Jerry Rice.....................................$5
19. Mark Rypien.................................$4
20. Deion Sanders $5
21. Phil Simms $3
22. Emmitt Smith $8
23. Lawrence Taylor $5
24. Derrick Thomas............................$4
25. Thurman Thomas $5
26. Steve Young $4

Chapter 15 ©

Auctions

Sports auctions offer all types of memorabilia for bidders.

How to buy through the mail

Sports Collectors Digest, as do all Krause Publications hobby publications, screens its advertisers to weed out dishonesty, but these guidelines are helpful when buying collectibles through the mail:

1) Read the entire ad carefully before you order.

2) Condition and authenticity of the merchandise should be guaranteed.

3) For quicker service, send a money order or certified check instead of a personal check.

4) Pack and unpack the items carefully; damaged or broken items can't always be blamed on the post office. If damaged product should arrive, take the entire contents to the post office and file a claim.

How to buy at auctions and through auction houses

1) Learn the bidding process; rules for buying vary from state to state.

2) Listen to the auctioneer for a while to determine nuances and his acknowledgements of bids; a scratch of your nose might mean you just bid.

3) Bidding may be done by voice or by hand raising.

4) Many auction houses do not take responsibility for the correctness of description, authenticity, genuineness or condition of the item. So, go early and look at the items in person. Check out the condition, size and whether the item has been repaired or restored.

5) Items are often sold "as is" and the house, in issuing catalogs, does not take responsibility or issue warranties regarding the description or physical condition, size, quality, rarity, importance or historical relevance, or errors.

6) The highest bid accepted is usually the buyer's, but disputes may result. If so, bidding is often reopened, but only between the two, with the highest bidder becoming the owner. Then it's his responsibility and risk for relocating the item. Sometimes the house will send the purchased property to a public warehouse for the account, risk and expense of the purchaser.

7) At unrestricted sales, or those without a reserve, the consigners of the items being sold are not supposed to bid. If they do bid back their own items, they still pay the full sales commission.

8) Most auctioneers reserve the right to refuse a bid if it does not match the item's value or is a nominal advance over the previous bid. He's looking to make the most on a bid. If the auctioneer decides an opening bid is below the reserve value for the article offered, he may reject the same and withdraw the article from the sale. A buyers premium, often 10 percent, is generally added on to the successful bid, and is payable by the purchaser as part of the total purchase price.

9) Get there early to browse, pick up a bidder's number, and get a good seat.

10) Local auctions will probably accept personal checks, but traveler's checks are wise for out-of-town auctions.

11) When dealing as a consignor, read the contract in its entirety before signing it and understand what you've just signed.

Telephone auctions

Convey the lot you wish to bid on and your absolute top bid. Normal bidding progresses with bids being raised by the regular 10 percent. When someone tops your current bid, the auctioneer automatically increases your bid by the mandatory 10 percent. This process continues until your absolute top bid is reached.

Often the times are designated and the bidding ends promptly, with no exceptions.

Pre-registration by potential bidders is usually required a few days in advance. A bidding number is obtained at that time and is later given when the auction occurs. Then the lots and absolute top bids for each are given and the process continues.

Bidders are generally discouraged from calling immediately after the auction to check on results. Winners are contacted within the next day; those wishing results may generally do so after the auction's deadline by sending an SASE for a prices realized list.

Absentee bids are encouraged, too, but require top limits on the bids for each lot. Lots are purchased for the absentee bidders at the lowest possible price under their top limit. For example: If you write in with an absentee top limit bid of $500 and the highest bid received by other phone bidders is $300, you win the lot for $330 - ($300 plus 10 percent) plus the 10 percent buyer's fee.

As O.J. Simpson dominated the media in 1994 and 1995, interest in his memorabilia increased, and values went up. Rod Hirsch's story in the July 29, 1994, issue of Sports Collectors Digest captured the essence of the O.J. Simpson phenomenon:

"As millions of television viewers sat glued to their screens and watched O.J. Simpson make the run of his life on a busy California freeway, savvy dealers and collectors watched prices for O.J. Simpson memorabilia spiral upwards.

Interest increases in Simpson memorabilia

Photos Courtesy Leland's

This O.J. Simpson memorabilia set sold for $165.

"Prior to, and immediately following his arrest for the murder of his ex-wife and a friend outside Nicole Simpson's condominium, there was a noticeable lurch upwards in demand for his rookie NFL card, signed publicity photos and jerseys.

"Just two days after the murder was reported, and two days before his desperate flight, far removed from his exploits on the gridiron for the Trojans of USC and the Buffalo Bills of the NFL, a red, white and blue jersey worn by the running back, emblazoned with his No. 32 and SIMPSON in large block letters, sold for $2,100 during a sports memorabilia auction by Wolffers of San Francisco. It was accompanied by a letter of authenticity."

Then, in the Nov. 11, 1994, issue of Sports Collectors Digest, Hirsch reported:

"Four days into the start if his murder trial last month, O.J. Simpson sat at the defense table in a Los Angeles courtroom with his team of high-priced lawyers interviewing potential jurors.

"As that tedious process wore on, a more animated gathering involving Simpson's links to his past glory was taking place up the California coast in Simpson's hometown of San Francisco during Richard Wolffers Auctions' latest sale of sports memorabilia.

"Selling for $800 was a red, white and blue Buffalo Bills helmet signed by Simpson in blue Sharpie, with the further notation "Juice #32" in his hand, along with the original autograph ticket. For $230, a bidder walked away with an official Wilson NFL Super Bowl XXVII football signed by O.J. Simpson in silver Sharpie. Simpson's signature, along with his notation #32 on a National League baseball, sold for $200.

"A complete 263-card set of 1970 Topps NFL football cards, including Simpson's rookie card, graded Very Good, sold for $150. An 8-by-10 color photo of Simpson, signed in blue Sharpie, capturing the record-setting rush in which he broke 2,000 yards for the season, sold for $200. A vertical

8-by-10 color profile shot of Simpson sitting on the sidelines, signed by Simpson with #32 in his hand, and a letter of authenticity, sold for $260. Simpson's signature, along with #32 in his hand, on the side of an NFL mini helmet, sold for $180."

Leland's Grand Slam auction, Nov. 19-20, 1994, in New York, also offered O.J. items. Krause Publications' February 1995 issue of Today's Collector reported:

"Among the more surprising lots at the Leland's sale was an autograph that Simpson signed just hours before the June 12 murder of his ex-wife Nicole. That afternoon Simpson, while attending his daughter's dance recital, signed the back of a ticket stub for a young fan as a souvenir of the event.

"Offered at the Leland's auction, the signed ticket sold for an amazing $3,850 - many times the value of a typical Simpson autograph. (Prior to the murder, a Simpson autograph generally sold in the $25-$35 range; after his arrest the value jumped to about $125).

"The winning bid obviously reflects the historical significance of this particular signature and the special circumstances surrounding it, but even the auction house was surprised by the final selling price, which more than doubled its high estimate."

An original game-used 1970s Simpson Buffalo Bills jersey, against an estimate of $3,500-$4,000, also sold for $3,850 during the auction. An O.J. Simpson memorabilia set sold for $165, against a pre-sale estimate of $300-$400. The ensemble includes a 26-piece action figure set by Shindana Toys, a 1968 football yearbook with Simpson on the cover, a 17x22 Hertz poster of Simpson in action, and eight 11x14 lobby cards from Simpson's 1976 movie "The Cassandra Crossing."

Leland's April 7, 1995, telephone auction featured an October 1994 letter on O.J. Simpson letterhead, written while Simpson was incarcerated in the Los Angeles County Jail. The letter thanks the writer for contributing to his defense fund. It read, in part, "I know that the truth and my innocence will prevail...Thanks for believing in me!" and was signed by Simpson. It included the original mailer with "O.J. Simpson c/o Los Angeles County Jail" as a return address. Against a reserve bid of $800, the letter sold for $1,289.

In addition to O.J. memorabilia, Leland's offered all kinds of vintage football, basketball and hockey memorabilia over the last year. In its Grand Slam auction, one of the largest sports auctions ever, the New York auction house netted more than $1.8 million from its more than 1,100 items up for bids, compared to a pre-auction estimate of $2 million.

Green Bay Packer Coach Vince Lombardi's 1965 championship ring sold for substantially more than its $18,000-$20,000 pre-sale estimate. The ring, obtained from Lombardi's daughter, sold for $33,000. A collection of four 8x10 photos featuring Lombardi at Fordham, St. Cecelia and in Green Bay, sold for $440. A legendary 9x7 black-and-white photo of the coach riding on the shoulders of guard Jerry Kramer after the team's Super Bowl I victory sold for $495.

A lot of 10 programs from the first Super Bowl sold for $2,310, while a complete collection of 26 press pins and two patches (used instead of pins for Super Bowls IV and V) sold for $3,740. A complete run of 28 Super Bowl programs sold for $2,090, while a program from Walter Payton's 275-yard rushing effort Nov. 20, 1977, in Chicago against the Minnesota Vikings, sold for $165.

A program from the first Monday Night Football game, between the New York Jets and Cleveland Browns Sept. 21, 1970, sold for $330, while a program from the Nov. 17, 1968, "Heidi Bowl" game between the Jets and Oakland Raiders, sold for $1,045. It's signed by 41 members of the Super Bowl III Champion Jets team, including Joe Namath.

A San Francisco 49ers "team of the 1980s" helmet, signed by 44 players from the "team of the decade," sold for $1,100. It includes signatures from Joe Montana, Jerry Rice, John Taylor, Roger Craig and Dwight Clark. Eric Dickerson's game-used Indianapolis Colts helmet sold for $770, while a 1920s aviator-style flat-top leather McAlister helmet with ear flaps and a primitive face mask sold for $990. A lot of eight leather football helmets sold for $3,575. It included two early 1900s flat tops, a 1920s aviator, a 1930s Wilson, a 1930s Rawlings, a 1930s MacGregor, a 1940s Wilson, and a 1930s kid's helmet with pads and pants.

Two 1930s Green Bay Packers cardboard advertising signs/schedules, each 12x18, sold for $330. One advises fans to "Don't Miss Seeing the Packers;" the other says "Get Your Tickets Early." A 30x24 Baltimore Memorial Stadium four-color metal road sign directing travelers to the stadium sold for $1,210, against a $500-$600 estimate. The sign pictures the stadium which housed the Colts and Orioles for 35 years. A 1940s 57x18 Shibe Park wooden ticket sign sold for $2,640, against an estimate of $1,500-$2,000. The sign, featuring a charging running back, instructs "Ticket Holders Enter Here" in yellow block letters.

Auctions

Running back Earl Campbell's baby blue Houston Oilers mesh jersey sold for $1,100, while a 1981 Seattle Seahawks home jersey for another Hall of Famer, Steve Largent, sold for $935. Joe Montana's game-used red San Francisco 49ers home jersey sold for $2,750.

Miami Dolphins running back Mercury Morris was also featured in the Grand Slam auction. Several items from the team's perfect 17-0 1972 season were up for bids. A leather Wilson football, with 35 signatures from members of that Super Bowl championship team, sold for $2,530. Morris' 9-inch award for gaining 1,000 yards rushing in 1972, presented to him by the National 1,000 Yard Club Foundation Inc. on June 19, 1973, sold for $1,100.

A trophy honoring Morris as the 1971 kickoff return leader sold for $1,650. The 14-inch award, featuring a silver-toned player on a black pedestal, is inscribed "Mercury Morris, Miami Dolphins, 1971 AFC Kick-Off Return Champion, 28.2 Yards Per Return, NFL Players Association." A 7-inch 1973 Pro Bowl award, a huge chunk of crystal bearing the NFL logo on a broad wooden base, sold for $550. It's inscribed "AFC-NFC Pro Bowl Game 1973, Eugene Morris."

Hockey memorabilia included several items used by the "Great One," Wayne Gretzky. A pair of Daoust skates he wore while with Edmonton sold for $4,950. Showing extensive game use, they had "99" stamped in white below the eyelets on both skates. A pair of game-used blue, orange and white Jofa gloves, worn while Gretzky was with the team in the 1980s, sold for $2,420, while an equipment bag, with an Oilers logo and "99" stenciled on it in three places, sold for $1,430. It also included used shoulder pads, unused elbow pads, and two Gretzky books.

A Gretzky point record presidential puck sold for $990. The puck was used for locker room photo sessions after he broke Gordie Howe's record. A bold "1,851" is painted in white on both sides of the framed practice puck, which features a classic photo of Gretzky celebrating, holding the puck.

Mark Messier's 1994 All-Star Game jersey, a teal and white Eastern Conference autographed jersey, with game patches and a Captain's C patch, sold for $4,950. Jean Ratelle's 1972 All-Star Game jersey, with his nameplate and number "19," sold for $4,400. Ratelle's New York Rangers dark blue snap-front jacket, with NHL and Rangers patches and Ratelle's name sewn inside, sold for $2,640.

Tony Esposito's 1976 game-used Chicago Blackhawks Wilson road jersey sold for $2,530, while his brother Phil's black Rawlings Boston Bruins warmup jacket sold for $935. Glenn Hall's 1967-68 St. Louis Blues home Rawlings jersey sold for $2,310. Mario Lemieux's 1987 Canada Cup blue Team Canada practice jersey, with #6 and his name on back, sold for $550. Goalie John Vanbiesbrouck's USA jersey, worn in the series while he faced the Soviets and Gretzky/Lemieux's Team Canada, sold for $660. A lot of nine Soviet Union practice jerseys, worn by several Russians, including Pavel Bure and Sergei Makarov, sold for $2,750.

An artist's recreation of goalie Ed Belfour's Chicago Blackhawks red mask sold for $770. It features screaming hawks with a broad wingspan and a wire cage from nose to eyebrows. An artist's recreation of Gerry Cheevers' white "Hannibal Lector" mask with black stitches sold for $275. Hall of Famer Terry Sawchuck's 1960s Cooper Trapper leather glove, showing tremendous game use, sold for $1,870, while his Custom CCM goalie stick, with "Sawchuck" on the shaft and half of the blade missing, sold for $605.

A pair of 1840s hockey skates, featuring hand-forged blades, leather straps and large screws to affix to boots, sold for $660, while a 1940s pair of game-used skates belonging to Hall of Famer Charlie Conacher sold for $1,100. A vintage pair of 1920s hockey gloves with a Stall & Dean "Puckmaster" emblem embossed on them sold for $330. An Art Ross NHL puck with its original box sold for $440. It featured an orange seal which says "Adopted by National Hockey League."

A 1927 Ottawa Senators 18k diamond ring with black onyx, the earliest known Stanley Cup championship ring, sold for $3,300. It's inscribed "1927" on one side and "CJD," for Cy Denneny, on the other, with "From the Citizens of Ottawa" on the inside. A 1969 St. Louis Blues Stanley Cup 18k ring, inscribed "West Division Champions" and engraved "Bill McCreary," sold for $1,760, while a 14-inch Stanley Cup championship trophy model, presented to players and team personnel of the 1978-79 Montreal Canadiens, sold for $2,750. It's inscribed "Club De Hockey Canadien 1978-79" and includes names such as Larry Robinson, Guy Lafleur and Jacques Lemaire.

A 1992-93 Stanley Cup Canadiens black and gold watch, created by Jostens, sold for $440. The watch, which included the original box, was given to players and team personnel. It's inscribed "Montreal Canadiens...Champions" and "Stanley Cup Centennial 1893-1993." Three watches obtained from a Chicago Bulls top executive were also sold, each with its original box. A Jostens' 1990-

These two Mercury Morris awards sold for $2,750.

91 World Champion Chicago Bulls watch, gold and black with a red Bulls logo in the center, given to a team executive, sold for $660. A 1992-93 championship watch with a red logo and three championship trophies sold for $1,045, while a lady's version of the same watch sold for $2,860.

A restored trophy given to Bulls star Michael Jordan when he was the 1984 John Wooden College Player of the Year sold for $6,600. The 18-inch high trophy, given by the Los Angeles Athletic Club annually to the outstanding collegiate player in the United States, has the names of seven winners, including Jordan's. The trophy, updated each year, was damaged and replaced after Jordan's name was added.

A 1969-70 World Champion New York Knickerbockers trophy, 3.5" in diameter, sold for $1,870. New York Mayor John Lindsay gave the pewter presentational bowl to Knicks team president Edward S. Irish. A 1965-66 World Champion Boston Celtics autographed program from the series between the Celtics and the Knicks sold for $440. It included signatures from Bill Russell, John Havlicek, Casey Jones and Don Nelson, plus two tickets and a Celtics schedule. A scored program from Wilt Chamberlain's first NBA game, Oct. 31, 1959, sold for $495.

Kareem Abdul-Jabbar's fisheye goggles, featuring tape around the bridge and ear pieces, sold for $1,650. David Robinson's 1990-91 game-worn Nike Air sneakers, signed by Robinson, sold for $605. A salesman's sample 1978 World Championship ring for another center, Wes Unseld, sold for $605. The ring, honoring the Washington Bullets, was inscribed "NBA World Champions...The Fat Lady Sings."

Seven green practice jackets worn by members of the 1985 NBA championship runners-up, the Boston Celtics, sold for $2,530. Included in the lot were jackets for Larry Bird, Kevin McHale, Robert Parish, Dennis Johnson, Danny Ainge, Scott Wedman and Cedric Maxwell. NBA game-used jerseys also did well in the auction. Larry Bird's 1986-87 Celtics home white jersey sold for $2,860, and included a pair of trunks.

Isiah Thomas' 1981-82 Detroit Pistons home rookie jersey and trunks sold for $1,320, while a Charles Barkley 1992-93 Phoenix Suns home jersey sold for $2,530. Marcus Haynes' 1960s Harlem Globetrotters #40 jersey sold for $1,045. Patrick Ewing's New York Knicks warmup jersey from the same season, signed "Patrick Ewing 33" in the collar, sold for $1,430, as did a Julius Erving 1977 Philadelphia 76ers warmup jersey.

Shaquille O'Neal's blue-and-yellow "Western" uniform from the movie "Blue Chips" didn't sell, but several movie-related posters did. A collection of 56 1930s football half-sheet posters, each 22x28, sold for $2,200. Included in the lot were 10 for "Jim Thorpe All-American," two 1936 "Fighting Youth" posters (with Jim Thorpe), three for the "Bob Mathias Story," four for Crazylegs (starring Elroy Hirsch), and one each for "Iron Major," "Rose Bowl Story," "Spirit of Notre Dame" (1950, featuring the Four Horsemen), "Triple Threat" (Baugh, Waterfield and Luckman), and "The Big Game" (1936, with eight All-Americans).

A collection of 36 14x36 football inserts sold for $1,320. The lot included four for "Jim Thorpe All-American," six for "Crazylegs," and one each for "Smith of Minnesota" (Bruce Smith), "Iron Major," "The Spirit of Notre Dame" and "Spirit of West Point" (with Blanchard and Davis).

A collection of 49 27x41 one-sheets sold for $2,750. Included in the lot of 1930s material were posters for "Triple Threat" (featuring 11 pros and Sammy Baugh), "While Thousands Cheer" (with Kenny Washington), "Hold 'Em Navy, Spirit of West Point," "Two Minutes to Play," "Iron Major" (two posters), "Cowboy Quarterback," "Spirit of Notre Dame," "Rose Bowl Story" and "Crazylegs."

A scarce 27x41 one-sheet of "Crazylegs" sold for $880. This poster, created for black neighborhoods, pictures "Great Negro Stars of the L.A. Rams" - Tank Younger, Deacon Towler, Night Train Lane and Woodley Lewis, plus Elroy Hirsch. A 27x41 one-sheet for "The New Halfback" sold for $550. It features a football player diving for glory, promoting Mack Sennett's late-1920s "All-Talking Comedy."

Leland's Feb. 24, 1995, telephone auction sold more than 600 sports-related collectibles. Football items included an autographed pair of Barry Sanders' game used Nike turf shoes, which sold for $393, while a 1990 Super Bowl champions New York Giants football sold for $787. The ball was signed by 20 players, including Lawrence Taylor and Phil Simms. A program from the 1958 championship game, which ended in a Baltimore Colts' sudden death overtime victory over the New York Giants, sold for $363.

Basketball items included Larry Bird's 1981 Boston Celtics shooting shirt, which sold for $1,100, and Patrick Ewing's 1987-88 game-used New York Knicks road jersey, which sold for the same amount. Michael Jordan's No. 9 "Dream Team" USA Olympic jersey sold for $980. It included autographs from all 12 members of the team. An LSU media guide, signed by "Pistol Pete" Maravich, sold for $294.

Hockey items included Mark Messier's game-used size 11 Edmonton Oilers hockey skates, which sold for $880, and Phil Esposito's Boston Bruins warmup jacket, which sold for $726. An autographed Stan Mikita game-used hockey stick sold for $1,210. A full ticket from the 1980 United States Olympic team's "Miracle On Ice" win against the Soviet Union sold for $732.

The company's March 31, 1995, telephone auction featured nearly 700 lots. Football items included the previously mentioned O.J. Simpson letter, and a 1969 Super Bowl III program, which sold for $380. The game featured Joe Namath leading his New York Jets to an improbable win against Johnny Unitas' Baltimore Colts. A 1962 Colts press pin sold for $110, while a Unitas Hartland statue, in Near Mint, sold for $363. A white-paneled Wilson football, signed by 30 members of the 1994 Dallas Cowboys, sold for $330.

During Leland's June 9, 1995, telephone auction, an early 1990s Wayne Gretzky Los Angeles Kings game-used jersey was the big-ticket item. The black and silver jersey sold for $6,655. A 1986 New York Giants Super Bowl championship ring brought the next highest winning bid, at $3,509. The salesman's sample features a miniature of the Super Bowl trophy in diamonds, set in a blue stone.

A collection of game-issued Riddell helmets for several World League of America teams sold for between $110 and $176 each. The teams included the Frankfurt Galaxy, the London Monarchs, the Montreal Machine, the New Jersey Knights, the Orlando Thunder, the Sacramento Surge, Barcelona Dragons and Birmingham Fire.

A 1980s Cleveland Browns helmet and jersey worn by Bernie Kosar sold for $733. Brett Hull's Calgary Flames rookie jersey, which featured the 1988 Olympics patch on the shoulder, sold for $1,815.

A 1962 NFL championship game tie-clasp press pin sold for $187. The blue, white and gold enamel pin was used for the game between the New York Giants and Green Bay Packers. A press tie clasp from Super Bowl III in 1969, featuring the Jets and Colts, sold for $444.

Leland's Heavy Hitters Auction
Jan. 15, 1992, in New York, N.Y.

Photos courtesy Leland's

Jim Brown's 1964 ring, Walt Frazier's 1970s New York Knicks uniform, Wayne Gretzky's Canada Cup jersey.

- Jim Brown's World Championship ring - a Mint platinum and diamond ring which says "Browns, World's Champions" on the face. One side has the score of the game (Browns 27, Colts 0, 1964 NFL); the other side says "Jim Brown" over a football helmet carved in platinum............................ $15,000-$20,000
- The first New York Giants program - from an Oct. 18, 1925, contest pitting Jim Thorpe and the Giants against Philadelphia, in Excellent condition..................................... $300-$400
- Walter Payton's last jersey - a Chicago Bears home white mesh, a Wilson size 44, from 1987, Payton's last year as a player. A "GSH" memorial sleeve and repair marks indicate game use................................ $1,200-$1,500
- Dallas Texans flag - an original red and yellow flag, 77" by 103," which hung in Kansas City's Municipal Stadium when the team moved. It says "American Football League Champions Dallas Texans 1962."......................$500-$600
- Wayne Gretzky Canada Cup jersey - a Gretzky 99 road red jersey worn during games leading up to this 1991 world hockey series. The jersey, with size 54 Maska tagging, shows game use and included a letter of authenticity from the Hockey Hall of Fame. .... $1,500-$2,000
- Eric Lindros Canada Cup jersey - a home white jersey which shows game use from an exhibition during this 1991 world hockey series. A letter of authenticity from the Hockey Hall of Fame was included with the jersey, which has Lindros' #88 on it.................... $1,200-$1,500
- Mario Lemieux jersey - a game-used home white Pittsburgh Penguins jersey from the 1988-89 season, obtained directly from the team. The CCM knit jersey has the appropriate tagging, including "Lemieux 66."...................
.... $2,500-$3,000
- Walt Frazier uniform - a New York Knicks home white worn during the 1970s, this Medalist Sand-Knit size 44 has "New York 10" on the front, and "Frazier 10" on the back. The jersey and pants, which included a letter from Frazier to the owner, show good game use. ...
.... $2,000-$2,500

Leland's Souvenirs auction
Feb. 20, 1993, in New York, N.Y.

- Vince Lombardi Super Bowl I Championship ring - a salesman's sample from Balfour, this ring has "World Champions 1966 Green Bay Packers" surrounding a diamond atop a football-shaped world, with sides featuring the NFL logo, a Packers helmet and "Lombardi." .... $600-$800
- Julius Erving ABA Championship ring - a salesman's sample in 10k, it sports the ABA logo in enamel with a gem in the center. The sides say "Erving 1974" and have the playoff record..................................... $1,800-$2,000
- Larry Bird game-used Boston Celtics jersey - from his final season in 1991-92, this home white, a size 48, has "Bird 33" in green on the back. .... $2,000-$2,500
- Julius Erving game-used Philadelphia 76ers jersey - from 1976-77, this one-year style home white Wilson, size 44, has tags and "Sixers 6" on the back............ $3,750-$4,250
- Larry Bird game-used sneakers - Celtic green Converse All-Stars, show game use from his first season................................... $800-$900
- Michael Jordan's autographed "Dream Team" sneakers - size 13 Nike Air Jordans, these game used shoes are white with red and black trim. .... $800-$1,000
- Michael Jordan autographed game-used sneakers - Nike Airs from 1986-87, these white with red and black trim have the Nike Air logo on the back and are autographed. .... $600-$800
- 1992-93 Chicago Bulls autographed warmup jacket - B.J. Armstrong's MacGregor Sand-Knit is signed by all 12 members of the team's second consecutive championship team, including Michael Jordan and Scottie Pippen... $600-$800
- Chicago Bulls banner - 98x31, this banner hung outside City Hall in Chicago after the Bulls won their second straight NBA championship. It has a Bulls logo and says "1992 NBA Championship Sweet Repeat, City of Chicago, Richard M. Daley, Mayor." .... $500-$600

Coach Frank Leahy's Notre Dame jacket.

- Tony Dorsett's 1976 University of Pittsburgh jersey - game used, worn during a game against Syracuse during his senior year, it has "Dorsett 33" on the back. .... $800-$1,000
- Bo Jackson Raiders game-used jersey - an extra large silver-and-black Goodman says "Jackson 34" across the back and is autographed. .... $1,000-$1,500
- Brian Piccolo game-used Chicago Bears jersey - a King O'Shea size 46, this jersey has #41 on the back and both sleeves and includes a letter of authenticity............. $2,000-$2,500
- Frank Leahy Notre Dame jacket - worn when he was the coach at Notre Dame, it's a heavy wool with a golden "ND" chenille logo and leather sleeves. .... $1,000-$1,500
- Hershey Bears stadium banner - 180x113, has magenta lettering on canvas which says "Pennsylvania Professional Hockey Championship 1944-45 Hershey Bears."..$300-$400
- John Davidson game-used New York Rangers goalie mask - worn circa 1980-81, was painted by noted facemask artist Greg Harrison in a "Lone Ranger" motif............... $1,200-$1,500

Photo courtesy Leland's

At left, the 1975 WFL Championship Trophy; at right, a 1950s Zamboni machine from Madison Square Garden. Below, a signed Boston Celtics parquet floor board.

Above, a lighted NBA sign from Madison Square Garden; below is a Julius Erving salesman's sample ABA championship ring. At right is a Hersey Bears stadium banner.

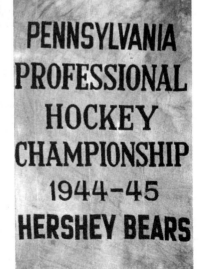

Leland's Doubleheader auction
Nov. 20-21, 1993, in New York, N.Y.

- 1957 Boston Celtics NBA Championship ring - striking gold salesman's sample has "1957 Celtics" and shamrocks on it. The face has "World Champions" engraved around a basketball. .... $700-$800
- 1958 Baltimore Colts NFL Championship ring - salesman's sample has a diamond and two blue stones in the center, with "Baltimore Colts World Champions" running around it. The side has a bucking horse inside a horseshoe, with "Colts 23 Giants 17" and 1958 in the horseshoe. .... $600-$800
- 1966-67 Bobby Hull Stanley Cup Championship ring - a salesman's sample with a large diamond in the center, surrounded by 12 smaller stones. The sides say "66 NHL 67 Champions, R. Hull" with a Blackhawks logo. .... $700-$900
- 1970 Johnny Unitas Super Bowl ring - salesman's sample, a 10k diamond in the center of a silver horseshoe, "Johnny Unitas 1970 Super Bowl V" along the side.$2,000-$2,500
- 1978 Wes Unseld Washington Bullets NBA Championship ring - Full-bodied basketball with diamond, surrounded by "NBA World Champions," also says "Unseld" and the "Fat Lady Sings," and includes a Bullets logo. ......
  .... $500-$700
- 1979 Terry Bradshaw Pittsburgh Steelers Super Bowl ring - Four diamonds on top, with "Pittsburgh 1979 World Champions" on top and "Super Bowl XIV 31-19" and "Steelers Bradshaw 12." .... $800-$1,000
- 1981 Larry Bird Boston Celtics World Championship ring - salesman's sample, has a diamond in the center, surrounded by a kelly green stone and "NBA World Champions." "Bird, Pride" is on the side, with a kelly green shamrock. .... $1,000-$1,200
- 1984 Philadelphia Stars USFL Championship ring - 10k with Stars logo and diamond in the center, "Philadelphia 1984 USFL Champions" around the rim, for defensive end "Moor." .... $2,500-$3,000

A salesman's sample of a 1970 Super Bowl ring for Johnny Unitas.

Photo courtesy Leland's

- 1986 Bill Parcell's New York Giants Super Bowl ring - salesman's sample has "Giants 1986 World Champions" engraved around a Super Bowl Trophy encrusted with diamonds, sides herald "Super Bowl XXI 39-20" and "Parcells 17-2." .... $5,000-$6,000
- 1987 Los Angeles Lakers NBA World Champions ring - presented to the team's Spanish announcer, it has five diamonds surrounded by "World Champion Lakers 1987" and "Castillo 72, 80, 82 and 85" on one side, with "Drive for Five" on the other, with a team logo in purple enamel. .... $4,000-$5,000
- 1924 Boston Bruins pocket watch - 10k gold relic is inscribed "Boston Hockey Club 1924. J.A. Langley Goal. Colonial Series." ....
  .... $1,000-$1,500
- Jim Thorpe Award - a gold football, presented to Thorpe by the Philadelphia Inquirer in 1950, is engraved "Jim Thorpe, America's Greatest Athlete of the Mid-Century" and has the paper's name on it. .... $2,000-$3,000
- 1975 WFL Championship Trophy - a gold and wood trophy with five football players on the top. The 30-inch tall trophy is engraved "Birmingham Americans, WFL 1974, World Bowl Champions Dec. 5, 1974." .... $1,000-$1,200

- 1982 NFL Players Association All-Star Game helmet and jersey - from the 1982 strike season, this set includes Earnest Gray's Riddell helmet with an NFL Players Association logo, and Vince Evans' white mesh jersey. The set included a letter of authenticity from the NFLPA. .... $500-$700
- Los Angeles Rams helmet collection of three - Riddell helmets used by Jim Everett, Henry Ellard and Flipper Anderson, they have the padding intact with full face guards and the player's names inside. .... $700-$900
- Chuck Bednarick Philadelphia Eagles jersey - green knit #60 from circa 1958, shows game use and includes a Topps card of him wearing the jersey. .... $2,000-$2,500
- Dan Fouts game-used San Diego Chargers jersey - this 1984 Sand-Knit blue mesh road jersey, size 48, has "Fouts 14" in gold on the back and a lightning bolt on each sleeve........ .... $1,000-$1,500
- Jack Ham Pittsburgh Steelers jersey - 1970s road black, with tags, shows game use and includes Ham's nameplate on the back and his autograph on the front. ..... $1,000-$1,200
- Charlie Joiner game-used San Diego Chargers jersey - road blue mesh, with "Joiner" on the back, has tagging, a Silver Anniversary patch, and a lightning bolt on each sleeve...... .... $700-$800
- Jim Kelly Houston Gamblers jersey - home black jersey shows game use from Kelly's tenure in the USFL, it's a Russell size 44 with #12 screened on the back in white. .... $1,200-$1,500
- Dan Marino game-used Miami Dolphins jersey - from 1990, this autographed, aqua mesh, Wilson size 48, road jersey has "Marino 13" on the back and a Dolphins logo on the cutoff sleeves. .... $1,000-$1,200
- Jerry Rice game-used San Francisco 49ers jersey - wine-colored road jersey from 1992, it's a Wilson size 46 with an NFL logo patch on the collar and "Rice 80" sewn in white on the back. .... $800-$1,000
- Gale Sayers 1971 Chicago Bears jersey - King-O-Shea size 46 shows game use, has #40 on front, sleeves and back. Sayers wrote

This jersey was used in the movie "The Longest Yard," starring Burt Reynolds.

"Game Used Jersey" on it and autographed it during the 1993 National Sports Collectors Convention in Chicago........... $2,500-$3,000
- Lawrence Taylor New York Giants game-used jersey - road white from 1985, with "Taylor 56" on back, this extra-length Champion jersey has tags and is autographed. .... $3,000-$3,500
- St. Louis Gunners football jersey - black wool from the NFL's dark ages, is white with a geometric gold post design. Worn by Swede Johnson, it includes Lowe and Campbell tag. .... $3,000-$3,500
- The "Longest Yard" jersey - black mesh worn by New York Giant Ernie Wheelright, who scored a touchdown in the movie. "Mean Machine 75" is on the back, along with fake blood. A clip of Burt Reynolds holding the jersey is also included. .... $400-$500
- Oakland Raiders collection of four jerseys - all are game-used Sand-Knits from the 1980s, worn by Cliff Branch (practice), Ray Guy, Ted Hendricks and Gene Upshaw. ...$1,200-$1,500
- Tony Dorsett equipment collection - includes a Russell size 42 1984 Dallas Cowboys white mesh game jersey with a 25th Anniversary patch, his Sun Bowl jacket, a University of Pittsburgh helmet, and a Dallas practice jersey. .... $1,200-$1,500

B.J. Armstrong's Bulls warmup.

Photos courtesy Leland's

Magic Johnson's Lakers uniform.

Larry Bird's Celtics warmup.

Michael Jordan's autographed shoes.

A VIP seat from Madison Square Garden.

Meadowlark Lemon's Globetrotters uniform.

418

- 1960 New York Titans autographed football - from the team's inaugural season, the white AFL ball has 36 signatures on it, including those from Wayne Fontes, Bulldog Turner and Don Maynard...................... $750-$1,000
- 1962 World Champion Green Bay Packers autographed football - an official Wilson "The Duke" ball, signed by 45 players, including Willie Davis, Forrest Gregg, Vince Lombardi, Ray Nitschke, Bart Starr and Jim Taylor. .... $1,000-$1,200
- Kansas City Chiefs Super Bowl I autographed football - official AFL autograph model signed by 35 members of the AFL championship team, including Bobby Bell, Buck Buchanan, Len Dawson, Hank Stram and Otis Taylor. .... $800-$1,000
- 1969 New York Jets Super Bowl Champions autographed football - a white Spalding AFL model with 39 signatures, including Emerson Boozer, Don Maynard, Joe Namath and Matt Snell....................................... $1,500-$1,750
- Super Bowl IV Champion Kansas City Chiefs autographed football - an official NFL autograph model with 40 signatures, including Buck Buchanan, Buddy Bell, Len Dawson, Willie Lanier, Hank Stram and Otis Taylor...
  .... $600-$800
- O.J. Simpson game-used Buffalo Bills helmet - from 1976, a white helmet with a red, white and blue Bill on each side, has a two-bar face guard and padding intact, plus #32 in faded black marker and a 1976 inspection sticker on it.............................. $2,500-$3,500
- Super Bowl XXV autographed helmet - a limited-edition silver Riddell, signed by 30 members of the New York Giants, including Ottis Anderson, Carl Banks, Jeff Hostetler, Dave Meggett, Phil Simms and Lawrence Taylor. .... $1,200-$1,500
- 1989 Super Bowl Champion San Francisco 49ers autographed helmet - Gold 49ers helmet with the "SF" logo on each side, has 50 signatures on it, including Roger Craig, Ronnie Lott, Joe Montana, Jerry Rice, John Taylor and Steve Young............. $1,800-$2,000
- 1933 Football pinball machine - 42x18x38, an early Genco, it works and features a colorful, high-kicking player on the front, with 10 balls for 5 cents. .... $1,000-$1,500

Photo courtesy Leland's

A 1933 football pinball machine.

- 1950s New York Giants down marker - 59" tall, has a twirling metal wheel on a solid pole in original multicolored paint, shows all four downs. .... $400-$500
- Super Bowl II referee jersey and apron - #46 jersey with black and gold apron, signed by its wearer "Super Bowl II Jan. 14, 1968, Tony Veteri #36.".............................. $500-$600
- 1950s Zamboni machine - 68x36x36, an original machine used by the New York Rangers at Madison Square Garden during the 1950s. This red/white/blue human-powered machine is made of steel with black rubber wheels. ....
  .... $500-$700

Auctions

Photos courtesy Leland's

At left, a Super Bowl XXV signed Giants helmet; at right, Kareem Abdul-Jabbar's goggles. Below, left, a 1992 Bulls championship banner.

At left, John Davidson's goalie mask; bottom left, Bobby Orr's Bruins sweater. Below right, Larry Bird's sneakers.

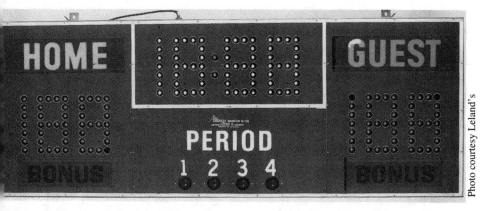

Madison Square Garden's basketball/hockey scoreboard.

- Madison Square Garden basketball and hockey scoreboard - 96x36x6, is a main side scoreboard by All American Scoreboard. Lighted digital has clock in the center, with Home, Visitor and Period scoring capacity.... .... $1,000-$1,500

- Trainer's table - a blue cushioned massage table used by the New York Knicks and New York Rangers, includes 15 rolls of tape, 25 white shin guards, 17 ice bags, two spit buckets, and three used pairs of Rangers hockey pants. .... $500-$750

- NHL All-Star Game banner - 98x31, two-sided banner autographed by 28 members of the Chicago Blackhawks, it hung in the streets of Chicago and says "Chicago Welcomes 42nd NHL All-Star Game." .... $600-$800

- NBA lighted sign - 72x30x12, has the Jerry West NBA logo, used for Knicks games and includes a similar sign picturing GE's worldwide locations........................ $1,000-$1,500

- Madison Square Garden VIP seat - elaborate, plus red-clothed upholstered folding seat, similar to those used in a movie theater, has a #1 brass plaque............................ $250-$300

- New York Knicks collection - includes a New York Knicks equipment bag, a basketball support pad (16x60), and 17 orange cushions (30x24 each) which went inside traveling teams' lockers............................. $150-$200

- Boston Celtics signed parquet floor board - 60x4, a complete section of the original parquet floor was removed and autographed by 17 members from the 1981-82 team, including Kevin McHale, Robert Parish, Larry Bird, Bill Fitch and Red Auerbach.. $1,500-$2,000

- Chicago Bulls banner - 98x31, this two-sided banner, which hung in the streets of Chicago, features a snorting bull and says "Chicago Bulls 1990-91 NBA Champs.".... $600-$800

- Michael Jordan banner - 98x31, this two-sided black-and-white banner shows Michael Jordan holding the team's first championship trophy and says "Comic Relief Salutes Michael Jordan. July 25, 1991.".... $400-$600

- Magic Johnson game-used Los Angeles Lakers jersey and trunks - from 1988-89, gold mesh home yellows, with "Johnson 32" on the jersey back in royal purple. Trunks have #32 stitched in them............. $3,750-$4,250.

- Julius Erving game-used Philadelphia 76ers jersey - 1983 home white mesh with "Sixers" across the front and "Erving 6" across the back, includes the tagging. ..... $2,500-$3,000

- Patrick Ewing's rookie New York Knicks jersey - game used in 1985-86, the blue Sand-Knit size 46 mesh jersey features Ewing's #33 and includes Cosby tags.. $2,500-$3,000

- Kevin McHale game-used Boston Celtics jersey - autographed home white knit, has "Celtics 32" on the front in kelly green and "McHale 32" on the back, with tags. .... $750-$1,000

Auctions

- Larry Bird game-used Boston Celtics warmup jacket - home white Sand-Knit with green nameplate on the back, shows game use from the 1987-88 season. .... $1,800-$2,000
- Moses Malone game-used Washington Bullets warmup jacket - from 1986-87, a red, white and blue Sand-Knit size 46 with tags and "Bullets" across the back....... $700-$800
- Chris Mullin Olympic basketball warmup - game-used blue from the gold medal round, has tagging and Mullin's uniform #13. .... $2,000-$2,500
- Michael Jordan game-used shooting shirt - from 1989-90, a road red Sand-Knit size 46 pullover with "Bulls" across the front and "Jordan 23" on the back. .... $3,000-$3,500
- Julius Erving game-used sneakers - size 15 white and red Converse All-Stars, have "Dr. J" stenciled on them, both are autographed. .. .. $800-$1,000
- Artis Gilmore game-used sneakers - size 18 white Nikes, with a red swoosh on the sides and "Artis" in red on the heels. .... $400-$500
- Michael Jordan game-used sneakers - autographed size 13 white Nikes, specifically crafted for his feet, they have the Air Jordan logo and #23 on leather straps... $800-$1,000
- Kareem Abdul-Jabbar autographed goggles - durable, clear plastic with an elastic headband and original tape replacement, worn by Jabbar in 1988............... $2,500-$3,000
- Meadowlark Lemon collection - includes "Quench" soft drink game-worn shorts, pants and jersey, which says "Meadowlark" and has lemons on it; two 1960s Harlem Globetrotters jackets with team logo embroidered on them; a Globetrotters coach's T-shirt, embroidered "George;" and three pairs of Adidas high tops in Globetrotter colors. .... $800-$1,200
- Ray Bourque game-used hockey stick - a black Sherwood, says "Hand-crafted Exclusively for Ray Bourque" on the shaft. .... $400-$500
- Stan Mikita game-used hockey stick - a 1960s Northland model, has original tape on the handle and blade and "Mikita" on the barrel in black...................................... $700-$900

- Bobby Orr game-used hockey stick - Sherwood Custom Pro model, still has tape on it, with "4 B. Orr" on it and "Made in Canada, Everett Square Sporting Goods." .... $1,000-$1,200
- 1931 Stanley Cup Champion Montreal Canadiens autographed stick - "Hand Made Special" from "Choquette Sports," it's signed by 20 Canadiens, including Howie Morenz, Sylvio Mantha and Aurel Joliat................... .... $1,000-$1,200
- Mark Messier game-used New York Ranger gloves - large, heavily-padded protective Louisville gloves, have an NHL logo on each and are signed "Mark Messier 93" in black. ... . $1,300-$1,500
- Bobby Orr sweater - cream-colored wool dress sweater with black and gold Boston Bruins trim, has "Bruins NHL" patch on the front. .... $2,000-$2,500
- Tony Esposito game-used Chicago Blackhawks jersey - Wilson size 44 home jersey with a Blackhawk logo on the front, and "Esposito" nameplate and #35 in black and red on the back, plus a game-used Esposito Northland hockey stick. .... $3,400-$3,700
- Mario Lemieux game-used Pittsburgh Penguins jersey - autographed home white jersey shows game use and has a giant Penguin logo and a captain's C patch, plus "Lemieux 66" on the back. .... $3,000-$3,500
- Frank Mahovlich game-used Detroit Red Wings jersey - from the late 1960s, this white jersey has red striping and the team logo on it, plus tags................................ $3,500-$4,000
- Bobby Orr's Oshawa Generals game-used jersey - this minor league jersey is a red cotton knit with "Oshawa Generals" sewn across the front, with a #2 on the back and a captain's "C" patch on the front................. $10,000-$12,000
- Dennis Potvin game-used New York Islanders jersey - a deep blue jersey with a captain's "C" patch on it, has "Potvin 5" on the back in white..................................... $1,500-$2,000
- Patrick Roy game-used NHL All-Star game jersey - a Maska 56 with burnt orange and black trim, includes NHL logo and Stanley Cup 100th anniversary patches and "ROY 33" on the back..................... $1,500-$2,000

Christie's East Sports Memorabilia auction
Oct. 17, 1992, in New York, N.Y.

Top photo, Jean Beliveau's game-used hockey stick. Above, Curly Neal's Globetrotters uniform. At left, a menu from Bill Russell's restaurant.

Photos courtesy Christie's East

- Johnny Unitas Bert Bell Award - this 39 1/2" by 39 1/2" award, which hung in the Baltimore Colt's corporate office, is given annually by the Maxwell Club of Philadelphia to the NFL's top player; Unitas won the award in 1959. The award, named after Commissioner Bell, has a large color photo of Unitas and a plaque at the bottom which reads: "John Constantine Unitas - Winner of the Bert Bell Award as the outstanding professional football player in the United States for the 1959 season. Presented to the Baltimore Colts by the Robert W. Maxwell Memorial Football Club, Philadelphia, Pennsylvania." ....$1,200-$1,400

- Bill Russell autographed restaurant menu - autographed two-page menu from Russell's original barbeque restaurant called "Slades," on Tremont Street in Boston. ...... $500-$700.

- 1972-73 Los Angeles Lakers World Championship ring - issued to Happy Hairston, this 14k yellow/gold ring, manufactured by Bal-

four, has a diamond in the center of a white gold basketball, surrounded by NBA Champions. "1972 NBA" is on one side, "H. Hairston, Los Angeles Lakers - 33 straight 69-13" is on the other side.............. $18,000-$20,000

- 1938 National League Championship Game program - program from the Oct. 11, 1938, game at the Polo Grounds pitting the New York Giants and the Green Bay Packers, features Giants team captain Mel Hein and is autographed by lineman Owen "Ox" Perry and Coach Steve Owen. .... $1,400-$1,600

- Jean Beliveau game-used hockey stick - early-1960s cracked CCM model, is a straight blade stick which is stamped "Beliveau 4 McNieces Montreal Canada." ...... $600-$800

- Curly Neal Harlem Globetrotters jersey - early-1970s Wilson size 42, this royal blue with red and white trim has "Harlem Globetrotters 22" on the front, with "Neal 22" and four stars on the back. .... $700-$900

Sotheby's Copeland Collection of Important Baseball Cards and Sports Memorabilia
March 22-23, 1991, in New York, N.Y.

- Football match covers - circa 1934, from Diamond Match Co. (second series football type I), these 124 different covers have red, green, blue or tan borders, with the striker intact, but they are folded out flat without the matches.. .... $1,500-$2,500
- Football match covers - circa 1936-38, from Diamond Match Co. (third series), these 105 different covers have red, green or tan borders, with sepia photos and strikers intact...... .... $1,000-$1,500
- Football Championship press pin collection - 12 different NFL and AFL Championship press pins, tie bars and a money clip. Includes NFL press pins for 1945, 1946, 1947, 1948 and 1960; NFL press tie bars for 1962, 1963,

1964; cuff links; a 1965 NFL Championship money clip; and 1970 AFL Championship tie bar. .... $5,000-$7,000
- Super Bowl press pins - complete run of 23 pins from 1967 through 1989, with cuff links to accompany the Super Bowl I pin. .... $6,000-$8,000
- Super Bowl ticket stubs - complete run of 22 tickets from 1967 through 1988, all are game used, with graphic fronts in full color. ....$2,000-$3,000
- Super Bowl programs - a complete run from #I to #XXI. .... $3,000-$4,000
- Super Bowl patches - woven and ornate patches, from Super Bowls 1-23, given to the press. .... $1,000-$1,500

Sotheby's Copeland Collection of Important Baseball Cards and Sports Memorabilia
March 13, 1993, in New York, N.Y.

- 1936-37 Madison Square Garden hockey poster - 11" by 17", this broadside shows a schedule of events at the Garden in November 1936 and pictures Hall of Famer Mervin "Red" Dutton of the New York Rangers. .... $1,500-$2,000
- Granger Pipe Tobacco hockey poster - 1930s 12 1/2" by 18 1/2" multi-color advertising sign featuring Harvey Jackson of the New York Americans. .... $400-$500
- CCM diecut advertising signs - 1) 1953 Bernard "Boom Boom" Geoffrion, "Winner of the Rookie of the Year Award 1952," 14", shows him in full color in his Montreal Canadiens uniform ($700-$900); 2) 1953 Sid Smith, "Winner of the Lady Byng Trophy 1952," 14 1/4", shows him in full color Toronto Maple Leafs uniform ($700-$900); 3) 1949 Elmer Lach, "Leading Scorer of the National Hockey League-Season 1947-48," 20 1/4", black-and-white of him in his Montreal Canadiens uniform ($600-$800); 4) 1949 Buddy O'Connor, "Winner of the Hart and Byng Trophies-Season 1947-48, The First

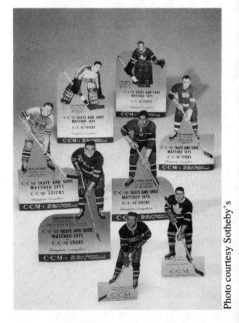

These CCM diecuts feature hockey stars.

424

Player in Hockey History to Win Trophies in the Same Season," 20 1/4", black-and-white of him in his New York Rangers uniform ($600-$800); 5) 1949 Carl Liscombe, "Leading Scorer American Hockey League-Season 1947-48," 20", black-and-white photo of him in his Providence Reds uniform ($500-$700); 6) 1949 Jim McFadden, "Winner of the Calder Trophy. The Most Outstanding Rookie of the National Hockey League Season 1947-48," 20", black-and-white of him in his Detroit Red Wings uniform ($600-$800); 7) 1949 Baz Bastien, "Winner of Goal Tending Honors American Hockey League-Season 1947-48," 18 1/2", black-and-white of him in his Pittsburgh Hornets uniform; 8) 1949 Turk Broda, "Winner of the Vezina Trophy-Season 1947-48," 19", black-and-white of him in his Toronto Maple Leafs uniform ....($600-$800).

- 1962-63 Maple Leaf Gardens/Toronto Maple Leafs Stanley Cup Champions commemorative calendar - 16 1/2" by 26", advertising "Smoke Export," each month has a Maple Leaf-related theme picture, and eight pages previewing the upcoming hockey season are also included............................ $700-$1,000

- 1943 NFL Championship Game program - from Wrigley Field in Chicago on Dec. 26, 1943, the game pitted the Chicago Bears against the Washington Redskins..................
.... $800-$1,000

- 1940 Chicago Bears World Championship gold pocket watch and chain - 10k gold, presented to the team by owner George Halas, this one was owned by team auditor M. Maraburda and is engraved on the back "M. Maraburda, Auditor, Chicago Bears 1940 World Champions," with an image of a football in the center. Still works. ....$1,500-$2,000

- Knute Rockne pin - 1920s 1 3/4" celluloid gold and blue button with an original gold and blue ribbon attached to a metal football and celluloid football player. .... $500-$600

- "The Galloping Ghost" movie poster with Red Grange - 1930s 28x42 poster made by Morgan Litho Corp. of Cleveland, Ohio, it's framed and shows Grange falling out of a bi-wing airplane. His name is in bold red letters. .... $1,000-$1,500

- Red Grange sheet music - dated 1928, entitled "I Never Believed in Lucky Numbers," has two photos of Grange on the cover and a facsimile autograph. .... $800-$1,000

- 1963 NFL Championship press tie bar - issued to the press for the 1963 NFL Championship game between the Chicago Bears and the New York Giants, has a football, listing the two team's names, inside of a rectangle which says "NFL Championship."................
.... $500-$600

- Bob Hayes game-used Dallas Cowboys jersey - size 46 road jersey, made by Southland Athletic Mfg. Co., has "Hayes 22" on the back in white. .... $600-$800

- Joe Namath game-used New York Jets jersey - circa 1967, the green cotton and nylon size 42 jersey has #12 on the front, with "Namath 12" on the back in white......... $4,000-$5,000

- 1969-70 Topps basketball rulers - complete set of 23, including Lew Alcindor, Wilt Chamberlain, Oscar Robertson and Jerry West, feature a cartoon drawing of the player standing next to a height chart. .... $700-$900

This broadside promotes a game featuring the Original Celtics.

- 1918-21 basketball broadside - using green ink on sturdy stock, this poster promotes a game to be played by the Original Celtics, World's Basketball Champions, and the Eber's Western New York Champions, and pictures Hall of Famer "Dutch" Dehnert. ......
.... $2,000-$3,000

Richard Wolffers Auctions Inc.
Feb. 18, 1993, in San Francisco

Photos courtesy Richard Wolffers Auction

At left, Kareem Abdul-Jabbar's Lakers warmup; at right, one he wore with the Bucks.

- Kareem Abdul-Jabbar's 1984 Los Angeles Lakers game-used jersey - purple Tiernan road with "Abdul-Jabbar 33" on the back, has the proper tagging. .... $2,750-$3,000
- Clyde Austin's late-1980s Harlem Globetrotters game-used jersey - Wilson mesh, size 40, with tags and "Austin 15" on the back........... .... $400-$500
- Charles Barkley's 1989 Philadelphia 76ers game used jersey - Sand-Knit road mesh, size 50, with tags and "Barkley 34" on the back... .... $1,250-$1,500
- Rick Barry's 1977-78 Golden State Warriors game-used jersey - autographed yellow home mesh by Sand-Knit, a size 42 with "Barry 24" on the back and proper tagging. .... $5,000-$6,000
- Larry Bird's 1991 Boston Celtics game-used jersey - home white Champion, with proper tagging and "Bird 33" on the back. .... $4,000-$5,000
- Bill Bradley's early-1970s New York Knicks game-used jersey - Sand-Knit, size 44, home white mesh with "Bradley 24" on the back, it's autographed. .... $8,000-$10,000

- Walter Davis' early-1980s Phoenix Suns game-used jersey - home white, with "Davis 6" on the back............................... $350-$400
- Artis Gilmore's mid-1980s San Antonio Spurs game-used jersey - black road mesh by Russell Athletic, a size 42 with "Gilmore 53" on the back and proper tagging. ... $500-$600
- Magic Johnson's mid-1980s Los Angeles Lakers game-used jersey - home yellow by Tiernan, autographed, with "Johnson 32" on the back. .... $4,500-$5,000
- Richard Jones' early-1970s Dallas Chaparrals game-used jersey - home white, Rawlings size 40, with tags and "Jones 33" on the back. .... $350-$400
- Michael Jordan's 1991 Chicago Bulls game-used jersey - autographed road red, Champion mesh, size 46, with proper tagging and "Jordan 23" on the back. .... $5,500-$6,000
- Kevin McHale's 1991 Boston Celtics game-used jersey - green road mesh, Champion size 48, with proper tagging and "McHale 32" on the back. .... $800-$1,000
- Cedric "Cornbread" Maxwell's early-1980s Boston Celtics game-used jersey - road green, cotton

knit by Sand-Knit, size 42 with "Maxwell 31" on the back and proper taggings. ....$400-$450

- Earl Monroe's 1988 New York Knicks charity game used jersey - autographed white Knicks home mesh by Sand-Knit, size 42, has proper tagging and "Monroe 15" on the back. .... $250-$300
- Willis Reed's 1989 New York Knicks charity game used jersey - autographed white Knicks home mesh by Sand-Knit, size 46, with proper tagging and "Reed 19" on the back. ... . $250-$300
- Pat Riley's 1974 Los Angeles Lakers game-used jersey - by Tiernan, purple road jersey has the proper tagging, with "Riley 12" on the back. .... $3,000-$3,500
- David Robinson's 1989-90 San Antonio Spurs game-used jersey - home white Sand-Knit, size 46, with proper tagging and "Robinson 50" on the back. .... $3,000-$3,500
- Bill Russell's mid-1950s Ararat Shrine College All-Star Game jersey - size 44, by Lowe & Campbell Athletic Goods, has his #6 on the front and a collar tag labeled "Bill Russell," the jersey is green and red on gold. .... $9,000-$10,000
- Cazzie Russell's 1985 Winston Legends All-Star game-used uniform - jersey and trunks by Spanjan, has proper tagging and "Russell 33" on the jersey back. .... $150-$175
- Isiah Thomas' 1991 Detroit Pistons game-used jersey - autographed blue road mesh, Champion size 40, with proper tagging and "Thomas 11" on the back. .... $700-$800
- Bill Walton's 1986-87 Boston Celtics game-used jersey - white home cotton by Sand-Knit, size 44 with proper tags and "Walton 5" on the back. .... $5,000-$6,000
- Jerry West's 1973 Los Angeles Lakers game-used jersey - by Tiernan, purple road jersey has tagging, with "West 44" on the back. .... $7,000-$8,000
- Dominique Wilkins' 1991 Atlanta Hawks game-used jersey - autographed red road mesh, Champion size 42, with proper tagging and "Wilkins 21" on the back. .... $1,000-$1,250
- Kareem Abdul-Jabbar's 1972 Milwaukee Bucks warmup jacket - Sand-Knit road, size 44, with tags and Abdul-Jabbar's name on the back. .... $4,000-$5,000

- Kareem Abdul-Jabbar's mid-1980s Los Angeles Lakers warmup jacket - yellow home warmup by Tiernan, has proper tagging and Abdul-Jabbar's name on the back. .... $2,000-$2,500
- Larry Bird's 1987 Boston Celtics warmup jacket - Sand-Knit road, size 46, with proper tagging and Bird's name on the back. .... $3,000-$3,500
- Hal Greer's 1964 USA World Tour satin warmup suit, jacket and pants - by Felco and Skinner, has "USA" on the back of the jacket and his number, 15, on a sleeve. .... $1,570-$2,000

This is a 1867 patent model football.

- Magic Johnson's 1988 Los Angeles Lakers warmup jacket - home yellow by Sand-Knit, size 46 with Johnson's name on the back and proper tagging. .... $3,000-$3,500
- 1867 patent model football - U.S. Patent Model No. 72722, from Dec. 31, 1867, with original pair of patent tags issued to Henry A. Alden for "covering for foot-balls." .... $25,000-$30,000

- 1967 Green Bay Packers autographed football - official MacGregor NFL ball, 45 signatures from this Super Bowl I championship team, including Willie Davis, Paul Hornung, Henry Jordan, Jerry Kramer, Vince Lombardi, Ray Nitschke, Bart Starr, Jim Taylor and Fuzzy Thurston................... $800-$1,000
- 1987 San Francisco 49ers autographed football - on a Wilson San Francisco 49ers World Champions football, 50 signatures from this Super Bowl championship team, including Dwight Clark, Roger Craig, Ronnie Lott, Joe Montana, Jerry Rice and John Taylor. ....
.... $700-$800
- Lance Alworth's late-1960s San Diego Chargers game-used jersey - blue home Rawlings, size 42, with proper tagging and "Alworth 19" on the back. ..... $4,000-$5,000
- George Blanda's 1974 Oakland Raiders game-used jersey - black home mesh by Sand-Knit, with proper tagging and "Blanda 16" on the back........................ $1,750-$2,000
- John Brodie's 1970 San Francisco 49ers game-used jersey - red home Wilson cotton, with proper taggings and "Brodie 12" on the back. .... $1,500-$1,750
- Dwight Clark's 1980-81 San Francisco 49ers game-used jersey - red home mesh by Wilson, with tags and "Clark 87" on the back. ....
.... $700-$800
- Bob Griese's late-1970s Miami Dolphins game-used jersey - white road mesh by Russell Athletic, with proper taggings and "Griese 12" on the back. .... $3,000-$3,500
- Hugh McElhenny's late-1950s San Francisco 49ers game-used jersey - white road, with proper taggings and his number, 39, on both sides...................................... $4,000-$5,000
- Joe Montana's 1981 San Francisco 49ers game-used jersey - red home mesh by Wilson, size 44, with proper tagging and "Montana 16" on the back.............. $3,500-$4,000
- Jerry Rice's 1989 San Francisco 49ers game-used jersey - red home by Wilson, size 46, with tags and crotch piece, "Rice 80" on the back. .... $1,500-$1,750
- Art Shell's mid-1970s Oakland Raiders game-used jersey - black home mesh by Sand-Knit, autographed, with proper tags and "Shell 78" on the back........... $3,000-$3,500

A 1990 autographed 49ers helmet.

- 1990 San Francisco 49ers team autographed football helmet - official 49ers helmet by Riddell, 42 signatures, including Roger Craig, Brent Jones, Ronnie Lott, Joe Montana, Jerry Rice, Keena Turner and Steve Young..............$1,500-$1,750

Photos courtesy Richard Wolffers Auctions

A Super Bowl XXIV trophy.

- 1990 Super Bowl XXIV San Francisco 49ers official crystal trophy - 8" trophy, #104 of a limited edition of 150, presented to players, coaches and management, lists the team's four Super Bowl wins............. $2,500-$3,000

Richard Wolffers Auctions Inc.
June 2, 1993, in San Francisco

- 1992 United States Olympic Gold Medal Team autographed basketball - official Spalding NBA ball, signed by all 12 members of the Dream Team: Charles Barkley, Larry Bird, Clyde Drexler, Patrick Ewing, Magic Johnson, Michael Jordan, Christian Laettner, Karl Malone, Chris Mullin, Scottie Pippen, David Robinson and John Stockton. .... $2,500-$3,000

- 1959-60 Boston Celtics autographed team photo - 8x10 sepia-toned photo signed by the entire championship team, including Hall of Famers Red Auerbach, Bob Cousy, Tom Heinsohn, K.C. Jones, Sam Jones, Bill Russell and Bill Sharman....................... $900-$1,000

- Kareem Abdul-Jabbar's 1971-72 Milwaukee Bucks game-used jersey - autographed white home cotton, "Abdul-Jabbar 33" is on the back. .... $5,000-$6,000

- Rick Barry's 1971 ABA East All-Star game-used jersey - red, white and blue jersey by Felco, has proper tagging and "Barry 24" on the back. .... $4,500-$5,000

- Wilt Chamberlain's 1970-71 Los Angeles Lakers game-used jersey - yellow home cotton by Tiernan, with proper tagging and "Chamberlain 13" on the back. .... $17,500-$20,000

- Dave DeBusschere's 1989 New York Knicks charity game used jersey - by MacGregor Sand-Knit, size 42, with proper tagging and "DeBusschere 22" on the back..... $250-$300

- Clyde Drexler's 1991 Portland Trail Blazers game-used jersey - white home mesh by Champion, size 44, with proper tagging and "Drexler 22" on the back........ $2,000-$2,500

- Julius Erving's 1984-85 Philadelphia 76ers game-used jersey - autographed home mesh by Wilson, size 40, with proper taggings and 'Erving 6' on the back. .... $3,000-$3,500

- Patrick Ewing's 1988 New York Knicks game-used jersey - road mesh by Sand-Knit and Cosby, size 46, with proper tagging and "Ewing 33" on the back. .... $2,500-$3,000

George Gervin's All-Star Game jersey.

- Larry Foust's 1959 Minneapolis Lakers game-used jersey - white home by Wilson, size 48, with proper tagging and "14" on the back. .... $3,500-$4,000

- George Gervin's 1979 NBA East All-Star game used jersey - cotton by Sand-Knit, size 40, with proper tagging and "Gervin 44" on the back. .... $1,400-$1,600

- Bobby Jones' 1977-78 Denver Nuggets game-used jersey - road mesh by Power, with proper tagging and "Jones 24" on the back.... .... $400-$500

- Maurice Lucas' 1981-82 New York Knicks game-used jersey - white home mesh by Sand-Knit and Cosby, size 46, with proper taggings and "Lucas 23" on the back............ .... $300-$350

Auctions

- Magic Johnson's mid-1980s Los Angeles Lakers game-used jersey - autographed purple road mesh by Tiernan, with proper tagging and "Johnson 32" on the back. .... $4,000-$4,500
- Michael Jordan's late-1980s Chicago Bulls game-used jersey - red road mesh by Sand-Knit, size 42, with proper taggings and "Jordan 23" on the back. .... $4,500-$5,000
- Moses Malone's 1988 Atlanta Hawks game-used jersey - home mesh by Sand-Knit, size 48 with proper taggings and "Malone 2" on the back. .... $1,000-$1,250
- Moses Malone's 1983 NBA East All-Star Game used jersey - mesh by Sand-Knit, size 46, with proper taggings and "Malone 2" on the back. .... $1,400-$1,600
- George McGinnis' 1977 NBA East All-Star Game used jersey - Sand-Knit mesh jersey, size 44, with taggings, with "McGinnis 30" on the back. .... $1,000-$1,250
- Robert Parish's 1991 Boston Celtics game-used jersey - white home mesh by Champion, size 48, with proper taggings and "Parish 00" on the back. .... $1,000-$1,200
- Oscar Robertson's 1971 Milwaukee Bucks game-used jersey - green road mesh by Sand-Knit, size 42, with proper tagging and "Robertson 1" on the back. .... $16,000-$18,000
- Bill Russell's mid-1960s World Tour game-used jersey - Wilson size 48, with tags, "U.S.A. 6 N.B.A." on the front, "Russell 6" on the back. .... $10,000-$12,500
- Isiah Thomas' 1984 NBA East All-Star Game used jersey - autographed mesh by Sand-Knit, size 42, with proper taggings and "Thomas 11" on the back. .... $2,000-$2,500
- Jerry West's 1970-71 Los Angeles Lakers game-used jersey - yellow home cotton by Tiernan, with proper tagging and "West 44" on the back. .... $9,000-$10,000
- Larry Bird's 1977 Indiana State University game-used home uniform - size 42 jersey by Sand-Knit, with "Indiana State 33" on the front, and trunks by Rawlings, with proper taggings. .... $14,000-$16,000
- Larry Bird's 1988 Boston Celtics game-used warmup jacket - Sand-Knit size 46, with proper tagging and Bird nameplate on the back. .... $2,500-$3,000

- Derrick Coleman's 1991 New Jersey Nets warmup jacket - Champion size 48, with proper tagging. .... $500-$600
- Brad Daugherty's 1988 Cleveland Cavaliers warmup jacket - size 48 by Sand-Knit, with proper tagging and Daugherty's name on the back. .... $400-$500

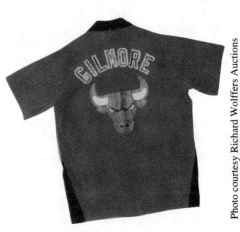

Artis Gilmore's Bulls warmup.

- Artis Gilmore's 1980 Chicago Bulls warmup jacket - Rawlings size 46, with proper tagging and "Gilmore" and a Bulls logo on the back.. .... $350-$400
- George McGinnis' 1976-77 Philadelphia 76ers warmup suit - jacket and pants by Pearson and Coane, size XL jacket has proper tagging. .... $400-$450
- Kevin McHale's 1991 Boston Celtics warmup jacket - green cotton road by Champion, size 46, with proper tagging and McHale nameplate on the back. .... $700-$800
- Earl Monroe's mid-1970s New York Knicks warmup suit - jacket and pants by Wilson, size 42 jacket has #15 in the collar and proper tagging. .... $2,750-$3,000
- Hakeem Olajuwon's 1987 Houston Rockets warmup suit - jacket and pants by Sand-Knit, with proper taggings, jacket is autographed... .... $800-$1,000
- Magic Johnson's 1990-91 Los Angeles Lakers reversible practice jersey - Champion size XL, autographed.................... $1,500-$1,750

- Michael Jordan's 1987 Chicago Bulls shooting shirt - Sand-Knit size 46, with proper tagging and "Jordan 23" on the back...................... .... $3,000-$3,500
- Michael Jordan's 1990-91 Chicago Bulls road warmup suit - jacket and pants by Champion, worn during the final NBA Championship Game on June 12, 1991, with proper tagging............................. $12,500-$15,000

Charles Barkley's 1992 Dream Team uniform.

Photo courtesy Richard Wolffers Auctions

- Charles Barkley's 1992 United States Olympic "Dream Team" mesh uniform - jersey, with "Barkley 14" on the back, and trunks by Champion, autographed shoes by Nike......... .... $22,500-$25,000
- Clyde Drexler's game-used "Dream Team" shoes - autographed Avia shoes, used during the 1992 Olympics in Barcelona................... ....$1,000-$1,200
- Michael Jordan's game-used "Dream Team" shoes - autographed Air Jordan shoes, with #23 on the back........................ $900-$1,000
- Christian Laettner's game-used "Dream Team" shoes - autographed Nike Air Hurache shoes, used in Barcelona. .... $900-$1,000

- Karl Malone's game-used "Dream Team" shoes - autographed LA Tech shoes with "Mailman" sewn on the back. ....$1,500-$1,750
- Chris Mullin's game-used "Dream Team" shoes - autographed Nike Airs used during the Olympics. .... $1,500-$1,750
- Scottie Pippen's game-used "Dream Team" shoes - autographed Nike Air shoes, used during the Olympics. .... $1,500-$1,750
- John Stockton's game-used "Dream Team" shoes - autographed Nike Air shoes, used in Barcelona.................................. $900-$1,000
- Rick Barry's 1970 ABA All-Star Game ring - 10k, features a red, white and blue ABA ball logo on the side. .... $3,000-$3,500.
- Tom Heinsohn's Boston Celtics travel bag - green bag by Converse, with "Tom Heinsohn Boston Celtics" sewn in white. .... $400-$500
- Marcus Allen's mid-1980s Los Angeles Raiders game-used jersey - white road mesh by Sand-Knit, size 42, with proper tagging and "Allen 32" on the back. ... $1,400-$1,600
- Terry Bradshaw's early-1970s Pittsburgh Steelers game-used jersey - road white, size 46, with proper tagging and "Bradshaw 12" on the back. .... $3,500-$4,000
- Earl Campbell's mid-1970s Houston Oilers game-used jersey - home mesh by Sand-Knit, size 48, with proper tagging and "Campbell 34" on the back...................... $1,400-$1,600
- Dave Casper's early-1980s Houston Oilers game-used jersey - home mesh by Sand-Knit, size 48, with proper taggings and "Casper 87" on the back. .... $1,400-$1,600
- Larry Csonka's circa 1974 Miami Dolphins game-used jersey - home mesh by Russell Athletic, autographed and with "Csonka 39" on the back. .... $2,500-$3,000
- Richard Dent's circa 1985 Chicago Bears game-used jersey - white road mesh by Wilson, size 48, with proper tagging and "Dent 95" on the back........................... $600-$700
- Tony Dorsett's late-1970s Dallas Cowboys game-used jersey - white home mesh by Southland, size 46, with proper tagging and "Dorsett 33" on the back. .... $1,400-$1,600
- John Elway's late-1980s Denver Broncos game-used jersey - white road mesh by Russell Athletic, size 46, with proper tagging and "Elway 7" on the back............. $800-$1,000

- Mel Gray's circa 1980 St. Louis Cardinals game-used jersey - white road mesh by Sand Knit, size 42, with proper tagging and "Gray 85" on the back .... $700-$800
- Franco Harris' early-1970s Pittsburgh Steelers game-used jersey - home black by Sand-Knit, size 46, with proper tagging and "Harris 32" on the back .... $2,000-$2,500
- Joe Kuharich's early-1940s St. Louis Cardinals game-used jersey - home size 46 by Champion, with proper tagging and #88 on the back. .... $1,000-$1,250
- Jim Lachey's 1992 Pro Bowl game-used jersey - mesh by Wilson for National Football Conference, size 48, with proper tagging and "Lachey 79" on the back. .... $700-$800
- Willie Lanier's mid-1970s Kansas City Chiefs game-used jersey - home mesh by Russell Southern, size 54, with proper tagging and "Lanier 63" on the back. .... $2,500-$3,000

Steve Largent's Seattle jersey.

- Steve Largent's 1987 Seattle Seahawks game-used jersey - blue home fishnet, size 42, with proper tagging and "Largent 80" on the back. .... $1,750-$2,000
- Eddie LeBaron's early-1960s Dallas Cowboys game-used jersey - road by Southland, size 44, with proper tagging and #14 on the back. .... $2,750-$3,000
- Floyd Little's mid-1970s Denver Broncos game-used jersey - home mesh by Sand-Knit, with proper tagging and "Little 44" on the back. .... $900-$1,000

- Dan Marino's circa 1989 Miami Dolphins game-used jersey - aqua home mesh by Wilson, size 46, with proper tagging and "Marino 13" on the back .... $1,500-$1,750
- Merlin Olsen's early-1970s Los Angeles Rams game-used jersey - white road cotton by Rawlings, size 52, with proper tagging and "Olsen 74" on the back. .... $3,500-$4,000
- Jim Otto's mid-1970s Oakland Raiders game-used jersey - black home mesh by Sand-Knit, with proper tagging and "Otto 00" on the back. .... $1,500-$1,750
- Alan Page's 1970 Minnesota Vikings game-used jersey - purple home cotton by Sand-Knit, size 50, with proper tags and "Page 88" on the back. .... $2,000-$2,500
- Jim Plunkett's early-1980s Los Angeles Raiders game-used jersey - white road mesh by Goodman, with proper tagging and "Plunkett 16" on the back .... $1,750-$2,000
- John Riggin's mid-1980s Washington Redskins game-used jersey - red home mesh by Goodman, with proper tagging and "Riggins 44" on the back .... $2,000-$2,500
- Gale Sayers' 1971 Chicago Bears game-used jersey - home mesh by Wilson, size 46, with proper tagging and "Sayers 40" on the back. . ... $3,000-$3,500
- Ken Stabler's 1976 Oakland Raiders game-used jersey - black home mesh by Sand-Knit, with proper tagging and "Stabler 12" on the back. .... $1,400-$1,600
- Roger Staubach's late-1970s Dallas Cowboys game-used jersey - blue road mesh by Southland, size 46, with proper tagging and "Staubach 12" on the back. .... $3,000-$3,500
- Lynn Swann's mid-1970s Pittsburgh Steelers game-used jersey - black home by Medalist Sand-Knit, with proper tagging and "Swann 88" on the back .... $2,000-$2,500
- Fran Tarkenton's early-1970s Minnesota Vikings game-used jersey - white road mesh by Sand-Knit, size 46, with proper tagging and "Tarkenton 10" on the back .... $3,500-$4,000
- Charlie Taylor's mid-1970s Washington Redskins game-used jersey - road mesh by Sand-Knit, with proper tagging and "C. Taylor 42" on the back. .... $3,500-$4,000

- Joe Theismann's 1982 Washington Redskins game-used jersey - white road mesh by Russell Athletic, size 40, with proper tagging and "Theismann 7" on the back. Worn during the 1982 Super Bowl. .... $3,500-$4,000
- Mike Webster's 1987 Pittsburgh Steelers game-used jersey - black home by Sand-Knit, size 48, with proper tagging and "Webster 52" on the back. .... $650-$750
- Randy White's circa 1980 Dallas Cowboys game-used jersey - white home mesh by Southland, with "R. White 54" on the back. ...
.... $2,000-$2,500

Joe Montana's ring.

- Joe Montana's 1981 San Francisco 49ers Super Bowl XVI World Championship ring - salesman's sample, has large diamond in the center, flanked by two smaller diamonds, circled by 14 others. .... $3,500-$4,000
- 1991 Super Bowl XXV crystal trophy - by Walton Engravers and Co., 5" by 3", #79 of 100 made, each head coach received one of these for the Super Bowl between the New York Giants and Buffalo Bills...... $400-$500

A signed Giants Super Bowl helmet.

- 1990-91 New York Giants Super Bowl Championship team autographed helmet - official Giants Riddell helmet with 39 signatures in silver, including O.J. Anderson, Jeff Hostetler, Bill Parcells and Lawrence Taylor.
....$800-#$1,000

A Vince Lombardi signed check.

- Vince Lombardi signed check - a 1959 Green Bay Packers Inc. check to Bart Starr for $193, endorsed on the back by Starr. ..... $200-$250

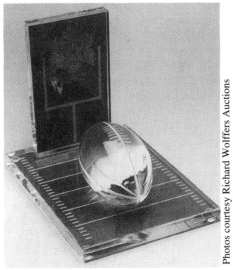

Photos courtesy Richard Wolffers Auctions

A Super Bowl XXVII trophy.

- 1993 Super Bowl XXVII official trophy produced for the Dallas Cowboys' victory - by Morgan, 6x7, #8 of 150 made... $800-$1,000

Superior Galleries
1993 Premiere Sports Auction
Feb. 27, 1993, in Beverly Hills, Calif.

- 1968 Pro Football Hall of Fame ring, Bronco Nagurski - 10k yellow/gold salesman's sample from Nagurski's induction in 1963, has a royal-blue stone on top with a Hall of Fame symbol embossed on it. .... $2,000-$2,500

- 1969 New York Jets Super Bowl Championship ring, Joe Namath - salesman's sample, has emerald-green football-shaped stone with seven cubic zirconia in the shape of a football mounted on top. .... $3,500-$4,000

- 1969 Kansas City Chiefs Super Bowl Championship ring, Jerry Mays - 14kt gold salesman's sample, has a burgundy stone on top with a large football-shaped cubic zirconia in the center. .... $2,500-$3,500

- Kansas City Chiefs World Championship gold money clip - 14k salesman's sample, yellow/gold money clip with a burgundy stone on top and a football-shaped cubic zirconia in the middle. .... $2,500-$3,000

- 1970 Baltimore Colts Super Bowl Championship ring, Johnny Unitas - 10k yellow gold salesman's sample, has a royal-blue stone with a horseshoe in the middle, with a cubic zirconia in its middle. .... $2,750-$3,200

- 1970 Dallas Cowboys NFC Championship ring - 10k white/gold salesman's sample, with a royal-blue stone and Texas five-pointed star, containing six cubic zirconia, in the middle. .... $3,500-$4,000

- 1971 Dallas Cowboys World Championship ring, Roger Staubach - 10k white/gold salesman's sample, has a cubic zirconia mounted on a midnight-blue Texas star. .... $4,500-$5,000

- 1972 Miami Dolphins World Championship Super Bowl ring, Joe Robbie - salesman's sample, has a skyblue stone on top with a cubic zirconia in the center, surrounded by more cubic zirconia. .... $3,000-$4,000

- 1974 Pittsburgh Steelers Super Bowl Championship ring, Joe Greene - 10k yellow/gold salesman's sample, has a black onyx stone with a cubic zirconia mounted in it. ....
.... $2,500-$3,000

A Minnesota Vikings championship ring.

- 1974 Minnesota Vikings NFC Championship ring, Bud Grant - 10k yellow/gold salesman's sample, amethyst stone with a gold Vikings head image on top, surrounded by 10 cubic zirconia. .... $2,500-$3,000

- 1975 Pittsburgh Steelers World Championship Super Bowl ring, Terry Bradshaw - salesman's sample has an image of the Lombardi Trophy in the middle, flanked by a cubic zirconia on each side. ... $2,500-$3,000

- 1975 Dallas Cowboys Super Bowl Championship ring, Mark Dennison - 10k white/gold salesman's sample with a skyblue stone in the middle and six diamonds forming a Texas star. .... $3,500-$4,500

- 1977 Dallas Cowboys Super Bowl Championship ring, Harvey Martin - 10k white/gold actual ring of the Super Bowl MVP, has 28 diamonds on a blue enameled Texas star. ......
.... $14,000-$16,000

- 1980 Philadelphia Eagles NFC Championship ring, Al Harris - salesman's sample has a Marquis diamond in the shape of a football, mounted on an emerald green rectangular stone. .... $3,000-$4,000

- 1981 San Francisco 49ers Super Bowl Championship ring, Joe Montana - 10k yellow/gold salesman's sample, several cubic zirconia form the shape of a football on top. ....
.... $3,500-$4,500

- 1981 Washington Redskins Super Bowl Championship ring, John Riggins - salesman's sample with a burgundy stone in a football shape on top, with cubic zirconia in a football shape embedded in it. .... $3,500-$4,000

- 1982 Miami Dolphins AFC Championship ring, Don Shula - 14k gold-plated salesman's sample has a skyblue stone with a cubic zirconia mounted in the center. .... $2,500-$3,000
- 1983 Los Angeles Raiders Super Bowl Championship ring, Dave Dalby - a real Super Bowl ring, but it does not have real diamonds in it; it has three giant football-shaped stones on top, mounted on black onyx. .... $10,000-$13,000
- 1983 Washington Redskins NFC Championship ring, John Riggins - 14k gold-plated salesman's sample, has a large rectangular burgundy stone with cubic zirconia mounted in it, with another synthetic stone mounted in the middle of that. .... $3,000-$3,500
- 1984 Miami Dolphins AFC Championship ring, Rick Roby - salesman's sample, 10 k yellow/gold has five real diamonds on top to commemorate five AFC Championships. .... $3,500-$4,500
- 1985 Chicago Bears Super Bowl Championship ring, William Perry - largest Super Bowl ring ever made, size 23, this salesman's sample is a 14k yellow/gold-plated ring with a traditional Chicago C made of cubic zirconia in the middle, circled by another ring of cubic zirconia. .... $4,500-$5,500
- 1985 New England Patriots AFC Championship ring, Raymond Berry - 10k yellow/gold salesman's sample with a football-shaped burgundy stone and a football shaped from cubic zirconia. .... $2,500-$3,000
- 1989 San Francisco 49ers Super Bowl Championship ring - salesman's sample with four cubic zirconia diamonds shaped like footballs surrounded by cubic zirconia making a larger football. .... $3,500-$4,000
- 1971 ABA Utah Stars Championship ring - 10k white/gold saleman's sample with a multi-colored enameled basketball "Utah Stars" shooting across and a cubic zirconia below. .... $1,500-$2,500
- 1982 Los Angeles Lakers NBA Championship ring - 10k white/gold salesman's sample, has a round amethyst stone with a cubic zirconia mounted on top. .... $3,000-$3,500
- 1984 Boston Celtics NBA World Championship ring - 10k yellow/gold salesman's sample has a green enamel shamrock with cubic zirconia mounted in the center. .... $3,000-$3,500
- 1985 Los Angeles Lakers World Championship ring, Magic Johnson - 10k yellow/gold salesman's sample, has a amethyst stone with a cubic zirconia basketball going into a cubic zirconia basketball hoop. .... $3,000-$4,000
- 1985 Los Angeles Lakers World Championship ring, Kareem Abdul-Jabbar - 10k yellow/gold salesman's sample, has a amethyst stone with a cubic zirconia basketball going into a cubic zirconia basketball hoop. .... $3,500-$4,000
- Los Angeles Lakers Team of the Decade ring (1980-89) - 10k yellow/gold salesman's sample with a cubic zirconia stone, represents five World Championships the team won in the 1980s. These rings were only given to season ticket holders. .... $1,200-$1,500
- 1986 NBA All-Star Game ring - salesman's sample has a dark-blue rectangular stone, embossed on top with a silver basketball. .... $1,000-$1,250
- 1978 Montreal Canadiens Stanley Cup Championship ring, Rick Chartraw - real, 14k yellow/gold, has several diamonds on top in a rectangle and a Stanley Cup on the side......... .... $3,500-$4,000
- 1979 Montreal Canadiens Stanley Cup Championship ring, Rick Chartraw - real ring, 14k yellow/gold, has a giant Stanley Cup mounted on top with four diamonds (two on each side, representing Stanley Cup wins in 1976, 1977, 1978 and 1979), and many small diamonds surrounding the Stanley Cup. .... $3,500-$4,500
- 1984 Edmonton Oilers Stanley Cup Championship ring, Rick Chartraw - real ring, 14k yellow/gold with a royal-blue stone that has a diamond mounted in the center. .... $4,000-$5,000
- Rick Chartraw's 1976-77 Stanley Cup Trophy - exact replica awarded to players and front office personnel, 13" silver trophy stands on a 1/2" black base and has the players' and office personnel's names engraved on it....................... $2,500-$3,000

Rick Chartraw's Prince of Wales Trophy.

• Rick Chartraw's 1977-78 Prince of Wales Trophy - 13" tall, silver trophy stands on a 2 1/2"

wooden base, with a plaque which reads "HRH Prince of Wales Trophy - Rick Chartraw." ....
....$1,200-$1,500

• 1976 New York Nets ABA Championship Trophy - 14" high, with a 15" diameter black ornately-cut base with four silver basketball players and a plaque which reads "NY Nets." A silver 12" diameter bowl, engraved "ABA Championship Award," rests on the base. .....
.... $3,500-$4,500

• San Francisco 49ers Super Bowl XXIV crystal trophy - 8" tall, number 83 of 150 made by Walton & Co., presented to a player, coach or front office personnel, it also commemorates the team's three other Super Bowl wins. ....
.... $2,500-$3,500

• Isiah Robertson's 1971 Rookie Trophy - 18" tall trophy on a 6 1/2" wooden base with a silver plaque which says "1971 Ye Old Rams Rookie of the Year Award Isiah Robertson."
.... $1,000-$1,500

• Isiah Robertson's 1972 Defensive Player of the Year Trophy - 15" silver trophy on a 5" wooden base with a silver plaque which says "1972 Ye Old Rams Defensive Player of the Year Isiah Robertson." .... $1,000-$1,500

Photos courtesy Superior Galleries

The Nets' ABA Championship Trophy and Isiah Robertson's Defensive Player of the Year award.

Superior Galleries Windy City Sports Auction
July 22-23, 1993, in Chicago

- Ed Belfour's rookie Chicago Blackhawks game-used jersey - front has Blackhawk logo, back has Belfour's name and #1, which he only wore during his rookie season................... $2,000-$2,500
- Bobby Clarke's early-1980s Philadelphia Flyers game-used jersey - Flyers logo and captain "C" patch on the front, with "Clarke 16" on the back...................... $1,200-$1,500
- Glenn Hall's game-used St. Louis Blues jersey - blue, with Blues logo on the front and #1 on the back. .... $4,000-$5,000
- Eric Lindros' Oshawa Generals Junior A Team replica jersey - autographed on the back, which says "Lindros 88.".... $350-$400
- Eric Lindros' 1991 Canada Cup game-used jersey - white Air-Knit CCM jersey with the Labatt's Canada Cup emblem on the front and "Lindros 88" on the back.........$2,500-$3,500
- Pit Martin's Chicago Blackhawks game-used sweater - has a Blackhawks logo on the front, with #7 on the back...................... $600-$800
- Bobby Orr's 1976-77 Chicago Blackhawks game-used jersey - home white with Blackhawks logo on the front and #4 on the back...
  .... $6,000-$8,000
- Gilbert Perreault's mid-1980s Buffalo Sabres game-used sweater - has the Buffalo logo and a captain "C" patch on the front, and "Perreault 11" on the back. .... $1,000-$1,200
- Manon Rheaume's Tampa Bay Lightning game-used practice jersey - worn during training camp and the exhibition season during her inaugural season, has the team logo on the front and #33 on the back.........$1,500-$2,500
- Ian Turnbull's mid-1970s Toronto Maple Leafs game-used sweater - Maple Leafs logo is on the front, "Turnbull 2" is on the back....
  .... $300-$400
- 1930s St. Louis Flyers AHL game-used jersey - red, white and blue jersey with the Flyers name on the front and #6 on the back.......
  .... $2,000-$3,000
- Early-1950s Chicago Blackhawks game-used sweater - features the barber pole stripes design, with the Blackhawks logo on the front and #15 on the back............... $1,500-$2,000

- 1960s St. Louis Braves ladies booster club jacket - a red lady's blazer with the Chicago Blackhawks logo on the front, the parent club of this farm team. .... $200-$300

Eric Lindros' game-used gloves.

- Eric Lindros' Philadelphia Flyers game-used gloves - Louisville models from his rookie season, have his name embroidered above each thumb. .... $1,500-$2,000
- Autographed Toronto Maple Leafs 1962-63 Stanley Cup Championship team hockey stick - signed by nine Hall of Famers, including George Armstrong, Johnny Bower, Tim Horton, Punch Imlach, Red Kelly, Frank Mahovlich, Bob Pulford and Allan Stanley...
  .... $1,000-$1,200
- Autographed New York Islanders Stanley Cup Championship hockey stick - Koho signed by all the members from the four Stanley Cup teams, including Mike Bossy, Clark Gillies, Bob Nystrom, Chico Resch, Billy Smith and Bryan Trottier. .... $800-$1,000
- 1944-45 Toronto Maple Leafs autographed miniature Stanley Cup Championship hockey stick - signed by the entire team, including

Hall of Famers Dave Schriner and Hap Day, given out at a souvenir victory dinner by the team, includes two black-and-white team photos. .... $400-$500
• 1950-51 Toronto Maple Leafs autographed miniature Stanley Cup Championship hockey stick - team signed, including signatures from Turk Broda, Ted Kennedy and Bill Barilko... .... $400-$600
• 1957-58 Montreal Canadiens autographed miniature Stanley Cup Championship hockey stick - CCM model signed by 13 players, including Jean Beliveau, Toe Blake, Boom Boom Geoffrion, Doug Harvey, Dicky Moore, Jacques Plante, Claude Pronovost and Rocket Richard. .... $200-$300
• Russian National Hockey Club hockey stick - signed by the entire 1966-67 Russian team, it's game used and was manufactured in Russia... ....$600-$800
• Bill Barber wooden blade pattern - from the Northland Co., serial number 4666, pattern was used to cut out his stick blades......... $200-$300
• John Bucyk wooden blade pattern - from the Northland Co., used as pattern to cut out his stick blades. .... $200-$300
• Phil Esposito wooden blade pattern - from the Northland Co., serial number 98002, used as a pattern to cut out his stick blades. ..... $200-$300

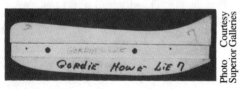

Photo Courtesy Superior Galleries

Gordie Howe's blade pattern.

• Gordie Howe wooden blade pattern - from the Northland Co., used as a pattern to cut out his stick blades. .... $500-$700
• Bobby Hull wooden blade pattern - from the Northland Co., serial number 954A, used as a pattern to cut out his stick blades....$400-$500
• Frank Mahovlich wooden blade pattern - from the Northland Co., serial number 6744, used as a pattern to cut out his stick blades. ..... $250-$350
• Bobby Orr wooden blade pattern - from the Northland Co., serial number 98005, used as a pattern to cut out his stick blades. ......$400-$600

• Brad Park wooden blade pattern - from the Northland Co., serial number 98024, used as a pattern to cut out his stick blades. .... $200-$300
• Denis Potvin wooden blade pattern - from the Northland Co., serial number 6L, used as a pattern to cut out his stick blades. .... $200-$300
• Gary Unger wooden blade pattern - from the Northland Co., serial number 5L957, used as a pattern to cut out his stick blades. .... $200-$300
• 1926 New York Rangers team photo - 8x32, framed black-and-white, taken in Toronto, shows the first Rangers team, including Hall of Famers Frank Boucher, Bill Cook, F.J. Cook and Ching Johnson, with autographs from both Cooks........................ $400-$600
• 1935 Chicago Black Hawks team photo - 11x14, framed and matted black-and-white, depicts the members of the 1935 team, including Hall of Famer Howie Morenz. ....$200-$300
• Autographed Hockey Hall of Fame book, 1974-75 - this book, available for purchase only from the Hockey Hall of Fame in Toronto, contains 142 signatures of all-time greats, including 98 Hall of Famers. .... $1,200-$1,500
• Autographed Gordie Howe/Wayne Gretzky Nike poster - color photo of the two, Mr. Hockey and the Great One, standing on the ice in front of a goalie's net. Howe has on a Detroit uniform, while Gretzky is in a Kings uniform....................................... $300-$400
• 1991 Team Canada Cup program - from the first Team Canada Cup series that Eric Lindros participated in, he and Wayne Gretzky signed the cover.......................... $100-$150
• 1931-32 Toronto Maple Leafs puzzle - features 10 Hall of Famers from this Stanley Cup Championship team, the puzzle, produced by General Motors of Canada is completed, framed and matted, and includes an original box with Happy Day on it. .... $400-$600
• 1954 Detroit Red Wings puzzle - 14x20, depicts the Stanley Cup winners posing in front of the trophy, and has been completed and glued to a cardboard backing.......... $300-$400
• 1947-48 Montreal Canadiens calendar - made by the Montreal Forum, it features the Stanley Cup championship team. .... $400-$500

A 1954 Red Wings puzzle.

- Clark Shaughnessy playbooks - twelve bound playbooks provide information on plays compiled by the Hall of Fame football coach, plus copies of some of his speeches and responses from several coaches to questions he had about plays. .... $1,000-$1,500

A 1947-48 Montreal Canadiens calendar.

- Clark Shaughnessy handwritten football plays - 100 football plays, done in the Hall of Famer's handwriting on 6x9 cards............$1,000-$1,500

Photos courtesy Superior Galleries

A Super Bowl XXVII neon sign.

- Super Bowl XXVII NFL sign - 5' by 5' actual neon sign which hung atop the entrance of the Rose Bowl in Pasedena before the game, green, blue, red and white neon lights combine to portray red roses in the background of a shield which reads "Super Bowl XXVII.".... $10,000-$12,000
- Autographed Hall of Fame football - Wilson white-paneled football signed by 21 players, including Len Dawson, Sam Huff, Dick Lane, Ray Nitschke, Merlin Olsen and Jack Tatum. .... $100-$200
- Limited-edition autographed Jerry Rice football - one of only 101 commemorative handpainted footballs produced in honor of his record-breaking 101st touchdown reception on Dec. 6, 1992, against the Miami Dolphins, includes a custom-made display case and a UPI photo of the catch.................. $400-$600
- Commemorative handpainted football autographed by Randall Cunningham - game ball from the Philadelphia Eagles 17-13 win against the Washington Redskins on Dec. 20, 1992.. $150-$200
- Commemorative handpainted football autographed by John Elway - game ball from the Denver Broncos' 16-10 win against the Seattle Seahawks on Sept. 15, 1991............$150-$200

Jerry Rice and Bo Jackson signed these handpainted footballs.

- Commemorative handpainted football auto-graphed by Jim Harbaugh - Chicago Bears game ball from Sept. 6, 1992, a 27-24 win against the Detroit Lions. .... $150-$200
- Commemorative handpainted football auto-graphed by Bo Jackson - touchdown ball from the Los Angeles Raiders' 23-20 win against the Denver Broncos on Dec. 2, 1990. ......$250-$350
- Commemorative handpainted football auto-graphed by Jim Kelly - game ball from the Buffalo Bills' 30-27 win over the Los Ange-les Raiders on Dec. 8, 1991. .... $150-$250
- Commemorative handpainted football auto-graphed by Dan Marino - game ball from Miami's 19-16 win against the Houston Oil-ers on Nov. 22, 1992. .... $150-$250
- Commemorative handpainted football auto-graphed by Warren Moon - game ball pre-sented to Moon after the Houston Oilers' 17-13 win over the Miami Dolphins on Oct. 20, 1991. .... $150-$250
- Commemorative handpainted football auto-graphed by Mark Rypien - Washington Red-skins game ball from a 16-13 win against the Houston Oilers on Nov. 3, 1991... $150-$250

- Commemorative handpainted football auto-graphed by Steve Young - game ball from the San Francisco 49ers' 41-3 win over the Atlanta Falcons on Nov. 9, 1992. ....$150-$250
- 1985 Chicago Bears autographed Super Bowl football - official Wilson NFL Super Bowl game ball signed by 34 members of the World Championship team, including Richard Dent, Mike Ditka, Willie Gault, Jim McMahon, Walter Payton, William Perry and Mike Sin-gletary... $500-$700
- Commemorative autographed Washington Redskins 1991-92 Super Bowl football - hand-painted to say "Redskins 1991-92 World Cham-pions" with the Super Bowl logo, features more than 40 signatures, including Art Monk, Mark Rypien and Rickey Sanders.............$350-$450
- Commemorative Super Bowl XX football autographed by Richard Dent - from the 1986 Super Bowl, a Chicago Bears 46-10 win over the New England Patriots. .... $800-$1,000.
- Commemorative Super Bowl XXVII football autographed by MVP Troy Aikman - handpaint-ed and inscribed "Troy Aikman MVP 1/31/93 Dallas vs. Buffalo 52-17." ....$1,000-$1,200

Dan Marino and Troy Aikmand signed these handpainted footballs.

A Kareem-Abdul Jabbar handpainted basketball.

- Kareem Abdul-Jabbar autographed commemorative handpainted basketball - an official NBA Spalding inscribed "MVP Kareem Abdul-Jabbar NBA Champions Los Angeles Lakers 1979-80" with the Lakers logo........... .... $400-$600
- 1983 Los Angeles Lakers autographed team basketball - official AMF Voit Los Angeles Lakers ball, signed by 11 members, including Kareem Abdul-Jabbar, Michael Cooper, Magic Johnson, Magic Johnson, Norm Nixon and Jamaal Wilkes........................ $700-$800
- Autographed 1987-88 Boston Celtics basketball - official green and white Spalding, featuring the team logo and 15 signatures, including Larry Bird, Robert Parish, Kevin McHale, Danny Ainge and Chris Ford. .... $400-$500
- 1989-90 Orlando Magic autographed basketball - official Spalding NBA ball signed by 21 members of this inaugural team, including Shaquille O'Neal........................ $300-$400
- Commemorative basketball autographed by the 1991-92 World Champion Chicago Bulls - handpainted basketball inscribed "World Champions Chicago Bulls," includes Michael Jordan, Scottie Pippen, Bill Cartwright and others. .... $550-$750

- 1992 Chicago Bulls autographed basketball - white-paneled Rawlings, has 12 signatures from this World Championship team, including Horace Grant, Bill Cartwright, Michael Jordan and Scottie Pippen. .... $400-$600
- Basketball autographed by the five starters on the 1993 Chicago Bulls - official Spalding basketball with a Bulls logo, has gold ink signatures from Scottie Pippen, Bill Cartwright, Michael Jordan, John Paxson and Horace Grant... $250-$350
- 1992 Olympic Dream Team replica basketball jersey collection - autographed replica jerseys from six players, half of the team, including Charles Barkley, Larry Bird, Clyde Drexler, Michael Jordan, Chris Mullin and Scottie Pippen........................ $1,200-$1,800
- Michael Jordan's autographed 1992 USA Olympic Basketball Team shoes - red, white and blue Air Jordan high tops, size 13, autographed................................. $1,000-$1,500

Photos courtesy Superior Galleries

A Bob Cousy ad for shoes.

- Bob Cousy advertisement piece - yellow and blue ad shows Bob Cousy recommending P-F Litenfast basketball shoes by B.F. Goodrich. .... $400-$600

Centerfield Collectibles Inc.

Centerfield Collectibles Inc., of Ambler, Pa., had several sports auctions over the last year which offered football, basketball and hockey memorabilia. Prices realized results from the company's Oct. 24-Nov. 4, 1994, "Non-World Series" 1,420-lot auction included:

- Mark Messier's 1993-94 game-used New York Rangers jersey, with Captain's C patch and NOB: $945
- 1969 Baltimore Colts autographed team football, with 32 members from this Super Bowl team, including Johnny Unitas: $440.
- Hakeem Olajuwon's game-used autographed Nike Air sneakers, size 18s worn in 1993: $779
- Autographed Joe Namath hand-painted football, commemorates the Jets' upset Super Bowl III victory over the Colts: $268.
- Bill Russell autographed basketball, official NBA Spalding: $471.
- O.J. Simpson Salvino statue, featuring him in his red and yellow USC uniform, hand-signed on a white base: $275.
- Autographed Clarence Weatherspoon game-used sneakers, Nike Air Huaraches, from his rookie season: $293.
- Magic Johnson autographed Forum floor piece, the 8x10 piece, obtained after the floor was resurfaced in the 1990s, included a purple Lakers gift box: $300.
- 1992 U.S. Olympic basketball team cartoon T-shirt, signed by nine members of the Dream Team: $279.
- A miniature University of Pittsburgh football helmet signed by Dan Marino: $253.
- Jack Kemp autographed baseball cap, a 1964 Buffalo Bills commemorative throwback style model: $161.
- Brett Hull game-used Easton aluminum hockey stick, taped on the blade and handle with #16 on the shaft: $336.
- New York Jets throwback-style Pro Line helmet, signed by Joe Namath, includes a mirrored case and name placard: $220.
- Drew Bledsoe's game-used Apex turf cleats, autographed on each toe: $385.
- Autographed O.J. Simpson 8x10 color photo of "The Juice" breaking the single-season rushing total record in 1973, framed and matted to measure 13x16: $200.
- Bart Starr hand-painted autographed football, commemorates the Green Bay Packers' first world championship: $316.
- Baltimore Colts mascot uniform, belonged to the horse who performed in the 1960s, it's autographed by more than 25 players, including Johnny Unitas, Art Donovan, Raymond Berry and Earl Morrall: $282.
- Walter Payton autographed Wilson NFL football: $165.
- Bo Jackson autographed Wilson NFL football: $103.

- Frank Gifford autographed Wilson NFL football: $275.
- Lawrence Taylor autographed Wilson NFL football: $162.
- Fran Tarkenton autographed Wilson football, white panel: $110.
- Joe Montana hand-painted autographed football, Super Bowl XVI: $550.
- Terry Bradshaw hand-painted autographed football, Super Bowl XIV: $389.
- Troy Aikman hand-painted autographed football, Super Bowl XXVII: $275.
- Autographed Monday Night Football announcers' football, white paneled Wilson, signed by Frank Gifford, Dan Dierdorf and Al Michaels: $141.
- 1994 Philadelphia Eagles team-signed football, triple white-paneled Wilson with 30 signatures, includes Randall Cunningham and Herschel Walker: $237.
- Kareem Abdul-Jabbar autographed Spalding basketball, indoor/outdoor model: $112.
- Bob Cousy autographed Spalding basketball, indoor/outdoor model: $119.
- Michael Jordan hand-painted autographed basketball, third NBA title: $333.
- Moses Malone autographed basketball, white-paneled Hall of Fame model: $55.
- Shaquille O'Neal autographed Spalding basketball, NBA model: $208.
- Chris Webber autographed Spalding basketball, indoor/outdoor model: $91.
- Walt Frazier autographed Spalding basketball, outdoor ball: $107.
- Magic Johnson autographed Spalding basketball, commemorative 1992 Orlando All-Star Game model, red/white/blue: $195.
- Michael Jordan autographed Spalding basketball, 1993 NBA Finals model: $440.
- 1920s football helmet, black MacGregor with little padding and cloth chinstrap: $202.
- Chicago Cardinals team-issued football helmet, MacGregor model: $389.
- Greg Coleman autographed Minnesota Vikings jersey, road purple with tags: $195.
- Reggie White team-issued Green Bay Packers white jersey, worn when he announced he'd signed with the team: $322.
- Shaquille O'Neal autographed Orlando Magic replica home jersey: $229.
- Bart Starr autographed Green Bay Packers replica jersey, white: $94.
- Dave Lapham game-used USFL jersey, New Jersey Generals home white: $150.

- Bill Bergey game-used Philadelphia Eagles jersey, road green: $564.
- Alan Page commemorative Minnesota Vikings "throwback" jersey, home white: $100.
- Ken Stabler commemorative Oakland Raiders "throwback" jersey, 1976 black: $81.
- Joe Namath commemorative New York Jets "throwback" jersey, 1968 white: $97.
- Ricky Watters autographed San Francisco 49ers replica jersey, road red: $125.
- Rodney Hampton autographed New York Giants replica jersey, road blue: $88.
- Steve Largent autographed Seattle Seahawks jersey, road blue: $165.
- Alexander Mogilny game-used Buffalo Sabres jersey, 1993-94 preseason use: $399.
- Denis Savard game-used Tampa Bay Lightning jersey, 1993-94 preseason use: $513.
- Eric Lindros autographed Philadelphia Flyers replica jersey, home white: $144.
- Lot of 14 Hockey Heroes Standups, including Bobby Clarke, Rick MacLeish, Dave Shultz: $55.
- Wayne Gretzky Pro Stars full cereal box, Canadian issue from General Mills: $84.
- Two Chicago Bulls Wheaties boxes, honoring third straight NBA title: $35.
- Lot of six Coca-Cola Super Bowl XXVIII bottles, includes colorful box holder: $40.
- 1992 hockey All-Star Game luggage bag, with the All-Star, NHL and Philadelphia Flyers logos, done in Flyers colors: $81.
- Troy Aikman autographed Super Bowl XXVIII seat cushion: $55.
- Dan Marino restaurant lot, from his restaurant in Florida, includes an 11x17 menu, two matches, napkins, two plastic drinking cups, a wine list and a late night lineup menu: $89.
- Steve Largent Wheaties box, 18-ounces: $61.
- Vince Lombardi library of six football training videos, includes the handbook which accompanies the set: $131.
- Lot of six Barry Sanders Starting Lineup figurines, includes 1991 and 1992 Headliners and regulars for 1990-93, all in original packages: $81.
- Lot of eight Dallas Cowboys Starting Lineup figurines, includes three of Troy Aikman and Emmitt Smith and two of Michael Irvin, all in original packages: $67.
- 1974 Pittsburgh Steelers World Champions pennant, commemorates the team's Super Bowl victory: $55.
- Wayne Gretzky autographed Sports Illustrated magazine, issue date 2/18/85: $61.
- Don Shula autographed Time magazine, during the team's 1972 season: $45.
- Lot of three Wayne Gretzky autographed pucks, official Los Angeles Kings pucks: $173.
- Lot of eight Philadelphia Flyers autographed pucks, on official team pucks, signers include Eric Lindros, Mark Recchi, Pelle Eklund, Kevin

Dineen, Dimitri Yushkevich, Michael Renberg and Tommy Soderstrom: $108.
- Lot of four Detroit Red Wings autographed pucks, on official team pucks, signers include Hall of Famers Gordie Howe, Ted Lindsay, Sid Abel and Red Kelly: $108.
- Lot of four Montreal Canadiens autographed pucks, on official team pucks, signers include Hall of Famers Bernie Geoffrion, Dickie Moore, Maurice Richard and Elmer Lach: $109.
- Lot of two Brett Hull autographed pucks, on official St. Louis Blues pucks: $80.
- Lot of three Mario Lemieux autographed pucks, on official Pittsburgh Penguins pucks: $150.
- Danny Ainge 1979 Sportscaster card, a two-sport card of him on the Toronto Blue Jays and Boston Celtics: $89.

Results from Centerfield Collectibles' Dec. 15-16, 1994, "Seasons Greatings" auction, which featured 1,335 lots, include:

- 1967 Green Bay Packers Super Bowl II championship autographed football, white-paneled ball signed by more than 20 members, including Bart Starr, Max McGee, Jim Taylor, Fuzzy Thurston and Herb Adderley: $354.
- Rick Barry game-used 1960s San Francisco Warriors jersey, with tags: $2,974.
- Official Olympic basketball signed by 12 members of the 1992 U.S. Dream Team, including Magic Johnson, Charles Barkley, Michael Jordan and Larry Bird: $921.
- O.J. Simpson autographed Salvino statue, one of 1,000 showing him in his Buffalo Bills white uniform: $242.
- Drazen Petrovic 1991 game-used New Jersey Nets jersey, with tags and NOB: $471.
- Danny Manning worn jersey, grey and maroon, used by Manning for a commercial at the beginning of an HBO movie titled "White Mile": $103.
- Johnny Unitas autographed Baltimore Colts replica jersey, 1960s model: $287.
- Nolan Cromwell 1980s game-used Pro Bowl jersey, red/white/blue NFC style: $293.
- Walter Tullis game-used New Jersey Generals USFL jersey: $138.
- Jerry Rice autographed Super Bowl XXIV commemorative football: $103.
- Barry Sanders autographed replica NFL football: $132.
- Dick Butkus autographed replica NFL football: $105.
- Super Bowl XXI commemorative Wilson NFL football, has Super Bowl logo, date, team names and site on it: $116.
- Kareem Abdul-Jabbar autographed basketball, official Spalding NBA leather ball: $158.
- Steve Yzerman autographed hockey stick, white Louisville TPS with his name screened on the shaft: $88.

443

Auctions

- Super Bowl XXIV commemorative poster, from the Louisiana Superdome, pictures Bourbon Street, 24x36 dry mounted: $15.
- Joe Namath Salvino statue: $389.
- Kareem Abdul-Jabbar Gartlan statue: $266.
- Mario Lemieux Salvino statue, black uniform: $193.
- Mario Lemieux Salvino statue, white uniform: $250.
- O.J. Simpson Salvino statue, Buffalo blue road uniform: $220.
- O.J. Simpson Salvino statue, USC uniform: $220.
- Wayne Gretzky Salvino statue, white uniform: $244.
- Lot of 16 Randall Cunningham Kenner Starting Lineup figurines: $61.
- Unused full ticket from Super Bowl XXVI in Minnesota, sealed in Lucite: $77.
- Super Bowl XXV seat cushion, given to fans attending the 1991 game in Tampa, with its packet of cards and goodies intact: $108.
- New York Jets record album, cover shows Joe Namath, record recaps the team's 1969 championship season: $50.
- 1981 "Mean Joe" Greene football pennant, says "One for the Thumb in '81," cartoon shows him wearing four Super Bowl rings: $25.
- 1960s Philadelphia 76ers pennant, red letters with a basketball player in action: $22.
- 1970 Pittsburgh Penguins pennant, blue with a Penguins logo in a circle: $25.
- Pittsburgh Steelers Super Bowl XIII pennant, black and gold with a team photo: $67.
- Lot of 53 basketball Sportscasters cards, including Pete Maravich, Jerry West, Dave Cowens and George Mikan: $61.
- Lot of 72 basketball Sportscasters cards, including Gale Sayers, O.J. Simpson, Johnny Unitas, Bob Griese, Tony Dorsett and Joe Namath: $85.
- Lot of 41 hockey Sportscasters cards, including Gordie Howe, Brad Park, Bobby Orr and Bobby Clarke: $50.

Results from Centerfield Collectibles' Feb. 16-17, 1995, "Spring Training" auction with 2,012 items included:

- Shaquille O'Neal game-used Orlando Magic road jersey, black with tags: $4,500.
- Reggie Lewis game-used 1988 Boston Celtics jersey, home white with tags, autographed: $733.
- President Gerald Ford autographed mini Michigan Wolverines helmet, Riddell model: $495.
- Magic Johnson game-used 1990-91 Los Angeles Lakers jersey, purple mesh with NOB: $2,100.
- Drew Bledsoe autographed New England Patriots helmet, team issued but not used: $385.
- Clyde Drexler 1989-90 Portland Trailblazers home shooting shirt, black nylon with NOB: $532.
- Michael Jordan Night autographed ticket, unused, from his retirement ceremony: $399.

- Michael Jordan autographed Nike Air high top sneakers, unused, size 13: $382.
- Kenny Stabler worn practice jersey, 1970s Sand-Knit Oakland Raiders: $195.
- Lynn Dickey game-used Green Bay Packers jersey, 1980s white: $142.
- Clyde Drexler game-used Portland Trailblazers shorts, white, from 1992-93: $121.
- John Elway autographed Denver Broncos jersey, NFL 75th anniversary style: $251.
- Kelvin Ramsey 1983 used New Jersey Nets warmup suit, with pants and tags: $83.
- Chris Dudley 1988 Cleveland Cavaliers warmup suit, with pants and tags: $116.
- Atlanta Falcons game-used Riddell football helmet, padding intact, player unknown: $117.
- Pittsburgh Steelers game-used Riddell football helmet, padding intact, player unknown: $518.
- Cleveland Browns game-used Riddell football helmet, padding intact, player unknown: $176.
- Warren Moon autographed mini Houston Oilers Riddell helmet: $149.
- Drew Bledsoe autographed mini Washington State Cougars Riddell helmet: $186.
- Jerry Rice/Steve Young autographed mini San Francisco 49ers Riddell helmet: $228.
- Jim Taylor/Paul Hornung autographed mini Green Bay Packers Riddell helmet: $117.
- Joe Montana autographed mini San Francisco 49ers Riddell helmet: $160.
- Emmitt Smith autographed mini Dallas Cowboys Riddell helmet: $165.
- Troy Aikman autographed mini Dallas Cowboys Riddell helmet: $157.
- Bart Starr hand-painted autographed football, Super Bowl II: $256.
- Len Dawson hand-painted autographed football, Super Bowl IV: $215.
- Chuck Howley hand-painted autographed football, Super Bowl V: $288.
- Roger Staubach hand-painted autographed football, Super Bowl VI: $259.
- Larry Csonka hand-painted autographed football, Super Bowl VIII: $363.
- Franco Harris hand-painted autographed football, Super Bowl IX: $225.
- Lynn Swann hand-painted autographed football, Super Bowl X: $256.
- Fred Biletnikoff hand-painted autographed football, Super Bowl XI: $150.
- Randy White/Harvey Martin hand-painted autographed football, Super Bowl XII: $227.
- Terry Bradshaw hand-painted autographed football, Super Bowl XIII: $400.
- Jim Plunkett hand-painted autographed football, Super Bowl XV: $177.
- Jim McMahon hand-painted autographed football, Super Bowl XX: $121.
- Ottis Anderson hand-painted autographed football, Super Bowl XXV: $627.

- Mark Rypien hand-painted autographed football, Super Bowl XXVI: $215.
- Joe Montana hand-painted autographed football, Super Bowl XIX: $253.
- Richard Dent hand-painted autographed football, Super Bowl XX: $165.
- Phil Simms hand-painted autographed football, Super Bowl XXI: $509.
- Doug Williams hand-painted autographed football, Super Bowl XXII: $212.
- Jerry Rice hand-painted autographed football, Super Bowl XXIII: $306.
- Joe Montana hand-painted autographed football, Super Bowl XXIV: $220.
- Glenn Robinson autographed Spalding basketball, indoor/outdoor model: $
- Shaquille O'Neal autographed basketball, official Spalding NBA leather ball: $119.
- Shawn Kemp autographed Spalding Olympic model basketball: $119.
- David Robinson autographed Spalding basketball, indoor/outdoor model: $145
- Dominique Wilkins autographed basketball, official Spalding NBA leather ball: $109.
- Grant Hill autographed basketball, official Spalding NBA leather ball: $237.
- Reggie Miller autographed basketball, official Spalding NBA leather ball: $146.
- John Stockton autographed basketball, official Spalding NBA leather ball: $176.
- Joe Dumars autographed basketball, official Spalding NBA leather ball: $125.
- 1984-85 Philadelphia 76ers pennant, 12x20, red/white/blue with players' names: $45.
- 1982-83 Philadelphia 76ers World Championship pennant, 12x30, red/white/blue: $61.
- 1969 New York Knicks pennant, 12x30, white/orange/blue: $45.
- 1970s Kansas City Kings pennant, 12x30, red/white/blue: $25.
- 1982 Tampa Bay Bandits USFL pennant, 12x30, white/red/black: $20.
- 1982 Denver Gold USFL pennant, 12x30, white/black/gold: $20.
- 1982 Chicago Blitz USFL pennant, 12x30, white/blue/red: $25.
- 1982 Houston Gamblers pennant, 12x30, white/red/black/grey: $40.
- Philadelphia Eagles Super Bowl XV pennant, 12x30, NFC Champions: $618.
- 1987 New York Giants Super Bowl XXI pennant, 12x30, with team photo: $25.
- 1967 New York Jets pennant, 12x30, green and white: $73.
- 1960s Washington Redskins pennant, 12x30, helmet design with arrow, yellow and red: $180.
- 1960s Chicago Bears pennant, 12x30, shows a helmet: $61.
- 1960s San Francisco 49ers pennant, 12x30, shows a helmet, red/white/gold: $37.

- 1970s Oakland Raiders pennant, 12x30, black/silver/white: $40.
- 1970s Minnesota Vikings pennant, 12x30, shows helmet: $25.
- 1970s Pittsburgh Steelers pennant, 12x30, gold/black/white: $45.
- 1970s Los Angeles Rams pennant, 12x30, white/blue/gold: $20.
- 1970s Washington Redskins pennant, 12x30, Indian head on helmet: $30.
- 1960s Green Bay Packers pennant, VG, 12x30, shows helmet: $50.
- 1967 Cleveland Browns pennant, 12x30, shows helmet: $45.
- 1967 Philadelphia Eagles pennant, 12x30, shows helmet: $61.
- 1967 Buffalo Bills pennant, 12x30, blue/red/white: $70.
- 1980s St. Louis Cardinals pennant, 12x30, red and white: $28.
- 1980s Philadelphia Flyers pennant, 12x30, lists players: $30.
- Cleveland Browns stadium flag from Veterans Stadium in Philadelphia, 6x8, brown banner with orange letters: $98.
- Lot of five Michael Jordan Valentine boxes from Cleo, 32 per box, unopened, Jordan on the cover: $35.
- Super Bowl XXIII seat cushion, from GTE, given to fans attending the game: $66.
- 1966 Philadelphia Eagles NFL game film, a 5-inch reel from the Sept. 2, 1966, game against the Washington Redskins, still in its metal case: $50.
- Joe Namath 1960s transistor radio, works, with box: $97.
- George Blanda's Monday Nite Touchdown football game, from 1972, with all pieces: $40.
- Lew Alcindor autographed Sports Illustrated, April 3, 1967, issue, "How Alcindor Paralyzed the NCAA," 13x17 framed: $35
- John Hannah autographed Super Bowl XX program cover, says "Hall of Fame Class of 1991:" $15.
- Lot of two Sporting News National Football League Guides, 1972 and 1973 issues: $20.
- Troy Aikman autographed Sports Illustrated magazine, Feb. 3, 1993, issue: $67.
- Joe Namath autographed Sports Illustrated magazine, Dec. 9, 1968, issue: $81.
- Walter Payton autographed Sports Illustrated magazine, Dec. 8, 1986, issue: $50.
- Joe Montana autographed Sports Illustrated magazine, Dec. 24, 1990, issue: $128.
- Joe Namath autographed Sports Illustrated magazine, Aug. 11, 1968, issue: $74.
- Terry Bradshaw autographed Sport magazine, August 1980 issue: $25.
- Brett Hull comic book, given away at participating McDonalds restaurants in the St. Louis area: $20.

445

Chapter 16

Miscellaneous

Football

1970 Clark Oil/Volpe
Chicago Bears

Clark Oil issued between six and nine cards for each of eight NFL teams in 1970. The cards, featuring drawings by artist Nicholas Volpe, are unnumbered and are presented alphabetically under their corresponding teams. Each card measures 7 1/2" by 9 15/16", unless the bottom tab containing a business reply card for Clark Oil and Refining Corp. is in tact; then they measure 7 1/2" by 14". The back of the drawing descibes the various mail-in offers Clark Oil was offering, such as posters and tumblers. The cards are generally found with the reply card in tact and are priced on that condition.

		NM	EX	VG
Complete Set (8):		35.00	17.50	10.50
Common Player:		4.00	2.00	1.25
(1)	Ron Bull	4.00	2.00	1.25
(2)	Dick Butkus	15.00	7.50	4.50
(3)	Lee Roy Caffey	4.00	2.00	1.25
(4)	Bobby Douglass	5.00	2.50	1.50
(5)	Dick Gordon	4.00	2.00	1.25
(6)	Bennie McRae	4.00	2.00	1.25
(7)	Ed O'Bradovich	4.00	2.00	1.25
(8)	George Seals	4.00	2.00	1.25

1970 Clark Oil/Volpe
Cincinnati Bengals

		NM	EX	VG
Complete Set (6):		30.00	15.00	9.00
Common Player:		3.00	1.50	.90
(1)	Bill Bergey	6.00	3.00	1.75
(2)	Jess Phillips	3.00	1.50	.90
(3)	Mike Reid	7.00	3.50	2.00
(4)	Paul Robinson	4.00	2.00	1.25
(5)	Bob Trumpy	8.00	4.00	2.50
(6)	Sam Wyche	7.00	3.50	2.00

1970 Clark Oil/Volpe
Cleveland Browns

		NM	EX	VG
Complete Set (7):		30.00	15.00	9.00
Common Player:		3.00	1.50	.90
(1)	Erich Barnes	3.00	1.50	.90
(2)	Gary Collins	4.00	2.00	1.25
(3)	Gene Hickerson	3.00	1.50	.90
(4)	Jim Houston	3.00	1.50	.90
(5)	Leroy Kelly	10.00	5.00	3.00
(6)	Ernie Kellerman	3.00	1.50	.90
(7)	Bill Nelsen	5.00	2.50	1.50

1970 Clark Oil/Volpe
Detroit Lions

		NM	EX	VG
Complete Set (9):		40.00	20.00	12.00
Common Player:		3.50	1.75	1.00
(1)	Lem Barney	8.00	4.00	2.50
(2)	Mel Farr	5.00	2.50	1.50
(3)	Larry Hand	3.50	1.75	1.00
(4)	Alex Karras	10.00	5.00	3.00
(5)	Mike Lucci	4.00	2.00	1.25
(6)	Bill Munson	4.00	2.00	1.25
(7)	Charlie Sanders	4.50	2.25	1.25
(8)	Tommy Vaughn	3.50	1.75	1.00
(9)	Wayne Walker	3.50	1.75	1.00

1970 Clark Oil/Volpe
Green Bay Packers

		NM	EX	VG
Complete Set (9):		40.00	20.00	12.00
Common Player:		4.00	2.00	1.25
(1)	Lionel Aldridge	4.00	2.00	1.25
(2)	Donny Anderson	4.50	2.25	1.25
(3)	Ken Bowman	4.00	2.00	1.25
(4)	Carroll Dale	4.00	2.00	1.25
(5)	Jim Grabowski	5.00	2.50	1.50
(6)	Ray Nitschke	10.00	5.00	3.00
(7)	Dave Robinson	6.00	3.00	1.75
(8)	Travis Williams	4.00	2.00	1.25
(9)	Willie Wood	8.00	4.00	2.50

1970 Clark Oil/Volpe
Kansas City Chiefs

		NM	EX	VG
Complete Set (9):		35.00	17.50	10.50
Common Player:		3.00	1.50	.90
(1)	Fred Arbanas	3.00	1.50	.90
(2)	Bobby Bell	6.00	3.00	1.75
(3)	Aaron Brown	3.00	1.50	.90
(4)	Buck Buchanan	6.00	3.00	1.75
(5)	Len Dawson	8.00	4.00	2.50
(6)	Jim Marsalis	3.00	1.50	.90
(7)	Jerry Mays	3.00	1.50	.90
(8)	Johnny Robinson	4.00	2.00	1.25
(9)	Jim Tyrer	4.00	2.00	1.25

1970 Clark Oil/Volpe
Minnesota Vikings

		NM	EX	VG
Complete Set (9):		40.00	20.00	12.00
Common Player:		3.50	1.75	1.00
(1)	Bill Brown	4.50	2.25	1.25
(2)	Fred Cox	3.50	1.75	1.00
(3)	Gary Cuozzo	3.50	1.75	1.00
(4)	Carl Eller	7.00	3.50	2.00
(5)	Jim Marshall	7.00	3.50	2.00
(6)	Dave Osborn	3.50	1.75	1.00
(7)	Alan Page	8.00	4.00	2.50
(8)	Mike Tingelhoff	5.00	2.50	1.50
(9)	Gene Washington	5.00	2.50	1.50

1970 Clark Oil/Volpe
St. Louis Cardinals

		NM	EX	VG
Complete Set (9):		30.00	15.00	9.00
Common Player:		3.50	1.75	1.00
(1)	Pete Beathard	4.00	2.00	1.25
(2)	John Gilliam	5.00	2.50	1.50
(3)	Jim Hart	7.00	3.50	2.00
(4)	Johnny Roland	3.00	1.50	.90
(5)	Jackie Smith	6.00	3.00	1.75
(6)	Larry Stallings	3.50	1.75	1.00
(7)	Roger Wehrli	5.00	2.50	1.50
(8)	Dave Williams	3.50	1.75	1.00
(9)	Larry Wilson	7.00	3.50	2.00

1986 DairyPak Cartons

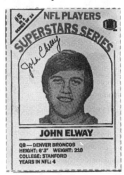

These cards were sponsored by various brands of milk across the country in 1986; different colors (purple, green, lavender, aqua, orange, red, light blue, dark blue, black and brown) were used for different sponsors. Each card is perforated and features a black-and-white head shot of the player, plus a facsimilie autograph and card number. Cards which have been cut from the milk carton measure 3 1/4" by 4 7/16", but generally are more valuable if they are left intact as a complete carton. The set was not licensed by the NFL, so no team logos are shown; the NFLPA, however, licensed the set. Below each card was an offer to receive a 24" by 32" poster featuring the 24 cards.

		MT	NM	EX
Complete Set (24):		65.00	49.00	26.00
Common Player:		1.25	.90	.50
1	Joe Montana	8.00	6.00	3.25
2	Marcus Allen	2.50	2.00	1.00
3	Art Monk	2.00	1.50	.80
4	Mike Quick	1.25	.90	.50

5	John Elway	3.00	2.25	1.25
6	Eric Hipple	1.25	.90	.50
7	Louis Lipps	1.25	.90	.50
8	Dan Fouts	2.00	1.50	.80
9	Phil Simms	2.00	1.50	.80
10	Mike Rozier	1.25	.90	.50
11	Greg Bell	1.25	.90	.50
12	Ottis Anderson	1.50	1.25	.60
13	Dave Krieg	1.75	1.25	.70
14	Anthony Carter	1.25	.90	.50
15	Freeman McNeil	1.25	.90	.50
16	Doug Cosbie	1.25	.90	.50
17	James Lofton	5.00	3.75	2.00
18	Dan Marino	5.00	3.75	2.00
19	James Wilder	1.25	.90	.50
20	Cris Collinsworth	1.50	1.25	.60
21	Eric Dickerson	4.00	3.00	1.50
22	Walter Payton	6.00	4.50	2.50
23	Ozzie Newsome	2.00	1.50	.80
24	Chris Hinton	1.25	.90	.50

1992 Dog Tags

These plastic dog tags were available as a boxed set from Chris Martin Enterprises Inc. Each tag has a color action photo on the front, with the player's name, position and team information at the bottom. The top of each dog tag has a Team NFL logo and a hole so it can be worn on a chain. Each back has a mug shot of the player, 1991 statistics and a recap of the 1991 season. A panel for an autograph is also included. The cards are numbered on both sides; cards 1-28 are team cards, while 29-76 are player cards. There were also five rookie tags made; they have a gold foil border stripe at the top, compared to the white stripe used for a regular player card. All cards have rounded borders.

		MT	NM	EX
Complete Set (81):		80.00	60.00	32.00
Common Player:		.50	.40	.20
1	Atlanta Falcons	.50	.40	.20
2	Buffalo Bills	.60	.45	.25
3	Chicago Bears	.50	.40	.20
4	Cincinnati Bengals	.50	.40	.20
5	Cleveland Browns	.50	.40	.20
6	Dallas Cowboys	.75	.60	.30
7	Denver Broncos	.50	.40	.20
8	Detroit Lions	.75	.60	.30
9	Green Bay Packers	.50	.40	.20
10	Houston Oilers	.50	.40	.20
11	Indianapolis Colts	.50	.40	.20
12	Kansas City Chiefs	.75	.60	.30
13	Los Angeles Raiders	.75	.60	.30
14	New England Patriots	.50	.40	.20
15	Miami Dolphins	.75	.60	.30
16	Minnesota Vikins	.50	.40	.20
17	New England Patriots	.50	.40	.20
18	New Orleans Saints	.50	.40	.20
19	New York Giants	.65	.50	.25
20	New York Jets	.50	.40	.20
21	Philadelphia Eagles	.50	.40	.20
22	Phoenix Cardinals	.60	.45	.25
23	Pittsburgh Steelers	.50	.40	.20
24	San Diego Chargers	.50	.40	.20
25	San Francisco 49ers	.75	.60	.30
26	Seattle Seahawks	.50	.40	.20
27	Tampa Bay Buccaneers	.50	.40	.20
28	Washington Redskins	.50	.40	.20
29	Chris Martin	1.00	.70	.40
30	Dan Marino	5.00	3.75	2.00
31	Chris Miller	1.50	1.25	.60
32	Deion Sanders	2.50	2.00	1.00
33	Jim Kelly	2.50	2.00	1.00
34	Thurman Thomas	3.00	2.25	1.25
35	Jim Harbaugh	1.25	.90	.50

36	Mike Singletary	1.00	.70	.40
37	Boomer Esiason	1.00	.70	.40
38	Anthony Munoz	1.50	1.25	.60
39	Bernie Kosar	1.00	.70	.40
40	Troy Aikman	6.00	4.50	2.50
41	Michael Irvin	3.50	2.75	1.50
42	Emmitt Smith	7.50	5.75	3.00
43	John Elway	3.00	2.25	1.25
44	Rodney Peete	1.50	1.25	.60
45	Sterling Sharpe	3.00	2.25	1.25
46	Haywood Jeffires	2.00	1.50	.80
47	Warren Moon	2.00	1.50	.80
48	Jeff George	2.00	1.50	.80
49	Christian Okoye	1.00	.70	.40
50	Derrick Thomas	2.00	1.50	.80
51	Howie Long	1.00	.70	.40
52	Ronnie Lott	1.25	.90	.50
53	Jim Everett	1.00	.70	.40
54	Mark Clayton	1.00	.70	.40
55	Anthony Carter	1.00	.70	.40
56	Chris Doleman	1.00	.70	.40
57	Andre Tippett	.85	.60	.35
58	Pat Swilling	1.00	.70	.40
59	Jeff Hostetler	1.50	1.25	.60
60	Lawrence Taylor	1.50	1.25	.60
61	Rob Moore	1.50	1.25	.60
62	Ken O'Brien	.75	.60	.30
63	Keith Byars	1.00	.70	.40
64	Randall Cunningham	2.00	1.50	.80
65	Johnny Johnson	2.00	1.50	.80
66	Timm Rosenbach	.75	.60	.30
67	Bubby Brister	.75	.60	.30
68	John Friesz	1.25	.90	.50
69	Jerry Rice	3.50	2.75	1.50
70	Steve Young	2.75	2.00	1.00
71	Dan McGwire	.75	.60	.30
72	Broderick Thomas	.75	.60	.30
73	Vinny Testaverde	1.00	.70	.40
74	Gary Clark	1.25	.90	.50
75	Mark Rypien	1.25	.90	.50
76	Neil Smith	1.00	.70	.40
1R	Dale Carter	1.50	1.25	.60
2R	Steve Emtman	1.50	1.25	.60
3R	David Klingler	3.00	2.25	1.25
4R	Tommy Maddox	2.50	2.00	1.00
5R	Vaughn Dunbar	1.50	1.25	.60

1993 Dog Tags

Chris Martin Enterprises Inc. increased its 1992 set total to 138 dog tags for its 1993 issue. Twenty-eight teams and 110 players are represented in the set, which did not have tags made for numbers 48 and 138. The cards are numbered on the back, which features a mug shot of the player, 1992 statistics, a player profile, biographical information and an autograph panel, all against a team color-coded background. The front of the plastic tag has a full-bleed action photo, along with the player's name at the bottom. "1993" and "Dog Tags" are stamped in gold foil at the top, near where a hole has been punched to allow the tag to be worn on a chain.

		MT	NM	EX
	Complete Set (138):	130.00	97.00	52.00
	Common Player:	.50	.40	.20
1	Atlanta Falcons	.60	.45	.25
2	Buffalo Bills	.50	.40	.20
3	Chicago Bears	.50	.40	.20
4	Cincinnati Bengals	.50	.40	.20
5	Cleveland Browns	.50	.40	.20
6	Dallas Cowboys	.75	.60	.30
7	Denver Broncos	.50	.40	.20
8	Detroit Lions	.50	.40	.20
9	Green Bay Packers	.60	.45	.25
10	Houston Oilers	.50	.40	.20
11	Indianapolis Colts	.50	.40	.20

12	Kansas City Chiefs	.50	.40	.20
13	Los Angeles Raiders	.75	.60	.30
14	Los Angeles Rams	.50	.40	.20
15	Miami Dolphins	.75	.60	.30
16	Minnesota Vikings	.50	.40	.20
17	New England Patriots	.50	.40	.20
18	New Orleans Saints	.65	.50	.25
19	New York Giants	.50	.40	.20
20	New York Jets	.50	.40	.20
21	Philadelphia Eagles	.65	.50	.25
22	Phoenix Cardinals	.50	.40	.20
23	Pittsburgh Steelers	.50	.40	.20
24	San Diego Chargers	.50	.40	.20
25	San Francisco 49ers	.75	.60	.30
26	Seattle Seahawks	.50	.40	.20
27	Tampa Bay Buccaneers	.50	.40	.20
28	Washington Redskins	.50	.40	.20
29	Steve Broussard	.50	.40	.20
30	Chris Miller	1.50	1.25	.60
31	Andre Rison	1.50	1.25	.60
32	Deion Sanders	2.00	1.50	.80
33	Cornelius Bennett	1.00	.70	.40
34	Jim Kelly	2.50	2.00	1.00
35	Bruce Smith	1.25	.90	.50
36	Thurman Thomas	2.50	2.00	1.00
37	Neal Anderson	.75	.60	.30
38	Mark Carrier	.75	.60	.30
39	Jim Harbaugh	.75	.60	.30
40	Alonzo Spellman	1.00	.70	.40
41	David Fulcher	.50	.40	.20
42	Harold Green	.75	.60	.30
43	David Klingler	1.50	1.25	.60
44	Carl Pickens	1.25	.90	.50
45	Bernie Kosar	1.00	.70	.40
46	Clay Matthews	1.25	.90	.50
47	Eric Metcalf	1.00	.70	.40
49	Troy Aikman	5.00	3.75	2.00
50	Michael Irvin	2.50	2.00	1.00
51	Russell Maryland	1.00	.70	.40
52	Emmitt Smith	6.00	4.50	2.50
53	Steve Atwater	.75	.60	.30
54	John Elway	4.00	3.00	1.50
55	Tommy Maddox	1.25	.90	.50
56	Shannon Sharpe	1.50	1.25	.60
57	Herman Moore	1.25	.90	.50
58	Rodney Peete	.75	.60	.30
59	Barry Sanders	4.00	3.00	1.50
60	Andre Ware	.75	.60	.30
61	Terrell Buckley	.75	.60	.30
62	Brett Favre	2.50	2.00	1.00
63	Sterling Sharpe	3.00	2.25	1.25
64	Reggie White	1.50	1.25	.60
65	Ray Childress	.90	.70	.35
66	Haywood Jeffires	1.25	.90	.50
67	Warren Moon	2.50	2.00	1.00
68	Lorenzo White	.75	.60	.30
69	Duane Bickett	.75	.60	.30
70	Quentin Coryatt	1.00	.70	.40
71	Steve Emtman	.80	.60	.30
72	Jeff George	1.50	1.25	.60
73	Dale Carter	1.00	.70	.40
74	Neil Smith	1.00	.70	.40
75	Derrick Thomas	2.50	2.00	1.00
76	Harvey Williams	1.25	.90	.50
77	Eric Dickerson	1.25	.90	.50
78	Howie Long	.75	.60	.30
79	Todd Marinovich	.50	.40	.20
80	Alexander Wright	.75	.60	.30
81	Flipper Anderson	.50	.40	.20
82	Jim Everett	.75	.60	.30
83	Cleveland Gary	.50	.40	.20
84	Chris Martin	.50	.40	.20
85	Irving Fryar	.85	.60	.35
86	Keith Jackson	1.25	.90	.50
87	Dan Marino	6.00	4.50	2.50
88	Louis Oliver	.50	.40	.20
89	Terry Allen	1.00	.70	.40
90	Anthony Carter	.50	.40	.20

		NM	EX	VG
91	Chris Doleman	.75	.60	.30
92	Rich Gannon	.60	.45	.25
93	Eugene Chung	.50	.40	.20
94	Marv Cook	.50	.40	.20
95	Leonard Russell	1.00	.70	.40
96	Andre Tippett	.75	.60	.30
97	Morten Anderson	.50	.40	.20
98	Vaughn Dunbar	.75	.60	.30
99	Rickey Jackson	.75	.60	.30
100	Sam Mills	.50	.40	.20
101	Derek Brown	.75	.60	.30
102	Lawrence Taylor	2.00	1.50	.80
103	Rodney Hampton	2.00	1.50	.80
104	Phil Simms	1.25	.90	.50
105	Johnny Mitchell	1.00	.70	.40
106	Rob Moore	1.00	.70	.40
107	Blair Thomas	.75	.60	.30
108	Browning Nagle	1.00	.70	.40
109	Eric Allen	.50	.40	.20
110	Fred Barnett	1.25	.90	.50
111	Randall Cunningham	2.00	1.50	.80
112	Herschel Walker	.75	.60	.30
113	Chris Chandler	.75	.60	.30
114	Randal Hill	1.00	.70	.40
115	Ricky Proehl	.75	.60	.30
116	Eric Swann	.75	.60	.30
117	Barry Foster	1.75	1.25	.70
118	Eric Green	1.25	.90	.50
119	Neil O'Donnell	1.50	1.25	.60
120	Rod Woodson	1.00	.70	.40
121	Marion Butts	1.00	.70	.40
122	Stan Humphries	1.75	1.25	.70
123	Anthony Miller	1.00	.70	.40
124	Junior Seau	1.50	1.25	.60
125	Amp Lee	1.00	.70	.40
126	Jerry Rice	4.00	3.00	1.50
127	Ricky Watters	2.25	1.75	.90
128	Steve Young	2.50	2.00	1.00
129	Brian Blades	.75	.60	.30
130	Cortez Kennedy	1.00	.70	.40
131	Dan McGwire	.75	.60	.30
132	John L. Williams	.75	.60	.30
133	reggie Cobb	1.00	.70	.40
134	Steve DeBerg	.50	.40	.20
135	Keith McCants	.75	.60	.30
136	Broderick Thomas	.75	.60	.30
137	Earnest Byner	.75	.60	.30
139	Mark Rypien	.50	.40	.20
140	Ricky Sanders	.75	.60	.30

1978 Marketcom Test

These unnumbered posters, featuring 32 NFL stars, measure 5 1/2" by 8 1/2". The fronts feature full-color photos, along with the player's name in the upper left corner. Marketcom, which produced the set, is listed in the lower right corner. The backs are blank.

		NM	EX	VG
Complete Set (32):		225.00	112.00	67.00
Common Player:		3.25	1.75	1.00
(1)	Otis Armstrong	6.00	3.00	1.75
(2)	Steve Bartkowski	9.00	4.50	2.75
(3)	Terry Bradshaw	25.00	12.50	7.50
(4)	Earl Campbell	25.00	12.50	7.50
(5)	Dave Casper	5.00	2.50	1.50
(6)	Dan Dierdorf	10.00	5.00	3.00
(7)	Dan Fouts	15.00	7.50	4.50
(8)	Tony Galbreath	3.25	1.75	1.00
(9)	Randy Gradishar	7.00	3.50	2.00
(10)	Bob Griese	12.00	6.00	3.50
(11)	Steve Grogan	5.00	2.50	1.50
(12)	Ray Guy	6.00	3.00	1.75
(13)	Pat Haden	8.00	4.00	2.50
(14)	Jack Ham	7.00	3.50	2.00
(15)	Cliff Harris	7.00	3.50	2.00
(16)	Franco Harris	8.00	4.00	2.50
(17)	Jim Hart	5.00	2.50	1.50

		NM	EX	VG
18	Ron Jaworski	5.00	2.50	1.50
19	Bert Jones	10.00	5.00	3.00
20	Jack Lambert	10.00	5.00	3.00
21	Reggie McKenzie	3.25	1.75	1.00
22	Karl Mecklenberg	7.00	3.50	2.00
23	Craig Morton	5.00	2.50	1.50
24	Dan Pastorini	3.25	1.75	1.00
25	Walter Payton	25.00	12.50	7.50
26	Lee Roy Selmon	5.00	2.50	1.50
27	Roger Staubach	25.00	12.50	7.50
28	Joe Theismann (misspelled Theisman)	9.00	4.50	2.75
29	Wesley Walker	7.00	3.50	2.00
30	Randy White	7.00	3.50	2.00
31	Jack Youngblood	12.00	6.00	3.50
32	Jim Zorn	5.00	2.50	1.50

1980 Marketcom

These white-bordered posters, measuring 5 1/2" by 8 1/2", feature 50 NFL stars. The player's name appears at the top of the card; Marketcom, the set's producer, is credited in the bottom lower right corner. A white facsimile autograph also appears on the card front. The back has the player's name at the top, and a card number on the bottom (Mini-Poster 1 of 50, etc.). Marketcom, of St. Louis, sold the posters in packs of five.

		NM	EX	VG
Complete Set (50):		25.00	12.50	7.50
Common Player:		.50	.25	.15
1	Ottis Anderson	1.00	.50	.30
2	Brian Sipe	.60	.30	.20
3	Lawrence McCutcheon	.60	.30	.20
4	Ken Anderson	1.25	.60	.40
5	Roland Harper	.50	.25	.15
6	Chuck Foreman	.75	.40	.25
7	Gary Danielson	.50	.25	.15
8	Wallace Francis	.50	.25	.15
9	John Jefferson	.75	.40	.25
10	Charlie Waters	.75	.40	.25
11	Jack Ham	1.00	.50	.30
12	Jack Lambert	1.25	.60	.40
13	Walter Payton	5.00	2.50	1.50
14	Bert Jones	1.00	.50	.30
15	Harvey Martin	.75	.40	.25
16	Jim Hart	.60	.30	.20
17	Craig Morton	.75	.40	.25
18	Reggie McKenzie	.50	.25	.15
19	Keith Wortman	.50	.25	.15
20	Otis Armstrong	.75	.40	.25
21	Steve Grogan	.75	.40	.25
22	Jim Zorn	.75	.40	.25
23	Bob Griese	2.00	1.00	.60
24	Tony Dorsett	2.00	1.00	.60
25	Wesley Walker	.75	.40	.25
26	Dan Fouts	2.00	1.00	.60
27	Dan Dierdorf	1.00	.50	.30

Miscellaneous

28	Steve Bartkowski	.75	.40	.25
29	Archie Manning	1.00	.50	.30
30	Randy Gradishar	.75	.40	.25
31	Randy White	1.25	.60	.40
32	Joe Theismann	2.00	1.00	.60
33	Tony Galbreath	.50	.25	.15
34	Cliff Harris	.75	.40	.25
35	Ray Guy	1.00	.50	.30
36	Dave Casper	.75	.40	.25
37	Ron Jaworski	.75	.40	.25
38	Greg Pruitt	.75	.40	.25
39	Ken Burrough	.60	.30	.20
40	Robert Brazile	.60	.30	.20
41	Pat Haden	1.00	.50	.30
42	Dan Pastorini	.60	.30	.20
43	Lee Roy Selmon	.75	.40	.25
44	Franco Harris	2.00	1.00	.60
45	Jack Youngblood	1.25	.60	.40
46	Terry Bradshaw	5.00	2.50	1.50
47	Roger Staubach	6.00	3.00	1.75
48	Earl Campbell	5.00	2.50	1.50
49	Phil Simms	3.00	1.50	.90
50	Delvin Williams	.50	.25	.15

1981 Marketcom

The 1981 Marketcom posters are the first set to include detailed information on the back of the poster. Along with biographical and statistical information for 1980 and for the player's career, a comprehensive summary of the player's accomplishments is provided. A poster number is also given. Each poster, measuring 5 1/2" by 8 1/2", has a full-color action photo of the player on the front, along with his facsimile signature. His name is listed in the upper left corner.

		MT	NM	EX
Complete Set (50):		32.00	24.00	13.00
Common Player:		.50	.40	.20
1	Ottis Anderson	.75	.60	.30
2	Brian Sipe	.60	.45	.25
3	Rocky Bleier	.75	.60	.30
4	Ken Anderson	1.00	.70	.40
5	Roland Harper	.50	.40	.20
6	Steve Furness	.50	.40	.20
7	Gary Danielson	.50	.40	.20
8	Wallace Francis	.60	.45	.25
9	John Jefferson	.60	.45	.25
10	Charlie Waters	.75	.60	.30
11	Jack Ham	.75	.60	.30
12	Jack Lambert	1.25	.90	.50
13	Walter Payton	5.00	3.75	2.00
14	Bert Jones	1.00	.70	.40
15	Harvey Martin	.75	.60	.30
16	Jim Hart	.75	.60	.30
17	Craig Morton	.75	.60	.30
18	Reggie McKenzie	.50	.40	.20
19	Keith Wortman	.50	.40	.20
20	Joe Greene	1.50	1.25	.60
21	Steve Grogan	.75	.60	.30
22	Jim Zorn	.75	.60	.30
23	Bob Griese	2.00	1.50	.80
24	Tony Dorsett	2.50	2.00	1.00
25	Wesley Walker	.75	.60	.30
26	Dan Fouts	2.00	1.50	.80
27	Dan Dierdorf	1.00	.70	.40
28	Steve Bartkowski	.75	.60	.30
29	Archie Manning	1.00	.70	.40
30	Randy Gradishar	.75	.60	.30
31	Randy White	1.25	.90	.50
32	Joe Theismann	2.00	1.50	.80
33	Tony Galbreath	.50	.40	.20
34	Cliff Harris	.75	.60	.30
35	Ray Guy	1.00	.70	.40
36	Joe Ferguson	.75	.60	.30
37	Ron Jaworski	.75	.60	.30
38	Greg Pruitt	.75	.60	.30

39	Ken Burrough	.60	.45	.25
40	Robert Brazile	.50	.40	.20
41	Pat Haden	1.00	.70	.40
42	Ken Stabler	2.00	1.50	.80
43	Lee Roy Selmon	.75	.60	.30
44	Franco Harris	2.00	1.50	.80
45	Jack Youngblood	1.25	.90	.50
46	Terry Bradshaw	6.00	4.50	2.50
47	Roger Staubach	6.00	4.50	2.50
48	Earl Campbell	4.00	3.00	1.50
49	Phil Simms	1.50	1.25	.60
50	Delvin Williams	.50	.40	.20

1982 Marketcom

These 50 mini posters from Marketcom are similar in design to the previous year's issue. Each poster is 5 1/2" by 8 1/2" and has a full-color action photo on the front, along with a facsimile signature in white letters. The backs are similar to the backs of the 1981 posters - they have a detailed career summary and biographical information, plus statistics for the player's career and 1981 season. In addition to a number, the back also says "St. Louis - Marketcom - Series C".

		MT	NM	EX
Complete Set (48):		175.00	100.00	85.00
Common Player:		2.00	1.50	.80
1	Joe Ferguson	2.50	2.00	1.00
2	Kellen Winslow	3.00	2.25	1.25
3	Jim Hart	2.50	2.00	1.00
4	Archie Manning	4.00	3.00	1.50
5	Earl Campbell	15.00	11.00	6.00
6	Wallace Francis	2.00	1.50	.80
7	Randy Gradishar	2.50	2.00	1.00
8	Ken Stabler	5.00	3.75	2.00
9	Danny White	3.00	2.25	1.25
10	Jack Ham	4.00	3.00	1.50
11	Lawrence Taylor	20.00	15.00	8.00
12	Eric Hipple	2.00	1.50	.80
13	Ron Jaworski	2.50	2.00	1.00
14	George Rogers	2.00	1.50	.80
15	Jack Lambert	5.00	3.75	2.00
16	Randy White	5.00	3.75	2.00
17	Terry Bradshaw	15.00	11.00	6.00
18	Ray Guy	3.00	2.25	1.25
19	Rob Carpenter	2.00	1.50	.80
20	Reggie McKenzie	2.00	1.50	.80
21	Tony Dorsett	7.50	5.75	3.00
22	Wesley Walker	2.50	2.00	1.00
23	Tommy Kramer	2.50	2.00	1.00
24	Dwight Clark	3.00	2.25	1.25
25	Franco Harris	5.00	3.75	2.00
26	Craig Morton	2.50	2.00	1.00
27	Harvey Martin	2.50	2.00	1.00
28	Jim Zorn	2.50	2.00	1.00
29	Steve Bartkowski	2.50	2.00	1.00
30	Joe Theismann	5.00	3.75	2.00
31	Dan Dierdorf	3.00	2.25	1.25
32	Walter Payton	20.00	15.00	8.00
33	John Jefferson	2.50	2.00	1.00
34	Phil Simms	5.00	3.75	2.00
35	Lee Roy Selmon	2.50	2.00	1.00
36	Joe Montana	35.00	26.00	14.00
37	Robert Brazile	2.00	1.50	.80
38	Steve Grogan	2.50	2.00	1.00
39	Dave Logan	2.00	1.50	.80
40	Ken Anderson	4.00	3.00	1.50
41	Richard Todd	2.50	2.00	1.00
42	Jack Youngblood	3.00	2.25	1.25
43	Ottis Anderson	3.00	2.25	1.25
44	Brian Sipe	2.50	2.00	1.00
45	Mark Gastineau	2.50	2.00	1.00
46	Mike Pruitt	2.00	1.50	.80
47	Cris Collinsworth	2.50	2.00	1.00
48	Dan Fouts	5.00	3.75	2.00

1974 Parker Pro Draft

These 50 cards were included inside a Parker Brothers board game called Pro Draft. The cards, featuring only offensive players, were produced by Topps and use the identical design as the 1974 Topps set. However, some differences can be noted on certain cards. Some of the game cards have 1972 statistics on the card backs, and others have different player poses on the front (#s 23, 49, 116, 124, 126 and 127). Players with an * have 1972 statistics. Card numbers in this set are identical to the card numbers the players have in the regular 1974 Topps set.

		NM	EX	VG
Complete Set (50):		75.00	37.00	22.00
Common Player:		1.00	.50	.30
4	Ken Bowman	1.00	.50	.30
6	Jerry Smith*	3.00	1.50	.90
7	Ed Podolak*	2.50	1.25	.70
9	Pat Matson	1.00	.50	.30
11	Frank Pitts*	2.00	1.00	.60
15	Winston Hill	1.00	.50	.30
18	Rich Coady*	2.00	1.00	.60
19	Ken Willard*	3.75	2.00	1.25
21	Ben Hawkins*	2.00	1.00	.60
23	Norm Snead* (vertical pose)	10.00	5.00	3.00
24	Jim Yarborough*	2.00	1.00	.60
28	Bob Hayes*	5.00	2.50	1.50
32	Dan Dierdorf	8.00	4.00	2.50
35	Essex Johnson*	2.00	1.00	.60
39	Mike Siani	1.00	.50	.30
42	Del Williams	1.00	.50	.30
43	Don McCauley*	2.00	1.00	.60
44	Randy Jackson*	2.00	1.00	.60
46	Gene Washington*	3.50	1.75	1.00
49	Bob Windsor* (vertical pose)	6.00	3.00	1.75
50	John Hadl*	4.00	2.00	1.25
52	Steve Owens*	4.00	2.00	1.25
54	Rayfield Wright*	2.00	1.00	.60
57	Milt Sunde*	2.00	1.00	.60
58	Bill Kilmer*	5.50	2.75	1.75
61	Rufus Mayes*	2.00	1.00	.60
63	Gene Washington*	2.50	1.25	.70
65	Eugene Upshaw	4.50	2.25	1.25
75	Fred Willis*	2.00	1.00	.60
77	Tom Neville	1.00	.50	.30
78	Ted Kwalick*	3.00	1.50	.90
80	John Niland*	2.00	1.00	.60
81	Ted Fritsch Jr.	1.00	.50	.30
83	Jack Snow*	3.00	1.50	.90
87	Mike Phipps*	3.00	1.50	.90
90	MacArthur Lane*	3.00	1.50	.90
95	Calvin Hill*	3.50	1.75	1.00
98	Len Rohde	1.00	.50	.30
101	Gary Garrison*	2.50	1.25	.70
103	Len St. Jean	1.00	.50	.30

107	Jim Mitchell*	2.00	1.00	.60
109	Harry Schuh	1.00	.50	.30
110	Greg Pruitt*	4.00	2.00	1.25
111	Ed Flanagan	1.00	.50	.30
113	Chuck Foreman*	6.00	3.00	1.75
116	Charlie Johnson* (vertical pose)	8.00	4.00	2.50
119	Roy Jefferson*	4.00	2.00	1.25
124	Forrest Blue (not All-Pro on card)	6.00	3.00	1.75
126	Tom Mack* (not All-Pro on card)	8.00	4.00	2.50
127	Bob Tucker* (not All-Pro on card)	6.00	3.00	1.75

1981 Shell Posters

The works of three different artists are featured on these 10 7/8" by 13 7/8" posters available at participating Shell Oil stations across the country in 1981. Each poster has a black-and-white drawing of the featured player, as rendered by either K. Atkins, Nick Galloway or Tanenbawm (these signatures are on the corresponding poster fronts). There are, however, some posters which were not signed by the artist (#s 7, 11, 12 and 93). The posters are listed alphabetically by teams, then alphabetically by players. Team sets consist of six posters. A national set of six posters was also made (Payton, Griffin, Logan, Pearson, Campbell and O. Anderson) and was available in markets where a pro team did not exist.

		MT	NM	EX
Complete Set (96):		400.00	300.00	160.00
Common Player:		4.00	3.00	1.50
(1)	William Andrews	5.00	3.75	2.00
(2)	Steve Bartkowski	7.00	5.25	2.75
(3)	Buddy Curry	3.50	2.75	1.50
(4)	Wallace Francis	5.00	3.75	2.00
(5)	Mike Kenn	5.00	3.75	2.00
(6)	Jeff Van Note	5.00	3.75	2.00
(7)	Mike Barnes	4.00	3.00	1.50
(8)	Roger Carr	4.00	3.00	1.50
(9)	Curtis Dickey	5.00	3.75	2.00
(10)	Bert Jones	7.00	5.25	2.75
(11)	Bruce Laird	4.00	3.00	1.50
(12)	Randy McMillan	5.00	3.75	2.00
(13)	Brian Baschnagel	4.00	3.00	1.50
(14)	Vince Evans	5.00	3.75	2.00
(15)	Gary Fencik	5.00	3.75	2.00
(16)	Roland Harper	4.00	3.00	1.50
(17)	Alan Page	9.00	6.75	3.50
(18)	Walter Payton	10.00	7.50	4.00
(19)	Ken Anderson	8.00	6.00	3.25
(20)	Ross Browner	5.00	3.75	2.00
(21)	Archie Griffin	4.00	3.00	1.50
(22)	Pat McInally	5.00	3.75	2.00
(23)	Anthony Munoz	8.00	6.00	3.25
(24)	Reggie Williams	5.00	3.75	2.00
(25)	Lyle Alzado	6.00	4.50	2.50
(26)	Joe DeLamielleure	4.00	3.00	1.50
(27)	Doug Dieken	4.00	3.00	1.50
(28)	Dave Logan	4.00	3.00	1.50
(29)	Reggie Rucker	5.00	3.75	2.00
(30)	Brian Sipe	5.00	3.75	2.00
(31)	Benny Barnes	4.00	3.00	1.50
(32)	Bob Breunig	4.00	3.00	1.50
(33)	D.D. Lewis	4.00	3.00	1.50
(34)	Harvey Martin	6.00	4.50	2.50
(35)	Drew Pearson	4.00	3.00	1.50
(36)	Rafael Septien	4.00	3.00	1.50
(37)	Al (Bubba) Baker	5.00	3.75	2.00
(38)	Dexter Bussey	4.00	3.00	1.50
(39)	Gary Danielson	5.00	3.75	2.00
(40)	Freddie Scott	4.00	3.00	1.50
(41)	Billy Sims	6.00	4.50	2.50
(42)	Tom Skladany	4.00	3.00	1.50

(43)	Robert Brazile	6.00	4.50	2.50
(44)	Ken Burrough	6.00	4.50	2.50
(45)	Earl Campbell	9.00	6.75	3.50
(46)	Leon Gray	5.00	3.75	2.00
(47)	Carl Mauck	5.00	3.75	2.00
(48)	Ken Stabler	8.00	6.00	3.25
(49)	Bob Baumhower	5.00	3.75	2.00
(50)	Jimmy Cefalo	5.00	3.75	2.00
(51)	A.J. Duhe	5.00	3.75	2.00
(52)	Nat Moore	6.00	4.50	2.50
(53)	Ed Newman	4.00	3.00	1.50
(54)	Uwe Von Schamann	4.00	3.00	1.50
(55)	Steve Grogan	7.00	5.25	2.75
(56)	John Hannah	4.50	3.50	1.75
(57)	Don Hasselbeck	4.00	3.00	1.50
(58)	Mike Haynes	6.00	4.50	2.50
(59)	Harold Jackson	5.00	3.75	2.00
(60)	Steve Nelson	4.00	3.00	1.50
(61)	Elois Grooms	5.00	3.75	2.00
(62)	Rickey Jackson	7.50	5.75	3.00
(63)	Archie Manning	8.00	6.00	3.25
(64)	Tommy Myers	5.00	3.75	2.00
(65)	Benny Ricardo	5.00	3.75	2.00
(66)	George Rogers	6.00	4.50	2.50
(67)	Harry Carson	7.00	5.25	2.75
(68)	Dave Jennings	4.00	3.00	1.50
(69)	Gary Jeter	4.00	3.00	1.50
(70)	Phil Simms	8.00	6.00	3.25
(71)	Lawrence Taylor	12.00	9.00	4.75
(72)	Brad Van Pelt	5.00	3.75	2.00
(73)	Greg Buttle	5.00	3.75	2.00
(74)	Bruce Harper	4.00	3.00	1.50
(75)	Joe Klecko	5.00	3.75	2.00
(76)	Randy Rasmussen	4.00	3.00	1.50
(77)	Richard Todd	5.00	3.75	2.00
(78)	Wesley Walker	6.00	4.50	2.50
(79)	Ottis Anderson	4.00	3.00	1.50
(80)	Dan Dierdorf	9.00	6.75	3.50
(81)	Mel Gray	5.00	3.75	2.00
(82)	Jim Hart	6.00	4.50	2.50
(83)	E.J. Junior	5.00	3.75	2.00
(84)	Pat Tilley	5.00	3.75	2.00
(85)	Jimmie Giles	5.00	3.75	2.00
(86)	Charley Hannah	4.00	3.00	1.50
(87)	Bill Kollar	4.00	3.00	1.50
(88)	David Lewis	4.00	3.00	1.50
(89)	Lee Roy Selmon	6.00	4.50	2.50
(90)	Doug Williams	5.00	3.75	2.00
(91)	Joe Lavender	4.00	3.00	1.50
(92)	Mark Moseley	5.00	3.75	2.00
(93)	Mark Murphy	4.00	3.00	1.50
(94)	Lemar Parrish	5.00	3.75	2.00
(95)	John Riggins	9.00	6.75	3.50
(96)	Joe Washington	5.00	3.75	2.00

6D	Otto Graham	6.00	3.00	1.75
7D	Chuck Bednarik	4.00	2.00	1.25
8D	Jim Taylor	3.00	1.50	.90
9D	Mel Hein	2.00	1.00	.60
10D	Eddie Price	1.50	.70	.45
11D	Sonny Randle	1.50	.70	.45
12D	Joe Perry	4.00	2.00	1.25
13D	Bob Waterfield	5.00	2.50	1.50
1H	NFL Logo	1.50	.70	.45
2H	Paul Hornung	5.00	2.50	1.50
3H	Johnny Unitas	10.00	5.00	3.00
4H	Doak Walker	5.00	2.50	1.50
5H	Tom Fears	3.00	1.50	.90
6H	Jim Thorpe	10.00	5.00	3.00
7H	Gino Marchetti	3.00	1.50	.90
8H	Claude Buddy Young	1.50	.70	.45
9H	Jim Benton	2.00	1.00	.60
10H	Jim Brown	12.00	6.00	3.50
11H	George Halas	1.50	.70	.45
12H	Sammy Baugh	4.00	2.00	1.25
13H	Bill Dudley	2.50	1.25	.70
1S	NFL Logo	1.50	.70	.45
2S	Eddie LeBaron	2.00	1.00	.60
3S	Don Hutson	3.50	1.75	1.00
4S	Clarke Hinkle	2.00	1.00	.60
5S	Charley Conerly	2.50	1.25	.70
6S	Earl Curly Lambeau	2.00	1.00	.60
7S	Sid Luckman	5.00	2.50	1.50
8S	Pete Pihos	2.00	1.00	.60
9S	Dante Lavelli	2.00	1.00	.60
10S	Norm Van Brocklin	4.00	2.00	1.25
11S	Cloyce Box	1.50	.70	.45
12S	Joe Schmidt	3.00	1.50	.90
13S	Elroy Hirsch	3.00	1.50	.90

1962 Topps Bucks

This 48-"card" set was issued one per wax pack in the 1962 Topps football issue. The 1 1/4 by 4 1/4 "cards" have a dollar bill motif with the player's head in the middle and his name underneath. Backs show the same motif, with the NFL and team logo encircled. The Topps Bucks were printed on this white paper.

1963 Stancraft Playing Cards

	NM	EX	VG
Complete Set (54):	100.00	50.00	30.00
Common Player:	1.50	.70	.45
1C	NFL Logo	1.50	.70	.45
2C	Johnny Blood McNally	2.00	1.00	.60
3C	Bobby Mitchell	3.00	1.50	.90
4C	Bill Howton	1.50	.70	.45
5C	Wilbur Fats Henry	2.00	1.00	.60
6C	Tony Canedeo	2.00	1.00	.60
7C	Bulldog Turner	3.00	1.50	.90
8C	Charlie Trippi	2.00	1.00	.60
9C	Tommy Mason	1.50	.70	.45
10C	Earl Dutch Clark	2.00	1.00	.60
11C	Y.A. Tittle	5.00	2.50	1.50
12C	Lou Groza	5.00	2.50	1.50
13C	Bobby Layne	6.00	3.00	1.75
1D	NFL Logo	1.50	.70	.45
2D	Frankie Albert	1.50	.70	.45
3D	Del Shofner	1.50	.70	.45
4D	Ollie Matson	4.00	2.00	1.25
5D	Mike Ditka	8.00	4.00	2.50

	NM	EX	VG
Complete Set (48):	400.00	200.00	120.00
Common Player:	4.50	2.25	1.35
1	J.D. Smith	4.50	2.25	1.35
2	Bart Starr	25.00	12.50	7.50
3	Dick James	4.50	2.25	1.35
4	Alex Webster	6.00	3.00	1.75
5	Paul Hornung	18.00	9.00	5.50
6	John David Crow	6.00	3.00	1.75
7	Jimmy Brown	60.00	30.00	18.00
8	Don Perkins	4.50	2.25	1.35
9	Bobby Walston	4.50	2.25	1.35
10	Jim Phillips	4.50	2.25	1.35
11	Y.A. Tittle	20.00	10.00	6.00
12	Sonny Randle	4.50	2.25	1.35
13	Jerry Reichow	4.50	2.25	1.35
14	Yale Lary	7.00	3.50	2.25
15	Buddy Dial	4.50	2.25	1.35
16	Ray Renfro	4.50	2.25	1.35
17	Norm Snead	4.50	2.25	1.35
18	Leo Nemellini	6.00	3.00	1.75
19	Hugh McElhenny	8.00	4.00	2.50

20	Eddie LeBaron	4.50	2.25	1.35
21	Bill Howton	4.50	2.25	1.35
22	Bobby Mitchell	9.00	4.50	2.75
23	Nick Pietrosante	4.50	2.25	1.35
24	John Unitas	30.00	15.00	9.00
25	Raymond Berry	9.00	4.50	2.75
26	Billy Kilmer	7.00	3.50	2.25
27	Lenny Moore	8.00	4.00	2.50
28	Tommy McDonald	4.50	2.25	1.35
29	Del Shofner	4.50	2.25	1.35
30	Jim Taylor	12.00	6.00	3.75
31	Joe Schmidt	7.00	3.50	2.25
32	Bill George	6.00	3.00	1.75
33	Fran Tarkenton	65.00	32.50	20.00
34	Willie Galimore	4.50	2.25	1.35
35	Bobby Layne	17.00	8.50	5.00
36	Max McGee	4.50	2.25	1.35
37	Jon Arnett	4.50	2.25	1.35
38	Lou Groza	10.00	5.00	3.00
39	Frank Varrichione	4.50	2.25	1.35
40	Milt Plum	4.50	2.25	1.35
41	Prentice Gault	4.50	2.25	1.35
42	Billy Wade	6.00	3.00	1.75
43	Gino Marchetti	7.00	3.50	2.25
44	John Brodie	10.00	5.00	3.00
45	Sonny Jurgensen	10.00	5.00	3.00
46	Clarence Peaks	4.50	2.25	1.35
47	Mike Ditka	20.00	10.00	6.00
48	John Henry Johnson	7.00	3.50	2.25

1968 Topps Posters

Sixteen players from both the AFL and NFL are included in this set. Posters, printed on paper, measure about 5" by 7" and were issued in gum packs, similar to the Topps baseball posters of the same year. A full-color posed action shot is on the front, with the players, name, team and position shown in an oval at the bottom of the front. Backs are blank.

		NM	EX	VG
	Complete Set (16):	50.00	25.00	15.00
	Common Player:	1.50	.75	.45
1	Johnny Unitas	9.00	4.50	2.75
2	Leroy Kelly	1.50	.75	.45
3	Bob Hayes	1.50	.75	.45
4	Bart Starr	5.00	2.50	1.50
5	Charley Taylor	1.50	.75	.45
6	Fran Tarkenton	4.50	2.25	1.35
7	Jim Bakken	1.50	.75	.45
8	Gale Sayers	6.00	3.00	1.75
9	Gary Cuozzo	1.50	.75	.45
10	Les Josephson	1.50	.75	.45
11	Jim Nance	1.50	.75	.45
12	Brad Hubbert	1.50	.75	.45
13	Keith Lincoln	1.50	.75	.45
14	Don Maynard	2.00	1.00	.60
15	Len Dawson	3.00	1.50	1.75
16	Jack Clancy	1.50	.75	.45

1968 Topps Stand-Ups

These 22 unnumbered card-size (2 1/2 by 3 1/2) issues were meant to be punched and folded in order to make it stand. Cards lose much of their value of they're not complete; obviously, not too many complete sets have been found. Cards show a head shot of the player, with his name beneath the photo. Backs are blank. Cards are listed below in alphabetical order.

		NM	EX	VG
	Complete Set (22):	225.00	115.00	67.50
	Common Player:	5.00	2.50	1.50
(1)	Sid Blanks	5.00	2.50	1.50
(2)	John Brodie	12.00	6.00	3.75

(3)	Jack Concannon	5.00	2.50	1.50
(4)	Roman Gabriel	7.00	3.50	2.25
(5)	Art Graham	5.00	2.50	1.50
(6)	Jim Grabowski	5.00	2.50	1.50
(7)	John Hadl	7.00	3.50	2.25
(8)	Jim Hart	7.00	3.50	2.25
(9)	Homer Jones	5.00	2.50	1.50
(10)	Sonny Jurgensen	15.00	7.50	4.50
(11)	Alex Karras	9.00	4.50	2.75
(12)	Billy Kilmer	7.00	3.50	2.25
(13)	Daryle Lamonica	5.00	2.50	1.50
(14)	Floyd Little	5.00	2.50	1.50
(15)	Curtis McClinton	5.00	2.50	1.50
(16)	Don Meredith	35.00	17.50	9.50
(17)	Joe Namath	85.00	42.50	25.00
(18)	Bill Nelsen	5.00	2.50	1.50
(19)	Dave Osborn	5.00	2.50	1.50
(20)	Willie Richardson	5.00	2.50	1.50
(21)	Frank Ryan	5.00	2.50	1.50
(22)	Norm Snead	5.00	2.50	1.50

1970 Topps posters

This 24-poster set was included one per pack in the first series of 1970 Topps football wax packs. The posters, which measure about 8" by 10", were folded several times; it's very difficult to find any in top condition.

		NM	EX	VG
	Complete Set (24):	50.00	25.00	15.00
	Common Player:	1.00	.50	.30
1	Gale Sayers	4.50	2.75	
2	Bobby Bell	3.00	1.50	.90
3	Roman Gabriel	3.25	1.65	1.00
4	Jim Tyrer	1.00	.50	.30
5	Willie Brown	3.00	1.50	.90
6	Carl Eller	3.00	1.50	.90
7	Tom Mack	1.50	.75	.45
8	Deacon Jones	3.00	1.50	.90
9	Johnny Robinson	1.00	.50	.30
10	Jan Stenerud	2.00	1.00	.60
11	Dick Butkus	5.00	2.50	1.50
12	Lem Barney	1.00	.50	.30
13	David Lee	1.00	.50	.30
14	Larry Wilson	2.00	1.00	.60
15	Gene Hickerson	1.00	.50	.30
16	Lance Alworth	3.00	1.50	.90
17	Merlin Olsen	3.00	1.50	.90
18	Bob Trumpy	2.00	1.00	.60
19	Bob Lilly	3.00	1.50	.90
20	Mick Tingelhoff	1.50	.75	.45
21	Calvin Hill	2.00	1.00	.60
22	Paul Warfield	3.00	1.50	.90
23	Chuck Howley	1.00	.50	.30
24	Bob Brown	1.00	.50	.30

1971 Topps Pin-Ups

These mini-posters (about 5 by 7 inches) were folded twice and inserted into wax packs. The front features a head shot of the player, with his name in bold capitals above the photo and his team in smaller type at the bottom. Backs howed a football field with side markers, as well as the accompanying instructions. Because these posters were folded, it's very difficult, if not impossible, to find any in Mint condition.

		NM	EX	VG
	Complete Set (32):	40.00	20.00	12.00
	Common Player:	.65	.32	.20
1	Gene Washington	.75	.37	.25
2	Andy Russell	.65	.32	.20
3	Harold Jackson	.65	.32	.20
4	Joe Namath	12.00	6.00	3.75
5	Fran Tarkenton	5.00	2.50	1.50
6	Dave Osborn	.65	.32	.20
7	Bob Griese	2.50	1.25	.75
8	Roman Gabriel	1.00	.50	.30
9	Jerry LeVias	.65	.32	.20
10	Bart Starr	5.00	2.50	1.50
11	Bob Hayes	1.00	.50	.30
12	Gale Sayers	5.50	2.25	1.10
13	O.J. Simpson	7.50	3.75	2.25
14	Sam Brunelli	.65	.32	.20
15	Jim Nance	.65	.32	.20
16	Bill Nelsen	.65	.32	.20
17	Sonny Jurgensen	2.50	1.25	.75
18	John Brodie	2.50	1.25	.75
19	Lance Alworth	1.50	.75	.45
20	Larry Wilson	1.00	.50	.30
21	Daryle Lamonica	.75	.37	.25
22	Dan Abramowicz	.65	.32	.20
23	Gene Washington (Minn.)	.65	.32	.20
24	Bobby Bell	1.50	.75	.45
25	Merlin Olsen	2.00	1.00	.60
26	Charlie Sanders	.65	.32	.20
27	Virgil Carter	.65	.32	.20
28	Dick Butkus	2.50	1.25	.75
29	Johnny Unitas	7.00	3.50	2.25
30	Tommy Nobis	.75	.37	.25
31	Floyd Little	.65	.32	.20
32	Larry Brown	.65	.32	.20

Basketball

1977 Dell Flipbooks

These 24-page booklets feature color action photos of the player which simulate motion when they are rifled through. Each shows a player demonstrating a basketball technique and includes player statistics. The booklets are 4" by 3 3/16" and were produced by Pocket Money Basketball Co.

		NM	EX	VG
	Complete Set (6):	140.00	70.00	42.00
	Common Player:	18.00	9.00	5.50
(1)	Kareem Abdul-Jabbar	45.00	22.00	13.50
(2)	Dave Cowens	18.00	9.00	5.50
(3)	Julius Erving	40.00	20.00	12.00
(4)	Pete Maravich	35.00	17.50	10.50
(5)	David Thompson	18.00	9.00	5.50
(6)	Bill Walton	25.00	12.50	7.50

1993 Kelloggs Postercards

Star Pics produced this 10-card set for Kelloggs to randomly insert cards in its 20-ounce boxes of Raisin Bran starting in January 1993. About one million of the set, subtitled "Kellogg's College Greats Postercards," were produced. The unnumbered cards measure 2 1/2" by 7" and are folded in half. One side has a color posed shot of the player in his college uniform, plus career highlights. The other side has a vertical 2 1/2" by 7" color photo of the player, with his name at the bottom. Two female collegiate stars were also included in the set.

		MT	NM	EX
	Complete Set (10):	20.00	15.00	8.00
	Common Player:	1.50	1.25	.60
(1)	Kareem Abdul-Jabbar	3.00	2.25	1.25
(2)	Teresa Edwards	1.50	1.25	.60
(3)	Christian Laettner	3.00	2.25	1.25
(4)	Danny Manning	1.50	1.25	.60
(5)	Cheryl Miller	1.50	1.25	.60
(6)	Harold Miner	5.00	3.75	2.00
(7)	Chris Mullin	2.00	1.50	.80
(8)	Scottie Pippen	3.00	2.25	1.25
(9)	David Robinson	3.00	2.25	1.25
(10)	Isiah Thomas	2.00	1.50	.80

1989 Magnetables

This officially-licensed NBA set features blank-backed magnets depicting stars from the league on the fronts. The set, produced by Phoenix Industries, is subtitled "Pro Sports." The unnumbered magnets, each measuring 1 7/8" by 2 15/16", were sold in convenience and food stores.

		MT	NM	EX
	Complete Set (34):	65.00	49.00	26.00
	Common Player:	1.00	.70	.40
(1)	Mark Aguirre	1.50	1.25	.60
(2)	Willie Anderson	1.50	1.25	.60
(3)	Charles Barkley	3.00	2.25	1.25
(4)	Larry Bird	3.00	2.25	1.25
(5)	Rolando Blackman	1.50	1.25	.60
(6)	Tom Chambers	1.50	1.25	.60
(7)	Clyde Drexler	3.00	2.25	1.25
(8)	Joe Dumars	2.00	1.50	.80
(9)	Dale Ellis	1.50	1.25	.60
(10)	Alex English	1.50	1.25	.60
(11)	Patrick Ewing	2.50	2.00	1.00
(12)	Roy Hinson	1.00	.70	.40
(13)	Kevin Johnson	3.00	2.25	1.25
(14)	Magic Johnson	3.00	2.25	1.25
(15)	Vinnie Johnson	1.25	.90	.50
(16)	Michael Jordan	4.00	3.00	1.50
(17)	Bernard King	1.50	1.25	.60
(18)	Bill Laimbeer	1.25	.90	.50
(19)	Karl Malone	2.50	2.00	1.00
(20)	Moses Malone	1.50	1.25	.60
(21)	Kevin McHale	1.50	1.25	.60
(22)	Chris Mullin	2.00	1.50	.80
(23)	Ken Norman	1.50	1.25	.60

(24)	Akeem Olajuwon	3.00	2.25	1.25
(25)	Chuck Person	1.50	1.25	.60
(26)	Mark Price	2.00	1.50	.80
(27)	Mitch Richmond	2.00	1.50	.80
(28)	Dennis Rodman	1.75	1.25	.70
(29)	Kenny Smith	1.25	.90	.50
(30)	Jon Sundvold	1.00	.70	.40
(31)	Isiah Thomas	2.00	1.50	.80
(32)	Kelly Tripucka	1.00	.70	.40
(33)	Dominique Wilkins	2.50	2.00	1.00
(34)	James Worthy	1.75	1.25	.70

1971 Mattel Instant Replay

These replay records recount actual thrilling games involving the players depicted. The discs, which were 2 3/8" in diameter, were sold in two packs of four (#s 1-4 and 5-8 were sold together). Mattel produced a toy record player, which required "D" batteries, to play the records. A display box with a record for Lew Alcindor was also produced. The complete set price below does not include a Bill Russell disc, available only in a "Sports Challenges" series four-pack.

		NM	EX	VG
Complete Set (9):		225.00	112.00	67.00
Common Player:		12.00	6.00	3.50
(1)	Elgin Baylor	20.00	10.00	6.00
(2)	Wilt Chamberlain	30.00	15.00	9.00
(3)	Jerry Lucas	12.00	6.00	3.50
(4)	Pete Maravich	25.00	12.50	7.50
(5)	John Havlicek	25.00	12.50	7.50
(6)	Willis Reed	12.00	6.00	3.50
(7)	Oscar Robertson	20.00	10.00	6.00
(8)	Jerry West	20.00	10.00	6.00
(9)	Lew Alcindor	50.00	25.00	15.00
(10)	Bill Russell	100.00	50.00	30.00

1990 NBA Hoops Action Photos

MICHAEL JORDAN

These 8" x 10" glossy cards were issued in February 1990. The first 22 cards were available nationally and locally. The rest were available locally in each NBA city, five per team. Card backs are unnumbered and contain player stats. The local players are listed alphabetically by team after the 22 national cards.

		MT	NM	EX
Complete Set (136):		50.00	37.00	20.00
1	Larry Bird	1.00	.70	.40
2	Charles Barkley	1.00	.70	.40
3	Tom Chambers	.50	.40	.20
4	Clyde Drexler	.75	.60	.30

5	Joe Dumars	.75	.60	.30
6	Dale Ellis	.50	.40	.20
7	Patrick Ewing	1.00	.70	.40
8	Magic Johnson	1.00	.70	.40
9	Kevin Johnson	.75	.60	.30
10	Michael Jordan	2.00	1.50	.80
11	Karl Malone	1.00	.70	.40
12	Moses Malone	.75	.60	.30
13	Kevin McHale	.75	.60	.30
14	Chris Mullin	1.00	.70	.40
15	Akeem Olajuwon	1.50	1.25	.60
16	Scottie Pippen	1.50	1.25	.60
17	Mark Price	1.00	.70	.40
18	David Robinson	1.50	1.25	.60
19	John Stockton	1.00	.70	.40
20	Isiah Thomas	1.00	.70	.40
21	Dominique Wilkins	1.00	.70	.40
22	James Worthy	1.00	.70	.40
23	Doc Rivers	.50	.40	.20
24	Spud Webb	.50	.40	.20
25	Kevin Willis	.50	.40	.20
26	Reggie Lewis	.50	.40	.20
27	Robert Parish	.75	.60	.30
28	Brian Shaw	.50	.40	.20
29	Muggsy Bogues	.50	.40	.20
30	Rex Chapman	.50	.40	.20
31	Dell Curry	.50	.40	.20
32	J.R. Reid	.50	.40	.20
33	Kelly Tripucka	.25	.20	.10
34	Bill Cartwright	.75	.60	.30
35	Horace Grant	.75	.60	.30
36	Stacey King	.50	.40	.20
37	Chucky Brown	.25	.20	.10
38	Brad Daugherty	.75	.60	.30
39	Craig Ehlo	.50	.40	.20
40	Larry Nance	.50	.40	.20
41	Rolando Blackman	.50	.40	.20
42	Brad Davis	.25	.20	.10
43	James Donaldson	.25	.20	.10
44	Derek Harper	.50	.40	.20
45	Roy Tapley	.50	.40	.20
46	Michael Adams	.50	.40	.20
47	Walter Davis	.50	.40	.20
48	Bill Hanzlik	.25	.20	.10
49	Todd Lichti	.25	.20	.10
50	Blair Rasmussen	.25	.20	.10
51	Bill Laimbeer	.50	.40	.20
52	Dennis Rodman	.50	.40	.20
53	John Salley	.50	.40	.20
54	Tim Hardaway	1.00	.70	.40
55	Rod Higgins	.25	.20	.10
56	Sarunas Marciulionis	.50	.40	.20
57	Mitch Richmond	.75	.60	.30
58	Sleepy Floyd	.50	.40	.20
59	Bucky Johnson	.25	.20	.10
60	Vernon Maxwell	.50	.40	.20
61	Otis Thorpe	.50	.40	.20
62	Vern Fleming	.25	.20	.10
63	Reggie Miller	1.00	.70	.40
64	Chuck Person	.50	.40	.20
65	Rik Smits	.50	.40	.20
66	LaSalle Thompson	.25	.20	.10
67	Benoit Benjamin	.25	.20	.10
68	Gary Grant	.25	.20	.10
69	Danny Manning	.75	.60	.30
70	Ken Norman	.50	.40	.20
71	Charles Smith	.50	.40	.20
72	A.C. Green	.50	.40	.20
73	Byron Scott	.50	.40	.20
74	Vlade Divac	.75	.60	.30
75	Sherman Douglas	.50	.40	.20
76	Kevin Edwards	.50	.40	.20
77	Glen Rice	.75	.60	.30

78	Rony Seikaly	.50	.40	.20
79	Billy Thompson	.25	.20	.10
80	Jay Humphries	.25	.20	.10
81	Brad Lohaus	.25	.20	.10
82	Ricky Pierce	.25	.20	.10
83	Alvin Robertson	.25	.20	.10
84	Jack Sikma	.25	.20	.10
85	Randy Breuer	.25	.20	.10
86	Tony Campbell	.25	.20	.10
87	Tyrone Corbin	.25	.20	.10
88	Sam Mitchell	.25	.20	.10
89	Pooh Richardson	.50	.40	.20
90	Mookie Blaylock	.25	.20	.10
91	Sam Bowie	.25	.20	.10
92	Lester Conner	.25	.20	.10
93	Roy Hinson	.25	.20	.10
94	Chris Morris	.25	.20	.10
95	Maurice Cheeks	.50	.40	.20
96	Mark Jackson	.50	.40	.20
97	Charles Oakley	.50	.40	.20
98	Gerald Wilkins	.50	.40	.20
99	Nick Anderson	.50	.40	.20
100	Michael Ansley	.25	.20	.10
101	Terry Catledge	.50	.40	.20
102	Sidney Green	.25	.20	.10
103	Sam Vincent	.25	.20	.10
104	Ron Anderson	.50	.40	.20
105	Mike Giminski	.25	.20	.10
106	Hersey Hawkins	.50	.40	.20
107	Rick Mahorn	.50	.40	.20
108	Jeff Hornacek	.75	.60	.30
109	Eddie Johnson	.50	.40	.20
110	Mark West	.25	.20	.10
111	Kevin Duckworth	.50	.40	.20
112	Jerome Kersey	.50	.40	.20
113	Terry Porter	.50	.40	.20
114	Buck Williams	.50	.40	.20
115	Antoine Carr	.50	.40	.20
116	Eric Leckner	.25	.20	.10
117	Ralph Sampson	.50	.40	.20
118	Lionel Simmons	.50	.40	.20
119	Wayman Tisdale	.75	.60	.30
120	Willie Anderson	.50	.40	.20
121	Terry Cummings	.75	.60	.30
122	Sean Elliott	.75	.60	.30
123	Rod Strickland	.50	.40	.20
124	Michael Cage	.25	.20	.10
125	Shawn Kemp	1.00	.70	.40
126	Xavier McDaniel	.50	.40	.20
127	Derrick McKey	.75	.60	.30
128	Thurl Bailey	.50	.40	.20
129	Mark Eaton	.50	.40	.20
130	Blue Edwards	.25	.20	.10
131	Harvey Grant	.50	.40	.20
132	Charles Jones	.25	.20	.10
133	Bernard King	.75	.60	.30
134	Darrell Walker	.25	.20	.10
135	John Williams	.25	.20	.10
136	Checklist	.75	.60	.30

1976 Superstar Socks

These 5" by 6 3/4" cards were used a promotion by Superstar Socks, which is written on the front of each card in a fancy design. The player is shown in a close-up color photo, along with his facsimile signature. "The Superstars Sock. Cushioned comfort. In thick luxurious COTTON" is also written on the front. Backs have a player biography and statistics. The unnumbered cards were used to clamp the socks together and had a hole punched through them so the socks could be hung on a display rod.

		NM	EX	VG
Complete Set (7):		800.00	400.00	240.00
Common Player:		100.00	50.00	30.00
(1)	Kareem Abdul-Jabbar	160.00	80.00	48.00
(2)	Nate Archibald	125.00	62.00	37.00
(3)	Rick Berry	125.00	62.00	37.00
(4)	Doug Collins	100.00	50.00	30.00
(5)	Spencer Haywood	100.00	50.00	30.00
(6)	Bob Lanier	125.00	62.00	37.00
(7)	Pete Maravich	135.00	67.00	40.00

1969 Topps Posters

This set of 23 posters (numbered to 24, but #5 was never issued) was issued one per wax pack of basketball cards. Printed on this paper stock, the posters (approximately 2 1/2 x 10 inches) showed a cartoon of the player and a "growth chart" showing his height at the left. Poster #5, which was to have depicted Bill Russell, was pulled. Because these posters were folded when inserted into the packs, it's impossible to find them in Mint condition.

		NM	EX	VG
Complete Set:		250.00	125.00	75.00
Common Player:		3.00	1.50	.90
1	Walt Bellamy	3.00	1.50	.90
2	Jerry West	25.00	12.50	7.50
3	Bailey Howell	3.00	1.50	.90
4	Elvin Hayes	10.00	5.00	3.00
6	Bob Rule	3.00	1.50	.90
7	Gail Goodrich	4.00	2.00	1.25
8	Jeff Mullins	3.00	1.50	.90
9	John Havlicek	15.00	7.50	4.50
10	Lew Alcindor	60.00	30.00	18.00
11	Wilt Chamberlain	50.00	25.00	15.00
12	Nate Thurmond	4.00	2.00	1.25
13	Hal Greer	4.00	2.00	1.25
14	Lou Hudson	3.00	1.50	.90
15	Jerry Lucas	5.00	2.50	1.50
16	Dave Bing	5.00	2.50	1.50
17	Walt Frazier	10.00	5.00	3.00
18	Gus Johnson	4.00	2.00	1.25
19	Willis Reed	10.00	5.00	3.00
20	Earl Monroe	10.00	5.00	3.00
21	Billy Cunningham	10.00	5.00	3.00
22	Wes Unseld	7.00	3.50	2.00
23	Bob Boozer	3.00	1.50	.90
24	Oscar Robertson	25.00	12.50	7.50

1969 Topps Rulers

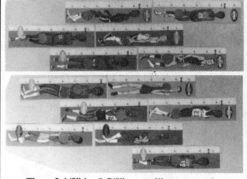

These 2 1/2" by 9 7/8" paper-like cartoon drawings were inserted in 1969-70 Topps wax packs. Ruler marks on the left side of the card tell how tall the player pictured is. The set was to be 24 cards, but card number 5 was never issued.

	NM	EX	VG
Complete Set (23):	400.00	200.00	120.00
1 Walt Bellamy	8.00	4.00	2.50
2 Jerry West	40.00	20.00	12.00
3 Bailey Howell	5.00	2.50	1.50
4 Elvin Hayes	20.00	10.00	6.00
5 Not Issued			
6 Bob Rule	5.00	2.50	1.50
7 Gail Goodrich	10.00	5.00	3.00
8 Jeff Mullins	5.00	2.50	1.50
9 John Havlicek	35.00	17.50	10.50
10 Lew Alcindor	100.00	50.00	30.00
11 Wilt Chamberlain	75.00	37.00	22.00
12 Nate Thurmond	10.00	5.00	3.00
13 Hal Greer	10.00	5.00	3.00
14 Lou Hudson	5.00	2.50	1.50
15 Jerry Lucas	15.00	7.50	4.50
16 Dave Bing	10.00	5.00	3.00
17 Walt Frazier	20.00	10.00	6.00
18 Gus Johnson	5.00	2.50	1.50
19 Willis Reed	15.00	7.50	4.50
20 Earl Monroe	15.00	7.50	4.50
21 Billy Cunningham	10.00	5.00	3.00
22 Wes Unseld	10.00	5.00	3.00
23 Bob Boozer	5.00	2.50	1.50
24 Oscar Robertson	35.00	17.50	10.50

1970 Topps Posters

One of these 24 posters was inserted into a wax pack of basketball cards. Printed on thin white paper stock, they feature an action shot of an NBA star, with his name in bold letters near the top. Since these 8x10 inch posters were folded several times to fit in the packs, it's impossible to find any in Mint condition.

	NM	EX	VG
Complete Set (24):	115.00	58.00	35.00
Common Player:	1.00	.50	.30
1 Walt Frazier	5.00	2.50	1.50
3 Willis Reed	5.00	2.50	1.50
4 Elvin Hayes	7.50	3.75	2.25
6 Oscar Robertson	10.00	5.00	3.00
7 Dave Bing	4.00	2.00	1.25
8 Jerry Sloan	1.00	.50	.30
10 Hal Greer	3.00	1.50	.90
13 Lew Alcindor	25.00	12.50	7.50
14 Chet Walker	1.25	.60	.40
15 Jerry West	10.00	5.00	3.00
16 Billy Cunningham	5.00	2.50	1.50
17 Wilt Chamberlain	20.00	10.00	6.00
18 John Havlicek	7.50	3.75	2.25

	NM	EX	VG
19 Lou Hudson	1.00	.50	.30
20 Earl Monroe	5.00	2.50	1.50
21 Wes Unseld	5.00	2.50	1.50
22 Connie Hawkins	1.50	.75	.45

1980 Topps Posters

These posters, which measure around 5" by 7", were folded and inserted into Topps wax packs of basketball cards. Posters feature one of 16 NBA teams and feature the same design as the basketball cards. Posters are printed on thin white paper.

	NM	EX	VG
Complete Set:	12.50	6.25	3.75
Common Team:	.75	.40	.25
1 Atlanta Hawks	.75	.40	.25
2 Boston Celtics	1.00	.50	.30
3 Chicago Bulls	.75	.40	.25
4 Cleveland Cavaliers	.75	.40	.25
5 Detroit Pistons	.75	.40	.25
6 Houston Rockets	.75	.40	.25
7 Indiana Pacers	.75	.40	.25
8 Los Angeles Lakers	1.00	.75	.40
9 Milwaukee Bucks	1.00	.75	.40
10 New Jersey Nets	.75	.40	.25
11 New York Knicks	1.00	.40	.25
12 Philadelphia 76ers	1.00	.40	.25
13 Phoenix Suns	.75	.40	.25
14 Portland Trail Blazers	.75	.40	.25
15 Seattle Sonics	.75	.40	.25
16 Washington Bullets	.75	.40	.25

Hockey

1993 American Licorice Sour Punch Caps

These cards, featuring two 1 1/2" diameter perforated discs, were included in specially-marked packages of Sour Punch Candy Straws. The cards, produced by the American Licorice Co., contained one player portrait disc and one Sour Punch flavor disc. The card, which is standard size, is numbered on the front; the back is blank. A promotional Bobby Hull cap was also produced. It is not numbered, but has a letter P on it.

	MT	NM	EX
Complete Set (8):	5.00	3.75	2.00
Common Player:	.25	.20	.10
1 Sour Apple Cap	.50	.40	.20
(Theoren Fleury)			
2 Blue Raspberry Cap	1.50	1.25	.60
(Guy Lafleur)			
3 Strawberry Cap	1.00	.70	.40
(Chris Chelios)			

4	Sour Apple Cap (Stan Mikita)	1.25	.90	.50
5	Strawberry Cap (Rocket Richard)	1.50	1.25	.60
6	Blue Raspberry Cap (Steve Thomas)	.25	.20	.10
7	Sour Punch Cap Logo (Checklist 1)	.25	.20	.10
8	Sour Punch Cap Logo (Checklist 2)	.25	.20	.10
P	Bobby Hull	1.00	.70	.40

1964 Coca-Cola Caps

These unnumbered caps are 1 1/8" in diameter and feature a mug shot on the front, plus the player's name, number, team and product, either Coke or Sprite. The Sprite caps are rarer, and are therefore more valuable. The bottle caps are listed alphabetically by team, then by player. Backs are blank. A plastic display rink for the caps was also produced.

		NM	EX	VG
Complete Set:		400.00	200.00	120.00
Common Player:		2.50	1.25	.70
(1)	Murray Balfour	2.50	1.25	.70
(2)	Leo Boivin	3.50	1.75	1.00
(3)	John Bucyk	7.50	3.75	2.25
(4)	Gary Dornhoefer	3.50	1.75	1.00
(5)	Reggie Fleming	2.50	1.25	.70
(6)	Ted Green	3.50	1.75	1.00
(7)	Tom Johnson	3.50	1.75	1.00
(8)	Eddie Johnston	3.50	1.75	1.00
(9)	Forbes Kennedy	2.50	1.25	.70
(10)	Orland Kurtenbach	3.50	1.75	1.00
(11)	Bobby Leiter	2.50	1.25	.70
(12)	Bob McCord	2.50	1.25	.70
(13)	Ab McDonald	2.50	1.25	.70
(14)	Murray Oliver	2.50	1.25	.70
(15)	Dean Prentice	3.50	1.75	1.00
(16)	Ron Schock	2.50	1.25	.70
(17)	Ed Westfall	3.50	1.75	1.00
(18)	Tom Williams	2.50	1.25	.70
(19)	John Brenneman	2.50	1.25	.70
(20)	Denis DeJordy	3.50	1.75	1.00
(21)	Phil Esposito	45.00	22.00	13.50
(22)	Glenn Hall	9.00	4.50	2.75
(23)	Billy Hay	2.50	1.25	.70
(24)	Wayne Hillman	2.50	1.25	.70
(25)	Bobby Hull	45.00	22.00	13.50
(26)	Al MacNeil	2.50	1.25	.70
(27)	Chico Maki	3.50	1.75	1.00
(28)	John McKenzie	2.50	1.25	.70
(29)	Stan Mikita	15.00	7.50	4.50
(30)	Doug Mohns	2.50	1.25	.70
(31)	Eric Nesterenko	3.50	1.75	1.00
(32)	Pierre Pilote	3.50	1.75	1.00
(33)	Doug Robinson	2.50	1.25	.70
(34)	Fred Stanfield	2.50	1.25	.70
(35)	Elmer Vasko	2.50	1.25	.70
(36)	Kenny Wharram	2.50	1.25	.70
(37)	Doug Barkley	2.50	1.25	.70
(38)	Gary Bergman	2.50	1.25	.70
(39)	Roger Crozier	3.50	1.75	1.00
(40)	Bill Gadsby	3.50	1.75	1.00
(41)	Paul Henderson	3.50	1.75	1.00
(42A)	#9 (Gordie Howe)	75.00	37.00	22.00
(42B)	#10 (Gordie Howe)	75.00	37.00	22.00
(43)	Larry Jeffrey	2.50	1.25	.70
(44)	Eddie Joyal	2.50	1.25	.70
(45)	Al Langlois	2.50	1.25	.70
(46)	Ted Lindsay	7.50	3.75	2.25
(47)	Parker MacDonald	2.50	1.25	.70
(48)	Bruce MacGregor	2.50	1.25	.70
(49)	Pit Martin	3.50	1.75	1.00
(50)	Ron Murphy	2.50	1.25	.70
(51)	Marcel Pronovost	3.50	1.75	1.00
(52)	Floyd Smith	2.50	1.25	.70
(53)	Norm Ullman	5.00	2.50	1.50
(54)	Ralph Backstrom	3.50	1.75	1.00
(55)	Dave Balon	2.50	1.25	.70
(56)	Jean Beliveau	18.00	9.00	5.50
(57)	Yvan Cournoyer	15.00	7.50	4.50
(58)	John Ferguson	3.50	1.75	1.00
(59)	Terry Harper	3.50	1.75	1.00
(60)	Ted Harris	2.50	1.25	.70
(61)	Bill Hicke	2.50	1.25	.70
(62)	Charlie Hodge	3.50	1.75	1.00
(63)	Jacques Laperriere	3.50	1.75	1.00
(64)	Claude Larose	2.50	1.25	.70
(65)	Claude Provost	2.50	1.25	.70
(66)	Henri Richard	6.00	3.00	1.75
(67)	Jim Richard	6.00	3.00	1.75
(68)	Bobby Rousseau	3.50	1.75	1.00
(69)	Jean-Guy Talbot	3.50	1.75	1.00
(70)	Gilles Tremblay	2.50	1.25	.70
(71)	J.C. Tremblay	3.50	1.75	1.00
(72)	Lou Angotti	2.50	1.25	.70
(73)	Arnie Brown	2.50	1.25	.70
(74)	Dick Duff	3.50	1.75	1.00
(75)	Val Fonteyne	2.50	1.25	.70
(76)	Rod Gilbert	6.00	3.00	1.75
(77)	Phil Goyette	2.50	1.25	.70
(78)	Vic Hadfield	3.50	1.75	1.00
(79)	Camille Henry	3.50	1.75	1.00
(80)	Harry Howell	3.50	1.75	1.00
(81)	Earl Ingarfield, Sr.	2.50	1.25	.70
(82)	Don Johns	2.50	1.25	.70
(83)	Don Marshall	2.50	1.25	.70
(84)	Jim Mikol	2.50	1.25	.70
(85)	Jim Neilson	2.50	1.25	.70
(86)	Bob Nevin	2.50	1.25	.70
(87)	Marcel Paille	2.50	1.25	.70
(88)	Jacques Plante	18.00	9.00	5.50
(89)	Rod Seiling	2.50	1.25	.70
(90A)	#9 (Andy Bathgate)	6.00	3.00	1.75
(90B)	#10 (Andy Bathgate)	6.00	3.00	1.75
(91)	Bob Baun	3.50	1.75	1.00
(92)	Johnny Bower	6.00	3.00	1.75
(93)	Carl Brewer	3.50	1.75	1.00
(94)	Kent Douglas	2.50	1.25	.70
(95)	Ron Ellis	3.50	1.75	1.00
(96)	Tim Horton	10.00	5.00	3.00
(97)	Red Kelly	7.50	3.75	2.25
(98)	Dave Keon	5.00	2.50	1.50
(99)	Frank Mahovlich	10.00	5.00	3.00
(100)	Don McKenney	2.50	1.25	.70
(101)	Dickie Moore	6.00	3.00	1.75
(102)	Bob Pulford	3.50	1.75	1.00
(103)	Terry Sawchuk	20.00	10.00	6.00
(104)	Eddie Shack	5.00	2.50	1.50
(105)	Allan Stanley	3.50	1.75	1.00
(106)	Ron Stewart	2.50	1.25	.70

1966 Coca-Cola Booklets

These 32-page booklets offer insights from the pros on how to play better hockey. For example, Henri Richard gives instructions on how to play offense at the forward position. Each "How To Play" booklet is 4 5/16" by 3 15/16" and has a four-color front, with a blue background and black letters. A facsimile autograph of the player offering the tip is also given. There were four booklets issued in English (A-D) and four in French (W-Z).

		NM	EX	VG
	Complete Set:	70.00	35.00	21.00
	Common Player:	15.00	7.50	4.50
A	How to Play Goal	20.00	10.00	6.00
	(Johnny Bower)			
B	How to Play Forward	20.00	10.00	6.00
	(Defensive)			
	(David Keon)			
C	How to Play Defence	15.00	7.50	4.50
	(Jacques Lapierrier)			
D	How to Play Forwrd	25.00	12.50	7.50
	(Offensive)			
	(Henri Richard)			
W	Comment les Buts	20.00	10.00	6.00
	(Johnny Bower)			
X	Comment Jouer a l avant	20.00	10.00	6.00
	(David Keon)			
Y	Comment Joere a la defense	15.00	7.50	4.50
	(Jacques Laperriere)			
Z	Comment Jouer a l avant	25.00	12.50	7.50
	(Henri Richard)			

1971 Colgate Heads

These player busts are unnumbered and measure 1 1/4" in height. The player's name is on the back of the head, which is created from molded beige plastic.

		NM	EX	VG
	Complete Set (16):	90.00	45.00	27.00
	Common Player:	2.50	1.25	.70
(1)	Yvan Cournoyer	7.50	3.75	2.25
(2)	Marcel Dionne	15.00	7.50	4.50
(3)	Ken Dryden	18.00	9.00	5.50
(4)	Paul Henderson	4.00	2.00	1.25
(5)	Guy Lafleur	18.00	9.00	5.50
(6)	Frank Mahovlich	10.00	5.00	3.00
(7)	Richard Martin	4.00	2.00	1.25
(8)	Bobby Orr	35.00	17.50	10.50
(9)	Brad Park	10.00	5.00	3.00
(10)	Jacques Plante	8.00	4.00	2.50
(11)	Jean Ratelle	7.50	3.75	2.25
(12)	Derek Sanderson	6.00	3.00	1.75
(13)	Dale Tallon	2.50	1.25	.70
(14)	Walter Tkaczuk	2.50	1.25	.70
(15a)	Norm Ullman	50.00	25.00	15.00
(15b)	Norm Ullman	6.00	3.00	1.75
(16)	Garry Unger	4.00	2.00	1.25

1992 Kellogg's Posters

These 9 1/4" by 14 1/8" posters were available in specially-marked boxes of Kellogg's Corn Flakes. Each was included in a cellophane wrapper and were folded eight times. They were not numbered, but 700,000 of each were made. The posters are bilingual, in French and English. The front has a full-color borderless action photo and includes the player's name, along with logos for the NHL and Kellogg's.

		MT	NM	EX
	Complete Set:	15.00	11.00	6.00
	Common Player:	3.00	2.25	1.25
(1)	"Man of Steel"	4.00	3.00	1.50
	(Mario Lemieux)			
(2)	"Power Broker"/"LA Super	4.00	3.00	1.50
	Star" (Mark Messier)			
(3)	"Robo Show"/"Le Coupe De	3.00	2.25	1.25
	Maitre" (Luc Robitaille)			
(4)	"Road Block"/"Le Baraque	4.00	3.00	1.50
	(Patrick Roy) (Goalie)			
(5)	"Frequent Flyer"/"Vol-Au-	3.00	2.25	1.25
	Vent" (Cornelius Rooster)			

1986 Kraft Posters

These posters, measuring 16" by 20", were available as a mail-in offer included on the posters' 1986-87 Kraft drawings cards. The fronts have a black-and-white charcoal illustration, done by either Jerry Hersh or Carlton McDiarmid. The backs are blank.

		MT	NM	EX
	Complete Set (81):	250.00	187.00	100.00
	Common Player:	3.00	2.25	1.25
1	Rejean Lemelin	3.00	2.25	1.25
2	Hakan Loob	3.00	2.25	1.25
3	Lanny McDonald	5.00	3.75	2.00
4	Joe Mullen	5.00	3.75	2.00
5	James Peplinski	3.00	2.25	1.25
6	Paul Reinhart	3.00	2.25	1.25
7	Doug Risebrough	3.00	2.25	1.25
8	Gary Suter	3.00	2.25	1.25
9	Mike Vernon	5.00	3.75	2.00
10	Carey Wilson	3.00	2.25	1.25
11	Glenn Anderson	5.00	3.75	2.00
12	Paul Coffey	5.00	3.75	2.00
13	Grant Fuhr	5.00	3.75	2.00
14	Wayne Gretzky	20.00	15.00	8.00
15	Michael Krushelnyski	3.00	2.25	1.25
16	Jari Kurri	3.00	2.25	1.25
17	Kevin Lowe	3.00	2.25	1.25
18	Mark Messier	7.50	5.75	3.00
19	Andrew Moog	5.00	3.75	2.00
20	Mark Napier	3.00	2.25	1.25
21	Guy Carbonneau	5.00	3.75	2.00
22	Chris Chelios	6.00	4.50	2.50
23	Kjell Dahlin	3.00	2.25	1.25
24	Bob Gainey	3.00	2.25	1.25
25	Gaston Gingras	3.00	2.25	1.25
26	Richard Green	3.00	2.25	1.25
27	Brian Hayward	3.00	2.25	1.25
28	Mike Lalor	3.00	2.25	1.25
29	Claude Lemieux	3.00	2.25	1.25
30	Craig Ludwig	3.00	2.25	1.25
31	Michael McPhee	3.00	2.25	1.25
32	Sergio Momesso	3.00	.60	1.25
33	Mats Naslund	3.00	2.25	1.25
34	Christopher Nilan	3.00	2.25	1.25
35	Stephane J.J. Richer	3.00	2.25	1.25
36	Larry Robinson	6.00	4.50	2.50
37	Patrick Roy	17.50	13.00	7.00
38	Brian Skrudland	5.00	3.75	2.00
39	Robert Smith	5.00	3.75	2.00
40	Petr Svoboda	5.00	3.75	2.00
41	Ryan Walter	3.00	2.25	1.25
42	Brent Ashton	3.00	2.25	1.25
43	Alain Cote	3.00	2.25	1.25
44	Mario Gosselin	3.00	2.25	1.25
45	Michel Goulet	5.00	3.75	2.00
46	Dale Hunter	3.00	2.25	1.25
47	Clint Malarchuk	3.00	2.25	1.25
48	Randy Moller	3.00	2.25	1.25
49	Pat Price	3.00	2.25	1.25
50	Anton Stastny	3.00	2.25	1.25
51	Peter Stastny	5.00	3.75	2.00
52	Wendel Clark	5.00	3.75	2.00
53	Russ Courtnall	4.00	3.00	1.50
54	Dan Daoust	3.00	2.25	1.25
55	Tom Fergus	3.00	2.25	1.25
56	Gary Leeman	3.00	2.25	1.25
57	Borje Salming	3.00	2.25	1.25
58	Greg Terrion	3.00	2.25	1.25
59	Steve Thomas	3.00	2.25	1.25
60	Richard Vaive	3.00	2.25	1.25
61	Ken Wregget	3.00	2.25	1.25
62	Richard Brodeur	3.00	2.25	1.25
63	Glen Cochrane	3.00	2.25	1.25
64	Doug Halward	3.00	2.25	1.25
65	Doug Lidster	3.00	2.25	1.25
66	Barry Pederson	3.00	2.25	1.25

67	Brent Peterson	3.00	2.25	1.25
68	Petri Skriko	3.00	2.25	1.25
69	Stanley Smyl	3.00	2.25	1.25
70	Patrik Sundstrom	3.00	2.25	1.25
71	Tony Tanti	3.00	2.25	1.25
72	Laurie Boschman	3.00	2.25	1.25
73	Randy Carlyle	4.00	3.00	1.50
74	Bill Derlago	3.00	2.25	1.25
75	Dale Hawerchuk	6.00	4.50	2.50
76	Paul MacLean	3.00	2.25	1.25
77	Mario Marois	3.00	2.25	1.25
78	Brian Mullen	3.00	2.25	1.25
79	Steve Penney	3.00	2.25	1.25
80	Thomas Steen	3.00	2.25	1.25
81	Perry Turnbull	3.00	2.25	1.25

1971 O-Pee-Chee Booklets

Each of these color comic booklets measure 2 1/2" by 3 1/2" and represent a mini biography, in French, of the featured player. The booklets were inserts in the 1971-72 O-Pee-Chee packs, but were also produced by Topps. The prices are generally the same for both versions, but the English booklets are easier to find. The booklet is numbered on the front; the back has a checklist of the complete set.

		NM	EX	VG
Complete Set (24):		75.00	37.00	22.00
Common Player:		1.25	.60	.40
1	Bobby Hull	12.00	6.00	3.50
2	Phil Esposito	6.00	3.00	1.75
3	Dale Tallon	1.25	.60	.40
4	Jacques Plante	5.00	2.50	1.50
5	Roger Crozier	1.25	.60	.40
6	Henri Richard	2.50	1.25	.70
7	Ed Giacomin	2.00	1.00	.60
8	Gilbert Perreault	2.00	1.00	.60
9	Greg Polis	1.25	.60	.40
10	Bobby Clarke	2.50	1.25	.70
11	Danny Grant	1.25	.60	.40
12	Alex Delvecchio	2.00	1.00	.60
13	Tony Esposito	2.50	1.25	.70
14	Garry Unger	1.25	.60	.40
15	Frank St. Marseille	1.25	.60	.40
16	Dave Keon	2.00	1.00	.60
17	Ken Dryden	10.00	5.00	3.00
18	Rod Gilbert	2.00	1.00	.60
19	Juha Widing	1.25	.60	.40
20	Orland Kurtenbach	1.25	.60	.40
21	Jude Drouin	1.25	.60	.40
22	Gary Smith	1.25	.60	.40
23	Gordie Howe	20.00	10.00	6.00
24	Bobby Orr	20.00	10.00	6.00

1971 O-Pee-Chee Posters

Each of these color pictures measures 10" by 18" and were folded to fit inside wax packs, two per pack. They were a separate issue, and were not inserts. Each poster is numbered on the front and includes a star which contains the player's name and team inside. A facsimilie autograph appears on most posters. The backs are blank.

		NM	EX	VG
Complete Set (24):		700.00	350.00	210.00
Common Player:		12.00	6.00	3.50
1	Bobby Orr	150.00	75.00	45.00
2	Bob Pulford	20.00	10.00	6.00
3	Dave Keon	25.00	12.50	7.50
4	Yvan Cournoyer	30.00	15.00	9.00
5	Dale Tallon	12.00	6.00	3.50
6	Richard Martin	12.00	6.00	3.50
7	Rod Gilbert	25.00	12.50	7.50
8	Tony Esposito	35.00	17.50	10.50
9	Bobby Hull	65.00	32.00	19.50
10	Red Berenson	12.00	6.00	3.50
11	Norm Ullman	25.00	12.50	7.50
12	Orland Kurtenbach	12.00	6.00	3.50
13	Guy Lafleur	70.00	35.00	21.00
14	Gilbert Perreault	30.00	15.00	9.00
15	Jacques Plante	35.00	17.50	10.50
16	Bruce Gamble	12.00	6.00	3.50
17	Walt McKechnie	12.00	6.00	3.50
18	Tim Horton	35.00	17.50	10.50
19	Jean Ratelle	25.00	12.50	7.50
20	Garry Unger	12.00	6.00	3.50
21	Phil Esposito	40.00	20.00	12.00
22	Ken Dryden	80.00	40.00	24.00
23	Gump Worsley	30.00	15.00	9.00
24	Club de Hockey	20.00	10.00	6.00

1980 Pepsico Caps

These unnumbered caps, arranged alphabetically by team and then by player, feature 20 players from each of the 20 Canadian NHL teams. The caps, found on Pepsi bottles, come in two sizes, depending on the size of the bottle. The top has the Pepsi logo; the inside of the cap has a head shot of the player and his team's city. The caps measure 1 1" in diameter. A plastic round display plaque was also available as a mail-in offer.

		NM	EX	VG
Complete Set (140):		175.00	87.00	52.00
Common Player:		1.50	.70	.45
(1)	Dan Bouchard	1.75	.90	.50
(2)	Guy Chouinard	1.75	.90	.50
(3)	Bill Clement	2.50	1.25	.70
(4)	Randy Holt	1.50	.70	.45
(5)	Ken Houston	1.50	.70	.45
(6)	Kevin LaVallee	1.50	.70	.45
(7)	Don Lever	1.50	.70	.45
(8)	Bob MacMillan	2.00	1.00	.60
(9)	Bradley Marsh	2.00	1.00	.60
(10)	Bob Murdoch	1.50	.70	.45
(11)	Kent Nilsson	2.00	1.00	.60
(12)	James Peplinski	1.50	.70	.45
(13)	Willi Plett	2.00	1.00	.60
(14)	Pekka Rautakillio	1.50	.70	.45
(15)	Paul Reinhart	2.00	1.00	.60
(16)	Pat Riggin	2.00	1.00	.60
(17)	Phil Russell	1.50	.70	.45
(18)	Brad Smith	1.50	.70	.45
(19)	Eric Vail	1.50	.70	.45
(20)	Bert Wilson	1.50	.70	.45
(21)	Glenn Anderson	3.50	1.75	1.00
(22)	Curt Brackenbury	1.50	.70	.45
(23)	Brett Callighen	1.50	.70	.45
(24)	Paul Coffey	8.00	4.00	2.50

	Player	NM	EX	VG
(25)	Lee Fogolin	1.50	.70	.45
(26)	Matti Hagman	1.50	.70	.45
(27)	John Hughes	1.50	.70	.45
(28)	Dave Hunter	1.50	.70	.45
(29)	Jari Kurri	6.00	3.00	1.75
(30)	Ron Low	2.00	1.00	.60
(31)	Kevin Lowe	2.00	1.00	.60
(32)	Dave Lumley	1.50	.70	.45
(33)	Blair McDonald	1.50	.70	.45
(34)	Mark Messier	17.00	8.50	5.00
(35)	Ed Mio	2.00	1.00	.60
(36)	Don Murdoch	1.50	.70	.45
(37)	Pat Price	1.50	.70	.45
(38)	Dave Semenko	2.00	1.00	.60
(39)	Risto Siltanen	1.50	.70	.45
(40)	Stan Weir	1.50	.70	.45
(41)	Keith Acton	1.50	.70	.45
(42)	Brian Englbom	1.50	.70	.45
(43)	Bob Gainey	2.50	1.25	.70
(44)	Gaston Gingras	1.50	.70	.45
(45)	Denis Herron	2.00	1.00	.60
(46)	Rejean Houle	1.50	.70	.45
(47)	Doug Jarvis	2.00	1.00	.60
(48)	Yvon Lambert	1.50	.70	.45
(49)	Rod Langway	3.00	1.50	.90
(50)	Guy Lapointe	3.00	1.50	.90
(51)	Pierre Larouche	2.50	1.25	.70
(52)	Pierre Mondou	1.50	.70	.45
(53)	Mark Napier	2.00	1.00	.60
(54)	Christopher Nilan	2.00	1.00	.60
(55)	Doug Risebrough	2.00	1.00	.60
(56)	Larry Robinson	4.00	2.00	1.25
(57)	Serge Savard	3.00	1.50	.90
(58)	Steve Shutt	3.00	1.50	.90
(59)	Mario Tremblay	2.00	1.00	.60
(60)	Douglas Wickenheiser	1.50	.70	.45
(61)	Serge Bernier	1.50	.70	.45
(62)	Kim Clackson	1.50	.70	.45
(63)	Real Cloutier	1.50	.70	.45
(64)	Andre Dupont	1.50	.70	.45
(65)	Robbie Ftorek	2.00	1.00	.60
(66)	Michel Goulet	6.00	3.00	1.75
(67)	Jamie Hislop	1.50	.70	.45
(68)	Dale Hoganson	1.50	.70	.45
(69)	Dale Hunter	2.50	1.25	.70
(70)	Pierre Lacroix	1.50	.70	.45
(71)	Garry Lariviere	1.50	.70	.45
(72)	Rich Leduc	1.50	.70	.45
(73)	John Paddock	2.00	1.00	.60
(74)	Michel Plasse	2.00	1.00	.60
(75)	Jacques Richard	1.50	.70	.45
(76)	Anton Stastny	2.00	1.00	.60
(77)	Peter Stastny	6.00	3.00	1.75
(78)	Marc Tardif	2.00	1.00	.60
(79)	Wally Weir	1.50	.70	.45
(80)	John Wensink	1.50	.70	.45
(81)	John Anderson	1.50	.70	.45
(82)	Laurie Boschman	1.50	.70	.45
(83)	Jiri Crha	1.50	.70	.45
(84)	Bill Derlago	1.50	.70	.45
(85)	Vitezslav Duris	1.50	.70	.45
(86)	Ron Ellis	1.50	.70	.45
(87)	Dave Farrish	1.50	.70	.45
(88)	Robert (Stewart) Gavin	2.00	1.00	.60
(89)	Pat Hickey	1.50	.70	.45
(90)	Dan Maloney	2.00	1.00	.60
(91)	Terry Martin	1.50	.70	.45
(92)	Barry Melrose	2.50	1.25	.70
(93)	Wilf Paiement	2.00	1.00	.60
(94)	Robert Picard	1.50	.70	.45
(95)	Jim Rutherford	2.50	1.25	.70
(96)	Rocky Saganiuk	1.50	.70	.45
(97)	Borje Salming	2.00	1.00	.60
(98)	Dave Shand	1.50	.70	.45
(99)	Ian Turnbull	1.50	.70	.45
(100)	Richard Vaive	2.50	1.25	.70
(101)	Brent Ashton	2.00	1.00	.60
(102)	Ivan Boldirev	1.50	.70	.45
(103)	Per-Olov Brasar	1.50	.70	.45
(104)	Richard Brodeur	2.50	1.25	.70
(105)	Jerry Butler	1.50	.70	.45
(106)	Colin Campbell	2.50	1.25	.70
(107)	Curt Fraser	1.50	.70	.45
(108)	Thomas Gradin	2.00	1.00	.60
(109)	Dennis Kearns	1.50	.70	.45
(110)	Rick Lanz	1.50	.70	.45
(111)	Lars Lindgren	1.50	.70	.45
(112)	Dave Logan	1.50	.70	.45
(113)	Mario Marois	1.50	.70	.45
(114)	Kevin McCarthy	1.50	.70	.45
(115)	Gerry Minor	1.50	.70	.45
(116)	Darcy Rota	1.50	.70	.45
(117)	Bobby Schmautz	1.50	.70	.45
(118)	Stanley Smyl	1.50	.70	.45
(119)	Harold Snepsts	2.00	1.00	.60
(120)	David Williams	2.00	1.00	.60
(121)	David Babych	2.00	1.00	.60
(122)	Al Cameron	1.50	.70	.45
(123)	Scott Campbell	1.50	.70	.45
(124)	Dave Christian	2.00	1.00	.60
(125)	Jude Drouin	1.50	.70	.45
(126)	Norm Dupont	1.50	.70	.45
(127)	Danny Geoffrion	1.50	.70	.45
(128)	Pierre Hamel	1.50	.70	.45
(129)	Barry Legge	1.50	.70	.45
(130)	Willy Lindstrom	1.50	.70	.45
(131)	Barry Long	1.50	.70	.45
(132)	Kris Manery	1.50	.70	.45
(133)	Jimmy Mann	1.50	.70	.45
(134)	Maurice Mantha	1.50	.70	.45
(135)	Markus Mattsson	1.50	.70	.45
(136)	Don Spring	2.00	1.00	.60
(137)	Douglas Small	1.50	.70	.45
(138)	Anders Steen	2.00	1.00	.60
(139)	Peter Sullivan	1.50	.70	.45
(140)	Ronald Wilson	1.50	.70	.45

1968 Post Cereal Marbles

These marbles were issued by Post Cereal in Canada and feature players from two Canadian teams - the Montreal Canadiens and Toronto Maple Leafs. The player's mug shot and name are featured on a disc inside the clear marble, which has a diameter of 3/4". A white plastic game board, shaped like a hockey rink, was also produced to display the marbles. Perforations could be punched out to put the marbles on the rink, which included the teams' and team logos. Players 1-15 are Canadiens; 16-30 are Maple Leafs.

		NM	EX	VG
	Complete Set (30):	140.00	70.00	42.00
	Common Player:	3.50	1.75	1.00
1	Ralph Backstrom	3.50	1.75	1.00
2	Jean Beliveau	17.00	8.50	5.00
3	Yvan Cournoyer	9.00	4.50	2.75
4	John Ferguson	3.50	1.75	1.00
5	Terry Harper	3.50	1.75	1.00
6	Ted Harris	3.50	1.75	1.00
7	Jacques Laperriere	6.00	3.00	1.75
8	Jacques Lemaire	8.00	4.00	2.50
9	Henri Richard	12.00	6.00	3.50
10	Bobby Rousseau	3.50	1.75	1.00
11	Serge Savard	7.00	3.50	2.00
12	Gilles Tremblay	3.50	1.75	1.00
13	J.C. Tremblay	5.00	2.50	1.50

14	Rogatien Vachon	7.00	3.50	2.00
15	Gump Worsley	12.00	6.00	3.50
16	Johnny Bower	8.00	4.00	2.50
17	Wayne Carleton	3.50	1.75	1.00
18	Ron Ellis	3.50	1.75	1.00
19	Bruce Gamble	3.50	1.75	1.00
20	Paul Henderson	5.00	2.50	1.50
21	Tim Horton	8.00	4.00	2.50
22	Dave Keon	8.00	4.00	2.50
23	Murray Oliver	3.50	1.75	1.00
24	Mike Pelyk	3.50	1.75	1.00
25	Pierre Pilote	6.00	3.00	1.75
26	Marcel Pronovost	6.00	3.00	1.75
27	Bob Pulford	6.00	3.00	1.75
28	Floyd Smith	3.50	1.75	1.00
29	Norm Ullman	8.00	4.00	2.50
30	Mike Walton	3.50	1.75	1.00

1981 Post Cereal
NHL Stars in Action

This die-cut standup set features thick cards which could be folded into "popup" action photos of the players. The cards were issued one per cello pack in specially-marked boxes of Post cereals (Alpha-Bits, Sugar-Crisp or Honeycomb). A display box was also produced to store the cards. It could hold all the cards and left room for one card to be displayed in its popup form. Each card has three panels to it. The first one has an NHL, NHLPA and team logo on it, along with the set name in French and English. The back has a color action photo of a player from the team designated on the front. The second panel has the standup photo of the player, with a facsimile signature at the bottom; the back is blank. The third panel has the player's name and stats from the previous season, in French and English. Team stats are also listed. The third panel's back has popup instructions in French and English.

		MT	NM	EX
Complete Set (28):		36.00	27.00	14.50
Common Player:		1.00	.70	.40
1	Raymond Bourque	7.00	5.25	2.75
2	Gilbert Perreault	3.00	2.25	1.25
3	Denis Savard	3.00	2.25	1.25
4	Dale McCourt	1.00	.70	.40
5	Robert Smith	1.00	.70	.40
6	Mike Bossy	3.00	2.25	1.25
7	Bobby Clarke	2.50	2.00	1.00
8	Randy Carlyle	1.00	.70	.40
9	Mike Palmateer	1.00	.70	.40
10	David Williams	1.00	.70	.40
11	Mark Howe	1.25	.90	.50
12	Marcel Dionne	2.50	2.00	1.00
13	Mike Liut	1.25	.90	.50
14	Barry Beck	1.00	.70	.40
15	Mark Messier	9.00	6.75	3.50
16	Larry Robinson	3.00	2.25	1.25
17	Real Cloutier	1.00	.70	.40
18	Borje Salming	1.50	1.25	.60
19	Morris Lukowich	1.00	.70	.40
20	Brett Callighen	1.00	.70	.40
21	George (Rob) Ramage	1.00	.70	.40
22	Wilf Paiement	1.00	.70	.40
23	Mario Tremblay	1.00	.70	.40
24	Robbie Ftorek	1.00	.70	.40
25	Stanley Smyl	1.00	.70	.40
26	David Babych	1.00	.70	.40
27	Willi Plett	1.00	.70	.40
28	Kent Nilsson	1.00	.70	.40

1992 Season's
Action Player Patches

These patches, made out of soft black cloth, were intended to be used on clothes. Each measures 3 1/8" by 4 3/8" and came individually wrapped in cellophane. The player's team name is above the action photo; the player's name, position and uniform are below it. The patch has an embroidered border in team colors. Patch 22 is a prototype and is not considered part of the set; it features Seasons company president Grant Mulvey, who used the patch as a handout. The patch backs are blank.

		MT	NM	EX
Complete Set (70):		200.00	150.00	80.00
Common Player:		2.50	2.00	1.00
1	Jeremy Roenick	5.00	3.75	2.00
2	Steve Larmer	2.50	2.00	1.00
3	Ed Belfour	4.00	3.00	1.50
4	Chris Chelios	3.00	2.25	1.25
5	Sergei Fedorov	5.00	3.75	2.00
6	Steve Yzerman	3.50	2.75	1.50
7	Tim Cheveldae	2.50	2.00	1.00
8	Bob Probert	2.50	2.00	1.00
9	Wayne Gretzky	8.00	6.00	3.25
10	Luc Robitaille	3.00	2.25	1.25
11	Tony Granato	2.50	2.00	1.00
12	Kelly Hrudey	2.50	2.00	1.00
13	Brett Hull	5.00	3.75	2.00
14	Curtis Joseph	4.00	3.00	1.50
15	Brendan Shanahan	3.50	2.75	1.50
16	Nelson Emerson	2.50	2.00	1.00
17	Raymond Bourque	4.00	3.00	1.50
18	Joseph Juneau	3.50	2.75	1.50
19	Andrew Moog	3.00	2.25	1.25
20	Adam Oates	4.00	3.00	1.50
21	Patrick Roy	6.00	4.50	2.50
22	(Grant Mulvey) (prototype)	4.00	3.00	1.50
23	Denis Savard	2.50	2.00	1.00
24	Gilbert Dionne	2.50	2.00	1.00
25	Kirk Muller	2.50	2.00	1.00
26	Mark Messier	5.00	3.75	2.00
27	Anthony Amonte	3.00	2.25	1.25
28	Brian Leetch	4.00	3.00	1.50
29	Mike Richter	4.00	3.00	1.50
30	Trevor Lindon	4.00	3.00	1.50
31	Pavel Bure	7.00	5.25	2.75
32	Cliff Ronning	3.00	2.25	1.25
33	Geoff Courtnall	3.00	2.25	1.25
34	Mario Lemieux	6.00	4.50	2.50
35	Jaromir Jagr	5.00	3.75	2.00
36	Tom Barrasso	3.00	2.25	1.25
37	Rick Tocchet	2.50	2.00	1.00
38	Eric Lindros	8.00	6.00	3.25
39	Rod Brind'Amour	2.50	2.00	1.00

40	Dominic Roussel	2.50	2.00	1.00
41	Mark Recchi	4.00	3.00	1.50
42	Pat LaFontaine	4.00	3.00	1.50
43	Donale Audette	2.50	2.00	1.00
44	Patrick Verbeek	2.50	2.00	1.00
45	John Cullen	2.50	2.00	1.00
46	Owen Nolan	2.50	2.00	1.00
47	Joe Sakic	4.00	3.00	1.50
48	Kevin Hatcher	2.50	2.00	1.00
49	Donald Beaupre	2.50	2.00	1.00
50	Scott Stevens	2.50	2.00	1.00
51	Chris Terreri	2.50	2.00	1.00
52	Scott Lachance	2.50	2.00	1.00
53	Pierre Turgeon	4.00	3.00	1.50
54	Grant Fuhr	3.00	2.25	1.25
55	Douglas Gilmour	5.00	3.75	2.00
56	Dave Manson	2.50	2.00	1.00
57	Bill Ranford	2.50	2.00	1.00
58	Troy Murray	2.50	2.00	1.00
59	Phil Housley	2.50	2.00	1.00
60	Allan MacInnis	4.00	3.00	1.50
61	Michael Vernon	3.00	2.25	1.25
62	Pat Falloon	4.00	3.00	1.50
63	Douglas Wilson	2.50	2.00	1.00
64	Jon Casey	2.50	2.00	1.00
65	Michael Modano	4.00	3.00	1.50
66	Kevin Stevens	3.50	2.75	1.50
67	Al Iafrate	2.50	2.00	1.00
68	Dale Hawerchuk	2.50	2.00	1.00
69	Igor Kravchuk	2.50	2.00	1.00
70	Wendel Clark	3.00	2.25	1.25
71	Kirk McLean	4.00	3.00	1.50

1962 Topps Hockey Bucks

These unnumbered bucks were folded and included one per wax pack of 1962-63 Topps cards. The front is green and includes a mug shot of the player and a facsimile autograph. The back is blank but has a patterned green background. Each buck measures 4 1/8" by 1 3/4".

	NM	EX	VG
Complete Set (24):	700.00	350.00	210.00
Common Player:	15.00	7.50	4.50
1 Leo Boivin	35.00	17.50	10.50
2 John Bucyk	35.00	17.50	10.50
3 Warren Godfrey	15.00	7.50	4.50
4 Ted Green	20.00	10.00	6.00
5 Don McKenney	15.00	7.50	4.50
6 Doug Mohns	20.00	10.00	6.00
7 Murray Oliver	15.00	7.50	4.50
8 Jerry Toppazzini	15.00	7.50	4.50
9 Reggie Fleming	15.00	7.50	4.50
10 Glenn Hall	45.00	22.00	13.50
11 Billy Hay	17.50	8.75	5.25
12 Bobby Hull	125.00	62.00	37.00
13 Ab McDonald	15.00	7.50	4.50
14 Stan Mikita	70.00	35.00	21.00
15 Pierre Pilote	35.00	17.50	10.50
16 Elmer Vasko	15.00	7.50	4.50
17 Dave Balon	15.00	7.50	4.50
18 Andy Bathgate	45.00	22.00	13.50
19 Andy Hebenton	15.00	7.50	4.50
20 Harry Howell	20.00	10.00	6.00
21 Earl Ingarfield	17.50	8.75	5.25
22 Al Langlois	17.50	8.75	5.25
23 Dean Prentice	20.00	10.00	6.00
24 Gump Worsley	45.00	22.00	13.50

1971 Topps Booklets

These booklets present a mini biography of the player featured within the eight pages. They were inserts in the 1971-72 Topps hockey packs and use the same design as those included in 1971-72 O-Pee-Chee packs, but are in English, not French like the O-Pee-Chee versions. The booklets are numbered on the front and have a checklist on the back. The values for each version are generally the same, but the Topps (English) booklets are more readily available. Each booklet is 2 1/2" by 3 1/2".

	NM	EX	VG
Complete Set (24):	45.00	22.00	13.50
Common Player:	1.00	.50	.30
1 Bobby Hull	7.50	3.75	2.25
2 Phil Esposito	4.50	2.25	1.25
3 Dale Tallon	1.00	.50	.30
4 Jacques Plante	3.00	1.50	.90
5 Roger Crozier	1.00	.50	.30
6 Henri Richard	1.75	.90	.50
7 Ed Giacomin	1.75	.90	.50
8 Gilbert Perreault	1.75	.90	.50
9 Greg Polis	1.00	.50	.30
10 Bobby Clarke	2.25	1.25	.70
11 Danny Grant	1.00	.50	.30
12 Alex Delvecchio	2.25	1.25	.70
13 Tony Esposito	1.50	.70	.45
14 Garry Unger	1.00	.50	.30
15 Frank St. Marseille	1.50	.70	.45
16 Dave Keon	3.00	1.50	.90
17 Ken Dryden	1.50	.70	.45
18 Rod Gilbert	1.00	.50	.30
19 Juha Widing	1.00	.50	.30
20 Orland Kurtenbach	1.00	.50	.30
21 Jude Drouin	1.00	.50	.30
22 Gary Smith	1.00	.50	.30
23 Gordie Howe	15.00	7.50	4.50
24 Bobby Orr	15.00	7.50	4.50

1980 Topps Team Posters

These 5" by 7" posters were folded so they could be inserted in 1980-81 Topps packs. Each poster front has a color photo of the team, with a white border. The team name is at the bottom of the poster; a hockey puck to the right contains the words "1979-80 Season." The front also has a poster number (1 of 16, etc.). Three NHL teams - Edmonton, Quebec and Winnipeg - were not represented in the set.

	NM	EX	VG
Complete Set (16):	17.00	8.50	5.00
Common Player:	1.25	.60	.40
1 New York Islanders	2.00	1.00	.60
2 New York Rangers	1.50	.70	.45
3 Philadelphia Flyers	1.50	.70	.45
4 Boston Bruins	2.00	1.00	.60
5 Hartford Whalers	3.00	1.50	.90
6 Buffalo Sabres	1.25	.60	.40
7 Chicago Blackhawks	1.50	.70	.45
8 Detroit Red Wings	1.50	.70	.45
9 Minnesota North Stars	1.25	.60	.40
10 Toronto Maple Leafs	2.00	1.00	.60
11 Montreal Canadiens	2.00	1.00	.60
12 Colorado Rockies	2.00	1.00	.60
13 Los Angeles Kings	1.25	.60	.40
14 Vancouver Canucks	1.50	.70	.45
15 St. Louis Blues	1.25	.60	.40
16 Washington Capitals	1.25	.60	.40

1985 7-11 Credit Cards

7-Eleven sponsored these 2 1/8" by 3 3/8" plastic credit cards. The front has closeup shots of two teammates, framed by a black background. The player's name, position and uniform number are below his picture in blue letters. The back has a 7-Eleven and team logo on one side, with a card number, too (1 of 25, etc.). The other side has a team history. Each side's information is framed by a red box. "NHL Collectors' Series" is printed along the bottom of the back, along with a 1985 Super Stars Sports copyright.

		MT	NM	EX
Complete Set (25):		30.00	22.00	12.00
Common Player:		.75	.60	.30
1	Raymond Bourque, Rick Middleton	1.50	1.25	.60
2	Tom Barrasso, Gilbert Perreault	1.00	.70	.40
3	Paul Reinhart, Lanny McDonald	1.00	.70	.40
4	Denis Savard, Doug Wilson	1.00	.70	.40
5	Ron Duguay, Steve Yzerman	2.50	2.00	1.00
6	Paul Coffey, Jari Kurri	2.00	1.50	.80
7	Ron Frances, Mike Liut	1.00	.70	.40
8	Marcel Dionne, Dave Taylor	1.25	.90	.50
9	Brian Bellows, Dino Ciccarelli	1.00	.70	.40
10	Larry Robinson, Guy Charbonneau	1.00	.70	.40
11	Mel Bridgman, Chico Resch	.75	.60	.30
12	Mike Bossy, Bryan Trottier	2.00	1.50	.80
13	Reijo Ruotsalainen, Barry Beck	.75	.60	.30
14	Tim Kerr, Mark Howe	.75	.60	.30
15	Mario Lemieux, Mike Bullard	20.00	15.00	8.00
16	Peter Stastny, Michel Goulet	2.00	1.50	.80
17	George (Rob) Ramage, Brian Sutter	.75	.60	.30
18	Rick Vaive, Borje Salming	.75	.60	.30
19	Patrik Sundstrom, Stan Smyl	.75	.60	.30
20	Rod Langway, Mike Gartner	1.00	.70	.40
21	Dale Hawerchuk, Paul MacLean	1.00	.70	.40
22	Stanley Cup Winners	.75	.60	.30
23	Prince of Wales; Trophy Winners	.75	.60	.30
24	Clarence S. Campbell; Bowl Winners	.75	.60	.30
25	Title Card: Superstar Collector's Series	.75	.60	.30

Football

Bookmarks

1992 Breyers bookmarks

These 2" by 8" bookmarks, featuring players from 11 NFL teams, were produced by Breyers to encourage youngsters to read. Each bookmark has a player photo superimposed against a yellow background which has open books incorporated into its design. A bookmark number, player profile and biographical information also appear on the front, which lists the player's name in a black stripe. The Breyers logo and "Reading Team" appear at the top, inside a scoreboard. The back has a sponsor logo, too, along with recommendations of books which can be found at the library. An American Library Association logo is also on the back.

The 11 teams and cities where the bookmarks were available are: Los Angeles Raiders (1-6), San Francisco 49ers (7-12), San Diego Chargers (13-18), Seattle Seahawks (19-24), New Orleans Saints (25-30), Kansas City Chiefs (31-36), Minnesota Vikings (37-42), Pittsburgh

Steelers (43-48), Indianapolis Colts (49-54), Dallas Cowboys (55-60) and Cleveland Browns (61-66). The bookmarks include coaches, cheerleaders and team cards.

	MT	NM	EX
Complete set (66):	100.00	75.00	40.00
Common player:	1.00	.70	.40
1. Greg Townsend	1.00	.70	.40
2. Steve Wisniewski	1.00	.70	.40
3. Art Shell	2.50	2.00	1.00
4. Jeff Jaeger	1.00	.70	.40
5. Lisa O'Day	2.00	1.50	.80
6. Los Angeles Raiders helmet and Super Bowl trophies	1.00	.70	.40
7. Jerry Rice	10.00	7.50	4.00
8. Don Griffin	1.00	.70	.40
9. John Taylor	2.50	2.00	1.00
10. Joe Montana	17.50	13.00	7.00
11. Mike Walter	1.00	.70	.40
12. San Francisco 49ers helmet	1.00	.70	.40
13. Junior Seau	3.00	2.25	1.25
14. John Friesz	2.00	1.50	.80
15. Ronnie Harmon	2.00	1.50	.80
16. Marion Butts	2.00	1.50	.80
17. Gill Byrd	1.00	.70	.40
18. San Diego Chargers helmet	1.00	.70	.40
19. Kelly Stouffer	1.00	.70	.40
20. John Kasay	1.00	.70	.40
21. Andy Heck	1.00	.70	.40
22. Jacob Green	1.50	1.25	.60
23. Eugene Robinson	1.00	.70	.40
24. Seattle Seahawks helmet	1.00	.70	.40
25. Pat Swilling	1.50	1.25	.60
26. Vaughan Johnson	1.00	.70	.40
27. Bobby Hebert	1.50	1.25	.60
28. Floyd Turner	1.00	.70	.40
29. Rickey Jackson	1.50	1.25	.60
30. New Orleans Saints helmet	1.00	.70	.40
31. Harvey Williams	2.00	1.50	.80
32. Derrick Thomas	3.00	2.25	1.25
33. Bill Maas	1.00	.70	.40
34. Tim Grunhard	1.00	.70	.40
35. Jonathan Hayes	1.00	.70	.40
36. Kansas City Chiefs mascot	1.00	.70	.40
37. Rich Gannon	1.50	1.25	.60
38. Tim Irwin	1.00	.70	.40
39. Audray McMillian	1.00	.70	.40
40. Gary Zimmerman	1.00	.70	.40
41. Hassan Jones	1.00	.70	.40
42. Minnesota Vikings helmet	1.00	.70	.40
43. Eric Green	1.50	1.25	.60
44. Louis Lipps	1.50	1.25	.60
45. Rod Woodson	2.00	1.50	.80
46. Merril Hoge	1.00	.70	.40
47. Gary Anderson	1.00	.70	.40
48. Pittsburgh Steelers emblem	1.00	.70	.40
49. Anthony Johnson	1.50	1.25	.60
50. Bill Brooks	2.00	1.50	.80
51. Jeff Herrod	1.00	.70	.40
52. Mike Prior	1.00	.70	.40
53. Jeff George	1.00	.70	.40
54. Ted Marchibroda	1.00	.70	.40
55. Troy Aikman	17.50	13.00	7.00
56. Jay Novacek	2.50	2.00	1.00
57. Emmitt Smith	20.00	15.00	8.00
58. Michael Irvin	6.00	4.50	2.50
59. Dorie Braddy	2.00	1.50	.80
60. Dallas Cowboys Super Bowl Trophy	1.00	.70	.40
61. Clay Matthews	1.50	1.25	.60
62. Tommy Vardell	2.00	1.50	.80
63. Eric Turner	1.00	.70	.40
64. Mike Johnson	1.50	1.25	.60
65. James Jones	1.00	.70	.40
66. Cleveland Browns helmet	1.00	.70	.40

JEFF GOSSETT
and the
**Los Angeles
Public Library**
recommend:

**Mufaro's
Beautiful
Daughter** by
John Steptoe, a
beautifully illustrated
folktale from
Zimbabwe that will
remind you of
Cinderella. You will
also enjoy **Yeh
Shen: A Cinderella
Story from Cina** by
Al-Ling Louie and
the original version,
available in many
beautiful editions.

Find these and
other entertaining
and helpful books
at your local
public library.

**6 – JEFF GOSSETT
Punter**

College: Eastern Illinois
Height: 6'2" Weight: 195
Born: January 25, 1957
Raiders: Two years

Pro: Third in the AFC in net punting
average with 35.7 yards and his
season high was 48 yards against
Denver. Jeff led AFC for punts inside
the 20 yard line with 27.

Personal: Born in Charleston, Illinois. Lettered in football, baseball
and basketball. Played in N.Y. Mets
system for two years.

Knudsen's Dairy bookmarks

Knudsen's Dairy in California has issued several bookmark sets featuring players from the Los Angeles Raiders, Los Angeles Rams, San Diego Chargers and San Francisco 49ers from 1989-91. Each 2" x 8" bookmark was used to promote reading by youngsters in each respective team's city. The bookmarks, distributed on a weekly basis during the football season by the cities' public libraries, feature reading tips on the back. Each front has a player picture, biographical data and player highlights. The back has sponsors' logos, reading tips and book reviews (except in 1989). The set from 1989 is numbered by the player's uniform number, while sets from 1990 are unnumbered; those players are listed alphabetically. Sets from 1991 are numbered consecutively, in groups of six.

1989 Knudsen's Los Angeles Raiders

	MT	NM	EX
Complete set (14):	25.00	18.50	10.00
Common player:	1.00	.70	.40
6. Jeff Gossett	1.00	.70	.40
13. Jay Schroeder	2.50	2.00	1.00
26. Vann McElroy	1.00	.70	.40
35. Steve Smith	2.00	1.50	.80
36. Terry McDaniel	1.00	.70	.40
70. Scott Davis	1.00	.70	.40
72. Doug Mosebar	1.00	.70	.40
75. Howie Long	2.50	2.00	1.00

76. Steve Wisniewski	1.00	.70	.40
81. Tim Brown	4.00	3.00	1.50
83. Willie Gault	2.00	1.50	.80
xx Mike Shanahan	10.00	7.50	4.00
xx Raiders/Super Bowl	1.00	.70	.40
xx Raiderettes	3.00	2.25	1.25

* Note: The Shanahan coach card was apparently withdrawn after he was fired.

1990 Knudsen Los Angeles Rams

	MT	NM	EX
Complete set (6):	20.00	15.00	8.00
Common player:	3.00	2.25	1.25
1. Henry Ellard	5.00	3.75	2.00
2. Jim Everett	5.00	3.75	2.00
3. Jerry Gray	3.00	2.25	1.25
4. Pete Holohan	3.00	2.25	1.25
5. Mike Lansford	3.00	2.25	1.25
6. Irv Pankey	3.00	2.25	1.25

1990 Knudsen/Sealtest New England Partiots

	MT	NM	EX
Complete set (6):	20.00	15.00	8.00
Common player:	3.00	2.25	1.25
1. Steve Grogan	5.00	3.75	2.00
2. Ronnie Lippett	4.00	3.00	1.50
3. Eric Sievers	3.00	2.25	1.25
4. Mosi Tatupu	4.00	3.00	1.50
5. Andre Tippett	5.00	3.75	2.00
6. Garin Veris	3.00	2.25	1.25

1990 Knudsen/Sealtest Philadelphia Eagles

	MT	NM	EX
Complete set (6):	12.00	9.00	4.75
Common player:	2.00	1.50	.80
1. David Alexander	2.00	1.50	.80
2. Eric Allen	2.50	2.00	1.00
3. Keith Byars	3.00	2.25	1.25
4. Randall Cunninham	5.00	3.75	2.00
5. Mike Pitts	2.00	1.50	.80
6. Mike Quick	2.50	2.00	1.00

1990 Knudsen San Diego Chargers

	MT	NM	EX
Compete set (6):	10.00	7.50	4.00
Common player:	1.00	.70	.40
1. Marion Butts	2.50	2.00	1.00
2. Anthony Miller	3.00	2.25	1.25
3. Leslie O'Neal	2.00	1.50	.80
4. Gary Plummer	1.00	.70	.40
5. Billy Ray Smith	1.00	.70	.40
6. Billy Joe Tolliver	2.00	1.50	.80

1990 San Francisco 49ers

	MT	NM	EX
Complete set (6):	20.00	15.00	8.00
Common player:	1.50	1.25	.60
1. Roger Craig	2.50	2.00	1.00
2. Ronnie Lott	3.00	2.25	1.25
3. Joe Montana	10.00	7.50	4.00
4. Jerry Rice	7.00	5.25	2.75
5. George Siefert	1.50	1.25	.60
6. Michael Walter	1.50	1.25	.60

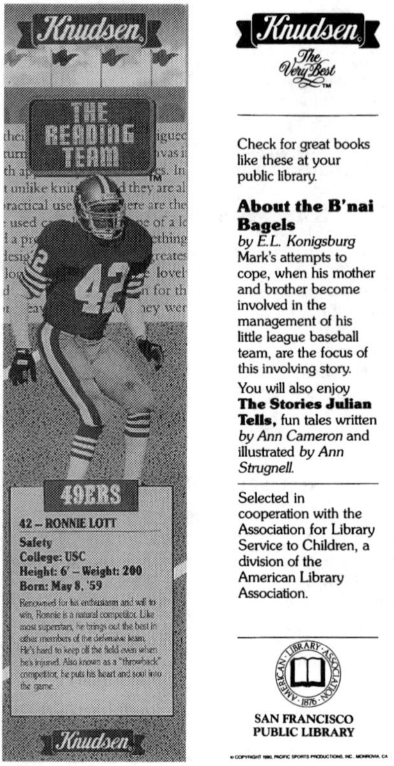
Knudsen
THE READING TEAM
49ERS
42 – RONNIE LOTT
Safety
College: USC
Height: 6' – Weight: 200
Born: May 8, '59
Renowned for his enthusiasm and will to win, Ronnie is a natural competitor. Like most superstars, he brings out the best in other members of the defensive team. He's hard to keep off the field even when he's injured. Also known as a "throwback" competitor, he puts his heart and soul into the game.
Knudsen
Knudsen
The Very Best
Check for great books like these at your public library.
About the B'nai Bagels
by E.L. Konigsburg
Mark's attempts to cope, when his mother and brother become involved in the management of his little league baseball team, are the focus of this involving story.
You will also enjoy The Stories Julian Tells, fun tales written by Ann Cameron and illustrated by Ann Strugnell.
Selected in cooperation with the Association for Library Service to Children, a division of the American Library Association.
SAN FRANCISCO PUBLIC LIBRARY

1991 Knudsen set

	MT	NM	EX
Complete set (18):	30.00	22.00	12.00
Common player:	1.00	.70	.40

San Diego Chargers

Complete set (6):	10.00	7.50	4.00
1. Gil Byrd	1.50	1.25	.60
2. Courtney Hall	1.00	.70	.40
3. Ronnie Harmon	1.50	1.25	.60
4. Anthony Miller	2.50	2.00	1.00
5. Joe Phillips	1.00	.70	.40
6. Junior Seau	3.00	2.25	1.25

Los Angeles Rams

Complete set (6):	7.50	5.75	3.00
7. Jim Everett	2.00	1.50	.80
8. Kevin Greene	1.50	1.25	.60
9. Damone Johnson	1.00	.70	.40
10. Tom Newberry	1.00	.70	.40
11. John Robinson	1.50	1.25	.60
12. Michael Stewart	1.00	.70	.40

San Francisco 49ers

Complete set (6):	15.00	11.00	6.00
13. Michael Carter	1.50	1.25	.60
14. Charles Haley	2.00	1.50	.80
15. Joe Montana	7.50	5.75	3.00
16. Tom Rathman	2.00	1.50	.80
17. Jerry Rice	5.00	3.75	2.00
18. George Seifert	1.00	.70	.40

Books/programs

- 1929 Spalding's "How to Play Football," by Walter Camp $45
- Roger Staubach 1957 Purcell High School Yearbook $295
- Hall of Fame Game program, Aug. 8, 1987, San Francisco 49ers vs. Kansas City Chiefs in Canton, Ohio, pictures the seven Hall of Fame inductees (Don Maynard, Jim Langer, Len Dawson, Larry Csonka, John Henry Johnson, Gene Upshaw and Joe Greene), signed by all seven $70
- 1969 Joe Namath Testimonial Dinner Banquet Program, from Beaver Falls, Pa., with Namath's picture on the front $55

Coke Caps

1964 Coca-Cola AFL All-Stars caps

These unnumbered caps, each measuring 1 1/8" in diameter, could be found under bottle caps of Coca-Cola products (Coke, Tab, Fresca) in participating cities with AFL teams. The cap has a Coke logo and a football on the outside; the player's mug shot, name, position and number were included on the inside of the cap. A Cap Saver sheet was also issued; caps could be affixed to the sheet. Completed sheets could be turned in for prizes.

Complete set NM (44):	$125.00
Common player:	$2.50
1) Tom Addison (Boston Patriots)	$2.50
2) Dalva Allen (Oakland Raiders)	$2.50
3) Lance Alworth (San Diego Chargers)	$15.00
4) Houston Antwine (Boston Patriots)	$2.50
5) Fred Arbanas (Kansas City Chiefs)	$3.00
6) Tony Banfield (Houston Oilers)	$2.50
7) Stew Barber (Buffalo Bills)	$2.50
8) George Blair (San Diego Chargers)	$2.50
9) Mel Branch (Kansas City Chiefs)	$2.50
10) Nick Buoniconti (Boston Patriots)	$10.00
11) Doug Cline (Houston Oilers)	$2.50
12) Eldon Danenhauer (Denver Broncos)	$2.50
13) Clem Daniels (Oakland Raiders)	$3.00
14) Larry Eisenhauer (Boston Patriots)	$2.50
15) Earl Faison (San Diego Chargers)	$2.50
16) Cookie Cilchrist (Buffalo Bills)	$5.00
17) Fred Glick (Houston Oilers)	$2.50
18) Larry Grantham (New York Jets)	$3.00
19) Ron Hall (Boston Patriots	$2.50
20) Charlie Hennigan (Houston Oilers)	$4.50
21) E.J. Holub (Kansas City Chiefs)	$3.00
22) Ed Husmann (Houston Oilers)	$2.50
23) Jack Kemp (Buffalo Bills)	$25.00
24) Dave Kocourek (San Diego Chargers)	$2.50
25) Keith Lincoln (San Diego Chargers)	$4.50
26) Charley Long (Boston Patriots)	$2.50
27) Paul Lowe (San Diego Chargers)	$4.50
28) Archie Matsos (Oakland Raiders)	$2.50
29) Jerry Mays (Kansas City Chiefs)	$3.00
30) Ron Mix (San Diego Chargers)	$6.00
31) Tom Morrow (Oakland Raiders)	$2.50
32) Billy Neighbors (Boston Patriots)	$3.00
33) Jim Otto (Oakland Raiders)	$6.00
34) Art Powell (Oakland Raiders)	$3.00
35) Johnny Robinson (Kansas City Chiefs)	$4.50
36) Tobin Rote (San Diego Chargers)	$4.50
37) Bob Schmidt (Houston Oilers)	$2.50

38) Tom Sestak (Buffalo Bills)................................$2.50
39) Billy Shaw (Buffalo Bills)...............................$2.50
40) Bob Talamini (Houston Oilers)......................$2.50
41) Lionel Taylor (Denver Broncos).....................$4.50
42) Jim Tyrer (Kansas City Chiefs).......................$3.00
43) Dick Westmoreland (San Diego Chargers).......$2.50
44) Fred Williamson (Oakland Raiders).................$5.00

1964 Coke NFL All-Stars caps

These unnumbered caps, each measuring 1 1/8" in diameter, could be found under bottle caps of Coca-Cola products (Coke, Tab, Fresca) in participating cities with NFL teams. The cap has a Coke logo and a football on the outside; the player's mug shot, name, position and number were included on the inside of the cap. A Cap Saver sheet was also issued; caps could be affixed to the sheet. Completed sheets could be turned in for prizes.

Complete set NM (44): $175.00
Common player: $2.50
1) Doug Atkins (Chicago Bears) $6.00
2) Terry Barr (Detroit Lions)...............................$2.50
3) Jim Brown (Cleveland Browns).......................$20.00
4) Roger Brown (Detroit Lions) $3.00
5) Roosevelt Brown (New York Giants) $6.00
6) Timmy Brown (Philadelphia Eagles).................$4.50
7) Bobby Joe Conrad (Chicago Bears) $3.00
8) Willie Davis (Green Bay Packers) $6.00
9) Bob DeMarco (St. Louis Cardinals)..................$2.50
10) Darrell Dess (New York Giants) $2.50
11) Mike Ditka (Chicago Bears)...........................$10.00
12) Bill Forester (Green Bay Packers)...................$3.00
13) Joe Fortunato (Chicago Bears) $2.50
14) Bill George (Chicago Bears) $6.00
15) Ken Gray (St. Louis Cardinals).......................$3.00
16) Forrest Gregg (Green Bay Packers) $6.00
17) Roosevelt Grier (Los Angeles Rams)...............$5.00
18) Henry Jordan (Green Bay Packers)..................$4.50
19) Jim Katcavage (New York Giants) $2.50
20) Jerry Kramer (Green Bay Packers) $5.00
21) Ron Kramer (Green Bay Packers) $3.00
22) Dick Lane (Detroit Lions)...............................$6.00
23) Dick Lynch (New York Giants) $3.00
24) Gino Marchetti (Baltimore Colts) $6.00
25) Tommy Mason (Minnesota Vikings) $3.00
26) Ed Meador (Los Angeles Rams) $3.00
27) Bobby Mitchell (Washington Redskins)...........$6.00
28) Larry Morris (Chicago Bears) $2.50
29) Merlin Olsen (Los Angeles Rams)...................$6.00
30) Jim Parker (Baltimore Colts)..........................$6.00
31) Jim Patton (New York Giants) $3.00
32) Myron Pottios (Pittsburgh Steelers) $3.00
33) Jim Ringo (Green Bay Packers) $3.00
34) Dick Schafrath (Cleveland Browns).................$3.00
35) Joe Schmidt (Chicago Bears) $6.00
36) Del Shofner (New York Giants) $4.50
37) Bob St. Clair (San Francisco 49ers) $6.00
38) Jim Taylor (Green Bay Packers) $7.50
39) Roosevelt Grier (Chicago Bears) $2.50
40) Y.A. Tittle (New York Giants) $10.00
41) John Unitas (Baltimore Colts)........................$17.50
42) Larry Wilson (St. Louis Cardinals)..................$6.00
43) Willie Wood (Green Bay Packers) $6.00
44) Abe Woodson (San Francisco 49ers) $3.00

In addition to the bottle caps made for AFL/NFL All-Stars in 1964, Coca-Cola issued 35 unnumbered caps each for three teams - Cleveland, Detroit and San Diego - and 36 for Boston. Each cap, measuring 1 1/8" in diameter, has mug shot of the player underneath the cork on the inside of the cap. The caps, available in the respective teams' cities during the football season,

were available with Coke, Fresca and Tab products. They could be identified by the football on the outside of the cap. Collectors who completed an entire set on a special Cap Saver sheet could redeem them for a prize. The sheet also had a section for unnumbered caps for each of the 14 NFL teams - Baltimore Colts, Chicago Bears, Cleveland Browns, Dallas Cowboys, Detroit Lions, Green Bay Packers, Los Angeles Rams, Minnesota Vikings, New York Giants, Philadelphia Eagles, Pittsburgh Steelers, San Francisco 49ers, St. Louis Cardinals and Washington Redskins. They generally are about $4-$5 each, with a complete set at $50.

1964 Boston Patriots

Complete set NM (36): $75.00
Common player:...$2.50
1) Jon Morris..$3.00
2) Don Webb..$2.50
3) Charles Long..$3.00
4) Tony Romeo $2.50
5) Bob Dee $2.50
6) Tom Addison..$3.00
7) Bob Yates..$2.50
8) Ron Hall..$2.50
9) undetermined
10) Jack Rudolph...$2.50
11) Don Oakes $2.50
12) Tom Yewcic $2.50
13) undetermined
14) undetermined
15) Larry Garron..$3.00
16) Dave Watson..$2.50
17) Art Graham $2.50
18) Babe Parilli $4.50
19) Jim Hunt...$2.50
20) Don McKinnon $2.50
21) Houston Antwine..$3.00
22) Nick Buoniconti $6.00
23) undetermined
24) Gino Cappelletti...$4.50
25) Chuck Shonta $2.50
26) Dick Felt $2.50
27) Mike Dukes...$2.50
28) Larry Eisenhauer..$3.00
29) Bob Schmidt $2.50
30) undetermined
31) J.D. Garrett...$2.50
32) Jim Whalen $2.50
33) Jim Nance...$4.50
34) undetermined
35) Lonnie Farmer $2.50
36) Boston Patriots Logo $2.50

1964 Cleveland Browns

Complete set NM (35): $100.00
Common player:...$2.50
1) Walter Beach $2.50
2) Larry Benz $2.50
3) Johnny Brewer...$2.50
4) Jim Brown..$20.00
5) John Brown..$2.50
6) Monte Clark..$4.50
7) Gary Collins...$4.50
8) Vince Costello $3.00
9) Ross Fitchner $2.50
10) Galen Fiss $2.50
11) Bob Franklin $2.50
12) Bob Gain..$2.50
13) Bill Glass $4.50
14) Ernie Green...$3.00

Miscellaneous

15) Lou Groza...$7.50
16) Gene Hickerson..$3.00
17) Jim Houston...$3.00
18) Tom Hutchinson..$2.50
19) Jim Kanicki..$2.50
20) Mike Lucci...$3.00
21) Dick Modzelewski..$3.00
22) John Morrow..$2.50
23) Jim Ninowski...$3.00
24) Frank Parker..$2.50
25) Bernie Parrish..$3.00
26) Frank Ryan..$5.00
27) Charles Scales..$2.50
28) Dick Schafrath...$3.00
29) Roger Shoals...$2.50
30) Jim Shorter..$2.50
31) Billy Truax..$3.00
32) Paul Warfield..$12.00
33) Ken Webb..$2.50
34) Paul Wiggin...$3.00
35) John Wooten...$3.00

1964 Detroit Lions

Complete set NM (35): $75.00
Common player: $2.50
1) Terry Barr.......................................$3.00
2) Carl Brettschneider...........................$2.50
3) Roger Brown....................................$3.00
4) Mike Bundra....................................$2.50
5) Ernie Clark......................................$2.50
6) Gail Cogdill....................................$3.00
7) Larry Ferguson.................................$2.50
8) Dennis Gaubatz................................$2.50
9) Jim Gibbons....................................$3.00
10) John Gonzaga.................................$2.50
11) John Gordy.....................................$3.00
12) Tom Hall..$2.50
13) Alex Karras....................................$7.50
14) Dick Lane......................................$6.00
15) Dan LaRose....................................$2.50
16) Yale Lary.......................................$6.00
17) Dick LeBeau...................................$4.50
18) Dan Lewis......................................$2.50
19) Garry Lowe.....................................$2.50
20) Bruce Maher....................................$2.50
21) Darris McCord.................................$2.50
22) Max Messner...................................$2.50
23) Earl Morrall....................................$5.00
24) Nick Pietrosante...............................$4.50
25) Milt Plum.......................................$4.50
26) Daryl Sanders..................................$2.50
27) Joe Schmidt....................................$6.00
28) Bob Sholtz.....................................$2.50
29) J.D. Smith......................................$2.50
30) Pat Studstill...................................$4.50
31) Larry Vargo....................................$2.50
32) Wayne Walker..................................$3.00
33) Tom Watkins...................................$3.00
34) Bob Whitlow...................................$2.50
35) Sam Williams..................................$2.50

1964 San Diego Chargers

Complete set NM (35): $75.00
Common player: $2.50
1) Chuck Allen.....................................$2.50
2) Lance Alworth................................$12.00
3) George Blair....................................$2.50
4) Frank Buncom...................................$3.00
5) Earl Faison......................................$3.00
6) Ken Graham.....................................$2.50
7) George Gross...................................$2.50

8) Sam Gruneisen..................................$2.50
9) John Hadl...$7.50
10) Dick Harris.....................................$3.00
11) Bob Jackson....................................$2.50
12) Emil Karas......................................$2.50
13) Dave Kocourek.................................$3.00
14) Ernie Ladd......................................$6.00
15) Bobby Lane.....................................$2.50
16) Keith Lincoln...................................$5.00
17) Paul Lowe.......................................$5.00
18) Jacque MacKinnon.............................$3.00
19) Gerry McDougall...............................$2.50
20) Charley McNeill...............................$4.50
21) Bob Mitinger...................................$2.50
22) Ron Mix...$6.00
23) Don Norton.....................................$3.00
24) Ernie Park......................................$2.50
25) Bob Petrich.....................................$2.50
26) Jerry Robinson.................................$3.00
27) Don Rogers.....................................$3.00
28) Tobin Rote......................................$4.50
29) Henry Schmidt.................................$2.50
30) Pat Shea...$2.50
31) Walt Sweeney...................................$3.00
32) Jimmy Warren..................................$2.50
33) Dick Westmoreland............................$2.50
34) Bud Whitehead.................................$2.50
35) Ernie White.....................................$2.50

1965 Coca-Cola
NFL All-Stars caps

These bottle caps, available in participating NFL cities, feature NFL All-Stars. The format and design are basically the same as Coke's prior issues, except these caps are numbered using a C prefix.

Complete set NM (34): $100.00
Common player:...................................$2.50
C37 Sonny Jurgensen (Washington Redskins)........$6.00
C38 Fran Tarkenton (Minnesota Vikings)............$10.00
C39 Frank Ryan (Cleveland Browns)....................$3.00
C40 John Unitas (Baltimore Colts)....................$10.00
C41 Tommy Mason (Minnesota Vikings)..............$3.00
C42 Mel Renfro (Dallas Cowboys).......................$4.50
C43 Ed Meador (Los Angeles Rams)....................$2.50
C44 Paul Krause (Washington Redskins)..............$4.50
C45 Irv Cross (Philadelphia Eagles)....................$3.00
C46 Bill Brown (Minnesota Vikings)...................$3.00
C47 Joe Fortunato (Chicago Bears).....................$2.50
C48 Jim Taylor (Green Bay Packers) $6.00
C49 John Henry Johnson (Pittsburgh Steelers).......$6.00
C50 Pat Fischer (St. Louis Cardinals)..................$2.50
C51 Bobby Boyd (Baltimore Colts) $2.50
C52 Terry Barr (Detroit Lions)...........................$2.50
C53 Charley Taylor (Washington Redskins)..........$7.50
C54 Paul Warfield (Cleveland Browns)................$7.50
C55 Pete Retzlaff (Philadelphia Eagles)...............$3.00
C56 Maxie Baughan (Philadelphia Eagles)...........$3.00
C57 Matt Hazeltine (San Francisco 49ers)............$2.50
C58 Ken Gray (St. Louis Cardinals)....................$2.50
C59 Ray Nitschke (Green Bay Packers).................$6.00
C60 Myron Pottios (Pittsburgh Steelers)..............$2.50
C61 Charlie Krueger (San Francisco 49ers)...........$2.50
C62 Deacon Jones (Los Angeles Rams)................$6.00
C63 Bob Lilly (Dallas Cowboys) $7.50
C64 Merlin Olsen (Los Angeles Rams).................$6.00
C65 Jim Parker (Baltimore Colts).......................$6.00
C66 Roosevelt Brown (New York Giants) $6.00
C67 Jim Gibbons (Detroit Lions) $2.50
C68 Mike Ditka (Chicago Bears) $10.00
C69 Willie Davis (Green Bay Packers) $6.00
C70 Aaron Thomas (New York Giants)................$2.50

1965 Coca-Cola bottle caps

In 1965, Coca-Cola issued caps for five teams - Buffalo (B), Detroit (C), New York Giants (G), New York Jets (J) and Washington Redskins (C). The caps follow the same format and concept as previous issues, but use letter prefixes for the numbers.

1965 Buffalo Bills

Complete set NM (35):	$75.00
Common player:	$2.50
B1 Ray Abbruzzese	$2.50
B2 Joe Auer	$2.50
B3 Stew Barber	$3.00
B4 Glenn Bass	$2.50
B5 Dave Behrman	$2.50
B6 Al Bemiller	$2.50
B7 Butch Byrd	$3.00
B8 Wray Carlton	$3.00
B9 Hagood Clarke	$2.50
B10 Jack Kemp	$25.00
B11 Oliver Dobbins	$2.50
B12 Elbert Dubenion	$5.00
B13 Jim Dunaway	$3.00
B14 Booker Edgerson	$2.50
B15 George Flint	$2.50
B16 Pete Gogolak	$4.50
B17 Dick Hudson	$3.00
B18 Harry Jacobs	$3.00
B19 Tom Keating	$3.00
B20 Tom Day	$3.00
B21 Daryle Lamonica	$7.50
B22 Paul Maguire	$5.00
B23 Roland McDole	$3.00
B24 Dudley Meredith	$2.50
B25 Joe O'Donnell	$2.50
B26 Willie Ross	$2.50
B27 Ed Rutkowski	$2.50
B28 George Saimes	$3.00
B29 Tom Sestak	$3.00
B30 Billy Shaw	$4.50
B31 Bob Smith	$2.50
B32 Mike Stratton	$3.00
B33 Gene Sykes	$2.50
B34 John Tracey	$3.00
B35 Ernie Warlick	$3.00

1965 Detroit Lions

Complete set NM (36):	$75.00
Common player:	$2.50
C1 Pat Studstill	$4.50
C2 Bob Whitlow	$2.50
C3 Wayne Walker	$3.00
C4 Tom Watkins	$3.00
C5 Jim Simon	$2.50
C6 Sam Williams	$2.50
C7 Terry Barr	$3.00
C8 Jerry Rush	$2.50
C9 Roger Brown	$3.00
C10 Tom Nowatzke	$3.00
C11 Dick Lane	$6.00
C12 Dick Compton	$2.50
C13 Yale Lary	$6.00
C14 Dick Lebeau	$4.50
C15 Dan Lewis	$3.00
C16 Wally Hilgenburg	$3.00
C17 Bruce Maher	$2.50
C18 Darris McCord	$3.00
C19 Hugh McInnis	$2.50
C20 Ernie Clark	$2.50
C21 Gail Cogdill	$3.00

C22 Wayne Rasmussen	$2.50
C23 Joe Don Looney	$12.00
C24 Jim Gibbons	$3.00
C25 John Gonzaga	$2.50
C26 John Gordy	$3.00
C27 Bobby Thompson	$3.00
C28 J.D. Smith	$3.00
C29 Earl Morrall	$5.00
C30 Alex Karras	$6.00
C31 Nick Pietrosante	$4.50
C32 Milt Plum	$4.50
C33 Daryl Sanders	$2.50
C34 Joe Schmidt	$6.00
C35 Bob Scholtz	$2.50
C36 Team logo	$2.50

1965 New York Giants

Complete set NM (35):	$75.00
Common player:	$2.50
G1 Joe Morrison	$3.00
G2 Dick Lynch	$3.00
G3 Andy Stynchula	$2.50
G4 Clarence Childs	$2.50
G5 Aaron Thomas	$2.50
G6 Mickey Walker	$2.50
G7 Bill Winter	$2.50
G8 Bookie Bolin	$2.50
G9 Tom Scott	$2.50
G10 John Lovetere	$2.50
G11 Jim Patton	$3.00
G12 Darrell Dess	$2.50
G13 Dick James	$2.50
G14 Jerry Hillebrand	$2.50
G15 Dick Pesonen	$2.50
G16 Del Shofner	$4.50
G17 Erich Barnes	$3.00
G18 Roosevelt Brown	$6.00
G19 Greg Larson	$2.50
G20 Jim Katcavage	$3.00
G21 Frank Lasky	$2.50
G22 Lou Slaby	$2.50
G23 Jim Moran	$2.50
G24 Roger Anderson	$2.50
G25 Steve Thurlow	$2.50
G26 Ernie Wheelwright	$3.00
G27 Gary Wood	$3.00
G28 Tony Dimidio	$2.50
G29 John Contoulis	$2.50
G30 Tucker Frederickson	$4.50
G31 Bob Timberlake	$3.00
G32 Chuck Mercein	$3.00
G33 Ernie Koy	$4.50
G34 Tom Costello	$2.50
G35 Homer Jones	$4.50

1965 New York Jets

Complete set NM (35):	$100.00
Common player:	$2.50
J1 Don Maynard	$6.00
J2 George Sauer	$4.50
J3 Cosmo Iacavazzi	$3.00
J4 Jim O'Mahoney	$2.50
J5 Matt Snell	$4.50
J6 Clyde Washington	$2.50
J7 Jim Turner	$3.00
J8 Mike Tailaferro	$3.00
J9 Marshall Starks	$2.50
J10 Mark Smolinski	$2.50
J11 Bob Schweickert	$2.50
J12 Paul Rochester	$2.50
J13 Sherman Plunkett	$3.00

J14 Gerry Philbin	$3.00
J15 Pete Perreault	$2.50
J16 Dainard Paulson	$2.50
J17 Joe Namath	$50.00
J18 Winston Hill	$3.00
J19 Dee Mackey	$2.50
J20 Curley Johnson	$3.00
J21 Mike Hudock	$2.50
J22 John Huarte	$4.50
J23 Gordy Holz	$2.50
J24 Gene Heeler	$4.50
J25 Larry Grantham	$3.00
J26 Dan Ficca	$2.50
J27 Sam DeLuca	$2.50
J28 Bill Baird	$2.50
J29 Ralph Baker	$2.50
J30 Wahoo McDaniel	$6.00
J31 Jim Evans	$2.50
J32 Dave Herman	$2.50
J33 John Schmitt	$2.50
J34 Jim Harris	$2.50
J35 Bake Turner	$3.00

1965 Washington Redskins

Complete set NM (36):	$60.00
Common player:	$2.50
C1 undetermined	
C2 Fred Mazurek	$2.50
C3 Lonnie Sanders	$2.50
C4 Jim Steffen	$2.50
C5 John Nisby	$2.50
C6 George Izo	$4.50
C7 Vince Promuto	$2.50
C8 John Sample	$3.00
C9 Pat Richter	$3.00
C10 Preston Carpenter	$2.50
C11 Sam Huff	$6.00
C12 Pervis Atkins	$3.00
C13 Fred Barnett	$2.50
C14 undetermined	
C15 Bill Anderson	$2.50
C16 undetermined	
C17 George Seals	$2.50
C18 undetermined	
C19 undetermined	
C20 undetermined	
C21 John Paluck	$2.50
C22 Fran O'Brien	$2.50
C23 Joe Rutgens	$2.50
C24 Rod Breedlove	$2.50
C25 undetermined	
C26 Bob Jencks	$3.00
C27 undetermined	
C28 Sonny Jurgensen	$7.50
C29 Bob Toneff	$2.50
C30 Charley Taylor	$6.00
C31 Bob Shiner	$2.50
C32 Bob Williams	$2.50
C33 undetermined	
C34 Ron Snidow	$2.50
C35 Paul Krause	$4.50
C36 Team logo	$2.50

1966 Coca-Cola
National NFL bottle caps

Complete set NM (70):	$175.00
Common player:	$2.50
1) Larry Wilson	$5.00
2) Frank Ryan	$3.00
3) Norm Snead	$3.00
4) Mel Renfro	$4.50

5) Timmy Brown	$3.00
6) Tucker Frederickson	$2.50
7) Jim Bakken	$2.50
8) Paul Krause	$4.50
9) Irv Cross	$3.00
10) Cornell Green	$2.50
11) Pat Fischer	$2.50
12) Bob Hayes	$4.50
13) Charley Taylor	$5.00
14) Pete Retzlaff	$2.50
15) Jim Ringo	$5.00
16) Maxie Baughan	$3.00
17) Chuck Howley	$3.00
18) John Wooten	$2.50
19) Bob DeMarco	$2.50
20) Dale Meinert	$2.50
21) Gene Hickerson	$2.50
22) George Andrie	$2.50
23) Joe Rutgens	$2.50
24) Bob Lilly	$6.00
25) Sam Silas	$2.50
26) Bob Brown	$3.00
27) Dick Schafrath	$2.50
28) Roosevelt Brown	$5.00
29) Jim Houston	$2.50
30) Paul Wiggin	$2.50
31) Gary Ballman	$2.50
32) Gary Collins	$3.00
33) Sonny Randle	$3.00
34) Charlie Johnson	$3.00
35) Cleveland Browns logo	$2.50
36) Green Bay Packers logo	$2.50
37) Herb Adderley	$5.00
38) Grady Alderman	$2.50
39) Doug Atkins	$5.00
40) Bruce Bosley	$2.50
41) John Brodie	$6.00
42) Roger Brown	$2.50
43) Bill Brown	$3.00
44) Dick Butkus	$7.50
45) Lee Roy Caffey	$2.50
46) John David Crow	$3.00
47) Willie Davis	$5.00
48) Mike Ditka	$7.50
49) Joe Fortunato	$2.50
50) John Gordy	$2.50
51) Deacon Jones	$5.00
52) Alex Karras	$5.00
53) Dick LeBeau	$2.50
54) Jerry Logan	$2.50
55) John Mackey	$5.00
56) Ed Meador	$2.50
57) Tommy McDonald	$3.00
58) Merlin Olsen	$5.00
59) Jimmy Orr	$3.00
60) Jim Parker	$5.00
61) Dave Parks	$3.00
62) Walter Rock	$2.50
63) Gale Sayers	$10.00
64) Pat Studstill	$2.50
65) Fran Tarkenton	$7.50
66) Mick Tingelhoff	$3.00
67) Bob Vogel	$2.50
68) Wayne Walker	$3.00
69) Ken Willard	$3.00
70) Willie Wood	$5.00

1966 Coca-Cola
AFL/NFL All-Stars bottle caps

These caps, each measuring 1 1/8" in diameter, could be found under bottle caps of Coca-Cola products (Coke, Tab, Fresca) in participating cities with AFL or NFL teams. The cap has a Coke logo and a football on the outside; the player's mug shot, name, position, number and AFL or NFL were included on the inside of the cap. A Cap Saver sheet, indicating cap numbers, was also issued; caps could be affixed to the sheet. Completed sheets could be turned in for prizes.

1966 AFL Stars

Complete set NM (34): $100.00
Common player: $2.50
C37 Babe Parilli (Boston Patriots) $3.00
C38 Mike Stratton (Buffalo Bills) $2.50
C39 Jack Kemp (Buffalo Bills) $17.50
C40 Len Dawson (Kansas City Chiefs) $7.50
C41 Fred Arbanas (Kansas City Chiefs) $2.50
C42 Bobby Bell (Kansas City Chiefs) $5.00
C43 Willie Brown (Oakland Raiders) $5.00
C44 Buck Buchanan (Kansas City Chiefs) $5.00
C45 Frank Buncom (San Diego Chargers) $2.50
C46 Nick Buoniconti (Boston Patriots) $4.50
C47 Gino Cappelletti (Boston Patriots) $3.00
C48 Eldon Danenhauer (Denver Broncos) $2.50
C49 Clem Daniels (Oakland Raiders) $3.00
C50 Leslie Duncan (San Diego Chargers) $3.00
C51 Willie Frazier (Kansas City Chiefs) $3.00
C52 Cookie Gilchrist (Miami Dolphins) $4.50
C53 Dave Grayson (Oakland Raiders) $2.50
C54 John Hadl (San Diego Chargers) $4.50
C55 Wayne Hawkins (Oakland Raiders) $2.50
C56 Sherrill Headrick (Kansas City Chiefs) $2.50
C57 Charlie Hennigan (Houston Oilers) $3.00
C58 E.J. Holub (Kansas City Chiefs) $3.00
C59 Curley Johnson (New York Jets) $2.50
C60 Keith Lincoln (San Diego Chargers) $3.00
C61 Paul Lowe (San Diego Chargers) $3.00
C62 Don Maynard (New York Jets) $5.00
C63 Jon Morris (Boston Patriots) $2.50
C64 Joe Namath (New York Jets) $20.00
C65 Jim Otto (Oakland Raiders) $5.00
C66 Dainard Paulson (New York Jets) $2.50
C67 Art Powell (Oakland Raiders) $3.00
C68 Walt Sweeney (San Diego Chargers) $2.50
C69 Bob Talamini (Houston Oilers) $2.50
C70 Lance Alworth (San Diego Chargers,
misspelled Alsworth) $7.50

1966 NFL Stars

Complete set NM (34): $100.00
Common player: $2.50
C37 Frank Ryan (Cleveland Browns) $3.00
C38 Timmy Brown (Philadelphia Eagles) $3.00
C39 Tucker Frederickson (New York Giants) $3.00
C40 Cornell Green (Dallas Cowboys) $3.00
C41 Bob Hayes (Dallas Cowboys) $4.50
C42 Charley Taylor (Washington Redskins) $5.00
C43 Pete Retzlaff (Philadelphia Eagles) $3.00
C44 Jim Ringo (Green Bay Packers) $5.00
C45 John Wooten (Cleveland Browns) $2.50
C46 Dale Meinert (St. Louis Cardinals) $2.50
C47 Bob Lilly (Dallas Cowboys) $7.50
C48 Sam Silas (St. Louis Cardinals) $2.50
C49 Roosevelt Brown (New York Giants) $5.00
C50 Gary Ballman (Pittsburgh Steelers) $3.00
C51 Gary Collins (Cleveland Browns) $3.00
C52 Sonny Randle (St. Louis Cardinals) $3.00
C53 Charlie Johnson (St. Louis Cardinals) $3.00
C54 Herb Adderley (Green Bay Packers) $5.00
C55 Doug Atkins (Chicago Bears) $5.00
C56 Roger Brown (Detroit Lions) $3.00
C57 Dick Butkus (Chicago Bears) $10.00
C58 Willie Davis (Green Bay Packers) $5.00

C59 Tommy McDonald (Los Angeles Rams) $3.00
C60 Alex Karras (Detroit Lions) $6.00
C61 John Mackey (Baltimore Colts) $5.00
C62 Ed Meador (Los Angeles Rams) $3.00
C63 Merlin Olsen (Los Angeles Rams) $6.00
C64 Dave Parks (San Francisco 49ers) $3.00
C65 Gale Sayers (Chicago Bears) $20.00
C66 Fran Tarkenton (Minnesota Vikings) $7.50
C67 Mick Tingelhoff (Minnesota Vikings) $3.00
C68 Ken Willard (San Francisco 49ers) $3.00
C69 Willie Wood (Green Bay Packers) $5.00
C70 Bill Brown (Minnesota Vikings) $3.00

1966 Coca-Cola bottle caps
1966 Atlanta Falcons

Complete set NM (36): $75.00
Common player: $2.50
C1 Tommy Nobis $6.00
C2 Ernie Wheelright $3.00
C3 Lee Calland $2.50
C4 Chuck Sieminski $2.50
C5 Dennis Claridge $2.50
C6 Ralph Heck $2.50
C7 Alex Hawkins $3.00
C8 Dan Grimm $2.50
C9 Marion Rushing $2.50
C10 Bobbie Johnson $2.50
C11 Bobby Franklin $2.50
C12 Bill McWatters $2.50
C13 Billy Lothridge $3.00
C14 Billy Martin $2.50
C15 Tom Wilson $2.50
C16 Dennis Murphy $2.50
C17 Randy Johnson $3.00
C18 Guy Reese $2.50
C19 Frank Marchlewski $2.50
C20 Don Talbert $4.00
C21 Errol Linden $2.50
C22 Dan Lewis $2.50
C23 Ed Cook $2.50
C24 Hugh McInnis $2.50
C25 Frank Lasky $2.50
C26 Bob Jencks $2.50
C27 Bill Jobko $2.50
C28 Nick Rassas $2.50
C29 Rob Riggle $2.50
C30 Ken Reaves $2.50
C31 Bob Sanders $2.50
C32 Steve Sloan $6.00
C33 Ron Smith $3.00
C34 Bob Whitlow $2.50
C35 Roger Anderson $2.50
C36 Falcons logo $2.50

1966 Baltimore Colts

Complete set NM (36): $75.00
Common player: $2.50
C1 Ted Davis $2.50
C2 Bobby Boyd $2.50
C3 Lenny Moore $6.00
C4 Jackie Burkett $3.00
C5 Jimmy Orr $4.50
C6 Andy Stynchula $2.50
C7 Mike Curtis $4.50
C8 Jerry Logan $2.50
C9 Steve Stonebreaker $3.00
C10 John Mackey $5.00
C11 Dennis Gaubatz $2.50
C12 Don Shinnick $3.00
C13 Dick Szymanski $2.50
C14 Ordell Braase $2.50

Miscellaneous

C15 Len Lyles.............................$2.50
C16 Rick Kestner........................$2.50
C17 Dan Sullivan........................$2.50
C18 Lou Michaels........................$3.00
C19 Gary Cuozzo $3.00
C20 Butch Wilson........................$2.50
C21 Willie Richardson $3.00
C22 Jim Welch $2.50
C23 Tony Lorick.........................$3.00
C24 Billy Ray Smith.....................$3.00
C25 Fred Miller $2.50
C26 Tom Matte...........................$4.50
C27 John Unitas.........................$12.00
C28 Glenn Ressler.......................$2.50
C29 Alvin Haymond.......................$2.50
C30 Jim Parker $5.00
C31 Butch Allison $2.50
C32 Bob Vogel...........................$2.50
C33 Jerry Hill $2.50
C34 Raymond Berry $6.00
C35 Sam Ball............................$2.50
C36 Colts logo $2.50

1966 Boston Patriots

Complete set NM (36) $75.00
Common player:..........................$2.50
C1 Jon Morris...........................$2.50
C2 Don Webb $2.50
C3 Charles Long $2.50
C4 Tony Romeo...........................$2.50
C5 Bob Dee..............................$2.50
C6 Tom Addison..........................$2.50
C7 Tom Neville $2.50
C8 Ron Hall $2.50
C9 White Graves.........................$2.50
C10 Ellis Johnson $2.50
C11 Don Oakes $2.50
C12 Tom Yewcic..........................$2.50
C13 Tom Hennessey.......................$2.50
C14 Jay Cunningham......................$2.50
C15 Larry Garron $2.50
C16 Justin Canale $2.50
C17 Art Graham $2.50
C18 Babe Parilli........................$3.00
C19 Jim Hunt............................$2.50
C20 Karl Singer.........................$2.50
C21 Houston Antwine $3.00
C22 Nick Buoniconti $5.00
C23 John Huarte.........................$4.50
C24 Gino Cappelletti....................$3.00
C25 Chuck Shonta $2.50
C26 Dick Felt...........................$2.50
C27 Mike Dukes $2.50
C28 Larry Eisenhauer....................$3.00
C29 Jim Fraser..........................$2.50
C30 Len St. Jean $2.50
C31 J.D. Garrett........................$2.50
C32 Jim Whalen $2.50
C33 Jim Nance...........................$4.50
C34 Dick Arrington $2.50
C35 Lonnie Farmer.......................$2.50
C36 Patriots logo $2.40

1966 Buffalo Bills

Complete set NM (36): $75.00
Common player: $2.50
B1 Bill Laskey $2.50
B2 Marty Schottenheimer.................$6.00
B3 Stew Barber $3.00
B4 Glenn Bass $2.50
B5 Remi Prudhomme $2.50

B6 Al Bemilller.........................$2.50
B7 Butch Byrd $3.00
B8 Wray Carlton $3.00
B9 Hagood Clarke........................$2.50
B10 Jack Kemp $25.00
B11 Charley Warner $2.50
B12 Elbert Dubenion $5.00
B13 Jim Dunaway $3.00
B14 Booker Edgerson $2.50
B15 Paul Costa..........................$3.00
B16 Henry Schmidt.......................$2.50
B17 Dick Hudson.........................$3.00
B18 Harry Jacobs........................$3.00
B19 Tom Janik...........................$2.50
B20 Tom Day.............................$3.00
B21 Daryle Lamonica.....................$6.00
B22 Paul Maguire $5.00
B23 Roland McDole $3.00
B24 Dudley Merideth $2.50
B25 Joe O'Donnell $2.50
B26 Charley Ferguson $2.50
B27 Ed Rutkowski........................$3.00
B28 George Saimes.......................$3.00
B29 Tom Sestak..........................$3.00
B30 Billy Shaw..........................$3.00
B31 Bob Smith...........................$2.50
B32 Mike Stratton.......................$3.00
B33 Gene Sykes..........................$2.50
B34 John Tracey.........................$3.00
B35 Ernie Warlick $3.00
B36 Bills logo..........................$2.50

1966 Cleveland Browns

Complete set NM (36): $75.00
Common player:..........................$2.50
C1 Jim Ninowski $3.00
C2 Leroy Kelly $6.00
C3 Lou Groza............................$6.00
C4 Gary Collins $3.00
C5 Bill Glass $3.00
C6 Dale Lindsey $2.50
C7 Galen Fiss $2.50
C8 Ross Fichtner........................$2.50
C9 John Wooten..........................$2.50
C10 Clifton McNeil $3.00
C11 Paul Wiggin.........................$3.00
C12 Gene Hickerson $3.00
C13 Ernie Green $3.00
C14 Mike Howell.........................$2.50
C15 Dick Schafrath $3.00
C16 Sidney Williams $2.50
C17 Frank Ryan $4.50
C18 Bernie Parrish $3.00
C19 Vince Costello $2.50
C20 John Brown $2.50
C21 Monte Clark.........................$3.00
C22 Walt Roberts........................$2.50
C23 Johnny Brewer.......................$2.50
C24 Walter Beach $2.50
C25 Dick Modzelewski....................$3.00
C26 Gary Lane...........................$2.50
C27 Jim Houston $3.00
C28 Milt Morin $3.00
C29 Erich Barnes $3.00
C30 Tom Hutchinson $2.50
C31 John Morrow $2.50
C32 Jim Kanicki $2.50
C33 Paul Warfield.......................$6.00
C34 Jim Garcia $2.50
C35 Walter Johnson $3.00
C36 Browns logo $3.00

1966 Dallas Cowboys

Complete set NM (36): $75.00
Common player: $2.50
C1 Mike Connelly..$2.50
C2 Tony Liscio $2.50
C3 Jethro Pugh..$4.50
C4 Larry Stephens $2.50
C5 Jim Colvin $2.50
C6 Malcolm Walker $2.50
C7 Danny Villanueva $3.00
C8 Frank Clarke...$3.00
C9 Don Meredith..$10.00
C10 George Andrie...$3.00
C11 Mel Renfro $5.00
C12 Pettis Norman..$3.00
C13 Buddy Dial $3.00
C14 Pete Gent $3.00
C15 Jerry Rhome $3.00
C16 Bob Hayes $5.00
C17 Mike Gaechter..$2.50
C18 Joe Bob Isbell..$2.50
C19 Harold Hays $2.50
C20 Craig Morton..$4.50
C21 Jake Kupp...$2.50
C22 Cornell Green $3.00
C23 Dan Reeves...$7.50
C24 Leon Donohue...$2.50
C25 Dave Manders $3.00
C26 Warren Livingston $2.50
C27 Bob Lilly $6.00
C28 Chuck Howley...$4.50
C29 Don Bishop $2.50
C30 Don Perkins $3.00
C31 Jim Boeke..$2.50
C32 Dave Edwards..$2.50
C33 Lee Roy Jordan $5.00
C34 Obert Logan $2.50
C35 Ralph Neely $3.00
C36 Cowboys logo $2.50

1966 Houston Oilers

Complete set NM (36): $75.00
Common player: $2.50
C1 Scott Appleton...$3.00
C2 George Allen..$3.00
C3 Don Floyd $3.00
C4 Ronnie Caveness..$2.50
C5 Jim Norton...$2.50
C6 Jackie Lee..$2.50
C7 George Blanda..$2.50
C8 Tony Banfield $3.00
C9 George Rice...$2.50
C10 Charley Tolar $3.00
C11 Bobby Jancik...$3.00
C12 Fred Glick $2.50
C13 Ode Burrell..$2.50
C14 Walt Suggs...$2.50
C15 Bob McLeod $2.50
C16 Johnny Baker..$2.50
C17 Danny Bradshaw $2.50
C18 Gary Cutsinger..$2.50
C19 Doug Cline $2.50
C20 Hoyle Granger..$3.00
C21 Bob Talamini..$2.50
C22 Don Trull..$3.00
C23 Charlie Hennigan $3.00
C24 Sid Blanks..$3.00
C25 Pat Holmes $2.50
C26 John Frongillo $2.50
C27 John Whitehorn...$2.50
C28 George Kinney..$2.50

C29 Charles Frazier $3.00
C30 Ernie Ladd..$5.00
C31 W.K. Hicks...$2.50
C32 Sonny Bishop $2.50
C33 Larry Elkins..$3.00
C34 Glen Ray Hines $3.00
C35 Bobby Maples $3.00
C36 Oilers logo $2.50

1966 Kansas City Chiefs

Complete set NM (36): $75.00
Common player:...$2.50
C1 E.J. Holub..$3.00
C2 Al Reynolds...$2.50
C3 Buck Buchanan $6.00
C4 Curt Merz..$7.50
C5 David Hill..$2.50
C6 Bobby Hunt $2.50
C7 Jerry Mays...$3.00
C8 Joe Gilliam $3.00
C9 Walt Corey $2.50
C10 Solomon Brannan $2.50
C11 Aaron Brown $3.00
C12 Bert Coan...$3.00
C13 Ed Budde $3.00
C14 Tommy Brooker $3.00
C15 Bobby Bell $6.00
C16 Smokey Stover $2.50
C17 Curtis McClinton...$3.00
C18 Jerrel Wilson $4.50
C19 Ron Burton $3.00
C20 Mike Garrett...$6.00
C21 Jim Tyrer $3.00
C22 Johnny Robinson $4.50
C23 Bobby Ply..$2.50
C24 Frank Pitts $2.50
C25 Ed Lothamer...$2.50
C26 Sherrill Headrick $3.00
C27 Fred Williamson..$5.00
C28 Chris Burford..$3.00
C29 Willie Mitchell $2.50
C30 Otis Taylor...$6.00
C31 Fred Arbanas $3.00
C32 Hatch Rosdahl $2.50
C33 Reg Carolan..$2.50
C34 Len Dawson..$7.50
C35 Pete Beathard..$4.50
C36 Chiefs logo $2.50

1966 Los Angeles Rams

Complete set NM (36): $75.00
Common player:...$2.50
C1 Tom Mack $3.00
C2 Tom Moore...$3.00
C3 Bill Munson..$3.00
C4 Bill George $5.00
C5 Joe Carollo...$2.50
C6 Dick Bass...$3.00
C7 Ken Iman...$2.50
C8 Charlie Cowam...$3.00
C9 Terry Baker $4.50
C10 Don Chuy $2.50
C11 Jack Pardee $4.50
C12 Lamar Lundy $3.00
C13 Bill Anderson $2.50
C14 Roman Gabriel $5.00
C15 Roosevelt Grier $4.50
C16 Billy Truax $3.00
C17 Merlin Olsen $5.00
C18 Deacon Jones...$5.00
C19 Joe Scibelli $2.50

Miscellaneous

C20 Marlin McKeever $3.00
C21 Doug Woodlief...$2.50
C22 Chuck Lamson $2.50
C23 Dan Currie..$2.50
C24 Maxie Baughan...$3.00
C25 Bruce Gossett $3.00
C26 Les Josephson $3.00
C27 Ed Meador..$3.00
C28 Anthony Guillory $2.50
C29 Irv Cross..$3.00
C30 Tommy McDonald...$3.00
C31 Bucky Pope...$3.00
C32 Jack Snow $4.50
C33 Joe Wendryhoski...$2.50
C34 Clancy Williams...$3.00
C35 Ben Wilson...$2.50
C36 Rams logo $2.50

1966 New York Giants

Complete set NM (35): $75.00
Common player: $2.50
G1 Joe Morrison $3.00
G2 Dick Lynch $3.00
G3 Pete Case $2.50
G4 Clarence Childs..$2.50
G5 Aaron Thomas...$2.50
G6 Jim Carroll $2.50
G7 Henry Carr $3.00
G8 Bookie Bolin $2.50
G9 Roosevelt Davis $2.50
G10 John Lovetere...$2.50
G11 Jim Patton $3.00
G12 Wendell Harris..$2.50
G13 Roger LaLonde $2.50
G14 Jerry Hillebrand $2.50
G15 Carl Lockhart $3.00
G16 Del Shofner..$4.50
G17 Earl Morrall..$5.00
G18 Roosevelt Brown...$5.00
G19 Greg Larson $2.50
G20 Jim Katcavage $3.00
G21 Smith Reed $2.50
G22 Lou Slaby...$2.50
G23 Jim Moran $2.50
G24 Bill Swain $2.50
G25 Steve Thurlow $2.50
G26 Olen Underwood...$2.50
G27 Gary Wood $3.00
G28 Larry Vargo..$3.00
G29 Jim Prestel..$2.50
G30 Tucker Frederickson $3.00
G31 Bob Timberlake $3.00
G32 Chuck Mercein...$3.00
G33 Ernie Koy $3.00
G34 Tom Costello...$2.50
G35 Homer Jones $3.00

1966 New York Jets

Complete set NM (35) $75.00
Common player: $2.50
J1 Don Maynard $5.00
J2 George Sauer...$3.00
J3 Paul Crane $2.50
J4 Jim Colclough $2.50
J5 Matt Snell $4.50
J6 Sherman Lewis $3.00
J7 Jim Turner $3.00
J8 Mike Taliaferro $3.00
J9 Cornell Gordon..$2.50
J10 Mark Smolinski $2.50
J11 Al Atkinson $3.00

J12 Paul Rochester...$2.50
J13 Sherman Plunkett $2.50
J14 Gerry Philbin $3.00
J15 Pete Lammons $3.00
J16 Dainard Paulson $2.50
J17 Joe Namath $25.00
J18 Winston Hill $2.50
J19 Dee Mackey...$2.50
J20 Curley Johnson $2.50
J21 Verlon Biggs..$3.00
J22 Bill Mathis..$3.00
J23 Carl McAdams $2.50
J24 Bert Wilder..$2.50
J25 Larry Grantham $3.00
J26 Bill Yearby $2.50
J27 Sam DeLuca $2.50
J28 Bill Baird $2.50
J29 Ralph Baker...$2.50
J30 Ray Abruzzese...$2.50
J31 Jim Hudson..$2.50
J32 Dave Herman...$2.50
J33 John Schmitt..$2.50
J34 Jim Harris..$2.50
J35 Bake Turner...$3.00

1966 Pittsburgh Steelers

Complete set NM (36): $75.00
Common player:..$2.50
C1 John Baker..$2.50
C2 Mike Lind...$3.00
C3 Ken Kortas..$2.50
C4 Willie Daniel...$2.50
C5 Roy Jefferson..$4.00
C6 Bob Hohn $2.50
C7 Dan James $2.50
C8 Gary Ballman $3.00
C9 Brady Keys...$2.50
C10 Charley Bradshaw $3.00
C11 Jim Bradshaw..$2.50
C12 Jim Butler...$2.50
C13 Paul Martha $4.00
C14 Mike Clark..$2.50
C15 Ray Lemek $2.50
C16 Clarence Peaks $3.00
C17 Theron Sapp $3.00
C18 Ray Mansfield $2.50
C19 Chuck Hinton $2.50
C20 Bill Nelsen..$4.50
C21 Rod Breedlove...$2.50
C22 Frank Lambert $2.50
C23 Ben McGee $2.50
C24 Myron Pottios $3.00
C25 John Campbell...$2.50
C26 Andy Russell $4.50
C27 Mike Sandusky..$2.50
C28 Bob Schmitz $2.50
C29 Riley Gunnels..$2.50
C30 Clendon Thomas $3.00
C31 Tommy Wade $2.50
C32 Dick Hoak $3.50
C33 Marv Woodson $2.50
C34 Bob Nichols..$2.50
C35 John Henry Johnson $6.00
C36 Steelers logo $2.50

1966 St. Louis Cardinals

Complete set NM (36): $75.00
Common player:..$2.50
C1 Pat Fischer $3.00
C2 Sonny Randle $3.00
C3 Joe Childress $2.50

C4 Dave Meggysey, misspelled Meggyesy $4.50
C5 Joe Robb $2.50
C6 Jerry Stovall $3.00
C7 Ernie McMillan $3.00
C8 Dale Meinert $2.50
C9 Irv Goode $2.50
C10 Bob DeMarco $3.00
C11 Mal Hammack $2.50
C12 Jim Bakken $4.00
C13 Bill Thornton $2.50
C14 Buddy Humphrey $2.50
C15 Bill Koman $2.50
C16 Larry Wilson $6.00
C17 Charles Walker $2.50
C18 Prentice Gautt $4.50
C19 Charlie Johnson, misspelled Charley $4.50
C20 Ken Gray $3.00
C21 Dave Simmons $3.00
C22 Sam Silas $2.50
C23 Larry Stallings $3.00
C24 Don Brumm $2.50
C25 Bobby Joe Conrad $3.00
C26 Bill Triplett $2.50
C27 Luke Owens $2.50
C28 Jackie Smith $5.00
C29 Bob Reynolds $2.50
C30 Abe Woodson $3.00
C31 Jimmy Burson $2.50
C32 Willis Crenshaw $2.50
C33 Billy Gambrell $2.50
C34 Ray Ogden $2.50
C35 Herschel Turner $2.50
C36 Cardinals logo $2.50

1966 San Francisco 49ers

Complete set NM (36): $75.00
Common player: $2.50
C1 Bernie Casey $4.50
C2 Bruce Bosley $3.00
C3 Kermit Alexander $3.00
C4 John Brodie $7.50
C5 Dave Parks $3.00
C6 Len Rohde $2.50
C7 Walter Rock $2.50
C8 George Mira $4.50
C9 Karl Rubke $2.50
C10 Ken Willard $3.00
C11 John David Crow, misspelled Crowe $4.50
C12 George Donnelly $2.50
C13 Dave Wilcox $4.50
C14 Vern Burke $2.50
C15 Wayne Swinford $2.50
C16 Elbert Kimbrough $2.50
C17 Clark Miller $2.50
C18 Dave Kopay $3.00
C19 Joe Cerne $2.50
C20 Roland Lakes $2.50
C21 Charlie Krueger $3.00
C22 Billy Kilmer $5.00
C23 Jim Johnson $5.00
C24 Matt Hazeltine $2.50
C25 Mike Dowdle $2.50
C26 Jim Wilson $2.50
C27 Tommy Davis $3.00
C28 Jim Norton $2.50
C29 Jack Chapple $2.50
C30 Ed Beard $2.50
C31 John Thomas $2.50
C32 Monty Stickles $3.00
C33 Kay McFarland $3.00
C34 Gary Lewis $2.50
C35 Howard Mudd $2.50
C36 49ers logo $2.50

1971 Coca-Cola Green Bay Packer bottle caps

This 22-cap set, sponsored by Coca-Cola, features members of the Green Bay Packers. Each player's face is printed in black below his picture. The unnumbered caps, which measure approximately 1 1/8" in diameter, are listed alphabetically.

Complete set NM (22): $20.00
Common player: $1.00
1) Ken Bowman $1.00
2) John Brockington $2.50
3) Bob Brown $1.50
4) Fred Carr $1.50
5) Jim Carter $1.00
6) Carroll Dale $1.50
7) Ken Ellis $1.00
8) Gale Gillingham $1.50
9) Dave Hampton $1.00
10) Doug Hart $1.00
11) Jim Hill $1.00
12) Dick Himes $1.00
13) Scott Hunter $1.50
14) MacArthur Lane $2.50
15) Bill Lueck $1.00
16) Al Matthews $1.00
17) Rich McGeorge $1.00
18) Ray Nitschke $5.00
19) Francis Peay $1.00
20) Dave Robinson $1.50
21) Alden Roche $1.00
22) Bart Starr $7.50

Cups/glasses/plates

- 1959 Baltimore Colts World Champions tall glasses, with 1959 schedule on back $25

- 1970s Bart Starr 6" Pizza Hut commemorative drinking glass, features black-and-white photo on one side and career highlights on the other $25

- 1970s Vince Lombardi/Curly Lambeau commemorative drinking glass, features green-and-white illustrations of the two Green Bay Packer coaches, with career milestones printed in yellow $25

- Early 1970s Vince Lombardi Pizza Hut commemorative 6" glass, features a black-and-white Lombardi photo and facsimile signature on one side, and a famous Lombardi quote on the other $25

- Green Bay Packers 4-ounce shot glass by Kessler, with 1969 Packer schedule on one side and a Wisonsin Badgers schedule on the other $12 (mb)

- Dallas Cowboys 4" glass, blue graphics of a player, #34, running with the ball, says Cowboys under his feet, late 1960s .... $15 (mb)

- Baltimore Colts 4 1/2" cocktail mug, blue print honors 1959 Western Division NFL Champions and lists games and scores .... $22 (mb)

- 1950s New York Giants 10 1/2" dinner plate with Giants logo, orange/black border $150

- 1970 Kansas City Chiefs commemorative Super Bowl plate, 18-ounce, #18 of 500, autographed by Hall of Famers Jan Stenerud, Buck Buchanan, Bobby Bell and Len Dawson $295

- Walter Payton 1980 Vienna Beef plastic cup .. $45

- Boston Patriots ceramic team-issued AFL tankard from the early 1960s $95

Miscellaneous

- Super Bowl XVII ceramic mug, Miami vs. Washington $45
- New York Giants 1986 Super Bowl XXI Champions coffee mug $35
- Super Bowl XXI paper plates, unopened $25
- New York Giants 1986 Super Bowl XXI commemorative signature plate, 9 1/2" $45
- 1940s New York Giants drinking glass $75
- Set of four Pittsburgh Steelers Super Bowl XIV/McDonald's glasses $100
- Super Bowl III mug, featuring Daily News sports page headline "No Impossible Dream: Jets 16, Colts 7" $75

Equipment/jerseys

- Official World Football League football $225
- circa 1920s football helmet, brown adult-sized, with felt lining still inside, this helmet was made before plastics and face guards existed, manufactured by S.R. & Co. $225
- Burt Reynolds' jersey from the movie "The Longest Yard," worn during the filming of Paramount's 1974 hit, the jersey is a Rawlings, size L, with #22 in white on both sides and "Mean Machine" in red on the back $600
- Evening Shade television show football uniform, jersey and pants for the "Mules" $75
- Los Angeles Raiders jersey #42 (Ronnie Lott), autographed by singer Michael Jackson, whose song "Bad" was used in television commericals to promote Lott $295

Food-related items

- 1983 Cleveland Browns Nu-Maid Margarine tubs, set of 5, including Doug Dieken, Dave Logan, Ozzie Newsome, Mike Pruitt and Clarence Scott $45
- Dallas Cowboys 1971 World Champions commemorative Pepsi bottles, 16-ounce $20
- 1981 Terry Bradshaw peanut butter jar, with him in uniform on the label $35
- 1980 Ken Stabler unopened Can-Snake Venom Cola $25

- 1981 7-Up Iron-ons, 9x10: Pat Haden (Rams) and Earl Campbell (Oilers) $6 each; Tony Dorsett (Cowboys) $7; Hollywood Henderson (Cowboys) $5
- 1972 Gatorade lids with team logos on the top: Cleveland Browns, Dallas Cowboys, Denver Broncos, Detroit Lions, Kansas City Chiefs, Miami Dolphins, New York Giants, New York Jets, Oakland Raiders, St. Louis Cardinals, San Diego Chargers and San Francisco 49ers, each $9
- 1977 Pittsburgh Steeler Ice Cream bags, 6x15, with Terry Bradshaw and Jack Lambert $15
- 1983 Pittsburgh Steelers butter tubs: L.C. Greenwood ($12), Jack Ham ($20), Mel Blount ($13), John Stallworth ($12), Franco Harris ($24) and Mike Webster ($15)

Milk Cartons

1963 Buffalo Bills Jones Dairy

These cardboard cards, 1" diameter perforated discs, were included on the sides of Jone Diary milk cartons. They are unnumbered and are often found off-centered. Each has a drawing of the player on it, with his last name below.

	NM	EX	VG
Complete set (40):	750.00	375.00	225.00
Common player:	15.00	7.50	4.50
1. Ray Abruzzese	15.00	7.50	4.50
2. Art Baker	15.00	7.50	4.50
3. Stew Barber	18.00	9.00	5.50
4. Glenn Bass	18.00	9.00	5.50
5. Dave Behrman	18.00	9.00	4.50
6. Al Bemiller	15.00	7.50	4.50
7. Wray Carlton	20.00	10.00	6.00
8. Carl Charon	15.00	7.50	4.50
9. Monte Crockett	18.00	9.00	5.50
10. Wayne Crow	15.00	7.50	4.50
11. Tom Day	15.00	7.50	4.50
12. Elbert Dubenion	20.00	10.00	6.00
13. Jim Dunaway	18.00	9.00	5.50
14. Booker Edgerson	15.00	7.50	4.50
15. Cookie Gilchrist	30.00	15.00	9.00
16. Dick Hudson	18.00	9.00	5.50
17. Frank Jackunas	15.00	7.50	4.50
18. Harry Jacobs	18.00	9.00	5.50
19. Jack Kemp	300.00	150.00	90.00
20. Roger Kochman	15.00	7.50	4.50
21. Daryle Lamonica	50.00	25.00	15.00
22. Charley Leo	15.00	7.50	4.50
23. Marv Matuszak	18.00	9.00	5.50
24. Bill Miller	15.00	7.50	4.50
25. Leroy Moore	15.00	7.50	4.50
26. Harold Olson	15.00	7.50	4.50
27. Herb Paterra	15.00	7.50	4.50
28. Ken Rice	15.00	7.50	4.50
29. Henry Rivera	15.00	7.50	4.50
30. Ed Rutkowski	18.00	9.00	5.50
31. George Saimes	20.00	10.00	6.00
32. Tom Sestak	20.00	10.00	6.00
33. Billy Shaw	20.00	10.00	6.00
34. Mike Stratton	20.00	10.00	6.00
35. Gene Sykes	15.00	7.50	4.50
36. John Tracey	18.00	9.00	5.50
37. Ernie Warlick	18.00	9.00	5.50
38. Willie West	20.00	10.00	6.00
39. Mack Yoho	18.00	9.00	5.50
40. Sid Youngman	18.00	9.00	5.50

1986 Buffalo Bills Sealtest milk cartons

In 1986, half-gallon Sealtest milk cartons in the Buffalo area included 3 5/8" by 7 5/" panels on the sides, featuring a Buffalo Bills player. Each panel had a black-and-white mug shot of the player, statistics, career highlights and biographical information. They are unnumbered and were included on vitamin D and 2% lowfat milk cartons.

	MT	MN	EX
Complete set (6):	17.00	12.50	6.75
Common player:	1.00	.70	.40
1. Greg Bell	4.00	3.00	1.50
2. Jerry Butler	3.00	2.25	1.25
3. Steve Freeman	1.00	.70	.40
4. Jim Kelly	10.00	7.50	4.00
5. Eugene Marve	1.00	.70	.40
6. Charles Romes	1.00	.70	.40

1964-69 Kansas City Chiefs Fairmont Dairy

From 1964-69, half-gallon Fairmont Dairy milk cartons in the Kansas City area included panels featuring members of the Kansas City Chiefs football team. The front has a mug shot of the player, with his name, position, jersey number and biographical information on the right. Below the picture and information is a schedule of the team's home game for a particular season. Because they were issued over several seasons, there are different sizes and colors used. The printing on the cards is either red or black, depending on the year of issue. Red cards measure 3 3/8" by 2 3/8" when cut; black cards measure 3 7/16" by 1 9/16" when cut. Complete cartons double the values listed below, which are for Near Mint, Excellent and Very Good. The cards are unnumbered and have blank backs.

	NM	EX	VG
Complete set (18):	1,200.00	600.00	350.00
Common player:	50.00	25.00	15.00
1. Fred Arbanas, red	60.00	30.00	18.00
2. Bobby Bell, red	100.00	50.00	30.00
3. Buck Buchanan, black	100.00	50.00	30.00
4. Chris Burford, black	60.00	30.00	18.00
5. Len Dawson, red	200.00	100.00	60.00
6. Dave Grayson, red	50.00	25.00	15.00
7. Abner Hayes, red	75.00	37.00	22.00
8. Sherrill Headrick, red	60.00	30.00	18.00
9. Bobby Hunt, red	50.00	25.00	15.00
10. Frank Jackson, red	50.00	25.00	15.00
11. Curtis McClinton, red	60.00	30.00	18.00
12. Bobby Ply, red	50.00	25.00	15.00
13. Al Reynolds, red	50.00	25.00	15.00
14. Johnny Robinson, red	75.00	37.00	22.00
15. Noland Smith, red	50.00	25.00	15.00
16. Smokey Stover, red	50.00	25.00	15.00
17. Otis Taylor	100.00	50.00	30.00
18. Jim Tyrer, red	60.00	30.00	18.00

1990-91 Los Angeles Raiders Main Street Dairy cartons

This set of six, issued on Main Street Dairy cartons in the Los Angeles area, features Raiders players. Each half-pint milk carton has a head shot of the player, the team logo and a safety tip. The cartons, unnumbered, are printed in three colors - brown (chocolate), red (vitamin D) and blue (2% lowfat). The cartons measure 4 1/2" x 6" when collapsed.

	MT	NM	EX
Complete set (6):	15.00	11.00	6.00
Common player:	2.50	2.00	1.00
1. Bob Golic, blue	3.50	2.75	1.50
2. Terry McDaniel, brown	2.50	2.00	1.00
3. Don Mosebar, red	2.50	2.00	1.00
4. Jay Schroeder, blue	4.00	3.00	1.50
5. Art Shell, red	4.00	3.00	1.50
6. Steve Wisniewski, brown	2.50	2.00	1.00

1991-92 Los Angeles Raiders Adohr Farms Dairy cartons

These half-pint milk cartons are quite similar to the 1990-91 Main Street Dairy cartons which featured Raiders players; Adohr Farms Dairy apparently bought out Main Street Dairy. Each carton, measuring 4 1/2" by 6" when collapsed, features a head shot, team logo and safety tip. The cartons, issued in the Los Angeles area, are printed in red and black and are unnumbered.

	MT	NM	EX
Complete set (10):	25.00	18.50	10.00
Common player:	2.50	2.00	1.00
1. Jeff Gossett	2.50	2.00	1.00
2. Ethan Horton	2.50	2.00	1.00
3. Jeff Jaeger	2.50	2.00	1.00
4. Ronnie Lott	5.00	3.75	2.00
5. Terry McDaniel	2.50	2.00	1.00
6. Don Mosebar	2.50	2.00	1.00
7. Jay Schroeder	4.00	3.00	1.50
8. Art Shell	4.00	3.00	1.50
9. Greg Townsend	3.50	2.75	1.50
10. Steve Wisniewski	2.50	2.00	1.00

1993-94 Los Angeles Raiders Adohr Farms Dairy cartons

Six Los Angeles Raiders were featured on half-pint vitamin D milk cartons from the Adohr Farms Dairy. The unnumbered cartons measure 4 1/2" by 6" when collapsed. Two million cartons were distributed to area schools and hospitals during the season. Each has a Raiders logo, head shot and saftey message on one side.

	MT	NM	EX
Complete set (6):	15.00	11.00	6.00
Common player:	2.50	2.00	1.00
1. Jeff Gossett	2.50	2.00	1.00
2. Ethan Horton	2.50	2.00	1.00
3. Terry McDaniel	2.50	2.00	1.00
4. Don Mosebar	2.50	2.00	1.00
5. Art Shell	4.00	3.00	1.50
6. Steve Wisniewski	2.50	2.00	1.00

1965 St. Louis Cardinals Big Red Biographies

Adams Dairy half-gallon milk cartons in the St. Louis area included these 3 1/16" by 5 9/16" Big Red Biographies cards on them. Each card front has a head shot of a member of the St. Louis team, with purple and orange printing that provides biographical and statistical information about the player. The cards are unnumbered and have blank backs. Complete milk cartons would double the value of the card listed below. Prices are for Near Mint, Excellent and Very Good.

Miscellaneous

	NM	EX	VG
Complete set (17):	800.00	400.00	250.00
Common player:	50.00	25.00	15.00
1. Monk Bailey	50.00	25.00	15.00
2. Jim Bakken	100.00	50.00	30.00
3. Jim Burson	50.00	25.00	15.00
4. Willis Crenshaw	60.00	30.00	18.00
5. Bob DeMarco	60.00	30.00	18.00
6. Pat Fischer	85.00	42.00	25.00
7. Billy Gambrell	50.00	25.00	15.00
8. Ken Gray	60.00	30.00	18.00
9. Irv Goode	50.00	25.00	15.00
10. Mike Melinkovich	50.00	25.00	15.00
11. Bob Reynolds	50.00	25.00	15.00
12. Marion Rushing	50.00	25.00	15.00
13. Carl Silvestri	50.00	25.00	15.00
14. Dave Simmons	60.00	30.00	18.00
15. Jackie Smith	100.00	50.00	30.00
16. Bill Thornton	50.00	25.00	15.00
17. Herschel Turner	50.00	25.00	15.00

Miscellaneous

- Kansas City Chiefs quarterback towel, with team logo, used and autographed by Joe Montana.....$250
- Roger Staubach brass statue, 16" tall, with brass base, he's scrambling, with ball tucked under his arm; #12 with Dallas Cowboys helmet.....$100 (mb)
- 1973 Minnesota Vikings NFC Championship ladies ring, by Jostens, 10K pinky ring made for a player's wife, has a miniature Norseman head in a purple oval ornamented by a gold chain encircling the oval.......$500
- Alex Karras Swiss-made wrist watch, made for the "Alex Karras Golf Classic for Cystic Fibrosis," has a caricature of Karras on it, works....$70
- 1926 Red Grange football box, pictures Grange running, with the quote "I believe this football fills a need of every American boy." 6 1/4" by 13 1/8" by 3".......$500
- Joe Namath counter display to collect coins for the Leukemia Society, 12x8 1/2 cardboard tent, facsimile autograph.......$40 (mb)
- 1969 Fortune Shoe premiums, 9x12, black-and-white prints of Roman Gabriel and Don Merideth, $45 each, Frank Ryan.......$40
- Joe Namath large 1970s store display for Dingo Boots, in original box.......$125
- 1993 Fruit of the Loom underwear, unopened, with Dan Marino Fleer card on top.......$39
- 1967 NFL plastic pennant set: "Pennants" are silk-screened into a 16x45 sheet of vinyl that, when cut in accordance with the instructions at the bottom, opens up to form a pennant set of the 16 NFL teams. The item was part of a redemption program for Coca-Cola bottle caps and was tied in with Ford Motor Co.'s annual Punt, Pass and Kick competition.......$50
- 1974 Jim Thorpe Hall of Fame coin, brass, silver dollar size, proof-like.......$18
- Glass ashtray from Alan Ameche's restaurant in Baltimore.......$75
- Minnesota Vikings 14" tin serving tray, with colorful helmet logo in the center and a yellow border.......$11 (mb)

- Jim Beam Pro Football Hall of Fame whiskey decanter, 1972.......$75
- New York Giants Bud Lite fluorescent bar light, 20x15.......$125
- 6x2 bus sign for Colts Night.......$100
- Deion Sanders Atlanta Falcons autographed T-shirt.......$75
- Washington Redskins helmet telephone, by Nardi Enterprises, just like the ones used at the NFL Draft, new in the box.......$259
- 1992 Freeman McNeil vs. NFL trial courtroom art, illustrations used in the historic trial granting free agency to NFL players, done by artists Rachel Ketchum or Steve Michaels for local Minneapolis television stations during their coverage of the case; each is done on 16x20 matboard (or smaller) and is signed by the artist; some have been signed in red Sharpie by the player depicted.
  1) Freeman McNeil, in suit, headshot, matted with beige border, autographed.......$295
  2) Gene Upshaw, on the witness stand, as a leader in the NFL's labor movement, autographed..$250
  3) Gene Upshaw, on the witness stand, being handed a document by lead lawyer James Quinn, autographed.......$195
  4) Don Majkowski, smaller, on the witness stand, being questioned by attorney Randy Vataha, a former player.......$75
  5) Niko Noga, on the witness stand, also shows the judge, the U.S. flag and seal, the lawyers and the front of the court room, matted with a blue border.......$150
- 1946 Football Highlights of the Year film, 16mm, in original decorative box.......$50
- 1975 World Football League unused tickets, nine different home games for the Memphis Southmen, Mint.......$50 (mb)
- Raymond Berry's 1964-65-66-67 original NFL Baltimore Colts contracts.......$300 each
- Raymond Berry cancelled check, $15, Lenny Moore cancelled check.......$10
- Don Shula Miami Herald record-breaking game headline edition newspaper, autographed.......$50
- O.J. Simpson hand-signed, typed letter to Brett Butler (Los Angeles Dodgers) on behalf of a charity event in 1991.......$295
- Oakland Raiders waste can, late 1970s.......$50
- Early-1960s AFL megaphone featuring team logos, cracked.......$45
- Early 1960s New York Giants megaphone, "Go With The Giants".......$135
- Joe Namath Body Building Kit, exercise kit with carrying bag, facsimile autograph.......$75
- 1984 Slurpee football coin advertising piece, 17 1/2" by 13 1/2", featuring Franco Harris.......$95
- New York Giants late-1960s WNEW advertising matchbook.......$25
- 1964 NFL lunchbox, Packers vs. Bears, Giants vs Browns, with thermos.......$150

Pins

- 1982/83 USFL pins, 2 1/4": Arizona Outlaws, Baltimore Stars, Birmingham Stallions, Denver Gold, Houston Gamblers, Jacksonville Bulls, Los Angeles Express, Memphis Showboats, Oakland Invaders, Orlando Renegades, Philadelphia Stars, Portland Breakers, San Antonio Gunslingers, Tampa Bay Bandits ....$8 each
- 1970s-80s NFL players, 3": Ottis Anderson, Terry Bradshaw, Scott Brunner, Dick Butkus, Todd Christianson, Tony Dorsett, Franco Harris, Phil Simms, Roger Staubach, Lawrence Taylor, Richard Todd, "Too Tall" Jones, Wesley Walker, Charlie Waters, Randy White, $12 each; Mark Gastineau, Ron Jaworski, Dave Jennings, Gary Jeter, Jack Youngblood ....$10 each
- Johnny Unitas Day 3" pin, from May 19, 1973, black-and-white photo.................................$65
- New York Giants "Yea Team" 3" pin.............$35
- Minnesota Vikings Super Bowl XI pin, 3 1/2" with ribbon $45
- Oakland Raiders Super Bowl XV pin, 3 1/2", from Jan. 25, 1981 ....$35

Pencils

- 1983 NFLPA pencils - $5 unless marked - Ken Anderson (Bengals), Ottis Anderson (Cardinals), Steve Bartkowski (Falcons), Brad Budde (Chiefs), Russell Erxleben (Saints), Vince Ferragamo (Rams, $8), Dan Fouts (Broncos), Mark Gastineau (Jets), Willie Gault (Bears), Ray Guy (Raiders), Franco Harris (Steelers, $15), Leroy Irvin (Rams), Tom Jackson (Broncos), Ron Jaworski (Eagles), John Jefferson (Chargers), Too Tall Jones (Cowboys), Joe Klecko (Jets), Jack Lambert (Steelers, $8), Mark Moseley (Redskins), Chuck Muncie (Chargers), Mike Pagel (Colts), Walter Payton (Bears, $10), Carl Roaches (Oilers), Lawrence Taylor (Giants, $8), Tommy Vigorito (Dolphins)

1988 NFLPA pencils

- Series I - Jim Everett (Rams, $9), Freeman McNeil (Jets, $12), Herschel Walker Cowboys, $13), Reggie White (Eagles, $15), Doug Williams (Redskins, $10)
- Series II - Ken Anderson (Bengals, $9), Willie Gault (Bears, $12), Too Tall Jones (Cowboys, $9), Joe Klecko (Jets, $9)

Posters

- Bart Starr poster for La Crosse Rubber Mills Co., with six different pictures of Bart Starr model sneakers and a photo of him in a passing pose, 9x22 1/2..$75 (mb)
- O.J. Simpson Hertz Rent-A-Car 17x22 color action poster, "Hertz Rents Fords and Other Fine Cars"...$10
- 1970s Drug Enforcement Administration 15x18 color posters, each has words of encouragement, a color photo and facsimile autograph: Roger

Staubach $17; Jim Robinson, Clarence Williams, Essex Johnson, Jack Snow, Joe Moore and Doug Buffone at $10 each; complete set of 7 for $49.95
- Joe Namath "Broadway Joe" autographed 16x20 Jets photo, mounted, with name plaque....$168.95
- Joe Namath 1976 stadium poster, 18x24, advertising the current week's issue of Pro! magazine sold for the game $25
- 1992 Minnesota Vikings "School is Cool" autographed 18x24 promotional poster, sponsored by the Vikings and Cub Foods supermarkets to recognize the value of education, signed in purple by six of the seven players featured: Hassan Jones, Steve Jordan, Randall McDaniel, Gary Zimmerman, David Huffman and Tim Irwin........................$30
- Super Bowl XXVI commemorative poster, full size poster features the artwork which appeared on the official Super Bowl game program...........$20
- 1993 Frito Lay posters: Bombs Away - Troy Aikman, Steve Young, Dan Marino, $5; Air Strike - Jerry Rice, Michael Irvin, Andre Rison, $4; Trench Warfare - Joe Montana, $4; Ground Assault - Barry Sanders, ...$3
- 1981 7-Up Earl Campbell poster $7
- 1989 Busch Beer Terry Bradshaw poster $5

Press passes/pins

- Dec. 22, 1968, tie-on press pass for the Oakland Raiders Western Division playoff game, 2 1/4x6 ....$17.50
- Jan. 21, 1968, tie-on NBC press pass for the AFL All-Star game..$15
- Jan. 17, 1970, NBC tie-on press pass for the AFL All-Star game at the Houston Astrodome.......$15
- Football Writers Association of America lapel pin, oval-shaped press pin with a gold football in the center, surrounded by a blue border and gold inscription $45
- Photo press pass from 12/16/73, Jets vs. Bills, when O.J. Simpson breaks rushing record with 2,003 yards..$125

1969 Green Bay Packers pins
Drenks Potato Chips

These unnumbered pins, issued in 1969, feature members of the Green Bay Packers. The pins are green, with a white football-shaped background that has a player mug shot in it. The team name is above the black-and-white photo; the player's name and position are listed below it. The pins measure 1 1/8" in diameter.

	NM	EX	VG
Complete set (20):	50.00	25.00	15.00
Common player:	1.00	.50	.30
1. Herb Adderly	5.00	2.50	1.50
2. Lionel Aldridge	1.50	.70	.45
3. Donny Anderson	2.00	1.00	.60
4. Ken Bowman	1.00	.50	.30
5. Carroll Dale	1.50	.70	.45
6. Willie Davis	5.00	2.50	1.50
7. Boyd Dowler	2.00	1.00	.60
8. Marv Fleming	2.00	1.00	.60

9. Gale Gillingham	1.50	.70	.45
10. Jim Grabowski	2.00	1.00	.60
11. Forrest Gregg	5.00	2.50	1.50
12. Don Horn	1.00	.50	.30
13. Bob Jeter	1.50	.70	.45
14. Henry Jordan	2.00	1.00	.60
15. Ray Nitschke	6.00	3.00	1.75
16. Elijah Pitts	1.50	.70	.45
17. Dave Robinson	2.00	1.00	.60
18. Bart Starr	10.00	5.00	3.00
19. Travis Williams	1.50	.70	.45
20. Willie Wood	5.00	2.50	1.50

Royal Crown Cola pop cans

These cans, issued around 1976-77 by Royal Crown Cola, feature mug shots of NFL players. The Walter Payton can leads the way at $14, while Joe Theismann is $12. Hall of Famers Paul Warfield, Terry Bradshaw and John Riggins are $10 each; Jack Lambert is $9. The rest are between $5-$8.

- Chicago Bears - Bob Avellini, Brian Baschnagel, Waymond Bryant, Doug Buffone, Wally Chambers, George Musso, Walter Payton, Bo Rather

- Cincinnati Bengals - Ken Anderson, Coy Bacon, Tommy Casanova, Boobie Clark, Archie Griffin, Jim LeClair, Rufus Mayes, Chip Myers, Ken Riley, Bob Trumpy

- Cleveland Browns - Don Cockroft, Clarence Darden, Tom DeLeone, John Garlington, Walter Johnson, Joe Jones, Cleo Miller, Greg Pruitt, Reggie Rucker, Paul Warfield

- Detroit Lions - Lem Barney, Larry Hand, J.D. Hill, Levi Johnson, Greg Landry, Jon Morris, Paul Naumoff, Charlie Sanders, Jim Yarbrough, Charlie West

- Green Bay Packers - John Brockington, Fred Carr, Lynn Dickey, Bob Hyland, Chester Marcol, Mike McCoy, Rich McGeorge, Steve Odom, Clarence Williams

- Kansas City Chiefs - Jim Lynch

- Minnesota Vikings - Bobby Bryant, Fred Cox, Carl Eller, Chuck Foreman, Paul Krause, Jeff Siemon, Ed White, Mick Tingelhoff, Nate Wright, Ron Yary

- New Orleans Saints - Archie Manning, Derland Moore

- New York Giants - John Hicks, Doug Van Horn

- New York Jets - Phil Wise

- Oakland Raiders - Dave Caster, Phil Villapiano

- Pittsburgh Steelers - Rocky Bleier, Terry Bradshaw, Roy Gerela, Joe Greene, Ernie Holmes, Jack Lambert, Ray Mansfield, Dwight White

- Washington Redskins - Mike Bragg, Eddie Brown, Bill Brundige, Dave Butz, Brad Dusek, Pat Fischer, Jean Fugett, Frank Grant, Len Hauss, Terry Hermeling, Calvin Hill, Ken Houston, Bob Kuziel, Joe Lavender, Mark Moseley, Brig Owens, John Riggins, Ron Saul, George Starke, Diron Talbert, Charley Taylor, Joe Theismann, Mike Thomas

Records

- 1958 Baltimore Colts vs. New York Giants recorded highlights from the actual broadcast between the two teams as they played for the world's professional football championship, on Dec. 28, 1958, at Yankee Stadium $60

- 1961 "Sounds of the Vikings" illustrated 7x7 record album and booklet, colorful purple and yellow low cover features coach Norm Van Brocklin and quarterback George Shaw; inside pages feature player sketches, photos and three vinyl records which can be played $50

- 1972 Paul Warfield: "How to Catch a Pass" instructional record, features a color action photo on the jacket cover; unopened $25

- 1972 Bob Griese: "How to Quarterback" instructional record, jacket cover features a color action photo, unopened... $25

- 1981 Minnesota Vikings "Farewell Season at the Met" LP, jacket has a fish-eye lens shot of Vikings helmet in the snow in an empy Met Stadium, record has 1981 season highlights narrated by Ray Scott...$25
- Baltimore Colts 45-rpm record "The Colt Songs," has two songs - "Let's Go You Colts" and "Go You Fighting Colts," white album cover with Colts helmet $20
- 1981 Jack Lambert football-shaped record, "Mad Man Jack," 33 1/3" rpm $95
- Jim Brown Tells It Like It Is, 33 1/3" record..$45
- 1976 Terry Bradshaw C&W 33 1/3" record, "I'm So Lonesome" $45

Schedules

- 1959 Chicago Bears brass schedule coin for Falstaff Bear..$10 (mb)
- 1970 Chicago Bears brass schedule coin from Johnny Walker Red................................... $8 (mb)
- 1961 AFL/NFL place mat, 14x10, with schedules for every team $6
- 1965 San Diego Chargers Hamms Beer pocket schedule..$40

1982 Sears Roebuck posters

These unnumbered 5" by 7" cards, featuring color action photos on the fronts, are similar to posters issued by Marketcom during the same time period. The player's name appears above the photo; a facsimile autograph is also on the front. The set's sponsor, Sears Roebuck, has its name on the card back; cards were available at participating stores in 1982. Biographical and statistical information is on the back, too, along with a career summary.

	MT	NM	EX
Complete set (11):	200.00	150.00	80.00
Common player:	7.50	5.75	3.00
1) Ken Anderson	12.50	9.50	5.00
2) Terry Bradshaw	25.00	18.50	10.00
3) Earl Campbell	30.00	22.00	12.00
4) Dwight Clark	7.50	5.75	3.00
5) Chris Collinsworth	7.50	5.75	3.00
6) Tony Dorsett	20.00	15.00	8.00
7) Dan Fouts	15.00	11.00	6.00
8) Franco Harris	20.00	15.00	8.00
9) Joe Montana	70.00	52.00	28.00
10) Walter Payton	30.00	22.00	12.00
11) Kellen Winslow	7.50	5.75	3.00

Sheet music

- 1933 sheet music for "You Gotta Be a Football Hero" to get along with the beautiful girls, by Sherman, Fields and Lewis, football art cover...........$20
- 1930 sheet music for "Football" by Freed & Brown, from the MGM movie "Good News" $20
- "Hail to the Redskins" sheet music.................$65
- 1960 Baltimore Colts sheet music for "Go You Fighting Colts," Colts player on the cover, music and words inside..$20

- "The Forward Pass" motion picture songsheet booklet, features football action and black-and-white photos of Douglas Fairbanks Jr., in football garb, and Loretta Young on the cover. Orange booklet contains sheet music for "Hello Baby," the theme song for the movie. Copyright 1930 by Remick Music..$35

Super Bowl memorabilia

- Super Bowl XXVI GTE seat cushion, with inserts, royal blue with attractive Super Bowl XXVI logo on one side and a GTE pouch on the other to hold inserts, which included a flip book featuring action scenes from the AFC and NFC Championship games, and Pro Set commemorative cards $50
- Super Bowl XXVI CBS Sports 7x17 nylon banner that was displayed in the end zone during the game, light blue border with "CBS Sports" and logo in royal blue in a white strips, with grommets to hang the banner..$250
- 1992 Super Bowl XXVI vendor's apron, with the Super Bowl logo on the front and storage pockets sewn-in at the bottom $25

Toys/games/puzzles

- 1980 Tudor team sets for electric football games, hand-painted 1"-high players in different poses, 11 per team, without bases: Buffalo Bills, Chicago Bears, Cincinnati Bengals, Cleveland Browns, Denver Broncos, Detroit Lions, Green Bay Packers, Miami Dolphins, New York Jets, Pittsburgh Steelers and San Francisco 49ers, each $25
- Atlanta Falcons, Baltimore Colts, Houston Oilers, Kansas City Chiefs, Los Angeles Rams, New England Patriots, San Diego Chargers, Seattle Seahawks, Tampa Bay Buccaneers, each.......$20
- 1983 Tonka NFL players action figures, still in original, sealed packages, with a decal sheet for uniform numbers, player is in uniform and base has a team logo on it: Atlanta Falcons, Baltimore Colts, Buffalo Bills, Cincinnati Bengals, Cleveland Browns, Denver Broncos, Detroit Lions, Green Bay Packers, Houston Oilers, Kansas City Chiefs, Los Angeles Rams, Miami Dolphins, New England Patriots, New Orleans Saints, New York Giants, New York Jets, Philadelphia Eagles, Pittsburgh Steelers, San Diego Chargers, San Francisco 49ers, Seattle Seahawks, St. Louis Cardinals, Tampa Bay Buccaneers and Washington Redskins, each $25
- 1985 Pocket Whoozit Sports picture game cards, featuring nine photos on each card, with three trivia questions on the back for each player. Cards with football-related people, and other significant hockey and basketball representatives include: George Blanda ($10, with Raymond Berry and Bob Cousy); Mel Blount/Jim Zorn ($4, with Turk Broda); Paul Bryant ($25); Chris Collinsworth/Bobby Layne ($12, with Adolph Rupp); Otto Graham ($6); Red Grange ($10); Franco Harris ($15, with Julius Erving); Mark Gastineau/Arnie Herber/Chuck Hughes/Freeman McNeil/Merlin Olsen/Steve Owen ($10); Elroy

Hirsch/Greasy Neale ($6, with the Stanley Cup and Art Ross); Sam Huff ($6, with Howie Morenz); Jack Kemp ($10); Doug Kotar/Tommy Kramer ($6); Earl Lambeau ($7); Frank Leahy/Mark Moseley ($5, with Rogie Vachon); Bob Lilly ($10, with Pop Warner); Ronnie Lott ($6); Sid Luckman ($6, with Bert Bell); Archie Manning/Buddy Young ($5, with Jack Sikma); Art Monk/Merlin Olsen ($6); Joe Montana ($25, with Paul Brown and John Wooden); Anthony Munoz/Rick Upchurch ($4); Alan Page ($10); Brian Piccolo ($16, with Mike Bossy); Vince Lombardi/Knute Rockne ($17, with James Naismith and Jim Thorpe); Roger Staubach ($10, with Wilt Chamberlain and Tom Gola); Charley Taylor/Phil Villapiano ($5).

SPORTS

- 1971 jigsaw puzzles, 16x20, 500 pieces, never opened box has full-color photo on the top: Roman Gabriel $45, Jim Plunkett, $40, Joe Namath $65
- 1980 Pittsburgh Steelers jigsaw puzzles, 11x17, vs. Houston Oilers: #1 Offense, with Terry Bradshaw and Mike Webster $30; #2 Defense, with L.C. Greenwood, Jack Lambert, Donnie Shell, Mike Wagner, etc. $30

Basketball

Advertisements

- 1970 Schaefer Bear New York Knicks poster, 15x18, says "The Knicks Have the Knack" $17.50

- Shaquille O'Neal six-pack of longneck Pepsi bottles, commemorating Shaq's first year in the NBA, each is filled and has a different phrase, found only in Orlando and includes two promotional cards $15
- Fruity Snack Boxes with Michael Jordan, Larry Bird or David Robinson............................ $9 each
- Michael Jordan valentine box with cards in the back $5
- Michael Jordan 1991 McDonald's picture stop watch.. $30
- Shaquille O'Neal life-size wooden standup display, with hoop and net, autographed $395
- 1973-74 Chicago Bulls Pabst cardboard standup display schedule, 18x14................................. $45
- Julius Erving late-1970s Sears Converse cardboard standup display $200
- Kevin McHale Papa Ginos cardboard standup display... $125
- 1981 Magic Johnson 7-Up card, 5 1/2" by 7 1/2" with statistics on the back....................... $35
- Clyde Lovellette 8 1/2x11 Spalding Sports Advisory Staff photo, with autograph $20
- Magic Johnson Miller Genuine Draft NBA All-Star Ballot display sign from the early 1990s, 17x21 1/2", Johnson autographed below his photo; Charles Barkley, Isiah Thomas and David Robinson photos are in the background $110

Books/yearbooks

- Terry Porter 1980 high school yearbook $35
- 1958 Union Oil Sports Club Booklet #5, Bill Russell, "Fine Points of Basketball Defense".................. $20
- 1972 Keds/Uniroyal Pete Maravich booklet, titled "Pass, Shoot, Rebound"................................. $25
- 1990 LSU yearbook, featuring Shaquille O'Neal $100
- 1967 LSU yearbook, featuring Pete Maravich $395
- 1955-56 Harlem Globetrotters yearbook $40
- 1959-60 Harlem Globetrotters yearbook $30
- Oscar Robertson's 1958, 1959 and 1960 University of Cincinnati yearbooks ...... $225 each
- 1992 Chicago phone book, with Michael Jordan on the cover, autographed.............................. $100
- 1928-29 Referee's Official Rule Book, leather cover which has Harry Norris' name imprinted in it...... $45

Calendars

- 1987 Boston Celtics calendar, world champions, with Kevin McHale, Robert Parish, Bill Walton... .... $20
- 1988 Boston Celtics calendar with Dennis Johnson $15
- 1989 Boston Celtics calendar with Larry Bird $15
- 1990 Boston Celtics calendar with Larry Bird, Kevin McHale and Robert Parish.................. $15
- 1991 Boston Celtics calendar with Kevin McHale $10

Collegiate memorabilia

- 1958, 1959 and 1960 University of Cincinnati yearbooks, each featuring Oscar Robertson ....
  ....$225 each
- UCLA Bruins/John Wooden 1975 commemorative 7-Up bottles, 16 ounces......................$20

Decals/stickers/patches

- Carolina Cougars 2 1/2" ABA decal..............$12
- 1994 Chicago Stadium patch, commemorates the Bulls and stadium's existence from 1929-94, this premium is still wrapped.................................$25
- Dallas Chaparrals 2 1/2" ABA cloth patch $15
- Denver Rockets 3 1/2" ABA window decal ...$15
- Kentucky Colonels 2 1/2" ABA cloth patch ...$15
- 1972-73 Los Angeles Lakers 2 1/2" cloth patch for the World Champions $15
- Los Angeles Stars ABA window sticker.........$15
- Memphis Pros 3 1/2" ABA decal....................$15
- New Orleans Buccaneers 3 1/2" ABA window decal...$15
- St. Louis Spirits 4" ABA window decal $20

Jewelry

- Kareem Abdul-Jabbar/Julius Erving "Clash of the Legends" Gartlan USA wristwatch, signed by both, $200, unsigned is $70
- 1968 Minnesota Pipers "ABA Champions" tie bar, for a team which never actually won the ABA Championship, but instead inherited the ABA's first championship team, the 1967-68 Pittsburgh Pipers, who relocated to Minneapolis for the 1968-69 season. $125
- Magic Johnson 1985 Los Angeles Lakers 10k championship salesman's sample ring.......$2,500
- Larry Bird 1984 Boston Celtics 10k championship salesman's sample ring $2,800
- 1992-93 Chicago Bulls Josten championship ring given to season ticket holders $295
- Michael Jordan 1991 Chicago Bulls 10k championship salesman's sample ring with diamonds $4,500

Milk cartons

1970-71 Chicago Bulls Hawthorne Milk cartons

These 3 1/4" by 3 3/8" perforated cards could be found on side panels of Hawthorne Milk cartons. Each card has a mug shot of a Chicago Bulls player framed with a white circle. The card background is printed in red. The unnumbered cards have blank backs. Two Bob Weiss cards were made; the larger one measures 4 11/16" by 2 7/8".

	NM	EX	VG
Complete set (6):	900.00	450.00	275.00
Common player:	100.00	50.00	30.00
1. Bob Love	200.00	100.00	60.00
2. Jerry Sloan	150.00	75.00	45.00

	NM	EX	VG
3. Jerry Sloan(red photo)	150.00	75.00	45.00
4. Chet Walker	200.00	100.00	60.00
5. Bob Weiss	100.00	50.00	30.00
6. Bob Weiss (l)	125.00	65.00	40.00

1968-69 Phoenix Suns Carnation Milk cartons

Carnation Milk cartons featured player photos on a side panel during the 1968-69 season. Each unnumbered card measures 3 1/2" by 7 1/2" and includes biographical information below the photo. The bottom of the panel promotes the team's sweepstakes for a chance to win one of 440 home game tickets. "Carnation Introduces Your Phoenix Suns" along with "Meet" and the player's name are also on the card. This practice continued with each subsequent set issued by Carnation.

	NM	EX	VG
Complete set (12):	900.00	450.00	275.00
Common player:	50.00	25.00	15.00
1. Jim Fox	50.00	25.00	15.00
2. Gail Goodrich	200.00	100.00	60.00
3. Gary Gregor	50.00	25.00	15.00
4. Neil Johnson	50.00	25.00	15.00
5. John Kerr	75.00	37.00	22.00
6. Dave Lattin	75.00	37.00	22.00
7. Stan McKenzie	50.00	25.00	15.00
8. McCoy McLemore	50.00	25.00	15.00
9. Dick Snyder	50.00	25.00	15.00
10. Dick Van Arsdale	100.00	50.00	30.00
11. Bob Warlick	50.00	25.00	15.00
12. George Wilson	50.00	25.00	15.00

1969-70 Phoenix Suns Carnation Milk cartons

These cartons feature blue-and-white drawings of a Phoenix Suns player in action, along with a head shot. The bottom of the unnumbered card, which measures 3 1/2" by 7 1/2", has a player tip in red type. Player statistics appeared on the opposite side panel of the player photos.

	NM	EX	VG
Complete set (10):	700.00	350.00	125.00
Common player:	50.00	25.00	15.00
1. Jerry Chambers	50.00	25.00	15.00
2. Jim Fox	50.00	25.00	15.00
3. Gail Goodrich	125.00	65.00	40.00
4. Connie Hawkins	200.00	100.00	60.00
5. Stan McKenzie	50.00	25.00	15.00
6. Paul Silas	100.00	50.00	30.00
7. Dick Snyder	50.00	25.00	15.00
8. Dick Van Arsdale	75.00	37.00	22.00
9. Neal Walk	50.00	25.00	15.00
10. Gene Williams	50.00	25.00	15.00

1970-71 Phoenix Suns Carnation Milk cartons

These cards feature profile shots against red or orange backgrounds. The unnumbered cards have blank backs and measure 3 1/2" by 7 1/2". A career summary appears below the player photo.

	NM	EX	VG
Complete set (10):	700.00	350.00	125.00
Common player:	50.00	25.00	15.00
1. Mel Counts	50.00	25.00	15.00
2. Lamar Green	50.00	25.00	15.00

3. Art Harris	50.00	25.00	15.00
4. Clem Haskins	75.00	37.00	22.00
5. Connie Hawkins	150.00	75.00	45.00
6. Gus Johnson	100.00	50.00	30.00
7. Otto Moore	50.00	25.00	15.00
8. Paul Silas	100.00	50.00	30.00
9. Dick Van Arsdale	75.00	37.00	22.00
10. Neal Walk	50.00	25.00	15.00

1971-72 Phoenix Suns Carnation Milk cartons

These cards follow the same format as Carnation's previous issues, except only five players are featured.

	NM	EX	VG
Complete set (5):	300.00	150.00	90.00
Common player:	40.00	20.00	12.00
1. Connie Hawkins	150.00	75.00	45.00
2. Otto Moore	40.00	20.00	12.00
3. Fred Taylor	40.00	20.00	12.00
4. Neal Walk	50.00	25.00	15.00
5. John Wetzel	50.00	25.00	15.00

1972-73 Phoenix Suns Carnation Milk cartons

Once again, Carnation Milk cartons featured side panels with photos of Phoenix Suns players. This time, however, the set included 12 members of the team.

	NM	EX	VG
Complete set (12):	700.00	350.00	125.00
Common player:	50.00	25.00	15.00
1. Mel Counts	50.00	25.00	15.00
2. Lamar Green	50.00	25.00	15.00
3. Clem Haskins	75.00	37.00	22.00
4. Connie Hawkins	150.00	75.00	45.00
5. Gus Johnson	100.00	50.00	30.00
6. Dennis Layton	50.00	25.00	15.00
7. Otto Moore	50.00	25.00	15.00
8. Fred Taylor	50.00	25.00	15.00
9. Dick Van Arsdale	75.00	37.00	22.00
10. Bill Van Breda Kolff	50.00	25.00	15.00
11. Neal Walk	50.00	25.00	15.00
12. John Wetzel	50.00	25.00	15.00

Miscellaneous

- 1994 New York Knicks tie-on media pass for NBA Playoff Game 4 at Madison Square Garden, Knicks vs. Chicago Bulls $12
- 1970 New York Nets Drink Tray, giveaway at a Nets game, has a large New York logo in red/white/blue.. $35
- 1994-95 Houston Rockets team autographed hardwood floor, framed, with Rockets logo in the center of the floor... $250
- 1957-58 St. Louis Hawks world champions commemorative mug, 5" tall, off-white porcelain with gold trim along the rim and handle, has a small gold banner above the Hawks logo which says "World Champions 1957-58" $125
- 1980s Los Angeles Lakers promotional drinking glass.. $5
- "Nothing But Net" hat, autographed by Charles Barkley, Larry Bird and Michael Jordan, $295, by Bird and Jordan $250
- 1973 New York Knickerbockers world champs artist's proof lithograph, signed by Bill Bradley, Dave DeBusschere, Walt Frazier, Red Holtzman, Jerry Lucas, Earl Monroe, Willis Reed and artist R.S. Simon; original, numbered edition sold for $995 while artist's proofs were $1,395; $500
- Original Forum basketball court, 8x10 piece of the floor, autographed by Magic Johnson $149.95, unsigned.. 65
- Chicago Stadium seat, free-standing wooden chair, red, from upper reaches of the stadium ......l $200
- Chicago Stadium free-standing chair used in the first two rows (players or elite ticket holders), large Bulls logo on the back cushion, seat has extra cushion, in Bulls colors $350
- Larry Bird Night magnet, Feb. 4, 1993 .... $20
- 1992 McDonald's Dream Team plastic cup of Michael Jordan $5
- 1973 Keds Pete Maravich shoe box and shoes, box is excellent, shoes were never worn; Maravich picture on the top of the box................................ $95
- Autographed Larry Bird 5x5 authentic piece of floor from Springs Valley High School where Bird played from 1971-74, includes certificate of authenticity $125
- 1980s Spalding Larry Bird Ball Bag Back Pack, green and white in the shape of a back pack with a shot of Bird on it and a facsimile autograph....$25
- Larry Bird retirement night bag, given out when Bird's number was retired on Feb. 3, 1993 .....$35
- Indiana Pacers ABA ceramic bank................. $75

Newspapers

- Houston Chronicle special championship headline edition, signed by Hakeem Olajuwon $40
- Boston Globe Larry Bird retirement issue, autographed by Bird $60
- Boston Herald 08/19/92 issue "Larry, It's been a Ball" retirement announcement....................... $25
- Michael Jordan's retirement press release, issued by Associated Press upon his retirement in 1993, a 3x9 piece of paper which came over the printer from NBC Studios in New York $15

Paper-related products

- 1953 Harlem Globetrotters red/white/blue stationery $19
- 1968-69 New York Nets "Official Theme Song" sheet music, with schedule $50
- 1967 Jimmy Walker's Detroit Pistons NBA contract, signed by Walker and Piston owner Fred Zollner, lot of three................................. $75
- 1981 official NBA All-Star ballot, including names of Danny Ainge, Larry Bird, Juilius Erving, Elvin Hayes, Kareem Abdul-Jabbar and Bill Walton $15
- Spalding 1991-92-93 Chicago Bulls commemorative folder, looks like a basketball, autographed by Michael Jordan................... $150

- 1980s Larry Bird Christmas postcard, features Bird wearing a Santa Claus cap while trimming a tree on the front, with a list of "thank yous" on the back to those who contributed to the "Make Them Smile" fund raiser $12
- New York Nets theme song, the sheet music for the Nets, includes musical score and lyrics, plus a schedule for the 1968-69 season, 3" by 7" with Nets logo $50
- Larry Bird Night retirement banner, given out the night of his retirement ceremony, replica of what hangs in the Boston Garden $30

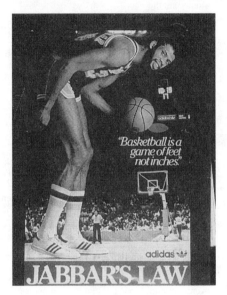

Posters

- 1970s Pete Maravich American Cancer Society poster, 12x16, Maravich's Atlanta Hawks vs. New York Knicks, says "I don't smoke cigarettes" $35
- Michael Jordan 1993 cardboard Gatorade store display, 20x28, says "Nothing Beats Gatorade" and is signed in black Sharpie "Best Wishes Michael Jordan" $85
- 1994 27x39 movie display poster for "Blue Chips," featuring Shaquille O'Neal $20
- Leroy Nieman All-Star game poster, signed by Julius Erving 99
- 1978 John Havlicek farewell poster, signed, $30, unsigned $10
- Larry Bird retirement poster $15
- 1980-81 Larry Bird Converse poster $20
- Boston Celtics Big Five poster, signed by Danny Ainge, Larry Bird, Dennis Johnson, Kevin McHale and Robert Parish $350
- 1980s Adidas poster featuring Kareem Abdul-Jabbar, "Basketball is a game of feet, not inches" $25

Costacos Brothers mini basketball posters

- $4 each: Charles Barkley, Jimmy Jackson, Larry Johnson, Karl Malone, David Robinson, John Stockton, Dominique Wilkins.
- $2.50 each: Stacey Augmon, Rex Chapman, Joe Dumars, Sean Elliott, Dale Ellis, Kendall Gill, Ron Harper, Dan Majerle, Sarunas Marciulionis, Dikembe Mutombo, Robert Pack, Mark Price, Mitch Richmond, Cliff Robinson, John Starks

Starline mini basketball posters

- $6 each: Michael Jordan, Jordan Bullseye, Bulls collage, Jordan collage, Jordan soaring, Licensed to Jam (M. Jordan), Secretary of Defense (M. Jordan), Michael Jordan (dunking vs. Lakers).
- $4 each: Larry Bird collage, Magic Show, Magic Johnson collage, Patrick Ewing, Charles Barkley (red), Charles Barkley (blue), Kevin McHale.

Programs/publications

- 1952-53 Harlem Globetrotters yearbook, signed by nine players, including Pop Gates, Boid Buie, Ducky Moore, Jess Caffy, Oris Hill and Phil Jefferson .. $100
- 1963 Harlem Globetrotters yearbook $100
- Oscar Robertson's 1966 "Play Better Basketball" publication $15
- 1977 John R. Wooden First Annual Award Dinner Banquet Program, for basketball's equivalent of the Heisman, this four-page program has a drawing of the John Wooden trophy on the front and a decorative yellow cord draped over the center of the booklet $30
- Jan. 30, 1994, Kevin McHale retirement program, with full ticket and replica banner, autographed ... $85
- Larry Bird retirement night program, sold at the ceremony, not through the mail $75
- 1954 World Series of Basketball, College All-Americans vs. Harlem Globetrotters, collegiates include Gene Shue, Frank Ramsey, Cliff Hagan and John Kerr. Globetrotters include Walter Dukes and Goose Tatum $60

Records

- Larry Bird 45-rpm record "The New State Bird," in his ISU uniform... $95
- 1971 NBA 25th Anniversary record album, documentary by Chris Schenkel, unopened.... $35
- 1976 Play-It Pro Dave Cowens, 12-minute record and 20-page booklet, in wrapper..................... $25
- 1969 NBA 25 Action Years, 33 1/3 lp........... $30
- The Big O, 45rpm record featuring Oscar Roberston on the picture sleeve $65
- Havlicek Stole the Ball, highlights from the Boston Celtics playoff and championship games from 1956-57 - 1965-66, narrated by Johnny Most $45

1978-79 Royal Crown Cola cards

Royal Crown Cola in the New England area offered one of these cards per six-pack in 1978-79. The 3 1/8" by 6" cards, part of a "Basketball Stars Collection," have the RC Cola logo, with a black-and-white player head shot below inside a basketball hoop's net. The player's name and biographical information are also included on the unnumbered card. No NBA or team logos appear on the cards.

	NM	EX	VG
Complete set (40):	1,500.00	750.00	450.00
Common player:	20.00	10.00	6.00
1. Kareem Abdul-Jabbar	125.00	65.00	40.00
2. Nate Archibald	50.00	25.00	15.00
3. Rick Barry	60.00	30.00	18.00
4. Jim Chones	20.00	10.00	6.00
5. Doug Collins	30.00	15.00	9.00
6. Dave Cowens	50.00	25.00	15.00
7. Adrian Dantley	30.00	15.00	9.00
8. Walter Davis	30.00	15.00	9.00
9. John Drew	20.00	10.00	6.00
10. Julius Erving	125.00	65.00	40.00
11. Walt Frazier	60.00	30.00	18.00
12. George Gervin	50.00	25.00	15.00
13. Artis Gilmore	40.00	20.00	12.00
14. Elvin Hayes	50.00	25.00	15.00
15. Dan Issel	60.00	30.00	18.00
16. Marques Johnson	25.00	12.50	7.50
17. Bernard King	40.00	20.00	12.00
18. Bob Lanier	40.00	20.00	12.00
19. Maurice Lucas	25.00	12.50	7.50
20. Pete Maravich	100.00	50.00	30.00
21. Bob McAdoo	25.00	12.50	7.50
22. George McGinnis	25.00	12.50	7.50
23. Eric Money	20.00	10.00	6.00
24. Earl Monroe	40.00	20.00	12.00
25. Calvin Murphy	40.00	20.00	12.00
26. Robert Parish	50.00	25.00	15.00
27. Billy Paultz	20.00	10.00	6.00
28. Jack Sikma	25.00	12.50	7.50
29. Ricky Sobers	20.00	10.00	6.00
30. David Thompson	30.00	15.00	9.00
31. Rudy Tomjanovich	40.00	20.00	12.00
32. Wes Unseld	40.00	20.00	12.00
33. Norm van Lier	25.00	12.50	7.50
34. Bill Walton	60.00	30.00	18.00
35. Marvin Webster	20.00	10.00	6.00
36. Scott Wedman	20.00	10.00	6.00
37. Paul Westphal	40.00	20.00	12.00
38. Jo Jo White	30.00	15.00	9.00
39. John Williamson	20.00	10.00	6.00
40. Brian Winters	20.00	10.00	6.00

Slides

1970s 2x2 slides, original and in color; presumably used for national TV broadcasts; $8 each unless marked.

- Atlanta Hawks - Andy Benson, Hubie Brown, John Drew, Cotton Fitzsimmons, Lou Hudson ($10)
- Boston Celtics - John Havlicek ($25), Don Nelson ($10), Paul Silas, Kevin Stacom, JoJo White ($12),
- Buffalo Braves - Bob McAdoo ($16), Jim McMillan, Tom McMillen ($13), Jack Ramsey, Randy Smith
- Chicago Bulls - John Mengelt, Dick Motta, Nate Thurmond ($10) Van Lier (2 different), Nick Weatherspoon
- Cleveland Cavaliers - Jim Brewer, Jim Chones, Bill Fitch, Campy Russell, Dick Snyder
- Detroit Pistons - M.L. Carr, Allen Eberhard, Bob Lanier ($20), Eric Money, Kevin Porter ($10, 2 different), Ralph Simpson
- Golden State Warriors - Rick Barry ($16), Derek Dickey, Chris Dudley, Larry McNeill, Robert Parish ($25), Clifford Ray, Phil Smith, Jamaal Wilkes ($10)
- Houston Rockets - John Egan, Moses Malone ($16), Mike Newlin, Eric Ratliff, Larry Siegfried, Rudy Tomjanovich ($12, 2 different)
- Indiana Pacers - Dave Robisch
- Kansas City Kings - Luc Allen, Sam Lacey, Bill Robinzine, Scott Wedman ($10)
- Los Angeles Lakers - Kareem Abdul-Jabbar ($35, 2 different), Corky Calhoun, Brad Davis, Jim McMillan, Cazzie Russell ($10), Bill Sharman ($16), Kermit Washington (two different), Jerry West $25, Jamaal Wilkes
- Milwaukee Bucks - Kareem Abdul-Jabbar ($35), Kent Benson ($10), Junior Bridgeman (2 different), Marques Johnson, David Meyers (2 different), Don Nelson, Elmore Smith
- New Jersey Nets - Jim Ard, Bill Melchionni, Albert Skinner, Brian Taylor, Dave Wohl,
- New Orleans Jazz - Gus Bailey, Pete Maravich ($35, 2 different), James McElroy, Otto Moore, Louis Nelson, Rick Roberson, Bud Stallworth, Nate Williams
- New York Knicks - Red Holtzman ($15), Bob McAdoo ($14), Tom McMillen ($12), Neal Walk
- Philadelphia 76ers - Doug Collins ($12, 2 different), Billy Cunningham ($13), George McGinnis ($14), Steve Mix, Gene Shue
- Phoenix Suns - Don Buse, Ron Lee, Stan McKenzie, Robert Warlick
- San Antonio Spurs - Coby Dietrick, Doug Moe, Billy Paultz
- Seattle Supersonics - Tom Burleson, Tommy Kron, Tom Meschery, Dorie Murray, Bruce Seals, Slick Watts
- Utah Stars - Ron Boone
- Virginia Squires - Jim Eakins
- Washington Bullets - Greg Ballard, Phil Chenier ($10), Bob Dandridge, Elvin Hayes ($16), Dick Motta, Leonard Robinson, Wes Unseld (2 different)

Standups

1973-74 Washington Bullets standups

These 12 player cards were distributed in an album to fans who attended a Bullets' game at the Capital Centre on Feb. 16, 1974. Six players were included on each 11 1/4" by 14" sheet; individual die-cut perforated cards measure 3 3/4" by 7 1/16" and feature a color photo of a player shooting or passing. The cards are un-numbered and are blank backed. They were issued by Johnny Pro Enterprises. Prices below are for individual cards, starting in Near Mint condition; a complete set intact, with the album, would triple the value.

	NM	EX	VG
Complete set (12):	30.00	15.00	9.00
Common player:	2.00	1.00	.60
1. Phil Chenier	4.00	2.00	1.25
2. Archie Clark	4.00	2.00	1.25
3. Elvin Hayes	15.00	7.50	4.50
4. Tom Kozelko	2.00	1.00	.60
5. Manny Leaks	2.00	1.00	.60
6. Louie Nelson	2.50	1.25	.70
7. Kevin Porter	3.00	1.50	.90
8. Mike Riordan	2.50	1.25	.70
9. Dave Stallworth	2.00	1.00	.60
10. Wes Unseld	10.00	5.00	3.00
11. Nick Weatherspoon	2.50	1.25	.70
12. Walt Wesley	2.00	1.00	.60

1992-93 Charlotte Hornets standups

These standups were available at participating Burger King restaurants in the Charlotte area during the 1992-93 season. Each standup has a purple back-ground and measures 4" by 8 7/8". A facsimile auto-graph appears on the front, along with logos for the set's sponsors (Burger King, Coca-Cola, WJZY Ra-dio and the team). The back also has the sponsors' logos, the player's name, statistics and biographical information. The standups were issued in four sets of three and were given away one set per customer.

	MT	NM	EX
Complete set (12):	10.00	7.50	4.00
Common player:	.25	.20	.10
1. Tony Bennett	.25	.20	.10
2. Dell Curry	.35	.25.	.14
3. Alonzo Mourning	5.00	3.75	2.00
4. Muggsy Bogues	.50	.40	.20
5. Mike Gminski	.25	.20	.10
6. Johnny Newman	.25	.20	.10
7. Kenny Gattison	.25	.20	.10
8. Kendall Gill	.50	.40	.20
9. David Wingate	.25	.20	.10
10. Sidney Green	.25	.20	.10
11. Larry Johnson	3.00	2.25	1.25
12. Kevin Lynch	.25	.20	.10

Ticket stubs

- San Antonio Spurs 1977 ABA Game 6 playoff ticket stubs ....$1.50 each
- Magic Johnson's first game as the Los Angeles Lakers head coach, dated March 27, 1994 ......$25
- Larry Bird retirement unused ticket, featuring Leroy Nieman portrait of Bird $495

Paper-related products

- 1974-75 New York Nets ABA World Champions ticket brochure, with Julius Erving action shot on the cover $45

Toys

- 1973 Wilt Chamberlain Coleco metal basketball game, featuring Chamberlain in his Los Angeles Lakers uniform, but missing the scoreboard display portion...$65
- 1970s APBA Pro Basketball Game, when the Kansas City Kings still existed, includes player cards for 22 teams, plus scoresheets..........$12.50
- 1960s Basketelle basketball game by Marx Toys, a colorful tin litho and 4x12 court where marbles are shot at a hoop....................................$15.75
- 1971 Milton Bradley Harlem Globetrotters board game, in the original box, features caricatures of the players, including Meadowlark Lemon, Curly Neal and Geese Ausbie $20
- 1971 jigsaw puzzles, 16x20, 500 pieces each, feature Wilt Chamberlain, Lew Alcindor vs. Chamberlain, or Pete Maravich.......$65-$75 each
- Michael Jordan frisbee from McDonald's.......$12
- 1977 Harlem Globetrotters View-Master, still sealed, three reels and booklet, in wrap..........$25
- NBA Pro Basketball 500-piece puzzle, 16x20, features Willis Reed vs. Lew Alcindor, or Walt Frazier vs. Jerry West....................................$45
- 1981 Julius Erving 18x24 550-piece puzzle, features Dr. J dunking on Larry Bird and Kevin McHale $85
- Late-1980s Charles Barkley 3" pin, as a Philadelphia 76er...$25

Trophies/awards

- Larry Johnson John Wooden Award, one of three made, it's almost two feet high and includes picutres of Johnson with the award, plus a signed John Wooden Gartlan statue $9,000
- Chris Mullin 1986 Classic Hall of Fame basketball award, has his name on the plate for being a participant in the game $450

UPI wire photos

1968-70 UPI photos; stamped on back "Please Credit"; 8x10 black-and-white; most posed head and shoulders shots.

- $3 each unless indicated: Jim Barnett (Rockets), Dave Bing (Detroit, $8), John Block (Rockets), Vince Boryla (Knicks, $7), Carl Braun (Knicks, $8), Bill Bridges (Hawks), Joe Caldwell (Hawks), Mel Counts (Lakers), Harry Gallatin, John Havlicek (Celtics, $15), Elvin Hayes (Rockets, $10), Bailey Howell (Celtics, $9), Toby Kimball (Rockets), Dick McGuire (Knicks, $15), Bill Russell (Cletics, $25), Satch Sanders (Celtics), Neal Walk (Florida), Chet Walker (Philadelphia, $10).

Hockey

Autographed baseballs

- Rob Blake autographed baseball $20
- Kelly Hrudey autographed baseball $25
- Brett Hull autographed baseball $30
- Jari Kurri autographed baseball $20

Christmas cards

- Chicago Blackhawks Christmas card, signed by Mike Keenan and the coaching staff $63
- 1973-74 Toronto Maple Leafs Christmas card, team photo and facsimile autographs $25
- Harold Ballard signed 1974 Toronto Maple Leafs Christmas card $150

Contracts

- Dave Dryden's 1969-70 NHL contract, autographed by Clarence Campbell, Tommy Ivan $150
- Phil Esposito's 1961 tryout agreement with the Chicago Blackhawks $800
- Phil Esposito's 1964-66 standard NHL contract with the Chicago Blackhawks $950
- Doug Harvey's 1966-67 standard NHL contract with Baltimore $950
- Jacques Lemaire's 1970-71 standard NHL contract with the Montreal Canadiens $650
- Ted Lindsay's 1957-58 standard NHL contract with the Chicago Blackhawks $650
- John Bucyk 1991 Boston Bruins payroll check $85

1975-76 Hockey Heroes Stand-ups

Players from five NHL teams are represented in this set of laminated cardboard stand-ups. Each unnumbered stand-up features a color action shot of a player from either Boston (1-7), Montreal (8-13), New York Islanders (14-19), Philadelphia (20-25) or Toronto (26-31). The Boston and Philadelphia stand-ups measure 15 1/2" by 8 3/4"; the others measure 13 1/2" by 7 1/2". The player's facsimile autograph appears at the bottom of each stand-up. The package the stand-ups are in says "Hockey Heroes Autographed Pin-up Standup Sportrophy."

	NM	EX	VG
Complete set (31):	150.00	75.00	45.00
Common player:	4.00	2.00	1.25
1) Gerry Cheevers	8.00	4.00	2.50
2) Terry O'Reilly	5.00	2.50	1.50
3) Bobby Orr	25.00	12.50	7.50
4) Brad Park	8.00	4.00	2.50
5) Jean Ratelle	7.00	3.50	2.00
6) Andre Savard	4.00	2.00	1.25
7) Gregg Sheppard	4.00	2.00	1.25
8) Yvan Cournoyer	7.00	3.50	2.00
9) Guy Lafleur	15.00	7.50	4.50
10) Jacques Lemaire	6.00	3.00	1.75
11) Peter Mahovlich	4.00	2.00	1.25
12) Doug Risebourgh	4.00	2.00	1.25
13) Larry Robinson	10.00	5.00	3.00
14) Billy Harris	4.00	2.00	1.25
15) Gerry Hart	4.00	2.00	1.25
16) Denis Potvin	7.00	3.50	2.00
17) Glenn Resch	6.00	3.00	1.75
18) Bryan Trottier	8.00	4.00	2.50
19) Ed Westfall	4.00	2.00	1.25
20) Bill Barber	6.00	3.00	1.75
21) Bobby Clarke	10.00	5.00	3.00
22) Reggie Leach	5.00	2.50	1.50
23) Rick MacLeish	6.00	3.00	1.75
24) Bernie Parent	8.00	4.00	2.50
25) Dave Schultz	6.00	3.00	1.75
26) Lanny MacDonald	8.00	4.00	2.50
27) Borje Salming	6.00	3.00	1.75
28) Darryl Sittler	8.00	4.00	2.50
29) Wayne Thomas	4.00	2.00	1.25
30) Errol Thompson	4.00	2.00	1.25
31) Dave Williams	5.00	2.50	1.25

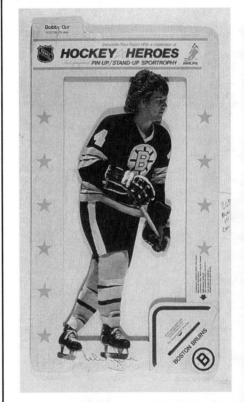

Hockey pucks

- Vancouver Canucks puck, blue/green/white rectangular logo with a hockey stick in the middle, reverse has the official Art Ross Official Converse NHL label .... $12 (minimum bid)
- St. Louis Blues game puck, with blue and white logo .... $12 (mb)
- 1940s Art Ross Tyler NHL game puck, logo on one side $295

- NHL Converse game pucks - New York Rangers, Montreal Canadiens, Detroit Red Wings, $50 each; Buffalo Sabres, Vancouver Canucks, St. Louis Blues ....$40 each
- NHL Viceroy game pucks - most teams each $20

Jewelry

- 1970 Boston Bruins Stanley Cup player's watch, Ted Green...$1,275
- 1981 Wayne Gretzky digital Remex watch, in original package $63
- 1946 Montreal Canadiens Stanley Cup player's ring, silver with letter................................$5,625

Matchbook covers

During the 1930s Diamond Match Co. of New York issued matchbooks with silver or tan backgrounds. The following, with silver backgrounds, have green and black bars running vertically from top to bottom on the left side. The player is in a posed position; the back has a career profile. 60 exist in this silver hockey set, including: Bill Cook $50; Red Jackson, Harold Oliver and Roy Worters $35 each; Jackie Beattie, Doug Brennan, Eddie Burke, Gerald Carson, Red Conn, Rosario Couture, Robert Davie, Cecil Dillon, Mervin Dutton, Normie Himes, Butch Keeling, Lloyd Klein, Joseph Lamb, Harold March, Rabbitt McVeigh, Murray Murdoch, George Patterson, Hal Picketts, Victor Ripley, Elwin Romnes, Johnny Sheppard, Art Somers and Chris Speyers $15 each.

Milk cartons

1972 Philadelphia Flyers milk cartons

These 3 5/8" by 7 1/2" panels could be found on the sides of half gallon cartons of Mighty Milk. Each panel has a player portrait in the middle, with a career summary below, all surrounded by a frame with rounded corners. Blue ink is used. Above the photo it says "Philadelphia Hockey Star" and gives the player's name. Ads for Mighty Milk and TV Channel 29 appear at the bottom of the card.

	NM	EX	VG
Complete set (7):	75.00	37.00	22.00
Common player:	10.00	5.00	3.00
1. Serge Bernier	10.00	5.00	3.00
2. Bobby Clarke	50.00	25.00	15.00
3. Gary Dornhofer	15.00	7.50	4.50
4. Doug Favell	17.00	8.50	5.00
5. Jean-Guy Gendron	10.00	5.00	3.00
6. Bill Lesuk	10.00	5.00	3.00
7. Ed Van Impe	10.00	5.00	3.00

1981-82 Buffalo Sabres milk cartons

Wilson Farms Dairy offered these 16 panels on the sides of its half-gallon milk cartons in 1981-82. Each panel, measuring 3 3/4" by 7 1/2", has an action photo with biographical and statistical information below it. A date and product/card number also appear on the card. The cartons were printed using three dif-ferent color variations - red, green and blue, depending on the grade of milk (2% milkfat or homogenized vitamin D). Each panel says "Kids! Collect Action Photos of the 1981-82 Buffalo Sabres" at the top.

	MT	NM	EX
Complete set (16):	125.00	95.00	50.00
Common player:	7.50	5.75	3.00
1. Craig Ramsey	7.50	5.75	3.00
2. John Van Boxmeer	7.50	5.75	3.00
3. Don Edwards	10.00	7.50	4.00
4. Gilbert Perreault	20.00	15.00	8.00
5. Alan Haworth	7.50	5.75	3.00
6. Jim Schoenfield	15.00	11.00	6.00
7. Richie Dunn	7.50	5.75	3.00
8. Bob Sauve	10.00	7.50	4.00
9. Bill Hajt	7.50	5.75	3.00
10. Larry Playfair	7.50	5.75	3.00
11. Tony McKegney	10.00	7.50	4.00
12. Mike Ramsey	10.00	7.50	4.00
13. Andre Savard	7.50	5.75	3.00
15. Ric Seiling	7.50	5.75	3.00
16. Yvon Lambert	7.50	5.75	3.00
17. Dale McCourt	10.00	7.50	4.00

1982-83 Buffalo Sabres milk cartons

These panels are slightly different than those issued in the previous year. They say "Kids! Clip and Save Exciting Tips and Pictures of Buffalo Sabres" at the top and are printed in blue, plus, the photos are head shots.

A hockey tip also appears at the bottom of the card.

	MT	NM	EX
Complete set (17):	125.00	95.00	50.00
Common player:	7.50	5.75	3.00
2. 1982-83 home schedule	15.00	11.00	6.00
3. Craig Ramsey	7.50	5.75	3.00
4. John Van Boxmeer	8.00	6.00	3.25
5. Lindy Ruff	7.50	5.75	3.00
6. Bob Sauve	8.00	6.00	3.25
7. Gilbert Perreault	20.00	15.00	8.00
8. Ric Seiling	7.50	5.75	3.00
9. Jacques Cloutier	8.00	6.00	3.25
10. Larry Playfair	7.50	5.75	3.00
11. Phil Housley	25.00	18.50	10.00
12. Mike Foligno	8.00	6.00	3.25
13. Tony McKegney	8.00	6.00	3.25
14. Dale McCourt	8.00	6.00	3.25
15. Mike Ramsey	8.00	6.00	3.25
16. Hannu Virta	7.50	5.75	3.00
17. Brent Peterson	7.50	5.75	3.00
18. Scott Bowman	20.00	15.00	8.00

Miscellaneous

- Phil Esposito mouthguard in original package, 1970s $25
- Phil Esposito can of hockey boot wax, late 1960s $40
- 1971-72 Boston Bruins Black Label Stanley Cup beer can bank..$45
- Square ceramic tiles featuring full-color action pictures of several players from the early 1960s, 6" each: Phil Goyette (Chicago) $20 (mb); Red Berenson (Chicago) $20 (mb); Andy Hebenton (Rangers) $20 (mb); Al Langlois (Rangers) $20 (mb); Doug Harvey (Rangers) $32 (mb).

489

- Bobby Orr coin/token issued by City of Parry Sound $32
- Bobby Orr medallion, issued circa 1974 .... $60
- Bobby Orr Zippo lighter, with "Go Bruins Go" slogan $80
- Pelle Lindbergh golf ball, "5th annual memorial tournament".......... $30
- Boston Bruins 1972 bumper sticker, "Get the Cup Back" $20
- Toronto Maple Leafs Gardens seat (actual seat from the arena).......... $300
- Bobby Hull 1960s instructional booklet on scoring goals $25
- John Bucyk Boston Bruins plastic ashtray, photo and facsimile autograph $21
- 1973-74 Boston Bruins 50th Anniversary jersey patch $35
- Jacques Plante typed letter to young goalie fan, signed $340
- 1985 Ronald McDonald's Wayne Gretzky buttons $11
- Mid-1980s Wayne Gretzky pillow cases $15
- Mark Messier framed "Traditions of Champions" print, 1,111 produced $390
- 1962-63 Toronto Maple Leafs souvenir serving tray, facsimile autographs $140

Plates

- 1989-90 Edmonton Oilers Stanley Cup champions plate $49
- Mark Messier autographed 8 1/4-inch plate, 3,000 produced by Enor $79

Posters/advertisements

- 1980s Wayne Gretzky 7-Up poster $10
- Wayne Gretzky Coca-Cola holiday ad display ... $20

Press kits

- 1981 Canada Cup press kit, 70 pages in a folder... .... $80
- Wayne Gretzky fan club kit, 1984, 12 pieces in a folder, with photos and a poster $120

Programs

- Jean Beliveau's 500th goal program from Feb. 11, 1971 .... $160
- Paul Coffey's 1st NHL goal program from Oct. 22, 1980 .... $80
- Bobby Hull's 500th goal program from Feb. 21, 1970 .... $120
- 1975-76 Pittsburgh Penguins vs. USSR program $30
- 1975-76 Chicago Blackhawks vs. USSR program $30
- 1981 or 1984 Canada Cup program $20

Records/videos/films

- Wayne Gretzky 45-rpm record, "Gretzky, Read All About 'Im", new $30
- Guy Lafleur 33 1/3 LP record, music and commentary $25
- 1971 NHL playoffs on 8-mm color film, in original package $63
- VHS video "Gretzky - Hockey My Way," 1986, new $20
- Wayne Gretzky, VHS video, "Above & Beyond," 1990 .... $20
- Bobby Orr's "The Two Sides of Bobby Orr" LP $20

Topps hockey card cartoons

- 1972-73 Topps hockey card cartoons original artwork, 2x3, purchased at and stamped with the official 1989 Topps Auction Stamp to authenticate them (mb was a minimum bid): #24 Jacques Plante, Maple Leafs, with card ($30mb); #35 Garry Unger, Blues, with card ($20mb); #50 Jean Ratelle, Rangers, with card ($30mb); #71 Frank St. Marseille, Blues, with card ($60mb); #88 Dave Keon, Maple Leafs, with card ($15mb); #90 Bobby Clarke, Flyers ($60); #107 Mike Pelyk, Maple Leafs, with card ($15mb); #147 Jack Egers, Blues, with card ($15mb).
- 1979-80 Topps cartoon original artwork, 4x6: #33 Garry Unger, Blues, with card ($20 mb); #57 Larry Patey, Blues, with card ($15mb); #109 Rick Kehoe, Penguins, with card ($15mb); #122 Jim Rutherford, Red Wings, with card ($15mb); #125 Bobby Clarke, Flyers ($60mb); #142 Wayne Babych, Blues, with card ($15mb); #153 Lanny McDonald, Maple Leafs, with card ($40mb); #173 Don Bolduc, Red Wings, with card ($15mb); #208 Ron Duguay, Rangers, with card ($20mb); #217 Bob Nystrom, Islanders, with card ($20mb).
- Original cartoon artwork from the back of Tim Horton's 1969-70 Topps hockey card $125
- Original cartoon artwork from the back of Ed Shack's 1971-72 Topps card $85

Miscellaneous, all three sports

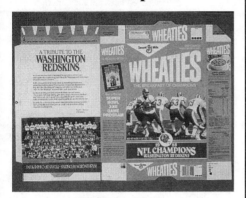

Cereal boxes
Wheaties

1995 NFL 75th Anniversary Wheaties $14.95
1995 Michael Jordan's Back Wheaties.................$19.95
1995 Boston Garden Wheaties $19.95
1995 San Francisco 49ers Super Bowl Wheaties ..$24.95
1995 Pro Football's 75th Anniversary Wheaties...$14.95
1994 Jerry Rice Wheaties $29.95
1994 Dallas Cowboys Wheaties $24.95
1993 Larry Bird Wheaties $34.95
1993 Dallas Cowboys Wheaties $24.95
1993 John Elway Wheaties..................................$29.95
1993 Micheal Jordan Wheaties, golfing $24.95
1993 Minnesota Vikings NFC Champions...........$39.95
1992 Chicago Bulls Wheaties..............................$19.95
1992 Pittsburgh Penguins Wheaties $29.95
1992 Pittsburgh Steelers Wheaties $24.95
1992 Barry Sanders Wheaties..............................$29.95
1992 Washington Redskins Wheaties $29.95
1992 Michael Jordan 1-ounce Wheaties...................$xx
1991 Michael Jordan 3/4-ounce Wheaties............$14.95
1991 Chicago Bulls 3/4-ounce Wheaties..............$14.95
1991 Joe Montana Wheaties................................$24.95
1991 New York Giants Wheaties $29.95
1991 Pittsburgh Penguins Wheaties $39.95
1988 Los Angeles Lakers Wheaties $49.95
1988 Steve Largent Wheaties $59.95
1988 Walter Payton Wheaties $39.95
1988 Washington Redskins Wheaties $39.95
1951 Johnny Lujack (football)..........................$60-$75
1951 George Mikan (basketball) ....$75-$100

Kellogg's Corn Flakes

1992 Larry Bird Olympic Corn Flakes.................$19.95
1992 David Robinson Olympic Corn Flakes.........$19.95
1992 USA basketball team $14.95
1983 Danny White, Dallas Cowboys....................$24.95

Kellogg's Frosted Mini Wheats

1992 Larry Bird Olympic Mini Wheats.................$24.95
1992 Karl Malone Olympic Mini Wheats $24.95
1992 Chris Mullin Olympic Mini Wheats.............$24.95
1992 David Robinson Olympic Mini Wheats $24.95
1992 John Stockton Olympic Mini Wheats..........$24.95

Honey Nut Crunch Raisin Bran
1982 Bob Griese, Miami Dolphins $24.95

Kellogg's Raisin Bran
1992 USA basketball team cartoon.......................$14.95

Postage stamps

Values are from the Official 1996 Blackbook Price Guide of United States Postage Stamps, 18th edition:

1) 1961 4-cent Dr. James Naismith - basketball founder, brown - Mint sheet for $8; block of 4 for 70 cents; unused stamp for 22 cents; used stamp for $16 cents.

2) 1969 6-cent Intercollegiate Football Centenary, red and green - Mint sheet for $13; block of 4 for $1.50; unused stamp for 40 cents; used stamp for 16 cents.

3) 1984 20-cent Jim Thorpe, black and white - Mint sheet for $30; block of 4 for $3; unused stamp for 70 cents; used stamp for 16 cents.

1974-75 Nabisco Sugar Daddy caricatures

In 1974 and 1975, specially-marked Sugar Daddy and Sugar Mama products included one of these 1 1/16" by 2 3/4" cards featuring a caricature of a sports star of that time. The cards were intended to be displayed on a 18" by 24" poster available by mail from Nabisco. The 1974 set, titled "Pro Faces" shows the athlete's head on a caricature body, with his name below. The 1975 set, titled Sugar Daddy All-Stars," is the same, except the player is standing against a red-white-and-blue starred flag background. The player's name is at the bottom, flanked by a star on each side. The numbered backs have statistics and biographical information, plus a stick-on area for applying the card to the poster. fb means football, bb means basketball, h means hockey.

1974 Nabisco Pro Faces

	NM	EX	VG
Complete set (25):	125.00	65.00	40.00
Common player:	2.50	1.25	.70
1. Roger Staubach (fb)	30.00	15.00	9.00
2. Floyd Little (fb)	4.50	2.25	1.25
3. Steve Owens (fb)	3.00	1.50	.90
4. Roman Gabriel (fb)	3.00	1.50	.90
5. Bobby Douglass (fb)	2.50	1.25	.70
6. John Gilliam (fb)	2.50	1.25	.90
7. Bob Lilly (fb)	7.50	3.75	2.25
8. John Brockington (fb)	3.00	1.50	.90
9. Jim Plunkett (fb)	5.00	2.50	1.50
10. Greg Landry (fb)	2.50	1.25	.70
11. Phil Esposito (h)	7.50	3.75	2.25
12. Dennis Hull (h)	3.00	1.50	.90
13. Reg Fleming (h)	2.50	1.25	.70
14. Garry Unger (h)	3.00	1.50	.90
15. Derek Sanderson (h)	4.50	2.25	1.25
16. Jerry Korab (h)	2.50	1.25	.70
17. Oscar Robertson (bb)	20.00	10.00	6.00
18. Spencer Haywood (bb)	4.50	2.25	1.25
19. Jo Jo White (bb)	4.50	2.25	1.25
20. Connie Hawkins (bb)	7.50	3.75	2.25
21. Nate Thurmond (bb)	5.00	2.50	1.50
22. Mickey Redmond (h)	3.00	1.50	.90
23. Chet Walker (bb)	4.50	2.25	1.25
24. Calvin Murphy (bb)	5.00	2.50	1.50
25. Kareem Abdul-Jabbar (bb)	25.00	12.50	7.50

491

1975 Sugar Daddy All-Stars

	NM	EX	VG
Complete set (25):	125.00	65.00	40.00
Common player:	2.50	1.25	.70
1. Roger Staubach (fb)	30.00	12.50	7.50
2. Floyd Little (fb)	4.50	2.25	1.25
3. Alan Page (fb)	5.00	2.50	1.50
4. Merlin Olsen (fb)	7.50	3.75	2.25
5. Wally Chambers (fb)	2.50	1.25	.70
6. John Gilliam (fb)	2.50	1.25	.70
7. Bob Lilly (fb)	7.50	3.75	2.25
8. John Brockington (fb)	3.00	1.50	.90
9. Jim Plunkett (fb)	5.00	2.50	1.50
10. Willie Lanier (fb)	5.00	2.50	1.50
11. Phil Esposito (h)	7.50	3.75	2.25
12. Dennis Hull (h)	3.00	1.50	.90
13. Brad Park (h)	5.00	2.50	1.50
14. Tom Lysiak (h)	2.50	1.25	.70
15. Bernie Parent (h)	5.00	2.50	1.50
16. Mickey Redmond (h)	3.00	1.50	.90
17. Jerry Sloan (bb)	4.50	2.25	1.25
18. Spencer Haywood (bb)	4.50	2.25	1.25
19. Bob Lanier (bb)	7.50	3.75	2.25
20. Connie Hawkins (bb)	7.50	3.75	2.25
21. Geoff Petrie (bb)	2.50	1.25	.70
22. Don Awrey (h)	2.50	1.25	.70
23. Chet Walker (bb)	4.50	2.25	1.25
24. Bob McAdoo (bb)	4.50	2.25	1.25
25. Kareem Abdul-Jabbar (bb)	25.00	12.50	7.50

1987 Quaker Chewy Granola Bar Posters

Marcus Allen	$25
Larry Bird	$35
Eric Dickerson	$15
Tony Dorsett	$25
Michael Jordan	$40
Walter Payton	$30

7-Eleven cups

These unnumbered white plastic cups feature color or line portraits of basketball and football players. In most cases, a facsimile signature appears below the portrait and above the player's name and team. All of the football players are helmetless.

The backs include some basic biographical information and a handful of career highlights. A 7-Eleven logo is at the top, while a team helmet is at the bottom. Basketball cups have the 7-Eleven logo, too, along with an NBA Players Association logo.

The football cups are not dated. The size of the print can be used to determine the year; the 1973 cups have larger type. The basketball cups, however, are dated; "1972" is wedged between the copyright logo and a Players Association logo.

Each cup stands 5 1/4" inches tall, and are 3 1/4" in diameter at the mouth, tapering down to two inches at the base. The cups are very susceptible to cracking, so don't put too much pressure on them, and leave them out of direct sunlight so they don't fade.

Checklists for the sets were available at the 7-Eleven stores when the cups were issued; baseball players were also produced in 1972-73. The checklist also advised "Important Kids! Hand Wash Only. Keep Out Of Dishwasher." It's best just to let the cups soak in water for a couple of hours, then rinse them off and let them air dry.

7-Eleven basketball cups (40)

Kareem Abdul-Jabbar	$35
Nate Archibald	$15
Rick Barry	$25
Dave Bing	$10
Austin Carr	$10
Wilt Chamberlain	$30
Dave DeBusschere	$12
Walt Frazier	$30
Gail Goodrich	$6
Hal Greer	$10
Happy Hairston	$6
John Havlicek	$30
Connie Hawkins	$8
Elvin Hayes	$15
Spencer Haywood	$15
Lou Hudson	$10
John Johnson	$6
Don Kojis	$6
Bob Lanier	$20
Kevin Loughery	$6
Jerry Lucas	$20
Pete Maravich	$35
Jack Marin	$6
Jim McMillian	$6
Jeff Mullins	$6
Geoff Petrie	$10
Abdul Rahman	$6
Willis Reed	$10
Oscar Robertson	$15
Paul Silas	$6
Jerry Sloan	$8
Elmore Smith	$6
Nate Thurmond	$7
Wes Unseld	$20
Dick Van Arsdale	$12
Tom Van Arsdale	$12
Chet Walker	$15
John Warren	$6
Jerry West	$25
Jo Jo White	$12

1972 7-Eleven football cups (60)

- Atlanta Falcons - Claude Humphrey ($4.50), George Kunz ($5.50)
- Baltimore Colts - Norm Bulaich ($5.50), Bill Curry ($5.50), Ted Hendricks ($5.50), Bubba Smith ($6.50), Rick Volk ($5.50)
- Buffalo Bills - O.J. Simpson
- Chicago Bears - Dick Butkus ($20)
- Cincinnati Bengals - Mike Reid ($6.50)
- Cleveland Browns - Leroy Kelly ($6.50), Milt Morin ($5.50)

- Dallas Cowboys - Chuck Howley ($6.50), Bob Lilly ($10), John Niland ($6.50), Mel Renfro ($5.50)
- Denver Broncos - Floyd Little ($6.50)
- Detroit Lions - Ed Flanagan ($4.50), Steve Owens ($4.50), Charlie Sanders ($5.50)
- Green Bay Packers - Gale Gillingham ($4.50)
- Houston Oilers - Elvin Bethea ($5.50), Ken Houston ($5.50)
- Kansas City Chiefs - Len Dawson ($6.50), Willie Lanier ($6.50), Jan Stenerud ($4.50), Jim Tyrer ($5.50)
- Los Angeles Rams - Willie Ellison ($4.50), Tom Mack ($5.50), Isiah Robertson ($4.50)
- Miami Dolphins - Larry Little ($5.50), Mercury Morris ($5.50), Bill Stanfill ($5.50)
- Minnesota Vikings - Paul Krause ($6.50), Alan Page ($10), Ron Yary ($5.50)
- New England Patriots - Jim Plunkett ($6.50)
- New Orleans Saints - Jake Kupp ($5.50), Del Williams ($5.50)
- New York Giants - Bob Tucker ($4.50)
- New York Jets - Winston Hill ($4.50)
- Oakland Raiders - Fred Biletnikoff ($10), Willie Brown ($5.50), Ray Chester ($5.50), Jim Otto ($10)
- Philadelphia Eagles - Bill Bradley ($4.50)
- Pittsburgh Steelers - Terry Bradshaw ($15), Joe Greene ($20), Andy Russell ($5.50)
- St. Louis Cardinals - Donny Anderson ($4.50), Jim Hart ($4.50)
- San Diego Chargers - Gary Garrison ($4.50), Walt Sweeney ($4.50)
- San Francisco 49ers - Cedric Hardman ($4.50), Ted Kwalick ($6.50), Gene Washington ($4.50), Dave Wilcox ($4.50)
- Washington Redskins - Larry Brown ($5.50), Roy Jefferson ($5.50), Sonny Jurgensen ($10)

1973 7-Eleven football cups (80)

- Atlanta Falcons - Art Malone ($4), Tommy Nobis ($5)
- Baltimore Colts - Ray May ($4), Don McCauley ($4), Tom Mitchell ($4), Bubba Smith ($7)
- Buffalo Bills - J.D. Hill ($5), Dennis Shaw ($4), O.J. Simpson ($15)
- Chicago Bears - Dick Butkus ($20), Bobby Douglass ($5), Randy Jackson ($4), Mac Percival ($5)
- Cincinnati Bengals - Ken Anderson ($7), Robert D. Johnson ($4), Bob Trumpy ($5)
- Cleveland Browns - Dale Lindsey ($4), Mike Phipps ($4), Bo Scott ($4)
- Dallas Cowboys - Walt Garrison ($5), Calvin Hill ($5), Bob Lilly ($10)
- Denver Broncos - Pete Duranko ($4), George Goeddeke ($4), Jim Turner ($5)
- Detroit Lions - Mel Farr ($4), Greg Landry ($7), Mike Lucci ($7)
- Green Bay Packers - John Brockington ($4), Scott Hunter ($4), Mike McCoy ($4)

- Houston Oilers - Jim Beirne ($4), Dan Pastorini ($7)
- Kansas City Chiefs - Buck Buchanan ($7), Jim Lynch ($4), Ed Podolak ($4), Otis Taylor ($5)
- Los Angeles Rams - Jim Bertelsen ($4), Larry Smith ($4), Jack Snow ($4), Jack Youngblood ($5)
- Miami Dolphins - Marlin Briscoe ($4), Larry Little ($7), Doug Swift ($4)
- Minnesota Vikings - Bob Berry ($4), Gary Larsen ($4), Ed Marinaro ($5), Jim Marshall ($5)
- New England Patriots - Larry Carwell ($4), Ron Sellers ($4)
- New Orleans Saints - Dan Ambramowicz ($5), Bob Gresham ($4)
- New York Giants - Ron Johnson ($4), Spider Lockhart ($4), Norm Snead ($5)
- New York Jets - Eddie Bell ($6), Rich Caster ($5), Don Maynard ($7)
- Oakland Raiders - Marv Hubbard ($5), Mike Siani ($10), Jack Tatum ($5), Phil Villipiano ($5)
- Philadelphia Eagles - Harold Jackson ($5), Leroy Keyes ($4), John Reaves ($5)
- Pittsburgh Steelers - Jack Ham ($7), Franco Harris ($7), Frank Lewis ($4)
- St. Louis Cardinals - Jackie Smith ($5), Roger Wehrli ($5)
- San Diego Chargers - Cid Edwards ($4), Mike Garrett ($4), Tim Rossovich ($4)
- San Francisco 49ers - Jimmy Johnson ($5), Steve Spurrier ($5), Bruce Taylor ($4), Ken Willard ($4)
- Washington Redskins - Larry Brown (5), Pat Fischer ($5), Chris Hanburger ($5)

Sports Illustrated posters

During the late 1960s and early 1970s, Sports Illustrated produced several posters featuring hockey, basketball, football and baseball players. These posters, made available through ads in the magazine, originally sold for only $1.50. But today some have reached as much as $200, including baseball stars Mickey Mantle and Roberto Clemente. The year listed behind the player's name is the year the poster was released. The year of release of some posters is unknown, so those posters are indicated by 1968-71.

Basketball (7)

Player, Year Issued	Value
Bill Bradley, 1968-71	$50-$75
Billy Cunningham, 1968-71	$10-$15
John Havlicek, 1968-71	$25-$35
Elvin Hayes, 1970	$25-$45
Spencer Haywood, 1971	$10-$15
Willis Reed, 1968-71	$15-$25
Oscar Robertson, 1971	$35-$50

Football (81)

Player, Year Issued	Value
Lance Alworth, 1968-71	$15-$25
Jim Bakken, 1968-71	$7-$10
Pete Banaszak, 1968-71	$10-$15
Lem Barney, 1968-71	$12-$15
Mike Battle, 1968-71	$7-$10

Fred Biletnikoff, 1968-71	$15-$20
George Blanda, 1968-71	$15-$25
John Brockington, 1968-71	$10-$15
John Brodie, 1968	$15-$25
Bill Brown, 1968-71	$7-$10
Larry Brown, 1968-71	$15-$20
Norm Bulaich, 1968-71	$7-$10
Dick Butkus, 1968-71	$50-$75
Vince Carter, 1968-71	$7-$10
Junior Coffey, 1968-71	$7-$10
Greg Cook, 1968-71	$7-$10
Larry Csonka, 1968-71	$15-$25
Mike Curtis, 1968-71	$12-$15
Ben Davidson, 1968-71	$10-$15
Len Dawson, 1968-71	$15-$25
Carl Eller, 1968-71	$15-$20
Mel Farr, 1969	$7-$10
Roman Gabriel, 1968	$10-$20
Mike Garrett, 1968-71	$7-$10
Jim Grabowski, 1968-71	$7-$15
Joe Greene, 1968-71	$15-$20
Bob Griese, 1968-71	$25-$35
John Hadl, 1969	$12-$15
Ben Hawkins, 1968-71	$7-$10
Bob Hayes, 1968-71	$10-$15
Rich Jackson, 1968-71	$7-$10
Charley Johnson, 1968-71	$7-$10
Ron Johnson, 1968-71	$7-$10
Deacon Jones, 1969	$12-$15
Homer Jones, 1969	$7-$10
Sonny Jurgenson, 1968	$25-$30
Joe Kapp, 1968-71	$10-$15
Alex Karras, 1970	$10-$15
Leroy Kelly, 1968-71	$10-$15
Jack Kemp, 1968	$25-$40
Billy Kilmer, 1968-71	$12-$15
Daryle Lamonica, 1968-71	$15-$20
Greg Landry, 1971	$10-$15
Bob Lilly, 1968-71	$15-$20
Floyd Little, 1968-71	$12-$15
Spider Lockhart, 1968-71	$7-$10
John Mackey, 1968	$12-$15
Archie Manning, 1968-71	$15-$20
Tom Matte, 1969	$7-$10
Don Maynard, 1968-71	$15-$20
Craig Morton, 1970	$10-$15
Jim Nance, 1968-71	$10-$15
Bill Nelson, 1970	$10-$15
Kent Nix, 1968-71	$7-$10
Ray Nitschke, 1968-71	$15-$20
Tommy Nobis, 1968-71	$12-$15
Joe Namath, 1968-71	$75-$100
Merlin Olsen, 1968-71	$25-$35
Alan Page, 1968-71	$15-$20
Jim Plunkett, 1971	$12-$15
Dan Reeves, 1968-71	$10-$15
Tim Roosovich, 1968-71	$7-$10
Andy Russell, 1968-71	$7-$10
Frank Ryan, 1968	$10-$12
George Sauer, 1968-71	$7-$10
Gale Sayers, 1968-71	$25-$35
Ron Sellers, 1968-71	$7-$10
Dennis Shaw, 1968-71	$7-$10
O.J. Simpson, 1968-71	$75-$100
Jackie Smith, 1968-71	$10-$15
Norm Snead, 1968-71	$10-$12
Matt Snell, 1968-71	$10-$15
Bart Starr, 1968-71	$25-$35
Roger Staubach, 1968-71	$50-$75
Charley Taylor, 1968-71	$15-$20
Otis Taylor, 1968-71	$15-$20

Paul Warfield, 1968-71	$15-$20
Gene Washington, 1968-71	$10-$15
George Webster, 1969	$7-$10
Larry Wilson, 1968-71	$15-$20
Marv Woodson, 1968-71	$7-$10

Hockey (10)

Player, Year Issued	Value
Red Berenson, 1970	$25-$35
Phil Esposito, 1971	$15-$25
Ed Giacomin, 1970	$12-$15
Vic Hadfield, 1968-71	$7-$10
Gordie Howe, 1968-71	$25-$40
Bobby Hull, 1968-71	$25-$50
Dave Keon, 1968-71	$7-$10
Bobby Orr, 1968-71	$25-$50
Derek Sanderson, 1968-71	$10-$15
Gump Worsley, 1968-71	$10-$15

Awards/Rings

Although each player, coach, front office personnel and team dignitary receives one, less than 100 rings are made for each championship team. This makes them quite rare and more valuable compared to other memorabilia.

Jostens, of Minneapolis, Minn., has created the majority of the rings designed for Super Bowl winners and conference championship teams. Each year the designs have become more expensive and complex; as more gold and diamonds are added to the design, the ring's value on the gold and precious gem market increases, too.

Jostens, which produced the ring for the Super Bowl I champion Green Bay Packers, also created the ring when the team won Super Bowl II. This ring has a one carat diamond in the center of the bezel, set between two half-carat diamonds. By comparison, the Chicago Bears Super Bowl XX ring has 40 diamonds on the bezel, including a half-carat diamond in the center surrounded by 13 .025 carat diamonds in the shape of the letter "C" bordered by 26 smaller diamonds.

It generally takes four to six weeks to design a ring. The teams often request special design elements or graphics, words or logos. The sides (the shank) often feature a year, a message, symbol, team/league logo or game score. Most of the Super Bowl rings are made of gold and contain diamonds, but some contain other stones, either natural or synthetic, in the team's colors.

Most of the championship rings which are listed for sale in advertisements are marked "salesman's sample." These rings have a serial number inside the band and were not created for a player, but rather for a salesman to market and advertise the rings. Instead of real diamonds, they generally contain a diamond look-alike, called cubic zirconia.

Rings are also created for players entering their respective sport's Hall of Fame. Balfour, of Attleboro, Mass., has created the majority of these rings.

The best places to find rings at memorabilia shows in larger cities, or for sale through auctions. Another alternative is to scan ads in pages of various hobby publications. Although they are generally on the high end of the monetary scale, rings offer a lasting memory from a championship season.

494

Rings

- Troy Aikman's 1992 Dallas Cowboys Super Bowl Champions ring, 14k gold-plated salesman's sample, has a star diamond in the center.... $4,195
- George Allen's 1972 Washington Redskins Super Bowl VII/NFC Championship ring, salesman's sample $1,995
- Lyle Alzado's 1979 Denver Broncos team ring, salesman's sample..................................... $1,250
- Terry Bradshaw's 1975 Pittsburgh Steelers Super Bowl X Championship ring, 10k yellow/gold salesman's sample, has Bradshaw's name on the side, with two sparkling diamonds mounted on the top between the Vince Lombardi trophy.... $2,950
- Terry Bradshaw's 1979 Pittsburgh Steelers Super Bowl Championship ring, 10k, four diamonds inside represent four Super Bowl wins, salesman's sample $3,695
- Joe Greene's 1974 Pittsburgh Steelers Super Bowl Championship ring, with diamond set in an antique black onyx stone, salesman's sample............. $2,000
- Bob Griese's 1971 Miami Dolphins Super Bowl VI/AFC Championship ring, 10k white/gold salesman's sample, has a diamond mounted in a grayish blue stone on top, Griese's name on the shank $2,950
- Jeff Hostetler's 1990 New York Giants Super Bowl Championship ring, 14k gold-plated salesman's sample, has two football-shaped diamonds in the center $4,250
- Jack Kemp's 1984 Buffalo Bills Honor Roll ring, 10k salesman's sample with a diamond set in a blue stone, given to Bills players who were inducted into the Hall of Fame.................. $1,295
- Joe Montana's 1981 San Francisco 49ers Super Bowl XVI Championship ring, 10k yellow/gold salesman's sample, 16 diamonds surround a diamond mounted in a huge football-shaped bezel, Montana's name is on the side.................. $3,750
- Joe Montana's 1988 San Francisco 49ers Super Bowl ring, 10k salesman's sample............. $4,250
- Craig Morton's 1977 Denver Broncos AFC Champions ring, 10k salesman's sample ... $2,250
- William Perry's 1985 Chicago Bears Super Bowl XXIII Championship ring, 10k salesman's sample, size 22 .... $4,500
- Jim Plunkett's 1980 Oakland Raiders Super Bowl XV Championship ring, 14k white gold, with 34 diamonds mounted on the top, salesman's sample $3,500
- John Riggins' 1983 Washington Redskins NFC Champions ring, 14k gold-plated salesman's sample, features a diamond-studded football with a ruby red stone in the center $1,595
- Joe Robbie's 1972 Miami Dolphins Super Bowl Championship ring, 10k salesman's sample, diamond set inside aquamarine stone........ $3,595
- O.J. Simpson's NFL Players Alumni ring, 10k gold salesman's sample, has a large, gold detailed football mounted on a huge football-shaped tiger's eye stone.. $2,100
- O.J. Simpson's 1980 Buffalo Bills Hall of Fame ring, 10k yellow gold salesman's sample, with a diamond mounted in a midnight blue stone on top.. $1,850
- Bart Starr's Green Bay Packer's Super Bowl I Championship ring, salesman's sample $2,750
- Hank Stram's 1969 Kansas City Chiefs Super Bowl IV Championship ring, 10k yellow/gold salesman's sample, has a football filled with sparkling diamonds mounted on a large burgundy stone...$3,500
- Roger Staubach's 1977 Dallas Cowboys Super Bowl Champions ring , 10k white/gold salesman's sample, with diamonds set inside blue stars surrounded by 22 diamonds.......................$3,500
- 1974 Minnesota Vikings NFC Champions ring, 10k $4,250
- 1975 Pittsburgh Steelers Super Bowl World Champions player's ring, 10k by Balfour $9,500
- 1981 Cincinnati Bengals AFC Championship ring, 10k salesman's sample.......................$2,250
- 1983 Oakland Raiders Super Bowl XVIII Championship player's ring, 14k $13,500
- 1983 Washington Redskins NFC Champs player's ring, 14k $6,500
- 1984 San Francisco 49ers Super Bowl XIX Championship ring, 10k yellow/gold salesman's sample, two diamonds as big as the footballs in the Vince Lombardi trophies, which are surrounded by other diamonds $3,500
- 1984 Philadelphia Stars USFL Championship ring, 14k gold-plated, has the team logo with a diamond set inside it, all set on a ruby stone $1,695
- 1987 Washington Redskins Super Bowl XXII Championship ring, a real player's ring, it includes its original presentation box, and a lady's ring, too; made for Dennis Woodberry, #46, whose name is on the inside of the 10k gold/yellow ring, which has 42 diamonds and 30 rubies; lady's ring has 16 diamonds $15,500
- 1989 San Francisco 49ers Super Bowl XXIV Championship ring, 10k yellow/gold salesman's sample, with 41 diamonds $3,850
- Rick Barry's 1970 ABA All-Star Game ring, a 10k yellow/gold ring with Barry's name on the shank; Barry gave the ring to basketball trainer Bob Travilini; "To Trav from R. Barry 1-24-70" is engraved on the inside $1,850
- Michael Jordan's 1986 All-Star game ring $2,095
- Jerry West's Hall of Fame basketball ring, a 10k yellow/gold salesman's sample, has West's name on one side and the Naismith Memorial Basketball Hall of Fame logo on the other; has a sparkling diamond mounted in a gold "Roman" reef, set on top of a ruby red stone $2,495
- Larry Bird's 1984 Boston Celtics NBA Championship ring, 10k salesman's sample $2,750
- Elvin Hayes' 1978 Washington Bullets NBA Championship ring, 10k salesman's sample $1,195
- Magic Johnson's 1985 Los Angeles Lakers NBA Championship ring, 10k salesman's sample $2,250
- Michael Jordan 1991 Chicago Bulls 10k ring, with diamonds, salesman's sample....................$4,500
- Isiah Thomas' 1990 Detroit Pistons NBA Championship ring, salesman's sample, has 20 diamonds surrounded by a large ruby red stone with another diamond in the middle..........$2,650

These salesman's samples were made for George Allen
(1972 season) and Johnny Unitas (1970 season).

- Jo Joe White's 1974 Boston Celtics NBA Championship ring, 10k white/gold salesman's sample, with a diamond in the center........ $3,195
- 1982 Los Angeles Lakers NBA Championship ring, 10k yellow/gold, has a deep purple stone on top with 14 diamonds surrounding a detailed Lakers logo mounted in the center............. $2,995
- 1985 Los Angeles Lakers NBA Championship ring, 14k with diamond $6,500
- 1976 Montreal Canadiens Stanley Cup Championship ring, 14k salesman's sample, has a diamond mounted in an ice blue hockey rink $1,650
- 1991 Pittsburgh Penguins Stanley Cup Championship ring, 10k, Mario Lemieux salesman's sample..................................... $3,850

Awards/Trophies

- George Mikan's 1949 NBA All-Star Classic's MVP award ....$8,500-$12,500
- Larry Bird's 1986-87 NBA Free Throw Percentage leader trophy, 2 feet tall, 16 inches wide, one inch thick; resembles the NBA All-Star MVP trophy; has a large etched basketball with an NBA Players Association logo etched into glass; weighs 15 pounds..................................... $4,995

- 1982 St. Louis Cardinals Super Bowl tournament jewelry; sets were given to players and coaches, contains a tournament pendant, cuff links, tie bar, stick pin, in original sterling box $795
- Dan Marino's 1984 Professional Athlete of the Year award, presented to him by the Florida Sports Writers Association and Florida Sportscasters Association, with letter from Marino $2,250
- Super Bowl XI Oakland Raiders, city of Oakland Super Bowl trophy, given to the players; given to Skip Thomas; autographed $2,495
- 1988 Heisman Trophy made for Barry Sanders; one of probably three to six which were produced....$29,995
- O.J. Simpson, USC Heisman Trophy; one of probably three to six produced $34,995
- George Halas Award (owner's trophy) for 1989 San Francisco 49ers NFC Championship $14,995
- Joe Montana Super Bowl XIX MVP Award, 18x24, has image of Montana's face and is engraved on the bottom "Joe Montana, San Francisco 49ers, MVP Super Bowl XIX, San Francisco 38 - Miami 16" given by owner Eddie DeBartolo to Montana, says "Joe - With all my thanks, Best wishes and Friendship, Eddie," autographed by Montana $7,500
- 1966 Kansas City Chiefs AFL Champs 10k pendant, with diamond $1,250

Beer cans

Over the last 40 years, more than 250 beer cans with sports-related themes have been issued. Generally, the cans feature team/player photos, drawings, schedules or stats in the design. The most appealing cans usually salute pro sports teams and their stars, but lower levels of competition have also been represented. At the professional level, teams from Chicago and Pittsburgh lead the way in appearances, in part because of the breweries serving these markets. Overall, there have been more than 70 football-related cans, while basketball and hockey each have more than 20.

Pro football teams and players represented include the Chicago Bears, Cincinnati Bengals, Dallas Cowboys, Pittsburgh Steelers, Mel Blount, Dick Butkus, Terry Bradshaw, Mike Ditka, Joe Greene, Jack Ham, Franco Harris, William "Pudge" Heffelfinger, Chuck Noll, Walter Payton and Art Rooney. Pro basketball teams represented include the Boston Celtics, Golden State Warriors, Milwaukee Bucks, Phoenix Suns and San Antonio Spurs; hockey teams include the Boston Bruins, Chicago Blackhawks, Detroit Red Wings, Minnesota North Stars/Dallas Stars, Philadelphia Flyers, Pittsburgh Penguins and San Jose Sharks. So far, no pro hockey or basketball players have been represented.

The National Brewing Co., in Phoenix, Ariz., issued what is considered the first true sports-related beer can, producing a can with the Phoenix Suns' 1969-70 basketball schedule on it. The Carling Brewery in Natick, Mass., also issued a Black Label Beer can to commemorate the Boston Bruins' Stanley Cup championship. Before this time, sports-related cans had generic designs featuring sports activities in general.

The 1969-70 Phoenix Suns schedule can is one of the scarcest and most difficult to obtain. Values for these cans approach three figures, while the 1970 Bruins can be had for $25-$30. Iron City cans from the 1970s are generally between $5-$8.

Places to search for beer cans include flea markets, antique shops and malls, along the roadside, at hunting camps and cabins, in old farms and at the town dump. There are also clubs to join, such as the Beer Can Collectors of America (in Fenton, Mo.) and the American Breweriana Association (in Pueblo, Colo.). Most collectors display empty cans, preferably opened from the bottom.

Football

Pittsburgh Brewing Co., Pittsburgh, Pa.

a) 1973, Iron City: "Pour it on Steelers;" 1972 results, 1973 schedule.
b) 1973, Iron City: Defense! Defense! Defense!; helmets with player numbers; 16 ounce.
c) 1973, Iron City: Pittsburgh Steeler offense; facsimile autographs.
d) 1973, Iron City: Pittsburgh Steeler defense; facsimile autographs.
e) 1974, Iron City Beer & Draft: Super Bowl winners 1967-74.
f) 1976, Iron City: Congratulations Super Steelers 1975; Pittsburgh 16, Minnesota 6.
g) 1976, Iron City: Steelers 1975 Super Bowl Champions; color team photo; 12 and 16 ounce.
h) 1977, Iron City: Steelers 1976 Super Bowl Champions; color team photo; 12 and 16 ounce.
i) 1977, Iron City: The 1976 Pittsburgh Steelers; color team photo.
j) 1980, Iron City: Super Super Super Steelers 1979; color team photo.
k) 1980, Iron City: The Team of the Decade - 1980 Pittsburgh; team photo.
l) 1981, Iron City: Pittsburgh's Pride; color team photo.
m) 1982, Iron City: Steelers 50 seasons.
n) 1983, Iron City: The Pittsburgh Steelers, Chuck Noll, Art Rooney.
o) 1984, Iron City: Super Steelers' autographs.
p) 1985, Iron City: Title Drive 1985 - Steelers.
q) 1986, Iron City: Two Great Traditions; Steeler autographs; 1st edition.
r) 1986, Iron City: Two Great Traditions; Steeler autographs; 2nd edition.
s) 1986, Iron City: Two Great Traditions; Steeler autographs; 3rd edition.
t) 1987, Iron City: Steeler Hall of Famers.
u) 1988, Iron City: Jack Ham; portrait and stats.
v) 1989, Iron City: Terry Bradshaw; 12 and 16 ounce.
w) 1989, Iron City: Mel Blount; 12 and 16 ounce.
x) 1990, Iron City: Joe Greene, Hall of Famer; 12 and 16 ounce.
y) 1990, Iron City: Franco Harris, 1990 Hall of Famer; 12 and 16 ounce.
z) 1992, Iron City: Two Great Traditions; Steeler autographs; 2nd edition; similar to the 1986 can, but this one has Art Rooney's signature at the top.
aa) 1993, Iron City: Chuck Noll, Hall of Famer; 12 and 16 ounce.

G. Heileman Brewing Co., La Crosse, Wis.

a) 1990, Old Style: Chicago Bears 1920-1989; first in a series; 16 ounce.
b) 1991, Old Style: Chicago's All-Time Greatest, Mike Ditka; second in a series; 16 ounce.
c) 1991, Old Style Light: Chicago's All-Time Greatest, Mike Ditka; third in a series; 16 ounce.
d) 1991, Old Style: Chicago's All-Time Greatest, Dick Butkus; fourth in a series; 16 ounce.
e) 1991, Old Style: Chicago's All-Time Greatest, Walter Payton; fifth in a series; 16 ounce.
f) 1991, Old Style Light: Chicago's All-Time Greatest, Walter Payton; sixth in a series; 16 ounce.

Hudepohl Brewing Co., Cincinnati, Ohio

a) 1987, Hu-Dey: "Who dey think bonna beat dem Bengals."
b) 1988, Hu-Dey: 14k Premium, 1988 Bengals schedule.
c) 1989, Hu-Dey: Bengals-AFC Champs; 1988-89 Super Bowl edition, 1988-89 results.

Miller Brewing Co., Milwaukee, Wis.

a) 1992, Miller Lite: Dallas Cowboys, Super Bowl; 16 ounce.
b) 1992, Miller Lite: Dallas Cowboys, Super Bowl; 16 ounce.
c) 1993, Miller Lite: 1993 Champions, Super Bowl XXVII, Dallas Cowboys.
d) 1993, Miller Lite: World Champions, Dallas Cowboys.
e) 1993, Miller Lite: Super Bowl XXVIII, Sun., Jan. 30, 1994.

Genesee Beer,

a) 1993: 1st Pro, William "Pudge" Heffelfinger.

Basketball

National Brewing Co., Phoenix, Ariz.

a) 1969-70, A-1 Beer: 1969-70 Phoenix Suns schedule; bank.
b) 1970-71, A-1 Beer: 1970-71 Phoenix Suns schedule; bank.
c) 1971-72, A-1 Beer: 1971-72 Phoenix Suns schedule; bank.
d) 1972-73, A-1 Beer: 1972-73 Phoenix Suns schedule; bank.
e) 1973-74, A-1 Beer: 1973-74 Phoenix Suns schedule; bank.
f) 1974-75, A-1 Beer: 1974-75 Phoenix Suns schedule; bank.
g) 1973-74, Colt 45 Malt Liquor: 1973-74 Golden State Warriors schedule; bank.
h) 1975-76, Colt 45 Malt Liquor: 1975-76 Phoenix Suns schedule, bank.
i) 1977, Tuborg Gold: 1977 Boston Celtics schedule; bank.
j) 1977-78, Tuborg Gold: 1977-78 Phoenix Suns home schedule.

G. Heileman Brewing Co., La Crosse, Wis.

a) 1982-83, Old Style: 1982-83 Milwaukee Bucks schedule; bank.
b) 1983-84, Old Style: 1983-84 Milwaukee Bucks schedule; bank.

Pittsburgh Brewing Co., Pittsburgh, Pa.

a) 1974, Iron City Beer & Draft: NBA Champions 1947-1974.

Lone Star Brewing Co., San Antonio, Texas

a) 1983-84, Lone Star Beer: San Antonio Spurs 1983-84 schedule.
b) 1984-85, Lone Star Beer: San Antonio Spurs 1984-85 schedule.

Hockey

Carling National Brewing Co., Phoenix, Ariz.

a) 1969-70, Black Label: Boston Bruins 1969-70.
b) 1971-72, Black Label: Boston Bruins 1971-72; bank.

Pittsburgh Brewing Co., Pittsburgh, Pa.

a) 1974, Iron City Beer & Draft: Stanley Cup Champions; listing.
b) 1974, Iron City: "Two Great Names on Ice, Penguins and Iron City."
c) 1982, Iron City: 1982 Pittsburgh Penguins; color team photo.
d) 1991, Iron City: "Workin' on a Cold Iron;" goalie; 12 and 16 ounce.
e) 1991, Iron City: Pittsburgh Penguins player in black #90 uniform.
f) 1991, Iron City: Salutes 1991 Stanley Cup Champions, 12 and 16 ounce.
g) 1991, Iron City: "Boys of Winter" 12 and 16 ounce.
h) 1993, IC Light: Pittsburgh Penguins back-to-back championships; "Go Pens. Go For The Hat Trick;" 12 and 16 ounce.
i) 1994, IC Light: "Go Pens. Bring Back the Cup;" 12 and 16 ounce.

G. Heileman Brewing Co., La Crosse, Wis.

a) 1991, Old Style: Salutes Chicago Blackhawks; white, 16 ounce.
b) 1991, Old Style Light: Salutes Chicago Blackhawks; silver, 16 ounce.
c) 1991, Old Style: Chicago Blackhawks highlights; 16 ounce.
d) 1993, Special Export: Minnesota North Stars/Dallas Stars; 16 ounce.

e) 1993, Special Export Light: Minnesota North Stars/Dallas Stars; 16 ounce.
f) 1993, Old Style: 1992-93 Chicago Blackhawks.
g) 1993, Old Style Light: 1992-93 Chicago Blackawks.

Adolph Coors Co., Denver, Colo.

a) 1992, Coors Light: Penguins Silver Anniversary; Penguin on silver background; 16 ounce.
b) 1992, Coors Light: Penguins Silver Anniversary; Penguin on a white background; 16 ounce.
c) 1993, Coors Light: Pittsburgh Penguins 1993-94 season; team logo; 16 ounce.

Miller Brewing Co., Milwaukee, Wis.

a) 1993, Miller Light: Detroit Red Wings 1993-94 season; team logo.
b) 1993, Miller Genuine Draft: Detroit Red Wings 1993-94 season; team logo.
c) 1993, Miller Genuine Draft: Philadelphia Flyers 1993-94 season; team logo.
d) 1993, Miller Genuine Draft: Boston Bruins 1993-94 season; team logo.
e) 1993, Miller Genuine Draft: San Jose Sharks 1993-94 season; team logo.

Phone cards

Several sports-related themes have been used on phone cards, which are prepaid cards offering callers an alternative from using coins. Through a phone card, the caller has purchased phone time in advance. A $10 card entitles the caller to $10 worth of long distance phone time.

The cards, similar to credit cards, have an 800-number and a personal identification number on the back; they are punched in before the telephone number is dialed. A computer voice informs the caller how much time remains on the card and calculates time as it is used. When the time is used up, the card can be thrown away or kept as a collectible.

The cards are collectibles for several reasons - they offer the same beauty and themes of stamps, the monetary value of coins and paper money, and the trading appeal of sports cards. Generally, the most desirable cards are those which feature images of popular people, places or events. The print runs are often limited, too.

Condition also plays a factor in how valuable the card is; if a card has been used it can not be considered to be in Mint condition. Cards tend to scratch easily, so it's wise to examine the surface closely.

New phone cards can be found in a growing number of places - hobby shops, bus stations, post offices, airport gift shops, or any high pedestrian traffic area. Generally, used cards are an affordable alternative for those who are starting a phone card collection.

Card	Date	Quantity	Value
ACMI Larry Bird $6 L card	May 1994	5,000	$15
ACMI Larry Bird $10 L card	May 1994	4,000	$17
ACMI Larry Bird $20 L card	May 1994	800	$50
ACMI Larry Bird $50 L card	May 1994	200	$60
ACMI Larry Bird $6 A card	Sept. 1994	5,000	$15
ACMI Larry Bird $10 A card	Sept. 1994	4,000	$13
ACMI Larry Bird $20 A card	Sept. 1994	800	$30
ACMI Larry Bird $50 A card	Sept. 1994	200	$75
ACMI Byron Scott $6 B card	Jan. 1995	2,000	$15
ACMI Byron Scott $10 B card	Jan. 1995	500	$15
ACMI Byron Scott $20 B card	Jan. 1995	200	$25
ACMI Byron Scott $50 B card	Jan. 1995	100	$60
ACMI Packer Hall of Fame Bart Starr $3 card	March 1994	2,500	$10
ACMI Packer Hall of Fame Bart Starr $7 card	March 1994	2,500	$12
ACMI Packer Hall of Fame Ray Nitschke $3 card	March 1994	2,500	$10
ACMI Packer Hall of Fame Ray Nitschke $7 card	March 1994	1,500	$12

Miscellaneous

AmeriVox issued two series of cards featuring legendary NFL quarterbacks.

ACMI Packer Hall of Fame Ray Nitschke $20 card	March 1994	700	$25
ACMI Packer Hall of Fame Vince Lombardi $3 card	March 1994	2,500	$10
ACMI Packer Hall of Fame Vince Lombardi $7 card	March 1994	1,500	$12
ACMI Packer Hall of Fame Willie Davis $3 card	March 1994	2,500	$10
ACMI Packer Hall of Fame Willie Davis $7 card	March 1994	1,500	$12
ACMI Packer Hall of Fame Lombardi/Starr $3 card	Nov. 1994	2,500	$10
ACMI Packer Hall of Fame Lombardi/Starr $7 card	Nov. 1994	1,500	$12
ACMI Packer Hall of Fame $7 set of 5	March 1994	1,500	$12
AmCall NFL Players Association set of 10	Aug. 1993	5,000	$200
AmCall Emmitt Smith $10 card	Aug. 1993	5,000	$95
AmCall Deion Sanders $10 card	Dec. 1994	5,000	$25
AmCall Michael Irvin $10 promo card	Sept. 1993	10,000	$30
AmCall Michael Irvin $10 promo 2-card set	Sept. 1993	10,000	$60
AmeriVox NFL Quarterback Legends Series I, five $10 cards			
(Terry Bradshaw, Johnny Unitas, Roger Staubach,			
Y.A. Tittle, Bart Starr)	Nov. 1993	2,000 each	$130
AmeriVox NFL Quarterback Legends Series II, five $10 cards			
(Sonny Jurgensen, Len Dawson, Bob Griese, George Blanda,			
Otto Graham)	Feb. 1994	2,000 each	$90
AT & T Steve Young/Snoopy 10m three-card set	Feb. 1995	15,000	$30
AT & T Steve Young/Snoopy 49m jumbo set	Feb. 1995	10,000	$40
Authentix Brian Leetch Stanley Cup MVP four-card set			
including one of 594 cards featuring artwork			
and autograph	Nov. 1994	594	$75

Classic/Sprint 4-Sport Marshall Faulk $1 ($15), $2 ($25), $4 ($100)
Classic/Sprint 4-Sport Jason Kidd $1 ($35), $2 ($100), $4 ($200)
Classic/Sprint 4-Sport Jeff O'Neill $1 ($5), $2 ($10), $4 ($30)
Classic/Sprint 4-Sport Glenn Robinson $1 ($15), $2 ($30), $4 ($100)
Classic 4-Sport Trent Dilfer $1 ($5), $2 ($10), $4 ($30)
Classic 4-Sport Ed Jovanovski $1 ($7), $2 ($14), $4 ($40)
Classic Assets I/Sprint Troy Aikman $2 ($12), $5 ($25), $100 ($250), 1m($5)
Classic Assets I/Sprint Drew Bledsoe $5 ($25), $100 ($250), 1m ($5)
Classic Assets I/Sprint Marshall Faulk $2 ($20), $25 ($100), 1m ($8)
Classic Assets I/Sprint Grant Hill $2 ($5), 1m ($2)
Classic Assets I/Sprint Jason Kidd $2 ($15), $5 ($30), $100 ($250), 1m ($6)
Classic Assets I/Sprint Donyell Marshall $2 ($12)
Classic Assets I/Sprint Alonzo Mourning $2 ($12), 1m ($4)
Classic Assets I/Sprint Shaquille O'Neal $2 ($15), $5 ($20), $25 ($100), 1m ($6)
Classic Assets I/Sprint Hakeem Olajuwon $5 ($20), $100 ($200)
Classic Assets I/Sprint Manon Rheaume $2 ($15)
Classic Assets I/Sprint Glenn Robinson $2 ($20), 1m ($8)
Classic Assets I/Sprint Dan Wilkinson 1m ($3)

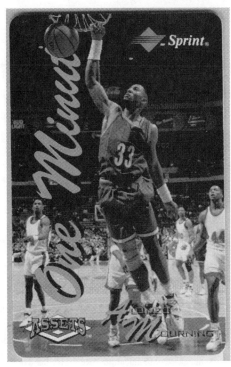

Classic Assets/Sprint has featured a wide array of stars on its phone cards.

Classic Assets I/Sprint Steve Young 1m ($7)
Classic Assets I Derrick Alexander $2 ($5), 1m ($2)
Classic Assets I Drew Bledsoe $2 ($12)
Classic Assets I Radek Bonk $2 ($5), 1m ($2)
Classic Assets I Marshall Faulk $25 ($80), 1m ($6)
Classic Assets I Charlie Garner $2 ($5), 1m ($2)
Classic Assets I Ed Jovanovski $2 ($8), 1m ($3)
Classic Assets I Antonio Langham $2 ($8), 1m ($3)
Classic Assets I Donyell Marshall 1m ($4)
Classic Assets I Eric Montross $2 ($2), 1m ($4)
Classic Assets I Alonzo Mourning 1m ($4)
Classic Assets I Shaquille O'Neal sample $25
Classic Assets I Hakeem Olajuwon $2 ($12), 1m ($4)
Classic Assets I Manon Rheaume 1m $5
Classic Assets I Jalen Rose $2 ($6), 1m ($3)
Classic Assets I Dan Wilkinson $2 ($8)
Classic Assets II/Sprint Anfernee Hardaway $2 ($11), $50 ($150), 1m ($5)
Classic Assets II/Sprint Shaquille O'Neal $2 ($13), $50 ($150), 1m ($5)
Classic Assets II/Sprint Jeff O'Neill $2 ($7), 1m ($3)
Classic Assets II/Sprint Emmitt Smith $2 ($17), $5 ($30), $50 ($200), $200 ($500), 1m ($8)
Classic Assets II Eric Fichaud 1m ($2)
Classic Assets II Juwan Howard $2 ($7), 1m ($3)
Classic Assets II Eddie Jones 1m ($2)
Classic Assets II Dikembe Mutombo 1m ($3)
Classic Assets II Manon Rheaume $2 ($7), 1m ($4)
Classic Assets II Isiah Rider $2 ($7), 1m ($3)
Classic Assets II Rashaan Salaam $2 ($13), $5 ($25), $200 ($300), 1m ($5)
Classic Assets II Emmitt Smith sample $2,000 ($25)
Classic Assets II Emmitt Smith sample error $75

Collector's Advantage Hakeem "The Dream" Olajuwon $3 card	Aug. 1994	10,000	$25
GTE Super Bowl XXIX helmets 49ers/Chargers	Jan. 1995	3,000	$40
GTE Super Bowl XXIX logo/football	Jan. 1995	3,000	$40
GTE Super Bowl XXIX "Hi, Mom" card, with Super Bowl logo	Jan. 1995	80,000	$60
GTE cards depicting helmets of the 15 NFC teams	July 1994	2,500	$150
GTE cards depicting helmets of the 15 AFC teams	July 1994	2,500	$150
GTS offers cards featuring the logos of each of the 26 NHL teams	Jan. 1994	5,000 each team	$15 each, set $300
GTS Basketball Hall of Fame set of 5 - Rick Barry, Hal Greer, Elvin Hayes, Bill Walton, 1st team photo	March 1995	2,000	$35
GTS "Miracle on Ice" five-card set - featuring the 1980 U.S. Olympic Hockey team	March 1995	2,000	$35
IDB Worldcomm Wayne Gretzky NHL all-time scorer $25 card	Jan. 1994	802	$50
Liberty/Quest Charles Barkley five card set	Oct. 1994	10,000	$75
Liberty/Quest Charles Barkley "Not Your Role Model" $3 card	Nov. 1994	1,200	$15
Liberty/Quest Pro Football Hall of Fame card $10 card	Jan. 1994	550	$40
Liberty/Quest Pro Football Hall of Fame card $25 card	Jan. 1994	550	$60
Sprint Monsters of the Gridiron $3 card	Jan. 1994	200,000	$55
Sprint Orlando Magic logo card	Nov. 1994	16,500	$55
USACard Jerry Rice "The Record Breaker" $10 card	Oct. 1994	5,000	$30
USACard Jerry Rice "The Record Breaker" $49 card	Oct. 1994	127	$300

Miscellaneous

1) Hall of Fame Dan Marino card (2,500), $40; 50 were signed, $175; test card, $150; proof card, $300.
2) INET/Clubhouse 49ers cheerleaders four-card set, $50.
3) Instacall Tony Dorsett $25 card.
4) LDDS Miami Heat 3-minute card, $25.
5) Millennium Telecommunications cards of Jalen Rose, Eric Montross, Donyell Marshall, Khalid Reeves, Eric Piatkowski, Billy McCaffrey.
6) NHLPA Four on Four Challenge - $20 cards, set of eight includes Patrick Roy, Brett Hull, Paul Kariya, Eric Lindros, Luc Robitaille, Jeremy Roenick, John Vanbiesbrouck and Doug Gilmour (2,500 per player).
7) Omni-Tel has issued cards for Drew Bledsoe, Vincent Brown, Cam Neely, the Boston Garden and Ray Bourque.
8) Schneider Communications "Rerun for the Roses," Wisconsin Badgers' 1994 football team.
9) Signature Rookies 1995 Hockey Auto-Phoenix set of 50 players, 3,000 autographed each.
10) Signature Rookies top five 1995 NFL rookies - Rashaan Salaam, Ki-Jana Carter, Kerry Collins, Michael Westbrook, Steve McNair - 2,500 five-card sets, 250 autographed sets.
11) Sprint/Gillette Final Four 35-card set, $85.
12) teleQuipe Heath Shuler three-card set (4,000).

Highland Mint Topps replica rookie cards

All exact size (2 1/2" by 3 1/2") Topps replica "Mint-Cards" contain 4.25 ounces of silver or bronze - or 24-karat gold plated on silver - and are individually numbered. Each card includes a certificate of authenticity signed by Topps' Sy Berger, considered the father of the modern day baseball card, and is packaged in a numbered album and a three-piece Lucite display.

The company, based in Melbourne, Fla., has produced the cards since 1992 at a suggested retail price per card of $50 for bronze cards, $235 for silver cards and $500 for gold cards. The limited-edition cards are officially licensed by Topps, the National Hockey League, the NHL Players Association, the National Football League, the NHL Players Association and the Quarterback Club (Highland Mint has also produced limited-edition cards for several baseball players).

In early 1995, after its contracts expired with Topps, the Highland Mint reached an agreement with Pinnacle Brands Inc. to produce replica hockey and football cards. (Note: availability figures were as of June 1995)

Player (replica)	Sport	Style	Mintage	Available	Value
Troy Aikman 1989 Topps	Football	Gold	375	No	$1,000
Troy Aikman 1989 Topps	Football	Silver	500	No	$500
Troy Aikman 1989 Topps	Football	Bronze	2,500	No	$125
Marcus Allen 1983 Topps	Football	Silver	309	Yes	$235
Marcus Allen 1983 Topps	Football	Bronze	1,305	Yes	$50
Jerome Bettis 1993 Topps	Football	Silver	625	Yes	$235
Jerome Bettis 1993 Topps	Football	Bronze	1,879	Yes	$50
Drew Bledsoe 1993 Topps	Football	Gold	375	No	$1,000
Drew Bledsoe 1993 Topps	Football	Silver	500	No	$400
Drew Bledsoe 1993 Topps	Football	Bronze	2,500	No	$100
Ray Bourque 1980 Topps	Hockey	Silver	274	Yes	$250
Ray Bourque 1980 Topps	Hockey	Bronze	747	Yes	$75
Pavel Bure 1992 Topps	Hockey	Silver	466	Yes	$250
Pavel Bure 1992 Topps	Hockey	Bronze	1,524	Yes	$75
John Elway 1984 Topps	Football	Silver	500	No	$300
John Elway 1984 Topps	Football	Bronze	2,434	Yes	$50
Marshall Faulk 1994 Topps	Football	Silver	572	Yes	$350
Marshall Faulk 1994 Topps	Football	Bronze	2,500	Yes	$75
Brett Favre 1992 Topps	Football	Silver	304	Yes	$235
Brett Favre 1992 Topps	Football	Bronze	1,042	Yes	$50
Sergei Fedorov 1991 Topps	Hockey	Silver	355	Yes	$275
Sergei Fedorov 1991 Topps	Hockey	Bronze	920	Yes	$75
Doug Gilmour 1985 Topps	Hockey	Silver	330	Yes	$275
Doug Gilmour 1985 Topps	Hockey	Bronze	907	Yes	$75
Wayne Gretzky 1979 Topps	Hockey	Silver	1,000	No	$850
Wayne Gretzky 1979 Topps	Hockey	Bronze	5,000	No	$150
Brett Hull 1988 Topps	Hockey	Silver	500	No	$350
Brett Hull 1988 Topps	Hockey	Bronze	1,497	Yes	$75
Michael Irvin 1989 Topps	Football	Silver	661	Yes	$350
Michael Irvin 1989 Topps	Football	Bronze	1,993	Yes	$75
Jaromir Jagr 1995 Pinnacle	Hockey	Silver	500	Yes	$235
Jaromir Jagr 1995 Pinnacle	Hockey	Bronze	2,500	Yes	$50
Michael Jordan 1994 Upper Deck	Baseball	Gold	500	No	$1,000
Michael Jordan 1994 Upper Deck	Baseball	Silver	1,000	Yes	$700
Michael Jordan 1994 Upper Deck	Baseball	Bronze	5,000	Yes	$125
Paul Karyia 1995 Pinnacle	Hockey	Silver	250	Yes	$235
Paul Karyia 1995 Pinnacle	Hockey	Bronze	1,500	Yes	$50
Jim Kelly 1987 Topps	Football	Silver	499	Yes	$275
Jim Kelly 1987 Topps	Football	Bronze	1,500	Yes	$50
Pat LaFontaine 1995 Pinnacle	Hockey	Silver	250	Yes	$235
Pat LaFontaine 1995 Pinnacle	Hockey	Bronze	1,500	Yes	$50
Mario Lemieux 1985 Topps	Hockey	Silver	1,000	No	$325
Mario Lemieux 1985 Topps	Hockey	Bronze	3,649	Yes	$75
Eric Lindros 1992 Topps	Hockey	Silver	810	Yes	$300
Eric Lindros 1992 Topps	Hockey	Bronze	2,687	Yes	$75
Dan Marino 1984 Topps	Football	Gold	375	No	$1,250
Dan Marino 1984 Topps	Football	Silver	500	No	$800
Dan Marino 1984 Topps	Football	Bronze	2,500	No	$175
Natrone Means 1993 Topps	Football	Silver	371	Yes	$235
Natrone Means 1993 Topps	Football	Bronze	2,111	Yes	$50
Mark Messier 1984 Topps	Hockey	Silver	230	Yes	$300
Mark Messier 1984 Topps	Hockey	Bronze	801	Yes	$75
Rick Mirer 1993 Topps	Football	Silver	750	Yes	$235
Rick Mirer 1993 Topps	Football	Bronze	2,450	Yes	$50
Mike Modano 1995 Pinnacle	Hockey	Silver	500	Yes	$235
Mike Modano 1995 Pinnacle	Hockey	Bronze	2,500	Yes	$50
Cam Neely 1995 Pinnacle	Hockey	Silver	250	Yes	$235

Miscellaneous

Cam Neely 1995 Pinnacle	Hockey	Bronze	1,500	Yes	$50
Felix Potvin 1992 Topps	Hockey	Silver	321	Yes	$250
Felix Potvin 1992 Topps	Hockey	Bronze	1,057	Yes	$75
Jeremy Roenick 1995 Pinnacle	Hockey	Silver	500	Yes	$235
Jeremy Roenick 1995 Pinnacle	Hockey	Bronze	2,500	Yes	$50
Patrick Roy 1986 Topps	Hockey	Silver	500	No	$300
Patrick Roy 1986 Topps	Hockey	Bronze	1,465	Yes	$75
Barry Sanders 1989 Topps	Football	Gold	375	No	$850
Barry Sanders 1989 Topps	Football	Silver	750	No	$300
Barry Sanders 1989 Topps	Football	Bronze	2,500	Yes	$75
Deion Sanders 1989 Topps	Football	Silver	430	Yes	$235
Deion Sanders 1989 Topps	Football	Bronze	1,186	Yes	$50
Teemu Selanne 1992 Topps	Hockey	Silver	200	Yes	$275
Teemu Selanne 1992 Topps	Hockey	Bronze	929	Yes	$75
Sterling Sharpe 1989 Topps	Football	Silver	330	Yes	$235
Sterling Sharpe 1989 Topps	Football	Bronze	1,159	Yes	$50
Emmitt Smith 1990 Topps	Football	Gold	375	No	$1,700
Emmitt Smith 1990 Topps	Football	Silver	750	No	$1,000
Emmitt Smith 1990 Topps	Football	Bronze	2,500	No	$250
Lawrence Taylor 1984 Topps	Football	Silver	750	Yes	$235
Lawrence Taylor 1984 Topps	Football	Bronze	1,664	Yes	$50
Steve Young 1986 Topps	Football	Gold	375	No	$750
Steve Young 1986 Topps	Football	Silver	500	No	$400
Steve Young 1986 Topps	Football	Bronze	2,500	No	$100
Steve Yzerman 1984 Topps	Hockey	Silver	336	Yes	$275
Steve Yzerman 1984 Topps	Hockey	Bronze	1,177	Yes	$75

Medallions produced include:

Troy Aikman	1994	Football	Silver	7,500	$40
Troy Aikman	1994	Football	Bronze	25,000	$10
Jerome Bettis	1994	Football	Silver	7,500	$25
Drew Bledsoe	1994	Football	Silver	7,500	$40
Drew Bledsoe	1994	Football	Bronze	25,000	$10
John Elway	1995	Football	Silver	7,500	$25
Marshall Faulk	1994	Football	Silver	7,500	$40
Michael Irvin	1995	Football	Silver	7,500	$25
Dan Marino	1994	Football	Silver	7,500	$45
Dan Marino	1994	Football	Bronze	25,000	$10
Natrone Means	1994	Football	Silver	7,500	$25
Rick Mirer	1994	Football	Silver	7,500	$25
Joe Montana	1995	Football	Gold	100	$1,350
Joe Montana	1995	Football	Silver	7,500	$25
Jerry Rice	1994	Football	Silver	7,500	$35
Jerry Rice	1994	Football	Bronze	25,000	$10
Barry Sanders	1994	Football	Silver	7,500	$30
Heath Shuler	1995	Football	Silver	7,000	$25
Emmitt Smith	1994	Football	Silver	7,500	$45
Emmitt Smith	1994	Football	Bronze	25,000	$15
Steve Young	1994	Football	Silver	7,500	$35
Pavel Bure	1994	Hockey	Silver	5,000	$20
Sergei Fedorov	1994	Hockey	Silver	5,000	$20
Brett Hull	1994	Hockey	Silver	5,000	$20
Mario Lemieux	1994	Hockey	Silver	5,000	$25
Eric Lindros	1995	Hockey	Silver	5,000	$20
Patrick Roy	1995	Hockey	Silver	5,000	$20
Teemu Selanne	1995	Hockey	Silver	5,000	$20

1977-79 Sportscaster cards

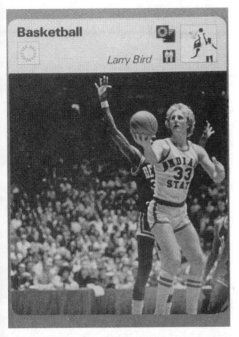

This massive set of full-color cards, which includes players from dozens of different sports - some of them very obscure - contains 2,184 different cards, making it one of the biggest sets of trading cards ever issued. Cards were issued in 91 series, 24 cards per series. These series are numbered from 01-88 and 101-103. The numbering in this list is the series first, followed by the card number in that series - i.e. 06-21 means the sixth series, card #21.

The set was available by mail subscription, at $1.89 plus postage per series. However, later series costs were increased to $2.69 per series. Each series was mailed to subscribers on approval and could be canceled at any time. A total set would have initially cost more than $170, plus postage.

Because the set was issued in series, and many collectors dropped out of the program before the end, cards in the higher series are especially scarce. This accounts for prices on some of the superstar cards, issued in early series, being lower than for some of the lesser-known players.

The initial promotion for the set included a filing tray with which to store cards. Subscribers who ordered three series at a time also received a six-page leaflet on a sports topic, such as - "Beyond Sports - The Winter Olympic Games," or "Basketball - The NBA," or "Track and Field - The Olympic Marathon."

A wide variety of sports (149 subjects) are represented in the set, ranging from 148 cards related to baseball, to ballooning, darts, Jui jitsu, polo and others represented by one card each. Some deal with the history of the sport, techniques, rules, equipment, star players, competitions, major sporting events, stadiums or international meets.

The cards measure 4 3/4-by-6 3/8 inches and have a color-coded band at the top corresponding to a particular sport. Cards can be sorted that way, or numerically by card number and series. A symbol is also used to depict what aspect of the sport is being represented (history, equipment, players), plus a second symbol is also used to indicate how the sports are played (indoor, outdoor, individual, team).

There were actually two manufacturers of the cards - Editions Recontre S.A. (Lausanne, Switzerland, for series 01-64) and Edito-Service S.A. (Geneva, Switzerland, for series 65-88 and 101-103).

The first seven series were printed in Italy and Japan; all the rest were done in Italy. There were some series also reprinted, creating resultant changes in titles, subjects, color-coding variations, text on the back, updated statistics, and picture variations.

Basketball

01-24 Basketball (Pete Maravich) $10
02-03 Basketball (Kareem Abdul-Jabbar) $6
02-09 Basketball (USA vs. USSR) $3
03-15 Basketball (Julius Erving) $5
04-12 Basketball (Bill Russell) $7.50
04-14 Basketball (Dave Cowens) $4
04-15 Basketball (Rick Barry) $3
05-10 Referee's Signals (Olympic Action) $2
05-19 1969-70 Knickerbockers
    (Knicks vs. Lakers) $3
06-08 The UCLA Dynasty (UCLA in Action) $3
06-21 Basketball (George McGinnis) $3
07-09 Refereeing (European Action) $2
07-12 A Laboratory Sport (USA vs. Russia) $2
07-13 Basketball (Walt Frazier) $5
07-20 Basketball (Wilt Chamberlain) $10
08-10 Basketball (Jerry West) $4
09-12 Basketball (Nate Archibald) $3
09-16 A Game for Giants (USA vs. Russia) $2.50
10-18 Basketball (John Havlicek) $4
11-24 UCLA vs. Houston (Lew Alcindor) $8
12-13 Basketball (Wes Unseld) $5
13-04 The European Championship Cup
    (Ignis Varese Tea) $2
13-10 Lakers Win 33 In A Row
    (Chamberlain/West) $5
14-18 Basketball (Oscar Robertson) $5
14-21 3-Guard Offense (Phil Chenier) $3
16-14 Basketball (Elgin Baylor) $5
18-20 Basketball (Jackie Chazalon) $2
19-14 Basketball (Bob Pettit) $5
20-21 24-Second Clock (76ers player) $2
21-14 Basketball (Clarence "Bevo" Francis) $2
22-08 Milwaukee Bucks 1970-71
    (Bucks vs. Knicks) $5
23-03 Basketball Lingo (Pete Maravich) $8
26-24 Basketball (Villeurbanne) $2
30-10 Fouls and Penalties (Hawks vs. Bulls) $2
30-12 Podoloff Cup (Kareem Abdul-Jabbar) $5
30-13 NBA All-Star Game (Randy Smith) $3
33-04 Pivot Play (Bill Walton) $10
34-14 Defenses (College action) $3
35-06 The Highest Scoring Game
    (Julius Erving) $7
36-08 Basketball (Artis Gilmore) $5
36-12 The Four Corner Offense
    (Bulls vs. Bullets) $3
36-22 The NCAA Tournament
    (Kentucky vs. Duke) $6
38-11 Basketball (Paul Westphal) $6
38-12 Biddy-Basket (Playground Game) $2
39-10 MacCabi of Tel Aviv (MacCabi team) $2
39-15 Basketball (Doug Collins) $3

Miscellaneous

40-07 Basketball (Marques Johnson) \$4
40-09 Basketball (Walter Davis) \$4
42-02 Basketball (Bernard King)..................\$3
43-01 The Washington Bullets
(Bullets vs. Sonics)................................\$2
43-18 Power Forward (Maurice Lucas)..........\$3
44-16 Basketball (Butch Lee)......................\$2
52-24 Basketball (Hank Luisetti)..................\$3
53-22 Basketball (Jack Sikma) \$3
54-15 Basketball (George Mikan) \$15
54-23 Basketball (Manuel Raga)..................\$2
55-18 Basketball (Leonard Robinson)...........\$3
56-11 Basketball (Marvin Webster) \$5
59-05 Basketball (David Thompson)............\$10
60-08 Basketball (Carol Blazejowski)...........\$6
62-09 Basketball (Calvin Murphy)............\$7.50
63-05 First TV Game (Burke Crotty).........\$2.50
63-20 Basketball (Austin Carr)....................\$6
64-04 Chinese Tour (Mu Tieh-Chu)............\$4
64-05 Olmpic Games Honors Tables
(USA vs. Russia)..................................\$6
64-24 Basketball (Three Officials) \$2.50
65-15 20,000-Point Club (Hal Greer)...........\$8
66-11 Basketball (Hall of Fame)..............\$3.50
67-02 Basketball (Nancy Lieberman).......\$7.50
67-11 Basketball (Bob Morse)....................\$4
73-03 Basketball (Rudy Tomjanovich) \$12
74-07 A Pro Oddity (Eric Money)................\$6
74-18 Basketball (Larry Bird) \$500
76-08 The Longest Shot (Rudy Williams)....\$10
76-14 Basketball (Inge Nissen) \$3
77-05 Basketball (Kevin Porter)..................\$9
77-21 Basketball (Nat Holman) \$12
78-02 Basketball (Earvin Johnson) \$325
78-24 Basketball (Dave Bing) \$7.50
79-10 Basketball (Ouliana Semenova) \$8
79-15 Basketball (Phil Ford) \$5
79-19 Women's Basketball League
(Randi Burick) \$10
81-02 Basketball (Lenny Wilkens).............\$20
82-02 Basketball (Moses Malone)..............\$20
82-15 Academic Basketball Team (Greg Kelser)..........\$10
83-07 Three-Point Field Goal (Louis Dampier).........\$15
83-17 Basketball (Dutch Dehnert)..............\$12
84-09 United Basketball Association
(Mike Riordan) \$15
85-15 Women's Draft (Pat Colasurdo).........\$10
85-22 F.P. Naismith Award (Scheib/Byrd) \$8
86-08 Baseball/Basketball (Danny Ainge)..............\$100
102-02 Basketball (Ray Meyer)..............\$17.50
103-04 Basketball (Ann Meyers)..............\$15

Beyond Sports

25-14 The NCAA (Basketball)....................\$2
61-10 Bill Bradley (Basketball)..................\$20
69-12 First Televised Football Games (Skip Walz)........\$7
72-21 Greg Pruitt (Football)......................\$5
80-23 Al McGuire (Basketball)..................\$15
83-23 Jack Kemp (Football)......................\$25
84-06 Fines (Doug Moe, basketball) \$10
86-06 Kiki and Ernie Vandeweghe (Basketball)........\$10
87-09 Madison Square Garden (Basketball)...........\$7.50
101-17 Pat Haden (Football) \$12

Football

01-15 Football (Johnny Unitas)..................\$10
01-20 Football (Jets vs. Colts)....................\$3
02-04 Football (George Blanda)..................\$5
03-07 Football (O.J. Simpson)....................\$25
03-20 Football (Joe Namath)......................\$7
05-23 Football (Gale Sayers)......................\$6
06-13 Football (Red Grange)......................\$6

06-18 Football (Jimmy Brown) \$6
07-15 Football (1967 Green Bay Packers)....\$3
08-06 Football (Fran Tarkenton) \$4
09-22 Football (The Rose Bowl) \$3
10-24 Football (Tony Dorsett)....................\$4
11-13 Football (Csonka/Kiick) \$5
12-06 A Very Warlike Game (Football action)...........\$2
12-09 Football (Joe Greene)......................\$5
13-06 Football (Archie Griffin) \$4
13-12 Miami vs. Kansas City (Garo Yepremian)........\$3
16-12 Football (Paul Hornung) \$10
17-01 Football (Jimmy Taylor)....................\$4
17-15 Football (Ken Stabler) \$7
20-20 Football (Ken Anderson) \$4
21-18 College All-Star Game
(All-Stars vs. Steelers)..........................\$3
22-16 Lingo (Redskins vs. Vikings) \$3
23-11 Football (Super Bowl) \$3
24-05 Football (Bert Jones) \$3
25-23 Football (Charley Taylor)..................\$4
26-14 Football (Walter Payton) \$8
27-06 Football (Packers vs. Bears)..............\$3
29-07 Defensive Formations (Harry Carson) \$7.50
29-16 NFL History (Packers/Browns)..........\$4
31-02 Trick Plays (Russ Francis)..................\$4
32-03 Offensive Alignments (UCLA in Action) \$5
33-01 Holding (Patriots vs. Raiders)............\$3
33-14 Football (Chuck Foreman)................\$5
33-22 Football (Gene Upshaw)..................\$10
34-18 Football (Preston Pearson)................\$5
35-18 Football (Jim Bakken) \$3
36-17 Goal Line Defense (Bills vs. Colts)....\$3
36-20 Two-Minute Offense (Ken Stabler)....\$8
37-15 Legal and Illegal Blocks (Blocking Action)...........\$2
37-17 Football (Lynn Swann)......................\$7
38-22 Football (Jack Youngblood)..............\$3
39-17 Ball Control (Packers vs. Chiefs) \$2
39-21 Grab Face Mask (Colts vs. Bills).......\$4
39-22 Football (Harvey Martin)..................\$6
40-04 Pass Interference (Bob Chandler)......\$4
40-10 Football (Rick Upchurch)..................\$4
42-13 Football (Curly Culp)........................\$4
42-24 Cheerleading (USC Cheerleaders)......\$2
43-12 Holding the Ball for Placement
(Wehrli/Bakken)..................................\$2
44-22 Punting (Ray Guy)............................\$4
44-24 Special Team Defense, Kick Return....\$2
45-04 Throwing the Ball (Bob Griese)..........\$7
45-09 Punt Returns (Len Barney)................\$6
46-01 NFL Draft (Bubba Smith)..................\$3
46-13 Kickoff Returns (Gale Sayers)............\$6
47-21 Football (Tom Jackson)....................\$7
50-01 Equipment (San Diego Charger) \$2
50-20 Football (Ernie Nevers) \$4
52-13 Football (Lydell Mitchell)..................\$7
53-10 The Sidelines (San Diego Charger) \$2
53-17 Great Moments (Sonny Jurgensen) \$7
54-14 Football (Joe Kapp) \$3
54-20 Football (Jim Thorpe)........................\$8
55-01 Football (Dave Casper)......................\$6
56-15 Football (Ray Guy)............................\$8
56-18 Great Moments (Joe Namath)............\$7
57-01 Football (Willie Lanier)......................\$5
59-02 Football (Roger Staubach)................\$12
61-20 Heisman Trophy (Earl Campbell) \$10
62-14 Football (Eddie Lee Ivery) \$6
63-02 17-0 Miami Dolphins (Griese/Csonka) \$10
63-16 Outland Award (Brad Shearer)..........\$4
64-11 Football (Harvard Stadium)..............\$5
64-19 Football (Floyd Little) \$6
65-24 Football (Franco Harris)..................\$10
66-07 Football (Four Horsemen) \$15
67-05 Football/Soccer (The Bahr Family)....\$4
68-06 Incredible Playoff (Bill Osmanski)....\$5
68-20 Football (John Cappelletti)................\$7
69-02 Football (Terry Bradshaw) \$15

70-10 Pro Bowl (Jan Stenerud)......................................$5
71-01 Football (Dave Jennings).............................$7
71-23 Football (Chuck Noll) $12
72-17 Football (Joe Paterno) $25
73-06 Football (Bear Bryant)..............................$25
75-02 Football (Nick Buoniconti) $8
76-05 NFL Hall of Fame (Canton, Ohio) $7
76-24 Football (Walter Camp All-American Team) $8
78-09 Football (Tom Landry)................................$20
78-20 Rating Passers (Dan Fouts) $12
79-22 College Football Hall of Fame
    (Ronald Reagan)..$15
80-19 Football (Jim Marshall)................................$10
81-18 Football (Dan Pastorini) $10
81-22 Football (Billy Sims)....................................$10
82-21 Football (Tom Cousineau)...............................$6
84-11 Stength Coaches (Carlos Alberto)....................$6
85-02 Barefoot Athletes (Tony Franklin)...............$7.50
85-10 Protecting the Quarterback (Craig Morton).........$10
85-20 Football (Lou Holtz).....................................$10
86-01 Grambling (Doug Williams) $7.50
88-11 Football (Ernie Davis)..................................$15
102-20 NCAA Records (Steve Owens)......................$8
103-01 Football (Jim Turner)..................................$10
103-16 Longest Runs (Jack Tatum)..........................$10

Ice Hockey

01-02 Ice Hockey (Bobby Orr)...............................$10
02-06 Ice Hockey (Gordie Howe) $15
02-13 The Stanley Cup (Cournoyer/Savard) $4
03-19 Ice Hockey (Phil and Tony Esposito)................$7
05-09 Ice Hockey (USA vs. Czechoslovakia)................$7
05-20 Ice Hockey (Bobby Hull)..............................$12
06-07 Ice Hockey (Gump Worsley) $7
07-08 Ice Hockey (1976 USSR team) $8
07-17 Ice Hockey (Brad Park).................................$7
10-14 Ice Hockey (Jean Beliveau)............................$7
11-19 Hat Trick (Bob Hodges)................................$3
12-15 World Championship (Czechs vs. USSR).............$8
12-22 Ice Hockey (Stan Mikita) $12
14-23 Ice Hockey (Ken Dryden) $8
15-13 Ice Hockey (Yvan Cournoyer) $7
17-09 Ice Hockey (Denis Potvin) $8
18-23 Ice Hockey (Garry Unger)..............................$8
19-15 World Championship (1977 Canadiens)............$4
21-12 The Equipment (Fussen) $2
27-24 National Hockey League

    (Blackhawks/Capitals)......................................$6
29-08 The Power Play (Phil Esposito)......................$12
31-03 Penalty Killing (Bobby Clarke)......................$10
33-03 Lines in the Ice (The Red Line).......................$2
35-03 Ice Hockey (The Spengler Cup)......................$2
38-07 The Seven Professional Trophies
    (Guy Lafleur)...$10
40-24 The Stanely Cup (Rangers vs. Blues).................$3
43-04 Major and Minor Penalties
    (Maple Leafs/Capitals) $2
43-06 Ice Hockey (Rogie Vachon) $4
44-03 Ice Hockey (Jaroslav Jirik)............................$2
44-20 Ice Hockey (Gerry Cheevers)..........................$3
45-13 Ice Hockey (Steve Shutt)...............................$3
46-14 In the Corners (Leafs/Capitals).......................$2
46-21 Ice Hockey (Bryan Trottier)............................$8
47-16 Trio Grande (Three Islander Stars)...................$8
47-18 Ice Hockey (Darryl Sittler).............................$6
50-03 Sticks (Bobby Hull).....................................$5
50-04 Ice Hockey (Facemasks)................................$5
51-01 Ice Hockey (1977 Czechoslovakia team)..........$3
51-18 Ice Hockey (Guy Lafleur)..............................$6
55-14 Ice Hockey (Jiri/Holik).................................$3
55-23 World Hockey Association (Bobby Hull)..............$4
56-05 Montreal Forum (Toronto/Montreal)................$5
60-12 Ice Hockey (Bobby Clarke)...........................$10
61-03 Lingo (Eddie Giacomin)................................$5
62-17 Ice Hockey (Lester Patrick).............................$6
63-09 Ice Hockey (The Howe Family) $20
64-16 Sudden Death (Pete Stemkowski) $5
67-21 Ice Hockey (Bill Chadwick)............................$5
70-06 Ice Hockey (Hall of Fame)..............................$4
71-04 Ice Hockey (The Abrahamson Brothers)..............$4
71-12 Ice Hockey (Hedberg/Nilsson).........................$5
73-01 USSR vs. NHL (game action) $7.50
73-11 Ice Hockey (1976 Czechoslovakia team).............$5
74-17 The 1978 WCH (USSR 1978 Champs).............$4
74-24 Vaclav Nedomansky (USSR vs. Czechs)............$5
76-03 NCAA Hockey Champions
    (Minnesota/North Dakota).................................$5
77-10 Ice Hockey (Wayne Gretzky).......................$250
77-24 Expansion (Whalers/Oilers)............................$5
78-04 Ice Hockey (Real Cloutier).............................$4
80-18 Ice Hockey (John Davidson) $8
81-19 Ice Hockey (Jacques Lemaire) $12
82-05 Ice Hockey (Scotty Bowman)..........................$15
82-23 Ice Hockey (Dave Dryden)...........................$7.50
102-14 Ice Hockey (Russian Team) $15
103-08 Ice Hockey (Alexander Yakushev)..................$8

Movie Posters

    Interest in movie posters continues to increase every day, with the potential to grow even more. Posters, in general, have caught the eye of top auction houses, with the likes of Dracula and King Kong posters fetching $77,000, a poster record, and $52,500 in a poster auction in 1994. Still, there's something for everyone, from those who seek to invest in their sports posters, to the budget-minded newcomers. In the general hobby, posters from the 1950s, '60s and '70s, and those featuring Hollywood legends (John Wayne, Marilyn Monroe), have the greatest demand among those seeking to invest in posters, while currently underpriced posters are those which feature established superstars who are still active (Clint Eastwood, Jack Nicholson). Horror films and science fiction are also popular among collectors. That leaves plenty of room for those who are targeting the sports niche. Although the posters below are upwards of

$500 in value, there are 27x41 sports posters from the 1970s and later which are less than $100, such as Blue Chips ($25), Wildcats ($10), Hoosiers, Heaven Can Wait ($15), Semi-Tough, The Longest Yard, and Slap Shot.

Miscellaneous

Football movie posters, all are linen backed 27x41 unless noted

Title Year	Stars	Price
The All-American, 1952	Tony Curtis, Mamie Van Doren	$400
Crazylegs, 1953	Elroy "Crazylegs" Hirsch, Lloyd Nolan	$500
Crazylegs, 1953 (22x28)		$350
The Guy Who Came Back, 1951	Paul Douglas, Joan Bennett	$200
Iron Major, 1943	Pat O'Brien, Ruth Warrick	$500
King of Gamblers, 1948	Janet Martin, William Wright	$400
King of the Texas Rangers-Chapter 3, 1941	Sammy Baugh, Duncan Renaldo	$500
North Dallas Forty, 1979	Nick Nolte, Mac Davis	$100
Over the Goal, 1937	June Travis, William Hopper	$500
Paper Lion, 1968	Alan Alda, Lauren Hutton	$150
The Quarterback, 1940	Wayne Morris, Virginia Dale	$500
The Rose Bowl Story, 1952	Marshall Thompson, Vera Miles	$300
Saturday's Hero, 1951	John Derek, Donna Reed	$250
The Spirit of West Point, 1947	Felix "Doc" Blanchard, Glenn Davis	$400
Triple Threat, 1948	Richard Crane, Gloria Henry	$500
Triple Threat, 1948 (22x28)		$350
Two Minute Warning, 1976	Charlton Heston, John Cassavates	$100

Basketball movie posters

The Big Fix, 1947	James Brown, Sheila Ryan	$300
Blue Chips, 1994	Nick Nolte, Shaq O'Neal	$25
The Fish That Saved Pittsburgh, 1979	Julius Erving, Meadowlark Lemon	$150
Go Man Go!, 1954	Harlem Globetrotters, Dane Clark	$275
Go Man Go!, 1954 (22x28)		$250
Go Man Go!, 1954 (14x36)		$250
The Harlem Globetrotters, 1951	Harlem Globetrotters, Thomas Gomez	$250
Kings of Basketball, 1940	St. John's basketball team (Joe Lapchick, F. Levane)	$500

Hockey movie posters

Gay Blades, 1946	Allan Lane, Jean Rogers	$300
White Lightning, 1953	Stanley Clements	$250

Artwork

Elaine's Fine Art and Sports Memorabilia, in New York, N.Y., Commemorative Sports Prints Inc., of Riderwood, Md., and Kelly Russell Studios Inc., of Minneapolis, Minn., all offer sports artwork. Kelly Russell Studios offers more than 250 limited-edition images from all four major sports, auto racing, wildlife and entertainment. Superstars such as Emmitt Smith and Wayne Gretzky have been featured by the studio. Each print is 11x14, with a double bevel-cut mat with three openings. One opening displays a larger lithographic print taken from original art, along with a smaller action photo and biographical information. (A team logo replaces the smaller photo on NBA prints). Each is numbered and limited to 12,500 prints. Prints can be purchased framed or unframed. The following list of items advertised in Sports Collectors Digest gives a representative sampling of values:

Football prints

The Coach (Tom Landry), by Daniel Smith, limited-edition 16 3/4x16 1/2 print, autographed......................$250
Friends (Michael Irvin and Emmitt Smith), by Vernon Wells, limited-edition 17x24 lithograph,
    autographed..$295
Dan Marino, by Anthony Douglas, limited-edition lithograph print of 750......................................$45
Joe Montana, by Anthony Douglas, limited-edition lithograph print of 750....................................$45
Joe Montana Tribute, by Daniel Smith, limted-edition 17x16 1/4 print, autographed.................................$395
Joe Namath, by Robert Hurst, limted-edition 24x30 lithograph...$225
O.J. Simpson, by Edgar Brown, oil on canvas, 48x36..$1,600
Emmitt Smith, by Anthony Douglas, limited-edition lithograph of 378 ....$45
Super Bowl MVPs, by Bernie Fuchs, 32x24 poster $45
Lawrence Taylor, by Ed LaPere, acrylic on illustration board, 13x10 1/2, autographed $350
Lawrence Taylor, Palmer Murphy, oil on canvas, 30x24..$1,500
Lawrence Taylor, by Frank Stapleton, limited edition, 38x25, autograped $225
Texas Toddlers (Emmitt Smith and Troy Aikman), by Kenneth Gatewood, 18x19 1/2......................................$35

Basketball prints

Baby Dream Team (Larry Bird, Charles Barkley, Michael Jordan, Magic Johnson and Patrick Ewing),
    by Kenneth Gatewood, 35 3/4x24..$50
Chairmen of the Boards (Charles Barkley, Shaquille O'Neal, Michael Jordan),
    by Kenneth Gatewood, 33 1/4x26 1/4..$45
Legacy I (Bill Russell, Bob Cousy, John Havlicek, Red Auerbach, Tom Heinsohn),
    by Ann Neilsen, limited edition print of 500, autographed by each $795

Hakeem Olajuwon, by Anthony Douglas, limited-edition of 300 lithographs, autographed $250
Pure Magic, by Brent Hayes, limited-edition 28x20 print, ...$300
Shaq Baby (Shaquille O'Neal), by Kenneth Gatewood, 25 3/4x19 1/2 ....$35

Hockey prints

Determination, by Paul Morin, limited-edition 19 1/4x32 print, autographed by Brian Leetch $300
Sergei Fedorov, by Ed Lapere, acrylic on illustration board, 12x9, ...$350

Newspapers

   Every pro sports team has had its name splashed across the front pages of the sports section, as have many of the athletes on those teams. These papers, which provide a glance back at history, also offer an affordable alternative for collectors. Significant historical moments or achievements which are captured in the headlines make the best collectibles, and the most valuable ones, too. They are also easier to find, compared with an average daily story about your favorite player or team. Value is determined by several factors, including what section features the story, and what paper. Was the story on the front page of the entire newspaper, or just the sports page? Are the photos game shots, or posed? Who's pictured? Is it a photo taken the day before, or is it a stock shot which has had repeated use? Condition plays a role in the value, too. Because of the high acidic content in the paper, and the fact newspapers were not meant to be saved, they deteriorate over time. Papers should be stored flat (unfolded) in Mylar and other acid-free materials. Vinyl holders should be avoided. Box Seat Collectibles, of Halesite, N.Y., is a leading dealer in newspapers with sports headlines and offers a catalog of its inventory. A representative sample of papers (unless noted, Des Moines Register sports sections, all having banner headlines) has been listed. Box Seat Collectibles can be reached at P.O. Box 2013, Halesite, N.Y., 11743.

Football

12-19-32 "Bears Win, 9-0, for Pro Crown," 1st NFL Championship Game.......................................$175
12-09-40 "Bears Overwhelm Redskins by Record Score!" New York Times.......................................$125
1951 "Rams Rally to Win Title, 24-17!" with action photo $50
03-29-53 "The Great Jim Thorpe Dies"...$40
01-04-54 "(Len) Dawson Star After 3 Big 10 Games"...$15
11-02-59 "(Jim) Brown's 5 Touchdowns Top Colts"...$50
01-29-60 "Twin Cities (Minnesota), Dallas added to NFL!"..$15
1962 Dallas Takes AFL Title over Houston, with action photo $50
11-29-64 "Bears Draft Illinois' Butkus, Kansas' Sayers!"...$50
12-13-66 "Heisman (Trophy) To Florida's (Steve) Spurrier" $15
01-02-67 "Chiefs, Packers In Super Bowl (I)!"...$75
10-31-67 "O.J. Simpson May Be Out for Season"...$40
1968 O.J. Simpson's USC Wins Rose Bowl, with Simpson photo $50
02-02-68 "Vince (Lombardi) Quits as Packer Coach!"...$35
09-23-68 "There's No Doubt, O.J.'s (Simpson) Top Runner"...$40
11-27-68 "O.J.'s (Simpson) Vigil Ends in Heisman Prize"...$60
01-28-69 "Bills to Draft O.J. (Simpson) - But What's the Price?"....................................$25
02-04-69 "(Vince) Lombardi: I'll Coach Redskins!"...$25
08-21-70 "(Rookie Terry) Bradshaw: 'Li'l Abner With Cleats'" $35
06-04-70 "Bears Bag (Walter) Payton, No. 1 Draft Choice"...$35
1971 Colts Win Super Bowl Over Dallas, many photos $40
01-19-71 "Jim Plunkett Wins Heisman Trophy"...$25
12-18-72 "O.J. (Simpson) Nails Rushing Crown"...$35
09-17-73 "Simpson Super!" Shatters NFL Rushing Record With 250 Yards"...............................$50
12-04-73 "Tab Frosh (Tony) Dorsett All-America"...$20
12-05-73 "John Cappelletti Wins Heisman Trophy"...$20
12-17-73 "O.J. Scampers to 2,003 Yards"...$50
01-02-74 "Greatest (Rose Bowl) Victory - Woody (Hayes)"...$25
01-17-74 "No. 1 Athlete: O.J. (Simpson) Over (Hank) Aaron" $150
11-24-75 "(Fran) Tarkenton Smashes Completion Record" $20
11-26-76 "'Juice' Sets Yardage Mark As Bills Bow"...$40
07-29-77 "(Gale) Sayers Hall of Famer Off Field, Too!"...$40
11-21-77 "It's Payton Place As Walter Sets Mark," New York Star-Gazette.............................$25
03-25-78 "O.J. Simpson Heads Home! Dealt to 49ers for 5 High Draft Picks"..........................$25
12-19-79 "Houston's (Earl) Campbell Named MVP"...$20
12-06-81 "(Marcus) Allen Wins Heisman Trophy"...$25
01-26-81 "Plunkett Passes Raiders To (Super Bowl XV) Title"...$40
01-05-82 "NFL Names (Ken) Anderson MVP"...$20
01-11-82 "49ers to the Super Bowl On 'The Catch'"...$60
01-12-82 "Montana Is One Solid 'Joe Cool'" $20
12-15-82 "Report (Bear) Bryant Will Resign Today as Alabama Coach" $20
12-16-82 "End of Era: Bear (Bryant) Retires At Alabama" $20
02-24-83 "Herschel Walker Signs with USFL"..$20
05-03-83 "Broncos Deal With Colts, Sign Elway" $20

07-18-83 "(Michigan) Panthers top (Philadelphia) Stars, 24-22, for 1st USFL Title".........................$25
01-23-84 "(Marcus) Allen Sparks 38-9 Raider (Super Bowl XVIII) Rampage" $40
03-06-84 "A Rich (Steve) Young Man: BYU Star Gets $40 Million Deal" $40
07-25-84 "Steelers' QB Bradshaw Retires" $25
12-03-84 "Marino's Record Day Spoiled By Raiders' Win" $25
12-10-84 "Eric the Great (Dickerson) Gains 2,007, Eclipsing O.J.!" Los Angeles Times $25
12-22-84 "Marino Named Most Valuable Player In NFL" $25
12-08-85 "(Bo) Jackson Edges (Chuck) Long For Heisman" $20
1985 "Montana Dismantles Dolphins" in Super Bowl XIX, action photos $40
01-27-86 "Number 1! Bears Shuffle to Title!" $35
08-19-86 "Bills Make (Jim) Kelly NFL's Richest Player" $15
12-04-88 "(Barry) Sanders Wins Heisman Vote Quietly" $25
02-28-89 "Emotional (Tom) Landry Says Goodbye to Cowboys" $15

Basketball

11-28-39 "Naismith Dies! Invented Basketball!" $15
09-25-54 "Mikan Retires as Pro Cager!"..$20
10-29-58 "Wilt (Chamberlain) Posts 24 (Points) While Trotter Mates Clown!" $25
10-25-59 "Wilt (Chamberlain) Hits 43 in Pro Debut" $25
11-16-60 "Laker Star (Elgin) Baylor Hits Record 71 (points)".......................................$20
11-04-62 "Wilt (Chamberlain) Scores 72 Points As Frisco Fails" $20
03-21-66 "Celtics' 9-Year Reign Ends!" Philadelphia wins division $20
03-18-68 "(Lew) Alcindor vs. (Elvin) Hayes In Rematch" NCAA tournament $20
07-06-68 "(Wilt) Chamberlain Traded to Lakers"...$20
03-29-69 "Lew (Alcindor) to Sign Bucks' Pact of $1 Million!".......................................$15
02-05-70 "(Bill) Russell Wins (Basketball Player of) Decade Honor" $15
03-18-70 "NBA Vote Picks (Willis) Reed as MVP"...$25
04-15-70 "Lew (Alcindor) Named Top (NBA) Rookie Unanimously" $25
05-08-71 "NBA, ABA Agree: We'll Merge!"..$10
01-24-73 "East (NBA All-) Stars Romp (104-84)!" $20
05-03-74 "(Bill) Walton To NBA!" $15
04-01-75 "(John) Wooden Goes Out On Top, 92-85"..$25
06-01-75 Darryl Dawkins Signs NBA Contract Out of High School".....................................$10
06-17-75 "Bucks Swap (Kareem Abdul-) Jabbar to Lakers!"..$15
03-31-81 "And Then There Was One: Indiana," Isiah Thomas and Indiana win NCAA title $25
05-28-81 "(Julius) Erving Named Most Valuable (Player) In NBA Ranks!" $15
11-26-81 "It's A First! Magic Johnson Gets Boss Fired"...$20
06-10-82 "It's Magic! Lakers Rule NBA Again"...$35
02-21-84 "College Basketball's Best: (Michael) Jordan!" $35
06-26-84 "(Larry) Bird Receives MVP Award"...$35
05-13-85 "NBA Lottery Gives Knicks 1st Choice In 1985 Draft".......................................$40
06-10-85 "NBA Champion Lakers End Boston Jinx" $40
06-20-86 "Len Bias Dies of Drug Overdose"..$15
04-19-87 "A Doctor (Julius Erving) With 'Class' Written All Over Him!" $50
06-15-87 "No Question: Lakers Coast to NBA Crown!"...$40
01-06-88 "Former Star (Pete) Maravich Dies At Game!" $10
02-08-88 "(Michael) Jordan Wears MVP Crown At All-Star Game!" $40
06-13-91 "High Five!" Bulls Are Champs!" $40
06-15-92 "2 For 2: Bulls Still Champs!"..$40
08-19-92 "Bird Decides To Hang Up His Sneakers! Larry, It's Been A Ball!"..........................$25
06-21-93 "Three-Mendous!" Bulls Win 3rd Straight NBA Championship!" $40

Hockey

04-14-33 "Crowd of 13,500 Sees Rangers Annex World's Hockey Championship" $50
04-17-61 "Chicago (Blackhawks) Win Stanley Cup" $25
04-29-69 "(Phil) Esposito is Most Valuable (Player)"...$35
06-01-70 "Star NHL Goalie (Terry) Sawchuck Dies of Heart Attack at 40"............................$10
05-19-71 "15th Stanley Cup to Canadiens"..$25
05-12-72 "Too Much (Bobby) Orr - Boston Wins Stanley Cup"..$40
05-20-74 "Surprise: Flyers NHL Champs!"...$25
05-25-80 "The Cup: Islanders Sitting On Top of the World" $20
02-25-82 "Gretzky Snaps NHL Record With 77th Goal! Tops Esposito"..................................$25
05-20-84 "Stanley Cup Belongs to Gretzky and Co.!"..$25
08-10-88 "Gretzky Traded to L.A. (Kings) In Stunner"..$20
10-16-89 "'Great One' (Gretzky) Nets NHL Point Mark" $25
06-22-91 "Bossy, Potvin Gain Fame" $10
03-24-94 "No. 99 Gets Goal 802 To Become No. 1 on List!" $10
06-15-94 "It's Ours! The Cup Comes Back to N.Y. after 54 Years" $15

Games

Parker Bros. Pro Draft combines the action of a game with football cards.

Generally, player or team-related games are in greater demand than generic games, while board games are more valuable than card games. Game values are also determined in part by age (older is more valuable); company (Milton Bradley and Parker Bros. are two of the top); graphics/illustrations (those with higher quality of lithography and highly-detailed, colorful illustrations, especially on the box, are more valuable); box and board style (wooden boxes are more valuable, then heavy cardboard; metal games are more valuable than cardboard ones); theme; the region in which the item is being sold; rarity; implements (game parts): and completeness (missing game cards or integral parts may drop a value by 50 percent). The American Game Collectors Association has archives of game instructions and can supply copies by contacting AGCA, 49 Brooks Ave., Lewiston, Maine 04240.

Condition is also a big factor in determining game values. Look for games which are in Very Good or Excellent condition - those which are not faded, water stained, covered with soot or mildew, and have all the parts and instructions.

The best places to find board games are at game conventions, collectibles shows, antique shops, flea markets, and through auction houses and hobby publications, such as Krause Publications' Toy Shop and Today's Collector publications. When buying sight-unseen through the mail, however, get as detailed of a description about condition beforehand, and inquire if the seller has a return policy if the material is not satisfactory.

Many games are repairable, but that's best left to an archivist or other professional who can clean your game using special materials such as acid-free glue and paper. Rubber cement thinner can be used to remove price stickers or tape on the outside box cover on games which are taped shut. Mildew can be cleaned with a bathroom mildew remover and a damp sponge, but test a small area first.

Games should be kept out of extremely cold or hot temperatures and places with wide temperature fluctuations. Direct sunlight, spotlights and other bright lights should be avoided, too, to prevent fading. Damp areas can cause mildew buildup, so a dehumidifier is recommended. Also, although stacking is not suggested, if you are going to stack your games, do so by cross-stacking them, alternating them vertically and horizontally, so that the weight of the games on top do not crush those underneath.

Note: Because so few exist in that condition, games from 1844-1945 are not priced in Mint condition. Prices fluctuate, too, oftentimes based on auction fever, which tends to drive prices up. Remember, value is what someone is willing to pay, not necessarily the selling price.

Football games

The Navy's Tom Hamilton was the subject of Parker Bros.' Pigskin game.

Name	Company	Year	VG	Ex	Mint
ABC Monday Night Football	Aurora	1972	$8	$30	$40
ABC Monday Night Football (Roger Staubach edition)	Aurora	1973	$10	$15	$50
All-American Foot Ball Game	Parker Bros.	1925	$100	$165	xxx
All-American Football Game	National Games	1935	$35	$55	xxx
All-American Football	Cadaco	1969	$35	$60	$90
Alpha Football Game	Replica Mfg. Co.	1940s	$75	$100	xxx
All-Star Electric Baseball and Football	Harrett-Gilmar	1955	$35	$60	$90
All-Star Football	Gardner & Co.	1950	$55	$90	$135
American Football Game	Ace Leather Goods Co.	1930	$70	$115	xxx
American Football Game	American News Co.	1930s	$60	$100	xxx
American Football Game	Intercollegiate Football Inc.	1935	$50	$75	xxx
America's Football	Trojan Games	1939	$55	$90	
APBA Pro League Football	APBA	1964	$50	$75	
	APBA	1970s	$35	$50	xxx
	APBA	1980s	$12	$20	$30
Art Lewis Football Game	Morgantown Game Co.	1955	$70	$115	$175
Bart Starr Quarterback Game		1960s	$175	$295	$450
Baseball, Football & Checkers	Parker Bros.	1957	$35	$60	$90
The Benson Football Game	Benson	1930s	$85	$140	xxx
Big League Manager Football	BLM	1965	$20	$35	$50
Big Payoff Payoff Enterprises Co.		1984	$6	$10	$15
Big Ten Football Game	Wheaties' Jack Armstrong Presents	1936	$55	$90	xxx
Big Time Colorado Football	B.J. Tall	1983	$6	$10	$15
Bo McMillan's Indoor Football	Indiana Game Co.	1939	$75	xxx	xxx
Booth's Pro Conference Football	Sher-Co	1977	$10	$15	$25
Bowl Bound!	Sports Illustrated	1973	$15	$25	$40
Bowl Bound!	Avalon Hill-Sports Illustrated	1978	$7	$10	$15

Boys Own Football Game	McLoughlin Bros.	1901	$325	$750	xxx
Challenge Football	Avalon Hill	xxx	$10	$15	$20
Chex Ches Football	Chex Ches Games	1971	$15	$25	$40
College Football	Milton Bradley	1945	$85	$125	xxx
Dan Kersteter's Classic Football	Big League Co.	xxx	$10	$20	xxx
Electric Football	Electric Game Co.	1930s	$55	$90	xxx
Elmer Layden's Scientific Football	Cadaco-Ellis	1936	$40	$80	xxx
F/11 Armchair Quarterback	James R. Hock	1964	$10	$20	xxx
First Down	TGP Games	1970	$50	$80	$125
Fobaga	American Football Co.	1942	$50	$75	xxx
Fooba-Roo Football Game	Memphis Plastic Ent.	1955	$25	$40	$65
Football	J. Pressman & Co.	1940s	$30	$45	xxx
Football	All-Fair	1946	$55	$80	xxx
Football (with baseball, basketball and hockey)	Samuel Lowe	1942	$50	$75	xxx
Football (Knapp Electro Game Set)	Knapp Co.	1929	$125	$205	xxx
Football	Wilder	1930s	$50	$80	xxx
Football	Parker Bros.	1898	$295	$495	xxx
Football-As-You-Like-It	Wayne W. Light	1940	$85	$145	xxx
Football, Baseball & Checkers	Parker Bros.	1948	$15	$45	$65
Football Fever	Hansen	1985	$20	$35	$50
Football Game (Princeton vs. Yale)	Parker Bros.	1910	$350	xxx	xxx
Football Strategy	Avalon Hill	1962	$8	$25	$45
Football Strategy	Avalon Hill, Sports Illustrated	1972	$3	$10	$15
Foto-Electric Football	Cadaco-Ellis	1950	$50	$75	xxx
Frank Cavanaugh's American Football	F. Cavanaugh Assoc.	1955	$25	$40	$60
Fut-Bal	The Fut-Bal Co.	1940s	$35	$60	xxx
The Game of Football	George A. Childs	1895	$350	xxx	xxx
The Game of Football	Parker Bros.	1892	$400	xxx	xxx
Game of Touchdown or Parlor Football	Union Mutual Life Insurance Premium	1897	$125	xxx	xxx
Goal Line Stand	Game Shop Inc.	1980	$12	$20	$30
Gregg Football Game	Albert A. Gregg	1924	$175	$285	xxx
Half-Time Football	Lakeside	1979	$5	$9	$15
Hit That Line, The All-American Football Game	La Rue Sales	1930s	$100	$165	xxx
Howard H. Jones (Collegiate Football)	Municipal Service	1932	$40	$100	xxx
Huddle All-American Football Game	xxx	1931	$100	$165	xxx
Indoor Football	Underwood	1919	$145	$250	xxx
Instant Replay	Parker Bros.	1987	$8	$13	$20
Intercollegiate Football	Hustler-Frantz	1923	$125	$245	xxx
Jerry Kramer's Instant Replay	Emd Enterprises	1970	$15	$25	$40
Jimmy the Greek Oddsmaker Football	Aurora	1974	$15	$25	$35
Jim Prentice Electric Football	Electric Game Co.	1940	$50	$75	xxx
The Johnny Unitas Football Game	Play-Rite	1960	$125	$150	xxx
Johnny Unitas' Football	Pro Mentor	1970	$25	$40	$65
J.R. Quarterback Football	Built Rite	1950s	$30	$45	xxx
Kellogg's Football Game	Kellogg's Premium	1936	$25	$40	xxx
Knute Rockne Football	Radio Sports	1940	$300	xxx	xxx
Linebacker Football	Linebacker Inc.	1990	$12	$20	$30
Los Angeles Rams Football Game	Zondine Game Co.	1930s	$175	$295	xxx
Monday Morning Quarterback	A.B. Zbinden	1963	$20	$35	$50
NBC Pro Playoff	NBC-Hasbro	1969	$25	$40	$65
The New Game, Touchdown	Hartford Mfg. Co.	1920	$100	xxx	xxx
NFL All-Pro Football	Ideal	1967	$20	$35	$50
NFL Armchair Quarterback	Trade Wind Inc.	1986	$8	$13	$20
NFL Franchise	Rohwood	1982	$10	$16	$25
NFL Game Plan	Tudor Games	1980	$6	$10	$15
NFL Play Action Tudor		1979	$7	$10	$15
NFL Quarterback	Tudor	1977	$14	$23	$35
NFL Strategy	Tudor Games	1935	$45	$70	xxx
NFL Strategy	Tudor	1976	$5	$16	$25
NFL Strategy	Tudor	1986	$6	$10	$15
Official Knute Rockne Football Game	Radio Sports	1930	$250	$400	xxx
Official National Football League Quarterback	Toy Craft	1965	$50	$75	xxx
Official NFL Football Game	Ideal	1968	$20	$30	$50
Official Radio Football	Toy Creations	1939	$45	$75	xxx
Ot-O-Win Football	Ot-O-Win Toys and Games	1920s	$55	$90	xxx
Parlor Football Game	McLoughlin Bros.	1890s	$525	$875	xxx
Paul Brown's Football Game	Trikilis	1947	$110	$180	$275
Paydirt!	Sports Illustrated	1973	$10	$16	$25
Paydirt!	Avalon Hill	1979	$10	$18	$30
Pigskin	Parker Bros.	1940	$75	$100	xxx
	Parker Bros.	1956	$30	$40	xxx
	Parker Bros.	1960	$20	$30	xxx

Miscellaneous

Pigskin, Tom Hamilton's Football	Parker Bros.	1946	$50	$75	xxx
Pigskin, Tom Hamilton's Football Game (stadium cover)	Parker Bros.	1934	$75	$100	xxx
Play Football	Whitman	1934	$55	$90	xxx
Playoff Football	Crestline Mfg. Co.	1970s	$20	$35	$50
Pocket Football	Toy Creations	1940	a	b	$35
Pocket Football	AMV Publishing	xxx	$5	$7	$10
Pro Bowl Live Action Football	Marx	1960s	$35	$65	$95
Pro Coach Football	Mastermind Sports		$30	$40	xxx
Pro Draft	Parker Bros.	1974	$15	$25	$40
Pro Football	Milton Bradley	1964	$25	$35	xxx
Pro Football	3M	1964	$15	$20	xxx
Pro Football Franchise	Ron Wood	1987	$10	$16	xxx
Pro Football	Strat-O-Matic	1968	$25	$35	xxx
		1960s cards	$15	$20	$30
		1970s cards	$10	$15	$20
		1980s cards	$6	$10	$15
Pro-Foto-Football	Cadaco	1977	$25	$40	$60
Pro-Foto-Football	Cadaco	1986	$8	$12	$18
Pro Franchise Football	Rohrwood Inc.	1987	$10	$16	$25
Pro Quarterback	Tod Lansing	1964	$20	$40	$60
Pro Quarterback	Championship Games	1965	a	b	$75
Pro Replay Football	Pro Replay	xxx	$15	$20	xxx
Quarterback	Littlefield Mfg. Co.	1914	$100	$165	xxx
Quarterback	Olympia Games	1914	$50	xxx	xxx
Quarterback Football Game	Transogram	1969	$25	$40	$65
Radio Football Game	Toy Creations	1939	$50	$80	$125
Razzle Dazzle Football Game	Texantics Unlimited	1954	$50	$80	$125
Razz-O Dazz-O Six Man Football	Gruhn & Melton	1938	$60	$100	xxx
Realistic Football	Match Play	1976	$15	$25	$35
Replay Pro Football	Replay Games	xxx	$30	$45	xxx
Roll-O Football	Supply Sales Co.	1923	$35	$60	xxx
Rose Bowl Championship Football Game	E.S. Lowe Co.	1940s	$40	$100	xxx
Rummy Football	Milton Bradley	1944	$35	$60	xxx
Samsonite Football	Samsonite	1969	$20	$35	$50
Scrimmage	SPI	1973	$15	$25	$35
Scrimmage	Scrimmage Inc.	1978	$5	$7	$12
Sod Buster	D. Santee	1980	$10	$16	$25
Sports Illustrated College Football	Time	1971	$8	$25	$40
Sports Illustrated Pro Football	Time	1970	$15	$25	$40
Stars on Stripes Football Game	Stars & Stripes Games Co.	1941	$55	$90	xxx
Statis-Pro Football	Statis-Pro	1970s	$25	$40	$65
Statis-Pro Football	Avalon Hill-Sports Illustrated	xxx	$5	$10	$15
Strat-O-Matic College Football	Strat-O-Matic	1976	$25	$40	$60
Super Coach TV Football	Coleco	1974	$25	$40	$65
Tackle	Tackle Game Co.	1933	$75	$115	xxx
Tackle-Lite	Saxon Toy Corp.	1940s	$50	$75	xxx
Talking Football	Mattel	1971	$12	$20	$30
Talking Monday Night Football	Mattel	1977	$8	$13	$20
T.H.E. Pro Football	T.H.E. Game Co.	xxx	$15	$25	$35
Thinking Man's Football	3M	1969	$15	$20	$30
	3M	1973	$10	$15	$20
Thrilling Indoor Football Game	Cronston Co.	1933	$70	$115	xxx
Top Pro Football Quiz Game	Ed-U-Cards	1970	$15	$25	$40
Touchdown	Cadaco	1937	$65	$110	xxx
Touchdown	Milton Bradley	1930s	$150	$250	xxx
Touchdown Football Game	Wilder Mfg. Co.	1920s	$100	$165	xxx
21st Century Football	Kerger Co.	1930	$55	$90	xxx
Va-Lo Football Card Game		1930s	$125	xxx	xxx
Varsitee Football Playing Cards	Kerger Co.	1938	$100	xxx	xxx
Varsity Football, PB	Kerger Co.	1925	$75	xxx	xxx
Varsity Football Game	Cadaco-Ellis	1942	$45	$75	xxx
	Cadaco-Ellis	1955	$25	$35	xxx
The VCR Quarterback Game	Interactive VCR Games	1986	$8	$13	$20
Vince Lombardi's Game	Research Games Inc.	1970	$20	$50	$75
Ward Cuff's Football Game	Continental Sales	1938	$125	$200	xxx
Whiz Football	Electric Game Co.	1945	$50	$75	xxx
Wilder's Football Game	Wilder Mfg. Co.	1930s	$50	$75	xxx
Wiry Dan's Electric Football Game	Harett-Gilmar	1953	$25	$40	$65
Yale Harvard Game	McLoughlin Bros.	1890	$1,050	$1,775	xxx
Yale-Harvard Football Game	La Velle Mfg. Co.	1922	$200	$300	xxx
Yale and Princeton Football Game	McLoughlin Bros.	1895	$575	$950	xxx

Basketball games

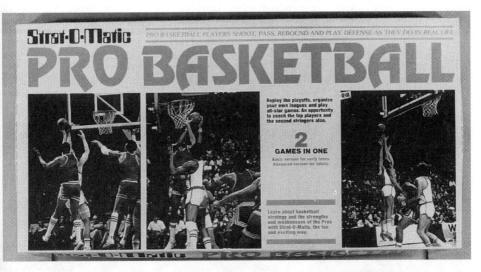

Strat-O-Matic games have provided youngsters hours of fun, using real-life players.

Name	Company	Year	VG	Ex	Mint
APBA Pro Basketball	APBA	xxx	$15	$25	$35
All American Basketball	Corey Games	1941	$55	$90	$135
All-Pro Basketball	Ideal	1969	$15	$25	$35
All Star Basketball	Gardner	1950s	$55	$90	$135
Basket (blue box)	Cadaco-Ellis	1938	$50	$75	$100
Basket (red/yellow box)	Cadaco-Ellis	1962	$35	$50	$65
Basket (photo cover)	Cadaco-Ellis	1969	$25	$35	$45
Basket (photo cover)	Cadaco-Ellis	1973	$25	$35	$45
Basketball, Harlem Globetrotters Official Edition	Cadaco-Ellis	1970s	$45	$75	$115
Basketball	Chaffee & Selchow	1898	$3,700	xxx	xxx
Basketball	Russell	1929	$150	$350	xxx
Basketball (with baseball, football, hockey)	Samuel Lowe	1942	$50	$75	xxx
Basketball, A Game (celluloid ball, hoop)	xxx	1903	$200	xxx	xxx
Basketball Card Game	Built-Rite Warren	1940s	$15	$25	xxx
Basketball Game	Warren Built-Rite	1950s	$20	$30	$45
Basketball Strategy	Avalon Hill-Sports Illustrated	xxx	$10	$15	$25
Big League Basketball	Baumgarten & Co.	1920s	$125	$200	xxx
Challenge Basketball All-Stars	Avalon Hill	xxx	$10	$16	$25
College Basketball	Cadaco-Ellis	1954	$20	$30	$55
Computer Basketball	Electric Data Controls Corp.	1969	$45	$75	$115
Fastbreak Basketball	Mickey Games	xxx	$25	$45	xxx
Harlem Globetrotters Game	Milton Bradley	1971	$30	$50	$75
Home Court Basketball (Home Court)	Charlie Eckman Photo	1954	$145	$250	$375
Junior Basketball Game	Rosebud Art Co.	1930s	$75	xxx	xxx
Let's Play Basketball	DMR	1965	$10	$15	$25
Mickey Mouse Basketball	Gardner	1950s	$55	$90	$135
Negamco Basketball	Nemadji Game Co.	1975	$10	$16	$25
Official Basketball Game	Toy Creations	1940	$55	$90	xxx
The Official Globetrotter Basketball	Meljak	1950s	$50	$85	xxx
Official NBA Basketball Game	Gerney Games	1970s	$40	$60	$75
Official Radio Basketball Game	Toy Creations	1939	$45	$75	xxx
Oscar Robertson's Pro Basketball Strategy	Research Games	1964	$70	$115	$175
Play Basketball with Bob Cousy	National Games	1950s	$115	$195	$295
Quarter Bouncers, Coin Foul Shot Game	Anderson & Association	1993	$15	$25	$35
Real-Life Basketball	Gamecraft	1974	$10	$16	$25
Samsonite Basketball	Samsonite	1969	$15	$25	$35
Sports Illustrated All Time All Star Basketball	Sports Illustrated	1973	$20	$35	$50

Miscellaneous

Sports Illustrated Pro Basketball	Avalon Hill	1981	$7	$10	$15
Star Basketball	Star Paper Products	1926	$125	$205	xxx
Swish	Jim Hawkers Games Mfg.	1948	$45	$75	$115
Tak-Tiks	Midwest Products	1939	$15	$25	xxx
Top Pro Basketball Quiz Game	Edu-Cards	1970	$15	$25	$40
Top Ten College Basketball	Top Ten Game Co.	1980	$10	$16	$25
Tru-Action Electric Basketball	Tudor	1961	$25	$50	$75
Ultimate College Basketball	Ultimate Game Co.	xxx	$35	$50	xxx
The VCR Basketball Game	Interactive VCR Games	1987	$6	$10	$15

Hockey games

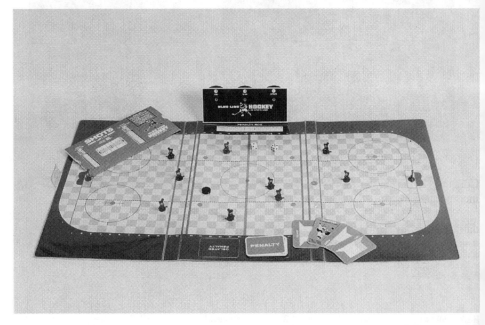

A Blue Line Hockey game in Mint condition can be worth up to $60.

Blue Line Hockey	3M	1968	$25	$40	$60
Box Hockey	Milton Bradley	xxx	$35	$50	xxx
Face-Off	Con-Fro Game Co.	xxx	$25	$35	xxx
Hoc-Key	Cadaco-Ellis	1958	$10	$35	$50
Ice Hockey	Milton Bradley	1942	$25	$40	xxx
The Katzenjammer Kids Hockey	Jaymar	1940s	$40	$65	xxx
NHL All-Pro Hockey	Ideal	1969	$10	$16	$25
NHL Strategy	Tudor	1976	$10	$35	$50
National Pro Hockey	Sports Action	1985	$15	$25	$35
Nip and Tuck Hockey	Parker Bros.	1928	$115	$195	xxx
Nok-Hockey	Carrom	1947	$20	$35	$55
Official Hockey	Toy Creations	1940	$50	$75	xxx
Play Hockey Fun with Popeye & Wimpy	Barnum Mfg.	1935	$205	$350	xxx
Power Play Hockey	Romac Ind.	1970	$30	$50	$75
Slapshot	Avalon Hill	1982	$5	$8	$12
Strat-O-Matic Hockey	Strat-O-Matic	1978	$35	$55	$85
Sure Shot Hockey	Ideal	1970	$15	$25	$40
Tit for Tat Indoor Hockey	Lemper Novelty Co.	1920s	$45	$75	xxx
Top Hockey Game	Coren Game Co.	1943	$50	$75	xxx
The VCR Hockey Game	Interactive VCR Games	1987	$5	$8	$12

Acknowledgments

Thanks to everyone at Krause Publications who somewhere along the process assisted in the creation of this book. These teammates especially deserve some extra credit and many thanks for their assistance, patience and cooperation:

Tom Payette, who followed the roadmaps to style this book, and Ethel Thulien, who did the pasteup work.

Those in the camera and scanning departments, for their assistance in the photography which appears in this book.

Allen West and Ross Hubbard, who used their creative talents to design the cover for this book.

Marge Larson, who input data, and Bonnie Tetzlaff, who coordinated the input and output of material for this book.

Sharon Korbeck, who assisted in pricing games for Chapter 16.

Tom Michael, who assisted in pricing hardcover books for Chapter 8.

Sports Collectors Digest's Tom Hultman, who provided bits and pieces for this book and helped compile autograph information for Chapter 1.

David Bushing, the author of Sports Collectors Digest's *Sports Equipment Price Guide*.

Dave Miedema, uniforms, and Mike Shannon, books, whose previous efforts for Sports Collectors Digest's second edition of *The Complete Guide to Baseball Memorabilia* were incorporated into this book. Dave's uniform terms have also appeared in SCD.

James Thompson, from Chicagoland Processing Enviromint, who sent in updated medallion information for Chapter 12.

About the Author

The author has been at Krause Publications for more than seven years, serving as the sports book editor for the last four years. During that time, he's worked on Krause Publications' annual and standard baseball card price guides and the Standard Catalog of Football, Basketball and Hockey Cards. He's edited *Team Baseballs, Getting Started in Card Collecting, Baseball Cards Questions and Answers*, SCD's *The Sports Card Explosion*, and the *All Sport Autograph Guide*; he's co-authored *Mickey Mantle Memorabilia* and Sports Collectors Digest's *Minor League Baseball Card Price Guide*; and he's written *101 Sports Card Investments* and both editions of *The Complete Guide to Baseball Memorabilia*. All of these books are under the Sports Collectors Digest banner and are available through Krause Publications.

Larson has been a collector for 25 years, primarily baseball cards and memorabilia. He does, however, have a wide array of football, basketball and hockey memorabilia - ranging from Green Bay Packer yearbooks and a "00" Packer bobbing head doll (which, after he dropped it on its head and cracked it, his brother said "good thing he's wearing a helmet"); to a 1970s Keds Sneakers Pete Maravich shoebox (the box, which, since he wore the shoes, now stores his electric football team players); to several 8x10 hockey photos. He'd like to personally get autographs of his two favorite goalies - Manon Rheaume and Lorne "Gump" Worsley - and hopes to see his nephews someday playing on the big league NHL ponds across the country...

Sources

The following sources have been used for information or to help determine prices:

Baker, Mark Allen. *Sports Collectors Digest's All Sport Autograph Guide.* Krause Publications, Iola, Wis. 1994.

Bushing, David. *Sports Collectors Digest's Sports Equipment Price Guide.* Krause Publications, Iola, Wis. 1995.

Case, Roger and Sharon Korbeck. *1996 Toys & Prices*, third edition. Krause Publications, Iola, Wis. 1995.

Hudgeons, Marc. *The Official 1996 Blackbook Price Guide of United States Postage Stamps*, 18th edition. Random House, New York, N.Y. 1995.

Larson, Mark K. *Sports Collectors Digest's Complete Guide to Baseball Memorabilia*, second edition. Krause Publications, Iola, Wis. 1994.

Malloy, Roderick A. *Malloy's Sports Collectibles Value Guide.* Wallace-Homestead Book Co., Radnor, Pa. 1993.

Rosen, Allen. *Mr. Mint's Insider's Guide to Investing in Baseball Cards and Collectibles.* Warner Books, New York, N.Y. 1991.

Also, for Chapter 16, Auctions, respective auction catalogs have been used for descriptions and photos for items in auctions by Sotheby's, Leland's, Richard Wolffers, Christie's East and Centerfield Collectibles Inc.

The December 1986 issue of *Sport* and the 35th anniversary issue of *Sports Illustrated*, from 1990, have been used to determine cover photos for those magazines.

Back issues of *Sports Collectors Digest* and Krause Publication's *Phone Card Collector* have also been used to compile checklists, determine values and provide background material. *Sports Collectors Digest's Standard Catalog of Football, Basketball and Hockey Cards*, published in 1995 by Krause Publications, was also used.

Information in the various chapters has been compiled from advertisments in *Sports Collectors Digest*. The dealers who specialize in these areas have been listed, but keep in mind that many from this list have a wide variety of memorabilia for sale, not just in the areas for which they are listed.

1) Autographs

Albersheim Autographs, 14755 Ventura Blvd., Suite 806, Sherman Oaks, Calif. 91403.

Anaconda Sports, P.O. Box 660, One Anaconda Drive, Lake Katrine, N.Y. 12449.

B&J Collectibles, 999 Airport Road, Unit 2, Lakewood, N.J. 08701.

California Numismatic Investments, 525 West Manchester Blvd., Inglewood, Calif. 90301.

Champion Sports Collectables Inc., 150 E. Santa Clara, Arcadia, Calif. 91006.

Dan's Dugout, 1303 Lavall Drive, Davidsonville, Md. 21035.

Gibraltar Trade Center North, 237 N. River Road, Mt. Clemens, Mich. 48043.

Greg Tucker Autographs, P.O. Box 909, Broken Arrow, Okla. 74013-0909.

M.D.'s Sports Connection, 280 Albright Drive, Loveland, Ohio 45140.

Ralph Paticchio, P.O. Box 129, Everett, Mass. 02149.

Rich Altman Hollywood Collectibles, 3942 North 46th Ave., Hollywood, Fla. 33021.

Schenker Promotions, 13B Chestnut Ct., Brielle, N.J. 08730.

The Score Board Inc., 1951 Old Cuthbert Road, Cherry Hill, N.J. 08034.
SLS, P.O. Box 640332, Oakland Gardens, N.Y. 11364.
Sport Card Heaven, 471 Orange Center Road, Orange, Conn. 06477.
The Sports Alley Inc., 15545 E. Whittier Blvd., Whittier, Calif. 90603.
Sports Collectors Store, 1040 LaGrange Road, LaGrange, Ill. 60525.
Vince's Baseball Cards, 306 Winthrop St., Taunton, Mass. 02780.

2) Uniforms

Ball Park Heroes, 1531 J Street, Bedford, Ind. 47421.
The Best of Baseball And All Sports, 980 Broadway, Suite 624, Thornwood, N.Y. 10594.
Broadway Rick's Strike Zone, 1840 North Federal Highway, Boynton Beach, Fla. 33435-2833.
California Sports Investments, 2785 Pacific Coast Highway, Suite #129, Torrance, Calif. 90505.
E&R Galleries, P.O. Box 15, New Rochelle, N.Y. 10804-0015.
The Man of Steal, 231 Market Place, Suite 212, San Ramon, Calif. 94583.
M.D.'s Sports Connection, 280 Albright Drive, Loveland, Ohio 45140.
Sebring Sports Inc., 427 Forks-of-the-River Parkway, Sevierville, Tenn. 37862.
The Sports Alley Inc., 15545 E. Whittier Blvd., Whittier, Calif. 90603.
Sports Heroes, 3 Westchester Plaza, Elmsford, N.Y. 10523.
Truly Unique, Box 28821, Gladstone, Mo. 64188.

3) Equipment

Ball Park Heroes, 1531 J Street, Bedford, Ind. 47421.
Broadway Rick's Strike Zone, 1840 North Federal Highway, Boynton Beach, Fla. 33435-2833.
California Sports Investments, 2785 Pacific Coast Highway, Suite #129, Torrance, Calif. 90505.
Chapel Hill Collection, 39 Adrian St., Greensburg, Pa. 15601.
E&R Galleries, P.O. Box 15, New Rochelle, N.Y. 10804-0015.
M.D.'s Sports Connection, 280 Albright Drive, Loveland, Ohio 45140.
PC Collectibles, West 124 Midland Ave., Paramus, N.J. 07652.
Sebring Sports Inc., 427 Forks-of-the-River Parkway, Sevierville, Tenn. 37862.
Spivak & Kraut Inc., 66 Jericho Road, Holland, Pa. 18966.
The Sports Alley Inc., 15545 E. Whittier Blvd., Whittier, Calif. 90603.

4) Statues/Figurines

All-Star Celebrity Collectibles, 1207 Nilgai Place, Ventura, Calif. 93003.
B&E Collectibles, 950 Broadway, Thornwood, N.Y. 10594.
Bill Daniels, 510 Indianapolis Ave., P.O. Box 607, Lebanon, Ind. 46052.
Bob McCann, 108 Village Green Drive, Gilbertsville, Pa. 19525.
Bob Rothschild, 5 Fillmore Drive, Clarksburg, N.J. 08510.
David Epstein Sports Collectibles, P.O. Box 4553, Metuchen, N.J. 08840-4553.
Down-Maine Limited, 2315 Griffin Road, Unit #1, Leesburg, Fla. 34748.
E&R Galleries, P.O. Box 15, New Rochelle, N.Y. 10804-0015.
Kirk's Cards, 6841 Pearl Road, Middleburg Heights, Ohio 44130.
The Minnesota Connection, 17773 Kenwood Trail, Lakeville, Minn. 55044.
PM Sportscards, P.O. Box 31011, Bloomington, Minn. 55431.
Romito Enterprises, 232 Elmtree Road, New Kensington, Pa. 15068.

5) Yearbooks/Media Guides

B&E Collectibles, 950 Broadway, Thornwood, N.Y. 10594.

E&R Galleries, P.O. Box 15, New Rochelle, N.Y. 10804-0015.
Phil's Collectibles, P.O. Box 95, Briarcliff Manor, N.Y. 10510-0095.

6) Programs

Alan Getz, 237 E. Valley Parkway, Escondido, Calif. 92025.
B&E Collectibles, 950 Broadway, Thornwood, N.Y. 10594.
Chicago Sportscards Ltd., P.O. Box 702, Wheeling, Ill. 60090.
Ed Taylor's Baseball Dreams, 982 Monterey St., San Luis Obispo, Calif. 93401.
E&R Galleries, P.O. Box 15, New Rochelle, N.Y. 10804-0015.
Lou Madden's Concord Collectibles, 15875 Greenway Hayden Loop, Suite 112, Scottsdale, Ariz. 85260.
Phil's Collectibles, P.O. Box 95, Briarcliff Manor, N.Y. 10510-0095.
Sports Collectors Store, 1040 LaGrange Road, LaGrange, Ill. 60525.
Sportsworld, 429 Broadway, Everett, Mass. 02149.

7) Periodicals

B&E Collectibles, 950 Broadway, Thornwood, N.Y. 10594.
Centerfield Collectibles Inc., P.O. Box 522, Ambler, Pa. 19002.
Chicago Sportscards Ltd., P.O. Box 702, Wheeling, Ill. 60090.
Ed Taylor's Baseball Dreams, 982 Monterey St., San Luis Obispo, Calif. 93401.
Ken Domonkos, P.O. Box 4177, River Edge, N.J. 07661.
Phil's Collectibles, P.O. Box 95, Briarcliff Manor, N.Y. 10510-0095.
Sports Collectors Store, 1040 LaGrange Road, LaGrange, Ill. 60525.

8) Books

B&E Collectibles, 950 Broadway, Thornwood, N.Y. 10594.
Bill Rosenthal's All Sports, 16617 Music Grove Court, Rockville, Md. 20853.
Bob Rothschild, 5 Fillmore Drive, Clarksburg, N.J. 08510.
The Brothers Green, David and Lawrence Green, 268 Wichita St., Shreveport, La. 71101.
R. Plapinger Baseball Books, P.O. Box 1062, Ashland, Ore. 97520.
Phil's Collectibles, P.O. Box 95, Briarcliff Manor, N.Y. 10510-0095.
Sports Collectors Store, 1040 LaGrange Road, LaGrange, Ill. 60525.

9) Commemoratives

Bill Daniels, 510 Indianapolis Ave., P.O. Box 607, Lebanon, Ind. 46052.
Gateway Stamp Co. Inc., P.O. Box D, Florissant, Mo. 63031-0040.
Goal Line Art Inc., P.O. Box 372, Ridley Park, Pa. 19078.
Historic Limited Editions, P.O. Box 1236, New Canaan, Conn. 06840.
Legends of Diamonds/Diamond Connection, 6740 E. 10 Mile Road, Center Line, Mich. 48015.

10) Pins

Allegheny Collectibles Ltd., P.O. Box 288, 613 Elm St., Tionesta, Pa. 16353.
Novak Enterprises, 1150 Cushing Circle #334, St. Paul, Minn. 55108.
Recollectics, P.O. Box 1011, Darien, Conn. 06820.

11) Tickets/Schedules

Ed Taylor's Baseball Dreams, 982 Monterey St., San Luis Obispo, Calif. 93401.
Lew Lipset, P.O. Box 137, Centereach, N.Y. 11720.
Novak Enterprises, 1150 Cushing Circle #334, St. Paul, Minn. 55108.

12) Medallions

Chicagoland Processing Enviromint, 501 W. Algonquin Road, Mt. Prospect, Ill. 60056.

14) Pennants

Kirk's Cards, 6841 Pearl Road, Middleburg Heights, Ohio 44130.

15) Auctions

Centerfield Collectibles Inc., P.O. Box 522, Ambler, Pa. 19002.
Christie's East, 219 East 67th St., New York, N.Y. 10021.
Leland's, 245 Fifth Ave., Suite 902, New York, N.Y. 10016.
Richard Wolffers Auctions Inc., 133 Kearny St., Suite 400, San Francisco, Calif. 94108.
Sotheby's, 1334 York Avenue at 72nd St., New York, N.Y. 10021.

16) Miscellaneous

Columbia City Collectibles Co., 830 S. Bluegrass Drive, Columbia City, Ind. 46725.
My Mom Threw Out My Baseball Cards, 143 North Washington St., North Attleboro, Mass. 02760.
TG Sports Enterprises, 99 Snelling Ave. N., St. Paul, Minn. 55104.

a) Rings/Awards

Out of this World Memorabilia, 1418 Brett Place, Suite 123, San Pedro, Calif. 90732.
The Ring Man, P.O. Box 18194, Philadelphia, Pa. 19116.
Truly Unique, Box 28821, Gladstone, Mo. 64188.

b) Highland Mint Topps replica rookie cards

The Highland Mint, 4100 North Riverside Drive, Melbourne, Fla. 32937.

c) Sportscaster cards

Ed Taylor's Baseball Dreams, 982 Monterey St., San Luis Obispo, Calif. 93401.
Kevin Savage Cards/Mid-America Sports, 3509 Briarfield Blvd., Maumee, Ohio 43537.
Mid-Atlantic Sports Cards Inc., 22 SCD South Morton Ave., Morton, Pa. 19070-1708.
Pro-Am Sports, 256 Chateau Place, Edmonton, Alberta, Canada T5T 1V3.
San Diego Sports Collectibles, 10639 Roselle St., Suite A, San Diego, Calif. 92121.

d) Music posters

Tary Enterprises Inc., 550 Kinderkamack Road, Oradell, N.J. 07649.

e) Newspapers

Box Seat Collectibles, P.O. Box 2013, Halesite, N.Y. 11743
Jim Lyons, 970 Terra Bella Ave., Suite 3, Mountain View, Calif. 94043.

f) Games

Carousel Card Coin & Collectibles, Rt. 1 Box 88e, Henderson, Minn. 56044.

YOUR NEWEST GUIDES TO SPORTS COLLECTIBLES

SPORTS EQUIPMENT PRICE GUIDE

Find pricing for collectible baseball, football, basketball and hockey equipment used from 1860 - 1960.

6"x9", 352 pgs., 500 photos

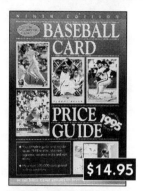

BASEBALL CARD PRICE GUIDE, 9th Ed.

Thorough and reliable pricing to evaluate your collection of modern baseball cards. Over 95,000 cards and 285,000 current values.

6"x9", 816 pgs., 1400 photos

PREMIUM INSERT SPORTS CARDS

Put a premium on your premium insert sports cards with updated prices from 1960 to date. 600 sets and 10,000 cards are included.

6"x9",, 400 pgs., 400 photos

COMPLETE GUIDE TO BOXING MEMORABILIA

Boxing fans can now identify, evaluate and authenticate all their boxing memorabilia with this new handy guide.

6"x9", 320 pgs., 300+ photos

All titles are softcover

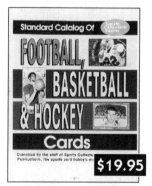

STANDARD CATALOG OF FOOTBALL, BASKETBALL & HOCKEY CARDS

One convenient catalog for three sports. Over 750 sets and 100,000 cards with updated pricing help to buy, sell, trade and evaluate your collection.

8-1/2"x11", 600 pgs., 500 photos

ALL SPORTS ALPHA-BETICAL PRICE GUIDE

Easily find prospects, stars, Hall of Famers and desirable players. 24,000 collectible cards from 725 popular players of 1948 to date, alphabetized, checklisted and priced here.

6"x9", 500 pgs., 725 photos

Shipping: Add $2.50 1st book, $1.50 each additional, $5.00 each foreign. WI residents add 5.5% sales tax.

Krause Publications

700 E. State St., Dept. KLB1
Iola, WI 54990-0001

Call in or send check or money order (payable to Krause Publications) today!

Charge Card Holders call toll-free
800-258-0929 Dept. KLB1

523

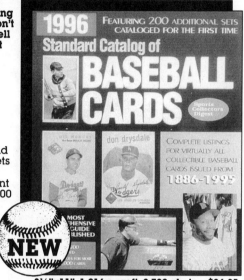